The United States Government Manual 2021

Lanham • Boulder • New York • London

Bernan Press does not claim copyright with U.S. government information.

Published by Bernan Press
An imprint of The Rowman & Littlefield Publishing Group, Inc.
4501 Forbes Boulevard, Suite 200, Lanham, Maryland 20706
www.rowman.com
800-865-3457

6 Tinworth Street, London SE11 5AL, United Kingdom

ISBN: 978-1-63671-091-4

♾™ The paper used in this publication meets the minimum requirements of American National Standard for Information Sciences—Permanence of Paper for Printed Library Materials, ANSI/NISO Z39.48-1992.

Preface

As the official handbook of the Federal Government, *The United States Government Manual* provides comprehensive information on the agencies of the legislative, judicial, and executive branches. The *Manual* also includes information on quasiofficial agencies; international organizations in which the United States participates; and boards, commissions, and committees.

A typical agency description includes a list of principal officials, a summary statement of the agency's purpose and role in the Federal Government, a brief history of the agency, including its legislative or executive authority, a description of its programs and activities, and a "Sources of Information" section. This last section provides information on consumer activities, contracts and grants, employment, publications, and many other areas of public interest.

Contents

DECLARATION OF INDEPENDENCE 1

CONSTITUTION OF THE UNITED STATES 5

CHART: The Government of the United States 21

LEGISLATIVE BRANCH
Congress... 25
    The Senate.. 27
    The House of Representatives 35
Architect of the Capitol... 50
Congressional Budget Office 53
Government Accountability Office 57
Government Publishing Office 60
Library of Congress... 65
    Congressional Research Service 70
United States Botanic Garden... 71

JUDICIAL BRANCH
The Supreme Court of the United States... 77
Lower Courts 80
    United States Courts of Appeals.. 80
    United States Court of Appeals for the Federal Circuit....................... 81
    United States District Courts.. 82
    Territorial Courts.. 82
    United States Court of International Trade... 83
    Judicial Panel on Multidistrict Litigation.. 83
Special Courts 84
    United States Court of Appeals for the Armed Forces 84
    United States Court of Appeals for Veterans Claims 84
    United States Court of Federal Claims.. 85
    United States Tax Court 85
Administrative Office of the United States Courts....................................... 86
Federal Judicial Center.. 90
United States Sentencing Commission 92

EXECUTIVE BRANCH
The President.. 99
The Vice President 102
The Executive Office of the President... 103
    White House Office 105
    Office of the Vice President 107

Council of Economic Advisers 108
Council on Environmental Quality 109
National Security Council 111
Office of Administration 112
Office of Management and Budget 113
Office of National Drug Control Policy 117
Office of Policy Development 119
    Domestic Policy Council 119
    National Economic Council 120
Office of Science and Technology Policy 121
Office of the United States Trade Representative 123

EXECUTIVE BRANCH: DEPARTMENTS

Department of Agriculture 127
Department of Commerce 149
    Bureau of Industry and Security 152
    Economic Development Administration 155
    Economics and Statistics Administration 156
    International Trade Administration 158
    Minority Business Development Agency 159
    National Oceanic and Atmospheric Administration 159
    National Telecommunications and Information Administration 164
    National Institute of Standards and Technology 165
    National Technical Information Service 166
    United States Patent and Trademark Office 167
Department of Defense 168
Department of the Air Force 175
Department of the Army 183
Department of the Navy 191
    United States Marine Corps 199
    United States Naval Academy 200
Defense Agencies 201
    Defense Advanced Research Projects Agency 201
    Defense Commissary Agency 201
    Defense Contract Audit Agency 202
    Defense Contract Management Agency 202
    Defense Finance and Accounting Service 203
    Defense Information Systems Agency 203
    Defense Intelligence Agency 204
    Defense Legal Services Agency 204
    Defense Logistics Agency 205
    Defense Security Cooperation Agency 205
    Defense Counterintelligence and Security Agency 206
    Defense Threat Reduction Agency 207
    Missile Defense Agency 207
    National Geospatial-Intelligence Agency 208
    National Security Agency / Central Security Service 208
    Pentagon Force Protection Agency 209
    Joint Service Schools 209
        Defense Acquisition University 209
        National Intelligence University 210
        National Defense University 210
        Uniformed Services University of the Health Sciences 212

Department of Education 214
    Federally Aided Corporations 219
        American Printing House for the Blind 219
        Gallaudet University 219
        Howard University 220
        National Technical Institute for the Deaf / Rochester Institute of Technology 221
Department of Energy 222
    Federal Energy Regulatory Commission 229
Department of Health and Human Services 232
    Administration for Children and Families 236
    Administration for Community Living 237
    Agency for Healthcare Research and Quality 237
    Agency for Toxic Substances and Disease Registry 238
    Centers for Disease Control and Prevention 239
    Centers for Medicare and Medicaid Services 241
    Food and Drug Administration 242
    Health Resources and Services Administration 243
    Indian Health Service 244
    National Institutes of Health 244
    Substance Abuse and Mental Health Services Administration 249
Department of Homeland Security 251
Department of Housing and Urban Development 260
Department of Justice 266
    Bureaus 272
        Bureau of Alcohol, Tobacco, Firearms and Explosives 272
        Bureau of Prisons 274
        Drug Enforcement Administration 275
        Federal Bureau of Investigation 277
        International Criminal Police Organization (INTERPOL)–Washington 279
        Office of Justice Programs 280
        United States Marshals Service 282
    Offices / Boards 283
        Executive Office for Immigration Review 283
        Foreign Claims Settlement Commission of the United States 285
        Office of Community Oriented Policing Services 286
        Office on Violence Against Women 286
        United States Parole Commission 287
Department of Labor 288
    Bureau of International Labor Affairs 296
    Bureau of Labor Statistics 297
    Employee Benefits Security Administration 299
    Employment and Training Administration 301
    Mine Safety and Health Administration 304
    Occupational Safety and Health Administration 306
    Veterans' Employment and Training Service 308
    Wage and Hour Division 309
    Women's Bureau 311
Department of State 314
Department of Transportation 328
    Federal Aviation Administration 333
    Federal Highway Administration 337
    Federal Motor Carrier Safety Administration 339
    Federal Railroad Administration 342
    Federal Transit Administration 345

Great Lakes Saint Lawrence Seaway Development Corporation................................ 349
Maritime Administration.. 351
National Highway Traffic Safety Administration 353
Pipeline and Hazardous Materials Safety Administration 356
Department of Veterans Affairs.. 359
Department of the Interior 366
Bureau of Indian Affairs.. 371
Bureau of Indian Education 374
Bureau of Land Management... 377
Bureau of Ocean Energy Management 382
Bureau of Reclamation.. 387
Bureau of Safety and Environmental Enforcement.. 392
National Park Service 394
Office of Surface Mining Reclamation and Enforcement.............................. 396
United States Fish and Wildlife Service... 398
United States Geological Survey.. 401
Department of the Treasury.. 404
Alcohol and Tobacco Tax and Trade Bureau.. 411
Bureau of Engraving and Printing.. 413
Bureau of the Fiscal Service... 415
Internal Revenue Service 417
Office of the Comptroller of the Currency 419
United States Mint... 422

EXECUTIVE BRANCH: INDEPENDENT AGENCIES
AND GOVERNMENT CORPORATIONS

Administrative Conference of the United States 425
Central Intelligence Agency.. 429
Commodity Futures Trading Commission... 431
Consumer Financial Protection Bureau.. 435
Consumer Product Safety Commission 439
Corporation for National and Community Service 443
Defense Nuclear Facilities Safety Board... 445
Environmental Protection Agency 447
Equal Employment Opportunity Commission 453
Export-Import Bank of the United States 458
Farm Credit Administration.. 461
Federal Communications Commission.. 464
Federal Deposit Insurance Corporation.. 469
Federal Election Commission... 473
Federal Housing Finance Agency... 474
Federal Labor Relations Authority 478
Federal Mine Safety and Health Review Commission 482
Federal Maritime Commission 484
Federal Mediation and Conciliation Service... 490
Federal Reserve System.. 494
Federal Retirement Thrift Investment Board 500
Federal Trade Commission 504
General Services Administration 508
Inter-American Foundation 514
Merit Systems Protection Board 516
National Aeronautics and Space Administration 518
National Archives and Records Administration 527

National Capital Planning Commission 535
National Credit Union Administration 538
National Foundation on the Arts and the Humanities 542
    National Endowment for the Arts 542
    National Endowment for The Humanities 544
    Institute of Museum and Library Services 546
National Labor Relations Board 549
National Mediation Board 552
National Railroad Passenger Corporation (AMTRAK) 554
National Science Foundation 556
National Transportation Safety Board 562
Nuclear Regulatory Commission 567
Occupational Safety and Health Review Commission 569
Office of Government Ethics 571
Office of Personnel Management 573
Office of the Director of National Intelligence 579
Overseas Private Investment Corporation 584
Peace Corps 585
Pension Benefit Guaranty Corporation 588
Postal Regulatory Commission 592
Railroad Retirement Board 593
Securities and Exchange Commission 598
Selective Service System 603
Small Business Administration 606
Social Security Administration 612
Surface Transportation Board 616
Tennessee Valley Authority 619
Trade and Development Agency 622
United States African Development Foundation 625
United States Agency for Global Media 628
United States Agency for International Development 632
United States Commission on Civil Rights 637
United States International Trade Commission 638
United States Office of Special Counsel 643
United States Postal Service 645

QUASI-OFFICIAL AGENCIES
Legal Services Corporation 655
Smithsonian Institution 658
    John F. Kennedy Center for the Performing Arts 667
    National Gallery of Art 669
    Woodrow Wilson International Center for Scholars 672
State Justice Institute 673
United States Holocaust Memorial Museum 675
United States Institute of Peace 680

INTERNATIONAL ORGANIZATIONS
African Development Bank 685
Asian Development Bank 687
European Bank for Reconstruction and Development 688
Inter-American Defense Board 689
Inter-American Development Bank 690
Inter-American Investment Corporation 691

International Monetary Fund 692
International Organization for Migration 695
Organization of American States.. 698
United Nations 701
World Bank Group 705
    International Bank for Reconstruction and Development... 709
    International Centre for Settlement of Investment Disputes 709
    International Development Association 710
    International Finance Corporation 711
    Multilateral Investment Guarantee Agency 713

Declaration of Independence

Action of Second Continental Congress, July 4, 1776

IN CONGRESS, JULY 4, 1776.

THE UNANIMOUS DECLARATION of the thirteen united STATES OF AMERICA,

WHEN in the Course of human events, it becomes necessary for one people to dissolve the political bands which have connected them with another, and to assume among the powers of the earth, the separate and equal station to which the Laws of Nature and of Nature's God entitle them, a decent respect to the opinions of mankind requires that they should declare the causes which impel them to the separation.

We hold these truths to be self-evident, that all men are created equal, that they are endowed by their Creator with certain unalienable Rights, that among these are Life, Liberty and the pursuit of Happiness.—That to secure these rights, Governments are instituted among Men, deriving their just powers from the consent of the governed,—That whenever any Form of Government becomes destructive of these ends, it is the Right of the People to alter or to abolish it, and to institute new Government, laying its foundation on such principles and organizing its powers in such form, as to them shall seem most likely to effect their Safety and Happiness. Prudence, indeed, will dictate that Governments long established should not be changed for light and transient causes; and accordingly all experience hath shewn, that mankind are more disposed to suffer, while evils are sufferable, than to right themselves by abolishing the forms to which they are accustomed. But when a long train of abuses and usurpations, pursuing invariably the same Object evinces a design to reduce them under absolute Despotism, it is their right, it is their duty, to throw off such Government, and to provide new Guards for their future security.—Such has been the patient sufferance of these Colonies; and such is now the necessity which constrains them to alter their former Systems of Government. The history of the present King of Great Britain is a history of repeated injuries and usurpations, all having in direct object the establishment of an absolute Tyranny over these States. To prove this, let Facts be submitted to a candid world.

He has refused his Assent to Laws, the most wholesome and necessary for the public good.

He has forbidden his Governors to pass Laws of immediate and pressing importance, unless suspended in their operation till his Assent should be obtained; and when so suspended, he has utterly neglected to attend to them.

He has refused to pass other Laws for the accommodation of large districts of people, unless those people would relinquish the right of Representation in the Legislature, a right inestimable to them and formidable to tyrants only.

He has called together legislative bodies at places unusual, uncomfortable, and distant from the depository of their public Records, for the sole purpose of fatiguing them into compliance with his measures.

He has dissolved Representative Houses repeatedly, for opposing with manly firmness his invasions on the rights of the people.

He has refused for a long time, after such dissolutions, to cause others to be elected; whereby the Legislative powers, incapable of Annihilation, have returned to the People at large for their exercise; the State remaining in the mean time exposed to all the dangers of invasion from without, and convulsions within.

He has endeavoured to prevent the population of these States; for that purpose obstructing the Laws for Naturalization of Foreigners; refusing to pass others to encourage their migrations hither, and raising the conditions of new Appropriations of Lands.

He has obstructed the Administration of Justice, by refusing his Assent to Laws for establishing Judiciary powers.

He has made Judges dependent on his Will alone, for the tenure of their offices, and the amount and payment of their salaries.

He has erected a multitude of New Offices, and sent hither swarms of Officers to harrass our people, and eat out their substance.

He has kept among us, in times of peace, Standing Armies without the Consent of our legislatures.

He has affected to render the Military independent of and superior to the Civil power.

He has combined with others to subject us to a jurisdiction foreign to our constitution, and unacknowledged by our laws; giving his Assent to their Acts of pretended Legislation:

For Quartering large bodies of armed troops among us:

For protecting them, by a mock Trial, from punishment for any Murders which they should commit on the Inhabitants of these States:

For cutting off our Trade with all parts of the world:

For imposing Taxes on us without our Consent:

For depriving us in many cases, of the benefits of Trial by Jury:

For transporting us beyond Seas to be tried for pretended offences

For abolishing the free System of English Laws in a neighbouring Province, establishing therein an Arbitrary government, and enlarging its Boundaries so as to render it at once an example and fit instrument for introducing the same absolute rule into these Colonies:

For taking away our Charters, abolishing our most valuable Laws, and altering fundamentally the Forms of our Governments:

For suspending our own Legislatures, and declaring themselves invested with power to legislate for us in all cases whatsoever.

He has abdicated Government here, by declaring us out of his Protection and waging War against us.

He has plundered our seas, ravaged our Coasts, burnt our towns, and destroyed the lives of our people.

He is at this time transporting large Armies of foreign Mercenaries to compleat the works of death, desolation and tyranny, already begun with circumstances of Cruelty & perfidy scarcely paralleled in the most barbarous ages, and totally unworthy the Head of a civilized nation.

He has constrained our fellow Citizens taken Captive on the high Seas to bear Arms against their Country, to become the executioners of their friends and Brethren, or to fall themselves by their Hands.

He has excited domestic insurrections amongst us, and has endeavoured to bring on the inhabitants of our frontiers, the merciless Indian Savages, whose known rule of warfare, is an undistinguished destruction of all ages, sexes and conditions.

In every stage of these Oppressions We have Petitioned for Redress in the most humble terms: Our repeated Petitions have been answered only by repeated injury. A Prince whose character is thus marked by every act which may define a Tyrant, is unfit to be the ruler of a free people.

Nor have We been wanting in attentions to our Brittish brethren. We have warned them from time to time of attempts by their legislature to extend an unwarrantable jurisdiction over us. We have reminded them of the circumstances of our emigration and settlement here. We have appealed to their native justice and magnanimity, and we have conjured them by the ties of our common kindred to disavow these usurpations, which, would inevitably interrupt our connections and correspondence. They too have been deaf to the voice of justice and of consanguinity. We must, therefore, acquiesce in the necessity, which denounces our Separation, and hold them, as we hold the rest of mankind, Enemies in War, in Peace Friends.

WE, THEREFORE, THE REPRESENTATIVES OF THE UNITED STATES OF AMERICA, in General Congress, Assembled, appealing to the Supreme Judge of the world for the rectitude of our intentions, do, in the Name, and by Authority of the good People of these Colonies, solemnly publish and declare, That these United Colonies are, and of Right ought to be FREE AND INDEPENDENT STATES; that they are Absolved from all Allegiance to the British Crown, and that all political connection between them and the State of Great Britain, is and ought to be totally dissolved; and that as Free and Independent States, they have full Power to levy War, conclude Peace, contract Alliances, establish Commerce, and to do all other Acts and Things which Independent States may of right do. And for the support of this Declaration, with a firm reliance on the protection of divine Providence, we mutually pledge to each other our Lives, our Fortunes and our sacred Honor.

The 56 signatures on the Declaration appear in the positions indicated:

Column 1

Georgia:
  Button Gwinnett
  Lyman Hall
  George Walton

Column 2

North Carolina:
  William Hooper
  Joseph Hewes
  John Penn
South Carolina:
  Edward Rutledge
  Thomas Heyward, Jr.
  Thomas Lynch, Jr.
  Arthur Middleton

Column 3

Massachusetts:
  John Hancock
Maryland:
  Samuel Chase
  William Paca
  Thomas Stone
  Charles Carroll of
  Carrollton
Virginia:
  George Wythe
  Richard Henry Lee
  Thomas Jefferson
  Benjamin Harrison
  Thomas Nelson, Jr.
  Francis Lightfoot Lee
  Carter Braxton

Column 4

Pennsylvania:
  Robert Morris
  Benjamin Rush
  Benjamin Franklin
  John Morton
  George Clymer
  James Smith
  George Taylor
  James Wilson
  George Ross
Delaware:
  Caesar Rodney
  George Read
  Thomas McKean

Column 5

New York:
  William Floyd
  Philip Livingston
  Francis Lewis
  Lewis Morris
New Jersey:
  Richard Stockton
  John Witherspoon
  Francis Hopkinson
  John Hart
  Abraham Clark

Column 6

New Hampshire:
  Josiah Bartlett
  William Whipple
Massachusetts:
  Samuel Adams
  John Adams
  Robert Treat Paine
  Elbridge Gerry
Rhode Island:
  Stephen Hopkins
  William Ellery
Connecticut:
  Roger Sherman
  Samuel Huntington
  William Williams
  Oliver Wolcott
New Hampshire:
  Matthew Thornton

For more information on the Declaration of Independence and the Charters of Freedom, see http://archives.gov/exhibits/charters/declaration.html

Constitution of the United States

Note: The following text is a transcription of the Constitution in its original form. Items that are hyperlinked/underlined have since been amended or superseded.

Preamble

WE THE PEOPLE of the United States, in order to form a more perfect union, establish justice, insure domestic tranquility, provide for the common defense, promote the general welfare, and secure the blessings of liberty to ourselves and our posterity, do ordain and establish this Constitution for the United States of America.

Article I

Section 1. All legislative powers herein granted shall be vested in a Congress of the United States, which shall consist of a Senate and House of Representatives.

Section 2. The House of Representatives shall be composed of members chosen every second year by the people of the several states, and the electors in each state shall have the qualifications requisite for electors of the most numerous branch of the state legislature.

No person shall be a Representative who shall not have attained to the age of twenty five years, and been seven years a citizen of the United States, and who shall not, when elected, be an inhabitant of that state in which he shall be chosen.

Representatives and direct taxes shall be apportioned among the several states which may be included within this union, according to their respective numbers, which shall be determined by adding to the whole number of free persons, including those bound to service for a term of years, and excluding Indians not taxed, three fifths of all other Persons. The actual Enumeration shall be made within three years after the first meeting of the Congress of the United States, and within every subsequent term of ten years, in such manner as they shall by law direct. The number of Representatives shall not exceed one for every thirty thousand, but each state shall have at least one Representative; and until such enumeration shall be made, the state of New Hampshire shall be entitled to chuse three, Massachusetts eight, Rhode Island and Providence Plantations one, Connecticut five, New York six, New Jersey four, Pennsylvania eight, Delaware one, Maryland six, Virginia ten, North Carolina five, South Carolina five, and Georgia three.

When vacancies happen in the Representation from any state, the executive authority thereof shall issue writs of election to fill such vacancies.

The House of Representatives shall choose their speaker and other officers; and shall have the sole power of impeachment.

Section 3. The Senate of the United States shall be composed of two Senators from each state, <u>chosen by the legislature thereof, for six years; and each Senator shall have one vote.</u>
<u>Immediately after they shall be assembled in consequence of the first election, they shall</u>
<u>be divided as equally as may be into three classes. The seats of the Senators of the first class</u>
<u>shall be vacated at the expiration of the second year, of the second class at the expiration</u>
<u>of the fourth year, and the third class at the expiration of the sixth year, so that one third</u>
<u>may be chosen every second year; and if vacancies happen by resignation, or otherwise,</u>
<u>during the recess of the legislature of any state, the executive thereof may make temporary</u>
<u>appointments until the next meeting of the legislature, which shall then fill such vacancies.</u>

No person shall be a Senator who shall not have attained to the age of thirty years, and been nine years a citizen of the United States and who shall not, when elected, be an inhabitant of that state for which he shall be chosen.

The Vice President of the United States shall be President of the Senate, but shall have no vote, unless they be equally divided.

The Senate shall choose their other officers, and also a President pro tempore, in the absence of the Vice President, or when he shall exercise the office of President of the United States.

The Senate shall have the sole power to try all impeachments. When sitting for that purpose, they shall be on oath or affirmation. When the President of the United States is tried, the Chief Justice shall preside: And no person shall be convicted without the concurrence of two thirds of the members present.

Judgment in cases of impeachment shall not extend further than to removal from office, and disqualification to hold and enjoy any office of honor, trust or profit under the United States: but the party convicted shall nevertheless be liable and subject to indictment, trial, judgment and punishment, according to law.

Section 4. The times, places and manner of holding elections for Senators and Representatives, shall be prescribed in each state by the legislature thereof; but the Congress may at any time by law make or alter such regulations, except as to the places of choosing Senators.

The Congress shall assemble at least once in every year, and such meeting shall <u>be on the first Monday in December,</u> unless they shall by law appoint a different day.

Section 5. Each House shall be the judge of the elections, returns and qualifications of its own members, and a majority of each shall constitute a quorum to do business; but a smaller number may adjourn from day to day, and may be authorized to compel the attendance of absent members, in such manner, and under such penalties as each House may provide.

Each House may determine the rules of its proceedings, punish its members for disorderly behavior, and, with the concurrence of two thirds, expel a member.

Each House shall keep a journal of its proceedings, and from time to time publish the same, excepting such parts as may in their judgment require secrecy; and the yeas and nays of the members of either House on any question shall, at the desire of one fifth of those present, be entered on the journal.

Neither House, during the session of Congress, shall, without the consent of the other, adjourn for more than three days, nor to any other place than that in which the two Houses shall be sitting.

Section 6. The Senators and Representatives shall receive a compensation for their services, to be ascertained by law, and paid out of the treasury of the United States. They shall in all cases, except treason, felony and breach of the peace, be privileged from arrest during their attendance at the session of their respective Houses, and in going to and returning from the same; and for any speech or debate in either House, they shall not be questioned in any other place.

No Senator or Representative shall, during the time for which he was elected, be appointed to any civil office under the authority of the United States, which shall have been created, or the emoluments whereof shall have been increased during such time: and no person holding any office under the United States, shall be a member of either House during his continuance in office.

Section 7. All bills for raising revenue shall originate in the House of Representatives; but the Senate may propose or concur with amendments as on other Bills.

Every bill which shall have passed the House of Representatives and the Senate, shall, before it become a law, be presented to the President of the United States; if he approve he shall sign it, but if not he shall return it, with his objections to that House in which it shall have originated, who shall enter the objections at large on their journal, and proceed to reconsider it. If after such reconsideration two thirds of that House shall agree to pass the bill, it shall be sent, together with the objections, to the other House, by which it shall likewise be reconsidered, and if approved by two thirds of that House, it shall become a law. But in all such cases the votes of both Houses shall be determined by yeas and nays, and the names of the persons voting for and against the bill shall be entered on the journal of each House respectively. If any bill shall not be returned by the President within ten days (Sundays excepted) after it shall have been presented to him, the same shall be a law, in like manner as if he had signed it, unless the Congress by their adjournment prevent its return, in which case it shall not be a law.

Every order, resolution, or vote to which the concurrence of the Senate and House of Representatives may be necessary (except on a question of adjournment) shall be presented to the President of the United States; and before the same shall take effect, shall be approved by him, or being disapproved by him, shall be repassed by two thirds of the Senate and House of Representatives, according to the rules and limitations prescribed in the case of a bill.

Section 8. The Congress shall have power to lay and collect taxes, duties, imposts and excises, to pay the debts and provide for the common defense and general welfare of the United States; but all duties, imposts and excises shall be uniform throughout the United States;

To borrow money on the credit of the United States;

To regulate commerce with foreign nations, and among the several states, and with the Indian tribes;

To establish a uniform rule of naturalization, and uniform laws on the subject of bankruptcies throughout the United States;

To coin money, regulate the value thereof, and of foreign coin, and fix the standard of weights and measures;

To provide for the punishment of counterfeiting the securities and current coin of the United States;

To establish post offices and post roads;

To promote the progress of science and useful arts, by securing for limited times to authors and inventors the exclusive right to their respective writings and discoveries;

To constitute tribunals inferior to the Supreme Court;

To define and punish piracies and felonies committed on the high seas, and offenses against the law of nations;

To declare war, grant letters of marque and reprisal, and make rules concerning captures on land and water;

To raise and support armies, but no appropriation of money to that use shall be for a longer term than two years;

To provide and maintain a navy;

To make rules for the government and regulation of the land and naval forces;

To provide for calling forth the militia to execute the laws of the union, suppress insurrections and repel invasions;

To provide for organizing, arming, and disciplining, the militia, and for governing such part of them as may be employed in the service of the United States, reserving to the states respectively, the appointment of the officers, and the authority of training the militia according to the discipline prescribed by Congress;

To exercise exclusive legislation in all cases whatsoever, over such District (not exceeding ten miles square) as may, by cession of particular states, and the acceptance of Congress, become the seat of the government of the United States, and to exercise like authority over all places purchased by the consent of the legislature of the state in which the same shall be, for the erection of forts, magazines, arsenals, dockyards, and other needful buildings;—And

To make all laws which shall be necessary and proper for carrying into execution the foregoing powers, and all other powers vested by this Constitution in the government of the United States, or in any department or officer thereof.

Section 9. The migration or importation of such persons as any of the states now existing shall think proper to admit, shall not be prohibited by the Congress prior to the year one thousand eight hundred and eight, but a tax or duty may be imposed on such importation, not exceeding ten dollars for each person.

The privilege of the writ of habeas corpus shall not be suspended, unless when in cases of rebellion or invasion the public safety may require it.

No bill of attainder or ex post facto Law shall be passed.

No capitation, or other direct, tax shall be laid, unless in proportion to the census or enumeration herein before directed to be taken.

No tax or duty shall be laid on articles exported from any state.

No preference shall be given by any regulation of commerce or revenue to the ports of one state over those of another: nor shall vessels bound to, or from, one state, be obliged to enter, clear or pay duties in another.

No money shall be drawn from the treasury, but in consequence of appropriations made by law; and a regular statement and account of receipts and expenditures of all public money shall be published from time to time.

No title of nobility shall be granted by the United States: and no person holding any office of profit or trust under them, shall, without the consent of the Congress, accept of any present, emolument, office, or title, of any kind whatever, from any king, prince, or foreign state.

Section 10. No state shall enter into any treaty, alliance, or confederation; grant letters of marque and reprisal; coin money; emit bills of credit; make anything but gold and silver coin a tender in payment of debts; pass any bill of attainder, ex post facto law, or law impairing the obligation of contracts, or grant any title of nobility.

No state shall, without the consent of the Congress, lay any imposts or duties on imports or exports, except what may be absolutely necessary for executing it's inspection laws: and the net produce of all duties and imposts, laid by any state on imports or exports, shall be for the use of the treasury of the United States; and all such laws shall be subject to the revision and control of the Congress.

No state shall, without the consent of Congress, lay any duty of tonnage, keep troops, or ships of war in time of peace, enter into any agreement or compact with another state, or with a foreign power, or engage in war, unless actually invaded, or in such imminent danger as will not admit of delay.

Article II

Section 1. The executive power shall be vested in a President of the United States of America. He shall hold his office during the term of four years, and, together with the Vice President, chosen for the same term, be elected, as follows:

Each state shall appoint, in such manner as the Legislature thereof may direct, a number of electors, equal to the whole number of Senators and Representatives to which the State may be entitled in the Congress: but no Senator or Representative, or person holding an office of trust or profit under the United States, shall be appointed an elector.

The electors shall meet in their respective states, and vote by ballot for two persons, of whom one at least shall not be an inhabitant of the same state with themselves. And they shall make a list of all the persons voted for, and of the number of votes for each; which list they shall sign and certify, and transmit sealed to the seat of the government of the United States, directed to the President of the Senate. The President of the Senate shall, in the presence of the Senate and House of Representatives, open all the certificates, and the votes shall then be counted. The person having the greatest number of votes shall be the President, if such number be a majority of the whole number of electors appointed; and if there be more than one who have such majority, and have an equal number of votes, then the House of Representatives shall immediately choose by ballot one of them for President; and if no person have a majority, then from the five highest on the list the said House shall in like manner choose the President. But in choosing the President, the votes shall be taken by States, the representation from each state having one vote; A quorum for this purpose shall consist of a member or members from two thirds of the states, and a majority of all the states shall be necessary to a choice. In every case, after the choice of the President, the person having the greatest number of votes of the electors shall be the Vice President. But if there should remain two or more who have equal votes, the Senate shall choose from them by ballot the Vice President.

The Congress may determine the time of choosing the electors, and the day on which they shall give their votes; which day shall be the same throughout the United States.

No person except a natural born citizen, or a citizen of the United States, at the time of the adoption of this Constitution, shall be eligible to the office of President; neither shall any person be eligible to that office who shall not have attained to the age of thirty five years, and been fourteen Years a resident within the United States.

In case of the removal of the President from office, or of his death, resignation, or inability to discharge the powers and duties of the said office, the same shall devolve on the Vice President, and the Congress may by law provide for the case of removal, death, resignation or inability, both of the President and Vice President, declaring what officer shall then act as President, and such officer shall act accordingly, until the disability be removed, or a President shall be elected.

The President shall, at stated times, receive for his services, a compensation, which shall neither be increased nor diminished during the period for which he shall have been elected, and he shall not receive within that period any other emolument from the United States, or any of them.

Before he enter on the execution of his office, he shall take the following oath or affirmation:—"I do solemnly swear (or affirm) that I will faithfully execute the office of President of the United States, and will to the best of my ability, preserve, protect and defend the Constitution of the United States."

Section 2. The President shall be commander in chief of the Army and Navy of the United States, and of the militia of the several states, when called into the actual service of the United States; he may require the opinion, in writing, of the principal officer in each of the executive departments, upon any subject relating to the duties of their respective offices, and he shall have power to grant reprieves and pardons for offenses against the United States, except in cases of impeachment.

He shall have power, by and with the advice and consent of the Senate, to make treaties, provided two thirds of the Senators present concur; and he shall nominate, and by and with the advice and consent of the Senate, shall appoint ambassadors, other public ministers and consuls, judges of the Supreme Court, and all other officers of the United States, whose appointments are not herein otherwise provided for, and which shall be established by law: but the Congress may by law vest the appointment of such inferior officers, as they think proper, in the President alone, in the courts of law, or in the heads of departments.

The President shall have power to fill up all vacancies that may happen during the recess of the Senate, by granting commissions which shall expire at the end of their next session.

Section 3. He shall from time to time give to the Congress information of the state of the union, and recommend to their consideration such measures as he shall judge necessary and expedient; he may, on extraordinary occasions, convene both Houses, or either of them, and in case of disagreement between them, with respect to the time of adjournment, he may adjourn them to such time as he shall think proper; he shall receive ambassadors and other public ministers; he shall take care that the laws be faithfully executed, and shall commission all the officers of the United States.

Section 4. The President, Vice President and all civil officers of the United States, shall be removed from office on impeachment for, and conviction of, treason, bribery, or other high crimes and misdemeanors.

Article III

Section 1. The judicial power of the United States, shall be vested in one Supreme Court, and in such inferior courts as the Congress may from time to time ordain and establish. The judges, both of the supreme and inferior courts, shall hold their offices during good behaviour, and shall, at stated times, receive for their services, a compensation, which shall not be diminished during their continuance in office.

Section 2. The judicial power shall extend to all cases, in law and equity, arising under this Constitution, the laws of the United States, and treaties made, or which shall be made, under their authority;—to all cases affecting ambassadors, other public ministers and consuls;—to all cases of admiralty and maritime jurisdiction;—to controversies to which the United States shall be a party;—to controversies between two or more states;—between a state and citizens of another state;—between citizens of different states;—between citizens of the same state claiming lands under grants of different states, and between a state, or the citizens thereof, and foreign states, citizens or subjects.

In all cases affecting ambassadors, other public ministers and consuls, and those in which a state shall be party, the Supreme Court shall have original jurisdiction. In all the other cases before mentioned, the Supreme Court shall have appellate jurisdiction, both as to law and fact, with such exceptions, and under such regulations as the Congress shall make.

The trial of all crimes, except in cases of impeachment, shall be by jury; and such trial shall be held in the state where the said crimes shall have been committed; but when not committed within any state, the trial shall be at such place or places as the Congress may by law have directed.

Section 3. Treason against the United States, shall consist only in levying war against them, or in adhering to their enemies, giving them aid and comfort. No person shall be convicted of treason unless on the testimony of two witnesses to the same overt act, or on confession in open court.

The Congress shall have power to declare the punishment of treason, but no attainder of treason shall work corruption of blood, or forfeiture except during the life of the person attainted.

Article IV

Section 1. Full faith and credit shall be given in each state to the public acts, records, and judicial proceedings of every other state. And the Congress may by general laws prescribe the manner in which such acts, records, and proceedings shall be proved, and the effect thereof.

Section 2. The citizens of each state shall be entitled to all privileges and immunities of citizens in the several states.

A person charged in any state with treason, felony, or other crime, who shall flee from justice, and be found in another state, shall on demand of the executive authority of the state from which he fled, be delivered up, to be removed to the state having jurisdiction of the crime.

No person held to service or labor in one state, under the laws thereof, escaping into another, shall, in consequence of any law or regulation therein, be discharged from such service or labor, but shall be delivered up on claim of the party to whom such service or labor may be due.

Section 3. New states may be admitted by the Congress into this union; but no new states shall be formed or erected within the jurisdiction of any other state; nor any state be formed by the junction of two or more states, or parts of states, without the consent of the legislatures of the states concerned as well as of the Congress.

The Congress shall have power to dispose of and make all needful rules and regulations respecting the territory or other property belonging to the United States; and nothing in this Constitution shall be so construed as to prejudice any claims of the United States, or of any particular state.

Section 4. The United States shall guarantee to every state in this union a republican form of government, and shall protect each of them against invasion; and on application of the legislature, or of the executive (when the legislature cannot be convened) against domestic violence.

Article V

The Congress, whenever two thirds of both houses shall deem it necessary, shall propose amendments to this Constitution, or, on the application of the legislatures of two thirds of the several states, shall call a convention for proposing amendments, which, in either case, shall be valid to all intents and purposes, as part of this Constitution, when ratified by the legislatures of three fourths of the several states, or by conventions in three fourths thereof, as the one or the other mode of ratification may be proposed by the Congress; provided that no amendment which may be made prior to the year one thousand eight hundred and eight shall in any manner affect the first and fourth clauses in the ninth section of the first article; and that no state, without its consent, shall be deprived of its equal suffrage in the Senate.

Article VI

All debts contracted and engagements entered into, before the adoption of this Constitution, shall be as valid against the United States under this Constitution, as under the Confederation.

This Constitution, and the laws of the United States which shall be made in pursuance thereof; and all treaties made, or which shall be made, under the authority of the United States, shall be the supreme law of the land; and the judges in every state shall be bound thereby, anything in the Constitution or laws of any State to the contrary notwithstanding.

The Senators and Representatives before mentioned, and the members of the several state legislatures, and all executive and judicial officers, both of the United States and of the several states, shall be bound by oath or affirmation, to support this Constitution; but no religious test shall ever be required as a qualification to any office or public trust under the United States.

Article VII

The ratification of the conventions of nine states, shall be sufficient for the establishment of this Constitution between the states so ratifying the same.

Signers

Done in convention by the unanimous consent of the states present the seventeenth day of September in the year of our Lord one thousand seven hundred and eighty seven and of the independence of the United States of America the twelfth. *In witness whereof We have hereunto subscribed our Names,*

G. Washington—Presidt.
and deputy from Virginia

New Hampshire	John Langdon
	Nicholas Gilman
Massachusetts	Nathaniel Gorham
	Rufus King
Connecticut	Wm: Saml. Johnson
	Roger Sherman
New York	Alexander Hamilton
New Jersey	Wil: Livingston
	David Brearly
	Wm. Paterson
	Jona: Dayton
Pennsylvania	B. Franklin
	Thomas Mifflin
	Robt. Morris
	Geo. Clymer
	Thos. FitzSimons
	Jared Ingersoll
	James Wilson
	Gouv Morris
Delaware	Geo: Read
	Gunning Bedford jun
	John Dickinson
	Richard Bassett
	Jaco: Broom
Maryland	James McHenry
	Dan of St Thos. Jenifer
	Danl Carroll
Virginia	John Blair—
	James Madison Jr.

North Carolina	Wm. Blount
	Richd. Dobbs Spaight
	Hu Williamson
South Carolina	J. Rutledge
	Charles Cotesworth Pinckney
	Charles Pinckney
	Pierce Butler
Georgia	William Few
	Abr Baldwin

Amendments

Note: The first ten Amendments were ratified December 15, 1791, and form what is known as the Bill of Rights.

Amendment 1

Congress shall make no law respecting an establishment of religion, or prohibiting the free exercise thereof; or abridging the freedom of speech, or of the press; or the right of the people peaceably to assemble, and to petition the government for a redress of grievances.

Amendment 2

A well regulated militia, being necessary to the security of a free state, the right of the people to keep and bear arms, shall not be infringed.

Amendment 3

No soldier shall, in time of peace be quartered in any house, without the consent of the owner, nor in time of war, but in a manner to be prescribed by law.

Amendment 4

The right of the people to be secure in their persons, houses, papers, and effects, against unreasonable searches and seizures, shall not be violated, and no warrants shall issue, but upon probable cause, supported by oath or affirmation, and particularly describing the place to be searched, and the persons or things to be seized.

Amendment 5

No person shall be held to answer for a capital, or otherwise infamous crime, unless on a presentment or indictment of a grand jury, except in cases arising in the land or naval forces, or in the militia, when in actual service in time of war or public danger; nor shall any person be subject for the same offense to be twice put in jeopardy of life or limb; nor shall be compelled in any criminal case to be a witness against himself, nor be deprived of life, liberty, or property, without due process of law; nor shall private property be taken for public use, without just compensation.

Amendment 6

In all criminal prosecutions, the accused shall enjoy the right to a speedy and public trial, by an impartial jury of the state and district wherein the crime shall have been committed, which district shall have been previously ascertained by law, and to be informed of the nature and cause of the accusation; to be confronted with the witnesses against him; to have compulsory process for obtaining witnesses in his favor, and to have the assistance of counsel for his defense.

Amendment 7

In suits at common law, where the value in controversy shall exceed twenty dollars, the right of trial by jury shall be preserved, and no fact tried by a jury, shall be otherwise reexamined in any court of the United States, than according to the rules of the common law.

Amendment 8

Excessive bail shall not be required, nor excessive fines imposed, nor cruel and unusual punishments inflicted.

Amendment 9

The enumeration in the Constitution, of certain rights, shall not be construed to deny or disparage others retained by the people.

Amendment 10

The powers not delegated to the United States by the Constitution, nor prohibited by it to the states, are reserved to the states respectively, or to the people.

Amendment 11

(Ratified February 7, 1795)

The judicial power of the United States shall not be construed to extend to any suit in law or equity, commenced or prosecuted against one of the United States by citizens of another state, or by citizens or subjects of any foreign state.

Amendment 12

(Ratified July 27, 1804)

The electors shall meet in their respective states and vote by ballot for President and Vice-President, one of whom, at least, shall not be an inhabitant of the same state with themselves; they shall name in their ballots the person voted for as President, and in distinct ballots the person voted for as Vice-President, and they shall make distinct lists of all persons voted for as President, and of all persons voted for as Vice-President, and of the number of votes for each, which lists they shall sign and certify, and transmit sealed to the seat of the government of the United States, directed to the President of the Senate;—The President of the Senate shall, in the presence of the Senate and House of Representatives, open all the certificates and the votes shall then be counted;—the person having the greatest number of votes for President, shall be the President, if such number be a majority of the whole number of electors appointed; and if no person have such majority, then from the persons having the highest numbers not exceeding three on the list of those voted for as President, the House of Representatives shall choose immediately, by ballot, the President. But in choosing the President, the votes shall be taken by states, the representation from each state having one vote; a quorum for this purpose shall consist of a member or members from two-thirds of the states, and a majority of all the states shall be necessary to a choice. And if the House of Representatives shall not choose a President whenever the right of choice shall devolve upon them, before the fourth day of March next following, then the Vice-President shall act as President, as in the case of the death or other constitutional disability of the President. The person having the greatest number of votes as Vice-President, shall be the Vice-President, if such number be a majority of the whole number of electors appointed, and if no person have a majority, then from the two highest numbers on the list, the Senate shall choose the Vice-President; a quorum for the purpose shall consist of two-thirds of the whole number of Senators, and a majority of the whole number shall be necessary to a choice. But no person constitutionally ineligible to the office of President shall be eligible to that of Vice-President of the United States.

Amendment 13

(Ratified December 6, 1865)

Section 1. Neither slavery nor involuntary servitude, except as a punishment for crime whereof the party shall have been duly convicted, shall exist within the United States, or any place subject to their jurisdiction.

Section 2. Congress shall have power to enforce this article by appropriate legislation.

Amendment 14

(Ratified July 9, 1868)

Section 1. All persons born or naturalized in the United States, and subject to the jurisdiction thereof, are citizens of the United States and of the state wherein they reside. No state shall make or enforce any law which shall abridge the privileges or immunities of citizens of the United States; nor shall any state deprive any person of life, liberty, or property, without due process of law; nor deny to any person within its jurisdiction the equal protection of the laws.

Section 2. Representatives shall be apportioned among the several states according to their respective numbers, counting the whole number of persons in each state, excluding Indians not taxed. But when the right to vote at any election for the choice of electors for President and Vice President of the United States, Representatives in Congress, the executive and judicial officers of a state, or the members of the legislature thereof, is denied to any of the male inhabitants of such state, being twenty-one years of age, and citizens of the United States, or in any way abridged, except for participation in rebellion, or other crime, the basis of representation therein shall be reduced in the proportion which the number of such male citizens shall bear to the whole number of male citizens twenty-one years of age in such state.

Section 3. No person shall be a Senator or Representative in Congress, or elector of President and Vice President, or hold any office, civil or military, under the United States, or under any state, who, having previously taken an oath, as a member of Congress, or as an officer of the United States, or as a member of any state legislature, or as an executive or judicial officer of any state, to support the Constitution of the United States, shall have engaged in insurrection or rebellion against the same, or given aid or comfort to the enemies thereof. But Congress may by a vote of two-thirds of each House, remove such disability.

Section 4. The validity of the public debt of the United States, authorized by law, including debts incurred for payment of pensions and bounties for services in suppressing insurrection or rebellion, shall not be questioned. But neither the United States nor any state shall assume or pay any debt or obligation incurred in aid of insurrection or rebellion against the United States, or any claim for the loss or emancipation of any slave; but all such debts, obligations and claims shall be held illegal and void.

Section 5. The Congress shall have power to enforce, by appropriate legislation, the provisions of this article.

Amendment 15

(Ratified February 3, 1870)

Section 1. The right of citizens of the United States to vote shall not be denied or abridged by the United States or by any state on account of race, color, or previous condition of servitude.

Section 2. The Congress shall have power to enforce this article by appropriate legislation.

Amendment 16

(Ratified February 3, 1913)

The Congress shall have power to lay and collect taxes on incomes, from whatever source derived, without apportionment among the several states, and without regard to any census or enumeration.

Amendment 17

(Ratified April 8, 1913)

The Senate of the United States shall be composed of two Senators from each state, elected by the people thereof, for six years; and each Senator shall have one vote. The electors in each state shall have the qualifications requisite for electors of the most numerous branch of the state legislatures.

When vacancies happen in the representation of any state in the Senate, the executive authority of such state shall issue writs of election to fill such vacancies: Provided, that the legislature of any state may empower the executive thereof to make temporary appointments until the people fill the vacancies by election as the legislature may direct.

This amendment shall not be so construed as to affect the election or term of any Senator chosen before it becomes valid as part of the Constitution.

Amendment 18

(Ratified January 16, 1919. Repealed December 5, 1933 by Amendment 21)

Section 1. After one year from the ratification of this article the manufacture, sale, or transportation of intoxicating liquors within, the importation thereof into, or the exportation thereof from the United States and all territory subject to the jurisdiction thereof for beverage purposes is hereby prohibited.

Section 2. The Congress and the several states shall have concurrent power to enforce this article by appropriate legislation.

Section 3. This article shall be inoperative unless it shall have been ratified as an amendment to the Constitution by the legislatures of the several states, as provided in the Constitution, within seven years from the date of the submission hereof to the states by the Congress.

Amendment 19

(Ratified August 18, 1920)

The right of citizens of the United States to vote shall not be denied or abridged by the United States or by any state on account of sex.
 Congress shall have power to enforce this article by appropriate legislation.

Amendment 20

(Ratified January 23, 1933)

Section 1. The terms of the President and Vice President shall end at noon on the 20th day of January, and the terms of Senators and Representatives at noon on the 3d day of January, of the years in which such terms would have ended if this article had not been ratified; and the terms of their successors shall then begin.

Section 2. The Congress shall assemble at least once in every year, and such meeting shall begin at noon on the 3d day of January, unless they shall by law appoint a different day.

Section 3. If, at the time fixed for the beginning of the term of the President, the President elect shall have died, the Vice President elect shall become President. If a President shall not have been chosen before the time fixed for the beginning of his term, or if the President elect shall have failed to qualify, then the Vice President elect shall act as President until a President shall have qualified; and the Congress may by law provide for the case wherein neither a President elect nor a Vice President elect shall have qualified, declaring who shall then act as President, or the manner in which one who is to act shall be selected, and such person shall act accordingly until a President or Vice President shall have qualified.

Section 4. The Congress may by law provide for the case of the death of any of the persons from whom the House of Representatives may choose a President whenever the right of choice shall have devolved upon them, and for the case of the death of any of the persons from whom the Senate may choose a Vice President whenever the right of choice shall have devolved upon them.

Section 5. Sections 1 and 2 shall take effect on the 15th day of October following the ratification of this article.

Section 6. This article shall be inoperative unless it shall have been ratified as an amendment to the Constitution by the legislatures of three-fourths of the several states within seven years from the date of its submission.

Amendment 21

(Ratified December 5, 1933)

Section 1. The eighteenth article of amendment to the Constitution of the United States is hereby repealed.

Section 2. The transportation or importation into any state, territory, or possession of the United States for delivery or use therein of intoxicating liquors, in violation of the laws thereof, is hereby prohibited.

Section 3. This article shall be inoperative unless it shall have been ratified as an amendment to the Constitution by conventions in the several states, as provided in the Constitution, within seven years from the date of the submission hereof to the states by the Congress.

Amendment 22

(Ratified February 27, 1951)

Section 1. No person shall be elected to the office of the President more than twice, and no person who has held the office of President, or acted as President, for more than two years of a term to which some other person was elected President shall be elected to the office of the President more than once. But this article shall not apply to any person holding the office of President when this article was proposed by the Congress, and shall not prevent any person who may be holding the office of President, or acting as President, during the term within which this article becomes operative from holding the office of President or acting as President during the remainder of such term.

Section 2. This article shall be inoperative unless it shall have been ratified as an amendment to the Constitution by the legislatures of three-fourths of the several states within seven years from the date of its submission to the states by the Congress.

Amendment 23

(Ratified March 29, 1961)

Section 1. The District constituting the seat of government of the United States shall appoint in such manner as the Congress may direct:
   A number of electors of President and Vice President equal to the whole number of Senators and Representatives in Congress to which the District would be entitled if it were a state, but in no event more than the least populous state; they shall be in addition to those

appointed by the states, but they shall be considered, for the purposes of the election of President and Vice President, to be electors appointed by a state; and they shall meet in the District and perform such duties as provided by the twelfth article of amendment.

Section 2. The Congress shall have power to enforce this article by appropriate legislation.

Amendment 24

(Ratified January 23, 1964)

Section 1. The right of citizens of the United States to vote in any primary or other election for President or Vice President, for electors for President or Vice President, or for Senator or Representative in Congress, shall not be denied or abridged by the United States or any state by reason of failure to pay any poll tax or other tax.

Section 2. The Congress shall have power to enforce this article by appropriate legislation.

Amendment 25

(Ratified February 10, 1967)

Section 1. In case of the removal of the President from office or of his death or resignation, the Vice President shall become President.

Section 2. Whenever there is a vacancy in the office of the Vice President, the President shall nominate a Vice President who shall take office upon confirmation by a majority vote of both Houses of Congress.

Section 3. Whenever the President transmits to the President pro tempore of the Senate and the Speaker of the House of Representatives his written declaration that he is unable to discharge the powers and duties of his office, and until he transmits to them a written declaration to the contrary, such powers and duties shall be discharged by the Vice President as Acting President.

Section 4. Whenever the Vice President and a majority of either the principal officers of the executive departments or of such other body as Congress may by law provide, transmit to the President pro tempore of the Senate and the Speaker of the House of Representatives their written declaration that the President is unable to discharge the powers and duties of his office, the Vice President shall immediately assume the powers and duties of the office as Acting President.

Thereafter, when the President transmits to the President pro tempore of the Senate and the Speaker of the House of Representatives his written declaration that no inability exists, he shall resume the powers and duties of his office unless the Vice President and a majority of either the principal officers of the executive department or of such other body as Congress may by law provide, transmit within four days to the President pro tempore of the Senate and the Speaker of the House of Representatives their written declaration that the President is unable to discharge the powers and duties of his office. Thereupon Congress shall decide the issue, assembling within forty-eight hours for that purpose if not in session. If the Congress, within twenty-one days after receipt of the latter written declaration, or, if Congress is not in session, within twenty-one days after Congress is required to assemble, determines by two-thirds vote of both Houses that the President is unable to discharge the powers and duties of his office, the Vice President shall continue to discharge the same as Acting President; otherwise, the President shall resume the powers and duties of his office.

Amendment 26

(Ratified July 1, 1971)

Section 1. The right of citizens of the United States, who are 18 years of age or older, to vote, shall not be denied or abridged by the United States or any state on account of age.

Section 2. The Congress shall have the power to enforce this article by appropriate legislation.

Amendment 27

(Ratified May 7, 1992)

No law, varying the compensation for the services of the Senators and Representatives, shall take effect, until an election of Representatives shall have intervened.

For more information on the Constitution and the Charters of Freedom, see http://archives.gov/exhibits/charters/constitution.html

THE GOVERNMENT OF THE UNITED STATES

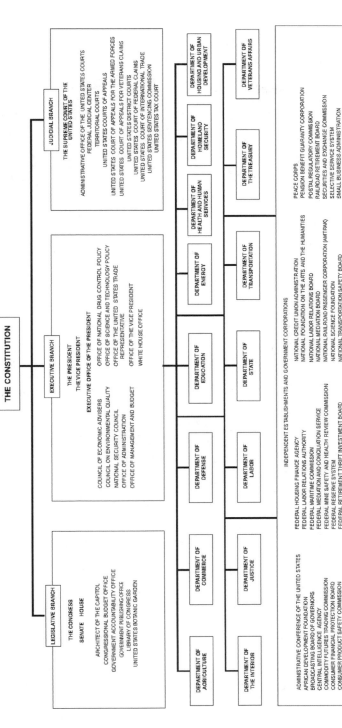

THE CONSTITUTION

LEGISLATIVE BRANCH

THE CONGRESS

SENATE   HOUSE

ARCHITECT OF THE CAPITOL
CONGRESSIONAL BUDGET OFFICE
GOVERNMENT ACCOUNTABILITY OFFICE
GOVERNMENT PUBLISHING OFFICE
LIBRARY OF CONGRESS
UNITED STATES BOTANIC GARDEN

EXECUTIVE BRANCH

THE PRESIDENT
THE VICE PRESIDENT

EXECUTIVE OFFICE OF THE PRESIDENT

COUNCIL OF ECONOMIC ADVISERS
COUNCIL ON ENVIRONMENTAL QUALITY
NATIONAL SECURITY COUNCIL
OFFICE OF ADMINISTRATION
OFFICE OF MANAGEMENT AND BUDGET

OFFICE OF NATIONAL DRUG CONTROL POLICY
OFFICE OF SCIENCE AND TECHNOLOGY POLICY
OFFICE OF THE UNITED STATES TRADE
REPRESENTATIVE
OFFICE OF THE VICE PRESIDENT
WHITE HOUSE OFFICE

JUDICIAL BRANCH

THE SUPREME COURT OF THE
UNITED STATES

ADMINISTRATIVE OFFICE OF THE UNITED STATES COURTS
FEDERAL JUDICIAL CENTER
TERRITORIAL COURTS
UNITED STATES COURTS OF APPEALS
UNITED STATES COURT OF APPEALS FOR THE ARMED FORCES
UNITED STATES COURT OF APPEALS FOR VETERANS CLAIMS
UNITED STATES DISTRICT COURTS
UNITED STATES COURT OF FEDERAL CLAIMS
UNITED STATES COURT OF INTERNATIONAL TRADE
UNITED STATES SENTENCING COMMISSION
UNITED STATES TAX COURT

DEPARTMENT OF AGRICULTURE

DEPARTMENT OF COMMERCE

DEPARTMENT OF DEFENSE

DEPARTMENT OF EDUCATION

DEPARTMENT OF ENERGY

DEPARTMENT OF HEALTH AND HUMAN SERVICES

DEPARTMENT OF HOMELAND SECURITY

DEPARTMENT OF HOUSING AND URBAN DEVELOPMENT

DEPARTMENT OF THE INTERIOR

DEPARTMENT OF JUSTICE

DEPARTMENT OF LABOR

DEPARTMENT OF STATE

DEPARTMENT OF TRANSPORTATION

DEPARTMENT OF THE TREASURY

DEPARTMENT OF VETERANS AFFAIRS

INDEPENDENT ESTABLISHMENTS AND GOVERNMENT CORPORATIONS

ADMINISTRATIVE CONFERENCE OF THE UNITED STATES
AFRICAN DEVELOPMENT FOUNDATION
BROADCASTING BOARD OF GOVERNORS
CENTRAL INTELLIGENCE AGENCY
COMMODITY FUTURES TRADING COMMISSION
CONSUMER FINANCIAL PROTECTION BUREAU
CONSUMER PRODUCT SAFETY COMMISSION
CORPORATION FOR NATIONAL AND COMMUNITY SERVICE
DEFENSE NUCLEAR FACILITIES SAFETY BOARD
ENVIRONMENTAL PROTECTION AGENCY
EQUAL EMPLOYMENT OPPORTUNITY COMMISSION
EXPORT-IMPORT BANK OF THE UNITED STATES
FARM CREDIT ADMINISTRATION
FEDERAL COMMUNICATIONS COMMISSION
FEDERAL DEPOSIT INSURANCE CORPORATION
FEDERAL ELECTION COMMISSION

FEDERAL HOUSING FINANCE AGENCY
FEDERAL LABOR RELATIONS AUTHORITY
FEDERAL MARITIME COMMISSION
FEDERAL MEDIATION AND CONCILIATION SERVICE
FEDERAL MINE SAFETY AND HEALTH REVIEW COMMISSION
FEDERAL RESERVE SYSTEM
FEDERAL RETIREMENT THRIFT INVESTMENT BOARD
FEDERAL TRADE COMMISSION
GENERAL SERVICES ADMINISTRATION
INTER-AMERICAN FOUNDATION
MERIT SYSTEMS PROTECTION BOARD
NATIONAL AERONAUTICS AND SPACE ADMINISTRATION
NATIONAL ARCHIVES AND RECORDS ADMINISTRATION
NATIONAL CAPITAL PLANNING COMMISSION

NATIONAL CREDIT UNION ADMINISTRATION
NATIONAL FOUNDATION ON THE ARTS AND THE HUMANITIES
NATIONAL LABOR RELATIONS BOARD
NATIONAL MEDIATION BOARD
NATIONAL RAILROAD PASSENGER CORPORATION (AMTRAK)
NATIONAL SCIENCE FOUNDATION
NATIONAL TRANSPORTATION SAFETY BOARD
NUCLEAR REGULATORY COMMISSION
OCCUPATIONAL SAFETY AND HEALTH REVIEW COMMISSION
OFFICE OF THE DIRECTOR OF NATIONAL INTELLIGENCE
OFFICE OF GOVERNMENT ETHICS
OFFICE OF PERSONNEL MANAGEMENT
OFFICE OF SPECIAL COUNSEL
OVERSEAS PRIVATE INVESTMENT CORPORATION

PEACE CORPS
PENSION BENEFIT GUARANTY CORPORATION
POSTAL REGULATORY COMMISSION
RAILROAD RETIREMENT BOARD
SECURITIES AND EXCHANGE COMMISSION
SELECTIVE SERVICE SYSTEM
SMALL BUSINESS ADMINISTRATION
SOCIAL SECURITY ADMINISTRATION
TENNESSEE VALLEY AUTHORITY
TRADE AND DEVELOPMENT AGENCY
UNITED STATES AGENCY FOR INTERNATIONAL DEVELOPMENT
UNITED STATES COMMISSION ON CIVIL RIGHTS
UNITED STATES INTERNATIONAL TRADE COMMISSION
UNITED STATES POSTAL SERVICE

Legislative Branch

LEGISLATIVE BRANCH

CONGRESS
ONE HUNDRED AND SEVENTEENTH CONGRESS
http://www.congress.gov

The Congress of the United States was created by Article I, section 1, of the Constitution, adopted by the Constitutional Convention on September 17, 1787, providing that "All legislative Powers herein granted shall be vested in a Congress of the United States, which shall consist of a Senate and House of Representatives."

The first Congress under the Constitution met on March 4, 1789, in the Federal Hall in New York City. The membership then consisted of 20 Senators and 59 Representatives.*

Congressional Record Proceedings of Congress are published in the Congressional Record, which is issued each day when Congress is in session. Publication of the Record began March 4, 1873. It was the first record of debate officially reported, printed, and published directly by the Federal Government. The Daily Digest of the Congressional Record, printed in the back of each issue of the Record, summarizes the proceedings of that day in each House and each of their committees and subcommittees, respectively. The Digest also presents the legislative program for each day and, at the end of the week, gives the program for the following week. Its publication was begun March 17, 1947.

Congressional Record (Bound), 1873–2016 https://www.govinfo.gov/app/collection/crecb

Congressional Record (Daily), 1994–Present https://www.govinfo.gov/app/collection/CREC

Sessions Article I, section 4, of the Constitution makes it mandatory that "The Congress shall assemble at least once in every Year. . . ." Under this provision,

also, the date for convening Congress was designated originally as the first Monday in December, "unless they shall by Law appoint a different Day." Eighteen acts were passed, up to 1820, providing for the meeting of Congress on other days of the year. From 1820 to 1934, however, Congress met regularly on the first Monday in December. In 1934 the 20th amendment changed the convening of Congress to January 3, unless Congress "shall by law appoint a different day." In addition, the President, according to Article II, section 3, of the Constitution "may, on extraordinary Occasions, convene both Houses, or either of them, and in Case of Disagreement between them, with Respect to the Time of Adjournment, he may adjourn them to such Time as he shall think proper. . . ." https://www.archives.gov/founding-docs/constitution-transcript#toc-section-4-

Powers of Congress Article I, section 8, of the Constitution defines the powers of Congress. Included are the powers to assess and collect taxes—called the chief power; to regulate commerce, both interstate and foreign; to coin money; to establish post offices and post roads; to establish courts inferior to the Supreme Court; to declare war; and to raise and maintain an army and navy. Congress is further empowered "To provide for calling forth the Militia to execute the Laws of the Union, suppress

---

*New York ratified the Constitution on July 26, 1788, but did not elect its Senators until July 15 and 16, 1789. North Carolina did not ratify the Constitution until November 21, 1789; Rhode Island ratified it on May 29, 1790.

Insurrections and repel Invasions;" and "To make all Laws which shall be necessary and proper for carrying into Execution the foregoing Powers, and all other Powers vested by this Constitution in the Government of the United States, or in any Department or Officer thereof." https://www. archives.gov/founding-docs/constitution-transcript#toc-section-8-

Amendments to the Constitution Another power vested in the Congress is the right to propose amendments to the Constitution, whenever two-thirds of both Houses shall deem it necessary. Should two-thirds of the State legislatures demand changes in the Constitution, it is the duty of Congress to call a constitutional convention. Proposed amendments shall be valid as part of the Constitution when ratified by the legislatures or by conventions of three-fourths of the States, as one or the other mode of ratification may be proposed by Congress.

Prohibitions Upon Congress Article I, section 9, of the Constitution also imposes prohibitions upon Congress. "The Privilege of the Writ of Habeas Corpus shall not be suspended, unless when in Cases of Rebellion or Invasion the public Safety may require it." A bill of attainder or an ex post facto law cannot be passed. No export duty can be imposed. Ports of one State cannot be given preference over those of another State. "No money shall be drawn from the Treasury, but in Consequence of Appropriations made by Law. . . ." No title of nobility may be granted. https://www. archives.gov/founding-docs/constitution-transcript#toc-section-9-

Rights of Members According to Article I, section 6, Members of Congress are granted certain privileges. In no case, except in treason, felony, and breach of the peace, can Members be arrested while attending sessions of Congress "and in going to and returning from the same. . . ." Furthermore, the Members cannot be questioned in any other place for remarks made in Congress. Each House may expel a Member of its body by a two-thirds vote. https://www. archives.gov/founding-docs/constitution-transcript#toc-section-6-

Enactment of Laws In order to become law, all bills and joint resolutions, except those proposing a constitutional amendment, must pass both the House of Representatives and the Senate and either be signed by the President or be passed over the President's veto by a two-thirds vote of both Houses of Congress. Section 7 of Article I states: "If any Bill shall not be returned by the President within ten Days (Sundays excepted) after it shall have been presented to him, the Same shall be a Law, in like Manner as if he had signed it, unless the Congress by their Adjournment prevent its Return, in which Case it shall not be a Law." When a bill or joint resolution is introduced in the House, the usual procedure for its enactment into law is as follows: assignment to House committee having jurisdiction; if favorably considered, it is reported to the House either in its original form or with recommended amendments; if the bill or resolution is passed by the House, it is messaged to the Senate and referred to the committee having jurisdiction; in the Senate committee the bill, if favorably considered, may be reported in the form as received from the House, or with recommended amendments; the approved bill or resolution is reported to the Senate, and if passed by that body, is returned to the House; if one body does not accept the amendments to a bill by the other body, a conference committee comprised of Members of both bodies is usually appointed to effect a compromise; when the bill or joint resolution is finally approved by both Houses, it is signed by the Speaker (or Speaker pro tempore) and the Vice President (or President pro tempore or acting President pro tempore) and is presented to the President; and once the President's signature is affixed, the measure becomes a law. If the President vetoes the bill, it cannot become a law unless it is re-passed by a two-thirds vote of both Houses.

The Senate

The Capitol, Washington, DC 20510
Phone, 202-224-3121. Internet,http://www.senate.gov

Constitutionally Mandated Officers	
President of the Senate / Vice President of the United States	KAMALA D. HARRIS
President pro tempore	PATRICK J. LEAHY
http://www.senate.gov/senators/leadership.htm	
Political Party Leaders	
Majority Leader—Democrat	CHARLES E. SCHUMER
Minority Leader—Republican	A. MITCHELL MCCONNELL
https://www.senate.gov/artandhistory/history/common/briefing/ Majority_Minority_Leaders.htm#3	
Senate-Elected Officers and Officials	
Chaplain	BARRY C. BLACK
Parliamentarian	ELIZABETH C. MACDONOUGH
SECRETARIES	
for the Majority	GARY B. MYRICK
for the Minority	ROBERT M. DUNCAN
for the Senate	SONCERIA BERRY
Sergeant at Arms	JENNIFER A. HEMINGWAY, ACTING
https://www.senate.gov/history/officers.htm	

The above list of key personnel was updated 3–2021.

Overview The Senate comprises 100 Members, 2 from each State. Senators are elected to serve for a term of 6 years. There are three classes of Senators, and a new class is elected every 2 years. Senators were originally chosen by the State legislatures. The 17th amendment, which became part of the Constitution in 1913, made their election a function of the people.

A Senator must be a resident of the State that he or she represents. A Senator also must be at least 30 years of age and have been a U.S. citizen for at least 9 years.
Officers The Vice President of the United States is the Presiding Officer of the Senate. In the Vice President's absence, the duties are taken over by a President pro tempore, elected by that body, or someone designated by the President pro tempore.

The positions of Senate Majority and Minority Leader have been in existence only since the early years of the 20th century. Leaders are elected at the beginning of each new Congress by a majority vote of the Senators in their political party. In cooperation with their party organizations, Leaders are responsible for the design and achievement of a legislative program. This involves managing the flow of legislation, expediting noncontroversial measures, and keeping Members informed regarding proposed action on pending business. Each Leader serves as an ex officio member of his party's policymaking and organizational bodies and is aided by an assistant floor leader (whip) and a party secretary.

The Secretary of the Senate, elected by vote of the Senate, performs the duties of the Presiding Officer of the Senate in the absence of the Vice President and pending the election of a President pro tempore. The Secretary is the custodian of the seal of the Senate, draws requisitions on the Secretary of the Treasury for moneys appropriated for the compensation of Senators, officers, and employees, and for the contingent expenses of the Senate, and is empowered to administer oaths to any officer of the Senate and to any witness produced before it. The Secretary's executive duties include certification of extracts from the Journal of the Senate; the attestation of bills and joint, concurrent, and Senate resolutions; in impeachment trials, issuance, under the authority of the Presiding Officer, of all orders, mandates, writs, and precepts authorized by the Senate; and certification to the President of the United States of the advice and consent of the Senate to ratification of treaties and the names of persons confirmed or rejected upon the nomination of the President.

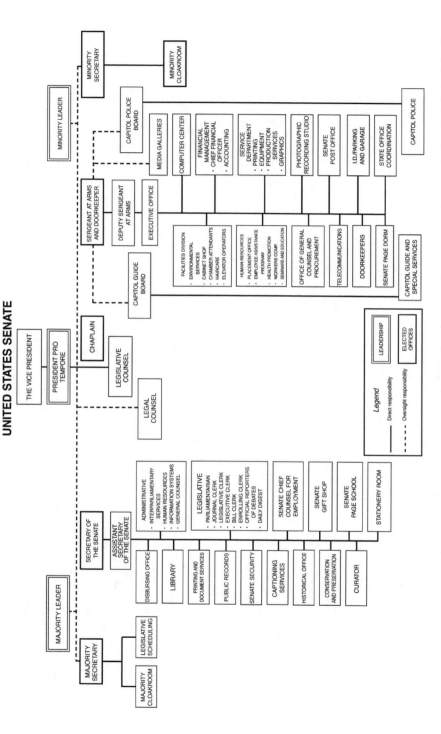

The Sergeant at Arms, elected by vote of the Senate, serves as the executive, chief law enforcement, and protocol officer and is the principal administrative manager for most support services in the Senate. As executive officer, the Sergeant at Arms has custody of the Senate gavel; enforces Senate rules and regulations as they pertain to the Senate Chamber, the Senate wing of the Capitol, and the Senate office buildings; and subject to the Presiding Officer, maintains order on the Senate floor, Chamber, and galleries. As chief law enforcement officer of the Senate, the Sergeant at Arms is authorized to maintain security in the Capitol and all Senate buildings, as well as to protect Senators; to arrest and detain any person violating Senate rules; and to locate absentee Senators for a quorum. The Sergeant at Arms serves as a member of the Capitol Police Board and as its chairman each odd year. As protocol officer, the Sergeant at Arms escorts the President and other heads of state or official guests of the Senate who are attending official functions in the Capitol; makes arrangements for funerals of Senators who die in office; and assists in planning the inauguration of the President and organizing the swearing-in and orientation programs for newly elected Senators.

Committees   The work of preparing and considering legislation is done largely by committees of both Houses of Congress. There are 16 standing committees in the Senate. The standing committees of the Senate are shown in the list below. In addition, there are two select committees in each House and various congressional commissions and joint committees composed of Members of both Houses. Each House may also appoint special investigating committees. The membership of the standing committees of each House is chosen by a vote of the entire body; members of other committees are appointed under the provisions of the measure establishing them.

Each bill and resolution is usually referred to the appropriate committee, which may report a bill out in its original form, favorably or unfavorably, recommend amendments, report original measures, or allow the proposed legislation to die in committee without action. http://www.senate.gov/general/common/generic/about_committees.htm

Standing Committees of the Senate

Committee	Chair	Website
Agriculture, Nutrition, and Forestry	Deborah A. Stabenow	http://www.agriculture.senate.gov
Appropriations	Patrick J. Leahy	http://www.appropriations.senate.gov
Armed Services	John F. Reed	http://www.armed-services.senate.gov
Banking, Housing, and Urban Affairs	Sherrod C. Brown	http://www.banking.senate.gov
Budget	Bernard Sanders	http://www.budget.senate.gov
Commerce, Science, and Transportation	Maria E. Cantwell	http://www.commerce.senate.gov
Energy and Natural Resources	Joseph A. Manchin III	https://www.energy.senate.gov
Environment and Public Works	Thomas R. Carper	https://www.epw.senate.gov
Finance	Ronald L. Wyden	https://www.finance.senate.gov
Foreign Relations	Robert Menendez	http://www.foreign.senate.gov
Health, Education, Labor, and Pensions	Patricia L. Murray	http://www.help.senate.gov
Homeland Security and Governmental Affairs	Gary C. Peters	https://www.hsgac.senate.gov
Indian Affairs	Brian E. Schatz	https://www.indian.senate.gov
Judiciary	Richard J. Durbin	https://www.judiciary.senate.gov
Rules and Administration	Amy J. Klobuchar	http://www.rules.senate.gov
Small Business and Entrepreneurship	Benjamin L. Cardin	http://www.sbc.senate.gov
Veterans' Affairs	R. Jon Tester	https://www.veterans.senate.gov

The above list of committee chairs was updated 2–2021. https://www.senate.gov/committees/committees_home.htm

Special Powers   Under the Constitution, the Senate is granted certain powers not accorded to the House of Representatives. The Senate approves or disapproves certain Presidential appointments by majority vote, and treaties must be concurred in by a two-thirds vote.

List of U.S. Senators

State	Expiration of Term—Party Affiliation	Contact Information
Alabama		
Richard C. Shelby	2023—Republican	http://www.shelby.senate.gov
Thomas H. Tuberville	2027—Republican	https://www.tuberville.senate.gov
Alaska		
Lisa A. Murkowski	2023—Republican	https://www.murkowski.senate.gov
Daniel S. Sullivan	2027—Republican	http://www.sullivan.senate.gov
Arizona		
Mark E. Kelly	2023—Democrat	https://www.kelly.senate.gov
Kyrsten Sinema	2025—Democrat	https://www.sinema.senate.gov
Arkansas		
John N. Boozman	2023—Republican	https://www.boozman.senate.gov
Thomas B. Cotton	2027—Republican	https://www.cotton.senate.gov
California		
Dianne Feinstein	2025—Democrat	http://www.feinstein.senate.gov
Alejandro Padilla	2023—Democrat	https://www.padilla.senate.gov
Colorado		
Michael F. Bennet	2023—Democrat	https://www.bennet.senate.gov
John W. Hickenlooper	2027—Democrat	https://www.hickenlooper.senate.gov
Connecticut		
Richard L. Blumenthal	2023—Democrat	https://www.blumenthal.senate.gov
Christopher S. Murphy	2025—Democrat	https://www.murphy.senate.gov
Delaware		
Thomas R. Carper	2025—Democrat	https://www.carper.senate.gov
Christopher A. Coons	2027—Democrat	https://www.coons.senate.gov
Florida		
Marco A. Rubio	2023—Republican	http://www.rubio.senate.gov
Richard L. Scott	2025—Republican	https://www.rickscott.senate.gov
Georgia		
T. Jonathan Ossoff	2027—Democrat	https://www.ossoff.senate.gov
Raphael G. Warnock	2023—Democrat	https://www.warnock.senate.gov
Hawaii		
Mazie K. Hirono	2025—Democrat	https://www.hirono.senate.gov
Brian E. Schatz	2023—Democrat	http://www.schatz.senate.gov
Idaho		
Michael D. Crapo	2023—Republican	http://www.crapo.senate.gov
James E. Risch	2027—Republican	http://www.risch.senate.gov
Illinois		
L. Tammy Duckworth	2023—Democrat	https://www.duckworth.senate.gov
Richard J. Durbin	2027—Democrat	http://www.durbin.senate.gov
Indiana		
Michael K. Braun	2025—Republican	https://www.braun.senate.gov
Todd C. Young	2023—Republican	https://www.young.senate.gov
Iowa		
Joni K. Ernst	2027—Republican	http://www.ernst.senate.gov
Charles E. Grassley	2023—Republican	http://www.grassley.senate.gov

List of U.S. Senators (*Continued*)

State	Expiration of Term—Party Affiliation	Contact Information
Kansas		
Roger W. Marshall	2027—Republican	https://www.marshall.senate.gov
Gerald W. Moran	2023—Republican	http://www.moran.senate.gov
Kentucky		
A. Mitchell McConnell	2027—Republican	http://www.mcconnell.senate.gov
Randal H. Paul	2023—Republican	https://www.paul.senate.gov
Louisiana		
William M. Cassidy	2027—Republican	http://www.cassidy.senate.gov
John N. Kennedy	2023—Republican	https://www.kennedy.senate.gov
Maine		
Susan M. Collins	2027—Republican	https://www.collins.senate.gov
Angus S. King, Jr.	2025—Independent	http://www.king.senate.gov
Maryland		
Benjamin L. Cardin	2025—Democrat	https://www.cardin.senate.gov
Christopher Van Hollen, Jr.	2023—Democrat	https://www.vanhollen.senate.gov
Massachusetts		
Edward J. Markey	2027—Democrat	http://www.markey.senate.gov
Elizabeth A. Warren	2025—Democrat	https://www.warren.senate.gov
Michigan		
Gary C. Peters	2027—Democrat	https://www.peters.senate.gov
Deborah A. Stabenow	2025—Democrat	http://www.stabenow.senate.gov
Minnesota		
Amy J. Klobuchar	2025—Democrat	https://www.klobuchar.senate.gov
Tina F. Smith	2027—Democrat	https://www.smith.senate.gov
Mississippi		
Cindy Hyde-Smith	2027—Republican	https://www.hydesmith.senate.gov
Roger F. Wicker	2025—Republican	https://www.wicker.senate.gov
Missouri		
Roy D. Blunt	2023—Republican	http://www.blunt.senate.gov
Joshua D. Hawley	2025—Republican	https://www.hawley.senate.gov/
Montana		
Steven D. Daines	2027—Republican	https://www.daines.senate.gov
R. Jon Tester	2025—Democrat	http://www.tester.senate.gov
Nebraska		
Debra S. Fischer	2025—Republican	http://www.fischer.senate.gov
Benjamin E. Sasse	2027—Republican	http://www.sasse.senate.gov
Nevada		
Catherine Cortez Masto	2023—Democrat	https://www.cortezmasto.senate.gov
Jacklyn S. Rosen	2025—Democrat	http://www.rosen.senate.gov
New Hampshire		
Margaret Wood Hassan	2023—Democrat	https://www.hassan.senate.gov
C. Jeanne Shaheen	2027—Democrat	https://www.shaheen.senate.gov
New Jersey		
Cory A. Booker	2027—Democrat	http://www.booker.senate.gov
Robert Menendez	2025—Democrat	https://www.menendez.senate.gov

List of U.S. Senators (*Continued*)

State	Expiration Of Term—Party Affiliation	Contact Information
New Mexico		
Martin T. Heinrich	2025—Democrat	http://www.heinrich.senate.gov
Benjamin R. Luján	2027—Democrat	https://www.lujan.senate.gov
New York		
Kirsten E. Gillibrand	2025—Democrat	https://www.gillibrand.senate.gov
Charles E. Schumer	2023—Democrat	https://www.schumer.senate.gov
North Carolina		
Richard M. Burr	2023—Republican	http://www.burr.senate.gov
Thomas R. Tillis	2027—Republican	https://www.tillis.senate.gov
North Dakota		
Kevin Cramer	2025—Republican	http://www.cramer.senate.gov
John H. Hoeven III	2023—Republican	https://www.hoeven.senate.gov
Ohio		
Sherrod C. Brown	2025—Democrat	https://www.brown.senate.gov
Robert J. Portman	2023—Republican	http://www.portman.senate.gov
Oklahoma		
James M. Inhofe	2027—Republican	http://www.inhofe.senate.gov
James Lankford	2023—Republican	https://www.lankford.senate.gov
Oregon		
Jeffrey A. Merkley	2027—Democrat	https://www.merkley.senate.gov
Ronald L. Wyden	2023—Democrat	https://www.wyden.senate.gov
Pennsylvania		
Robert P. Casey, Jr.	2025—Democrat	https://www.casey.senate.gov
Patrick J. Toomey	2023—Republican	http://www.toomey.senate.gov
Rhode Island		
John F. Reed	2027—Democrat	https://www.reed.senate.gov
Sheldon Whitehouse	2025—Democrat	https://www.whitehouse.senate.gov
South Carolina		
Lindsey O. Graham	2027—Republican	https://www.lgraham.senate.gov
Timothy E. Scott	2023—Republican	https://www.scott.senate.gov
South Dakota		
M. Michael Rounds	2027—Republican	https://www.rounds.senate.gov
John R. Thune	2023—Republican	https://www.thune.senate.gov
Tennessee		
Marsha W. Blackburn	2025—Republican	https://www.blackburn.senate.gov
William F. Hagerty IV	2027—Republican	https://www.hagerty.senate.gov
Texas		
John Cornyn III	2027—Republican	https://www.cornyn.senate.gov
R. Edward Cruz	2025—Republican	https://www.cruz.senate.gov
Utah		
Michael S. Lee	2023—Republican	https://www.lee.senate.gov
W. Milton Romney	2025—Republican	http://www.romney.senate.gov
Vermont		
Patrick J. Leahy	2023—Democrat	https://www.leahy.senate.gov
Bernard Sanders	2025—Independent	https://www.sanders.senate.gov

List of U.S. Senators (*Continued*)

State	Expiration Of Term—Party Affiliation	Contact Information
Virginia		
Timothy M. Kaine	2025—Democrat	http://www.kaine.senate.gov
Mark R. Warner	2027—Democrat	http://www.warner.senate.gov
Washington		
Maria E. Cantwell	2025—Democrat	https://www.cantwell.senate.gov
Patricia L. Murray	2023—Democrat	http://www.murray.senate.gov
West Virginia		
Shelley Moore Capito	2027—Republican	https://www.capito.senate.gov
Joseph A. Manchin III	2025—Democrat	http://www.manchin.senate.gov
Wisconsin		
Tammy S. Baldwin	2025—Democrat	https://www.baldwin.senate.gov
Ronald H. Johnson	2023—Republican	https://www.ronjohnson.senate.gov
Wyoming		
John A. Barrasso III	2025—Republican	https://www.barrasso.senate.gov
Cynthia M. Lummis	2027—Republican	https://www.lummis.senate.gov

Information on Senate.gov may be more accurate and current. The Above List of 100 Senators was Updated 2–2021. Republicans are 50; Democrats are 48; Independents are 2; and there are no vacancies. https://www.senate.gov/senators/index.htm; https://www.senate.gov/general/contact_information/senators_cfm.cfm?OrderBy=state&Sort=ASC

Sources of Information

Art   The Senate's collections of ephemera, decorative art, graphic art, paintings, and sculpture can be viewed online. https://www.senate.gov/art/art_hist_home.htm | Email: curator@sec.senate.gov

Biographical Directory   The online "Biographical Directory of the United States Congress, 1774–Present," allows visitors to search for Members of Congress— past and present—by first or last name, political affiliation, position, State, or year or Congress. http://bioguide.congress.gov/biosearch/biosearch.asp

Books by Senators   A bibliography of books that Senators who are currently serving in the U.S. Congress have written is available online. https://www.senate.gov/senators/BooksWrittenbySittingSenators.htm

Campaign Finance   The Federal Election Commission maintains a campaign finance database that contains information on candidates, including senatorial candidates, who file reports with the Commission. Users of the online "Candidate and Committee Viewer" can sort data and download them. The data presentations consist of biennial summaries, report summaries, and report images and downloads. http://www.fec.

gov/finance/disclosure/candcmte_info.shtml?tabIndex=1

Campaign Websites   The Library of Congress maintains a database of "Archived Web Sites" that includes thousands of official campaign websites. Former senatorial candidates' websites are part of this collection. https://www.loc.gov/websites

Career Opportunities   Information on fellowships, internships, and job openings is available online. http://www.senate.gov/visiting/employment.htm

Chaplains of the Senate   Nine of the first ten Senate Chaplains were Episcopalian; one was Presbyterian. Based on a simple denominational count, the history of the Senate chaplaincy has been dominated by Episcopalians (19), Methodists (17), and Presbyterians (14). The total number of chaplains who have filled the office of Senate Chaplain to date is 62. https://www.senate.gov/artandhistory/history/common/briefing/Senate_Chaplain.htm

Children's Books   Links to educational resources are available on the Senate's website. https://www.senate.gov/reference/bibliography/kids/kids.shtml

Committees   Information on Senate committees is available online. http://www.senate.gov/committees/committees_home.htm

Congressional Directory   Prepared by the Joint Committee on Printing, the "Congressional Directory" is the official directory of the U.S. Congress. The Directory contains a short biography of each Member of the Senate; committee memberships, terms of service, administrative assistants and secretaries, and room and telephone numbers for Senators; lists of court officials, military establishments, and other Federal departments and agencies, including District of Columbia government officials, governors of States and territories, foreign diplomats, and members of the press, radio, and television galleries. https://www.govinfo.gov/app/collection/CDIR

Congressional Record   Starting with the year 1995, the official record of the proceedings and debates of the U.S. Congress is available on Congress.gov. https://www.congress.gov/congressional-record

Starting with the year 1994, the official record of the proceedings and debates of the U.S. Congress is available on the Government Publishing Office's govinfo website. https://www.govinfo.gov/app/collection/crec

Contact Information   The address for sending postal correspondence to a Senator or Senate committee is available online. Secretary of the Senate: Phone, 202-224-2115. U.S. Capitol switchboard: Phone, 202-224-3121. https://www.senate.gov/general/contacting.htm

Phone numbers, postal addresses, and online forms are available for contacting a Senator. http://www.senate.gov/senators/contact

An online list of States also provides web forms for contacting a Senator via email. http://www.senate.gov/senators/states.htm

Glossary   A Senate glossary is available online. http://www.senate.gov/reference/glossary.htm

History   The Senate Historical Office has told the history of the Senate, from the First Federal Congress of 1789 through the early 21st century; explained its traditions; described the individuals who served in its Chamber, and examined the major issues that confronted these national leaders. http://www.senate.gov/pagelayout/history/a_three_section_with_teasers/Explore_Senate_

History.htm | Email: historian@sec.senate.gov

How To . . .   Many congressional and other Government documents are available online. The Senate's website has resources that explain how to find materials related to the Senate and the general legislative process. https://www.senate.gov/reference/howto.htm

Legislation / Records   Research guides and resources are available online. http://www.senate.gov/legislative/legislative_home.htm

Member Profiles   The "Members of the U.S. Congress" database contains profiles for Senators who have held office since 1973 or were still serving in the 93d Congress. Users of the database can filter profiles by chamber, Congress, political affiliation, and State or U.S. Territory. A Member profile includes the following: dates of service, State represented, party affiliation, and a picture when available, as well as a link to the Member's entry in the "Biographical Directory of the United States Congress, 1774–Present" and a link to remarks made in the "Congressional Record." A profile also includes the list of legislation that the Member sponsored and cosponsored. https://www.congress.gov/members

Publications   The "Congressional Directory," the "Senate Manual," and telephone directory for the U.S. Senate are available from the Government Publishing Office's bookstore. Phone, 202-512-0132. https://bookstore.gpo.gov/agency/congress-legislative-branch | Email: mainbks@gpo.gov

States Represented by Senators   The "States in the Senate" web page provides a short description of each State's history in the U.S. Senate. http://www.senate.gov/states/statesmap.htm

Statistics / Lists   Statistics on and lists regarding a variety of topics—including cloture, nominations, roll call votes, Senate history, senators, and much more—are available online. https://www.senate.gov/reference/stats_and_lists.htm

Websites   More information on legislation and the U.S. Senate is available on Congress.gov. https://www.congress.gov

More information also is available on the Government Publishing Office's govinfo website. https://www.govinfo.gov

The above Sources of Information for the Senate were updated 2–2021.

The House of Representatives

The Capitol, Washington, DC 20515
Phone, 202-225-3121. Internet, http://www.house.gov

Constitutionally Mandated Officer
Speaker of the House   NANCY P. PELOSI
https://www.speaker.gov

Political Party Leaders
Majority Leader   STENY H. HOYER
Minority Leader   KEVIN O. MCCARTHY
https://www.house.gov/leadership

Appointed Officials
General Counsel   DOUGLAS N. LETTER
Historian   MATTHEW A. WASNIEWSKI
Inspector General   MICHAEL PTASIENSKI
Parliamentarian   JASON A. SMITH
https://history.house.gov/People/Appointed-Officials/Appointed-
Officials/

Elected Officers
Chaplain   MARGARET G. KIBBEN
Chief Administrative Officer   CATHERINE L. SZPINDOR
Clerk   CHERYL L. JOHNSON
Sergeant at Arms   TIMOTHY P. BLODGETT
https://www.house.gov/the-house-explained/officers-and-organizations

The above list of key personnel was updated 3–2021.

Overview   The House of Representatives comprises 435 Representatives. The number representing each State is determined by population, but every State is entitled to at least one Representative. Members are elected by the people for 2-year terms, all terms running for the same period. Representatives must be residents of the State from which they are chosen. In addition, a Representative must be at least 25 years of age and must have been a citizen for at least 7 years.

A Resident Commissioner from Puerto Rico (elected for a 4-year term) and Delegates from American Samoa, the District of Columbia, Guam, the Northern Mariana Islands, and the Virgin Islands complete the composition of the Congress of the United States. Delegates are elected for a term of 2 years. The Resident Commissioner and Delegates may take part in the floor discussions, but have no vote in the full House. They do, however, vote in the committees to which they are assigned.
Officers   The Presiding Officer of the House of Representatives, the Speaker, is elected by the House. The Speaker may designate any

Member of the House to act in the Speaker's absence.

The House leadership is structured essentially the same as the Senate, with the Members in the political parties responsible for the election of their respective leader and whips.

The elected officers of the House of Representatives include the Clerk, the Sergeant at Arms, the Chief Administrative Officer, and the Chaplain.

The Clerk is custodian of the seal of the House and administers the primary legislative activities of the House. These duties include accepting the credentials of the Members-elect and calling the Members to order at the commencement of the first session of each Congress; keeping the Journal; taking all votes and certifying the passage of bills; and processing all legislation. Through various departments, the Clerk is also responsible for floor and committee reporting services; legislative information and reference services; the administration of House reports pursuant to House rules and certain legislation including the Ethics in Government Act and the Lobbying Disclosure Act of 1995; and the distribution of House documents. The Clerk is also charged with supervision of the offices vacated by Members due to death, resignation, or expulsion.

The Sergeant at Arms maintains the order of the House under the direction of the Speaker and is the keeper of the Mace. As a member of the U.S. Capitol Police Board, the Sergeant at Arms is the chief law enforcement officer for the House and serves as Board Chairman each even year. The ceremonial and protocol duties parallel those of the Senate Sergeant at Arms and include arranging the inauguration of the President of the United States, Joint Sessions of Congress, visits to the House of heads of state, and funerals of Members of Congress. The Sergeant at Arms enforces the rules relating to the privileges of the Hall of the House, including admission to the galleries, oversees garage and parking security of the House, and distributes all House staff identification cards.

Committees   The work of preparing and considering legislation is done largely by committees of both Houses of Congress. There are 19 standing committees in the House of Representatives. The standing committees of the House of Representatives are shown in the list below. In addition, there are two select committees in the House and various congressional commissions and joint committees composed of Members of both Houses. Each House may also appoint special investigating committees. The membership of the standing committees of each House is chosen by a vote of the entire body; members of other committees are appointed under the provisions of the measure establishing them.

Each bill and resolution is usually referred to the appropriate committee, which may report a bill out in its original form, favorably or unfavorably, recommend amendments, report original measures, or allow the proposed legislation to die in committee without action.

Standing Committees of the House of Representatives

Committee	Chair	Website
Agriculture	David A. Scott	http://agriculture.house.gov
Appropriations	Rosa L. DeLauro	http://appropriations.house.gov
Armed Services	D. Adam Smith	https://armedservices.house.gov
Budget	John A. Yarmuth	http://budget.house.gov
Education and Labor	Robert C. Scott	https://edlabor.house.gov
Energy and Commerce	Frank J. Pallone, Jr.	https://energycommerce.house.gov
Ethics	Theodore E. Deutch	http://ethics.house.gov
Financial Services	Maxine M. Waters	http://financialservices.house.gov
Foreign Affairs	Gregory W. Meeks	https://foreignaffairs.house.gov
Homeland Security	Bennie G. Thompson	https://homeland.house.gov
House Administration	Zoe Lofgren	https://cha.house.gov
Judiciary	Jerrold L. Nadler	https://judiciary.house.gov
Natural Resources	Raúl M. Grijalva	http://naturalresources.house.gov
Oversight and Reform	Carolyn B. Maloney	https://oversight.house.gov
Rules	James P. McGovern	https://rules.house.gov
Science, Space, and Technology	Eddie B. Johnson	https://science.house.gov
Small Business	Nydia M. Velázquez	http://smallbusiness.house.gov
Transportation and Infrastructure	Peter A. DeFazio	http://transportation.house.gov
Veterans' Affairs	Mark A. Takano	https://veterans.house.gov
Ways and Means	Richard E. Neal	https://waysandmeans.house.gov

The above list of committee chairs was updated 2–2021. https://www.house.gov/committees

Special Powers   The House of Representatives is granted the power of originating all bills for the raising of revenue. Both Houses of Congress act in impeachment proceedings, which, according to the Constitution, may be instituted against the President, Vice President, and all civil officers of the United States. The House of Representatives has the sole power of impeachment, and the Senate has the sole power to try impeachments.

List of U.S. Representatives

State / District	District—Party Affiliation	Contact Information
Alabama		
Jerry L. Carl, Jr.	01—Republican	https://carl.house.gov
F. Barry Moore	02—Republican	https://barrymoore.house.gov
Michael D. Rogers	03—Republican	https://mikerogers.house.gov
Robert B. Aderholt	04—Republican	https://aderholt.house.gov
Morris J. Brooks, Jr.	05—Republican	https://brooks.house.gov
Gary J. Palmer	06—Republican	https://palmer.house.gov
Terrycina A. Sewell	07—Democrat	https://sewell.house.gov
Alaska		
Donald E. Young	At Large—Republican	http://donyoung.house.gov
American Samoa		
Amata Coleman Radewagen	Delegate—Republican	https://radewagen.house.gov
Arizona		
Thomas C. O'Halleran	01—Democrat	https://ohalleran.house.gov
Ann L. Kirkpatrick	02—Democrat	https://kirkpatrick.house.gov
Raúl M. Grijalva	03—Democrat	https://grijalva.house.gov
Paul A. Gosar	04—Republican	http://gosar.house.gov
Andrew S. Biggs	05—Republican	https://biggs.house.gov
David Schweikert	06—Republican	https://schweikert.house.gov
Ruben M. Gallego	07—Democrat	https://rubengallego.house.gov
Debra Kay Lesko	08—Republican	https://lesko.house.gov
Gregory J. Stanton	09—Democrat	https://stanton.house.gov
Arkansas		
Eric A. Crawford	01—Republican	https://crawford.house.gov
J. French Hill	02—Republican	https://hill.house.gov
Stephen A. Womack	03—Republican	https://womack.house.gov
Bruce E. Westerman	04—Republican	https://westerman.house.gov
California		
Douglas L. LaMalfa	01—Republican	http://lamalfa.house.gov
Jared W. Huffman	02—Democrat	https://huffman.house.gov
John R. Garamendi	03—Democrat	https://garamendi.house.gov
Thomas M. McClintock	04—Republican	https://mcclintock.house.gov
Michael C. Thompson	05—Democrat	https://mikethompson.house.gov
Doris O. Matsui	06—Democrat	https://matsui.house.gov
Amerish B. Bera	07—Democrat	https://bera.house.gov
Jay P. Obernolte	08—Republican	https://obernolte.house.gov
Gerald M. McNerney	09—Democrat	https://mcnerney.house.gov
Joshua K. Harder	10—Democrat	https://harder.house.gov
Mark J. DeSaulnier	11—Democrat	https://desaulnier.house.gov
Nancy P. Pelosi	12—Democrat	https://pelosi.house.gov
Barbara J. Lee	13—Democrat	https://lee.house.gov
K. Jacqueline Speier	14—Democrat	https://speier.house.gov
Eric M. Swalwell	15—Democrat	https://swalwell.house.gov
James M. Costa	16—Democrat	https://costa.house.gov
Ro Khanna	17—Democrat	https://khanna.house.gov
Anna G. Eshoo	18—Democrat	https://eshoo.house.gov
Zoe Lofgren	19—Democrat	https://lofgren.house.gov

List of U.S. Representatives (*Continued*)

State / District	District—Party Affiliation	Contact Information
James V. Panetta	20—Democrat	https://panetta.house.gov
David G. Valadao	21—Republican	https://valadao.house.gov
Devin G. Nunes	22—Republican	https://nunes.house.gov
Kevin O. McCarthy	23—Republican	https://kevinmccarthy.house.gov
Salud O. Carbajal	24—Democrat	https://carbajal.house.gov
Michael Garcia	25—Republican	https://mikegarcia.house.gov
Julia A. Brownley	26—Democrat	https://juliabrownley.house.gov
Judy M. Chu	27—Democrat	https://chu.house.gov
Adam B. Schiff	28—Democrat	https://schiff.house.gov
Antonio Cárdenas	29—Democrat	https://cardenas.house.gov
Bradley J. Sherman	30—Democrat	https://sherman.house.gov
Peter R. Aguilar	31—Democrat	https://aguilar.house.gov
Grace F. Napolitano	32—Democrat	https://napolitano.house.gov
Ted W. Lieu	33—Democrat	https://lieu.house.gov
Jimmy Gomez	34—Democrat	https://gomez.house.gov
Norma J. Torres	35—Democrat	https://torres.house.gov
Raul Ruiz	36—Democrat	https://ruiz.house.gov
Karen R. Bass	37—Democrat	https://bass.house.gov
Linda T. Sánchez	38—Democrat	https://lindasanchez.house.gov
Young Kim	39—Republican	https://youngkim.house.gov
Lucille Roybal-Allard	40—Democrat	https://roybal-allard.house.gov
Mark A. Takano	41—Democrat	https://takano.house.gov
Kenneth S. Calvert	42—Republican	http://calvert.house.gov
Maxine M. Waters	43—Democrat	https://waters.house.gov
Nanette Diaz Barragán	44—Democrat	https://barragan.house.gov
Katherine M. Porter	45—Democrat	https://porter.house.gov
J. Luis Correa	46—Democrat	https://correa.house.gov
Alan S. Lowenthal	47—Democrat	http://lowenthal.house.gov
Michelle Steel	48—Republican	https://steel.house.gov
Michael T. Levin	49—Democrat	https://mikelevin.house.gov
Darrell Issa	50—Republican	https://issa.house.gov
Juan C. Vargas	51—Democrat	http://vargas.house.gov
Scott H. Peters	52—Democrat	http://scottpeters.house.gov
Sara Jacobs	53—Democrat	https://sarajacobs.house.gov
Colorado		
Diana L. DeGette	01—Democrat	http://degette.house.gov
Joseph D. Neguse	02—Democrat	https://neguse.house.gov
Lauren Boebert	03—Republican	https://boebert.house.gov
Kenneth R. Buck	04—Republican	https://buck.house.gov
Douglas L. Lamborn	05—Republican	http://lamborn.house.gov
Jason A. Crow	06—Democrat	https://crow.house.gov
Edwin G. Perlmutter	07—Democrat	https://perlmutter.house.gov
Connecticut		
John B. Larson	01—Democrat	https://larson.house.gov
Joseph D. Courtney	02—Democrat	https://courtney.house.gov
Rosa L. DeLauro	03—Democrat	https://delauro.house.gov
James A. Himes	04—Democrat	https://himes.house.gov
Jahana F. Hayes	05—Democrat	https://hayes.house.gov
Delaware		
Lisa Blunt Rochester	At Large—Democrat	https://bluntrochester.house.gov

List of U.S. Representatives (*Continued*)

State / District	District—Party Affiliation	Contact Information
District of Columbia		
Eleanor Holmes Norton	Delegate—Democrat	https://norton.house.gov
Florida		
Matthew L. Gaetz II	01—Republican	https://gaetz.house.gov
Neal P. Dunn	02—Republican	https://dunn.house.gov
Kathryn Cammack	03—Republican	https://cammack.house.gov
John H. Rutherford	04—Republican	https://rutherford.house.gov
Alfred J. Lawson, Jr.	05—Democrat	https://lawson.house.gov
Michael G. Waltz	06—Republican	https://waltz.house.gov
Stephanie N. Murphy	07—Democrat	https://stephaniemurphy.house.gov
William J. Posey	08—Republican	http://posey.house.gov
Darren M. Soto	09—Democrat	https://soto.house.gov
Valdez Butler Demings	10—Democrat	https://demings.house.gov
Daniel A. Webster	11—Republican	http://webster.house.gov
Gus M. Bilirakis	12—Republican	https://bilirakis.house.gov
Charlie J. Crist, Jr.	13—Democrat	https://crist.house.gov
Katherine A. Castor	14—Democrat	http://castor.house.gov
C. Scott Franklin	15—Republican	https://franklin.house.gov
Vernon G. Buchanan	16—Republican	https://buchanan.house.gov
W. Gregory Steube	17—Republican	https://steube.house.gov
Brian J. Mast	18—Republican	https://mast.house.gov
Byron Donalds	19—Republican	https://donalds.house.gov
Alcee L. Hastings	20—Democrat	http://alceehastings.house.gov
Lois J. Frankel	21—Democrat	http://frankel.house.gov
Theodore E. Deutch	22—Democrat	http://teddeutch.house.gov
Deborah Wasserman Schultz	23—Democrat	https://wassermanschultz.house.gov
Frederica S. Wilson	24—Democrat	https://wilson.house.gov
Mario R. Díaz-Balart	25—Republican	http://mariodiazbalart.house.gov
Carlos A. Gimenez	26—Republican	https://gimenez.house.gov
Maria E. Salazar	27—Republican	https://salazar.house.gov
Georgia		
Earl L. Carter	01—Republican	http://buddycarter.house.gov
Sanford D. Bishop, Jr.	02—Democrat	http://bishop.house.gov
A. Drew Ferguson IV	03—Republican	https://ferguson.house.gov
Henry C. Johnson, Jr.	04—Democrat	https://hankjohnson.house.gov
Nikema Williams	05—Democrat	https://nikemawilliams.house.gov
Lucia K. McBath	06—Democrat	https://mcbath.house.gov
Carolyn Bourdeaux	07—Democrat	https://bourdeaux.house.gov
J. Austin Scott	08—Republican	https://austinscott.house.gov
Andrew S. Clyde	09—Republican	https://clyde.house.gov
Jody B. Hice	10—Republican	https://hice.house.gov
Barry D. Loudermilk	11—Republican	http://loudermilk.house.gov
Richard W. Allen	12—Republican	http://allen.house.gov
David A. Scott	13—Democrat	http://davidscott.house.gov
Marjorie T. Greene	14—Republican	https://greene.house.gov
Guam		
Michael F.Q. San Nicolas	Delegate—Democrat	https://sannicolas.house.gov
Hawaii		
Edward E. Case	01—Democrat	https://case.house.gov
Kaialiʻi Kahele	02—Democrat	https://kahele.house.gov

List of U.S. Representatives (*Continued*)

State / District	District—Party Affiliation	Contact Information
Idaho		
Russell M. Fulcher	01—Republican	https://fulcher.house.gov
Michael K. Simpson	02—Republican	http://simpson.house.gov
Illinois		
Bobby L. Rush	01—Democrat	http://rush.house.gov
Robin L. Kelly	02—Democrat	https://robinkelly.house.gov
Marie Newman	03—Democrat	https://newman.house.gov
Jesús G. García	04—Democrat	https://chuygarcia.house.gov
Michael B. Quigley	05—Democrat	https://quigley.house.gov
Sean T. Casten	06—Democrat	https://casten.house.gov
Danny K. Davis	07—Democrat	https://davis.house.gov
S. Raja Krishnamoorthi	08—Democrat	https://krishnamoorthi.house.gov
Janice D. Schakowsky	09—Democrat	https://schakowsky.house.gov
Bradley S. Schneider	10—Democrat	https://schneider.house.gov
William G. Foster	11—Democrat	http://foster.house.gov
Michael J. Bost	12—Republican	https://bost.house.gov
Rodney L. Davis	13—Republican	http://rodneydavis.house.gov
Lauren Underwood	14—Democrat	https://underwood.house.gov
Mary E. Miller	15—Republican	https://marymiller.house.gov
Adam D. Kinzinger	16—Republican	http://kinzinger.house.gov
Cheryl C. Bustos	17—Democrat	https://bustos.house.gov
Darin M. LaHood	18—Republican	https://lahood.house.gov
Indiana		
Frank J. Mrvan	01—Democrat	https://mrvan.house.gov
Jacqueline S. Walorski	02—Republican	http://walorski.house.gov
James E. Banks	03—Republican	https://banks.house.gov
James R. Baird	04—Republican	https://baird.house.gov
Victoria Spartz	05—Republican	https://spartz.house.gov
Gregory J. Pence	06—Republican	https://pence.house.gov
André D. Carson	07—Democrat	http://carson.house.gov
Larry D. Bucshon	08—Republican	https://bucshon.house.gov
Joseph A. Hollingsworth III	09—Republican	https://hollingsworth.house.gov
Iowa		
Ashley E. Hinson	01—Republican	https://hinson.house.gov
Mariannette J. Miller-Meeks	02—Republican	https://millermeeks.house.gov
Cynthia L. Axne	03—Democrat	https://axne.house.gov
Randall L. Feenstra	04—Republican	https://feenstra.house.gov
Kansas		
Tracey R. Mann	01—Republican	https://mann.house.gov
Jacob A.J. LaTurner	02—Republican	https://laturner.house.gov
Sharice L. Davids	03—Democrat	https://davids.house.gov
Ronald G. Estes	04—Republican	https://estes.house.gov
Kentucky		
James R. Comer	01—Republican	https://comer.house.gov
S. Brett Guthrie	02—Republican	https://guthrie.house.gov
John A. Yarmuth	03—Democrat	https://yarmuth.house.gov
Thomas H. Massie	04—Republican	https://massie.house.gov
Harold D. Rogers	05—Republican	https://halrogers.house.gov
Garland H. Barr IV	06—Republican	https://barr.house.gov

List of U.S. Representatives (*Continued*)

State / District	District—Party Affiliation	Contact Information
Louisiana		
Stephen J. Scalise	01—Republican	http://scalise.house.gov
(vacancy)	02—	https://
G. Clay Higgins	03—Republican	https://clayhiggins.house.gov
J. Michael Johnson	04—Republican	https://mikejohnson.house.gov
(Julia Letlow—	05—Republican	https://
Representative-elect)		
Garret N. Graves	06—Republican	https://garretgraves.house.gov
Maine		
Chellie M. Pingree	01—Democrat	https://pingree.house.gov
Jared F. Golden	02—Democrat	https://golden.house.gov
Maryland		
Andrew P. Harris	01—Republican	http://harris.house.gov
C.A. Dutch Ruppersberger	02—Democrat	http://ruppersberger.house.gov
John P. Sarbanes	03—Democrat	https://sarbanes.house.gov
Anthony G. Brown	04—Democrat	https://anthonybrown.house.gov
Steny H. Hoyer	05—Democrat	https://hoyer.house.gov
David J. Trone	06—Democrat	https://trone.house.gov
Kweisi Mfume	07—Democrat	https://mfume.house.gov
Jamin B. Raskin	08—Democrat	https://raskin.house.gov
Massachusetts		
Richard E. Neal	01—Democrat	https://neal.house.gov
James P. McGovern	02—Democrat	http://mcgovern.house.gov
Lori L. Trahan	03—Democrat	https://trahan.house.gov
Jacob D. Auchincloss	04—Democrat	https://auchincloss.house.gov
Katherine M. Clark	05—Democrat	https://katherineclark.house.gov
Seth W. Moulton	06—Democrat	http://moulton.house.gov
Ayanna S. Pressley	07—Democrat	https://pressley.house.gov
Stephen F. Lynch	08—Democrat	http://lynch.house.gov
William R. Keating	09—Democrat	https://keating.house.gov
Michigan		
John W. Bergman	01—Republican	https://bergman.house.gov
William P. Huizenga	02—Republican	http://huizenga.house.gov
Peter J. Meijer	03—Republican	https://meijer.house.gov
John R. Moolenaar	04—Republican	https://moolenaar.house.gov
Daniel T. Kildee	05—Democrat	http://dankildee.house.gov
Frederick S. Upton	06—Republican	http://upton.house.gov
Timothy L. Walberg	07—Republican	http://walberg.house.gov
Elissa B. Slotkin	08—Democrat	https://slotkin.house.gov
Andrew S. Levin	09—Democrat	https://andylevin.house.gov
Lisa C. McClain	10—Republican	https://mcclain.house.gov
Haley M. Stevens	11—Democrat	https://stevens.house.gov
Deborah A. Dingell	12—Democrat	https://debbiedingell.house.gov
Rashida H. Tlaib	13—Democrat	https://tlaib.house.gov
Brenda L. Lawrence	14—Democrat	https://lawrence.house.gov
Minnesota		
James L. Hagedorn	01—Republican	https://hagedorn.house.gov
Angela D. Craig	02—Democrat	https://craig.house.gov
Dean B. Phillips	03—Democrat	https://phillips.house.gov

List of U.S. Representatives (*Continued*)

State / District	District—Party Affiliation	Contact Information
Betty L. McCollum	04—Democrat	http://mccollum.house.gov
Ilhan A. Omar	05—Democrat	https://omar.house.gov
Thomas E. Emmer, Jr.	06—Republican	https://emmer.house.gov
Michelle L. Fischbach	07—Republican	https://fischbach.house.gov
Peter A. Stauber	08—Republican	https://stauber.house.gov
Mississippi		
J. Trent Kelly	01—Republican	https://trentkelly.house.gov
Bennie G. Thompson	02—Democrat	https://benniethompson.house.gov
Michael P. Guest	03—Republican	https://guest.house.gov
Steven M. Palazzo	04—Republican	http://palazzo.house.gov
Missouri		
Cori A. Bush	01—Democrat	https://bush.house.gov
Ann L. Wagner	02—Republican	http://wagner.house.gov
W. Blaine Luetkemeyer	03—Republican	http://luetkemeyer.house.gov
Vicky J. Hartzler	04—Republican	https://hartzler.house.gov
Emanuel Cleaver II	05—Democrat	http://cleaver.house.gov
Samuel B. Graves, Jr.	06—Republican	https://graves.house.gov
William H. Long	07—Republican	https://long.house.gov
Jason T. Smith	08—Republican	https://jasonsmith.house.gov
Montana		
Matthew M. Rosendale, Sr.	At Large—Republican	https://rosendale.house.gov
Nebraska		
Jeffrey L. Fortenberry	01—Republican	https://fortenberry.house.gov
Donald J. Bacon	02—Republican	https://bacon.house.gov
Adrian M. Smith	03—Republican	http://adriansmith.house.gov
Nevada		
A. Costandina Titus	01—Democrat	https://titus.house.gov
Mark E. Amodei	02—Republican	https://amodei.house.gov
Suzanne K. Lee	03—Democrat	https://susielee.house.gov
Steven A. Horsford	04—Democrat	https://horsford.house.gov
New Hampshire		
Christopher C. Pappas	01—Democrat	https://pappas.house.gov
Ann McLane Kuster	02—Democrat	http://kuster.house.gov
New Jersey		
Donald W. Norcross	01—Democrat	https://norcross.house.gov
Jefferson H. Van Drew	02—Republican	https://vandrew.house.gov
Andrew Kim	03—Democrat	https://kim.house.gov
Christopher H. Smith	04—Republican	http://chrissmith.house.gov
Joshua S. Gottheimer	05—Democrat	https://gottheimer.house.gov
Frank J. Pallone, Jr.	06—Democrat	https://pallone.house.gov
Tomasz P. Malinowski	07—Democrat	https://malinowski.house.gov
Albio B. Sires	08—Democrat	https://sires.house.gov
William J. Pascrell, Jr.	09—Democrat	http://pascrell.house.gov
Donald M. Payne, Jr.	10—Democrat	http://payne.house.gov
R. Michelle Sherrill	11—Democrat	https://sherrill.house.gov
Bonnie Watson Coleman	12—Democrat	https://watsoncoleman.house.gov
New Mexico		
(vacancy)	01—	https://
S. Yvette Herrell	02—Republican	https://herrell.house.gov

List of U.S. Representatives (*Continued*)

State / District	District—Party Affiliation	Contact Information
Teresa I. Leger Fernandez	03—Democrat	https://fernandez.house.gov
New York		
Lee M. Zeldin	01—Republican	https://zeldin.house.gov
Andrew R. Garbarino	02—Republican	https://garbarino.house.gov
Thomas R. Suozzi	03—Democrat	https://suozzi.house.gov
Kathleen M. Rice	04—Democrat	http://kathleenrice.house.gov
Gregory W. Meeks	05—Democrat	http://meeks.house.gov
Grace Meng	06—Democrat	http://meng.house.gov
Nydia M. Velázquez	07—Democrat	https://velazquez.house.gov
Hakeem S. Jeffries	08—Democrat	http://jeffries.house.gov
Yvette D. Clarke	09—Democrat	https://clarke.house.gov
Jerrold L. Nadler	10—Democrat	http://nadler.house.gov
Nicole Malliotakis	11—Republican	https://malliotakis.house.gov
Carolyn B. Maloney	12—Democrat	http://maloney.house.gov
Adriano D. Espaillat	13—Democrat	https://espaillat.house.gov
Alexandria Ocasio-Cortez	14—Democrat	https://ocasio-cortez.house.gov
Ritchie J. Torres	15—Democrat	https://ritchietorres.house.gov
Jamaal Bowman	16—Democrat	https://bowman.house.gov
Mondaire Jones	17—Democrat	https://jones.house.gov
Sean P. Maloney	18—Democrat	http://seanmaloney.house.gov
Antonio Delgado	19—Democrat	https://delgado.house.gov
Paul D. Tonko	20—Democrat	https://tonko.house.gov
Elise M. Stefanik	21—Republican	https://stefanik.house.gov
Claudia Tenney	22—Republican	https://tenney.house.gov
Thomas W. Reed II	23—Republican	https://reed.house.gov
John M. Katko	24—Republican	https://katko.house.gov
Joseph D. Morelle	25—Democrat	https://morelle.house.gov
Brian M. Higgins	26—Democrat	http://higgins.house.gov
Christopher L. Jacobs	27—Republican	https://jacobs.house.gov
North Carolina		
George K. Butterfield	01—Democrat	http://butterfield.house.gov
Deborah K. Ross	02—Democrat	https://ross.house.gov
Gregory F. Murphy	03—Republican	https://gregmurphy.house.gov
David E. Price	04—Democrat	https://price.house.gov
Virginia A. Foxx	05—Republican	http://foxx.house.gov
Kathy A. Manning	06—Democrat	https://manning.house.gov
David C. Rouzer	07—Republican	https://rouzer.house.gov
Richard L. Hudson, Jr.	08—Republican	https://hudson.house.gov
J. Daniel Bishop	09—Republican	https://danbishop.house.gov
Patrick T. McHenry	10—Republican	http://mchenry.house.gov
D. Madison Cawthorn	11—Republican	https://cawthorn.house.gov
Alma S. Adams	12—Democrat	http://adams.house.gov
Theodore P. Budd	13—Republican	https://budd.house.gov
North Dakota		
Kelly Armstrong	At Large—Republican	https://armstrong.house.gov
Northern Mariana Islands		
Gregorio K.C. Sablan	Delegate—Democrat	http://sablan.house.gov
Ohio		
Steven J. Chabot	01—Republican	http://chabot.house.gov
Brad R. Wenstrup	02—Republican	http://wenstrup.house.gov

List of U.S. Representatives (*Continued*)

State / District	District—Party Affiliation	Contact Information
Joyce B. Beatty	03—Democrat	http://beatty.house.gov
James D. Jordan	04—Republican	http://jordan.house.gov
Robert E. Latta	05—Republican	http://latta.house.gov
William L. Johnson	06—Republican	http://billjohnson.house.gov
Robert B. Gibbs	07—Republican	https://gibbs.house.gov
Warren E. Davidson	08—Republican	https://davidson.house.gov
Marcia C. Kaptur	09—Democrat	https://kaptur.house.gov
Michael R. Turner	10—Republican	https://turner.house.gov
(vacancy)	11—	https://
W. Troy Balderson	12—Republican	https://balderson.house.gov
Timothy J. Ryan	13—Democrat	http://timryan.house.gov
David P. Joyce	14—Republican	https://joyce.house.gov
Steven E. Stivers	15—Republican	http://stivers.house.gov
Anthony Gonzalez	16—Republican	https://anthonygonzalez.house.gov
Oklahoma		
Kevin R. Hern	01—Republican	https://hern.house.gov
Markwayne Mullin	02—Republican	http://mullin.house.gov
Frank D. Lucas	03—Republican	http://lucas.house.gov
Thomas J. Cole	04—Republican	https://cole.house.gov
Stephanie I. Bice	05—Republican	https://bice.house.gov
Oregon		
Suzanne M. Bonamici	01—Democrat	http://bonamici.house.gov
Cliff S. Bentz	02—Republican	https://bentz.house.gov
Earl Blumenauer	03—Democrat	https://blumenauer.house.gov
Peter A. DeFazio	04—Democrat	http://defazio.house.gov
W. Kurt Schrader	05—Democrat	http://schrader.house.gov
Pennsylvania		
Brian K. Fitzpatrick	01—Republican	https://fitzpatrick.house.gov
Brendan F. Boyle	02—Democrat	https://boyle.house.gov
Dwight E. Evans	03—Democrat	https://evans.house.gov
Madeleine C. Dean	04—Democrat	https://dean.house.gov
Mary Gay Scanlon	05—Democrat	https://scanlon.house.gov
Christina J. Houlahan	06—Democrat	https://houlahan.house.gov
Susan E. Wild	07—Democrat	https://wild.house.gov
Matthew A. Cartwright	08—Democrat	https://cartwright.house.gov
Daniel P. Meuser	09—Republican	https://meuser.house.gov
Scott G. Perry	10—Republican	https://perry.house.gov
Lloyd K. Smucker	11—Republican	https://smucker.house.gov
Frederick B. Keller	12—Republican	https://keller.house.gov
John P. Joyce	13—Republican	https://johnjoyce.house.gov
Guy L. Reschenthaler	14—Republican	https://reschenthaler.house.gov
Glenn W. Thompson	15—Republican	https://thompson.house.gov
George J. Kelly, Jr.	16—Republican	https://kelly.house.gov
Conor J. Lamb	17—Democrat	https://lamb.house.gov
Michael F. Doyle	18—Democrat	https://doyle.house.gov
Puerto Rico		
Jenniffer A. González-Colón	Resident Commissioner—Republican	https://gonzalez-colon.house.gov
Rhode Island		
David N. Cicilline	01—Democrat	http://cicilline.house.gov

List of U.S. Representatives (*Continued*)

State / District	District—Party Affiliation	Contact Information
James R. Langevin	02—Democrat	http://langevin.house.gov
South Carolina		
Nancy R. Mace	01—Republican	https://mace.house.gov
Addison G. Wilson	02—Republican	http://joewilson.house.gov
Jeffrey D. Duncan	03—Republican	http://jeffduncan.house.gov
William R. Timmons	04—Republican	https://timmons.house.gov
Ralph W. Norman, Jr.	05—Republican	https://norman.house.gov
James E. Clyburn	06—Democrat	http://clyburn.house.gov
H. Thompson Rice, Jr.	07—Republican	http://rice.house.gov
South Dakota		
Dustin M. Johnson	At Large—Republican	https://dustyjohnson.house.gov
Tennessee		
Diana L. Harshbarger	01—Republican	https://harshbarger.house.gov
Timothy F. Burchett	02—Republican	https://burchett.house.gov
Charles J. Fleischmann	03—Republican	http://fleischmann.house.gov
Scott E. DesJarlais	04—Republican	https://desjarlais.house.gov
James H.S. Cooper	05—Democrat	http://cooper.house.gov
John W. Rose	06—Republican	https://johnrose.house.gov
Mark E. Green	07—Republican	https://markgreen.house.gov
David F. Kustoff	08—Republican	https://kustoff.house.gov
Stephen I. Cohen	09—Democrat	https://cohen.house.gov
Texas		
Louis B. Gohmert, Jr.	01—Republican	https://gohmert.house.gov
Daniel R. Crenshaw	02—Republican	https://crenshaw.house.gov
N. Vancampen Taylor	03—Republican	https://vantaylor.house.gov
Patrick E. Fallon	04—Republican	https://fallon.house.gov
Lance Gooden	05—Republican	https://gooden.house.gov
(vacancy)	06—	—
Elizabeth P. Fletcher	07—Democrat	https://fletcher.house.gov
Kevin P. Brady	08—Republican	http://kevinbrady.house.gov
Alexander N. Green	09—Democrat	http://algreen.house.gov
Michael T. McCaul	10—Republican	http://mccaul.house.gov
August L. Pfluger	11—Republican	https://pfluger.house.gov
Kay M. Granger	12—Republican	http://kaygranger.house.gov
Ronny L. Jackson	13—Republican	https://jackson.house.gov
Randy K. Weber, Sr.	14—Republican	http://weber.house.gov
Vicente Gonzalez	15—Democrat	https://gonzalez.house.gov
Veronica Escobar	16—Democrat	https://escobar.house.gov
Peter A. Sessions	17—Republican	https://sessions.house.gov
Sheila Jackson Lee	18—Democrat	http://jacksonlee.house.gov
Jodey Cook Arrington	19—Republican	https://arrington.house.gov
Joaquin Castro	20—Democrat	https://castro.house.gov
Charles E. Roy	21—Republican	https://roy.house.gov
Troy E. Nehls	22—Republican	https://nehls.house.gov
E. Anthony Gonzalez	23—Republican	https://gonzales.house.gov
Elizabeth A. Van Duyne	24—Republican	https://vanduyne.house.gov
J. Roger Williams	25—Republican	http://williams.house.gov
Michael C. Burgess	26—Republican	http://burgess.house.gov
Michael J. Cloud	27—Republican	https://cloud.house.gov
Enrique R. Cuellar	28—Democrat	http://cuellar.house.gov

List of U.S. Representatives (*Continued*)

State / District	District—Party Affiliation	Contact Information
Sylvia R. Garcia	29—Democrat	https://sylviagarcia.house.gov
Eddie B. Johnson	30—Democrat	http://ebjohnson.house.gov
John R. Carter	31—Republican	https://carter.house.gov
Colin Z. Allred	32—Democrat	https://allred.house.gov
Marc A. Veasey	33—Democrat	http://veasey.house.gov
Filemón B. Vela, Jr.	34—Democrat	https://vela.house.gov
Lloyd A. Doggett II	35—Democrat	https://doggett.house.gov
Brian Babin	36—Republican	http://babin.house.gov
Utah		
Blake D. Moore	01—Republican	https://blakemoore.house.gov
Christopher D. Stewart	02—Republican	http://stewart.house.gov
John R. Curtis	03—Republican	https://curtis.house.gov
C. Burgess Owens	04—Republican	https://owens.house.gov
Vermont		
Peter F. Welch	At Large—Democrat	https://welch.house.gov
Virgin Islands		
Stacey E. Plaskett	Delegate—Democrat	https://plaskett.house.gov
Virginia		
Robert J. Wittman	01—Republican	http://wittman.house.gov
Elaine G. Luria	02—Democrat	https://luria.house.gov
Robert C. Scott	03—Democrat	http://bobbyscott.house.gov
A. Donald McEachin	04—Democrat	https://mceachin.house.gov
Robert G. Good	05—Republican	https://good.house.gov
Benjamin L. Cline	06—Republican	https://cline.house.gov
Abigail D. Spanberger	07—Democrat	https://spanberger.house.gov
Donald S. Beyer, Jr.	08—Democrat	http://beyer.house.gov
H. Morgan Griffith	09—Republican	http://morgangriffith.house.gov
Jennifer L. Wexton	10—Democrat	https://wexton.house.gov
Gerald E. Connolly	11—Democrat	https://connolly.house.gov
Washington		
Suzan K. DelBene	01—Democrat	https://delbene.house.gov
Richard R. Larsen	02—Democrat	http://larsen.house.gov
Jaime L. Herrera Beutler	03—Republican	http://herrerabeutler.house.gov
Daniel M. Newhouse	04—Republican	https://newhouse.house.gov
Cathy A. McMorris Rodgers	05—Republican	http://mcmorris.house.gov
Derek C. Kilmer	06—Democrat	https://kilmer.house.gov
Pramila Jayapal	07—Democrat	https://jayapal.house.gov
Kimberly M. Schrier	08—Democrat	https://schrier.house.gov
D. Adam Smith	09—Democrat	https://adamsmith.house.gov
Marilyn Strickland	10—Democrat	https://strickland.house.gov
West Virginia		
David B. McKinley	01—Republican	https://mckinley.house.gov
Alexander X. Mooney	02—Republican	https://mooney.house.gov
Carol D. Miller	03—Republican	https://miller.house.gov
Wisconsin		
Bryan G. Steil	01—Republican	https://steil.house.gov
Mark Pocan	02—Democrat	http://pocan.house.gov
Ronald J. Kind	03—Democrat	https://kind.house.gov
Gwendolynne S. Moore	04—Democrat	https://gwenmoore.house.gov

List of U.S. Representatives (*Continued*)

State / District	District—Party Affiliation	Contact Information
Scott L. Fitzgerald	05—Republican	https://fitzgerald.house.gov
Glenn S. Grothman	06—Republican	http://grothman.house.gov
Thomas P. Tiffany	07—Republican	https://tiffany.house.gov
Michael J. Gallagher	08—Republican	https://gallagher.house.gov
Wyoming		
Elizabeth L. Cheney	At Large—Republican	https://cheney.house.gov

The Above List of 435 Representatives was Updated 3–2021. Democrats are 219; Republicans are 211; and 5 districts do not have a Representative. The Resident Commissioner and Delegates are not counted as Members. https://www.house.gov/representatives

Information on the Office of the Clerk's website may be more accurate and current. | https://clerkpreview.house.gov/Members#MemberProfiles. Information on House.gov may be more accurate and current. | https://www.house.gov/representatives. Information on the Office of the Clerk's website may be more accurate and current. | https://clerkpreview.house.gov/Members#MemberProfiles

Sources of Information

Additional Resources   The "House of Representatives Resources" web page contains links that allow easy access to calendars, committee assignments, current House floor activities, directories, documents, profiles, statistics, texts of bills, the Office of the Clerk and the House Library, and information on committee meetings, House history, precedents, procedures, rules, salaries, Speakers of the House, vacancies, and information for those who are planning a visit to the U.S. Capitol. https://www.congress.gov/help/house-of-representatives

Art Competition   Each spring, the Congressional Institute sponsors a nationwide high school visual art competition to recognize and encourage artistic talent. Students submit their entries to their Representative's office, and panels of district artists select the winning artwork, which is displayed at the U.S. Capitol for 1 year. http://www.house.gov/content/educate/art_competition

Campaign Finance   The Federal Election Commission maintains a campaign finance database that contains information on candidates, including congressional candidates, who file reports with the Commission. Users of the online "Candidate and Committee Viewer" can sort data and download them. The data presentations consist of biennial summaries, report summaries, and report images and downloads. http://www.fec.gov/finance/disclosure/candcmte_info.shtml?tabIndex=1

Campaign Websites   The Library of Congress maintains a "Web Archives" that includes thousands of official campaign websites. Former congressional candidates' websites are part of this collection. https://www.loc.gov/websites

Career Opportunities   The House Vacancy Announcement and Placement Service assists House Members, committees, and leadership by posting job vacancies and maintaining a resume bank. The Service provides confidential referral of resumes when House offices request them. Information on submitting a resume is available online. http://www.house.gov/content/jobs/members_and_committees.php To apply for positions with House organizations, read the individual vacancy announcements and follow the instructions. http://www.house.gov/content/jobs/vacancies.php

Committees   Information on House committees is available on House.gov. http://www.house.gov/committees

Additional information is available on the Office of the Clerk's website. http://clerk.house.gov/committee_info/index.aspx

Congressional Record   Starting with the year 1995, the official record of the proceedings and debates of the U.S. Congress is available on Congress.gov. https://www.congress.gov/congressional-record

Starting with the year 1994, the official record of the proceedings and debates of the U.S. Congress is available on the Government Publishing Office's govinfo website. https://www.govinfo.gov/app/collection/crec

Contact the Clerk   Additional information on the House of Representatives is available from the Clerk, U.S. Capitol, Room H-154, Washington, DC 20515-6601. Phone, 202-225-7000. https://clerkpreview.house.gov/About#OverviewContact | Email: info.clerkweb@mail.house.gov

Directories   The website House.gov has a directory that contains the committee assignment, congressional district, name, phone number, political affiliation, and room number of each Member of the U.S. House of Representatives, as well as the Uniform Resources Locator (URL) that leads to his or her website. http://www.house.gov/representatives

The online "Biographical Directory of the United States Congress, 1774–Present," allows visitors to search for Members of Congress—past and present—by first or last name, political affiliation, position, State, or year or Congress. http://bioguide.congress.gov/biosearch/biosearch.asp

Present and former Members of Congress have control numbers associated with their records in the "Biographical Directory of the United States Congress." Member IDs or "BioGuide IDs" serve as metadata within Congress.gov and legislative documents that the Government Publishing Office publishes. https://www.congress.gov/help/field-values/member-bioguide-ids

Find a Representative   A Zip code-based search tool is available on House.gov for locating a representative. http://www.house.gov/representatives/find

Frequently Asked Questions (FAQs)   The Office of the Clerk has posted answers to general legislative questions and to more specific questions related to members and committees. https://clerkpreview.house.gov/Help#MemberFAQs

Glossaries   The Office of the Clerk's website has a short glossary for children. https://kids-clerk.house.gov/high-school/glossary.html

House.gov has a glossary of terms for readers of congressional records. http://history.house.gov/Records-and-Research/FAQs/Congressional-Glossary/

House.gov features a glossary of records management terms. http://history.house.gov/Records-and-Research/FAQs/Records-Glossary/

The "Statement of Disbursements" is a quarterly public report of all receipts and expenditures for U.S. House of Representatives committees, leadership, Members, and officers and offices. To help the general public read this report, House.gov maintains an online glossary. https://www.house.gov/the-house-explained/open-government/statement-of-disbursements/glossary-of-terms

History   The House of Representative's "History, Art and Archives" website features resources and a trove of information, including online collections, exhibitions, publications, and records. http://history.house.gov | Email: history@mail.house.gov

In 2015, the "History, Art & Archives" team presented 10 favorite historical highlights and blog posts. Its selection had an eclectic character and includes highlights on a lavaliere of diamonds, the protective power of a thrice-folded newspaper, the House gym, an amendment to abolish the U.S. Senate, national weather forecasts, possums, dueling in the House, hunting dogs on the floor, a titanic story of love and courage, and a very kissable man. https://history.house.gov/Blog/2015/May/5-20-Top-Ten/

Learning About the House   The Office of the Clerk's website features educational and entertaining information on the legislative branch of the Government for students of all ages. Its "Kids in the House" site explains the role of the House of Representatives, describes the legislative process, and covers House history. https://kids-clerk.house.gov

Adults seeking to learn about commissions, committees, House history, House leadership, Representatives, rules, or a Representative's schedule may benefit from "The House Explained" section on House.gov. http://www.house.gov/content/learn

Member Profiles   The "Members of the U.S. Congress" database contains profiles for Representatives who have held office since 1973 or were still serving in the 93d Congress. Users of the database can filter profiles by chamber, Congress, political affiliation, and State or U.S. Territory. A Member profile includes the following: dates of service, district number and State, party affiliation, and a picture when available, as well as a link to the Member's entry in the "Biographical Directory of the United States Congress, 1774–Present" and a link to remarks made in the "Congressional Record." A profile also includes the list of legislation that the Member sponsored and cosponsored. https://www.congress.gov/members

The Office of the Clerk's website also maintains a database of Member profiles. https://clerkpreview.house.gov/Members#MemberProfiles

Most-Viewed Bills   The top ten most-viewed bills list is compiled each Monday and posted on the Congress.gov website. https://www.congress.gov/resources/display/content/Most-Viewed+Bills

Oath of Office   The constitutional oath of office requires each Member of Congress to swear or affirm that he or she will support and defend the U.S. Constitution against foreign and domestic enemies; bear faith and allegiance to the Constitution; take this obligation freely, with neither mental reservation nor purpose of evasion; and discharge the duties of the office well and faithfully. https://clerkpreview.house.gov/Members#MemberOaths

Party Seats / Vacancies   The Office of the Clerk's "House at a Glance" page keeps a tally of the number of Democratic, Independent, Libertarian, Republican, and vacant seats in the House of Representatives. https://clerk.house.gov/#view-at-a-glance

People Search   The "History, Art, and Archives" section on the House.gov website has a versatile tool that allows users to search a comprehensive database containing biographical information on Members of the House of Representatives and on nonmember officers like chaplains, clerks, parliamentarians, sergeants at arms, and others. https://history.house.gov/People/Search

Publications   The Congressional Directory, Rules and Manual of the House of Representatives, and telephone directory for the House of Representatives are available from the Government Publishing Office's bookstore. Phone, 202-512-0132. https://bookstore.gpo.gov/agency/congress-legislative-branch | Email: mainbks@gpo.gov

Schedule   The House's schedule and related resources are available in the "Legislative Activity" section on House.gov. http://www.house.gov/legislative

Site Map   House.gov features a site map that allows visitors to look for a specific topic or to browse content that aligns with their interests. http://www.house.gov/content/site_tools/sitemap.php

Vacancies   The Office of the Clerk posts recent resignations, deaths, and other separations from the House of Representatives on its "Current Vacancies" web page. Vacancies are grouped according to congressional session, and the page includes the results of recent special elections that have been held to fill vacancies. http://clerk.house.gov/member_info/vacancies.aspx?pr=house&%3Bvid=130

The above Sources of Information for the House of Representatives were updated 2–2021.

Architect of the Capitol

U.S. Capitol Building, Washington, DC 20515
Phone, 202-228-1793. Internet, http://www.aoc.gov

Architect of the Capitol	THOMAS J. CARROLL III, ACTING
Deputy Architect of the Capitol	(VACANCY)

Directors
Communications and Congressional Relations	ERIN COURTNEY, ACTING
Safety, Fire and Environmental Programs	PATRICIA WILLIAMS
General Counsel	JASON BALTIMORE

https://www.aoc.gov/organization/acting-architect

Jurisdictions Reporting to the Architect

Chief Executive Officer for Visitor Services	
U.S. Capitol Visitor Center	BETH PLEMMONS

https://www.aoc.gov/jurisdiction/capitol-visitor-center

Executive Director	
U.S. Botanic Garden	SAHARAH MOON CHAPOTIN

https://www.aoc.gov/jurisdiction/botanic-garden

Operations	
Chief Operating Officer	(VACANCY)
Chief Officers	
Administrative	WILLIAM R. O'DONNELL
Financial	JONATHAN KRAFT, ACTING
Director	
Planning and Project Management	PETER W. MUELLER JURISDICTIONS REPORTING TO THE CHIEF OPERATING OFFICER

Directors	
Capitol Grounds and Arboretum	JAMES KAUFMANN
Capitol Police Buildings, Grounds and Security	VAL HASBERRY, ACTING
Capitol Power Plant	CHRISTOPHER POTTER
Facility Manager	
Supreme Court Building and Grounds	JOSEPH A. CAMPBELL
Superintendents	
Capitol Building	MARK REED
House Office Buildings	MICHELLE KAYON, ACTING
Library Buildings and Grounds	ANTONIO M. EDMONDS
Senate Office Buildings	LAWRENCE BARR, ACTING

https://www.aoc.gov/organizational-directory

Office of Inspector General	
Inspector General	CHRISTOPHER P. FAILLA

https://www.aoc.gov/oig/inspector-general

The above list of key personnel was updated 10–2019.

The Architect of the Capitol maintains the U.S. Capitol and the buildings and grounds of the Capitol campus.

Establishment and Organization

The origins of the office of the Architect of the Capitol (AOC) may be traced to the act of July 16, 1790, that established "the temporary and permanent seat of the Government of the United States" (1 Stat. 130). https://www.loc.gov/law/help/statutes-at-large/1st-congress/session-2/c1s2ch28.pdf

The title Architect of the Capitol is the official title of both the agency and the person who heads it. The act of August 15, 1876, that made "appropriations for the legislative, executive, and judicial expenses of the Government . . . and for other purposes" established permanent authority for the care and maintenance of the U.S. Capitol (19 Stat. 147). https://www.loc.gov/law/help/statutes-at-large/44th-congress/session-1/c44s1ch287.pdf

Prior to 1989, the President selected the Architect for an unlimited term and without any formal action by Congress. An act of November 21, 1989, that made "appropriations for the Legislative Branch . . . and for other purposes" changed the procedure. This statute, which is also cited as the "Legislative Branch Appropriations Act, 1990," stipulates that the President appoints the Architect of the Capitol for a term of 10 years, by the advice and with the consent of the Senate, from a list of at least three candidates whom a congressional commission recommends (103 Stat. 1068). Upon confirmation by the Senate, the Architect becomes an official of the legislative branch as an officer of Congress. The Architect is eligible for reappointment at the end of his or her 10-year term. While overseeing the agency, the Architect also serves as the Acting Director of the U.S. Botanic Garden. https://www.govinfo.gov/content/pkg/STATUTE-103/pdf/STATUTE-103-Pg1041.pdf

The Congressional Research Service prepared the report "Architect of the Capitol: Appointment, Duties, and Current Issues," which includes a section on the statutory evolution of the Architect's office. Mildred Amer, a specialist on the Congress, of the Government and Finance Division, prepared the report in October of 2008. https://www.everycrsreport.com/reports/RL32820.html

An organizational directory is available online. https://www.aoc.gov/organizational-directory

Activities

The Architect of the Capitol serves the Congress and Supreme Court in its capacity as the builder and steward of the landmark buildings and grounds of Capitol Hill. AOC employees preserve and maintain the art, historic buildings, monuments, and gardens on the Capitol campus. Comprising more than 2,000 employees and providing around-the-clock service, the AOC team creates a safe environment and inspiring experiences for those who visit or work on Capitol Hill.

The agency oversees the operations and care of more than 17.4 million square feet of facilities, 580 acres of grounds, and thousands of works of art. The Capitol campus accommodates 30,000 daily occupants and hosts more than 3 million visitors annually. https://www.aoc.gov/defining-aoc

Sources of Information

Architecture   A trove of information on columns, materials, styles, and more is available on the AOC website. https://www.aoc.gov/architecture

Art   The AOC website includes pages on AOC art stories, artists, art by State, decorative arts, paintings and murals, and sculptures, as well as on African Americans, Native Americans, and women in art. https://www.aoc.gov/art

Blog   AOC experts write on the architecture, art, and work on the Capitol Hill. http://www.aoc.gov/blog

Business Opportunities   Information for contractors and small businesses—delivery instructions, procedures, procurement opportunities, and programs—is accessible online. https://www.aoc.gov/procurement

Career Opportunities   The AOC relies heavily on architects, carpenters, electricians, engineers, gardeners, masons, mechanics, painters and plasterers, plumbers, and sheet metal workers to maintain the U.S. Capitol and the buildings and grounds of the surrounding campus. https://www.aoc.gov/careers

In 2018, the AOC ranked 9th among 27 midsize Government agencies in the Best Places To Work Agency Rankings. http://bestplacestowork.org/BPTW/rankings/detail/AC00

Events   The AOC website contains pages of events associated with the U.S. Capitol and Botanic Garden. Events include Christmas tree displays, concerts, lying in state, Presidential Inaugurations, and State of the Union addresses. https://www.aoc.gov/capitol-campus-events

Facts   Capitol Hill facts are posted on the AOC website. https://www.aoc.gov/facts/capitol-hill

Gallery   A multimedia gallery is available online. https://www.aoc.gov/multimedia-gallery

Grounds   Frederick L. Olmsted planned the late 19th-century expansion and landscaping of the Capitol Grounds. Olmsted, who also designed Central Park in New York City, was regarded as the most talented American landscape architect of his day. The "About the Grounds" web page features an informative 4-minute video on his plan for the U.S. Capitol. https://www.aoc.gov/capitol-grounds/about-grounds

History   President George Washington appointed commissioners to provide buildings and accommodations for Congress. The commissioners hired the French artist and engineer Major Pierre Charles L'Enfant, a Revolutionary War veteran, to lay out the new city. They also staged a competition for the design of the Capitol. Dr. William Thornton's entry won the competition. To learn more about the first "architect of the capitol" and the Architects that followed, visit the AOC's history web pages. https://www.aoc.gov/about-aoc/history-architect

Map   A map of Capitol Hill is available online. https://www.aoc.gov/us-capitol-map

News   The AOC posts news and notices on its website. https://www.aoc.gov/news

Oversight   The Office of the Inspector General from the AOC posts reports and data on Oversight.gov, a text-searchable repository of reports that Federal Inspectors General publish. The Council of the Inspectors General on Integrity and Efficiency operates and maintains the website to increase public access to independent and authoritative information on the Federal Government. https://oversight.gov

Planning a Visit   Information on accessibility services, activities, tours, visiting hours, and where to shop and eat is available online. http://www.aoc.gov/plan-your-visit

Projects   The AOC never lacks things to preserve or restore. Visit the "Projects" web page to learn about ongoing work. https://www.aoc.gov/projects

Publications   The AOC publishes a variety of publications that are accessible online. https://www.aoc.gov/publications

Site Map   The website map allows visitors to look for specific topics or to browse content that aligns with their interests. https://www.aoc.gov/sitemap

Social Media   The AOC has a Facebook account. https://www.facebook.com/ArchitectoftheCapitol

The AOC tweets announcements and other newsworthy items on Twitter. https://twitter.com/uscapitol

The AOC posts videos on its YouTube channel. https://www.youtube.com/user/AOCgov

Trees   Approximately 890 trees surround the Capitol Building on Capitol Square, and more than 4,300 trees grow throughout the 274-acre Capitol Grounds. A tree map is available on the "Trees on Capitol Grounds" web page. https://www.aoc.gov/trees

The Sources of Information were updated 10–2019.

Congressional Budget Office

Second and D Streets SW., Washington, DC 20515
Phone, 202-226-2600. Internet, http://www.cbo.gov

Office of the Director

Director	Phillip L. Swagel
Deputy Director	Mark P. Hadley
General Counsel	(vacancy)
Senior Advisor	Robert A. Sunshine
Associate Directors	
Communications	Deborah Kilroe
Economic Analysis	Wendy Edelberg
	Jeffrey Kling
Legislative Affairs	Leigh Angres

Other Divisions

Assistant Directors	
Budget Analysis	Theresa A. Gullo
Financial Analysis	Sebastien Gay
Health, Retirement, and Long-Term Analysis	David Weaver
Macroeconomic Analysis	Jeffrey F. Werling
Assistant Director, Microeconomic Studies	Joseph Kile
National Security	David E. Mosher
Tax Analysis	John McClelland
Chief Administrative Officer	
Management, Business, and Information Services	Joseph E. Evans, Jr.

https://www.cbo.gov/about/organization-and-staffing

The above list of key personnel was updated 7–2019.

The Congressional Budget Office independently analyzes budgetary and economic issues to support the congressional budget process.

The Congressional Budget Office (CBO) was established by the Congressional Budget Act of 1974 (2 U.S.C. 601), which also created a procedure by which the Congress considers and acts on the annual Federal budget. This process enables the Congress to have an overview of the Federal budget and to make overall decisions on spending and taxation levels and on the deficit or surplus these levels generate. https://www.cbo.gov/about/founding

Activities

The CBO assists the congressional budget committees with drafting and enforcing the annual budget resolution, which serves as a blueprint for total levels of Government spending and revenues in a fiscal year. Once completed, the budget resolution guides the action of other congressional committees in drafting subsequent spending and revenue legislation within their jurisdiction.

To support this process, the CBO makes budgetary and economic projections, analyzes the proposals set forth in the President's budget request, and details alternative spending and revenue options for lawmakers to consider. The CBO also provides cost estimates of bills approved by congressional committees and tracks the progress of spending and revenue legislation in a scorekeeping system. CBO cost estimates and scorekeeping help the budget committees determine whether the budgetary effects of individual proposals are consistent with the most recent spending and revenue targets.

Upon congressional request, the CBO also produces reports analyzing specific policy

Organization Chart   July 2019

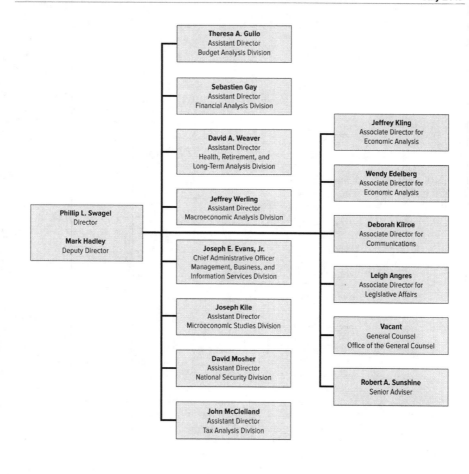

and program issues that are significant for the budget. In keeping with the Office's nonpartisan role, its analyses do not include policy recommendations, and they routinely disclose their underlying assumptions and methods. This open and nonpartisan stance has been instrumental in preserving the credibility of the Office's analyses. https://www.cbo.gov/about/products/RecurringReports

Analysis of the President's Budget   The CBO estimates the budgetary impact of the proposals in the President's budget using its own economic forecast and assumptions. The CBO's independent reestimate allows Congress to compare the administration's spending and revenue proposals with the CBO's baseline projections and other proposals using a consistent set of economic and technical assumptions. https://www.cbo.gov/about/products#2

Baseline Budget Projections and Economic Forecasts   Each year, the CBO issues reports on the budget and economic outlook that cover the 10-year period used in the congressional budget process. Those reports present and explain the CBO's baseline budget projections and economic forecast, which are generally based on current law regarding Federal spending and revenues. The reports also describe the differences between the current projections and previous ones, compare the CBO's economic forecast with those of other forecasters, and show the budgetary impact of some alternative policy assumptions. https://www.cbo.gov/about/products#1

Budgetary and Economic Policy Issues   The CBO also analyzes specific program and policy issues that affect the Federal budget and the economy. Generally, requests for these analyses come from the chair or ranking minority member of a committee or subcommittee or from the leadership of either party in the House or Senate. https://www.cbo.gov/topics/reports-policy-options

Cost Estimates for Bills   The CBO provides cost estimates of every bill to show how it would affect spending or revenues over the next 5 or 10 years, depending on the type of spending involved. The CBO also provides informal estimates at the committee level and other stages in the legislative process. https://www.cbo.gov/publication/54437

Federal Mandates   As required by the Unfunded Mandates Reform Act of 1995, the CBO analyzes the costs that proposed legislation would impose on State, local, and tribal governments and on the private sector. The CBO produces mandate statements with its cost estimates for each committee-approved bill. https://www.cbo.gov/about/products#7

Scorekeeping   The CBO provides the budget and appropriations committees with frequent tabulations of congressional action affecting spending and revenues. Those scorekeeping reports provide information on whether legislative actions are consistent with the spending and revenue levels set by the budget resolution. https://www.cbo.gov/about/products#9

Sources of Information

Blog   The CBO maintains an active blog. https://www.cbo.gov/blog

Business Opportunities   The CBO posts answers to questions that vendors frequently ask. https://www.cbo.gov/about/business-opportunities | Email: procurementservices@cbo.gov

Career Opportunities   CBO employees and interns analyze public policies and their budgetary and economic effects, work with policy analysis experts, support the Congress, and provide nonpartisan and objective analysis. To carry out these activities, the agency relies on professionals with superior academic backgrounds and experience in defense, environmental and resource, financial, health, and labor economics; industrial organization; macroeconomics; public finance; and public-policy analysis. https://www.cbo.gov/about/careers | Email: careers@cbo.gov

According to the Partnership for Public Service, the CBO is an outstanding place to work in the Federal Government. Among 29 small agencies, it placed 3d in the 2018 Best Places To Work rankings. http://bestplacestowork.org/rankings/detail/CB00

Climate   In "Expected Costs of Damage From Hurricane Winds and Storm-Related Flooding" (April 2019), the CBO reports: "Without limits on emissions, the rise in sea levels is predicted to accelerate in the second half of this century . . . . Those increases, along with other changes caused by warming (such as increases in droughts and the spread of certain invasive species), will adversely affect economic output in the future and have other negative effects that are not captured by change in GDP (such as decreases in biodiversity)." https://www.cbo.gov/topics/climate-and-environment/climate-change

Contact Information   The nature of the inquiry determines the best way to contact the agency. The "Contact Information" page has specific contact information for Members of Congress and congressional staff, members of the public, representatives of the media, job candidates, vendors and contractors, and for those wanting to leave a comment about the CBO website. https://www.cbo.gov/about/contact

Cost Estimates   The Congress relies on CBO cost estimates for implementing budget enforcement rules and procedures. https://www.cbo.gov/cost-estimates

Defense Budget   The CBO analyzes the possible consequences of planned reductions in funding for the military's force structure and acquisitions. It also studies the budgetary implications of Department of Defense plans, including military personnel, weapon systems, and operations plans. https://www.cbo.gov/topics/defense-and-national-security/defense-budget

Frequently Asked Questions (FAQs)   The CBO posts answers to the most common questions that people ask. https://www.cbo.gov/faqs

Glossary   The glossary is available online in Portable Document Format (PDF). It defines terms that are commonly used in CBO reports. Many of the entries conform to those published in "A Glossary of Terms Used in the Federal Budget Process" (Government Accountability Office, 2005). https://www.cbo.gov/publication/42904

History   The CBO was birthed in the crucible of conflict: President Richard M. Nixon had threatened to withhold congressional appropriations for programs whose activities diverged from his policies. Members of Congress responded by enacting the Congressional Budget and Impoundment Control Act of 1974. This law reasserted Congress's constitutional control over the budget and created new legislative institutions for implementing the new budget process. One of these institutions was a new legislative-branch agency. To learn more, visit the CBO "History" web page. https://www.cbo.gov/about/history

Information Products   CBO informational, nonpartisan products include baseline projections for selected programs, budget and economic data, and major recurring reports. https://www.cbo.gov/about/products

Interactive Tools / Workbooks   The "Interactives" web page allows visitors to simulate a variety of budget-relevant scenarios and explore their potential costs. For example, the "Force Structure Tool" determines the costs and capabilities of customized plans for the Armed Forces. https://www.cbo.gov/interactives

Nuclear Forces Costs   The CBO projects the 10-year costs of nuclear forces every 2 years. The report of January 2019 contains projections for the period from 2019 to 2028. https://www.cbo.gov/publication/54914

Organizational Chart   The CBO posts its organizational chart in Portable Document Format (PDF) for viewing and downloading. https://www.cbo.gov/system/files/2019-07/CBO-Organization-Chart-2019-07.pdf

Press Center   The most recent CBO news is available online. Each Thursday, the agency posts a list of key publications that are likely to be released during the coming week or soon thereafter. https://www.cbo.gov/about/press-center

Social Media   The CBO has a SlideShare account. https://www.slideshare.net/cbo

The CBO tweets announcements and other newsworthy items on Twitter. https://twitter.com/uscbo

The CBO posts videos on its YouTube channel. https://www.youtube.com/uscbo

Ten Things To Know   The CBO has posted the 10 most important things that it wants people to know about the agency. https://www.cbo.gov/about/10-things-to-know

Topics   The Topics web page allows visitors to browse subjects ranging from agriculture to veterans' issues. https://www.cbo.gov/topics

Transparency   By prioritizing its commitment to transparency, the CBO seeks to promote better understanding of its work, to help people gauge the potential change

in estimates when policies or circumstances differ, and to enhance the credibility of its analyses and processes. https://www.cbo. gov/about/transparency
Visiting Scholars   The CBO welcomes applications from analysts and scholars

in all fields; however, it has a special interest in collaborating with experts in macroeconomics and financial, health, and public economics. https://www. cbo.gov/about/careers/visitingscholars | Email: careers@cbo.gov

The Sources of Information were updated 7–2019.

Government Accountability Office
441 G Street NW., Washington, DC 20548
Phone, 202-512-3000. Internet, http://www.gao.gov

Comptroller General of the United States	GENE L. DODARO
STAFF OFFICES—Managing Directors	
Congressional Relations	ORICE WILLIAMS BROWN
Opportunity and Inclusiveness	EDDA EMMANUELLI-PEREZ
Public Affairs	CHARLES YOUNG
Strategic Planning and External Liaison	JAMES-CHRISTIAN BLOCKWOOD
http://www.gao.gov/cghome/gdbiog.html	
Chief Operating Officer	KATHERINE A. SIGGERUD
Chief Quality Officer	TIMOTHY P. BOWLING
Managing Director of the Continuous Process Improvement Office	PATRICIA MCCLURE
Mission Teams—Managing Directors	
Applied Research and Methods	NANCY KINGSBURY
Contracting and National Security Acquisitions	MICHELE MACKIN
Defense Capabilities and Management	CATHLEEN A. BERRICK
Education, Workforce, and Income Security	BARBARA D. BOVBJERG
Financial Management and Assurance	J. LAWRENCE MALENICH
Financial Markets and Community Investment	LAWRANCE EVANS, JR.
Forensic Audits and Investigative Service	JOHANA R. AYERS
Health Care	A. NICOLE CLOWERS
Homeland Security and Justice	CHARLES M. JOHNSON, JR.
Information Technology and Cybersecurity	VALERIE MELVIN
International Affairs and Trade	THOMAS MELITO
Natural Resources and Environment	MARK E. GAFFIGAN
Physical Infrastructure	DANIEL BERTONI
Strategic Issues	J. CHRISTOPHER MIHM
Chief Administrative Officer / Chief Financial Officer	KARL J. MASCHINO
Deputy Chief Administrative Officer	PAUL R. JOHNSON
GENERAL COUNSEL	THOMAS H. ARMSTRONG
Deputy General Counsel / Ethics Counselor	(VACANCY)
Inspector General	ADAM TRZECIAK
http://www.gao.gov/about/workforce/igbio.html	

The key personnel table was updated 2–2019. *https://www.gao.gov/about/careers/our-teams/*

The Government Accountability Office helps the Congress fulfill its constitutional responsibilities and heightens the Federal Government's accountability and performance.

The Government Accountability Office (GAO) is an independent, nonpartisan agency that works for the Congress. The agency is known as the "congressional watchdog" because it investigates how the Federal Government spends taxpayer dollars. The Budget and Accounting Act of 1921 (31 U.S.C. 702) established the General Accounting Office. Eighty three years later, it was renamed the Government Accountability Office pursuant to the GAO Capital Reform Act of 2004 (31 U.S.C. 702 note).

Activities

The GAO gathers information that the Congress uses to determine how effective executive branch agencies are at carrying out their missions. Its efforts routinely center on answering basic questions: Are Government programs meeting their objectives? Are they providing services of value to the public? Ultimately, the GAO ensures that the Government is accountable to the American people.

To help Senators and Representatives make informed policy decisions, the GAO provides them with accurate, balanced, and timely information. The Office supports congressional oversight by evaluating Government policies and programs; auditing agency operations to ensure effective, efficient, and appropriate spending of Federal funds; investigating allegations of illegal and improper activities; and issuing legal decisions and opinions.

With virtually the entire Federal Government subject to its review, the GAO issues a steady stream of products, including hundreds of reports and testimonies by GAO officials each year. Its reports, which are often called "blue books," meet short-term, immediate needs for information on a wide range of Government operations. These reports help Members of Congress better understand emerging, long-term issues whose effects are far-reaching. The GAO saves billions of American tax dollars by supporting improvements in Government operations and thoughtfulness in legislative actions. http://www.gao.gov/about

Sources of Information

At a Glance   The "GAO at a Glance" web page offers a profile of the agency, including information on the scope and nature of its activities. http://www.gao.gov/about/gglance.html

Bid Protests   Bidders or other interested parties may protest Federal Government procurement contracts. The GAO provides an inexpensive and expeditious forum for the resolution of these protests. Two search tools are available on the "Bid Protests" web page. One allows users to search and access all published bid protest decisions; the other allows users to search the bid protest docket to find status information on cases filed within the past 12 months. http://www.gao.gov/legal/bid-protests/search | Email: ProtestFinder@gao.gov

Blog   The GAO's website features "WatchBlog: Following the Federal Dollar." To receive electronic notifications of new posts, sign up by entering an email address in the appropriate text box on the "WatchBlog" web page. https://blog.gao.gov

Career Opportunities   The GAO relies on attorneys, communications analysts, criminal investigators, economists, financial auditors, information technology analysts, and other professionals to carry out its mission. http://www.gao.gov/careers/index.html

The GAO offers an intern program for students. Appointments for intern positions are 10–16 weeks in length and normally held during summer months. A student must be enrolled on at least a half-time basis, as determined by his or her college or university. A GAO student intern receives an appointment on a nonpermanent basis; however, after completing 400 hours of service and meeting degree requirements, he or she may be eligible for a permanent position. Internships are open to undergraduate and graduate students. http://www.gao.gov/careers/student.html

According to the Partnership for Public Service, the GAO is an outstanding place to work in the Federal Government. Among 27 midsize agencies, it placed fourth in the 2018 Best Places To Work rankings. http://bestplacestowork.org/BPTW/rankings/detail/GA00

Find an Expert   The "Find an Expert" web page is useful for identifying a subject matter expert as a potential speaker for an organizational event. The list of experts includes names, as well as areas of expertise, email addresses, and telephone numbers. https://www.gao.gov/about/contact-us/find-an-expert

FraudNet   FraudNet helps people report suspicion of abuse, fraud, waste, or mismanagement of Federal funds to the appropriate authorities. It refers allegations to Federal, State, and local law enforcement, and to Offices of Inspector General, when appropriate; it supports congressional investigation and audit requests; it provides audit and investigative leads to GAO staff; and it offers support to government at all levels for establishing and operating hotlines. Phone, 800-424-5454. Fax, 202-512-3086. http://www.gao.gov/fraudnet | Email: fraudnet@gao.gov

Freedom of Information Act (FOIA)   The GAO is not subject to the FOIA; however, it discloses information in accordance with the spirit of the Act, while remaining true to its duties and functions as an agency whose primary responsibility is to the Congress. Fax, 202-512-5806. http://www.gao.gov/about/freedom_of_information_act | Email: RecordsRequest@gao.gov

Frequently Asked Questions (FAQs)   The GAO posts answers to general questions about its legal decisions. http://www.gao.gov/legal/more/about

Good Governance   The Center for Audit Excellence promotes good governance and builds the capacity of domestic and international accountability organizations. It provides high-quality training, technical assistance, and related products and services. http://www.gao.gov/resources/centerforauditexcellence/overview

History   After the signing of the armistice agreement of November 11, 1918, the hostilities of the First World War ended. Although the United States had entered the war late as a combatant, it transported millions of troops and their equipment to the Western Front to support the Allies. Wartime spending inflated the national debt, and Congress needed reliable information and enhanced expenditure control. In 1921, to improve managing the Nation's affairs, Congress passed the Budget and Accounting Act. To learn more about this piece of legislation and the role that a new agency was playing in Federal financial management, visit "The History of GAO" web pages. http://www.gao.gov/about/history

Key Issues   The "Key Issues" web pages allow visitors to explore the GAO's work on a range of national issues by agency or topic. The agency's most relevant reports are highlighted on these web pages. http://www.gao.gov/key_issues/overview#t=0

Organizational Chart   The GAO's organizational chart is available on its website. http://www.gao.gov/about/workforce/orgchart.html

Podcast Gallery   Recorded, hosted, and produced by GAO staff, the "Watchdog Report" features interviews with agency officials on significant issues and new reports. http://www.gao.gov/multimedia/podcast

Press Releases   The GAO posts press releases online. https://www.gao.gov/about/press-center/press-releases/

Publications   Most GAO products and publications are available online, free of charge. Charges for printed copies cover the printing, shipping, and handling costs. Phone, 202-512-6000 or 866-801-7077. TDD, 202-512-2537. http://www.gao.gov/ordering.htm

The GAO's website allows visitors to browse reports and testimonies by date and topic and by agency alphabetically or hierarchically. http://www.gao.gov/browse/date/week

The "Principles of Federal Appropriations Law," also known as the "Red Book," is a multivolume treatise on Federal fiscal law. It provides text discussions with references to specific legal authorities to illustrate legal principles, their applications, and exceptions. These references include GAO decisions and judicial decisions, opinions, statutory provisions, and other relevant sources. http://www.gao.gov/legal/red-book/overview

Recommendations Database   The recommendations database contains report recommendations that still need to be addressed. GAO's recommendations help congressional and agency leaders prepare for appropriations and oversight activities, as well as improve Government operations. Recommendations remain open until designated as "closed-implemented" or "closed-not implemented." The general public may browse or search open recommendations online. http://www.gao.gov/recommendations

Reports / Testimonies   The GAO posts an alphabetical listing of significant reports and testimonies each month. https://www.gao.gov/reports-testimonies/month-in-review/top-ten/

Resources   The GAO website features resources that auditors and others promoting accountability may find useful. http://www.gao.gov/resources/auditors/overview

The GAO website features resources that Members of Congress and and their staff may find useful. http://www.gao.gov/resources/congress/overview

The GAO website features resources that Federal agency managers may find useful. http://www.gao.gov/resources/federal_managers/overview

The GAO website features resources that journalists may find useful. http://www.gao.gov/resources/journalists/overview

The GAO website features resources—search tips for locating GAO products on its website, information on using the data and images contained in them, suggestions for additional informational sources—that researchers may find useful. http://www.gao.gov/resources/researchers/overview

Site Map   The website map allows visitors to look for specific topics or to browse content that aligns with their interests. http://www.gao.gov/sitemap.html

Social Media   The GAO uses social media tools—Facebook, Flickr, LinkedIn, Twitter, YouTube—to make its work more accessible to both Congress and the general public. https://www.gao.gov/about/contact-us/stay-connected/

Telephone Directory   The "Organizational Telephone Directory" (January 2019), a resource that the agency updates often, contains GAO personnel contact information. It is available online in Portable Document Format (PDF). http://www.gao.gov/about.gao/phonebook/orgphonebook.pdf

Updates   A subscription form is available on the GAO's website to sign up for email updates on the latest reports. Daily or monthly electronic updates are options, too, as well as notifications about correspondence, reports, and testimony that fall within a specific topic area. http://www.gao.gov/subscribe/index.php

Video Gallery   The GAO website features a video collection that is diverse and extensive, educational and informative. http://www.gao.gov/multimedia/video/#video_id=679942

Widgets   Snippets of HTML code for embedding small news widgets that refresh automatically are available on the GAO website. Pasting the code into the desired location on a website makes the most recent reports and testimonies and legal decisions from GAO locally accessible. http://www.gao.gov/widgets_reports_and_legal.html http://www.gao.gov/about/contact.html | Email: contact@gao.gov

For further information, contact the Office of Public Affairs, Government Accountability Office, 441 G Street NW., Washington, DC 20548. Phone, 202-512-4800.

Government Publishing Office

732 North Capitol Street NW., Washington, DC 20401
Phone, 202-512-1800. Internet, http://www.gpo.gov

Director	HUGH N. HALPERN
Deputy Director	PATRICIA COLLINS
Equal Employment Opportunity Managing Director https://www.gpo.gov/who-we-are/our-agency/leadership	(VACANCY)

Administration

Chief Administrative Officer	(VACANCY)
Administrative Services Manager	RICHARD G. DAVIS, ACTING
Chief Officers	
Acquisition	LORNA E. BAPTISTE-JONES
Human Capital	DAN M. MIELKE
Information	WESAM MUSA FINANCE

Chief Financial Officer	William L. Boesch, Jr. Legal
General Counsel	Kerry L. Miller
Associate General Counsel—Labor Relations	Melissa Hatfield Operations
Deputy Director	Patricia Collins
Managing Directors	
Official Journals of Government	Gregory Estep, Acting
Plant Operations	John W. Crawford
Security and Intelligent Documents	Stephen G. LeBlanc
Customer Services	Sandra K. MacAfee Public Access
Superintendent of Documents	Laurie Hall
Library Services and Content Management Managing Director	Laurie Hall
Publications and Information Sales Chief	Lisa L. Williams Security Services
Chief Security Officer	LaMont R. Vernon Strategy
Chief of Staff	Richard G. Davis, Acting
Chief Officers	
Technology	Richard G. Davis
Public Relations	Gary Somerset
Specialists	
Congressional Relations	James McCarthy
Employee Communications	Gary Somerset
Inspector General https://www.gpo.gov/who-we-are/our-agency/inspector-general/overview-and-hotline	Michael P. Leary

The above list of key personnel was updated 9–2021.
The Government Publishing Office produces, procures, and disseminates printed and electronic publications of the Congress, executive departments, and Federal agencies and establishments

Establishment and Organization

On June 23, 1860, the U.S. Congress passed Joint Resolution 25 in "Relation to the Public Printing" (12 Stat. 117). It empowered the Superintendent of Public Printing to execute the printing and binding that the Senate and House of Representatives, the executive and judicial departments, and the Court of Claims authorized. It also directed the Superintendent "to contract for the erection or purchase of the necessary buildings, machinery, and materials for that purpose." The Government Printing Office opened for business on March 4, 1861, the same day that President Abraham Lincoln was sworn into office and a few weeks after the first salvos of the American Civil War, when Confederate guns bombarded Fort Sumter in Charleston Harbor. https://www.loc.gov/law/help/statutes-at-large/36th-congress/c36.pdf

On December 17, 2014, President Barack Obama approved Public Law 113–235, which is commonly cited as the "Consolidated and Further Continuing Appropriations Act, 2015." Section 1301 of that law (128 Stat. 2537) redesignated the Government Printing Office as the Government Publishing Office (GPO). Congress changed the name to reflect the prominent role that the GPO plays in providing access to Government information in digital formats. https://www.congress.

Government Publishing Office

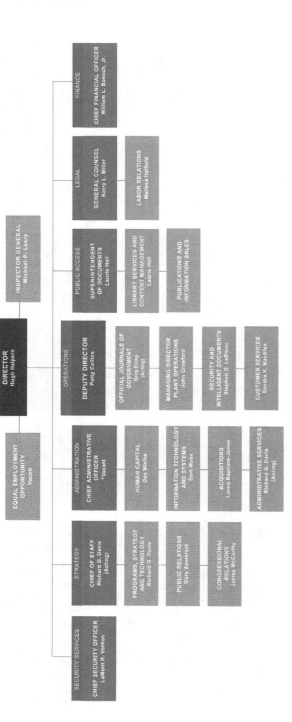

DIRECTOR
Hugh Halpern

INSPECTOR GENERAL
Michael P. Leary

EQUAL EMPLOYMENT OPPORTUNITY
Vacant

FINANCE
CHIEF FINANCIAL OFFICER
William L. Boesch, Jr.

LEGAL
GENERAL COUNSEL
Kerry L. Miller

LABOR RELATIONS
Melissa Hatfield

PUBLIC ACCESS
SUPERINTENDENT OF DOCUMENTS
Laurie Hall

LIBRARY SERVICES AND CONTENT MANAGEMENT
Laurie Hall

PUBLICATIONS AND INFORMATION SALES

OPERATIONS
DEPUTY DIRECTOR
Patty Collins

OFFICIAL JOURNALS OF GOVERNMENT
Greg Estep
(Acting)

MANAGING DIRECTOR
PLANT OPERATIONS
John Crawford

SECURITY AND INTELLIGENT DOCUMENTS
Stephen G. LeBlanc

CUSTOMER SERVICES
Sandra K. MacAfee

ADMINISTRATION
CHIEF ADMINISTRATIVE OFFICER
Vacant

HUMAN CAPITAL
Dan Mielke

INFORMATION TECHNOLOGY AND SYSTEMS
Sam Musa

ACQUISITIONS
Lorna Baptiste-Jones

ADMINISTRATIVE SERVICES
Richard G. Davis
(Acting)

STRATEGY
CHIEF OF STAFF
Richard G. Davis
(Acting)

PROGRAMS, STRATEGY AND TECHNOLOGY
Richard G. Davis

PUBLIC RELATIONS
Gary Somerset

CONGRESSIONAL RELATIONS
James McCarthy

SECURITY SERVICES
CHIEF SECURITY OFFICER
LaMont R. Vernon

gov/113/plaws/publ235/PLAW-113publ235.pdf

By the advice of the Senate, the President nominates "a suitable person" as the Director; with its consent, the President appoints him or her "to take charge of and manage" the agency (44 U.S.C. 301). https://uscode.house.gov/view.xhtml?req=granuleid:USC-prelim-title44-section301&num=0&edition=prelim

The agency's organizational chart is available in Portable Document Format (PDF) for viewing and downloading on the "Leadership" web page. https://www.gpo.gov/docs/default-source/leadership-pdf-file/gpo-organizational-chart_july-2021.pdf

Statutory Authorities   Duties of the GPO are defined in 44 U.S.C. https://uscode.house.gov/view.xhtml?path=/prelim@title44&edition=prelim

Activities

Headquartered in Washington, DC, with a total employment of approximately 1,580, the Office is responsible for the production and distribution of information products and services for the three branches of the Federal Government. It is the Federal Government's primary centralized resource for producing, procuring, cataloging, indexing, authenticating, disseminating, and preserving the official information products of the U.S. Government in digital and tangible forms.

While many of the informational products, such as the "Congressional Record" and "Federal Register," are produced at the main GPO plant, most of the Government's printing is done in partnership with America's printing industry. The Office procures 75 percent of all printing orders through private sector vendors across the country, competitively buying products and services from thousands of businesses in all 50 States. The contracts cover the entire spectrum of printing and publishing services and are suitable for companies of all sizes.

The agency disseminates Federal information products through a sales program, a nationwide distribution network of Federal depository libraries, the Federal Digital System (FDsys), and the free U.S. Government information service known as govinfo, which is replacing FDsys. The

public can already access hundreds of thousands of Federal Government document titles by visiting the govinfo website. https://www.gpo.gov/who-we-are/our-agency/mission-vision-and-goals

Sources of Information

Annual Reports / Budget Submissions   An annual report archives and budget submission archives are available on the "Congressional Relations" web page. https://www.gpo.gov/who-we-are/our-agency/congressional-relations

Archived Records   The records of the GPO are referenced in the "Guide to Federal Records in the National Archives of the United States." The Guide is accessible online, and GPO records have been assigned to Record Group 149. https://www.archives.gov/research/guide-fed-records/groups/149.html

Ben's Guide   An educational website for children and young adults, Ben's Guide has learning adventures for the apprentice level (ages 4–8), journeyperson level (ages 9–13), and master level (ages 14 and older). https://bensguide.gpo.gov

Blog   "Government Book Talk" offers reviews of new and popular publications, talking about forthcoming and out-of-print books. The blog spotlights the variety of Government publications that are available and the scope of their influence. https://govbooktalk.gpo.gov

Bookstore   Printed copies of many documents, ranging from Supreme Court opinions to reports from the Bureau of Labor Statistics, may be purchased. To order in person, visit the GPO Main Bookstore at 710 North Capitol Street NW., Washington, DC (corner of North Capitol Street NW. and G Street), 8 a.m.–4 p.m. To order online, use the link below. To order by phone or inquire about an order, call 866-512-1800 or 202-512-1800 (Washington, DC–metropolitan area), 8 a.m.–5:30 p.m., eastern standard time. All orders require prepayment by an American Express, Discover/NOVUS, MasterCard, or VISA credit card; check or money order; or Superintendent of Documents (SOD) deposit account, which customers who purchase Government products on a recurring basis can open

with the GPO. Fax, 202-512-2104. https://
bookstore.gpo.gov | Email: contactcenter@
gpo.gov

Business Opportunities   GPO procurement
services teams post open term contract and
one-time bid solicitations online. https://
www.gpo.gov/how-to-work-with-us/vendors/
contract-opportunities

Small purchase solicitations are posted
on the "Quick Quote" website. https://
contractorconnection.gpo.gov/OpenJobs.
aspx

Career Opportunities   The GPO provides
other Government agencies with services
for the printing, publishing, distribution,
and storage of digital content. To deliver
these services successfully, it relies
on creative, energetic, and talented
professionals representing diverse trades and
administrative fields. https://www.gpo.gov/
who-we-are/careers/how-to-apply

**Catalog of U.S. Government Publications
(CGP)**   The CGP is a searchable Federal
publications catalog that contains
descriptive information on recent and
historical publications, as well as links to
some complete documents. Users may
search the catalog by agency, keywords,
subject, and title. https://catalog.gpo.
gov/F?RN=785806650

Congressional Record   The "Congressional
Record" (CR) is the official record of
the proceedings and debates of the U.S.
Congress. When the U.S. Congress is in
session, it is published daily. The CR's
publication history started in 1873 and
continues to the present. The first link leads
to CR bound editions from 1873 to 2016.
https://www.govinfo.gov/app/collection/crecb

CR electronic editions 1994–2020 https://
www.govinfo.gov/app/collection/CREC

Congressional Relations   The Office
of Congressional Relations responds to
congressional inquiries and requests. Phone,
202-512-1991. Fax, 202-512-1293. https://
www.gpo.gov/who-we-are/our-agency/
congressional-relations

Contact Information   The "Contact
Us" web page is laden with hyperlinked
resources. An electronic form allows various
categories of online visitors to submit an
inquiry to GPO staff. https://ask.gpo.gov/s/

**Federal Depository Library Program
(FDLP)**   Libraries that participate in the

FDLP maintain a basic collection of key
sources of information for supporting the
general public's right to know about the
essential activities and workings of the
Federal Government. https://www.fdlp.gov/
requirements-guidance/collections-and-
databases/1442-basic-collection

Federal Lawmaking   An outline of the
Federal lawmaking process—starting with
the introduction of a bill by a Member of
the Congress, continuing through its passage
by both Chambers, and culminating in the
President's approval—is available online in
Portable Document Format (PDF). https://
www.gpo.gov/docs/default-source/media-kit-
files/how-a-bill-becomes-a-Law.pdf

Federal Register   Documents that the
GPO recently published in the Federal
Register are accessible online. https://www.
federalregister.gov/agencies/government-
publishing-office

Govinfo   Free public access to the full
text of official publications from the three
branches of the Federal Government is
available at govinfo. The website also serves
as a standards-compliant preservation
repository, offers advanced search engine
capabilities, and functions as a content
management system to control digital
content throughout its lifecycle. https://www.
govinfo.gov

History   The GPO opened for business
several weeks before Confederate artillery
opened fire on a Federal fort in Charleston
Harbor. Within 18 months of the first salvo,
the GPO had readied one of the most
significant documents in American history
for President Abraham Lincoln's signature.
To learn more about the 1862 war order that
acted as a precursor to the Emancipation
Proclamation of 1863, watch the video
"Lincoln and His Printers: GPO in the Civil
War." https://www.gpo.gov/who-we-are/our-
agency/history

A GPO timeline and short history of
making electronic Government information
accessible to the public is available online.
https://www.govinfo.gov/about/history

Media Kit   The GPO media kit contains
links to access resources and to download
information that may be useful for reporters
and Federal agency customers. It also has
a list of links providing easy access to the
agency's social media sites. For additional

information, contact the Public Relations team. Phone, 202-512-1957. https://www.gpo.gov/who-we-are/news-media/media-kit
News / Press Releases   The GPO posts the latest news and maintains a news archive, from 1997 to the present, on its website. Phone, 202-512-1957. Fax, 202-512-1998. https://www.gpo.gov/who-we-are/news-media/news-and-press-releases
Offices / Distribution Centers   Contact information for nationwide offices and the Laurel, MD, and Pueblo, CO, distribution centers is available on the GPO website. https://www.gpo.gov/who-we-are/our-agency/office-locations
Oversight   The Office of the Inspector General from the GPO posts reports and data on Oversight.gov, a text-searchable repository of reports that Federal

Inspectors General publish. The Council of the Inspectors General on Integrity and Efficiency operates and maintains the website to increase public access to independent and authoritative information on the Federal Government. https://oversight.gov
Social Media   The GPO maintains a presence on six social media sites: Facebook, Twitter, YouTube, LinkedIn, Instagram, and Pinterest. Links to these sites are listed together in one location on the "Media Kit" web page. https://www.gpo.gov/who-we-are/news-media/media-kit
Style Manual   An official guide to the form and style of Federal Government publishing is available online. https://www.govinfo.gov/content/pkg/GPO-STYLEMANUAL-2016/pdf/GPO-STYLEMANUAL-2016.pdf

The Sources of Information were updated 9–2021.

Library of Congress
101 Independence Avenue SE., Washington, DC 20540
Phone, 202-707-5000. Internet, http://www.loc.gov

Librarian of Congress	CARLA D. HAYDEN
Deputy Librarian for Institutional Advancement	ROBERT R. NEWLEN
Chief of Staff	ELIZABETH C. MORRISON
Chief Operating Officer	EDWARD R. JABLONSKI
General Counsel	ELIZABETH PUGH
Inspector General	KURT W. HYDE
Chief Communications Officer	ROSWELL M. ENCINA
Director of Human Resources Services	RACHEL BOUMAN
Director of Congressional Research Service	MARY B. MAZANEC
Associate Librarian for Library Services	J. MARK SWEENEY
Director of National International Outreach	JANE MCAULIFFE
Law Librarian of Congress	JANE F. SÁNCHEZ
Acting Register of Copyrights	KARYN A. TEMPLE CLAGGETT

Library of Congress Trust Fund Board

Chair (Librarian of Congress)	CARLA D. HAYDEN
(Fiscal Assistant Secretary of the Treasury)	DAVID A. LEBRYK
(Chair, Joint Committee on the Library)	GREGG HARPER
(Vice Chair, Joint Committee on the Library)	RICHARD SHELBY
Member	KATHLEEN L. CASEY
Member	J. RICHARD FREDERICKS
Member	THOMAS GIRARDI
Member	CHRISTOPHER G. LONG
Member	SHEILA MARCELO

Member	GEORGE MARCUS
Member	JOHN MILLER
Member	(VACANCY)
Member	(VACANCY)
Member	(VACANCY)

The Library of Congress is the national library of the United States, offering diverse materials for research, including the world's most extensive collections in areas such as American history, music, and law.

The Library of Congress was established by Act of April 24, 1800 (2 Stat. 56), appropriating $5,000 "for the purchase of such books as may be necessary for the use of Congress . . . ." The Library's scope of responsibility has been widened by subsequent legislation (2 U.S.C. 131-168d). The Librarian, appointed by the President with the advice and consent of the Senate, directs the Library.

The Library's first responsibility is service to Congress. Its Congressional Research Service provides Congress with legislative research and analysis that is authoritative, confidential, objective, and timely during all stages of the legislative process. The Library's Congress.gov Web site serves as a source of legislative information for both Congress and the general public. https://www.congress.gov

As the Library has developed, its range of service has expanded to include the entire governmental establishment and the public at large. The Library serves as a national library for the United States, and its online presence makes it a global resource. https://www.loc.gov/about

Activities

Collections The Library's extensive collections are universal in scope. They include books, serials, and pamphlets on every subject and in more than 470 languages, and research materials in many formats, including maps, photographs, manuscripts, motion pictures, and sound recordings. Among them are the most comprehensive collections of books outside Asia and the former Soviet Union; the largest collection of published aeronautical literature; and the most extensive collection of books in the Western Hemisphere.

The manuscript collections relate to various aspects of American history and civilization and include the personal papers of most of the Presidents from George Washington to Calvin Coolidge. The music collections contain volumes and pieces—manuscript and published—from classic works to the newest popular compositions. Other materials available for research include maps and views; photographic records; recordings, prints, drawings, and posters; government documents, newspapers, and periodicals; and motion pictures, microforms, audio and video tapes, and digital and online materials. https://www.loc.gov/discover

Reference Resources Admission to the various research facilities of the Library is free. The Library's reading rooms are open to persons age 16 and older. Readers must register by presenting valid photo identification with a current address. For some collections, there are additional requirements. While priority is given to inquiries about special materials or to unique resources, the Library provides helpful responses to all inquirers. Online reference service is also available through the "Ask a Librarian" Web page. http://www.loc.gov/rr

Copyrights With the enactment of the second general revision of the U.S. copyright law by Act of July 8, 1870 (16 Stat. 212–217), all activities relating to copyright, including deposit and registration, were centralized in the Library of Congress. The Copyright Act of 1976 (90 Stat. 2541) brought all forms of copyrightable authorship, both published and unpublished, under a single statutory system which gives authors protection upon creation of their works. Exclusive rights granted to authors under the statute include the right to reproduce and prepare derivative works, distribute copies or phonorecords, perform and display the work publicly, and in the case of sound recordings, to perform the work publicly by means of a digital audio transmission. Works eligible for copyright include literary works (books and periodicals), musical works, dramatic works, pantomimes and choreographic works, pictorial, graphic, and sculptural works, motion pictures, sound recordings, vessel hull designs, mask works, and architectural works.

The Copyright Office serves as a National registry for creative works, registering more than 500,000 claims annually. It is also a major source of acquisitions for the Library's collections. Most paper information is also accessible on its Web site. http://www.copyright.gov

Extension of Service   The Library offers duplication services; the sale of sound recordings, cataloging data and tools; the exchange of duplicates with other institutions; development of classification schemes; preparation of bibliographic lists for Government and research; maintenance and publication of cooperative publications; and publication of catalogs, bibliographic guides, and lists, and texts of original manuscripts and rare books. It has items for circulation in traveling exhibitions; books in Braille, as well as "talking books on the Internet, and books on tape. The Library distributes electronic materials and provides research and analytical services for a fee. The Library also manages the following programs: centralized and cooperative cataloging; cataloging-in-publication for unpublished books; interlibrary loan system; and the U.S. International Standard Serial Number (ISSN) Center.

Furthermore, the Library provides for the following: the preparation of bibliographical lists responsive to the needs of Government and research; the maintenance and the publication of cooperative publications; the publication of catalogs, bibliographical guides, and lists, and of texts of original manuscripts and rare books in the Library of Congress; the circulation in traveling exhibitions of items from the Library's collections; the provision of books in Braille, electronic access to Braille books on the Internet, "talking books," and books on tape for the blind and the physically handicapped

through more than 100 cooperating libraries throughout the Nation; the distribution of its electronic materials via the Internet; and the provision of research and analytical services on a fee-for-service basis to agencies in the executive and judicial branches. https://www.loc.gov/services

American Folklife Center   The American Folklife Center was established in the Library of Congress by Act of January 2, 1976 (20 U.S.C. 2102 et seq.). It supports, preserves, and presents American folklife by receiving and maintaining folklife collections, scholarly research, field projects, performances, exhibitions, festivals, workshops, publications, and audiovisual presentations. The Center administers the Veterans History Project, which records and preserves the first-person accounts of war veterans. It collaborates with the Smithsonian Institution's National Museum of African American History and Culture to maintain the Civil Rights History Project and its resulting collection of interviews with leaders and participants in the Civil Rights movement. The Center also maintains and administers the American Folklife Center Archive, which is an extensive multi-format collection of ethnographic materials from this country and around the world, and serves as the national repository for folk-related field recordings, manuscripts, and other unpublished materials. The Archive also contains the collections of StoryCorps, a program to record and collect oral histories from people from all walks of life.

The Center's reading room contains over 4,000 books and periodicals; a sizable collection of magazines, newsletters, unpublished theses, and dissertations; field notes; and many textual and some musical transcriptions and recordings. Information on the Center's blog, social media, publications, and collections is available online. https://www.loc.gov/folklife

For further information, call 202-707-5510.

Center for the Book   The Center was established in the Library of Congress by an Act of October 13, 1977 (2 U.S.C. 171 et seq.), to stimulate public interest in books, reading, and libraries, and to encourage the study of books and print culture. The Center promotes and explores the vital role of books, reading, and libraries, nationally and internationally. As a partnership between the Government and the private sector, the Center for the Book depends on tax-deductible contributions from individuals and corporations to support its programs.

The Center's activities are directed toward the general public and scholars. The overall program includes reading promotion projects with television and radio networks, symposia, lectures, exhibitions, special events, and publications. More than 80 national education and civic organizations participate in the Center's annual reading promotion campaign.

The Center provides leadership for 52 affiliated State—including the District of Columbia and the Virgin Islands—centers for the book and nonprofit reading-promotion partners. It oversees the Library's read.gov Web site, administers the Library's Young Readers Center and its Poetry and Literature Center, and plays a key role in the Library's annual National Book Festival. The Center also administers the position of Poet Laureate Consultant in Poetry, as well as, in collaboration with the Children's Book Council, the position of the National Ambassador for Young People's Literature. http://www.read.gov/cfb | Email: cfbook@loc. gov

For further information, contact the Center for the Book. Phone, 202-707-5221. Fax, 202-707-0269.

National Film Preservation Board   The National Film Preservation Board, established by the National Film Preservation Act of 1988 (102 Stat. 1785) and reauthorized by the National Film Preservation Act of 2005 (2 U.S.C. 179l note), serves as a public advisory group to the Librarian of Congress. The Board works to ensure the survival, conservation, and increased public availability of America's film heritage, including advising the Librarian on the annual selection of films to the National Film Registry and counseling the Librarian on development and implementation of the national film preservation plan. https://www.loc.gov/ programs/national-film-preservation-board/ about-this-program

For further information, call 202-707-5912.

National Sound Recording Preservation Board   The National Recording Preservation

Board, established by the National Recording Preservation Act of 2000 (2 U.S.C. 1701 note) reviews nominated sound recordings for inclusion in the National Recording Registry and advises the Librarian on the inclusion of such recordings in the Registry to preserve sound recordings that are culturally, historically, or aesthetically significant. The Board comprises three major components: a National Recording Preservation Advisory Board, which brings together experts in the field; a National Recording Registry; and a fundraising foundation, all of which are conducted under the auspices of the Library of Congress. The Board implements a national plan for the long-term preservation and accessibility of the Nation's audio heritage. The national recording preservation program sets standards for future private and public preservation efforts in conjunction with the Library's National Audio-Visual Conservation Center in Culpeper, VA. https://www.loc.gov/ programs/national-recording-preservation-board/about-this-program

For further information, call 202-707-5856.

Preservation   The Library provides technical information related to the preservation of library and archival material. The Library's Preservation Directorate includes three preservation science laboratories, a Center for the Library's Analytical Science Samples, and a Collections Recovery Room. Information on publications and various preservation and conservation topics is available online. http://www.loc.gov/rr/ askalib/ask-preserv.html

For further information, call 202-707-1840.

Sources of Information

Books for the Blind and Physically Handicapped   Braille and talking books and magazines, including music materials, are distributed through more than 100 regional and subregional libraries to residents of the United States and its territories who are blind or have a physical disability. Eligible Americans living abroad are also able to participate. Users may also register for the Braille and Audio Reading Download (BARD) online service, enabling them to use the BARD mobile app to read on smart devices. Information is available from the National Library Service for the Blind and Physically Handicapped, Library of Congress, 1291 Taylor Street NW., Washington, DC 20542-4960. Phone, 202-707-5100 or 1-888-NLS-READ (1-888-657-7323). http://www.loc.gov/ThatAllMayRead | Email: nls@loc.gov

Business Opportunities To learn about business opportunities, visit the "Doing Business With the Library" Web page. http://www.loc.gov/about/doing-business-with-the-library

Cataloging Distribution Services Cataloging and bibliographic information in the form of microfiche catalogs, book catalogs, magnetic tapes, CD-ROM cataloging tools, bibliographies, and other technical publications is distributed to libraries and other institutions. Information about ordering materials is available from the Cataloging Distribution Service, Library of Congress, Washington, DC 20541-4910. Phone, 202-707-6100. TDD, 202-707-0012. Fax, 202-707-1334. Email, cdsinfo@mail. loc.gov. Card numbers for new publications and Electronic Preassigned Control Numbers for publishers are available from the Cataloging in Publication Division, Library of Congress, Washington, DC 20541-4910. Phone, 202-707-6345.

Copyright Services Information about the copyright law (title 17 of the U.S. Code), the method of securing copyright, and copyright registration procedures may be obtained by writing to the Copyright Office, Library of Congress, 101 Independence Avenue SE., Washington, DC 20559-6000. Phone, 202-707-3000. Registration application forms may be ordered by calling the forms hotline at 202-707-9100. Copyright records may be researched and reported by the Copyright Office for a fee; for an estimate, call 202-707-6850. Members of the public may use the copyright card catalog in the Copyright Office without charge. The database of Copyright Office records cataloged from January 1, 1978, to the present is available online at http://cocatalog.loc.gov/. The Copyright Information Office is located in Room LM-401, James Madison Memorial Building, 101 Independence Avenue SE., Washington, DC 20559-6000. It is open to the public Monday through Friday, 8:30 a.m. to 5 p.m., except for Federal holidays. http://www.loc.gov/copyright

Employment The Library offers many opportunities for those seeking employment, fellowships or internships, or volunteer positions. Job vacancy announcements and application information are posted online and also available from the Employment Office, Room LM-107, 101 Independence Avenue SE., Washington, DC 20540. Phone, 202-707-4315. http://www.loc.gov/hr/employment

Duplication Services Copies of manuscripts, prints, photographs, maps, and book material not subject to copyright and other restrictions are available for a fee. Order forms for photo reproduction and price schedules are available from Duplication Services, Library of Congress, 101 Independence Avenue SE., Washington, DC 20540-4570. Phone, 202-707-5640. http://www.loc.gov/duplicationservices

Exhibitions Throughout the year, the Library offers free exhibitions featuring items from its collections. Library exhibitions may be viewed Monday through Saturday, 8:30 a.m. to 4:30 p.m., in the Thomas Jefferson Building. For more information, call 202-707-4604. To view current and past exhibitions online, use the link below. http://www.loc.gov/exhibits

Federal Agency Research Services Federal agencies can procure research and analytical products on foreign and domestic topics using the collections of the Library of Congress through the Federal Research Division. Science, technology, humanities, and social science research are conducted by staff specialists exclusively on behalf of Federal agencies on a fee-for-service basis. Research requests should be directed to the Federal Research Division, Marketing Office, Library of Congress, Washington, DC 20540-4840. Phone, 202-707-9133. Fax, 202-707-3920. https://www.loc.gov/rr/frd

Publications Library of Congress publications are available online. The Library of Congress Magazine (LCM) is published 6 times a year and may be viewed online at http://www.loc.gov/lcm/. The calendar of public events is also available online at www.loc.gov/loc/events and is available by mail to persons within 100 miles of Washington, DC. To be added to the calendar mailing list, send a request to Office Systems Services, Mail and Distribution Management Section, Library of Congress,

101 Independence Avenue SE., Washington, DC 20540-9441 or send an email to pao@loc.gov. http://www.loc.gov/visit/shopping

Reference and Bibliographic Services   Guidance is offered to readers in identifying and using the material in the Library's collections, and reference service is provided to those with inquiries who have exhausted local, State, and regional resources. Persons requiring services that cannot be performed by the Library staff can be supplied with names of private researchers who work on a fee-for-service basis. Requests for information should be directed to the Reference Referral Service, Library of Congress, 101 Independence Avenue SE., Washington, DC 20540-4720. Phone, 202-707-5522. Fax, 202-707-1389. Questions may also be submitted online at the "Ask a Librarian" Web site. http://www.loc.gov/rr/askalib

Research and Reference Services in Science and Technology   Requests for reference services should be directed to the Science, Technology, and Business Division, Library of Congress, Science Reference Section, 101 Independence Avenue SE., Washington, DC 20540-4750. Phone, 202-707-5639. http://www.loc.gov/rr/scitech

Tours   Guided tours of the Library are available on weekdays, 10:30 a.m.–3:30 p.m., and on Saturdays at 10:30 and 11:30 a.m. and at 1:30 and 2:30 p.m. For more information on scheduling a tour for a group of 10 or more, contact the Visitor Services Office. Phone, 202-707-0919. https://www.loc.gov/visit/tours; http://www.loc.gov | Email: pao@loc.gov

For further information, contact the Public Affairs Office, Library of Congress, 101 Independence Avenue SE., Washington, DC 20540-8610. Phone, 202-707-2905. Fax, 202-707-2905. Fax, 202-707-9199.

Congressional Research Service

101 Independence Avenue SE., Washington, DC 20540
Phone, 202-707-5000

Director	MARY B. MAZANEC
Deputy Director	T.J. HALSTEAD

The above list of key personnel was updated 12–2020. *https://www.loc.gov/crsinfo/about/ofc-dir.html*

The Congressional Research Service provides high quality research, analysis, information, and confidential consultation to help the U.S. Congress carry out its legislative, representational and oversight duties.

Establishment and Organization

In 1914, President Woodrow Wilson approved a law to to establish a separate department within the Library of Congress. That department was named the Legislative Reference Service, and its purpose was to serve the legislative needs of the U.S. Congress. https://www.loc.gov/crsinfo/about/history.html

With the Legislative Reorganization Act of 1970, the U.S. Congress changed the name of the Legislative Reference Service to the Congressional Research Service (CRS) and expanded its statutory obligations. https://www.loc.gov/crsinfo/about/history.html

The CRS is organized into five research divisions: American Law; Domestic Social Policy; Foreign Affairs, Defense and Trade; Government and Finance; and Resources, Science and Industry. Research support services are given to the policy experts in each of the five divisions by the Knowledge Services Group. https://www.loc.gov/crsinfo/research/

The Office of the Director and other infrastructure offices oversee long-term goals and provide management and administrative support.

The CRS has about 600 employees who are based in Washington, DC. More than 400 of them are attorneys, information professionals, and policy analysts working in one of the five research divisions. https://www.loc.gov/crsinfo/about/structure.html

Activities

The CRS provides comprehensive research and analysis on all legislative and oversight issues of interest to the U.S. Congress. The CRS assists Congress by responding to specific questions and by preparing reports on legislative topics in anticipation of questions and emerging issues. The CRS works with Members, committees, and congressional staff to identify and clarify policy problems and assess the implications of proposed policy alternatives. CRS experts play a role in every stage of the legislative process. http://www.loc.gov/crsinfo/about

Sources of Information

Annual Reports   The CRS posts its annual reports on the "About CRS" webs page. https://www.loc.gov/crsinfo/about/
Career Opportunities   The CRS hires motivated and talented individuals who can contribute to its unique role in supporting the U.S. Congress. To carry out the CRS's mission, the research divisions rely on attorneys, information professionals, and policy analysts, whose expertise falls within a variety of disciplines. Those disciplines include defense, economics, education, energy, environmental protection, foreign affairs, healthcare, homeland security, immigration, law, public administration, science, and technology. https://www.loc.gov/crsinfo/opportunities/
Contact Information   The "Contact Us" web page contains an electronic comment and question form. CRS staff responds to questions about employment and specific job listings. CRS staff works exclusively for the U.S. Congress; therefore, they do not respond to inquiries pertaining to other subjects. https://www.loc.gov/crsinfo/contact/
History   To mark the centennial of the CRS, communications specialist Cory V. Langley complied the article "CRS at 100—Informing the Legislative Debate Since 1914." The article was published in the May and June 2014 issue of "Library of Congress Magazine," pages 14–18. Accompanying the article is a CRS timeline that runs from 1914 though 2014. https://www.loc.gov/lcm/pdf/LCM_2014_0506.pdf
Reports   CRS reports are accessible on the website Congress.gov. A search tool is available on the "Search CRS Reports" web page. https://crsreports.congress.gov/
Values   All queries from Members of Congress and exchanges between them and CRS staff are confidential; all CRS services and products are authoritative; and to the maximum extent that human nature allows, CRS analyses are objective and nonpartisan. https://www.loc.gov/crsinfo/about/values.html

The Sources of Information were updated 12–2020.

United States Botanic Garden

Office of Executive Director, 245 First Street SW., Washington, DC 20024
Phone, 202-226-8333. Internet, http://www.usbg.gov | Email: usbg@aoc.gov

Conservatory, 100 Maryland Avenue SW., Washington, DC 20001

Production Facility, 4700 Shepherd Parkway SW., Washington, DC 20032
Phone, 202-226-4780

Acting Director

(vacancy)
https://www.aoc.gov/organization/acting-architect

Executive Director

Saharah Moon Chapotin
https://www.usbg.gov/staff/saharah-moon-chapotin-phd

The above list of key personnel was updated 10–2019.
The United States Botanic Garden demonstrates the essential contribution that plants make aesthetically, culturally, ecologically, economically, and therapeutically, to the well-being of humankind, and it supports partnerships, nationally and internationally, by fostering exchanges of information and ideas.

Establishment and Organization

The U.S. Botanic Garden (USBG) has a long root that runs deep in the soil of the Nation's history. On October 21, 1796, while addressing some gentlemen in a letter from Mount Vernon, President George Washington conceived that "a Botanical Garden would be a good appendage to the Institution of a University" in the "Federal City." Twenty-four years later, that conception blossomed, when President James Madison helped establish a botanic garden in the U.S. Capital under the auspices of the Columbian Institute, a society dedicated to promoting the arts and sciences. This early botanic collection served as the core of what would grow to become the Nation's future botanic garden. https://founders.archives.gov/?q=%20 Author%3A%22Washington%2C%20 George%22&s=1211311113&r=2118

The U.S. Congress also supported establishing a national botanic garden. By an act of August 26, 1842, it made provision for the safekeeping and arrangement of dried and living specimens that Lieutenant Charles Wilkes's expedition had collected while exploring the Pacific Rim. Congress enacted that the enlarged collection should be placed under the stewardship of its Joint Committee on the Library and that it should be kept in the upper room of the Patent Office (5 Stat. 534). http://www.loc.gov/ law/help/statutes-at-large/27th-congress/ session-2/c27s2ch205.pdf

When the old Patent Office was expanded in 1849, a new location for the plants and greenhouse had to be found. Congress again intervened and, by an act of May 15, 1850, funded the construction of a new greenhouse and the collection's removal and relocation to a "suitable site on the public grounds" of the Capitol. The Joint Committee on the Library, with supervision from the Commissioner of Public Buildings, managed the project (9 Stat. 427). A new national botanic garden opened on the National Mall, at the west end of the Capitol Grounds, later that year. http://www.loc. gov/law/help/statutes-at-large/31st-congress/ session-1/c31s1ch10.pdf

By 1856—the collection had been named officially the United States Botanic Garden, Congress was providing an annual appropriation for its upkeep, and the Joint Committee on the Library had assumed responsibility for both its direction and maintenance. To satisfy the McMillan Commission's plan for a large, open mall, the USBG relocated one block south, to its present site, in 1933. The Joint Committee on the Library maintains oversight of the USBG through the Architect of the Capitol, who holds the title of Acting Director. https://www. usbg.gov/brief-history-us-botanic-garden

Activities

The USBG highlights botanical diversity worldwide and informs people about plants' aesthetic, cultural, ecological, economic, and therapeutic significance. The agency promotes appreciation of plants and stimulates interest in botany through artistic plant displays, education programs, exhibits, and curation of a large plant collection. It supports conservation by serving as a repository for endangered plant species. It also encourages the exchange of ideas and disseminates mission-relevant information to national and international visitors and policymakers. https://www.usbg.gov/about-us

Three USBG sites are open year-round to the public: the Conservatory, the National Garden, and Bartholdi Park. The production facility is periodically open for public programs and tours. https://www.usbg.gov/ hours-and-location-0

Sources of Information

America's Agricultural Experience   Based on a meeting that the U.S. Botanic Garden helped to organize of the Nation's leading agricultural and botanical educators, "Agriculture and the Future of Food: The Role of Botanic Gardens" presents a series of educational narratives that promote the reconnection of people and plants through the American agricultural experience. The document is available online in Portable Document Format (PDF). https://www. usbg.gov/sites/default/files/attachments/ agriculture_and_the_future_of_food_-_the_ role_of_botanic_gardens.pdf

Calendar of Events   The USBG offers children and family programs, lectures, special tours, and workshops, as well as free theater, concerts, cooking demonstrations, and more. An events calendar is posted on the "Programs and Events" page, and a Portable Document Format (PDF) version is available for downloading. https://www.usbg.gov/programs-and-events

Carbon Footprint   A small step can lead to a big change. A carbon, or ecological, footprint helps demonstrate the effect that lifestyle has on Earth systems. Most people can reduce their carbon footprint (i.e., the amount of emitted greenhouse gases that lifestyle governs) by shifting to sustainable practices and products. The USBG posted a list of suggestions for developing a more sustainable lifestyle, a lifestyle that leaves behind a smaller carbon footprint. The list includes suggestions for bottled water, coffee grounds, driving less, eating locally, junk mail, planting trees, plastic bags, and washing clothes. https://www.usbg.gov/know-your-impact

Career Opportunities   Information on career and volunteer opportunities is available online. https://www.usbg.gov/opportunities-us-botanic-garden

Contact Information   The USBG welcomes feedback: comments, concerns, and questions. Got a growing plant question? Select the "Plant Hotline" option in the "Inquiry Type" field of the electronic comment form. https://www.usbg.gov/contact-us-botanic-garden

Exhibits   The USBG creates exhibits that not only delight and educate visitors, but that inspire them to become more active and better stewards of the plants supporting life on Earth. It posts Information on current and upcoming exhibits online. https://www.usbg.gov/exhibits

Factsheets   Gardening factsheets are available online. https://www.usbg.gov/gardening-fact-sheets-0

Kids   The USBG is a child-friendly living plant museum.https://www.usbg.gov/kids-are-welcome-us-botanic-garden

Land Development and Management   An interdisciplinary partnership led by the USBG, American Society of Landscape Architects, and the Lady Bird Johnson Wildflower Center, the Sustainable Sites Initiative™ improves land development and management practices with a voluntary rating system for sustainable land design, construction, and maintenance practices.

Architects, designers, developers, engineers, landscape architects, policymakers, and others use SITES to align land development and management with sustainable design. SITES supports the creation of ecologically resilient communities, and it benefits property owners, local and regional communities and their economies, as well as the environment. Certification covers development projects on land where buildings are absent or present. http://www.sustainablesites.org

Landscaping   A collaboration between the USBG and the Lady Bird Johnson Wildflower Center, Landscape For Life™ promotes an approach to landscaping that respects nature. Irrespective of location—downtown, suburbia, or the farm—every landscape or garden can protect and even restore the environment, without sacrificing visual appeal. The Landscape for Life website contains a trove of information—getting started, materials, human health, plants, soil, and water—for transforming an environmentally ambivalent landscape into a healthy, sustainable one. http://landscapeforlife.org

Living Collections Database   An online tool is available to search the USBG's living collections database. https://www.usbg.gov/search-collection

Native Plant Recommendations   The USBG posts lists of selected plants to grow in the garden. The lists are available in Portable Document Format (PDF) for downloading. https://www.usbg.gov/national-garden-native-plant-recommendations

Plant Hotline   Questions about a garden plant? Call the Plant Hotline. Phone, 202-226-4785.

Pollinators   Learn about the role birds and bees, as well as other creatures like bats, beetles, butterflies, flies, moths, and even wasps, play in the life cycle of plants. https://www.usbg.gov/pollinator-information

Production Facility   The production facility opens periodically for public programs and tours. An annual open house allows visitors to meet the gardeners, ask questions, and explore the facility. https://www.usbg.gov/us-botanic-garden-production-facility

Rare and Endangered Plants   USBG experts bank seeds of rare plants, introduce rare plants to the horticultural trade, maintain live specimens, and study wild plants at risk of endangerment or extinction. The website maintains a gallery of plants whose threat levels are vulnerable, threatened, and endangered. https://www.usbg.gov/gardens/rare-and-endangered-plants-gallery

Site Map   The website map allows visitors to look for specific topics or to browse content that aligns with their interests. https://www.usbg.gov/sitemap

Social Media   The USBG has a Facebook account. https://www.facebook.com/usbotanicgarden

The Sources of Information were updated 10–2019.

Staff Directory   Approximately 65 employees work at the USBG in four divisions: Administration, Horticulture, Operations, and Public Programs. https://www.usbg.gov/staff-directory

Visitor Guide   More than a million visitors come to see the USBG each year. A visitor guide is available in Arabic, Chinese, English, French, German, Italian, Japanese, Korean, Russian, and Spanish. https://www.usbg.gov/visit

Judicial Branch

JUDICIAL BRANCH

In Memoriam: Justice Ruth Bader Ginsburg 1933–2020

The Supreme Court of the United States
United States Supreme Court Building, One First Street NE., Washington, DC 20543
Phone, 202-479-3000. Internet, http://www.supremecourt.gov

Members

Chief Justice of the United States	JOHN G. ROBERTS, JR.
Associate Justice	CLARENCE THOMAS
Associate Justice	STEPHEN G. BREYER
Associate Justice	SAMUEL A. ALITO, JR.
Associate Justice	SONIA M. SOTOMAYOR
Associate Justice	ELENA KAGAN
Associate Justice	NEIL M. GORSUCH
Associate Justice	BRETT M. KAVANAUGH
Associate Justice	AMY C. BARRETT

https://www.supremecourt.gov/about/biographies.aspx

Officers

Counselor to the Chief Justice	JEFFREY P. MINEAR
Clerk	SCOTT S. HARRIS
Court Counsel	ETHAN V. TORREY
Curator	CATHERINE E. FITTS
Director of Information Technology	ROBERT J. HAWKINS
Librarian	LINDA S. MASLOW
Marshal	(VACANCY)
Public Information Officer	KATHLEEN L. ARBERG
Reporter of Decisions	(VACANCY)

The above list of officers was updated 1–2021. https://www.supremecourt.gov/about/about.aspx

Article III, section 1, of the Constitution of the United States provides that "[t]he judicial Power of the United States, shall be vested in one supreme Court, and in such inferior Courts as the Congress may from time to time ordain and establish."

The Supreme Court of the United States was created on the basis of this constitutional provision and by authority of the Judiciary Act of September 24, 1789 (1 Stat. 73), which President George Washington approved. The Supreme Court was organized on February 2, 1790. https://www.loc.gov/law/help/statutes-at-large/1st-congress/session-1/c1s1ch20.pdf

Article III, section 2, of the Constitution defines the jurisdiction of the Supreme Court. https://www.archives.gov/founding-docs/constitution-transcript#toc-article-iii-

The Supreme Court comprises the Chief Justice of the United States and such number of Associate Justices as may be fixed by Congress (28 U.S.C. 1). Currently, the total number of Associate Justices has been fixed at eight. Six Justices are needed for a quorum. If more than three of the nine Justices are unable to participate in a case, the Supreme Court lacks the authority to render a decision. https://uscode.house.gov/view.xhtml?path=/prelim@title28/part1/chapter1&edition=prelim

The President nominates the Justices with the advice and consent of the Senate. Article III, section 1, of the Constitution further provides that "[t]he Judges, both of the supreme and inferior Courts, shall hold their Offices during good Behaviour, and shall, at stated Times, receive for their Services, a Compensation, which shall not be diminished during their Continuance in Office."

In the performance of its functions, the Court is assisted by nine court officers: the Clerk, the Counselor to the Chief Justice, the Court Counsel, the Curator, the Director of Information Technology, the Librarian, the Marshal, the Public Information Officer, and the Reporter of Decisions. https://www.supremecourt.gov/about/about.aspx

Appellate Jurisdiction   The Constitution has given authority to the Congress to pass statutes that confer appellate jurisdiction upon the Supreme Court. The basic statute that is effective at this time, in conferring and controlling jurisdiction of the Supreme Court, may be found in 28 U.S.C. 1251, 1253, 1254, 1257-1259, and various special statutes. Congress has no authority to change the original jurisdiction of this Court. https://uscode.house.gov/view.xhtml?path=/prelim@title28/part4/chapter81&edition=prelim

Court Term   The term of the Court begins on the first Monday in October and lasts until the first Monday in October of the next year. Over the course of a term, approximately 10,000 petitions are filed for cases to be briefed before the Court. Moreover, each year, about 1,200 applications, which can be acted upon by a single Justice while serving in the capacity of a Circuit Justice, are filed. http://www.supremecourt.gov/about/procedures.aspx

Rulemaking   From time to time, Congress has conferred upon the Supreme Court power to prescribe rules of procedure to be followed by the lower courts of the United States.

Sources of Information

Archived Records   The "Guide to Federal Records in the National Archives of the United States" indicates that records belonging to the Supreme Court of the United States have been assigned to record group 267. https://www.archives.gov/research/guide-fed-records/groups/267.html

Art Collections   The Supreme Court has been acquiring artwork since the 1830s. Today, it continues to add to its three collections of decorative art, fine art, and graphic art. These collections include antique furniture, busts, engravings, historic furnishings, lithographs, miniatures, photographs, and portraits. https://www.supremecourt.gov/about/historicCollections.aspx

Audio Recordings   Recordings of oral arguments become publicly accessible at the end of each argument week. A listener has the option to download the audio files or to hear the arguments on the Supreme Court's website. Recordings are listed by case name, docket number, and the date of oral argument. https://www.supremecourt.gov/oral_arguments/argument_audio/2018

Calendars / Lists   Supreme Court calendars and argument calendars, as well as day call and hearing lists, are posted in Portable Document Format (PDF) for viewing and downloading. https://www.supremecourt.gov/oral_arguments/calendarsandlists.aspx

Career Opportunities   The Supreme Court posts vacancy announcements. It also has programs for docents, fellows, and interns. https://www.supremecourt.gov/jobs/jobs.aspx

Chief and Associate Justices A Chief Justices list and Associate Justices list are available on the "Justices 1789 to Present" web page. The lists include all of the Justices who have served on the Supreme Court. https://www.supremecourt.gov/about/members_text.aspx

A timeline of Chief and Associate Justices is also available. https://www.supremecourt.gov/about/members.aspx

Constitutional Interpretation See the cornerstone address of Chief Justice Charles E. Hughes: "The Republic Endures and This Is the Symbol of Its Faith." https://www.supremecourt.gov/about/constitutional.aspx

Contact Information General contact information is available on the "Contact Us" web page. The Public Information Office receives general questions that are not time sensitive. https://www.supremecourt.gov/contact/contactus.aspx | Email: pio@supremecourt.gov

Docket Search The online docket database contains information on the status of cases filed since the beginning of the 2001 Term. https://www.supremecourt.gov/docket/docket.aspx

The engrossed dockets from 1791 to 1995 have been scanned by the National Archives from its microfilm collection and are available in its catalog. https://catalog.archives.gov/id/1524561

Exhibitions The Office of the Curator creates exhibitions to highlight the work and history of the Nation's highest court, the lives of individual Justices, and the architecture of the Supreme Court building. Exhibitions are self-guided and located on the ground floor of the building. http://www.supremecourt.gov/visiting/exhibition.aspx

Frequently Asked Questions (FAQs) The Supreme Court posts answers to FAQs online. https://www.supremecourt.gov/about/faq.aspx

The Public Information Office has answered questions that reporters often ask in its "Reporter's Guide to Applications Pending Before The Supreme Court of the United States." https://www.supremecourt.gov/publicinfo/reportersguide.pdf | Email: pio@supremecourt.gov

Gift Shop The Supreme Court Historical Society Gift Shop is accessible online and located on the ground floor of the Supreme Court building. Merchandise ranges from books, folders, statues, and woven throws to jewelry, learning games, scarves, ties, and writing instruments. The shop is open Monday–Friday, from 9 a.m. to 4:25 p.m., excluding Federal Holidays. Phone, 888-539-4438. http://supremecourtgifts.org/ | Email: giftshop@supremecourthistory.org

Granted and Noted Cases List Annual lists are posted in Portable Document Format (PDF) for viewing and downloading. The earliest of the lists starts with the October term of 2007. https://www.supremecourt.gov/orders/grantednotedlists.aspx

History The Supreme Court Historical Society, a private nonprofit organization, collects and preserves the history of the Supreme Court. Incorporated in the District of Columbia in 1974, its founder Chief Justice Warren E. Burger served as the first honorary chairman. The Society is headquartered in the Opperman House in Washington, DC, where it maintains The Goldman Library. The books housed therein comprise one of the finest collections of Court histories, Justices' writings, and judicial biographies. The library also has materials relating to U.S. attorneys general, solicitors, and Presidents. http://supremecourthistory.org/index.html

Indigent Petitioners The "Guide for Filing In Forma Pauperis Cases" assists litigants who may lack the financial resources to pay the filing fee or to submit booklet-format documents under Court Rule 33.1. https://www.supremecourt.gov/casehand/guideforIFPcases2019.pdf

Links The Supreme Court's website has links to other Internet sources of information on the Federal Government, the Judiciary, and the Supreme Court. https://www.supremecourt.gov/links/links.aspx

Minutes of the Court The "Journal of the Supreme Court" contains the official minutes. It reflects the disposition of each case, identifies the court whose judgment is under review, lists the cases argued that day and the attorneys who presented oral argument, contains miscellaneous announcements by the Chief Justice from the bench, and names the attorneys who have been admitted to

the bar of the Supreme Court. https://www.
supremecourt.gov/orders/journal.aspx
Press Releases   Press releases are posted
online. https://www.supremecourt.gov/
publicinfo/press/pressreleases.aspx
Reports on the Federal Judiciary   "Year-
End Reports on the Federal Judiciary,"
which the current and former Chief Justices
have prepared, are posted on the Supreme
Court's website. Starting with the year 2000,
most of the reports are available in Portable
Document Format (PDF) for viewing and
downloading. https://www.supremecourt.
gov/publicinfo/year-end/year-endreports.aspx
Search Tips   Use the search tips to refine
a search and find more specific results on
the Supreme Court's website. https://www.
supremecourt.gov/search_help.aspx
Seating To Hear Oral Arguments   All
oral arguments are open to the public.
Seating is limited and on a first-come,
first-seated, basis. Before a session begins,
two lines form on the plaza in front of the
building. One line is for those attending
an entire argument; the other, a 3-minute
line, is for those observing the Court in
session for a brief period of time. https://
www.supremecourt.gov/oral_arguments/
courtroomseating.aspx

The Sources of Information were updated 1–2021.

Site Map   The site map allows visitors to
look for specific information or to browse
content that aligns with their interests.
https://www.supremecourt.gov/sitemap.aspx
Slip Opinions   Slip opinions are posted
within minutes after the Justices issue their
opinions. They remain posted until the
opinions for the entire term are published
in the bound volumes of the "United States
Reports." A slip opinion comprises the
majority or principal opinion, concurring or
dissenting opinions, and a prefatory syllabus
summarizing the decision. https://www.
supremecourt.gov/opinions/slipopinion/18
Speeches   Speeches of current and former
Supreme Court Justices are available online.
https://www.supremecourt.gov/publicinfo/
speeches/speeches.aspx
Visiting the Court   The Supreme Court
building is open to the public Monday–
Friday, from 9:00 a.m. to 4:30 p.m,
excluding Federal holidays. http://www.
supremecourt.gov/visiting/visiting.aspx
   Maps and brochures are available
online. The visitors' guide and map are
available in translation: Chinese, French,
German, Japanese, Russian, and Spanish.
https://www.supremecourt.gov/visiting/
mapsandbrochures.aspx

Lower Courts

Article III of the Constitution declares, in
section 1, that the judicial power of the
United States shall be invested in one
Supreme Court and in "such inferior Courts
as the Congress may from time to time
ordain and establish." The Supreme Court

has held that these constitutional courts ". . .
share in the exercise of the judicial power
defined in that section, can be invested with
no other jurisdiction, and have judges who
hold office during good behavior, with no
power in Congress to provide otherwise."

United States Courts of Appeals

The courts of appeals are intermediate
appellate courts created by act of March
3, 1891 (28 U.S.C. ch. 3), to relieve the
Supreme Court of considering all appeals
in cases originally decided by the Federal
trial courts. They are empowered to review
all final decisions and certain interlocutory
decisions (18 U.S.C. 3731; 28 U.S.C.
1291, 1292) of district courts. They also are

empowered to review and enforce orders
of many Federal administrative bodies. The
decisions of the courts of appeals are final
except as they are subject to review on writ
of certiorari by the Supreme Court.
   The United States is divided geographically
into 12 judicial circuits, including the
District of Columbia. Each circuit has a court
of appeals (28 U.S.C. 41, 1294). Each of the

50 States is assigned to one of the circuits. The territories and the Commonwealth of Puerto Rico are assigned variously to the first, third, and ninth circuits. There is also a Court of Appeals for the Federal Circuit, which has nationwide jurisdiction defined by subject matter. At present each court of appeals has from 6 to 28 permanent circuit judgeships (179 in all), depending upon the amount of judicial work in the circuit. Circuit judges hold their offices during good behavior as provided by Article III, section 1, of the Constitution. The judge senior in commission who is under 70 years of age (65 at inception of term), has been in office at least 1 year, and has not previously been chief judge, serves as the chief judge of the circuit for a 7-year term. One of the Justices of the Supreme Court is assigned as circuit justice for each of the 13 judicial circuits. Each court of appeals normally hears cases in panels consisting of three judges but may sit en banc with all judges present.

The judges of each circuit (except the Federal Circuit) by vote determine the size of the judicial council for the circuit, which consists of the chief judge and an equal number of circuit and district judges. The council considers the state of Federal judicial business in the circuit and may "make all necessary and appropriate orders for [its] effective and expeditious administration . . ." (28 U.S.C. 332).

The chief judge of each circuit may summon periodically a judicial conference of all judges of the circuit, including members of the bar, to discuss the business of the Federal courts of the circuit (28 U.S.C. 333). The chief judge of each circuit and a district judge elected from each of the 12 geographical circuits, together with the chief judge of the Court of International Trade, serve as members of the Judicial Conference of the United States, over which the Chief Justice of the United States presides. This is the governing body for the administration of the Federal judicial system as a whole (28 U.S.C. 331).

To obtain a complete list of judges, court officials, and official stations of the United States Courts of Appeals for the Federal Circuit, as well as information on opinions and cases before the court, consult the Judicial Circuit Web sites listed below.

Circuit	URL
District of Columbia Circuit	http://www.cadc.uscourts.gov
First Circuit	http://www.ca1.uscourts.gov
Second Circuit	http://www.ca2.uscourts.gov
Third Circuit	http://www.ca3.uscourts.gov
Fourth Circuit	http://www.ca4.uscourts.gov
Fifth Circuit	http://www.ca5.uscourts.gov
Sixth Circuit	http://www.ca6.uscourts.gov
Seventh Circuit	http://www.ca7.uscourts.gov
Eighth Circuit	http://www.ca8.uscourts.gov
Ninth Circuit	http://www.ca9.uscourts.gov
Tenth Circuit	http://www.ca10.uscourts.gov
Eleventh Circuit	http://www.ca11.uscourts.gov

United States Court of Appeals for the Federal Circuit

This court was established under Article III of the Constitution pursuant to the Federal Courts Improvement Act of 1982 (28 U.S.C. 41, 44, 48), as successor to the former United States Court of Customs and Patent Appeals and the United States Court of Claims. The jurisdiction of the court is nationwide (as provided by 28 U.S.C. 1295) and includes appeals from the district courts in patent cases; appeals from the district courts in contract, and certain other civil actions in which the United States is a defendant; and appeals from final decisions of the U.S. Court of International Trade, the U.S. Court of Federal Claims, and the U.S. Court of Appeals for Veterans Claims. The jurisdiction of the court also includes the review of administrative rulings by the Patent and Trademark Office, U.S. International Trade Commission, Secretary of Commerce, agency boards of contract appeals, and the Merit Systems Protection Board, as well as rulemaking of the Department of Veterans Affairs; review of decisions of the U.S. Senate Committee on Ethics concerning discrimination claims of Senate employees; and review of a final order of an entity to be designated by the President concerning discrimination claims of Presidential appointees.

The court consists of 12 circuit judges. It sits in panels of three or more on each case and may also hear or rehear a case en banc. The court sits principally in Washington, DC, and may hold court wherever any court of appeals sits (28 U.S.C. 48). http://www.cafc. uscourts.gov

United States District Courts

The Nation's district courts are the trial courts of general Federal jurisdiction. These courts resolve disputes by determining the facts and applying legal principles to decide which party is right. Each State has at least one district court, and large States have as many as four. There are 89 district courts in the 50 States, plus one in the District of Columbia and another in the Commonwealth of Puerto Rico. Three other U.S. Territories also have courts that hear Federal cases: Guam and the Northern Mariana and Virgin Islands.

At present, each district court has from 2 to 28 Federal district judgeships, depending upon the amount of judicial work within its territory. Only one judge is usually required to hear and decide a case in a district court, but in some limited cases it is required that three judges be called together to comprise the court (28 U.S.C. 2284). The judge senior in commission who is under 70 years of age (65 at inception of term), has been in office for at least 1 year, and has not previously been chief judge, serves as chief judge for a 7-year term. There are 645 permanent district judgeships in the 50 States and 15 in the District of Columbia. There are seven district judgeships in Puerto Rico. District judges hold their offices during good behavior as provided by Article III, section 1, of the Constitution. However, Congress may temporary judgeships for a court with the provision that when a future vacancy occurs in that district, such vacancy shall not be filled. Each district court has one or more United States magistrate judges and bankruptcy judges, a clerk, a United States attorney, a United States marshal, probation officers, court reporters, and their staffs. The jurisdiction of the district courts is set forth in title 28, chapter 85, of the United States Code and at 18 U.S.C. 3231.

Cases from the district courts are reviewable on appeal by the applicable court of appeals. http://www.uscourts.gov/ about-federal-courts/court-role-and-structure

Territorial Courts

Pursuant to its authority to govern the Territories (Art. IV, sec. 3, clause 2, of the Constitution), Congress has established district courts in the territories of Guam and the Virgin Islands. The District Court of the Canal Zone was abolished on April 1, 1982, pursuant to the Panama Canal Act of 1979 (22 U.S.C. 3601 note). Congress has also established a district court in the Northern Mariana Islands, which is administered by the United States under a trusteeship agreement with the United Nations. These Territorial courts have jurisdiction not only over the subjects described in the judicial article of the Constitution, but also over many local matters that, within the States, are decided in State courts. The District Court of Puerto Rico, by contrast, is established under Article III, is classified like other "district courts," and is called a "court of the United States" (28 U.S.C. 451). There is one judge each in Guam and the

Northern Mariana Islands, and two in the Virgin Islands. The judges in these courts are appointed for terms of 10 years. http://www. uscourts.gov/about-federal-courts/court-role-and-structure

For further information concerning the lower courts, contact the Administrative Office of the United States Courts, Thurgood Marshall Federal Judiciary Building, One Columbus Circle NE., Washington, DC 20544. Phone, 202-502-2600.

United States Court of International Trade

This court was originally established as the Board of United States General Appraisers by act of June 10, 1890, which conferred upon it jurisdiction theretofore held by the district and circuit courts in actions arising under the tariff acts (19 U.S.C. ch. 4). The act of May 28, 1926 (19 U.S.C. 405a), created the United States Customs Court to supersede the Board; by acts of August 7, 1939, and June 25, 1948 (28 U.S.C. 1582, 1583), the court was integrated into the United States court structure, organization, and procedure. The act of July 14, 1956 (28 U.S.C. 251), established the court as a court of record of the United States under Article III of the Constitution. The Customs Court Act of 1980 (28 U.S.C. 251) constituted the court as the United States Court of International Trade.

The Court of International Trade has jurisdiction over any civil action against the United States arising from Federal laws governing import transactions. This includes classification and valuation cases, as well as authority to review certain agency determinations under the Trade Agreements Act of 1979 (19 U.S.C. 2501) involving antidumping and countervailing duty matters. In addition, it has exclusive jurisdiction of civil actions to review determinations as to the eligibility of workers, firms, and communities for adjustment assistance under the Trade Act of 1974 (19 U.S.C. 2101). Civil actions commenced by the United States to recover customs duties, to recover on a customs bond, or for certain civil penalties alleging fraud or negligence are also within the exclusive jurisdiction of the court.

The court is composed of a chief judge and eight judges, not more than five of whom may belong to any one political party. Any of its judges may be temporarily designated and assigned by the Chief Justice of the United States to sit as a court of appeals or district court judge in any circuit or district. The court has a clerk and deputy clerks, a librarian, court reporters, and other supporting personnel. Cases before the court may be tried before a jury. Under the Federal Courts Improvement Act of 1982 (28 U.S.C. 1295), appeals are taken to the U.S. Court of Appeals for the Federal Circuit, and ultimately review may be sought in appropriate cases in the Supreme Court of the United States.

The principal offices are located in New York, NY, but the court is empowered to hear and determine cases arising at any port or place within the jurisdiction of the United States. http://www.cit.uscourts.gov

For further information, contact the Clerk, United States Court of International Trade, One Federal Plaza, New York, NY 10278-0001. Phone, 212-264-2814.

Judicial Panel on Multidistrict Litigation

The Panel, created by act of April 29, 1968 (28 U.S.C. 1407), and consisting of seven Federal judges designated by the Chief Justice from the courts of appeals and district courts, is authorized to temporarily transfer to a single district, for coordinated or consolidated pretrial proceedings, civil actions pending in different districts that involve one or more common questions of fact. http://www.jpml.uscourts.gov

For further information, contact the Clerk, Judicial Panel on Multidistrict Litigation, Room G–255, Thurgood Marshall Federal Judiciary Building, One Columbus Circle NE., Washington, DC 20002-8041. Phone, 202-502-2800.

SPECIAL COURTS
United States Court of Appeals for the Armed Forces

450 E Street NW., Washington, DC 20442-0001
Phone, 202-761-1448. Fax, 202-761-4672. Internet, http://www.armfor.uscourts.gov

This court was established under Article I of the Constitution of the United States pursuant to act of May 5, 1950, as amended (10 U.S.C. 867). Subject only to certiorari review by the Supreme Court of the United States in a limited number of cases, the court serves as the final appellate tribunal to review court-martial convictions of all the Armed Forces. It is exclusively an appellate criminal court, consisting of five civilian judges who are appointed for 15-year terms by the President with the advice and consent of the Senate.

The court is called upon to exercise jurisdiction to review the record in all cases extending to death; certified to the court by a Judge Advocate General of one of the Armed Forces; or petitioned by accused who have received a sentence of confinement for 1 year or more and/or a punitive discharge.

The court also exercises authority under the All Writs Act (28 U.S.C. 1651(a)).

In addition, the judges of the court are required by law to work jointly with the senior uniformed lawyer from each of the Armed Forces and two members of the public appointed by the Secretary of Defense to make an annual comprehensive survey, to report annually to the Congress on the operation and progress of the military justice system under the Uniform Code of Military Justice, and to recommend improvements wherever necessary.

Sources of Information

Career Opportunities Job openings and available clerkships are posted online. http://www.armfor.uscourts.gov/newcaaf/ employment.htm; http://www.armfor. uscourts.gov/newcaaf/contact.htm

For further information, contact the Clerk, United States Court of Appeals for the Armed Forces, 450 E Street NW., Washington, DC 20442-0001. Phone, 202-761-1448. Fax, 202-761-4672.

United States Court of Appeals for Veterans Claims

Suite 900, 625 Indiana Avenue NW., Washington, DC 20004-2950
Phone, 202-501-5970. Fax, 202-501-5848. Internet, http://www.uscourts.cavc.gov

The United States Court of Appeals for Veterans Claims, a court of record under Article I of the Constitution, was established on November 18, 1988 (38 U.S.C. 7251) and given exclusive jurisdiction to review decisions of the Board of Veterans' Appeals. Appeals concern veteran disability benefits, dependent educational assistance, survivor benefits, and pension benefits claims. In addition to its review authority, the Court has contempt authority, as well as the authority to compel action by the Secretary of Veterans Affairs, the authority to grant a petition for extraordinary relief under the All Writs Act (28 U.S.C. 1651), and the authority to make attorney fee determinations under the Equal Access to Justice Act (28 U.S.C. 2412). Decisions of the Court of Appeals for Veterans

Claims are subject to review by the United States Court of Appeals for the Federal Circuit on questions of law and on writ of certiorari by the United States Supreme Court.

The Court consists of nine judges whom the President appoints with the advice and consent of the Senate for 15-year terms. One of the judges serves as chief judge.

The Chief Judge generally conducts a judicial conference every 2 years. The primary purpose of the conference, which involves the active participation of members of the legal community, attorneys, and practitioners admitted to practice before the Court, is to consider the business of the Court and to recommend means of improving the administration of justice within the Court's jurisdiction.

The Court is located in Washington, DC, but it is a court of national jurisdiction and may sit at any location within the United States.

Opinions issued by the Court, case information, and a current list of judges and officials of the United States Court of Appeals for Veterans Claims are available online.

Sources of Information

Employment Job opportunities are posted online. http://www.uscourts.cavc.gov/employment.php; http://www.uscourts.cavc.gov/contact.php

For further information, contact the Clerk, United States Court of Appeals for Veterans Claims, Suite 900, 625 Indiana Avenue NW., Washington, DC 20004-2950. Phone, 202-501-5970. Fax, 202-501-5848

United States Court of Federal Claims

717 Madison Place NW., Washington, DC 20439
Phone, 202-357-6400. Internet, http://www.uscfc.uscourts.gov

The United States Court of Federal Claims has jurisdiction over claims seeking money judgments against the United States. A claim must be founded upon the Constitution, an act of Congress, an Executive order, a contract with the United States, or Federal regulations. Judges are appointed by the President for 15-year terms, subject to Senate confirmation.

Appeals are to the U.S. Court of Appeals for the Federal Circuit.

Sources of Information

Career Opportunities Information on job opportunities and internships is available online. http://www.uscfc.uscourts.gov/job-opportunitiesemployment http://www.uscfc.uscourts.gov/court-directory

For further information, contact the Clerk's Office, United States Court of Federal Claims, 717 Madison Place NW., Washington, DC 20439. Phone, 202-357-6400.

United States Tax Court

400 Second Street NW., Washington, DC 20217-0002
Phone, 202-521-0700. Internet, http://www.ustaxcourt.gov

The United States Tax Court is a court of record under Article I of the Constitution of the United States (26 U.S.C. 7441). The court was created as the United States Board of Tax Appeals by the Revenue Act of 1924 (43 Stat. 336). The name was changed to the Tax Court of the United States by the Revenue Act of 1942 (56 Stat. 957). The Tax Reform Act of 1969 (83 Stat. 730) established the court under Article I and then changed its name to the United States Tax Court.

The court comprises 19 judges who are appointed by the President to 15-year terms and subject to Senate confirmation. The court also has varying numbers of both senior judges (who may be recalled by the chief judge to perform further judicial duties) and special trial judges (who are appointed by the chief judge and may hear and decide

a variety of cases). The court's jurisdiction is set forth in various sections of title 26 of the U.S. Code.

The offices of the court and its judges are in Washington, DC. However, the court has national jurisdiction and schedules trial sessions in more than 70 cities in the United States. Each trial session is conducted by one judge, senior judge, or special trial judge. Court proceedings are open to the public and are conducted in accordance with the court's rules of practice and procedure and the rules of evidence applicable in trials without a jury in the U.S. District Court for the District of Columbia. A fee of $60 is charged for the filing of a petition. Practice before the court is limited to practitioners admitted under the court's rules of practice and procedure.

Decisions entered by the court, other than decisions in small tax cases, may be appealed to the regional courts of appeals and, thereafter, upon the granting of a writ of certiorari, to the Supreme Court of the United States. At the option of petitioners, simplified procedures may be used in small tax cases. Small tax cases are final and not subject to review by any court. http://www.ustaxcourt.gov/about.htm

Sources of Information

Career Opportunities   Vacancy announcements and information on the court's law clerk program are available online. http://www.ustaxcourt.gov/employment.htm

Forms   Applications, certificates, notices, and other forms can be completed online and then printed. http://www.ustaxcourt.gov/forms.htm

Taxpayer Information   An online guide provides information—not legal advice—that may be helpful for those representing themselves before the Tax Court. It answers frequent questions that taxpayers ask and explains the process of filing a petition to begin a Tax Court case and things that occur before, during, and after trial. It also features a glossary. http://www.ustaxcourt. gov/taxpayer_info_intro.htm | Email: info@ustaxcourt.gov http://www.ustaxcourt.gov/phone.htm

For further information, contact the Office of the Clerk of the Court, United States Tax Court, 400 Second Street NW., Washington, DC 20217-0002. Phone, 202-521-0700.

Administrative Office of the United States Courts

One Columbus Circle NE., Washington, DC 20544
Phone, 202-502-2600. Internet, http://www.uscourts.gov

Director	James C. Duff
Deputy Director	Lee Ann Bennett

Associate Directors

Departments	
Administrative Services	James R. Baugher
Program Services	Mary Louise Mitterhoff
Technology Services	Joseph R. Peters, Jr.

Officers

Defender Services	Cait T. Clarke
Judicial Conference Secretariat	Katherine H. Simon
Judicial Integrity	Jill Langley
Legislative Affairs	David T. Best
Public Affairs	David A. Sellers
General Counsel	Sheryl L. Walter

https://www.uscourts.gov/statistics-reports/profile-administrative-office-us-courts-annual-report-2019

The above list of key personnel was updated 8–2020.

The Administrative Office of the United States Courts supports and serves the nonjudicial, administrative business of the United States Courts.

Establishment

On August 7, 1939, President Franklin D. Roosevelt approved Public Law 76–299, which provided "for the administration of the United States courts" (53 Stat. 1223). The new statute included an effective date:

90 days after its approval by the President (53 Stat. 1226). On November 6, 1939, the Administrative Office of the United States Courts (AOUSC) was established. https://www.loc.gov/law/help/statutes-at-large/76th-congress/session-1/c76s1ch501.pdf

On June 25, 1948, President Harry S. Truman approved Public Law 80–773, which "revised, codified, and enacted into law" 28 U.S.C. The law provided for the annual summoning of the chief judges of the judicial circuits by the Chief Justice of the United States to the newly named Judicial Conference of the United States, at which the Chief Justice presides (62 Stat. 902). It also described the general duties of the AOUSC Director, who serves as "the administrative officer of the courts, and under the supervision and direction of the Judicial Conference of the United States" (62 Stat. 914). https://www.loc.gov/law/help/statutes-at-large/80th-congress/session-2/c80s2ch646.pdf

The Chief Justice of the United States, after consultation with the Judicial Conference, appoints the Director and Deputy Director of the AOUSC.

Statutory Authorities

Codified statutory material on the "Judiciary and Judicial Procedure" has been assigned to 28 U.S.C. Part III, which deals with court officers and employees, comprises chapters 41–58. https://uscode.house.gov/view.xhtml?path=/prelim@title28/part3&edition=prelim

"Chapter 41—Administrative Office of United States Courts," which comprises sections 601–613, has been assigned to 28 U.S.C. https://uscode.house.gov/view.xhtml?path=/prelim@title28/part3/chapter41&edition=prelim

Activities

The AOUSC provides a range of administrative, financial, legal, legislative, management, technology, and program support services to Federal courts. Judicial Conference committees, with input from the courts, advise the AOUSC as it develops the annual judiciary budget for approval by the U.S. Congress and the President. The AOUSC also carries out Judicial Conference policies. Providing staff support and counsel to the Judicial Conference and its committees is a primary responsibility of the AOUSC. http://www.uscourts.gov/about-federal-courts/judicial-administration

Administering the Courts

The Director is the administrative officer of the courts of the United States—except of the Supreme Court. Under the guidance of the Judicial Conference of the United States, the Director supervises all administrative matters relating to the offices of clerks and other clerical and administrative personnel of the courts; examines the state of the dockets of the courts, secures information as to the courts' need of assistance, and prepares statistical data and reports each quarter and transmits them to the chief judges of the circuits; submits an activities report of the Administrative Office and the courts' state of business to the annual meeting of the Judicial Conference of the United States; fixes the compensation of court employees whose compensation is not otherwise fixed by law; regulates and pays annuities to widows and surviving dependent children of judges; disburses moneys appropriated for the maintenance and operation of the courts; examines accounts of court officers; regulates travel of judicial personnel; provides accommodations and supplies for the courts and their clerical and administrative personnel; establishes and maintains programs for the certification and utilization of court interpreters and the provision of special interpretation services in the courts; and performs such other duties as may be assigned by the Supreme Court or the Judicial Conference of the United States.

The Director also prepares and submits the budget of the courts, which the Office of Management and Budget transmits to Congress without change. http://www.uscourts.gov/about-federal-courts/judicial-administration

Bankruptcy According to the Bankruptcy Amendments and Federal Judgeship Act of 1984 (28 U.S.C. 151), the bankruptcy judges for each judicial district constitute a unit of the district court known as the bankruptcy court. The courts of appeals appoint bankruptcy judges in such numbers as authorized by Congress. These judges serve for a term of 14 years as judicial officers of the district courts.

This act placed jurisdiction in the district courts over all cases under title 11, United States Code, and all proceedings arising in or related to cases under that title (28 U.S.C. 1334). The district court may refer such cases and proceedings to its bankruptcy judges (as authorized by 28 U.S.C. 157).

The Director of the Administrative Office recommends to the Judicial Conference the duty stations of bankruptcy judges and the places they hold court, surveys the need for additional bankruptcy judgeships to be recommended to Congress, and determines the staff needs of bankruptcy judges and the clerks of the bankruptcy courts. http://www.uscourts.gov/services-forms/bankruptcy

Federal Magistrate Judges   The Director of the Administrative Office exercises general supervision over administrative matters in offices of U.S. magistrate judges, compiles and evaluates statistical data relating to such offices, and submits reports thereon to the Judicial Conference. The Director reports annually to Congress on the business that has come before U.S. magistrate judges and also prepares legal and administrative manuals for the magistrate judges. In compliance with the act, the Administrative Office conducts surveys of the conditions in the judicial districts to make recommendations as to the number, location, and salaries of magistrate judges. The Judicial Conference then determines their number, location, and salaries, subject to the availability of appropriated funds. https://www.uscourts.gov/judges-judgeships/about-federal-judges

Probation / Pretrial Services   The Administrative Office exercises general supervision of the accounts and practices of the Federal probation offices, which are subject to primary control by the respective district courts that they serve. The Administrative Office publishes, in cooperation with the Department of Justice's Bureau of Prisons, the "Federal Probation Journal." This online, quarterly publication presents current thought, research, and practice in corrections, community supervision, and criminal justice.

In accordance with the Pretrial Services Act of 1982 (18 U.S.C. 3152), the Director establishes pretrial services in the district courts. The offices of these district courts report information on pretrial release of persons charged with Federal offenses and supervise such persons who are released to their custody. http://www.uscourts.gov/services-forms/probation-and-pretrial-services

Representation   The Criminal Justice Act (18 U.S.C. 3006A) establishes the procedure for the appointment of private panel attorneys in Federal criminal cases for individuals who are unable to afford adequate representation, under plans adopted by each district court. The act also permits the establishment of Federal public defender or Federal community defender organizations by the district courts in districts where at least 200 persons annually require the appointment of counsel. Two adjacent districts may be combined to reach this total.

Each defender organization submits to the Director of the Administrative Office an annual report of its activities along with a proposed budget or, in the case of community defender organizations, a proposed grant for the coming year. The Director is responsible for the submission of the proposed budgets and grants to the Judicial Conference for approval. The Director also makes payments to the defender organizations out of appropriations in accordance with the approved budgets and grants, as well as compensating private counsel appointed to defend criminal cases in the United States courts. http://www.uscourts.gov/services-forms/defender-services

Sources of Information

Archived Records   The "Guide to Federal Records in the National Archives of the United States" indicates that Administrative Office records have been assigned to record group 116. https://www.archives.gov/research/guide-fed-records/groups/116.html

Business Opportunities   The Federal Acquisition Regulation does not apply to procurement within the Federal judiciary. Judiciary procurement policies are the responsibility of the Procurement Management Division within the Administrative Office and are issued in the "Guide to Judiciary Policy" (volume 14—Procurement). https://www.uscourts.gov/services-forms/business-opportunities

Career Opportunities   To help carry out its mission, the Federal Judiciary relies on attorneys, interpreters, information technology experts, probation officers, and other skilled professionals. https://www.uscourts.gov/careers

Contact Information   Postal correspondence should be sent to the Administrative Office of the United States Courts, One Columbus Circle NE., Washington, DC 20544. The "Contact Us" web page also allows online visitors to send an electronic message. https://www.uscourts.gov/contact-us

eJuror Program   The national eJuror program allows a potential juror to respond online to his or her jury qualification questionnaire. Using the eJuror service, a potential juror may revise personal information, check when he or she needs to report for jury service, submit a request for an excuse or deferral, and select an alternate time to serve. https://www.uscourts.gov/services-forms/jury-service/national-ejuror-program

Electronic Filing   Attorneys and others may submit files online using the Federal courts' Case Management and Electronic Case Files system. http://www.uscourts.gov/courtrecords/electronic-filing-cmecf

Email Updates   A subscriber receives notifications by email when new information is available, including news, newsletters, specific website content, and other alerts. https://www.uscourts.gov/email-updates

Federal Courts   The Federal court finder search tool allows online visitors to find a Federal court by location or court name, including appellate, bankruptcy, district, probation, and pretrial office, or Federal defender organization. https://www.uscourts.gov/federal-court-finder/search

Federal Register   Documents that the Administrative Office published in the Federal Register are accessible online. https://www.federalregister.gov/agencies/administrative-office-of-united-states-courts

Forms   National Federal court forms are accessible online. National court forms can be used in all Federal courts. Each Federal court also maintains its own local court forms. https://www.uscourts.gov/services-forms/forms

Frequently Asked Questions (FAQs)   nswers to FAQs on the Federal Judiciary are available online. http://www.uscourts.gov/frequently-asked-questions-faqs

Glossaries   A glossary of legal terms is available online. http://www.uscourts.gov/glossary

A glossary of common legal terms is also available in the 50-page publication "Understanding the Federal Courts," starting on page 29. https://www.uscourts.gov/sites/default/files/understanding-federal-courts.pdf

Judicial Vacancies   Judicial vacancies on the U.S. Court of Appeals, U.S. Court of Federal Claims, U.S. Court of International Trade, U.S. District Courts, and U.S. Supreme Court are posted online. https://www.uscourts.gov/judges-judgeships/judicial-vacancies

Law Day   "Your Vote, Your Voice, Our Democracy: The 19th Amendment at 100" is the theme of Law Day 2020. https://www.uscourts.gov/about-federal-courts/educational-resources/annual-observances/law-day

News   Judiciary news is available online. https://www.uscourts.gov/judiciary-news

Public Access to Court Electronic Records (PACER)   The online PACER service allows account holders to search and locate appellate, district, and bankruptcy court case and docket information. A person may register for an account, using the "Find a Case (PACER)" web page. https://www.uscourts.gov/court-records/find-case-pacer

Publications   The Federal judiciary and Administrative Office produce publications for the Congress, the public, and others to educate and inform about the work of the courts. http://www.uscourts.gov/statistics-reports/publications

Social Media   The Administrative Office tweets announcements and other newsworthy items on Twitter. https://twitter.com/uscourts

The Administrative Office posts videos on its YouTube channel. https://www.youtube.com/user/uscourts

Statistical Data   Statistical data on the business of the Federal Judiciary are available online. http://www.uscourts.gov/statistics-reports/caseload-statistics-data-tables

Understanding Federal Courts   The AOUSC developed the 50-page publication "Understanding the Federal Courts" as an introduction to the Federal judicial system, its organization and administration, and its relationship to the legislative and executive branches of the Government. The publication is available in Portable Document Format (PDF) for viewing and downloading. https://www.uscourts.gov/sites/default/files/understanding-federal-courts.pdf

The Sources of Information were updated 8–2020.

Federal Judicial Center

Thurgood Marshall Federal Judiciary Building, One Columbus Circle NE., Washington, DC 20002-8003
Phone, 202-502-4000. Internet, http://www.fjc.gov

Director	JOHN S. COOKE
Deputy Director	CLARA J. ALTMAN

Division Directors

Education	DANA K. CHIPMAN
Research	JAMES B. EAGLIN

Office Directors

Administration	NANCY PAYNE
Federal Judicial History	(VACANCY)
International Judicial Relations	MIRA GUR-ARIE
Information Technology	ESTHER DEVRIES

https://www.fjc.gov/about/senior-staff

Board of the Federal Judicial Center

Chief Justice of the United States*	JOHN G. ROBERTS, JR.
Bankruptcy Judge	BARBARA J. HOUSER
Circuit Judges	DUANE BENTON
	DAVID S. TATEL
District Judges	CURTIS L. COLLIER
	KIMBERLY J. MUELLER
	GEORGE Z. SINGAL
Magistrate Judge	TIMOTHY A. BAKER
Director of the Administrative Office of the U.S. Courts **	JAMES C. DUFF

*The Chief Justice chairs the Board of the Federal Judicial Center. ** The Director of the Administrative Office is an ex officio member of the Board. https://www.fjc.gov/about/board-members

The above list of key personnel was updated 10–2019.

The Federal Judicial Center is the judicial branch's agency for policy research and continuing education.

Establishment and Organization

On December 20, 1967, President Lyndon B. Johnson approved Public Law 90–219, "an act to provide for the establishment of a Federal Judicial Center [FJC], and for other purposes." The FJC was established "to further the development and adoption of improved judicial administration in the courts of the United States" (81 Stat. 664). https://www.govinfo.gov/content/pkg/STATUTE-81/pdf/STATUTE-81-Pg664.pdf

The FJC's statutory duties are described in chapter 42, sections 620–629, of 28 U.S.C. https://uscode.house.gov/browse/prelim@title28/part3/chapter42&edition=prelim

The Board of the FJC determines the agency's basic policies and activities. The Board comprises the Chief Justice of the United States, who permanently chairs of the Board by statute; two circuit judges of the U.S. courts of appeals; three judges of the U.S. district courts; one bankruptcy judge; and one magistrate judge. The Judicial Conference of the United States elects these eight members of the Board for 4-year terms. The ninth member is the Director of the Administrative Office of the United States Courts, who serves on Board in a permanent capacity. An elected member may serve only for one four-year term on the Board. https://www.fjc.gov/about/statute

The FJC does not post an organizational chart on its website.

Activities
The organization of the FJC reflects its primary statutory mandates. The Education Division plans education and produces training—including curriculum packages for in-district training, in-person programs, publications, video programs, and web-based programs and resources—for judges and court staff. The Research Division examines and evaluates current and alternative Federal court practices and policies. Its research assists Judicial Conference committees in developing policy recommendations. The research also supports the FJC's educational programs. The Federal Judicial History Office helps courts and other parties study and preserve Federal judicial history. The International Judicial Relations Office provides information to judicial and legal officials from foreign countries and informs Federal judicial personnel of developments in international law and other court systems that may affect their work. Two units of the Director's Office—the Editorial and Information Services Office and the Information Technology Office—provide editorial and design assistance, organization and dissemination of FJC resources, and technology. https://www.fjc.gov/about

Sources of Information

Annual Reports Annual Reports, from 1969 to the present, are available to download as Portable Document Format (PDF) files. https://www.fjc.gov/content/annual-reports

Archived Judicial Records The FJC record group does not currently have a description associated with it in the "Guide to Federal Records in the National Archives of the United States." The Guide is accessible online, and FJC records have been assigned to Record Group 516. https://www.archives.gov/research/guide-fed-records/groups/000.html

The National Archives does maintain a "Judicial Records" web page that contains information and resources for identifying and locating Federal court documents within its holdings. These documents comprise records of hearings and trials of Federal jurisdiction. https://www.archives.gov/research/court-records/archives.html

Biographical Directory of Judges The directory includes the biographies of judges appointed by the President to serve during good behavior since 1789 on the U.S. district courts, U.S. courts of appeals, Supreme Court of the United States, and U.S. Court of International Trade, as well as the former U.S. circuit courts, Court of Claims, U.S. Customs Court, and U.S. Court of Customs and Patent Appeals. Also included are judges who received presidential recess appointments to the above named courts but were not confirmed by the Senate to serve during good behavior. https://www.fjc.gov/history/judges

Career Opportunities The FJC posts job openings online. Contact the Human Resources Office for more information. Phone, 202-502-4165. https://www.fjc.gov/about/job-vacancies | Email: personnel@fjc.gov

Contact Information The "Contact Us" page has fax and phone numbers for FJC offices and divisions. https://www.fjc.gov/about/contact-us

Educational Materials Materials that the FJC produces as part of its educational programs for judges and court employees are accessible online. https://www.fjc.gov/education

Environmental Law The FJC published "International Environmental Law: A Guide for Judges" (2015) that Roger R. Martella, Jr., and James W. Coleman wrote. The guide introduces judges to some of the major areas of international environmental law and examines how the law might arise in Federal litigation involving climate change, hazardous chemicals and materials, protected species, water pollution, air pollution, environmental disaster response, and transborder enforcement of environmental regulations. It also discusses the sources of international environmental laws, such as bilateral investment treaties, international standards and standard-setting organizations, and multilateral trade agreements. The FJC regards the content of the guide as responsible and valuable, but it does not reflect the policy or recommendations of the FJC Board. https://

www.fjc.gov/content/309707/international-environmental-law-guide-judges

History   Questions about the history of the Federal judiciary? Submit them to the experts at the Federal Judicial History Office. Phone, 202-502-4180. Fax, 202-502-4077. https://www.fjc.gov/history | Email: history@fjc.gov

Nearly 600 images of historic Federal courthouses and other buildings that have served as the meeting places of Federal courts are available online. https://www.fjc.gov/history/courthouses

Timelines of the structure of the Federal courts, jurisdiction of the Federal courts, administration of the Federal courts, and cases that shaped the them are posted online. https://www.fjc.gov/history/timeline

Integrated Database   Under a working arrangement with the Administrative Office of the U.S. Courts, The FJC provides public access to its Integrated Data Base, which contains data on civil case and criminal defendant filings and terminations in the district courts, as well as bankruptcy court and appellate court case information. https://www.fjc.gov/research/idb

Publications   The online catalog contains records of FJC publications: manuals, monographs, reference guides, and research reports. A bibliographic record, which includes abstract or description, author and title, and additional information, is available for each item. Phone, 202-502-4153.

Fax, 202-502-4077. https://www.fjc.gov/publications | Email: publications@fjc.gov

Reports / Studies   The FJC posts studies that were published in the past on its website in Portable Document Format (PDF) for downloading. Its Research Division conducted them. Some Center reports are not published or made publicly available due to restrictions in place from the source of the research request. https://www.fjc.gov/research/reports-and-studies

Resources on Law and Practice   The "Special Topics" web page provides online access to curated collections of FJC resources on discrete areas of law and judicial practice. https://www.fjc.gov/research/special-topics

Site Map   The website map allows visitors to look for specific topics or to browse content that aligns with their interests. https://www.fjc.gov/sitemap

Teaching Resources   Teaching and civic outreach resources are available online. https://www.fjc.gov/education/civic-education-about-courts

Visiting Foreign Judicial Fellows   Foreign judges, court officials, and scholars may apply for the opportunity to conduct research at the FJC on topics concerning the administration of justice in the United States. https://www.fjc.gov/content/visiting-foreign-judicial-fellows-program

The Sources of Information were updated 10–2019.

United States Sentencing Commission

Suite 2-500, One Columbus Circle NE., Washington, DC 20002-8002
Phone, 202-502-4500. Internet, http://www.ussc.gov

Chair	WILLIAM H. PRYOR, JR., ACTING
Vice Chair	(VACANCY)
Vice Chair	(VACANCY)
Vice Chair	(VACANCY)
Commissioner	CHARLES R. BREYER
Commissioner	RACHEL E. BARKOW
Commissioner	DANNY C. REEVES
Commissioner	WIILIAM H. PRYOR, JR.
Commissioner (ex officio)	JONATHAN WROBLEWSKI
Commissioner (ex officio)	J. PATRICIA WILSON SMOOT
Staff Director	KENNETH P. COHEN
Director, Office of Administration and Planning	SUSAN M. BRAZEL

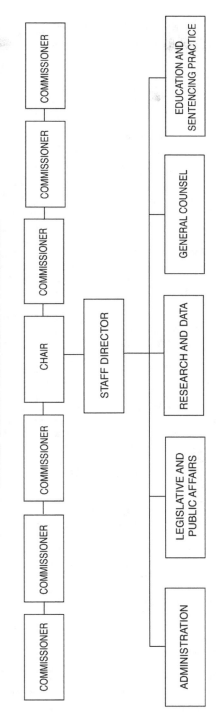

UNITED STATES SENTENCING COMMISSION

- COMMISSIONER
- COMMISSIONER
- COMMISSIONER
- COMMISSIONER
- CHAIR
- COMMISSIONER
- COMMISSIONER
- COMMISSIONER

STAFF DIRECTOR

- ADMINISTRATION
- LEGISLATIVE AND PUBLIC AFFAIRS
- RESEARCH AND DATA
- GENERAL COUNSEL
- EDUCATION AND SENTENCING PRACTICE

Director, Office of Education and Sentencing Practice	RAQUEL WILSON
Director, Office of Legislative and Public Affairs	CHRISTINE M. LEONARD
Director, Office of Research and Data	GLENN R. SCHMITT
General Counsel	KATHLEEN C. GRILLI

The United States Sentencing Commission develops sentencing guidelines and policies for the Federal court system.

The United States Sentencing Commission was established as an independent agency in the judicial branch of the Federal Government by the Sentencing Reform Act of 1984 (28 U.S.C. 991 et seq. and 18 U.S.C. 3551 et seq.). The Commission establishes sentencing guidelines and policies for the Federal courts, advising them of the appropriate form and severity of punishment for offenders convicted of Federal crimes.

The Commission comprises seven voting members and two nonvoting members. The President appoints the voting members with the advice and consent of the Senate for 6-year terms. The President also appoints one of the voting members as the Chair and designates three others as Vice Chairs.

The Commission evaluates the effects of the sentencing guidelines on the criminal justice system, advises Congress on the modification or enactment of statutes pertaining to criminal law and sentencing matters, establishes a research and development program on sentencing issues, and performs other related duties.

In executing its duties, the Commission promulgates and distributes to Federal courts and to the U.S. probation system guidelines for determining sentences to be imposed in criminal cases, general policy statements regarding the application of guidelines, and policy statements on the appropriate use of probation and supervised release revocation provisions. These sentencing guidelines and policy statements are intended to support the principles of just punishment, deterrence, incapacitation, and rehabilitation; provide fairness in meeting the purposes of sentencing; avoid unwarranted disparity; and reflect advancement in the knowledge of human behavior as it relates to the criminal justice process.

The Commission also provides training, conducts research on sentencing-related

issues, and serves as an information resource for Congress, criminal justice practitioners, and the public. http://www.ussc.gov/about

Sources of Information

Education   The Commission offers courses that fulfill continuing legal education requirements in several jurisdictions. http://www.ussc.gov/education/training-resources/continuing-legal-education

Career Opportunities   The Commission posts job announcements on its Web site. http://www.ussc.gov/employment

Guidelines Manual   The current "USSC Guidelines Manual" is available in Portable Document Format on the Commission's Web site. An electronic archive of the yearly manual starts with the year 1987. http://www.ussc.gov/guidelines/2015-guidelines-manual/archive

Helpline   Attorneys, judges, and probation officers who have questions may call the Commission's helpline for assistance. The helpline also handles data requests. Its hours of operations are 8:30 a.m.–5 p.m., eastern standard time, Monday–Friday, excluding Federal holidays. Phone, 202-502-4545.

News   Press releases are available on the Commission's Web site. http://www.ussc.gov/about/news/press-releases

The Commission also posts amicus curiae briefs, reports, speeches, statements, and testimonies online. http://www.ussc.gov/about/news/testimony-speeches/speeches-and-submissions

Publications   A topical index of publications is available online. http://www.ussc.gov/research/topical-index-publications

Reports   The Commission posts reports to the Congress on its Web site. http://www.ussc.gov/research/reports-congress

Annual overviews of Federal criminal cases are available online. http://www.ussc.gov/topic/year-review

The Office of Research and Data publishes periodic reports on Federal sentencing practices. The reports include information on the types of crimes committed, offenders who commit those crimes, the punishments imposed, and the manner in which the sentencing guidelines were applied. http://www.ussc.gov/topic/data-reports

Site Map   The Web site map allows visitors to look for specific topics or to browse content that aligns with their interests. http://www.ussc.gov/sitemap

Updates   An online subscription form is available to sign up for regular email updates from the USSC. http://www.ussc.gov/sign-regular-updates http://www.ussc.gov | Email: pubaffairs@ussc.gov

For further information, contact the Office of Legislative and Public Affairs, U.S. Sentencing Commission, Suite 2–500, One Columbus Circle NE., Washington, DC 20002-8002. Phone, 202-502-4500.

Executive Branch

EXECUTIVE BRANCH: THE PRESIDENT

The President
1600 Pennsylvania Avenue NW., Washington, DC 20500

The President of the United States
https://www.whitehouse.gov/administration/president-biden

JOSEPH R. BIDEN, JR.

First Lady of the United States
https://www.whitehouse.gov/administration/dr-jill-biden

JILL T. BIDEN

The above list of key personnel was updated 1–2021.

Establishment
The U.S. Constitution vests the President with the executive power of the Federal Government. It stipulates that the President will hold his (or her) office for a term of 4 years and will serve the duration of this term together with the Vice President (ART. II, Sec. 1). https://www.archives.gov/founding-docs/constitution-transcript#toc-section-1--2

Constitutional and Statutory Authorities
The second article of the Constitution addresses the "executive Power" and "Office" of the President. https://www.archives.gov/founding-docs/constitution-transcript#toc-article-ii-

In addition to the powers set forth in the U.S. Constitution, the statutes have conferred specific authority and responsibility covering a range of matters upon the President. Subject matter affecting the President is codified in 3 U.S.C. Title 3 contains four chapters that currently remain in effect: "Presidential Elections and Vacancies"; "Office and Compensation of President"; "Delegation of Functions"; and "Extension of Certain Rights and Protections to Presidential

Offices." https://uscode.house.gov/view.xhtml?path=/prelim@title3&edition=prelim

Activities
The President serves as the administrative head of the Government's executive branch, which includes over 55 permanent independent agencies and Government corporations, as well as the 15 executive departments.

The President is the Commander in Chief of the Army and Navy (and Air Force). The President also has the power, by the advice and with the consent of the Senate, to make treaties and to appoint the Justices of the U.S. Supreme Court, U.S. Ambassadors, and other consuls, officers, and public ministers (ART. II, Sec. 2). https://www.archives.gov/founding-docs/constitution-transcript#toc-section-2--2

The Cabinet comprises the Vice President and the heads of the 15 executive departments. These department heads include the Secretaries of Agriculture, Commerce, Defense, Education, Energy, Health and Human Services, Homeland Security, Housing and Urban Development,

Interior, Labor, State, Transportation, Treasury, and Veterans Affairs, plus the Attorney General. https://www.whitehouse.gov/administration/cabinet

The Cabinet, which is a creation of custom and tradition and which dates back to the administration of President George Washington, functions at the pleasure of the President. Cabinet members advise the President on topics that relate to the duties of their respective appointments. In the language of the Constitution: The President "may require the Opinion, in writing, of the principal Officer in each of the executive Departments, upon any Subject relating to the Duties of their respective Offices" (ibid.). https://www.archives.gov/founding-docs/constitution-transcript#toc-section-2--2

Sources of Information

Cabinet   In addition to the Vice President and heads of the 15 executive departments, President Biden's Cabinet includes the White House Chief of Staff, the U.S. Ambassador to the United Nations, the Director of National Intelligence, and the U.S. Trade Representative, as well as the heads of the Environmental Protection Agency, Office of Management and Budget, Council of Economic Advisers, Office of Science and Technology Policy, and Small Business Administration. https://www.whitehouse.gov/administration/cabinet

Compilation of Presidential Documents (CPD)   This collection of Presidential documents comprises the official publications of materials that the White House Press Secretary has released. The Office of the Federal Register publishes the CPD, and the Government Publishing Office maintains the collection on its govinfo web site. https://www.govinfo.gov/app/collection/CPD

Contact the President   An electronic message box is available on the "Contact Us" web page. https://www.whitehouse.gov/contact

COVID–19   The "COVID–19" web page contains a description of the response that the Biden–Harris Administration has adopted for mitigating the Nation's ongoing health and economic crisis. https://www.whitehouse.gov/priorities/covid-19

Español   A short biography of President Biden is available in Spanish. https://www.whitehouse.gov/es/administracion/presidente-biden

Executive Branch   "The Executive Branch" web page includes a section describing the responsibilities and powers of the President. https://www.whitehouse.gov/about-the-white-house/our-government/the-executive-branch

Farewell Addresses   The Our Documents initiative is a cooperative effort in which the National Archives and Records Administration (NARA) participates. As part of the initiative, NARA has selected 100 milestone documents from American history. Among those select documents are two Presidential farewell addresses, one of which was given by President Dwight D. Eisenhower in 1961. https://www.ourdocuments.gov/doc.php?flash=false&doc=90&page=transcript

President George Washington's farewell address to the people of the United States—which he did not publicly deliver, but which was published first on September 19, 1796, in the "Philadelphia Daily American Advertiser"—is among the 100 milestone American documents that the National Archives and Records Administration has compiled. Since 1893, the Senate has observed the first President's birthday by having one of its Members read his farewell address aloud. https://www.govinfo.gov/content/pkg/GPO-CDOC-106sdoc21/pdf/GPO-CDOC-106sdoc21.pdf

First Families   Profiles of former first families and of the Biden family are available online. https://www.whitehouse.gov/about-the-white-house/first-families

Immediate Priorities   The immediate priorities of the Biden-Harris Administration center on relief for American families and other related actions. The agenda of priorities includes bringing the pandemic under control, providing economic assistance, addressing the steadily increasing adverse effects of climate change, and further advancing racial equity and civil rights. President Biden also has prioritized reforming the Nation's immigration system and improving America's international standing. https://www.whitehouse.gov/priorities

Legislation The "Legislation" web page is a convenient resource for seeing recent pieces of legislation that the President signed into law. https://www.whitehouse.gov/briefing-room/legislation

Libraries / Museums The National Archives and Records Administration oversees Presidential libraries and museums, which are repositories for Presidential papers, records, and historical materials. https://www.archives.gov/presidential-libraries

Nominations The website congress.gov has a large searchable database that allows users to apply filters and limit search results. One of the search options is "Nominations" (i.e., Presidential nominations that require Senate approval for confirmation). https://www.congress.gov

Pardons / Commutations The Department of Justice's Office of the Pardon Attorney maintains a list of Presidential pardons and commutations on its "Clemency Recipients" web page. The list starts with pardons and commutations that President Richard M. Nixon granted and ends with those that were granted by President Donald J. Trump. . https://www.justice.gov/pardon/clemency-recipients

Policy and Supporting Positions Published after each Presidential election, by either the Senate Committee on Homeland Security and Governmental Affairs or the House Committee on Oversight and Reform, the "Plum Book" lists thousands of Federal civil service leadership and support positions that may be subject to noncompetitive appointment, nationwide. https://www.govinfo.gov/collection/plum-book?path=/GPO/United%20States%20Government%20Policy%20and%20Supporting%20Positions%20%2528Plum%20Book%2529

Presidential Actions President Biden's announcements, Executive orders, memorandums, and proclamations are posted online. https://www.whitehouse.gov/presidential-actions

Presidents Present and Past To learn more about the current President and the men who occupied the Oval Office in the past,

visit the "Presidents" web page. https://www.whitehouse.gov/about-the-white-house/presidents

Press Briefings The White House posts press briefings on its website. https://www.whitehouse.gov/briefing-room/press-briefings

Shared Heritage Travel Itinerary The Heritage Education Services of the National Park Service (NPS), in partnership with the NPS Office of Tourism, White House Historical Association, and National Conference of State Historic Preservation Officers, produced the American Presidents "Discover Our Shared Heritage Travel Itinerary." The travel itinerary helps visitors explore the lives and contributions of 43 American Presidents. It includes places that American Presidents knew during their lifetimes and that now honor their public service. https://www.nps.gov/nr/travel/presidents/list_of_sites.html

Social Media The White House has a Facebook account. https://www.facebook.com/WhiteHouse

The White House tweets announcements and other newsworthy items on Twitter. https://twitter.com/whitehouse

Speeches / Remarks President Biden's speeches and remarks are posted online. https://www.whitehouse.gov/briefing-room/speeches-remarks

Statements / Releases Announcements, factsheets, readouts of phone conversations, and statements are posted on the White House website. https://www.whitehouse.gov/briefing-room/statements-releases

Travels Abroad Starting with President Theodore Roosevelt and his visit to Panama, the Department of State's Office of the Historian maintains a "Travels Abroad of the President" web page. https://history.state.gov/departmenthistory/travels/president

White House Grounds The White House and the grounds that surround it are the home of the President and First Family and serve as a museum of American history. https://www.whitehouse.gov/about-the-white-house/the-grounds

The Sources of Information were updated 12–2021.

THE VICE PRESIDENT

The Vice President https://www.whitehouse.gov/administration/vice-president-harris	KAMALA D. HARRIS
Second Gentleman of the United States https://www.whitehouse.gov/administration/douglas-emhoff	DOUGLAS C. EMHOFF

The above list of key personnel was updated 1–2021.

Establishment

The U.S. Constitution stipulates that while occupying his (or her) office for a term of 4 years, the President will serve the duration of that term together with the Vice President (ART. II, Sec. 1). https://www.archives.gov/founding-docs/constitution-transcript#toc-section-1--2

Constitutional and Statutory Authorities

The Vice President is mentioned in two articles of the U.S. Constitution: Article I, Section 3, and Article II, Sections 1 and 4. https://www.archives.gov/founding-docs/constitution-transcript

The contents of the 12th, 20th, and 25th Amendments directly affect the office and responsibilities of the Vice President. https://www.archives.gov/founding-docs/amendments-11-27#toc-amendment-xii

In addition to the powers set forth in the U.S. Constitution, the statutes have conferred specific authority and responsibility, covering a range of matters, upon the President and Vice President. Subject matter affecting both the President and Vice President is codified in 3 U.S.C. https://uscode.house.gov/view.xhtml?path=/prelim@title3&edition=prelim

Activities

The executive functions of the Vice President include participation in Cabinet meetings. https://www.whitehouse.gov/administration/cabinet

Public Law 81–216, which is also cited as the National Security Act Amendments of 1949, changed the composition of the National Security Council to include the Vice President (63 Stat. 579). http://www.loc.gov/law/help/statutes-at-large/81st-congress/session-1/c81s1ch412.pdf

By an Act that was approved on August 10, 1846, to establish the Smithsonian Institution, the Vice President serves as a regent on the Board of Regents of the Smithsonian Institution (9 Stat. 103). http://www.loc.gov/law/help/statutes-at-large/29th-congress/session-1/c29s1ch178.pdf

Pursuant to Article II, Section 1, the powers and duties of the Presidency devolve on the Vice President in the case of the President's death, inability to discharge the office's powers and duties, or removal from office. https://www.archives.gov/founding-docs/constitution-transcript#toc-section-1--2

The Vice President also fills a legislative role as President of the Senate. In this capacity, the Vice President had been expected to preside at regular sessions of the Senate and cast votes only to break ties. From the vice-presidency of John Adams in 1789 to that of Richard Nixon in the 1950s, presiding over the Senate was the chief function of the Vice President. Each one had an office in the Capitol, received staff support and office expenses through the legislative appropriations, and rarely was invited to participate in executive activities, including Cabinet meetings. In 1961, Vice President Lyndon B. Johnson moved his chief office from the Capitol to the White House, directed his attention to executive functions, and started attending Senate sessions only at critical times. His actions changed the traditional role of the Vice President, and those changes continue in effect today. https://www.senate.gov/artandhistory/history/common/briefing/President_Pro_Tempore.htm#1

Sources of Information

Contact Information The website of the United States Senates has a "Suite and Telephone List" (JUN 2021) that is accessible from its "Contacting U.S. Senators" web page. The list is posted in Portable Document Format (PDF) for viewing and downloading. Vice President Kamala D. Harris is the first entry on the list. Phone, 202-224-2424. https://www.senate.gov/general/resources/pdf/senators_phone_list.pdf

Biography   A brief biographical description of Vice President Harris is part of the "Biographical Directory of the United States Congress, 1774–Present." https://bioguideretro.congress.gov/Home/MemberDetails?memIndex=H001075

A short biography of Vice President Harris is available in Spanish. https://www.whitehouse.gov/es/administracion/vicepresidenta-harris

Executive Branch   "The Executive Branch" web page includes a section describing the responsibilities and powers of the Vice President. https://www.whitehouse.gov/about-the-white-house/our-government/the-executive-branch

Immediate Priorities   The immediate priorities of the Biden-Harris Administration

center on relief for American families and other related actions. The agenda of priorities includes bringing the pandemic under control, providing economic assistance, addressing the steadily increasing adverse effects of climate change, and further advancing racial equity and civil rights. Reforming the Nation's immigration system and improving America's international standing are also part of the Biden-Harris Administration's list of priorities. https://www.whitehouse.gov/priorities

President of the Senate   Vice President Harris also serves in a constitutionally mandated capacity as the President of the Senate. https://www.senate.gov/senators/leadership.htm

Service Academy Nominations   The Vice President is authorized to nominate candidates to the U.S. Military, Naval, and Air Force Academies, but cannot make nominations to the U.S. Merchant Marine Academy and does not nominate to the U.S. Coast Guard Academy. https://www.whitehouse.gov/service-academy-nominations

The Sources of Information were updated 9–2021.

THE EXECUTIVE OFFICE OF THE PRESIDENT

The White House, 1600 Pennsylvania Avenue NW., Washington, DC 20500; http://www.whitehouse.gov

Annual Report to Congress on White House Office Personnel

The report carries a date of July 1, 2021, and it discloses the status (e.g., employee or detailee), salary, pay basis, and title of staff members who are associated with the Executive Office of the President. https://www.whitehouse.gov/wp-content/uploads/2021/07/July-1-2021-Report-Final.pdf

Establishment and Organization

On April 3, 1939, President Franklin D. Roosevelt approved Public Law 76–19, which is also cited as the Reorganization Act of 1939. The Act reorganized Government agencies to save money: "The Congress hereby declares that by reason of continued national deficits

beginning in 1931 it is desirable to reduce substantially Government expenditures and that such reduction may be accomplished . . . by proceeding immediately under the provisions of this Act" (53 Stat. 561). The reorganization sought to reduce expenditures and maintain efficient operation of Government; to increase efficiency of the operations of Government as much as possible within the revenues available; to group, coordinate, and consolidate Government agencies according to major purposes; to reduce the number of agencies through consolidation and termination; and to eliminate overlap and duplication. http://www.loc.gov/law/help/statutes-at-large/76th-congress/session-1/c76s1ch36.pdf

On June 7, 1939, President Roosevelt approved Public Resolution 76–20, which acknowledged that "reorganization plan numbered I" had been submitted to the U.S. Congress on April 25, 1939, and that "reorganization plan numbered II" had been submitted on May 9, 1939. The joint resolution made the provisions of these two reorganization plans effective on July 1, 1939. http://www.loc.gov/law/help/statutes-at-large/76th-congress/session-1/c76s1ch193.pdf

Under authority of the Reorganization Act of 1939, the President's two reorganization plans transferred various agencies to the Executive Office of the President. The contents of Reorganization Plan I and Reorganization Plan II of 1939 are codified in the appendix of 5 U.S.C. https://uscode.house.gov/view.xhtml?path=/prelim@title5/title5a/node84&edition=prelim

The National Archives published President Roosevelt's two reorganization plans that he had prepared and transmitted to the Senate and the House of Representatives, the first on April 25 and the second on May 9, in the Federal Register (4 FR 2727–2733) on July 1, 1939. https://www.govinfo.gov/content/pkg/FR-1939-07-01/pdf/FR-1939-07-01.pdf

On September 8, 1939, President Franklin D. Roosevelt signed an order that established five standing divisions of the Executive Office of the President and defined their functions and duties. The National Archives published Executive Order No. 8248 in the Federal Register (4 FR 3864) 4 days later. https://www.govinfo.gov/content/pkg/FR-1939-09-12/pdf/FR-1939-09-12.pdf

Presidents have continued to use Executive orders, reorganization plans, and legislative initiatives for reorganizing the Executive Office of the President to make its composition compatible with their administrative goals. https://www.whitehouse.gov/about-the-white-house/the-executive-branch

Regulatory Authorities   Rules and regulations that are associated with the Executive Office of the President are codified in the first chapter, sections 100–199, of 3 CFR. https://www.ecfr.gov/cgi-bin/text-idx?SID=6d49df89015aa267bedec9a29f6a2662&mc=true&tpl=/ecfrbrowse/Title03/3chapterI.tpl

Sources of Information

Archived Records   The "Guide to Federal Records in the National Archives of the United States" indicates that records of organizations in the Executive Office of the President have been assigned to record group 429. https://www.archives.gov/research/guide-fed-records/groups/429.html

Career Opportunities   Applicants seeking noncareer positions may contact the Biden-Harris Administration by using an electronic form. https://www.whitehouse.gov/get-involved/join-us

Information on the White House Fellows program is available online. https://www.whitehouse.gov/get-involved/fellows

Contact Information   Phone numbers for leaving comments and calling the White House switchboard and visitor's office are available on the "How You Can Write or Call the White House" web page. An email link that leads to an electronic message form is also available on the web page, as well as instructions for writing a letter, addressing the envelope, and sending it by postal mail. https://www.whitehouse.gov/get-involved/write-or-call

Disclosures   Strict rules govern the conduct of executive branch appointees and require every appointee in an executive branch agency to sign an ethics pledge. A waiver is permitted in cases where the literal application of the pledge is inconsistent with its purposes or is not in the public interest. Waivers that have been granted are posted online. https://www.whitehouse.gov/disclosures

On January 20, 2021, President Joseph R. Biden, Jr., signed "Executive Order 13989—Ethics Commitments by Executive Branch Personnel". This Executive Order was published in the Federal Register on January 25, 2021. https://www.govinfo.gov/content/pkg/DCPD-202100058/pdf/DCPD-202100058.pdf

Federal Register   Significant documents and documents that the Executive Office of the President recently published in the Federal Register are accessible online. https://www.federalregister.gov/agencies/executive-office-of-the-president

Social Media   The White House has a Facebook account. https://www.facebook.com/WhiteHouse

The White House tweets announcements and other newsworthy items on Twitter. https://twitter.com/whitehouse

Staff Salaries   In June or July of 2021, the Biden-Harris Administration's first Annual report to Congress on White House Personnel for 2021 should be available in Portable Document Format (PDF) for viewing and downloading. The report contains professional information (e.g., name, status, salary, pay basis, and position title) about people who are associated with the Executive Office of the President. A link will be provided below after the report is released to the public.

The above Sources of Information were updated 3–2021.

White House Office

1600 Pennsylvania Avenue NW., Washington, DC 20500
Phone, 202-456-1414. Internet, http://www.whitehouse.gov

Chief of Staff	RONALD A. KLAIN
National Security Advisor	JACOB J. SULLIVAN
White House Counsel	DANA A. REMUS
Deputy National Security Advisor	ELIZABETH D. SHERWOOD-RANDALL
Press Secretary	JENNIFER R. PSAKI
To The First Lady	
Chief of Staff	JULISSA REYNOSO PANTALEÓN
Senior Advisor	ANTHONY BERNAL
Advisors	
Senior Advisors	MICHAEL C. DONILON
	CEDRIC L. RICHMOND
Homeland Security	ELIZABETH D. SHERWOOD-RANDALL
National Climate	REGINA A. MCCARTHY
Science	ERIC S. LANDER
Assistants to The President	
	KATHERINE J. BEDINGFIELD
	ANTHONY R. BERNAL
	BRIAN C. DEESE
	JENNIFER B. DILLON
	MICHAEL C. DONILON
	ANNE E. FILIPIC
	JONATHAN J. FINER
	RONALD A. KLAIN
	REGINA A. MCCARTHY
	JENNIFER R. PSAKI
	BRUCE N. REED
	DANA A. REMUS
	CEDRIC L. RICHMOND
Domestic Policy	SUSAN E. RICE
Special Assistants	
Climate and Science Agency Personnel	JEFFREY MAROOTIAN
Climate Policy	DAVID J. HAYES
Economic Policy	JOELLE GAMBLE
Immigration	TYLER MORAN

Deputy Chiefs of Staff

JENNIFER B. DILLON
BRUCE N. REED

Directors
Communications
Intergovernmental Affairs
Legislative Affairs
Management and Administration
Oval Office Operations
Presidential Correspondence
Presidential Personnel
Public Engagement
Speechwriting
White House Military Office
White House Personnel

KATHERINE J. BEDINGFIELD
JULIE RODRIGUEZ
LOUISA TERRELL
ANNE FILIPIC
ANNIE TOMASINI
EVA KEMP
CATHERINE M. RUSSELL
CEDRIC L. RICHMOND
VINAY REDDY
MAJU VARGHESE
CATHERINE RUSSELL

Speechwriters

AMBER MACDONALD
JEFFREY NUSSBAUM

The above list of key personnel was updated 7–2021. The updating process remains in progress.

The White House Office serves the President in the performance of the many detailed activities incident to his immediate office.

Establishment
On September 8, 1939, President Frankzin D. Roosevelt signed an order that established the divisions of the Executive Office of the President and defined their functions and duties. The National Archives published Executive Order No. 8248 in the Federal Register (4 FR 3864) 4 days later. The President's order established the White House Office as one of five divisions within the Executive Office. It also defined the Office's duties and functions as "to serve the President in an intimate capacity in the performance of the many detailed activities incident to his immediate office." https://www.govinfo.gov/content/pkg/FR-1939-09-12/pdf/FR-1939-09-12.pdf

Activities
The President's staff facilitates and maintains communication with the Congress, the heads of executive agencies, the press and other information media, and the general public. The various Assistants to the President aid the President in such matters as he or she may direct.

Sources of Information

Archived Records   The "Guide to Federal Records in the National Archives of the United States" indicates that White House Office records have been assigned to record group 130. https://www.archives.gov/research/guide-fed-records/groups/130.html
Career Opportunities   The White House Fellows program offers gifted and highly motivated young Americans firsthand experience with the process of governing the Nation and a sense of personal involvement in the leadership of society. https://www.whitehouse.gov/get-involved/fellows | Email: whitehousefellows@who.eop.gov
Coronavirus Disease 2019 (COVID–19)   The Biden-Harris Administration is responding to the public health and economic crisis that the COVID-19 outbreak continues to cause. The President is pushing for action by the Federal Government to help protect and support caregivers, families, first responders, small-businesses owners, and others whose health or economic stability has been affected

adversely. https://www.whitehouse.gov/
priorities/covid-19
Ethics Pledge A list of waiver certifications
for White House Office employees is posted
in Portable Document Format (PDF), for
viewing and downloading, at the bottom
of the "Disclosures" web page, under the

heading "Ethics Pledge Waivers." https://
www.whitehouse.gov/disclosures
Federal Register Documents that the
White House Office published in the Federal
Register are accessible online. https://www.
federalregister.gov/agencies/the-white-house-
office

The above Sources of Information were updated 1–2021.

Editorial Note:
A dedicated website for the Office of the Vice President is not available.

Office of the Vice President

Eisenhower Executive Office Building, Washington, DC 20501
Phone, 202-456-7549. Internet, http://www.whitehouse.gov/people/mike-pence/

Chief of Staff to the Vice President	HARTINA FLOURNOY
Advisors to the Vice President	
Domestic Policy	ROHINI KOSOGLU
National Security	NANCY MCELDOWNEY
Chief Spokeswoman	SYMONE SANDERS
Director of Communications	ASHLEY ETIENNE

The above list of key personnel was updated 1–2021.

Establishment
From the vice-presidency of John Adams
in 1789 to that of Richard Nixon in the
1950s, presiding over the Senate was
the Vice President's chief function. Each
Vice President maintained an office in
the Capitol, received staff support and
office expenses through the legislative
appropriations, and rarely was invited to
participate in executive activities, including
Cabinet meetings. In 1961, Vice President
Lyndon B. Johnson moved his chief office
from the Capitol to the White House,
directed his attention to executive functions,
and started attending Senate sessions only
at critical times. His actions changed the
traditional role of the Vice President and his
office, and those changes continue in effect
today. https://www.senate.gov/artandhistory/
history/common/briefing/President_Pro_
Tempore.htm#1

Activities
The Office of the Vice President supports
the Vice President's in his or her executive

and legislative roles. Within the executive
branch of Government, the Vice President
holds a position of second in command;
within the legislative branch, he or she
serves as President of the Senate. The
Office's staff develops policy options on
a variety of issues, ranging from tax and
healthcare policy to foreign policy and
national security. Its staff also works with
Senators and Representatives to promote the
President's legislative priorities in the U.S.
Congress.

The Office also handles the Vice
President's correspondence, events,
scheduling, speechwriting, and travel.
https://www.whitehouse.gov/get-involved/
internships/presidential-departments

Sources of Information

Career Opportunities The following Offices
within the Office of the Vice President offer
opportunities for young men and women:
Administration, Advance for the Vice President,
Communications, Counsel to the Vice

President, Intergovernmental Affairs, Scheduling for the Vice President, and the Office of the Second Lady. The Departments of Domestic Policy and of Legislative Affairs also participate in the internship program. https://www.whitehouse.gov/get-involved/internships/ | Email: intern_application@who.eop.gov

The above Sources of Information were updated 1–2021.

Ethics Pledge   A list of waiver certifications for Office of the Vice President employees is posted in Portable Document Format (PDF), for viewing and downloading, at the bottom of the "Disclosures" web page, under the heading "Ethics Pledge Waivers." https://www.whitehouse.gov/disclosures

Council of Economic Advisers

Seventeenth and Pennsylvania Avenue NW., Washington, DC 20502
Phone, 202-456-4779. Internet, http://www.whitehouse.gov/cea

Chair	CECILIA E. ROUSE
Members	JARED BERNSTEIN
	HEATHER M. BOUSHEY

The above list of key personnel was updated 3–2021.

The Council of Economic Advisers analyzes and appraises the national economy to make policy recommendations to the President.

Establishment and Organization
On February 20, 1946, President Harry S. Truman signed Public Law 79–304, which is also cited as the Employment Act of 1946. The Act "created in the Executive Office of the President a Council of Economic Advisers" (60 Stat. 24). http://www.loc.gov/law/help/statutes-at-large/79th-congress/session-2/c79s2ch33.pdf

On June 1, 1953, President Dwight D. Eisenhower prepared a reorganization plan and transmitted it to the U.S. Congress on June 1, 1953. Reorganization Plan No. 9 of 1953 became effective 2 months later on August 1st and was published in the Federal Register on August 3d. https://www.govinfo.gov/content/pkg/FR-1953-08-04/pdf/FR-1953-08-04.pdf

The Council continues to function under the Employment Act of 1946 and Reorganization Plan No. 9 of 1953 (5 U.S.C. app.). https://uscode.house.gov/view.xhtml?req=granuleid:USC-prelim-title5a-node84-leaf142&num=0&edition=prelim

Public Law 112–166, which also is cited as the Presidential Appointment Efficiency and Streamlining Act of 2011, affected the appointment process of Council members.

The Council comprises three members: one of whom serves as the Chair and another of whom serves as the Vice Chair. The President appoints the Chair by the advice and with the consent of the Senate. The President designates one of the members as Vice Chair, who acts as the Chair in his or her absence. Each Council member, "as a result of training, experience, and attainments," should be "exceptionally qualified to analyze and interpret economic developments, to appraise programs and activities of the Government . . . and to formulate and recommend national economic policy to promote full employment, production, and purchasing power under free competitive enterprise" (126 Stat. 1287–1288). https://www.govinfo.gov/content/pkg/STATUTE-126/pdf/STATUTE-126.pdf

Statutory Authorities
Statutory subject matter affecting the Council of Economic Advisers is codified in "Chapter 21—National Policy on Employment and Productivity" of 15 U.S.C. Section 1023 is dedicated to the Council of Economic Advisers. https://uscode.house.gov/view.xhtml?req=granuleid:USC-prelim-title15-se

ction1023&num=0&edition=prelim#source credit

Activities
The Council analyzes the national economy and its various sectors; advises the President on economic developments; appraises the economic programs and policies of the Federal Government; recommends policies for economic growth and stability to the President; assists in the preparation of the President's economic reports to the U.S. Congress; and prepares the "Annual Report of the Council of Economic Advisers." https://www.whitehouse.gov/cea

The above Sources of Information were updated 1–2021.

Sources of Information

Archived Records   The "Guide to Federal Records in the National Archives of the United States" indicates that records of the Council of Economic Advisers have been assigned to record group 459. https://www.archives.gov/research/guide-fed-records/groups/459.html

Documents   The Government Publishing Office's govinfo website includes the Council of Economic Advisers in the list of executive branch authors on its "Browse by Government Author" web page. https://www.govinfo.gov/app/browse/author

Council on Environmental Quality

722 Jackson Place NW., Washington, DC 20503
Phone, 202-395-5750 or 202-456-6224. Fax, 202-456-2710. Internet, http://www.whitehouse.gov/ceq

Chair	BRENDA MALLORY
Members	(VACANCY)
	(VACANCY)
Chief of Staff	MATTEW LEE-ASHLEY, ACTING
General Counsel	JUSTIN PIDOT
Special Assistant	SARA JORDAN
Federal Chief Sustainability Officer	ANDREW MAYOCK
Senior Directors	
Building Emissions	MARK CHAMBERS
Emissions	AUSTIN BROWN
Environmental Justice	CECILIA MARTINEZ
Lands	MATTEW LEE-ASHLEY
National Environmental Policy Act (NEPA) Oversight	JAYNI HEIN
Water	SARA GONZALEZ-ROTHI

The above list of key personnel was updated 4–2021.

The Council on Environmental Quality formulates and recommends national policies and initiatives for improving the environment.

Establishment and Organization
On January 1, 1970, President Richard M. Nixon approved Public Law 91–190, which also is cited as the National Environmental Policy Act of 1969. The Act established "a national policy for the environment" and provided "for the establishment of a Council on Environmental Quality" (83 Stat. 852). It created the Council (CEQ)

in the Executive Office of the President. The CEQ is composed of three members, whom the President appoints by the advice and with the consent of the Senate. The President designates one of the members to serve as the Chair. Each Council member is required to be "exceptionally well qualified to analyze and interpret environmental trends and information of all kinds . . . to formulate and recommend national policies to promote the improvement of the quality of the environment" (83 Stat. 854). https://www.govinfo.gov/content/pkg/STATUTE-83/pdf/STATUTE-83-Pg852.pdf

On April 3, 1970, President Richard M. Nixon approved Public Law 91–224, which also is cited as the Environmental Quality Improvement Act of 1970. The Act established the Office of Environmental Quality (OEQ) in the Executive Office of the President. The CEQ Chair also serves as the Director of the OEQ. The President also appoints, by the Senate's advice and with its consent, the OEQ's deputy director (84 Stat. 114). The Office provides professional and administrative support for the Council. The CEQ and OEQ are referred to, collectively, as the Council on Environmental Quality. https://www.govinfo.gov/content/pkg/STATUTE-84/pdf/STATUTE-84-Pg91.pdf

Statutory and Regulatory Authorities
Statutory subject matter affecting the Council on Environmental Quality is codified in "Chapter 55—National Environmental Policy" of 42 U.S.C. Sections 4341–4347 are dedicated to the Council on Environmental Quality. https://uscode.house.gov/view.xhtml?path=/prelim@title42/chapter55&edition=prelim

Statutory subject matter affecting the Office of Environmental Quality is codified in "Chapter 56—Environmental Quality Improvement" of 42 U.S.C. Section 4372 is dedicated to the Office of Environmental Quality. https://uscode.house.gov/view.xhtml?path=/prelim@title42/chapter56&edition=prelim

Codified rules and regulations associated with the Council on Environmental Quality have been assigned to chapter V of 40 CFR, parts 1500–1599. https://www.ecfr.gov/cgi-bin/text-idx?SID=3332dfb05e2ecdfa883fa40713ac3de3&mc=true&tpl=/ecfrbrowse/Title40/40chapterV.tpl

Activities
The Council develops policies that bring together the Nation's economic, social, and environmental priorities to improve Federal decisionmaking. As required by NEPA, the CEQ also evaluates, coordinates, and mediates Federal activities. It advises and

assists the President on both national and international environmental policy matters. It oversees Federal agency and departmental implementation of NEPA.

The CEQ's Office of Federal Sustainability coordinates policy to promote energy and environmental sustainability across Federal Government operations. The Federal Government manages more than 350,000 buildings, operates more than 600,000 vehicles, and purchases annually more than $500 billion in goods and services. https://www.sustainability.gov/index.html

Sources of Information

Archived Records The "Guide to Federal Records in the National Archives of the United States" indicates that records of the CEQ have been assigned to record group 580; however, that group does not have a description associated with it. https://www.archives.gov/research/guide-fed-records/index-numeric/501-to-600.html

The "Guide to Federal Records in the National Archives of the United States" indicates that records of the organizations in the Executive office of the President have been assigned to record group 429. Within that record group, the records of the Citizens' Advisory Committee on Environmental Quality (CACEQ) are located in subgroup 429.3. The CACEQ was established on May 29, 1969, and its members advised the newly established Environmental Quality Council. https://www.archives.gov/research/guide-fed-records/groups/429.html

Contact Information Contact information for the Office of Federal Sustainability is available on the "Contact Us" page of its website. https://www.sustainability.gov/contact.html | Email: sustainability@ceq.eop.gov

Federal Register Significant documents and documents that the CEQ recently published in the Federal Register are accessible online. https://www.federalregister.gov/agencies/council-on-environmental-quality

Freedom of Information Act (FOIA) The FOIA gives a person a right to request access to Federal agency records or information. An agency must disclose records that any person properly requests in writing. Pursuant to one or more of nine exemptions and three

exclusions that the Act contains, a Federal agency may withhold certain records or parts of them. The FOIA applies only to Federal agencies and does not create a right of access to records held by the U.S. Congress, the courts, State or local government agencies, and private entities. The CEQ maintains an online requester service center.
News The White House posts news items on energy and the environment.
Sustainability The Federal Government is the Nation's largest energy consumer,

managing over 350,000 buildings and operating over 600,000 vehicles. By increasing operational efficiency, Federal agencies reduce waste, save taxpayer dollars, lessen harmful effects on ecosystems, and support cleaner air, land, and water. Governmentwide performance data on sustainability goals are available on the website of the Office of Federal Sustainability. https://www.sustainability.gov/performance.html | Email: sustainability@ceq.eop.gov

The above Sources of Information were updated 1–2021.

National Security Council

Eisenhower Executive Office Building, Washington, DC 20504
Phone, 202-456-1414. Internet, http://www.whitehouse.gov/nsc

Statutory Members

Chair	JOSEPH R. BIDEN, JR.
https://www.whitehouse.gov/administration/president-biden	
https://www.defense.gov/Our-Story/Meet-the-Team/Secretary-of-Defense	LLOYD J. AUSTIN III
https://www.whitehouse.gov/administration/vice-president-harris	KAMALA D. HARRIS
https://www.state.gov/secretary	ANTONY J. BLINKEN
Statutory Advisors	
https://www.dni.gov/index.php/who-we-are/leadership/director-of-national-intelligence	AVRIL HAINES
https://www.jcs.mil/Leadership/Article-View/Article/1974872/gen-mark-a-milley	GEN. MARK A. MILLEY, USA

Standing Participants

Chief of Staff to the President	RONALD A. KLAIN
Counsel to the President	DANA A. REMUS
Director of the National Economic Council	BRIAN C. DEESE
National Security Advisor	JACOB J. SULLIVAN
Secretary of the Treasury	JANET L. YELLEN
U.S. Representative to the United Nations	LINDA THOMAS-GREENFIELD
https://www.whitehouse.gov/nsc	

The above list of key personnel was updated 3–2021.

Establishment and Organization

On July 26, 1947, President Harry S. Truman signed Public Law 80–253, which is also cited as the National Security Act of 1947. By enacting this legislation, the U.S. Congress sought "to provide for the establishment of integrated policies and procedures for the departments, agencies, and functions of the Government relating to the national security; to provide three

military departments for the operation and administration of the Army, the Navy . . . and the Air Force, with their assigned combat and service components; to provide for their authoritative coordination and unified direction under civilian control but not to merge them; to provide for the effective strategic direction of the armed forces and for their operation under unified control and for their integration into an efficient team of land, naval, and air forces." The law established "a council to be known as the National Security Council" and stipulated that the President should preside over its meetings (61 Stat. 496). http://www.loc.gov/law/help/statutes-at-large/80th-congress/session-1/c80s1ch343.pdf

The National Security Council (NSC) was placed in the Executive Office of the President by Reorganization Plan No. 4 of 1949 (5 U.S.C. app.). https://uscode.house.gov/view.xhtml?req=granuleid:USC-prelim-title5a-node84-leaf100&num=0&edition=prelim

The statutory members (PL 81–216) of the NSC—in addition to the President, who chairs the Council—are the Vice President and the Secretaries of State and Defense (63 Stat. 579). The Chairman of the Joint Chiefs of Staff is the statutory military adviser to the NSC, and the Director of National Intelligence serves as its intelligence adviser. The Secretary of the Treasury, the U.S. Representative to the United Nations, the Assistant to the President for National Security Affairs, the Assistant to the President for Economic Policy, and the Chief of Staff to the President are invited to all meetings of the NSC. The Attorney General and the Director of National Drug Control Policy are invited to attend meetings pertaining to their jurisdictions, and other officials are invited, as appropriate. http://www.loc.gov/law/help/statutes-at-large/81st-congress/session-1/c81s1ch412.pdf

Statutory and Regulatory Authorities
Codified content on the National Security Council from Section 101 of the National Security Act of 1947 was formerly located in "Chapter 15—National Security" of 50 U.S.C.and classified editorially as section 402. That content has been subsequently transferred to "Chapter 44—National Security" of 50 U.S.C. and editorially reclassified as section 3021. https://uscode.house.gov/view.xhtml?path=/prelim@title50/chapter44/subchapter1&edition=prelim

NSC rules and regulations are codified in 32 CFR 2100–2199. Within title 32, sections 2100–2199 constitute "Chapter XXI—National Security Council." https://www.ecfr.gov/cgi-bin/text-idx?SID=6df20eda89deafaa9405f41122a78691&mc=true&tpl=/ecfrbrowse/Title32/32chapterXXI.tpl

Activities
The NSC advises and assists the President, in conjunction with the National Economic Council, with the integration of all aspects of national security policy—domestic, economic, foreign, intelligence, and military—that affects the United States. https://www.whitehouse.gov/nsc

Sources of Information

Archived Records The "Guide to Federal Records in the National Archives of the United States" indicates that NSC records have been assigned to record group 273. https://www.archives.gov/research/guide-fed-records/groups/273.html

Federal Register Documents that the NSC published in the Federal Register are accessible online. https://www.federalregister.gov/agencies/national-security-council

The Sources of Information above were updated 2–2021.

Editorial Note:
A dedicated website for the Office of Administration is not available.

Office of Administration

Eisenhower Executive Office Building, 1650 Pennsylvania Avenue, NW., Washington, DC 20503
Phone, 202-456-2861.

Director   ANNE E. FILIPIC

The above list of key personnel was updated 7–2021.

Establishment and Organization

The origins of the Office of Administration lie in Reorganization Plan No. 1 of 1977, which President James E. Carter prepared and transmitted to the Senate and House of Representatives on July 15 of that same year. The new office was created to "provide components of the Executive Office of the President with such administrative services as the President shall from time to time direct." https://uscode.house.gov/view. xhtml?req=granuleid:USC-prelim-title5a-node84-leaf183&num=0&edition=prelim

On December 12, 1977, President Carter signed Executive Order 12028 and formally established the Office of Administration within the Executive Office of the President. That Executive order was published in the Federal Register on December 14, 1977 (42 FR 62895). Transfers of records, property, personnel, and unexpended balances of appropriations to the Office of Administration became effective on April 1, 1978. https://www.govinfo.gov/content/pkg/FR-1977-12-14/pdf/FR-1977-12-14.pdf

The activities of the Director are subject to the direction or approval of the President. The Director organizes the Office of Administration, employs its staff, contracts for supplies and services, and carries out other duties that the President, as head of the Office, might do. In his or her capacity as the chief administrative officer of the Office, the Director ensures that it provides units within the Executive Office of the President with common administrative support and services.

The above Sources of Information were updated 7–2021.

Activities

The Office of Administration is exclusively dedicated to providing uniform administrative support and services to all units that constitute the Executive Office of the President—except for services that are provided primarily in direct support of the President. The Office does, however, upon request, assist the White House Office with providing administrative services that are primarily in direct support of the President (42 FR 62895).

The common administrative support and services that the Office provides fall within the following general administrative areas: personnel management (e.g., equal employment opportunity programs); financial management; data processing; library, records, and information; and office and operations (e.g., graphics, mail, messenger, printing and duplication, procurement, supply, and word processing); and other support or services that can achieve savings and efficiency through centralization (ibid). https://www.govinfo.gov/content/pkg/FR-1977-12-14/pdf/FR-1977-12-14.pdf

Sources of Information

Federal Register   Documents that the Office of Administration published in the Federal Register are accessible online. https://www.federalregister.gov/agencies/administration-office-executive-office-of-the-president

---

Office of Management and Budget

New Executive Office Building, Washington, DC 20503
Phone, 202-395-3080. Internet, http://www.whitehouse.gov/omb

Director	SHALANDA D. YOUNG, ACTING
Deputy Director	SHALANDA D. YOUNG
Deputy Director for Management	JASON S. MILLER
General Counsel	SAMUEL R. BAGENSTOS

Assistant Directors
Budget
Legislative Reference
Management and Operations

Heads of Statutory Offices

Administrators
Electronic Government and Information Technology
Federal Procurement Policy
Information and Regulatory Affairs

Controller
Federal Financial Management

The above list of key personnel was updated 7–2021. The updating process remains in progress.

The Office of Management and Budget assists the President in discharging budgetary, management, and other responsibilities; develops, coordinates, oversees, and implements Federal Government policies affecting financial management and procurement, rules and regulations, and information and statistics; and promotes better program and administrative management, develops measures for agency-performance, and improves coordination of operations within the executive branch.

Establishment and Organization

On April 3, 1939, President Franklin D. Roosevelt approved Public Law 76–19, which also is cited as the Reorganization Act of 1939 (53 Stat. 561). Pursuant to the Act, President Roosevelt prepared an appropriate plan of reorganization. https://www.loc.gov/law/help/statutes-at-large/76th-congress/session-1/c76s1ch36.pdf

Reorganization Plan No. 1 of 1939 transferred the Bureau of the Budget and its functions and personnel from the Department of the Treasury to the Executive Office of the President. President Roosevelt submitted the plan to the Senate and House of Representatives on April 25. https://uscode.house.gov/view.xhtml?req=granuleid:USC-prelim-title5a-node84-leaf86&num=0&edition=prelim

On July 1, 1939, the National Archives published President Roosevelt's reorganization plan in the Federal Register (4 FR 2727). The Bureau of the Budget was the forerunner of the Office of Management and Budget (OMB). https://www.govinfo.gov/content/pkg/FR-1939-07-01/pdf/FR-1939-07-01.pdf

Pursuant to the provisions of chapter 9 of 5 U.S.C., President Richard M. Nixon prepared Reorganization Plan No. 2 of 1970 and submitted it to the Senate and House of Representatives on March 12. The plan redesignated the Bureau of the Budget as the OMB. https://uscode.house.gov/view.xhtml?req=granuleid:USC-prelim-title5a-node84-leaf177&num=0&edition=prelim

On May 23, 1970, the National Archives published the reorganization plan in the Federal Register (35 FR 7959). https://www.govinfo.gov/content/pkg/FR-1970-05-23/pdf/FR-1970-05-23.pdf

Pursuant to Reorganization Plan No. 2 of 1970, President Nixon issued Executive Order 11541 on July 1, 1970. The Executive order prescribed the duties of the newly designated OMB and was published the next day, in the Federal Register (35 FR 10737). https://www.govinfo.gov/content/pkg/FR-1970-07-02/pdf/FR-1970-07-02.pdf

Statutory and Regulatory Authorities

Codified statutory material on money and finance has been assigned to 31 U.S.C. Chapter 5, which comprises sections 501–522, of that title is dedicated to statutory material affecting the OMB. https://uscode.house.gov/view.xhtml?path=/prelim@title31/subtitle1/chapter5&edition=prelim

"Subtitle A—Office of Management and Budget Guidance for Grants and Agreements," which comprises parts 1–299, has been assigned to 2 CFR. https://www.ecfr.gov/cgi-bin/text-idx?SID=76703d9ac3361ee46fdf902194fd8a1f&mc=true&tpl=/ecfrbrowse/Title02/2subtitleA.tpl

"Chapter III—Office of Management and Budget," which comprises parts 1300–1399,

Office of Management and Budget

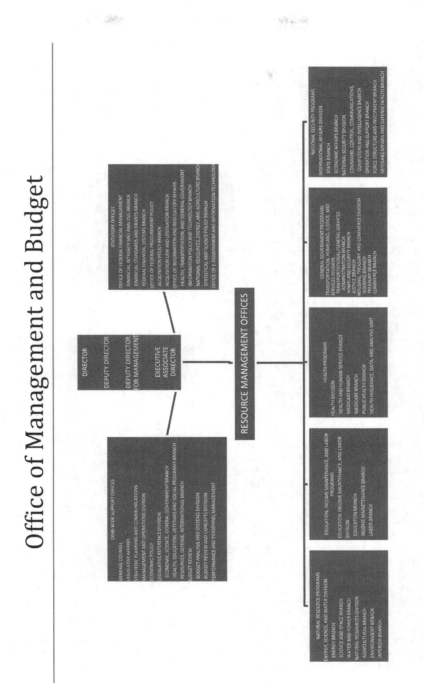

DIRECTOR

DEPUTY DIRECTOR

DEPUTY DIRECTOR FOR MANAGEMENT

EXECUTIVE ASSOCIATE DIRECTOR

STATUTORY OFFICES
OFFICE OF FEDERAL FINANCIAL MANAGEMENT
FINANCIAL INTEGRITY AND ANALYSIS BRANCH
FINANCIAL STANDARDS AND GRANTS BRANCH
FEDERAL FINANCIAL SYSTEMS BRANCH
OFFICE OF FEDERAL PROCUREMENT POLICY
ACQUISITION POLICY BRANCH
ACQUISITION LAW AND LEGISLATION BRANCH
OFFICE OF INFORMATION AND REGULATORY AFFAIRS
HEALTH, TRANSPORTATION, AND GENERAL GOVERNMENT
INFORMATION POLICY AND TECHNOLOGY BRANCH
NATURAL RESOURCES, ENERGY, AND AGRICULTURE BRANCH
STATISTICAL AND SCIENCE POLICY BRANCH
OFFICE OF E-GOVERNMENT AND INFORMATION TECHNOLOGY

OMB-WIDE SUPPORT OFFICES
GENERAL COUNSEL
LEGISLATIVE AFFAIRS
STRATEGIC PLANNING AND COMMUNICATIONS
MANAGEMENT AND OPERATIONS DIVISION
ECONOMIC POLICY
LEGISLATIVE REFERENCE DIVISION
ECONOMIC, SCIENCE, GENERAL GOVERNMENT BRANCH
HEALTH, EDUCATION, VETERANS AND SOCIAL PROGRAMS BRANCH
RESOURCES, DEFENSE, INTERNATIONAL BRANCH
BUDGET REVIEW
BUDGET ANALYSIS AND SYSTEMS DIVISION
BUDGET REVIEW AND CONCEPTS DIVISION
PERFORMANCE AND PERSONNEL MANAGEMENT

RESOURCE MANAGEMENT OFFICES

NATURAL RESOURCE PROGRAMS
ENERGY, SCIENCE, AND WATER DIVISION
ENERGY BRANCH
SCIENCE AND SPACE BRANCH
WATER AND POWER BRANCH
NATURAL RESOURCES DIVISION
AGRICULTURAL BRANCH
ENVIRONMENT BRANCH
INTERIOR BRANCH

EDUCATION, INCOME MAINTENANCE, AND LABOR PROGRAMS
EDUCATION, INCOME MAINTENANCE, AND LABOR DIVISION
EDUCATION BRANCH
INCOME MAINTENANCE BRANCH
LABOR BRANCH

HEALTH PROGRAMS
HEALTH DIVISION
HEALTH AND HUMAN SERVICE BRANCH
MEDICAID BRANCH
MEDICARE BRANCH
PUBLIC HEALTH BRANCH
HEALTH INSURANCE, DATA, AND ANALYSIS UNIT

GENERAL GOVERNMENT PROGRAMS
TRANSPORTATION, HOMELAND, JUSTICE, AND SERVICES DIVISION
TRANSPORTATION BRANCH
ADMINISTRATION BRANCH
HOMELAND SECURITY BRANCH
JUSTICE BRANCH
HOUSING, TREASURY, AND COMMERCE DIVISION
HOUSING BRANCH
TREASURY BRANCH
COMMERCE BRANCH

NATIONAL SECURITY PROGRAMS
INTERNATIONAL AFFAIRS DIVISION
STATE BRANCH
ECONOMIC AFFAIRS BRANCH
NATIONAL SECURITY DIVISION
COMMAND, CONTROL, COMMUNICATIONS, COMPUTERS AND INTELLIGENCE BRANCH
OPERATION AND SUPPORT BRANCH
FORCE STRUCTURE AND INVESTMENT BRANCH
VETERANS AFFAIRS AND DEFENSE HEALTH BRANCH

has been assigned to 5 CFR. That CFR title contains codified rules and regulations whose contents deal with the subject of administrative personnel. https://www.ecfr.gov/cgi-bin/text-idx?SID=be579a84626d26223245cc3a9139c7d9&mc=true&tpl=/ecfrbrowse/Title05/5chapterIII.tpl

Activities
The OMB's principle functions are diverse and many. They include assisting the President with the development of more effective Government and its maintenance by reviewing the organizational structure and management procedures of the executive branch; assisting with the development of efficient coordinating mechanisms for the implementation of Government activities and the expansion of interagency cooperation; assisting the President with preparation of the budget and formulation of the Government's fiscal program; supervising and controlling the administration of the budget; assisting the President with clearing and coordinating departmental advice on proposed legislation and with making recommendations to effect Presidential action on legislative enactments; assisting with the development of regulatory reform proposals and programs for paperwork reduction; assisting with the consideration, clearing, and preparation of proposed Executive orders and proclamations; planning and developing information systems that provide the President with program performance data; planning, conducting, and promoting evaluation efforts that help the President assess program efficiency, performance, and objectives; improving the efficiency and effectiveness of the procurement processes by guiding procurement policies, procedures, regulations, and use of forms; and informing the President of the progress of Government agency activities with respect to proposed, initiated, and completed work, together with the relative timing of work between agencies of the Government—to the end that the work programs of executive branch agencies may be coordinated and that the moneys the U.S. Congress appropriates may be expended with economy, barring overlapping and duplication of effort.

Sources of Information

Archived Records   The "Guide to Federal Records in the National Archives of the United States" indicates that OMB records have been assigned to record group 051. https://www.archives.gov/research/guide-fed-records/groups/051.html

Career Opportunities   In 2019, the OMB ranked 6th among 28 small Government agencies in the Partnership for Public Service's Best Places To Work Agency Rankings. https://bestplacestowork.org/rankings/detail/BO00

Chief Financial Officers Council   The Chief Financial Officers Act of 1990 (PL 101–576) established the Chief Financial Officers Council. The OMB's deputy director for management serves as the chair of the Council. The General Services Administration and the OMB jointly manage its website. https://www.cfo.gov/about-the-council

Circulars   The OMB posts information and instructions that it issues to Federal agencies on its "Circulars" web page. https://www.whitehouse.gov/omb/information-for-agencies/circulars

Contact   Postal correspondence should be addressed to the Office of Management and Budget, 725 Seventeenth Street NW., Washington, DC 20503. Information and directory assistance are available. Phone, 202-395-3080. https://www.whitehouse.gov/omb

Congressional inquiries may be made by phone. Phone, 202-395-4790. Congressional correspondence may be sent by facsimile. Fax, 202-395-3729.

Media inquiries may be made by email, facsimile, or phone. Fax, 202-395-3888. Phone, 202-395-7254.

Email: media@omb.eop.gov

Council of the Inspectors General on Integrity and Efficiency (CIGIE)   The Inspector General Reform Act of 2008 (PL 110–409) established the CIGIE as an independent entity within the executive branch. The OMB's deputy director for management serves as the executive chair of the Council. https://www.ignet.gov/content/cigie-governing-documents

Federal Register   Significant documents and documents that the OMB recently published in the Federal Register are accessible online. https://www.federalregister.gov/agencies/management-and-budget-office

Freedom of Information Act (FOIA) To any person, the FOIA gives a statutory right for obtaining access to Government information in the records of executive branch agencies. This right to access has limits, when any of nine exemptions that are contained within the statute shield the requested information from disclosure. Information on how to submit a FOIA request is available online. The OMB's FOIA Requester Service Center also provides assistance. Phone, 202-395-3642. Email: OMBFOIA@omb.eop.gov

Many OMB documents are freely available online and do not require a FOIA request for gaining access to them. These documents are called "proactive disclosures" because the OMB proactively posts them online. Documents that are disclosed in the interest of transparency and documents that have been requested frequently under the FOIA are examples of proactive disclosures. Before submitting a FOIA request, an information seeker should browse the holdings of the OMB's electronic FOIA library to see if the desired information has been posted already.

Frequently Asked Questions (FAQs) The OMB's Office of Information and Regulatory Affairs posts answers to FAQs that deal with regulations, rules, and the process of making rules, on the website reginfo.gov. https://www.reginfo.gov/public/jsp/Utilities/faq.myjsp

President's Budget Past budgets of former Presidents are available in Portable Document Format (PDF) for viewing and downloading. https://www.whitehouse.gov/omb/budget

Publications The U.S. Government Bookstore, which the Government Publishing Office maintains on its website, has many publications that deal with Federal deficits, Government budgets, and the Nation's economic outlook. https://bookstore.gpo.gov/catalog/budget-economy | Email: mainbks@gpo.gov

Sequestration The OMB posts sequestration reports on whitehouse.gov. https://www.whitehouse.gov/omb/legislative/sequestration-reports-orders

The above Sources of Information were updated 2–2021.

Office of National Drug Control Policy

Executive Office of the President, Washington, DC 20503
Phone, 202-395-6700. Fax, 202-395-6708. Internet, http://www.ondcp.gov

Director	REGINA M. LABELLE, ACTING
Deputy Director	REGINA M. LABELLE
Chief of Staff	MARIO MORENO
General Counsel	ROBERT KENT
Senior Policy Analyst	TOM HILL ASSOCIATE DIRECTORS
Legislative Affairs	ANNE SOKOLOV
Outreach	ARIEL BRITT

The above list of key personnel was updated 3–2021. The updating process remains in progress.

The Office of National Drug Control Policy helps the President establish his National Drug Control Strategy objectives, priorities, and policies and makes budget, program, and policy recommendations affecting National Drug Control Program agencies.

Establishment and Organization

On November 18, 1988, President Ronald W. Reagan approved Public Law 100–690 "to prevent the manufacturing, distribution, and use of illegal drugs, and for other purposes" (102 Stat. 4181). The 365-page piece of legislation contained a number of shorter acts, including the National

Narcotics Leadership Act of 1988, which established the Office of National Drug Control Policy (ONDCP) in the Executive Office of the President and became effective January 21, 1989 (102 Stat. 4189). At the head of the new Office, the Act placed a Director who is assisted by a Deputy Director for Demand Reduction and a Deputy Director for Supply Reduction. The Act also created a Bureau of State and Local Affairs within the Office (102 Stat. 4181). https://www.govinfo.gov/content/pkg/STATUTE-102/pdf/STATUTE-102-Pg4181.pdf

On October 21, 1998, President William J. Clinton approved Public Law 105–277, which made "omnibus consolidated and emergency appropriations" (112 Stat. 2681). The 920-page piece of legislation included the Office of National Drug Control Policy Reauthorization Act of 1998 (112 Stat. 2681–670). This Act of reauthorization created the new position of Deputy Director of National Drug Control Policy to assist the ONDCP Director (112 Stat. 2681–672). https://www.govinfo.gov/content/pkg/STATUTE-112/pdf/STATUTE-112-Pg2681.pdf

On December 29, 2006, President George W. Bush approved Public Law 109–469, which also is cited as the Office of National Drug Control Policy Reauthorization Act of 2006 (120 Stat. 3502). This Act of reauthorization made amendments to the earlier Act of 1998 and contained the following reporting provision: "The Deputy Director for Demand Reduction, the Deputy Director for Supply Reduction, and the Deputy Director for State, Local, and Tribal Affairs shall report directly to the Deputy Director of the Office of National Drug Control Policy" (120 Stat. 3505). https://www.govinfo.gov/content/pkg/STATUTE-120/pdf/STATUTE-120-Pg3502.pdf

On October 24, 2018, President Donald J. Trump approved Public Law 115–271, which also is cited as the "SUPPORT for Patients and Communities Act" (132 Stat. 3894). This 250-page piece of legislation included the Substance Abuse Prevention Act of 2018 (132 Stat. 4110), which reauthorized the ONDCP, expanded its mandate, and made other changes. https://www.govinfo.gov/content/pkg/PLAW-115publ271/pdf/PLAW-115publ271.pdf

The President appoints the ONDCP Director by the advice and with the consent of the Senate. The President also appoints the Deputy Director. Both of these appointees serve at the pleasure of the President. https://uscode.house.gov/view.xhtml?path=/prelim@title21/chapter22&edition=prelim

Statutory and Regulatory Authorities
Codified statutory material on food and drugs has been assigned to 21 U.S.C. Subchapter I, which comprises sections 1501–1509 of chapter 20, of that title, and is dedicated to statutory material affecting the ONDCP. https://uscode.house.gov/view.xhtml?path=/prelim@title21/chapter20/subchapter1&edition=prelim

Codified statutory material on food and drugs has been assigned to 21 U.S.C. Chapter 22, which comprises sections 1701–1715 of that title and is dedicated to statutory material affecting national drug control policy. https://uscode.house.gov/view.xhtml?path=/prelim@title21/chapter22&edition=prelim

"Chapter III—Office of National Drug Control Policy," which comprises parts 1400–1499, has been assigned to 21 CFR. That CFR title contains codified rules and regulations whose content deals with the subjects of food and drugs. https://www.ecfr.gov/cgi-bin/text-idx?SID=eadabaf406c904d7d3d6cdeb5ae6a7ec&mc=true&tpl=/ecfrbrowse/Title21/21chapterIII.tpl

Activities
The Director establishes policies, objectives, priorities, and performance measurements for the National Drug Control Program. Each year, the Director promulgates the President's National Drug Control Strategy, other related drug control strategies, supporting reports, and a program budget that the President submits to Congress. The Director advises the President on necessary changes in the organization, management, budgeting, and personnel allocation of Federal agencies that monitor drug activities. The Director also notifies Federal agencies if their policies do not comply with their responsibilities under the National Drug Control Strategy. The ONDCP also has direct programmatic responsibility for the High

Intensity Drug Trafficking Areas (HIDTA) program and the Drug-Free Communities (DFC) support program.

The HIDTA program is a Federal grant program that the ONDCP administers. The program provides resources to Federal, State, local, and Tribal agencies for coordinating activities to address drug production and trafficking in designated areas nationwide.

The DFC support program is a Federal grant program that the ONDCP administers. The program provides grants to community coalitions for strengthening the local infrastructure to reduce drug use among youth and to maintain the reductions that are achieved.

Sources of Information

Archived Records   The "Guide to Federal Records in the National Archives of the United States" indicates that records of the ONDCP have been assigned to record group 581; however, that group does not have a description associated with it. https://www.

The above Sources of Information were updated 2–2021.

archives.gov/research/guide-fed-records/index-numeric/501-to-600.html#page-header

Career Opportunities   The ONDCP posts employment opportunities on USAJobs.gov. https://www.usajobs.gov

Federal Register   Significant documents and documents that the ONDCP recently published in the Federal Register are accessible online. https://www.federalregister.gov/agencies/office-of-national-drug-control-policy

Freedom of Information Act (FOIA)   To any person, the FOIA gives a statutory right for obtaining access to Government information in the records of executive branch agencies. This right to access has limits, when any of nine exemptions that are contained within the statute shield the requested information from disclosure. Information on how to submit a FOIA request is available online. The ONDCP's FOIA Requester Center also provides assistance. Phone, 202-395-6622. Fax, 202-395-5543. Email: FOIA@ondcp.eop.gov

---

Office of Policy Development

The Office of Policy Development comprises the Domestic Policy and the National Economic Councils, which advise and assist the President in the formulation, coordination, and implementation of domestic and economic policy. The Office of Policy Development also supports other policy development and implementation activities as directed by the President.

Sources of Information

Federal Register   A document that the Office of Policy Development published in

the Federal Register is accessible online. https://www.federalregister.gov/agencies/office-of-policy-development

Editorial Note:

A dedicated website for the Domestic Policy Council is not available.

Domestic Policy Council

Room 469, Eisenhower Executive Office Building, Washington, DC 20502
Phone, 202-456-5594. Internet, https://https://www.whitehouse.gov/administration/eop/dpc

Domestic Policy Council	
Director	SUSAN E. RICE
Deputy Directors	
Economic Mobility	CARMEL MARTIN

Health and Veterans Affairs	Christen L. Young
Immigration	Esther Olavarria
Racial Justice and Equality	Catherine Lhamon

The above list of key personnel was updated 2–2021.

On August 16, 1993, President William J. Clinton signed Executive Order 12859 to establish the Domestic Policy Council (DPC). The DPC oversees development and implementation of the President's domestic policy agenda, and it ensures coordination and communication among the heads of relevant Federal offices and agencies. https://www.govinfo.gov/content/pkg/WCPD-1993-08-23/pdf/WCPD-1993-08-23-Pg1638.pdf

Editorial Note:
A dedicated website for the National Economic Council is not available.

National Economic Council
Room 235, Eisenhower Executive Office Building, Washington, DC 20502
Phone, 202-456-2800. Internet, https://https://www.whitehouse.gov/administration/eop/nec

National Economic Council

Director	Brian C. Deese
Deputy Directors	Sameera Fazili
	David C. Kamin
	Bharat R. Ramamurti
Chief of Staff	Leandra English

The above list of key personnel was updated 7–2021.

On January 25, 1993, President William J. Clinton signed Executive Order 12835 to establish the National Economic Council (NEC). The NEC coordinates the economic policymaking process and advises the President on economic policy. The NEC also ensures that economic policy decisions and programs remain consistent with the President's stated goals, and it monitors the implementation of the President's economic goals. https://www.govinfo.gov/content/pkg/WCPD-1993-02-01/pdf/WCPD-1993-02-01-Pg95.pdf

Sources of Information

Federal Register   Documents that the NEC has published in the Federal Register are accessible online. https://www.federalregister.gov/agencies/national-economic-council

History   The William J. Clinton Presidential Library posted video footage of President Clinton signing Executive Order 12835 and giving remarks on the establishment of the NEC. The signing and the remarks took place on on January 25, 1993. The President singled out the efforts of Robert E. Rubin, who served as the NEC's first Director after leaving the Goldman Sachs Group, Inc., in 1992. https://www.youtube.com/watch?v=39XBertis9A

The above Sources of Information were updated 7–2021.

Office of Science and Technology Policy

Eisenhower Executive Office Building, 1650 Pennsylvania Avenue NW., Washington, DC 20502
Phone, 202-456-4444. Fax, 202-456-6021. Internet, http://www.ostp.gov

Director	ERIC S. LANDER
Chief of Staff	KEI KOIZUMI
Directors	
Communications	
Legislative Affairs	NARDA JONES
Assistant Director	
Assistant Director	
General Counsel	

Office of the Chief Technology Officer

Chief Technology Officer

Environment and Energy Division

Assistant Directors
Clean Energy and Transportation
Climate Adaptation and Ecosystems
Climate Resilience and Information
Climate Resilience and Land Use
Climate Science
Earth Observations
Environmental Health
Natural Disaster Resilience
Polar Sciences
Space Weather

National Security and International Affairs Division

Assistant Directors
Biosecurity and Emerging Technologies
Cybersecurity
Cybersecurity Strategy
Defense Programs
Global Security
Special Programs

Science Division

Assistant Directors
Bioethics and Privacy
Broadening Participation
Education and Learning Science
Education and Physical Sciences
Research Infrastructure
Scientific Data and Information

Technology and Innovation Division

Assistant Directors
Behavioral Science
Biological Innovation
Civil and Commercial Space
Education and Telecommunications Innovation

Entrepreneurship
Innovation for Growth
Learning and Innovation
Nanotechnology and Advanced Materials
Open Innovation

Budget and Administration

Councils

President's Council of Advisors on Science and Technology
Executive Director

National Science And Technology Council
Executive Director

Directors
National Nanotechnology Coordination Office
Networking and Information Technology Research and Development
   National Coordination Office
U.S. Global Change Research Program National Coordination Office
U.S. Group on Earth Observation Program

The above list of key personnel was updated 7–2021. The updating process remains in progress.

The Office of Science and Technology Policy (OSTP) was established within the Executive Office of the President by the National Science and Technology Policy, Organization, and Priorities Act of 1976 (PL 94–282). https://www.govinfo.gov/content/pkg/STATUTE-90/pdf/STATUTE-90-Pg459.pdf

The Office supports the President by serving as a source of engineering, scientific, and technological analysis and judgment on plans, policies, and programs of the Federal Government. OSTP experts advise the President on scientific and technological matters that affect areas of national concern like the economy, environment, foreign relations, health, and national security; evaluate the effectiveness, quality, and scale of the Federal effort in science and technology; advise and assist the President, the Office of Management and Budget, and Federal agencies throughout the Federal budget development process; and help the President with leading and coordinating the Federal Government's research and development programs. https://www.whitehouse.gov/ostp

Sources of Information

Archived Records   The "Guide to Federal Records in the National Archives of the United States" indicates that OSTP records have been assigned to record group 364. https://www.archives.gov/research/guide-fed-records/groups/359.html?_ga=2.140748923.870523185.1612200813-2031726786.1611773339

Contact Information   The "Contact OSTP" web page has information for contacting the Office by email, phone, and postal mail. https://www.whitehouse.gov/ostp/contact

Federal Register   Documents that the OSTP recently published in the Federal Register are accessible online. https://www.federalregister.gov/agencies/science-and-technology-policy-office

Freedom of Information Act (FOIA)   Instructions for submitting a FOIA request are available online. https://www.whitehouse.gov/ostp/legal | Email: ostpfoia@ostp.eop.gov

Reports   National Science and Technology Council reports from 2009–2016 are posted online. https://obamawhitehouse.archives.gov/administration/eop/ostp/nstc/docsreports

The above Sources of Information were updated 7–2021.

Office of the United States Trade Representative
600 Seventeenth Street NW., Washington, DC 20508
Phone, 202-395-3230. Internet, http://www.ustr.gov

United States Trade Representative https://ustr.gov/about-us/biographies-key-officials	KATHERINE C. TAI
Assistant U.S. Trade Representatives	
Administration	FRED AMES
Africa	CONSTANCE HAMILTON
Agricultural Affairs and Commodity Policy	JULIE CALLAHAN
China Affairs	TERRENCE J. MCCARTIN
Congressional Affairs	JAN BEUKELMAN
Environment and Natural Resources	KELLY K. MILTON
Europe and the Middle East	L. DANIEL MULLANEY
Innovation and Intellectual Property	DANIEL LEE
Intergovernmental Affairs	SIRAT ATTAPIT
Japan, Korea, and Asia Pacific Economic Cooperation (APEC) Affairs	MICHAEL BEEMAN
Labor	LEWIS KARESH
Media and Public Affairs	ADAM HODGE
Monitoring and Enforcement	JUAN A. MILLAN
Private Sector Engagement	(VACANCY)
Public Engagement	JULIE GREEN
Services and Investment	DANIEL BAHAR
Small Business, Market Access and Industrial Competitiveness	JAMES SANFORD
South and Central Asia	CHRISTOPHER WILSON
Southeast Asia and the Pacific	KARL EHLERS
Textiles	WILLIAM D. JACKSON
Trade Policy and Economics	EDWARD GRESSER
Western Hemisphere	DANIEL WATSON
World Trade Organization (WTO) and Multilateral Affairs https://ustr.gov/about-us/organization	DAWN SHACKLEFORD

The above list of key personnel was updated 3–2021.

The United States Trade Representative formulates trade policy for and directs all trade negotiations of the United States.

The Office of the U.S. Trade Representative (USTR) was created as the Office of the Special Representative for Trade Negotiations by Executive Order 11075 of January 15, 1963 (28 FR 473–475). https://www.govinfo.gov/content/pkg/FR-1963-01-18/pdf/FR-1963-01-18.pdf

The Trade Act of 1974 (PL 93–618) established the Office of the USTR as an agency of the Executive Office of the President charged with administering the trade agreements program. https://www.govinfo.gov/content/pkg/STATUTE-88/pdf/STATUTE-88-Pg1978-2.pdf

The Office sets and administers overall trade policy. The USTR heads the Office and serves as the President's principal adviser, negotiator, and spokesperson on international trade and investment issues. The Representative acts as the chief representative of the United States in all General Agreement on Tariffs and Trade activities; in Organization for Economic Cooperation and Development discussions, meetings, and negotiations that deal primarily with commodity issues and trade; in U.N. Conference on Trade and Development negotiations and other

Office of the U.S. Trade Representative

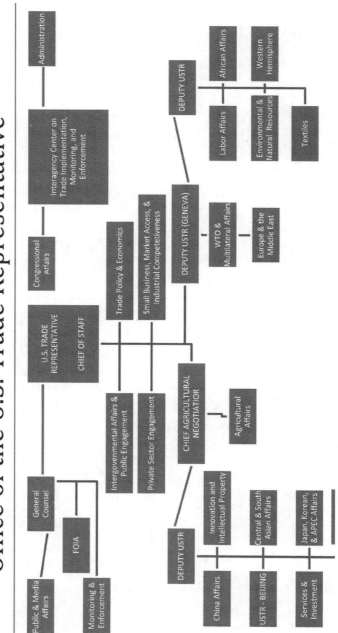

multilateral institution negotiations that deal primarily with commodity issues and trade; in other bilateral and multilateral negotiations that deal primarily with commodities or trade, including East-West trade; in negotiations under sections 704 and 734 of the Tariff Act of 1930 (19 U.S.C. 1671c and 1673c); and in negotiations on direct investment incentives and disincentives and on bilateral investment issues concerning barriers to investment.

The Omnibus Trade and Competitiveness Act of 1988 codified these authorities and added additional authority, including the implementation of section 301 actions that enforce U.S. rights under international trade agreements.

The USTR serves as a Cabinet-level official with the rank of Ambassador and reports directly to the President. The Chief Agricultural Negotiator and three Deputy U.S. Trade Representatives also hold the rank of Ambassador—two of the deputies are located in Washington, DC, and the other serves in Geneva, Switzerland.

The USTR is also an ex officio member on the boards of directors of the Export-Import Bank and the Overseas Private Investment Corporation. The Representative also serves on the National Advisory Council on International Monetary and Financial Policy. https://ustr.gov/about-us

Sources of Information

Archived Records The "Guide to Federal Records in the National Archives of the United States" indicates that USTR records have been assigned to record group 364. https://www.archives.gov/research/guide-fed-records/groups/364.html
Blog "Tradewinds" is the official blog of the USTR. https://ustr.gov/tradewinds
Contact Information Email addresses and phone numbers are available on the "Contact Us" web page.

Members of the media may contact the Press Office to find answers to questions, to obtain information, or to schedule interviews. https://ustr.gov/about-us/policy-offices/press-office
Factsheets The USTR releases factsheets on trade issues. https://ustr.gov/about-us/policy-offices/press-office/fact-sheets

Federal Register Documents that the Office of the USTR recently published in the Federal Register are accessible online. https://www.federalregister.gov/agencies/trade-representative-office-of-united-states
Freedom of Information Act (FOIA) Requests must be made in writing: Freedom of Information Officer, Office of the U.S. Trade Representative, 1724 F Street NW., Washington, DC 20508. Security procedures can slow down mail receipt and processing. Sending a request by email or fax avoids security-related delays. To facilitate finding the desired information, a record description must contain key details—author, date, recipient, subject matter, title or name. The Office of the USTR operates a FOIA requester service center. Phone, 202-395-3419. Fax, 202-395-9458. https://ustr.gov/about-us/reading-room/foia | Email: FOIA@ustr.eop.gov

The electronic FOIA Library contains information that is made available on a routine basis to the public. It also features documents that are frequently requested under the FOIA. This collection of online documents continues to grow as records in which the public expresses an interest are added. https://ustr.gov/about-us/reading-room/freedom-information-act-foia/foia-library
History In 1963, President John F. Kennedy created a new Office of the Special Trade Representative in the Executive Office of the President and designated two new Deputies, one in the Nation's capital and the other in Geneva, Switzerland. The rest of the story is available on the website of the Office of the USTR. https://ustr.gov/about-us/history
Key Issues The Office of the USTR focuses it's trade policy on 14 issue areas: agriculture, economy and trade, enforcement, environment, government procurement, industry and manufacturing, intellectual property, labor, preference programs, services and investment, small business, textiles and apparel, trade and development, and trade organizations. https://ustr.gov/issue-areas
Map The United States has trade relations with more than 200 countries, territories, and regional associations worldwide. https://ustr.gov/countries-regions

Organization Structure   The Office of the USTR does not have an organizational chart posted on its website; however, the "Organization Structure" web page does provide an outline of its structure that is based on five organizational lines of activities. https://ustr.gov/about-us/organization/organization-structure

Press Releases   The Office of the USTR posts press releases on its website. https://ustr.gov/about-us/policy-offices/press-office/press-releases

Reports / Publications   The Office of the USTR posts reports and publications on its website. https://ustr.gov/about-us/policy-offices/press-office/reports-and-publications

Social Media   The Office of the USTR has a presence on social media: Flickr, Twitter, Vimeo, and YouTube. https://ustr.gov/tradewinds/social

The above Sources of Information were updated 1–2021.

EXECUTIVE BRANCH: DEPARTMENTS

DEPARTMENT OF AGRICULTURE

1400 Independence Avenue SW., Washington, DC 20250
Phone, 202-720-2791. Internet, http://www.usda.gov

Secretary of Agriculture   TOM VILSACK
Deputy Secretary
https://www.usda.gov/our-agency/about-usda/our-secretary

MISSION AREAS

https://www.usda.gov/our-agency/about-usda/mission-areas

Farm Production and Conservation

Under Secretary
Deputy Under Secretary
Administrator, Farm Service Agency
Chief, Natural Resources Conservation Service
Administrator, Risk Management Agency
https://www.usda.gov/media/press-releases/2017/06/16/perdue-
    names-leadership-acting-roles-usda-reorganization-takes

Food, Nutrition and Consumer Services

Under Secretary
Deputy Under Secretary
Administrator, Food and Nutrition Service
Director, Center for Nutrition Policy and Promotion
https://www.usda.gov/media/press-releases/2017/07/19/secretary-
    perdue-announces-new-leadership-food-nutrition-and

Food Safety

Under Secretary
Deputy Under Secretary

Administrator, Food Safety and Inspection Service
https://www.fsis.usda.gov/wps/portal/informational/aboutfsis/
    agency-leadership

Marketing and Regulatory Programs

Under Secretary

Administrator, Agricultural Marketing Service
Administrator, Animal and Plant Health Inspection Service
Administrator, Grain Inspection, Packers and Stockyards
    Administration

https://www.ams.usda.gov/about-ams/our-leadership/under-secretary-greg-ibach

Natural Resources and Environment

Under Secretary
Deputy Under Secretary

Chief, Forest Service
https://www.fs.fed.us/about-agency/newsroom/leadership-biographies

Research, Education and Economics

Under Secretary
Deputy Under Secretary

Administrator, Agricultural Research Service
Administrator, Economic Research Service
Administrator, National Agricultural Statistics Service
Director, National Agricultural Library
Director, National Institute of Food and Agriculture
https://www.ree.usda.gov/about-ree/biographies

Rural Development

Assistant to the Secretary

Adminstrator, Rural Business-Cooperative Service
Administrator, Rural Housing Service
Administrator, Rural Utilities Service
https://www.rd.usda.gov/about-rd/leadership
Trade and Foreign Agricultural Affairs

Under Secretary
Deputy Under Secretary

Administrator, Farm Agricultural Service
https://www.fas.usda.gov/about-fas/leadership

Office Heads

Assistant Secretary for Administration
Assistant Secretary for Civil Rights

Chief Economist
Chief Financial Officer
Chief Information Officer
Chief Scientist

Deputy Assistant Secretary for Congressional Relations
Deputy Assistant Secretary for External and Intergovernmental Affairs

Director, Advocacy and Outreach
Director, Budget and Program Analysis
Director, Communications
Director, National Appeals Division
Director, Tribal Relations

General Counsel
https://www.usda.gov/our-agency/staff-offices
Inspector General
https://www.usda.gov/oig

USDA
Organization Chart

Secretary
Deputy Secretary

- Inspector General
- General Counsel
- Office of the Chief Financial Officer
- Office of the Chief Economist
- Office of the Executive Secretariat
- Office of Budget and Program Analysis

- Assistant Secretary for Civil Rights
- Assistant Secretary for Congressional Relations
- Assistant Secretary for Administration

- Office of Communications
- Office of Tribal Relations
- Office of Partnerships and Public Engagement
  - Higher Education
  - Strategic Initiatives
  - 2601 Grants
- Office of Hearings and Appeals
- Office of the Chief Information Officer

Under Secretary for Farm Production and Conservation
- FPAC Business Center
- Farm Service Agency
- Risk Management Agency
- Natural Resources Conservation Service

Under Secretary for Food, Nutrition and Consumer Services
- Food and Nutrition Service

Under Secretary for Food Safety
- Food Safety and Inspection Service

Under Secretary for Marketing and Regulatory Programs
- Agricultural Marketing Service
- Animal and Plant Health Inspection Service

Under Secretary for Natural Resources and Environment
- Forest Service

Under Secretary for Rural Development
- Rural Housing Service
- Rural Utility Service
- Rural Business Cooperative Service

Under Secretary for Research, Education and Economics
- Office of the Chief Scientist
- Agricultural Research Service
- National Agricultural Statistical Service
- National Institute of Food and Agriculture
- Economic Research Service

Under Secretary for Trade and Foreign Agricultural Affairs
- Foreign Agricultural Service
- U.S. Codex Office

USDA is an equal opportunity provider, employer, and lender.

UPDATED 10/19/21 This organization chart displays the names of USDA offices, agencies, and mission areas. Each office, agency, and mission area is placed within a cell connected by lines to show the structure and hierarchy (Under Secretary, Deputy Secretary, or Secretary) for which they fall under. An HTML version that lists USDA Agencies and Offices and USDA Mission Areas is also available on usda.gov. The Secretary's Memorandum 1076-031 was signed August 12, 2019 effectuating a change to Rural Development.

[For the Department of Agriculture statement of organization, see the Code of Federal Regulations, Title 7, Part 2]

The Department of Agriculture develops agricultural markets, fights hunger and malnutrition, conserves natural resources, and ensures food quality standards.

The Department of Agriculture (USDA) was created by an act of Congress on May 15, 1862 (7 U.S.C. 2201). In carrying out its work in the program mission areas, the USDA relies on the support of departmental administration staff, as well as on the Offices of Communications, Congressional Relations, the Chief Economist, the Chief Financial Officer, the Chief Information Officer, the General Counsel, and the Inspector General. http://www.usda.gov/wps/portal/usda/usdahome?navid=USDA150

Farm and Foreign Agricultural Services
This mission area centers on helping America's farmers and ranchers deal with the unpredictable nature of weather and markets. These services deliver commodity, conservation, credit, disaster, and emergency assistance programs to strengthen and stabilize the agricultural economy. http://www.usda.gov/wps/portal/usda/usdahome?navid=USDA_MISSION_AREAS

Farm Service Agency (FSA)   The Farm Service Agency administers farm commodity, disaster, and conservation programs for farmers and ranchers. It also makes and guarantees farm emergency, ownership, and operating loans through a network of State and county offices. http://www.fsa.usda.gov/index

Commodity Credit Corporation   The Commodity Credit Corporation, an agency and instrumentality of the United States within the USDA, is under the supervision of the Secretary of Agriculture. The Corporation does not have any employees, but relies on various Federal agencies, principally those in the USDA, to conduct its operations. It carries out a wide array of functions as authorized by the Commodity Credit Corporation Charter Act and as specifically authorized by the Congress in numerous statutes. Corporation funds are used to offer marketing assistance loans to producers of certain commodities, fund conservation programs to protect or enhance natural resources, support the export of agricultural commodities, provide humanitarian

assistance abroad, and further economic progress in developing countries. http://www.fsa.usda.gov/about-fsa/structure-and-organization/commodity-credit-corporation/index

Commodity Operations   FSA facilitates the purchase, storage, transportation, and disposition of U.S.-origin commodities acquired as a result of commodity loan forfeiture or through procurement for humanitarian food aid programs. FSA administers the United States Warehouse Act, which authorizes the Secretary of Agriculture to license warehouse operators who store agricultural products. The FSA also enters into agreements with warehouse operators to store commodities owned by the Commodity Credit Corporation or pledged by farmers as security for Commodity Credit Corporation marketing assistance loans. http://www.fsa.usda.gov/about-fsa/structure-and-organization/commodity-operations/index

Conservation Programs   FSA's conservation programs include the Conservation Reserve Program, which is the Federal Government's largest environmental improvement program on private lands. It safeguards millions of acres of topsoil from erosion, improves air quality, increases wildlife habitat, and reduces water runoff and sedimentation. In return for planting a protective cover of grass or trees on environmentally sensitive land, participants receive an annual rental payment. Cost-share payments are available to help establish conservation practices such as the planting of native grass, trees, windbreaks, or plants that improve water quality and give shelter and food to wildlife. http://www.fsa.usda.gov/FSA/webapp?area=home&subject=copr&topic=landing

Farm Commodity Programs   FSA manages farm safety net programs for America's farmers and ranchers. Its Commodity Credit Corporation stabilizes, supports, and protects farm income and prices; helps maintain balanced and adequate supplies of agricultural commodities; and aids in their orderly distribution. http://www.fsa.usda.

gov/about-fsa/structure-and-organization/ commodity-credit-corporation/index

Farm Loan Programs FSA makes and guarantees loans to family farmers and ranchers to purchase farmland and finance agricultural production. These programs offer credit on reasonable rates and terms to farmers—those who have suffered financial setbacks from natural disasters, those with limited resources for establishing and maintaining profitable farming operations, and beginners. http://www.fsa.usda.gov/ programs-and-services/farm-loan-programs/ index

Noninsured Crop Disaster Assistance Program The Noninsured Crop Disaster Assistance Program gives financial assistance to producers of noninsurable crops when yields are low, inventory is lost, or natural disasters prevent planting. http://www.fsa. usda.gov/programs-and-services/disaster-assistance-program/noninsured-crop-disaster-assistance/index

Other Emergency Assistance In counties that are declared disaster areas, low-interest loans for eligible farmers help cover physical and production losses. Eligible producers can be compensated for crop losses, livestock feed losses, tree damage, and for the cost of rehabilitating certain farmlands damaged by natural disaster. http://www. fsa.usda.gov/programs-and-services/disaster-assistance-program/index

For further information, contact the Office of External Affairs, Farm Service Agency, Department of Agriculture, Stop 0506, 1400 Independence Avenue SW., Washington, DC 20250. Phone, 202-720-7807. Or, contact the Information Division, Foreign Agricultural Service, Department of Agriculture, Stop 1004, 1400 Independence Avenue SW., Washington, DC 20250. Phone, 202-720-7115. Fax, 202-720-1727.

Foreign Agricultural Service (FAS) The Foreign Agricultural Service improves foreign market access for U.S. products, builds new markets, improves the competitive position of U.S. agriculture in the global marketplace, and provides food aid and technical assistance to foreign countries.

FAS has the primary responsibility for USDA's activities in the areas of international marketing, trade agreements and negotiations, and the collection and analysis of international statistics and market information. It also administers the USDA's export credit guarantee and food aid programs. FAS helps increase income and food availability in developing nations by mobilizing expertise for agriculturally led economic growth.

FAS also enhances U.S. agricultural competitiveness through a global network of agricultural economists, marketing experts, negotiators, and other specialists. FAS agricultural counselors, attaches, trade officers, and locally employed staff are stationed in over 93 countries to support U.S. agricultural interests and cover 171 countries.

In addition to agricultural affairs offices in U.S. embassies, trade offices operate in a number of key foreign markets. They function as service centers for U.S. exporters and foreign buyers seeking market information.

Reports prepared by FAS overseas offices cover changes in policies and other developments that could affect U.S. agricultural exports. FAS staff in U.S. embassies worldwide assess U.S. export marketing opportunities and respond to the daily informational needs of those who develop, initiate, monitor, and evaluate U.S. food and agricultural policies and programs.

The Service also maintains a worldwide agricultural reporting system based on information from U.S. agricultural traders, remote sensing systems, and other sources. Analysts in Washington, DC, prepare production forecasts, assess export marketing opportunities, and track changes in policies affecting U.S. agricultural exports and imports.

FAS programs help U.S. exporters develop and maintain markets for hundreds of food and agricultural products, from bulk commodities to brand-name items. Formal market promotion activities are carried out chiefly in cooperation with agricultural trade associations, State-regional trade groups, small businesses, and cooperatives that plan, manage, and contribute human and financial resources to these efforts. The Service also advises exporters on locating buyers and provides assistance through a variety of other methods, including supporting U.S. participation in trade shows and single-industry exhibitions each year. http://www.fas.usda.gov

For further information, contact the Public Affairs Division, Foreign Agricultural Service, Stop 1004, 1400

Independence Avenue SW., Department of Agriculture, Washington, DC 20250-1004. Phone, 202-720-7115. Fax, 202-720-1727.

Risk Management Agency (RMA)   The Risk Management Agency, on behalf of the Federal Crop Insurance Corporation (FCIC), oversees and administers the Federal crop insurance program under the Federal Crop Insurance Act.

Federal crop insurance is offered to qualifying producers through 16 private sector crop insurance companies. Under the Standard Reinsurance Agreement (SRA), RMA provides reinsurance, pays premium subsidies, reimburses insurers for administrative and operating expenses, and oversees the financial integrity and operational performance of the delivery system. RMA bears much of the noncommercial insurance risk under the SRA, allowing insurers to retain commercial insurance risks or reinsure those risks in the private market.

In 2016, the Federal crop insurance program provided producers with more than $100 billion in protection. Twenty-five insurance plans are available, covering over 550 varieties of crops, 37 reinsured privately developed products, and 18 RMA-developed pilot programs in various stages of operation.

RMA also works closely with the private sector to find innovative ways to expand coverage. The expansion affects risk protection for specialty crops, livestock and forage, and rangeland and pasture. Thus, RMA is able to reduce the need for ad hoc disaster assistance, while providing coverage for production declines that result from adverse weather in many areas.

Additional information is available on the RMA Web site, which features agency news, State profiles, publications, and announcements on current issues. It also has summaries of insurance sales, pilot programs, downloadable crop policies, and agency-sponsored events. Online tools, calculators, and applications are also part of the Web site. http://www.rma.usda.gov

For further information, contact the Office of the Administrator, Risk Management Agency, Department of Agriculture, Stop 0801, 1400 Independence Avenue SW., Washington, DC 20250. Phone, 202-690-2803.

Food, Nutrition and Consumer Services   The mission area of the food, nutrition, and consumer services centers on harnessing the Nation's agricultural abundance to reduce hunger and improve health in the United States. Its agencies administer Federal domestic nutrition assistance programs and the Center for Nutrition Policy and Promotion, which links scientific research to the nutrition needs of consumers through science-based dietary guidance, nutrition policy coordination, and nutrition education. http://www.usda.gov/wps/portal/usda/usdahome?navid=USDA_MISSION_AREAS

Center for Nutrition Policy and Promotion (CNPP)   The Center for Nutrition Policy and Promotion improves the health and well-being of Americans by developing and promoting dietary guidance that links the latest evidence-based scientific research to consumers' nutrition needs. Initiatives range from setting Federal dietary guidance to consumer-based nutrition education (MyPlate), to cutting-edge personalized electronic tools (SuperTracker), to "report cards" on the status of the American diet. https://www.choosemyplate.govhttps://www.supertracker.usda.govhttp://www.cnpp.usda.gov

For further information, contact the Office of Public Information, Center for Nutrition Policy and Promotion, Suite 200, 1120 20th Street NW., Washington, DC 20036-3406. Phone, 202-418-2312.

Food and Nutrition Service (FNS)   The Food and Nutrition Service administers the USDA domestic nutrition assistance programs, serving one in four Americans in the course of a year. The FNS works in partnership with States and local agencies to increase food security and reduce hunger by providing children and low-income people with access to food, a healthy diet, and nutrition education. http://www.fns.usda.gov

FNS administers the following nutrition assistance programs:

The Supplemental Nutrition Assistance Program (SNAP) gives nutrition assistance to millions of eligible low-income individuals and families, and it provides economic benefits to communities. SNAP is the largest program in the domestic hunger safety net. FNS also works with State partners and the retail community to improve program administration and ensure program integrity. http://www.fns.usda.gov/snap/supplemental-nutrition-assistance-program-snap

The Special Supplemental Nutrition Program for Women, Infants, and Children (WIC) provides Federal grants to States for supplemental foods, health care referrals, and nutrition education for low-income pregnant, breastfeeding, and nonbreastfeeding postpartum women, and to infants and children up to age 5 who are found to be at nutritional risk. WIC and the Seniors' Farmers' Market Nutrition Programs provide WIC participants and senior citizens with increased access to fresh produce through coupons to purchase fresh fruits and vegetables from authorized farmers. http://www.fns.usda.gov/wic/women-infants-and-children-wic

The Farmers' Market Nutrition Program is linked to WIC, which provides supplemental foods, health care referrals, and nutrition education at no cost to low-income pregnant, breastfeeding, and nonbreastfeeding post partum women, and to infants and children who are up to 5 years of age and found to be at nutritional risk. http://www.fns.usda.gov/fmnp/wic-farmers-market-nutrition-program-fmnp

The Senior Farmers' Market Nutrition Program awards grants to States, U.S. Territories, and federally recognized Indian tribal governments for coupons that low-income seniors can use to purchase eligible foods at farmers' markets, roadside stands, and community-supported agriculture programs. http://www.fns.usda.gov/sfmnp/senior-farmers-market-nutrition-program-sfmnp

The Commodity Supplemental Food Program improves the health of low-income pregnant and breastfeeding women, nonbreastfeeding mothers up to 1 year postpartum, infants, and children up to age 6. The program supplements their diets with nutritious USDA commodity foods. It also provides food and administrative funds to States to supplement the diets of these groups. http://www.fns.usda.gov/csfp/commodity-supplemental-food-program-csfp

School districts and independent schools that choose to take part in the National School Lunch Program receive cash subsidies and donated commodities from the USDA. In return, they must serve lunches that meet Federal requirements and must offer free or reduced-price lunches to

eligible children. School food authorities can also be reimbursed for snacks served to children through age 18 in afterschool educational or enrichment programs. http://www.fns.usda.gov/nslp/national-school-lunch-program-nslp

The School Breakfast Program operates like the National School Lunch Program. School districts and independent schools that choose to take part in the breakfast program receive cash subsidies from the USDA for each meal they serve. In return, they must serve breakfasts that meet Federal requirements and must offer free or reduced-price breakfasts to eligible children. http://www.fns.usda.gov/sbp/school-breakfast-program-sbp

The Special Milk Program provides milk to schoolchildren and children in childcare institutions who do not participate in other Federal meal service programs. The program reimburses schools for the milk that they serve. Schools in the National School Lunch or School Breakfast Programs may participate so that milk is available to prekindergarten and kindergarten children who may not have access to school meal programs. http://www.fns.usda.gov/smp/special-milk-program

The Child and Adult Care Food Program helps child and adult care institutions and family or group day care homes provide nutritious foods to promote the health and wellness of young children, older adults, and chronically impaired disabled persons. http://www.fns.usda.gov/cacfp/child-and-adult-care-food-program

The Summer Food Service Program ensures that low-income children receive nutritious meals when they are not attending school. http://www.fns.usda.gov/sfsp/summer-food-service-program-sfsp

The Emergency Food Assistance Program helps low-income and elderly Americans access free emergency food and nutrition assistance. The program provides food and administrative funds to States to supplement the diets of these groups. http://www.fns.usda.gov/tefap/emergency-food-assistance-program-tefap

The Food Distribution Program on Indian Reservations helps low-income households—including the elderly living on Indian reservations—and Native American families residing in designated areas in Oklahoma and near reservations elsewhere to access USDA foods. http://www.fns.usda. gov/fdpir/food-distribution-program-indian-reservations-fdpir

The Fresh Fruit and Vegetable Program helps make fruits and vegetables available to students free of charge, during the schoolday, in participating elementary schools. The program is a tool for reducing childhood obesity: It exposes schoolchildren to fresh produce that they otherwise might not have the opportunity to sample. http://www.fns.usda.gov/ffvp/fresh-fruit-and-vegetable-program

For further information, contact the Public Information Officer, Food and Nutrition Service, Department of Agriculture, 3101 Park Center Drive, Alexandria, VA 22302. Phone, 703-305-2286.

Food Safety

This mission area centers on the labeling and packaging, safety, and wholesomeness of the Nation's commercial supply of egg, poultry, and meat. It also contributes significantly to the President's Council on Food Safety and has helped coordinate a nationwide food safety strategic plan. http://www.usda.gov/wps/portal/usda/usdahome?navid=USDA_MISSION_AREAS

Food Safety and Inspection Service (FSIS)   The Food Safety and Inspection Service was established by the Secretary of Agriculture on June 17, 1981, pursuant to authority contained in 5 U.S.C. 301 and Reorganization Plan No. 2 of 1953 (5 U.S.C. app.). FSIS monitors the Nation's commercial supply of meat, poultry, and processed egg products. http://www.fsis.usda.gov/wps/portal/fsis/home

Meat, Poultry, and Processed Egg Products Inspection   FSIS is the public health regulatory agency in the U.S. Department of Agriculture that ensures commercial meat, poultry, and processed egg products are safe, wholesome, accurately labeled, and properly packaged. FSIS enforces the Federal Meat Inspection Act (FMIA), the Poultry Products Inspection Act (PPIA), and the Egg Products Inspection Act (EPIA), which require Federal inspection and regulation of meat, poultry, and processed egg products prepared for distribution in commerce for use as human food. FSIS is also responsible

for administering the Humane Methods of Slaughter Act, which requires that livestock are handled and slaughtered humanely at the FSIS-inspected establishment.

FSIS administers FMIA, PPIA, and EPIA by developing and implementing data-driven regulations, including inspection, testing, and enforcement activities for the products under FSIS's jurisdiction. In addition to mandatory inspection of meat, poultry, and processed egg products, FSIS tests samples of these products for microbial and chemical residues to monitor trends for enforcement purposes and to understand, predict, and prevent contamination. FSIS also ensures that only meat, poultry, and processed egg products that meet U.S. requirements are imported into the United States, and it certifies meat, poultry, and processed egg products for export.

FSIS also monitors meat, poultry, and processed egg products throughout storage, distribution, and retail channels, and it ensures regulatory compliance to protect the public, including detention of products, voluntary product recalls, court-ordered seizures of products, administrative suspension and withdrawal of inspection, and referral of violations for criminal and civil prosecution. To protect against intentional contamination, the Agency conducts food defense activities, as well.

FSIS maintains a toll-free Meat and Poultry Hotline (phone, 888-674-6854; TTY, 800-256-7072) and chat feature to answer questions in English and Spanish about the safe handling of meat, poultry, and egg products. The Hotline's hours are weekdays, from 10 a.m. to 4 p.m., EST, year round. An extensive selection of food safety messages in English and Spanish is available at the same number at all hours of the day. Questions can also be submitted anytime to MPHotline.fsis@usda.gov.

"Ask Karen," an online virtual representative, provides answers to consumer questions on preventing foodborne illness, safe food handling and storage, and safe preparation of meat, poultry, and egg products (http://www.fsis.usda.gov/wps/portal/informational/askkaren). http://www.fsis.usda.gov

For further information, contact the Assistant Administrator, Office of Public Affairs and Consumer

Education, Department of Agriculture, 1400 Independence Avenue SW., Washington, DC 20250. Phone, 202-720-3884.

Marketing and Regulatory Programs

The scope of the marketing and regulatory mission area includes marketing and regulatory programs other than those concerned with food safety. http://www.usda.gov/wps/portal/usda/usdahome?navid=USDA_MISSION_AREAS

Agricultural Marketing Service (AMS) The Agricultural Marketing Service was established by the Secretary of Agriculture on April 2, 1972, under the authority of Reorganization Plan No. 2 of 1953 (5 U.S.C. app.) and other authorities. The Service facilitates the fair and efficient marketing of U.S. agricultural products. It supports agriculture through a variety of programs: cotton and tobacco; dairy; fruit and vegetable; livestock, poultry, and seed; organic products; transportation and marketing, and science and technology. The Service's activities support American agriculture in the global marketplace and help ensure the availability of wholesome food. http://www.ams.usda.gov

Audit and Accreditation Services AMS audit and accreditation programs give producers and suppliers of agricultural products the opportunity to assure customers of their ability to provide consistent quality products and services. The AMS verifies their documented programs through independent, third-party audits. AMS audit and accreditation programs are voluntary and paid through hourly user-fees. http://www.ams.usda.gov/services/auditing

Commodity Purchasing The AMS purchases a variety of domestically produced and processed commodity food products through a competitive process involving approved vendors. The purchasing supports American agriculture by providing an outlet for surplus products and encouraging domestic consumption of domestic foods. The wholesome, high quality products, collectively called USDA Foods, are delivered to schools, food banks, and households across the country and constitute a vital component of the Nation's food safety net. http://www.ams.usda.gov/selling-food

Farmers Markets / Direct-to-Consumer Marketing The AMS regularly collects data and analyzes farmers market operations and other direct-to-consumer marketing outlets—Community Supported Agriculture, food hubs, on-farm markets—to help market managers, planners, and researchers better understand the effect of these outlets on food access and local economic development, and to help the public find sources of fresh, local food. http://www.ams.usda.gov/services/local-regional

Grades / Standards USDA grade shields, official seals, and labels are symbols of the quality and integrity of American agricultural products. Large-volume buyers such as grocery stores, military institutions, restaurants, and foreign governments benfit from the quality grades and standards because they serve as as a common "language" that simplifies business transactions. http://www.ams.usda.gov/AMSv1.0/standards

Grant Programs The AMS administers a series of grant programs that make over $100 million available to support a variety of agricultural activities, including the specialty crop industry and local and regional food system expansion. These grant programs improve domestic and international opportunities for growers and producers and help support rural America. http://www.ams.usda.gov/services/grants

Laboratory Testing and Approval Services The AMS oversees the National Science Laboratories (NSL), a fee-for-service lab network. NSL scientists and technicians conduct chemical, microbiological, and biomolecular analyses on food and agricultural commodities. The network provides testing services for AMS commodity programs, other USDA agencies, Federal and State agencies, research institutions, private sector food and agricultural industries, and the U.S. military. The AMS also approves or accredits labs to perform testing services in support of domestic and international trade. At the request of industry, other Federal agencies, or foreign governments, it develops and administers laboratory approval programs to verify that the analysis of food and agricultural products meet country or customer-specified requirements. http://www.ams.usda.gov/services/lab-testing

Marketing Agreements and Orders   Marketing agreements and orders are initiated by industry to stabilize markets for dairy products, fruits, vegetables, and specialty crops. An agreement is binding only for handlers who sign the agreement. Marketing orders are a binding regulation for the entire industry in the specified geographical area, once the producers and the Secretary of Agriculture have approved it. http://www.ams.usda.gov/rules-regulations/moa

Market News   Market News issues thousands of reports each year, providing the agricultural industry with important wholesale, retail, and shipping data. The reports give farmers, producers, and other agricultural businesses the information they need to evaluate market conditions, identify trends, make purchasing decisions, monitor price patterns, evaluate transportation equipment needs, and accurately assess movement. http://www.ams.usda.gov/market-news

National Organic Program   The National Organic Program is a regulatory program housed within the AMS. It develops national standards for organically-produced agricultural products. The "USDA ORGANIC" seal means that a product met consistent and uniform standards. USDA organic regulations do not address food safety or nutrition. Organic production integrates cultural, biological, and mechanical practices to increase cycling of resources, biodiversity, and ecological balance. http://www.ams.usda.gov/about-ams/programs-offices/national-organic-program

Pesticide Data Program   The Pesticide Data Program (PDP) monitors pesticide residue nationwide. It produces the most comprehensive pesticide residue database in the Nation. The PDP administers the sampling, testing, and reporting of pesticide residues on agricultural commodities in the U.S. food supply—with an emphasis on those commodities regularly consumed by infants and children. The AMS implements the program in cooperation with State agriculture departments and other Federal agencies. The Environmental Protection Agency relies on PDP data to assess dietary exposure, and Food and Drug Administration and other government experts use them for making informed decisions. http://www.ams.usda.gov/datasets/pdp

Plant Variety Protection Program   The Plant Variety Protection Office protects the intellectual property of breeders of new seed and tuber varieties. Implementing the Plant Variety Protection Act, the Office examines new applications and grants certificates that protect varieties for 20 or 25 years. Certificate owners have exclusive rights to market and sell their varieties, manage the use of their varieties by other breeders, and benefit from legal protection of their work. http://www.ams.usda.gov/services/plant-variety-protection

Regulatory Programs   The AMS administers several regulatory programs designed to protect producers, handlers, and consumers of agricultural commodities from financial loss or personal injury resulting from careless, deceptive, or fraudulent marketing practices. These regulatory programs encourage fair trading practices in the marketing of fruits and vegetables, and they require accuracy in seed labeling and in advertising. The AMS also enforces the Country of Origin Labeling law, which requires retailers—full-line grocery stores, supermarkets, club warehouse stores—to notify their customers with information regarding the source of certain foods. http://www.ams.usda.gov/rules-regulations

Research and Promotion Programs   The AMS monitors certain industry-sponsored research, promotion, and information programs authorized by Federal laws. These programs give farmers and processors a means to finance and operate various research, promotion, and information activities for agricultural products. http://www.ams.usda.gov/rules-regulations/research-promotion

Quality Grading / Inspections   Nearly 600 grade standards have been established for some 230 agricultural commodities to help buyers and sellers trade on agreed-upon quality levels. Standards are developed with assistance from individuals outside the Department, particularly from those involved with the industries directly affected. The AMS also participates in developing international commodity standards to facilitate trade. Grading and classing services are provided to certify the grade and quality of products. These grading services are provided to buyers and sellers of live cattle, swine, sheep, meat, poultry, eggs, rabbits, fruits, vegetables, tree nuts, peanuts, dairy products, tobacco, and other miscellaneous food products. Classing services are provided to buyers and sellers of cotton and cotton products. These services are mainly voluntary and are provided upon request and for a fee. The AMS is also responsible for testing seed. http://www.ams.usda.gov/services/grading

Transportation Research and Analysis The Transportation Services Division (TSD) of the AMS serves as the definitive source for economic analysis of agricultural transportation. TSD experts support domestic and international agribusinesses by giving technical assistance and releasing reports and offering analysis. They track developments in truck, rail, barge, and ocean transportation and provide information on and analysis of these modes of moving food from farm to table, from port to market. http://www.ams.usda.gov/services/transportation-analysis

For further information, contact the Public Affairs Staff, Agricultural Marketing Service, Department of Agriculture, Room 3933, South Agriculture Building, Stop 0273, 1400 Independence Ave, SW., Washington, DC 20250. Phone, 202-720-8998.

Animal and Plant Health Inspection Service (APHIS) [For the Animal and Plant Health Inspection Service statement of organization, see the Code of Federal Regulations, Title 7, Part 371]

The Animal and Plant Health Inspection Service was originally established in 1972 and reestablished by the Secretary of Agriculture on March 14, 1977, pursuant to authority contained in 5 U.S.C. 301 and Reorganization Plan No. 2 of 1953 (5 U.S.C. app.). The APHIS was established to conduct regulatory and control programs to protect and improve animal and plant health for the benefit of agriculture and the environment. In cooperation with State governments, industry stakeholders, and other Federal agencies, the APHIS works to prevent the entry and establishment of foreign animal and plant pests and diseases. It also regulates certain genetically engineered organisms and supports healthy international agricultural trade and exports of U.S. agricultural products. The agency also works to ensure the humane treatment of certain animals and carries out research and operational activities to mitigate damage caused by birds, rodents, and other wildlife. https://www.aphis.usda.gov/wps/portal/aphis/home

Animal Care Animal Care upholds and enforces the Animal Welfare Act and the Horse Protection Act. The Animal Welfare Act requires that federally established standards of care and treatment be provided for certain warmblooded animals bred for commercial sale, used in research, transported commercially, or publicly exhibited. The Horse Protection Act seeks to end soring by preventing sored horses from participating in auctions, exhibitions, sales, and shows. The Center for Animal Welfare collaborates with other animal welfare entities to help the USDA build partnerships domestically and internationally, improve regulatory practices, and develop outreach, training, and educational resources. Animal Care's emergency response component provides national leadership on the safety and well-being of pets during disasters—supporting animal safety during emergencies is a significant factor in ensuring the well-being of pet owners. https://www.aphis.usda.gov/wps/portal/aphis/ourfocus/animalwelfare

Biotechnology Regulatory Services To protect plant health, Biotechnology Regulatory Services implements APHIS regulations affecting the importation, movement, and field release of genetically engineered plants and certain other genetically engineered organisms that may pose a risk to plant health. The APHIS coordinates these responsibilities along with the other designated Federal agencies as part of the Federal coordinated framework for the regulation of biotechnology. https://www.aphis.usda.gov/wps/portal/aphis/ourfocus/biotechnology

International Services APHIS protects the health and value of American agriculture and natural resources. Its International Services supports this mission in an international environment. The Services collaborate with foreign partners to control pests and diseases, facilitate safe agricultural trade, ensure effective and efficient management of internationally-based programs, and invest in international capacity-building with foreign counterparts to build technical and regulatory skills that prevent diseases and pests from spreading. https://www.aphis.usda.gov/wps/portal/aphis/ourfocus/internationalservices

Plant Protection and Quarantine   APHIS oversees Plant Protection and Quarantine. The program protects U.S. agriculture and natural resources against the entry, establishment, and spread of economically and environmentally significant pests. It also facilitates the safe trade of agricultural products. https://www.aphis.usda.gov/wps/portal/aphis/ourfocus/planthealth

Veterinary Services   Veterinary Services supports APHIS' efforts to protect and improve the health, quality, and marketability of the Nation's animals, animal products, and veterinary biologics. The Service is organized strategically into four sections: surveillance, preparedness, and response; national import export services; science, technology, and analysis; and program support services. https://www.aphis.usda.gov/wps/portal/aphis/ourfocus/animalhealth

Wildlife Services   Wildlife Services provides Federal leadership and expertise for resolving conflicts between wildlife and people to allow coexistence. It conducts program delivery, research, and other activities through regional and State offices, the National Wildlife Research Center and field stations, as well as through national programs. Contact the APHIS customer service call center for more information. Phone, 844-820-2234. https://www.aphis.usda.gov/wps/portal/aphis/ourfocus/wildlifedamage

For further information, contact Legislative and Public Affairs, Animal and Plant Health Inspection Service, Department of Agriculture, 1400 Independence Avenue SW., Washington, DC 20250. Phone, 202-799-7030.

Grain Inspection, Packers and Stockyards Administration (GIPSA)   The Grain Inspection, Packers and Stockyards Administration was established in 1994 to facilitate the marketing of livestock, poultry, meat, cereals, oilseeds, and related agricultural products, and to promote fair and competitive trading practices for the overall benefit of consumers and American

agriculture. The Packers and Stockyards Program protects fair trade practices, financial integrity, and competitive markets for livestock, meat, and poultry. The Federal Grain Inspection Service facilitates the marketing of U.S. grains, oilseeds, and related agricultural products through its grain inspection and weighing system. The Service also maintains the integrity of the grain marketing system by developing unbiased grading standards and methods for assessing grain quality. http://www.gipsa.usda.gov

Inspection   The United States Grain Standards Act requires most U.S. export grain to be inspected. At export port locations, GIPSA or State agencies that have been delegated authority by the Administrator carry out inspections. For domestic grain marketed at inland locations, the Administrator designates private and State agencies to provide official inspection services upon request. Both export and domestic services are provided on a fee-for-service basis. http://www.gipsa.usda.gov/fgis/inspectionservices.aspx

Methods Development   GIPSA's methods development activities include applied research or tests to produce new or improved techniques for measuring grain quality. Examples include knowledge gained through the study of how to establish real-time grain inspection, develop reference methods in order to maintain consistency and standardization in the grain inspection system, as well as the comparison of different techniques for evaluation of end-use quality in wheat.

Packers and Stockyards Activities   GIPSA prohibits deceptive, discriminatory, and unfair practices by market agencies, dealers, stockyards, packers, swine contractors, and live poultry dealers in the livestock, meat packing, and poultry industries. According to the provisions of the Packers and Stockyards Act, it fosters fair competition and ensures payment protection for growers and farmers through regulatory activities: investigating alleged violations of the act, auditing regulated entities, verifying the accuracy of scales, and monitoring industry trends to protect consumers and members of the livestock, meat, and poultry industries. The Administration also has certain responsibilities derived from the Truth-in-Lending and the Fair Credit Reporting Acts. GIPSA carries out the Secretary's responsibilities under section 1324 of the Food Security Act of 1985 pertaining to State-established central filing systems to prenotify buyers, commission merchants, and selling agents of security interests against farm products. GIPSA administers the section of the act commonly referred to as the "Clear Title" provision and certifies qualifying State systems. http://www.gipsa. usda.gov/psp/psp.aspx

Standardization Official inspections of grains, oilseeds, and other agricultural and processed commodities are based on established official U.S. standards. The inspections also rely on sound, proven, and standardized procedures, techniques, and equipment. The official standards and accompanying procedures, techniques, and equipment produce consistent test results and services, from elevator to elevator and State to State. http://www.gipsa.usda.gov/fgis/standardprocedures.aspx

Weighing GIPSA or State agencies that have been delegated authority the Administrator officially weigh U.S. export grain at port locations. For domestic grain marketed at inland locations, GIPSA or designated private or State agencies provide the weighing services. Weighing services are provided on a fee-for-service basis. http://www.gipsa.usda.gov/fgis/weighingservices.aspx

For further information, contact the Grain Inspection, Packers, and Stockyards Administration, Department of Agriculture, 1400 Independence Avenue SW., Washington, DC 20250. Phone, 202-720-0219.

Natural Resources and Environment

This mission area centers on stewardship of 75 percent of the Nation's total land area. The USDA's operating philosophy in this mission area places a premium on collaboration with diverse partners and on the health and sustainability of ecosystems to maximize stewardship of the Nation's natural resources. This approach ensures that the necessary requirements for maintaining healthy and sustainable systems are in balance with people's priorities and the products and services that they desire. http://www.usda.gov/wps/portal/usda/usdahome?navid=USDA_MISSION_AREAS

Forest Service (FS) [For the Forest Service statement of organization, see the Code of Federal Regulations, Title 36, Part 200.1]

In 1876, Congress created the Office of Special Agent in the Department of Agriculture to assess the condition of the forests in the United States. The Forest Service was created decades later by the Transfer Act of February 1, 1905 (16 U.S.C. 472), which transferred the Federal forest reserves and the responsibility for their management to the USDA from the Department of the Interior. The mission of the Forest Service is to achieve quality land management under the sustainable, multiple-use management concept to meet the diverse needs of people. The Service advocates a conservation ethic in promoting the health, productivity, diversity, and beauty of forests and associated lands; listens to people and responds to their diverse needs in making decisions; protects and manages the National Forests and Grasslands to best demonstrate the sustainable, multiple-use management concept; provides technical and financial assistance to State, tribal, and private forest landowners, encouraging them to become better stewards and quality land managers; helps cities and communities improve their natural environment by planting trees and caring for their forests; provides international technical assistance and scientific exchanges to sustain and enhance global resources and to encourage quality land management; assists States and communities in using the forests wisely to promote rural economic development and a quality rural environment; develops and disseminates scientific and technical knowledge that helps protect, manage, and improve use of forests and rangelands; and offers employment, training, and educational opportunities to the unemployed, underemployed, disadvantaged, elderly, and youth. http://www.fs.fed.us

Forest Research The Service performs basic and applied research to develop the scientific information and technology needed to protect, manage, use, and sustain the natural resources of the Nation's forests and rangelands, including those on private and tribal lands. Its forest research strategy focuses on three major program components: understanding the structure and functions of forest and range ecosystems; understanding how people perceive and value the protection, management, and use of natural resources; and determining which protection, management, and utilization practices are most suitable for sustainable production and use of natural resources worldwide. http://www.fs.fed.us/research/research-topics

National Forest System   Using the principles of multiple-use and sustained yield, the Service manages 154 National Forests, 20 National Grasslands, 1 tall grass prairie, and 8 national monuments on approximately 193 million acres of land in 44 States, the U.S. Virgin Islands, and Puerto Rico. The Nation's need for wood and paper products must be balanced against the other vital, renewable resources or benefits that the National Forests and Grasslands provide: recreation and natural beauty, wildlife habitat, livestock forage, and water supplies. As a guiding principle, the Service tries to achieve greatest good for the greatest number in the long run.

These lands are managed to promote resiliency against catastrophic wildfire, epidemics of disease and insect pests, erosion, and other threats. Burned areas receive emergency seeding treatment to prevent massive erosion and stream siltation. Roads and trails are built where needed to give the public access to outdoor recreation areas and provide scenic drives and hikes. Picnic, camping, skiing, water sport and other recreational areas feature facilities for public convenience and enjoyment. Vegetative management methods protect the land and streams, ensure rapid renewal of the forest, provide food and cover for wildlife and fish, and mitigate human impact on scenic and recreation assets. Local communities benefit from activities on National Forest lands. These lands also provide needed oil, gas, and minerals. Millions of livestock and game animals benefit from improved rangelands. The National Forests serve as a refuge for many species of endangered birds, animals, and fish. Some 34.6 million acres are set aside as wilderness and 175,000 acres as primitive areas where timber will not be harvested. http://www.fs.fed.us/managing-land/national-forests-grasslands

State and Private Forestry   The State and Private Forestry organization of

the Forest Service reaches across the boundaries of National Forests to States, tribes, communities, and nonindustrial private landowners. The organization is the Federal leader in giving technical and financial assistance to landowners and resource managers to help sustain the Nation's forests and protect communities and the environment from wildland fires. National priorities for State and private forestry promote four core actions: conserving and managing working forest landscapes for multiple values and uses, protecting forests from threats, enhancing public benefits from trees and forests, and increasing organizational effectiveness. The State and Private Forestry organization supports sustainable stewardship of non-Federal forest land nationwide, including 423 million acres of private forest land, 69 million acres of State forest land, 18 million acres of tribal forests, and over 130 million acres of urban and community forests. The organization offers leadership in wildland fire management, operations, methods development, risk mapping, forest products utilization, and advanced survey and monitoring, as well as geospatial technologies. http://www.fs.fed.us/spf

Natural Resources Conservation Service (NRCS)   [For the Natural Resources Conservation Service statement of organization, see the Code of Federal Regulations, Title 7, Parts 600 and 601]

The Natural Resources Conservation Service, formerly known as the Soil Conservation Service, helps America's farmers, ranchers, and other private landowners develop and implement voluntary efforts to conserve and protect the Nation's natural resources. http://www.nrcs.usda.gov/wps/portal/nrcs/site/national/home

Agricultural Conservation Easement Program   The Agricultural Conservation Easement Program helps conserve agricultural lands and wetlands by offering financial and technical assistance. Under the program's Agricultural Land Easements component, NRCS supports Indian tribes, State and local governments, and nongovernmental organizations in their efforts to protect working agricultural lands and to limit agricultural land use for nonagricultural purposes. Under the program's Wetlands Reserve Easements component, NRCS supports efforts to restore, protect, and enhance enrolled wetlands. http://www.nrcs.usda.gov/wps/portal/nrcs/main/national/programs/easements/acep

Agricultural Management Assistance   Agricultural Management Assistance, by giving financial and technical assistance to agricultural producers, encourages them to incorporate conversation practices into their farming operations to improve water management and quality, to reduce erosion, and to mitigate risk through production diversification. The assistance supports producers' in their efforts to plant trees for windbreaks, construct irrigation structures, use integrated pest management, and transition to organic farming. NRCS administers the program's conservation components, while AMS and RMA handle the others. http://www.nrcs.usda.gov/wps/portal/nrcs/main/national/programs/financial/ama

Conservation Stewardship Program   The Conservation Stewardship Program helps agricultural producers maintain and improve their existing conservation systems and adopt additional conservation practices that address resource concerns of high priority. Participants earn program payments for conservation performance: Payments are directly proportional to performance. The program offers two types of payments through 5-year contracts: annual payments for adopting new conservation practices and maintaining current ones, and supplemental payments for initiating a resource-conserving crop rotation. Producers may be able to renew a contract if they met the obligations of the initial contract and agree to achieve additional conservation goals. http://www.nrcs.usda.gov/wps/portal/nrcs/main/national/programs/financial/csp

Conservation Technical Assistance   Conservation Technical Assistance makes conservation technology and the delivery system needed to achieve the benefits of a healthy and productive landscape available to land users. The program reduces the loss of soil from erosion; offers solutions for agricultural waste management, air quality, soil, and water conservation and quality problems; mitigates potential water, sedimentation, or drought damage; improves fish and wildlife habitat; assists others in facilitating changes

in land use for natural resource protection and sustainability; and increases the long term sustainability of all lands—cropland, forestland, grazing lands, coastal lands, and developing or developed lands. Technical Assistance supports clients in their efforts to address concerns and problems and explore opportunities related to the use of natural resources. NRCS staff and the employees of other agencies or entities under the technical supervision of NRCS provide the assistance. http://www.nrcs.usda.gov/wps/portal/nrcs/main/national/programs/technical/cta

Emergency Watershed Protection Program   The Emergency Watershed Protection Program safeguards lives and property in jeopardy due to sudden watershed impairment caused by natural disasters. Emergency assistance includes quickly establishing a protective plant cover on denuded land and stream banks, opening dangerously restricted channels, and repairing diversions and levees. To be eligible for assistance under this program, an emergency area does not need to be declared a national disaster area. NRCS may bear up to 75 percent of the construction cost of emergency measures. The remaining cost must come from local sources. Funding is subject to Congressional approval. http://www.nrcs.usda.gov/wps/portal/nrcs/main/national/programs/landscape/ewpp

Environmental Quality Incentives Program   The Environmental Quality Incentives Program assists agricultural producers by offering contracts up to a maximum term of 10 years in length. These contracts provide financial assistance for planning and implementing conservation practices that address natural resource concerns and for improving air, animal, plant, soil, water, and related resources on agricultural land and nonindustrial private forestland. Sixty percent of the available funds are for conservation activities related to livestock production. The program also helps producers meet Federal, State, tribal and local environmental regulations. http://www.nrcs.usda.gov/wps/portal/nrcs/main/national/programs/financial/eqip

Healthy Forests Reserve Program   The Healthy Forests Reserve Program helps landowners restore, enhance, and protect forestland resources on private lands through easements, 30-year contracts, and 10-year cost-share agreements. The program supports the efforts of landowners to promote the recovery of endangered or threatened species, increase plant and animal biodiversity, and improve carbon sequestration. http://www.nrcs.usda.gov/wps/portal/nrcs/main/national/programs/easements/forests

National Cooperative Soil Survey   The National Cooperative Soil Survey, a nationwide partnership of Federal, State, regional, and local agencies and private entities and institutions, works cooperatively to investigate, inventory, document, classify, interpret, disseminate, and publish soil information. It informs the public about the uses and capabilities of local soils. The published survey for a county or other designated area includes maps and interpretations that are essential for farm planning, other private land use decisions, and governmental policy development and resource planning. http://www.nrcs.usda.gov/wps/portal/nrcs/main/soils/survey/partnership/ncss

Plant Materials Program   The Plant Materials Program selects conservation plants and develops innovative planting technology for addressing natural resource challenges and maintaining healthy and productive farms and ranches. It focuses on using plants as a natural solution for conservation issues and reestablishing ecosystem function; collects, selects, and releases grasses, legumes, wildflowers, trees and shrubs, working with commercial, private, public, and tribal partners and land managers to apply new plant-based conservation methods; provides plant materials and new applied technologies for national initiatives; offers plant solutions to fight invasive species, heal lands damaged by natural disasters, reduce drought effects, promote air and water quality, and produce alternative energy; and assists Native American tribes with producing and protecting culturally significant plants. http://www.nrcs.usda.gov/wps/portal/nrcs/main/plantmaterials/about

Regional Conservation Partnership Program   The Regional Conservation Partnership Program promotes coordination between NRCS and its partners for the delivery of conservation assistance to producers and landowners. NRCS assists producers through partnership agreements and program contracts or easement agreements. The program combines the authorities of four previous programs: the Cooperative Conservation Partnership Initiative, the Agricultural Water Enhancement, the Chesapeake Bay Watershed, and the Great Lakes Basin Programs. http://www.nrcs.usda.gov/wps/portal/nrcs/main/national/programs/farmbill/rcpp

Small Watershed Program   The Small Watershed Program relies on local government sponsors to help participants solve natural resource and related economic problems on a watershed basis. Projects include efforts to protect watersheds, prevent floods, control erosion and sedimentation, improve water supply and quality, enhance fish and wildlife habitat, create and restore wetlands, and support public recreation in watersheds of 250,000 or fewer acres. The program offers both financial and technical assistance. Through the Small Watershed Program, NRCS maps flood hazard areas, solves local flooding problems, evaluates potential greenbelts along streams, develops guidelines for erosion control and runoff management, helps farmers control erosion in high priority watersheds, and improves the water quality of ground water and water bodies. http://www.nrcs.usda.gov/wps/portal/nrcs/detail/nd/programs/?cid=nrcs141p2_001682

Snow Survey and Water Supply Forecasts   The Snow Survey is conducted by NRCS to make information on future water supplies available to residents of Alaska and Western States. At more than 1,800 mountain sites, NRCS personnel collect and analyze data on snowpack depth and its water equivalent to estimate annual water availability, spring runoff, and summer streamflows. Federal and State agencies, organizations, and individuals rely on these forecasts for agricultural production, fish and wildlife management, municipal and industrial water supply, urban development, flood control, recreation power generation, and water quality management. The National Weather Service includes the forecasts in their river forecasting function. http://www.nrcs.usda.gov/wps/portal/nrcs/main/national/water/snowsurvey

Watershed Surveys and Planning   The Watershed Surveys and Planning program supports Federal, State, and local agencies and tribal governments in their efforts to protect watersheds from damage caused by erosion, floodwater, and sediment and to conserve and develop water and land resources. The program addresses a number of resource concerns: agricultural drought problems, municipal and industrial water needs, rural development, upstream flood damages, water quality and conservation, wetland and water storage capacity, and water needs for fish, wildlife, and forest-based industries. http://www.nrcs.usda.gov/wps/portal/nrcs/main/national/programs/landscape/wsp

Research, Education and Economics

This mission area centers on creating, applying, and transferring knowledge and technology to make available affordable food and fiber, ensure food safety and nutrition, and support rural development and people's natural resource needs. The creation, application, and transfer of this knowledge and technology are achieved by conducting integrated national and international research and by providing information, education, and statistical programs and services. http://www.usda.gov/wps/portal/usda/usdahome?navid=USDA_MISSION_AREAS

Agricultural Research Service (ARS)   The Agricultural Research Service conducts research on agricultural problems of high national priority. It provides information access and dissemination to ensure high-quality, safe food and other agricultural products; to assess the nutritional needs of Americans; to sustain a competitive agricultural economy; to enhance the natural resource base and the environment; and to promote economic opportunities for rural citizens, communities, and society as a whole.

Research activities are carried out at 96 domestic locations, including Puerto Rico and the U.S. Virgin Islands, and five overseas locations. ARS conducts much of this research in cooperation with partners in State universities and experiment stations, other Federal agencies, and private organizations. National Programs, headquartered in Beltsville, MD, plans and coordinates the research programs, and five area offices carry out the day-to-day management of the respective programs for specific field locations.

The National Agricultural Library, the primary resource in the United States for information on food, agriculture, and natural resources, serves as an electronic gateway to a widening array of scientific literature, printed text, and agricultural images. The library supports the USDA and a broad customer base of policymakers, agricultural specialists, research scientists, and the general public. It works with other agricultural libraries and institutions to advance open and democratic access specifically to the Nation's agricultural knowledge and to agricultural information in general. http://www.nal.usda.gov

For further information, contact the Agricultural Research Service, Department of Agriculture, 1400 Independence Avenue SW., Washington, DC 20250. Phone, 202-720-3656. Fax, 202-720-5427.

The National Institute of Food and Agriculture (NIFA)   The National Institute of Food and Agriculture invests in and advances agricultural education, extension, and research to address societal challenges. The Institute works with academic institutions, land-grant universities, and other science organizations nationwide. With its partners and customers, NIFA promotes a global system of research, extension, and higher education in the food and agricultural sciences and related environmental and human sciences for the good of people, communities, and the Nation.

The Institute collaborates with scientists, policymakers, experts, and educators in organizations worldwide to find innovative solutions to pressing local and global problems. Scientific discovery and application advance the competitiveness of American agriculture, strengthen the U.S. economy, make the Nation's food supply safer, improve the nutrition and well-being of American citizens, sustain natural resources and the environment, and build energy independence. Partnering with other Federal science agencies, NIFA also makes important contributions to science policy decisionmaking. http://nifa.usda.gov

For further information, contact the Communications Staff, The National Institute of Food and Agriculture, Department of Agriculture, 1400 Independence Avenue SW., Washington, DC 20250-2207. Phone, 202-720-4651. Fax, 202-690-0289.

Economic Research Service (ERS)   The Service informs and strengthens public and private decisionmaking on economic and policy issues affecting agriculture, food, rural development, and the environment. ERS also serves as a primary source of economic information and research in the USDA.

Using a variety of means, ERS disseminates economic information and research results. It produces agency-published research reports, economic briefs, data products, and market analysis and outlook reports. "Amber Waves," its award-winning online magazine features articles on the economics of food, farming, natural resources, and rural America (www.ers.usda.gov/amber-waves). The ERS Web site allows access to all agency products, and it connects users directly with ERS analysts. The agency delivers oral briefings, written staff analyses, and congressionally mandated studies to executive and legislative branch policymakers and program administrators. Its experts also write articles for professional journals and present papers at academic conferences and meetings. http://www.ers.usda.gov

For further information, contact the Information Services Division, Economic Research Service, Department of Agriculture, 1400 Independence Avenue SW., Washington, DC 20250. Phone, 202-694-5100. Fax, 202-245-4781.

National Agricultural Statistics Service (NASS)   The National Agricultural Statistics Service prepares estimates and reports on production, supply, price, chemical use, and other items necessary for the orderly operation of the U.S. agricultural economy.

NAAS reports include statistics on field crops, fruits and vegetables, dairy, cattle, hogs, sheep, poultry, aquaculture, and related commodities or processed products. Estimates concern farm numbers, farm production expenditures, agricultural chemical use, prices received by farmers for products sold, prices paid for commodities and services, indexes of prices received and paid, parity prices, farm employment, and farm wage rates.

NASS prepares these estimates through a complex system of sample surveys of producers, processors, buyers, and others associated with agriculture. Information is gathered by mail, electronic data reporting, telephone, and personal interviews.

The Service conducts the Census of Agriculture, which is taken every 5 years and provides comprehensive data on the agricultural economy down to the county level. It also conducts follow-on studies on aquaculture, irrigation, horticultural energy, and organic agriculture.

NASS performs reimbursable survey work and statistical consulting services for other Federal and State agencies. It also helps other countries develop agricultural data systems by offering technical assistance. http://www.nass.usda.gov

For further information, contact the Customer Service Center, National Agricultural Statistics Service, Department of Agriculture, 1400 Independence Avenue SW., Washington, DC 20250-2000. Phone, 202-720-3878.

Rural Development

The rural development mission area centers on increasing the economic opportunities of rural Americans and improving their quality of life. To achieve these goals, the USDA creates and fosters cooperative relationships among Government, industry, and communities. As a capital investment bank, the USDA provides financing for rural housing and community facilities, business and cooperative development, telephone and high-speed Internet access, and electric, water, and sewer infrastructure. Approximately 3,400 employees in 47 State offices and 477 field offices administer rural development loan and grant programs at the local level. http://www.usda.gov/wps/portal/usda/usdahome?navid=USDA_MISSION_AREAS

Advanced Biofuel Repayment Program   The program provides payments to producers to support and expand production of advanced biofuels refined from sources other than corn kernel starch. http://www.rd.usda.gov/programs-services/advanced-biofuel-payment-program

Biorefinery, Renewable Chemical, and Biobased Product Manufacturing Assistance Program   This program assists in the development, construction, and retrofitting of new and emerging technologies for developing advanced biofuels, renewable chemicals, and biobased product manufacturing by giving loan guarantees. http://www.rd.usda.gov/programs-services/biorefinery-renewable-chemical-and-biobased-product-manufacturing-assistance

Business and Industry Guaranteed Loan Program This program creates jobs and stimulates the rural economy by financially backing rural businesses. It bolsters the existing private credit structure through the guaranteeing of loans for rural businesses, allowing private lenders to increase the credit that they extend. Borrowers use loan proceeds for working capital, machinery and equipment, buildings, real estate, and certain types of debt refinancing. A borrower may be a cooperative organization, corporation, partnership, nonprofit corporation, Native American tribe, federally recognized tribal group, public body, or individual. http://www.rd.usda.gov/programs-services/business-industry-loan-guarantees

Cooperative Programs USDA Cooperative Programs is the Nation's major source for information on cooperatives. Its library of more than 150 co-op publications—many of which are available in hardcopy, as well as online—range from co-op primers, such as "Co-ops 101," to reports on technical topics, such as "Tax Law for Cooperatives," to reports focusing on co-op economic theory, such as "The Nature of the Cooperative." These publications may be accessed on the "Publications for Cooperatives" Web page. http://www.rd.usda.gov/programs-services/all-programs/cooperative-programs

Delta Health Care Services Grant Program This program provides financial assistance to meet ongoing health needs in the Delta Region through cooperation among health care professionals, institutions of higher education, research institutions, and others in the Delta Region. http://www.rd.usda.gov/programs-services/delta-health-care-services-grants

Intermediary Relending Program This program provides capital to rural areas through low-interest and direct loans made to nonprofit corporations, public agencies, Native American groups, and certain corporations (intermediaries). These intermediaries establish revolving loan funds so they can relend the money to businesses in economically and socially disadvantaged rural communities. The process creates a source of capital that promotes job growth and economic development. http://www.rd.usda.gov/programs-services/intermediary-relending-program

Repowering Assistance Program This program funds up to 50 percent of the total eligible costs for biorefineries to install renewable biomass systems for heating and power or to produce new energy from renewable biomass. http://www.rd.usda.gov/programs-services/repowering-assistance-program

Rural Business Development Grant Program This program provides grants for rural projects that promote small and emerging business development, business incubators, employment, and related adult education programs. It also provides grants for sustainable economic development in rural communities with exceptional needs. Recipients use the grants to fund community- and technology-based economic development projects, feasibility studies, leadership and entrepreneur training, rural business incubators, and long-term business strategic planning. Eligible organizations include Native American tribes, nonprofit corporations, and rural public entities. http://www.rd.usda.gov/programs-services/rural-business-development-grants

Rural Business-Cooperative Service To meet business credit needs in underserved rural areas, USDA's Rural Business-Cooperative Service provides loan guarantees, direct loans, and grants to rural businesses, cooperatives, farmers, and ranchers, often in partnership with private sector lenders. The following is a list and description of USDA's Rural Development business and cooperative programs. http://www.rd.usda.gov/about-rd/agencies/rural-business-cooperative-service

Rural Cooperative Development Grant Program This program improves rural economic conditions by assisting individuals and businesses in the startup, expansion or operational improvement of rural cooperatives and other mutually-owned businesses through Cooperative

Development Centers. http://www.rd.usda.gov/programs-services/rural-cooperative-development-grant-program

Rural Economic Development (RED) Loan and Grant Program   The RED Loan and Grant programs provide funding to rural projects through local utility organizations. Under the loan program, USDA gives zero-interest loans that local utilities pass through to local businesses for projects that create and retain employment in rural areas. Under the grant program, USDA gives grant funds to local utility organizations that use them to establish revolving loan funds. http://www.rd.usda.gov/programs-services/rural-economic-development-loan-grant-program

Rural Energy for America Program   Grant recipients assist rural small businesses and agricultural producers by conducting and promoting energy audits and assisting in the development of renewable energy. http://www.rd.usda.gov/programs-services/rural-energy-america-program-energy-audit-renewable-energy-development-assistance

Rural Housing Programs   USDA Rural Development improves the quality of life in rural America. Its Rural Housing Service offers loans, grants, and loan guarantees to support essential services such as housing, economic development, health care, first-responder equipment and personnel, and water, electric and communications infrastructure. It also helps rural residents buy or rent safe and affordable housing, and make home repairs to improve safety and to create healthier living environments. http://www.rd.usda.gov/about-rd/agencies/rural-housing-service

Rural Microentrepreneur Assistance Program   This program makes loans and gives grants to Microenterprise Development Organizations. These organizations then provide microloans for microenterprise startups and growth through a rural microloan revolving fund. They also offer training and technical assistance to microloan borrowers and microentrepreneurs. http://www.rd.usda.gov/programs-services/rural-microentrepreneur-assistance-program

Rural Utilities Programs   USDA Rural Development strengthens rural economies and makes life better for Americans living in rural areas. Its Rural Utilities Service administers programs that provide infrastructure or infrastructure improvements to nonurban communities. These programs include water and waste treatment and electric power and telecommunications services. Utilities programs connect residents to the global community and its economy by increasing access to broadband and 21st-century telecommunications services, funding sustainable renewable energy development and conservation, financing reliable and affordable electric systems, working to integrate electric smart grid technologies, and developing reliable and affordable rural water and wastewater systems. http://www.rd.usda.gov/about-rd/agencies/rural-utilities-service

Socially-Disadvantaged Groups Grant Program   This program gives technical assistance to small socially-disadvantaged agricultural producers in rural areas. http://www.rd.usda.gov/programs-services/socially-disadvantaged-groups-grant

Value-Added Producer Grant Program   This program helps agricultural producers engage in value-added activities related to the processing and marketing of bio-based, value-added products. The program is designed to generate new products, create and expand marketing opportunities, and increase producer income. http://www.rd.usda.gov/programs-services/value-added-producer-grants

For further information, contact the Rural Development Legislative and Public Affairs Staff, Department of Agriculture, Stop 0705, 1400 Independence Avenue SW., Washington, DC 20250-0320. Phone, 202-690-0498.

Sources of Information

Ask the Expert   This tool helps Web site visitors locate the answers to their USDA-related questions. http://www.usda.gov/wps/portal/usda/usdahome?navid=ASK_EXPERT2

A–Z Index   The USDA Web site has a topical index that is arranged in alphabetical order. http://www.usda.gov/wps/portal/usda/usdahome?navid=AZ_INDEX

Blog   The USDA Web site features a blog that includes contributions on conservation, energy, food and nutrition, forestry, knowing your farmer and your food, rural development, and other topics. http://blogs.usda.gov

Business Opportunities   Marketing to the USDA can be a daunting task. To assist businessmen and women who seek to sell their products and services to the agency, the USDA has collected all of the necessary information and packaged it in one place— in the "Doing Business with USDA Kit" (2005 edition). http://www.dm.usda.gov/procurement/business/index.htm

The USDA awards over 50 percent of eligible contracting dollars to small businesses nationwide. Information on contracting or subcontracting opportunities, attending small business outreach events, or how to do business with the USDA is available on the "Office of Small and Disadvantaged Business Utilization" Web site. Phone, 202-720-7117. http://www.dm.usda.gov/smallbus/index.php

Career Opportunities   For information on vacant positions within the USDA and opportunities for students, recent graduates, and veterans, visit the "Careers and Jobs" Web page. http://www.usda.gov/wps/portal/usda/usdahome?navid=CAREERS

In 2017, the USDA ranked 7th among 18 large agencies in the Partnership for Public Service's Best Places To Work Agency Rankings. http://bestplacestowork.org/BPTW/rankings/detail/AG00

Freedom of Information Act (FOIA)   Departmental Management oversees the USDA's FOIA program. Twenty-one USDA FOIA officers at the mission area and agency levels work to increase Government transparency through proactive disclosures and the use of technology. http://www.dm.usda.gov/foia

Agency reading rooms are updated frequently and contain commonly requested records. Information seekers should visit the relevant reading rooms before submitting a FOIA request. http://www.dm.usda.gov/foia/agencyfoia.htm

The FOIA public access link (PAL) is a web portal that allows information seekers to create and submit a FOIA request and to check its status. Registration, which requires creating a user name and password, is the first step for using PAL. https://efoia-pal.usda.gov/palMain.aspx

Glossary   The USDA maintains a glossary of agency acronyms. http://www.usda.gov/wps/portal/usda/usdahome?navid=glossary#top

Newsroom   Announcements, factsheets, reports, and statements are accessible

online. http://www.usda.gov/wps/portal/usda/usdahome?navid=NEWSROOM

Open Government   The USDA supports the Open Government initiative by promoting the principles of collaboration, participation, and transparency. http://www.usda.gov/wps/portal/usda/usdahome?navid=USDA_OPEN

Organic Agriculture   The USDA is committed to increasing organic agriculture. It operates many programs that serve the growing organic sector. The USDA Organic Seal, which has been in use nearly 15 years, is a leading global standard. Visit the "Organic Agriculture" Web pages to learn more. http://www.usda.gov/wps/portal/usda/usdahome?navid=organic-agriculture

Instructions for becoming a certified organic operation are available online. https://www.ams.usda.gov/services/organic-certification/faq-becoming-certified

To receive "USDA Organic Insider" updates via email, use the online subscription form. https://visitor.r20.constantcontact.com/manage/optin/ea?v=001tanuLSmJHqsq1D840Z7eyw%3D%3D

Organizational Chart   The USDA's organizational chart is available in Portable Document Format (PDF) for viewing and downloading. https://www.usda.gov/sites/default/files/documents/usda-organization-chart.pdf

Plain Language   In support of the Plain Writing Act of 2010, USDA editors and writers strive to provide the public with information that is clear, understandable, and useful in forms, instructions, letters, notices, and publications. If a USDA document or content on the Department's Web site is unclear or difficult to understand, contact the USDA via email. http://www.usda.gov/wps/portal/usda/usdahome?navid=PLAIN_WRITING | Email: plainlanguage@osec.usda.gov

Program Discrimination   The Office of the Assistant Secretary for Civil Rights investigates and resolves complaints of discrimination in programs operated or assisted by the USDA. Information on what to include in a letter of complaint is available online. For information on the discrimination complaint process, contact the information research service in the Office of the Assistant Secretary. Phone, 202-260-1026 or 866-632-9992. Federal Relay Service, 800-877-

8339 (English) or 800-845-6136 (Spanish). https://www.ascr.usda.gov/filing-program-discrimination-complaint-usda-customer | Email: CR-INFO@ascr.usda.gov

Reports   Agency reports, data, and forecasts and outlooks are accessible online. http://www.usda.gov/wps/portal/usda/usdahome?navid=AGENCY_REPORTS

Site Map   The Web site map allows visitors to look for specific topics or to browse for topics that align with their interests. http://www.usda.gov/wps/portal/usda/usdahome?navtype=FT&navid=SITE_MAP

Snarge   Birds and other animals occasionally collide with airborne aircraft and planes moving on the ground. These collisions are called wildlife strikes, and snarge is the remaining residue after impact. To learn about efforts to reduce wildlife strikes, visit the Animal and Plant Health Inspection Service's (APHIS) wildlife strike web page. https://www.aphis.usda.gov/aphis/ourfocus/wildlifedamage/programs/SA_Airport

Watch the USDA's video to see how bird parts and snarge are collected, reported, shipped, and identified. https://www.youtube.com/watch?v=_OhJXexmmTg&list=PLF1BE3AC34367E99E

Social Media   The USDA tweets announcements, events, and other newsworthy items on Twitter. https://twitter.com/usda

Speakers   Contact the nearest USDA office or county extension agent. In the District of Columbia, contact the Office of Communications, U.S. Department of Agriculture, 1400 Independence Avenue SW., Washington, DC 20250. Phone, 202-720-4623. http://www.usda.gov/wps/portal/usda/usdahome?navid=OC_MEDIA_COMMS

Whistleblower Hotline   To file a complaint of alleged improprieties—employee misconduct, conflicts of interest, criminal activity, mismanagement or wasteful use of funds, workplace violence—visit the "OIG Hotline" Web page and use the "Submit a Complaint" feature. Or, contact a regional office or the Office of the Inspector General, U.S. Department of Agriculture, P.O. Box 23399, Washington, DC 20026. Phone, 800-424-9121 or 202-690-1622. TDD, 202-690-1202. Fax, 202-690-2474. http://www.usda.gov/oig/hotline.htm

Wood Pellets   European Union (EU) policies requiring renewable energy sources and energy associated with low greenhouse gas emissions are affecting wood products manufacturing and forests in the United States. Wood pellet production is on the rise as export to the EU increases. The primary U.S. exporting region is the South. To learn more about this topic, see the "Effect of Policies on Pellet Production and Forests in the U.S. South," which was published by the Southern Research Station of the U.S. Forest Service in December of 2014. https://www.srs.fs.usda.gov/pubs/gtr/gtr_srs202.pdf http://www.usda.gov/wps/portal/usda/usdahome?navid=CONTACT_US

For further information concerning the Department of Agriculture, contact the Office of Communications, Department of Agriculture, 1400 Independence Avenue SW., Washington, DC 20250. Phone, 202-720-4623.

DEPARTMENT OF COMMERCE

Fourteenth Street and Constitution Avenue NW., Washington, DC 20230
Phone, 202-482-2000. Internet, http://www.doc.gov

Office of The Secretary	
Secretary of Commerce	GINA M. RAIMONDO
Deputy Secretary	DON GRAVES
https://www.commerce.gov/about/leadership/gina-m-raimondo	
Office Heads Reporting to the Secretary and Deputy Secretary	
Assistant Secretaries	
Administration	WYNN W. COGGINS, ACTING
Legislative and Intergovernmental Affairs	(VACANCY)
Chief Officers	
Financial	WYNN W. COGGINS, ACTING
Information	(VACANCY)
General Counsel	LESLIE KIERNAN
https://www.commerce.gov/about/leadership?q=/about/ leadership&page=1	
Inspector General	PEGGY E. GUSTAFSON
https://www.commerce.gov/bureaus-and-offices/os/inspector-general	
Office Heads Reporting to the Chief of Staff	
Chief of Staff	MIKE HARNEY
Directors of Offices	
Business Liaison	LAURA O'NEILL
Executive Secretariat	(VACANCY)
Policy and Strategic Planning	(VACANCY)
Public Affairs	GABRIELA CASTILLO
The White House Liaison	(VACANCY)
https://www.commerce.gov/bureaus-and-offices	
Heads of Bureaus and Offices	
Under Secretaries	
Economic Affairs	(VACANCY)
Industry and Security	JEREMY PELTER, ACTING
Under Secretaries of Commerce	
Intellectual Property	DREW HIRSHFELD, ACTING
International Trade	DIANE FARRELL, ACTING
Oceans and Atmosphere	RICHARD W. SPINRAD
Standards and Technology	JAMES K. OLTHOFF
Assistant Secretaries of Commerce	
Communications and Information	EVELYN REMALEY, ACTING
Economic Development	ALEJANDRA Y. CASTILLO
National Director	
Minority Business Development Agency	MIGUEL ESTIÉN, ACTING

The above list of key personnel was updated 8–2021.

DEPARTMENT OF COMMERCE

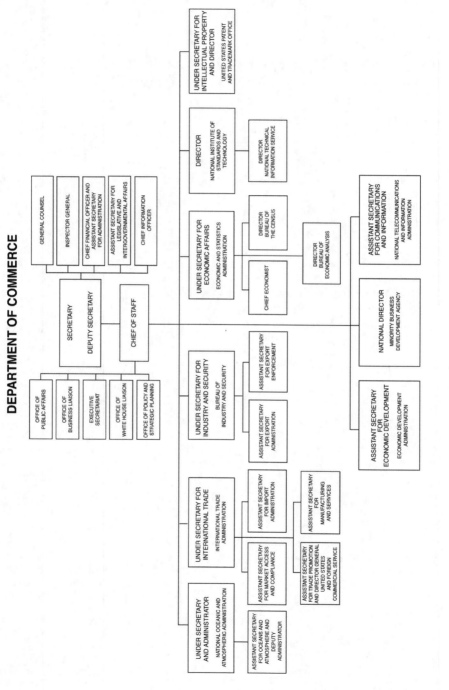

The Department of Commerce promotes the Nation's domestic and international trade, economic growth, and technological advancement by fostering free enterprise worldwide, supporting fair trade, compiling social and economic statistics, protecting Earth's physical resources, granting patents and registering trademarks, and assisting small and minority-owned businesses.

Establishment and Organization

The Department of Commerce was designated as such by act of March 4, 1913 (15 U.S.C. 1501). The act reorganized the Department of Commerce and Labor, created by act of February 14, 1903 (15 U.S.C. 1501), by transferring labor activities into a new, separate Department of Labor.

The "2020 Annual Performance Report" and "2022 Annual Performance Plan," which are combined into a single document, are posted on the DOC website. On page 4 of the introduction, a chart representing the DOC's organizational structure may be found. https://www.commerce.gov/files/fy-2022-annual-performance-plan-and-fy-2020-annual-performance-report

The "Bureaus and Offices" web page provides links that lead to the various web pages belonging to those bureaus and offices. https://www.commerce.gov/bureaus-and-offices

Statutory and Regulatory Authorties

Rules and regulations that affect commerce and foreign trade and that are associated with the DOC are codified and have been assigned to 15 CFR. https://www.ecfr.gov/cgi-bin/text-idx?SID=249848b7d71bf886fd9b4f1823873a43&mc=true&tpl=/ecfrbrowse/Title15/15tab_02.tpl

Activities

The DOC ensures fair trade, provides data to support commerce and constitutional democracy, and fosters innovation by setting standards and conducting foundational research and development. The DOC makes helpful tools available to entrepreneurs who and companies that are based in the United States. Programs, such as the Decennial Census, the National Weather Service, National Oceanic and Atmospheric Administration Fisheries, and the Foreign Commercial Service, are the providers of these tools. The DOC also oversees ocean and coastal navigation, participates in the negotiation of bilateral trade agreements, and enforces laws that ensure fairness for American businesses and workers. https://www.commerce.gov/about

Sources of Information

A–Z Index The Census Bureau has posted an alphabetical index of its website's content. https://www.census.gov/about/index.html

Business Opportunities The industry liaison helps business owners, contractors, and others seeking opportunities to work with the DOC. https://www.commerce.gov/oam/vendors/vendor-engagement

Career Opportunities For information on internships and career opportunities throughout the Department, visit the "Career Opportunities and Internships" Web page. https://www.commerce.gov/work-with-us/careers

In 2020, the DOC ranked 5th among 17 large Government agencies in the Partnership for Public Service's Best Places To Work Agency Rankings. https://bestplacestowork.org/rankings/detail/?c=CM00

Census The 2020 Census is a record of every person living in the United States and the five U.S. Territories. https://www.census.gov/programs-surveys/decennial-census/decade/2020/2020-census-main.html

Contact Information The "Contact Us" web page has the DOC's mailing address and main phone number. It also has links that lead to additional points of contact and DOC bureaus and agencies. https://www.commerce.gov/about/contact-us

Data / Reports The DOC collects, stores, and analyzes a wealth of information, including data on the Nation's economy, population, and environment. https://www.commerce.gov/data-and-reports

Economic Development Information The Economic Development Administration maintains a clearinghouse for economic development information on its Web site. http://www.eda.gov

Environment   The National Oceanic and Atmospheric Administration conducts research and gathers data on the atmosphere, oceans, space, and Sun, and it applies this knowledge to science and public service: warning of dangerous weather, charting seas and skies, guiding the use and protection of ocean and coastal resources, and improving stewardship of the environment. For more information, contact the Office of Communications, National Oceanic and Atmospheric Administration, Room 6013, Fourteenth Street and Constitution Avenue NW., Washington, DC 20230. Phone, 202-482-6090. Fax, 202-482-3154. http://www.noaa.gov

Federal Register   Significant documents and documents that the DOC recently published in the Federal Register are accessible online. https://www.federalregister.gov/agencies/commerce-department

Inspector General Hotline   The Office of Inspector General promotes economy, efficiency, and effectiveness and prevents and detects fraud, waste, abuse, and mismanagement in departmental programs and operations. To file a complaint, contact the Hotline, Inspector General, Complaint Intake Unit, Mail Stop 7886, 1401 Constitution Avenue, NW., Washington, DC 20230. Phone, 202-482-2495 or 800-424-5197. TTD, 202-482-5923 or 856-860-6950. Fax, 855-569-9235. http://www.oig.doc.gov | Email: hotline@oig.doc.gov

The Sources of Information were updated 8–2021.

Bureau of Industry and Security

Department of Commerce, Washington, DC 20230
Phone, 202-482-2721. Internet, http://www.bis.doc.gov

Industry and Security

Under Secretary	JEREMY PELTER, ACTING
Deputy Under Secretary	JEREMY PELTER
Chief Counsel	OPHER SHWEIKI, ACTING

https://www.commerce.gov/about/leadership
Export

Assistant Secretaries

Administration	MATTHEW S. BORMAN, ACTING
Enforcement	KEVIN J. KURLAND, ACTING

https://www.bis.doc.gov/index.php/about-bis/organization/senior-management-team

---

The above list of key personnel was updated 9–2021.

The Bureau of Industry and Security ensures an effective export control and treaty compliance system and promotes the Nation's strategic leadership in technology to strengthen national security, advance U.S. foreign policy, and achieve economic objectives.

Establishment and Organization
The Bureau of Export Administration, which was later renamed the Bureau of Industry and Security (BIS), was established within the Department of Commerce on October 1, 1987.

On March 10, 1988, the Department of Commerce issued Department Organization Order 10–16. It set forth the scope of authority and the functions of the new Under Secretary for Export Administration. A copy of the order was published in the Federal Register on June 7, 1988 (53 FR 20881). https://www.govinfo.gov/content/pkg/FR-1988-06-07/pdf/FR-1988-06-07.pdf

The Department of Commerce used an internal organization order to change the name of the Bureau of Export Administration to the BIS on April 18, 2002. The nomenclature change was published as a final rule in the Federal Register on April 26, 2002 (67 FR 20630). https://www.govinfo.gov/content/pkg/FR-2002-04-26/pdf/02-10166.pdf

The BIS posts an organization chart on its website. https://www.bis.doc.gov/index.php/about-bis/organization

Activities

The BIS advances U.S. national security, foreign policy, and economic objectives. The Bureau ensures an effective export control and treaty compliance system and promotes U.S. leadership in strategic technologies. The BIS maintains and strengthens adaptable, efficient, and effective export controls and treaty compliance systems. It also is involved with international export control regimes, often playing a lead role. https://www.commerce.gov/bureaus-and-offices/bis

Export Administration The Office of the Assistant Secretary for Export Administration is responsible for export licenses, treaty compliance, treaty obligations relating to weapons of mass destruction, and the defense industrial and technology base. The Office regulates the export of dual-use items requiring licenses for national security, nonproliferation, foreign policy, and short supply; ensures that approval or denial of license applications is consistent with economic and security concerns; promotes an understanding of export control regulations within the business community; represents the Department in interagency and international forums relating to export controls, particularly in multilateral regimes; monitors the availability of industrial resources of national defense; analyzes the impact of export controls on strategic industries; and assesses the security consequences of certain foreign investments. https://www.bis.doc.gov/index.php/regulations/export-administration-regulations-ear

Export Enforcement The Office of the Assistant Secretary for Export Enforcement enforces dual-use export controls. This enables exporters to take advantage of legal export opportunities while ensuring that illegal exports will be detected and either prevented or investigated and sanctioned. The Office also ensures prompt, aggressive action against restrictive trade practices; and conducts cooperative enforcement activities on an international basis. Export Enforcement also enforces U.S. antiboycott laws and regulations by advising U.S. exporters on potential prohibited requests contained in foreign contracts; investigating violations such as the furnishing of boycott-related information, refusing to deal with blacklisted businesses; and pursuing criminal and administrative sanctions for violations. https://www.bis.doc.gov/index.php/enforcement

Sources of Information

Additional Programs The "Add'l Programs" web page provides convenient access to information on technology evaluation, strategic industries and economic security, chemical weapons, and nuclear fuel cycle-related activities. https://www.bis.doc.gov/index.php/other-areas

Archived Records The "Guide to Federal Records in the National Archives of the United States" indicates that records of the Bureau of Export Administration have been assigned to record group 476. The Administration was renamed the BIS in 2002. Record group 476 does not have a description that currently is associated with it. https://www.archives.gov/research/guide-fed-records/index-numeric/401-to-500.html

Boycott Requests The Office of Antiboycott Compliance posts recent examples of boycott requests that have been reported. The list of prohibited conditions is illustrative and not exhaustive. https://www.bis.doc.gov/index.php/all-articles/7-enforcement/1755-examples-of-recent-boycott-related-requests

Career Opportunities BIS career opportunities are posted on USAJobs, which is a free web-based job board that serves as the Federal Government's official source of Federal job listings and employment opportunity information. https://www.usajobs.gov

In 2020, the BIS ranked 136th among 411 agency subcomponents in the Partnership for

Public Service's Best Places To Work Agency Rankings. https://bestplacestowork.org/rankings/detail/?c=CM67

Commerce Control List   Export control classification numbers are helpful for determining whether or not a Department of Commerce-issued export license is needed for exporting a particular export item. https://www.bis.doc.gov/index.php/regulations/commerce-control-list-ccl

Commerce Country Chart   The BIS has posted an overview of the commerce control list and the commerce country chart. https://www.bis.doc.gov/index.php/documents/regulations-docs/federal-register-notices/federal-register-2014/1033-738-supp-1/file

Contact Information   Forms and telephone numbers are available on the "Contact Us" web page. https://www.bis.doc.gov/index.php/about-bis/contact-bis

Descriptions of BIS activities and contact information for its program offices are available online. https://www.bis.doc.gov/index.php/program-offices

Data   The "BIS Data Portal" web page allows access to datasets that are relevant for analyzing exports and licensing. https://www.bis.doc.gov/data-portal

Electronic Code of Federal Regulations (e-CFR)   Title 15 of the e-CFR is dedicated to rules and regulations on commerce and foreign trade. https://www.ecfr.gov/cgi-bin/text-idx?SID=713f591c01d176fc38d7d3cc23a07ffd&mc=true&tpl=/ecfrbrowse/Title15/15tab_02.tpl

Enforcement Resources   Descriptions of the sentinel program and outreach program, as well as links to enforcement resources, are available online. https://www.bis.doc.gov/index.php/compliance-a-training/export-management-a-compliance/enforcement-resources

Federal Register   Significant documents and documents that the BIS recently published in the Federal Register are accessible online. https://www.federalregister.gov/agencies/industry-and-security-bureau

Freedom of Information Act (FOIA)   The FOIA is a Federal freedom of information law. It allows a person the right to request access to Federal agency records that are maintained by agencies within the Government's executive branch. After receiving a written request, an agency must disclose the requested information; however, some records may be shielded from disclosure by one or more of nine FOIA exemptions or by one of three special law enforcement record exclusions. https://efoia.bis.doc.gov

Frequently Asked Questions (FAQs)   The BIS posts answers to a lot of questions on its "FAQs" web page. https://www.bis.doc.gov/index.php/policy-guidance/faqs

Links to Resources   The "Resource Links" web page has contact information for and links to other Government departments and agencies whose activities include export control. The web page also has links to Federal agencies that offer trade promotion information and other related services. https://www.bis.doc.gov/index.php/about-bis/resource-links

Newsroom   The newsroom has information on the Bureau's current activities, as well as historical records and speeches by and testimony from senior managers. https://www.bis.doc.gov/index.php/about-bis/newsroom

Press Releases   The BIS posts press releases. https://www.bis.doc.gov/index.php/about-bis/newsroom/press-releases

Publications   Publications that are available online include the BIS's Annual Report to Congress, the guidance on the Commerce Department's Reexport Controls, and the Exporter User Manual and Licensing FAQ. http://www.bis.doc.gov/index.php/about-bis/newsroom/publications

Regulations   Subscribers to the "Export Administration Regulations" can stay informed of the latest rules. Phone, 301-208-0700 (ext. 112). https://www.bis.doc.gov/index.php/regulations/order-a-hard-copy-of-the-ear | Email: pubs@ocr-inc.com

The "Recently Published Regulations" web page contains helpful links to regulatory publications that are electronic. https://www.bis.doc.gov/index.php/regulations

Social Media   The BIS tweets announcements and other newsworthy items on Twitter. https://twitter.com/BISgov

Statistical Reports   The BIS posts statistical reports on its website. https://www.bis.doc.gov/index.php/statistical-reports

The above Sources of Information were updated 9–2021.

Economic Development Administration

Department of Commerce, Washington, DC 20230
Phone, 202-482-5081. Internet, http://www.eda.gov

Assistant Secretary of Commerce for Economic Development	ALEJANDRA Y. CASTILLO
Deputy Assistant Secretary	DENNIS ALVORD
Chief Operating Officer	DENNIS ALVORD
https://eda.gov/about/leadership	

The above list of key personnel was updated 9–2021.

The Economic Development Administration (EDA) was created in 1965 under the Public Works and Economic Development Act (42 U.S.C. 3121) as part of an effort to target Federal resources to economically distressed areas and to help develop local economies in the United States. It was mandated to assist rural and urban communities that were outside the mainstream economy and that lagged in economic development, industrial growth, and personal income.

EDA provides grants to States, regions, and communities nationwide to generate wealth and minimize poverty by promoting an attractive business environment for private capital investment and higher skill, higher wage jobs through capacity building, planning, infrastructure, research grants, and strategic initiatives. Through its grant program, EDA uses public sector resources to cultivate an environment where the private sector risks capital and job opportunities are created. https://www.eda.gov/about

Sources of Information

Annual Reports The EDA posts annual reports on its website. https://eda.gov/annual-reports

Archived Records The "Guide to Federal Records in the National Archives of the United States" indicates that EDA records have been assigned to record group 378. https://www.archives.gov/research/guide-fed-records/groups/378.html

Career Opportunities The EDA posts information on permanent career and term job opportunities on its website. https://eda.gov/careers/opportunities

In 2020, the EDA ranked 114th among 411 agency subcomponents in the Partnership for Public Service's Best Places To Work Agency Rankings. https://bestplacestowork.org/rankings/detail/?c=CM52

Contact Information Phone numbers for EDA headquarters and its six regional offices are posted online. The Office of Public Affairs handles media inquiries. Phone, 202-482-4085. http://www.eda.gov/contact

Disaster Recovery Support The EDA supports disaster recovery and resiliency efforts. Media posts highlight EDA assistance to communities that are recovering from years of disasters and EDA efforts to increase the resiliency of those communities. https://eda.gov/disaster-recovery/clips

Federal Register Significant documents and documents that the EDA recently published in the Federal Register are accessible online. https://www.federalregister.gov/agencies/economic-development-administration

Newsroom The "Newsroom" web page provides convenient access to blog posts, newsletters, press releases, success stories, Twitter tweets, and the latest news. https://www.eda.gov/news

Programs / Initiatives The EDA administrates programs that support the economic development of communities. It also leads initiatives involving multiple agencies. https://eda.gov/programs

Resources The EDA maintains a resources directory on its "Resources" web page. https://eda.gov/resources

Social Media The EDA has a Facebook account. https://www.facebook.com/eda.commerce

The EDA tweets announcements and other newsworthy items on Twitter. https://twitter.com/US_EDA

The EDA posts videos on its YouTube channel. https://www.youtube.com/user/EDACommerce

The above Sources of Information were updated 9–2021.

Economics and Statistics Administration

Department of Commerce, Washington, DC 20230
Phone, 202-482-3727. Internet, http://www.esa.doc.gov

Under Secretary For Economic Affairs https://www.commerce.gov/about/leadership	(VACANCY)
Bureau Directors	
Economic Analysis https://www.commerce.gov/bureaus-and-offices/bea	MARY BOHMAN, ACTING
U.S. Census https://www.commerce.gov/bureaus-and-offices/census	RONALD S. JARMIN, ACTING [ROBERT SANTOS—CONFIRMED BY SENATE; SWEARING-IN FORTHCOMING]

The above list of key personnel was updated 11–2021.

The Economics and Statistics Administration (ESA), headed by the Under Secretary for Economic Affairs, has three principal components: the Office of the Chief Economist, the Bureau of the Census, and the Bureau of Economic Analysis. ESA develops policy options, analyzes economic developments, manages economic data systems, and produces a major share of U.S. economic and demographic statistics, including the national economic indicators. The Under Secretary is the chief economic adviser to the Secretary and provides leadership and executive management for the Office of the Chief Economist and the Bureaus of Economic Analysis and of the Census. http://www.esa.gov/content/about-economics-statistics-administration

Bureau of Economic Analysis

[For the Bureau of Economic Analysis statement of organization, see the Federal Register of Dec. 29, 1980, 45 FR 85496]

The Bureau of Economic Analysis (BEA) provides the most accurate, relevant, and timely economic accounts data in an objective and cost-effective manner. BEA's economic statistics offer a comprehensive picture of the U.S. economy. BEA prepares national, regional, industry, and international accounts that present essential information on such issues in the world economy.

BEA's national economic statistics provide a comprehensive look at U.S. production, consumption, investment, exports and imports, and income and saving. The international transactions accounts provide

information on trade in goods and services (including the balance of payments and trade), investment income, and government and private finances. In addition, the accounts measure the value of U.S. international assets and liabilities and direct investment by multinational companies.

The regional accounts provide data on total and per capita personal income by region, State, metropolitan area, and county, and on gross State product. The industry economic account provides a detailed view of the interrelationships between U.S. producers and users and the contribution to production across industries. http://www.bea.gov | Email: customerservice@bea.gov

For further information, contact the Public Information Office, Bureau of Economic Analysis, Department of Commerce, Washington, DC 20230. Phone, 202-606-9900. Fax, 202-606-5310.

Bureau of the Census

[For the Bureau of the Census statement of organization, see the Federal Register of Sept. 16, 1975, 40 FR 42765]

The Bureau of the Census was established as a permanent office by act of March 6, 1902 (32 Stat. 51). The major functions of the Census Bureau are authorized by the Constitution, which provides that a census of population shall be taken every 10 years, and by laws codified as title 13 of the United States Code. The law also provides that the information collected by the Census Bureau from individual persons, households, or establishments be kept strictly confidential and be used only for statistical purposes.

The Census Bureau is responsible for the decennial censuses of population and housing; the quinquennial censuses of State and local governments, manufacturers, mineral industries, distributive trades, construction industries, and transportation; current surveys that provide information on many of the subjects covered in the censuses at monthly, quarterly, annual, or other intervals; compilation of current statistics on U.S. foreign trade, including data on imports, exports, and shipping; special censuses at the request and expense of State and local government units; publication of estimates and projections of the population; publication of current data on population and housing characteristics; and current reports on manufacturing, retail and wholesale trade, services, construction, imports and exports, State and local government finances and employment, and other subjects.

The Census Bureau makes available statistical results of its censuses, surveys, and other programs to the public through the Internet, mobile applications, and other media. The Bureau also prepares special tabulations sponsored and paid for by data users. It also produces statistical compendia, catalogs, guides, and directories that are useful in locating information on specific subjects. Upon request, the Bureau makes searches of decennial census records and furnishes certificates to individuals for use as evidence of age, relationship, or place of birth. A fee is charged for searches. http://www.census.gov | Email: PIO@census.gov

For further information, contact the Public Information Office, Bureau of the Census, Department of Commerce, Washington, DC 20233. Phone, 301-763-3030. Fax, 301-763-3762.

Office of the Chief Economist
The economists and analysts of the Office of the Chief Economist analyze domestic

and international economic developments and produce in-depth reports, factsheets, briefings, and social media postings. These tools cover policy issues and current economic events, as well as economic and demographic trends. Department of Commerce and White House policymakers, American businessmen, State and local governments, and news organizations worldwide rely on these tools. http://www.esa.gov/content/chief-economist

Sources of Information
Archived Records The "Guide to Federal Records in the National Archives of the United States" indicates that BEA records have been assigned to record group 375. https://www.archives.gov/research/guide-fed-records/groups/375.html?_ga=2.203325393.1312685709.163 4330345-1378874314.1634330345

The "Guide to Federal Records in the National Archives of the United States" indicates that Census Bureau records have been assigned to record group 029. https://www.archives.gov/research/guide-fed-records/groups/029.html?_ga=2.256758347.1312685709.1634 330345-1378874314.1634330345
Career Opportunities Visit the "Working at BEA" web page to learn about a career that involves economic analysis for measuring and better understanding the U.S. economy. https://www.bea.gov/about/working-at-bea

Visit the "Census Careers" web page to explore a career with one of the most important statistical organizations in the world. http://www.census.gov/about/census-careers.html
Learning Center The BEA maintains an online learning center. https://www.bea.gov/resources/learning-center
Library The Census Bureau collection formats include audio, images, mobile apps, video, and publications. https://www.census.gov/library.html

The above Sources of Information were updated 10–2021.

International Trade Administration

Department of Commerce, Washington, DC 20230
Phone, 202-482-3917. Internet, http://www.trade.gov

Under Secretary for International Trade	DIANE FARRELL, ACTING
Assistant Secretaries	
Enforcement and Compliance	CHRISTIAN MARSH, ACTING
Global Markets	DALE N. TASHARSKI, ACTING
Industry and Analysis	ANNE DRISCOLL, ACTING
Director General	
U.S. and Foreign Commercial Service	DALE N. TASHARSKI, ACTING

The above list of key personnel was updated 10–2021. https://www.trade.gov/ita-senior-staff

The International Trade Administration (ITA) was established on January 2, 1980, by the Secretary of Commerce to promote world trade and to strengthen the international trade and investment position of the United States.

The International Trade Administration's statement of organization was published in the Federal Register on January 25, 1980 (45 FR 6148). https://www.govinfo.gov/content/pkg/FR-1980-01-25/pdf/FR-1980-01-25.pdf

The Under Secretary for International Trade heads the ITA, coordinating all issues concerning trade promotion, international commercial policy, market access, and trade law enforcement. The Administration is responsible for U.S. Government nonagricultural trade operations, and it supports the U.S. Trade Representative's efforts to negotiate trade policy. http://www.trade.gov/about.asp

Enforcement / Compliance   The Office of Enforcement and Compliance defends American industry against injurious and unfair trade practices by administering U.S. antidumping and countervailing duty trade laws. The Office also ensures the proper administration of foreign trade zones and advises the Secretary on establishment of new ones; oversees the administration of the Department's textiles program; and administers programs governing watch assemblies and other statutory import programs. http://www.trade.gov/enforcement

Global Markets   The Global Markets unit assists and advocates for U.S. businesses in international markets. Relying on a network of trade promotion and policy professionals located in over 70 countries and 100 U.S.

locations, the unit promotes U.S. exports, especially those of small and medium-sized enterprises; advances and protects U.S. commercial interests overseas; and attracts investment from abroad into the United States. http://www.trade.gov/markets

Industry / Analysis   The Manufacturing and Services unit advises on domestic and international trade and investment policies affecting the competitiveness of U.S. industry. It also researches and analyzes manufacturing and services. Based on this analysis and interaction with U.S. industry, the unit Secretary develops strategies, policies, and programs to strengthen U.S. industry competitiveness domestically and globally. The unit manages an integrated program that includes industry and economic analysis, trade policy development and multilateral, regional, and bilateral trade agreements for manufactured goods and services; administers trade arrangements with foreign governments in product and service areas; and develops and provides business information and assistance to the United States on its rights and opportunities under multilateral and other agreements. http://www.trade.gov/industry

Sources of Information

Data   Trade data and export and import statistics are available online. http://www.trade.gov/data.asp

Employment   For information on career opportunities, visit the "Jobs" Web page. http://www.trade.gov/jobs

Publications   The ITA has an online bookstore. http://www.trade.gov/publications http://www.trade.gov/contact.asp

For further information, contact the International Trade Administration, Department of Commerce, Washington, DC 20230. Phone, 202-482-3917.

Minority Business Development Agency

Department of Commerce, Washington, DC 20230
Phone, 202-482-2332. Internet, http://www.mbda.gov

National Director   ALEJANDRA Y. CASTILLO
National Deputy Director   ALBERT K. SHEN

[For the Minority Business Development Agency statement of organization, see the Federal Register of Mar. 17, 1972, 37 FR 5650, as amended]

The Minority Business Development Agency was established by Executive order in 1969. The Agency develops and coordinates a national program for minority business enterprise.

The Agency was created to help minority businesses achieve effective and equitable participation in the American free enterprise system and overcome social and economic disadvantages that limited past participation. The Agency provides policies and leadership supporting a partnership of business, industry, and government with the Nation's minority businesses.

Business development services are provided to the minority business community through three vehicles: the minority business opportunity committees, which disseminate information on business opportunities; the minority business development centers, which provide management and technical assistance and other business development services; and electronic commerce, which includes a Web site that shows how to start a business and use the service to find contract opportunities.

The Agency promotes and coordinates the efforts of other Federal agencies in assisting or providing market opportunities for minority business. It coordinates opportunities for minority firms in the private sector. Through such public and private cooperative activities, the Agency promotes the participation of Federal, State, and local governments, and business and industry in directing resources for the development of strong minority businesses. http://www.mbda.gov/main/who-mbda/about-minority-business-development-agency

Sources of Information

Internships   Information on student eligibility and how to apply is available online. http://www.mbda.gov/main/intern-program

Library   An online research library serves as a repository for factsheets, reports, statistical data, and other publications. http://www.mbda.gov/pressroom/research-library

Newsletter   A free, monthly newsletter is accessible online. http://www.mbda.gov/newsletter

Speakers   For information on scheduling a speaker for an organized event, visit the "Speaker Request Form" Web page. http://www.mbda.gov/main/mbda-speaker-request-form http://www.mbda.gov/contact

For further information, contact the Office of the National Director, Minority Business Development Agency, Department of Commerce, Washington, DC 20230. Phone, 202-482-2332.

National Oceanic and Atmospheric Administration

Department of Commerce, Washington, DC 20230
Phone, 202-482-2985. Internet, http://www.noaa.gov

Administrator   RICHARD W. SPINRAD
Deputy Administrator   JANET L. COIT, ACTING

Assistant Administrators
National Marine Fisheries Service   JANET L. COIT
Satellite and Information Services   STEPHEN M. VOLZ

Chief Operating Officer	Benjamin P. Friedman
Chief Scientist	Craig N. McLean, Acting
General Counsel	Walker B. Smith
Chief of Staff	Karen H. Hyun
https://www.noaa.gov/about-our-agency	

The above list of key personnel was updated 1–2022.

The National Oceanic and Atmospheric Administration seeks to understand and predict changes in climate and weather and changes that affect coasts and oceans; shares its knowledge and information with others; and conserves and manages coastal and marine ecosystems and resources.

Establishment and Organization

On October 3, 1970, Reorganization Plan No. 4 of 1970 (5 U.S.C. app.) formed the National Oceanic and Atmospheric Administration (NOAA).

NOAA posts an organizational chart at the bottom of its "Organization" web page, in Portable Document Format (PDF), for viewing and downloading. https://www.noaa.gov/about/organization

NOAA published its statement of functions, organization, and delegation of authority in the Federal Register on February 13, 1978 (43 FR 6128). https://www.govinfo.gov/content/pkg/FR-1978-02-13/pdf/FR-1978-02-13.pdf

Activities

Science, service, and stewardship characterize NOAA's mission. Its researchers, scientists, and technicians study the atmosphere, the ocean, and the ecosystems associated with them; they integrate research and analysis; they observe and monitor; and they use modeling to predict the future state of complex systems. NOAA serves academic institutions, businesses, communities, and ordinary people by communicating and sharing its data, information, knowledge, and research. NOAA also applies its institutional know-how and science assets to the conservation and management of coastal and marine ecosystems and resources. The agency regulates and sustains marine fisheries and ecosystems, protects endangered species, restores habitats and ecosystems, conserves marine sanctuaries, responds to environmental emergencies, and assists with

disaster recovery. https://www.noaa.gov/about-our-agency

Marine and Aviation Operations   The Office of Marine and Aviation Operations manages the aviation safety, the small boat, and the NOAA diving programs. It also operates a fleet of specialized ships and aircraft that collect data and carry out research to support NOAA's mission, the Global Earth Observation System, and the Integrated Ocean Observing System—including flying "hurricane hunter" aircraft into the most turbulent storms to collect data critical for research. http://www.omao.noaa.gov/about.html

For further information, contact Office of Marine and Aviation Operations, Suite 500, 8403 Colesville Rd., Silver Spring, MD 20910. Phone, 301-713-7600. Fax, 301-713-1541.

National Coastal Resources   The National Ocean Service helps balance the Nation's use of coastal resources through research, management, and policy. The Service monitors the health of U.S. coasts by examining how human use and natural events affect coastal ecosystems. Coastal communities rely on the Service for information on natural hazards so they can reduce or eliminate destructive effects of coastal hazards. The Service assesses the damage caused by hazardous material spills and tries to restore or replace the affected coastal resources. The Service also protects beaches, water quality, wetlands, and wildlife. It provides a wide range of navigational products and data that help vessels move safely through U.S. waters, and it supplies the basic information for establishing the latitude, longitude, and

The page intentionally left blank

elevation framework necessary for the Nation's mapping, navigation, positioning, and surveying activities. https://oceanservice. noaa.gov/

For further information, contact the National Ocean Service, Room 13231, SSMC 4, 1305 East-West Highway, Silver Spring, MD 20910. Phone, 301-713-3074. Fax, 301-713-4307.

National Environmental Satellite, Data, and Information The National Environmental Satellite, Data, and Information Service operates the Nation's civilian geostationary and polar-orbiting environmental satellites. It also manages the largest collection of atmospheric, climatic, geophysical, and oceanographic data in the world. The Service develops and provides, through various media, environmental data for forecasts, national security, and weather warnings to protect life and property. These data are also used for energy distribution, global food supplies development, natural resources management, and rescuing downed pilots and mariners in distress. https://www.nesdis.noaa.gov/

For further information, contact the National Environmental Satellite, Data, and Information Service, 1335 East-West Highway, Silver Spring, MD 20910-3283. Phone, 301-713-3578. Fax, 301-713-1249.

National Marine Fisheries The National Marine Fisheries Service supports the management, conservation, and sustainable development of domestic and international living marine resources and the protection and restoration of ecosystems. The Service helps assess the stock of the Nation's multi-billion-dollar marine fisheries, protect marine mammals and threatened species, conserve habitats, assist trade and industry, and conduct fishery enforcement activities. http://www.nmfs.noaa.gov

For further information, contact the National Marine Fisheries Service, 1315 East-West Highway, Silver Spring, MD 20910. Phone, 301-713-2239. Fax, 301-713-1940.

National Weather The National Weather Service (NWS) provides weather, water, and climate warnings and forecasts and data for the United States, its territories, and adjacent waters and ocean areas. Government agencies, the private sector, the general public, and the global community rely on NWS data and products to protect

life and property. Working with partners in Government, academic and research institutions, and private industry, the Service responds to the needs of the American public through its products and services. NWS data and information support aviation, maritime activities, and other sectors of the economy, as well as wildfire suppression. The Service also helps national security efforts with long- and short-range forecasts, air quality and cloud dispersion forecasts, and broadcasts of warnings and critical information over the 800-station NOAA Weather Radio network. http://www.weather.gov

For further information, contact the National Weather Service–Executive Affairs, 1325 East-West Highway, Silver Spring, MD 20910-3283. Phone, 301-713-0675. Fax, 301-713-0049.

Oceanic and Atmospheric Research The Office of Oceanic and Atmospheric Research conducts research on air quality and composition, climate variability and change, weather, and coastal, marine, and Great Lakes ecosystems. The Office uses its own laboratories and offices to run research programs in atmospheric, coastal, marine, and space sciences, as well as relying on networks of university-based programs across the country. http://www.oar.noaa.gov

For further information, contact the Office of Oceanic and Atmospheric Research, Room 11458, 1315 East-West Highway, Silver Spring, MD 20910. Phone, 301-713-2458. Fax, 301-713-0163.

Sources of Information

Archived Records The "Guide to Federal Records in the National Archives of the United States" indicates that NOAA records have been assigned to record group 370. https://www.archives.gov/research/guide-fed-records/groups/370.html

Arctic Report Cards Every year, NOAA publishes an Arctic Report Card as part of its efforts to track recent environmental changes relative to historical records. In December of 2021, NOAA released its most up-to-date version of the Arctic Report Card. https://www.arctic.noaa.gov/Report-Card/Report-Card-2021

NOAA released a 4-minute video synopsis of the updated report card. The video's narration opens and closes with these words: "The Arctic, an ancient ecosystem, is disappearing before our eyes. . . . All these disruptions are the direct result of a climate straining under the heat-trapping burden of greenhouse gas pollution. The time to face this monumental challenge is now." This year's report card notes the fall in numbers of iconic species like the ice-dependent polar bear and the rise in numbers of new species like beavers, whose engineering activities create wetlands. The report card also notes the nearly complete loss of old Arctic sea ice. Without the barricading presence of thick sea ice, ships and the industrial activities that they support are becoming more common in the Arctic. The effects include more garbage adrift and more pollution on shore, as well as higher levels of marine noise. Plastics and toxic chemicals are lethal threats to marine mammals such as seals, walrus, and whales. Undermining the food security of native communities, marine noise drives these magnificent mammals from their preferred habitats, which also are traditional hunting areas for indigenous hunters. https://www.youtube.com/watch?v=_WbWjLUTvZM

Atmospheric Carbon Dioxide   Adding to the data record that C. David Keeling of the Scripps Institution of Oceanography started in 1958, NOAA continues to measure atmospheric carbon at the Mauna Loa Observatory in Hawaii. https://gml.noaa.gov/ccgg/trends/

The Earth System Research Laboratory's Global Monitoring Division has posted a 4-minute video showing 800,000 years of atmospheric carbon dioxide history. https://www.esrl.noaa.gov/gmd/ccgg/trends/history.html

Atmospheric Methane   The Earth System Research Laboratory's Global Monitoring Division has been measuring methane since 1983 at a globally distributed network of air sampling sites. https://esrl.noaa.gov/gmd/ccgg/trends_ch4

A recent NOAA study (APR 2019) concludes that long term measurements show little evidence for large increases in total U.S. methane emissions over the past decade. https://research.noaa.gov/article/ArtMID/587/ArticleID/2453/US-methane-emissions-flat-since-2006-despite-increased-oil-and-gas-activity-study

Career Opportunities   A career at NOAA is a mission-oriented experience that centers on protecting natural resources, safeguarding the public, and strengthening the economy. https://www.noaa.gov/work-with-us

In 2020, NOAA ranked 111th among 411 agency subcomponents in the Partnership for Public Service's Best Places To Work Agency Rankings. https://bestplacestowork.org/rankings/detail/CM54

Climate Change   The Carbon Cycle Greenhouse Gases research area operates the global greenhouse gas reference network. Researchers measure the atmospheric distribution and trends of the main causes of climate change: carbon dioxide (CO_2); methane (CH_4); nitrous oxide (N_2O); and carbon monoxide (CO) because it is an indicator of air pollution. https://gml.noaa.gov/ccgg/

"The Power of Greenhouse Gases" web page presents examples of the excess heat that the Earth system is retaining. The amount of excess heat is sufficiently large to force climate change on a regional and global scale. https://www.esrl.noaa.gov/gmd/ccgg/ghgpower

Contact Information   The "Contact Us" web page has contact information and other frequently requested resources. https://www.noaa.gov/contact-us

Federal Register   Significant documents and documents that NOAA recently published in the Federal Register are accessible online. https://www.federalregister.gov/agencies/national-oceanic-and-atmospheric-administration

Freedom of Information Act (FOIA)   Any person has a right to obtain access to Federal agency records; however, some records, or portions of them, may be shielded from disclosure by one of nine FOIA exemptions or by one of three special law enforcement exclusions. https://www.noaa.gov/information-technology/foia

Before submitting a FOIA request, an information seeker should search the electronic reading room to determine if the desired information is in the public domain. https://www.noaa.gov/organization/information-technology/foia-reading-room

Maritime Archaeology   Visit the "Maritime Archaeology" web page to learn about discovering shipwrecks and safeguarding them. https://www.noaa.gov/topic-tags/maritime-archaeology

Monthly Climate Report   The report of August 13, 2021, carried the headline "It's official: July was Earth's hottest month on record." https://www.noaa.gov/topic-tags/monthly-climate-report

Nautical Charts   NOAA has posted the entire suite of U.S. coastal and Great Lakes charts on its "Charting" page for download. https://www.noaa.gov/charting

NOAA Nationwide   NOAA facilities—as well as personnel and the activities and programs they manage—are located throughout the Nation in various States and Territories. https://www.noaa.gov/legislative-and-intergovernmental-affairs/noaa-in-your-state-territory

Podcast   The NOAA Ocean podcast explores topics ranging from coastal science to coral reefs with ocean experts. https://oceanservice.noaa.gov/podcast

Social Media   NOAA relies on social media to share information and to promote understanding of its science, service, and stewardship-oriented mission. https://www.noaa.gov/stay-connected

Staff Directory   The NOAA staff directory is available online. https://nsd.rdc.noaa.gov

Weather   The NOAA Weather Radio All Hazards network broadcasts continuous weather information nationwide from the nearest National Weather Service office. The network broadcasts official Weather Service forecasts, warnings, watches, and other hazard information around the clock every day. https://www.weather.gov/nwr

NOAA's Sources of Information were updated 1–2022.

National Telecommunications and Information Administration

Department of Commerce, Washington, DC 20230
Phone, 202-428-1840. Internet, http://www.ntia.doc.gov

Assistant Secretary, Communications and Information / Administrator   LAWRENCE E. STRICKLING
Deputy Assistant Secretary, Communications and Information   ANGELA SIMPSON

[For the National Telecommunications and Information Administration statement of organization, see the Federal Register of June 5, 1978, 43 FR 24348]

The National Telecommunications and Information Administration (NTIA) was established in 1978 by Reorganization Plan No. 1 of 1977 (5 U.S.C. app.) and Executive Order 12046 of March 27, 1978 (3 CFR, 1978 Comp., p. 158), by combining the Office of Telecommunications Policy of the Executive Office of the President and the Office of Telecommunications of the Department of Commerce to form a new agency reporting to the Secretary of Commerce. NTIA operates under the authority of the National Telecommunications and Information Administration Organization Act (47 U.S.C. 901).

NTIA serves as the principal executive branch adviser to the President on telecommunications and information policy; develops and presents U.S. plans and policies at international communications conferences and related meetings; prescribes policies for and manages Federal use of the radio frequency spectrum; serves as the principal Federal telecommunications research and engineering laboratory—NTIA's Institute for Telecommunication Sciences; promotes broadband deployment and adoption through BroadbandUSA (www2.ntia.doc.gov); and assists the First Responder Network Authority (www.firstnet.gov) develop and operate a nationwide broadband network dedicated to public safety. https://www.ntia.doc.gov/about

Sources of Information

Employment   To see current NTIA career opportunities on USAJobs, click on the link below, scroll down, and select "NTIA Jobs." https://www.ntia.doc.gov/about

Publications   Since 1954, NTIA and its predecessors have published several hundred technical reports and memoranda, special publications, contractor reports, and other information products. For more information, call the Office of Spectrum Management in Washington, DC, at 202-482-1850. Or, contact the publications officer at the Institute for Telecommunication Sciences–Department of Commerce, 325 Broadway, MC ITS.D, Boulder, CO 80305.

Phone, 303-497-3572. https://www.ntia.doc.gov/publications
Speakers   A speaker request form is available online. https://www.ntia.doc.gov/webform/speaker-request
Telecommunications Research   For information on telecommunications research and engineering services, visit the "Institute for Telecommunication Sciences" Web page. Phone, 303-497-3571. http://www.its.bldrdoc.gov | Email: info@its.bldrdoc.gov https://www.ntia.doc.gov/contact

For further information, contact the National Telecommunications and Information Administration, Department of Commerce, Washington, DC 20230. Phone, 202-482-1551.

National Institute of Standards and Technology

100 Bureau Drive, Gaithersburg, MD 20899
Phone, 301-975-2000. Internet, http://www.nist.gov

Under Secretary, Standards And Technology / Director   WILLIE E. MAY

The National Institute of Standards and Technology (NIST) operates under the authority of the National Institute of Standards and Technology Act (15 U.S.C. 271), which amends the Organic Act of March 3, 1901 (ch. 872), which created the National Bureau of Standards (NBS) in 1901. In 1988, the Congress renamed NBS as NIST and expanded its activities and responsibilities. http://www.nist.gov/timeline.cfm

NIST is a nonregulatory Federal agency within the Department of Commerce. To carry out its mission, NIST relies on research laboratories, user facilities, innovative manufacturing programs, and its participation in collaborative institutes and centers. NIST research laboratories conduct world-class research to advance the Nation's technological infrastructure and help U.S. companies improve products and services. The Baldrige Performance Excellence

Program (www.nist.gov/baldrige) also helps them and other organizations increase operational performance and quality. NIST user facilities include the Center for Nanoscale Science and Technology (www.nist.gov/cnst) and NIST Center for Neutron Research (www.ncnr.nist.gov). http://www.nist.gov/programs-projects.cfm

Sources of Information

Employment   For information on career opportunities, visit the "Careers at NIST" Web page. http://www.nist.gov/ohrm/careers.cfm
Publications   The "Journal of Research of the National Institute of Standards and Technology" and other publications are available online. http://www.nist.gov/nvl/nist_publications.cfm http://www.nist.gov/public_affairs/contact.cfm | Email: inquiries@nist.gov

For further information, contact the National Institute of Standards and Technology, 100 Bureau Drive, Mail Stop 1070, Gaithersburg, MD 20899-1070. Phone, 301-975-6478. Fax, 301-926-1630.

National Technical Information Service

5301 Shawnee Road, Alexandria, VA 22312
Phone, 703-605-6050. Fax, 888-584-8332. Internet, http://www.ntis.gov

Director   AVI BENDER

The National Technical Information Service (NTIS) is the largest central resource for business-related, engineering, Government-funded, scientific, and technical information available. For more than 60 years, the Service has assured businesses, Government, universities, and the public timely access to approximately 3 million publications covering over 350 subject areas. The Service supports the Department of Commerce's mission by providing access to information that stimulates innovation and discovery. The Service receives no appropriations and recovers its costs through fees charged for products and services.

The NTIS promotes economic growth, progress, and science and information. On behalf of the Secretary of Commerce, the Service operates a permanent clearinghouse of scientific and technical information and makes it readily available to industry, business, and the general public—codified as chapter 23 of Title 15 of the United States Code (15 U.S.C. 1151-1157). The Service collects scientific and technical information; catalogs, abstracts, indexes, and permanently archives the information; disseminates information through electronic and other media; and provides information processing services to other Federal agencies.

NTIS also provides information management services to other Federal agencies to help them interact with and better serve the information needs of their own constituents. It develops, plans, evaluates, and implements business strategies for information management and dissemination services and Internet-based service business opportunities for Federal agencies; uses new and existing technologies to ensure optimal access to Government online information services; and manages service projects using in-house capabilities and through joint public-private partnerships. NTIS provides eTraining and Knowledge Management, Web services and cloud computing, distribution and fulfillment, digitization and scanning services for Federal Government agencies. http://www.ntis.gov/about

Sources of Information

Employment   Approximately 150 NTIS employees work in Northern Virginia. The Service hires professionals with skills in administration, information technology, and program management. https://www.usajobs.gov

Freedom of Information Act (FOIA)   The Office of Director handles Freedom of Information Act (FOIA) requests. The FOIA contact reviews, coordinates, and responds to requests within 20 days under the requirements of the Freedom of Information Act. http://www.ntis.gov/about/FOIA

Products   For general information or to place a telephone order, call the Customer Contact Center, 8 a.m.–6 p.m., eastern standard time. Phone, 800-553-6847. TDD, 703-487-4639. Fax, 703-605-6900. http://www.ntis.gov/products | Email: info@ntis.gov

Services   To learn more about NTIS information services for Federal agencies, call the Office of Federal Services at 703-605-6800. http://www.ntis.gov/services | Email: obdinfo@ntis.gov http://www.ntis.gov/about/contact

For further information, contact the National Technical Information Service, 5301 Shawnee Road, Alexandria, VA 22312. Phone, 703-605-6000 or 800-553-6847.

United States Patent and Trademark Office

600 Dulany Street, Alexandria, VA 22314
Phone, 571-272-8700. Internet, http://www.uspto.gov

Under Secretary, Intellectual Property / Director	MICHELLE K. LEE
Deputy Under Secretary, Intellectual Property / Deputy Director	RUSSELL D. SLIFER

[For the Patent and Trademark Office statement of organization, see the Federal Register of Apr. 14, 1975, 40 FR 16707]

The United States Patent and Trademark Office (USPTO) was established by the act of July 19, 1952 (35 U.S.C. 1) "to promote the progress of science and useful arts, by securing for limited times to authors and inventors the exclusive right to their respective writings and discoveries" (U.S. Constitution Art. I, sec. 8). The commerce clause provides the constitutional basis for the registration of trademarks.

USPTO examines and issues patents. There are three major patent categories: utility patents, design patents, and plant patents. USPTO also issues statutory invention registrations and processes international patent applications.

Through the registration of trademarks, USPTO assists businessmen and women in protecting their investments, promoting goods and services, and safeguarding consumers against confusion and deception in the marketplace. A trademark includes any distinctive word, name, symbol, device, or any combination thereof adopted and used or intended to be used by a manufacturer or merchant to identify his or her goods or services and distinguish them from those manufactured or sold by others. Trademarks are examined by the Office for compliance with various statutory requirements to prevent unfair competition and consumer deception.

In addition to the examination of patent and trademark applications, issuance of patents, and registration of trademarks, USPTO advises and assists government agencies and officials in matters involving all domestic and global aspects of intellectual property. USPTO also promotes an understanding of intellectual property protection.

USPTO provides public access to patent, trademark, and related scientific and technical information. Patents and trademarks may be reviewed and searched online or at designated Patent and Trademark Depository Libraries.

There are 80 Patent and Trademark Depository Libraries located within the United States and Puerto Rico. Additionally, USPTO's Scientific and Technical Information Center in Alexandria, VA, houses over 120,000 volumes of scientific and technical books in various languages; 90,000 bound volumes of periodicals devoted to science and technology; the official journals of 77 foreign patent organizations; and over 40 million foreign patents on paper, microfilm, microfiche, and CD–ROM. http://www.uspto.gov/about-us

Sources of Information

Data Monthly summaries for patents data and quarterly summaries for trademark data are available online. http://www.uspto.gov/learning-and-resources/statistics

Employment Information on employment opportunities is available on the "Careers" Web page. http://careers.uspto.gov

Patents Information on getting started and applying for and maintaining a patent is available online. http://www.uspto.gov/patent

Publications The "Official Gazette" journal, "Inventors Eye" newsletter, and other publications are accessible online. http://www.uspto.gov/learning-and-resources/official-gazette http://www.uspto.gov/learning-and-resources/newsletter-archives http://www.uspto.gov/about-us/news-updates

Speakers A speaker request form is available online. http://www.uspto.gov/about-us/organizational-offices/office-chief-communications-officer/speaker-request-form

Trademarks Information on getting started and applying for and maintaining a trademark is available online. http://www.uspto.gov/trademark http://www.uspto.gov/about-us/organizational-offices/office-chief-communications-officer

For further information, contact the Office of the Chief Communications Officer, United States Patent and Trademark Office, 600 Dulany Street, Alexandria, VA 22314. Phone, 571-272-8400.

DEPARTMENT OF DEFENSE

Office of the Secretary, The Pentagon, Washington, DC 20301-1155
Phone, 703-545-6700. Internet, http://www.defense.gov

Secretary of Defense — LLOYD AUSTIN
Deputy Secretary of Defense
Under Secretary of Defense for Acquisition, Technology and
  Logistics
Under Secretary of Defense Comptroller / Chief Financial
  Officer
Under Secretary of Defense for Intelligence
Under Secretary of Defense for Personnel and Readiness
Under Secretary of Defense for Policy

Principal Deputy Under Secretary of Defense Comptroller /
  DOD Chief Financial Officer
Principal Deputy Under Secretary of Defense for Acquisition,
  Technology and Logistics
Principal Under Secretary of Defense for Intelligence
Principal Under Secretary of Defense for Personnel and
  Readiness
Principal Under Secretary of Defense for Policy

Assistant Secretary of Defense for Acquisition
Assistant Secretary of Defense for Asian and Pacific Security
  Affairs
Assistant Secretary of Defense for Health Affairs
Assistant Secretary of Defense for Homeland Defense and
  Global Security
Assistant Secretary of Defense for International Security Affairs
Assistant Secretary of Defense for Legislative Affairs
Assistant Secretary of Defense for Logistics and Materiel
  Readiness
Assistant Secretary of Defense for Manpower and Reserve
  Affairs
Assistant Secretary of Defense for Nuclear, Chemical, and
  Biological Defense Programs
Assistant Secretary of Defense for Operational Energy Plans
  and Programs
Assistant Secretary of Defense for Personnel and Readiness
Assistant Secretary of Defense for Research and Engineering
Assistant Secretary of Defense for Special Operations/Low-
  Intensity Conflict

Chief Information Officer
Chief Operating Officer

Director, Administration and Management
Director, Cost Assessment and Program Evaluation
Director, Operational Test and Evaluation

168

General Counsel
Inspector General

Assistant to the Secretary of Defense for Public Affairs
Deputy Chief Management Officer

Joint Chiefs of Staff

Chair
Vice Chair
Senior Enlisted Advisor to the Chair

Chief of Naval Operations
Chief of Staff, Air Force
Chief of Staff, Army
Chief of the National Guard Bureau
Commandant of the Marine Corps

[For the Department of Defense statement of organization, see the Code of Federal Regulations, Title 32, Chapter I, Subchapter R]

The Department of Defense provides the military forces needed to deter war and protect national security. Under the President, the Secretary of Defense directs and exercises authority and control over the separately organized Departments of the Air Force, the Army, and the Navy; over the Joint Chiefs of Staff; over the combatant commands; and over defense agencies and field activities.

The National Security Act Amendments of 1949 redesignated the National Military Establishment as the Department of Defense (DOD) and established it as an executive department (10 U.S.C. 111) headed by the Secretary of Defense.

Structure The Department of Defense is composed of the Office of the Secretary of Defense; the military departments and the military services within those departments; the Chairman of the Joint Chiefs of Staff and the Joint Staff; the combatant commands; the defense agencies; DOD field activities; and such other offices, agencies, activities, and commands as may be established or designated by law or by the President or the Secretary of Defense.

Each military department is separately organized under its own Secretary and functions under the authority, direction, and control of the Secretary of Defense. The Secretary of each military department is responsible to the Secretary of Defense for the operation and efficiency of his department. Orders to the military departments are issued through the Secretaries of these departments or their designees, by the Secretary of Defense, or under authority specifically delegated in writing by the Secretary of Defense or provided by law.

The commanders of the combatant commands are responsible to the President and the Secretary of Defense for accomplishing the military missions assigned to them and exercising command authority over forces assigned to them. The operational chain of command runs from the President to the Secretary of Defense, to the commanders of the combatant commands. The Chairman of the Joint Chiefs of Staff functions within the chain of command by transmitting the orders of the President or the Secretary of Defense to the commanders of the combatant commands.

Office of the Secretary of Defense

Secretary of Defense The Secretary of Defense is the principal defense policy adviser to the President and is responsible for the formulation of general defense policy and policy related to DOD and for the execution of approved policy. Under

DEPARTMENT OF DEFENSE

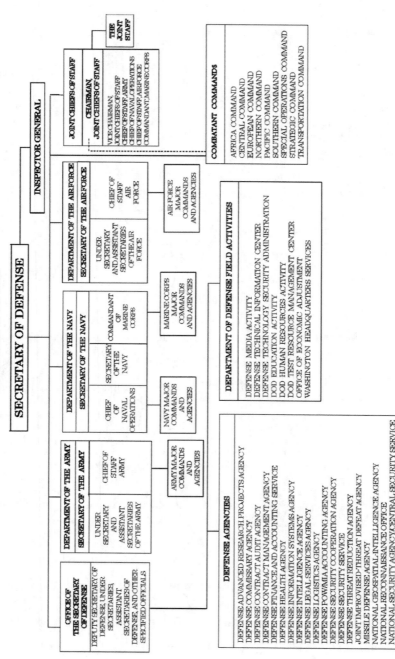

the direction of the President, the Secretary exercises authority, direction, and control over the Department of Defense. http://www.defense.gov/osd

Acquisition, Technology and Logistics   The Under Secretary of Defense for Acquisition, Technology and Logistics is the principal staff assistant and adviser to the Secretary of Defense for all matters relating to the DOD Acquisition System; research and development; modeling and simulation; systems engineering; advanced technology; developmental test and evaluation; production; systems integration; logistics; installation management; military construction; procurement; environment, safety, and occupational health management; utilities and energy management; business management modernization; document services; and nuclear, chemical, and biological defense programs. http://www.acq.osd.mil

Intelligence   The Under Secretary of Defense for Intelligence is the principal staff assistant and adviser to the Secretary and Deputy Secretary of Defense for intelligence, intelligence-related matters, counterintelligence, and security. The Under Secretary of Defense for Intelligence supervises all intelligence and intelligence-related affairs of DOD.

Networks and Information Integration   The Assistant Secretary of Defense for Networks and Information Integration is the principal staff assistant and adviser to the Secretary and Deputy Secretary of Defense for achieving and maintaining information superiority in support of DOD missions, while exploiting or denying an adversary's ability to do the same. The Assistant Secretary of Defense for Networks and Information Integration also serves as the Chief Information Officer. http://dodcio.defense.gov

Personnel and Readiness   The Under Secretary of Defense for Personnel and Readiness is the principal staff assistant and adviser to the Secretary of Defense for policy matters relating to the structure and readiness of the total force. Functional areas include readiness; civilian and military personnel policies, programs, and systems; civilian and military equal opportunity programs; health policies, programs, and activities; Reserve component programs,

policies, and activities; family policy, dependents' education, and personnel support programs; mobilization planning and requirements; language capabilities and programs; and the Federal Voting Assistance Program. The Under Secretary of Defense for Personnel and Readiness also serves as the Chief Human Capital Officer. http://prhome.defense.gov

Policy   The Under Secretary of Defense for Policy is the principal staff assistant and adviser to the Secretary of Defense for policy matters relating to overall international security policy and political-military affairs and represents the Department at the National Security Council and other external agencies involved with national security policy. The Under Secretary's areas of activity include homeland defense; NATO affairs; foreign military sales; arms limitation agreements; international trade and technology security; regional security affairs; special operations and low-intensity conflict; stability operations; integration of departmental plans and policies with overall national security objectives; drug control policy, requirements, priorities, systems, resources, and programs; and issuance of policy guidance affecting departmental programs. http://policy.defense.gov

Special Staff   A special staff assists the Secretary and Deputy Secretary of Defense. This special staff of assistants includes the Assistant Secretaries of Defense for Legislative Affairs and for Public Affairs; the Under Secretary of Defense (Comptroller), who also functions as the Chief Financial Officer; the General Counsel; the Inspector General; the Assistant to the Secretary of Defense for Intelligence Oversight; the Directors of Administration and Management, of Operational Test and Evaluation, of Business Transformation, of Net Assessment, of Program Analysis and Evaluation; and other officers whom the Secretary of Defense determines are necessary to help carry out his or her duties and responsibilities. http://www.defense.gov/About-DoD/Leaders

Joint Chiefs of Staff

The Joint Chiefs of Staff consist of the Chairman, the Vice Chairman, the Chief of Staff of the Army, the Chief of Naval

Operations, the Chief of Staff of the Air Force, and the Commandant of the Marine Corps. The Chairman of the Joint Chiefs of Staff is the principal military adviser to the President, the National Security Council, and the Secretary of Defense. The other members of the Joint Chiefs of Staff are military advisers who may provide additional information upon request from the President, the National Security Council, or the Secretary of Defense. They may also submit their advice when it does not agree with that of the Chairman. Subject to the authority of the President and the Secretary of Defense, the Chairman of the Joint Chiefs of Staff is responsible for assisting the President and the Secretary of Defense in providing strategic direction and planning for the Armed Forces; making recommendations for the assignment of responsibilities within the Armed Forces; comparing the capabilities of American and allied Armed Forces with those of potential adversaries; preparing and reviewing contingency plans that conform to policy guidance; preparing joint logistic and mobility plans; and recommending assignment of logistic and mobility responsibilities.

The Chairman, while so serving, holds the grade of general or admiral and outranks all other officers of the Armed Forces.

The Vice Chairman of the Joint Chiefs performs duties assigned by the Chairman, with the approval of the Secretary of Defense. The Vice Chairman acts as Chairman when there is a vacancy in the office of the Chairman or in the absence or disability of the Chairman. The Vice Chairman, while so serving, holds the grade of general or admiral and outranks all other officers of the Armed Forces except the Chairman of the Joint Chiefs of Staff. http://www.jcs.mil

Joint Staff   The Joint Staff, under the Chairman of the Joint Chiefs of Staff, assists the Chairman and the other members of the Joint Chiefs of Staff in carrying out their responsibilities.

The Joint Staff is headed by a Director who is selected by the Chairman in consultation with the other members of the Joint Chiefs of Staff and with the approval of the Secretary of Defense. Officers assigned to serve on the Joint Staff are selected by the Chairman

in approximately equal numbers from the Army, Navy, Marine Corps, and Air Force. http://www.jcs.mil/About.aspx

Combatant Commands

The combatant commands are military commands with broad continuing missions maintaining the security and defense of the United States against attack; supporting and advancing the national policies and interests of the United States and discharging U.S. military responsibilities in their assigned areas; and preparing plans, conducting operations, and coordinating activities of the forces assigned to them in accordance with the directives of higher authority. The operational chain of command runs from the President to the Secretary of Defense, to the commanders of the combatant commands. The Chairman of the Joint Chiefs of Staff serves as the spokesman for the commanders of the combatant commands, especially on the administrative requirements of their commands. http://www.defense.gov/Sites/Unified-Combatant-Commands

Field Activities

Counterintelligence Field Activity   The DOD Counterintelligence Field Activity was established in 2002 to build a Defense counterintelligence (CI) system that is informed by national goals and objectives and supports the protection of DOD personnel and critical assets from foreign intelligence services, foreign terrorists, and other clandestine or covert threats. The desired end is a transformed Defense CI system that integrates and synchronizes the counterintelligence activities of the military departments, defense agencies, Joint Staff, and combatant commands.

Defense Health Agency   The Defense Health Agency (DHA) manages the activities of the Military Health System. It is also the market manager for the National Capital Region enhanced Multi-Service Market, which includes Walter Reed National Military Medical Center and Fort Belvoir Community Hospital. http://www.dha.mil

Defense Media Activity   Defense Media Activity (DMA) gathers Defense news and information from all departmental levels and reports that news and information to DOD audiences worldwide through American Forces Network online, radio, television, and through publications. DMA reports news on individual airmen, marines, sailors, soldiers, and DOD civilian employees to the American public through the Hometown News Service. DMA provides World Wide Web infrastructure and services for DOD organizations. It collects, processes, and stores DOD imagery products created by the Department and makes them available to the American public. It trains the Department's public affairs and visual information military and civilian professionals. DMA also operates Stars and Stripes, a news and information organization, free of Government editorial control and censorship, for military audiences overseas. http://www.dma.mil

Defense Prisoner of War / Missing in Action Accounting Agency   The Defense POW / MIA Accounting Agency (DPAA) provides centralized management of prisoner of war and missing personnel affairs within the DOD. DPAA's primary responsibilities include leadership for and policy oversight over all efforts to account for Americans still missing from past conflicts and the recovery of and accounting for those who may become isolated in hostile territory in future conflicts. DPAA also provides administrative and logistical support to the U.S.-Russia Joint Commission on POW / MIAs, conducts research and analysis to help resolve cases of those unaccounted for, examines DOD documents for possible public disclosure, and maintains viable channels of communications on POW / MIA matters between the DOD and Congress, the families of the missing, and the American public. http://www.dpaa.mil

Defense Technical Information Center   The Defense Technical Information Center (DTIC) is a field activity in the Office of the Under Secretary of Defense for Acquisition, Technology and Logistics. It operates under the authority, direction, and control of the Director of Defense Research and Engineering. DTIC provides defense scientific and technical information, offers controlled access to defense information, and designs and hosts more than 100 DOD Web sites. DTIC's collections include technical reports, summaries of research

in progress, independent research and development material, defense technology transfer agreements, and DOD planning documents. http://www.dtic.mil/dtic/about/about.html

Defense Technology Security Administration   The Defense Technology Security Administration (DTSA) is the central DOD point of contact for development and implementation of technology security policies governing defense articles and services and dual-use commodities. DTSA administers the development and implementation of DOD technology security policies on international transfers of defense-related goods, services, and technologies. It does so to ensure that critical U.S. military technological advantages are preserved, transfers that could prove detrimental to U.S. security interests are controlled and limited, weapons of mass destruction and their means of delivery do not proliferate, diversion of defense-related goods to terrorists is prevented, legitimate defense cooperation with foreign friends and allies is supported, and the health of the defense industrial base is assured. http://www.dtsa.mil/SitePages/default.aspx

Education Activity   The Department of Defense Education Activity (DODEA) was established in 1992. It consists of two subordinate organizational entities: the Department of Defense Dependents Schools (DODDS) and the Department of Defense Domestic Dependent Elementary and Secondary Schools (DDESS). DODEA formulates, develops, and implements policies, technical guidance, and standards for the effective management of Defense dependents education activities and programs. It also plans, directs, coordinates, and manages the education programs for eligible dependents of U.S. military and civilian personnel stationed overseas and stateside; evaluates the programmatic and operational policies and procedures for DODDS and DDESS; and provides education activity representation at meetings and deliberations of educational panels and advisory groups. http://www.dodea.edu/Americas

Human Resources Field Activity   The Department of Defense Human Resources Activity (DODHRA) enhances the operational effectiveness and efficiency of a host of dynamic and diverse programs supporting the Office of the Under Secretary of Defense for Personnel and Readiness. The Field Activity supports policy development, performs cutting-edge research and expert analysis, supports readiness and reengineering efforts, manages the largest automated personnel data repositories in the world, prepares tomorrow's leaders through robust developmental programs, supports recruiting and retaining the best and brightest, and delivers both benefits and critical services to warfighters and their families. http://www.dhra.mil/website/index.shtml

Office of Economic Adjustment The Office of Economic Adjustment (OEA) assists communities that are adversely affected by base closures, expansions, or realignments and Defense contract or program cancellations. OEA provides technical and financial assistance to those communities and coordinates other Federal agencies' involvement through the Defense Economic Adjustment Program. http://www.oea.gov

Test Resource Management The Test Resource Management Center (TRMC) is a DOD Field Activity under the authority, direction, and control of the Under Secretary of Defense for Acquisition, Technology and Logistics. The Center develops policy, plans for, and assesses the adequacy of the major range and test facility base to provide adequate testing in support of development, acquisition, fielding, and sustainment of defense systems. TRMC develops and maintains the test and evaluation resources strategic plan, reviews the proposed DOD test and evaluation budgets, and certifies the adequacy of the proposed budgets and whether they provide balanced support of the strategic plan. TRMC manages the Central Test and Evaluation Investment Program, the Test and Evaluation Science and Technology Program, and the Joint Mission Environment Test Capability Program. http://www.acq.osd.mil/dte-trmc

Washington Headquarters Services Washington Headquarters Services (WHS), established as a DOD Field Activity on October 1, 1977, is under the authority and control of the Deputy Chief Management Officer. WHS provides a range of administrative and operational services to the Office of the Secretary of Defense, specified DOD components, the general public, and for Federal Government activities. WHS services include contracting and procurement; data systems and information technology support; Defense facilities, directives and records, and financial management; enterprise information technology infrastructure, human resource, legal, library, and personnel security services; evaluation and planning functions; Pentagon renovation and construction; and support for advisory boards and commissions. http://www.whs.mil

Sources of Information

Budget Data The Defense Technical Information Center (DTIC) sponsors a Web site that features congressional budget data pertaining to the DOD. The DTIC posts data from each budget report once it is filed and made available on the Library of Congress' Web site. The data are accessible in Portable Document Format (PDF) and Excel spreadsheet format. http://www.dtic.mil/congressional_budget

Business Opportunities Information on and resources for acquisition, business, contracting, and subcontracting opportunities are available on the DOD's Web site. http://www.defense.gov/Resources/Contract-Resources

The Office of Small Business Programs supports the participation of small businesses in the acquisition of goods and services for the DOD. http://www.acq.osd.mil/osbp

Career Opportunities The DOD employs over 718,000 civilian personnel. For additional information on applying for DOD job opportunities, contact Washington Headquarters Services–Human Resources Servicing Team. Phone, 614-692-0252. https://dod.usajobs.gov

Dictionary The Defense Technical Information Center's Web site features the "DOD Dictionary of Military and Associated Terms," which is commonly called the "DOD Dictionary." The dictionary facilitates communication and mutual understanding within the DOD, with external Federal agencies, and between the United States and its international partners by standardizing military and associated terminology. http://www.dtic.mil/doctrine/dod_dictionary

Freedom of Information Act (FOIA) Approved by President Lyndon B. Johnson in 1966, the statute generally provides that any person has the right to request access to Federal agency information or records. Upon receiving a written request, the Federal agency holding the desired document or record must disclose it. Some records, however, are shielded from disclosure by one of the FOIA's nine exemptions or three exclusions. http://open.defense.gov/Transparency/FOIA.aspx

History A short history of the Pentagon, from construction to completion, is available on the Pentagon Tours Office's Web site. https://pentagontours.osd.mil/Tours/construction.jsp

Joint Chiefs of Staff The Joint Chiefs of Staff maintain a Web site. http://www.jcs.mil

News The DOD posts news releases on its Web site. http://www.defense.gov/News/News-Releases

Plain Language The DOD aims to write documents in readable English by adhering to Federal plain language guidelines. http://www.dtic.mil/whs/directives/plainlanguage.html

Popular Resources A page of popular DOD resources is available on the DOD Web site. http://www.defense.gov/Resources

Social Media The DOD tweets announcements and other newsworthy items on Twitter. https://twitter.com/DeptofDefense

The DOD has a Facebook account. https://www.facebook.com/DeptofDefense

The DOD posts videos on its YouTube channel. https://www.youtube.com/user/DODvClips/featured

Site Index The Web site index allows visitors to look for specific topics or to browse content that aligns with their interests. http://www.defense.gov/Site-Index

Speakers Civilian and military officials from the DOD are available to speak to public and private sector groups interested in defense-related topics, including the global war on terrorism. Requests for speakers should be addressed to the Director for Community Relations and Public Liaison, 1400 Defense Pentagon, Room 2C546, Washington, DC 20310-1400.

Today in the DOD The "Today in the Department of Defense" Web page features contracts, news and casualty releases, photos, press advisories, speeches, and transcripts on a daily basis. http://www.defense.gov/Today-in-DoD

Tours For information on guided tours of the Pentagon, contact the Pentagon Tours Office. Phone, 703-697-1776. http://pentagontours.osd.mil | Email: osd.pentagon.pa.mbx.pentagon-tours-schedule@mail.mil

Web Sites A list of DOD Web site links is available online. http://www.defense.gov/Military-Services/DoD-Websites

An A–Z list of DOD Web site links is available online. http://www.defense.gov/Military-Services/A-Z-List http://www.defense.gov/Contact

For further information concerning the Department of Defense, contact the Director, Directorate for Public Inquiry and Analysis, Office of the Assistant Secretary of Defense for Public Affairs, 1400 Defense Pentagon, Washington, DC 20301-1400. Phone, 703- 697-9312.

Department of the Air Force

1690 Air Force Pentagon, Washington, DC 20330-1670
Phone, 703-697-6061. Internet, http://www.af.mil

Air Force Secretariat

Secretary of The Air Force	Dr. Heather A. Wilson
Under Secretary of the Air Force	Lisa S. Disbrow
Administrative Assistant	Patricia J. Zarodkiewicz
Auditor General	Daniel F. McMillin
General Counsel	Joseph M. McDade, Jr.

Information Dominance and Chief Information Officer (A6)	Lt. Gen. William J. Bender
Inspector General	Lt. Gen. Anthony J. Rock
Legislative Liaison	Maj. Gen. Steven L. Basham
Assistant Secretary, Acquisition	Darlene Costello
Assistant Secretary, Financial Management and Comptroller	Doug Bennett
Assistant Secretary, Installations, Environment, and Energy	Richard K. Hartley
Assistant Secretary, Manpower and Reserve Affairs	Daniel R. Sitterly
Deputy Under Secretary for Management	Marilyn M. Thomas
Deputy Under Secretary, International Affairs	Heidi H. Grant
Deputy Under Secretary, Space	Winston Beauchamp
Director, Air Force Small Business Programs	Mark S. Teskey
Director, Public Affairs	Brig. Gen. Edward W. Thomas, Jr.

Air Staff

Chief of Staff	Gen. David L. Goldfein
Vice Chief of Staff	Gen. Stephen W. Wilson
Chief Master Sergeant of the Air Force	CMSAF Kaleth O. Wright
Assistant Vice Chief of Staff	Lt. Gen. Stayce D. Harris
Judge Advocate General	Lt. Gen. Christopher F. Burne
Surgeon General	Lt. Gen. Mark A. Ediger
Chief of Air Force Reserve	Lt. Gen. Maryanne Miller
Chief of Chaplains	Maj. Gen. Dondi Constin
Chief of Safety	Maj. Gen. Andrew Mueller
Chief of Staff, Strategic Deterrence and Nuclear Integration (A10)	Lt. Gen. Jack Weinstein
Chief Scientist	Greg L. Zacharias
Deputy Chief of Staff, Intelligence, Surveillance and Reconnaissance (A2)	Lt. Gen. VeraLinn Jamieson
Deputy Chief of Staff, Logistics, Engineering and Force Protection (A4)	Lt. Gen. John B. Cooper
Deputy Chief of Staff, Manpower, Personnel and Services (A1)	Lt. Gen. Gina Grosso
Deputy Chief of Staff, Operations, Plans and Requirements (A3)	Lt. Gen. Mark C. Nowland
Deputy Chief of Staff, Strategic Plans and Programs (A5/8)	Lt. Gen. Jerry D. Harris, Jr.
Director, Air Force Sexual Assault Prevention and Response	Maj. Gen. James C. Johnson
Director, Air National Guard	Lt. Gen. L. Scott Rice
Director, History and Museums Policies and Programs	Walter A. Grudzinskas
Director, Studies and Analyses, Assessments (A9)	Kevin E. Williams
Director, Test and Evaluation	Devin Cate

Major Commands

Air Combat Command	Gen. James M. Holmes
Air Education and Training Command	Lt. Gen. Darryl L. Roberson
Air Force Global Strike Command	Gen. Robin Rand
Air Force Materiel Command	Gen. Ellen M. Pawlikowski
Air Force Reserve Command	Lt. Gen. Maryanne Miller

Air Force Space Command	Gen. John W. Raymond
Air Force Special Operations Command	Lt. Gen. Marshall B. Webb
Air Mobility Command	Gen. Carlton D. Everhart II
Pacific Air Forces	Gen. Terrence J. O'Shaughnessy
U.S. Air Forces in Europe	Gen. Tod D. Wolters

The Department of the Air Force defends the United States by providing air, space, and cyberspace capabilities.

The Department of the Air Force (USAF) was established as part of the National Military Establishment by the National Security Act of 1947 (61 Stat. 502) and came into being on September 18, 1947. The National Security Act Amendments of 1949 redesignated the National Military Establishment as the Department of Defense, established it as an executive department, and made the Department of the Air Force a military department within the Department of Defense (63 Stat. 578). The Department of the Air Force is separately organized under the Secretary of the Air Force. It operates under the authority, direction, and control of the Secretary of Defense (10 U.S.C. 8010). The Department comprises the Office of the Secretary of the Air Force, the Air Staff, and field organizations.

Secretary   The Secretary and Secretariat Staff oversee matters of organization, training, logistical support, maintenance, welfare of personnel, administrative, recruiting, research and development, and other activities that the President or Secretary of Defense prescribes. http://www.af.mil/AboutUs/AirForceSeniorLeaders/SECAF.aspx

Air Staff   The Air Staff assists the Secretary, the Under Secretary, the Assistant Secretaries, and the Chief of Staff in carrying out their responsibilities.

Field Organizations   The major commands, field operating agencies, and direct reporting units constitute the field organizations of the Air Force. They are organized primarily on a functional basis in the United States and on a geographic basis overseas. These commands are responsible for accomplishing certain phases of the Air Force's worldwide activities. They also organize, administer, equip, and train subordinate elements to accomplish assigned missions.

Major Commands: Continental U.S. Commands

Air Combat Command   The Air Combat Command operates CONUS-based, combat-coded fighter and attack aircraft. It organizes, trains, equips, and maintains combat-ready forces for rapid deployment and employment while ensuring strategic air defense forces are ready to meet the challenges of peacetime air sovereignty and wartime air defense. http://www.acc.af.mil

Air Education and Training Command   The Air Education and Training Command recruits, assesses, commissions, educates, and trains Air Force enlisted and officer personnel. It provides basic military training, initial and advanced technical training, flying training, and professional military and post-secondary education. The Command also conducts Air Force security assistance, joint, medical service, and readiness training. http://www.aetc.af.mil

Air Force Global Strike Command   The Air Force Global Strike Command is responsible for the Nation's three intercontinental ballistic missile wings; the Air Force's bomber force, including the B–1, B–2, and B–52 wings; the Long Range Strike Bomber program; and operational and maintenance support to organizations within the nuclear enterprise. http://www.afgsc.af.mil

Air Force Materiel Command   The Air Force Materiel Command delivers expeditionary capabilities through research, development, test, evaluation, acquisition, modernization, and sustainment of aerospace weapon systems throughout their life cycles. Those weapon systems include Air Force fighter, bomber, cargo, and attack fleets and armament. They also include net-centric command and control assets; intelligence, surveillance, and reconnaissance assets; and combat support

Department of the Air Force

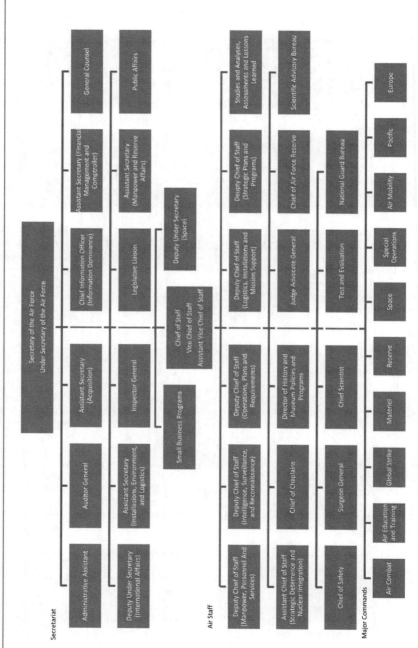

information systems. The command oversees basic research and development that support air, space, and cyberspace capabilities. The command relies on an integrated, efficient life cycle management approach to ensure the best possible support to warfighters. http://www.afmc.af.mil

Air Force Reserve Command   The Air Force Reserve Command provides the Air Force with approximately 14 percent of the total force and approximately 4 percent of the manpower budget. Reservists support air, space, and cyberspace superiority; command and control; global integrated intelligence surveillance reconnaissance; global precision attack; nuclear deterrence operations; special operations; rapid global mobility; and personnel recovery. They also perform aircraft flight testing, space operations, and aerial port operations, as well as communications, civil engineer, military training, mobility support, security forces, services, and transportation missions. http://www.afrc.af.mil

Air Force Space Command   The Air Force Space Command provides space and cyberspace capabilities such as missile warning, space control, spacelift, satellite operations, and designated cyberspace activities. http://www.afspc.af.mil

Air Force Special Operations Command   The Air Force Special Operations Command provides the air component of U.S. Special Operations Command. The command deploys specialized air power and delivers special operations combat power wherever and whenever needed. It provides agile combat support, combat search and rescue, information warfare, precision aerospace fires, psychological operations, and specialized aerospace mobility and refueling to unified commands. http://www.afsoc.af.mil

Air Mobility Command   The Air Mobility Command provides airlift, air refueling, special air missions, and aeromedical evacuation for U.S. forces. It also airlifts forces to theater commands to support wartime tasking. http://www.amc.af.mil

Major Commands: Overseas Commands

Pacific Air Forces   The Pacific Air Forces deliver rapid and precise air, space, and cyberspace capabilities to protect the United States, its territories, and its allies and partners; provide integrated air and missile warning and defense; promote interoperability throughout the Pacific area of responsibility; maintain strategic access and freedom of movement across all domains; and posture to respond across the full spectrum of military contingencies to restore regional security. http://www.pacaf.af.mil

U.S. Air Forces in Europe   The U.S. Air Forces in Europe (USAFE) execute the Air Force, European Command, and Africa Command missions with forward-based air power and infrastructure to conduct and enable theater and global operations. The USAFE direct air operations in a theater that spans three continents, covers more than 19 million square miles, contains 104 independent states, produces more than a quarter of the world's gross domestic product, and comprises more than a quarter of Earth's population. http://www.usafe.af.mil

Field Operating Agencies

Air Force Agency for Modeling and Simulation   The Air Force Agency for Modeling and Simulation provides seamless integration of cross-functional live, virtual, and constructive operational training environments that allow war fighters to maximize performance and optimize decisionmaking. The agency works with combatant commands, major commands, the Air Force Reserve Command, the Air National Guard, the Air Force headquarters, direct reporting units, and field operating agencies to provide the necessary development and implementation standards for common access and interoperability within the live, virtual, and constructive domains for efficient and secure global operations. http://www.afams.af.mil

Air Force Audit Agency   The Air Force Audit Agency provides all levels of Air Force management with independent, objective, and quality audit services by reviewing and promoting operational economy, effectiveness, and efficiency; evaluating programs and activities to achieve intended results; and assessing and improving financial reporting. http://www.afaa.af.mil

Air Force Cost Analysis Agency   The Air Force Cost Analysis Agency performs nonadvocate cost analyses for major space, aircraft, and information system programs. The agency supports the departmentwide cost analysis program by developing and maintaining cost-estimating tools, techniques, and infrastructure. It provides guidance, analytical support, quantitative risk analyses, and special studies to improve long-range planning, force structure, analysis of alternatives, and lifecycle cost analyses.

Air Force Flight Standards Agency   The Air Force Flight Standards Agency performs worldwide inspection of airfields, navigation systems, and instrument approaches. It provides flight standards to develop Air Force instrument requirements and certifies procedures and directives for cockpit display and navigation systems. It also provides air traffic control and airlift procedures and evaluates air traffic control systems and airspace management procedures.

Air Force Historical Research Agency   The Air Force Historical Research Agency serves as a repository for Air Force historical records and maintains research facilities for scholars and the general public. http://www.afhra.af.mil/index.asp

Air Force Inspection Agency   The Air Force Inspection Agency provides independent inspection, evaluation, oversight, training and analysis to improve the effectiveness and efficiency of the Air Force. http://www.af.mil/AboutUs/FactSheets/Display/tabid/224/Article/104564/air-force-inspection-agency.aspx

Air Force Legal Operations Agency   The Air Force Legal Operations Agency includes all senior defense, senior trial, appellate defense, and Government counsel in the Air Force, as well as all Air Force civil litigators who defend the Air Force against civil lawsuits that claim damages and seek other remedies in contracts, environmental, labor, and tort litigation.

Air Force Manpower Analysis Agency   The Air Force Manpower Analysis Agency provides analysis and develops tools for helping Air Force and Department of Defense senior leaders make decisions affecting total force manpower requirements. The agency supports the Under Secretary of the Air Force for Management's efforts to improve processes and carries out departmentwide transformation initiatives. It also oversees human capital planning and training to develop and sustain manpower-specific capabilities at adequate levels. http://www.af.mil/AboutUs/FactSheets/Display/tabid/224/Article/104598/air-force-manpower-agency.aspx

Air Force Medical Operations Agency   The Air Force Medical Operations Agency assists the Air Force Surgeon General in developing plans, programs, and policies for aerospace medicine, bioenvironmental engineering, clinical investigations, family advocacy, health promotion, military public health, quality assurance, radioactive material management, and the medical service. http://www.airforcemedicine.af.mil/afmoa

Air Force Medical Support Agency   The Air Force Medical Support Agency provides consultative support and policy development for the Air Force Surgeon General in medical force management. It also supports ground and air expeditionary medical capabilities used in global, homeland security, and force health protection, as well as all aspects of medical and dental services, aerospace medicine operations, and medical support functions.

Air Force Mortuary Affairs Operations   The Air Force Mortuary Affairs Operations, a field operating agency of the Deputy Chief of Staff for Manpower, Personnel and Services, works to support the entire Department of Defense and other Federal entities ensuring dignity, honor and respect to the fallen, and care, service, and support to their families. http://www.mortuary.af.mil

Air Force Office of Special Investigations   The Air Force Office of Special Investigations identifies, exploits, and neutralizes criminal, terrorist, and intelligence threats to the U.S. Air Force, Department of Defense, and U.S. Government. Its primary responsibilities are criminal investigations and counterintelligence services. It also protects critical technologies and information, detects and mitigates threats, provides global specialized services, conducts major criminal investigations, and offensively engages foreign adversaries and threats. http://www.osi.af.mil

Air Force Operations Group   The Air Force Operations Group collects, processes, analyzes, and communicates information, enabling situational awareness of USAF operations worldwide. This awareness facilitates timely, responsive, and effective decisionmaking by senior USAF leaders and combatant commanders.

Air Force Personnel Center   The Air Force Personnel Center ensures that commanders around the world have enough skilled Air Force personnel to carry out the mission. The center also runs programs affecting the entire life cycle of military and civilian Air Force personnel from accession through retirement. http://www.af.mil/AboutUs/FactSheets/Display/tabid/224/Article/104554/air-force-personnel-center.aspx

Air Force Program Executive Offices   The Air Force Program Executive Offices (PEOs) oversee the execution of a program throughout its entire lifecycle. While the PEOs are not part of USAF headquarters, they report on acquisition and program-specific issues directly to the Air Force Service Acquisition Executive and the Assistant Secretary of the Air Force for Acquisition. Air Force PEOs are currently responsible for diverse programs in a range of areas: aircraft, command and control and combat support systems, Joint Strike Fighter, and weapons. http://ww3.safaq.hq.af.mil/organizations/index.asp

Air Force Public Affairs Agency   The Air Force Public Affairs Agency manages the Air Force media center. The center collects, archives, and distributes Air Force imagery; manages licensing and branding of Air Force trademarks; provides policy guidance and oversight for the Air Force's Web site and social media programs; operates the Air Force's official social media program; composes original musical arrangements for Air Force regional bands; and develops training curricula and requirements for the Air Force's nearly 6,000 public affairs practitioners. http://www.publicaffairs.af.mil

Air Force Review Boards Agency   The Air Force Review Boards Agency manages various military and civilian appellate processes for the Secretary of the Air Force. http://www.af.mil/AboutUs/FactSheets/Display/tabid/224/Article/104511/air-force-review-boards-agency.aspx

Air Force Safety Center   The Air Force Safety Center promotes safety to reduce the number and severity of mishaps. It also supports combat readiness by developing, implementing, executing, and evaluating Air Force aviation, ground, weapons, nuclear surety, space, and system programs. http://www.safety.af.mil

Air National Guard Readiness Center   The Air National Guard Readiness Center performs the operational and technical tasks associated with manning, equipping, and training Air National Guard units to meet required readiness levels. http://www.angrc.ang.af.mil

National Air and Space Intelligence Center   The National Air and Space Intelligence Center (NASIC) assesses foreign air and space threats. It creates integrated, predictive intelligence in the domains of air, space, and cyberspace to support military operations, force modernization, and policymaking. NASIC analyzes data on foreign aerospace forces and weapons systems to determine performance characteristics, capabilities, vulnerabilities, and intentions. These assessments are used to shape national security and defense policies. NASIC personnel also play a role in weapons treaty negotiations and verification. http://www.nasic.af.mil

Direct Reporting Units

Air Force District of Washington   The Air Force District of Washington supports Headquarters Air Force and other Air Force units in the National Capital Region. http://www.afdw.af.mil

Air Force Operational Test and Evaluation Center   The Air Force Operational Test and Evaluation Center plans and conducts test and evaluation procedures to determine operational effectiveness and suitability of new or modified USAF systems and their capacity to meet mission needs. http://www.afotec.af.mil

U.S. Air Force Academy   The U.S. Air Force Academy provides academic and military instruction and experience to prepare future USAF career officers. The Academy offers Bachelor of Science degrees in 31 academic majors, and upon completion, graduates receive commissions as second lieutenants. http://www.usafa.af.mil

Sources of Information

Employment   Members of the Air Force civilian service work side by side with active duty airmen. They are a diverse group of professionals: contract specialists, engineers, human resources specialists, intelligence experts, mechanics, scientists, teachers, and more. https://afciviliancareers.com/content/home-air-force-civilian-service

Factsheets   Factsheets contain current information and statistics on Air Force careers, organizations, inventory, and equipment—including aircraft and weapons. http://www.af.mil/AboutUs/FactSheets.aspx | Email: DMAPublicAffairs@mail.mil

Freedom of Information Act (FOIA)   The Freedom of Information and Privacy Act Office manages the policy and procedural guidance for the Freedom of Information Act (FOIA), Privacy Act (PA) and Quality of Information (QIP) programs in accordance with applicable laws. http://www.foia.af.mil/Welcome.aspx

Links to FOIA requester service centers are available online. The service centers are grouped, by base and by command, in two lists. http://www.foia.af.mil/Offices

Frequently Asked Questions (FAQs)   The Air Force provides answers to FAQs on its web-site. http://www.af.mil/Questions.aspx

History   For over a century, the Air Force has relied on the bravery and skill of American airmen to protect the United States in the air, space, and cyberspace. An overview of that history is available online. https://www.airforce.com/mission/history

Inspector General (IG)   The IG receives and investigates complaints of abuse, fraud, and waste involving Air Force personnel or programs. http://www.af.mil/InspectorGeneralComplaints.aspx | Email: usaf.ighotline@mail.mil

Intelligence, Surveillance, and Reconnaissance (ISR)   The Air Force's web-site features a section dedicated to ISR activities and news. http://www.af.mil/ISR.aspx

Joining the Air Force   To learn about its mission, how to join, and about educational, training, and career opportunities that

enlistment offers, visit the Air Force's recruitment Web site. https://www.airforce.com/how-to-join

Medal of Honor   Members of the Air Force and its predecessor organizations have earned Medals of Honor. The medal is awarded for conspicuous gallantry and intrepidity at the risk of life above and beyond the call of duty. http://www.af.mil/MedalofHonor.aspx

News   The Air Force posts announcements, art, commentaries, news items, and photos on its Web site. Air Force TV and radio news are also accessible online. http://www.af.mil/News.aspx | Email: DMAPublicAffairs@mail.mil

"Air Force Magazine" is posted online. Beginning in January 2013, full issues are available. Beginning in November 2015, HTML5 versions are available . http://www.airforcemag.com/MagazineArchive/Pages/default.aspx

Reading List   The Air Force Chief of Staff's annual reading list (2016) is available on the Department's Web site. An archives of the reading list, starting with the year 2007, is also available online. http://static.dma.mil/usaf/csafreadinglist/01_books.html

Sexual Assault   The "Sexual Assault Prevention and Response" (SAPR) Web page has information, policies, and reports on sexual assault, as well as links leading to additional resources within the Department of Defense (DOD) community and to external resources. http://www.af.mil/SAPR.aspx

The "SAPR" Web page also provides access to the Safe Helpline—an anonymous, confidential, and free crisis support service for DOD community members who have been affected by sexual assault. Phone, 877-995-5247. https://www.safehelpline.org/about-dod-safe-helpline

Social Media   The Air Force has a blog and maintains a social media presence on Facebook, Flickr, Instagram, Twitter, and YouTube. The Web site provides shortcuts to the different platforms as well as social media resources. http://www.af.mil/AFSites/SocialMediaSites.aspx

Strategic Documents   The site contains various "CSAF Focus Area", and other strategic documents in Portable Document Format (PDF). http://www.af.mil/Airpower4America.aspx

Suicide Prevention   The "Suicide Prevention" Web page promotes resources like the ACE (Ask, Care, and Escort) Card and provides access, by phone or confidential online chat, to the Military Crisis Line. Phone, 800-273-8255. http://www.af.mil/SuicidePrevention.aspx

Web sites   A directory of all registered Air Force Web sites is available online. http://www.af.mil/ContactUs.aspx

For further information concerning the Department of the Air Force, contact the Office of the Director of Public Affairs, Department of the Air Force, 1690 Air Force Pentagon, Washington, DC 20330-1670. Phone, 703-697-6061. http://www.af.mil/ContactUs.aspx

For further information concerning the Department of the Air Force, contact the Office of the Director of Public Affairs, Department of the Air Force, 1690 Air Force Pentagon, Washington, DC 20330-1670. Phone, 703-697-6061.

Department of the Army

The Pentagon, Washington, DC 20310
Phone, 703-695-6518. Internet, http://www.army.mil

Executive Office

Secretary of the Army	ROBERT SPEER, ACTING
Under Secretary of the Army	KARL F. SCHNEIDER, ACTING
Administrative Assistant to the Secretary of the Army	GERALD B. O'KEEFE
Auditor General	ANNE L. RICHARDS
Deputy Under Secretary of the Army	THOMAS E. HAWLEY
Director, Small Business Programs	TOMMY L. MARKS
Executive Director, Army National Military Cemeteries	PATRICK K. HALLINAN
General Counsel	(VACANCY)
Inspector General	LT. GEN. DAVID E. QUANTOCK
Assistant Secretary of the Army, Acquisition, Logistics and Technology	STEFFANIE EASTER
Assistant Secretary of the Army, Civil Works	JO-ELLEN DARCY
Assistant Secretary of the Army, Financial Management / Comptroller	ROBERT M. SPEER
Assistant Secretary of the Army, Installations, Energy and Environment	KATHERINE G. HAMMACK
Assistant Secretary of the Army, Manpower and Reserve Affairs	DEBRA S. WADA
Chief Information Officer (G–6)	MAJ. GEN. BRUCE T. CRAWFORD
Chief of Legislative Liaison	MAJ. GEN. LAURA E. RICHARDSON
Chief of Public Affairs	BRIG. GEN. OMAR J. JONES IV

Office of the Chief of Staff

Chief of Staff of the Army	GEN. MARK A. MILLEY
Vice Chief of Staff of the Army	GEN. DANIEL B. ALLYN
Director of the Army Staff	LT. GEN. GARY H. CHEEK
Vice Director of the Army Staff	STEVEN J. REDMANN

Army Staff

Sergeant Major of the Army	SMA DANIEL A. DAILEY
Chief of the National Guard Bureau	GEN. JOSEPH LENGYEL
Assistant Chief of Staff, Installation Management	LT. GEN. GWEN BINGHAM
Chief of Army Reserve	LT. GEN. CHARLES D. LUCKEY
Chief of Chaplains	MAJ. GEN. PAUL K. HURLEY

Chief of Engineers	Lt. Gen. Todd T. Semonite
Director, Army National Guard	Lt. Gen. Timothy J. Kadavy
Judge Advocate General	Lt. Gen. Flora D. Darpino
Provost Marshal General	Maj. Gen. Mark S. Inch
Surgeon General	Lt. Gen. Nadja Y. West
Deputy Chiefs of Staff	
Financial Management (G–8)	Lt. Gen. John M. Murray
Intelligence (G–2)	Lt. Gen. Robert P. Ashley, Jr.
Logistics (G–4)	Lt. Gen. Gustave F. Perna
Operations (G–3/5/7)	Lt. Gen. Joseph Anderson
Personnel (G–1)	Lt. Gen. James C. McConville

Commands

Commanding Generals	
U.S. Army Forces Command	Gen. Robert B. Abrams
U.S. Army Materiel Command	Gen. Gustave F. Perna
U.S. Army Training and Doctrine Command	Gen. David G. Perkins

Army Service Component Commands

Commanding Generals	
U.S. Army Africa / Southern European Task Force	Maj. Gen. Joseph P. Harrington
U.S. Army Central	Lt. Gen. Michael X. Garrett
U.S. Army Europe	Lt. Gen. Ben Hodges
U.S. Army North	Lt. Gen. Jeffrey S. Buchanan
U.S. Army Pacific	Gen. Robert B. Brown
U.S. Army South	Maj. Gen. Clarence K.K. Chinn
U.S. Army Military Surface Deployment and Distribution Command	Maj. Gen. Susan A. Davidson
U.S. Army Space and Missile Defense Command/Army Strategic Command	Lt. Gen. David L. Mann
U.S. Army Special Operations Command	Lt. Gen. Kenneth E. Tovo

Direct Reporting Units

Commandant, U.S. Army War College	Maj. Gen. William E. Rapp
Commander, Second Army	Lt. Gen. Edward C. Cardon
Commander, U.S. Army Accessions Support Brigade	Col. Janet R. Holliday
Director, U.S. Army Acquisition Support Center	Craig A. Spisak
Executive Director, Arlington National Cemetery	Patrick K. Hallinan
Superintendent, U.S. Military Academy	Lt. Gen. Robert L. Caslen, Jr.
Commanding Generals	
U.S. Army Corps of Engineers	Lt. Gen. Todd T. Semonite
U.S. Army Criminal Investigation Command	Maj. Gen. Mark S. Inch
U.S. Army Installation Management Command	Lt. Gen. Kenneth R. Dahl
U.S. Army Intelligence and Security Command	Maj. Gen. Christopher S. Ballard
U.S. Army Medical Command	Lt. Gen. Nadja Y. West
U.S. Army Military District of Washington	Maj. Gen. Bradley A. Becker
U.S. Army Reserve Command	Lt. Gen. Charles D. Luckey
U.S. Army Test and Evaluation Command	Maj. Gen. Daniel L. Karbler

The Department of the Army equips, organizes, and trains active duty and reserve forces to maintain peace and security and to defend the Nation; administers programs to mitigate erosion and flooding, to develop water resources, to improve waterway navigation, and to protect the environment; and provides military and natural disaster relief assistance to Federal, State, and local government agencies.

DEPARTMENT OF THE ARMY

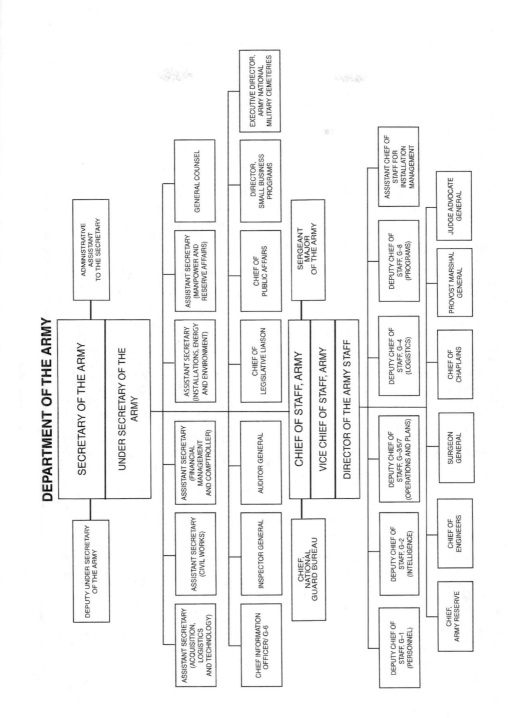

The Continental Congress established the American Continental Army, now called the United States Army, on June 14, 1775, more than a year before the Declaration of Independence. The Department of War was established as an executive department at the seat of Government by act approved August 7, 1789 (1 Stat. 49). The Secretary of War was established as its head. The National Security Act of 1947 (50 U.S.C. 401) created the National Military Establishment, and the Department of War was designated the Department of the Army. The title of its Secretary became Secretary of the Army (5 U.S.C. 171). The National Security Act Amendments of 1949 (63 Stat. 578) provided that the Department of the Army be a military department within the Department of Defense.

Secretary

The Secretary of the Army is the senior official of the Department of the Army. Subject to the direction, authority, and control of the President as Commander in Chief and of the Secretary of Defense, the Secretary of the Army is responsible for and has the authority to conduct all affairs of the Department of the Army, including its organization, administration, operation, efficiency, and such other activities as may be prescribed by the President or the Secretary of Defense as authorized by law. https://www.army.mil/leaders/sa

For further information, call 703-695-2422.

Army Staff

The Army Staff is the Secretary of the Army's military staff. It makes preparations for deploying the Army, including recruiting, organizing, supplying, equipping, training, mobilizing, and demobilizing it, to support the Secretary or the Chief of Staff in his or her executive capacity; investigates and reports on the efficiency of the Army and its preparation for military operations; acts as the agent of the Secretary of the Army and the Chief of Staff in coordinating the action of all organizations of the Department of the Army; and performs other nonstatutory duties that the Secretary of the Army may prescribe.

Program Areas

Civil Functions   Civil functions of the Department of the Army include the administration of Arlington and the U.S. Soldiers' and Airmen's Home National Cemeteries and the Civil Works Program—the Nation's principal Federal water resources development activity involving dams, reservoirs, levees, harbors, waterways, locks, and other engineering structures. http://www.army.mil/asacw

History   This area includes advisory and coordination service provided to the Army Secretariat and staff on all historical matters: the formulation and execution of the Army historical program, the maintenance of the organizational history of Army units, the preparation and publication of histories that the Army requires, and historical properties. http://www.history.army.mil | Email: usarmy. mcnair.cmh.mbx.answers@mail.mil

Installations   This area consists of policies, procedures, and resources for the management of installations to ensure the availability of efficient and affordable base services and infrastructure in support of military missions. It includes the identification and validation of resource requirements, the review of facilities requirements and stationing, and program and budget development and justification. Other activities include support for base operations; base realignment and closure; competitive sourcing; energy security and sustainability; environmental programs; housing; military construction; morale, recreation, and welfare; and real property maintenance and repair. https://www.army. mil/info/organization/unitsandcommands/commandstructure/imcom

Intelligence   This area includes management of Army intelligence with responsibility for policy formulation, planning, programming, budgeting, evaluation, and oversight of intelligence activities. The Army Staff is responsible for monitoring relevant foreign intelligence developments and foreign disclosure; imagery, signals, human, open-source, measurement, and signatures intelligence; counterintelligence; threat models and simulations; and security countermeasures. https://www.army.mil/inscom/?from=org

Medical This area includes management of health services for the Army and as directed for other services, agencies, and organizations; health standards for Army personnel; health professional education and training; career management authority over commissioned and warrant officer personnel of the Army Medical Department; medical research, materiel development, testing, and evaluation; policies concerning health aspects of Army environmental programs and prevention of disease; and planning, programming, and budgeting for Armywide health services. https://www.army.mil/armymedicine/?from=org

Military Operations and Plans This includes Army forces strategy formation; mid-range, long-range, and regional strategy application; arms control, negotiation, and disarmament; national security affairs; joint service matters; net assessment; politico-military affairs; force mobilization, demobilization, and planning; programming structuring, development, analysis, requirements, and management; operational readiness; overall roles and missions; collective security; individual and unit training; psychological operations; information operations; unconventional warfare; counterterrorism; operations security; signal security; special plans; equipment development and approval; nuclear and chemical matters; civil affairs; military support of civil defense; civil disturbance; domestic actions; command and control; automation and communications programs and activities; management of the program for law enforcement, correction, and crime prevention for military members of the Army; special operations forces; foreign language and distance learning; and physical security.

Reserve Components This area includes management of individual and unit readiness and mobilization for Reserve Components, which consist of the Army National Guard and U.S. Army Reserve. https://www.army.mil/reserve/?from=org

Religious This area includes departmentwide management of religious and moral leadership and chaplain support activities; religious ministrations, religious education, pastoral care, and counseling for Army military personnel; liaison with ecclesiastical agencies; chapel construction requirements and design approval; and career management of clergymen serving in the Chaplains Corps. http://www.army.mil/chaplaincorps

Army Commands
U.S. Army Forces
Command Headquartered at Fort Bragg, NC, U.S. Army Forces Command (FORSCOM) prepares conventional forces to provide a sustained flow of trained and ready land power to combatant commanders in defense of the Nation at home and abroad. https://www.army.mil/info/organization/unitsandcommands/commandstructure/forscom/?from=org

For further information, contact the FORSCOM Public Affairs Office. Phone, 910-570-7200.

U.S. Army Materiel Command U.S. Army Materiel Command (AMC) is the Army's premier provider of materiel readiness—technology, acquisition support, materiel development, logistics power projection, and sustainment—to the total force across the spectrum of joint military operations. Headquartered at Redstone Arsenal, Alabama, AMC's missions include the development of weapon systems, advanced research on future technologies, and maintenance and distribution of spare parts and equipment. AMC works closely with program executive offices, industry, academia, and other Military Services and Government agencies to develop, test, and acquire equipment that soldiers and units need to accomplish their missions. https://www.army.mil/info/organization/unitsandcommands/commandstructure/amc/?from=org

For further information, contact the AMC Public Affairs Office. Phone, 256-450-7978.

U.S. Army Training and Doctrine
Command Headquartered in Fort Eustis, VA, U.S. Army Training and Doctrine Command (TRADOC) develops, educates, and trains soldiers, civilians, and leaders; supports unit training; and designs, builds, and integrates a versatile mix of capabilities, formations, and equipment to strengthen the U.S. Army as a force of decisive action. https://www.army.mil/tradoc/?from=org

For further information, contact the TRADOC Public Affairs Office. Phone, 757-501-5876.

Army Service Component Commands

U.S. Army Africa / Southern European Task Force   U.S. Army Africa (USARAF) / Southern European Task Force (SETAF) is the Army service component command for U.S. Africa Command. It supports U.S. Africa Command operations, employs Army forces as partners, builds sustainable capacity, and supports the joint force to disrupt transnational threats and promote regional security in Africa. http://www.usaraf.army.mil

For further information, contact the USARAF / SETAF Public Affairs Office. Phone, 011-39-0444-71-8341 or 8342.

U.S. Army Central   U.S. Army Central (ARCENT) shapes the U.S. Central Command area of responsibility in 20 countries through forward land power presence and security cooperation engagements that ensure access, build partner capacity, and develop relationships. ARCENT also provides flexible options and strategic depth to the U.S. combatant commander and sets the conditions for improved regional security and stability. http://www.arcent.army.mil | Email: usarmy.shaw.usarcent.mbx.public-affairs@mail.mil

For further information, contact the USARCENT Public Affairs Office. Phone, 803-885-8266.

U.S. Army Europe   U.S. Army Europe (USAREUR) provides the principal land component for U.S. European Command throughout a 51-country area. As the U.S. Army's largest forward-deployed expeditionary force, USAREUR supports NATO and U.S. bilateral, multinational, and unilateral objectives. It supports U.S. Army forces in the European Command area; receives and assists in the reception, staging, and onward movement and integration of U.S. forces; establishes, operates, and expands operational lines of communication; ensures regional security, access, and stability through presence and security cooperation; and supports U.S. combatant commanders and joint and combined commanders. http://www.eur.army.mil

For further information, contact the USAREUR Public Affairs Office. Phone, 011-49-611-143-537-0005 or 0006.

U.S. Army North   U.S. Army North (USARNORTH) supports U.S. Northern Command, the unified command responsible for defending the U.S. homeland and coordinating defense support of civil authorities. USARNORTH helps maintain readiness to support homeland defense, civil support operations, and theater security cooperation activities. http://www.arnorth.army.mil | Email: usarmy.jbsa.arnorth.list.pao-owner@mail.mil

For further information, contact the USARNORTH Public Affairs Office. Phone, 210-221-0015.

U.S. Army South   U.S. Army South (ARSOUTH) is the Army service component command of U.S. Southern Command. ARSOUTH conducts security cooperation and responds to contingencies as part of a whole-of-government approach in conjunction with partner national armies in the U.S. Southern Command area of responsibility, which encompasses 31 countries and 15 areas of special sovereignty in Central and South America and the Caribbean. These activities counter transnational threats and strengthen regional security in defense of the homeland. ARSOUTH maintains a deployable headquarters at Fort Sam Houston, Texas, where it conducts strategic and operational planning. http://www.arsouth.army.mil | Email: usarmy.jbsa.arsouth.mbx.pao@mail.mil

For further information, contact the ARSOUTH Public Affairs Office. Phone, 210-295-6739.

U.S. Army Pacific   U.S. Army Pacific (USARPAC) prepares the force for unified land operations, responds to threats, sustains and protects the force, and builds military relationships that develop partner defense capacity to contribute to the stability and security of the U.S. Pacific Command area of responsibility. USARPAC commands soldiers in an area spanning from the Northwest Coast and Alaska to the Asia-Pacific region, including Japan. Since September 11, 2001, USARPAC soldiers have played a vital role in homeland defense for Alaska and Hawaii, Guam, and Japan, as well as in supporting operations with our allies elsewhere in the region. https://www.army. mil/info/organization/unitsandcommands/ commandstructure/usarpac/?from=org

For further information, contact USARPAC Public Affairs. Phone, 808-438-9761.

U.S. Army Military Surface Deployment and Distribution Command

U.S. Army Military Surface Deployment and Distribution Command (SDDC) delivers world-class, origin-to-destination distribution. It is the Army service component command of the U.S. Transportation Command and a subordinate command to the Army Materiel Command. This relationship links the Transportation Command's joint deployment and distribution enterprise with the Army Materiel Command's materiel enterprise. The SDDC also partners with the commercial transportation industry as the coordinating link between Department of Defense surface transportation requirements and the capability industry provides. http://www. sddc.army.mil

For further information, contact the SDDC Public Affairs Office. Phone, 618-220-6284.

U.S. Army Space and Missile Defense Command / Army Strategic Command

U.S. Army Space and Missile Defense Command (SMDC / ARSTRAT) conducts space and missile defense operations and provides planning, integration, control, and coordination of Army forces and capabilities in support of U.S. Strategic Command missions. SMDC / ARSTRAT also supports space, high-altitude, and global missile defense modernization efforts; serves as the Army operational integrator for global missile defense; and conducts mission-related research and development to support the Army's statutory responsibilities. http://www.army. mil/info/organization/unitsandcommands/ commandstructure/smdc

For further information, contact the SMDC Public Affairs Office. Phone, 256-955-3887.

U.S. Army Special Operations Command

U.S. Army Special Operations Command (USASOC) administers, deploys, educates, equips, funds, mans, mobilizes, organizes, sustains, and trains Army special operations forces to carry out missions worldwide, as directed. These special and diverse military operations support regional combatant commanders, American ambassadors, and other agencies. https:// www.army.mil/usasoc/?from=orghttp://www. soc.mil | Email: pao@soc.mil

For further information, contact the USASOC Public Affairs Office. Phone, 910-432-6005.

Sources of Information

Business Opportunities For information on contract procurement policies and procedures, contact the Deputy Assistant Secretary of the Army, Procurement. Phone, 703-695-2488. http://www.micc.army.mil/ contracting-offices.asp

Assistance for small businesses and minority educational institutions to increase participation in the Army contracting program is available through the Office of Small Business Programs. Phone, 703-697-2868. Fax, 703-693-3898. http://www.micc. army.mil/small-business.asp

Cemeteries Arlington National Cemetery is one of the two national military cemeteries that the Army maintains. This cemetery is the final resting place for more than 400,000 active duty servicemembers, veterans, and their families. For more information, visit its Web site or contact the cemetery. Phone, 877-907-8585. http://www. arlingtoncemetery.mil

The U.S. Soldiers' and Airmen's Home National Cemetery is one of the two national military cemeteries that the Army maintains. This cemetery is the final resting place for more than 14,000 veterans, including those that fought in the Civil War. For more information, visit its Web site or contact the Superintendent. Phone, 877-907-8585. http://www.nps.gov/nr/travel/national_ cemeteries/district_of_columbia/us_soldiers_ and_airmens_home_national_cemetery.html

Environment Information is available from the U.S. Army Environmental Command. https://aec.army.mil

Information is also available from the Office of the Deputy Assistant Secretary of the Army for Environment, Safety and Occupational Health. http://www.asaie. army.mil/Public/ESOH

The Army Environmental Policy Institute posts publications on its Web site. "Army Water Security Strategy" (DEC 2011), the results of the first comprehensive study of Army water security management, is available in Portable Document Format (PDF). "Quantifying the Army Supply Chain Water Bootprint" (DEC 2011), an initial step to quantify the amount of water used by suppliers to produce the goods and services that the Army procures through the supply chain, is also available in PDF. http://www.aepi.army.mil

Employment   More than 330,000 Army civilians work in a wide range of diverse professions. These professionals are not active duty military, but serve as an integral part of the Army team to support the defense of the Nation. http://armycivilianservice.com

Films   Address loan requests for Army-produced films to the Visual Information Support Centers of Army installations. Unclassified Army productions are available for sale from the National Audiovisual Center, National Technical Information Service, 5301 Shawnee Road, Alexandria, VA 22312. Phone, 800-553-6847. http://www.ntis.gov/Index.aspx | Email: orders@ntis.gov

Freedom of Information Act (FOIA)   Contact the appropriate information management officer associated with the Army installation or activity managing the desired information. Information is also available on the Records Management and Declassification Agency's Web site. https://www.rmda.army.mil

Frequently Asked Questions (FAQs)   The Army posts answers to FAQs on its Web site. https://www.army.mil/faq

Gold Star Survivors   All Gold Star family members have made a sacrifice to the Nation. The Army recognizes that no one gives more for the Nation than a family member of the fallen. Gold Star Mother's and Family's Day is the last Sunday of September, and Gold Star Spouses Day is April 5. https://www.army.mil/goldstar

History   "Army History" magazine, the professional bulletin of Army history, is available online in Portable Document Format (PDF). http://www.history.army.mil/news/2016/160900a_armyHistoryMag.html

A directory of Army museums is available on the Center of Military History's Web site. http://www.history.army.mil/museums/directory.html

The Office of Historic Properties and Partnerships raises awareness of and explores and tests creative uses for the Army's historic buildings. Its staff also promotes partnerships between the Army and nonprofit organizations, public or private, to preserve, renovate, and restore. http://www.asaie.army.mil/Public/IH/OHP/ohp.htm

Joining the Army   Information on Army life, assignments, benefits, pay, and enlisting or joining in other capacities is available online. Phone, 888-550-2769. http://www.goarmy.com

National Guard   The National Guard responds to domestic emergencies, counterdrug efforts, overseas combat missions, reconstruction missions, and more. The President or a State governor can call on the Guard in a moment's notice. Guard soldiers hold civilian jobs or attend college while maintaining their military training on a part-time basis, and their primary area of operation is their home state. https://www.nationalguard.com

Public Affairs / Community Relations   For official Army and community relations information, contact the Office of the Chief of Public Affairs. Phone, 703-695-0616. Automated assistance is available after normal work hours. Phone, 201-590-6575. http://www.army.mil/info/institution/publicAffairs

Publications   To request a publication, contact either the proponent listed on the title page of the document or the information management officer of the Army activity that publishes the desired publication. If the requester does not know which Army activity published the document, contact the Publishing Division, Army Publishing Directorate. Phone, 703-693-1557. http://www.army.mil/media/publications

Official texts published by Headquarters, Department of the Army, are available from the National Technical Information Service. Phone, 888-584-8332. http://www.ntis.gov

Ranks   Descriptions of officer, warrant officer, and enlisted ranks are available on the Army Web site. https://www.army.mil/symbols/armyranks.html

Reading List   The U.S. Army Chief of Staff's professional reading list comprises three categories—Armies at war: battles and campaigns; the Army profession; and strategy and the strategic environment—and is accessible online. http://www.history.army.mil/html/books/105/105-1-1/index.html

Research The Research, Development and Engineering Command is the Army's technology leader and largest technology developer. Its Web site features news on and resources related to long-range research and development plans for materiel requirements and objectives. Phone, 443-395-4006 (Public Affairs) or 3922 (Media Relations). http://www.army.mil/info/organization/unitsandcommands/commandstructure/rdecom

Reserve Officers' Training Corps (ROTC) Available at over 1,100 colleges and universities nationwide, the ROTC offers merit-based scholarships that can cover the full cost of tuition and open educational opportunities. http://www.goarmy.com/rotc.html

Site Index The Army's Web site features an A–Z index. https://www.army.mil/info/a-z

Specialized Careers Information on how to become an Army chaplain, the chaplain candidate program, and chaplain corps careers and jobs is available online and from the U.S. Army Recruiting Command. Phone, 877-437-6572. http://www.goarmy.com/chaplain

Health care professionals serving as officers in the Army's medical department benefit from a wide range of opportunities and financial incentives. http://www.goarmy.com/amedd.html

Members of the Army Judge Advocate General's corps often represent soldiers during courts-martial; however, they also engage in a wider range of legal activities that include civil litigation, international law, labor law, and tort claims. For more information, contact the Army Judge Advocate Recruiting Office. Phone, 866-276-9524. http://www.goarmy.com/jag

The Army relies on talented musicians to assist with military ceremonies, boost morale, and provide entertainment. http://www.goarmy.com/band.html

Speakers The Public Affairs Office nearest the event can help provide local Army speakers. The Office of the Chief of Public Affairs can assist with scheduling a general officer to address Army matters at public forums. To request a general officer speaker, writer to the Office of the Chief of Public Affairs, ATTN: Community Relations, Division (Speaker Request), 1500 Army Pentagon, Washington, DC 20310-1500. A lead time of at least 60–90 days is required. Phone, 703-614-1107. http://www.army.mil/comrel/assetrequests

U. S. Military Academy West Point has been educating, training, and inspiring U.S. Army leaders for more than 200 years. The academy offers a 47-month leader-development program of academic rigor, military discipline, and physical challenges with adherence to a code of honor. http://www.usma.edu | Email: admissions-info@usma.edu http://www.army.mil/info/institution/publicAffairs

For further information concerning the Department of the Army, contact U.S. Army Public Affairs, Community Relations Division, Office of the Chief of Public Affairs, 1500 Army Pentagon, Washington, DC 20310-1500.

Department of the Navy

The Pentagon, Washington, DC 20350
Phone, 703-697-7391. Internet, http://www.navy.mil

Secretary of the Navy	SEAN J. STACKLEY, ACTING
Under Secretary of the Navy	THOMAS P. DEE, ACTING
Assistant Secretaries	
Energy, Installations and Environment	STEVEN R. ISELIN, ACTING
Financial Management / Comptroller	JOSEPH B. MARSHALL JR., ACTING
Manpower and Reserve Affairs	ROBERT L. WOODS, ACTING
Research, Development and Acquisition	ALLISON F. STILLER
Auditor General	DONJETTE L. GILMORE, ACTING
Chief Information Officer	ROBERT FOSTER
Chief of Information	REAR ADM. DAWN CUTLER, ACTING

Chief of Legislative Affairs	REAR ADM. CRAIG S. FALLER
Chief of Naval Research	REAR ADM. DAVID J. HAHN
Director, Naval Criminal Investigative Service	ANDREW L. TRAVER
General Counsel	ANNE M. BRENNAN, Acting
Judge Advocate General	VICE ADM. JAMES W. CRAWFORD III
Naval Inspector General	VICE ADM. HERMAN SHELANSKI
Deputy Under Secretary of the Navy (Management)	SCOTT W. LUTTERLOH
Director, Sexual Assault Prevention and Response Office	JILL VINES LOFTUS
Chief of Naval Operations	ADMIRAL JOHN M. RICHARDSON
Vice Chief of Naval Operations	ADMIRAL BILL MORAN
Master Chief Petty Officer of the Navy	STEVEN S. GIORDANO

Naval Operations

Chief of Naval Operations	ADM. JOHN M. RICHARDSON
Vice Chief of Naval Operations	ADM. WILLIAM F. MORAN

Deputy Chiefs of Naval Operations

Fleet Readiness and Logistics	VICE ADM. DIXON SMITH
Information Dominance	VICE ADM. JAN TIGHE
Integration of Capabilities and Resources	VICE ADM. WILLIAM LESCHER
Manpower, Personnel, Training Education	VICE ADM. ROBERT P. BURKE
Operations, Plans and Strategy	VICE ADM. JOHN C. AQUILINO

Directors

Naval Intelligence	VICE ADM. JAN TIGHE
Naval Nuclear Propulsion Program	ADM. JAMES F. CALDWELL
Navy Staff	VICE ADM. JAMES G. FOGGO
Test and Evaluation and Technology Requirements / Chief of Naval Research	REAR ADM. DAVID J. HAHN

Chief of Chaplains of the Navy	REAR ADM. MARGARET G. KIBBEN
Chief of Naval Reserve	VICE ADM. LUKE MCCOLLUM
Master Chief Petty Officer of the Navy	STEVEN GIORDANO
Oceanographer of the Navy / Navigator of the Navy	REAR ADM. TIMOTHY C. GALLAUDET
Surgeon General of the Navy	VICE ADM. C. FORREST FAISON III

Shore Establishment

Chief of Naval Operations	ADM. JOHN M. RICHARDSON

Commanders

Naval Air Systems Command	VICE ADM. PAUL GROSKLAGS
Naval Education and Training Command	REAR ADM. MICHAEL S. WHITE
Naval Facilities Engineering Command	REAR ADM. KATE L. GREGORY
Naval Legal Service Command	REAR ADM. JOHN G. HANNINK
Naval Meteorology and Oceanography	REAR ADM. TIMOTHY C. GALLUDET
Naval Network Warfare Command	CAPT. JOHN W. CHANDLER
Naval Sea Systems Command	VICE ADM. THOMAS MOORE
Naval Supply Systems Command	REAR ADM. JONATHAN A. YUEN
Naval Warfare Development Command	REAR ADM. BRET C. BATCHELDER
Navy Installations Command	VICE ADM. DIXON SMITH
Space and Naval Warfare Systems Command	REAR ADM. DAVID H. LEWIS

Chief, Bureau of Medicine and Surgery	VICE ADM. C. FORREST FAISON III
Chief, Naval Personnel	VICE ADM. ROBERT P. BURKE
Director, National Maritime Intelligence-Integration Office / Commander, Office of Naval Intelligence	REAR ADM. ELIZABETH L. TRAIN

Director, Strategic Systems Program	REAR ADM. TERRY J. BENEDICT
Superintendent, U.S. Naval Academy	VICE ADM. WALTER E. CARTER, JR.

Operating Forces

Commanders

U.S. Fleet Forces Command	ADM. PHILIP S. DAVIDSON
Pacific Fleet	ADM. SCOTT H. SWIFT
Military Sealift Command	REAR ADM. DEE L. MEWBOURNE
Naval Forces Central Command	VICE ADM. KEVIN M. DONEGAN
Naval Forces Europe	ADM. MICHELLE J. HOWARD
Naval Reserve Forces Command	REAR ADM. THOMAS W. LUSCHER
Naval Special Warfare Command	REAR ADM. TIMOTHY SZYMANSKI
Operational Test and Evaluation Force	REAR ADM. JEFFREY R. PENFIELD

[For the Department of the Navy statement of organization, see the Code of Federal Regulations, Title 32, Part 700]

The Department of the Navy protects the United States and its interests by the prosecution of war at sea, including the seizure or defense of advanced naval bases with the assistance of its Marine Corps component; supports the forces of all military departments of the United States; and safeguards freedom of the seas.

The United States Navy was founded on October 13, 1775, when Congress enacted the first legislation creating the Continental Navy of the American Revolution. The Department of the Navy and the Office of Secretary of the Navy were established by act of April 30, 1798 (10 U.S.C. 5011, 5031). For 9 years prior to that date, by act of August 7, 1789 (1 Stat. 49), the Secretary of War oversaw the conduct of naval affairs.

The National Security Act Amendments of 1949 provided that the Department of the Navy be a military department within the Department of Defense (63 Stat. 578).

The President appoints the Secretary of the Navy as the head of the Department of the Navy. The Secretary is responsible to the Secretary of Defense for the operation and efficiency of the Navy (10 U.S.C. 5031). The Department of the Navy includes the U.S. Coast Guard when it is operating as a Service in the Navy.

Secretary The Secretary of the Navy is the head of the Department of the Navy, responsible for the policies and control of the Department of the Navy, including its organization, administration, functioning, and efficiency. The members of the Secretary's executive administration assist in the discharge of the responsibilities of the Secretary of the Navy. http://www.navy.mil/secnav

Legal The Office of the Judge Advocate General provides all legal advice and related services throughout the Department of the Navy, except for the advice and services provided by the General Counsel. It also provides legal and policy advice to the Secretary of the Navy on military justice, ethics, administrative law, claims, environmental law, operational and international law and treaty interpretation, and litigation involving these issues. The Judge Advocate General provides technical supervision for the Naval Justice School at Newport, RI. http://www.navy.mil/local/jag/index.asp

For further information, contact the Office of the Judge Advocate General, Department of the Navy, Washington Navy Yard, Suite 3000, 1322 Patterson Avenue SE., Washington Navy Yard, DC 20374-5066. Phone, 202-685-5190.

Criminal Investigations The Naval Criminal Investigative Service investigates and neutralizes criminal, terrorist, and foreign intelligence threats to the United States Navy and Marine Corps. To carry out its mission, the Service relies on the professionalism and law enforcement expertise of administrative support personnel, forensic specialists, intelligence analysts, investigators, military personnel, security specialists, special agents, and technical investigative specialists. http://www.ncis.navy.mil

DEPARTMENT OF THE NAVY

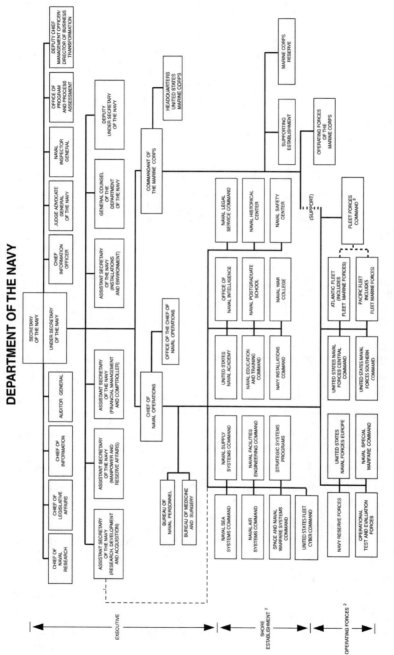

1 Systems commands and SSP report to ASN (RDA) for acquisition matters only.
2 Also includes other Echelon 2 commands and subordinate activities under the command or supervision of the designated organizations.
3 For Interdeployment Training Cycle purposes. Commander, Fleet Forms Command Controls LANFLT and PACFLT assets.

For further information, contact the Naval Criminal Investigative Service, 27130 Telegraph Road, Quantico, VA 22134. Phone, 877-579-3648.

Research   The Office of Naval Research initiates, coordinates, plans, and promotes naval research, including the coordination of research and development conducted by other agencies and offices in the Department of the Navy. The Office researches, develops, and delivers decisive naval capabilities by investing in a balanced portfolio of promising scientific research, innovative technology, and talent. It also manages and controls activities within the Department concerning copyrights, inventions, manufacturing technology, patents, royalty payments, small businesses, and trademarks. http://www.onr.navy.mil | Email: onrpublicaffairs@navy.mil

For further information, contact the Public Affairs Office, Office of Naval Research, One Liberty Center, 875 North Randolph Street, Arlington, VA 22203-1995. Phone, 703-696-5031.

Operating Forces   Operating forces carry out operations that enable the Navy to meet its responsibility to uphold and advance the national policies and interests of the United States. These forces include the several fleets; seagoing, fleet marine, and other assigned Marine Corps forces; the Military Sealift Command; Naval Reserve forces; and other forces and activities that the President or the Secretary of the Navy may assign. The Chief of Naval Operations administers and commands the operating forces of the Navy.

The Atlantic Fleet is composed of ships, submarines, and aircraft that operate throughout the Atlantic Ocean and Mediterranean Sea.

The Naval Forces Europe includes forces assigned by the Chief of Naval Operations or made available from either the Pacific or Atlantic Fleet to operate in the European theater.

The Pacific Fleet is composed of ships, submarines, and aircraft operating throughout the Pacific and Indian Oceans.

The Military Sealift Command provides ocean transportation for personnel and cargo of all components of the Department of Defense and, as authorized, for other Federal agencies; operates and maintains underway replenishment ships and other vessels providing mobile logistic support to elements of the combatant fleets; and operates ships in support of scientific projects and other programs for Federal agencies.

Other major commands of the operating forces of the Navy are the Naval Forces Central Command, Operational Test and Evaluation Force, Naval Special Warfare Command, and Naval Reserve Force. http://www.navy.mil/navydata/organization/orgopfor.asp

Activities

Air Systems   The Naval Air Systems Command provides full life-cycle support of naval aviation aircraft, weapons, and systems operated by Sailors and Marines. This support includes research, design, development, and systems engineering; acquisition; test and evaluation; training facilities and equipment; repair and modification; and in-service engineering and logistics support. The Command comprises eight "competencies" or communities of practice: program management, contracts, research and engineering, test and evaluation, logistics and industrial operations, corporate operations, comptroller, and counsel. The Command also supports the affiliated naval aviation program executive officer and the assigned program managers, who are responsible for meeting the cost, schedule, and performance requirements of their assigned programs. It is the principal provider for the Naval Aviation Enterprise, while contributing to every warfare enterprise in the interest of national security. http://www.navair.navy.mil

For further information, contact the Commander, Naval Air Systems Command, 47123 Buse Road, Building 2272, Suite 540, Patuxent River, MD 20670-1547. Phone, 301-757-7825.

Coast Guard   The Commandant of the Coast Guard reports to the Secretary of the Navy and the Chief of Naval Operations when the Coast Guard is operating as a service in the Navy and represents the Coast Guard before the Joint Chiefs of Staff. During such service, Coast Guard operations are integrated and uniform with Department of the Navy operations to the maximum extent possible. The Commandant of the

Coast Guard organizes, trains, prepares, and maintains the readiness of the Coast Guard for the performance of national defense missions as directed. The Commandant also maintains a security capability; enforces Federal laws and regulations on and under the high seas and waters subject to the jurisdiction of the United States; and develops, establishes, maintains, and operates aids to maritime navigation, as well as ice-breaking and rescue facilities, with due regard to the requirements of national defense. http://www.uscg.mil

Computers and Telecommunications   Naval Network Warfare Command operates the Navy's networks to achieve effective command and control through optimal alignment, common architecture, mature processes, and functions and standard terminology. The command enhances the Navy's network security posture and improves IT services through standardized enterprise-level management, network information assurance compliance, enterprise management, and root cause and trend analysis. Naval Network Warfare Command also delivers enhanced space products to operating forces by leveraging Department of Defense, national, commercial, and international space capabilities. The command serves as the Navy's commercial satellite operations manager; it executes tactical-level command and control of Navy networks and leverages Joint Space capabilities for Navy and Joint Operations. http://www.public.navy.mil/fcc-c10f/nnwc/Pages/default.aspx

For further information, contact Public Affairs, Naval Network Warfare Command, 112 Lake View Parkway, Suffolk, VA 23435. Phone, 757-203-0205.

Education and Training   The Naval Education and Training Command provides shore-based education and training for Navy, certain Marine Corps, and other personnel; develops specifically designated education and training afloat programs for the fleet; provides voluntary and dependents education; and participates with research and development activities in the development and implementation of the most effective teaching and training systems and devices for optimal education and training. http://www.navy.mil/local/cnet/ | Email: pnsc.netc.pao@navy.mil

For further information, contact the NETC Office of Public Affairs, 250 Dallas Street, Pensacola, FL 32508-5220. Phone, 850-452-4858.

Facilities   The Naval Facilities Engineering Command provides material and technical support to the Navy and Marine Corps for shore facilities, real property and utilities, fixed ocean systems and structures, transportation and construction equipment, energy, environmental and natural resources management, and support of the naval construction forces. http://www.navy.mil/local/navfachq

For further information, contact the Commander, Naval Facilities Engineering Command and Chief of Civil Engineers, Washington Navy Yard, 1322 Patterson Avenue SE., Suite 1000, Washington, DC 20374-5065. Phone, 202-685-1423.

Intelligence   The Office of Naval Intelligence ensures the fulfillment of the intelligence requirements and responsibilities of the Department of the Navy. http://www.oni.navy.mil | Email: pao@nmic.navy.mil

For further information, contact the Office of Public Affairs, Office of Naval Intelligence, Department of the Navy, 4251 Suitland Road, Washington, DC 20395-5720. Phone, 301-669-5670.

Manpower   The Bureau of Naval Personnel directs the procurement, distribution, administration, and career motivation of the military personnel of the regular and reserve components of the U.S. Navy to meet the quantitative and qualitative manpower requirements determined by the Chief of Naval Operations. http://www.navy.mil/cnp/index.asp

For further information, contact the Bureau of Naval Personnel, Department of the Navy, Federal Office Building 2, Washington, DC 20370-5000.

Medicine   The Bureau of Medicine and Surgery directs the medical and dental services for Navy and Marine Corps personnel and their dependents; administers the implementation of contingency support plans and programs to effect medical and dental readiness capability; provides medical and dental services to the fleet, fleet marine force, and shore activities of the Navy; and ensures cooperation with civil authorities in matters of public health disasters and other emergencies. http://www.med.navy.mil

For further information, contact the Bureau of Medicine and Surgery, Department of the Navy, 2300 E Street NW., Washington, DC 20373-5300. Phone, 202-762-3211.

Oceanography The Naval Meteorology and Oceanography Command and the Naval Observatory are responsible for the science, technology, and engineering operations that are essential to explore the ocean and the atmosphere and to provide astronomical data and time for naval and related national objectives. To that end, the naval oceanographic program studies astrometry, hydrography, meteorology, oceanography, and precise time. http://www.usno.navy.mil/ USNO

For further information, contact the Commander, Naval Meteorology and Oceanography Command, 1100 Balch Boulevard, Stennis Space Center, MS 39529-5005. Phone, 228-688-4384. Internet, http://www.navmetoccom.navy.mil. Or, contact the Oceanographer of the Navy, U.S. Naval Observatory, 3450 Massachusetts Avenue NW., Washington, DC 20392-1800. Phone, 202-762-1026.

Sea Systems The Naval Sea Systems Command provides material support to the Navy and Marine Corps and to the Departments of Defense and Transportation for ships, submarines, and other sea platforms, shipboard combat systems and components, other surface and undersea warfare and weapons systems, and ordnance expendables not specifically assigned to other system commands. http://www.navsea.navy.mil | Email: nssc_public_affairs@navy.mil

For further information, contact the Office of Public Affairs, Naval Sea Systems Command, 1333 Isaac Hull Avenue SE., Washington Navy Yard, DC 20376-1010. Phone, 202-781-4123.

Space and Naval Warfare The Space and Naval Warfare Systems Command develops, delivers, and sustains advanced cyber capabilities for naval warfighters. It helps provide the hardware and software needed to executive Navy missions. With nearly 10,000 active military and civilian professionals worldwide, the Command is at the forefront of research, engineering, and acquisition relevant for keeping U.S. military forces connected around the globe. http://www.spawar.navy.mil

For further information, contact the Commander, Space and Naval Warfare Systems Command, 4301 Pacific Highway, San Diego, CA 92110-3127. Phone, 619-524-3428.

Strategic Systems The Office of Strategic Systems Programs provides development, production, and material support to the Navy for fleet ballistic missile and strategic weapons systems, security, training of personnel, and the installation and direction of necessary supporting facilities. http://www.ssp.navy.mil

For further information, contact the Director, Strategic Systems Programs, Department of the Navy, Nebraska Avenue Complex, 287 Somers Court NW., Suite 10041, Washington, DC 20393-5446. Phone, 202-764-1608.

Supply Systems The Naval Supply Systems Command provides supply management policies and methods and administers related support service systems for the Navy and Marine Corps. http://www.navy.mil/local/navsup | Email: navsuphqQuestions@navy.mil

For further information, contact the Commander, Naval Supply Systems Command, 5450 Carlisle Pike, P.O. Box 2050, Mechanicsburg, PA 17055-0791. Phone, 717-605-3565.

Warfare Development The Navy Warfare Development Command plans and coordinates experiments employing emerging operational concepts; represents the Department of the Navy in joint and other service laboratories and facilities and tactical development commands; and publishes and disseminates naval doctrine. http://www.navy.mil/local/nwdc

For further information, contact the Commander, Navy Warfare Development Command, 686 Cushing Road, Sims Hall, Newport, RI 02841. Phone, 401-841-2833.

Sources of Information

Business Opportunities "Open for Business," a short video that gives an overview of the Navy's buying activities and small business programs, is available online. For more information, contact the Office of Small Business Programs. Phone, 202-685-6485. http://www.secnav.navy.mil/smallbusiness/Pages/video-openforbusiness.aspx | Email: osbp.info@navy.mil

Civilian Employment The possibilities of a civilian career at the Department of the Navy are many and diverse. They include a full range of occupations: from aircraft mechanic to pipefitter, from electrician to engineer, from zoologist to physician, and more. The Navy offers hundreds of different occupations nationwide and around the world. http://www.secnav.navy.mil/donhr/Pages/Default.aspx | Email: donhrfaq@navy.mil

Environment For information on Navy and Marine Corps environmental protection and natural resources management programs, contact the Deputy Assistant Secretary–Environment, 1000 Navy Pentagon, Room 4A674, Washington, DC 20350-1000. Phone, 703-614-5493. http://www.secnav.navy.mil/eie/Pages/Environment.aspx

The "U.S. Navy Climate Change Roadmap" (April 2010) is available in Portable Document Format (PDF) online. http://www.navy.mil/navydata/documents/CCR.pdf

The Navy has posted its environmental goals and descriptions of its strategies to achieve them. http://greenfleet.dodlive.mil/environment

Glossary The origins of Navy terminology section explains nautical terminology that has become a part of everyday English. http://www.navy.mil/navydata/traditions/html/navyterm.html

Joining the Navy Unparalleled opportunities, challenges, and experiences motivate bright and skilled people to join. America's Navy offers careers and jobs that match many backgrounds and interests. Hundreds of distinct roles in dozens of professional fields are part of what the Navy has to offer. http://www.navy.com/joining.html

Naval Oceanography Portal The U.S. Naval Meteorology and Oceanography Command provides information from the ocean depths to the distant reaches of space to meet the needs of civilian and the military

and scientific communities. http://www.usno.navy.mil

The U.S. Naval Observatory offers a wide range of astronomical data and products, and it serves as the official source of time for the Department of Defense and as the official source of a standard of time for the entire United States. http://www.usno.navy.mil/USNO

"The Sky This Week" is a weekly set of pictures and descriptions of the planets, sky, and stars. http://www.usno.navy.mil/USNO/tours-events/sky-this-week/the-sky-this-week

News The Navy posts recent headline news stories on its Web site. http://www.navy.mil/listStories.asp?x=2

An online subscription form is available to sign up for updates from the Navy news service. https://service.govdelivery.com/accounts/USNAVYDMA/subscriber/new

"All Hands" magazine is an electronic publication for sailors by sailors. It features articles, imagery, information, and videos that are relevant to sailors and their families. http://www.navy.mil/ah_online

Research Programs Research programs of the Office of Naval Research cover a broad spectrum of scientific fields. The research is primarily for the needs of the Navy and Marine Corps, but some of these programs conduct research that has relevance for the general public. For information on specific research programs, contact the Office of Naval Research–Public Affairs, One Liberty Center 875 N. Randolph Street, Arlington, VA 22203-1995. Phone, 703-696-5031. http://www.onr.navy.mil

Ships The Navy operates and relies on many types of ships to carry out its mission. Descriptions of these different ships—aircraft carriers, amphibious assault ships, cruisers, destroyers, littoral combat ships, and submarines—are available online. http://www.navy.mil/navydata/our_ships.asp

Site Index An A–Z information index is available on the Navy's Web site. http://www.navy.mil/navydata/infoIndex.asp?id=A
http://www.navy.mil/submit/contacts.asp

For further information concerning the Navy, contact the Office of Information, Department of the Navy, 1200 Navy Pentagon, Washington, DC 20350-1200. For press inquiries, phone 703-697-7391 or 703-697-5342.

United States Marine Corps

Commandant of the Marine Corps, Headquarters, U.S. Marine Corps, 3000 Pentagon, Washington, DC 20380-1775
Phone, 703-614-2500. Internet, http://www.marines.mil

Commandant of The Marine Corps	GEN. ROBERT B. NELLER
Assistant Commandant of the Marine Corps	GEN. GLENN M. WALTERS
Sergeant Major of the Marine Corps	SGT. MAJ. RONALD L. GREEN

The Continental Congress established the United States Marine Corps by resolution on November 10, 1775. Marine Corps composition and functions are detailed in 10 U.S.C. 5063.

The Marine Corps, which is part of the Department of the Navy, is the smallest of the Nation's combat forces. It also is the only service that the Congress has tasked specifically to be able to fight in the air, on land, and at sea. Although Marines fight in each of these dimensions, they are primarily a maritime force linked with the Navy, moving from the sea to fight on land.

The Marine Corps conducts entry-level training for its enlisted marines at two bases: Marine Corps Recruit Depot, Parris Island, SC; and Marine Corps Recruit Depot, San Diego, CA. Officer candidates are evaluated at Officer Candidate School, Marine Corps Combat Development Command, Quantico, VA. Marines train to be first on the scene to respond to attacks on the United States or its interests and to acts of political violence against Americans abroad, to provide disaster relief and humanitarian assistance, and to evacuate Americans from foreign countries.

Sources of Information

DSTRESS Line   The DSTRESS Line offers an around-the-clock anonymous phone, live chat, and referral service. The call center is staffed with veteran Marines, Fleet Marine Force Navy Corpsmen who were previously attached to the Marine Corps, Marine spouses and other family members, and licensed behavioral health counselors trained in Marine Corps culture. DSTRESS Line is designed to help callers improve overall fitness and to develop the necessary skills for coping with the challenges of life in the Marine Corps. Phone, 877-476-7734. http://www.usmc-mccs.org/

index.cfm/services/support/dstress-line | Email: dstressline@usmc.mil
Electronic Publications   Authentic and current digital versions of publications issued by Headquarters Marine Corps staff agencies, major commands, and other Department of Defense and Federal agencies are available online. http://www.marines.mil/News/Publications
Freedom of Information Act (FOIA)   Procedures for requesting records that the U.S. Marine Corps controls are available online. Phone, 703-614-4008. http://www.hqmc.marines.mil/Agencies/USMC-FOIA | Email: hqmcfoia@usmc.mil
Marine Corps Bands   Marine Corps bands perform at ceremonies, concerts, festivals, parades, professional sporting events, and other public events. Marine Corps bands perform six types of ensembles: brass/woodwind quintet, bugler, ceremonial band, concert band, jazz combo, and jazz/show band. Phone, 504-697-8184. http://www.marines.mil/Community-Relations/Asset-Requests/Band | Email: smb.mfr.pao.comrel@usmc.mil
News   The Marine Corps posts press releases on its Web site. http://www.marines.mil/News/Press-Releases

Marines TV is accessible via the Marine Corps Web site. http://www.marines.mil/News/Marines-TV
Reading List   The Commandant's professional reading list is available online. http://guides.grc.usmcu.edu/content.php?pid=408059&sid=3340387 | Email: Reading@usmc.mil
Sexual Assault   The Marine Corps' Sexual Assault Prevention and Response program lowers the incidence of sexual assault through preventative strategies and provides care to victims of the crime. http://www.usmc-mccs.org/index.cfm/services/support/sexual-assault-prevention

The Safe Helpline provides anonymous and confidential support for sexual assault survivors in the military. Phone, 877-995-5247. https://safehelpline.org

Silent Drill Platoon   The Marine Corps Silent Drill Platoon is a 24-Marine rifle platoon that performs a precision drill exhibition. This disciplined platoon exemplifies the professionalism associated with the U.S. Marine Corps. It first performed in the Sunset Parades of 1948 and received such a favorable response that it became a regular part of the parades at Marine Barracks, Washington, DC. Performance requests for the Silent Drill Platoon should be made 30–90 days prior to the event. Phone, 504-697-8184. http://www.marines.mil/Community-Relations/Asset-Requests/Silent-Drill-Platoon | Email: smb.mfr.pao.comrel@usmc.mil

Site Map   The Web site map allows visitors to look for specific topics or to browse content that aligns with their interests. http://www.marines.mil/Home/SiteMap.aspx

Social Media   The Marine Corps maintains a social media presence and supports online communities where people can go to share and collect information and stories. http://www.marines.mil/News/Social-Media

Speakers   The Marine Corps supports speaking engagements for community events nationwide, ranging from small-town civic organizations to big-city national conventions. The Marine Corps In the Community program helps business executives, educators, members of civic organizations, conference organizers, and others make contact with a Marine Corps public speaker. Phone, 504-697-8184. http://www.marines.mil/Community-Relations/Asset-Requests/Speakers | Email: smb.mfr.pao.comrel@usmc.mil

Tattoo Regulations   The Marine Corps tattoo policy seeks to balance personal taste with the high standards of professional military appearance and heritage. The Marine Corps Bulletin 1020 (June 2016) explains the current tattoo policy, which replaces previous guidance on the subject. http://www.marines.mil/Tattoos.aspx

Unit Directory   A complete list of Marine Corps units with links to their respective web pages is available online. http://www.marines.mil/Units.aspx http://www.marines.mil/Contact-Us

For further information regarding the Marine Corps, contact the Director of Public Affairs, Headquarters, U.S. Marine Corps, 2 Navy Annex–Pentagon 5D773, Washington, DC 20380-1775. Phone, 703-614-1492.

United States Naval Academy

Annapolis, MD 21402-5018
Phone, 410-293-1500. Internet, http://www.usna.edu

Superintendent	Vice Adm. Walter E. Carter, Jr., USN
Commandant of Midshipmen	Col. Stephen E. Liszewski, USMC

The U.S. Naval Academy is the undergraduate college of the Naval Service. Through its comprehensive 4-year program, which stresses excellence in academics, physical education, professional training, conduct, and honor, the Academy prepares young men and women morally, mentally, and physically to be professional officers in the Navy and Marine Corps. All graduates receive a Bachelor of Science degree in 1 of 19 majors. https://www.usna.edu/About/index.php

Sources of Information

Armel-Leftwich Visitor Center   From March to December, the visitor center is open daily,

9 a.m.–5 p.m. During January and February, the visitor center is open on weekdays, 9 a.m.–4 p.m. The gift shop, however, is open on the weekends, 9 a.m.–5 p.m. http://www.usnabsd.com/for-visitors | Email: tourinfo@usna.edu

A–Z Index   The Naval Academy's Web site has an alphabetical index to help visitors search for information or browse topics of interest. https://www.usna.edu/TOC/index.php

Career Opportunities   Six sources of employment are associated with the Naval Academy and its supporting organizations. https://www.usna.edu/Employment

Naval Academy Preparatory School   The Naval Academy Preparatory School prepares midshipman candidates for success at the U.S. Naval Academy. The 10-month course of instruction, August– May, centers on preparation in Chemistry, English Composition, Information Technology, Mathematics, and Physics. Phone, 401-841-6966 (administration). Phone, 401-841-2947 (academics). https:// www.usna.edu/NAPS

Naval Academy Store   All Profits support the brigade of midshipmen. http:// navyonline.com
Nimitz Library   An online tool is available to search the library's collection of articles, books, ebooks, and journals. Phone, 410-293-6945. https://www.usna.edu/Library | Email: askref@usna.edu https://www.usna. edu/Contact

For further information concerning the U.S. Naval Academy, contact the Superintendent, U.S. Naval Academy, 121 Blake Road, Annapolis, MD 21402-5018.

DEFENSE AGENCIES
Defense Advanced Research Projects Agency

675 North Randolph Street, Arlington, VA 22203-2114
Phone, 703-526-6630. Internet, http://www.darpa.mil

Director	VICTORIA COLEMAN
Deputy Director	PETER HIGHNAM
https://www.darpa.mil/about-us/people	

The Sources of Information were updated 12–2020.

The Defense Advanced Research Projects Agency is a separately organized agency within the Department of Defense and is under the authority, direction, and control of the Under Secretary of Defense (Acquisition, Technology and Logistics). The Agency serves as the central research and development organization of the Department of Defense with a primary responsibility to maintain U.S. technological superiority over potential adversaries. It pursues imaginative and innovative research and development projects, and conducts demonstration projects that represent technology appropriate for joint programs, programs in support of deployed forces, or selected programs of the military departments. To this end, the Agency arranges, manages, and directs the performance of work connected with assigned advanced projects by the military departments, other Government agencies, individuals, private business entities, and educational or research institutions, as appropriate. http://www.darpa.mil

For further information, contact the Defense Advanced Research Projects Agency, 675 North Randolph Street, Arlington, VA 22203-2114. Phone, 703-526-6630.

Defense Commissary Agency

1300 E Avenue, Fort Lee, VA 23801-1800
Phone, 804-734-8720. Internet, http://www.commissaries.com

Director / Chief Executive Officer	WILLIAM F. MOORE
Deputy Director / Chief Operating Officer	MICHAEL J. DOWLING
https://www.commissaries.com/our-agency/deca-organization	

The Sources of Information were updated 12–2020.

The Defense Commissary Agency (DeCA) was established in 1990 and is under the authority, direction, and control of the Under Secretary of Defense for Personnel and Readiness and the operational supervision of the Defense Commissary Agency Board of Directors.

DeCA provides an efficient and effective worldwide system of commissaries that sell quality groceries and household supplies at low prices to members of the Armed Services community. This benefit satisfies customer demand for quality products and delivers exceptional savings while enhancing the military community's quality of life. DeCA works closely with its employees, customers, and civilian business partners to satisfy its customers and to promote the commissary benefit. The benefit fosters recruitment, retention, and readiness of skilled and trained personnel.

Sources of Information

Employment information is available at www.commissaries.com or by calling the following telephone numbers: employment (703-603-1600); small business activities (804-734-8000, extension 4-8015/4-8529); contracting for resale items (804-734-8000, extension 4-8884/4-8885); and contracting for operations support and equipment (804-734-8000, extension 4-8391/4-8830). http://www.commissaries.com

For further information, contact the Defense Commissary Agency, 1300 E Avenue, Fort Lee, VA 23801-1800. Phone, 804-734-8720

Defense Contract Audit Agency

8725 John J. Kingman Road, Suite 2135, Fort Belvoir, VA 22060-6219
Phone, 703-767-3265. Internet, http://www.dcaa.mil | Email: dcaaweb@dcaa.mil

Director   ANITA F. BALES
https://www.dcaa.mil/Portals/88/FY2019%20DCAA%20Report%20to%20Congress.
   pdf?ver=XKAncoiKefo8TD5eh-OCxQ%3d%3d

The Sources of Information were updated 4–2020.

The Defense Contract Audit Agency (DCAA) was established in 1965 and is under the authority, direction, and control of the Under Secretary of Defense (Comptroller)/Chief Financial Officer. DCAA performs all necessary contract audit functions for DOD and provides accounting and financial advisory services to all Defense components responsible for procurement and contract administration. These services are provided in connection with the negotiation, administration, and settlement of contracts and subcontracts to ensure taxpayer dollars are spent on fair and reasonable contract prices. They include evaluating the acceptability of costs claimed or proposed by contractors and reviewing the efficiency and economy of contractor operations. Other Government agencies may request the DCAA's services under appropriate arrangements.

DCAA manages its operations through five regional offices responsible for approximately 104 field audit offices throughout the United States and overseas. Each region is responsible for the contract auditing function in its assigned area. Point of contact information for DCAA regional offices is available at www.dcaa.mil. http://www.dcaa.mil | Email: dcaaweb@dcaa.mil

For further information, contact the Executive Officer, Defense Contract Audit Agency, 8725 John J. Kingman Road, Suite 2135, Fort Belvoir, VA 22060-6219. Phone, 703-767-3265.

Defense Contract Management Agency

3901 A Avenue, Fort Lee, VA 23801
Phone, 804-734-0814. Internet, http://www.dcma.mil

Director   Lt. Gen. David G. Bassett, USA
Deputy Director   John M. Lyle
http://www.dcma.mil/About-Us   9

The Sources of Information were updated 12–2020.

The Defense Contract Management Agency (DCMA) was established by the Deputy Secretary of Defense in 2000 and is under the authority, direction, and control of the Under Secretary of Defense (Acquisition, Technology, and Logistics). DCMA is responsible for DOD contract management in support of the military departments, other DOD components, the National Aeronautics and Space Administration, other designated Federal and State agencies, foreign governments, and international organizations, as appropriate. http://www.dcma.mil

For further information, contact the Office of General Counsel, Defense Contract Management Agency, 3901 A Avenue, Fort Lee, VA 23801. Phone, 804-734-0814.

Defense Finance and Accounting Service

4800 Mark Center Drive, Suite 08J25-01, Alexandria, VA 22350-3000
Phone, 571-372-7883. Internet, http://www.dfas.mil

Director	AUDREY Y. DAVIS
Principal Deputy Director	(VACANCY)
https://www.dfas.mil/Pressroom/dfasleadership	

The above list of key personnel was updated 12–2020.

The Defense Finance and Accounting Service (DFAS) was established in 1991 under the authority, direction, and control of the Under Secretary of Defense (Comptroller)/Chief Financial Officer to strengthen and reduce costs of financial management and operations within DOD. DFAS is responsible for all payments to servicemembers, employees, vendors, and contractors. It provides business intelligence and finance and accounting information to DOD decisionmakers. DFAS is also responsible for preparing annual financial statements and the consolidation, standardization, and modernization of finance and accounting requirements, functions, processes, operations, and systems for DOD. http://www.dfas.mil

For further information, contact Defense Finance and Accounting Service Corporate Communications, 4800 Mark Center Drive, Suite 08J25-01, Alexandria, VA 22350-3000. Phone, 571-372-7883.

Defense Information Systems Agency

P.O. Box 549, Command Building, Fort Meade, MD 20755
Phone, 301-225-6000. Internet, http://www.disa.mil | Email: dia-pao@dia.mil

Director	VICE ADM. NANCY A. NORTON, USN
Executive Deputy Director	ANTHONY MONTEMARANO
http://www.disa.mil/About/Our-Leaders	

The above list of key personnel was updated 12–2020.

The Defense Information Systems Agency (DISA), established originally as the Defense Communications Agency in 1960, is under the authority, direction, and control of the Assistant Secretary of Defense (Networks and Information Integration). DISA is a combat support agency responsible for planning, engineering, acquiring, fielding, operating, and supporting global net-centric solutions to serve the needs of the President, Vice President, Secretary of Defense, and other DOD components. http://www.disa.mil | Email: dia-pao@dia.mil

For further information, contact the Public Affairs Office, Defense Information Systems Agency, P.O. Box 549, Command Building, Fort Meade, MD 20755. Phone, 301-225-6000.

Defense Intelligence Agency

200 MacDill Boulevard, Washington DC 20340-5100
Phone, 202-231-0800. Internet, http://www.dia.mil | Email: dia-pao@dia.mil

Director	Lt. Gen. Scott D. Berrier, USA
Deputy Director	Suzanne L. White
http://www.dia.mil/About/Leadership	

The above list of key personnel was updated 12–2020.

The Defense Intelligence Agency (DIA) was established in 1961 and is under the authority, direction, and control of the Under Secretary of Defense for Intelligence. DIA provides timely, objective, and cogent military intelligence to warfighters, force planners, as well as defense and national security policymakers. DIA obtains and reports information through its field sites worldwide and the Defense Attache System; provides timely intelligence analysis; directs Defense Human Intelligence programs; operates the Joint Intelligence Task Force for Combating Terrorism and the Joint Military Intelligence College; coordinates and facilitates Measurement and Signature Intelligence activities; manages and plans collections from specialized technical sources; manages secure DOD intelligence networks; and coordinates required intelligence support for the Secretary of Defense, Joint Chiefs of Staff, Combatant Commanders, and Joint Task Forces. http://www.dia.mil | Email: dia-pao@dia.mil

For further information, contact the Public Affairs Office, Defense Intelligence Agency, 200 MacDill Boulevard, Washington DC 20340-5100. Phone, 202-231-0800.

Defense Legal Services Agency

The Pentagon, Washington, DC 20301-1600
Phone, 703-695-3341. Internet, http://www.dod.mil/dodgc

Director / General Counsel of the Department of Defense	Paul C. Ney, Jr.
https://ogc.osd.mil/gc_bio.html	
Principal Deputy General Counsel of the Department of Defense	William S. Castle
https://ogc.osd.mil/dgc_bio.html	

The above list of key personnel was updated 12–2020.

The Defense Legal Services Agency (DLSA) was established in 1981 and is under the authority, direction, and control of the General Counsel of the Department of Defense, who also serves as its Director. DLSA provides legal advice and services for specified DOD components and adjudication of personnel security cases for DOD and other assigned Federal agencies and departments. It also provides technical support and assistance for development of the Department's legislative program; coordinates positions on legislation and Presidential Executive orders; provides a centralized legislative and congressional document reference and distribution point for the Department; maintains the Department's historical legislative files; and administers programs governing standards of conduct and alternative dispute resolution. https://ogc.osd.mil/index.html

For further information, contact the Administrative Office, Defense Legal Services Agency, Room 3A734, Washington, DC 20301-1600. Phone, 703-697-8343.

Defense Logistics Agency

8725 John J. Kingman Road, Suite 2533, Fort Belvoir, VA 22060-6221
Phone, 703-767-5264. Internet, http://www.dla.mil

Director	VICE ADM. MICHELLE C. SKUBIC
Vice Director	MICHAEL D. SCOTT
http://www.dla.mil/Leaders.aspx	

The above list of key personnel was updated 12–2020.

The Defense Logistics Agency (DLA) is under the authority, direction, and control of the Under Secretary of Defense for Acquisition, Technology, and Logistics. DLA supports both the logistics requirements of the military services and their acquisition of weapons and other materiel. It provides logistics support and technical services to all branches of the military and to a number of Federal agencies. DLA supply centers consolidate the requirements of the military services and procure the supplies in sufficient quantities to meet their projected needs. DLA manages supplies in eight commodity areas: fuel, food, clothing, construction material, electronic supplies, general supplies, industrial supplies, and medical supplies. Information on DLA's field activities and regional commands is available at www.dla.mil/ataglance.aspx.

Sources of Information

Career Opportunities For the Washington, DC, metropolitan area, all inquiries and applications concerning job recruitment programs should be addressed to Human Resources, Customer Support Office, 3990 East Broad Street, Building 11, Section 3, Columbus, OH, 43213-0919. Phone, 877-352-4762. http://www.dla.mil/Careers.aspx

Environmental Program For information on the environmental program, contact the Staff Director, Environmental and Safety, Defense Logistics Agency, Attn: DSS-E, 8725 John J. Kingman Road, Fort Belvoir, VA 22060-6221. Phone, 703-767-6278.

Procurement / Small Business Activities For information on procurement and small business activities, contact the Director, Small and Disadvantaged Business Utilization, Defense Logistics Agency, Attn: DB, 8725 John J. Kingman Road, Fort Belvoir, VA 22060-6221. Phone, 703-767-0192. http://www.dla.mil/DoingBusinessWithDLA.aspx

Surplus Sales Program Questions concerning this program should be addressed to DOD Surplus Sales, International Sales Office, 74 Washington Avenue North, Battle Creek, MI 49017-3092. Phone, 877-352-2255. http://dispositionservices.dla.mil/sales/Pages/default.aspx http://www.dla.mil

For further information, contact the Defense Logistics Agency, 8725 John J. Kingman Road, Fort Belvoir, VA 22060-6221. Phone, 703-767-5264.

Defense Security Cooperation Agency

201 Twelfth Street South, Suite 203, Arlington, VA 22202-5408
Phone, 703-604-6605. Internet, http://www.dsca.mil | Email: info@dsca.mil

Director	HEIDI H. GRANT
Deputy Director	CARA L. ABERCROMBIE, ACTING
https://www.dsca.mil/about-dsca/leadership	

The above list of key personnel was updated 12–2020.

The Defense Security Cooperation Agency (DSCA) was established in 1971 and is under the authority, direction, and control of the Under Secretary of Defense (Policy).

DSCA provides traditional security assistance functions such as military assistance, international military education and training, and foreign military sales. DSCA also has program management responsibilities for humanitarian assistance, demining, and other DOD programs. http://www.dsca.mil | Email: info@dsca.mil

For further information, contact the Defense Security Cooperation Agency, 201 Twelfth Street South, Suite 203, Arlington, VA 22202-5408. Phone, 703-604-6605.

Defense Counterintelligence and Security Agency

27130 Telegraph Road, Quantico, VA 22134
Phone, 703-617-2352. Internet, http://www.dss.mil

Director	WILLIAM K. LIETZAU
https://www.dcsa.mil/About-Us/Leadership/Bio-Display/ Article/1822359/william-k-lietzau	
Assistant Directors	
Background Investigations	CHRISTY K. WILDER
Critical Technology Protection	DAVID STAPLETON
https://www.dcsa.mil/about/leadership	

The above list of key personnel was updated 12–2020.

The Defense Counterintelligence and Security Agency (DCSA) is under the authority, direction, and control of the Under Secretary of Defense for Intelligence. It protects America's trusted workforce and trusted real and virtual workspaces. The DCSA joins two missions: personnel vetting and critical technology protection. Vetting personnel and protecting technology are supported by counterintelligence and training, education, and certification functions. The DCSA services over 100 Federal entities, oversees 10,000 cleared companies, and conducts approximately 2 million background investigations each year.

The DCSA ensures the safeguarding of classified information used by contractors on behalf of the DOD and other executive branch agencies under the National Industrial Security Program. It oversees the protection of conventional arms, munitions, and explosives in the custody of DOD contractors; evaluates the protection of selected private sector critical assets and infrastructures; and recommends measures needed to maintain operations identified as vital to the DOD. The agency makes clearance determinations for industry and provides support services for DOD Central Adjudicative Facilities. It provides security education, training, and proactive awareness programs for military, civilian, and cleared industry to enhance their proficiency and awareness of DOD security policies and procedures. The DCSA also integrates counterintelligence principles into security countermeasures missions and supports the national counterintelligence strategy. https://www.dcsa.mil/abouthttps://www.dcsa.mil/contact/pao | Email: dcsa.quantico.dcsa-hq.mbx.pa@mail.mil

For further information, contact the Defense Counterintelligence and Security Agency, Office of Public Affairs, 27130 Telegraph Road, Quantico, VA 22134. Phone, 571-305-6562.

Defense Threat Reduction Agency

8725 John J. Kingman Road, MS 6201, Fort Belvoir, VA 22060-6201
Phone, 703-767-7594. Internet, http://www.dtra.mil

Director	VAYL S. OXFORD
https://www.dtra.mil/About/DTRADirector	
Deputy Director	MAJ. GEN. ANTONIO M. FLETCHER, USA
https://www.dtra.mil/About/DTRA-Leadership/	
Deputy-Director-for-Combat-Support	

The above list of key personnel was updated 12–2020.

The Defense Threat Reduction Agency (DTRA) was established in 1998 and is under the authority, direction, and control of the Under Secretary of Defense for Acquisition, Technology, and Logistics. DTRA's mission is to reduce the threat posed by weapons of mass destruction (WMD). DTRA covers the full range of WMD threats (chemical, biological, nuclear, radiological, and high explosive), bridges the gap between the warfighters and the technical community, sustains the nuclear deterrent, and provides both offensive and defensive technology and operational concepts to warfighters. DTRA reduces the threat of WMD by implementing arms control treaties and executing the Cooperative Threat Reduction Program. It uses combat support, technology development, and chemical-biological defense to deter the use and reduce the impact of such weapons. DTRA also prepares for future threats by developing the technology and concepts needed to counter new WMD threats and adversaries. https://www.dtra.mil/WhoWeArehttp://www.dtra.mil

For further information, contact the Public Affairs Office, Defense Threat Reduction Agency, 8725 John J. Kingman Road, MS 6201, Fort Belvoir, VA 22060-5916. Phone, 703-767-7594. Email, dtra.publicaffairs@dtra.mil.

Missile Defense Agency

5700 Eighteenth Street, Bldg 245, Fort Belvoir, VA 22060-5573
Phone, 703-695-6420. Email: mda.info@mda.mil

Director	VICE ADM. JON A. HILL, USN
https://www.mda.mil/global/documents/pdf/Hill.pdf	
Executive Director	LAURA M. DESIMONE
https://www.mda.mil/global/documents/pdf/orgcht(002).pdf	

[For the Missile Defense Agency statement of organization, see the Code of Federal Regulations, Title 32, Part 388]

The above list of key personnel was updated 12–2020.

The Missile Defense Agency's (MDA) mission is to establish and deploy a layered ballistic missile defense system to intercept missiles in all phases of their flight and against all ranges of threats. This capability will provide a defense of the United States, deployed forces, and allies. The MDA is under the authority, direction, and control of the Under Secretary of Defense for Acquisition, Technology, and Logistics. It manages and directs DOD's ballistic missile defense acquisition programs and enables the Services to field elements of the overall system as soon as practicable. The MDA develops and tests technologies and, if necessary, uses prototype and test assets to provide early capability. Additionally, MDA improves the effectiveness of deployed capabilities by implementing new technologies as they become available or when the threat warrants an accelerated capability. https://www.mda.mil/about/ about.htmlhttps://www.mda.mil/contactus/contact.html | Email: mda.info@mda.mil

For further information, contact the Human Resources Directorate, Missile Defense Agency, 5700 Eighteenth Street, Bldg 245, Fort Belvoir, VA 22060-5573. Phone, 703-695-6420. Email, mda.info@mda.mil.

National Geospatial-Intelligence Agency

7500 Geoint Drive, MS N73-OCCAE, Springfield, Virginia 22150
Phone, 571-557-7300. Internet, http://www.nga.mil

Director https://www.nga.mil/about/1596227427521_Vice_ Admiral_Robert_D_Sharp_Director_.html	VICE ADM. ROBERT D. SHARP, USN
Deputy Director https://www.nga.mil/about/1596228141343_Dr_ Stacey_A_Dixon_Deputy_Director_.html	STACEY A. DIXON

The above list of key personnel was updated 12–2020.

The National Geospatial-Intelligence Agency (NGA), formerly the National Imagery and Mapping Agency, was established in 1996 and is under the authority, direction, and control of the Under Secretary of Defense for Intelligence. NGA is a DOD combat support agency and a member of the national intelligence community. NGA's mission is to provide timely, relevant, and accurate geospatial intelligence in support of our national security. Geospatial intelligence means the use and analysis of imagery to describe, assess, and visually depict physical features and geographically referenced activities on the Earth. Headquartered in Bethesda, MD, NGA has major facilities in the Washington, DC, Northern Virginia, and St. Louis, MO, areas with NGA support teams worldwide. https://www.nga.mil/contact/1595419637908_Contact_Us.html | Email: publicaffairs@nga.mil

For further information, contact the Public Affairs Office, National Geospatial-Intelligence Agency,. 7500 Geoint Drive, MS N73-OCCAE, Springfield, Virginia 22150. Phone, 571-557-7300.

National Security Agency / Central Security Service

Fort Meade, MD 20755-6248
Phone, 301-688-6524. Fax, 301-688-6198. Internet, http://www.nsa.gov

Director https://www.nsa.gov/About-Us/Current-Leadership/Article- View/Article/1596277/paul-m-nakasone/	GEN. PAUL M. NAKASONE, USA
Deputy Director https://www.nsa.gov/About-Us/Current-Leadership/Article- View/Article/1596282/george-c-barnes/	GEORGE C. BARNES

The above list of key personnel was updated 12–2020.

The National Security Agency (NSA) was established in 1952 and the Central Security Service (CSS) was established in 1972. NSA/CSS is under the authority, direction, and control of the Under Secretary of Defense for Intelligence. As the Nation's cryptologic organization, NSA/CSS employs the Nation's premier codemakers and codebreakers. It ensures an informed, alert, and secure environment for U.S. warfighters and policymakers. The cryptologic resources of NSA/CSS unite to provide U.S. policymakers with intelligence information derived from America's adversaries while protecting U.S. Government signals and information systems from exploitation by those same adversaries. https://www.nsa.gov/what-we-dohttps://www.nsa.gov/about/contact-us | Email: nsapao@nsa.gov

For further information, contact the Public Affairs Office, National Security Agency/Central Security Service, Fort Meade, MD 20755-6248. Phone, 301-688-6524. Fax, 301-688-6198.

Pentagon Force Protection Agency

9000 Defense Pentagon, Washington, DC 20301
Phone, 703-697-1001. Internet, http://www.pfpa.mil

Director	DANIEL P. WALSH, ACTING

https://www.pfpa.mil/Our-Agency/Leadership/Dr-Daniel-P-Walsh

Executive Directors	
Law Enforcement	CHRISTOPHER BARGERY
Security Integration and Technology	JAMES A. DAY

https://www.pfpa.mil/Our-Agency/Leadership

The above list of key personnel was updated 12–2020.

The Pentagon Force Protection Agency (PFPA) was established in May 2002 in response to the events of September 11, 2001, and subsequent terrorist threats facing the DOD workforce and facilities in the National Capital Region (NCR). PFPA is under the authority, direction, and control of the Director, Administration and Management, in the Office of the Secretary of Defense. PFPA provides force protection, security, and law enforcement for the people, facilities, infrastructure, and other resources at the Pentagon and for DOD activities and facilities within the NCR that are not under the jurisdiction of a military department. Consistent with the national strategy on combating terrorism, PFPA addresses threats, including chemical, biological, and radiological agents, through a strategy of prevention, preparedness, detection, and response to ensure that the DOD workforce and facilities in the NCR are secure and protected. https://www.pfpa.mil/Our-Agency/Our-Mission-Visionhttps://www.pfpa.mil/Contact

For further information, contact the Pentagon Force Protection Agency, 9000 Defense Pentagon, Washington, DC 20301. Phone, 703-697-1001.

JOINT SERVICE SCHOOLS
Defense Acquisition University

9820 Belvoir Road, Fort Belvoir, VA 22060-5565
Phone, 703-805-2764. Internet, http://www.dau.mil

President	JAMES P. WOOSLEY

https://www.dau.edu/about/Documents/DAU_James%20Woolsey%20Bio_20170222.pdf

Vice President	FRANK L. KELLEY

https://www.dau.edu/about/p/Mission-Organization

The above list of key personnel was updated 12–2020.

The Defense Acquisition University (DAU), established pursuant to the Defense Acquisition Workforce Improvement Act of 1990 (10 U.S.C. 1701 note), serves as the DOD center for acquisition, technology, and logistics training; performance support; continuous learning; and knowledge sharing. DAU is a unified structure with five regional campuses and the Defense Systems Management College-School of Program Managers, which provides executive and international acquisition training. DAU's mission is to provide the training, career management, and services that enable the acquisition, technology, and logistics community to make smart business decisions and deliver timely and affordable capabilities to warfighters. https://www.dau.edu/abouthttps://www.dau.edu/about/p/Contact-Us

For further information, contact the Public Affairs Office, Defense Acquisition University, 9820 Belvoir Road, Fort Belvoir, VA 22060-5565. Phone, 703-805-5412.

National Intelligence University

MAIN CAMPUS: Intelligence Community Campus—Bethesda, MD
Phone, 301-243-2093. Internet, http://ni-u.edu/wp

President	J. Scott Cameron
https://ni-u.edu/wp/about-niu/leadership-2/office-of-the-president	
Executive Vice President / Provost	Terrence Markin
https://ni-u.edu/wp/about-niu/leadership-2	

The above list of key personnel was updated 12–2020.

The National Intelligence University, formerly the Joint Military Intelligence College, was established in 1962. The College is a joint service interagency educational institution serving the intelligence community and operates under the authority of the Director, Defense Intelligence Agency. Its mission is to educate military and civilian intelligence professionals, conduct and disseminate relevant intelligence research, and perform academic outreach regarding intelligence matters. The College is authorized by Congress to award the bachelor of science in intelligence, master of science and technology intelligence, and master of science of strategic intelligence. Courses are offered to full-time students in a traditional daytime format and for part-time students in the evening, on Saturday, and in an executive format (one weekend per month and a 2-week intensive summer period). https://ni-u.edu/wp/about-niuhttps://ni-u.edu/wp/contact | Email: niuadmit@dodiis.mil

For further information, contact the Office of Enrollment and Student Services, National Intelligence University, Roberdeau Hall, Washington, DC 20511. Phone, 301-243-2094. Fax, 301-227-7067.

National Defense University

300 Fifth Avenue, Building 62, Fort Lesley J. McNair, DC 20319-5066
Phone, 202-685-2649. Internet, http://www.ndu.edu

College of Information and Cyberspace
Internet, http://cic.ndu.edu

College of International Security Affairs
Internet, http://cisa.ndu.edu

Joint Forces Staff College
Internet, http://jfsc.ndu.edu

National War College
Internet, http://nwc.ndu.edu

The Eisenhower School for National Security and Resource Strategy
Internet, http://es.ndu.edu

President	VICE ADM. FRITZ ROEGGE, USN
https://www.ndu.edu/About/Leadership/Article-View/	
Article/1314417/vice-admiral-fritz-roegge-usn	
Provost	ALAN DRIMMER
Senior Vice President	ARNOLD CHACON
Chancellors	
College of Information and Cyberspace	CASSANDRA C. LEWIS, ACTING
College of International Security Affairs	JOHN HOOVER, ACTING
Commandants	
Joint Forces Staff College	
National War College	
The Eisenhower School for National Security and Resource	
Strategy	
https://www.ndu.edu/About/Leadership	

The above list of key personnel was updated 12–2020.

National Defense University

The mission of the National Defense University is to prepare military and civilian leaders from the United States and other countries to evaluate national and international security challenges through multidisciplinary educational and research programs, professional exchanges, and outreach.

The National Defense University was established in 1976 and comprises the following colleges and programs: The Eisenhower School for National Security and Resource Strategy, National War College, Joint Forces Staff College, College of Information and Cyberspace (formerly, Information Resources Management College), College of International Security Affairs, Institute for National Strategic Studies, Center for the Study of Weapons of Mass Destruction, Center for Technology and National Security Policy, International Student Management Office, Joint Reserve Affairs Center, CAPSTONE, Security of Defense Corporate Fellows Program, NATO Education Center, Institute for National Security Ethics and Leadership, Center for Joint Strategic Logistics Excellence, Center for Applied Strategic Leaders, and Center for Complex Operations. http://www.ndu.edu

For further information, contact the Human Resources Directorate, National Defense University, 300 Fifth Avenue, Building 62, Fort Lesley J. McNair, DC 20319-5066. Phone, 202-685-2169.

College of Information and Cyberspace

After a Joint Staff request, in response to a continually changing national security environment, which includes new cyberspace and information related challenges, the Information Resources Management College was renamed the College of Information and Cyberspace (CIC). The change was confirmed by law in the Fiscal Year 2017 National Defense Authorization Act. The CIC offers educational activities, services, and programs for preparing information professionals to play critical roles in national security in the Age of Information. https://cic.ndu.edu/Contact/Contact-Us/ | Email: CICOSS@ndu.edu

For further information, contact the Office of Student Services, College of Information and Cyberspace, 300 Fifth Avenue, Building 62, Fort McNair, DC 20319-5066. Phone, 202-685-6300.

College of International Security Affairs

The College of International Security Affairs (CISA) is one of NDU's five colleges. CISA educates students from across the international, interagency, and interservice communities. CISA's primary areas of concentration include counterterrorism, conflict management of stability of operations, homeland security, and defense and international security studies. CISA is also home to NDU's International Counterterrorism Fellowship Program. http://cisa.ndu.edu

For further information, contact the Office of Academic Affairs, College of International Security Affairs, 260 Fifth Avenue, Building 64, Fort McNair, DC 20319-5066. Phone, 202-685-7774.

Joint Forces Staff College   The Joint Forces Staff College (JFSC) is an intermediate- and senior-level joint college in the professional military education system dedicated to the study of the principles, perspectives, and techniques of joint operational-level planning and warfare. The mission of JFSC is to educate national security professionals in the planning and execution of joint, multinational, and interagency operations in order to instill a primary commitment to joint, multinational, and interagency teamwork, attitudes, and perspectives. The College accomplishes this mission through four schools: the Joint Advanced Warfighters School, the Joint and Combined Warfighting School, the Joint Continuing and Distance Education School, and the Joint Command, Control, and Information Operations School. http://jfsc.ndu.edu

For further information, contact the Public Affairs Officer, Joint Forces Staff College, 7800 Hampton Boulevard, Norfolk, VA 23511-1702. Phone, 757-443-6212. Fax, 757-443-6210.

National War College   The National War College provides education in national security policy to selected military officers and career civil service employees of Federal departments and agencies concerned with national security. It is the only senior service college with the primary mission of offering a course of study that emphasizes national security policy formulation and the planning and implementation of national strategy. Its 10-month academic program is an issue-centered study in U.S. national security. The elective program is designed to permit each student to tailor his or her academic experience to meet individual professional development needs. http://nwc.ndu.edu

For further information, contact the Office of Administration, National War College, 300 D Street SW., Building 61, Fort McNair, DC 20319-5078. Phone, 202-685-3674.

The Eisenhower School for National Security and Resource Strategy   The Dwight D. Eisenhower School for National Security and Resource Strategy provides graduate level education to senior members of the U.S. Armed Forces, Government civilians, foreign nationals, and professionals from the private industrial sector. The School prepares students to contribute to national security strategy and policy, emphasizing the evaluation, marshaling, and managing of national resources. Students who fulfill the degree requirements receive a Master of Science degree in national resource strategy. http://es.ndu.edu/Home.aspx

For further information, contact the Director of Operations, Dwight D. Eisenhower School for National Security and Resource Strategy, 408 Fourth Avenue, Building 59, Fort McNair, DC 20319-5062. Phone, 202-685-4333.

Uniformed Services University of the Health Sciences

4301 Jones Bridge Road, Bethesda, MD 20814-4799
Phone, 301-295-3190. Internet, http://www.usuhs.mil

President
https://www.usuhs.edu/sites/default/files/
  media/vpe/pdf/thomas_richard_w_edit_17_
  nov_2020.pdf
	Maj. Gen. Richard W. Thomas, USA (retired)

Senior Vice Presidents for University Programs	
Southern Region	Lt. Gen. Thomas W. Travis, USAF (retired)
Western Region	Rear Adm. William Roberts, USN (retired)
https://www.usuhs.edu/pres/leadership	

The above list of key personnel was updated 12–2020.

Authorized by act of September 21, 1972 (10 U.S.C. 2112), the Uniformed Services University of the Health Sciences was established to educate career-oriented medical officers for the Military Departments and the Public Health Service. The University currently incorporates the F. Edward Hebert School of Medicine (including graduate and continuing education programs) and the Graduate School of Nursing.

Students are selected by procedures recommended by the Board of Regents and prescribed by the Secretary of Defense. The actual selection is carried out by a faculty committee on admissions and is based upon motivation and dedication to a career in the uniformed services and an overall appraisal of the personal and intellectual characteristics of the candidates without regard to sex, race, religion, or national origin. Applicants must be U.S. citizens.

Medical school matriculants will be commissioned officers in one of the uniformed services. They must meet the physical and personal qualifications for such a commission and must give evidence of a strong commitment to serving as a uniformed medical officer. The graduating medical student is required to serve a period of obligation of not less than 7 years, excluding graduate medical education.

Students of the Graduate School of Nursing must be commissioned officers of the Army, Navy, Air Force, or Public Health Service prior to application. Graduate nursing students must serve a commitment determined by their respective service. http://www.usuhs.mil

For further information, contact the President, Uniformed Services University of the Health Sciences, 4301 Jones Bridge Road, Bethesda, MD 20814-4799. Phone, 301-295-3013.

DEPARTMENT OF EDUCATION

400 Maryland Avenue SW., Washington, DC 20202
Phone, 202-401-2000. TTY, 800-437-0833. Internet, http://www.ed.gov

Secretary of Education	MIGUEL CARDONA
Deputy Secretary	CINDY MARTEN
Under Secretary	JAMES KVAAL

Office of the Secretary
Assistant Deputy Secretary and Director, Office of English
   Language Acquisition
Assistant Deputy Secretary, Office of Innovation and
   Improvement
Assistant Secretary, Office for Civil Rights
Assistant Secretary, Office of Communication and
   Outreach
Assistant Secretary, Office of Elementary and Secondary
   Education
Assistant Secretary, Office of Legislation and
   Congressional Affairs
Assistant Secretary, Office of Planning, Evaluation and
   Policy Development
Assistant Secretary, Office of Special Education and
   Rehabilitative Services
Chief of Staff
Director, International Affairs Office
Director, Institute of Education Sciences
Inspector General

Office of the Deputy Secretary
Assistant Secretary, Office of Management
Chief Financial Officer
Chief Information Officer
Director, Office of Educational Technology
General Counsel

Office of the Under Secretary
Assistant Secretary, Office of Career, Technical, and Adult
   Education
Assistant Secretary, Office of Postsecondary Education
Chief Operating Officer for Federal Student Aid
Director, Center for Faith-Based and Neighborhood
   Partnerships
Executive Director, White House Initiative on American
   Indian and Alaska Native Education
Executive Director, White House Initiative on Asian
   Americans and Pacific Islanders
Executive Director, White House Initiative on Educational
   Excellence for African Americans

Executive Director, White House Initiative on Educational
  Excellence for Hispanic Americans
Executive Director, White House Initiative on Historically
  Black Colleges and Universities

The Department of Education ensures equal access to education; promotes educational excellence; and administers, coordinates, and makes policy for most Federal assistance to education with the aim of raising levels of student achievement and readiness for the global future.

The Department of Education was created by the Department of Education Organization Act (20 U.S.C. 3411) and is administered under the supervision and direction of the Secretary of Education. http://www2.ed.gov/about/landing.jhtml?src=ln

Secretary   The Secretary of Education advises the President on education plans, policies, and programs of the Federal Government and serves as the chief executive officer of the Department, supervising all Department activities, providing support to States and localities, and focusing resources to ensure equal access to educational excellence throughout the Nation. http://www2.ed.gov/about/offices/list/os/index.html?src=oc

Activities

Career, Technical, and Adult Education   The Office of Career, Technical, and Adult Education (OCTAE) administers grant, contract, and technical assistance programs for vocational-technical education and for adult education and literacy. It promotes programs that enable adults to acquire the basic literacy skills necessary to function in today's society. The Office also helps students acquire challenging academic and technical skills and prepare for high-skill, high-wage, and high-demand occupations in the 21st-century global economy. OCTAE provides national leadership and works to strengthen the role of community colleges in expanding access to postsecondary education for youth and adults in advancing workforce development. http://www2.ed.gov/about/offices/list/ovae/index.html

Education Sciences   The Institute of Education Sciences was formally established by the Education Sciences Reform Act of 2002 (20 U.S.C. 9501 note). The Institute includes national education centers focused on research, special education, statistics, and evaluation and is the mechanism through which the Department supports the research activities needed to improve education policy and practice. https://ies.ed.gov

Elementary and Secondary Education   The Office of Elementary and Secondary Education directs, coordinates, and formulates policy relating to early childhood, elementary, and secondary education. Included are grants and contracts to State educational agencies and local school districts, postsecondary schools, and nonprofit organizations for disadvantaged, migrant, and Indian children; enhancement of State student achievement assessment systems; improvement of reading instruction; economic impact aid; technology; safe and healthy schools; and after-school learning programs. The Office also focuses on improving K–12 education, providing children with language and cognitive development, early reading, and other readiness skills, and improving the quality of teachers and other instructional staff. http://www2.ed.gov/about/offices/list/oese/index.html

English Language Acquisition   The Office of English Language Acquisition helps children who are limited in their English, including immigrant children and youth, attain English proficiency, develop high levels of academic attainment in English, and meet the same challenging State academic content and student academic achievement standards that all children are expected to meet. http://www2.ed.gov/about/offices/list/oela/index.html

Federal Student Aid   Federal Student Aid partners with postsecondary schools and financial institutions to deliver programs and services that help students finance their education beyond high school. This includes

DEPARTMENT OF EDUCATION

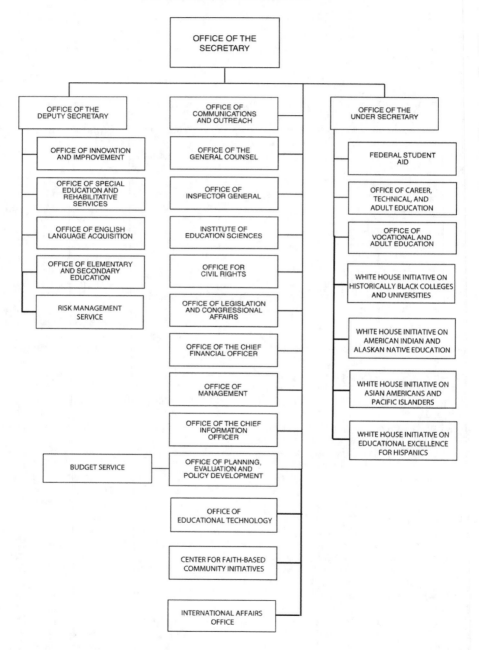

administering postsecondary student financial assistance programs authorized under Title IV of the Higher Education Act of 1965, as amended. https://studentaid.ed.gov

Innovation and Improvement The Office of Innovation and Improvement (OII) oversees competitive grant programs that support innovations in the educational system and disseminates the lessons learned from these innovative practices. OII administers, coordinates, and recommends programs and policy for improving the quality of activities designed to support and test innovations throughout the K–12 system in areas such as parental choice, teacher quality, use of technology in education, and arts in education. OII encourages the establishment of charter schools through planning, start-up funding, and approaches to credit enhancement for charter school facilities. OII also serves as the Department's liaison and resource to the nonpublic education community. http://innovation.ed.gov

Postsecondary Education The Office of Postsecondary Education (OPE) formulates Federal postsecondary education policy and administers programs that address critical national needs in support of the mission to increase access to quality postsecondary education. OPE develops policy for Federal student financial programs and support programs that reach out to low-income, first-generation college students and communities. OPE also supports programs that strengthen the capacity of colleges and universities serving a high percentage of disadvantaged students and improve teacher quality. OPE recognizes accrediting agencies that monitor academic quality, promote innovation in higher education, and expand American educational resources for international studies and services. http://www2.ed.gov/about/offices/list/ope/index.html

Special Education and Rehabilitative Services The Office of Special Education and Rehabilitative Services (OSERS) provides leadership and resources to help ensure that people with disabilities have equal opportunities to learn, work, and live as fully integrated and contributing members of society. OSERS has three components: The Office of Special Education Programs administers the Individuals with Disabilities

Education Act legislation, which helps States meet the early intervention and educational needs of infants, toddlers, children, and youth with disabilities. The Rehabilitation Services Administration supports State vocational rehabilitation, independent living, and assistive technology programs that provide people with disabilities the services, technology, and job training and placement assistance they need to gain meaningful employment and lead independent lives. The National Institute on Disability and Rehabilitation Research supports research and development programs that improve the ability of individuals with disabilities to work and live in a barrier-free, inclusive society. OSERS also supports Gallaudet University, the National Technical Institute for the Deaf, the American Printing House for the Blind, and the Helen Keller National Center. http://www2.ed.gov/about/offices/list/osers/index.html

Sources of Information

Blog "Homeroom" is the official blog of the Department of Education. http://blog.ed.gov

Business Opportunities Contact the Office of Small and Disadvantaged Business Utilization. Phone, 202–245–6301. http://www.ed.gov/fund/contract-opportunities.html

College Scorecard The Department of Education's Web site features a tool to help college bound students find colleges and universities based upon their location, size, and the programs and degrees that they offer. https://collegescorecard.ed.gov

Data / Statistics Information on school accreditation and data on the academic achievement of U.S. students are available on the "Data and Research" Web page. The National Center for Education Statistics collects and analyzes data related to education. Phone, 202–403–5551. http://www2.ed.gov/rschstat/landing.jhtml?src=pn http://nces.ed.gov

Career Opportunities For information on employment and the college recruitment program, contact Human Capital and Client Services. Phone, 202–401–0553. http://www.ed.gov/jobs

Freedom of Information Act (FOIA) The FOIA generally provides that any person has the right to request access to Federal agency records or information; all agencies of the Government are required to disclose records upon receiving a written request for them; nine exemptions to the FOIA protect certain records from disclosure; and three special protection provisions or record exclusions authorize Federal law enforcement agencies, under exceptional circumstances, to exclude records from FIOA requirements. The Federal FOIA does not provide access to records held by State or local government agencies, or by private businesses or individuals. http://www2.ed.gov/policy/gen/leg/foia/foiatoc.html?src=ft

Before submitting a request, browse the electronic FOIA Library and search the Department of Education's Web site. The desired records and information may be immediately available online and not require a FOIA request to access them. http://www2.ed.gov/policy/gen/leg/foia/readingroom.html

Frequently Asked Questions (FAQs)   The Department of Education provides answers to FAQs on its Web site. https://answers.ed.gov/ics/support/default.asp?deptID=28025&_referrer=http://www.ed.gov/&src=ft

Glossaries   The Department of Education's Web site features a glossary of reading terms. https://lincs.ed.gov/research/Glossary.html

The Department of Education's Web site features a glossary of terms related to Federal student aid. https://studentaid.ed.gov/sa/glossary

The Department of Education's Web site features a glossary of terms related to education research. http://www.ies.ed.gov/ncee/wwc/Glossary

The Department of Education's Web site features a glossary of terms related to education statistical standards. http://nces.ed.gov/statprog/2002/glossary.asp

Language Assistance   Education resources for Spanish speakers are available on the Department's Web site. http://www2.ed.gov/espanol/bienvenidos/es/index.html?src=ft

Free language assistance services—Chinese, Korean, Spanish, Vietnamese, Tagalog—are available to the public. Phone,

800-872-5327. http://www.ed.gov/notices/english-la | Email: Ed.Language.Assistance@ed.gov

News   The Department of Education posts media advisories, press releases, and speeches on its Web site. http://www.ed.gov/news

Press releases in Spanish are also available on the Department's Web site. http://www2.ed.gov/espanol/news/pressreleases/index.html

Open Government   The Department of Education supports the Open Government initiative by promoting the principles of collaboration, participation, and transparency. http://www2.ed.gov/about/open.html | Email: opengov@ed.gov

Plain Language   Department of Education writers and editors are committed to using Federal plain language guidelines. Publishing clear, useful information on programs and services is a priority and an ongoing effort. To comment on the clarity of a written product or to offer a suggestion for improvement, please communicate via email. http://www.ed.gov/plain-language | Email: plainwriting@ed.gov

Regional Offices   Each regional office serves as a center for the dissemination of information and provides technical assistance to State and local educational agencies and other institutions and individuals interested in Federal educational activities. Offices are located in Boston, MA; New York, NY; Philadelphia, PA; Atlanta, GA; Chicago, IL; Cleveland, OH; Dallas, TX; Kansas City, MO; Denver, CO; San Francisco, CA; and Seattle, WA. http://www2.ed.gov/about/contacts/gen/regions.html

Site Map   The Web site map allows visitors to look for specific topics or to browse content that aligns with their interests. http://www2.ed.gov/help/site/map/sitemap.jsp

Student Loans   Information on student loans is available online. http://www2.ed.gov/fund/grants-college.html?src=pn http://www2.ed.gov/about/contacts/gen/index.html

For further information, contact the Information Resources Center, Department of Education, Room 5E248 (FB–6), 400 Maryland Avenue SW., Washington, DC 20202. Phone, 800-872-5327.

Federally Aided Corporations
American Printing House for the Blind

P.O. Box 6085, Louisville, KY 40206
Phone, 502-895-2405. Internet, http://www.aph.org

President CRAIG MEADOR
Chair of the Board JANE HARDY

Founded in 1858 as a nonprofit organization, the American Printing House for the Blind (APH) received its Federal charter in 1879 when Congress passed the Act to Promote Education of the Blind. This Act designates APH as the official supplier of educational materials adapted for students who are legally blind and who are enrolled in formal educational programs below the college level. Materials produced and distributed by APH include textbooks in Braille and large type, educational tools such as Braille typewriters and computer software and hardware, teaching aides such as tests and performance measures, and other special supplies. The materials are distributed through allotments to the States to programs serving individuals who are blind. http://www.aph.org/about

Sources of Information

Business Opportunities Requests for proposals are posted online. http://www.aph.org/rfp
Employment The APH is the world's largest manufacturer of products for people who are blind and visually impaired. It is a drug-free workplace: New hires must pass a drug screening test and background check. http://www.aph.org/careers http://www.aph.org/contact

For further information, contact the American Printing House for the Blind, P.O. Box 6085, Louisville, KY 40206. Phone, 502-895-2405.

Gallaudet University

800 Florida Avenue NE., Washington, DC 20002
Phone, 202-651-5000. Internet, http://www.gallaudet.edu

President T. ALAN HURWITZ
Chair, Board of Trustees HEATHER HARKER

Gallaudet University received its Federal charter in 1864 and is currently authorized by the Education of the Deaf Act of 1986, as amended. Gallaudet is a private, nonprofit educational institution providing elementary, secondary, undergraduate, and continuing education programs for persons who are deaf. The University offers a traditional liberal arts curriculum for students who are deaf and graduate programs in fields related to deafness for students who are deaf and students who are hearing. Gallaudet also conducts a wide variety of basic and applied deafness research and provides public service programs for persons who are deaf and for professionals who work with persons who are deaf.

Gallaudet University is accredited by a number of organizations, among which are the Middle States Association of Colleges and Secondary Schools, the National Council for Accreditation of Teacher Education, and the Conference of Educational Administrators of Schools and Programs for the Deaf. http://www2.gallaudet.edu/attend-gallaudet/about-gallaudet
Laurent Clerc National Deaf Education Center Gallaudet's Laurent Clerc National Deaf Education Center operates elementary and secondary education programs on the main campus of the University. These programs are authorized by the Education of the Deaf Act of 1986 (20 U.S.C. 4304,

as amended) for the primary purpose of developing, evaluating, and disseminating model curricula, instructional strategies, and materials in order to serve individuals who are deaf or hard of hearing. The Education of the Deaf Act requires the programs to include students preparing for postsecondary opportunities other than college and students with a broad spectrum of needs, such as students who are academically challenged, come from non-English-speaking homes, have secondary disabilities, are members of minority groups, or are from rural areas. http://www.gallaudet.edu/clerc-center.html

Model Secondary School for the Deaf   The school was established by act of October 15, 1966, which was superseded by the Education of the Deaf Act of 1986. The school provides day and residential facilities for secondary-age students from across the United States from grades 9 to 12, inclusively. http://www.gallaudet.edu/mssd.html

Kendall Demonstration Elementary School   The school became the Nation's first demonstration elementary school for the deaf by the act of December 24, 1970

(20 U.S.C. 695), which was also later superseded by the Education of the Deaf Act of 1986. The school is a day program for students from the Washington, DC, metropolitan area from the age of onset of deafness to age 15, inclusively, but not beyond the eighth grade or its equivalent. http://www.gallaudet.edu/kdes.html

Sources of Information

Campus Tour   A virtual tour of the University's campus is available online. http://www.gallaudet.edu/visitors-center/virtual-tour.html

Employment   Serving deaf and hard of hearing students from many different backgrounds, Gallaudet University seeks to develop a workforce that reflects its diversity. The University is an equal employment opportunity and affirmative action employer, and it encourages members of traditionally underrepresented groups, persons with disabilities, veterans, and women to apply for vacancies. http://www.gallaudet.edu/hrs/employment-opportunities.html http://www.gallaudet.edu/about-gallaudet/contact-us.html

For further information, contact the Public Relations Office, Gallaudet University, 800 Florida Avenue NE., Washington, DC 20002. Phone, 202-651-5505.

Howard University

2400 Sixth Street NW., Washington, DC 20059
Phone, 202-806-6100. Internet, http://www.howard.edu

President   WAYNE A.I. FREDERICK

Howard University was established by Congress by the act of March 2, 1867 (14 Stat. 438). It offers instruction in 12 schools and colleges, as follows: the colleges of arts and sciences; dentistry; engineering, architecture, and computer sciences; medicine; pharmacy, nursing, and allied health sciences; the graduate school; the schools of business; communications; divinity; education; law; and social work. In addition, Howard University has research institutes, centers, and special programs in the following areas: cancer, child development,

computational science and engineering, international affairs, sickle cell disease, and the national human genome project. https://www2.howard.edu/about/howard-glance

Sources of Information

Employment   Information is available on the "Career Opportunities" Web page. https://www2.howard.edu/about/careers

Libraries   The Howard University Libraries are accessible online. http://library.howard.edu/library https://www2.howard.edu/contact

For further information, contact the Office of University Communications, Howard University, 2400 Sixth Street NW., Washington, DC 20059. Phone, 202-806-0970.

National Technical Institute for the Deaf / Rochester Institute of Technology

52 Lomb Memorial Drive, Rochester, NY 14623
Phone, 585-475-6317. Internet, http://www.ntid.rit.edu

President, Rochester Institute of Technology   WILLIAM W. DESTLER
President, National Technical Institute for the Deaf / Vice   GERARD J. BUCKLEY
   President, Rochester Institute of Technology

The National Technical Institute for the Deaf (NTID) was established by act of June 8, 1965 (20 U.S.C. 681) to promote the employment of persons who are deaf by providing technical and professional education. The National Technical Institute for the Deaf Act was superseded by the Education of the Deaf Act of 1986 (20 U.S.C. 4431, as amended). The U.S. Department of Education contracts with the Rochester Institute of Technology (RIT) for the operation of a residential facility for postsecondary technical training and education for individuals who are deaf. The purpose of the special relationship with the host institution is to give NTID's faculty and students access to more facilities, institutional services, and career preparation options than could be provided otherwise by a national technical institute for the deaf operating independently.

NTID offers a variety of technical programs at the certificate, diploma, and associate degree levels. Degree programs include majors in business, engineering, science, and visual communications. In addition, NTID students may participate in approximately 200 educational programs available through RIT.

NTID also conducts applied research in occupational- and employment-related aspects of deafness, communication assessment, demographics of NTID's target population, and learning processes in postsecondary education. In addition, NTID conducts training workshops and seminars related to deafness. These workshops and seminars are offered nationwide to professionals who employ, work with, teach, or serve persons who are deaf. http://www.ntid.rit.edu/about

Sources of Information

Campus Tour   A virtual tour of the college's campus is available online. http://www.ntid.rit.edu/virtual-tour http://www.ntid.rit.edu/contact

For further information, contact the Rochester Institute of Technology, National Technical Institute for the Deaf, Department of Recruitment and Admissions, Lyndon Baines Johnson Building, 52 Lomb Memorial Drive, Rochester, NY 14623-5604. Phone, 716-475-6700.

DEPARTMENT OF ENERGY

1000 Independence Avenue SW., Washington, DC 20585
Phone, 202-586-5000. Internet, http://www.energy.gov

Secretary of Energy	JENNIFER M. GRANHOLM
Deputy Secretary	DAVID M. TURK
Chief of Staff	TARAK SHAH
Ombudsman	(VACANCY)
https://www.energy.gov/leadership	
Under Secretary of Energy	(VACANCY)
Associate Under Secretary for Environment, Health, Safety and Security	MATTHEW MOURY
Director of Project Management	PAUL BOSCO

Nuclear Security

Under Secretary	JILL HRUBY

National Nuclear Security Administration

Administrator	JILL HRUBY
Principal Deputy Administrator	FRANK A. ROSE
Deputy Administrators	
Defense Nuclear Nonproliferation	COREY HINDERSTEIN
Defense Programs	CHARLES P. VERDON
Naval Reactors	ADM. JAMES F. CALDWELL, USN
Associate Administrators	
Acquisition and Project Management	ROBERT B. RAINES
Counterterrorism and Counterproliferation	JAY TILDEN
Defense Nuclear Security	JEFFREY R. JOHNSON
Emergency Operations	JOHN JUSKIE, ACTING
External Affairs	HOWARD DICKENSON, ACTING
Information Management	JAMES WOLFF
Management and Budget	FRANK J. LOWERY
Safety, Infrastructure and Operations	KENNETH SHEELY, ACTING
Chief Information Officer	JAMES WOLFF
Chief of Defense Nuclear Security	JEFFREY R. JOHNSON
General Counsel	TIMOTHY P. FISCHER
https://www.energy.gov/nnsa/person/jill-hruby	

Science and Energy

Under Secretary	KATHLEEN HOGAN, ACTING
Assistant Secretaries	
Cybersecurity, Energy Security, and Emergency Response	(VACANCY)
Electricity	PATRICIA HOFFMAN, ACTING
Energy Efficiency and Renewable Energy	(VACANCY)
Fossil Energy and Carbon Management	JENNIFER WILCOX, ACTING

Nuclear Energy	KATHRYN D. HUFF, ACTING
Chief Commercialization Officer	VANESSA Z. CHAN

Directors of Offices

Arctic Energy	GEORGE ROE
Artificial Intelligence and Technology	CHERYL INGSTAD
Clean Energy Demonstrations	(VACANCY)
Indian Energy Policy and Programs	WAHLEAH JOHNS
Loan Programs	JIGAR SHAH
Science	J. STEPHEN BINKLEY, ACTING
Technology Transitions	VANESSA Z. CHAN
Office of Electricity	
Assistant Secretary	PATRICIA HOFFMAN, ACTING

Power Marketing Administrators

Bonneville	JOHN HAIRSTON
Southeastern	VIRGIL G. HOBBS III
Southwestern	MICHAEL WECH
Western Area	TRACEY LeBEAU

https://www.energy.gov/oe/our-organization
Staff and Program Offices

Assistant Secretaries

Congressional and Intergovernmental Affairs	ALI NOURI
Environmental Management	(VACANCY)
International Affairs	ANDREW LIGHT
Chief Administrative Judge	POLI A. MARMOLEJOS

Chief Officers

Financial	(VACANCY)
Human Capital	ERIN MOORE
Information	ANN DUNKIN

Directors of Offices

Advanced Research Projects Agency—Energy	(VACANCY)
Economic Impact and Diversity	ANN AUGUSTYN, ACTING
Enterprise Assessments	JOHN E. DUPUY
Hearings and Appeals	POLI A. MARMOLEJOS
Intelligence and Counterintelligence	STEVEN K. BLACK
Legacy Management	CARMELO MELENDEZ
Management	INGRID C. KOLB
Policy	CARLA FRISCH, ACTING *
Public Affairs	DAVID A. MAYORGA
Small and Disadvantaged Business Utilization	PAUL E. ROSS, ACTING
General Counsel	(VACANCY)

* Acting Executive Director https://www.energy.gov/offices
U.S. Energy Information Administration

Administrator	STEPHEN NALLEY, ACTING
Deputy Administrator	STEPHEN NALLEY

https://www.eia.gov/about/senior_executive_bios.php

Inspector General	TERI L. DONALDSON

https://www.energy.gov/ig/leadership

The above list of key personnel was updated 1–2022.

The Department of Energy addresses the Nation's energy, environmental, and nuclear challenges, using transformative science and technology to ensure national security and prosperity.

Establishment and Organization
On August 4, 1977, President James E. Carter approved Public Law 95–91, which also is cited as the "Department of Energy Organization Act." President Carter made remarks about the new law (S. 826) on the same day that he approved it. https://www.energy.gov/management/august-4-1977-president-carter-signs-department-energy-organization-act

The President's remarks on signing S. 826, which also is cited as the "Department of Energy Organizational Act," were included in the "Public Papers of the Presidents of the United States." The public papers of "Jimmy Carter" for the year 1977 are collected in two books. Book II (25 JUN–31 DEC) is available on the Government Publishing Office's govinfo website in Portable Document Format (PDF) for downloading. The relevant section of the remarks is found on pages 1411 and 1412. https://www.govinfo.gov/app/details/PPP-1977-book2

The new statute consolidated the major Federal energy functions into one Cabinet-level department. It established "a Department of Energy in the executive branch by the reorganization of energy functions within the Federal Government in order secure effective management to assure a coordinated national energy policy" (91 Stat. 565). https://www.govinfo.gov/content/pkg/STATUTE-91/pdf/STATUTE-91-Pg565.pdf

On September 13, 1977, President Carter signed Executive Order 12009, which was published 2 days later in the Federal Register (42 FR 46267). Pursuant to the order, the Department of Energy Organization Act became effective on October 1st of that same year. https://www.govinfo.gov/content/pkg/FR-1977-09-15/pdf/FR-1977-09-15.pdf

By the advice and with the consent of the Senate, the President appoints the Secretary who serves as the top administrator at the Department of Energy. https://uscode.house.gov/view.xhtml?req=granuleid:USC-prelim-title42-section7131&num=0&edition=prelim

The "Offices" web page provides convenient access to information on DOE offices, centers, power administrations, and component agencies, as well as to online resources that are associated with some of them. https://www.energy.gov/offices

On the "About Us" web page, below the contact information, a hyperlink for the DOE's organization chart is available. The organization chart also may be viewed in Portable Document Format (PDF) and downloaded as a PDF file. https://www.energy.gov/about-us

Statutory and Regulatory Authorities
Title 42 of the United States Code (U.S.C.) is dedicated to the topic of "The Public Health and Welfare." Statutory material that affects the Department of Energy has been codified and assigned to Chapter 84 of 42 U.S.C. Chapter 84 runs from sections 7101 to 7385s-16. https://uscode.house.gov/view.xhtml?path=/prelim@title42/chapter84&edition=prelim

Rules and regulations that address the topic of energy have been codified and assigned to Title 10 of the Code of Federal Regulations (10 CFR 1–1899). https://www.ecfr.gov/current/title-10

Rules and regulations that are associated with the Department of Energy have been assigned to Chapter II of 10 CFR. https://www.ecfr.gov/current/title-10/chapter-II

Additional rules and regulations that are associated with the Department of Energy have been assigned to Chapter III of 10 CFR. https://www.ecfr.gov/current/title-10/chapter-III

The general provisions of the Department of Energy have been codified and assigned to Chapter X of 10 CFR. https://www.ecfr.gov/current/title-10/chapter-X

Activities and Programs
In 2022, the DOE will mark its 45th anniversary. The DOE is a cabinet-level department whose activities and programs are as important as they are diverse. The DOE brought together for the first time, within one Federal agency, two programmatic traditions that had coexisted within the Government. One tradition

constituted the defense responsibilities that included the design, construction, and testing of nuclear weapons originating with the effort to build the first atomic bomb during the Second World War. The other tradition comprised a loose amalgamation of energy-related programs that were scattered throughout the Federal Government. The presence of these two traditions remains palpable in the range of activities and programs of today's DOE.

Energy Economy The national economy benefits from robust investments in energy technologies. These investments stimulate the creation of new jobs. The DOE both supports proven energy technologies and funds and promotes energy technologies of the future. It also partners with private- and public-sector organizations to spread and accelerate the implementation of these technologies. https://www.energy.gov/energy-economy

The DOE guides legislators and policymakers through the complexities and details of energy related issues. It serves as a liaison among Federal agencies, Members of Congress, and State, local, and tribal governments. It also assists American Indian Tribes and Alaska Native villages with energy development, capacity building, electrification of lands and homes, and reducing energy costs. https://www.energy.gov/energy-economy/state-local-government

Research / Innovation The DOE is aptly described as a research and science agency that participates aggressively in the innovation economy. The Department stimulates the growth of basic and applied scientific research and the discovery and the development of new clean energy technologies. The DOE regards scientific innovation as a cornerstone of the Nation's economic prosperity and, therefore, prioritizes innovation in its research and science programs. It also fosters collaboration and cooperation among governmental organizations, industries, and universities to create a capacious scientific ecosystem and to invigorate it. https://www.energy.gov/science-innovation

The DOE's Loan Programs Office finances comprehensive and large-scale energy infrastructure projects nationwide. https://www.energy.gov/lpo/about-us-home

The Advanced Research Projects Agency–Energy (ARPA–E) supports the development of energy technologies that have high potential and broad application before they are ready for investment from the private sector. https://arpa-e.energy.gov/about

The DOE's 17 National Laboratories serve as regional drivers of economic growth for States and communities nationwide. Among the world's science institutions, the National Laboratories constitute a unique ecosystem of intellectual assets and pooled knowledge. https://www.energy.gov/national-laboratories

Safety / Security The DOE helps to protect national security. Its responsibilities include cleaning up the adverse environmental consequences of developing nuclear weapons and of nuclear energy research, supporting nuclear nonproliferation, ensuring the security of the Nation's nuclear weapons stockpile, providing training tools and procedures for emergency response and preparedness, managing the Strategic Petroleum Reserve, investing in protections against cyber and physical attacks on energy infrastructure, and conducting programs to ensure worker health and safety. https://www.energy.gov/national-security-safety

The DOE safely and cost-effectively transports and disposes of low-level wastes, decommissions and decontaminates old facilities, remediates contaminated soil and groundwater, and secures and stores nuclear material in stable and secure locations to protect national security. https://www.energy.gov/national-security-safety/environmental-cleanup

The National Nuclear Security Administration ensures the integrity and safety of the Nation's nuclear weapons, advances nuclear nonproliferation, and promotes international nuclear safety. https://www.energy.gov/nnsa/nuclear-security-nonproliferation

The DOE works closely with its public and private sector partners to secure the Nation's critical energy infrastructure against all hazards, to reduce the risk of disruptive events, and to respond to energy disruptions that could jeopardize national security, public health and safety, and the national economy. DOE response activities include hurricane response, extreme weather and wildfire response, and cyber incident response. https://www.energy.gov/ceser/emergency-response-hub

The DOE has contingency plans for mitigating the effects of extreme petroleum supply interruptions. The Office of Petroleum Reserves (OPR) acquires, stores, distributes, and manages emergency petroleum stocks. The OPR maintains the operational readiness of three emergency stockpiles: the Strategic Petroleum Reserve, the Northeast Home Heating Oil Reserve, and the Northeast Gasoline Supply Reserve (NGSR). In the event of a natural disaster or other national emergency, the Nation can draw from these emergency stockpiles to keep crude oil and other petroleum products in steady supply. https://www.energy.gov/fecm/office-petroleum-reserves

The DOE leads the Federal Government's effort to mitigate the potentially catastrophic effects of cybersecurity attacks on the energy sector. It also ensures the cybersecurity and resilience of all energy infrastructure that is associated with the DOE enterprise. https://www.energy.gov/national-security-safety/cybersecurity

DOE health and safety programs help to protect workers and the public from the hazards associated with departmental operations. Former and current DOE Federal, contract, and subcontract workers benefit from health and safety policies, program tools, and assistance resources. https://www.energy.gov/ehss/health-and-safety

The Energy Employees Occupational Illness Compensation Program Act (EEOICPA) provides compensation and medical benefits to employees—including contractors, subcontractors, and some vendors—who worked at certain DOE facilities. The Department of Labor (DOL) handles the adjudication of issues involving all claims for benefits under the EEOICPA . Alongside the Departments of Justice (DOJ) and Health and Human Services (HHS), the DOE supports the DOL as it adjudicates these issues. https://www.energy.gov/ehss/services/worker-health-and-safety/energy-employees-occupational-illness-compensation-program

Saving Money / Lowering Energy Consumption   The DOE maintains a website that is dedicated to helping consumers to use energy more efficiently

and to adopt renewable forms of energy. These consumers include builders and renovators, commuters and drivers, families, homeowners, landscapers, and renters. Energy Saver is the DOE's premier consumer resource for ideas on how to lower energy consumption and save money and for learning about renewable energy technologies that are applicable at home. https://www.energy.gov/energysaver/energy-saver

Sources of Information

Analysis / Statistics   The U.S. Energy Information Administration is the statistical and analytical agency within the DOE. It is the Nation's premier source of energy information. By law, its data, analyses, and forecasts are independent of approval by any other officer or employee of the Federal Government. https://www.eia.gov/about/mission_overview.php

Archived Records   The "Guide to Federal Records in the National Archives of the United States" indicates that DOE records have been assigned to record group 434. https://www.archives.gov/research/guide-fed-records/groups/434.html

Business Opportunities   To learn about the Office of Small and Disadvantaged Business Utilization and its mission or to find information on the services that it offers and its programs, visit its website. Phone, 202-586-7377. http://www.energy.gov/osdbu/office-small-and-disadvantaged-business-utilization | Email: smallbusiness@hq.doe.gov

Useful external links for small businesses are available on the Office of Small and Disadvantaged Business Utilization's website in its "Small Business Toolbox." https://www.energy.gov/osdbu/small-business-toolbox/useful-links-and-faq

Career Opportunities   The DOE offers career opportunities that span a broad, diverse range of professions: accounting and contracting, administration, business, communications and information technology, computer science, engineering, mathematics, national security and international affairs, public affairs, science and technology, and more. Most Federal jobs require U.S. citizenship;

however, noncitizens may apply for some opportunities at the National Laboratories. http://www.energy.gov/jobs/jobs

Information on opportunities for students and recent graduates, veterans, and those with disabilities is available on the DOE website. For more information, contact the Chief Human Capital Officer. Phone, 202-586-1234. http://www.energy.gov/jobs/services/students-recent-graduates

In 2020, the DOE ranked 11th among 25 midsize Government agencies in the Partnership for Public Service's Best Places To Work Agency Rankings. https://bestplacestowork.org/rankings/detail/?c=DN00

Climate Change   Mitigating the effects of climate change is on the DOE's top-priorities list. Global temperatures continue to rise; therefore, drought, heat waves, wildfires, and high demand for electricity will put additional stress on the Nation's energy infrastructure. The leading cause of power outages and fuel supply disruption in the United States is severe weather. As the Earth System continues on this current heating trajectory, Climate scientists predict that severe weather events will become more destructive and disruptive. Visit the "Climate Change" web pages to learn more about how the DOE is responding to this growing threat. https://www.energy.gov/science-innovation/climate-change

The Energy Exascale Earth System Model (E3SM) Project is a state-of-the-science Earth system modeling, simulation, and prediction project. Relying on DOE laboratory resources, the E3SM Project helps to meet the science needs of the Nation and the mission needs of the DOE. https://e3sm.org

Title 10 of the Code of Federal Regulations (CFR) is dedicated to rules and regulations that are associated with energy. Chapter II of that title is dedicated to the "Department of Energy." Subchapter B, which runs from section 300.01 to 300.13, is dedicated to "Climate Change." https://www.ecfr.gov/current/title-10/chapter-II/subchapter-B/part-300?toc=1

Contact Information   Email addresses, phone numbers, and the DOE's postal address are available on the "Contact Us" web page. https://www.energy.gov/contact-us

Energy Calculator   When deciding whether or not to invest in more energy efficiency, a consumer can benefit from knowing electricity usages and the associated costs. The online energy use calculator estimates annual energy use and costs associated with operating appliances and home electronics. http://energy.gov/energysaver/estimating-appliance-and-home-electronic-energy-use

Energy Explained   The U.S. Energy Information Administration has an online guide for understanding energy. https://www.eia.gov/energyexplained/index.php

Energy Kids   The U.S. Energy Information Administration maintains an award-winning website for children and teachers. The website "energy KIDS" answers the question: What is energy? It has web pages that describe sources of energy and that provide a historical overview of energy. A glossary, energy calculators, games and activities, and a section for teachers are also available on "energy KIDS." https://www.eia.gov/kids

Energy Simulation Software   EnergyPlus is cross-platform, free, and open-source software that runs on the Windows, Mac OS X, and Linux operating systems. It is a whole building energy simulation program that architects, engineers, and researchers use to model energy consumption and water use in buildings. The DOE's Building Technologies Office funded the development of EnergyPlus, and the National Renewable Energy Laboratory manages it. https://energyplus.net

Federal Register   Significant documents and documents that the DOE recently published in the Federal Register are accessible online. https://www.federalregister.gov/agencies/energy-department

Freedom of Information Act (FOIA)   The Office of Management administers policies, procedures, and programs to ensure DOE compliance with the FOIA. The FOIA gives information seekers a right to access DOE records; however, the Department may determine that releasing certain information would harm an interest that one or more of the nine FOIA exemptions shields or that doing so would violate the law. After receiving a properly submitted FOIA request, the DOE must provide the requester with copies of the relevant documents and records, or portions of them, that he or she is entitled to access under the law. https://www.energy.gov/management/freedom-information-act

The FOIA requires that certain documents be made available to the public for inspection and copying. This requirement pertains to agencies of the executive branch of the Federal Government. If the FOIA Reading Room does not contain the document, or record, that you seek, please be at liberty to submit an official FOIA request. Before submitting that request, please make sure that the desired information is not part of the electronic reading room's collection and, therefore, already immediately available online without a fee. https://www.energy.gov/management/foia-reading-room | Email: foia-central@hq.doe.gov

Genomics   A very important development in the field of biology within the past 100 years was the Human Genome Project (HGP), the 10-year Government-led effort that culminated in the first complete sequencing of a human genome in 2000. The HGP launched the field of genomics, transformed medicine, and pretty much birthed the modern biotechnology industry. The original idea and impetus for the HGP came from the DOE's Office of Science, which was then known as the Office of Energy Research. At the time, the sequencing of a whole human genome was considered a nearly impossible task. With the historical experience of large scientific endeavors that had started with the Manhattan Project, Office of Science personnel had the confidence that the task could be accomplished with sufficient Government resources. Interest in better understanding the genetic effects of radiation exposure stimulated the DOE's initial interest in undertaking this bold initiative. https://www.energy.gov/science/initiatives/genomics

Geothermal Energy   The Geothermal Technologies Office released the report "GeoVision: Harnessing the Heat Beneath Our Feet (MAY 2019)." https://www.energy.gov/eere/geothermal/geovision | Email: GeoVision@ee.doe.gov

Glossaries   The Bioenergy Technologies Office maintains an online biomass glossary. Its short descriptions are intended to help students and researchers understand biomass terminology. http://www.energy.gov/eere/bioenergy/glossary

The waterpower program maintains an online hydropower glossary. It is intended to help readers understand terminology associated with hydroturbine and hydropower plant components. http://www.energy.gov/eere/water/glossary-hydropower-terms

The Office of Legacy management maintains an online glossary. https://www.energy.gov/lm/glossary

The U.S. Energy Information Administration maintains a glossary on its website. https://www.eia.gov/tools/glossary

History   The DOE history timeline allows easy access to information on the Department's history and its predecessor agencies. The timeline includes links to press releases, reports, speeches, and other documentation. https://www.energy.gov/lm/doe-history/doe-history-timeline

Landscaping for Energy Efficiency   A well-designed landscape adds beauty to a home. Landscaping also can reduce cooling and heating costs. A shrub, tree, or vine can bring the coolness of shade, absorb the force of wind, and lower energy bills. Thoughtfully positioned trees can reduce the energy that a typical household uses by as much as 25 percent. https://www.energy.gov/energysaver/landscaping-energy-efficient-homes

Maps   The Office of Energy Efficiency and Renewable Energy posts National Renewable Energy Laboratory maps that illustrate a variety of energy-related topics and trends: alternative fueling stations, carbon capture, climate vulnerabilities, per capita energy expenditure, renewable energy production, solar energy potential, and more. https://www.energy.gov/eere/photos/collection-nrel-maps

Climate change is a threat to America's energy infrastructure in every region of the country: Alaska, Hawaii, Midwest, Northeast, Northern Great Plains, Northwest, Southeast, Southern Great Plains, Southwest, and Puerto Rico. The DOE website has an interactive map that illustrates the potential of climate change to disrupt the Nation's energy systems. https://www.energy.gov/articles/map-how-climate-change-threatens-america-s-energy-infrastructure-every-region

National Laboratories   For more than 60 years, these Laboratories have been leading institutions for scientific innovation in the United States. To learn more about the Ames Laboratory, Princeton Plasma Physics Laboratory, Thomas Jefferson National Accelerator Facility, and the other 14 National Laboratories, visit the DOE's "About the National Labs" web page. https://www.energy.gov/national-laboratories

News   The newsroom web page offers easy access to news and speeches, as well as to the "Energy Blog" and the "Direct Current" podcast. https://www.energy.gov/newsroom

Office of Inspector General (OIG)   The early alert system uses a distribution list for informing subscribers of significant press releases, publications, and reports the moment that the OIG posts them online. Subscription is free and available to anyone who has an interest in the OIG's work and an email address. http://www.energy.gov/ig/subscription-information | Email: ignewmedia@hq.doe.gov

Open Government   The DOE supports the Open Government initiative to create a more open and transparent Government by promoting the principles of collaboration, participation, and transparency. http://www.energy.gov/open-government | Email: open@hq.doe.gov

Postclosure Responsibilities   The Office of Legacy Management serves the public interest by fulfilling the DOE's postclosure responsibilities and ensuring the future protection of human health and the environment. https://www.energy.gov/lm/services

Renewable Energy   The steady expansion of the U.S. renewable energy sector suggests that a clean energy revolution is underway nationwide. https://www.energy.gov/clean-energy

Scientific and Technical Information   The Office of Scientific and Technical Information (OSTI) advances science and sustains technological creativity by making research and development findings available to and useful for DOE researchers and the public. The OSTI website provides access to DOE science resources and to U.S. Federal science (Science.gov) and global science (WorldWideScience.org) information. https://www.osti.gov/search-tools

Social Media   The DOE has a Facebook page. https://www.facebook.com/energygov

The DOE tweets announcements and other newsworthy items on Twitter. https://twitter.com/energy

The DOE posts videos on its YouTube channel. https://www.youtube.com/user/USdepartmentofenergy

Each of the 17 National Laboratories has its own YouTube channel. https://www.youtube.com/c/EnergyGov/channels?view=49&shelf_id=1

The Sources of Information were updated 02–2022.

Federal Energy Regulatory Commission

888 First Street NE., Washington, DC 20426
Phone, 202-502-8004. Internet, http://www.ferc.gov

Commissioners
Chair

RICHARD GLICK
MARK C. CHRISTIE
ALLISON CLEMENTS
JAMES DANLY
WILLIE L. PHILLIPS

https://www.ferc.gov/about/commission-members
The above list of Commissioners was updated 12–2021.

Senior Staff

Chief Administrative Law Judge
General Counsel

CARMEN A. CINTRON
MATTHEW CHRISTIANSEN

Office Directors	
Administrative Litigation	JOHN KROEGER
Electric Reliability	DAVID ORTIZ, ACTING
Energy Infrastructure Security	JOSEPH H. McCLELLAND
Energy Market Regulation	JETTE GEBHART
Energy Policy and Innovation	JIGNASA GADANI
Energy Projects	TERRY L. TURPIN
Enforcement	JANELBURDICK
Executive Director	ANTON C. PORTER
External Affairs	SARAH VENUTO
Secretary	KIMBERLY D. BOSE

https://www.ferc.gov/commission-members-senior-staff/
  commission-members-and-senior-staff

The above list of key personnel was updated 12–2021.

The Federal Energy Regulatory Commission helps consumers obtain efficient, reliable, and sustainable energy services at fair and reasonable rates through regulatory and market means.

Organization

The Federal Energy Regulatory Commission (FERC) is an independent agency within the Department of Energy that regulates the interstate transmission of electricity, natural gas, and oil. The Commission comprises five members whom the President appoints with the advice and consent of the Senate. FERC Commissioners serve 5-year terms and have an equal vote on regulatory matters. The President designates one member to serve as both the Commission's Chair and its administrative head. https://www.ferc.gov/what-ferc

An organizational chart and brief descriptions of the main activities of each office are posted online. https://www.ferc.gov/offices

Activities

Under the authority of the Federal Power, the Natural Gas, and the Interstate Commerce Acts, the FERC regulates the interstate transmission of electricity, natural gas, and oil. That authority also includes review of proposals to build interstate natural gas pipelines, natural gas storage facilities, and liquefied natural gas terminals, and licensing of nonfederal hydropower dams.

The FERC enforces regulatory requirements by imposing civil penalties and other means, monitors and investigates energy markets, and protects the reliability of the high voltage interstate transmission system through mandatory reliability standards. https://www.ferc.gov/about/what-ferc/what-ferc-does

Sources of Information

Archived Records   The "Guide to Federal Records in the National Archives of the United States" indicates that FERC records have been assigned to record group 138. https://www.archives.gov/research/guide-fed-records/groups/138.html

Career Opportunities   The FERC relies on accountants and auditors, attorneys, economists, energy industry analysts, engineers, environmental biologists, human resources specialists, information technology specialists, management analysts, and other professionals to carry out its mission. https://www.ferc.gov/about/careers

In 2020, the FERC ranked 3d among 25 midsize Government agencies in the Partnership for Public Service's Best Places To Work Agency Rankings. https://bestplacestowork.org/rankings/detail/?c=DR00

Contact Information   Email addresses and phone and fax numbers are available on the "Key Contacts" web page. https://www.ferc.gov/about/contact-us/key-contacts

Data Sources   The FERC posts sources of data on its website. https://www.ferc.gov/industries-data/resources/data-sources

Document Classes Table The FERC has a critical energy/electric infrastructure information (CEII) related document classes table on its website. https://www.ferc.gov/enforcement-legal/ceii/related-document-classes

Federal Register Significant documents and documents that the FERC recently published in the Federal Register are accessible online. https://www.federalregister.gov/agencies/federal-energy-regulatory-commission

FERC Online This electronic portal to dockets and documents provides an easy and efficient way to communicate and to do business with the FERC. https://www.ferc.gov/ferc-online/overview

Freedom of Information Act (FOIA) The FOIA gives a person the right to request public access to Federal agency records and information. The agency must release the records upon receiving a written FOIA request, except in cases that one of nine FOIA exemptions or one of three FOIA exclusions shields the records or parts of them from disclosure. https://www.ferc.gov/enforcement-legal/foia | Email: foia-ceii@ferc.gov

The FERC maintains an electronic reading room. Before submitting a formal FOIA request in writing, an information seeker should review the contents of the reading room to determine whether or not the information or record that they seek has been released in the public domain. https://www.ferc.gov/enforcement-legal/foia/reading-room-material

Frequently Asked Questions (FAQs) The FERC posts answers to FAQs. https://www.ferc.gov/about/what-ferc/frequently-asked-questions-faqs

The Sources of Information were updated 12–2021.

Glossary The FERC maintains a glossary of terms that are frequently used on its website. https://www.ferc.gov/about/what-ferc/about/glossary

The FERC maintains a market assessments glossary. https://www.ferc.gov/industries-data/market-assessments/overview/glossary

The FERC maintains an online list of acronyms and initialisms. https://www.ferc.gov/about/what-ferc/about/acronyms

News Releases The FERC posts news releases and headlines. https://www.ferc.gov/news-events/news/news-releases-headlines

Public Participation Citizens who may be affected by a proposed natural gas or hydroelectric project that the Commission regulates have certain rights. These rights range from seeing project correspondence to becoming an intervener and appealing FERC decisions in Federal court. https://www.ferc.gov/industries-data/resources/how-get-involved

Request a Speaker The FERC website has an electronic form on its "Speaker Request" web page. https://www.ferc.gov/about/contact-us/speaker-request

Site Map The website map allows visitors to look for specific topics or to browse content that aligns with their interests. https://www.ferc.gov/sitemap

Social Media The FERC has a Facebook account. https://www.facebook.com/FERC.gov

The FERC tweets announcements and other newsworthy items on Twitter. https://twitter.com/ferc

The FERC posts videos on its YouTube channel. https://www.youtube.com/c/FercGov-energy

DEPARTMENT OF HEALTH AND HUMAN SERVICES

200 Independence Avenue SW., Washington, DC 20201
Phone, 202-690-6343. Internet, http://www.hhs.gov

Secretary of Health and Human Services	XAVIER BECERRA
Deputy Secretary	
Chief of Staff	

Chair, Departmental Appeals Board
Chief Administrative Law Judge, Office of Medicare Hearings
  and Appeals
Executive Secretary
General Counsel
Inspector General
National Coordinator for Health Information Technology
Surgeon General

Assistant Secretaries
Administration
Financial Resources
Global Affairs
Health
Legislation
Planning and Evaluation
Preparedness and Response
Public Affairs

Directors
Center for Faith-Based and Neighborhood Partnerships
Office for Civil Rights
Office of Health Reform
Office of Intergovernmental and External Affairs
https://www.hhs.gov/about/leadership/index.html

The Department of Health and Human Services strengthens the public health and welfare of the American people by making affordable and quality health care and childcare accessible, ensuring the safety of food products, preparing for public health emergencies, and advancing the diagnosis, treatment, and curing of life-threatening illnesses.

The Department of Health and Human Services (HHS) was created as the Department of Health, Education, and Welfare on April 11, 1953 (5 U.S.C. app.).
Secretary The Secretary of Health and Human Services advises the President on health, welfare, and income security plans, policies, and programs of the Federal Government and directs Department staff in carrying out the programs and activities of the Department and promotes general public understanding of the Department's goals, programs, and objectives. http://www.hhs. gov/about/leadership/index.html#secretary
Office of Intergovernmental and External Affairs The Office of Intergovernmental and External Affairs (IEA) supports the Secretary by serving as the primary liaison between the Department and external stakeholders and governments at the State,

DEPARTMENT OF HEALTH AND HUMAN SERVICES
CENTERS FOR DISEASE CONTROL AND PREVENTION (CDC)

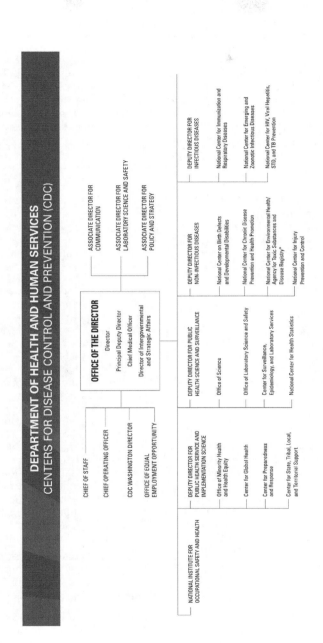

OFFICE OF THE DIRECTOR
Director
Principal Deputy Director
Chief Medical Officer
Director of Intergovernmental and Strategic Affairs

CHIEF OF STAFF

CHIEF OPERATING OFFICER

CDC WASHINGTON DIRECTOR

OFFICE OF EQUAL EMPLOYMENT OPPORTUNITY

ASSOCIATE DIRECTOR FOR COMMUNICATION

ASSOCIATE DIRECTOR FOR LABORATORY SCIENCE AND SAFETY

ASSOCIATE DIRECTOR FOR POLICY AND STRATEGY

NATIONAL INSTITUTE FOR OCCUPATIONAL SAFETY AND HEALTH

DEPUTY DIRECTOR FOR PUBLIC HEALTH SERVICE AND IMPLEMENTATION SCIENCE

Office of Minority Health and Health Equity

Center for Global Health

Center for Preparedness and Response

Center for State, Tribal, Local, and Territorial Support

DEPUTY DIRECTOR FOR PUBLIC HEALTH SCIENCE AND SURVEILLANCE

Office of Science

Office of Laboratory Science and Safety

Center for Surveillance, Epidemiology, and Laboratory Services

National Center for Health Statistics

DEPUTY DIRECTOR FOR NON-INFECTIOUS DISEASES

National Center on Birth Defects and Developmental Disabilities

National Center for Chronic Disease Prevention and Health Promotion

National Center for Environmental Health/Agency for Toxic Substances and Disease Registry*

National Center for Injury Prevention and Control

DEPUTY DIRECTOR FOR INFECTIOUS DISEASES

National Center for Immunization and Respiratory Diseases

National Center for Emerging and Zoonotic Infectious Diseases

National Center for HIV, Viral Hepatitis, STD, and TB Prevention local, territorial, and tribal levels. The Office facilitates communication regarding HHS initiatives as they relate to external stakeholders and governments at the State, local, territorial, and tribal levels. The IEA both represents the State, territorial, and tribal perspective in the process of Federal policymaking and clarifies the Federal perspective to State, territorial and tribal representatives. http://www.hhs.gov/intergovernmental

For further information, contact the Office of Intergovernmental and External Affairs. Phone, 202-690-6060.

Office of the Assistant Secretary for Preparedness and Response

The Office of the Assistant Secretary for Preparedness and Response (ASPR) provides national leadership in the prevention of, preparation for, and response to the adverse health effects of public health emergencies and disasters. It acts as the primary advisor to the HHS Secretary on bioterrorism and other public health emergency matters, strengthens the Nation's health and response systems, and enhances national health security. The ASPR leads a collaborative policy approach to the Department's preparedness, response, and recovery portfolio. It works with partners across Federal, State, local, tribal, and international bodies, in communities, and in the private sector to promote a unified and strategic approach to the challenges of public health and medical preparedness, response, and recovery through programs like the Hospital Preparedness Program. The ASPR coordinates public health and medical support available from across the Federal Government to help prepare communities and to augment local capabilities of overwhelmed communities during and after disasters, which includes providing medical professionals through the ASPR's National Disaster Medical System and the Medical Reserve Corps. The ASPR provides an integrated, systematic approach to the advanced development and acquisition of the necessary vaccines, drugs, therapies, and diagnostic tools for public health medical emergencies. It also coordinates within the Department and among Federal

partners on the policy, prioritization, funding, acquisition, and distribution of these medical countermeasures. In addition, offices within the ASPR coordinate within the division, within the Department and with Federal, State, local, territorial, tribal and international bodies on emergency communications, science preparedness, and administrative management to support decisionmakers in emergencies. http://www.phe.gov/preparedness/pages/default.aspx

For further information, contact the Office of the Assistant Secretary for Preparedness and Response. Phone, 202-205-2882.

Office of the Assistant Secretary for Health

The Office of the Assistant Secretary for Health (ASH) comprises 12 offices and 10 Presidential and secretarial advisory committees. The Assistant Secretary for Health heads the Office and serves as the Secretary's senior public health advisor. ASH provides assistance in implementing and coordinating secretarial decisions for the Public Health Service and coordination of population-based health clinical divisions; provides oversight of research conducted or supported by the Department; implements programs that provide population-based public health services; and provides direction and policy oversight, through the Office of the Surgeon General, for the Public Health Service Commissioned Corps. ASH administers a wide array of interdisciplinary programs related to disease prevention, health promotion, the reduction of health disparities, women's health, HIV/AIDS, vaccine programs, physical fitness and sports, bioethics, population affairs, blood supply, research integrity, and human research protections. http://www.hhs.gov/ash

For further information, contact the Office of the Assistant Secretary for Health. Phone, 202-690-7694.

Sources of Information

A–Z Index   The HHS Web site features an alphabetical index to help visitors search for specific topics or browse content that aligns with their interests. http://www.hhs.gov/az/a/index.html

Bullying   The HHS manages StopBullying. gov, a Web site that provides resources for defining, preventing, and responding to bullying, and for identifying who may be at risk. The Web site also features sections for children and teens, educators, parents, and communities. https://www.stopbullying.gov

Information on identifying, preventing, and reporting cyberbullying is also available on the Web site. https://www.stopbullying. gov/cyberbullying/index.html

Business Opportunities   The HHS relies on its contractors and grantees to help protect the health of Americans and provide essential human services. http://www.hhs. gov/grants/index.html#contract

The Office of Small and Disadvantaged Business Utilization helps develop and implement outreach programs to raise awareness of HHS contracting opportunities within the small business community. For information on programs, contact the Office of Small and Disadvantaged Business Utilization. Phone, 202-690-7300. http:// www.hhs.gov/asfr/ogapa/osbdu

Civil Rights   The Office for Civil Rights improves people's health and well-being, ensures equal access to health care and services without discrimination, and protects the privacy and security of people's health information. For information on enforcement of civil rights laws, contact the Director, Office for Civil Rights, 200 Independence Avenue SW.,Room 515–F Washington, DC 20201. Phone, 800-368-1019. TDD, 800-537-7697. http://www.hhs.gov/ocr/civilrights

Departmental Appeals Board   For information, contact the Departmental Appeals Board Immediate Office, MS 6127, Wilbur J. Cohen Building, 330 Independence Avenue SW., Room G–644, Washington, DC 20201. Phone, 202-565-0200. http://www.hhs.gov/dab

Career Opportunities   For information on training opportunities and opportunities for recent graduates and students or to view current job openings, visit the "Why a Career at HHS?" Web page. http://www.hhs. gov/about/careers/index.html

Freedom of Information Act (FOIA)   The FOIA allows individuals to request access to Federal agency records. The statute contains, however, nine exemptions that exempt some records or portions of them from disclosure.

The Assistant Secretary for Public Affairs also serves as the Agency Chief FOIA Officer. http://www.hhs.gov/foia | Email: hhs.acfo@ hhs.gov

Frequently Asked Questions (FAQs)   The HHS posts answers to FAQs on its Web site. http://www.hhs.gov/answers

Glossary   In the world of organ donation and transplantation, terms are used and topics discussed that many may not recognize. The OrganDonor.gov Web site features a glossary of organ donation terms. http://www.organdonor.gov/about/facts-terms/terms.html

Inspector General   Contact the Office of Inspector General, Wilbur J. Cohen Building, 330 Independence Avenue SW., Washington, DC 20201. http://oig.hhs.gov

To report fraud, waste, or abuse in Department programs, contact the Office of Inspector General, OIG Hotline Operations, P.O. Box 23489, L'Enfant Plaza Station, Washington, DC 20026-3489. TIPS Line, 800-447-8477. OIG Fugitive Line, 888-476-4453. TTY, 800-377-4950. Fax, 800-223-8164. https://forms.oig.hhs.gov/ hotlineoperations

Medicare Hearings / Appeals   For information on Medicare hearings before administrative law judges, regarding Medicare coverage and payment determinations that Medicare contractors, Medicare Advantage Organizations, or Part D plan sponsors have made, as well as information on determinations related to Medicare beneficiary eligibility and entitlement, Part B late enrollment penalties, and income-related monthly adjustment amounts that the Social Security Administration has made, contact the Office of Medicare Hearings and Appeals. Phone, 703-235-0635 or 855-556-8475. http:// www.hhs.gov/omha | Email: medicare. appeals@hhs.gov

Open Government   The HHS supports the Open Government initiative by promoting the principles of collaboration, participation, and transparency. http://www.hhs.gov/open/ index.html

Privacy Rights   For information on the HIPAA privacy, security, and breach notification rules or the Patient Safety Act, contact the Office for Civil Rights. Phone,

800-368-1019. TDD, 800-537-7697. http://www.hhs.gov/ocr/privacy

Public Health Service Commissioned Corps Officer Program   Information on the Commissioned Corps Officer programs is available at the Public Health Service Commissioned Corps Officer Web site. http://www.usphs.gov

Regional Offices   Visit the "Regional Offices" Web page for contact information. http://www.hhs.gov/about/agencies/regional-offices

Support Services (Fee-for-Service Activities)   The Program Support Center provides support services to all components of the Department and Federal agencies worldwide. For information concerning fee-for-service activities in the areas of acquisitions, occupational health, information technology support and security, human resource systems, financial management, and administrative operations, contact the Program Support Center, 5600 Fishers Lane, Rockville, MD 20857. Phone, 301-443-0034. http://www.psc.gov

Surgeon General   For information on the benefits of active living, healthy eating, mental and emotional well-being, and tobacco-free living, visit the "Surgeon General" Web site. Phone, 240-276-8853. http://www.surgeongeneral.gov http://www.hhs.gov/contactus.html

For further information, contact the U.S. Department of Health and Human Services, 200 Independence Avenue SW., Washington, DC 20201. Phone, 877-696-6775.

Administration for Children and Families

330 C Street SW., Washington, DC 20201
Phone, 202-401-9200. Internet, http://www.acf.hhs.gov

Assistant Secretary for Children and Families	MARK GREENBERG, ACTING
Chief of Staff	S. JEFFREY HILD

The Administration for Children and Families administers programs and provides advice to the Secretary on issues relevant to children, youth, and families; child support enforcement; community services; developmental disabilities; family assistance; Native American assistance; and refugee resettlement. http://www.acf.hhs.gov/about/what-we-do

Sources of Information

Career Opportunities   The Administration employs professionals with diverse academic and social backgrounds in a broad range of career fields and positions. http://www.acf.hhs.gov/about/jobs-contracts

History   The Administration for Children and Families was created on April 15, 1991. A short history of the Administration is available on its Web site. http://www.acf.hhs.gov

Homelessness   The Administration's Web site features information on its programs and services for the homeless and for those at risk of becoming homeless. http://www.acf.hhs.gov/program-topics/homelessness

Hotlines   The Administration supports nationwide crisis hotlines for child abuse, domestic violence, human trafficking, and runaways. The Health Insurance Marketplace Call Center assists callers with choosing coverage that provides the best protection and benefits for them and family members, as well as for their businesses. http://www.acf.hhs.gov/acf-hotlines

Lesbian, Gay, Bisexual, and Transgender (LGBT) Assistance   The Administration's Web site features information on its programs and services for the LGBT community, especially for LGBT families and youth. http://www.acf.hhs.gov/program-topics/lgbt-0

News   The Administration posts press releases on its Web site. http://www.acf.hhs.gov/media/press

Programs / Services   The Administration's Web site features a page showcasing by topic the programs and services that it provides to support families, children, individuals, and communities.

Topics include children and youth, communities, emergency response and recovery, families, financial security, global populations, Hispanic outreach, homelessness, human trafficking, LGBT, Native Americans and tribes, and unaccompanied children. http://www.acf. hhs.gov/program-topics http://www.acf. hhs.gov/media/program-contacts

For further information, contact the Administration for Children and Families, 330 C Street SW., Washington, DC 20201. Phone, 202-401-9200.

Administration for Community Living

330 C Street SW., Washington, DC 20201
Phone, 202-401-4634. TTY, 800-877-8339. Internet, http://www.acl.gov

Administrator	Mary Lazare, Acting
Principal Deputy Administrator	Mary Lazare, Acting

The Administration for Community Living administers programs and advises the Secretary on issues relevant to people with disabilities, their families and caregivers, and the independence, well-being, and health of older adults. https://acl.gov/About_ACL/Index.aspx

Sources of Information

Blog The Administration's Blog presents diverse perspectives on trends and issues related to older adults and people with disabilities. https://acl.gov/NewsRoom/blog/Index.aspx
Data / Statistics Data and statistics on older adults, as well as on persons with intellectual, physical, and developmental disabilities, are available on the Administration's Web site. https://acl.gov/Data_Outcomes/Index.aspx

Elder Care Services The elder care locator is a public service that provides information on services for older adults and their families. Online chat with an information specialist is also available Monday–Friday, 9 a.m.–8 p.m., eastern time. Phone, 800-677-1116. http://www.eldercare.gov/Eldercare.NET/Public/Index.aspx
Employment For information on employment opportunities, visit the "Career Opportunities" Web page. http://www.acl.gov/About_ACL/CareerOpportunities/Index.aspx
Help / Resources The Administration's Web site features resources for connecting caregivers, families, older adults, people with disabilities, and professionals to Federal, national, and local programs and information. https://acl.gov/Get_Help/Index.aspx http://www.acl.gov

For further information, contact the Administration for Community Living, 330 C Street SW., Washington, DC 20201. Phone, 202-401-4634. TTY, 800-877-8339.

Agency for Healthcare Research and Quality

5600 Fishers Lane, Rockville, MD 20857
Phone, 301-427-1364. Internet, http://www.ahrq.gov

Director	ANDREW BINDMAN
Deputy Director	SHARON B. ARNOLD

The Agency for Healthcare Research and Quality produces evidence to make health care affordable, equitable, more accessible, of a higher quality, and safer. It also works within the Department of Health and Human Services and with other partners to ensure that the evidence is understood and used. http://www.ahrq.gov/cpi/about/profile/index.html

Sources of Information

Data   Statistical portraits of health care delivery in the United States are available on the Agency's Web site. http://www.ahrq.gov/research/data/index.html

Career Opportunities   For information on employment opportunities, visit the "Job Opportunities" Web page. http://www.ahrq.gov/cpi/about/careers/index.html

Frequently Asked Questions (FAQs)   The Agency posts answers to FAQs on is Web site. https://info.ahrq.gov

Site Map   The Web site map allows visitors to look for specific topics or to browse content that aligns with their interests. http://www.ahrq.gov/sitemap.html http://www.ahrq.gov

For further information, contact the Agency for Healthcare Research and Quality, 5600 Fishers Lane, Rockville, MD 20857. Phone, 301-427-1364.

Agency for Toxic Substances and Disease Registry

MS E–61, 4770 Buford Highway NE., Atlanta, GA 30341
Phone, 770-488-0604. Internet, http://www.atsdr.cdc.gov

Administrator	Brenda Fitzgerald

The Agency for Toxic Substances and Disease Registry (ATSDR), as part of the Public Health Service, tries to prevent exposure to toxic substances—exposure to substances from wastesites, unplanned releases, and other pollution sources present in the environment—which produces adverse health effects and diminishes the quality of life. https://www.atsdr.cdc.gov/about/index.html

Sources of Information

A–Z Index   The Agency's Web site features an alphabetical index to help visitors search for specific topics or browse content that aligns with their interests. https://www.atsdr.cdc.gov/az/a.html

ATSDR in 60 Seconds   The ATSDR protects people from the health effects of chemical exposures. The Agency's Web site features the 60-second video "Dangerous Discovery" that communicates the importance of its mission. https://www.atsdr.cdc.gov/videos/ATSDR_DangerousDiscovery_h264.mp4

Internships / Training   Information on internships and educational and training opportunities is available on the ATSDR Web site. http://www.atsdr.cdc.gov/environmentaleducation.html

Toxic Frequently Asked Questions (ToxFAQs)   ToxFAQs features a series of summaries on hazardous substances that the Agency's Division of Toxicology developed. ATSDR toxicological profiles and public health statements are the sources of information on which the series relies. Each factsheet serves as a guide that is quick to read and easy to understand. ToxFAQs also answers FAQs on exposure to hazardous substances that are encountered near wastesites and their effects on human health. https://www.atsdr.cdc.gov/toxfaqs/index.asp

Toxic Substances Portal   The portal offers convenient access to the most relevant information on toxic substances and their effects on human health. The portal's Web pages feature an alphabetical ordering of documents on specific substances, toxicological information by health effect or chemical class, and toxicological information for specific audiences (community members, emergency responders, toxicological and health professionals, and health care providers). https://www.atsdr.cdc.gov/substances/index.asp http://www.atsdr.cdc.gov

For further information, contact the Agency for Toxic Substances and Disease Registry, 4770 Buford Highway NE., Atlanta, GA 30341. Phone, 770-488-0604.

Centers for Disease Control and Prevention

1600 Clifton Road, Atlanta, GA 30333
Phone, 800-232-4636. Internet, http://www.cdc.gov

Director	ROCHELLE WALENSKY
Principal Deputy Director	DEBRA HOURY
https://www.cdc.gov/about/leadership.htm	

The above list of key personnel was updated 3–2020.

Establishment and Organization
On July 1, 1946, the Communicable Disease Center opened its doors in Atlanta, GA, with the goal of stopping the spread of malaria nationwide. With a budget of $10 million, its employees numbered fewer than 400. Shovels, sprayers, and trucks were among the most important tools for slowing the disease's spread. https://www.cdc.gov/about/history/index.html

The CDC posts its organizational chart online in Portable Document Format for viewing and downloading. https://www.cdc.gov/about/pdf/organization/cdc-org-chart.pdf

Activities
The Centers for Disease Control and Prevention (CDC), as part of the Public Health Service, protects the public health of Americans by leading the national effort to prevent and manage diseases and other preventable conditions and by responding to public health emergencies. Within the CDC, the following five directorates lead efforts to diagnose, prevent, and treat public health hazards.

Infectious Diseases Research and Policies   The CDC oversees three infectious disease national centers. The National Center for Emerging and Zoonotic Infectious Diseases focuses on diseases that have been known for many years, emerging diseases, and zoonotic diseases (i.e., those that spread from animals to people). The National Center for HIV/AIDS, Viral Hepatitis, STD and TB Prevention eliminates, prevents, and controls disease, disability, and death caused by human immunodeficiency virus infection/acquired immunodeficiency syndrome, non-HIV retroviruses, viral hepatitis, other sexually transmitted diseases, and tuberculosis. The National Center for Immunization and Respiratory Diseases mitigates the effects of disease, which include disability and death, through immunization and by controlling respiratory and related diseases. https://www.cdc.gov/ddid/centers.html

Occupational Safety and Health   The National Institute for Occupational Safety and Health conducts research to reduce worker illness and injury and to advance worker well-being; promotes safe and healthy workers through interventions, recommendations, and building capacity to address hazards; and enhances worker safety and health through collaborations that are global in scope. http://www.cdc.gov/NIOSH

Noncommunicable Diseases Prevention   The CDC's current noninfectious disease priorities include marijuana use outcomes that affect health, mental health, and the prevention of nonoccupational hearing loss. Its noninfectious disease services are provided by four national centers: the National Center on Birth Defects and Developmental Disabilities; the National Center for Chronic Disease Prevention and Health Promotion; the National Center for Environmental Health / Agency for Toxic Substances and Disease Registry; and the National Center for Injury Prevention and Control. https://www.cdc.gov/about/leadership/leaders/ondieh.html

Public Health Preparedness and Response   The Center for Preparedness and Response helps the Nation prepare for and respond to urgent public health threats by providing strategic direction, coordination, and support for CDC's terrorism preparedness and emergency response activities. http://www.cdc.gov/phpr

Public Health Science and Surveillance   The Public Health Science and Surveillance services—which include the National Center for Health Statistics and the Center for Surveillance, Epidemiology, and Laboratory Services (CSELS)—lead the effort in promoting and facilitating science, surveillance, standards, and policies for reducing the burden of diseases in the United States and abroad. The CSELS promotes collaboration among health professionals globally; supports educational, training, and professional opportunities in epidemiology and public health science; maintains datasets and manages and preserves specimens; facilitates the sharing of health information; and reports on emerging public health problems. Within the CDC, the Office of Laboratory Science and Safety oversees and coordinates critical laboratory policies and operations; the Office of Science serves as the CDC's authority on scientific quality, integrity, and innovation. https://www.cdc.gov/ddphss

Public Health Service and Implementation Science   One office and three centers lead the national effort to promote and facilitate science programs and policies for identifying and responding to domestic and global public health threats. These four components are the Center for Global Health; Center for Preparedness and Response; Center for State, Tribal, Local and Territorial Support; and the Office of Minority Health and Health Equity. https://www.cdc.gov/about/leadership/leaders/ddphsis.html

Sources of Information

A–Z Index   An alphabetical subject index helps visitors navigate the content of the CDC's website. https://www.cdc.gov/az/a.html?CDC_AA_refVal=https%3A%2F%2Fwww.cdc.gov%2Faz%2Findex.html

Career Opportunities   The CDC is the leading national public health protection agency in the United States. It relies on professionals with scientific and nonscientific expertise to protect Earth's human population from the threat of deadly diseases like Ebola, HIV/AIDS, influenza, malaria, and tuberculosis. Most scientific and technical positions at the CDC are filled through the Commissioned Corps of the Public Health Service, a uniformed service of the U.S. Government. http://jobs.cdc.gov

In 2019, the CDC ranked 81st among 420 agency subcomponents in the Partnership for Public Service's Best Places To Work Agency Rankings. https://bestplacestowork.org/rankings/detail/HE39

Contact Information   The "Contact CDC–INFO" web page has CDC phone numbers and an electronic form for contacting the agency. https://wwwn.cdc.gov/dcs/ContactUs/Form

Coronavirus Disease 2019 (COVID–19)   Guidance on prevention and treatment of COVID–19, as well as updates on the virus and information for specific groups like healthcare professionals and travelers, is available on the CDC website. https://www.cdc.gov/coronavirus/2019-nCoV/index.html

Disease of the Week   The "Disease of the Week" Web page features key facts on, prevention tips for, and a quiz to test one's knowledge of common, serious diseases. http://www.cdc.gov/dotw

Freedom of Information Act (FOIA)   The CDC posts answers to frequently asked FOIA questions online. http://www.cdc.gov/od/foia/faqs/index.htm | Email: FOIARequests@cdc.gov

The CDC posts frequently requested agency records in its electronic reading room. http://www.cdc.gov/od/foia/reading/records/index.htm

Frequently Asked Questions (FAQs)   The CDC posts answers to FAQs on its website. https://www.cdc.gov/cdc-info/ask-cdc.html?CDC_AA_refVal=https%3A%2F%2Fwww.cdc.gov%2Fcdc-info%2Ffaqs.html

History   Some of the CDC's most important contributions to public health are described on the "CDC Timeline" web page. https://www.cdc.gov/museum/timeline/index.html

Influenza (Flu)   Information on and resources for influenza are available on the CDC website. https://www.cdc.gov/flu/index.htm

Language Assistance   Information on language assistance services is available online for readers of Arabic, Chinese, Farsi, French, German, Haitian Creole, Italian, Japanese, Korean, Polish, Portuguese, Russian, Spanish, Tagalog, and Vietnamese speakers. https://www.cdc.gov/other/language-assistance.html

Library   The Stephen B. Thacker CDC Library helps the advancement of science and public health and safety through information. It provides a full range of information services and products to support public health research, policy, and action. The Library, which comprises the headquarters library in Atlanta and six branches, serves CDC employees nationwide, as well as employees working in international locations. http://www.cdc.gov/library

Museum   The David J. Sencer CDC Museum features award-winning permanent and changing exhibitions that focus on public health topics, as well as on the history of the CDC. The museum is located in Atlanta, GA, and admission is free. It is open to the public on weekdays, excluding Federal holidays. Phone, 404-639-0830. http://www.cdc.gov/museum/index.htm

Podcasts   The Public Health Media Library's online holdings include recent and featured CDC podcasts. https://tools.cdc.gov/medialibrary/index.aspx#/landing/mediatype/Podcast/language/english/page/1/sort/desc/group/0

Publications   Many publications are accessible on the CDC's website. https://www.cdc.gov/publications

Sources of Information for the CDC were updated 3–2020.

Reports   The monthly report "CDC Vital Signs" is released on the first Tuesday of every month. Past editions have addressed topics like colorectal and breast cancer screening, obesity, alcohol and tobacco use, HIV testing, motor vehicle safety, cardiovascular disease, teen pregnancy and infections associated with health care, foodborne disease, and more. The report is also available in Spanish. http://www.cdc.gov/vitalsigns

The CDC prepares the "Morbidity and Mortality Weekly Report," which it uses for scientific publication of accurate, authoritative, objective, reliable, timely, and useful public health information and recommendations. Educators, epidemiologists and other scientists, physicians and nurses, public health practitioners, and researchers and laboratorians regularly read the report. https://www.cdc.gov/mmwr/index.html | Email: mmwrq@cdc.gov

Social Media   The CDC maintains a robust social media presence online. Digital tools are also accessible on its "Social Media at CDC" web page. https://www.cdc.gov/socialmedia

Travel Health Notices   The CDC posts travel health notices on its Web site. http://wwwnc.cdc.gov/travel/notices

Centers for Medicare and Medicaid Services

7500 Security Boulevard, Baltimore, MD 21244
Phone, 410-786-3000. Internet, http://www.cms.gov

Administrator	ANDREW SLAVITT, ACTING
Principal Deputy Administrator	PATRICK H. CONWAY, ACTING
Chief Operating Officer / Chief of Staff	MANDY COHEN

The Centers for Medicare and Medicaid Services (CMS) provides health coverage to more than 100 million people through Medicare, Medicaid, the Children's Health Insurance Program, and the Health Insurance Marketplace. The CMS seeks to strengthen and modernize the Nation's health care system, to provide access to high quality care and improved health at lower costs. https://www.cms.gov/About-CMS/About-CMS.html

Sources of Information

Blog   The CMS maintains an official blog on its Web site. https://blog.cms.gov

Career Opportunities   For information on career opportunities, visit the "Careers at CMS" Web page. https://www.cms.gov/About-CMS/Career-Information/CareersatCMS/index.html

Forms   Many CMS forms are accessible on the agency's Web site. https://www.cms.

gov/Medicare/CMS-Forms/CMS-Forms/CMS-Forms-List.html

Frequently Asked Questions (FAQs) The CMS posts answers to FAQs on its Web site. https://questions.cms.gov

Glossary The CMS maintains a glossary that explains terms found on its Web site. https://www.cms.gov/apps/glossary

History The CMS Web site features the agency's program history. https://www.cms.gov/About-CMS/Agency-Information/History/index.html

Medicaid The CMS manages the Medicaid.gov Web site. https://www.medicaid.gov

Medicare The CMS manages the Medicare.gov Web site. https://www.medicare.gov

The Medicare Coverage Database contains all national coverage determinations and local coverage determinations, local articles, and proposed national coverage determination decisions. The database also includes several other types of national coverage policy-related documents, including national coverage analyses, coding analyses for labs, Medicare Evidence Development and Coverage Advisory Committee proceedings, and Medicare coverage guidance documents. https://www.cms.gov/medicare-coverage-database

The CMS manages the "STOP Medicare Fraud" Web site. To report Medicare fraud, call 800-447-8477. TTY, 800-377-4950. https://www.stopmedicarefraud.gov/index.html

Newsroom The CMS posts news items on its Web site. https://www.cms.gov/Newsroom/Newsroom-Center.html

Social Media The CMS tweets announcements and other newsworthy items on Twitter. https://twitter.com/cmsgov

The CMS posts videos on its YouTube channel. https://www.youtube.com/user/CMSHHSgov http://www.cms.gov

For further information, contact the Centers for Medicare and Medicaid Services, Department of Health and Human Services, 7500 Security Boulevard, Baltimore, MD 21244. Phone, 410-786-3000.

Food and Drug Administration

10903 New Hampshire Avenue, Silver Spring, MD 20993
Phone, 888-463-6332. Internet, http://www.fda.gov

Commissioner	Scott Gottlieb
Chief of Staff	Lauren Silvis

The Food and Drug Administration (FDA) protects the public health by ensuring the safety, security, and efficacy of human and veterinary drugs, biological products, medical devices, the Nation's food supply, cosmetics, and products that emit radiation. The FDA also advances the public health by accelerating innovations to make medicines more effective and by providing the public with accurate, science-based information on medicines and food to improve health. The agency plays a significant role in the Nation's counterterrorism capability by ensuring the security of the food supply. http://www.fda.gov/AboutFDA/default.htm

Sources of Information

Animal and Veterinary Recalls The FDA posts animal and veterinary recall information—brand name, date of recall, company name, product description, and the reason or problem—on its Web site. http://www.fda.gov/AnimalVeterinary/SafetyHealth/RecallsWithdrawals/default.htm

A–Z Index The FDA's Web site features an alphabetical index to help visitors search for specific topics or browse content that aligns with their interests. http://www.fda.gov/SiteIndex/default.htm

Career Opportunities The FDA relies on attorneys, biologists, chemists, consumer safety officers, engineers, information technology specialists, medical officers, microbiologists, pharmacists, pharmacologists, statisticians, and other professionals to carry out its mission. http://www.fda.gov/AboutFDA/WorkingatFDA/default.htm

Cigarettes The FDA describes cigarettes with three words: attractive, addictive, and deadly. Cigarettes are designed to be attractive and addictive. The FDA's infographic "How a Cigarette is Engineered" explains the role design plays in attraction and addiction. http://www.fda.gov/TobaccoProducts/NewsEvents/ucm529397.htm

Cosmetics   The FDA posts answers to the questions that consumers frequently ask about cosmetic safety and regulation. http://www.fda.gov/Cosmetics/ResourcesForYou/Consumers/ucm2005206.htm

Foodborne Illnesses   The FDA regulates human and animal food. It posts information on recent foodborne illness outbreaks on its Web site. http://www.fda.gov/Food/RecallsOutbreaksEmergencies/Outbreaks/default.htm

Recalls / Safety Alerts   Information gathered from press releases and other public notices on certain recalls of FDA-regulated products is available online. http://www.fda.gov/Safety/Recalls/default.htm http://www.fda.gov

For further information contact the Food and Drug Administration, 10903 New Hampshire Avenue, Silver Spring, MD 20993. Phone, 888-463-6332.

Health Resources and Services Administration

5600 Fishers Lane, Rockville, MD 20857
Phone, 301-443-3376. Internet, http://www.hrsa.gov

Administrator	George Sigounas
Deputy Administrator	Diana Espinosa

The Health Resources and Services Administration (HRSA) improves access to health care by strengthening the health care workforce, building healthy communities, and achieving health equity. HRSA programs make health care accessible to people who are geographically isolated or economically or medically vulnerable. It supports the training of health professionals, the distribution of providers to areas where they are needed most, and improvements in health care delivery. The agency also oversees organ, bone marrow, and cord blood donations; compensates individuals harmed by vaccination; and maintains databases that protect against health care abuse, fraud, malpractice, and waste. https://www.hrsa.gov/about/index.html

Sources of Information

Data   The HRSA maintains an online data warehouse. https://datawarehouse.hrsa.gov

Career Opportunities   The HRSA posts career opportunities on its Web site. https://www.hrsa.gov/hr/

Freedom of Information Act (FOIA)   The FOIA requires the HRSA to disclose documents or records that any person properly requests in writing. Certain documents or records, or parts of them, may be protected, however, from disclosure by one of the nine exemptions contained in the statute. https://www.hrsa.gov/foia/index.html

Organ Donation and Transplantation   The HRSA manages the OrganDonor.gov Web site, which provides the public with U.S. Government information on organ donation and transplantation. http://organdonor.gov/index.html

Social Media   The HRSA tweets announcements and other newsworthy items on Twitter. https://twitter.com/HRSAgov

The HRSA has a Facebook account. https://www.facebook.com/HRSAgov

The HRSA posts videos on its YouTube channel. https://www.youtube.com/user/HRSAtube/videos http://www.hrsa.gov/about/contact

For further information, contact the Office of Communications, Health Resources and Services Administration, 5600 Fishers Lane, Rockville, MD 20857. Phone, 301-443-3376.

Indian Health Service

5600 Fishers Lane Rockville, MD 20857
Phone, 301-443-3593. Internet, http://www.ihs.gov

Director	(VACANCY)
Principal Deputy Director	MICHAEL WEAHKEE
Deputy Director	CHRISTOPHER BUCHANAN

The Indian Health Service, as part of the Public Health Service, provides a comprehensive health services delivery system for American Indians and Alaska Natives. It helps Native American tribes develop their health programs; facilitates and assists tribes in coordinating health planning and obtaining and utilizing health resources available through Federal, State, and local programs, in operating comprehensive health programs and evaluating them; and provides comprehensive health care services, including hospital and ambulatory medical care, preventive and rehabilitative services, and development of community sanitation facilities. https://www.ihs.gov/aboutihs

Sources of Information

A–Z Index   The Indian Health Service's Web site features an alphabetical index to help visitors search for specific topics or browse content that aligns with their interests. https://www.ihs.gov/atoz/a/

Career Opportunities   For information on employment, visit the "Career Opportunities" Web page. https://www.ihs.gov/careeropps

Freedom of Information Act (FOIA)   The Indian Health Service's Web site features an electronic FOIA requester center. https://www.ihs.gov/FOIA

Newsroom   The Newsroom features announcements, congressional testimony, factsheets, press releases, and speeches. https://www.ihs.gov/newsroom | Email: newsroom@ihs.gov

Social Media   The Indian Health Service has a Facebook account. https://www.facebook.com/IndianHealthService

The Indian Health Service posts videos on its YouTube channel. https://www.youtube.com/user/IHSgov/feed http://www.ihs.gov/contact

For further information, contact the Management Policy and Internal Control Staff, Indian Health Service, 5600 Fishers Lane Rockville, MD 20857. Phone, 301-443-3593.

National Institutes of Health

1 Center Drive, Bethesda, MD 20892
Phone, 301-496-4000. Internet, http://www.nih.gov

Director	FRANCIS S. COLLINS
Principal Deputy Director	LAWRENCE A. TABAK

The National Institutes of Health (NIH) support biomedical and behavioral research domestically and abroad, conduct research in NIH laboratories and clinics, train research scientists, and develop and disseminate credible, science-based health information to the public. https://www.nih.gov/about-nih/what-we-do

Aging   The National Institute on Aging (NIA) conducts and supports research on the aging process, age-related diseases, and other special problems and needs of older people. It is also the lead NIH Institute for research on age-related cognitive change and Alzheimer's disease. The NIA provides information on aging to the scientific community, health care providers, and the public. http://www.nia.nih.gov

For further information, contact the National Institute on Aging. Phone, 301-496-1752.

Alcohol Abuse and Alcoholism   The National Institute on Alcohol Abuse and Alcoholism leads the national effort to reduce alcohol-related problems by conducting and supporting biomedical and behavioral research into the causes, consequences, prevention, and treatment of alcohol-use disorders. http://www.niaaa.nih.gov

For further information, contact the National Institute on Alcohol Abuse and Alcoholism. Phone, 301-443-3885.

Allergy and Infectious Diseases The National Institute of Allergy and Infectious Diseases conducts and supports research to study the causes of infectious diseases and immune-mediated diseases and to develop better means of preventing, diagnosing, and treating these diseases. http://www.niaid.nih.gov

For further information, contact the National Institute of Allergy and Infectious Diseases. Phone, 866-284-4107 or 301-496-5717.

Arthritis and Musculoskeletal and Skin Diseases The National Institute of Arthritis and Musculoskeletal and Skin Diseases supports research on the causes, treatment, and prevention of arthritis and musculoskeletal and skin diseases; the basic and clinical training of scientists to carry out this research; and the dissemination of information on research progress. http://www.niams.nih.gov

For further information, contact the National Institute of Arthritis and Musculoskeletal and Skin Diseases. Phone, 877-226-4267 or 301-496-8190.

Behavioral and Social Sciences Research The Office of Behavioral and Social Sciences Research supports and coordinates health-related behavioral and social sciences research that the NIH conducts or supports, and it integrates these sciences within the larger NIH research enterprise. It also communicates and disseminates research findings to stakeholders within and outside the Federal Government, thereby increasing understanding and improving treatment and prevention of disease. https://obssr.od.nih.gov

For further information, contact the Office of Behavioral and Social Sciences Research. Phone, 301-402-1146.

Biomedical Imaging and Bioengineering The National Institute of Biomedical Imaging and Bioengineering supports research, training, and the dissemination of research advances for accelerating the development and application of biomedical technologies to improve the detection, treatment, and prevention of disease. It integrates the physical and engineering sciences with the life sciences to advance basic research and medical care. http://www.nibib.nih.gov

For further information, contact the National Institute of Biomedical Imaging and Bioengineering. Phone, 301-496-3500.

Cancer The National Cancer Institute (NCI) is the Federal Government's principal agency for cancer research and training. It coordinates the National Cancer Program, which conducts and supports research, training, health information dissemination, and other activities associated with diagnosing, preventing, treating, and finding the cause of cancer and with the continuing care of cancer patients and their families. http://www.cancer.gov

For further information, contact the Cancer Information Service. Phone, 800-422-6237.

Center for Information Technology The Center for Information Technology provides, coordinates, and manages information technology to advance computational science. http://www.cit.nih.gov

For further information, contact the Center for Information Technology. Phone, 301-496-5703.

Child Health and Human Development The Eunice Kennedy Shriver National Institute of Child Health and Human Development conducts and supports basic, clinical, and epidemiological research on the reproductive, rehabilitative, neurobiological, developmental, and behavioral processes that determine the health of children, adults, families, and communities. http://www.nichd.nih.gov

For further information, contact the Eunice Kennedy Shriver National Institute of Child Health and Human Development. Phone, 800-370-2943.

Clinical Center The Clinical Center is the clinical research hospital for the NIH. By doing clinical research, investigators translate laboratory discoveries into better treatments, therapies, and interventions to improve the Nation's health. The Center conducts clinical and laboratory research and trains future clinical investigators. Nearly 500,000 volunteers from across the Nation have participated in clinical research studies since the Center opened in 1953. About 1,500 clinical research studies are currently in progress. http://clinicalcenter. nih.gov

For further information, contact the Clinical Center. Phone, 301-496-4000.

Communications   The Office of Communications and Public Liaison communicates information on consumer health, scientific results, and NIH accomplishments, issues, and research and training programs to the public, media, scientific and medical communities, and other interested groups. http://www.nih. gov/institutes-nih/nih-office-director/office-communications-public-liaison

For further information, contact the Office of Communications and Public Liaison. Phone, 301-496-5787

Complementary and Integrative Health   The National Center for Complementary and Integrative Health defines the utility and safety of complementary and integrative health interventions and their roles in improving health and health care. This science-based information helps the public, health care professionals, and health policymakers make decisions on the use and integration of complementary and integrative health approaches. https://nccih.nih.gov

For further information, contact the National Center for Complementary and Integrative Health. Phone, 888-644-6226.

Deafness and Other Communication Disorders   The National Institute on Deafness and Other Communication Disorders conducts and supports biomedical and behavioral research and training on normal and disordered processes of hearing, balance, taste, smell, voice, speech, and language. The Institute also makes science-based health information publicly available, and it supports efforts to create devices that substitute for lost or impaired sensory and communication function. http://www.nidcd. nih.gov | Email: NIDCDinfo@nidcd.nih.gov

For further information, contact the National Institute on Deafness and Other Communication Disorders. Phone, 800-241-1044. TTY, 800-241-1055.

Dental and Craniofacial Research   The National Institute of Dental and Craniofacial Research funds research on dental, oral, and craniofacial health and disorders. It also conducts research in its own laboratories and clinic, supports research training, and promotes the timely transfer of research-based knowledge and its implications for health to researchers, to health professionals, to patients, and to the general public. http://www.nidcr.nih.gov

For further information, contact the National Institute of Dental and Craniofacial Research. Phone, 301-496-4261.

Diabetes and Digestive and Kidney Diseases   The National Institute of Diabetes and Digestive and Kidney Diseases conducts, supports, and coordinates research and research training. It also offers science-based information on diabetes and other endocrine and metabolic diseases; on digestive diseases, nutritional disorders, weight control, and obesity; and on kidney, urologic and blood diseases. https://www. niddk.nih.gov

For further information, contact the National Institute of Diabetes and Digestive and Kidney Diseases. Phone, 301-496-3583.

Drug Abuse   The National Institute on Drug Abuse supports and conducts basic and clinical research on drug use, its consequences, and the underlying neurobiological, behavioral, and social mechanisms. The Institute also ensures effective translation and dissemination of scientific findings to improve the prevention and treatment of substance-use disorders, and it works at raising the public's awareness that addiction is a type of brain disorder. http://www.drugabuse.gov

For further information, contact the National Institute on Drug Abuse. Phone, 877-643-2644.

Environmental Health Sciences   The National Institute of Environmental Health Sciences supports research that explores how the environment affects people's health. Its research centers on environmental exposures and understanding their effects on human biology and health with an emphasis on disease and disability prevention. The Institute also houses the national toxicology program, a cross-agency organization that coordinates toxicity testing across the Federal Government. http://www.niehs.nih.gov

For further information, contact the National Institute of Environmental Health Sciences. Phone, 919-541-3345.

Eye and Vision Diseases The National Eye Institute conducts, fosters, and supports research on the causes, natural history, prevention, diagnosis, and treatment of disorders of the eye and visual system. It also directs the National Eye Health Education Program. http://www.nei.nih.gov

For further information, contact the National Eye Institute. Phone, 301-496-5248.

Fogarty International Center The Fogarty International Center addresses global health challenges through innovative and collaborative research and training programs. It also supports and advances the NIH mission through international partnerships. http://www.fic.nih.gov

For further information, contact the Fogarty International Center. Phone, 301-496-2075.

General Medical Sciences The National Institute of General Medical Sciences (NIGMS) supports basic research that increases understanding of biological processes and lays the foundation for advances in disease diagnosis, treatment, and prevention. NIGMS-funded scientists investigate how living systems work at a range of levels, from molecules and cells to tissues, to whole organisms and populations. The Institute also supports research in clinical areas, primarily those that affect multiple organ systems. To assure the vitality and productivity of the research enterprise, the NIGMS provides leadership in training the next generation of scientists, in diversifying the scientific workforce, and in developing research capacities throughout the country. http://www.nigms.nih.gov

For further information, contact the National Institute of General Medical Sciences. Phone, 301-496-7301.

Heart, Lung, and Blood Diseases The National Heart, Lung, and Blood Institute provides leadership for a global program in sleep disorders, blood resources, and diseases of the heart, blood vessels, blood, and lungs. It conducts, fosters, and supports a comprehensive program of basic research, clinical investigations and trials, observational and implementation science studies, as well as demonstration and education projects. http://www.nhlbi.nih.gov

For further information, contact the National Heart, Lung, and Blood Institute. Phone, 301-592-8573.

Human Genome Research The National Human Genome Research Institute supports research to uncover the role that the genome plays in human health and disease; studies on the ethical, legal, and social implications of genomics research for individuals, families, and communities; and the application of genomics research to medical care. http://www.genome.gov

For further information, contact the National Human Genome Research Institute. Phone, 301-402-0911.

Library of Medicine The National Library of Medicine, the world's largest biomedical library, serves as the Nation's principal medical information source, providing medical library services and extensive online information resources to scientists, practitioners, and the general public. It conducts, fosters, and supports research and training in biomedical informatics and supports development and dissemination of clinical terminology standards. http://www.nlm.nih.gov

For further information, contact the National Library of Medicine. Phone, 301-496-6308.

Mental Health The National Institute of Mental Health works to transform the understanding and treatment of mental illnesses. Through basic and clinical research, it advances the prevention, recovery, and cure of mental conditions that disable many Americans. http://www.nimh.nih.gov

For further information, contact the National Institute of Mental Health. Phone, 866-615-6464.

Minority Health and Health Disparities The National Institute on Minority Health and Health Disparities leads scientific research to improve minority health and eliminate health disparities. The Institute plans, reviews, coordinates, and evaluates all minority health and health disparities research and activities of the NIH; conducts and supports research on minority health and health disparities; promotes and supports the training of a diverse research workforce; translates and disseminates research information; and fosters innovative collaborations and partnerships. http://www.nimhd.nih.gov

For further information, contact the National Institute on Minority Health and Health Disparities. Phone, 301-402-1366.

Neurological Disorders and Stroke   The National Institute of Neurological Disorders and Stroke works to better understand the brain and spinal cord and to use that knowledge to mitigate the effects of neurological disease. It conducts, promotes, coordinates, and guides research and training on the causes, prevention, diagnosis, and treatment of neurological disorders and stroke. It also supports basic, translational, and clinical research in related scientific areas. http://www.ninds.nih.gov

For further information, contact the National Institute of Neurological Disorders and Stroke. Phone, 301-496-5751.

Nursing Research   The National Institute of Nursing Research supports clinical and basic research and research training to build the scientific foundation for clinical practice, to prevent disease and disability, to manage and eliminate symptoms caused by illness, to enhance end-of-life and palliative care, and to train the next generation of nurse scientists. http://www.ninr.nih.gov

For further information, contact the National Institute of Nursing Research. Phone, 301-496-0207.

Program Coordination, Planning, and Strategic Initiatives   The Division of Program Coordination, Planning, and Strategic Initiatives coordinates trans-NIH programs, planning, and strategic scientific initiatives in the Office of the NIH Director. The Division includes major programmatic offices that coordinate and support research and research infrastructure. The Division also serves as a portfolio analysis resource, coordinates evaluation reporting and agency activities under the Government Performance and Results Act, and supports science education partnership awards. http://dpcpsi.nih.gov

For further information, contact the Division of Program Coordination, Planning, and Strategic Initiatives. Phone, 301-402-9852.

Scientific Review   The Center for Scientific Review (CSR) organizes the peer review groups that evaluate the majority of grant applications submitted to the NIH. These groups include experienced and respected researchers from across the country and abroad. Since 1946, CSR has ensured that NIH grant applications receive fair, independent, expert, and timely reviews—free from inappropriate influences—so the NIH can fund the most promising research. CSR also receives all incoming applications and assigns them to the appropriate Centers and Institutes that fund grants. http://public.csr.nih.gov

For further information, contact the Center for Scientific Review. Phone, 301-435-1111.

Translational Sciences   The National Center for Advancing Translational Sciences focuses on what is common across diseases and the translational process. The Center emphasizes innovation and deliverables, relying on data and new technologies to develop, demonstrate, and disseminate advances in translational science that tangibly improve human health. https://ncats.nih.gov

For further information, contact the National Center for Advancing Translational Sciences. Phone, 301-435-0888.

Sources of Information

Employment   For information on employment opportunities, visit the "Jobs at NIH" Web page. http://www.jobs.nih.gov

Events   The NIH posts upcoming events on its Web site. https://www.nih.gov/news-events/events

Freedom of Information Act (FOIA)   The FOIA gives a right to access documents or records in the possession of the Federal Government to any person. The Government may withhold, however, information pursuant to the statute's nine exemptions and three exclusions. For more information, contact the NIH FOIA Office. Phone, 301-496-5633. Fax, 301-402-4541. https://www.nih.gov/institutes-nih/nih-office-director/office-communications-public-liaison/freedom-information-act-office | Email: nihfoia@mail.nih.gov

Frequently Asked Questions (FAQs)   The NIH posts answers to FAQs on its Web site. https://www.nih.gov/about-nih/frequently-asked-questions

History   The story of the agency begins in 1887, and a brief retelling of it is available online. https://www.nih.gov/about-nih/who-we-are/history

The DeWitt Stetten, Jr., Museum of Medical Research, also known as the NIH Stetten Museum, preserves and interprets the material culture of the NIH's scientific work through physical and virtual exhibits. https://history.nih.gov/museum/index.html

News   The NIH posts news releases on its Web site. https://www.nih.gov/news-events/news-releases

The monthly newsletter "NIH News In Health" features practical consumer health news and information that is based on NIH research. https://newsinhealth.nih.gov

Social Media   The NIH tweets announcements and other newsworthy items on Twitter. https://twitter.com/NIH

The NIH has a Facebook account. https://www.facebook.com/nih.gov

The NIH posts videos on its YouTube channel. https://www.youtube.com/user/nihod

Spanish   Important health information is available in Spanish. https://salud.nih.gov

Staff Directory   The NIH enterprise directory allows users to search for staff members by email address, name, or phone number. https://ned.nih.gov/search

Visitor Information   Maps and information on access and security, parking, tours, the campus shuttle, and more are available on the NIH Web site. https://www.nih.gov/about-nih/visitor-information

Weight Management   The National Institute of Diabetes and Digestive and Kidney Diseases' Web site has a trove of weight management information and resources. https://www.niddk.nih.gov/health-information/weight-management

The online body weight planner allows users to make personalized calorie and physical activity plans for reaching a target weight within a specific time period—and for maintaining it afterwards. https://www.niddk.nih.gov/health-information/health-topics/weight-control/body-weight-planner/Pages/bwp.aspx https://www.nih.gov/about-nih/contact-us

For further information, contact the National Institutes of Health, 1 Center Drive, Bethesda, MD 20892. Phone, 301-496-4000.

Substance Abuse and Mental Health Services Administration

5600 Fishers Lane Rockville, MD 20857
Phone, 240-276-2130. Internet, http://www.samhsa.gov

Administrator	KANA ENOMOTO, ACTING
Chief of Staff	TOM CODERRE

The Substance Abuse and Mental Health Services Administration mitigates the effects of substance abuse and mental illness on communities nationwide. It provides national leadership, serving as a voice for behavioral health; funds State and local service agencies through grants and formulas; collects data and makes available surveillance reports on the effect of behavioral health on Americans; leads efforts to offer public education on mental illness and substance abuse prevention, treatment, and recovery; regulates and oversees

national behavioral health programs; and promotes practice improvement in community-based, primary, and specialty care settings. http://www.samhsa.gov/about-us

Sources of Information

Blog   The Administration's Web site features a blog. https://blog.samhsa.gov

Data   The Administration maintains five collections of data: Center for Behavioral Health Statistics and Quality reports, client level data, mental health facilities data, population data, and substance abuse facilities data. http://www.samhsa.gov/data

Career Opportunities   For information on career opportunities, visit the "Jobs and Internships" Web page. http://www.samhsa.gov/about-us/jobs-internships

Help / Treatment   Resources for help and treatment are available on the Administration's Web site. http://www.samhsa.gov/find-help

KSOC–TV   KSOC–TV is a web-based technical assistance program featuring behavioral health experts discussing leading issues in children's mental health. http://www.samhsa.gov/children/multimedia

Newsroom   Press announcements, quarterly newsletters, and media highlights of initiatives and other activities are available in the newsroom. http://www.samhsa.gov/newsroom

Offices / Centers   The agency's offices and centers provide leadership and assistance for quality behavioral health services, as well as support States, territories, tribes, communities, and local organizations through grants and contract awards. Contact information for these offices and centers is available online. http://www.samhsa.gov/about-us/who-we-are/offices-centers

Publications   Hundreds of publications are available on the Administration's Web site. http://store.samhsa.gov

Site Map   The Web site map allows visitors to look for specific topics or to browse content that aligns with their interests. http://www.samhsa.gov/sitemap

Social Media   The Administration uses various forms of social media to connect with the Internet community and engage people. http://www.samhsa.gov/social-media/social-media-accounts

Suicide Prevention   The Administration funds the National Suicide Prevention Lifeline. Phone, 800-273-8255. http://suicidepreventionlifeline.org/?WT_ac=AD20110315NSPL#

Treatment Services Locator   The behavioral health treatment services locator is a confidential and anonymous source of information for persons seeking treatment facilities in the United States or U.S. Territories for substance abuse, addiction, mental health problems, or a combination of the three. Phone, 800-662-4357. TDD, 800-487-4889. https://findtreatment.samhsa.gov

Underage Drinking   Underage drinking accounts for 11 percent of all the alcohol consumed in the United States. Alcohol is the most widely misused substance among America's youth. The Administration disseminates information on the dangers of underage drinking and offers prevention tips. http://www.samhsa.gov/underage-drinking-topic http://www.samhsa.gov/about-us/contact-us

For further information, contact the Substance Abuse and Mental Health Services Administration, 5600 Fishers Lane Rockville, MD 20857, Rockville, MD 20857. Phone, 240-276-2130.

DEPARTMENT OF HOMELAND SECURITY

Washington, DC 20528
Phone, 202-282-8000. Internet, http://www.dhs.gov

Secretary of Homeland Security	ALEJANDRO MAYORKAS
Deputy Secretary	JOHN TIEN

Chief of Staff
Executive Secretary
Military Advisor
https://www.dhs.gov/leadership

Office of the Secretary

Undersecretary
Strategy, Policy, and Plans

Assistant Secretaries
Legislative Affairs
Partnership and Engagement
Public Affairs

Chief Privacy Officer
Citizenship and Immigration Services Ombudsman
Civil Rights and Civil Liberties Officer
General Counsel
https://www.dhs.gov/office-secretary

Operational and Support Components

Under Secretaries
Intelligence and Analysis
Management
Science and Technology

Administrators
Federal Emergency Management Agency
Transportation Security Administration

Assistant Secretary
Countering Weapons of Mass Destruction

Chief Officers
Chief Financial Officer
Chief Information Officer

Directors
Cybersecurity and Infrastructure Security Agency
Federal Law Enforcement Training Centers
Operations Coordination
U.S. Citizenship and Immigration Services

U.S. Immigration and Customs Enforcement
U.S. Secret Service

U.S. Coast Guard Commandant
U.S. Customs and Border Protection Commissioner
https://www.dhs.gov/operational-and-support-components
Office of Inspector General
Inspector General
https://www.oig.dhs.gov/about/meetActingIG

The above list of key personnel was updated 8–2020.

The Department of Homeland Security prevents terrorism and enhances security, manages the Nation's borders, administers immigration laws, safeguards cyberspace, and ensures resilience in the wake of disaster.

Establishment and Organization
On November 25, 2002, President George W. Bush approved Public Law 107–296, which is also cited as the "Homeland Security Act of 2002" to establish the Department of Homeland Security (DHS). Sixty days after its enactment, on January 24, 2003, the law became effective (116 STAT. 2142). https://www.govinfo.gov/content/pkg/STATUTE-116/pdf/STATUTE-116-Pg2135.pdf

By the advice and with the consent of the Senate, the President appoints the Secretary of Homeland Security, who heads the Department and has direction, authority, and control over it (116 STAT. 2142). The Secretary develops and coordinates a comprehensive strategy to protect the Nation from terrorist attacks. These efforts are undertaken in coordination with Federal, State, local, international, and private sector partners. The Secretary also advises the President on border management and protection, cyberspace security, administration and enforcement of immigration laws, intelligence analysis and infrastructure protection, science and technology for countering weapons of mass destruction, and resilience after a disastrous event.

Title 6 of the U.S. Code contains codified subject matter that affects domestic security. Its six chapters are named: 1) "Homeland Security Organization"; 2) "National Emergency Management"; 3) "Security and Accountability for Every Port"; 4) "Transportation Security"; 5) "Border Infrastructure and Technology Modernization"; and 6) "Cybersecurity." https://uscode.house.gov/view.xhtml?path=/prelim@title6&edition=prelim

Rules and regulations that affect domestic security are codified in title 6 of the Code of Federal Regulations (CFR). Chapter I, parts 1–199, deals with the "Department of Homeland Security, Office of the Secretary." https://www.ecfr.gov/cgi-bin/text-idx?SID=c4691da41d68a6d8d63e570daa7abec6&mc=true&tpl=/ecfrbrowse/Title06/6chapterI.tpl

Title 5, chapter XCVII, part 9701, of the CFR is dedicated to the "Department of Homeland Security Human Resources Management System." https://www.ecfr.gov/cgi-bin/text-idx?SID=79801535510dc623dfd64869e36a7d0e&mc=true&node=pt5.3.9701&rgn=div5

The DHS posts an organizational chart on its "Organizational Chart" web page. A Portable Document Format (PDF) file of the chart is available for viewing and downloading. https://www.dhs.gov/organizational-chart

Administration
Citizenship / Immigration   The Office of the Citizenship and Immigration Services Ombudsman improves the quality of citizenship and immigration services that are delivered to the public by providing individual case assistance. The Offices also makes recommendations for improving the U.S. Citizenship and Immigration Services' administration of immigration benefits. http://www.dhs.gov/topic/cis-ombudsman | Email: cisombudsman@hq.dhs.gov

Civil Rights / Liberties The Office for Civil Rights and Civil Liberties ensures that while the DHS secures the Nation, it also preserves individual liberty, fairness, and equality under the law. The Office promotes respect for civil rights and civil liberties in policymaking and implementation; advises DHS leadership and personnel, and State and local partners; communicates with communities and individuals whose civil rights and civil liberties may be affected by DHS activities, informing them about policies and avenues of redress and bringing appropriate attention to their experiences and concerns within the Department; investigates civil rights and liberties complaints filed by the public regarding DHS policies or activities, or actions taken by DHS personnel; and leads DHS equal employment opportunity programs and promotes workforce diversity and merit system principles. http://www.dhs.gov/office-civil-rights-and-civil-liberties

Department of Defense Coordination The Military Advisor counsels and supports the Secretary and Deputy Secretary on matters relating to policy, procedures, preparedness activities, and operations involving the DHS and the Department of Defense. http://www.dhs.gov/about-office-military-advisor

Executive Support The Office of the Executive Secretary directly supports the Secretary and Deputy Secretary and provides related support to leadership and management agencywide. The Office's activities are diverse, including accurate and timely dissemination of information and written communications to the Secretary and Deputy Secretary from throughout the DHS and its homeland security partners . http://www.dhs.gov/office-executive-secretary

Internal Audits / Investigations The Office of Inspector General conducts and supervises audits, investigations, and inspections relating to DHS programs and operations. The Office examines, evaluates, and, where necessary, critiques DHS operations and activities. It recommends ways for the agency to carry out its responsibilities in more economical, efficient, and effective ways. The Office also reviews recommendations regarding existing and proposed legislation and regulations affecting DHS programs and operations. https://www.oig.dhs.gov

Legal Compliance The Office of General Counsel ensures that departmental activities comply with applicable legal requirements. The Office provides legal advice on matters affecting national security, immigration, litigation, international law, maritime safety and security, transportation security, border security law, cybersecurity, fiscal and appropriations law, environmental law, and on matters affecting many more subjects. It also ensures that DHS efforts to secure the Nation are consistent with the civil rights and civil liberties of its citizens and follow the rule of law. The Office also provides legal services in several areas where the law intersects with the achievement of mission goals, such as the coordination of rulemaking activities, managing interdepartmental clearance of proposed legislation, and providing legal training for law enforcement officers. http://www.dhs.gov/office-general-counsel

Legislative Affairs The Office of Legislative Affairs serves as primary liaison to Members of Congress and their congressional staff. The Office responds to inquiries from Congress; notifies it about DHS initiatives, policies, and programs; and keeps the agency's senior leaders informed about the activities of Congress. The Office also participates in the Senate confirmation process of each DHS nominee whom the President nominates. http://www.dhs.gov/about-office-legislative-affairs

Partnership / Engagement The Office of Partnership and Engagement includes the following offices and programs: the Office for State and Local Law Enforcement, Private Sector Office, Office of Academic Engagement, Committee Management Office, Homeland Security Advisory Council, Homeland Security Academic Advisory Council, Blue Campaign, and the "If You See Something, Say Something" public awareness campaign. The Office comprises stakeholder engagement offices that communicate with State, local, tribal, and territorial governments, and with law enforcement, the private sector, academia, and Federal advisory committees. These offices coordinate DHS programs and policies with these same stakeholders. The Office also serves as the liaison between these stakeholders and the Office of the Secretary. It promotes an integrated national approach to homeland security by coordinating and advancing Federal interaction with external stakeholders, and it continues the homeland security dialogue with those partners and with the national associations representing them. http://www.dhs.gov/partnership-engagement

Privacy   The Privacy Office safeguards the collection, disclosure, and use of personally identifiable information and departmental information. It ensures that appropriate access to information is consistent with the core values, mission, and vision of DHS. The Office also implements the agency's policies to defend and protect the individual rights, liberties, and information interests of U.S. citizens. The Office has oversight of privacy and disclosure policy matters, including compliance with the Privacy Act of 1974, the Freedom of Information Act, and the completion of statements addressing the effect of new programs and systems on privacy, as required by the E-Government Act of 2002 and the Homeland Security Act of 2002. http://www.dhs.gov/privacy-office | Email: privacy@dhs.gov

Public Affairs   The Office of Public Affairs coordinates the public affairs activities of DHS components and offices. It also serves as the Federal Government's lead public information office during a national emergency or disaster. The Office is the point of contact for members of the news media, representatives of organizations, and the general public who seek information on DHS policies, procedures, programs, services, and statistics. The Office assists the Secretary with strategic and internal communications and with all matters of public affairs. http://www.dhs.gov/office-public-affairs

Strategy / Policy / Plans   The Office of Strategy, Policy, and Plans advises the Secretary and Deputy Secretary, develops policy and represents the DHS in interagency fora, coordinates and unifies policy positions, leads and coordinates international engagement and negotiations, operates the REAL ID and Visa Waiver programs, leads the development of operational and resource allocation guidance, develops strategies and operational plans, and collects and maintains and reports immigration data. https://www.dhs.gov/office-policy

Operations and Support

Citizenship / Immigration   The Unites States Citizenship and Immigration Services (USCIS) administers the Nation's legal immigration system. Operating primarily by fee funding, it ensures that information and decisions on citizenship and immigration benefits are provided to applications and petitioners in an accurate, consistent, courteous, professional, and timely manner that is consistent with national security. USCIS also strengthens the integrity of the Nation's legal immigration system by combating the unauthorized practice of immigration law, by helping to combat unauthorized employment in the workplace, and by deterring, detecting, and pursuing immigration-related fraud. http://www.uscis.gov

Customs / Border Protection   The U.S. Customs and Border Protection secures America's borders to protect the public from dangerous people and materials, while enabling legitimate trade and travel to enhance the Nation's global economic competitiveness. http://www.cbp.gov

Cybersecurity / Infrastructure Security   The Cybersecurity and Infrastructure Security Agency (CISA) builds the Nation's capacity to defend against cyber attacks and works with the Federal Government to provide cybersecurity tools, incident response services, and assessment capabilities to safeguard the networks that support the essential operations of partner departments and agencies. The Agency coordinates security and resilience efforts, using trusted partnerships across the private and public sectors, and delivers technical assistance and assessments to Federal stakeholders and to infrastructure owners and operators nationwide. Working with stakeholders nationwide, CISA conducts extensive outreach to support and strengthen the ability of emergency responders and relevant government officials to communicate in the event of a natural disaster, act of terrorism, or other man-made disaster. https://www.dhs.gov/cisa/about-cisa

Emergency Management Federal Emergency Management Agency (FEMA) administers a nationwide, risk-based, and comprehensive emergency management system of preparedness, protection, response, recovery, and mitigation. The goal is to reduce the loss of life and property and to protect the Nation from all hazards, including natural disasters, acts of terrorism, and other man-made disasters. FEMA coordinates programs to improve the effectiveness of emergency response providers at all levels of the government, initiates proactive mitigation activities, and manages the National Flood Insurance Program and U.S. Fire Administration. It also leads Government continuity planning, guidance, and operations for the Federal executive branch to minimize the disruption of essential operations and to guarantee enduring constitutional governance. http://www.fema.gov

Immigration / Customs Enforcement U.S. Immigration and Customs Enforcement (ICE) is the principal investigative arm of DHS. It promotes homeland security and public safety through the criminal and civil enforcement of Federal laws governing border control, customs, immigration, and trade. https://www.ice.gov

Intelligence / Analysis The Office of Intelligence and Analysis, as a member of the U.S. Intelligence Community, is the nexus between the Nation's intelligence apparatus and DHS components and other State, local, and private sector partners. The Office ensures that information is gathered from all relevant DHS field operations and other State, local, and private sector partners and that this information is shared with appropriate stakeholders to produce accurate, timely, and actionable analytical intelligence products and services. https://www.dhs.gov/office-intelligence-and-analysis

Law Enforcement Training The Federal Law Enforcement Training Centers (FLETC) is the Nation's largest provider of law enforcement training. It offers career-long training to law enforcement professionals to help them fulfill their responsibilities safely and proficiently. Under a collaborative training model, FLETC's Federal partner organizations provide training unique to their missions, while FLETC provides training in areas common to all law enforcement officers: driving, firearms, investigations, legal training, and tactics. https://www.fletc.gov

Management The Directorate for Management is responsible for accounting and finance, appropriations, budget, expenditure of funds, and procurement; equipment, facilities, property, and other material resources; human resources, personnel, and their security; identification and tracking of performance measurements relating to the responsibilities of the agency, and information technology and communication systems. The Directorate ensures that DHS employees have well-defined responsibilities and that managers and their employees have effective means of communicating with one another, with other governmental and nongovernmental bodies, and with the public they serve. http://www.dhs.gov/directorate-management

Maritime Safety / Security The U.S. Coast Guard (USCG) is the principal Federal agency responsible for maritime safety, security, and environmental stewardship in U.S. ports and waterways. The USCG protects and defends more than 100,000 miles of coastline and inland waterways and safeguards an exclusive economic zone that stretches from north of the Arctic Circle to south of the equator, from Puerto Rico to Guam. The USCG is a member of the Intelligence Community and one of the five Armed Services. It is also a first response and humanitarian service provider that aids people in distress or impacted by natural and man-made disasters both at sea and ashore. It is a law enforcement and regulatory agency with broad legal authorities associated with bridge administration, hazardous materials shipping, maritime transportation, oil spill response, pilotage, and vessel construction and operation. https://www.work.uscg.mil

Nuclear Terrorism The Domestic Nuclear Detection Office focuses solely on preventing nuclear terrorism, in coordination with domestic and international partners, by improving deterrence, detection, response, and attribution. The Office coordinates development of the global nuclear detection architecture with partners from the private sector and local, State,

Federal, and international governments. The Office develops, acquires, and supports the deployment of mechanisms to detect and report attempts to import, possess, store, transport, develop, or use unauthorized nuclear and other radioactive material in the United States. The Office also serves as steward of an enduring national technical nuclear forensics capability and leads efforts to improve national nuclear forensics expertise. Working with the international community, it promotes the development of nuclear detection architectures and nuclear forensics guidance. http://www.dhs.gov/domestic-nuclear-detection-office

Operations Coordination   The Office of Operations Coordination provides decision support and enables the Secretary's execution of responsibilities across the homeland security enterprise by promoting situational awareness and information sharing, integrating and synchronizing strategic operations, and administering the DHS continuity program. At the strategic level, the Office provides a joint operations coordination capability to support DHS operational decision making, departmental leadership, and participation in interagency operations throughout the homeland security enterprise and across all mission areas. http://www.dhs.gov/office-operations-coordination

Presidential Protection / Safeguarding Financial and Payment Systems   The U.S. Secret Service carries out a dual mission of protection and investigation. It protects the President, Vice President, and their families; major Presidential and Vice Presidential candidates; visiting heads of state and government; and National Special Security Events, as well as the White House and other designated buildings within the Washington, DC, area. The Secret Service also safeguards the Nation's financial infrastructure and payment systems to preserve the integrity of the economy. http://www.secretservice.gov

Science / Technology   The Science and Technology Directorate is the primary research and development arm of the agency. The Directorate provides Federal, State, and local officials with protective technology and capabilities. Its strategic objectives are developing and deploying systems to prevent, detect, and mitigate

the consequences of biological, chemical, explosive, nuclear, and radiological attacks; develop equipment, protocols, and training procedures for response and recovery; enhance the agency's and other Federal, State, local, and tribal government's technical capabilities to fulfill their homeland security-related functions; and develop technical standards and establish certified laboratories to evaluate homeland security and emergency responder technologies for SAFETY Act certification. http://www.dhs.gov/science-and-technology/our-work

Transportation Security   The Transportation Security Administration protects the Nation's transportation systems to ensure freedom of movement for people and commerce. https://www.tsa.gov

Sources of Information

A–Z Index   The DHS website has an alphabetical index of topics to help visitors navigate its content. https://www.dhs.gov/dhsgov-z-index

Archived Records   The general records of the Department of Homeland Security and the records of the U.S. Citizenship and Immigration Services, U.S. Immigration and Customs Enforcement, and U.S. Customs and Border Protection are referenced in the "Guide to Federal Records in the National Archives of the United States." The Guide is accessible online, and these records have been assigned respectively to Record Groups 563 and 566–568. None of these record groups has a description associated with it. https://www.archives.gov/research/guide-fed-records/index-numeric/501-to-600.html#page-header

Audits / Inspections / Evaluations   The Office of the Inspector General (OIG) posts reports on its website. Starting with the year 2003, the OIG's archives of audits, inspections, and evaluations cover the following areas of oversight: border security, counterterrorism, cybersecurity, disaster recovery, immigration, management, and transportation security. https://www.oig.dhs.gov/reports/audits-inspections-and-evaluations

Blog   The DHS maintains a blog on its website. https://www.dhs.gov/news-releases/blog?field_news_type_tid=588

Career Opportunities   The DHS is one of the largest agencies in the Federal Government. It offers career opportunities in the areas of immigration and travel security, law enforcement, mission support, and prevention and response. To carry out its mission, the agency relies on attorneys, contract specialists, engineers, intelligence analysts, K–9 officers, pilots, scientists, and many other types of experts and professionals. https://www.dhs.gov/homeland-security-careers

In 2019, the DHS ranked 17th among 17 large Government agencies in the Partnership for Public Service's Best Places To Work Agency Rankings. https://bestplacestowork.org/rankings/detail/HS00

Climate Preparedness and Resilience   FEMA's web page on climate change helps visitors learn more about the agency's resources and other Federal Government resources that support climate preparedness and resilience. https://www.fema.gov/climate-change

In "Best Practices & Key Considerations for Enhancing Federal Facility Security and Resilience to Climate-Related Hazards" (2015), the Interagency Security Committee identified threats posed by climate change to the assets, missions, operations, and workforce of the Federal Government. It also provided guidance and security planning considerations for agencies housed in nonmilitary Federal facilities. This document's main purpose is to identify short- and long-term strategies for enhancing physical security and resilience in the face climate-related threats. https://www.dhs.gov/publication/isc-climate-related-hazards-best-practices

Contact Information   Contact information for DHS headquarters, DHS components, and specific programs of interest is available on the "Direct Contact Information" web page. https://www.dhs.gov/direct-contact-information

The "Department White Pages" is a listing of key contacts that are organized by component. The listing includes email addresses and phone numbers. https://www.dhs.gov/department-white-pages

Current Issues   The "In Focus" web page brings together in one place key current issues that fall within the scope of the Department's mission. https://www.dhs.gov/focus

Data   The DHS and its components provide Internet access to statistical reports and datasets: Coast Guard maritime information, Customs and Border Protection intellectual property rights recordations, Federal Emergency Management Agency disaster declarations, immigration data, and more. https://www.dhs.gov/topic/data

Flood Insurance Rate Maps (FIRMs)   Flooding can occur anywhere in the United States; however, certain areas are prone to serious flooding. To help communities understand their risk, flood maps or FIRMs have been created to show the locations of high-risk, moderate-to-low risk, and undetermined-risk areas. Banks, citizens, insurance agents, and all levels of government rely on FIRMs to determine whether flood insurance is required. https://msc.fema.gov/portal

Freedom of Information Act (FOIA)   To any person, the FOIA gives a statutory right for obtaining access to Government information in the records of executive branch agencies. This right to access is limited, however, when the requested information is shielded from disclosure by any of nine exemptions contained within the statute. Instructions for submitting a FOIA request or filing a Privacy Act request and information on other FOIA-related matters are available on the DHS website. https://www.dhs.gov/how-submit-foia-request

The DHS maintains a FOIA library on its website. Information seekers should avail themselves of this online resource to determine if the desired record is immediately available and readily accessible without the additional effort of filing a FOIA request. https://www.dhs.gov/foia-library

Frequently Requested Pages   Links to the most requested pages on the DHS website are collected in place for convenience. https://www.dhs.gov/frequently-requested-pages

Green Card   A person may obtain authorization to live and work in the United States on a permanent basis in several ways: A family member or employer in the United States may sponsor the Green Card applicant; refugee or asylee status and other humanitarian programs offer additional pathways; and, in some cases, a person may be eligible to file on his or her own initiative for permanent residency. https://www.dhs. gov/how-do-i/get-green-card

How Do I?   The DHS website features a comprehensive section that arranges answers to "how do I" questions according to audience: DHS employees, businessmen and women, travelers, and the general public. Entrepreneurs can learn how to apply for grants, find forms for exporting and importing, and verify employment eligibility; travelers can learn how to check wait times at airports and border crossings; and members of the public can learn how to adopt a child internationally, become a citizen, check the status of an immigration case, prepare for a disaster, and report cyber incidents and suspicious activity. https:// www.dhs.gov/how-do-i

Keywords   The DHS website features a long list of keywords that are linked to pages containing information on the DHS, its components, and its mission. https://www. dhs.gov/keywords

Multilingual Resources   The Office of Civil Rights and Civil Liberties identifies documents containing information that is particularly important to diverse communities of limited English proficiency. These documents are often translated into Arabic, Chinese, French, Haitian-Creole, Portuguese, Russian, Somali, Spanish, and Vietnamese. https://www.dhs.gov/dhs-multilingual-resources

National Terrorism Advisories   Terrorism advisories that remain in effect and archived copies of ones that have expired are posted on the National Terrorism Advisory System web page. https://www.dhs.gov/national-terrorism-advisory-system

Naturalization   Congress has established the requirements that a foreign citizen or national must fulfill to receive U.S. citizenship. The process of being granted citizenship is known as naturalization. The U.S. Citizenship and Immigration Services' website offers resources for those seeking citizenship through naturalization. https:// www.uscis.gov/us-citizenship/citizenship-through-naturalization

News   The DHS posts audio items, congressional testimony, factsheets, photos and videos, press releases, and speeches on its website. It also posts news items on

national security in Spanish. https://www. dhs.gov/news

Open Government   The DHS supports the Open Government initiative by promoting the principles of collaboration, participation, and transparency. https://www.dhs.gov/open-government

Operational Components   The DHS comprises 10 operational components: the U.S. Department of Homeland Security, Cybersecurity and Infrastructure Security Agency (CISA), U.S. Customs and Border Protection (CBP), Federal Emergency Management Agency (FEMA), Federal Law Enforcement Training Center (FLETC), U.S. Immigration and Customs Enforcement (ICE), U.S. Secret Service (USSS), Transportation Security Administration (TSA), U.S. Coast Guard (USCG), and U.S. Citizenship and Immigration Services (USCIS). The DHS website offers easy access to each of their home pages. https://www.dhs.gov/dhs-component-websites

Policy Facts   The information on the regularly updated "Myth vs. Fact" web page responds to misleading characterizations of DHS policies in the public domain. https:// www.dhs.gov/myth-vs-fact?utm_source=hp_ carousel&utm_medium=web&utm_ campaign=dhsgov

Publications   The DHS publications library contains brochures, guidance and policy papers, guidelines, program regulations, reports, strategies, and more. https://www. dhs.gov/publications

Report Cyber Incidents   To protect the Nation's cybersecurity, the DHS has organizations dedicated to collecting information and reporting on cyber incidents, phishing, malware, and other vulnerabilities. https://www.dhs.gov/how-do-i/report-cyber-incidents

Site Links   The "Site Links" web page offers easy access to some of the most helpful resources on the DHS web site. https://www. dhs.gov/site-links

Site Map   The website map allows visitors to look for specific topics or to browse content that aligns with their interests. https://www.dhs.gov/sitemap

Social Media   The DHS maintains accounts on Facebook, Flickr, Instagram, and Twitter. An online subscription form also is available to sign up for email updates. https://www. dhs.gov/social-media-directory

Topics   The "Topics" web page offers convenient access to content that has been arranged topically. https://www.dhs.gov/topics
Transportation Security   The "Transportation Security" web page provides information on transportation and travel: aviation security, cargo screening, domestic travel, electronic passports, visas, and more. https://www.dhs.gov/topic/transportation-security
Travel Alerts   The DHS website offers convenient access to alerts and wait times: airport security checkpoint wait times from the Transportation Security Administration, airport wait times from the U.S. Customs

and Border Protection, international travel warnings from the Department of State, and health alerts from the Centers for Disease Control and Prevention. https://www.dhs.gov/travel-alerts
White House Fence   The White House complex fence is in the process of being redesigned. The proposal for the new fence is accessible on the website of the U.S. Secret Service. See the Fine Arts Commission's 35-page presentation (JUN 2016) of the "White House Complex Fence—Phase 1." https://www.secretservice.gov/data/about/faqs/WH-Fence-updated-CFA-061616.pdf

The Sources of Information were updated 1–2020.

DEPARTMENT OF HOUSING AND URBAN DEVELOPMENT

451 Seventh Street SW., Washington, DC 20410
Phone, 202-708-1422. Internet, http://www.hud.gov

Secretary	MARCIA L. FUDGE
https://www.hud.gov/about/leadership/marcia_fudge	
Deputy Secretary	ADRIANNE TODMAN
https://www.hud.gov/about/leadership/Adrianne_Todman	
Offices Reporting to the Secretary	
Chief Officers	
Financial	(VACANCY)
Information	ELIZABETH NIBLOCK
Director	
Small and Disadvantaged Business Utilization	JEAN LIN PAO
General Counsel	(VACANCY)
https://www.hud.gov/about/leadership	
Inspector General	RAE OLIVER DAVIS
https://www.hudoig.gov/about-hud-oig/organization-staff/ inspector-general-immediate-office/rae-oliver-davis	
Offices Reporting to the Chief of Staff	
Chief of Staff	JENNIFER C. JONES
Assistant Secretaries	
Congressional and Intergovernmental Relations	(VACANCY)
Public Affairs	ADDIE WHISENANT
Director	
Faith-Based and Neighborhood Partnerships	DERRICK HARKINS
https://www.hud.gov/contact/principal_directory	
Offices Reporting to the Deputy Secretary	
Assistant Secretaties	
Administration	(VACANCY)
Community Planning and Development	(VACANCY)
Fair Housing and Equal Opportunity	JEANINE WORDEN, ACTING
Field Policy and Management	(VACANCY)
Housing	JANET GOLRICK, ACTING
Policy Development and Research	(VACANCY)
Public and Indian Housing	(VACANCY)
Chief Officers	
Administrative	(VACANCY)
Human Capital	MONICA MATTHEWS
Procurement	RONALD C. FLOM

Commissioner		Janet Golrick, Acting
Federal Housing		(vacancy)

Directors
Equal Employment Opportunity — Tami Wright, Acting
Lead Hazard Control and Healthy Homes — Michelle Miller, Acting
https://www.hud.gov/program_offices
Government National Mortgage Association—Ginnie Mae

President — (vacancy)
https://www.ginniemae.gov/about_us/who_we_are/pages/
  executive_leadership.aspx

The above list of key personnel was updated 8–2021.

The Department of Housing and Urban Development oversees housing needs nationwide, ensures fair housing opportunities, and creates strong, sustainable, and inclusive communities.

Establishment and Organization
On September 9, 1965, President Lyndon B. Johnson approved Public Law 89–174, which is also cited as the Department of Housing and Urban Development Act. As part of the statute's declaration of purpose, Congress declared that "the general welfare and security of the Nation and the health and living standards of our people require . . . sound development of the Nation's communities and metropolitan areas in which the vast majority of its people live and work." To support this requirement of sound development, Congress established "an executive department to be known as the Department of Housing and Urban Development [HUD]" (79 Stat. 667). https://www.govinfo.gov/content/pkg/STATUTE-79/pdf/STATUTE-79-Pg667.pdf

Statutory material that governed HUD's establishment and that continues to affect the appointment and supervision of the Secretary of HUD and his or her general duties is codified and assigned to section 3532 of 42 U.S.C. https://uscode.house.gov/view.xhtml?req=granuleid:USC-prelim-title42-section3532&num=0&edition=prelim

Rules and regulations that affect the Office of the Secretary have been codified and assigned to Subtitle A (parts 0–99) of 24 CFR. https://www.ecfr.gov/cgi-bin/text-idx?SID=5bb98a110aae0aa5ef135b4529083902&mc=true&tpl=/ecfrbrowse/Title24/24subtitleA.tpl

By the advice and with the consent of the Senate, the President appoints the Secretary of HUD. The Secretary supervises and directs the administration of the Department (79 Stat. 667). https://www.hud.gov/about/hud_secretary/powersec

HUD's department structure is presented like an organizational chart in its "Fiscal Year 2020 Annual Performance Report" on page 9. The Report was published in January of 2021. https://www.hud.gov/sites/dfiles/CFO/documents/HUD_FY20_Annual_Performance_Report_1-15-21.pdf

HUD's program offices are listed alphabetically and hyperlinked on the "Program Offices" web page. https://www.hud.gov/program_offices

Statutory and Regulatory Authorities
"The Public Health and Welfare" is the general topic of statutory material that has been codified and assigned to 42 U.S.C. Chapter 44 (sections 3531–3550) is dedicated to the "Department of Housing and Urban Development." https://uscode.house.gov/view.xhtml?path=/prelim@title42/chapter44&edition=prelim

Rules and regulations that affect housing and urban development have been codified and assigned to 24 CFR. https://www.ecfr.gov/cgi-bin/text-idx?SID=5bb98a110aae0aa5ef135b4529083902&mc=true&tpl=/ecfrbrowse/Title24/24tab_02.tpl

Program Areas
HUD administers various programs to facilitate its six core functions: insuring mortgages for single-family and multifamily dwellings and extending loans for home

improvement and for the purchasing of mobile homes; channeling funds from investors to the mortgage industry through the Government National Mortgage Association–Ginnie Mae; making direct loans for construction or rehabilitation of housing projects that benefit the elderly and handicapped; providing Federal housing subsidies for low- and moderate-income families; giving community development grants to States and communities; and promoting and enforcing fair housing and equal housing opportunity. https://www.hud.gov/topics

Community Planning and Development   The Office of Community and Planning Development administers grant programs to help communities plan and finance growth and development, to increase their governing capacity, and to shelter and provide services for the homeless. The Office is responsible for implementing Community Development Block Grant (CDBG) programs for entitlement communities; the State- and HUD-administered Small Cities Program; community development loan guarantees; special purpose grants for insular areas and historically black colleges and universities; Appalachian Regional Commission grants; the Home Investment in Affordable Housing Program, which provides Federal assistance for housing rehabilitation, tenant-based assistance, first-time homebuyers, and new construction when a jurisdiction is determined to need new rental housing; the Department's programs to address homelessness; the John Heinz Neighborhood Development Program; community outreach partnerships; the joint community development plan that assists institutions of higher education working in concert with State and local governments to undertake activities under the CDBG program; community adjustment and economic diversification planning grants; empowerment zones and enterprise communities; efforts to improve the environment; and community planning and development efforts of other departments and agencies, public and private organizations, private industry, financial markets, and international organizations. http://portal.hud.gov/hudportal/HUD?src=/program_offices/comm_planning

For further information, contact the Office of Community Planning and Development. Phone, 202-708-2690.

Fair Housing / Equal Opportunity   The Office of Fair Housing and Equal Opportunity administers fair housing laws and regulations prohibiting discrimination in public and private housing; equal opportunity laws and regulations prohibiting discrimination in HUD-assisted housing and community development programs; the fair housing assistance grants program to provide financial and technical assistance to State and local government agencies to implement local fair housing laws and ordinances; and the Community Housing Resources Boards program to provide grants for fair housing activities, including outreach and education, identification of institutional barriers to fair housing, and telephone hotlines for complaints. http://portal.hud.gov/hudportal/HUD?src=/program_offices/fair_housing_equal_opp

For further information, contact the Office of Fair Housing and Equal Opportunity. Phone, 202-708-4252.

Government National Mortgage Association–Ginnie Mae   Ginnie Mae is a Government corporation that makes housing affordable for millions of low- and moderate-income earners by channeling capital into the Nation's housing markets. The Ginnie Mae guaranty allows mortgage lenders to obtain a higher price when selling their mortgage loans in the secondary mortgage market. Lenders can then use the proceeds of these sales to fund new mortgage loans. Without that liquidity, lenders would have to keep all loans in their own portfolios and would not have adequate capital for making new loans. Ginnie Mae guarantees investors the timely payment of principal and interest on mortgage-backed securities that are backed by federally insured or federally guaranteed loans—loans insured by the Federal Housing Administration or guaranteed by the Department of Veterans Affairs. Other guarantors, or issuers, of loans that are eligible as collateral for Ginnie Mae mortgage-backed securities include HUD's Office of Public and Indian Housing and the Department of Agriculture's Rural Development. Ginnie Mae securities are the only mortgage-backed securities to carry the full faith and credit guaranty of the U.S.

Government. http://www.ginniemae.gov/pages/default.aspx

For further information, contact the Government National Mortgage Association. Phone, 202-708-0926.

Housing The Office of Housing oversees aid for construction and financing of new and rehabilitated housing and for preservation of existing housing. The Office underwrites single-family, multifamily, property improvement, and manufactured home loans; administers special purpose programs designed for the elderly, handicapped, and chronically mentally ill; administers housing assistance programs for low-income families having difficulties affording standard housing; administers grants to fund resident ownership of multifamily house properties; and protects consumers against fraudulent land development and promotional practices. http://portal.hud.gov/hudportal/HUD?src=/program_offices/housing

For further information, contact the Office of Housing. Phone, 202-708-3600.

Lead Hazard Control / Healthy Homes The Office of Lead Hazard Control and Healthy Homes is responsible for lead hazard control policy development, abatement, training, regulations, and research. Activities of the Office include increasing public and building-industry awareness of the dangers of lead-based paint poisoning and the options for detection, risk reduction, and abatement; encouraging the development of safer, more effective, and less costly methods for detection, risk reduction, and abatement; and encouraging State and local governments to develop lead-based paint programs covering contractor certification, hazard reduction, financing, enforcement, and primary prevention, including public education. http://portal.hud.gov/hudportal/HUD?src=/program_offices/healthy_homes

For further information, contact the Office of Lead Hazard Control and Healthy Homes. Phone, 202-755-1785.

Public and Indian Housing The Office of Public and Indian Housing administers public and Indian housing programs; assists technically and financially with planning, developing, and managing low-income projects; subsidizes the operations of public housing agencies (PHAs) and Indian housing authorities (IHAs) and provides procedures for reviewing the management of public housing agencies; administers the comprehensive improvement assistance and comprehensive grant programs for modernizing low-income housing projects; administers programs for resident participation, resident management, home ownership, economic development and supportive services, and drug-free neighborhood programs; protects low-income tenants from lead-based paint poisoning by requiring PHAs and IHAs to comply with HUD regulations for the testing and removal of lead-based paint; implements and monitors program requirements related to program eligibility and admission of families to public and assisted housing, as well as tenant income and rent requirements for continued occupancy; administers the HOPE VI and vacancy reduction programs; administers voucher and certificate programs and the Moderate Rehabilitation Program; coordinates all departmental housing and community development programs for Indian and Alaskan Natives; and awards grants to PHAs and IHAs for the construction, acquisition, and operation of public and Indian housing projects. http://portal.hud.gov/hudportal/HUD?src=/program_offices/public_indian_housing/ih

For further information, contact the Office of Public and Indian Housing. Phone, 202-708-0950.

Sources of Information

A–Z Index An alphabetical index is available on the HUD website to help visitors search for specific topics or browse content that aligns with their interests. https://www.hud.gov/siteindex/quicklinks

Archived Records HUD records are referenced in the "Guide to Federal Records in the National Archives of the United States." The Guide is accessible online, and HUD records have been assigned to Record Group 207. https://www.archives.gov/research/guide-fed-records/groups/207.html

Bibliographic Database The HUD USER bibliographic database contains more than 10,000 full-abstract citations to research reports, articles, books, monographs, and data sources in housing policy, building technology, economic development, urban planning, and a host of other relevant fields. https://www.huduser.gov/portal/bibliodb/pdrbibdb.html

Business Opportunities   To learn about contracting opportunities, programs, and resources, use the link below. The Office of the Chief Procurement Officer can provide additional information. Phone, 202-708-1290. TDD, 202-708-1455. https://www.hud.gov/program_offices/cpo

Career Opportunities   Information on career opportunities—including opportunities for veterans, students, and people with disabilities—is available online. Information is also available from the Personnel Division at the nearest regional office and from the Office of Human Resources in Washington, DC. Phone, 202-708-0408. https://www.hud.gov/program_offices/administration/careers

In 2020, HUD ranked 14th among 25 midsize Government agencies in the Partnership for Public Service's Best Places To Work Agency Rankings. https://bestplacestowork.org/rankings/detail/?c=HU00

Climate Change Resilience   The Office of Economic Development oversees HUD's preparations to mitigate the effects of climate change on it's mission, operations, and programs. This includes promoting greater capacity in and more utilization of resilient approaches to community development at the local, regional, and State levels. https://www.hud.gov/program_offices/economic_development/resilience/about | Email: EconomicDevelopment@hud.gov

Contact Information   Contact information is available on the "Contact Us" web page. https://www.hud.gov/contact

Data / Research   The Office of Policy Development and Research posts datasets, publications, research, and information on initiatives on its "HUD User" website. https://www.huduser.gov/portal/home.html

Employee Locater   To locate a HUD employee or to send a HUD employee an email, visit the "Search for HUD Employees" web page. An automated phone locator service is also available. Phone, 202-708-1112. TDD, 202-708-1455. http://peoplesearch.hud.gov/po/i/netlocator

En Español   HUD posts information in Spanish on its website. https://www.hud.gov/espanol

Federal Register   Significant documents and documents that HUD recently published in the Federal Register are accessible online. https://www.federalregister.gov/agencies/housing-and-urban-development-department

Several phone numbers are available on the "Información en Español" web page. https://www.hud.gov/directory/800/parainformacion

Field Offices   Visit HUD's online local office directory to find contact information for its field offices. https://www.hud.gov/program_offices/field_policy_mgt/localoffices

Freedom of Information Act (FOIA)   To any person, the FOIA gives a statutory right for obtaining access to Government information in the records of executive branch agencies. This right to access is limited, however, when the requested information is shielded from disclosure by any of nine exemptions contained within the statute. https://www.hud.gov/program_offices/administration/foia

Many HUD documents are available online. Before submitting a written request, click on the "Frequently Requested Materials" and "E–FOIA Reading Room" links on HUD's FOIA web page to see if the desired information is immediately accessible, free of charge. Phone, 202-708-3054. https://www.hud.gov/program_offices/administration/foia/frequentrequestedmaterials

Frequently Asked Questions (FAQs)   Answers to FAQs are posted online. https://www.hud.gov/faqs

Glossary   The Government National Mortgage Association (Ginnie Mae) maintains a glossary on its website. https://www.ginniemae.gov/Pages/Glossary.aspx

HUD maintains a list of frequently used terms and acronyms on its website. https://www.hud.gov/about/acronyms

History   In the aftermath of assassination that outraged communities of color and sparked protest and violence in American cities, President Lyndon B. Johnson approved Title VIII of the Civil Rights Act of 1968, commonly referred to as the Fair Housing Act. Signing "into law the promises of a century" was his description of that moment. The promises of this legislation included outlawing most housing discrimination and giving enforcement responsibility to HUD. To learn more about HUD's history of overseeing and coordinating Federal housing programs and enforcing fair housing practices, visit the "HUD History" web page. https://www.hud.gov/about/hud_history

Hotline The Office of the Inspector General maintains the Hotline to report fraud, mismanagement, and waste. Phone, 202-708-4200 or 800-347-3735. TDD, 202-708-2451. http://www.hudoig.gov/hotline | Email: hotline@hudoig.gov

Housing Choice Voucher (HCV) The HCV program is the Federal Government's main program to help low-income families, the elderly, and the disabled find and afford decent, safe, and sanitary housing in the private market. https://www.hud.gov/program_offices/public_indian_housing/programs/hcv/about/fact_sheet

Human Stories "The Humans of HUD" web page allows visitors to meet the men and women whom HUD serves. The page contains brief narratives and short videos. https://www.hud.gov/humansofhud

Library The library is located at HUD headquarters in Washington, DC. Visitors must schedule an appointment to use the library. It is open weekdays, except Federal holidays, from 9:30 a.m. to 5 p.m. Phone, 202-402-2680.

Organizational Directory An organization directory of HUD's headquarters is available online. https://www.hud.gov/directory/director

Press Room HUD posts press releases, remarks, speeches, statements, and testimonies on its website. https://www.hud.gov/press

Program Offices The "Program Offices" web page provides links for easy access to program information. https://www.hud.gov/program_offices

Property Disposition For single-family properties, contact the Chief Property Officer at the nearest HUD regional office or the Property Disposition Division. Phone,

202-708-0614. For multifamily properties, contact the Regional Housing Director at the nearest HUD regional office or the Property Disposition Division. Phone, 202-708-0614. https://www.hud.gov/topics/homes_for_sale

Regional Organization Map HUD is organized in 10 regions, each of which a regional administrator manages. A field office director manages each field office within a region. Field office directors report to the appropriate regional administrator. https://www.hud.gov/localoffices/regions

Publications Information on bibliographies, forms, grant applications, handbooks, technical guidance for programs, and other publications, is posted online. These publications are described on the "HUD Handbooks, Forms, and Publications" web page. https://www.hud.gov/program_offices/administration/handbks_forms

Resources The "Resources" web page has a list of helpful links in alphabetical order. https://www.hud.gov/resources

Site Map The website map allows visitors to look for specific topics or to browse content that aligns with their interests. https://www.hud.gov/siteindex

Social Media HUD's social media directory provides links to all of its official blogs and social media platforms on Facebook, Flickr, Instagram, Twitter, and YouTube. https://www.hud.gov/program_offices/public_affairs/socialmedia

State Information The "State Information" web page allows visitors to access online informational resources that States provide. People who are searching for resources that address homelessness and other related topics should explore how State-level organizations and government agencies may be able to help. https://www.hud.gov/states

Veteran Homelessness The "Veteran Homelessness" page lists HUD homeless programs and initiatives that are available to veterans and veteran service providers. The web page also has policy guidance, publications, resources, and relevant links to other agencies and organizations. https://www.hudexchange.info/homelessness-assistance/resources-for-homeless-veterans

The above Sources of Information were updated 8–2021.

DEPARTMENT OF JUSTICE

950 Pennsylvania Avenue NW., Washington, DC 20530
Phone, 202-514-2000. Internet, http://www.justice.gov

Attorney General	Merrick B. Garland
Deputy Attorney General	Lisa O. Monaco
https://www.justice.gov/ag/staff-profile/meet-attorney-general	
Associate Attorney General	Vanita Gupta
Solicitor General	Brian H. Fletcher, Acting
Assistant Attorneys General for Divisions	
Antitrust	Richard A. Powers, Acting
Civil	Brian Boynton, Acting
Civil Rights	Kristen Clarke
Criminal	Kenneth A. Polite, Jr.
Environment and Natural Resources	Todd S. Kim
Justice Management—Administration	Lee J. Lofthus
National Security	(vacancy)
Tax	David A. Hubbert, Acting
https://www.justice.gov/agencies/chart	
Assistant Attorneys General for Offices	
Legal Counsel	Dawn E. Johnsen, Acting
Legal Policy	Kevin Jones, Acting
Legislative Affairs	(vacancy)
Directors of Components	
Community Relations Service	Gerri L. Ratliff, Acting
Organized Crime Drug Enforcement Task Forces	Adam W. Cohen
Directors of Executive Offices	
U.S. Attorneys	Monty Wilkinson
U.S. Trustee Program	Clifford J. White III
Directors of Offices	
Information Policy	Bobak Talebian
Pardon Attorney	Rosalind Sargent-Burns, Acting
Professional Responsibility	Jeffrey R. Ragsdale
Professional Responsibility Advisory	Stacy Ludwig
Public Affairs	Anthony Coley
Tribal Justice	Tracy Toulou
https://www.justice.gov/agencies/alphabetical-listing-components-programs-initiatives	
Inspector General	Michael E. Horowitz
https://oig.justice.gov/about/meet-ig.htm	

The above list of key personnel was updated 8–2021.

Department of Justice

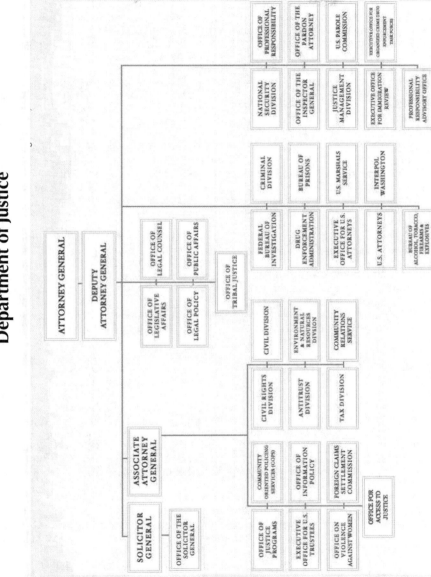

ATTORNEY GENERAL

DEPUTY ATTORNEY GENERAL

SOLICITOR GENERAL

OFFICE OF THE SOLICITOR GENERAL

ASSOCIATE ATTORNEY GENERAL

OFFICE OF LEGISLATIVE AFFAIRS

OFFICE OF LEGAL POLICY

OFFICE OF LEGAL COUNSEL

OFFICE OF PUBLIC AFFAIRS

OFFICE OF TRIBAL JUSTICE

OFFICE OF JUSTICE PROGRAMS

EXECUTIVE OFFICE FOR U.S. TRUSTEES

OFFICE ON VIOLENCE AGAINST WOMEN

OFFICE FOR ACCESS TO JUSTICE

COMMUNITY ORIENTED POLICING SERVICES (COPS)

OFFICE OF INFORMATION POLICY

FOREIGN CLAIMS SETTLEMENT COMMISSION

CIVIL RIGHTS DIVISION

ANTITRUST DIVISION

TAX DIVISION

CIVIL DIVISION

ENVIRONMENT & NATURAL RESOURCES DIVISION

COMMUNITY RELATIONS SERVICE

FEDERAL BUREAU OF INVESTIGATION

DRUG ENFORCEMENT ADMINISTRATION

EXECUTIVE OFFICE FOR U.S. ATTORNEYS

U.S. ATTORNEYS

BUREAU OF ALCOHOL, TOBACCO, FIREARMS & EXPLOSIVES

CRIMINAL DIVISION

BUREAU OF PRISONS

U.S. MARSHALS SERVICE

INTERPOL WASHINGTON

NATIONAL SECURITY DIVISION

OFFICE OF THE INSPECTOR GENERAL

JUSTICE MANAGEMENT DIVISION

EXECUTIVE OFFICE FOR IMMIGRATION REVIEW

PROFESSIONAL RESPONSIBILITY ADVISORY OFFICE

OFFICE OF PROFESSIONAL RESPONSIBILITY

OFFICE OF THE PARDON ATTORNEY

U.S. PAROLE COMMISSION

EXECUTIVE OFFICE FOR ORGANIZED CRIME DRUG ENFORCEMENT TASK FORCES

The Department of Justice enforces the law and defends national interests according to the law; ensures public safety against domestic and foreign threats; provides Federal leadership in preventing and controlling crime; seeks just punishment for those who have behaved unlawfully; and ensures fair and impartial administration of justice for all American citizens.

Establishment and Organization

On September 23, 1789, when the U.S. Congress was assembled in the City of New York, President George Washington approved "an Act for allowing certain Compensation . . . to the Attorney General of the United States." This statute, which is often called the Judiciary Act of 1789, established the Office of the Attorney General. http://www.loc.gov/law/help/statutes-at-large/1st-congress/session-1/c1s1ch18.pdf

The increased amount of litigation involving the United States after the Civil War necessitated the retention of private attorneys, until the U.S. Congress established the Department of Justice to handle the legal business of the Nation. https://www.justice.gov/history/timeline/150-years-department-justice#event-1195101

On June 22, 1870, President Ulysses S. Grant approved "an Act to establish the Department of Justice" (16 Stat. 162). The statute established the Department of Justice (DOJ) as "an executive department of the government of the United States . . . of which the Attorney-General shall be the head." The statute also established, within the DOJ, the office of Solicitor General: "an officer learned in the law, to assist the Attorney-General in the performance of his duties." The Solicitor General represents the interests of the United States before the Nation's Supreme Court. The statute became effective on July 1, 1870, and gave the DOJ control over all Federal law enforcement and all criminal prosecutions and civil suits in which the United States has an interest. http://www.loc.gov/law/help/statutes-at-large/41st-congress/session-2/c41s2ch150.pdf

Under the leadership of the Attorney General, the DOJ comprises approximately 40 separate component organizations with approximately 116,000 employees. The DOJ's headquarters are in Washington, DC, and the Department conducts most of its work through field locations nationwide and others that are overseas.

The DOJ posts its organizational chart online. https://www.justice.gov/agencies/chart

The DOJ posts its "Organization, Mission, and Functions Manual" online. https://www.justice.gov/jmd/organization-mission-and-functions-manual

Statutory and Regulatory Authorities

Statutory material whose subject matter affects the DOJ is codified in "Part II—Department of Justice" (parts 501–599B) in 28 U.S.C. https://uscode.house.gov/view.xhtml?path=/prelim@title28/part2&edition=prelim

Rules and regulations dealing with judicial administration are codified in 28 CFR. Chapter I (parts 0.1–200.1)) of that same CFR title contains subject matter associated with the DOJ. https://www.ecfr.gov/cgi-bin/text-idx?gp=&SID=4bc7cb17c5a411037d7efbd9fe3a2c32&mc=true&tpl=/ecfrbrowse/Title28/28chapterI.tpl

Activities

Administration of Bankruptcy Cases   The DOJ oversees the administration of bankruptcy cases and private trustees through its U.S. Trustee Program. This national program has broad administrative, regulatory, and litigation and enforcement authorities to promote the integrity and efficiency of the bankruptcy system for the benefit of creditors, debtors, and the public. https://www.justice.gov/ust

Coordination of Enforcement With Intelligence   The DOJ participates in the fight against terrorism and against other national security threats. The National Security Division (NSD) ensures that prosecutors and law enforcement agencies coordinate with intelligence attorneys and the intelligence community and that they share a unity of purpose to strengthen the effectiveness of the Federal Government's threat response. The NSD's major areas of responsibility include counterespionage, counterterrorism, foreign investment, intelligence operations and intelligence-related litigation, policy and other legal issues, oversight and reporting, and victims of terrorism. https://www.justice.gov/jmd/organization-mission-and-functions-manual-national-security-division

Criminal Investigation   The DOJ participates in the fight against crime. Its major investigative agencies—the Bureau of Alcohol, Tobacco, Firearms and Explosives; the Drug Enforcement Administration; and the Federal Bureau of Investigation—prevent and deter crime and arrest people who are suspect of criminal activity. https://www.justice.gov/agencies/alphabetical-listing-components-programs-initiatives

Incarceration / Rehabilitation   The Federal Bureau of Prisons supports public safety by confining Federal lawbreakers in the controlled environments of prisons and community-based facilities. Prisons and community-based facilities are appropriately secure, cost-efficient, humane, and safe. Work and other self-improvement opportunities are available to help offenders become law-abiding citizens. https://www.bop.gov

Litigation   The DOJ litigating divisions enforce Federal criminal and civil laws, including antitrust, civil justice, civil rights, environmental, and tax statutes. https://www.justice.gov/agencies/alphabetical-listing-components-programs-initiatives

Prosecution / Representation   U.S. Attorneys serve as the Nation's principal litigators, prosecuting offenders and representing the Federal Government in court. They conduct most of the trial work for cases in which the United States is a party. U.S. Attorneys have three statutory responsibilities: prosecution of criminal cases brought by the Federal Government; prosecution and defense of civil cases in which the United States is a party; and the collection of debts that are owed the Federal Government and that are administratively uncollectible. https://www.justice.gov/usao/mission

Protecting the Federal Judiciary   The U.S. Marshals Service occupies a central position in the Federal justice system. It serves as the enforcement arm of the Federal courts and is involved in virtually every Federal law enforcement initiative. Deputy U.S. marshals and criminal investigators form the backbone of the agency. They protect the Federal judiciary, apprehend Federal fugitives, seize property acquired by criminals through illegal activities, house and transport Federal prisoners, and operate the witness security program. https://www.justice.gov/jmd/organization-mission-and-functions-manual-united-states-marshals-service

Recommendations for Executive Clemency   The Office of the Pardon Attorney receives and reviews all petitions requesting executive clemency for Federal offenses, conducts the necessary investigations, and prepares recommendations to the President for the review and signature of the Deputy Attorney General. It provides policy guidance for the conduct of clemency proceedings and the standards for decision. It respond to inquiries from clemency applicants, their representatives, public groups, Members of Congress, various Federal, State, and local officials, and others concerning clemency petitions and the clemency process. It also maintains contacts with DOJ officials, the Counsel to the President, and other Government officials to advise them on clemency matters as requested. https://www.justice.gov/jmd/organization-mission-and-functions-manual-office-pardon-attorney

State, Tribal, and Local Assistance   The DOJ gives assistance to State, tribal, and local governments. The Office of Justice Programs (OJP) provides Federal leadership in developing the Nation's capacity to prevent and control crime, administer justice, and assist crime victims. The OJP partners with Federal, State, local, and tribal agencies, as well as with national, community-based, and nonprofit organizations, to develop, implement, and evaluate criminal and juvenile justice programs. The Office of Community Oriented Policing Services develops programs that respond to the emerging needs of State, local, and tribal law enforcement and helps shift its focus onto preventing, rather than reacting to, crime and disorder; develops training and technical assistance to enhance law enforcement officers' problem-solving and community interaction skills; promotes collaboration between law enforcement and community members for developing crime prevention initiatives; and provides responsive and cost-effective service delivery to grant recipients. The Community Relations Service provides services for conflicts and tensions arising from differences of race, color, or national origin. It is the only Federal service mandated to help State and local government agencies, public and private organizations, and community groups resolve and prevent community racial conflicts through mediation, conciliation, and other methods of conflict resolution. https://www.justice.gov/jmd/organization-mission-and-functions-manual

Sources of Information

Americans with Disabilities   The Civil Rights Division operates an Americans with Disabilities Act (ADA) information line. Phone, 800-514-0301. TDD, 800-514-0383. The ADA.gov website has a "Topics of Interest" web page. https://www.ada.gov/topics_of_interest.htm

Archived Records   The "Guide to Federal Records in the National Archives of the United States" indicates that DOJ records have been assigned to record group 060. https://www.archives.gov/research/guide-fed-records/groups/060.html

Asset Sales   As part of the asset forfeiture program, the U.S. Marshals Service maintains a web page that is dedicated to assets that are currently available for purchase. https://www.usmarshals.gov/assets/sales.htm

Blogs   DOJ staff members post their blogs online. https://www.justice.gov/blogs

Budget / Performance / Strategy   Budget factsheets, budget submissions, budget summaries, financial reports, performance plans, performance reports, performance summaries, and strategic plans are posted on the "Budget and Performance" web page. https://www.justice.gov/doj/budget-and-performance

Business Opportunities   For information on business opportunities, grants, and small and disadvantaged business utilization, visit the "Business" web page. https://www.justice.gov/business

Career Opportunities   The DOJ relies on people with various educational and professional backgrounds and who have diverse skills and talents to carry out its mission. Career opportunities that the DOJ offers include accountant, attorney, auditor, budget analyst, contract specialist, correctional officer, criminal investigator, financial manager, forensic scientist, human resource specialist, information technology technician, intelligence researcher, legal assistant, paralegal specialist, safety and occupational health specialist, and more. http://www.justice.gov/careers

The "Legal Careers" web page contains information for law students and entry-level and experienced attorneys. http://www.justice.gov/legal-careers

In 2020, the DOJ ranked 13th among 17 large Government agencies in the Partnership for Public Service's Best Places To Work Agency Rankings. https://bestplacestowork.org/rankings/detail/?c=DJ00

Components / Programs / Initiatives   The DOJ has a list of components, programs, and initiatives on its "Alphabetical Listing of Components, Programs, and Initiatives" web page. Each entry is hyperlinked and provides convenient access to the website of the respective component, program, or initiative. https://www.justice.gov/agencies/alphabetical-listing-components-programs-initiatives

Contact Information   An electronic "Contact Us Form" is available on the DOJ's "Contact Us" web page. General contact information also is available on the same page. https://www.justice.gov/contact-us

Office of Public Affairs contact information is posted for media inquiries. https://www.justice.gov/opa/contact-office

Crime Data   The Bureau of Justice Statistics collects, analyzes, publishes, and disseminates information on crime, criminal offenders, victims of crime, and the operation of justice systems at all levels of government. These data are critical to the efforts of Federal, State, and local policymakers to prevent crime and to ensure that justice is administered efficiently and evenhandedly. https://bjs.ojp.gov

En Español   The DOJ posts information in Spanish on its "Justice.gov En Español" web pages. https://www.justice.gov/espanol

Federal Register Significant documents and documents that the DOJ recently published in the Federal Register are accessible online. https://www.federalregister.gov/agencies/justice-department

Forms The DOJ posts an electronic forms list that can be sorted by form title or by agency. This list does not include forms for the Federal Bureau of Prisons or for the Bureau of Alcohol, Tobacco, Firearms and Explosives. Those forms are available on the Bureaus' websites. https://www.justice.gov/forms

Freedom of Information Act (FOIA) The FOIA gives the right to request access to records from a Federal agency. Any person may submit a request for access to Government records (i.e., a FOIA request). Federal agencies are required to disclose information requested under the FOIA, unless that information is shielded from disclosure because it falls under one of nine exemptions protecting interests such as personal privacy, national security, or law enforcement. The DOJ manages the website FOIA.gov, which serves as the Federal Government's central website for FOIA-related matters. https://www.foia.gov

The DOJ maintains an electronic FOIA Library. The library contains DOJ documents, including documents that belong to components of the DOJ. The DOJ proactively discloses documents, and these documents are accessible without submitting a FOIA request. Before making a formal FOIA request, an information seeker should search the FOIA library to rule out the possibility that the DOJ or one of its components already has disclosed the desired information proactively. https://www.justice.gov/oip/foia-library

Glossary The Offices of the U.S. Attorneys web page has a legal terms glossary that defines over 100 of the most common legal terms in simple language. https://www.justice.gov/usao/justice-101/glossary

History Historical information on the Attorneys General of the United States, the Department's motto and seal, and the art and architecture of the Robert F. Kennedy Department of Justice Building is available online. https://www.justice.gov/about/history

Housing Discrimination To report an incident of housing discrimination, contact the Civil Rights Division's housing and civil enforcement section. Phone, 800-896-7743. http://www.justice.gov/crt/housing-and-civil-enforcement-section | Email: fairhousing@usdoj.gov

Immigrant and Employee Rights The Civil Rights Division operates a worker hotline. Phone, 800-255-7688. TDD, 800-237-2515. It also has a hotline for employers. Phone, 800-255-8155. TTY, 800-237-2515. The hotlines allow workers and employers to work directly with Immigrant and Employee Rights staff to resolve potential immigration-related employment disputes, informally and quickly, without contested litigation. Language interpretation services are available upon request. http://www.justice.gov/crt/hotline-technical-assistance-referral-agencies

Initiatives / Programs / Subject Matter Areas Initiatives and programs in which the DOJ participates and subject matter areas that it handles are listed on the "Topics" web page. https://www.justice.gov/topics

Judicial Encroachment Former Attorney General Jefferson B. Sessions delivered remarks to the Heritage Foundation in October of 2018 on judicial encroachment. In those remarks, he said: "Federal district court judges are not empowered to fashion immigration policy, combat climate change, solve the opioid crisis, or run police departments. The Legislative and Executive branches . . . are the constitutionally authorized branches to do these things, and if these branches haven't done so to the satisfaction of an unaccountable judge, it's not because they need judicial expertise or advice." https://www.justice.gov/opa/speech/attorney-general-jeff-sessions-delivers-remarks-heritage-foundation-judicial-encroachment

Justice Manual The current and official version of the "Justice Manual" is available online. The manual was previously known as the "United States Attorneys' Manual." In 2018, it was comprehensively revised and renamed. The "Justice Manual" serves as an internal guide within the DOJ. https://www.justice.gov/jm/justice-manual

News The DOJ posts press releases on its website. https://www.justice.gov/news

Open Government The Department supports the Open Government initiative by promoting the principles of collaboration, participation, and transparency. https://www.justice.gov/open

Pardons / Commutations   The Office of the Pardon Attorney maintains a list of Presidential pardons and commutations on its "Clemency Recipients" web page. The list starts with pardons and commutations that President Richard M. Nixon granted and ends with those that were granted by the former or current President. https://www.justice.gov/pardon/clemencyrecipients

Publications   DOJ reports and publications are accessible and arranged alphabetically online. https://www.justice.gov/publications/usdoj-resources-publications-alphabetical-list

The Office of the Attorney General maintains a web page of "Selected Publications." https://www.justice.gov/ag/selected-publications

The Sources of Information were updated 8–2021.

Reading Rooms   Reading rooms are located in Washington, DC, at the Department of Justice, Tenth Street and Constitution Avenue NW., and at the National Institute of Justice, 633 Indiana Avenue NW., and in Falls Church, VA, at the Board of Immigration Appeals, 5107 Leesburg Pike. Phone, 202-514-3775.

Social Media   The DOJ and its component agencies rely on social media for providing information in additional places and in more ways. The DOJ uses various social media accounts to share news, to make information and services more widely available, and to increase Government transparency. https://www.justice.gov/social

---

BUREAUS
Bureau of Alcohol, Tobacco, Firearms and Explosives
99 New York Avenue NE., Washington, DC 20226
Phone, 202-648-8500. Internet, http://www.atf.gov

Director	Marvin G. Richardson, Acting
Deputy Director	Marvin G. Richardson
https://www.atf.gov/about-atf/executive-staff	

The above list of key personnel was updated 8–2021.

The Bureau of Alcohol, Tobacco, Firearms and Explosives protects the public from crimes involving arson, explosives, firearms, and the diversion of alcohol and tobacco products; regulates lawful commerce in explosives and firearms; and supports law enforcement, public safety, and industry partners worldwide.

Establishment and Organization
On June 6, 1972, Acting Secretary of the Treasury Charles E. Walker signed an order affecting the Department's organization and procedure. Order No. 221 transferred "the functions, powers and duties of the Internal Revenue Service arising under laws relating to alcohol, tobacco, firearms, and explosives (including the Alcohol, Tobacco and Firearms Division of the Internal Revenue Service), to the Bureau of Alcohol, Tobacco and Firearms . . . which is hereby established." On June 10, 1972, Treasury Department Order 221 was published as a notice in the Federal Register (37 FR 11696). https://www.govinfo.gov/content/pkg/FR-1972-06-10/pdf/FR-1972-06-10.pdf

On November 25, 2002, President George W. Bush approved Public Law 107–296, which also may be cited as the Homeland Security Act of 2002, "to establish the Department of Homeland Security, and for other purposes" (116 Stat. 2135). One of the other purposes was to separate the functions of the Bureau of Alcohol, Tobacco and Firearms (ATF). The alcohol and tobacco excise tax functions and regulations remained within the Department of the Treasury, and a new bureau became responsible for them. The Act also transferred ATF firearms and explosives functions to the Department of Justice and made the newly established Bureau of Alcohol, Tobacco, Firearms, and Explosives (ATFE) responsible for them (116 Stat. 2274). https://www.govinfo.gov/content/pkg/STATUTE-116/pdf/STATUTE-116-Pg2135.pdf

The ATFE posts an organizational chart on its website. https://www.atf.gov/about/organization-structure

Statutory and Regulatory Authorities

"Subchapter XI—Department of Justice Divisions" is part of "Chapter 1—Homeland Security Organization" in 6 U.S.C. Parts 531–533 contain codified statutory material associated with the transfer of the ATFE to the Department of Justice. https://uscode.house.gov/view.xhtml?path=/prelim@title6/chapter1/subchapter11&edition=prelim

Rules and regulations that affect firearms and ammunition, explosives, alcohol and tobacco, and explosive license and permit proceedings are codified in chapter II, parts 400–799, of 27 CFR. https://www.ecfr.gov/cgi-bin/text-idx?SID=c5bb1cb9dbe3c7d2134a728d6b30c7ea&mc=true&tpl=/ecfrbrowse/Title27/27chapterII.tpl

Activities

The ATFE enforces Federal criminal laws and regulates the firearms and explosives industries. Directly and through partnerships, the ATFE investigates and deters violent crime involving arson, firearms and explosives, and trafficking of alcohol and tobacco products. The Bureau provides training and support to its Federal, State, local, and international law enforcement partners and works primarily in 25 field divisions nationwide, including Puerto Rico, the U.S. Virgin Islands, and Guam. It also has foreign offices in Canada, El Salvador, Mexico, and Europe. https://www.atf.gov/about/what-we-do

Sources of Information

Archived Records The "Guide to Federal Records in the National Archives of the United States" indicates that ATFE records have been assigned to record group 436. https://www.archives.gov/research/guide-fed-records/groups/436.html

Career Opportunities ATFE employees conduct criminal investigations and regulate the firearms and explosives industries. They also assist other law enforcement agencies, help to prevent terrorism, reduce violent crime, and protect the public in a manner that is consistent with the Constitution and the laws of the United States. https://www.atf.gov/careers

In 2020, the ATFE ranked 23d among 411 agency subcomponents in the Partnership for Public Service's Best Places To Work Agency Rankings. https://bestplacestowork.org/rankings/detail/?c=TR40

Contact Information Contact information for media inquiries is available on the "Media and Congressional Contacts" web page. https://www.atf.gov/news/media-and-congressional-contacts

Data / Statistics The ATFE maintains a comprehensive collection of agency-related data from national surveys, State-based surveys, other collected license statistics, and other data sources. The data reflect trends in commerce, firearms, and use of Federal services in the United States. https://www.atf.gov/resource-center/data-statistics

Federal Register Significant documents and documents that the ATFE recently published in the Federal Register are accessible online. https://www.federalregister.gov/agencies/alcohol-tobacco-firearms-and-explosives-bureau

Freedom of Information Act (FOIA) The FOIA provides that a person may request access to Federal agency records or information. The ATFE must disclose records that any person properly requests in writing. Pursuant to one or more of nine exemptions and three exclusions that the Act contains, a Federal agency may withhold certain records or parts of them. The FOIA applies only to Federal agencies and does not create a right of access to records held by the U.S. Congress, the courts, State or local government agencies, and private entities. https://www.atf.gov/resource-center/freedom-information-act-foia

Frequently Asked Questions (FAQs) The ATFE posts answers to FAQs on its "Questions and Answers" web page. https://www.atf.gov/questions-and-answers

History A history timeline is available on the ATFE website. https://www.atf.gov/our-history/atf-history-timeline

Social Media The ATFE maintains accounts on Facebook, Instagram, Twitter, and YouTube. https://www.atf.gov/news/social-media

The Sources of Information were updated 8–2021.

Bureau of Prisons

320 First Street NW., Washington, DC 20534
Phone, 202-307-3198. Internet, http://www.bop.gov

Director	Michael Carvajal
Deputy Director	Gene Beasley
https://www.bop.gov/about/agency/leadership.jsp	

The above list of key personnel was updated 8–2021.

The BOP was established in 1930 to provide more progressive and humane care for Federal inmates, to professionalize the prison service, and to ensure consistent and centralized administration of the 11 Federal prisons in operation at that time. Today, the Bureau comprises more than 100 institutions and 6 regional offices. The Bureau has its headquarters, also known as Central Office, in Washington, DC. The Central Office is divided into 10 divisions, including the National Institute of Corrections.

The Correctional Programs Division (CPD) is responsible for inmate classification and programming, including psychology and religious services, substance abuse treatment, case management, and programs for special needs offenders. CPD provides policy direction and daily operational oversight of institution security, emergency preparedness, intelligence gathering, inmate discipline, inmate sentence computations, receiving and discharge, and inmate transportation, as well as coordinating international treaty transfers and overseeing the special security needs of inmates placed in the Federal Witness Protection Program. CPD administers contracts and intergovernmental agreements for the confinement of offenders in community-based programs, community corrections centers, and other facilities, including privately managed facilities. CPD staff is also involved in the Bureau's privatization efforts.

The Industries, Education, and Vocational Training Division oversees Federal Prison Industries, or UNICOR, which is a wholly owned Government corporation that provides employment and training opportunities for inmates confined in Federal correctional facilities. Additionally, it is responsible for oversight of educational, occupational, and vocational training and leisure-time programs, as well as those related to inmate release preparation.

The National Institute of Corrections (NIC) provides technical assistance, training, and information to State and local corrections agencies throughout the country, as well as the Bureau. It also provides research assistance and documents through the NIC Information Center. https://www.bop.gov/about/agency

Sources of Information

A–Z Index   An alphabetical subject index helps visitors navigate the website's content. https://www.bop.gov/website/a_to_z_topics.jsp

Archived Records   The "Guide to Federal Records in the National Archives of the United States" indicates that BOP records have been assigned to record group 129. https://www.archives.gov/research/guide-fed-records/groups/129.html

Business Opportunities   Information is available on the "Let's Do Business" web page. http://www.bop.gov/business

Career Opportunities   Job openings are posted online. For additional career-related information, contact any regional or field office or the Central Office, 320 First Street NW., Washington, DC 20534. Phone, 202-307-3082. http://www.bop.gov/jobs

In 2020, the BOP ranked 387th among 411 agency subcomponents in the Partnership for Public Service's Best Places To Work Agency Rankings. https://bestplacestowork.org/rankings/detail/?c=DJ03

Contact Information   The BOP has a "Contact Us" web page. https://www.bop.gov/contact

Federal Register   Significant documents and documents that the BOP recently published in the Federal Register are accessible online. https://www.federalregister.gov/agencies/prisons-bureau

Find an Inmate   The Department's website features a search tool for locating Federal inmates who were incarcerated after 1981. https://www.bop.gov/inmateloc

Freedom of Information Act (FOIA)   Enacted in 1966, the FOIA took effect on July 4, 1967. The law gives a right to obtain access to Federal agency records to any person, except a fugitive from the law. Some records, or portions of them, are shielded, however, from disclosure by one or more of nine statutory exemptions or by specific harm that disclosure may cause. https://www.bop.gov/foia/index.jsp#tabs-0 | Email: ogc_efoia@bop.gov

The BOP posts records online. Before filing a formal FOIA request, an information seeker should visit the BOP's "Freedom of Information" web page and view the records section to ensure that the desired information is not already freely accessible. https://www.bop.gov/foia/index.jsp#tabs-1

Locations   The "Our Locations" web page features a list of locations, a search tool that requires the facility's name, and location maps (national, regional, type of facility). https://www.bop.gov/locations

Population Statistics   Federal inmate population statistics are online. https://www.bop.gov/about/statistics/population_statistics.jsp

Reading Room   The reading room is located at the Bureau of Prisons, 320 First Street NW., Washington, DC 20534. Phone, 202-307-3029.

The Sources of Information were updated 8–2021.

Resources by Audience   Resources to help Bureau of Prisons staff and their families access frequently used services are online. https://www.bop.gov/resources/employee_resources.jsp

Resources to help former inmates make the transition from incarceration to normal life within a community are online. https://www.bop.gov/resources/former_inmate_resources.jsp

The Attorney General and the Secretary of Health and Human Services provide health management guidelines for infectious disease prevention, detection, and treatment of inmates and correctional employees who are exposed to infectious diseases in correctional facilities. https://www.bop.gov/resources/health_care_mngmt.jsp

Resources to help qualified media representatives visit institutions and gather information on programs and activities or conduct interviews are online. https://www.bop.gov/resources/media_resources.jsp

Resources to help victims or witnesses of Federal crimes find information on complaint procedures, notifications, and payments are online. https://www.bop.gov/resources/victim_resources.jsp

Site Map   The website map allows visitors to look for specific topics or to browse for content that aligns with their interests. https://www.bop.gov/website/site_map.jsp

Social Media   The BOP has a Facebook account. https://www.facebook.com/BOPCareers

The BOP tweets announcements and other newsworthy items on Twitter. https://twitter.com/officialfbop

---

Drug Enforcement Administration

8701 Morrissette Drive, Springfield, VA 22152
Phone, 202-307-1000. Internet, http://www.dea.gov/index.shtml

Administrator	ANNE MILGRAM
Principal Deputy Administrator	PRESTON L. GRUBBS
https://www.dea.gov/about/dea-leadership	

The above list of key personnel was updated 8–2021.

The Drug Enforcement Administration (DEA) is the lead Federal agency in enforcing narcotics and controlled substances laws and regulations. The DEA also enforces the Federal money laundering and bulk currency smuggling statutes when the funds involved in the transactions or smuggling are derived from the sale of narcotics. It was created in July 1973 by Reorganization Plan No. 2 of 1973 (5 U.S.C. app.). https://www.dea.gov/history

The DEA enforces the provisions of the controlled substances and chemical diversion and trafficking laws and regulations of the United States, operating on a worldwide basis. It presents cases to the criminal and civil justice systems of the United States—or any other competent jurisdiction—on those significant organizations and their members involved in cultivation, production, smuggling, distribution, laundering of proceeds, or diversion of controlled substances appearing in or destined for illegal traffic in the United States. The DEA disrupts and dismantles these organizations by arresting their members, confiscating their drugs, and seizing their assets; and it creates, manages, and supports enforcement-related programs—domestically and internationally—to reduce the availability of and demand for illicit controlled substances.

The DEA's responsibilities include: investigation of major narcotic, chemical, drug-money laundering, and bulk currency smuggling violators who operate at interstate and international levels; seizure and forfeiture of assets derived from, traceable to, or intended to be used for illicit drug trafficking; seizure and forfeiture of assets derived from or traceable to drug-money laundering or the smuggling of bulk currency derived from illegal drugs; enforcement of regulations governing the legal manufacture, distribution, and dispensing of controlled substances; management of an intelligence program that supports drug investigations, initiatives, and operations worldwide; coordination with Federal, State, and local law enforcement authorities and cooperation with counterpart agencies abroad; assistance to State and local law enforcement agencies in addressing their most significant drug and drug-related

violence problems; leadership and influence over international counterdrug and chemical policy and support for institution building in host nations; training, scientific research, and information exchange in support of drug traffic prevention and control; and education and assistance to the public community on the prevention, treatment, and dangers of drugs. https://www.dea.gov/mission

The DEA maintains liaison with the United Nations, INTERPOL, and other organizations on matters relating to international narcotics control programs. It has 239 domestic offices in 23 Divisions nationwide, and 91 foreign offices in 68 countries. https://www.dea.gov/domestic-divisions

Sources of Information

Archived Records   The "Guide to Federal Records in the National Archives of the United States" indicates that DEA records have been assigned to record group 170. https://www.archives.gov/research/guide-fed-records/groups/170.html

Asset Forfeiture   The DEA posts public notices of forfeiture in Portable Document Format (PDF) for viewing and downloading on the Department of Justice's forfeiture.gov website. https://www.forfeiture.gov

Business Opportunities   The DEA obtains supplies and services through its Office of Acquisition and Relocation Management. The Office acquires supplies and services for local needs and all DEA agency-level procurements. DEA field activities also have procurement authority, but it is limited. https://www.dea.gov/resources/doing-business-dea | Email: deasmallbusinessprogram@usdoj.gov

Career Opportunities   For career information, contact the nearest DEA field division recruitment office. The DEA also posts information on its "Careers" web page. https://www.dea.gov/careers

In 2020, the DEA ranked 96th among 411 agency subcomponents in the Partnership for Public Service's Best Places To Work Agency Rankings. https://bestplacestowork.org/rankings/detail/?c=DJAA

Contact Information   The DEA posts contact information on its "Contact Us" web page. https://www.dea.gov/who-we-are/contact-us | Email: info@dea.gov

Contact information for each of the DEA's 23 domestic divisions is available online. https://www.dea.gov/divisions

Controlled Substances Act Registration For information on registration under the Controlled Substances Act, contact the Office of Diversion Control, 8701 Morrissette Drive, Springfield, VA 22152. Phone: 800-882-9539. http://www.deadiversion.usdoj.gov/drugreg/index.html | Email: DEA.Registration.Help@usdoj.gov

Data / Statistics The DEA posts data and statistics online. https://www.dea.gov/resources/data-and-statistics

Federal Register Significant documents and documents that the DEA recently published in the Federal Register are accessible online. https://www.federalregister.gov/agencies/drug-enforcement-administration

Freedom of Information Act (FOIA) The FOIA gives a right for public access to Government records. A FOIA request must be submitted in writing. The DEA generally follows the FOIA guidelines that the Department of Justice has adopted. https://www.dea.gov/foia

Museum The DEA Museum and visitors' center are located in Arlington, VA. The museum posts virtual exhibits on its deamuseum.org website. Phone, 202–307–3463. https://deamuseum.org/exhibits

The Sources of Information were updated 8–2021.

Press Releases The DEA posts press releases online. https://www.dea.gov/what-we-do/news/press-releases

Publications The DEA posts various types of documents and publications online. https://www.dea.gov/resources/documents?field_document_document_type_value=Publication

Resources The "Resources" web page provides convenient access to data and statistics, drug information, Freedom of Information Act guidance, media galleries, and publications. https://www.dea.gov/resources

Social Media The DEA maintains Facebook, Instagram, LinkedIn, and Twitter accounts. A social media directory is part of the "Contact Us" web page. https://www.dea.gov/who-we-are/contact-us | Email: DEA.Public.Affairs@usdoj.gov

Victim Witness Assistance Victims' rights laws resulted in the implementation of the victim witness assistance program. These laws provide for fair and just treatment of crime victims, immediate emergency treatment, and referrals to appropriate adult and child service agencies. The Department of Justice also gives guidance to Federal law enforcement agencies through the Attorney General's guidelines for victim witness assistance. https://www.dea.gov/resources/vwap | Email: VWAP.DEA@usdoj.gov

Federal Bureau of Investigation

935 Pennsylvania Avenue NW., Washington, DC 20535
Phone, 202-324-3000. Internet, http://www.fbi.gov

Director	CHRISTOPHER A. WRAY
Deputy Director	PAUL M. ABBATE
https://www.fbi.gov/about/leadership-and-structure

The above list of key personnel was updated 8–2021.

The Federal Bureau of Investigation (FBI) is the Department of Justice's principal investigative arm. It is primarily charged with gathering and reporting facts, locating witnesses, and compiling evidence in cases involving Federal jurisdiction. It also provides law enforcement leadership and assistance to State and international law enforcement agencies.

The FBI was established in 1908 by the Attorney General, who directed that Department of Justice investigations be handled by its own staff. The Bureau is charged with investigating all violations of Federal law except those that have been assigned by legislative enactment or otherwise to another Federal agency. Its jurisdiction includes a wide range of responsibilities in the national security, criminal, and civil fields. Priority has been assigned to areas such as counterterrorism, counterintelligence, cybercrimes, internationally and nationally organized crime and drug-related activities, and financial crimes.

The FBI also offers cooperative services to local, State, and international law enforcement agencies. These services include fingerprint identification, laboratory examination, police training, the Law Enforcement Online communication and information service for use by the law enforcement community, the National Crime Information Center, and the National Center for the Analysis of Violent Crime.

Sources of Information

Archived Records   The "Guide to Federal Records in the National Archives of the United States" indicates that FBI records have been assigned to record group 065. https://www.archives.gov/research/guide-fed-records/groups/065.html

Career Opportunities   The FBI relies on professionals with diverse expertise and skills to analyze data for the intelligence community, safeguard national security, and support the structure of the Bureau. Information on career opportunities, including student internships, is available online. https://www.fbijobs.gov

In 2020, the FBI ranked 223d among 411 agency subcomponents in the Partnership for Public Service's Best Places To Work Agency Rankings. https://bestplacestowork.org/rankings/detail/?c=DJ02

Contact Information   The "Contact Us" web page provides convenient access to information for contacting FBI headquarters, field offices, and overseas offices. https://www.fbi.gov/contact-us

Members of the public may report a violation of U.S. Federal law or suspected terrorism or criminal activity to the FBI. https://www.fbi.gov/tips

Crime Statistics   The Uniform Crime Reporting program generates reliable statistics for use in law enforcement. It also releases information that is relevant for students of criminal justice, researchers, the media, and the public. The program has

been generating crime statistics since 1930. The crime reporting program includes data from more than 18,000 city, university and college, county, State, Tribal, and Federal law enforcement agencies. Agencies participate voluntarily and submit their crime data either through a State UCR program or directly to the FBI's UCR Program. https://www.fbi.gov/services/cjis/ucr

Federal Register   Significant documents and documents that the FBI recently published in the Federal Register are accessible online. https://www.federalregister.gov/agencies/federal-bureau-of-investigation

Freedom of Information Act (FOIA)   The FOIA provides that a person may request access to Federal agency records or information. The FBI must disclose records that any person properly requests in writing. Pursuant to one or more of nine exemptions and three exclusions that the Act contains, a Federal agency can withhold certain records or parts of them. The FOIA applies only to Federal agencies and does not create a right of access to records held by the U.S. Congress, the courts, State or local government agencies, and private entities. https://www.fbi.gov/services/information-management/foipa

The FBI's electronic FOIA library, which contains nearly 7,000 documents and other media that have been scanned from paper and made into more accessible digital copies, is named the "Vault." The library includes new files that have been released to the public, but never added to the FBI website; dozens of records previously posted on the FBI website, but removed when requests diminished; files from the previous FBI FOIA Library; and new and previously unreleased files. https://vault.fbi.gov

Frequently Asked Questions (FAQs)   The FBI posts answers to FAQs. https://www.fbi.gov/about/faqs

History   The FBI posted a brief agency history on its website. https://www.fbi.gov/history

Most Wanted   The FBI maintains the official "Ten Most Wanted Fugitives" list on its website. https://www.fbi.gov/wanted/topten

News   The FBI posts top news stories, press releases, podcasts, radio broadcasts, speeches, and Tweets on its "News" web page. https://www.fbi.gov/news

Publications The FBI's training division maintains the "Law Enforcement Bulletin" website. https://leb.fbi.gov

The FBI maintains an extensive "Reports and Publications" database. https://www.fbi.gov/stats-services/publications

Resources The "Resources" web page provides convenient access to information on business opportunities and victim services. It also has links to featured publications and frequently requested forms and services. https://www.fbi.gov/resources

The Sources of Information were updated 8–2021.

Safe Online Surfing The FBI maintains a "Safe Online Surfing" website for children. https://www.fbi.gov/fbi-kids

Services Services that the FBI provides are presented on a single "Services" web page. https://www.fbi.gov/services

Social Media The FBI started its presence on social media in 2008. Today, the Bureau has dozens of pages and sites. https://www.fbi.gov/news/fbi-social-media-sites

International Criminal Police Organization (INTERPOL)–Washington

Department of Justice, Washington, DC 20530
Phone, 202-616-9000. Fax, 202-616-8400. Internet, http://www.justice.gov/interpol-washington

Director MICHAEL A. HUGHES
https://www.justice.gov/interpol-washington/meet-leadership

The above list of key personnel was updated 8–2021.

INTERPOL–Washington is a separate component under the supervision of the Deputy Attorney General and comanaged with the Department of Homeland Security. It provides an essential communications link between the U.S. police community and their counterparts in the foreign member countries.

INTERPOL is an association of 190 countries that promotes mutual assistance among law enforcement authorities to prevent and suppress international crime. With no police force of its own, INTERPOL has no powers of arrest or search and seizure and, therefore, relies on the law enforcement authorities of its member countries. Each member country is required to have a national central bureau, such as INTERPOL–Washington, to act as the primary point of contact for police affairs. INTERPOL serves as a channel of communication for its member countries to cooperate in the investigation and prosecution of crime; provides a forum for discussions, working group meetings, and symposia to help police focus on specific areas of criminal activity affecting their countries; and issues

information and maintains databases—supplied and used by member countries—on crime, fugitives, humanitarian concerns, missing persons, and stolen passports and vehicles.

INTERPOL–Washington has permanent staff and detailed special agents from numerous Federal law enforcement agencies. It is organized into seven divisions: the Alien and Fugitive, Counterterrorism, Drug, Economic Crimes, Human Trafficking and Child Protection, State and Local Police Liaison, and Violent Crimes Divisions.

Sources of Information

Career Opportunities Information on career opportunities is available online. http://www.justice.gov/interpol-washington/employment

Contact Information The "Contact the Agency" web page contains a postal address for INTERPOL–Washington. https://www.justice.gov/interpol-washington/contact-agency

Freedom of Information Act (FOIA) The FOIA gives any person a right to access

Government records. A request for information must be submitted in writing. INTERPOL–Washington, U.S. National Central Bureau, generally follows the guidelines that the Department of Justice has set forth in its FOIA reference guide.

The Sources of Information were updated 8–2021.

https://www.justice.gov/interpol-washington/interpol-washington-foia

Frequently Asked Questions (FAQs)   INTERPOL posts answers to FAQs. https://www.justice.gov/interpol-washington/frequently-asked-questions

---

Office of Justice Programs

810 Seventh Street NW., Washington, DC 20531
Phone, 202-307-0703. Internet, http://www.ojp.gov | Email: askojp@ojp.usdoj.gov

Assistant Attorney General	AMY L. SOLOMON, ACTING
Principal Deputy Assistant Attorney General	AMY L. SOLOMON
https://www.ojp.gov/about/offices/office-assistant-attorney-general-oaag	

The above list of key personnel was updated 8–2021.

The Office of Justice Programs (OJP) was established by the Justice Assistance Act of 1984 (42 U.S.C. 3711) and reauthorized in 1994 and 2005 to provide Federal leadership, coordination, and assistance needed to make the Nation's justice system more efficient and effective in preventing and controlling crime. OJP is responsible for collecting statistical data and conducting analyses; identifying emerging criminal justice issues; developing and testing promising approaches to address these issues; evaluating program results; and disseminating these findings and other information to State and local governments. https://www.ojp.gov/about

The OJP is comprised of the following bureaus and offices: the Bureau of Justice Assistance provides funding, training, and technical assistance to State and local governments to combat violent and drug-related crime and help improve the criminal justice system; the Bureau of Justice Statistics is responsible for collecting and analyzing data on crime, criminal offenders, crime victims, and the operations of justice systems at all levels of government; the National Institute of Justice sponsors research and development programs, conducts demonstrations of innovative approaches to improve criminal justice, and develops new

criminal justice technologies; the Office of Juvenile Justice and Delinquency Prevention provides grants and contracts to States to help them improve their juvenile justice systems and sponsors innovative research, demonstration, evaluation, statistics, replication, technical assistance, and training programs to increase the Nation's understanding of and improve its response to juvenile violence and delinquency; the Office for Victims of Crime administers victim compensation and assistance grant programs and provides funding, training, and technical assistance to victim service organizations, criminal justice agencies, and other professionals to improve the Nation's response to crime victims; and the Office of Sex Offender Sentencing, Monitoring, Apprehending, Registering, and Tracking (SMART) maintains the standards of the Sex Offender Registration and Notification Act as defined by the Adam Walsh Act. The SMART Office also provides technical assistance and supports innovative and best practices in the field of sex offender management.

Sources of Information

Archived Records   The "Guide to Federal Records in the National Archives of the United States" indicates that Law

Enforcement Assistance Administration (LEAA) records have been assigned to record group 423. The OJP is one of the LEAA's successor agencies. https://www.archives.gov/research/guide-fed-records/groups/423.html

Blog OJP Blog posts highlight OJP programs, as well as Department of Justice initiatives that support OJP's mission. https://www.ojp.gov/news/ojp-blogs/2020-ojp-blogs

Career Opportunities The OJP relies on accountants, attorneys, grant and project managers, information technology specialists, policy advisors, public affairs specialists, researchers, scientists, statisticians, writers and editors, and many other professionals to carry out its mission. https://www.ojp.gov/about/jobs

In 2020, the OJP ranked 337th among 411 agency subcomponents in the Partnership for Public Service's Best Places To Work Agency Rankings. https://bestplacestowork.org/rankings/detail/?c=DJ07

Congressional Resources Resources for Members of Congress and their staff are posted on the "For Congress" web page. https://www.ojp.gov/congress | Email: OJPCongressionalAffairs@usdoj.gov

Contact The "Contact Us" web page has a mailing address, as well as email addresses and phone numbers. https://www.ojp.gov/contact | Email: askojp@ncjrs.gov

The OJP has a "For Media" web page that also contains contact information. https://www.ojp.gov/news/for-media

Federal Register Significant documents and documents that the OJP recently published in the Federal Register are accessible online. https://www.federalregister.gov/agencies/justice-programs-office

Freedom of Information Act (FOIA) Enacted in 1966, the FOIA took effect on July 4, 1967. The law gives a right to obtain access to Federal agency records to any person, except a fugitive from the law. Some records, or portions of them, are shielded, however, from disclosure by one or more of nine statutory exemptions or by specific harm that disclosure may cause. https://www.ojp.gov/program/freedom-information-act/overview

Juvenile Justice / Delinquency Prevention The Office of Juvenile Justice and Delinquency Prevention publishes the bimonthly electronic newsletter "OJJDP News @ a Glance." This award winning newsletter highlights office activities, funding opportunities, publications, Tribal connections, and upcoming events. https://ojjdp.ojp.gov/news/newsletter

News Releases News releases are posted on the OJP website. https://www.ojp.gov/news/news-releases

Publications The OJP posts publications on its website. https://www.ojp.gov/news/publications

Social Media The OJP has social media accounts. The "Social Media" web page provides convenient access to all of them: Facebook, LinkedIn, Twitter, and YouTube. https://www.ojp.gov/news/social-media

State Administering Agencies The OJP awards formula grants directly to State governments, which then set priorities and allocate funds within their respective States. https://www.ojp.gov/funding/state-administering-agencies/overview

Topics The "All Topics" web page provides convenient access to information on American Indian and Alaska Native Affairs, civil rights, corrections, courts, juvenile justice, law enforcement, research and statistics and evaluation, substance abuse and crime, technology to fight crime, and victims of crime. https://www.ojp.gov/topics/all-topics

Training / Technical Assistance The OJP offers training on and technical assistance with financial management, grant writing, and other subjects that are relevant to criminal and juvenile justice professionals and victim service providers. https://www.ojp.gov/training-and-technical-assistance

Virtual Library the National Criminal Justice Reference Service (NCJRS) is an informational resource that supports policy, program development, and research. The NCJRS Virtual Library contains bibliographic information on and abstracts of more than 230,000 collection resources and over 80,000 online materials. https://www.ojp.gov/ncjrs/virtual-library

The Sources of Information were updated 8–2021.

United States Marshals Service

Department of Justice, Washington, DC 20530
Phone, 703-740-1699. Internet, http://www.usmarshals.gov

Director https://www.usmarshals.gov/contacts/leadership.html	DONALD W. WASHINGTON
Deputy Director https://www.usmarshals.gov/contacts/index.html	JEFFREY R. TYLER

The above list of key personnel was updated 8–2021.

The United States Marshals Service (USMS) is the Nation's oldest Federal law enforcement agency, having served as a vital link between the executive and judicial branches of the Government since 1789. The USMS performs tasks that are essential to the operation of virtually every aspect of the Federal justice system. https://www.usmarshals.gov/duties/factsheets/overview.pdf

The USMS has these responsibilities: providing support and protection for the Federal courts, including security for 800 judicial facilities and nearly 2,000 judges and magistrates, as well as countless other trial participants such as jurors and attorneys; apprehending the majority of Federal fugitives; operating the Federal Witness Security Program and ensuring the safety of endangered Government witnesses; maintaining custody of and transporting thousands of Federal prisoners annually; executing court orders and arrest warrants; managing and selling seized property forfeited to the Government by drug traffickers and other criminals and assisting the Justice Department's asset forfeiture program; responding to emergency circumstances, including civil disturbances, terrorist incidents, and other crisis situations through its Special Operations Group; restoring order in riot and mob-violence situations; providing housing, transportation, and medical care of federal detainees; and operating the USMS Training Academy.

Sources of Information

Archived Records   The "Guide to Federal Records in the National Archives of the United States" indicates that USMS records have been assigned to record group 527.

https://www.archives.gov/research/guide-fed-records/groups/527.html

Notable references to USMS activities also are found in the following National Archives record groups: 021 (records of Federal courts); 060 (letters received by the Department of Justice); 118 (records of U.S. Attorneys, and formerly U.S. Marshals); and 206 (records of the Solicitor of the Treasury). https://www.usmarshals.gov/history/records_assistance.htm

Business Opportunities   The USMS posts products and services that it purchases. https://www.usmarshals.gov/business/index.html

Career Opportunities   The USMS relies on administrative personnel, aviation enforcement officers, deputy U.S. Marshals, detention enforcement officers, and other professionals to carry out its mission. https://www.usmarshals.gov/careers/index.html

In 2020, the USMS ranked 92d among 411 agency subcomponents in the Partnership for Public Service's Best Places To Work Agency Rankings. https://bestplacestowork.org/rankings/detail/?c=DJ08

Contact   The "U.S. Marshals Service Contacts" web page contains a lot of names, phone numbers, and titles. https://www.usmarshals.gov/contacts/index.html

The USMS posts contact information for its district offices. https://www.usmarshals.gov/contacts/districts.html

Factsheets   The USMS posts factsheets on its website. https://www.usmarshals.gov/duties/factsheets/index.html

Federal Register   Documents that the USMS recently published in the Federal Register are accessible online. https://www.federalregister.gov/agencies/united-states-marshals-service

Freedom of Information Act (FOIA) To any person, the FOIA gives a statutory right for obtaining access to Government information in the records of executive branch agencies. This right to access is limited, however, when the requested information is shielded from disclosure by any of nine exemptions contained within the statute. Phone, 703-740-3943. https://www.usmarshals.gov/foia/index.html | Email: usms.foia@usdoj.gov

The USMS maintains an electronic reading room. Before submitting a FOIA request, seekers of information should search the reading room's holdings to verify that the desired information is not already accessible, free of charge and without delay. https://www.usmarshals.gov/readingroom/files.html

The Sources of Information were updated 8–2021.

History A historical timeline of the USMS is available online. https://www.usmarshals.gov/history/timeline.html

Most Wanted The USMS posts information on its 15 most-wanted fugitives. The USMS considers these individuals armed and dangerous. Phone, 800-336-0102. https://www.usmarshals.gov/investigations/most_wanted/index.html

News The USMS posts news releases. https://www.usmarshals.gov/news/index.html

Site Map The USMS website index allows visitors to look for specific topics or to browse content that aligns with their interests. https://www.usmarshals.gov/site_map/index.html

OFFICES / BOARDS
Executive Office for Immigration Review

Falls Church, VA 22041
Phone, 703-305-0289. Internet, http://www.usdoj.gov/eoir

Director	JEAN KING, ACTING

https://www.justice.gov/eoir/staff-profile/meet-the-director

The above list of key personnel was updated 8–2021.

The Executive Office for Immigration Review (EOIR), under a delegation of authority from the Attorney General, is charged with adjudicating matters brought under various immigration statutes before its three administrative tribunals: the Office of the Chief Immigration Judge, the Board of Immigration Appeals, and the Office of the Chief Administrative Hearing Officer.

The Office of the Chief Immigration Judge provides overall direction for more than 300 immigration judges located in 58 immigration courts throughout the Nation. Immigration judges are responsible for conducting formal administrative proceedings and act independently in their decision-making capacity. Their decisions are administratively final, unless appealed or certified to the BIA.

In removal proceedings, an immigration judge determines whether an alien should be removed or allowed to remain in the United States. Judges are located throughout the United States, and each judge has jurisdiction to consider various forms of relief available under the law.

The Board of Immigration Appeals (BIA) has nationwide jurisdiction to hear appeals from certain decisions made by immigration judges and by district directors of the Department of Homeland Security (DHS). In addition, the BIA is responsible for hearing appeals involving disciplinary actions against attorneys and representatives before DHS and EOIR.

Decisions of the BIA are binding on all DHS officers and immigration judges unless modified or overruled by the Attorney General or a Federal court. All BIA decisions are subject to judicial review in Federal court. The majority of appeals reaching the BIA involve orders of removal and applications for relief from removal. Other cases before the BIA include petitions to classify the status of alien relatives for the issuance of preference immigrant visas, fines imposed upon carriers for the violation of the immigration laws, and motions for reopening or reconsideration of decisions previously rendered.

The Office of the Chief Administrative Hearing Officer (OCAHO) is headed by a Chief Administrative Hearing Officer (CAHO), who is responsible for the general supervision and management of administrative law judges (ALJs). OCAHO ALJs preside at hearings that are mandated by provisions of immigration law concerning allegations of unlawful employment of aliens, employment eligibility verification violations ("employer sanctions), unfair immigration-related employment practices, and immigration document fraud. ALJ decisions in employer sanctions and document fraud cases may be reviewed by the CAHO and the Attorney General, and all OCAHO cases may be appealed to the appropriate U.S. Circuit Court of Appeals.

Sources of Information

Archived Records   The "Guide to Federal Records in the National Archives of the United States" indicates that EOIR records have been assigned to record group 582. The guide does not contain, however, a description that is currently associated with this record group. https://www.archives.gov/research/guide-fed-records/index-numeric/501-to-600.html
Contact   Phone numbers and email and postal addresses are available on the "Contact EOIR" web page. https://www.justice.gov/eoir/contact-eoir | Email: PAO.EOIR@usdoj.gov
Federal Register   Significant documents and documents that the EOIR recently published

in the Federal Register are accessible online. https://www.federalregister.gov/agencies/executive-office-for-immigration-review
Forms   The "EOIR Forms" web page has most of the forms that one needs for filing with the Board of Immigration Appeals, the Immigration Courts, and the Office of the Chief Administrative Hearing Officer. https://www.justice.gov/eoir/forms
Freedom of Information Act (FOIA)   To any person, the FOIA gives a statutory right for obtaining access to Government information in the records of executive branch agencies. This right to access is limited, however, when the requested information is shielded from disclosure by any of nine exemptions contained within the statute. The EOIR maintains four electronic libraries: archived resources, frequently requested agency records, proactive disclosures, and reference materials. Before submitting a FOIA request, an information seeker should browse these library collections to verify that the desired information is not available, immediately and free of charge. https://www.justice.gov/eoir/freedom-information-act-foia
Immigration Courts   An alphabetical list of immigration courts, which are arranged by State and by cities within a State, is available online. https://www.justice.gov/eoir/eoir-immigration-court-listing
Legal Representation   The "Find Legal Representation" web page has resources for those seeking representation. https://www.justice.gov/eoir/find-legal-representation
Library   A virtual law library that serves as a complement to the Law Library and Immigration Research Center is available online. https://www.justice.gov/eoir/virtual-law-library
Social Media   The EOIR has a Facebook account. https://www.facebook.com/doj.eoir

The EOIR tweets announcements and other newsworthy items on Twitter. https://twitter.com/DOJ_EOIR

The Sources of Information were updated 8–2021.

Foreign Claims Settlement Commission of the United States

Suite 6002, 600 E Street NW., Washington, DC 20579
Phone, 202-616-6975. Fax, 202-616-6993. Internet, http://www.justice.gov/fcsc

Commissioner	SYLVIA M. BECKER
Commissioner	PATRICK HOVAKIMIAN
https://www.justice.gov/fcsc	

The above list of key personnel was updated 8–2021.

The Foreign Claims Settlement Commission of the United States is a quasi-judicial, independent agency within the Department of Justice, which adjudicates claims of U.S. nationals against foreign governments, either under specific jurisdiction conferred by Congress or the Department of State or pursuant to international claims settlement agreements. The decisions of the Commission are final and are not reviewable under any standard by any court or other authority. Funds for payment of the Commission's awards are derived from congressional appropriations, international claims settlements, or the liquidation of foreign assets in the United States by the Departments of Justice and the Treasury.

The Commission also has authority to receive, determine the validity and amount, and provide for the payment of claims by members of the U.S. Armed Services and civilians held as prisoners of war or interned by a hostile force in Southeast Asia during the Vietnam conflict or by the survivors of such servicemembers and civilians.

The Commission is also responsible for maintaining records and responding to inquiries related to the various claims programs it has conducted against the Governments of Albania, Bulgaria, China, Cuba, Czechoslovakia, Egypt, Ethiopia, the Federal Republic of Germany, the German Democratic Republic, Hungary, Iran, Italy, Panama, Poland, Romania, the Soviet Union, Vietnam, and Yugoslavia, as well as those authorized under the War Claims Act of 1948 and other statutes.

Sources of Information

Career Opportunities General information on career opportunities is available on the Department of Justice's "Careers" web page. For additional information on attorney positions, contact the Office of the Chief Counsel, 600 E Street NW., Suite 6002, Washington, DC 20579. Phone, 202-616-6975. http://www.justice.gov/careers

Contact Information The Commission may be contacted by sending electronic or postal mail. Addresses are posted on the "Contact the Commission" web page. https://www.justice.gov/fcsc/contact-commission | Email: info.FCSC@usdoj.gov

Publications Annual reports, starting with the year 2008, are available on the "Publications" web page. http://www.justice.gov/fcsc/publications

Reading Room The reading room is located at 600 E Street NW., Washington, DC 20579. Phone, 202-616-6975.

The Sources of Information were updated 8–2021.

Office of Community Oriented Policing Services

935 N. Street NE., Washington, DC 20530
Phone, 202-514-2058. Internet, http://www.cops.usdoj.gov

Director	ROBERT CHAPMAN, ACTING

https://m.facebook.com/DOJCOPS/photos/a.180221468674
  616/4732389816791069/?_se_imp=0vbs31vCvpgh7MTD3

The above list of key personnel was updated 8–2021.

The Office of Community Oriented Policing Services (COPS) was established to assist law enforcement agencies in enhancing public safety through the implementation of community policing strategies. The Office gives assistance by providing training to enhance law enforcement officers' problem-solving and community interaction skills and helping law enforcement and community members develop initiatives to prevent crime; increasing the number of law enforcement officers directly interacting with communities; and supporting the development of new technologies to shift law enforcement's focus to preventing crime and disorder within communities.

Sources of Information

Career Resources   The "Dispatch" is a monthly electronic newsletter. The article "Ten Recruiting Tips for Finding Good Officers" ran in the SEP 2019 issue. https://cops.usdoj.gov/html/dispatch/09-2019/recruitment.html

The "Dispatch" article "Surviving the Job" ran in the DEC 2019 issue. https://cops.usdoj.gov/html/dispatch/12-2019/surviving.html

Contact Information https://cops.usdoj.gov/contactcops | Email: askcopsRC@usdoj.gov

The Sources of Information were updated 8–2021.

Grants and Funding   COPS grants and funding opportunities support State, local, and tribal law enforcement efforts to advance community policing. Current applicant and grantee information—announcements, fiscal year grant programs, current funding opportunities, and resources for grantees—is available online. https://cops.usdoj.gov/grants

News   The "News" web page provides easy access to photo galleries, press releases, " the podcast series "The Beat," the video series "What's New in Blue, and the Office's news feed. https://cops.usdoj.gov/news

Resources   COPS is a valuable resource for smart approaches to preventing and reducing crime. COPS works with researchers, practitioners, and trailblazers to implement effective strategies in the field. https://cops.usdoj.gov/resources

Training / Technical Assistance   Resources for training and technical assistance are available on the COPS website. https://cops.usdoj.gov/training-technical-assistance

Social Media   COPS has a Facebook account. https://www.facebook.com/DOJCOPS

COPS tweets announcements and other newsworthy items on Twitter. https://twitter.com/COPSOffice

Office on Violence Against Women

145 N Street NE., Suite 10W–121, Washington, DC 20530
Phone: 202-307-6026. Internet, http://www.justice.gov/ovw

Director	ALLISON RANDALL, ACTING

https://www.justice.gov/ovw/about-office

The above list of key personnel was updated 8–2021.

The Office on Violence Against Women (OVW) was established in 1995 to reduce violence against women through the implementation of the Violence Against Women Act. The Office administers financial and technical assistance to communities that are developing programs, policies, and practices to end domestic and dating violence, sexual assault, and stalking.

Sources of Information

Employment Information on employment and internship opportunities is available online. http://www.justice.gov/ovw/careers
Publications Portable Document Format (PDF) files of selected publications are available online. http://www.justice.gov/ovw/selected-publications http://www.justice.gov/ovw/contact-office | Email: ovw.info@usdoj.gov

For further information, contact the Office on Violence Against Women, 145 N Street NE., Suite 10W–121, Washington, DC, 20530. Phone, 202-307-6026.

United States Parole Commission

90 K Street NE., Washington, DC 20530
Phone, 202-346-7000. Internet, http://www.usdoj.gov/uspc

Chair https://www.justice.gov/uspc/about-commission	Patricia K. Cushwa, Acting

The above list of key personnel was updated 8–2021.

The U.S. Parole Commission (USPC) makes parole release decisions for eligible Federal and District of Columbia prisoners; authorizes methods of release and conditions under which release occurs; prescribes, modifies, and monitors compliance with the terms and conditions governing offenders' behavior while on parole or mandatory or supervised release; issues warrants for violation of supervision; determines probable cause for the revocation process; revokes parole, mandatory, or supervised release; releases from supervision those offenders who are no longer a risk to public safety; and promulgates the rules, regulations, and guidelines for the exercise of USPC's authority and the implementation of a national parole policy.

USPC has sole jurisdiction over the following: Federal offenders who committed offenses before November 1, 1987; DC Code offenders who committed offenses before August 5, 2000; DC Code offenders sentenced to a term of supervised release; Uniform Code of Military Justice offenders who are in Bureau of Prison's custody; transfer treaty cases; and State probationers and parolees in the Federal Witness Protection Program.

Sources of Information

Freedom of Information Act (FOIA) The Commission maintains an online FOIA library. Information on Freedom of Information Act requests is available online. http://www.justice.gov/uspc/freedom-information-act-foia/foia-library http://www.justice.gov/uspc/freedom-information-act-foia | Email: USPC.FOIA@usdoj.gov
Reading Room The reading room is located at 90 K Street NE., Washington, DC 20530. Phone, 202-346-7000. http://www.justice.gov/uspc/contact-commission

For further information, contact the U.S. Parole Commission, Department of Justice, 90 K Street NE., Washington, DC 20530. Phone, 202-346-7000.

DEPARTMENT OF LABOR

200 Constitution Avenue NW., Washington, DC 20210
Phone, 202-693-6000. Internet, http://www.dol.gov

Secretary of Labor	MARTIN J. WALSH
Deputy Secretary	JULIE A. SU

https://www.dol.gov/agencies/osec

Chairs of Boards
Administrative Review
Benefits Review
Employees' Compensation Appeals

Chief Administrative Law Judge

Chief Information Officer

Directors
Centers for Faith and Opportunity Initiative
Executive Secretariat
Office of Public Liaison

Ombudsman for the Energy Employees Occupational Illness
 Compensation Program
https://www.dol.gov/general/dol-agencies

Administrator
Wage and Hour Division

Assistant Secretaries
Administration and Management
Congressional and Intergovernmental Affairs
Disability Employment Policy
Employee Benefits Security
Employment and Training
Mine Safety and Health
Occupational Safety and Health
Policy
Public Affairs
Veterans' Employment and Training

Chief Financial Officer

Commissioner
Labor Statistics

Deputy Undersecretary
International Affairs

Director
Women's Bureau

Office Directors
Federal Contract Compliance Programs

Department of Labor

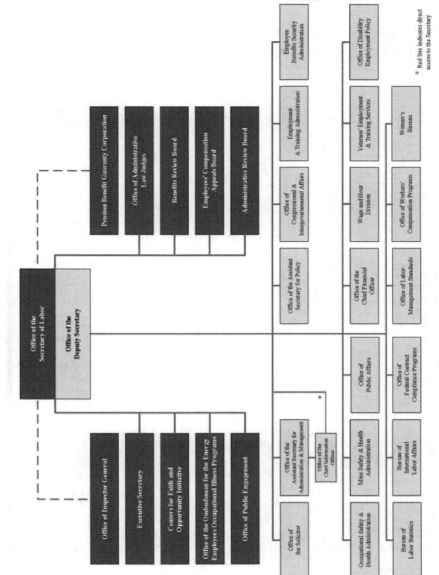

Office of the Secretary of Labor

Office of the Deputy Secretary

Pension Benefit Guaranty Corporation

Office of Administrative Law Judges

Benefits Review Board

Employees' Compensation Appeals Board

Administrative Review Board

Office of Inspector General

Executive Secretary

Centers for Faith and Opportunities Initiative

Office of the Ombudsman for the Energy Employees Occupational Illness Programs

Office of Public Engagement

Office of the Assistant Secretary for Policy

Office of Congressional & Intergovernmental Affairs

Employment & Training Administration

Employee Benefits Security Administration

Office of Disability Employment Policy

Veterans' Employment & Training Services

Wage and Hour Division

Office of the Chief Financial Officer

Women's Bureau

Office of Workers' Compensation Programs

Office of Labor-Management Standards

Office of the Solicitor

Office of the Assistant Secretary for Administration & Management

Office of the Chief Information Officer *

Office of Public Affairs

Office of Federal Contract Compliance Programs

Mine Safety & Health Administration

Bureau of International Labor Affairs

Occupational Safety & Health Administration

Bureau of Labor Statistics

* Red line indicates direct access to the Secretary

Labor-Management Standards
Workers' Compensation Programs

Solicitor of Labor
https://www.dol.gov/general/contact/contact-phonekeypersonnel

Inspector General
https://www.oig.dol.gov/digbio.htm

The above list of key personnel was updated 10–2020.

The Department of Labor promotes the welfare of job seekers, wage earners, and retirees by improving working conditions, advancing opportunities for profitable employment, protecting retirement and health care benefits, matching workers to employers, strengthening free collective bargaining, and tracking changes in economic indicators on a national scale.

Establishment and Organization

On March 4, 1913, President William H. Taft approved Public Law 62–426, which "created an executive department in the Government to be called the Department of Labor, with a Secretary of Labor, who shall be the head thereof, to be appointed by the President, by and with the advice and consent of the Senate." The Act also stated the purpose of the new Department of Labor (DOL): "to foster, promote, and develop the welfare of the wager earners of the United States, to improve their working conditions, and to advance their opportunities for profitable employment" (37 Stat. 736). http://www.loc.gov/law/help/statutes-at-large/62nd-congress/session-3/c62s3ch141.pdf

The U.S. Congress first established a Bureau of Labor in the Department of the Interior. President Chester A. Arthur approved the legislative action on June 27, 1884. The Act placed the new Bureau "under the charge of a Commissioner of Labor . . . [who] shall collect information upon the subject of labor, its relation to capital, the hours of labor, and the earnings of laboring men and women, and the means of promoting their material, social, intellectual, and moral prosperity" (23 Stat. 60 and 61). http://www.loc.gov/law/help/statutes-at-large/48th-congress/Session%201/c48s1ch127.pdf

Four years later, the U.S. Congress acted again, establishing the Bureau of Labor as an independent department without executive rank. On June 13, 1888, President Grover Cleveland approved the law to make

room "at the seat of Government [for] a Department of Labor, the general design and duties of which shall be to acquire and diffuse among the people of the United States useful information on subjects connected with labor, in the most general and comprehensive sense of that word, and especially upon its relation to capital, the hours of labor, the earnings of laboring men and women, and the means of promoting their material, social, intellectual, and moral prosperity." http://www.loc.gov/law/help/statutes-at-large/50th-congress/session-1/c50s1ch389.pdf

Fifteen years later, it returned to the status of a bureau within an expanded department that now acquired executive rank. On February 14, 1903, President Theodore Roosevelt approved Public Law 57–87, which established "an executive department to be known as the Department of Commerce and Labor" (32 Stat. 825). http://www.loc.gov/law/help/statutes-at-large/57th-congress/session-2/c57s2ch552.pdf

The DOL posts its organizational chart online. https://www.dol.gov/general/aboutdol/orgchart

The DOL relies on a number of offices and agencies to carry out its mission. These components are organized into major program areas, and an Assistant Secretary or other official heads each of them. https://www.dol.gov/general/dol-agencies

Statutory and Regulatory Authorities

Statutory material on matters of "Labor" is codified in 29 U.S.C. https://uscode.house.gov/browse/prelim@title29&edition=prelim

Rules and regulations associated with the Office of the Secretary of Labor are codified in subtitle A, parts 0–99, of 29 CFR. https://www.ecfr.gov/cgi-bin/text-idx?SID=b05b0c24dcef5daf53fdf059f2fdfd28&mc=true&tpl=/ecfrbrowse/Title29/29cfrv1_02.tpl#0

Rules and regulations that relate to "Labor" are codified in subtitle B, 100–4999, of 29 CFR. https://www.ecfr.gov/cgi-bin/text-idx?SID=b05b0c24dcef5daf53fdf059f2fdfd28&mc=true&tpl=/ecfrbrowse/Title29/29subtitleB.tpl

Activities

The DOL administers a variety of Federal labor laws to guarantee workers' rights to fair, safe, and healthy working conditions, including minimum hourly wage and overtime pay, protection against employment discrimination, and unemployment insurance. The Secretary advises the President on the development and execution of policies and the administration and enforcement of laws relating to wage earners, their working conditions, and their employment opportunities.

Administrative Law   Administrative law judges from the Office of Administrative Law Judges preside over formal adversarial hearings involving labor-related matters: the Longshore and Harbor Workers' Compensation, the Defense Base, the Black Lung Benefits, the McNamara O'Hara Service Contract, and the Davis Bacon Act; environmental, transportation, and securities whistleblower protection laws; permanent and temporary immigration; child labor law violations; employment discrimination; training; seasonal and migrant workers; and Federal construction and service contracts. The Office is comprised of headquarters in Washington, D.C. and seven district offices. Its judges are nonpolitical appointees: They are appointed under and guaranteed decisional independence by the Administrative Procedure Act. The Administrative Review Board or Benefits Review Board typically reviews appeals of the decisions made by the Office's judges. Depending upon the statute at issue, appeals then go to Federal district or appellate courts and, ultimately, may go to the U.S. Supreme Court. http://www.oalj.dol.gov

Administration and Management   The Office of the Assistant Secretary for Administration and Management is responsible for the development and promulgation of policies, standards, procedures, systems, and materials related to the resource and administrative management of the Department and for the execution of such policies and directives at Headquarters and in the field. http://www.dol.gov/oasam

Audits / Investigations   The Office of Inspector General (OIG) conducts audits to review the economy, effectiveness, efficiency, and integrity of all DOL programs and operations, including those performed by its contractors and grantees. The Inspector General works to answer the following types of questions: Do Department programs and operations comply with the applicable laws and regulations; are departmental resources being utilized efficiently and economically; and are DOL programs achieving their intended results? The Office also conducts administrative, civil, and criminal investigations relating to violations of Federal laws, regulations, or rules—including violations committed by DOL contractors and grantees—as well as investigations of allegations of misconduct on the part of DOL employees. In addition, the OIG has an "external" program function to conduct criminal investigations to combat the influence of labor racketeering and organized crime in the nation's labor unions. The OIG conducts labor racketeering investigations in three areas: employee benefit plans, labor-management relations, and internal union affairs. The OIG also works with other law enforcement partners on human trafficking matters. http://www.oig.dol.gov

Communications / Public Affairs   The Office of Public Affairs (OPA) directs and coordinates all public and employee communications activities. The Assistant Secretary of the Office acts as the chief adviser to the Secretary of Labor and his or her Deputy Secretary and to the agency heads and departmental staff for developing and implementing strategies that engage and connect with the public and educate it about the work and mission of the Department.

The Assistant Secretary also acts as the Secretary's chief adviser on crisis communications. The OPA serves as the first point of contact for news media inquiries, as the clearance and dissemination point for DOL public-facing materials, and it develops and maintains the Department's Web-based, audiovisual, and contact center communications. The OPA also administers "lock ups" when sensitive economic data are released to the press under an embargo. https://www.dol.gov/general/contact/media-contact

Disability Employment Policy   The Office of Disability Employment Policy (ODEP) is the only non-regulatory federal agency that promotes policies and coordinates with employers and all levels of government to increase workplace success for people with disabilities. ODEP helps employers foster inclusive workplaces where all employees can contribute and succeed, and works to improve government workforce systems so people with disabilities can secure good jobs and excel in the workplace. http://www.dol.gov/odep

Energy Employees Occupational Illness Compensation   The Office of the Ombudsman for the Energy Employees Occupational Illness Compensation Program was established in 2004 under Part E of the Energy Employees Occupational Illness Compensation Program Act (EEOICPA), as amended (42 U.S.C. 7385s-15). The EEOICPA is a system of Federal payments to compensate certain nuclear workers for occupational illnesses caused by exposure to toxic substances. This small and independent Office is headed by the Ombudsman, whom the Secretary of Labor appoints. It provides information to claimants on the benefits available under Parts B and E of the EEOICPA and issues annual reports to Congress detailing the complaints, grievances, and requests for assistance that the Office receives. http://www.dol.gov/eeombd

Federal Contract Compliance   The Office of Federal Contract Compliance Programs administers and enforces three equal employment opportunity laws: Executive Order 11246, Section 503 of the Rehabilitation Act of 1973, and the Vietnam Era Veterans' Readjustment Assistance Act of 1974. As amended, these laws prohibit Federal contractors and subcontractors

from discriminating based on race, color, religion, sex, sexual orientation, gender identity, national origin, disability, or status as a protected veteran. Executive Order 11246 prohibits Federal contractors and subcontractors, with limited exceptions, from taking adverse employment actions against applicants and employees for asking about, discussing, or sharing information on their pay or the pay of their coworkers. These laws also require Federal contractors and subcontractors to take affirmative action to ensure equal employment opportunity. http://www.dol.gov/ofccp | Email: OFCCP-Public@dol.gov

Labor-Management Standards   The Office of Labor-Management Standards (OLMS) administers and enforces most provisions of the Labor-Management Reporting and Disclosure Act of 1959 (LMRDA). The LMRDA primarily promotes union democracy and financial integrity in private sector labor unions through standards for union officer elections and union trusteeships and safeguards for union assets. Additionally, the LMRDA promotes labor union and labor-management transparency through reporting and disclosure requirements for labor unions and their officials, employers, labor relations consultants, and surety companies.

OLMS also administers provisions of the Civil Service Reform Act of 1978 and the Foreign Service Act of 1980, which extend comparable protections to Federal labor unions. OLMS does not have jurisdiction over unions representing solely state, county, or municipal employees. In addition, the Division of Statutory Programs (DSP) administers DOL responsibilities under the Federal Transit Act by ensuring that fair and equitable arrangements protecting mass transit employees are in place before the release of Federal transit grant funds. http://www.dol.gov/olms

Legal Services   The Office of the Solicitor of Labor (SOL) provides comprehensive legal services to help the Department achieve its mission. More specifically, the Solicitor serves dual roles in the Department. The Solicitor is the Department's chief enforcement officer, pursuing affirmative litigation on behalf of the Secretary before administrative law judges, review boards and commissions, and in the Federal district courts and courts of appeals. The Solicitor is also the Department's general counsel, assisting in the development of regulations, standards, and legislative proposals; providing legal opinions and advice on all of the Department's activities; advising the Solicitor General on Supreme Court litigation; and coordinating with the Department of Justice, as appropriate, to defend the Department in litigation. http://www.dol.gov/sol

Policy / Rulemaking   The Office of the Assistant Secretary for Policy advises and assists the Secretary, Deputy Secretary, and Department on policy development, policy evaluation, regulation, and legislation that improve the lives of workers, retirees, and their families. The Office also serves as the DOL's regulatory policy officer and regulatory reform officer to ensure that the Department complies with the regulatory and guidance development requirements of Executive Order 12866, as amended, Executive Order 13777, and any other related Office of Management and Budget circular or bulletin. The Office leads special initiatives and manages department-wide and interdepartmental activities. In its capacity as the DOL's policy innovation arm, it invests in research and analysis of current and emerging labor issues. https://www.dol.gov/agencies/oasp

Workers' Compensation   The Office of Workers' Compensation Programs (OWCP) protects workers who are injured or become ill on the job by making decisions on claims, paying benefits, and helping workers return to their jobs. OWCP administers eight major disability compensation statutes: the Federal Employees' Compensation Act; the Longshore and Harbor Workers' Compensation Act; the Defense Base Act (DBA); the Nonappropriated Fund Instrumentalities Act; the Outer Continental Shelf Lands Act; the War Hazards Compensation Act; the Black Lung Benefits Act; and the Energy Employees Occupational Illness Compensation Act. OWCP serves specific employee groups that are covered under the relevant statutes and regulations by mitigating the financial burden resulting from workplace injury or illness and promoting return to work when appropriate. Dependents or survivors may also be eligible for benefits. http://www.dol.gov/owcp

Boards

Administrative Review   The Administrative Review Board (ARB) consists of five members appointed by the Secretary. It issues final agency decisions for appeals cases under a wide range of worker protection laws, including the Service Contract Act (SCA) and the Davis Bacon Act (DBA). The appeals cases primarily address environmental, transportation, and securities whistleblower protection; H-1B immigration provisions; child labor law violations; employment discrimination; job training; seasonal and migrant workers. The Board's cases generally arise upon appeal from decisions of Department of Labor Administrative Law Judges (OALJ) or the Administrator of the Department's Wage and Hour Division (WHD). Depending upon the statute at issue, the parties may appeal the Board's decisions to Federal district or appellate courts and, ultimately, to the U.S. Supreme Court. http://www.dol.gov/arb/welcome.html

Benefits Review   The Benefits Review Board (BRB) consists of five members appointed by the Secretary. In 1972, Congress created the Board to review and issue decisions on appeals of workers' compensation cases arising under the Longshore and Harbor Workers' Compensation Act, and its extensions, and the Black Lung Benefits amendments to the Federal Coal Mine Safety Act of 1969. Board decisions may be appealed to the U.S. Courts of Appeals and to the U.S. Supreme Court. http://www.dol.gov/brb/welcome.html

Employees' Compensation Appeals   The Employees' Compensation Appeals Board (ECAB) is a five-member quasi-judicial body appointed by the Secretary and delegated exclusive jurisdiction by Congress to hear and make final decisions on appeals filed by Federal workers arising under the Federal Employees' Compensation Act (FECA). The Board was created by Reorganization Plan No. 2 of 1946 (60 Stat. 1095). The Board's decisions are not reviewable and are binding upon the Office of Workers' Compensation Programs (OWCP). http://www.dol.gov/ecab/welcome.html

Sources of Information

A–Z Index   The DOL website features an alphabetical index to help visitors search for information or browse topics of interest. https://www.dol.gov/general/siteindex

Agencies / Programs   The DOL carries out its mission through a number of offices and agencies, which are organized into major program areas. An Assistant Secretary, Director, or other official oversees each of these offices and agencies. https://www.dol.gov/general/dol-agencies

Archived Records   The "Guide to Federal Records in the National Archives of the United States" indicates that DOL records have been assigned to record group 174. https://www.archives.gov/research/guide-fed-records/groups/174.html

Business Opportunities   The Office of Acquisition Services is the primary procurement office for the DOL national office. It carries out most contracting, grants, and related activities. The Office procures a variety of goods and services on a recurring basis: auditors, expert witnesses, moving services, printing and graphics, support services, technical studies, and video productions. It also acts as the central procurement center for the Department's information technology needs. Phone, 202-693-4570. https://www.dol.gov/agencies/oasam/centers-offices/office-of-the-senior-procurement-executive/office-of-acquisition-services

The Office of Small and Disadvantaged Business Utilization administers the DOL's small business program in accordance with the Small Business Act. It seeks to ensure a fair share of procurement opportunities for small businesses, as well as for Historically Underutilized Business Zone (HUBZone) certified, service-disabled veteran-owned, small disadvantaged, and woman-owned small businesses. Phone, 202-603-7299 or 866-487-2365. https://www.dol.gov/agencies/oasam/centers-offices/office-of-the-senior-procurement-executive/office-of-small-and-disadvantaged-business-utilization

Career Opportunities   Each year, the DOL hires hundreds of professionals to help carry out its mission. These new employees enrich the Department by bringing with them a vast range of knowledge and skills. A sample of their areas of expertise include accounting and auditing, computer programming, criminal investigation, engineering, health inspection, industrial hygiene, personnel

management, and statistics. https://www.dol.gov/general/jobs

In 2019, the DOL ranked 17th among 25 midsize Government agencies in the Partnership for Public Service's Best Places To Work Agency Rankings. https://bestplacestowork.org/rankings/detail/DL00

Contact Information   Email addresses, phone numbers, and postal addresses are available on the "Contact Us" web page. https://www.dol.gov/general/contact

Contact information for representatives of the media is available on the DOL website. They should direct their inquiries to the Office of Public Affairs. Phone, 202-693-4676 (main line). Phone, 202-577-5744 (after-hours). https://www.dol.gov/general/contact/media-contact

Federal Register   Significant documents and documents that the DOL recently published in the Federal Register are accessible online. https://www.federalregister.gov/agencies/labor-department

Find It!   The "Find It" web page allows online visitors to look for information by audience or by topic. Available on the same page are the following internal links: A–Z index, DOL agencies, DOL forms, DOL services by location, and top 20 requested items. https://www.dol.gov/general/findit

Freedom of Information Act (FOIA)   The FOIA provides that a person may request access to Federal agency records or information. The DOL must disclose records that any person properly requests in writing. Pursuant to one or more of nine exemptions and three exclusions that the Act contains, a Federal agency can withhold certain records or parts of them. The FOIA applies only to Federal agencies and does not create a right of access to records held by the U.S. Congress, the courts, State or local government agencies, and private entities. https://www.dol.gov/general/foia | Email: foiarequests@dol.gov

The DOL maintains a departmentwide electronic library. Before submitting a FOIA request, a requester should browse or search the holdings of the online library to ensure that the desired information is not already accessible, immediately and free of charge. https://www.dol.gov/general/foia/readroom

Frequently Asked Questions (FAQs)   The DOL posts answers to FAQs on its website. http://webapps.dol.gov/dolfaq/dolfaq.asp

Glossary   The OIG maintains a glossary of terms related to its activities and mission. https://www.oig.dol.gov/hotlineterms.htm
History   A Defeated and departing incumbent, President William Howard Taft reluctantly approved Public Law 62–426 to establish the Department of Labor on March 4, 1913. To learn more of the story, read Judson MacLaury's online article "A Brief History: The U.S. Department of Labor." https://www.dol.gov/general/aboutdol/history/webannalspage

The "Online History Sources" web page has links to historical resources that are available on the DOL website and those of its subagencies. https://www.dol.gov/general/aboutdol/history/hiswebesources
Minimum Wage   The DOL website has a list of DOL web pages that deal with the topic of minimum wage. The Wage and Hour Division administers and enforces the Federal minimum wage law. https://www.dol.gov/general/topic/wages/minimumwage
News   The DOL posts press releases on its website. https://www.dol.gov/newsroom/releases
Open Government   The DOL has an Open Government plan to support making Government more accountable, responsive, and transparent . https://www.dol.gov/open
Plain Language   The DOL is committed to producing documents whose content complies with Federal plain language guidelines. It trains its employees and has adopted an oversight process to ensure the use of plain language in any document that is necessary for obtaining Federal Government benefits or services or filing taxes, provides information on Federal Government benefits or services, or explains to the public how to comply with a requirement that the Federal Government administers or enforces. https://www.dol.gov/general/plainwriting
Popular Topics   The DOL website features a "Topics" page with links for convenient access to popular material. https://www.dol.gov/general/topic
Public Disclosure   The Office of Labor-Management Standards maintains an online disclosure room where online visitors can search for union annual financial reports starting with the year 2000; view and print reports filed by unions, union officers and employees, employers, and labor relations consultants starting with the year 2000; and order copies of reports for the years prior to 2000. Certain collective bargaining agreements are also available. OLMS has public disclosure room: 200 Constitution Avenue NW., Room N–1519, Washington, DC 20210, which offers the same materials. http://www.unionreports.gov | Email: OLMS-Public@dol.gov
Social Media   The DOL has a Facebook account. https://www.facebook.com/departmentoflabor

The DOL tweets announcements and other newsworthy items on Twitter. https://twitter.com/USDOL

The DOL posts videos on its YouTube channel. https://www.youtube.com/user/USDepartmentofLabor
Spanish   The DOL supports the Hispanic workforce. An online list highlights some of the Department's Spanish resources. This list is intended for English-speakers who are looking for information in Spanish to share with the Hispanic community. https://www.dol.gov/general/topic/spanish-speakingtopic
Unemployment Insurance Relief   The DOL has created a web page that is dedicated to providing information on unemployment insurance relief during the COVID–19 pandemic. https://www.dol.gov/coronavirus/unemployment-insurance
Wirtz Labor Library   The library maintains an online card catalog of holdings added to the library after January of 1975. The online catalog also includes collections of historical significance: for example, the Folio and James Taylor Collections. The library is open to the public from 8:15 a.m. to 4:45 p.m. on weekdays, excluding Federal holidays. If the purpose of a visit is to access research material, contact the library in advance: Wirtz Labor Library, 200 Constitution Avenue NW., Frances Perkins Building, Room N–2445, Washington, DC 20210. Phone, 202-693-6600. https://www.dol.gov/agencies/oasam/centers-offices/business-operations-center/library | Email: library@dol.gov

The Sources of Information were updated 9–2020.

Bureau of International Labor Affairs
200 Constitution Avenue NW., Washington, DC 20210
Phone, 202-693-4770. Internet, http://www.dol.gov/ilab

Deputy Under Secretary	(VACANCY)
Associate Deputy Undersecretary	MARK A. MITTELHAUSER
Chief of Staff	GRANT LEBENS
https://www.dol.gov/agencies/ilab/about-us/organization	

The above list of key personnel was updated 10–2020. https://www.dol.gov/general/contact/contact-phonekeypersonnel

The Bureau of International Labor Affairs promotes a fair competitive environment for workers in the United States and other countries worldwide.

The Bureau of International Labor Affairs (ILAB) promotes a fair global playing field for workers and businesses in the United States by enforcing trade commitments; strengthening labor standards; and combating international child labor, forced labor, and human trafficking. ILAB combines trade and labor monitoring and enforcement, policy engagement, technical assistance, and research to carry out the Department of Labor's international responsibilities. https://www.dol.gov/agencies/ilab/our-work

Sources of Information

Archived Records   The "Guide to Federal Records in the National Archives of the United States" indicates that ILAB records have been assigned to record group 174.5. https://www.archives.gov/research/guide-fed-records/groups/174.html#174.5

Career Opportunities   ILAB relies on professionals with backgrounds in development economics and comparative labor law, as well as with firsthand experience designing and implementing international technical assistance programs. https://www.dol.gov/agencies/ilab/about-us/careers-at-ilab

In 2019, ILAB ranked 356th among 420 agency subcomponents in the Partnership for Public Service's Best Places To Work Agency Rankings. https://bestplacestowork.org/rankings/detail/DLBL

Hotline   The Interagency Labor Committee for Monitoring and Enforcement maintains a web-based hotline that allows for the receipt of confidential information from affected and concerned parties, regarding labor issues involving countries of the United States-Mexico-Canada Agreement. https://www.dol.gov/agencies/ilab/our-work/trade/labor-rights-usmca/hotline

News   ILAB-related news is posted on the Department of Labor's website. https://www.dol.gov/newsroom/releases?agency=34

Projects   ILAB grants help prevent and stop abusive labor practices like the use of child labor and forced labor and human trafficking. ILAB-funded projects also promote compliance by trade partners' with the labor requirements of U.S. trade agreements and preference programs. https://www.dol.gov/agencies/ilab/projects

Reports / Publications   ILAB conducts and funds research, whose results it relies on to inform the design and implementation of policy and programs. https://www.dol.gov/agencies/ilab/research-impact-evaluation

Workers' Rights   The International Labor Organization (ILO) has identified "fundamental principles and rights at work." All ILO members are obligated to respect these principles and rights and promote them. https://www.dol.gov/agencies/ilab/our-work/workers-rights

The Sources of Information were updated 9–2020.

Bureau of Labor Statistics

2 Massachusetts Avenue NE., Washington, DC 20212
Phone, 202-691-7800; 800-877-8339 (TDD). Internet, http://www.bls.gov

Commissioner	WILLIAM W. BEACH
Deputy Commissioner	WILLIAM J. WIATROWSKI
https://www.bls.gov/bls/senior_staff/home.htm	

The above list of key personnel was updated 10–2020. https://www.dol.gov/general/contact/contact-phonekeypersonnel

The Bureau of Labor Statistics measures labor market activity, working conditions, price changes, and productivity in the Nation's economy to support decision making in both the public and private sectors.

The Bureau of Labor Statistics (BLS) was established, in the Department of the Interior, as the Bureau of Labor by the act of June 27, 1884 (23 Stat. 60). It was renamed the Bureau of Labor Statistics by the act of March 4, 1913 (37 Stat. 737). The BLS measures labor market activity, working conditions, and price changes in the economy. It also collects, analyzes, and disseminates essential economic information to support public and private decisionmaking.

The Bureau strives to have its data satisfy a number of criteria, including: relevance to current social and economic issues, timeliness in reflecting today's rapidly changing economic conditions, accuracy and consistently high statistical quality, and impartiality in both subject matter and presentation.

Basic data are published in news releases on a monthly, quarterly, and annual basis. Basic data also are published in bulletins, reports, special publications, and periodicals. Regional offices issue additional reports and releases that often contain content of local or regional relevance. https://www.bls.gov/bls/infohome.htm

Sources of Information

A–Z Index The BLS website has an A–Z index to help visitors navigate its content. https://www.bls.gov/bls/topicsaz.htm

Announcements The BLS posts announcements on its website. https://www.bls.gov/bls/announcement.htm

Archived Records The "Guide to Federal Records in the National Archives of the United States" indicates that BLS records have been assigned to record group 257. https://www.archives.gov/research/guide-fed-records/groups/257.html

Blog The official BLS blog is called "Commissioner's Corner." https://blogs.bls.gov/blog

Calculators The "Databases, Tables, and Calculators by Subject" web page has an inflation calculator that allows users to calculate change in the buying power of the dollar over the years. An injury and illness calculator allows users to calculate injury and illness incidence rates for a specific establishment or firm and to compare those rates with the averages for the Nation, for States, and for the sector of industry to which the establishment or firm belongs. https://www.bls.gov/data/#calculators

Career Opportunities To carry out its mission, the BLS relies on professionals who have diverse educational backgrounds, skills, and training. The agency relies heavily on the work of economists, information technology specialists, and mathematical statisticians. https://www.bls.gov/jobs/home.htm

In 2019, the BLS ranked 93d among 420 agency subcomponents in the Partnership for Public Service's Best Places To Work Agency Rankings. https://bestplacestowork.org/rankings/detail/DLLS

Contact Information The "Information and Help" web page has an electronic form for requesting information and asking questions. Postal correspondence should be addressed to the U.S. Bureau of Labor Statistics, Postal Square Building, 2 Massachusetts Avenue NE., Washington, DC 20212–0001. Phone,

202-691-5200; Federal Relay Service, 800-877-8339. https://data.bls.gov/forms/opb.htm?/home.htm

Contact information for the eight BLS regional offices is available online: Atlanta, 404-331-3415; Boston, 617-565-2327; Chicago, 312-353-1880; Dallas, 972-850-4800; Kansas City, 816-285-7000; New York, 646-264-3600; Philadelphia, 215-597-3282; and San Francisco, 415-625-2270. https://www.bls.gov/regions/contacts.htm

Data Sources   Much of the information (e.g., databases and historical news release tables) that the BLS publishes is available from the "Databases, Tables, and Calculators by Subject" web page. https://www.bls.gov/data | Email: blsdata_staff@bls.gov

Some BLS data are available only through the home pages of individual programs—rather than from the "Databases, Tables, and Calculators by Subject" web page. These programs are listed on the "Subject Areas" page. For example, tables of employment projections data are available through the "Employment Projections" page; American time use survey data are available through the "American Time Use Survey" page; and national longitudinal surveys data are available through the "National Longitudinal Surveys" page. https://www.bls.gov/bls/proghome.htm

Certain BLS program data are available in compressed ZIP files. Some of these files are accessible on download.bls.gov. Other ZIP files may be located by starting at the home page of a specific program. https://download.bls.gov/pub/time.series/compressed/tape.format

Economic Summaries   The BLS regional information offices produce economic summaries that are organized by State and posted in Portable Document Format (PDF) for viewing and downloading. Each summary presents a sampling of economic information on benefits, employment, prices, spending, wages, and unemployment for a particular area (e.g., Boston or Sacramento). https://www.bls.gov/regions/economic-summaries.htm

Economy at a Glance   The "Economy at a Glance" web page has at-a-glance economic tables for many metropolitan areas nationwide. https://www.bls.gov/eag

Monthly and quarterly economic data for the Nation are also posted in an at-a-glance format. https://www.bls.gov/eag/eag.us.htm

Educational Resources   The "K–12" web pages include games and quizzes, sections for students and their teachers, a history timeline, and biographies of former Commissioners. https://www.bls.gov/k12

Federal Register   Significant documents and documents that the BLS recently published in the Federal Register are accessible online. https://www.federalregister.gov/agencies/labor-statistics-bureau

Finding Data   The "BLS Data Finder 1.1" web page has a search tool that uses the conjunction "and" as the default search operator. This feature produces display results that contain all of the search terms. To find data that contains a particular combination of terms, the user must separate the terms by inserting the conjunction "or" between them. https://beta.bls.gov/dataQuery/search

Frequently Asked Questions (FAQs)   The BLS posts answers to FAQs. https://www.bls.gov/bls/faqs.htm

Glossary   The BLS has a glossary on its website. https://www.bls.gov/bls/glossary.htm

History   The Bureau has been collecting data and crunching numbers for over 135 years. Over its long history, the BLS started out as the Bureau of Labor and part of the Department of the Interior; became an independent department for nearly 15 years; was incorporated into the former Department of Commerce and Labor; and was transferred to the newly created Department of Labor in 1913. To learn more of the story, visit the "BLS History" section. https://www.bls.gov/bls/history/home.htm

News   The BLS posts economic news releases, some of which are released on a monthly, quarterly, and annual basis. https://www.bls.gov/bls/newsrels.htm#latest-releases

Publications   The BLS publishes bulletins and reports and economic news releases. Its major publications include "Beyond the Numbers," "Career Outlook," "Monthly Labor Review," "Occupational Outlook Handbook," "The Economics Daily", and "Spotlight on Statistics." https://www.bls.gov/opub

Regional Information   Economic data and statistics according to geographic areas are available on the "Regional Information Offices" page. https://www.bls.gov/bls/regnhome.htm

Research Papers   The Office of Survey Methods Research maintains an online research paper database. https://www.bls.gov/osmr/research-papers

Resources   BLS economists, information technology specialists, and mathematical statisticians place a premium on accuracy, currency, innovation, objectivity, relevancy, and transparency. They strive to invest BLS datasets and informational products with these qualities, which help make them useful to a variety of audiences: business leaders, consumers, developers, economists, educators, investors, job seekers, members of the media, policymakers, researchers, and students. https://www.bls.gov/audience | Email: blsdata_staff@bls.gov

Select Datasets and Indices   The "Top Picks" web page allows easy access to the most requested price indices, as well as to the most requested employment, compensation, and productivity data tables. https://data.bls.gov/cgi-bin/surveymost?bls

A "Help and Tutorials" page is dedicated to the "Top Picks" application. https://www.bls.gov/help/hlpmrs.htm

Site Map   The BLS website map allows visitors to look for specific topics or to browse content that aligns with their interests. https://www.bls.gov/bls/sitemap.htm

Social Media   The BLS tweets announcements and other newsworthy items on Twitter. https://twitter.com/BLS_gov

The BLS posts videos on its YouTube channel. https://www.youtube.com/channel/UCijn3WBpHtx4AvSya7NER9Q

Statistical Websites   The "Statistical Sites on the World Wide Web" allows easy access to a collection of Internet sites that are not administered by the BLS. https://www.bls.gov/bls/other.htm

The Sources of Information were updated 9–2020.

Employee Benefits Security Administration

Department of Labor, Washington, DC 20210
Phone, 866-444-3272. Internet, http://www.dol.gov/ebsa

Assistant Secretary	JEANNE K. WILSON, ACTING
Principal Deputy Assistant Secretary	JEANNE K. WILSON
Deputy Assistant Secretaries	
National Office Operations / Chief Operating Officer	TIMOTHY D. HAUSER
Regional Office Operations	AMY J. TURNER
https://www.dol.gov/agencies/ebsa/about-ebsa/about-us/organization-chart#section1	

The above list of key personnel was updated 10–2020. https://www.dol.gov/general/contact/contact-phonekeypersonnel

The Employee Benefits Security Administration assures the security of the retirement, health, and other workplace related benefits of American workers and their families.

The Employee Benefits Security Administration (EBSA) educates and assists the over 154 million participants in and beneficiaries of approximately 710,000 private retirement plans, 2.4 million health plans, and similar numbers of other welfare benefit plans. The EBSA balances proactive enforcement with compliance assistance and supports enrollees and beneficiaries by developing effective regulations; assisting and educating fiduciaries, plan sponsors, service providers, and workers; and enforcing the law. https://www.dol.gov/agencies/ebsa/about-ebsa/about-us/what-we-do

Sources of Information

Ask EBSA   EBSA's workers and families assistance web page provides accessible information on programs and services, answers to frequently asked questions, and assistance where a health or retirement benefit has been denied inappropriately. https://www.dol.gov/agencies/ebsa/about-ebsa/ask-a-question/ask-ebsa

Career Opportunities   In 2019, the EBSA ranked 229th among 420 agency subcomponents in the Partnership for Public Service's Best Places To Work Agency Rankings. https://bestplacestowork.org/rankings/detail/DLPW

Contact Information   The "Regional Offices" web page has contact information for EBSA regional and district offices. https://www.dol.gov/agencies/ebsa/about-ebsa/about-us/regional-offices

Employee Retirement Income Security Act of 1974 (ERISA)   ERISA is a Federal law that sets minimum standards for most voluntarily established retirement and health plans in private industry. This statute provides protection for individuals who are enrolled in these plans. The Department of Labor has a web page that it has dedicated to the ERISA. https://www.dol.gov/general/topic/health-plans/erisa

On September 2, 1974, President Gerald R. Ford approved Public Law 93–406, which is also cited as the "Employee Retirement Income Security Act of 1974." Senators and Representatives of the U.S. Congress wrote this 207-page piece of legislation "to provide for pension reform" (88 Stat. 829). https://www.govinfo.gov/content/pkg/STATUTE-88/pdf/STATUTE-88-Pg829.pdf

En Español   The EBSA posts information in Spanish on its website. https://www.dol.gov/agencies/ebsa/es/about-ebsa/our-activities/informacion-en-espanol

ERISA Advisory Council   The membership of the council is posted on the "ERISA Advisory Council" web page. The council posts issue statements on the same page. https://www.dol.gov/agencies/ebsa/about-ebsa/about-us/erisa-advisory-council

The Sources of Information were updated 9–2020.

ERISA Advisory Council reports are posted online.

Factsheets   The EBSA posts factsheets. https://www.dol.gov/agencies/ebsa/about-ebsa/our-activities/resource-center/fact-sheets

Federal Register   Significant documents and documents that the EBSA recently published in the Federal Register are accessible online. https://www.federalregister.gov/agencies/employee-benefits-security-administration

Forms   The EBSA posts forms and filing instructions online. https://www.dol.gov/agencies/ebsa/employers-and-advisers/plan-administration-and-compliance/reporting-and-filing/forms

Frequently Asked Questions (FAQs)   The EBSA posts answers to frequently asked questions. https://www.dol.gov/agencies/ebsa/about-ebsa/our-activities/resource-center/faqs

History   The EBSA administers and enforces the fiduciary, reporting, and disclosure provisions of the first title of the Employee Retirement Income Security Act of 1974 (ERISA). The histories of the ERISA and EBSA are tightly intertwined. https://www.dol.gov/agencies/ebsa/about-ebsa/about-us/history-of-ebsa-and-erisa

Information for Researchers   EBSA researchers expand the knowledge of employee benefits and their role in meeting the Nation's economic security needs. https://www.dol.gov/agencies/ebsa/researchers

Key Topics   The EBSA website features a page with links to key topics: health and other employee benefits, reporting and filing, and retirement. https://www.dol.gov/agencies/ebsa/key-topics

News   The EBSA posts news items on the Department of Labor's website. https://www.dol.gov/newsroom/releases?agency=37&state=All&topic=All&year=all

Publications   The EBSA distributes booklets, factsheets, and pamphlets on employer responsibilities and employee rights under the Employee Retirement Income Security Act. A list of publications is available online or from the Office of Outreach, Education, and Assistance. Phone, 866-444-3272. http://www.dol.gov/agencies/ebsa/about-ebsa/our-activities/resource-center/publications

Employment and Training Administration

Department of Labor, Washington, DC 20520
Phone, 877-872-5627. Internet, http://www.doleta.gov

Assistant Secretary	JOHN P. PALLASCH
Deputy Assistant Secretaries	MATTHEW HUNTER
	NANCY ROONEY
	AMY SIMON

https://www.dol.gov/agencies/eta/about

The above list of key personnel was updated 10–2020. https://www.dol.gov/general/contact/contact-phonekeypersonnel

The Employment and Training Administration helps the U.S. labor market function more efficiently by providing job training, employment, labor market information, and income maintenance services.

Activities

In addition to training, employment, information, and services, which are provided primarily through State and local workforce development systems, the Employment and Training Administration (ETA) also administers programs to enhance employment opportunities and promote business prosperity. https://www.dol.gov/agencies/eta/program-areas

Apprenticeships   The Office of Apprenticeship oversees the National Apprenticeship System, sets standards for apprenticeship, and assists States, industry, and labor in developing apprenticeship programs that meet required standards, while promoting equal opportunity and safeguarding the welfare of apprentices. https://www.dol.gov/agencies/eta/apprenticeship

For more information, call 202-693-2796.

Contracts Management   The Office of Contracts Management advises the Assistant Secretary of the ETA, in a manner that is consistent with Federal statutes and regulations, on mission-critical procurement matters. The Office applies procurement services to ETA organizational components to address business challenges with best practices and cost-effective solutions. http://www.doleta.gov/contracts

For further information, call 202-693-3110.

Financial Administration   The Office of Financial Administration (OFA) manages all ETA fiscal resources for programs and activities for which funds are appropriated through the Office's functions of accounting, budget, and financial system oversight. The Office provides budgetary, accounting, audit, and internal control management. It coordinates with the departmental budget center and the Office of the Chief Financial Officer to provide financial management that supports carrying out the ETA's mission. https://www.dol.gov/agencies/eta/budget

For further information, call 202-693-3162.

Foreign Labor Certification   The Office of Foreign Labor Certification (OFLC) carries out the delegated responsibility of the Secretary of Labor under the Immigration and Nationality Act, as amended, concerning the admission of foreign workers into the United States for employment. In carrying out this responsibility, the Office administers temporary nonimmigrant and permanent labor certification programs through the ETA's national processing centers that are located in Chicago and Atlanta.

The OFLC also administers nationally the issuance of employer-requested prevailing wage determinations through the ETA's National Prevailing Wage and Helpdesk Center, which is located in Washington, DC. Prevailing wage determinations are issued for use in all nonagricultural temporary labor certification programs and the permanent labor certification program. https://www.dol.gov/agencies/eta/foreign-labor

For more information, call 202-693-3010.

Grants Management The Office of Grants Management provides grants management expertise to ETA offices and stakeholders throughout the life cycle of a grant. The Office delivers centralized grants administration and policy expertise to support pre-award, award, period of performance, audit resolution, and closeout of ETA Federal assistance awards. https://www.dol.gov/agencies/eta/grants

For further information, call 202-693-2800.

Job Training Job Corps is the largest nationwide residential career training program in the Nation and has been operating for more than half a century. The program helps eligible young people who are 16–24 years old complete their high school education, trains them for meaningful careers, and assists them with obtaining employment. https://www.dol.gov/agencies/eta/jobcorps

For further information, call 202-693-3000.

Policy Development and Research The Office of Policy Development and Research (OPDR) supports ETA policies and investments to improve the public workforce system by analyzing, formulating, and recommending legislative changes and options for policy initiatives. The Office coordinates the ETA's legislative and regulatory activities and their interactions with international organizations and foreign countries. The OPDR maintains the ETA's portion of the Department of Labor's regulatory agenda and disseminates advisories and publications. The Office provides the ETA with strategic approaches to improve performance and outcomes through research, demonstrations, and evaluation of its major programs. The Office manages the Workforce Investment Act performance accountability reporting system; oversees the maintenance of wage record exchange systems for State and other grantees; coordinates the development of the ETA's operating plan; and disseminates workforce program performance results. The OPDR also provides policy guidance on and technical assistance for the Worker Adjustment and Retraining Notification Act. https://www.dol.gov/agencies/eta/policy

For further information, call 202-693-3700.

Trade Adjustment Assistance The Office of Trade Adjustment Assistance (TAA) administers a workers assistance program for those who have lost or may lose their jobs because of foreign trade. The TAA program provides reemployment services and allowances for eligible individuals. https://www.dol.gov/agencies/eta/tradeact

For further information, call 202-693-3560.

Unemployment Compensation The Office of Unemployment Insurance provides national leadership, oversight, policy guidance, and technical assistance to the Federal-State unemployment compensation system. The Office also interprets Federal legislative requirements. https://oui.doleta.gov/unemploy/aboutoui.asp

For more information, call 202-693-3029.

Workforce Investment The Office of Workforce Investment implements an integrated national workforce investment system that supports economic growth and provides workers with information, advice, job search assistance, supportive services, and training for employment. The Office also helps employers hire skilled workers. https://www.dol.gov/agencies/eta/workforce-investment

For further information, call 202-693-3980.

Sources of Information

Archived Records The "Guide to Federal Records in the National Archives of the United States" indicates that ETA records have been assigned to record group 369. https://www.archives.gov/research/guide-fed-records/groups/369.html

Advisories The ETA uses its advisory system to disseminate its interpretations of Federal laws; procedural, administrative, management, and program direction; and other information to the States, direct grant recipients, and other interested parties. https://wdr.doleta.gov/directives

Career Opportunities In 2019, the ETA ranked 369th among 420 agency subcomponents in the Partnership for Public Service's Best Places To Work Agency Rankings. https://bestplacestowork.org/rankings/detail/DLET

Contact Information ETA contact information is available on its website. https://www.dol.gov/agencies/eta/contact | Email: eta.webportal@dol.gov

Contact information for the ETA's six regional offices is available online. https://www.dol.gov/agencies/eta/regions

Data The Division of Research and Evaluation posts datasets for public use on the ETA's website. https://www.dol.gov/agencies/eta/research/public-use-datasets

The Office of Unemployment Insurance posts unemployment insurance data as part of the ETA's contribution to the Department of Labor's collection and publication of data. https://oui.doleta.gov/unemploy/DataDashboard.asp

The Office of Foreign Labor Certification posts employment-based immigration data on the ETA's website. Three main categories are used to organize the data: selected statistics that provide cumulative quarterly data by major immigration program; cumulative quarterly and fiscal year releases of program disclosure data; and historical fiscal year annual program and performance report information. https://www.dol.gov/agencies/eta/foreign-labor/performance

The Office of Trade Adjustment Assistance posts charts, statistics, and other information on the ETA's website. Three main categories are used to organize the data: petitions and determinations, participants, and financial. https://www.dol.gov/agencies/eta/tradeact/data

Federal Register Significant documents and documents that the ETA recently published in the Federal Register are accessible online. https://www.federalregister.gov/agencies/employment-and-training-administration

Job Corps An online directory has contact information for the Office of Job Corps, including the national Job Corps hotline and phone numbers and email addresses for Office of the Administrator staff. It also allows convenient access to information for contacting Job Corps regional offices. https://www.dol.gov/agencies/eta/jobcorps/contact

Job Seekers The ETA posts resources for job seekers on its website. https://www.dol.gov/agencies/eta/job-seekers

Library A large repository of information is available online from the "ETA Library"

web page. https://www.dol.gov/agencies/eta/reports

National Agricultural Workers Survey This employment-based and random-sample survey of U.S. crop workers brings together demographic, employment, and health data that are collected during face-to-face interviews. https://www.dol.gov/agencies/eta/national-agricultural-workers-survey

News The ETA posts news releases on the Department of Labor's website. https://www.dol.gov/newsroom/releases?agency=39&state=All&topic=All&year=all

Rapid Response Services Rapid Response is designed to respond to layoffs and plant closings by quickly coordinating services and providing immediate aid to companies and their affected workers. Rapid Response teams work with employers and employee representatives to quickly maximize public and private resources to minimize disruptions associated with job loss. https://www.dol.gov/agencies/eta/layoffs

Reducing Recidivism The Reentry and Employment Opportunities—Adult Program strengthens urban communities through an employment-centered program of mentoring, job training, and other comprehensive transitional services. Helping former inmates find employment when they return to their communities reduces recidivism. https://www.dol.gov/agencies/eta/reentry

Research The research publication database provides access to a collection of research and evaluation reports. The ETA commissioned the research and evaluation reports to help guide the workforce investment system in administering effective programs that enhance employment opportunity and business. https://wdr.doleta.gov/research/eta_default.cfm

Veterans The ETA website has a section dedicated to veterans. It offers resources for veteran who are job seekers and for providers of employment and training programs. https://www.dol.gov/agencies/eta/jobs-for-veterans-act

Youth Services A section of the ETA's website is dedicated to youth programs and services. https://www.dol.gov/agencies/eta/youth

The Sources of Information were updated 9–2020.

Mine Safety and Health Administration

201 12th Street South, Suite 400, Arlington, Virginia 22202
Phone, 202-693-9400. Internet, http://www.msha.gov

Assistant Secretary	DAVID G. ZATEZALO
Deputy Assistant Secretaries	
Operations	PATRICIA W. SILVEY
Policy	WAYNE D. PALMER
https://www.msha.gov/about/leadership	

The above list of key personnel was updated 10–2020. https://www.dol.gov/general/contact/contact-phonekeypersonnel

The Mine Safety and Health Administration works to prevent mine-related deaths, illnesses, and injuries and promotes safe and healthy work environments.

Establishment and Organization

On November 9, 1977, President James E. Carter approved Public Law 95–164, which is also cited as the Federal Mine Safety and Health Amendments Act of 1977. This statute amended the Federal Coal Mine Health and Safety Act of 1969 (PL 91–173), including its short title, which was changed to the Federal Mine Safety and Health Act of 1977 (91 Stat. 1290). https://www.govinfo.gov/content/pkg/STATUTE-91/pdf/STATUTE-91-Pg1290.pdf

The Federal Mine Safety and Health Act of 1977 created the Mine Safety and Health Administration (MSHA) in 1978 by transferring the Federal mine safety program and its functions from the Department of the Interior to the Department of Labor. https://www.msha.gov/about/history

The MSHA is organized into program areas. https://www.msha.gov/about/program-areas

The MSHA posts its organizational chart online in Portable Document Format (PDF) for viewing and downloading. https://www.msha.gov/sites/default/files/Organizational_Charts/OAS-Org-Chart.pdf

Statutory and Regulatory Authorities

"Chapter 22—Mine Safety and Health" has been assigned to 30 U.S.C. https://uscode.house.gov/view.xhtml?path=/prelim@title30/chapter22&edition=prelim

Rules and regulations that are associated with the MSHA are assigned to the first chapter of 30 CFR. The chapter includes parts 1–199. https://www.ecfr.gov/cgi-bin/text-idx?SID=2f9b3d9dbb071240550f37 a930d0135d&mc=true&tpl=/ecfrbrowse/Title30/30cfrv1_02.tpl#0

Activities

The MSHA helps protect the Nation's miners by promoting healthy and safe work environments for them. It works toward the elimination of fatal mining accidents, the reduction of the frequency and severity of accidents, and the minimization of health hazards through enforcement of mandatory safety and health standards in the mining industry. It also provides technical, educational, and other assistance, including the testing and approval of equipment for use in the industry, to mine operators. The MSHA cooperates with industry, labor, and other Federal and State agencies to improve safety and health conditions for miners. https://www.msha.gov/about

Sources of Information

Archived Records The "Guide to Federal Records in the National Archives of the United States" indicates that MSHA records have been assigned to record group 433. That record group does not have a description that is associated with it. https://www.archives.gov/research/guide-fed-records/groups/000.html

Career Opportunities Information on employment opportunities is available online. http://www.msha.gov/about/careers

In 2019, the MSHA ranked 260th among 420 agency subcomponents in the Partnership for Public Service's Best

Places To Work Agency Rankings. https://bestplacestowork.org/rankings/detail/DLMS

Contact Information   The "Contact MSHA" web page has emergency and general contact information. https://www.msha.gov/about/contact-msha | Email: AskMSHA@dol.gov

Data Sources / Calculators   The "Data Sources and Calculators" web page allows convenient access to a range of mine safety and health data (e.g., information on accidents, air sampling, employment, injuries, illnesses, inspections, production totals, and violations). Compliance calculator tools can be used to illuminate the history of key health and safety violations of a mine. https://www.msha.gov/data-reports/data-sources-calculators

Educational Resources   The MSHA posts training and educational resources on its website. https://www.msha.gov/training-education

The National Mine Health and Safety Academy conducts education and training programs in health and safety and related subjects for Federal mine inspectors and other government mining and industry personnel. https://arlweb.msha.gov/PROGRAMS/MineAcademy/Academy.asp

Federal Register   Significant documents and documents that the MSHA recently published in the Federal Register are accessible online. https://www.federalregister.gov/agencies/mine-safety-and-health-administration

Frequently Asked Questions (FAQs)   The MSHA posts answers to FAQs on rulemaking. https://www.msha.gov/rulemaking-frequently-asked-questions

Historical Statutes / Legislative History   The "Laws" web page has key historical statutes and their legislative history. https://www.msha.gov/regulations/laws

Library   The MSHA digital library's holdings include accident reports, images, photographs, and research material. https://arlweb.msha.gov/TRAINING/LIBRARY/mshaPortal/index.html

Media Gallery   Online visitors may browse or search historical photographs and videos, including mine training and health training videos. https://www.msha.gov/news-media/media-gallery

Mine Disasters   Five or more fatalities define a mining disaster. The National Institute for Occupational Safety and Health posts data tables that summarize all U.S. mining disasters from 1839 to the present. Starting with the year 1900, graphs are also available. https://www.cdc.gov/niosh/mining/statistics/minedisasters.html

News / Media   The MSHA posts alerts and hazards, announcements, congressional testimonies, events, news releases, photographs and videos, and speeches on its website. https://www.msha.gov/news-media

Reports   Current and historical preliminary accident reports, fatalgrams, and fatal investigation reports for metal, nonmetal, and coal mines are accessible on the MSHA website. Quarterly and annual summaries of mining fatalities along with associated best practices and preventative recommendations are also accessible. https://www.msha.gov/data-reports/fatality-reports

Part 50 of Title 30 of the Code of Federal Regulations (30 CFR 50) requires mine operators to notify the MSHA when accidents occur and to investigate those accidents, while restricting disturbance of accident-related areas. Part 50 also requires mine operators to file reports on accidents, occupational injuries, and occupational illnesses, as well as employment and coal production data. https://www.msha.gov/data-reports/reports

Resources / Tools   The MSHA posts mine emergency operations information, miners' resources, and technical resources on its "Resources and Tools" web page. https://www.msha.gov/support-resources/resources-tools

Spanish   In the top right corner of the MSHA's home page are an Español option and an Inglés option. Using these options, visitors to the website can toggle between content in either language. https://www.msha.gov

State Mining Agencies   A list of links to the websites of State mining agencies is available on the MSHA website. https://www.msha.gov/support-resources/external-mining-resources/state-mining-agencies

Statistics   The "Statistics" web page allows easy access to numbers on mine employment and coal production; the most frequently cited standards (i.e., regulatory violations) by year, mine type, and industry group; and graphs, maps, and tables that The National Institute for Occupational Safety and Health has created to summarize a range of information on employees, fatalities, injuries, and mines. https://www.msha.gov/data-reports/statistics

The Sources of Information were updated 9–2020.

Targeted Inspections   The MSHA conducts targeted inspections each month at mines that merit increased attention and enforcement due to their poor compliance history or particular compliance concerns. Each month's inspection results are posted online. https://www.msha.gov/monthly-targeted-inspection-results

---

Coronavirus Disease 2019 (COVID–19): For employee and employer Coronavirus pandemic information, which includes links to interim guidance and other resources for preventing exposure to and infection with the virus, go to https://www.osha.gov/SLTC/covid-19.

Occupational Safety and Health Administration

Department of Labor, Washington, DC 20210
Phone, 800-321-6742. Internet, http://www.osha.gov

Assistant Secretary	JAMES FREDERICK, ACTING
Deputy Assistant Secretaries	AMANDA EDENS
	JAMES FREDERICK
Chief of Staff	LEAH FORD
https://www.osha.gov/aboutosha	

The above list of key personnel was updated 5–2021. https://www.dol.gov/general/contact/contact-phonekeypersonnel

Establishment and Organization
The Occupational Safety and Health Administration (OSHA) was created pursuant to the Occupational Safety and Health Act of 1970 (29 U.S.C. 651 et seq.). https://www.govinfo.gov/content/pkg/STATUTE-84/pdf/STATUTE-84-Pg1590.pdf

OSHA posts an organizational chart online in Portable Document Format (PDF) for viewing and downloading. https://www.osha.gov/html/OSHAorgchart.pdf

Activities
OSHA assures safe and healthful working conditions for men and women by promulgating common sense, protective health, and safety standards; enforcing workplace safety and health rules; providing training, outreach, education, and assistance to workers and employers in their efforts to control workplace hazards; prevent work-related injuries, illnesses, and fatalities; and

partnering with States that run their own OSHA-approved programs. https://www.osha.gov/aboutosha

Sources of Information

A–Z Index   An alphabetized topical index is available on the OSHA website to help visitors find information. https://www.osha.gov/a-z

Archived Records   The "Guide to Federal Records in the National Archives of the United States" indicates that OSHA records have been assigned to record group 100. https://www.archives.gov/research/guide-fed-records/groups/100.html

Career Opportunities   In 2019, OSHA ranked 196th among 420 agency subcomponents in the Partnership for Public Service's Best Places To Work Agency Rankings. https://bestplacestowork.org/rankings/detail/DLSH

Contact Information   OSHA posts contact information on its "Contact Us" web page. https://www.osha.gov/contactus

Coronavirus Disease 2019 (COVID–19)   The OSHA has posted a "COVID–19" web page containing employee and employer Coronavirus pandemic information that includes links to interim guidance and other resources for reducing exposure and preventing infection. https://www.osha.gov/SLTC/covid-19

Federal Register   Significant documents and documents that OSHA recently published in the Federal Register are accessible online. https://www.federalregister.gov/agencies/occupational-safety-and-health-administration

File a Complaint   Information on how to file a safety and health complaint and an electronic complaint form are available on the OSHA website. Phone, 800-321-6742. https://www.osha.gov/workers/file_complaint.html

Freedom of Information Act (FOIA)   The OSHA is required to disclose records that are properly requested in writing by any person. An agency may withhold information pursuant to one or more of nine exemptions and three exclusions contained in the FOIA. The act applies only to Federal agencies and does not create a right of access to records held by Congress, the courts, State or local government agencies, and private entities. https://www.osha.gov/foia

Frequently Asked Questions (FAQs)   The OSHA posts answers to FAQs online. https://www.osha.gov/faq

Injury and Illness Data   The OSHA website has a searchable, establishment-specific database for establishments that provided OSHA with valid data from 1996 through 2011. https://www.osha.gov/pls/odi/establishment_search.html

Workplace injury, illness, and fatality statistics are available on the OSHA website. https://www.osha.gov/oshstats/work.html

Make a Report   Employers must notify OSHA when an employee is killed on the job or suffers a work-related amputation, hospitalization, or loss of an eye. A fatality must be reported within 8 hours; an amputation, in-patient hospitalization, or eye loss must be reported within 24 hours.

An employer should be prepared to supply the name of the business, the names of employees who were affected, the location and time of the incident, a brief description of the incident, and a contact person and phone number. https://www.osha.gov/report.html

Map   A "Heat Fatalities Map" shows the locations of outdoor worker heat-related deaths between 2008 and 2014. https://www.osha.gov/SLTC/heatillness/map.html

A nationwide map of enforcement cases with initial penalties above $40,000 is available online. https://www.osha.gov/enforcement/toppenalties/bystate

News   The OSHA newsroom has a collection of quick links for relevant news sources. https://www.osha.gov/news

The "What's New" web page features news items that are organized chronologically. https://www.osha.gov/whatsnew.html

Newsletter   OSHA's online newsletter has the latest news on compliance assistance, enforcement actions, outreach activities, rulemaking, and training and educational resources. https://www.osha.gov/quicktakes

Offices   A complete listing of OSHA regional and area offices is available online. http://www.osha.gov/html/RAmap.html

OSHA Card   Facts on obtaining an OSHA card are available online. https://www.osha.gov/dte/oshacardfacts.html

Publications   OSHA publications are accessible online. https://www.osha.gov/pls/publications/publication.html

Social Media   OSHA tweets announcements and other newsworthy items on Twitter. https://twitter.com/OSHA_DOL

Spanish   In the top right corner of the OSHA's home page are an Español option and an Inglés option. Using these options, visitors to the website can toggle between content in Spanish or English. https://www.osha.gov

Training / Education   Stand-alone, interactive, web-based training tools—eTools and the eMatrix—are available on the OSHA website. These tools are highly illustrated and utilize graphical menus. https://www.osha.gov/dts/osta/oshasoft/index.html

Prevention video training tools (v-tools) on construction hazards are available on the OSHA website. These videos show how workers can be injured suddenly or even killed on the job. The videos assist those who are in the construction industry with identifying, reducing, and eliminating

hazards. The videos are presented in clear, accessible vocabulary; show common construction worksite activities; and most are 2–4 minutes long. https://www.osha.gov/dts/vtools/construction.html

The Sources of Information were updated 10–2020.

Veterans' Employment and Training Service

Department of Labor, Washington, DC 20210
Phone, 866-487-2365. Internet, http://www.dol.gov/vets

Assistant Secretary	JOHN LOWRY III
Deputy Assistant Secretaries	
Operations and Management	J. SAM SHELLENBERGER
Policy	(VACANCY)
Chief of Staff	JONATHAN VANDERPLAS

https://www.dol.gov/agencies/vets/about

The above list of key personnel was updated 10–2020. https://www.dol.gov/general/contact/contact-phonekeypersonnel

The Veterans' Employment and Training Service helps America's veterans, servicemembers, and their spouses who are eligible prepare for careers; provides them with employment resources and expertise; protects their employment rights; and promotes their employment opportunities.

On March 24, 1983, former Secretary of Labor Raymond J. Donovan signed Order 4–83, which redesignated the Office of the Assistant Secretary of Labor for Veterans Employment as the Veterans' Employment and Training Service. The Secretary's order of redesignation was published in the Federal Register on April 1, 1983 (48 FR 14092). https://www.govinfo.gov/content/pkg/FR-1983-04-01/pdf/FR-1983-04-01.pdf

The Veterans' Employment and Training Service (VETS) administers employment and training programs and compliance activities that help veterans and servicemembers succeed in their civilian careers. VETS also administers the jobs for veterans State grant program, which gives grants to States to fund personnel who are dedicated to serving the employment needs of veterans. VETS field staff works closely with and gives technical assistance to State employment workforce agencies to ensure that veterans receive priority of service and gain meaningful employment. VETS has two competitive grants programs: the homeless veterans

reintegration program and the incarcerated veterans transition program. VETS also helps servicemembers who are separating from the Armed Forces prepare for the civilian labor market.

VETS has three compliance programs: the Federal contractor program, veterans' preference in Federal hiring, and the Uniformed Services Employment and Reemployment Rights Act of 1994 (USERRA). With respect to the Federal contractor program, VETS promulgates regulations and oversees the program by helping contractors comply with their affirmative action and reporting obligations. Although the Office of Personnel Management administers and interprets statutes and regulations that govern veterans' preference in Federal hiring, VETS investigates allegations that veterans' preference rights have been violated. https://www.dol.gov/agencies/vets/about

In addition, VETS preserves servicemembers' employment and reemployment rights through its administration and enforcement of USERRA. VETS conducts investigations of alleged violations, and it carries out a USERRA outreach program. https://www.govinfo.gov/content/pkg/STATUTE-108/pdf/STATUTE-108-Pg3149.pdf

Sources of Information

Career Opportunities In 2019, the VETS ranked 227th among 420 agency subcomponents in the Partnership for Public Service's Best Places To Work Agency Rankings. https://bestplacestowork.org/rankings/detail/DLVE
Contact Information A national office directory is available online. https://www.dol.gov/agencies/vets/about/nationaloffice

A regional and State directory is available online. https://www.dol.gov/vets/aboutvets/regionaloffices/map.htm
Find Employment The "Find a Job" web page has resources to help veterans find employment. https://www.dol.gov/agencies/vets/veterans/findajob
Federal Register Significant documents and documents that VETS recently published in the Federal Register are accessible online. https://www.federalregister.gov/agencies/veterans-employment-and-training-service
Freedom of Information Act (FOIA) Any person has the right to request access to Federal agency records or information.

The Sources of Information were updated 10–2020.

VETS is required to disclose records that are properly requested in writing by any person. An agency may withhold information pursuant to nine exemptions and three exclusions contained in the FOIA. The act applies only to Federal agencies and does not create a right of access to records held by Congress, the courts, or by State or local government agencies. A FOIA request should be submitted to the appropriate national or regional VETS office by email, fax, or mail. The subject line, cover page, or envelope should be clearly labeled "Freedom of Information Act Request." The content of the request should indicate that it is a FOIA request, and it should contain as much information as possible describing the record or records being sought. https://www.dol.gov/agencies/vets/about/foia
Frequently Asked Questions (FAQs) VETS posts answers to FAQs on its website. https://www.dol.gov/vets/resources/faqs.htm

The Department of Labor posts answers to FAQs regarding veterans on its website. https://webapps.dol.gov/dolfaq/dolfaqbytopic.asp?topicID=12&topictitle=Veterans
Grants Information on grants and other opportunities is available online. http://www.dol.gov/vets/resources/grants.htm
News / Media VETS posts news releases and public service announcements on its website. https://www.dol.gov/vets/news.htm

---

Wage and Hour Division

Department of Labor, Washington, DC 20210
Phone, 866-487-9243. Internet, http://www.dol.gov/whd

Administrator	Cheryl M. Stanton
Deputy Administrator	Susan Boone
Chief of Staff	Michael Stojsavljevich

https://www.dol.gov/agencies/whd/about/organizational-chart#Keypersonnel

---

The above list of key personnel was updated 10–2020. https://www.dol.gov/general/contact/contact-phonekeypersonnel

The Wage and Hour Division protects and enhances the welfare of the Nation's workers by promoting and achieving compliance with labor standards.

Establishment and Organization

On June 25, 1938, President Franklin D. Roosevelt approved Public Law 75–718, which also is cited as the Fair Labor Standards Act of 1938. Among its findings, the U.S. Congress noted that the existence "in industries engaged in commerce or in the production of goods for commerce, of labor conditions detrimental to the maintenance of the minimum standard of living necessary for health, efficiency, and general well-being of workers" causes these adverse labor conditions to spread and perpetuate, burdens commerce and the free flow of goods, undermines fair competition, leads to disputes that burden and obstruct commerce and the free flow of goods, and interferes with the commercial marketing of goods (52 Stat. 1060). https://www.loc.gov/law/help/statutes-at-large/75th-congress/session-3/c75s3ch676.pdf

The statute also "created in the Department of Labor a Wage and Hour Division [WHD] which shall be under the direction of an Administrator" who "shall be appointed by the President, by and with the advice and consent of the Senate" (52 Stat. 1061).

Secretary Frances Perkins's order of October 15, 1942, established the Wage and Hour and Public Contracts Divisions (WHPCD) by consolidating the WHD and the Public Contracts Division to administer Federal minimum wage, overtime pay, and child labor laws. https://www.archives.gov/research/guide-fed-records/groups/155.html

In 1967, the Wage and Labor Standards Administration (WLSA) was established in the Department of Labor to direct and coordinate Federal wage and labor standards programs. On May 5, 1969, by secretarial order, the WHPCD was assigned to the WLSA.

On November 8, 2009, the Employments Standards Administration was dissolved into its four constituent components: The WHD, the Office of Federal Contract Compliance Programs, the Office of Workers' Compensation Programs, and the Office of Labor Management Standards. Authorities were delegated and responsibilities were assigned to the Administrator of the WHD (74 FR 58836). https://www.govinfo.gov/content/pkg/FR-2009-11-13/pdf/FR-2009-11-13.pdf

The WHD posts an organizational chart on its website. https://www.dol.gov/agencies/whd/about/organizational-chart

Statutory and Regulatory Authorities

"Chapter 8—Fair Labor Standards" has been assigned to 29 U.S.C. Title 29 is dedicated to codified statutory material that affects labor. https://uscode.house.gov/view.xhtml?path=/prelim@title29/chapter8&edition=prelim

"Subtitle B—Regulations Relating to Labor" has been assigned to 29 CFR. The fifth chapter (sections 500–899) of that subtitle is dedicated to the WHD. https://www.ecfr.gov/cgi-bin/text-idx?SID=efbbc65896d0d414403dfadb6f5d8d83&mc=true&tpl=/ecfrbrowse/Title29/29cfrv3_02.tpl#0

Activities

The WHD enforces Federal minimum wage, overtime pay, recordkeeping, and child labor law requirements of the Fair Labor Standards Act. The WHD also enforces the Migrant and Seasonal Agricultural Worker Protection Act, the Employee Polygraph Protection Act, the Family and Medical Leave Act, wage garnishment provisions of the Consumer Credit Protection Act, and a number of employment standards and worker protections as provided in several immigration-related statutes. Additionally, the WHD administers and enforces the prevailing wage requirements of the Davis Bacon Act and the Service Contract Act and other statutes applicable to Federal contracts for construction and for the provision of goods and services. https://www.dol.gov/agencies/whd/about

Sources of Information

Archived Records   The "Guide to Federal Records in the National Archives of the United States" indicates that WHD records have been assigned to record group 155. https://www.archives.gov/research/guide-fed-records/groups/155.html

Career Opportunities   In 2019, the WHD ranked 170th among 420 agency subcomponents in the Partnership for Public

Service's Best Places To Work Agency Rankings. https://bestplacestowork.org/rankings/detail/DLWH

Contact Information The WHD posts contact information on its "Contact Us" web page. https://www.dol.gov/agencies/whd/contact

Evaluations / Studies The WHD posts evaluations and studies on its website in Portable Document Format (PDF). https://www.dol.gov/whd/resources/evaluations.htm

Federal Register Significant documents and documents that the WHD recently published in the Federal Register are accessible online. https://www.federalregister.gov/agencies/wage-and-hour-division

File a Complaint Instructions for filing a complaint are available online. Phone, 866-487-9243. https://www.dol.gov/agencies/whd/contact/complaints

Freedom of Information Act (FOIA) The WHD is required to disclose records that are properly requested in writing by any person. The WHD may withhold information pursuant to nine exemptions and three exclusions contained in the FOIA. The WHD does not require a special FOIA request form. A request must reasonably describe the desired record. Providing its name or title is not mandatory, but the more specific the record description, the more likely that WHD staff can locate it. A FOIA request must be made in writing and may be submitted by courier service, email, fax, or postal mail. https://www.dol.gov/whd/foia/index.htm

History The WHD has posted a historical summary on its website. https://www.dol.gov/agencies/whd/about/history

News The WHD posts national and State news releases. https://www.dol.gov/newsroom/releases/whd

Offices Contact information for WHD area, district, and regional offices is available on the "WHD Local Offices" web page. https://www.dol.gov/whd/america2.htm

Resources Resources for workers are available on the WHD website. https://www.dol.gov/whd/workers.htm

Resources for employers are available on the WHD website. https://www.dol.gov/whd/foremployers.htm

Resources for State and local governments are available on the WHD website. https://www.dol.gov/whd/forstatelocalgovernments.htm

The Sources of Information were updated 10–2020.

Women's Bureau

Department of Labor, Washington, DC 20210
Phone, 202-693-6710. Internet, http://www.dol.gov/wb

Director	Laurie Todd-Smith
Chief of Staff	Jillian Rogers
Deputy Director of Operations	Joan Harrigan-Farrelly

https://www.dol.gov/agencies/wb/about

The above list of key personnel was updated 10–2020. https://www.dol.gov/general/contact/contact-phonekeypersonnel

The Women's Bureau develops policies and standards and conducts inquiries to safeguard the interests of working women, to advocate for their equality and the economic security of their families, and to promote quality work environments.

Establishment and Organization

On June 5, 1920, President Woodrow Wilson signed Public Law 66–259, which established "a bureau to be known as the Women's Bureau" in the Department of Labor. The Director of the Women's Bureau (WB) may not be a man, but is required by law to be a woman whom the President appoints by the advice and with the consent of the Senate. The U.S. Congress assigned the following duty to the WB: "to formulate standards and policies which shall promote the welfare of wage-earning women, improve their working conditions, increase their efficiency, and advance their opportunities for profitable employment." The WB has "authority to investigate and report" to the Department of Labor ""upon all matters pertaining to the welfare of women in industry." http://www.loc.gov/law/help/statutes-at-large/66th-congress/session-2/c66s2ch248.pdf

Activities

The Bureau identifies, researches, and analyzes topics that are relevant for working women; pioneers policies and programs to address those topics; and enhances public education and outreach efforts to raise awareness on key issues and developments affecting women in the workforce. https://www.dol.gov/wb/overview.htm

Sources of Information

Archived Records   The "Guide to Federal Records in the National Archives of the United States" indicates that WB records have been assigned to record group 086. https://www.archives.gov/research/guide-fed-records/groups/086.html

Centennial Anniversary   One of the Department of Labor's longest-serving agencies, the WB celebrates its centennial anniversary throughout the year 2020. https://www.dol.gov/newsroom/releases/wb/wb20200128

Contact Information   The WB has a toll-free phone number: 800-827-5335. Phone, 202-693-6710. Fax, 202-693-6725 https://www.dol.gov/agencies/wb/contact | Email: womens.bureau@dol.gov

Data / Statistics   Current and historical statistics on a broad range of topics and subpopulations of women in the labor force are available online. http://www.dol.gov/wb/stats/stats_data.htm

Federal Register   Significant documents and documents that the WB recently published in the Federal Register are listed under the Department of Labor. https://www.federalregister.gov/agencies/labor-department

Freedom of Information Act (FOIA)   The FOIA gives a right to access Federal Government records to any person. The FOIA is designed to make Government actions and operations more transparent. It applies to existing records and does not require an agency to create new records for compliance. The FOIA also does not require an agency to collect information that it does not have or to do research or analyze data to fulfill a request. Certain records, or parts of them, may be exempt from disclosure by the Act if one of nine exemptions shields their content. https://www.dol.gov/agencies/wb/foia

Grants   The Women in Apprenticeship and Nontraditional Occupations grant expands pathways for women to enter all industries and assume leadership roles in them. https://www.dol.gov/agencies/wb/grants/wanto-grants

Re-Employment, Support, and Training for the Opioid Related Epidemic grants help women who have been affected by the opioid crisis to rejoin the workforce. https://www.dol.gov/agencies/wb/grants/restore

History   Before the outbreak of the First World War, 75% of all women who worked in manufacturing made apparel or its materials, food, or tobacco products. The war changed the U.S. economy and how women participated in it: their numbers in the industrial workforce increased and the range of occupations open to them expanded, even though women remained concentrated in clerical occupations, domestic and personal service, and factory work. The Second World War, accelerated technological advancements, and changes in social attitude have created a different reality today. To learn more about the ever changing employment situation of women in the U.S. workforce and the role that the WB has played in shaping it for the better, visit the "History: An Overview 1920–2020" web page. https://www.dol.gov/agencies/wb/about/history

Maps   The "Equal Pay and Pay Transparency Protections" map is interactive and displays information on Federal and State equal pay and pay transparency protections for workers. https://www.dol.gov/agencies/wb/equal-pay-protections

The "Employment Protections for Workers Who Are Pregnant or Nursing" map is interactive and displays information on Federal and State employment protections against pregnancy discrimination, provisions for pregnancy accommodation, and workplace breastfeeding rights. https://www.dol.gov/agencies/wb/pregnant-nursing-employment-protections

Newsletter The "WB Updates Newsletter" is available online. https://www.dol.gov/agencies/wb/news/newsletter

Press Releases The Bureau posts press releases online. https://www.dol.gov/newsroom/releases/wb

Regional Offices A complete listing of WB regional offices is available online. http://www.dol.gov/wb/info_about_wb/regions/regional_offices.htm

The Sources of Information were updated 10–2020.

Resources The WB posts Federal resources for women on its website. https://www.dol.gov/agencies/wb/federal-agency-resources

"Meeting in a Box" is a communication resource that allows the WB to share information about its current activities, while also providing messaging tools for the general public. This communications resource includes a presentation slide deck with notes, factsheet, and talking points. It offers tools for conducting a meeting, incorporating information into speeches, or incorporating messages as part of a meeting presentation. A tool may be used singly as a stand-alone piece, or in combination, depending on the audience and setting. https://www.dol.gov/agencies/wb/meetinginabox

DEPARTMENT OF STATE

2201 C Street NW., Washington, DC 20520
Phone, 202-647-4000. Internet, http://www.state.gov

Secretary of State   Anthony Blinken

Counselor of the Department
Executive Secretary
https://www.state.gov/biographies/michael-r-pompeo

Deputy Secretary of State

Director, Office of U.S. Foreign Assistance
https://www.state.gov/biographies/stephen-biegun

Deputy Secretary of State for Management and Resources

Bureaus Reporting to the Secretary

Assistant Secretaries
Intelligence and Research
Legislative Affairs

Offices Reporting to the Secretary

Ambassadors-At-Large
Coordinating U.S. Government Activities to Combat HIV/AIDS
Global Women's Issues

Directors
Civil Rights
Policy Planning

Chief of Protocol
Legal Adviser

Special Envoys and Representatives Reporting to the Secretary

Presidential Envoys
Global Coalition to Defeat ISIS
Hostage Affairs

Representatives
Afghanistan Reconciliation
Global Health Diplomacy
Iran
North Korea
Syria Engagement
Venezuela
https://www.state.gov/bureaus-offices/bureaus-and-offices-
  reporting-directly-to-the-secretary

Arms Control and International Security

Undersecretary

Assistant Secretaries
Arms Control, Verification and Compliance
International Security and Nonproliferation
Political–Military Affairs
https://www.state.gov/bureaus-offices/under-secretary-for-arms-
  control-and-international-security-affairs
Civilian Security, Democracy, and Human Rights

Undersecretary

Ambassadors–At–Large
Counterterrorism and Countering Violent Extremism
Global Criminal Justice
International Religious Freedom
Monitoring and Combating Trafficking in Persons

Assistant Secretaries
Conflict and Stabilization Operations
Democracy, Human Rights, and Labor
International Narcotics and Law Enforcement Affairs
Population, Refugees, and Migration
https://www.state.gov/bureaus-offices/under-secretary-for-civilian-
  security-democracy-and-human-rights
Economic Growth, Energy, and the Environment

Undersecretary

Assistant Secretaries
Economic and Business Affairs
Energy Resources
Oceans and International Environmental and Scientific Affairs

Chief Economist
Science and Technology Adviser to the Secretary
https://www.state.gov/bureaus-offices/under-secretary-for-
  economic-growth-energy-and-the-environment

Management

Undersecretary

Assistant Secretaries
Administration
Consular Affairs
Diplomatic Security
Information Resource Management

Chief Officers
Information
Medical

Directors
Budget and Planning
Foreign Missions
Foreign Service Institute
Global Financial Services
Global Talent
Management Strategy and Solutions
Medical Services
Overseas Buildings Operations

Comptroller
Director General of the Foreign Service
https://www.state.gov/bureaus-offices/under-secretary-for-
    management/bureau-of-administration
Political Affairs

Undersecretary

Assistant Secretaries
African Affairs
East Asian and Pacific Affairs
European and Eurasian Affairs
International Organization Affairs
Near Eastern Affairs
South and Central Asian Affairs
Western Hemisphere Affairs
https://www.state.gov/bureaus-offices/under-secretary-for-
    political-affairs
Public Diplomacy and Public Affairs

Undersecretary

Assistant Secretaries
Global Public Affairs
Educational and Cultural Affairs
https://www.state.gov/bureaus-offices/under-secretary-for-public-
    diplomacy-and-public-affairs

United States Mission to the United Nations
799 United Nations Plaza, New York, NY 10017

Ambassadors
Representative of the U.S.A.
Deputy Representative of the U.S.A.
United Nations Management and Reform
https://usun.usmission.gov/our-leaders

Inspector General
https://www.stateoig.gov/about/IG

The above list of key personnel was updated 6–2020.

The Department of State advises the President on issues of foreign policy; supports democracy, freedom, and prosperity for all people; and fosters conditions that favor stability and progress worldwide.

Establishment and Organization
The First Congress of the United States held its first session in the City of New York, starting on March 4, 1789, and ending on September 29, 1789. By act of July 27, 1789 (Statute I, Ch. IV), which President George Washington signed, the U.S. Congress enacted the establishment of an executive department "to be denominated the Department of Foreign Affairs." https://

www.loc.gov/law/help/statutes-at-large/1st-congress/c1.pdf
    During the same session, by act of September 15, 1789 (Statute I, Ch. XIV), which President George Washington also signed, the First Congress renamed the Department of Foreign Affairs as the Department of State, and its principal officer became known as the Secretary of State. https://www.loc.gov/law/help/statutes-at-large/1st-congress/c1.pdf

Department of State

August 2021

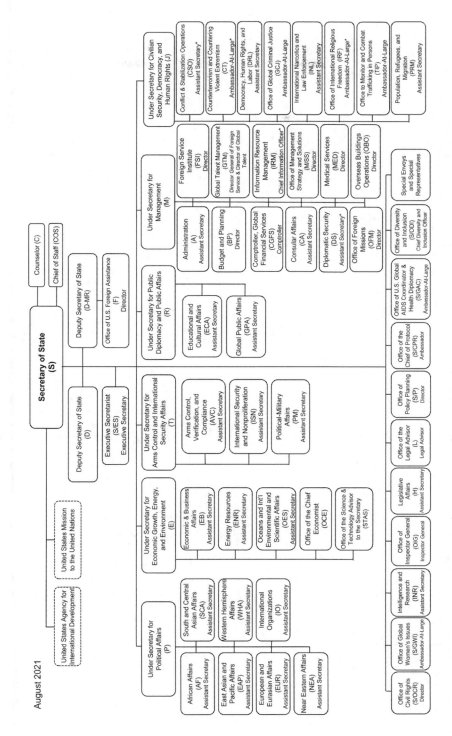

Subject matter on the establishment and organization of the Department of State is consolidated and codified in Title 22, Chapter 38, of the U.S. Code (Sec. 2651 and 2651a). https://uscode.house.gov/view.xhtml?path=/prelim@title22/chapter38&edition=prelim

By the advice and with the consent of the Senate, the President appoints the Secretary of State, the Deputy Secretary of State, and the Deputy Secretary of State for Management and Resources. By the Senate's advice and with its consent, the President also appoints, up to a maximum of six, the Department's Undersecretaries (22 USC 2651a). https://uscode.house.gov/view.xhtml?req=granuleid:USC-prelim-title22-section2651a&num=0&edition=prelim

The Department of State's statement of organization is found in 22 CFR 5. https://www.ecfr.gov/cgi-bin/text-idx?SID=9fcaa112da47aad8595acce6fd09ca0e&mc=true&node=pt22.1.5&rgn=div5

The Department's organizational chart is available in Portable Document Format (PDF) for viewing and downloading. https://www.state.gov/department-of-state-organization-chart

Activities

The Secretary of State directs, coordinates, and supervises U.S. foreign relations and the interdepartmental activities of the U.S. Government abroad. The Secretary ranks first in importance among the President's foreign affairs advisers, serves as a Cabinet member and on the National Security Council, and oversees State Department operations, including the Foreign Service. http://www.state.gov/secretary

The future of the United States depends on the relations that its has with other countries. The U.S. Foreign Service is the principal cultivator of those relations. Trained representatives stationed worldwide provide the President and the Secretary of State with many of the building blocks from which foreign policy is constructed. These representatives also offer recommendations to help guide the process of policy building.

Ambassadors are the personal representatives of the President and report to the President through the Secretary of State. Ambassadors have full responsibility for implementation of U.S. foreign policy by U.S. Government personnel within their country of assignment, except those who are under military commands. Responsibilities include negotiating agreements between the United States and the host country, explaining and disseminating official U.S. policy, and maintaining cordial relations with that country's government and people.

Administration   The Bureau of Administration provides support programs and services to Department of State operations worldwide, as well as programs and services to other U.S. Government agencies represented at U.S. Embassies and consulates. These functions include administrative policy; domestic emergency management; management of owned or leased facilities in the United States; procurement, supply, travel, and transportation support; classified pouch, unclassified pouch, and domestic mail distribution; official records, publishing, library, and foreign language interpreting and translating services; and support to the schools abroad that educate dependents of U.S. Government employees assigned to diplomatic and consular missions. Direct services to the public include authenticating documents used abroad for legal and business purposes; responding to requests under the Freedom of Information and Privacy Acts; providing the electronic reading room for public reference to State Department records; and determining use of the diplomatic reception rooms of the Harry S. Truman headquarters building in Washington, DC. https://www.state.gov/about-us-bureau-of-administration

For further information, contact the Bureau of Administration. Phone, 202-485-7000.

Arms Control, Verification, and Compliance   The Bureau of Arms Control, Verification and Compliance is responsible for ensuring and verifying compliance with international arms control, nonproliferation, and disarmament agreements and commitments. The Bureau also leads negotiation and implementation efforts with respect to strategic arms control, most recently the new START Treaty and conventional forces in Europe. The Bureau is the principal policy representative to the intelligence community with regard to verification and compliance matters and uses this role to promote, preserve, and enhance key collection and analytic capabilities and to ensure that intelligence verification, compliance, and implementation requirements are met. The Bureau staffs and manages treaty implementation commissions, creates negotiation and implementation policy for agreements and commitments, and develops policy for future arms control, nonproliferation, and disarmament arrangements. It also provides secure government-to-government communication linkages with foreign treaty partners. The Bureau is also responsible for preparing verifiability assessments on proposals and agreements, and reporting these to Congress as required. The Bureau also prepares the "President's Annual Report to Congress on Adherence to and Compliance With Arms Control, Nonproliferation, and Disarmament Agreements and Commitments," as well as the reports required by the Iran, North Korea, and Syria Nonproliferation Act. http://www.state.gov/t/avc

For further information, contact the Bureau of Arms Control, Verification and Compliance. Phone, 202-647-6830. Fax, 202-647-1321.

Budget and Planning   The Bureau of Budget and Planning manages budgeting and resource management for operation accounts. https://www.state.gov/bureaus-offices/under-secretary-for-management/bureau-of-budget-and-planning

For further information, contact the Bureau of Budget and Planning. Phone, 202-647-8517.

Comptroller and Global Financial Services   The Bureau of the Comptroller and Global Financial Services, led by the Chief Financial Officer, integrates strategic planning, budgeting, and performance to secure departmental resources. The Bureau manages all departmental strategic and performance planning; global financial services, including accounting, disbursing, and payroll; issuance of financial statements and oversight of the Department's management control program; coordination of national security resources and remediation of vulnerabilities within the

Department's global critical infrastructure; and management of the International Cooperative Administrative Support Services Program. http://www.state.gov/m/cgfs

For further information, contact the Bureau of the Comptroller and Global Financial Services. Phone, 703-875-4364.

Conflict and Stabilization Operations   The Bureau of Conflict and Stabilization Operations advances U.S. national security by driving integrated, civilian-led efforts to prevent, respond to, and stabilize crises in priority states, setting conditions for long-term peace. The Bureau emphasizes sustainable solutions guided by local dynamics and actors and promotes unity of effort, strategic use of scarce resources, and burden sharing with international partners. http://www.state.gov/j/cso

For further information, contact the Bureau of Conflict Stabilization Operations. Phone, 202-663-0299.

Consular Affairs   The Bureau of Consular Affairs is responsible for the protection and welfare of American citizens and interests abroad; the administration and enforcement of the provisions of the immigration and nationality laws insofar as they concern the Department of State and Foreign Service; the issuance of passports and visas; and related services. Approximately 18 million passports a year are issued by the Bureau's Office of Passport Services at the processing centers in Portsmouth, NH, and Charleston, SC, and the regional agencies in Boston, MA; Chicago, IL; Aurora, CO; Honolulu, HI; Houston, TX; Los Angeles, CA; Miami, FL; New Orleans, LA; New York, NY; Philadelphia, PA; San Francisco, CA; Seattle, WA; Norwalk, CT; Detroit, MI; Minneapolis, MN; and Washington, DC. In addition, the Bureau helps secure America's borders against entry by terrorists or narcotraffickers, facilitates international adoptions, and supports parents whose children have been abducted abroad. http://travel.state.gov/content/travel/en.html

More information is available online at the Bureau of Consular Affairs.

Counterterrorism   The Bureau of Counterterrorism leads the Department in the U.S. Government's effort to counter terrorism abroad and secure the United States against foreign terrorist threats. To carry out its mission, the Bureau develops and implements counterterrorism strategies, promotes international cooperation on counterterrorism issues, serves as the Department's key link on counterterrorism to the Department of Homeland Security, focuses efforts to counter violent extremism, and develops international partner counterterrorism capacity. http://www.state.gov/j/ct

For further information, contact CT's Office of Public Affairs. Phone, 202–647–1845.

Democracy, Human Rights, and Labor   The Bureau of Democracy, Human Rights, and Labor (DRL) is responsible for developing and implementing U.S. policy on democracy, human rights, labor, religious freedom, monitoring and combating anti-Semitism, and advocating for inclusion of people with disabilities. DRL practices diplomatic engagement and advocacy to protect human rights and strengthen democratic institutions. Working with governments, civil society, and multilateral organizations to support democratic governance and human rights, the Bureau also participates in multi-stakeholder initiatives to encourage multinational corporations to adhere to human rights standards of conduct, including the elimination of child labor. DRL fulfills the USG reporting responsibilities on human rights and democracy, producing the annual "Country Reports on Human Rights Practices," the annual "International Religious Freedom" report, and the "Advancing Freedom and Democracy" report. Providing targeted program assistance through the Human Rights and Democracy Fund and other funding streams, the Bureau works to protect human rights and strengthen democratic institutions around the world. DRL programs help prosecute war criminals, promote religious freedom, support workers' rights, encourage accountability in governance, as well as facilitate freedom of expression and freedom to access information on the Internet. The Bureau also has a Congressionally mandated responsibility to ensure that foreign military assistance and training is not provided to

gross violators of human rights. DRL leads the Secretary of State's Task Force on Global Internet Freedom. http://www.state.gov/j/drl

For further information, contact the Bureau of Democracy, Human Rights, and Labor. Phone, 202–647–2126.

Diplomatic Security   The Bureau of Diplomatic Security provides a secure environment to promote U.S. interests at home and abroad. The Bureau's mission includes protecting the Secretary of State and other senior Government officials, resident and visiting foreign dignitaries, and foreign missions in the United States; conducting criminal, counterintelligence, and personnel security investigations; ensuring the integrity of international travel documents, sensitive information, classified processing equipment, and management information systems; the physical and technical protection of domestic and overseas facilities of the Department of State; providing professional law enforcement and security training to U.S. and foreign personnel; and a comprehensive, multifaceted overseas security program serving the needs of U.S. missions and resident U.S. citizens and business communities. Through the Office of Foreign Missions, the Bureau regulates the domestic activities of the foreign diplomatic community in the areas of taxation, real property acquisitions, motor vehicle operation, domestic travel, and customs processing. http://www.state.gov/m/ds

For further information, contact the Bureau of Diplomatic Security Office of Public Affairs. Phone, 571–345–2502.

Economic and Business Affairs   The Bureau of Economic and Business Affairs (EB) promotes international trade, investment, economic development, and financial stability on behalf of the American people. EB works to build prosperity and economic security at home and abroad by implementing policy related to the promotion of U.S. trade, investment and exports, international development and reconstruction, intellectual property enforcement, terrorism financing and economic sanctions, international communications and information policy, and aviation and maritime affairs. EB formulates and carries out U.S. foreign economic policy and works to sustain a more democratic, secure, and prosperous world. http://www. state.gov/e/eb

For further information, contact the Bureau of Economic and Business Affairs. Phone, 202-647-9204.

Educational and Cultural Affairs The Bureau of Educational and Cultural Affairs administers the principal provisions of the Mutual Educational and Cultural Exchange Act (the Fulbright-Hays Act), including U.S. international educational and cultural exchange programs. These programs include the prestigious Fulbright Program for students, scholars, and teachers; the International Visitor Leadership Program, which brings leaders and future leaders from other countries to the United States for consultation with their professional colleagues; and professional, youth, sports, and cultural exchanges. Programs are implemented through cooperative relationships with U.S. nongovernmental organizations that support the Bureau's mission. http://exchanges.state.gov

For further information, contact the Bureau of Educational and Cultural Affairs. Phone, 202-632-6445. Fax, 202-632-2701.

Energy Resources The Bureau of Energy Resources (ENR) leads the State Department in the U.S. Government's promotion of U.S. and international energy policy. ENR works to ensure that international energy markets are secure and predictable in order to mitigate potential disruptions, while also working with international partners to diversify U.S. energy supplies. The Bureau also seeks to encourage the transformation of United States and world production and consumption of energy to confront the limits of a hydrocarbon-based society and rapid increases in energy demand. ENR works to promote good governance, transparency, and reform of energy sectors globally, which will help broaden energy access, further ensure stable energy supplies, and reduce political instability. http://www.state.gov/e/enr

For further information, contact the Bureau of Energy Resources. Phone, 202-647-3423.

Foreign Service Institute The Foreign Service Institute of the Department of

State is the Federal Government's primary foreign affairs-related training institution. In addition to the Department of State, the Institute provides training for more than 47 other Government agencies. The Institute has more than 700 courses, including some 70 foreign language courses, ranging in length from 1 day to 2 years. The courses are designed to promote successful performance in each professional assignment, to ease the adjustment to other countries and cultures, and to enhance the leadership and management capabilities of the foreign affairs community. https://www.state.gov/bureaus-offices/under-secretary-for-management/foreign-service-institute

For further information, contact the Foreign Service Institute. Phone, 703-302-7144. Fax, 703-302-7152.

Information Resource Management The Bureau of Information Resource Management (IRM) provides the Department with the information technology it needs to carry out U.S. diplomacy in the information age. The IRM Bureau is led by the Department's Chief Information Officer. IRM establishes effective information resource management planning and policies; ensures availability of information technology systems and operations, including information technology contingency planning, to support the Department's diplomatic, consular, and management operations; exercises management responsibility to ensure the Department's information resources meet the business requirements of the Department and provide an effective basis for knowledge sharing and collaboration within the Department and with other foreign affairs agencies and partners; exercises delegated approving authority for the Secretary of State for the development and administration of the Department's computer and information security programs and policies. http://www.state.gov/m/irm

For further information, contact the Bureau of Information Resource Management. Phone, 202-647-2977.

Inspector General The Office of Inspector General (OIG) conducts independent audits, inspections, and investigations to promote effective management, accountability, and positive change in the Department of State, the Broadcasting Board of Governors (BBG), and the foreign affairs community. OIG provides leadership to promote integrity, efficiency, effectiveness, and economy; prevents and detects waste, fraud, abuse, and mismanagement; identifies vulnerabilities and recommends constructive solutions; offers expert assistance to improve Department and BBG operations; communicates timely, useful information that facilitates decision-making and achieves measurable gains; and keeps the Department, BBG, and Congress informed. https://oig.state.gov

For further information, contact the Office of Inspector General. Phone, 202-663-0340.

Intelligence and Research   The primary mission of the Bureau of Intelligence and Research (INR) is to harness intelligence to serve U.S. diplomacy. Drawing on all-source intelligence, INR provides value-added independent analysis of events to Department policymakers, ensures that intelligence activities support foreign policy and national security purposes, and serves as the focal point in the Department for ensuring policy review of sensitive counterintelligence and law enforcement activities. The Bureau also analyzes geographical and international boundary issues. INR is a member of the U.S. Intelligence Community and serves as the Community's Executive Agent for Analytical Outreach. http://www.state.gov/s/inr

For further information, contact the Bureau of Intelligence and Research. Phone, 202-647-1080.

International Narcotics and Law Enforcement   The Bureau of International Narcotics and Law Enforcement Affairs (INL) is responsible for developing policies and managing programs to combat and counter international narcotics production and trafficking, and for strengthening law enforcement and other rule of law institutional capabilities outside the United States. The Bureau also directs narcotics control coordinators at posts abroad and provides guidance on narcotics control, justice sector reform, and anticrime matters to the chiefs of missions. It supports the development of strong, sustainable criminal justice systems as well as training for police force and judicial officials. INL works closely with a broad range of other U.S. Government agencies. http://www.state.gov/j/inl

For further information, contact the Bureau of International Narcotics and Law Enforcement Affairs. Phone, 202-647-2545. Fax, 202-736-4045.

International Organizations   The Bureau of International Organization Affairs provides guidance and support for U.S. participation in international organizations and conferences and formulates and implements U.S. policy toward international organizations, with particular emphasis on those organizations which make up the United Nations system. It provides direction in the development, coordination, and implementation of U.S. multilateral policy. http://www.state.gov/p/io

For further information, contact the Bureau of International Organization Affairs. Phone, 202-647-9600. Fax, 202-736-4116.

International Security and Nonproliferation   The Bureau of International Security and Nonproliferation (ISN), is responsible for managing a broad range of nonproliferation, counterproliferation, and arms control functions. ISN leads U.S. efforts to prevent the spread of weapons of mass destruction (nuclear, radiological, chemical, and biological weapons) related materials, and their delivery systems. It is responsible for spearheading efforts to promote international consensus on weapons of mass destruction proliferation through bilateral and multilateral diplomacy; addressing weapons of mass destruction proliferation threats posed by nonstate actors and terrorist groups by improving physical security, using interdiction and sanctions, and actively participating in the Proliferation Security Initiative; coordinating the implementation of key international treaties and arrangements, working to make them relevant to today's security challenges; working closely with the U.N., the G–8, NATO, the Organization for the Prohibition of Chemical Weapons, the International Atomic Energy Agency, and other international institutions and organizations to reduce and eliminate the threat posed by weapons of mass destruction; and supporting efforts of foreign partners to prevent, protect against, and respond to the threat or use of weapons of mass destruction by terrorists. http://www.state.gov/t/isn

For further information, contact the Bureau of International Security and Nonproliferation. Phone, 202-647-9868. Fax, 202-736-4863.

Legal Adviser The Office of the Legal Adviser advises the Secretary of State and other Department officials on all domestic and international legal matters relating to the Department of State, Foreign Service, and diplomatic and consular posts abroad. The Office's lawyers draft, negotiate, and interpret treaties, international agreements, domestic statutes, departmental regulations, Executive orders, and other legal documents; provide guidance on international and domestic law; represent the United States in international organization, negotiation, and treaty commission meetings; work on domestic and foreign litigation affecting the Department's interests; and represent the United States before international tribunals, including the International Court of Justice. http://www.state.gov/s/l

For further information, contact the Office of the Legal Adviser. Phone, 202-647-9598.

Legislative Affairs The Bureau of Legislative Affairs coordinates legislative activity for the Department of State and advises the Secretary, the Deputy, as well as the Under Secretaries and Assistant Secretaries on legislative strategy. The Bureau facilitates effective communication between State Department officials and the Members of Congress and their staffs. Legislative Affairs works closely with the authorizing, appropriations, and oversight committees of the House and Senate, as well as with individual Members that have an interest in State Department or foreign policy issues. The Bureau also manages Department testimony before House and Senate hearings, organizes Member and staff briefings, facilitates congressional travel to overseas posts for Members and staff throughout the year, reviews proposed legislation, and coordinates Statements of Administration Policy on legislation

affecting the conduct of U.S. foreign policy. The Legislative Affairs staff advises individual Bureaus of the Department on legislative and outreach strategies and coordinates those strategies with the Secretary's priorities. https://www.state.gov/bureaus-offices/bureaus-and-offices-reporting-directly-to-the-secretary/bureau-of-legislative-affairs

For further information, contact the Bureau of Legislative Affairs. Phone, 202-647-1714.

Medical Services The Office of Medical Services (MED) develops, manages, and staffs a worldwide primary health care system for U.S. Government employees and their eligible dependents residing overseas. In support of its overseas operations, MED approves and monitors the medical evacuation of patients, conducts pre-employment and in-service physical clearance examinations, and provides clinical referral and advisory services. MED also provides for emergency medical response in the event of a crisis at an overseas post. https://www.state.gov/bureaus-offices/under-secretary-for-management/bureau-of-medical-services

For further information, contact the Office of Medical Services. Phone, 202-663-1649. Fax, 202-663-1613.

Oceans and International Environmental and Scientific Affairs The Bureau of Oceans and International Environmental and Scientific Affairs (OES) serves as the foreign policy focal point for international oceans, as well as environmental and scientific efforts. OES projects, protects, and promotes U.S. global interests in these areas by articulating U.S. foreign policy, encouraging international cooperation, and negotiating treaties and other instruments of international law. The Bureau serves as the principal adviser to the Secretary of State on international environment, science, and technology matters and takes the lead in coordinating and brokering diverse interests in the interagency process, where the development of international policies or the negotiation and implementation of relevant international agreements are concerned. The Bureau seeks to promote the peaceful exploitation of outer space, develop and coordinate policy on international health issues, encourage government-to-government scientific cooperation, and prevent the destruction and degradation of the planet's natural resources and the global environment. http://www.state.gov/e/oes

For further information, contact the Bureau of Oceans and International Environmental and Scientific Affairs. Phone, 202-647-3004.

Overseas Buildings Operations The Bureau of Overseas Buildings Operations (OBO) directs the worldwide overseas buildings program for the Department of State and the U.S. Government community serving abroad under the authority of the chiefs of mission. Along with the input and support of other State Department bureaus, foreign affairs agencies, and Congress, OBO sets worldwide priorities for the design, construction, acquisition, maintenance, use, and sale of real properties and the use of sales proceeds. OBO also serves as the Single Real Property Manager of all overseas facilities under the authority of the chiefs of mission. http://overseasbuildings.state.gov

For further information, contact the Bureau of Overseas Buildings Operations. Phone, 703-875-4131. Fax, 703-875-5043.

Political-Military Affairs The Bureau of Political-Military Affairs is the principal link between the Departments of State and Defense and is the Department of State's lead on operational military matters. The Bureau provides policy direction in the areas of international security, security assistance, military operations, defense strategy and policy, counterpiracy measures, and defense trade. Its responsibilities include coordinating the U.S. Government's response to piracy in the waters off the Horn of Africa, securing base access to support the deployment of U.S. military forces overseas, negotiating status of forces agreements, coordinating participation in coalition combat and stabilization forces, regulating arms transfers, directing military assistance to U.S. allies, combating illegal trafficking in small arms and light weapons, facilitating the education and training of international peacekeepers and foreign military personnel, managing humanitarian mine action programs, and assisting other countries in reducing the availability of

man-portable air defense systems. http://www.state.gov/t/pm

For further information, contact the Bureau of Political-Military Affairs. Phone, 202-647-9022. Fax, 202-736-4413.

Population, Refugees, and Migration The Bureau of Population, Refugees, and Migration directs the Department's population, refugee, and migration policy development. It administers U.S. contributions to international organizations and nongovernmental organizations for humanitarian assistance- and protection-related programs on behalf of refugees, conflict victims, and internally displaced persons. The Bureau oversees the annual admissions of refugees to the United States for permanent resettlement, working closely with the Department of Homeland Security, the Department of Health and Human Services, and various State and private voluntary agencies. It coordinates U.S. international population policy and promotes its goals through bilateral and multilateral cooperation. It works closely with the U.S. Agency for International Development, which administers U.S. international population programs. The Bureau also coordinates the Department's international migration policy through bilateral and multilateral diplomacy. The Bureau oversees efforts to encourage greater participation in humanitarian assistance and refugee resettlement on the part of foreign governments and uses humanitarian diplomacy to increase access and assistance to those in need in the absence of political solutions. https://www.state.gov/bureaus-offices/under-secretary-for-civilian-security-democracy-and-human-rights/bureau-of-population-refugees-and-migration

For further information, contact the Bureau of Population, Refugees, and Migration. Phone, 202-453-9339. Fax, 202-453-9394.

Protocol The Chief of Protocol is the principal adviser to the U.S. Government, the President, the Vice President, and the Secretary of State on matters of diplomatic procedure governed by law or international custom and practice. The Office is responsible for arranging visits of foreign chiefs of state, heads of government, and other high officials to the United States; organizing credential presentations of newly arrived Ambassadors, as presented to the President and to the Secretary of State; operating the President's guest house, Blair House; organizing delegations representing the President at official ceremonies abroad; conducting official ceremonial functions and public events; interpreting the official order of precedence; conducting outreach programs of cultural enrichment and substantive briefings of the Diplomatic Corps; accrediting of over 118,000 embassy, consular, international organization, and other foreign government personnel, members of their families, and domestics throughout the United States; determining entitlement to diplomatic or consular immunity; publishing of diplomatic and consular lists; resolving problems arising out of diplomatic or consular immunity, such as legal and police matters; and approving the opening of embassy and consular offices in conjunction with the Office of Foreign Missions. http://www.state.gov/s/cpr

For further information, contact the Office of the Chief of Protocol. Phone, 202-647-1735. Fax, 202-647-1560.

Public Affairs The Bureau of Public Affairs (PA) supports U.S. foreign policy goals and objectives, advances national interests, and enhances National security by informing and influencing domestic and global public opinion about American interaction with the rest of the world. In addition, PA works to help Americans understand the importance of foreign affairs by conducting press briefings for the domestic and foreign press, pursuing media outreach by other means, arranging townhall meetings and community speakers, and preparing historical studies on U.S. diplomacy and foreign affairs matters. http://www.state.gov/r/pa

For further information, contact the Bureau of Public Affairs. Phone, 202-647-6575.

Sources of Information

Air Quality Worldwide AirNow–Department of State collects air quality monitoring data globally from U.S. embassies and consulates. https://airnow.gov/index.cfm?action=airnow.global_summary

Archived Records The records of the Department are referenced in the "Guide to Federal Records in the National Archives of the United States." The Guide is accessible online, and its records belong to Record Group 059. https://www.archives.gov/research/guide-fed-records/groups/059.html

Art in Embassies (AIE) The Department's AIE program stimulates cross-cultural dialogue and mutual understanding through the visual arts and artist exchanges. The program develops and presents approximately 60 exhibitions per year and has installed over 70 permanent art collections in the Department's diplomatic facilities in over 200 venues in 189 countries. https://art.state.gov

Blog "DipNote," the Department of State's official blog, offers first-person perspectives from U.S. Government employees who are working to shape and sustain a peaceful, prosperous, just, and democratic world and to foster stability and progress for people of every nation. https://blogs.state.gov

Business Opportunities Direct Line allows U.S. businessmen and women to hear directly from U.S. Ambassadors and economic and commercial experts at Embassies and consulates in over 190 countries. Direct line can help U.S. businessmen and women identify promising market sectors and U.S. exporters capitalize on new opportunities. https://www.state.gov/direct-line-for-american-business

The Office of Small and Disadvantaged Business Utilization works with industry partners, the acquisition corps, and program offices to increase prime and subcontracting opportunities for U.S. small businesses. Phone, 703-875-6822. http://www.state.gov/s/dmr/sdbu/index.htm

Career Opportunities To learn about joining the Civil Service, becoming a Foreign Service Specialist, the Consular Fellows Program, and other opportunities, visit the "Job Seekers" web page. Information of interest to students, recent graduates, veterans, and persons with disabilities is also accessible online. State Department personnel are available to answer questions on Federal workdays, 8:30 a.m.–4:30 p.m., eastern standard time. Phone, 202-663-2176. https://www.state.gov/job-seekers

In 2019, the Department of State ranked 13th among 17 large agencies in the Partnership for Public Service's Best Places To Work Agency Rankings. http://bestplacestowork.org/rankings/detail/ST00

Climate Change   The Office of Global Change implements and manages U.S. international policy on climate change. It also represents the United States in negotiations under the United Nations Framework Convention on Climate Change and in other international fora that focus on the topic, including the International Civil Aviation Organization and the International Maritime Organization. https://www.state.gov/bureaus-offices/under-secretary-for-economic-growth-energy-and-the-environment/bureau-of-oceans-and-international-environmental-and-scientific-affairs/office-of-global-change

Contact Information   An online visitor to the website may submit a question, using the electronic form on the "Contact Us" web page. https://register.state.gov/contactus/contactusform

DIPLOMATS@work   This experience provides insight into the distinct responsibilities of Foreign Service Officers in each of the five career tracks during a crisis situation in Vendurasaca, a fictitious country designed to represent an overseas location in which a U.S. embassy or consulate is located https://careers.state.gov/daw/diplomats-at-work

Embassies   Contact information for U.S. Embassies, consulates, and diplomatic missions worldwide is available online. https://www.usembassy.gov

Emergencies Abroad   The Bureau of Consular Affairs posts information for emergency travel-related situations abroad. https://travel.state.gov/content/travel/en/international-travel/emergencies.html

Federal Register   Significant documents, from 1995 (volume 60) to the present, and recent documents that the Department has published in the Federal Register are available online. https://www.federalregister.gov/agencies/state-department

Foreign Affairs Manual (FAM) / Foreign Affairs Handbooks (FAHs)   The (FAM) and (FAHs) are a single, comprehensive, and authoritative source for the Department's organization structures, policies, and procedures that govern the operations of the State Department, the Foreign Service, and, when applicable, other Federal agencies. The FAM, which centers on policy, and the FAHs, which center on procedures, convey codified information to Department staff and contractors, enabling them to carry out their responsibilities in accordance with statutory, executive, and Department mandates. https://fam.state.gov

Freedom of Information Act (FOIA)   To request records, write to the Director, Office of Information Programs and Services, A/GIS/IPS/RL, Department of State, SA–2, Washington, DC 20522-8100. For more information, contact the FOIA Requester Service Center. Phone, 202-261-8484. https://foia.state.gov/Default.aspx

The Department of State maintains an online reading room that contains over 220,000 documents. Before submitting a FOIA request, search the reading room to see if the desired document is accessible immediately and free of charge. https://foia.state.gov/Search/Search.aspx

Frequently Asked Questions (FAQs)   The Department of State posts answers to FAQs. https://careers.state.gov/faqs

The Office of the Historian posts answers to FAQs on its website. https://history.state.gov/about/faq

Geographic Bureaus   The geographic bureaus, which include the Bureaus of African, East Asian and Pacific, European and Eurasian, Near Eastern, South and Central Asian, and Western Hemisphere Affairs handle foreign affairs activities worldwide. https://www.state.gov/bureaus-offices/under-secretary-for-political-affairs

History   The Office of the Historian maintains an online guide to the United States' history of recognition, diplomatic, and consular relations by country. The database begins with the year 1776. https://history.state.gov/countries | Email: history@state.gov

The Office of the Historian also maintains an online index to diplomatic archives worldwide. https://history.state.gov/countries/archives | Email: history@state.gov

International Adoptions   For information on adoption of foreign children by private U.S. citizens, contact the Office of Children's Issues, Bureau of Consular

Affairs, Department of State, SA–29, 2201 C Street NW., Washington, DC 20520-4818. Phone, 888-407-4747 or 202-501-4444 (international). http://travel.state.gov/content/adoptionsabroad/en.html

Open Government The Department of State supports the Open Government initiative by promoting collaboration, participation, and transparency. https://www.state.gov/open-government-initiative

Passports Information on the application process for a new passport and on the renewal process for an expiring passport is available online. Lost or stolen passports may be reported online. Phone, 877-487-2778. TDD/TTY, 888-874-7793 https://travel.state.gov/content/travel/en/passports.html | Email: NPIC@state.gov

Press Releases The Office of the Spokesperson releases factsheets, media notes, notices to the press, and statements on a daily basis. https://www.state.gov/press-releases

Programs by State State Department programs affect American communities. The "Department of State by State" web pages describe some of the effects by offering State-by-State statistics. https://www.state.gov/department-of-state-by-state

Publications The Bureau of Human Resources publishes "State Magazine" monthly, except bimonthly in July and August. The magazine has an informative character and should not be regarded as

The Sources of Information were updated 6–2020.

authority for official action. Views and opinions expressed in "State Magazine" are not necessarily those of the Department of State. https://statemag.state.gov | Email: statemagazine@state.gov

Social Media The "Press" web page presents links to the Department's social media accounts under the "Join Us" section heading. Using the "Press" web page, a visitor can access easily the official blog "Dipnote," Facebook, Flickr, Instagram, Twitter, YouTube, and a form for subscribing to email updates. https://www.state.gov/press

Telephone Directory The Department's telephone directory can be accessed online. https://www.state.gov/telephone-directory

Tips for U.S. Travelers Information for Americans traveling abroad—including a traveler's checklist and tips on destinations, personal safety, health, and other topics—is available online from the Bureau of Consular Affairs. http://travel.state.gov/content/passports/english/go.html

Travel Advisories and Alerts The Bureau of Consular Affairs website posts travel advisories, alerts, and other information to help Americans travel safely abroad. http://travel.state.gov/content/passports/en/alertswarnings.html

Visas For information on visas for foreigners wishing to enter the United States, visit the Bureau of Consular Affairs online or call 603-334-0700. http://nvc.state.gov

DEPARTMENT OF TRANSPORTATION

1200 New Jersey Avenue SE., Washington, DC 20590
Phone, 202-366-4000. Internet, http://www.dot.gov

Secretary of Transportation	PETER P.M. BUTTIGIEG
Deputy Secretary	POLLY E. TROTTENBERG
Chief of Staff	LAURA SCHILLER
Under Secretary of Transportation for Policy	CARLOS MONJE, JR.

https://www.transportation.gov/office-of-secretary

Assistant Secretaries

Administration	PHILIP A. MCNAMARA
Aviation and International Affairs	CAROL A. PETSONK*
Finance and Budget	VICTORIA B. WASSMER*
Governmental Affairs	MOHSIN SYED*
Research and Technology	ROBERT C. HAMPSHIRE*
Transportation Policy	CHRISTOPHER COES*

Chief Officers

Financial	(VACANCY)
Legal	JOHN E. PUTNAM, ACTING
General Counsel	JOHN E. PUTNAM, ACTING*
Principal Deputy Assistant Secretary or Deputy Assistant Secretary	

https://www.transportation.gov/mission/meet-key-officials

Heads of Administrations

Federal Aviation	STEVE DICKSON
Federal Highways	STEPHANIE POLLACK, ACTING
Federal Motor Carrier Safety	MEERA JOSHI*
Federal Railroads	AMIT BOSE*
Federal Transit	NURIA FERNANDEZ
Maritime	LUCINDA LESSLEY, ACTING
National Highway Traffic Safety	STEVEN CLIFF, ACTING
Pipeline and Hazardous Materials Safety	TRISTAN BROWN, ACTING
Great Lakes St. Lawrence Seaway Development	CRAIG H. MIDDLEBROOK**
Deputy Administrator	

https://www.transportation.gov/administrations

Heads of Offices

Directors

Civil Rights	IRENE MARION
Executive Secretariat	JUSTINE HONG
Intelligence, Security and Emergency Response	RICHARD M. CHÁVEZ
Public Affairs	DANI SIMONS
Small and Disadvantaged Business Utilization	SHELBY M. SCALES

328

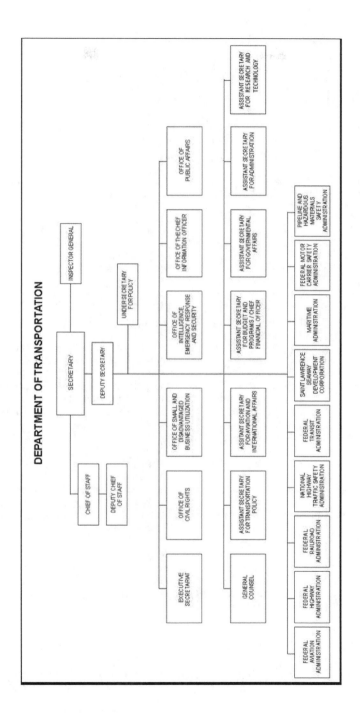

DEPARTMENT OF TRANSPORTATION

Chief Information Officer   CORDELL SCHACHTER
https://www.transportation.gov/policy/key-officials

Inspector General   ERIC J. SOSKIN
https://www.oig.dot.gov/about-oig/inspector-general

The above list of key personnel was updated 9–2021.

The Department of Transportation establishes national transportation policy for highway planning and construction, motor carrier safety, urban mass transit, railroads, aviation, and the safety of waterways, ports, highways, and pipelines.

Establishment and Organization
On October 15, 1966, President Lyndon B. Johnson approved Public Law 89–670, which also is cited as the Department of Transportation Act, "to establish a Department of Transportation [DOT] and for other purposes." The U.S. Congress had found that the establishment of a DOT was necessary "to assure the coordinated, effective administration of the transportation programs of the Federal Government; to facilitate the development and improvement of coordinated transportation service, to be provided by private enterprise to the maximum extent feasible; to encourage cooperation of Federal, State, and local governments, carriers, labor, and other interested parties toward the achievement of national transportation objectives; to stimulate technological advances in transportation; to provide general leadership in the identification and solution of transportation problems; and to develop and recommend to the President and the Congress for approval national transportation policies and programs to accomplish these objectives with full and appropriate consideration of the needs of the public, users, carriers, industry, labor, and the national defense." It also contained the following declaration of national policy: "Special effort should be made to preserve the natural beauty of the countryside and public park and recreation lands, wildlife and waterfowl refuges, and historic sites" (80 Stat. 931). The Nation's DOT had its first official day of operation on April 1, 1967. https://www.govinfo.gov/content/pkg/STATUTE-80/pdf/STATUTE-80-Pg931.pdf

The President appoints the Secretary of Transportation by the advice and with the consent of the Senate (80 Stat. 931). The Secretary, who serves as the principal adviser to the President in all Federal transportation program matters, administers the DOT. The Under Secretary for Policy serves as a principal policy adviser to the Secretary and provides leadership in policy development for the Department.

The DOT's statement of organization has been assigned to subpart A of part 1 in 49 CFR. https://www.ecfr.gov/cgi-bin/text-idx?SID=e53320fbfd2ae88a9b5ab278d4b5c6bd&mc=true&node=pt49.1.1&rgn=div5#sp49.1.1.a

The DOT posts its organization chart online. https://www.transportation.gov/org-chart

Statutory and Regulatory Authorities
Statutory material affecting the DOT has been codified and assigned to subtitle I of 49 U.S.C. https://uscode.house.gov/view.xhtml?path=/prelim@title49/subtitle1&edition=prelim

Regulatory material on the subject of transportation has been codified and assigned to 49 CFR. https://www.ecfr.gov/cgi-bin/text-idx?gp=&SID=e53320fbfd2ae88a9b5ab278d4b5c6bd&mc=true&tpl=/ecfrbrowse/Title49/49tab_02.tpl

Activities
Aviation and International Affairs   The Office of the Assistant Secretary for Aviation and International Affairs develops, reviews, and coordinates policy for international transportation and develops, coordinates, and implements policy on economic regulation of the airline industry. The Office licenses U.S. and foreign carriers to serve in international air transportation and conducts carrier fitness determinations for carriers serving the United States. The Office participates in negotiations with foreign

governments to develop multilateral and bilateral aviation and maritime policies on international transportation and trade and to coordinate cooperative agreements for the exchange of scientific and technical information. The Office also resolves complaints of unfair competitive practices in domestic and international air transportation, establishes international and intra-Alaska mail rates, determines the disposition of requests for approval and immunization from the antitrust laws of international aviation agreements, and administers the essential air service program. https://www.transportation.gov/policy/assistant-secretary-aviation-international-affairs

Drug and Alcohol Policy and Compliance The Office of Drug and Alcohol Policy and Compliance ensures that the Secretary's national and international drug and alcohol policies and goals are developed and implemented in a consistent, efficient, and effective manner within the transportation industry. Experts from the Office advise, counsel, and give recommendations on drugs and alcohol, as they pertain to the DOT and testing within the industry, to the Secretary. https://www.transportation.gov/odapc

Intelligence, Security and Emergency Response The Office of Intelligence, Security and Emergency Response ensures development, coordination, and execution of plans and procedures for the DOT to balance transportation security requirements with safety, mobility, and the Nation's economic needs. The Office monitors the Nation's transportation network on a continuous basis; advises the Secretary on incidents affecting transportation systems; leads on issues of national preparedness, response, and transportation security; briefs the Secretary on transportation-related intelligence; performs the DOT's National Response Framework Emergency Support Function responsibilities; coordinates departmental participation in emergency preparedness and response exercises under the National Training and Exercise Program; administers the DOT's Continuity of Government and Continuity of Operations programs; and serves as the DOT representative for emergency planning for civil aviation support to NATO and

other allies. https://www.transportation.gov/mission/administrations/intelligence-security-emergency-response

Transportation Policy The Office of the Assistant Secretary for Transportation Policy analyzes, develops, articulates, and reviews policies and plans for all transportation modes. It also develops, coordinates, and evaluates public policy on safety, energy, and environmental initiatives that affect air, surface, marine, and pipeline transportation. It maintains policy and economic oversight of DOT regulatory programs and legislative initiatives. The Office also analyzes the economic and institutional implications of current and emerging transportation policy issues, transportation infrastructure finances, and new transportation technologies. https://www.transportation.gov/policy/assistant-secretary-transportation-policy

Research and Technology The Office of the Assistant Secretary for Research and Technology (OST–R) was created by title I, division L, of the Department of Transportation Appropriations Act, 2014 (49 USC 112 note), which transferred the authorities, functions, personnel, and powers and duties of the former Research and Innovative Technology Administration to the OST–R. The Office coordinates, facilitates, and reviews DOT research and development programs and activities; performs transportation statistics research, analysis, and reporting; and promotes innovative technologies for improving transportation systems. The OST–R is composed of the staff from the Bureau of Transportation Statistics, the Volpe National Transportation Systems Center, the Transportation Safety Institute, and the Office of Research, Development, and Technology. https://www.transportation.gov/administrations/assistant-secretary-research-and-technology/office-assistant-secretary-research-0

Sources of Information

Administrations The "Our Administrations" web page provides convenient access to the home pages of the DOT's Administrations. https://www.transportation.gov/administrations

Archived Records The "Guide to Federal Records in the National Archives of the

United States" indicates that DOT records have been assigned to record group 398. https://www.archives.gov/research/guide-fed-records/groups/398.html

Aviation Consumer Protection   For information on air travelers' rights or for assistance in resolving consumer problems with providers of commercial air transportation services, contact the Consumer Affairs Division. Phone, 202-366-2220. https://www.transportation.gov/airconsumer

The Office of Aviation Enforcement and Proceedings publishes the "Air Travel Consumer Report" each month. The report makes information on the quality of airline services accessible to consumers. Issues of the consumer report are posted on the DOT website in Portable Document Format (PDF). Phone, 202-366-2220. TTY, 202-366-0511. https://www.transportation.gov/individuals/aviation-consumer-protection/air-travel-consumer-reports

Blog   The DOT's official blog is titled "Destinations." https://www.transportation.gov/blog/Destinations-by-DOT

Build America Bureau   The "Project Highlights" web page features 20 narratives that summarize the development process of specific new-build transportation public-private partnerships. Each narrative covers the partnership's conception through to its financial closing and construction. https://www.transportation.gov/buildamerica/projects/project-highlights | Email: BuildAmerica@dot.gov

Business Opportunities   Information on small business assistance, small business loans for women, and small business loans for veterans, as well as additional resources like DOT procurement forecasts, are available on the Office of Small and Disadvantaged Business Utilization's website. https://www.transportation.gov/content/office-small-and-disadvantaged-business-utilization

Career Opportunities   The DOT employs administrators and managers, air traffic controllers, aviation safety specialists, clerical staff, electronics maintenance technicians, and engineers—aeronautical, automotive, civil, electrical, highway, and general. For further information, contact the Office of the Secretary–Human Resource Operations, 1200 New Jersey Avenue SE.,

Room W75–340, Washington, DC 20590. Phone, 202-366-9391 or 800-525-2878. https://www.transportation.gov/careers

In 2020, the DOT ranked 3d among 17 large agencies in the Partnership for Public Service's Best Places To Work Agency Rankings. https://bestplacestowork.org/rankings/detail/?c=TD00

In 2020, the Office of the Inspector General ranked 83d among 411 agency subcomponents in the Partnership for Public Service's Best Places To Work Agency Rankings. https://bestplacestowork.org/rankings/detail/?c=TD12

Civil Rights   For information on equal employment opportunity, nondiscrimination in DOT employment and transportation services, or the Department's disadvantaged business enterprise certification appeals program, contact the Director, Departmental Office of Civil Rights. Phone, 202-366-4648. https://www.transportation.gov/civil-rights

Climate Change   On July 14, 2009, former Secretary of Transportation Ray LaHood read a statement before the U.S. Senate's Committee on Environment and Public Works. As part of his statement, the Secretary said: "Addressing VMT [vehicle-miles-traveled] growth plays a key role in decreasing transportation related GHG [greenhouse gas] emissions and should be included in overall efforts to prevent climate change. . . . transportation infrastructure will also face climate impacts such as rising sea levels, changing precipitation patterns, and temperature fluctuations. The need for adaptation is unavoidable. To ensure the continued integrity of the nation's transportation system, transportation infrastructure decisions must adequately consider forecasted effects and impacts from climate change." https://www.transportation.gov/testimony/transportations-role-climate-change-and-greenhouse-gases

Conferences / Events   The DOT has placed on one web page a list of links for conference and event pages that are found on the websites of various DOT Administrations, the Office of Drug and Alcohol Policy and Compliance, the Office of Small and Disadvantaged Business Utilization, and the Volpe Center. https://www.transportation.gov/mission/conferences-and-events

Contact Information The "Contact Us" web page contains the DOT's postal address and customer service center's hours and phone number, as well as directions to DOT headquarters and links leading to additional contact information for DOT Administrations. https://www.transportation.gov/contact-us

Federal Register Significant documents and documents that the DOT recently published in the Federal Register are accessible online. https://www.federalregister.gov/agencies/transportation-department

Freedom of Information Act (FOIA) The FOIA gives information seekers the right to access DOT records, unless the Department determines that releasing the information would harm an interest that one or more of the nine FOIA exemptions shields or that releasing the information would violate the law. After receiving a properly submitted FOIA request, the DOT must provide the requester with copies of the relevant documents and records, or portions of them, that he or she is entitled to access under the law. https://www.transportation.gov/foia

Improving the U.S. Transportation System The DOT Secretary has prioritized innovation through engagement with emerging technologies, maintenance of the Nation's infrastructure, and the safety of Americans when they travel. https://www.transportation.gov/priorities

Infographics The Volpe Center's "Our Impact Through Infographics" web page communicates concisely, both textually and graphically, how the Center has advanced transportation innovation for the public good. https://www.volpe.dot.gov/our-work/infographics

Motor Vehicle Safety To report vehicle safety problems, get motor vehicle and highway safety information, or request consumer information publications, visit the National Highway Traffic Safety Administration's SafeCar.gov website or call its vehicle safety hotline. Phone, 888-327-4236. TTY, 800-424-9153. Reports also may be filed online. http://www.safercar.gov

Newsroom The DOT posts press releases on its website. https://www.transportation.gov/newsroom

Plain Language The Plain Writing Act of 2010 improves "the effectiveness and accountability of Federal agencies to the public by promoting clear Government communication that the public can understand and use." The DOT is committed to helping its employees write clearly. https://www.transportation.gov/regulations/plain-language

Policy Initiatives The DOT posts current policy initiatives on its website. https://www.transportation.gov/policy-initiatives

National Transportation Library The Library makes transportation-related data, reports, research, and reference services accessible. https://ntl.bts.gov/ntl

Social Media The DOT has a YouTube channel and maintains Facebook, Instagram, LinkedIn, and Twitter accounts. https://www.transportation.gov/social

The above Sources of Information were updated 9–2021.

Federal Aviation Administration

800 Independence Avenue SW., Washington, DC 20591
Phone, 202-366-4000. Fax, 866-835-5322. Internet, http://www.faa.gov

Administrator	STEVE DICKSON
Deputy Administrator	A. BRADLEY MIMS
Chief of Staff	ANGELA H. STUBBLEFIELD

https://www.faa.gov/about/key_officials

The above list of key personnel was updated 10–2021.

Establishment and Organization

The Federal Aviation Administration (FAA), formerly the Federal Aviation Agency, was established by the Federal Aviation Act of 1958 (72 Stat. 731). https://www.govinfo.gov/content/pkg/STATUTE-72/pdf/STATUTE-72-Pg731.pdf

The Administration became a component of the Department of Transportation in 1967, pursuant to the Department of Transportation Act (49 U.S.C. 106). https://www.govinfo.gov/content/pkg/STATUTE-80/pdf/STATUTE-80-Pg931.pdf

The FAA posts an organizational chart on its "Offices" web page in Portable Document Format (PDF) for viewing and downloading. https://www.faa.gov/about/office_org/

Activities

The FAA regulates civil aviation and U.S. commercial space transportation, maintains and operates air traffic control and navigation systems for civil and military aircraft, and develops and administers programs involving aviation safety and the National Airspace System. https://www.faa.gov/about/mission/

Air Navigation Facilities The FAA locates and positions, constructs or installs, maintains, operates, and assures the quality of Federal air navigation electronic and visual aids. At flight service stations, airport traffic control towers, and air route traffic control centers, the Administration operates and maintains computer systems, radar facilities, and voice-data communications and visual display equipment. http://www.faa.gov/about/safety_efficiency

Airport Programs The Administration maintains a national plan of airport requirements, administers a grant program for development of public-use airports to assure and improve safety and to meet current and future airport capacity needs, evaluates the environmental effects of airport development, and administers an airport noise compatibility program. It also develops standards for and technical guidance on airport planning, design, operations, and safety and provides grants to assist public agencies in airport system and master planning and airport development and improvement. http://www.faa.gov/airports

Airspace and Air Traffic Management FAA activities center on the safe and efficient utilization of the navigable airspace. To achieve this goal, the Administration operates a network of airport traffic control towers, air route traffic control centers, and flight service stations. It develops air traffic rules and regulations and allocates airspace use. It also provides air traffic security control that meets national defense requirements. http://www.faa.gov/air_traffic

Civil Aviation Abroad Under the Federal Aviation Act of 1958 and the International Aviation Facilities Act (49 U.S.C. app. 1151), the FAA promotes aviation safety and supports civil aviation abroad. FAA experts exchange aeronautical information with foreign counterparts; certify foreign airmen, mechanics, and repair shops; provide technical aid and training; negotiate bilateral airworthiness agreements with other countries; and participate in international conferences. http://www.faa.gov/about/safety_efficiency

Commercial Space Transportation The Administration regulates and supports the U.S. commercial space transportation industry. It licenses commercial space launch facilities and private sector launches of space payloads on expendable vehicles. It also sets insurance requirements for the protection of persons and property and ensures that space transportation activities comply with U.S. domestic and foreign policy. http://www.faa.gov/about/office_org/headquarters_offices/ast/about

Registration The Aircraft Registry establishes and maintains the record of every U.S. civil aircraft. Buyers seeking information on aircraft they want to acquire, banks that finance aircraft purchases, aviation historians, and law enforcement and security agencies rely on the registry. An aircraft record contains information on the aircraft's registered owner, its airworthiness, and on recorded aircraft security interests. http://www.faa.gov/licenses_certificates/aircraft_certification/aircraft_registry/about_aircraft_records

Research, Engineering, and Development The research, engineering, and development activities of the FAA provide the systems, procedures, facilities, and devices needed for a safe and efficient air navigation and air traffic control system for civil aviation and air defense. The Administration also performs an aeromedical research function: It applies knowledge gained from its research program and the work of others to improve civil aviation safety and the safety, health, and efficiency of FAA employees. The Administration also supports the development and testing of aircraft and their parts. http://www.faa.gov/data_research/research

Safety Regulation The FAA issues and enforces regulations and minimum standards affecting the manufacture, operation, and maintenance of aircraft. It also certifies airmen and airports that serve air carriers. http://www.faa.gov/about/safety_efficiency

Test and Evaluation The FAA tests and evaluates specified items such as aviation systems, subsystems, equipment, devices, materials, concepts, or procedures at any phase in the cycle of their development from conception to acceptance, to implementation. At key decision points, it also carries out assigned independent testing.

Other Programs The FAA administers the Aviation Insurance Program, which provides insurance products to cover U.S. domestic air transportation industry needs that are not adequately met by the commercial insurance market. The Administration develops specifications for the preparation of aeronautical charts. It also publishes current information on airways and airport service; issues technical publications for the improvement of in-flight safety, airport planning and design, and other aeronautical activities; and serves as the executive administration for the operation and maintenance of the DOT automated payroll and personnel systems. http://www.faa.gov/about/office_org/headquarters_offices/apl/aviation_insurancehttp://www.faa.gov/air_traffic/flight_info/aeronav

Sources of Information

A–Z Index The FAA website features an alphabetical index to help visitors browse its content or search for information. https://www.faa.gov/quick_reference

Aircraft Registry The FAA maintains a registry that allows users to search aircraft registration information online. https://www.faa.gov/licenses_certificates/aircraft_certification/aircraft_registry

Airlines The Air Traffic Control System Command Center website features a list of links for the Web sites of airlines. http://www.fly.faa.gov/FAQ/Airline_Links/airline_links.jsp

Airmen Certification The FAA posts answers to frequently asked questions dealing with airmen certification on its website. https://www.faa.gov/licenses_certificates/airmen_certification/airmen_FAQ

Archived Records The "Guide to Federal Records in the National Archives of the United States" indicates that FAA records have been assigned to record group 237. https://www.archives.gov/research/guide-fed-records/groups/237.html

Business Opportunities Registration with the System for Award Management is required for doing business with the FAA. https://sam.gov/content/home

The Small Business Office administers programs that assist small businesses, small businesses that are owned and controlled by socially and economically disadvantaged individuals, women-owned small businesses, and service-disabled veteran-owned small businesses, with FAA procurement opportunities. https://sbo.faa.gov/Home.cfm

Career Opportunities The FAA offers civil aviation career opportunities in air traffic control, acquisition, contracts, engineering, information technology, safety and security, and other fields. https://www.faa.gov/jobs/career_fields

In 2020, the FAA ranked 119th among 411 agency subcomponents in the Partnership for Public Service's Best Places To Work Agency Rankings. http://bestplacestowork.org/BPTW/rankings/detail/TD03

Contact the FAA Information for finding the appropriate point of contact or reporting an issue to the FAA is available on the "Contact" web page. https://www.faa.gov/contact

Contact information for field and regional offices is available on the "National Engagement and Regional Administration" web page. https://www.faa.gov/about/office_org/headquarters_offices/arc/

Data / Research The FAA conducts research on commercial and general aviation. It posts information on how the research is carried out, the resulting data and statistics, and grant data and funding information. https://www.faa.gov/data_research

Federal Register Significant documents and documents that the FAA recently published in the Federal Register are accessible online.

https://www.federalregister.gov/agencies/federal-aviation-administration

Flight Delays   The FAA's Air Traffic Control System Command Center provides status information, which is not flight specific, for general airport conditions nationwide. http://www.fly.faa.gov/flyfaa/usmap.jsp

Flying With Pets   The "Flying With Pets" web page has information and relevant links for flying with a pet or service animal. https://www.faa.gov/travelers/fly_pets/

Email, personal digital assistants (PDAs), pagers, phones, and wireless devices can be used to monitor the real-time operating status of the Nation's largest airports and receive delay information from the FAA. https://www.fly.faa.gov/ais/jsp/ais.jsp

Freedom of Information Act (FOIA)   To any person, the FOIA gives a statutory right for obtaining access to Government information in the records of executive branch agencies. This right to access is limited, however, when the requested information is shielded from disclosure by one or more of nine exemptions that are contained within the statute. https://www.faa.gov/foia

FAA posts a lot of information on its website. Before making a formal FOIA request, search the records that are immediately available, particularly the contents of the FAA's electronic FOIA library. The desired information already may be accessible. https://www.faa.gov/foia/electronic_reading_room

Frequently Asked Questions (FAQs)   The FAA posts answers to FAQs on its website. https://faa.custhelp.com

Glossary   The Air Traffic Control System Command Center maintains a glossary of air traffic control management acronyms and terms. http://www.fly.faa.gov/FAQ/Acronyms/acronyms.jsp

International Travel   The "International Travel" web page has information and resources for those preparing to fly abroad. https://www.faa.gov/travelers/international_travel/

History   A timeline of aerospace history is available on the FAA website. The timeline starts on December 17, 1903, with Orville and Wilbur Wright's first self-propelled airplane flight. https://www.faa.gov/about/history/timeline

Newsroom   The FAA posts factsheets, news items and updates, press releases, speeches, and testimonies on its website. https://www.faa.gov/newsroom

NextGen   NextGen is a series of interlinked programs, portfolios, systems, policies, and procedures. It uses advanced technologies and capabilities for improving the operation of the National Airspace System. https://www.faa.gov/nextgen

Report a Drone   Please report a drone that is being operated dangerously or used to commit a crime to local law enforcement first responders. Please report a drone that is being operated in a manner that flouts FAA rules to a local FAA flight standards district office. An unauthorized drone operator may be penalized or criminally charged. https://www.faa.gov/uas/contact_us/report_uas_sighting/

Social Media   The FAA has a Facebook account. https://www.facebook.com/FAA

The FAA tweets announcements and other newsworthy items on Twitter. https://twitter.com/faanews

The FAA posts videos on its YouTube channel. https://www.youtube.com/user/FAAnews

Wildlife Strikes   Aircraft and wildlife in the United States collide on occasion. Wildlife strikes almost always involve birds; however, the FAA also has received reports of alligator, bat, coyote, deer, skunk, and turtle strikes. The most frequently struck birds are gulls, but ducks and geese cause more damage per strike. The FAA's National Wildlife Strike Database contains the information needed for telling the full story of collisions involving aircraft and animals. http://wildlife.faa.gov

The wildlife strike reporting system helps the FAA collect the information used to build the National Wildlife Strike Database. An online form is available for submitting a strike report. https://wildlife.faa.gov/add

The Sources of Information were updated 10–2021.

Federal Highway Administration

1200 New Jersey Avenue SE., Washington, DC 20590
Phone, 202-366-0650. Internet, http://www.fhwa.dot.gov

Administrator	STEPHANIE POLLACK, ACTING
Deputy Administrator	STEPHANIE POLLACK
Executive Director	THOMAS D. EVERETT
https://fhwaapps.fhwa.dot.gov/foisp/hqphone.do	

The above list of key personnel was updated 9–2021.

The Federal Highway Administration (FHWA) was established as an agency of the Department of Transportation by the Department of Transportation Act (49 U.S.C. 104). Title 23 of the United States Code and other supporting legislation authorize the Administration's various activities.

The FHWA improves mobility on our Nation's highways through national leadership, innovation, and program delivery. The Administration works with Federal, State, and local agencies as well as with other stakeholders and partners to maintain and improve the National Highway System, which includes the Interstate System and other roads of importance for national defense and mobility. The FHWA works to increase the National Highway System's safety and to minimize its traffic congestion. The FHWA ensures that America's roads and highways remain safe, technologically up-to-date, and environmentally friendly.

Through surface transportation programs, innovative and traditional financing mechanisms, and new types of pavement and operational technology, the FHWA helps people and goods move more efficiently throughout the Nation. The Administration also improves the efficiency of highway and road connections to other modes of transportation. The Federal-aid Highway Program's budget is primarily divided between Federal-aid funding and the Federal Lands Highway Program. http://www.fhwa. dot.gov/about

Activities

Federal-aid Highway Program   The Federal-Aid Highway Program supports State highway systems, providing financial assistance for the construction, maintenance and operations of the Nation's 3.9 million-mile highway network, which includes the Interstate Highway System, primary highways, and secondary local roads. The FHWA implements the Federal-aid Highway Program in cooperation with State and local governments. http://www.fhwa.dot.gov/ federal-aidessentials/federalaid.cfm

Federal Lands Highway Program   The Office of Federal Lands Highway promotes effective, efficient, and reliable administration for a coordinated program of Federal public roads and bridges; protects and enhances the Nation's natural resources; and gives transportation access to Native Americans. The Office provides financial resources and engineering assistance for public roads that meet the transportation needs of Federal and Indian lands. These services are provided in all 50 States, Puerto Rico, U.S. Territories, and the District of Columbia through the Office's Headquarters and its eastern, central, and western Federal Lands Highway division offices. http://flh. fhwa.dot.gov/about

Sources of Information

All-American Roads / National Scenic Byways   America's Byways—which include the National Scenic Byways and All-American Roads—is an umbrella term referring to the collection of 150 roads that the Secretary of Transportation selects for inclusion based on distinctiveness and diverseness. http://www.fhwa.dot.gov/ byways

Business Opportunities   FHWA programs generate a large number of contracting and procurement opportunities. http://www. fhwa.dot.gov/about/business.cfm

The Office of Acquisition and Grants Management manages most FHWA contracting opportunities. Phone, 202-366-4232. http://www.fhwa.dot.gov/aaa

Career Opportunities The FHWA operates offices throughout the country and hires professionals with expertise in a variety of fields to carry out its mission. http://www.fhwa.dot.gov/careers

The FHWA consistently ranks high among agency subcomponents in the Partnership for Public Service's Best Places To Work Agency Rankings. http://bestplacestowork.org/BPTW/rankings/detail/TD04

Core Topics The "Core Highway Topics" Web page features a topical, alphabetical list. The topics are categorized according to nine headings: environment, Federal and Indian lands, highway funding, international, research and technologies, road operations and congestion, roads and bridges, road users, and safety. http://www.fhwa.dot.gov/resources/topics

Environment The "Air Quality and Climate Change Highlights" newsletter is available on the FHWA Web site. https://www.fhwa.dot.gov/environment/sustainability/newsletter/index.cfm

Federal-Aid Essentials Federal-aid Essentials offers an online library of informational videos and resources for local public agencies. Each video addresses a single topic and condenses the complex regulations and requirements of the Federal-aid Highway Program into basic concepts and illustrated examples. http://www.fhwa.dot.gov/federal-aidessentials

Field and Division Offices The FHWA comprises a headquarters office in Washington, DC; a Federal-aid division office in each State, Puerto Rico, and the District of Columbia; four metropolitan offices—Chicago, Los Angeles, New York City, Philadelphia—that serve as extensions of the corresponding Federal-aid division offices; and three Federal Lands Highway division offices. http://www.fhwa.dot.gov/about/field.cfm

Freedom of Information Act (FOIA) The FOIA establishes a presumption that records in the possession of agencies and departments of the Federal Government's executive branch are available to the public. The statute sets standards for determining when Government records must be made available and which records

may be withheld. It also gives information seekers specific legal rights and provides administrative and judicial remedies when access is denied. Most importantly, the FOIA requires that Federal agencies provide, to the fullest extent possible, access to and disclosure of information pertaining to the Government's business. http://www.fhwa.dot.gov/foia

The FHWA maintains an electronic FOIA reading room. It contains records that are often requested under the statute. http://www.fhwa.dot.gov/foia/err.cfm

Glossary The FHWA Web site features a glossary of transportation planning terms and acronyms. https://www.fhwa.dot.gov/planning/glossary

History The FHWA Web site features a general highway history. http://www.fhwa.dot.gov/infrastructure/history.cfm

Infrastructure The FHWA's Web site offers a trove of information on the following infrastructure topics: asset management, bridges and structures, construction, design, Federal-aid Program administration, Federal-aid programs and special funding, geotechnical, hydraulics, pavement, preservation, and transportation performance management. http://www.fhwa.dot.gov/infrastructure

Libraries The FHWA research library is located in the Turner-Fairbank Highway Research Center in McLean, VA. It is open on weekdays, excluding Federal holidays, 7:30–4 p.m. Phone, 202-493-3172. Fax, 202-493-3495. http://www.fhwa.dot.gov/research/library/ | Email: fhwalibrary@dot.gov

Each FHWA office maintains accessibility information that relates to its own program. The accessibility resource library supports the effort to organize information relating to the Americans with Disabilities Act and other accessibility resources that may affect FHWA projects. http://www.fhwa.dot.gov/accessibility

Newsroom The FHWA posts press releases, as well as photos and videos, speeches and testimony, on its Web site and YouTube channel. http://www.fhwa.dot.gov/briefingroom

Resource Center / Technical Service Teams The FHWA's technical service teams are organized into 12 activity areas:

air quality, civil rights, construction and program management, environment and realty, finance services, geotechnical, hydraulics, operations, pavement and materials, planning, safety and design, and structures. Contact information for these teams and information on their activities, products, and services are available online in the Resource Center. http://www.fhwa.dot. gov/resourcecenter/index.cfm

Social Media   The FHWA tweets announcements and other newsworthy items on Twitter. https://twitter.com/USDOTFHWA

The FHWA maintains a page on Facebook. https://www.facebook.com/ FederalHighwayAdmin

The FHWA posts videos on its YouTube channel. https://www.youtube.com/user/ USDOTFHWA

Staff Directories   The headquarters organizational directory, key field personnel directory, and Washington headquarters fax numbers are available on the FHWA's Web site. http://www.fhwa.dot.gov/about/staff.cfm

Sustainability   The FHWA provides technical assistance to local, regional, and State transportation agencies to help them enhance sustainability, improve resilience, and reduce energy use and emissions on the Nation's highway system. https://www.fhwa. dot.gov/environment/sustainability/index. cfm http://www.fhwa.dot.gov/contact

For further information, contact the Federal Highway Administration, Office of Public Affairs, 1200 New Jersey Avenue, SE., Washington, DC 20590. Phone, 202-366-0660.

Federal Motor Carrier Safety Administration

1200 New Jersey Avenue SE., Washington, DC 20590
Phone, 202-366-2519. Internet, http://www.fmcsa.dot.gov

Administrator	(VACANCY)
Deputy Administrator	MEERA JOSHI
https://www.fmcsa.dot.gov/mission/leadership	

The above list of key personnel was updated 9–2021.

Establishment and Organization

The Federal Motor Carrier Safety Administration (FMCSA) was established within the Department of Transportation on January 1, 2000, pursuant to the Motor Carrier Safety Improvement Act of 1999 (113 Stat. 1750). https://www.govinfo.gov/ content/pkg/STATUTE-113/pdf/STATUTE-113-Pg1748.pdf

Statutory material that affects the organization of the FMCSA has been codified in the United States Code (U.S.C.) and assigned to 49 U.S.C. 113. https://uscode.house.gov/view. xhtml?req=granuleid:USC-prelim-title49-section113&num=0&edition=prelim

Activities

Formerly a part of the Federal Highway Administration, the FMCSA reduces commercial motor vehicle-related fatalities and injuries. Administration activities increase the safety of motor carrier operations by enforcing safety regulations— targeting high-risk commercial drivers and carriers; improving safety information systems and commercial motor vehicle technologies; strengthening equipment and operating standards; and increasing safety awareness. When carrying out these activities, the Administration works with representatives of the motor carrier industry, labor safety interest groups, and Federal, State, and local enforcement agencies. https://www.fmcsa.dot.gov/mission/about-us

Commercial Licensing   The FMCSA develops standards to test and license commercial motor vehicle drivers. https:// www.fmcsa.dot.gov/registration/commercial-drivers-license

Data / Analysis   The FMCSA collects and disseminates data on motor carrier safety and directs resources to improve motor carrier safety. https://www.fmcsa.dot.gov/

safety/data-and-statistics/motor-carrier-safety-progress-reports

Regulatory Compliance / Enforcement   The FMCSA operates a program to improve safety performance and remove high-risk carriers from the Nation's highways. https://www.fmcsa.dot.gov/regulations

Research / Technology   The FMCSA coordinates research and development to improve the safety of motor carrier operations and commercial motor vehicles and drivers. https://www.fmcsa.dot.gov/safety/research-and-analysis/active-research-projects

Safety Assistance   The FMCSA provides States with financial assistance for roadside inspections and other commercial motor vehicle safety programs. https://www.fmcsa.dot.gov/safety

Other Activities   The FMCSA supports the development of unified motor carrier safety requirements and procedures throughout North America. It participates in international technical organizations and committees to help share best-practices in motor carrier safety worldwide. It enforces regulations ensuring safe highway transportation of hazardous materials and maintains a task force for identifying and investigating household goods carriers that exhibit an unmistakable pattern of consumer abuse.

Sources of Information

Archived Records   The "Guide to Federal Records in the National Archives of the United States" indicates that FMCSA records have been assigned to record group 557. That record group, however, does not have a description that is associated with it. https://www.archives.gov/research/guide-fed-records/groups/000.html

Bicyclists / Pedestrians   Bicyclists and pedestrians share roads with large trucks and buses. The FMCSA website has resources that address safety issues affecting riders, walkers, and drivers. https://www.fmcsa.dot.gov/safety/resources-bicyclists-and-pedestrians

Career Opportunities   The FMCSA posts job announcements on the USAJobs website. Application tips, information for students and recent graduates, and reasons for pursuing a career at the FMCSA are available on its website. Phone, 800-832-5660. https://www.fmcsa.dot.gov/careers

In 2020, the FMCSA ranked 138th among 411 agency subcomponents in the Partnership for Public Service's Best Places To Work Agency Rankings. https://bestplacestowork.org/rankings/detail/?c=TD17

Certified Medical Examiners   Inclusion in the National Registry of Certified Medical Examiners is limited to medical professionals who complete training and pass an exam on the FMCSA's physical qualification standards. https://www.fmcsa.dot.gov/regulations/national-registry/national-registry-certified-medical-examiners

Commercial Carriers   The FMCSA website has resources to help carrier companies with registration and safety and regulatory matters. https://www.fmcsa.dot.gov/resources-for-carrier-companies

The FMCSA website has resources—regulatory information and safety publications—to make complying with regulations easier for passenger carriers and to help them operate more safely. https://www.fmcsa.dot.gov/safety/passenger-safety/passenger-carrier-safety-information

Commercial Drivers   The FMCSA website has resources for drivers who want to increase safety and who may need help them with the registration and licensing processes. https://www.fmcsa.dot.gov/resources-for-drivers

Company Safety Records   The FMCSA maintains websites that provide convenient access to safety-related information. To perform a search, a user must know a company's name, USDOT number, or motor carrier number. https://www.fmcsa.dot.gov/safety/company-safety-records

Contact Information   The "Contact Us" web page has a table that contains email addresses, phone numbers, and web forms. https://www.fmcsa.dot.gov/contact-us

Data / Statistics   The annual "Pocket Guide to Large Truck and Bus Statistics" highlights the FMCSA's role in collecting and analyzing data on large trucks and buses. The pocket guide is a compilation of statistics from the overall state of the industry to enforcement activity, details on traffic violations and other incidents, the costs of crashes, and more.

https://www.fmcsa.dot.gov/safety/data-and-statistics/commercial-motor-vehicle-facts

The Analysis Division compiles the information used for "Large Truck and Bus Crash Facts," an annual report containing descriptive statistics on fatal, injurious, and property-damage-only crashes involving large trucks and buses. https://www.fmcsa.dot.gov/safety/data-and-statistics/large-truck-and-bus-crash-facts

Federal Register Significant documents and documents that the FMCSA recently published in the Federal Register are accessible online. https://www.federalregister.gov/agencies/federal-motor-carrier-safety-administration

Freedom of Information Act (FOIA) The FMCSA supports efforts to create a more open and transparent Federal Government. Accordingly, it conscientiously carries out the requirements of the FOIA. The FMCSA ensures that nonexempt documents or records are accessible to anyone who properly files a FOIA request. Phone, 202-366-2960. Fax, 202-385-2335. https://www.fmcsa.dot.gov/foia | Email: foia@fmcsa.dot.gov

The FMCSA's electronic reading room contains frequently requested records, as well as final opinions and orders, policy statements, and staff manuals. https://www.fmcsa.dot.gov/foia/foia-electronic-reading-room

Frequently Asked Questions (FAQs) The FMCSA posts answers to FAQs on its website. https://www.fmcsa.dot.gov/faq

Grants State and local government agencies in the 50 States and the District of Columbia, as well as in American Samoa, Guam, Puerto Rico, and the Northern Mariana and the U.S. Virgin Islands may apply for safety grant funding. https://www.fmcsa.dot.gov/mission/grants

Look Before You Book The FMCSA website has resources for those making travel plans and for those looking to charter a bus for a sporting event, field trip, or other group activity. Safety tips and information, software applications (apps) to research bus operators, and information on reporting

safety violations are available on the "Look Before You Book" web pages. https://www.fmcsa.dot.gov/safety/passenger-safety/bus-passengers-look-you-book

Bus travel safety kits for seniors, students, and those traveling to faith-based events are available on "Look Before You Book." https://www.fmcsa.dot.gov/safety/look-you-book/consumer-safety-resources

Newsroom The FMCSA posts events, news releases, speeches, and testimony on its website. https://www.fmcsa.dot.gov/newsroom

Protect Your Move The "Protect Your Move" web pages have a trove of information on and resources for planning a move, selecting a mover, and filing a moving fraud complaint. https://www.fmcsa.dot.gov/protect-your-move

Safety Violations Safety, service, or discrimination issues involving a bus or truck or moving company or a cargo tank facility? If so, file a complaint on the National Consumer Complaint Database website or by phone on weekdays, 8 a.m.–8 p.m., eastern time. Phone, 888-368-7238. https://nccdb.fmcsa.dot.gov/nccdb/home.aspx

Service Centers / Field Offices Contact information for service centers and field offices is available on the FMCSA website. Phone, 800-832-5660. https://www.fmcsa.dot.gov/mission/field-offices

Social Media The FMCSA tweets announcements and other newsworthy items on Twitter. https://twitter.com/fmcsa

The FMCSA has a Facebook account. https://www.facebook.com/FMCSA

USDOT Numbers The FMCSA website features an interactive tool that can determine whether or not a commercial vehicle requires a USDOT number. https://www.fmcsa.dot.gov/registration/do-i-need-usdot-number

Veterans The FMCSA helps veterans find employment in the motor carrier industry. Several provisions in the Fixing America's Surface Transportation (FAST) Act support this effort. https://www.fmcsa.dot.gov/fastact/veteran-drivers

The above Sources of Information were updated 9–2021.

Federal Railroad Administration

1200 New Jersey Avenue, SE., West Building, Washington, DC 20590
Phone, 202-493-6014. Internet, http://www.fra.dot.gov

Administrator	(VACANCY)
Deputy Administrator	AMIT BOSE
https://railroads.dot.gov/about-fra/organization/vacant-administrator	

The above list of key personnel was updated 09–2021.

Establishment and Organization

The Federal Railroad Administration (FRA) was created pursuant to section 3(e)(1) of the Department of Transportation Act of 1966 (49 U.S.C. 103). https://www.govinfo.gov/content/pkg/STATUTE-80/pdf/STATUTE-80-Pg931.pdf

The FRA posts its organizational chart in Portable Document Format (PDF) on its website for viewing and downloading. https://railroads.dot.gov/about-fra/organization/organization-chart

Activities

The Administration promulgates and enforces rail safety regulations, administers railroad financial assistance programs, conducts research and development to improve railroad safety and national rail transportation policy, provides for the rehabilitation of Northeast Corridor rail passenger service, and consolidates Government support of rail transportation activities. https://railroads.dot.gov/about-fra/about-fra

Passenger and Freight Services   The FRA's passenger rail activities include administering Federal grants and loans to Amtrak, Alaska Railroad, and high-speed rail; supporting the Secretary of Transportation in his or her role as a member of Amtrak's board of directors; providing guidance and analysis of intercity passenger rail services and high-speed rail. https://railroads.dot.gov/rail-network-development/passenger-rail/passenger-rail

Its freight rail activities include supporting current freight rail market share and growth and developing strategies to attract 50 percent of all shipments 500 miles or more to intermodal rail. The Administration's Office of Railroad Policy and Development implements programs that provide financial support, research and development, and analysis and guidance for the freight rail industry and its stakeholders. https://railroads.dot.gov/rail-network-development/freight-rail-overview

Railroad Safety   The Administration administers and enforces the Federal laws and regulations that promote railroad safety, and it exercises jurisdiction over all areas of rail safety under the Rail Safety Act of 1970—track maintenance, inspection standards, equipment standards, operating practices. Railroad and related industry equipment, facilities, and records are inspected and required reports are reviewed. The Administration also educates the public about safety at highway rail grade crossings and the danger of trespassing on rail property. https://railroads.dot.gov/railroad-safety

Research / Development   The FRA's research and development program relies on basic and applied research and on the development of innovations and solutions to ensure the efficient, reliable, and safe movement of people and goods. Safety is the principal driver of the research and development program. https://railroads.dot.gov/research-development/research-development-and-technology

Transportation Test Center   The Administration tests and evaluates conventional and advanced railroad systems and components at the Transportation Test Center, Inc. Private sector companies and the Governments of Canada, Japan, and the United States use the facility to study the operation of conventional and advanced systems under controlled conditions. Amtrak tests new high-speed locomotives and trains at the Center, and the Federal Transit Administration uses it for testing urban rapid transit vehicles. https://railroads.dot.gov/

FEDERAL RAILROAD ADMINISTRATION

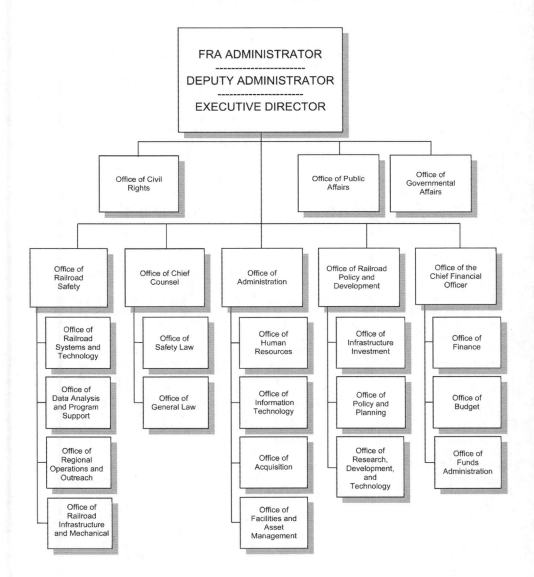

program-areas/testing-facilities-equipment/
testing-facilities-equipment

Sources of Information

Archived Records   The "Guide to Federal
Records in the National Archives of the
United States" indicates that FRA records
have been assigned to record group 399.
https://www.archives.gov/research/guide-fed-
records/groups/399.html
Business Opportunities   The "How To Do
Business with the FRA" web page explains
the steps of becoming eligible for doing
business with the FRA and of identifying
business opportunities that the FRA has to
offer. The web page also has a database of
small business vendors. https://railroads.dot.
gov/resource-center/how-do-business-fra/
how-do-business-fra
Career Opportunities   The FRA relies
heavily on railroad safety inspectors—
hazardous materials, motive power and
equipment, operating practices, signals and
train control, and track inspectors—to carry
out its mission. Safety inspectors inspect for
compliance with Federal laws, regulations,
rules, and standards; conduct accident
investigations and report on their findings;
and seek correction of unsafe conditions.
They also testify as expert witnesses in
civil suits. These jobs require skill in
evaluation, factfinding, and report writing;
comprehension and application of technical
and regulatory standards; an ability to build
rapport with individuals and organizations;
and knowledge of methods used in
installation, operation, and maintenance or
manufacturing of railroad equipment and
systems. https://railroads.dot.gov/resource-
center/jobs/job-vacancies

In 2020, the FRA ranked 206th among 411
agency subcomponents in the Partnership for
Public Service's Best Places To Work Agency
Rankings. https://bestplacestowork.org/
rankings/detail/?c=TD05
Contact Information   Email addresses
and phone numbers are available on the
"Contact Us" web page. https://railroads.dot.
gov/about-fra/contact-us
Electronic Library (eLibrary)   An eLibrary
offers convenient access to all the
documents that are posted on the FRA's

public website. https://railroads.dot.gov/
elibrary-search
Environmental Reviews   The FRA posts a
list of environmental projects that require the
FRA to pursue an environmental assessment
or environmental impact statement or both
an assessment and a statement. https://
railroads.dot.gov/rail-network-development/
environment/environmental-reviews
Federal Register   Significant documents and
documents that the FRA recently published
in the Federal Register are accessible online.
https://www.federalregister.gov/agencies/
federal-railroad-administration
Freedom of Information Act (FOIA)   Any
person—U.S. citizens, foreign nationals, as
well as those representing organizations,
associations, and universities—can file a
FOIA request. All FOIA requests must be
submitted in writing and are processed
in the Office of Chief Counsel at FRA
headquarters in Washington, DC. https://
railroads.dot.gov/freedom-information-act-
foia | Email: FRAFOIA@dot.gov

To comply with the Electronic Freedom of
Information Act (E–FOIA) Amendments of
1996, agencies must make some categories
of records available to the public on an
ongoing basis. https://railroads.dot.gov/
resource-center/freedom-information-act/
electronic-reading-room
Horn Noise   Noise from transportation
systems, including rail operations, often
has adverse environmental effects. The FRA
posts answers to frequently asked questions
on horn noise. https://railroads.dot.gov/
environment/noise-vibration/horn-noise-faq
Maps   The "Maps—Geographic Information
System" web page has interactive safety and
trespassers casualty maps. https://railroads.
dot.gov/maps-and-data/maps-geographic-
information-system/maps-geographic-
information-system
Media Relations   The Office of
Communications handles media relations.
https://railroads.dot.gov/about-fra/
communications/communications
News   The FRA posts news items on its
website. https://railroads.dot.gov/newsroom
Railroad Crossings / Trespassing   FRA
programs have helped to reduce the number
of railroad crossing and trespassing fatalities
by 60% over the last two decades. The

Railroad Crossing Safety and Trespasser Prevention Division seeks to continue this trend. Information on and resources for railroad crossing safety and preventing trespassing along railroad rights-of-way are available online. https://railroads.dot.gov/highway-rail-crossing-and-trespasser-programs/railroad-crossing-safety-trespass

Railroad Safety The Office of Safety Analysis posts railroad safety information—data related to railroad accidents and incidents, including highway-rail grade crossing accidents, rail equipment accidents, and employee injuries and illnesses—on its website. https://safetydata.fra.dot.gov/OfficeofSafety/Default.aspx

The FRA has a new safety data website. https://railroads.dot.gov/forms-guides-publications/guides/interacting-new-fra-safety-data-website

The FRA monitors the occurrence of train accidents and incidents and investigates serious events to determine their cause and to assess compliance with safety laws and regulations. Detailed information on

these investigations is available on the FRA's website. https://railroads.dot.gov/railroad-safety/accident-data-reporting-and-investigations

Operation Lifesaver, Inc., is a nonprofit organization and a rail safety education leader. https://oli.org/about-us

Research / Development The Office of Research and Development is organized into four divisions and works in 10 program areas. An online table shows where the four divisions and 10 program areas intersect with the most frequent causes of railroad accidents and incidents. https://railroads.dot.gov/research-development/program-areas/program-areas

Social Media The FRA posts photographs and tweets announcements and other newsworthy items on Twitter. https://twitter.com/USDOTFRA

The FRA has a Facebook page. https://www.facebook.com/USDOTFRA

The FRA posts videos on its YouTube channel. https://www.youtube.com/user/usdotfra

The above Sources of Information were updated 9–2021.

Federal Transit Administration

1200 New Jersey Avenue SE., Washington, DC 20590
Phone, 202-366-4043. Internet, http://www.fta.dot.gov

Administrator — Nuria Fernandez
Deputy Administrator — (vacancy)
Executive Director — Matthew J. Welbes
https://www.transit.dot.gov/about/officials/officials

[For the Federal Transit Administration statement of organization, see the Code of Federal Regulations, Title 49, Part 601]

The above list of key personnel was updated 9–2021.

The Federal Transit Administration (FTA), formerly the Urban Mass Transportation Administration, was established as an operating administration of the U.S. Department of Transportation by section 1 of Reorganization Plan No. 2 of 1968 (5 U.S.C. app. 1), effective July 1, 1968. The FTA helps America's communities by developing improved public transportation and providing financial assistance to State and local governments to finance public

transportation systems and carry out national transit goals and policy. https://www.transit.dot.gov/about-fta

Programs

Alternatives Analysis The Alternatives Analysis program provides grants to help identify public transportation needs and the costs and benefits of various transportation strategies for a defined travel corridor. The results of these studies may be the selection of a locally preferred transportation alternative, which is the first step for developing viable projects for possible future funding under the New Starts and Small Starts program. http://www.fta.dot.gov/grants/13094_7395.html

For further information, call the Office of Program Management. Phone, 202-366-2053.

Capital Investment   The Capital Investment program helps finance the acquisition, construction, reconstruction, and improvement of facilities and equipment for public transportation service in urban areas. The Capital Investment program makes available three types of funds: fixed guideway modernization funds for rolling stock renewal, safety-related improvements, and signal and power modernization; new and small starts funds for construction of new fixed guideway systems or extensions to existing fixed guideway systems or corridor based rapid bus systems; and bus and bus facilities funds for the acquisition of buses and rolling stock, ancillary equipment, and the construction of bus facilities. http://www.fta.dot.gov/12304.html

For further information, call the Office of Program Management. Phone, 202-366-2053.

Clean Fuels Grants   The Clean Fuels Grants program helps nonattainment and maintenance areas achieve or maintain the National Ambient Air Quality Standards for ozone and carbon monoxide, and it supports emerging clean fuel and advanced propulsion technologies for transit buses and markets for those technologies. The program funds purchasing or leasing clean fuel buses, including buses that employ a lightweight composite primary structure and vans for use in revenue service; constructing or leasing clean fuel bus facilities, including electrical recharging facilities and related equipment; and projects involving clean fuel, biodiesel, hybrid electric, or zero emissions technology buses. http://www.fta.dot.gov/cleanfuels

For further information, call the Office of Program Management. Phone, 202-366-2053.

Elderly Persons and Persons With Disabilities   The Transportation for Elderly Persons and Persons With Disabilities program provides financial assistance

to private nonprofit agencies for the transportation needs of elderly persons and persons with disabilities in places where public services are unavailable, insufficient, or inappropriate; to public bodies approved by the State to coordinate services for elderly persons or persons with disabilities; and to public bodies that certify to the Governor that no nonprofit corporation or association is readily available in an area to provide the service. Funds are allocated by formula to the States. Local organizations apply for funding through a designated State agency. http://www.fta.dot.gov/grants/13093_3556.html

For further information, call the Office of Program Management. Phone, 202-366-2053.

Job Access and Reverse Commuting   The Job Access and Reverse Commute program addresses the transportation challenges faced by welfare recipients and low-income persons seeking or maintaining employment. The program provides capital and planning and operating expenses for projects that transport low income individuals to and from jobs and employment-related activities and for projects that support reverse commuting. Many new entry level jobs are located in suburban areas: Low-income individuals have difficulty accessing these jobs from their inner city, urban, or rural neighborhoods. Many entry level-jobs also require working late or on weekends when conventional transit services are either reduced or nonexistent. Many employment related-trips also are complex, involving multiple destinations. http://www.fta.dot.gov/grants/13093_3550.html

For further information, call the Office of Program Management. Phone, 202-366-2053.

New Freedom   The New Freedom formula grants program supports new public transportation services that surpass the requirements of the Americans with Disabilities Act (ADA) of 1990. The program makes capital and operating funding available to private nonprofit organizations, State and local governmental authorities, and operators of public transportation services, including private operators of public transportation services. Eligible projects must benefit individuals with disabilities: Projects must assist them with transportation—including transportation to and from jobs and employment services—and remove barriers to transportation. http://www.fta.dot.gov/grants/13093_3549.html

For further information, call the Office of Program Management. Phone, 202-366-2053.

Nonurban Area Assistance The Other Than Urbanized Areas formula grants program provides funding to States to support public transportation in rural areas—with populations under 50,000. The program enhances people's access in nonurbanized areas to health care, shopping, education, employment, public services, and recreation; assists in the maintenance, development, improvement, and use of public transportation systems in nonurbanized areas; encourages and facilitates the most efficient use of all transportation funds used to provide passenger transportation in nonurbanized areas through the coordination of programs and services; helps develop and support intercity bus transportation; and promotes the participation of private transportation providers in nonurbanized transportation. http://www.fta.dot.gov/grants/13093_3555.html

For further information, call the Office of Program Management. Phone, 202-366-2053.

Planning The Office of Planning and Environment supports the development of information that Federal, State, and local officials use to make transportation investment decisions. With FHWA partners, the Office co-administers a national planning program that provides funding, guidance, oversight, and technical support to State and local transportation agencies. The FTA's 10 region offices and FHWA's 52 division offices work to convey the program to State and local governments and other transportation agencies. http://www.fta.dot.gov/about/12347.html

For further information, call the Office of Planning and Environment. Phone, 202-366-4033.

Research and Technology The FTA conducts research, development, demonstration, deployment, and evaluation projects to improve public transportation

services. The FTA administers the Bus Testing, International Public Transportation, National Research and Technology, and Transit Cooperative Research Programs. Through the Transit Investments for Greenhouse Gas and Energy Reduction (TIGGER) program, the Administration works with public transportation agencies to implement new strategies for lowering greenhouse gas emissions and to reduce energy use within transit operations. The FTA has five priority research areas: bicycles and transit, bus rapid transit, environmental sustainability, livable and sustainable communities, and state of good repair. https://www.transit.dot.gov/about/research-innovation

For further information, call the Office of Research, Demonstration and Innovation. Phone, 202-366-4052.

Rural Transit Assistance The Rural Transit Assistance Program provides a funding source to help design and implement training and technical assistance projects and other support services tailored to meet the needs of transit operators in nonurbanized areas. States, local governments, and providers of rural transit services can receive program funds. States may use the funds to support nonurbanized transit activities in four areas: training, technical assistance, research, and related support services. http://www.fta.dot.gov/grants/13093_3554.html

For further information, call the Office of Program Management. Phone, 202-366-2053.

Safety The Office of Transit Safety and Oversight administers a national safety program and oversees compliance with it. Based on FTA legislative, policy, and regulatory requirements, the program helps further the nationwide provision of transit service that is equitable, reliable, and safe. http://www.fta.dot.gov/tso.html

For further information, call the Office of Transit Safety and Oversight. Phone, 202-366-1783.

Training and Technical Assistance The Administration funds the National Transit Institute at Rutgers, The State University of New Jersey. Working with the Institute, the FTA develops and offers training courses on transit operations, planning, workforce performance, and productivity. Institute courses are offered at locations nationwide on a variety of subjects. Current course offerings are posted online. http://www.ntionline.com/courses/list.php

For further information, call the Office of Research, Demonstration and Innovation. Phone, 202-366-4052.

Transit in Parks   The Paul S. Sarbanes Transit in Parks Program provides funding for alternative transportation projects in and around National Parks and other Federal recreation areas. Alternative transportation includes bicycle, ferry, pedestrian trail, shuttle bus, and other forms of public or nonmotorized transportation. These projects reduce congestion, protect sensitive natural and cultural treasures, and enhance visitor experience. Funding is awarded through a competitive process to units of Federal land management agencies and to State, local and tribal government agencies. http://www.fta.dot.gov/transitinparks

For further information, call the Office of Program Management. Phone, 202-366-2053.

Sources of Information

Business Opportunities   Procurement-related information and resources are available on the FTA Web site. https://www.transit.dot.gov/funding/procurement/procurement

Career Opportunities   FTA fills vacancies in its Washington, DC, headquarters and regional offices. The FTA relies on attorneys, congressional relations specialists, engineers, environmental specialists, planners, program management specialists, research program specialists, and other professionals to carry out its mission. https://www.transit.dot.gov/about/jobs/jobs

In 2016, the FTA ranked 228th among 305 agency subcomponents in the Partnership for Public Service's Best Places To Work Agency Rankings. http://bestplacestowork.org/BPTW/rankings/detail/TD09

Environmental Justice   The FTA posts answers to questions related to environmental justice on its Web site. https://www.transit.dot.gov/regulations-and-guidance/environmental-programs/environmental-justice/environmental-justice-faqs

Events   The FTA has a calendar of events on its Web site. https://www.transit.dot.gov/about/events

Freedom of Information Act (FOIA)   The FOIA grants public access to the content of certain records that are held by the offices, agencies, corporations, administrations, commissions, boards, and services of the Federal Government's executive branch. Some records that contain sensitive commercial, governmental, and personal information are protected from disclosure. https://www.transit.dot.gov/foia/foia-requests | Email: FTA.FOIA@dot.gov

The FTA maintains an electronic reading room. Before submitting a FOIA request, information seekers should search for the desired document or record in the reading room to determine whether it is accessible immediately, without charge. https://www.transit.dot.gov/foia/foia-electronic-reading-room

Glossary   The FTA maintains a National Transit Database glossary on its Web site. https://www.transit.dot.gov/ntd/national-transit-database-ntd-glossary

Grants   The FTA provides grants to local public transit systems. It invests billions of dollars each year to support and to expand public transit services. It provides annual formula grants to transit agencies nationwide, as well as discretionary funding in competitive processes. https://www.transit.dot.gov/funding/grants/grant-programs

History   A brief history of mass transit is available on the FTA Web site. https://www.transit.dot.gov/about/brief-history-mass-transit

National Transit Database   U.S. transit ridership has grown by more than 20 percent in the last decade. To keep track of the industry and provide public information and statistics as growth continues, the National Transit Database records the asset, financial, and operating conditions of transit systems. Phone, 888-252-0936. https://www.transit.dot.gov/ntd | Email: NTDhelp@dot.gov

News   The FTA posts news releases on its Web site. https://www.transit.dot.gov/about/news

Regional Offices   Contact information for the 10 regional offices is available on the FTA's Web site. https://www.transit.dot.gov/about/regional-offices/regional-offices

Research / Innovation   Research projects assess new operational processes, expand public-private partnerships, fund demonstration grants for low or no emissions buses, improve traveler experiences, and test systems that monitor safety. Research and innovation reports and publications are available on the FTA Web site. https://www.transit.dot.gov/research-innovation/research-innovation-reports-and-publications

Social Media   The FTA maintains a channel on YouTube, as well as accounts on Facebook, LinkedIn, and Twitter. https://www.transit.dot.gov/about/news/social-media

Updates   A subscription form is available on the FTA Web site to sign up for email updates. https://public.govdelivery.com/accounts/USDOTFTA/subscriber/new http://www.fta.dot.gov/newsroom/13006.html

For further information, contact the Federal Transit Administration, Office of Communications and Congressional Affairs, 1200 New Jersey Avenue SE., Washington, DC 20590. Phone, 202-366-4043.

Great Lakes Saint Lawrence Seaway Development Corporation

55 M Street SE., Suite 930, Washington, DC 20003.
Phone, 202-366-0091; 202-366-7147. Internet, http://www.seaway.dot.gov

Departmental Postal Address: Great Lakes Saint Lawrence Seaway Development Corporation, 1200 New Jersey Avenue SE., Washington, DC 20590. Email: slsdc@dot.gov

Postal and Physical Address: Great Lakes Saint Lawrence Seaway Development Corporation–Operations, 180 Andrews Street, Massena, NY 13662. Phone, 315-764-3200; 315-764-3235

Policy Headquarters—Washington, DC

Administrator	(VACANCY)
Deputy Administrator	CRAIG H. MIDDLEBROOK

Operational Headquarters—Massena, NY

Associate Administrator, Seaway Operations   GARY CROOT
https://www.seaway.dot.gov/about/meet-our-team

The above list of key personnel was updated 03–2021.

The Great Lakes Saint Lawrence Seaway Development Corporation (GLSLSDC) was established by the Saint Lawrence Seaway Act of May 13, 1954 (33 U.S.C. 981-990) and became an operating administration of the DOT in 1966.

The GLSLSDC, working jointly with the Saint Lawrence Seaway Management Corporation (SLSMC) of Canada, operates and maintains a safe, reliable, and efficient deep draft waterway between the Great Lakes and the Atlantic Ocean. It ensures the safe transit of commercial and noncommercial vessels through the two U.S. locks and the navigation channels of the Saint Lawrence Seaway System and engages in economic and trade development activities to stimulate trade and employment in the eight States of the Great Lakes region. The GLSLSDC and SLSMC work together on all matters related to rules and regulations, overall operations, vessel inspections, traffic control, navigation aids, safety, operating dates, and trade development programs.

The Great Lakes-Saint Lawrence Seaway System extends from the Atlantic Ocean to the Lake Superior ports of Duluth and Superior, a distance of 2,342 miles. The Corporation's main customers are vessel owners and operators, Midwest States and Canadian Provinces, Great Lakes port communities, shippers and receivers of domestic and international cargo, and the maritime and related service industries of the Great Lakes and Saint Lawrence Seaway systems. https://www.seaway.dot.gov/about/what-does-slsdc-do

Sources of Information

Career Opportunities The GLSLSDC relies on professionals with expertise in administration, engineering, information technology, management, marine operations, public policy, and other fields. https://www.seaway.dot.gov/about/careers-slsdc

Contact Information Information for contacting the GLSLSDC by email, postal mail, and phone is posted online. https://www.seaway.dot.gov/about/contact-us

Freedom of Information Act (FOIA) Any person has the right to a copy of certain records possessed by the Government's executive administrations, agencies, boards, commissions, corporations, offices, and services. Some records, however, are protected from disclosure. https://www.seaway.dot.gov/publications/electronic-reading-room

Grants The GLSLSDC has an easy-to-use Federal grants toolkit that offers a snapshot of the essential information, resources, and tools needed to identify Federal agencies and processes offering financial assistance to maritime stakeholders seeking to carry out environmental, infrastructural, intermodal, and other development projects. https://www.seaway.dot.gov/publications/slsdc-federal-grants-toolkit

Map An interactive map of vessels transiting the Great Lakes-St. Lawrence Seaway System is available online. https://www.seaway.dot.gov/explore/interactive-shipping-map-and-shipping-schedule

News The SLSDC's quarterly newsletter "Seaway Compass" is available online. It features current information and recent news on the Great Lakes-St. Lawrence Seaway System. https://www.seaway.dot.gov/publications/seaway-compass

Publications The "Great Lakes-St. Lawrence Seaway System Directory" is a comprehensive publication on the ports and shipping-related businesses that are critical throughout the region and beyond.

It features extensive photography and serves as an excellent resource for readers who are interested in the Great Lakes Seaway maritime industry. https://www.seaway.dot.gov/publications/seaway-system-directory

The GLSLSDC's marketing brochure offers comprehensive information on the waterway and its significance to the Great Lakes region. It is available online in Portable Document Format (PDF). https://www.seaway.dot.gov/publications/slsdc-marketing-brochure

Reports The GLSLSDC posts annual reports on its website. https://www.seaway.dot.gov/publications/annual-reports

The GLSLSDC posts Asset Renewal Program reports on its website. https://www.seaway.dot.gov/publications/asset-renewal-program-reports

Social Media The GLSLSDC maintains a Facebook account. https://www.facebook.com/USDOTSLSDC

Studies The "Environmental and Social Impacts of Marine Transport in the Great Lakes-St. Lawrence Seaway Region" study provides marine stakeholders, transportation planners, and government policymakers with an assessment of the potential environmental and social consequences that could occur if cargo carried by marine vessels on the Seaway navigation system shifted to rail and road modes of transport. https://www.seaway.dot.gov/publications/social-impact-study

Visitors' Center The Seaway Visitors' Center at the Eisenhower Lock provides tourists and ship watchers with an observation deck where they can view commercial vessels and cruise ships transiting the lock. Each year, hundreds of ships from all over the globe make thousands of transits through the St. Lawrence Seaway. They carry a wide variety of cargoes: coal, grains, iron ore, steel, steel slabs, stone, and more. https://www.seaway.dot.gov/explore/visitors-center

The Sources of Information were updated 3–2021.

Maritime Administration

1200 New Jersey Avenue SE., Washington, DC 20590
Phone, 202-366-5807. Fax, 800-996-2723. Internet, http://www.marad.dot.gov

Administrator	LUCINDA LESSLEY, ACTING
Deputy Administrator	LUCINDA LESSLEY
https://www.maritime.dot.gov/about-us/office-administrator/key-personnel	

The above list of key personnel was updated 11–2021.

MARAD develops and promotes the U.S. merchant marine and its operations and oversees emergency merchant ship operations.

Establishment

The Maritime Administration (MARAD) was established by Reorganization Plan No. 21 of 1950 (5 U.S.C. app.). The Maritime Act of 1981 (46 U.S.C. 1601) transferred the Maritime Administration to the DOT.

MARAD manages programs that help develop and promote the U.S. merchant marine and its operations. It also organizes and directs emergency merchant ship operations.

Activities

MARAD serves as the DOT's waterborne transportation agency. Its programs promote waterborne transportation use, the seamless integration of waterborne transportation with other parts of the transportation system, and U.S. merchant marine viability. The Administration's activities involve ships and shipping, shipbuilding, port operations, vessel operations, national security, safety, and the environment. It also maintains the health of the merchant marine—commercial mariners, vessels, and intermodal facilities contribute significantly to national security. The Administration, therefore, supports current mariners, helps educate future mariners, and informs Americans about the maritime industry and how it benefits them. Recently, the Administration realigned its functions to be more effective as an industry promoter and to focus more attention on the environment and safety.

MARAD administers the Maritime Security Program, which maintains a core fleet of U.S.-flag, privately-owned ships that operate in international commerce. Under agreement, these ships are available to provide needed capacity, during war and national emergencies, to meet Department of Defense requirements.

It also administers the Ready Reserve Force program to facilitate deployment of U.S. military forces—rapidly and worldwide. The Force primarily supports transport of Army and Marine Corps unit equipment and combat support equipment. The Force also supports initial resupply during the critical surge period before commercial ships become available. The program provides nearly one-half of the Government-owned surge sealift capability. https://www.maritime.dot.gov/about-us

Sources of Information

Archived Records The "Guide to Federal Records in the National Archives of the United States" indicates that MARAD records have been assigned to record group 357. https://www.archives.gov/research/guide-fed-records/groups/357.html
Business Opportunities To learn about doing business with MARAD, visit its "Business Services and Products" web page. https://www.maritime.dot.gov/about-us/marad-business-services-products
Career Opportunities The "Mariners" web page has information on becoming a mariner and mariner opportunities. https://www.maritime.dot.gov/outreach/mariners

The six maritime academies and U.S. Merchant Marine Academy educate students for service as officers in the U.S. Merchant Marine, U.S. Armed Forces, and Nation's intermodal transportation system. https://www.maritime.dot.gov/education/

maritime-academies/maritime-academies | Email: careersafloat@dot.gov

In 2020, MARAD ranked 228th among 411 agency subcomponents in the Partnership for Public Service's Best Places To Work Agency Rankings. https://bestplacestowork.org/rankings/detail/?c=TD13

Contact Information   MARAD posts contact information on its "Maritime Contact Information" web page. https://cms.marad.dot.gov/about-us/maritime-contact-information

Data / Statistics   The "Data and Reports" web pages contain data that are organized into four broad categories: historical datasets, U.S.–international trade, U.S. vessel movements and port calls, and vessel fleet lists. The Office of Policy and Plans publishes statistical and economic analyses and reports on a variety of maritime transportation topics. https://www.maritime.dot.gov/data-reports | Email: data.marad@dot.gov

Federal Register   Significant documents and documents that MARAD recently published in the Federal Register are accessible online. https://www.federalregister.gov/agencies/maritime-administration

Freedom of Information Act (FOIA)   Enacted in 1966, the FOIA took effect on July 4, 1967. The Act gives a right for accessing Federal agency records to any person, except a fugitive from the law. Some records, or portions of them, are shielded from disclosure by one or more of nine statutory exemptions or by specific harm that disclosure could cause. The Electronic Freedom of Information Act Amendments of 1996 require Federal agencies to use electronic information technology to expand access to and availability of FOIA documents. MARAD posts contact information for its FOIA officer and FOIA public liaison on its "Freedom of Information Act Contacts" web page. https://www.maritime.dot.gov/about-us/foia/freedom-information-act-contacts | Email: FOIA.Marad@dot.gov

The agency maintains an online document library. Before submitting a FOIA request, browse its electronic reading room or search for the desired information to determine if it is accessible, immediately and free of charge, without submitting a formal FOIA request. https://www.marad.dot.gov/about-us/foia/electronic-reading-room

Frequently Asked Questions (FAQs)   MARAD posts answers to FAQs on its website. https://www.marad.dot.gov/about-us/frequently-asked-questions

Glossary   The "Glossary of Shipping Terms—2008" contains abbreviations, acronyms, initialisms, and words that its compilers selected from the rich vocabulary of the shipping business. https://www.maritime.dot.gov/sites/marad.dot.gov/files/docs/resources/3686/glossaryfinal.pdf

History   The MARAD vessel history database has information on vessels that have been or remain part of the National Defense Reserve Fleet and other vessels that were at one time owned, operated, or in the custody of MARAD or one of its predecessor agencies. Each database entry includes one or more images of vessel status cards—paper index cards that tell the story of a ship's career in Government service—and additional information when it is available. https://vesselhistory.marad.dot.gov/ShipHistory/ShipList?pageNumber=1&matchFromStart=True | Email: marad.history@dot.gov

Maps   A map of MARAD gateway offices is available on the "Gateway Offices" web page. https://www.maritime.dot.gov/about-us/gateway-offices/gateway-offices

MARAD maintains a deepwater port location and status map online. The "Deepwater Ports Map" web page has links to information on applications that are under review, that have been approved or disapproved, and that have been withdrawn. https://www.maritime.dot.gov/ports/deepwater-ports-and-licensing/deepwater-ports-map

Marine Environment   In a three-page special report "Marine Environment—Protecting the World's Waters," Carolyn E. Junemann and Koichi Yoshida discuss the following topics: anti-fouling systems, cooperation with the International Maritime Organization, oil booms, port waste, and underwater sound. https://www.maritime.dot.gov/sites/marad.dot.gov/files/docs/environment-security-safety/office-environment/606/isofocus12-04-ensr-marineenvironment.pdf

Marine Highway Routes The Marine Highway system comprises 25 marine highway routes serving as extensions of the surface transportation system. https://www.maritime.dot.gov/sites/marad.dot.gov/files/docs/grants-finances/marine-highways/3061/marine-highway-route-descriptions-8-14-2019.pdf

Maritime Advisory System U.S. maritime alerts provide basic information—date and time, incident type, location—on reported maritime security threats to U.S. maritime industry interests. In some situations, an alert may be issued to refute unsubstantiated claims. To be added to the electronic distribution list for U.S. maritime alerts and advisories, email the request to MARAD security. https://www.maritime.dot.gov/office-security/msci-portal/maritime-security-communications-industry-msci-web-portal | Email: MaradSecurity@dot.gov

Newsroom Congressional testimonies, news items, and speeches are available online. https://www.maritime.dot.gov/newsroom

Ship Disposal MARAD's website has information on four methods for disposing of a ship: artificial reefing, domestic recycling, ship donations, and naval sink at sea live-fire training exercises (SINKEX). https://www.maritime.dot.gov/national-defense-reserve-fleet/ship-disposal-program/ship-disposal-program

Social Media MARAD has a Facebook account. https://www.facebook.com/DOTMARAD

MARAD tweets announcements and other newsworthy items on Twitter. https://twitter.com/DOTMARAD

Video Archives A video archives is available on MARAD's website. https://www.maritime.dot.gov/outreach/maritime-administration-video-archives

Virtual Ship Tours Virtual tours inside cargo and crew spaces and engine rooms are part of MARAD's website. https://www.maritime.dot.gov/history/artifact-program/exhibits

A virtual tour of the NS Savannah, the world's first nuclear-powered merchant ship, which was launched in 1959 as part of the Atoms for Peace Program, is available online. https://maritime.org/tour/savannah

The Sources of Information were updated 11–2021.

National Highway Traffic Safety Administration

1200 New Jersey Avenue SE., Washington, DC 20590
Phone, 202-366-9550. Fax, 888-327-4236. Internet, http://www.nhtsa.gov

Administrator	STEVEN CLIFF, ACTING
Deputy Administrator	(VACANCY)
Executive Director	JACK DANIELSON
https://www.nhtsa.gov/about-nhtsa/nhtsa-leadership	

[For the National Highway Traffic Safety Administration statement of organization, see the Code of Federal Regulations, Title 49, Part 501]

The above list of key personnel was updated 9–2021.

The National Highway Traffic Safety Administration (NHTSA) was established by the Highway Safety Act of 1970 (23 U.S.C. 401 note) to reduce the number of deaths, injuries, and economic losses resulting from motor vehicle crashes on the Nation's highways.

The Administration administers motor vehicle and related equipment safety performance programs; co-administers the State and community highway safety program; regulates the Corporate Average Fuel Economy program; issues Federal Motor Vehicle Safety Standards (FMVSS) that prescribe safety features and levels of safety-related performance for vehicles and vehicular equipment; rates the safety of passenger vehicles in the New Car Assessment Program; monitors and participates in international vehicle safety forums to harmonize the FMVSS where appropriate; investigates and prosecutes odometer fraud; administers the National Driver Register Program; conducts studies and operates programs to reduce economic losses in motor vehicle crashes and repairs; performs studies, conducts demonstration projects, and issues regulations requiring manufacturers to provide motor vehicle consumer information; promotes programs to reduce impaired driving, to reduce risky driver behaviors, and to increase seat belt use; and issues theft prevention standards for passenger motor vehicles.

Activities

Research and Program Development   The Administration helps develop motor vehicle and highway safety program standards. It analyzes data and researches, develops, tests, and evaluates motor vehicles, motor vehicle equipment, and advanced technologies, and it collects and analyzes crash data. NHTSA activities are broad in scope with respect to safety: The Administration encourages industry to adopt advanced motor vehicle safety designs, increases public awareness of safety issues, and provides a base for vehicle safety information. http://www.nhtsa.gov/Research

Regional Operations and Program Delivery   The NHTSA administers State highway safety grant programs that the Safe, Accountable, Flexible, Efficient Transportation Equity Act: A Legacy for Users authorized. The Highway Safety formula grant program provides funds to States, Indian nations, and the territories each year to support safety programs, particularly in the following priority areas: data and traffic records, emergency medical services, impaired driving, motorcycle safety, occupant protection, pedestrian and bicycle safety, police traffic services, roadway safety, and speed control. Incentive grants are also used to encourage States to implement effective data improvement, impaired driving, motorcycle safety, and occupant protection programs. https://www.nhtsa.gov/highway-safety-grants-program

Rulemaking   The Administration issues FMVSS that prescribe safety features and levels of safety-related performance for vehicles and vehicular equipment. The Administration participates in the United Nations World Forum for the Harmonization of Vehicle Regulations (WP.29). It also oversees the New Car Assessment Program and the Government's Five Star Safety Rating Program, which evaluates the safety performance of light trucks, passenger cars, vans, and child seats (https://www.nhtsa.gov/ratings). These evaluations are highly publicized—star ratings must be visible on the price labels of new vehicles. The Administration also educates consumers on topics such as driving while distracted, as well as the proper use of vehicle safety features and child restraint seats. To promote fuel economy, it manages a program establishing and revising fleet average fuel economy standards for passenger car and light truck manufacturers (https://www.nhtsa.gov/laws-regulations/corporate-average-fuel-economy). The Administration also runs an antitheft program. Under this program the NHTSA issues rules requiring that certain passenger motor vehicles meet parts-marking requirements, and it calculates and publishes annual motor vehicle theft rates. https://www.nhtsa.gov/laws-regulations

Enforcement   The Administration's Office of Enforcement assures that all new vehicles sold in the U.S. meet applicable FMVSS. Under its compliance program, the Office conducts random tests and collects consumer complaints to identify and investigate problems with motor vehicles and vehicular equipment. If a vehicle or equipment suffers from a safety-related defect or does not meet all applicable FMVSS, the Office seeks a recall, which requires manufacturers to notify owners and to remedy the defect free of charge. The Office monitors recalls to ensure that owners are notified in a timely manner and that the scope of the recall and the remedy are adequate. The Office also assures that all motor vehicles subject to the Corporate Average Fuel Economy (CAFE) regulations meet their respective targets, and it enforces violations of Federal odometer fraud regulations by criminally prosecuting offenders. https://www.nhtsa.gov/recalls

National Center for Statistics and Analysis   The NHTSA maintains a collection of scientific and technical information on motor vehicle safety. It also operates the National Center for Statistics and Analysis, whose activities include the development and maintenance of national highway-crash data collection systems and related statistical and economic analyses. The public and the private sector and universities and Federal, State, and local agencies rely on these motor vehicle safety information resources for documentation. https://www.nhtsa.gov/research-data/national-center-statistics-and-analysis-ncsa

Communications and Consumer Information The Office of Communications and Consumer Information develops, directs, and implements communication strategies based on NHTSA policy and programs, including campaigns to support high visibility enforcement efforts. It promotes safety messages for NHTSA vehicle-related issues. The Office also manages NHTSA Web sites and the toll-free Vehicle Safety Hotline. Information received from calls to the hotline forms the basis of investigations, which can lead to recalls if safety-related defects are identified. http://www.trafficsafetymarketing.gov/ciot

Sources of Information

Car Seats A car seat glossary is available on the Parents Central Web site. http://www.safercar.gov/parents/CarSeats/Car-Seat-Glossary-of-Terms.htm?view=full

The car seat finder is an online tool that uses date of birth, height, and weight to find a car seat type that properly fits a child. http://www.safercar.gov/cpsApp/crs/index.htm

Career Opportunities Information on job openings is available on the "Jobs at NHTSA" Web page. http://www.nhtsa.gov/Jobs

In 2016, the NHTSA ranked 290th among 305 agency subcomponents in the Partnership for Public Service's Best Places To Work Agency Rankings. http://bestplacestowork.org/BPTW/rankings/detail/TD10

Data The NHTSA posts factsheets, reports, research notes, statistics, and studies on its Web site. https://www.nhtsa.gov/research-data

Driving Safety The NHTSA Web site features a trove of safety information and resources. Disabled, older, and teen drivers, as well as motorcyclists and others can find Web pages dedicated to improving their driving habits and addressing their safety needs. http://www.nhtsa.gov/Driving-Safety

Events The NHTSA hosts meetings and forums to explore new approaches to highway safety. Information and materials from these event are available online. https://www.nhtsa.gov/events

Freedom of Information Act (FOIA) The NHTSA is required to disclose records that are properly requested in writing by any person. A Government agency may withhold information pursuant to one or more of nine exemptions and three exclusions contained in the FOIA. The act applies only to Federal agencies and does not give a right of access to records held by Congress, the courts, State or local government agencies, and private entities. https://www.nhtsa.gov/about-nhtsa/foia

The NHTSA maintains an electronic reading room. Before submitting a FOIA request, an information seeker should search for the desired document or record in the reading room to determine whether it may be available immediately, without charge. The NHTSA also operates a service center for answering FOIA-related questions. Phone, 202-366-2870. https://www.nhtsa.gov/about-nhtsa/electronic-reading-room

News The NHTSA posts press releases on its Web site. http://www.nhtsa.gov/About-NHTSA/Press-Releases

The NHTSA posts speeches, press events, and testimonies on its Web site. https://www.nhtsa.gov/speeches-presentations

Publications The NHTSA disseminates information on traffic safety programs in "Traffic Techs." The publication, starting with the year 1995, is available online. Staring with the years 2005 and 2006, "Traffic Techs" becomes available in Portable Document Format (PDF). http://www.nhtsa.gov/About-NHTSA/Traffic-Techs | Email: TrafficTech@dot.gov

Recalls The Recalls Spotlight monitors high-profile recalls and provides resources finding and addressing vehicle recalls. http://www.safercar.gov/rs/index.html

The NHTSA's Web site features a search tool that allows the user to enter a vehicle's identification number (VIN) to learn whether it has been repaired as part of a safety recall in the last 15 years. http://www-odi.nhtsa.dot.gov/owners/SearchSafetyIssues

Regional Offices Contact information for the NHTSA's 10 regional offices is available on the "Regional Offices" Web page. http://www.nhtsa.gov/nhtsa/whatis/regions

Research The Office of Vehicle Safety Research strategizes, plans, and implements research programs to reduce crashes, fatalities, and injuries. The NHTSA's Web site contains a trove of information related to these programs. http://www.nhtsa.gov/Research

Resources for Parents The Parents Central Web site features resources to help parents protect their children and educate them on car and road safety and becoming

responsible drivers. http://www.safercar.gov/parents/index.htm

Vehicle Safety The NHTSA Web site features a trove of information on and resources for vehicle safety. Topics include defects and recalls, odometer fraud, theft protection, and tires. http://www.nhtsa.gov/Vehicle-Safety

To report suspected safety defects in vehicles, vehicle equipment, and child restraint seats, call the Vehicle Safety Hotline. English- and Spanish-speaking representatives are available on weekdays, excluding Federal holidays. Phone, 888-327-4236. TTY, 800-424-9153. https://www-odi.nhtsa.dot.gov/VehicleComplaint https://www.nhtsa.gov/about-nhtsa/contact-us

For further information, contact the National Highway Traffic Safety Administration, Office of Communications and Consumer Information, 1200 New Jersey Avenue SE., Washington, DC 20590. Phone, 202-366-9550.

Pipeline and Hazardous Materials Safety Administration

1200 New Jersey Avenue SE., Washington, DC 20590
Phone, 202-366-4433. Internet, http://www.phmsa.dot.gov

Administrator	(VACANCY)
Deputy Administrator	TRISTAN BROWN
Executive Director	HOWARD W. MCMILLAN
https://www.phmsa.dot.gov/about/key-officials	

The above list of key personnel was updated 11–2021.

The Pipeline and Hazardous Materials Safety Administration (PHMSA) was established on February 20, 2005. It is responsible for hazardous materials transportation and pipeline safety.

Hazardous Materials

The Office of Hazardous Materials Safety develops and issues regulations for the safe and secure transportation of hazardous materials by all modes, except bulk transportation by water. The regulations cover shipper and carrier operations, packaging and container specifications, and hazardous materials definitions. The Office provides training and outreach to help shippers and carriers meet hazardous material regulatory requirements. The Office enforces regulations other than those applicable to a single mode of

transportation. It manages a fee-funded grant program to help States plan for hazardous materials emergencies and to assist them and Indian tribes with training for hazardous materials emergencies. The Office also maintains a national safety program to safeguard food and other products from contamination during motor or rail transportation. http://www.phmsa.dot.gov/hazmat/info-center | Email: phmsa.hm-infocenter@dot.gov

For further information, call the Hazardous Materials Information Center. Phone, 800-467-4922.

Pipelines

The Office of Pipeline Safety (OPS) ensures the safety, security, and environmental protection of the Nation's pipeline transportation system. The Office establishes and enforces safety and environmental standards for pipeline transportation of gas and hazardous liquids. The Office analyzes data, educates and trains, promotes damage prevention, and conducts research and development for pipeline safety. Through OPS administered grants, States that voluntarily assume regulatory jurisdiction of pipelines can receive funding for up to 50 percent of the costs for their intrastate pipeline safety programs. OPS engineers inspect most interstate pipelines and other facilities not covered by State programs. In accordance with the Oil Pollution Act of 1990, the Office also approves and tests oil pipeline spill response plans. http://phmsa.dot.gov/pipeline

For further information, call the Pipeline Safety Information Center. Phone, 202-366-4595. Fax, 202-493-2311.

Sources of Information

Business Opportunities Information on the acquisition vehicles that the PHMSA uses to fulfill the requirements for goods and services of its program offices is available online. https://www.phmsa.dot.gov/about-phmsa/working-phmsa/phmsa-business-opportunities

Career Opportunities The PHMSA relies on accident investigators, accountants, attorneys, auditors, budget analysts, economists, engineers, finance analysts, geographic information systems specialists, grant specialists, human resource specialists, information technology specialists, and other professionals to carry out its mission. http://www.phmsa.dot.gov/careers

In 2020, the PHMSA ranked 322d among 411 agency subcomponents in the Partnership for Public Service's Best Places To Work Agency Rankings. https://bestplacestowork.org/rankings/detail/?c=TD16

Data / Statistics The Office of Pipeline Safety makes available data on federally regulated and State regulated natural gas pipelines, hazardous liquid pipelines, and liquefied natural gas plants. The operators of these pipeline facilities report this data in accordance with PHMSA pipeline safety regulations. The PHMSA provides downloads of the raw data, yearly summaries, multiyear

trends of safety performance metrics, and inventories tracking the removal of aging and other higher-risk infrastructure. https://www.phmsa.dot.gov/data-and-statistics/pipeline/data-and-statistics-overview

Environmental Justice The PHMSA website provides information for promoting environmental justice and ensuring nondiscrimination in communities. https://www.phmsa.dot.gov/about-phmsa/civil-rights/environmental-justice

Freedom of Information Act (FOIA) The FOIA establishes the public's right to obtain information from Federal Government agencies. Any person may file a FOIA request, including citizens and foreign nationals, as well as associations, organizations, and universities. https://www.phmsa.dot.gov/foia

Frequently Asked Questions (FAQs) The PHMSA posts answers to FAQs on its website. https://www.phmsa.dot.gov/about-phmsa/phmsa-faqs

Glossaries The PHMSA website has an inspection activity glossary. https://www.phmsa.dot.gov/pipeline/inspections/inspection-activity-glossary

The PHMSA has posted a list of definitions that are associated with safe travel. https://www.phmsa.dot.gov/safe-travel/definitions

Hazardous Materials The Hazardous Materials Information Center can provide assistance with applying the hazardous materials regulations (49 CFR Parts 100–185), can provide information on hazardous materials transportation and rulemakings, receives reports of violations of the hazardous materials regulations, can provide copies of recent Federal Register publications or Department of Transportation special permits, can provide copies of training materials, and receives requests for formal letters of interpretation. https://www.phmsa.dot.gov/standards-rulemaking/hazmat/hazardous-materials-information-center | Email: phmsa.hm-infocenter@dot.gov

History Millions of miles of transportation pipelines deliver the energy products that the American public uses to keep homes and businesses running. While rare, pipeline incidents can be fatal and cost millions of dollars in property damage. The Office of Pipeline Safety participated in the investigations of major pipeline incidents in San Bruno, CA; Allentown, PA; and Marshall, MI. In its commitment to safety awareness and outreach, the Office offers a historical look at high-profile pipeline incidents. https://www.phmsa.dot.gov/safety-awareness/pipeline/historical-pipeline-incidents

Library The resources library contains an accessible collection of public documents related to the safe transport of hazardous materials. https://www.phmsa.dot.gov/resources

The Sources of Information were updated 11–2021.

Mapping System The National Pipeline Mapping System public map viewer is a Web-based application designed to assist the general public with displaying and querying data related to gas transmission and hazardous liquid pipelines, liquefied natural gas plants, and breakout tanks under the jurisdiction of the PHMSA. https://www.npms.phmsa.dot.gov/Default.aspx

Newsroom The PHMSA posts news items online. https://www.phmsa.dot.gov/newsroom

DEPARTMENT OF VETERANS AFFAIRS

810 Vermont Avenue NW., Washington, DC 20420
Phone, 202-461-4800. Internet, http://www.va.gov

Office of the Secretary

Secretary of Veterans Affairs   Denis R. McDonough
Deputy Secretary

Chief of Staff
https://www.va.gov/opa/bios/secva.asp

Administrations
Executive in Charge
Health

Under Secretaries
Benefits
Memorial Affairs
https://www.va.gov/opa/bios/index.asp

Staff Offices
Assistant Secretaries
Congressional and Legislative Affairs
Enterprise Integration
Human Resources and Administration
Information and Technology / Chief Information Officer
Management / Chief Financial Officer
Public and Intergovernmental Affairs

Executive Directors
Accountability and Whistleblower Protection
Acquisition, Logistics, and Construction

Chair, Board of Veterans' Appeals
Chief Veterans Experience Officer
General Counsel
https://www.va.gov/landing_organizations.htm

Office of Inspector General
Inspector General
https://www.va.gov/oig/about/inspector-general.asp

The Department of Veterans Affairs operates programs benefiting Veterans and members of their families: It offers education opportunities and rehabilitation services and provides compensation payments for disabilities or death related to military service, home loan guaranties, pensions, burials, and health care that includes the services in clinics, medical centers, community living centers (which replace nursing home)s, and home- and community-based settings.

The Department of Veterans Affairs (VA) was established as an executive department by the Department of Veterans Affairs Act (38 U.S.C. 201 note). It is comprised of three organizations that administer Veterans programs: the Veterans Health Administration, the Veterans Benefits Administration, and the National Cemetery Administration. Each organization has field facilities and a central office component. Staff offices support the overall function of the Department and its Administrations. http://www.va.gov/landing2_about.htm

Activities

Acquisition, Logistics, and Construction   The Office of Acquisition, Logistics, and Construction (OALC) is a multifunctional organization responsible for directing the acquisition, logistics, construction, and leasing functions within the VA. The Executive Director, OALC, is also the Chief Acquisition Officer for the VA. http://www.va.gov/OALC

Cemeteries   The National Cemetery Administration (NCA) is responsible for the management and oversight of 135 national cemeteries in the United States and Puerto Rico, as well as 33 soldiers' lots, Confederate cemeteries, and monument sites. Burial in a national cemetery is available to eligible veterans, certain members of reserve components, and their spouses and dependent children. At no cost to the family, a national cemetery burial includes the gravesite, graveliner, opening and closing of the grave, headstone or marker, and perpetual care as part of a national shrine. If an eligible veteran is buried in an unmarked grave in a private cemetery anywhere in the world, NCA will provide a headstone or marker. A Government-furnished headstone or marker may be provided for eligible Veterans who died on or after Nov. 1, 1990 and whose grave is marked with a privately purchased headstone. A Government-furnished medallion may be provided for eligible Veterans who served on or after Apr. 6, 1917 and whose grave is marked with a privately purchased headstone or marker. NCA's Veterans Cemetery Grants Program provides funds to State and tribal governments to establish, expand, or improve veterans'

cemeteries. NCA issues Presidential Memorial Certificates to honor the memory of deceased veterans who are eligible for burial in a national cemetery. http://www.cem.va.gov

Congressional and Legislative Affairs   The mission of the Office of the Assistant Secretary for Congressional and Legislative Affairs (OCLA) is to improve the lives of Veterans and their families by advancing pro-Veteran legislation and maintaining responsive and effective communications with Congress. OCLA coordinates the Department's activities with Congress. It is the Department's focal point for interactions and engagements with Members of Congress, authorization committees, and personal staff. Additionally, the Office is the Department's liaison with the Government Accountability Office (GAO). https://www.va.gov/oca/

Faith-Based and Neighborhood Partnerships   The mission of the Center for Faith-Based and Neighborhood Partnerships (CFBNP) is to develop partnerships with, provide relevant information to, and expand participation of faith-based, nonprofit, and community/neighborhood organizations in VA programs in order to better serve the needs of Veterans, their families, survivors, caregivers, and other beneficiaries. https://www.va.gov/cfbnpartnerships/

Field Facilities   The Department's operations are handled through the following field facilities: cemeteries, medical centers, outpatient clinics, community living centers, domiciliaries, and regional offices. Cemeteries provide burial services to Veterans, their spouses, and dependent children. Medical centers provide eligible beneficiaries with medical and other health care services equivalent to those provided by private sector institutions, augmented in many instances by services to meet the special requirements of Veterans. Outpatient clinics provide the most common outpatient services, including health and wellness visits, without the hassle of visiting a larger medical center. Community Living Centers (CLC) are skilled nursing facilities, often referred to as nursing homes. Veterans with chronic stable conditions such as dementia, those requiring rehabilitation or those who need comfort and care at the end of life are served within one of our 135 Community Living Centers. Domiciliaries provide a variety of care to Veterans who suffer from a wide range of medical, psychiatric, vocational, educational, or social problems and illnesses in a safe, secure, homelike environment. VHA continues to expand the network of outpatient clinics to include more rural locations, putting access to care closer to home.

Regional offices grant benefits and services provided by law for Veterans, their dependents, and beneficiaries within an assigned territory; furnish information regarding VA benefits and services; adjudicate claims and make awards for disability compensation and pension; conduct outreach and information dissemination; provide support and assistance to various segments of the Veteran population to include former prisoners of war, minorities, the homeless, women, and elderly Veterans; supervise payment of VA benefits to incompetent beneficiaries; provide vocational rehabilitation and employment training; administer educational benefits; guarantee loans for purchase, construction, or alteration of homes; process grants for specially adapted housing; process death claims; and assist Veterans in exercising rights to benefits and services. https://www.va.gov/directory/guide/home. asp

Health Services The Veterans Health Administration (VHA) is the largest integrated health care system in the United States. It provides hospital, long-term services and support in community living centers (which replace nursing homes)- and home- and community- based settings, domiciliary, and outpatient medical and dental care and community care to eligible Veterans of the Armed Forces. In addition to providing health care, VHA performs research, and assists in the education and training of physicians, dentists, and many other health care professionals through its affiliations with educational institutions and organizations. As of March 2017, VHA treated over 8.76 million patients in over 1,700 sites of care. VHA has 1,247 health care facilities, including 170 VA Medical Centers and 1,067 outpatient sites of care of varying complexity (VHA outpatient clinics).

In addition, VA purchases medical care when needed from community providers including long-term services and supports in community nursing homes, State Veterans Homes, and in home and community based settings. In 2016, VA hospitals had about 621,520 inpatient admissions and provided nearly 84 million outpatient visits. In addition to care delivered in the VA system, VA also delivers care to millions of Veterans in the community. The number of women Veterans receiving health care from VA more than tripled between 2000 and 2016, growing from 160,000 in 2000 to 475,000. VA hospitals provide more public data about quality and safety than any health care system in the world and held academic affiliations with more than 1,800 educational institutions. More than 123,552 health care students receive clinical training at a VA facility each year.

Historically, VHA has been at the forefront of medical research. The first electronic health record, cardiac pacemaker, bionic ankle, and successful liver transplant were all developed at VA. VA has also developed new drugs and treatments for acquired immune deficiency syndrome/ human immunodeficiency virus, diabetes, Alzheimer's disease, and osteoporosis. Currently, VHA medical centers provide a wide range of services including traditional services such as primary care, surgery, critical care, mental health, orthopedics, pharmacy, radiology and physical therapy. Additional medical and surgical specialty services, including audiology & speech pathology, dermatology, dental, geriatrics, neurology, palliative medicine, oncology, podiatry, prosthetics, urology, vision care and extended care services; such as facility and community based long-term services and supports and hospice care are available. Some medical centers also offer advanced services such as organ transplants and plastic surgery. VA is also using Telehealth and Telemedicine to improve access to care, especially in remote areas. http://www. va.gov/HEALTH

Management The Advisory Committee Management Office (ACMO) provides administrative and management support to the Department's 29 Federal Advisory Committees (as of July 2017). VA's advisory committees solicit advice and recommendations from outside experts and the public concerning programs for which the Department is responsible for by law. http://www.va.gov/ADVISORY

Minority Veterans   The Center for Minority Veterans (CMV), established by the Veterans' Benefits Improvement Act of 1994, identifies barriers to benefits and health care access, promotes awareness of minority Veteran-related issues, develops strategies for improving minority Veterans' participation in existing VA programs, The CMV focuses on the unique and special needs of African Americans, Hispanics, Asian Americans, Pacific Islanders, and Native Americans, which include American Indians, Native Hawaiians, and Alaska Natives. http://www.va.gov/centerforminorityveterans

Small and Disadvantaged Business Utilization   The Office of Small and Disadvantaged Business Utilization (OSDBU) is the Department's principal liaison to the Small Business Administration (SBA), the Department of Commerce, the General Services Administration (GSA), and the Office of Federal Procurement Policy for matters dealing with small and disadvantaged business activities. OSDBU's mission is to enable Veterans to gain access to economic opportunity by leveraging the federal procurement system and expanding participation of procurement-ready small businesses. http://www.va.gov/osdbu

Survivors Assistance   Office of Survivors Assistance (OSA) provides support to survivors of Veterans by identifying and informing them of the benefits and services offered by VA. https://www.va.gov/survivors/

Veterans' Appeals   The Board of Veterans' Appeals (BVA) renders final decisions on behalf of the Secretary on appeals from decisions of local VA offices. The Board reviews all appeals for entitlement to Veterans' benefits, including claims for service connection, increased disability ratings, total disability ratings, pension, insurance benefits, educational benefits, home loan guaranties, vocational rehabilitation, dependency and indemnity compensation, health care delivery, and fiduciary matters. The Board has jurisdiction over appeals arising from the VA regional offices, VA medical centers, the National

Cemetery Administration, and the Office of General Counsel. The Board's mission is to conduct hearings and issue timely, understandable, and quality decisions for Veterans and other appellants in compliance with the requirements of law. Final BVA decisions are appealable to the U.S. Court of Appeals for Veterans Claims. http://www.bva.va.gov

Veterans Benefits   VBA provides information, advice, and assistance to Veterans, their dependents, beneficiaries, representatives, and others applying for VA benefits. It also cooperates with the Department of Labor and other Federal, State, and local agencies in developing employment opportunities for Veterans and referrals for assistance in resolving socioeconomic, housing, and other related problems.

VBA's Compensation and Pension and Fiduciary Services are responsible for adjudicating claims for disability compensation and pension, specially adapted housing, accrued benefits, adjusted compensation in death cases, reimbursement for headstones or markers, allowances for automobiles and special adaptive equipment, special clothing allowances, emergency officers' retirement pay, Survivors' claims for death compensation, dependency and indemnity compensation, death pension, burial and plot allowances, forfeiture determinations, and a benefits protection program for minors and incompetent adult beneficiaries.

VBA's Education Service administers VA education benefits to Veterans, Servicemembers, National Guard members, Selected Reserve members, and eligible dependents. These benefits provide financial assistance for attending institutions of higher learning, non-college degree programs, on-the-job and apprenticeship training, flight training, distance learning, correspondence training, national testing programs, licensing and certifications, entrepreneurship training, work-study programs, and co-op training. Education Service also performs compliance surveys to ensure that approved programs are compliant with pertinent laws. Additional information is available at www.benefits.va.gov/gibill.

VBA's Insurance Service operates for the benefit of Servicemembers, Veterans, and their beneficiaries. Customers can reach Insurance Service through the VA Insurance Center (phone, 800-669-8477). The Insurance Center performs a complete range of activities necessary to operate national life insurance programs. Activities include maintenance of individual accounts, underwriting functions, life and death insurance claims awards, and other insurance-related transactions for multiple insurance programs. The Insurance Center administers the Veterans Mortgage Life Insurance Program for those disabled Veterans who receive a VA grant for specially adapted housing, and the Service-Disabled Veterans Insurance program for Veterans who receive a service-connected disability rating. In addition, Insurance Service oversees the Servicemembers' Group Life Insurance (SGLI) and Veterans' Group Life Insurance Programs, as well as the Family Servicemembers' Group Life Insurance and SGLI Traumatic Injury Protection programs.

VBA's Loan Guaranty Service is responsible for administering operations that include establishing the eligibility of Veterans for the program; ensuring VA credit, income, and appraisal requirements are met; managing a panel of appraisers and establishing a property value; approving grants for specially adapted housing; supervising the construction of new residential properties; making direct loans to Native American Veterans to acquire a home on trust land; servicing and liquidating defaulted loans; and disposing of real estate acquired as the consequence of defaulted loans.

VBA's Vocational Rehabilitation and Employment Service (VR&E) program provides assistance to Veterans and Servicemembers with service-connected disabilities and an employment handicap, to prepare for, obtain, and maintain suitable employment. For those persons who are severely disabled and suitable employment is not an option, assistance may be provided to allow each person to live more independently. Through VA's VR&E program, individuals may benefit from individual support, vocational counseling, evaluation of interest, aptitudes and abilities, training, employment assistance, and other rehabilitation services. In some cases, rehabilitation services are available to spouses and children of totally and permanently disabled Veterans as well as Survivors of certain deceased Veterans.

Under 38 U.S.C. Chapter 18, VR&E provides vocational training and rehabilitation services to children with spina bifida having a parent who served in the Republic of Vietnam during the Vietnam era or who served in certain military units in or near the demilitarized zone in Korea between September 1, 1967 and August 31, 1971.

The Appeals Management Office assumes responsibility for and authority over all VBA appeals-related program policy, planning, budgeting, staffing, and other operational control as a separate entity under the VBA Principal Deputy Under Secretary for Benefits (PDUSB). This office works closely with the Board of Veterans Appeals to better service Veterans and their families. http://www.benefits.va.gov/benefits

Women Veterans The Center for Women Veterans (CWV), established by the Veterans' Benefits Improvement Act of 1994, monitors and coordinates VA's health care, benefits, services, and programs for women Veterans. CWV advocates a cultural transformation within VA and the general public to recognize the service and contributions of women Veterans and women in the military, and raises awareness of the responsibility to treat women Veterans with dignity and respect. The CWV Director serves as the primary advisor to the SECVA on all matters related to policy, legislation, programs, issues, and initiatives affecting women Veterans. http://www.va.gov/WOMENVET

Sources of Information

A–Z Index The "Veterans Health A–Z Index" includes frequent inquiries, popular subjects, and topics of critical importance to veterans and their caregivers. https://www.va.gov/health/topics

Blog "VAntage Point" is the VA's official blog. http://www.blogs.va.gov/VAntage | Email: blog.dalcbdt@va.gov

Business Opportunities The VA purchases goods and services on the national, regional, and local level from large and small businesses. Each VA facility has a local acquisition office that handles its procurement process. http://www.va.gov/oal/business/dbwva.asp | Email: dalcbdt@va.gov

The VA has the authority to award set-aside and sole source contracts to service-disabled veteran-owned small businesses and to veteran-owned small businesses. This procurement authority extends the reach of the agency's mission of caring for the Nation's veterans. Phone, 866-584-2344. https://www.va.gov/osdbu/verification/ | Email: osdbu@va.gov

Career Opportunities   The VA employs over 300,000 people in hundreds of professions. To fulfill its mission, the VA relies on claims examiners, dentists, management analysts, nurses, occupational therapists, optometrists, pharmacists, physical therapists, physician assistants, physicians, secretaries, and many additional types of professionals. www.vacareers.gov

In 2017, the VA ranked 17th among 18 large agencies in the Partnership for Public Service's Best Places To Work Agency Rankings. https://bestplacestowork.org/rankings/detail/VA00

Data / Statistics   The National Center for Veterans Analysis and Statistics posts reports, statistics, surveys, and other information on its website. https://www.va.gov/vetdata | Email: vancvas@va.gov

Freedom of Information Act (FOIA)   The FOIA requires that Federal agencies disclose records that information seekers request; however, some records or parts of them may be shielded from disclosure by one or more of nine statutory exemptions. A FOIA request should be sent by email, fax, or postal mail to the appropriate VA component where the desired document or record is kept. http://www.va.gov/oig/foia

If the information requester does not know which office or component maintains the desired document or record, he or she should contact the Director, FOIA Service, (005R1C), 810 Vermont Avenue NW., Washington, DC 20420. Phone, 877-750-3642. Fax 202-273-0487. https://www.oprm.va.gov/docs/foia/VACO_FOIA_Offices_Contact_List.pdf

Glossaries   The VA website has a health benefits glossary. https://www.va.gov/HEALTHBENEFITS/resources/glossary.asp

The VA National Center for Patient Safety has a glossary of patient safety terms on its website. http://www.patientsafety.va.gov/professionals/publications/glossary.asp

Gravesite Locator   The "National Cemetery Administration" website has a burial information database that is updated each day. The online locator allows users to search for the burial locations of veterans and their family members in VA National Cemeteries, State veterans cemeteries, and various other military and Department of Interior cemeteries, as well as for the interment sites of veterans who were buried in private cemeteries and whose graves are marked with Government grave markers. http://gravelocator.cem.va.gov/index.html

History   The Continental Congress of 1776 encouraged enlistments during the Revolutionary War by providing pensions to disabled soldiers. More than 210 years later, the 40th President of the United States elevated the Veterans Administration to a cabinet-level executive department. The promotion brought with it a new name: the Department of Veterans Affairs. To learn more about the history of the most comprehensive veterans assistance system in world, visit the "VA History" web page. https://www.va.gov/about_va/vahistory.asp?

Homeless Veterans   Information and resources to help a homeless veteran find a home are available on the VA website. https://www.va.gov/homeless

Locations   This page provides a facility locator that allows users to search for VHA facilities by state or territory, street address, type of facility, and distance. https://www.va.gov/directory/guide/division.asp?dnum=1

Media Room   The VA posts news releases online. http://www.va.gov/opa/pressrel

The VA posts speeches online. http://www.va.gov/opa/speeches

My Health   The "My HealtheVet" website provides information and tools for veterans to partner with their health care team and improve health care management. The website allows veterans to refill VA prescriptions, track their delivery, and view medication lists; to monitor approaching VA appointments and receive reminders; to communicate online with health care teams; and to access medical records and add information to them. Phone, 877-327-0022.

TTY, 800-877-8339. https://www.myhealth.va.gov/mhv-portal-web/home

Office of Inspector General (OIG) Public documents and information are available on the OIG's website. Complaints may be sent to the VA Inspector General (53E), P.O. Box 50410, Washington, DC 20091-0410. Hotline phone, 800-488-8244. http://www.va.gov/oig/default.asp | Email: page.vaoighotline@va.gov

Organizational Chart The VA's "2017 Functional Organizational Manual—version 4.0" is available online in Portable Document Format (PDF). The Department's organizational chart may be seen on page 2. https://www.va.gov/landing_organizations.htm

Our Doctors The "Federation of State Medical Boards" website has an online directory that allows users to search for information about physicians. http://www.docinfo.org/#/search/query

Posttraumatic Stress Disorder (PTSD) The National Center for PTSD is the world's leading PTSD and traumatic stress research and educational center. The website's home page has a helpful short video titled "What Is PTSD?" to explain the disorder. Information voice mail, 802-296-6300. https://www.ptsd.va.gov/

Public Affairs / News Media Contact the nearest regional Office of Public Affairs: Atlanta (404-929-5880); Chicago (312-980-4235); Dallas (817-385-3720); Denver (303-914-5855); Los Angeles (310-268-4207); New York (212-807-3429); or Washington, DC (202-530-9360). Representatives of the national media may prefer contacting the Office of Public Affairs in the VA Central Office, 810 Vermont Avenue NW., Washington, DC 20420. Phone, 202-461-7400. http://www.va.gov/opa

Publications Information on books, factsheets, and other publications is available on the "Office of Public and Intergovernmental Affairs" website. http://www.va.gov/opa/publications

Site Map The website map allows visitors to look for specific topics or to browse content that aligns with their interests. http://www.va.gov/site_map.htm

Social Media To see all of the VA's social media accounts, visit the "Social Media Directory" web page. https://www.va.gov/opa/socialmedia.asp

Sports Programs / Special Events Having fun together by participating in adaptive sports improves health, creates new friends, and elevates the quality of life. Many sports opportunities are available to veterans of all ages and abilities. To get started, visit the "National Veterans Sports Programs and Special Events" website and speak with your VA clinical team about getting involved. https://www.blogs.va.gov/nvspse/ | Email: sports4vets@va.gov

Veterans Service Organizations The VA maintains an online directory of veterans services organizations in Portable Document Format (PDF). For further information, contact the Office of Public and Intergovernmental Affairs, Department of Veterans Affairs, 810 Vermont Avenue NW., Washington, DC 20420. Phone, 202-273-6000. http://www.va.gov/vso

Women Veterans Call Center Women veterans, as a demographic, underutilize VA benefits and services. The main reason seems to be a lack of awareness that they are eligible recipients. https://www.womenshealth.va.gov/WOMENSHEALTH/ProgramOverview/wvcc.asp http://www.va.gov/opa

For further information, contact the Office of Public and Intergovernmental Affairs, Department of Veterans Affairs, 810 Vermont Avenue NW., Washington, DC 20420. Phone, 202-273-6000.

DEPARTMENT OF THE INTERIOR

1849 C Street NW., Washington, DC 20240
Phone, 202-208-3100. Internet, http://www.doi.gov

Secretary of the Interior	DEB HAALAND
Deputy Secretary	
https://www.doi.gov/whoweare/secretary-bernhardt	

Assistant Secretaries
Fish and Wildlife and Parks
Indian Affairs
Insular and International Affairs
Land and Minerals Management
Policy, Management and Budget
Water and Science
https://www.doi.gov/interior-leadership

Other Officers
Chief Information Officer
https://www.doi.gov/ocio/about/leadership

Solicitor
https://www.doi.gov/sites/doi.gov/files/uploads/m-37055.pdf

Special Trustee for American Indians
https://www.doi.gov/ost/about_us/organization
Office of the Inspector General

Inspector General
https://www.doioig.gov/about-us/inspector-general

The Department of the Interior protects America's heritage and natural resources, honors its cultures and tribal communities, and supplies energy for powering its future.

Establishment and Organization

On March 3, 1849, President James K. Polk approved an act that created the Department of the Interior (DOI) by transferring the Office of Indian Affairs and the General Land, the Patent, and the Pension Offices to a new department. The head of that new department was, and still is, called the Secretary of the Interior. The President appoints the Secretary by the advice of the Senate and with its consent. http://www.loc.gov/law/help/statutes-at-large/30th-congress/session-2/c30s2ch108.pdf

The Secretary of the Interior supervises the public business of the following agencies and subjects: Alaska Railroad, Alaska Road Commission, bounty-lands, Bureau of Land Management, U.S. Bureau of Mines, Bureau of Reclamation, division of Territories and Island Possessions, Fish and Wildlife Service, U.S. Geological Survey, Indians, National Park Service, petroleum conservation, and public lands and the mines that are on those lands (43 U.S.C. 1457). The Secretary reports directly to the President. https://uscode.house.gov/view.

xhtml?req=granuleid:USC-prelim-title43-section1457&num=0&edition=prelim

The DOI was reorganized by Reorganization Plan No. 3 of 1950, as amended (5 U.S.C. app.). https://uscode.house.gov/view.xhtml?req=granuleid:USC-prelim-title5a-node84-leaf107&num=0&edition=prelim

A more recent reorganization has created 12 unified administrative regions to improve coordination among bureaus, effectiveness of relationships with its partners, and customer service. The reorganization delegates authority and accountability closer to field operations and places a greater emphasis on local decision making. https://www.doi.gov/employees/reorg

This reorganization started under the direction of former Secretary Ryan K. Zynke, who led the DOI from March 2, 2017, through January 2, 2019. The reorganization, which became final on August 22, 2018, established unified interior region boundaries that are based on watersheds and generally follow State lines to simplify coordination with external partners. https://www.doi.gov/employees/reorg/unified-regional-boundaries

The "Strategic Plan for Fiscal Years 2018–2022" includes the DOI's organization chart on page 6. https://www.doi.gov/sites/doi.gov/files/uploads/fy2018-2022-strategic-plan.pdf

Statutory and Regulatory Authorities

Statutory material on the establishment of the DOI, the duties of its Secretary and Deputy Secretary, and other topics that affect departmental operations and activities are codified in chapter 31, sections 1451–1476a, of 43 U.S.C. https://uscode.house.gov/view.xhtml?path=/prelim@title43/chapter31&edition=prelim

Rules and regulations associated with the Office of the Secretary of the Interior are codified in subtitle A, parts 1–199, of 43 CFR. https://www.ecfr.gov/cgi-bin/text-idx?SID=2dff2e4675b2891abcf7c9eb0078703c&mc=true&tpl=/ecfrbrowse/Title43/43cfrv1_02.tpl#0

Mission Areas

A set of six mission areas offers a window on DOI activities that are top priorities through the year 2022. They are discussed in detail in the "Strategic Plan for Fiscal Years 2018–2022" on pages 15–47.

Conserving Land and Water The DOI conserves America's lands and waters for the benefit, enjoyment, and use of current and future generations. The DOI's nine technical bureaus rely on the best science that is available, efficient decision-making processes, improved land use planning, modern natural resource management techniques, partnerships, and technology and engineering to balance stewardship with public lands use and the development of natural resources that are part of those lands, including fish species and wildlife. https://www.doi.gov/stewardship

Expanding Outdoor Recreation and Access Every year, more than 330 million people from across the country and around the world visit the national parks. Millions more visit other public lands that the DOI also manages. The DOI works to make outdoor recreation opportunities on public lands more accessible. The DOI's multiple-use policy of land management allows Americans to fish and hunt on public lands, as well as boat, camp, climb, hike, view wildlife, and engage in other outdoor activities. https://www.doi.gov/recreation

Fulfilling Trust and Insular Responsibilities The DOI upholds the U.S. Government's unique trust responsibilities by fostering government-to-government relationships that exist between the Federal Government and federally recognized Tribes. It also upholds those responsibilities by providing services to individual American Indians and Alaskan Natives. https://www.doi.gov/ost/whatwedo/

The U.S. Government also has important relationships with the affiliated insular areas, which include the Territories of American Samoa, Guam, the U.S. Virgin Islands, and the Commonwealth of the Northern Mariana Islands. The DOI administers and oversees Federal assistance to the three Freely Associated States, which comprise the two Republics of Palau and the Marshall Islands and the Federated States of Micronesia. https://edit.doi.gov/oia/what-we-do

Generating Revenue From Utilization of Natural Resources The DOI provides access to and manages energy resources like coal, gas, oil, and woody biomass on public lands, as well as Outer Continental Shelf energy resources like gas and oil. It also provides access to and manages other public land resources like nonenergy minerals, rangelands suitable for grazing, and timber from forests. By responsibly using public lands for extracting resources to achieve multiple use and economic benefits for the Nation, the DOI supports American energy dominance. https://www.doi.gov/sites/doi.gov/files/uploads/fy2019_bib_dh005.pdf

Modernizing Organization and Infrastructure   The DOI seeks to ensure more effective operations and service delivery through coordinated organizational alignments in the field, across bureaus, and with other Federal and non-Federal partners, and by putting a larger fraction of DOI employees in the field to serve the public. Expediting environmental analysis and compliance, reducing the cost of space, collocating offices for convenient public service and improved interagency coordination, and common regional boundaries are potential ways to modernize the DOI's infrastructure and improve its effectiveness. https://www.doi.gov/sites/doi.gov/files/site-page/many-bureaus-one-mission.pdf

Protecting People and the Border   Inherent in the DOI's management responsibilities of public lands is protecting employees and visitors. Ensuring employee and public safety requires the resources of multiple bureaus and offices covering four disciplines: emergency management, law enforcement, natural hazards science, and wildland fire. Depending on the season, approximately 3,500–4,000 law enforcement officers, rangers, and other employees patrol vast areas of public lands, national parks, wildlife refuges, and Indian communities. They protect people and natural, cultural, and heritage resources from illegal activities.

The U.S. Geological Survey protects lives by monitoring natural hazards like earthquakes, environmental health hazards, landslides, and volcanoes, and by issuing warnings of their potential threat levels. Wildland fires endanger lives and damage property. The Office of Wildland Fire coordinates with the DOI's land management bureaus and the U.S. Forest Service to prevent, respond to, and manage the damage and loss that wildfires cause. The Office of Wildland Fire also shares wildfire management responsibilities with Mexico along the southern border.

The DOI manages land on the Canadian border and the Mexican border, and the Department has a presence in the Pacific, where Americans are exposed to risk from Asia. A considerable amount of DOI land abuts Mexico. Accordingly, DOI law enforcement officers work in partnership with the U.S. Customs and Border Patrol, Immigration and Customs Enforcement, Drug Enforcement Agency, and Tribal, State, and local governments, to address illegal immigration, trafficking in drugs and in guns, and to mitigate these activities' consequences, which adversely affect DOI lands and community partners.

Sources of Information

A–Z Additional Resources   The additional resources index contains links to resources that DOI employees may find helpful. https://www.doi.gov/employees/additional-resources

Abandoned Mines   Abandoned mine lands are lands, waters, and surrounding watersheds that extraction or beneficiation has contaminated, scarred, or done both. Beneficiation refers to the treatment (i.e., processing) of raw materials (e.g. coal, ores, and minerals) to change their chemical or physical properties. Abandoned mine lands include areas where mining or processing activity has ceased. The Abandoned Mine Lands (AML) Portal is a partnership that comprises Federal, State, and local efforts to reduce the environmental and health risks of abandoned mines through awareness, education, and action. The DOI participates in the AML Portal. https://www.abandonedmines.gov/federal-partners

Archived Records   The "Guide to Federal Records in the National Archives of the United States" indicates that Office of the Secretary of the Interior records have been assigned to record group 048. https://www.archives.gov/research/guide-fed-records/groups/048.html

Blog   "People, Land, and Water" is the DOI's official blog. https://www.doi.gov/blog

Bureaus / Offices The DOI employs resource-management professionals, scientists, and other experts in its nine technical bureaus. https://www.doi.gov/bureaus

In addition to the nine technical bureaus, a number of offices fall under the Offices of the Secretary and Assistant Secretary; Office of Policy, Management, and Budget; Office of the Solicitor; and Office of the Inspector General. https://www.doi.gov/bureaus/offices

Business Opportunities The DOI supports the transition to a clean energy economy and stimulates local economic growth through stewardship. The DOI also procures goods and services from American businesses. The DOI relies on them for bridge, irrigation system, office building, reservoir, road, school, and other types of maintenance. More information is available from the Office of Acquisition and Property Management. Phone, 202-513-7554. https://www.doi.gov/pam

Career Opportunities Information to assist persons with disabilities, students and recent graduates, veterans, and others who are interested in career opportunities is available on the DOI's website. https://www.doi.gov/joinus

In 2019, the DOI ranked 10th among 17 large agencies in the Partnership for Public Service's Best Places To Work Agency Rankings. https://bestplacestowork.org/rankings/detail/IN00

Climate Change Changes in climate are creating new challenges for communities and resource managers nationwide. The U.S. Geological Survey's Climate Adaptation Science Centers help managers of ecosystems, fish, and wildlife better understand the effects of these changes and strategically plan for and adapt to them. https://nccwsc.usgs.gov

Contact Information The DOI has included an electronic feedback form on its "Contact Interior" web page. The DOI also may be contacted by email, phone, or postal correspondence. The contact information is available online. https://www.doi.gov/contact-us

Deepwater Horizon The DOI continues to play a major role in restoration efforts associated with the Deepwater Horizon oil spill that occurred in the Gulf of Mexico in 2010. https://www.doi.gov/deepwaterhorizon

Federal Register Significant documents, from 1995 (volume 60) to the present, and recent documents that the DOI and its subagencies have published in the Federal Register are available online. https://www.federalregister.gov/agencies/interior-department

Freedom of Information Act (FOIA) Thirteen bureaus and offices support the DOI's FOIA operations. Its website features a single web page that allows convenient access to those bureaus and offices and to their electronic FOIA libraries. From the same web page, an information seeker may file a request, track the status of a request, learn about the FOIA program's structure, and review FOIA-related guidance and resources. Please note: the Department and its bureaus and offices post a great deal of information online; therefore, an information seeker should visit the appropriate electronic libraries and search for the desired information before submitting a FOIA request. That information already may be accessible, immediately and without charge. https://www.doi.gov/foia

Frequently Asked Questions (FAQs) The DOI has posted answers to FAQs about its reorganization. https://www.doi.gov/employees/reorg/faq

History On March 3, 1849, the last day of the 30th Congress, a bill was passed to create a department to manage the Nation's internal development and the welfare of its people. The responsibilities of the new Department were diverse and came to include the colonization of freed slaves in Haiti, exploration of western wilderness, oversight of the District of Columbia jail, regulation of territorial governments, management of hospitals and universities, and more. To explore the rich history of the "Department of Everything Else"—just about everything else that fell outside the purview of the Departments of Foreign Affairs, War, and the Treasury—visit the "History of the Department of the Interior" web page. https://www.doi.gov/whoweare/history

"There are no words that can tell the hidden spirit of the wilderness that can reveal its mystery, its melancholy and its charm. The Nation behaves well if it treats the natural resources as assets which it must turn over to the next generation increased and not impaired in value. These words belong to President Theodore Roosevelt, a man who loved the outdoors. To learn about the important role this President played in the history of American conservation, visit the "Theodore Roosevelt's Legacy" web page. https://www.doi.gov/blog/theodore-roosevelts-legacy

Library   The Interior Library's holdings and its reference and research services support the mission of the Department and its agencies and bureaus. Its holdings cover American history, geology, law, national parks, Native American culture and history, nature, and public lands and wildlife management. The library offers subscription databases and other online data sources that give Interior employees and external researchers nationwide access. A holdings catalog and descriptions of educational programs and training opportunities are available on the library's website. Phone, 202-208-5815. https://www.doi.gov/library | Email: library@ios.doi.gov

Museum   The Interior Museum offers exhibits on the history and mission of the Department. Programs highlight bureau management of cultural and natural resources. Museum guides conduct tours of the Interior Building's New Deal era art and architecture. Phone, 202-208-4743. https://www.doi.gov/interiormuseum

News   The Department posts press releases online. https://www.doi.gov/pressreleases

The DOI posts news and headlines of the week in video format on the "This Week at Interior" web page. https://www.doi.gov/video/twai

Open Government   The Department of the Interior supports the Open Government initiative by promoting the principles of collaboration, participation, and transparency. Beyond meeting Open Government requirements, the agency intends to create better relationships between citizens and their Government; to become better at understanding citizens' demands for services and more responsive to their needs; to accelerate the rate of

innovation by leveraging public knowledge; to increase the Department's ability to carry out its mission more effectively and efficiently by transparently engaging the public in decisionmaking; and to encourage the development of Open Government programs. https://www.doi.gov/open | Email: open@ios.doi.gov

Priorities   The "Our Priorities" web page lists the DOI's top 10 priorities. https://www.doi.gov/ourpriorities

Regulatory Reform   President Donald J. Trump has placed an emphasis on reforming rules and regulations that negatively affect the U.S. economy while doing little to help the environment. https://www.doi.gov/regulatory-reform

Site Map   The website map allows visitors to look for specific topics or to browse content that aligns with their interests. https://www.doi.gov/sitemap

Social Media   The DOI maintains a facebook account. https://www.facebook.com/USInterior

The DOI tweets announcements and other newsworthy items on Twitter. https://twitter.com/interior

The DOI posts videos on its YouTube channel. https://www.youtube.com/user/USInterior

Sustainability Programs   The Department of the Interior is dedicated to conserving and protecting the Nation's natural and cultural resources now and for future generations. Its employees are passionate about their stewardship responsibility for the resources and properties that they manage for the American People. https://www.doi.gov/stewardship

Water Conservation   The WaterSMART program improves water conservation and helps water-resource managers make sound decisions about water use. It identifies strategies to ensure that this and future generations will have sufficient supplies of clean water for drinking, economic activities, ecosystem health, and recreation. The program also identifies adaptive measures to address climate change and its effect on future water demands. https://www.doi.gov/watersmart

The Sources of Information were updated 12–2019.

Bureau of Indian Affairs

Department of the Interior, 1849 C Street NW., Washington, DC 20240
Phone, 202-208-3710. Internet, http://www.bia.gov/bia

Director *   DARRYL LACOUNTE
https://www.bia.gov/as-ia/opa/online-press-release/assistant-secretary-
   sweeney-names-darryl-lacounte-director-bureau-of-indian-affairs

* The Director reports to the Assistant Secretary of Indian Affairs.

The above list of key personnel was updated 5–2020.

*The Bureau of Indian Affairs enhances the quality of life, promotes economic opportunity,
and protects and improves the trust assets of American Indians, Indian tribes, and Alaska
Natives.*

Establishment and Organization
Secretary of War John C. Calhoun
established the Bureau of Indian Affairs (BIA)
on March 11, 1824, to oversee and carry
out the Federal Government's trade and
treaty relations with tribes. The BIA remains
the oldest Department of the Interior (DOI)
agency in continuous existence and one of
the oldest in the Federal government. The
DOI formally adopted Bureau of Indian
Affairs (BIA) as the agency's official name
on September 17, 1947. Prior to that time,
it was referred to as the Indian office, Indian
bureau, Indian department, and Indian
service. https://www.doi.gov/blog/193rd-
anniversary-bureau-indian-affairs

On March 3, 1849, President James K.
Polk approved an act that transferred the
"supervisory and appellate powers now
exercised by the Secretary of the War
Department, in relation to all the acts of
the Commissioner of Indian Affairs," to the
Secretary of the Interior, who now headed
the newly created DOI. http://www.loc.gov/
law/help/statutes-at-large/30th-congress/
session-2/c30s2ch108.pdf

The Bureau's organizational chart is
available in Portable Document Format
(PDF) for viewing and downloading. https://
www.indianaffairs.gov/sites/bia.gov/files/
uploads/bia/bia-org-chart.pdf

Statutory and Regulatory Authorities
Statutory material affecting the BIA is
codified in 25 U.S.C. 1–17 (chapter 1).
https://uscode.house.gov/view.xhtml?path=/
prelim@title25/chapter1&edition=prelim

Rules and regulations that affect Indians
are codified in 25 CFR. Parts 1–299 contain
rules and regulations that are associated
with the Bureau of Indian Affairs. Parts
900–999 contain rules and regulations that
are associated with the Bureau of Indian
Affairs and with the Department of Health
and Human Service's Indian Health Service.
https://www.ecfr.gov/cgi-bin/text-idx?SID=2d
ff2e4675b2891abcf7c9eb0078703c&mc=tru
e&tpl=/ecfrbrowse/Title25/25tab_02.tpl

Activities
The BIA's mission centers on fulfilling
its trust responsibilities and promoting
self-determination on behalf of federally
recognized tribal governments, American
Indians, and Alaska Natives. The BIA
provides services to members of 573
federally recognized Indian Tribes in the 48
contiguous United States and Alaska—nearly
two million American Indians and Alaska
Natives. https://www.bia.gov/bia

The BIA serves the federally recognized
Tribes through four Offices:

The Office of Indian Services operates
the BIA's general assistance, disaster relief,
Indian child welfare, tribal government,
Indian self-determination, and reservation
roads programs. https://www.bia.gov/bia/ois

The Office of Justice Services directly
operates or funds law enforcement, tribal
courts, and detention facilities on Federal
Indian lands. https://www.bia.gov/bia/ojs

The Office of Trust Services works with
tribes and individual American Indians and
Alaska Natives in the management of their

Bureau of Indian Affairs

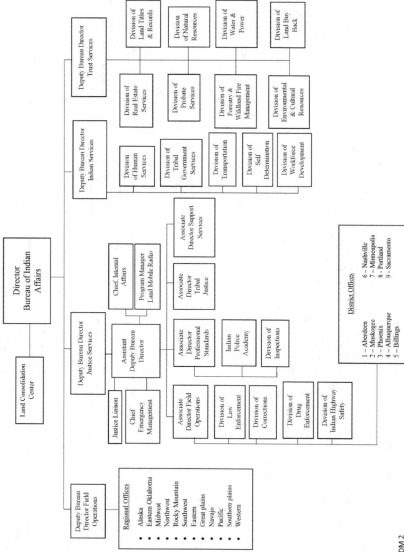

130 DM 2

trust lands, assets, and resources. https://www.bia.gov/bia/ots

Lastly, the Office of Field Operations oversees 12 regional offices and 83 agencies that carry out the mission of the BIA at the tribal level. The regional offices and agencies administer delivery of program services to the federally recognized Tribes, to individual Indians, and to Alaska Natives, either directly or through contracts, grants or compacts. https://www.bia.gov/regional-offices

Sources of Information

Archived Records The "Guide to Federal Records in the National Archives of the United States" indicates that Bureau of Indian Affairs records have been assigned to record group 075. https://www.archives.gov/research/guide-fed-records/groups/075.html

Career Opportunities BIA job opportunities, common job documents, and hiring information for American Indian and Alaska Native veterans are available online. https://www.bia.gov/Jobs/index.htm

In 2019, the BIA ranked 349th among 420 agency subcomponents in the Partnership for Public Service's Best Places To Work Agency Rankings. https://bestplacestowork.org/rankings/detail/IN06

Contact Information The BIA posts its mailing address and fax and phone numbers on the Indian Affairs' website on the "Contact Us" web page. https://www.bia.gov/contact-us

Estate Planning The American Indian Probate Reform Act of 2004 (AIPRA) made changes to the way trust or restricted land and property is inherited. It also made changes that affected land management and purchases. The BIA website has information that explains how AIPRA affects wills and inheritance. https://www.bia.gov/bia/ots/dres/estate-planning

Federal Register Significant documents, from 1995 (volume 60) to the present, and recent documents that the BIA has published in the Federal Register are available online. https://www.federalregister.gov/agencies/indian-affairs-bureau

Freedom of Information Act (FOIA) The FOIA establishes a presumption that the public may access records in the possession of Federal agencies. The Act is based on the principle of openness in government and generally provides that a person has a right of access to Federal agency records. This right of access is restricted, however, by nine exemptions and three special law enforcement record exclusions that shield certain records, or parts of them, from disclosure. More information on the FOIA and instructions for submitting a request to access BIA records are available on the Indian Affairs website. https://www.bia.gov/as-ia/foia | Email: foia@bia.gov

Before submitting a FOIA request in writing with the FOIA officer, the requester should check that the information being sought is not already in the public domain. The DOI maintains FOIA libraries that include the following record types and resources: final opinions made in the adjudication of cases; policy statements and interpretations that the DOI has adopted, but not published in the Federal Register; administrative staff manuals and staff instructions that affect a member of the public; records that have been requested repeatedly by submitters of FOIA requests or records that the DOI anticipates will be requested repeatedly in the future; an index of frequently requested records; and links to other related sites and reference materials. https://www.doi.gov/foia/library

Frequently Asked Questions (FAQs) Indian Affairs posts answers to FAQs on its website. https://www.bia.gov/frequently-asked-questions

Library Frequently requested documents and links are accessible on the Indian Affairs website in the electronic document library. https://www.bia.gov/bia/document-library

Maps The Office of Trust Services' Branch of Geospatial Support (BGS) posts web maps and static maps, as well as downloadable data, on the Indian Affairs' website. The BGS provides geographic information systems software, training, and system support for the management of natural resources on Indian lands. Phone, 877-293-9494. https://biamaps.doi.gov | Email: geospatial@bia.gov

"Indian Lands of Federally Recognized Tribes of the United States" is available on the Office of Trust Services' "Division of Land Titles and Records" web page. The Office's web team posted the map file in

Portable Document Format (PDF) for viewing and downloading. https://www.bia.gov/sites/bia.gov/files/assets/bia/ots/webteam/pdf/idc1-028635.pdf

The "National Climate Assessment—Indigenous People's Resilience Actions" map, which is posted on the Office of Trust Services' website, provides an overview of indigenous people's actions to prepare for changes in climate by taking steps to increase resilience. https://biamaps.doi.gov/nca/

Programs / Services   Federally recognized Tribes look to the BIA for a range of services. The "Programs and Services" web page, which is accessible on the Indian Affairs' website, provides information about them. https://www.bia.gov/programs-services

Regional Offices   Contact information for the 12 BIA regional offices is available online. https://www.bia.gov/regional-offices

Regulations in Development   The "Regulations and Other Documents in Development" web page, which is part of the Indian Affairs' website, allows visitors to monitor the progress of regulations that are in development, under review, or in development and under review. https://www.bia.gov/as-ia/raca/regulations-and-other-documents-in-development

The Sources of Information were updated 12–2019.

Site Map   The site map, which is part of the Indian Affairs' website, allows visitors to look for specific topics or to browse content that aligns with their interests. https://www.bia.gov/sitemap

Social Media   The BIA posts content on Facebook. https://www.facebook.com/USIndianAffairs

The BIA tweets announcements and other newsworthy items on Twitter. https://twitter.com/USIndianAffairs

Tribal Leaders Directory   The directory, which is part of the Indian Affairs' website, provides contact information for each federally recognized Tribe, as well as for the leadership of the BIA. The electronic and interactive map-based directory contains information on each BIA region and agency that provides services to a specific Tribe. https://www.bia.gov/tribal-leaders-directory

Wildland Fire Management   Indian Affairs posted a collection of fire prevention and education videos on wildland fire management in Indian country on its website. Note that not all of the videos in the collection were produced by the BIA. https://www.bia.gov/bia/ots/dfwfm/bwfm/Video-Library

Bureau of Indian Education

Department of the Interior, 1849 C Street NW., Washington, DC 20240
Phone, 202-208-3710. Internet, http://www.bie.edu

Director *   Tony L. Dearman
https://www.bie.edu/cs/groups/webteam/documents/text/
    idc2-092903.pdf

* The Director reports to the Assistant Secretary of Indian Affairs.

The above list of key personnel was updated 5–2020.

The Bureau of Indian Education provides educational opportunities for eligible American Indian and Alaska Native elementary, secondary, and postsecondary students from federally recognized Tribes

Establishment and Organization
To reflect the parallel purpose and organizational structure that the BIE has in relation to other programs within the Office of the Assistant Secretary–Indian Affairs, the Office of Indian Education Programs was renamed the Bureau of Indian Education (BIE) by departmental manual release no. 3721 of August 29, 2006. https://www.bia.gov/bie

Nearly 95 years earlier, President Warren G. Harding approved Public Law 67–85, which is also referred to as the Snyder Act of 1921, to authorize the BIA, under the supervision of the Secretary of the Interior, to "direct, supervise, and expend such moneys as Congress may from time to time appropriate, for the benefit, care, and assistance of the Indians throughout the United States for the following purposes . . ." One of those purposes was for the "general support and civilization, including education." Since the passage of the Snyder Act of 1921, three major legislative actions have restructured the Bureau of Indian Affairs (BIA) with regard to educating American Indians. http://www.loc.gov/law/help/statutes-at-large/67th-congress/Session%201/c67s1ch115.pdf

On June 18, 1934, the day on which President Franklin D. Roosevelt approved Public Law 73–383, which is also referred to as the Indian Reorganization Act of 1934 and the Wheeler-Howard Act, the longstanding Federal policy of acculturating and assimilating Indian people through a boarding school system ended. The new law introduced the teaching of Indian history and culture in BIA schools. http://www.loc.gov/law/help/statutes-at-large/73rd-congress/session-2/c73s2ch576.pdf

On January 4, 1975, President Gerald R. Ford approved Public Law 93–638, which is also cited as the Indian Self-Determination and Education Assistance Act of 1975, "to establish a program of assistance to upgrade Indian education" and "to support the right of Indian citizens to control their own educational activities." The law allows federally recognized Tribes to contract with the BIA for the operation of Bureau-funded schools and to determine education programs suitable for their children. https://www.govinfo.gov/content/pkg/STATUTE-88/pdf/STATUTE-88-Pg2203.pdf

On November 1, 1978, President James E. Carter approved Public Law 95–561, which is also cited as the Education Amendments of 1978. Additional amendments followed: Public Laws 98–511, 99–99, and 100–297. These legislative actions provided direct funding to tribally operated schools, empowered Indian school boards, permitted local hiring of teachers and staff, and created a direct line of authority between the Education Director and the Assistant Secretary of Indian Affairs. https://www.govinfo.gov/content/pkg/STATUTE-92/pdf/STATUTE-92-Pg2143.pdf

The BIE organizational chart is part of the organizational chart of Indian Affairs. https://www.indianaffairs.gov/sites/bia.gov/files/OrgChartFY18Greenbook.pdf

Statutory and Regulatory Authorities

Rules and regulations affecting Indians and their education are codified in 25 CFR 30–47 (subchapter E). https://www.ecfr.gov/cgi-bin/text-idx?SID=7954367ce0b81d96674d6b175d0dea54&mc=true&tpl=/ecfrbrowse/Title25/25CIsubchapE.tpl

Activities

The BIE provides quality education opportunities from early childhood throughout adulthood, in accordance with the Tribes' needs for cultural and economic well-being, and in keeping with the diversity of Indian Tribes and Alaska Native villages as distinct cultural and governmental entities. The BIE considers the whole person as it carries out its mission, taking into account the cultural, mental, physical, and spiritual aspects of the person within the contexts of family and Tribe or Alaska Native village. https://www.ecfr.gov/cgi-bin/text-idx?SID=317c41e73ba08bd8f84a0dbdfba8a9c3&mc=true&node=pt25.1.32&rgn=div5#se25.1.32_13

The BIE educates over 45,000 American Indian and Alaska Native children at 183 elementary and secondary schools on 64 reservations in 23 States. The Bureau operates 53 of these schools. The other 130 schools are tribally operated. The BIE oversees two postsecondary schools: Haskell Indian Nations University in Lawrence, KS, and Southwestern Indian Polytechnic Institute in Albuquerque, NM. It also funds the Navajo and United Tribes Technical Colleges. https://www.bia.gov/bie

Sources of Information

Archived Records The "Guide to Federal Records in the National Archives of the United States" indicates that Bureau of Indian Affairs records have been assigned to record group 075. "Records of the Education Division 1874–1972" are part of that record group. https://www.archives.gov/research/guide-fed-records/groups/075.html

Career Opportunities   American Indian children deserve a quality education—and that starts with highly qualified, dedicated staff and educators. The BIE employs nearly 4,500 professionals in careers that offer unique and diverse cultural and lifestyle experiences. Phone, 505-563-5304. https://www.bie.edu/Jobs/index.htm | Email: staffing@bie.edu

Contact Information   The "Contact Us" web page has addresses and phone numbers for contacting the BIE. https://www.bie.edu/ContactUs/index.htm

The Human Resources Office maintains a web page with contact information. https://www.bie.edu/HR/Contact/index.htm

The BIE "National Staff Directory" (APR 2019) is available in Portable Document Format (PDF) for viewing and downloading. https://www.bie.edu/cs/groups/xbie/documents/text/idc2-093307.pdf

Divisions / Programs   The BIE website features a web page with a list of the agency's divisions and programs and links to their websites. https://www.bie.edu/Programs/index

Freedom of Information Act (FOIA)   The FOIA establishes a presumption that the public may access records in the possession of Federal agencies. The Act is based on the principle of openness in government and generally provides that a person has a right of access to Federal agency records. This right of access is restricted, however, by nine exemptions and three special law enforcement record exclusions that shield certain records, or parts of them, from disclosure. More information on the FOIA and instructions for submitting a request to access BIE records are available on the Indian Affairs website. https://www.bia.gov/as-ia/foia | Email: foia@bia.gov

Before submitting a FOIA request in writing with the FOIA officer, the requester should check that the information being sought is not already in the public domain. The DOI maintains FOIA libraries that include the following record types and resources: final opinions made in the adjudication of cases; policy statements and interpretations that the DOI has adopted,

but not published in the Federal Register; administrative staff manuals and staff instructions that affect a member of the public; records that have been requested repeatedly by submitters of FOIA requests or records that the DOI anticipates will be requested repeatedly in the future; an index of frequently requested records; and links to other related sites and reference materials. https://www.doi.gov/foia/library

Frequently Asked Questions (FAQs)   The BIE posts answers to FAQs on its website. https://www.bie.edu/HR/FAQ/index.htm

News   The BIE posts news items on its website. https://www.bie.edu/NewsEvents/index.htm

Reports   Performance and special education reports and school report cards are accessible online. https://www.bie.edu/HowAreWeDoing/index.htm

Resources   BIE education line officers, school superintendents, principals, teachers, and staff can access program guidance, handbooks, templates, and training provided in various formats—WebEx or PowerPoint—to refresh professional skills. These online documents and presentations are provided to supplement staff training throughout the school year. https://www.bie.edu/Resources/index.htm

Scholarships   The BIE website provides information on scholarship opportunities for American Indian students. https://www.bie.edu/ParentsStudents/Grants/index.htm

Schools   Contact information for schools that the BIE oversees is available online. https://www.bie.edu/Schools/index.htm

Site Map   The website map allows visitors to look for specific topics or to browse content that aligns with their interests. https://www.bie.edu/SiteMap/index.htm

Social Media   The BIE maintains a Facebook account. https://www.facebook.com/Bureauofindianeducation

The BIE tweets announcements and other newsworthy items on Twitter. https://twitter.com/BureauIndianEdu

Tribal Resources   A directory of external resources to support tribes is accessible on the BIE website. The directory file is in Portable Document Format for viewing and downloading. https://www.bie.edu/Resources/index.htm

The Sources of Information were updated 12–2019.

Bureau of Land Management

Department of the Interior, 1849 C Street NW., Washington, DC 20240
Phone, 202-208-3710. Internet, http://www.bie.edu

Director *   (VACANCY)
https://www.blm.gov/leadership

---

* The Director reports to the Assistant Secretary of Land and Minerals Management.

The above list of key personnel was updated 7–2021.

The Bureau of Land Management sustains the health, diversity, and productivity of public lands for the use and enjoyment of present and future generations.

Establishment and Organization
President Harry S. Truman prepared and transmitted to the U.S. Congress a plan of reorganization that created the Bureau of Land Management (BLM). Section 403 of reorganization plan no. 3 of 1946 consolidated the General Land Office with the Grazing Service to establish the Bureau of Land Management. The plan became effective on July 16, 1946. https://uscode.house.gov/view.xhtml?req=granuleid:USC-prelim-title5a-node84-leaf93&num=0&edition=prelim

On October 21, 1976, President Gerald R. Ford approved the Federal Land Policy and Management Act of 1976 (PL 94–579) to establish public land policy; to establish guidelines for its administration; to provide for the management, protection, development, and enhancement of the public lands; and for other purposes" (90 STAT. 2743). In the law, Congress declared that national policy governing the management of public lands "be on the basis of multiple use and sustained yield." https://www.govinfo.gov/content/pkg/STATUTE-90/pdf/STATUTE-90-Pg2743.pdf

The BLM posts its organization chart online. https://www.blm.gov/about/organization-chart

Statutory and Regulatory Authorities
Laws that affect public lands are codified in 43 U.S.C. Chapter 1 of that title contains codified material that is associated with the BLM. https://uscode.house.gov/view.xhtml?path=/prelim@title43/chapter1&edition=prelim

Rules and regulations that affect public lands and that are associated with the BLM are codified in 43 CFR 1000–9999 (subtitle B, ch. II). The codified subjects include forest, general, land resource, minerals, and range management; preservation and conservation; recreation programs; and technical services. https://www.ecfr.gov/cgi-bin/text-idx?SID=5167eb7d8c784969301611a596a7818a&mc=true&tpl=/ecfrbrowse/Title43/43chapterII.tpl

Activities
The BLM sustains the diversity, health, and productivity of America's public lands for the benefit of present and future generations through a mandate of multiple-use and sustained-yield. It manages 1 of every 10 acres of land across the United States, about 245 million acres of land, most of which is located in Alaska and 11 other Western States. The Bureau also manages about 30 percent, or 700 million acres, of the Nation's subsurface mineral estate. The BLM oversees conventional and renewable energy development, livestock grazing, recreation, and timber harvesting, and it protects cultural, historical, and natural resources. Many of these resources are found on National Conservation Lands, a subset of BLM lands that are federally designated, that cover 32 million acres, and that include 260 wilderness areas and 28 national monuments. https://www.blm.gov/programs

A number of energy resources are accessible on public lands. The BLM supports a diversified energy approach that includes coal, oil and gas, strategic minerals, as well as renewable energy resources like geothermal, solar, wind, and woody biomass. A diversified approach strengthens the Nation's energy security,

Bureau of Land Management

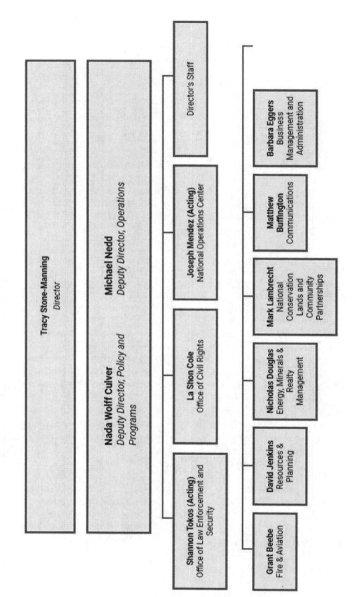

Tracy Stone-Manning
Director

Nada Wolff Culver
Deputy Director, Policy and Programs

Michael Nedd
Deputy Director, Operations

Director's Staff

Shannon Tokos (Acting)
Office of Law Enforcement and Security

La Shon Cole
Office of Civil Rights

Joseph Mendez (Acting)
National Operations Center

Grant Beebe
Fire & Aviation

David Jenkins
Resources & Planning

Nicholas Douglas
Energy, Minerals & Realty Management

Mark Lambrecht
National Conservation Lands and Community Partnerships

Matthew Buffington
Communications

Barbara Eggers
Business Management and Administration

strengthens its energy infrastructure, and stimulates job creation. To serve industry and the American public, the BLM is making energy development easier on public lands by reviewing and streamlining business processes. https://www.blm.gov/programs/energy-and-minerals

The Bureau manages livestock on 155 million acres of land, administering nearly 18,000 permits and leases held by ranchers who graze mostly cattle and sheep. https://www.blm.gov/programs/natural-resources/rangelands-and-grazing

Under the Wild Free-Roaming Horses and Burros Act of 1971, it also manages herds of wild horses and burros on public rangelands. https://www.blm.gov/whb

Recreation is also part of the BLM's portfolio. Birdwatchers, campers, hang gliders, horseback riders, hunters, mountain bikers, photographers, whitewater rafters, and visitors to cultural and natural heritage sites recreate on hundreds of millions of acres of public lands. The Bureau estimates that it receives approximately 62 million recreational visits per year. https://www.blm.gov/programs/recreation

The BLM manages habitat for over 300 wildlife, fish, and plant species that are listed as threatened or endangered under the Endangered Species Act and 12 species identified as candidates for listing. Public lands that the BLM manages offer the best opportunity for recovery of some rare or listed plant and animal species because their unique requirements for survival can be met only on Federal lands. https://www.blm.gov/programs/fish-and-wildlife/threatened-and-endangered

The Federal Land Policy and Management Act (FLPMA) of 1976 authorizes the Secretary of the Interior to stand up a law enforcement body to enforce Federal laws and regulations affecting public lands and their resources. As a result, the BLM has been given specific resource protection and law enforcement responsibilities that further the FLPMA's public lands management policy of multiple use. The Bureau's law enforcement program helps ensure public safety, while supporting its multiple-use mission. Law enforcement officers investigate vandalism and looting, support emergency responders, and maintain a safe environment for visitors to the public lands and for BLM employees. https://www.blm.gov/programs/public-safety-and-fire/law-enforcement

The BLM carries out a broad range of actions to protect the public, natural landscapes, wildlife habitat, and recreational areas from wildfire. The BLM's national fire and aviation program consists of community assistance and protection, fire prevention through education, fire suppression, preparedness, predictive services, prescribed fire, and vegetative fuels management. https://www.blm.gov/programs/fire-and-aviation

The BLM's lands, realty and cadastral survey program manages public land transactions: purchases and acquisitions, sales and exchanges, withdrawals, leases and permits, right-of-way authorizations, and, cadastral (i.e., mapping) survey services. From enabling energy development, to permitting commercial filming, to defining boundaries and maintaining public land records, BLM professionals regard the public lands as working landscapes, and they manage them for the benefit of current and future generations. The BLM's mission—which is built on the principles of multiple-use and sustained yield—requires the agency to promote commerce, conservation, and recreation on public lands. https://www.blm.gov/programs/lands-and-realty

The Bureau's broad management responsibilities require balancing public land uses and protection of public land resources. Working with State and local and tribal governments, stakeholder groups, and the public, the BLM creates land use plans, referred to as Resource Management Plans, to guide decisions for approved uses of and actions affecting public lands. https://www.blm.gov/programs/planning-and-nepa

Sources of Information

Adoption Schedule The BLM offers wild horses and burros for adoption or purchase at events nationwide throughout the year. The most current adoption event schedule is accessible online. https://www.blm.gov/programs/wild-horse-and-burro/adoption-and-sales/events

Archived Records   The "Guide to Federal Records in the National Archives of the United States" indicates that BLM records have been assigned to record group 049. https://www.archives.gov/research/guide-fed-records/groups/049.html

Artist-in-Residence Program   Residencies of 6–8 weeks are available in several Western States for painters, photographers, potters, sculptors, and other artists. https://www.blm.gov/get-involved/artist-in-residence/about-the-program

Business Opportunities   The BLM procures a wide array of goods and services. https://www.blm.gov/services/acquisition/contracting

Stewardship contracting refers to trading forest products for land management and services. In exchange for thinning the forest and keeping the trees to sell, for example, a contractor or an organization performs service-work that helps to achieve key land management goals like improving wildlife habitat or reestablishing native plant species. The intent of stewardship is to improve, maintain, or restore forest or rangeland health; restore or maintain water quality; improve fish and wildlife habitat; and reduce danger from wildfires. https://www.blm.gov/programs/natural-resources/forests-and-woodlands/stewardship-contracting

Career Opportunities   The BLM relies on people with diverse skills and from various professional backgrounds—business, engineering, fire management, law enforcement, science, and other fields—to manage the Nation's public lands and resources. https://www.blm.gov/careers

In 2020, the BLM ranked 322d among 411 agency subcomponents in the Partnership for Public Service's Best Places To Work Agency Rankings. https://bestplacestowork.org/rankings/detail/?c=IN05

Climate Change   Climate change presents challenges to the BLM as it manages inland freshwater ecosystems (e.g., lakes, rivers, streams, wetlands) and coastal wetlands. Researchers project the disappearance of cold-water fish from large areas of their current geographic ranges as streams become more sporadic and warmer; the expansion of the ranges of warm-water fish as surface waters warm; and more frequent and widespread algal blooms that adversely affect water quality. https://www.blm.gov/programs/fish-and-wildlife/fisheries-and-aquatics/about-the-program

Contact Information   Contact information is available online. https://www.blm.gov/office/national-office

Data Resources   The BLM regularly gathers, maintains, and publishes data to inform stakeholders and the general public. These data include detailed information on the commercial uses of the public lands; recreational activities and revenues; wild horse and burro management; cadastral (i.e., mapping) surveys; conservation of rangeland resources and 870 special units (e.g., wilderness areas); and the socioeconomic effects of public land management. https://www.blm.gov/about/data

Federal Register   Significant documents, from 1995 (volume 60) to the present, and recent documents that the BLM has published in the Federal Register are available online. https://www.federalregister.gov/agencies/land-management-bureau

Freedom of Information Act (FOIA)   The FOIA gives the right to request access to BLM records to anyone. In response to a FOIA request, the BLM will disclose the desired information, unless this right of access is restricted by one of nine exemptions or three special law enforcement record exclusions that shield certain records, or parts of them, from disclosure. More information on the FOIA and instructions for submitting a request are available on the BLM website. Phone, 202-912-7650. https://www.blm.gov/about/foia | Email: blm_wo_foia@blm.gov

Before submitting a records request in writing to the FOIA officer, the requester should check that the information being sought is not already publicly accessible. The BLM maintains an electronic FOIA reading room where it posts records that have been released into the public domain in response to previous requests. https://www.blm.gov/about/foia/foia-reading-room

General Land Office Records   The General Land Office Records website allows visitors to access Federal land conveyance records for the Public Land States (i.e., States created out of the public domain). The website contains images of more than five million Federal land title records that were issued since 1820. It also has images related to survey plats and field notes dating back to 1810. https://www.blm.gov/services/land-records

Geographic Information System (GIS) Data BLM Navigator serves as a centralized location for accessing project, State, and national geospatial data. https://navigator.blm.gov/home

The Landscape Approach Data Portal is a one-stop source for geospatial data, maps, models, and reports that BLM's landscape initiatives have produced. https://landscape.blm.gov/geoportal/catalog/main/home.page

History A timeline that is structured around the enactment of land management legislation is available online. Specific public laws have guided the BLM's mission, and the passage of the Federal Land Policy and Management Act of 1976 was the culmination of that process of policymaking. https://www.blm.gov/about/history/timeline

Information Center The "Information Center" web page has links to BLM policy, congressional testimony, Federal Register, live events, magazines and newsletters, notices, Office of Civil Rights, press releases, public room (brochures, maps, reports), and social media web pages. https://www.blm.gov/media

Kids Giving young people the opportunity to learn outdoors and recreate on public lands promotes the development of the next generation of public land stewards and conservation leaders. https://www.blm.gov/kids

Library The library has professional staff who can assist BLM employees nationwide. The library staff is also available to assist members of the general public seeking BLM publications and information. The library offers a range of resources and services that include journals, databases, publications, subject guides, and an online library catalog. https://www.blm.gov/learn/blm-library | Email: blm_library@blm.gov

Management The BLM manages public lands in accordance with the Federal Land Policy and Management Act of 1976. https://www.blm.gov/about/how-we-manage

The BLM manages one in every 10 acres of land in the United States, and approximately 30 percent of the Nation's

minerals. These lands and their minerals are found in each of the 50 States in diverse ecosystems like arctic tundra, deserts, forests, mountains, and grasslands. https://www.blm.gov/about/what-we-manage

Maps Map and geospatial products inform BLM decision making. These maps and products are becoming more accessible online. https://www.blm.gov/maps

Paleontology The BLM manages more than 245 million acres of public lands where Deinonychus, Edmontosaurus, Pentaceratops, and Stegosaurus once roamed. To learn more, visit the BLM's "Paleontology" web pages. https://www.blm.gov/paleontology

Recreation The National Conservation Lands program offers online recreational guides for a convenient connection to public lands. https://www.blm.gov/visit

The BLM website provides resources for mountain bikers. These resources include the BLM Top 20 Mountain Biking Opportunities list and interactive mountain biking maps for trails on BLM lands. https://www.blm.gov/programs/recreation/mountainbike

Social Media The BLM uses digital media tools to connect people with public lands and to keep people informed about activities on them. https://www.blm.gov/media/social-media

Statistics Tables and spreadsheets with data that include the numbers of BLM-administered oil and gas leases, of applications for permit to drill, and of oil and gas wells are accessible on the BLM website. Most of the statistics presented cover Fiscal Years 1988–2015. https://www.blm.gov/about/data/public-land-statistics

Timber Sales The availability of timber for harvest depends on the age and condition of the timber, land status, and public demand, as well as on other land use considerations. https://www.blm.gov/programs/natural-resources/forests-and-woodlands/timber-sales

Woody Biomass Woody biomass is used to produce electricity and products like furniture, paper, and wood for housing. https://www.blm.gov/programs/natural-resources/forests-and-woodlands/biomass-and-bioenergy

The Sources of Information were updated 7–2021.

Bureau of Ocean Energy Management

Department of the Interior, 1849 C Street NW., Washington, DC 20240-0001
Phone, 202-208-6474. Internet, http://www.boem.gov

Director *   AMANDA LEFTON
https://www.boem.gov/about-boem/boem-leadership

* The Director reports to the Assistant Secretary of Land and Minerals Management.

The above list of key personnel was updated 7–2021.

The Bureau of Ocean Energy Management manages development of U.S. Outer Continental Shelf energy and mineral resources in a way that is environmentally and economically responsible.

Establishment and Organization

In April of 2010, the Deepwater Horizon oil rig explosion and resulting oil spill in the Gulf of Mexico exposed inadequacies in the Federal offshore energy regulatory system. In response to the disaster, former Secretary of the Interior Kenneth L. Salazar issued two secretarial orders. On May 19, 2010, he issued Order 3299 "to separate and reassign the responsibilities that had been conducted by the Minerals Management Service [MMS] into new management structures that will improve the management, oversight, and accountability of activities on the Outer Continental Shelf [OCS]." https://www.doi.gov/sites/doi.gov/files/elips/documents/3299a2-establishment_of_the_bureau_of_ocean_energy_management_the_bureau_of_safety_and_environmental_enforcement_and_the_office_of_natural_resources_revenue.pdf

Within the Department of the Interior, Order 3299 initiated the establishment of the new Bureau of Ocean Energy Management (BOEM), whose director would report to the Assistant Secretary–Land and Minerals Management. The order also initiated the establishment of the new Bureau of Safety and Environmental Enforcement (BSEE), whose director also would report to the same Assistant Secretary. A third new agency, the Office of Natural Resources Revenue, formerly the MMS's minerals revenue management program, would be established within the Department, and its director would report to a different Assistant Secretary. https://www.boem.gov/about-boem/reorganization/reorganization-former-mms

On June 18, 2010, former Secretary Salazar issued Order 3302, which announced that the MMS would be renamed the Bureau of Ocean Energy Management, Regulation and Enforcement (BOEMRE) for the duration of the reorganization period. https://www.doi.gov/sites/doi.gov/files/elips/documents/3302_-change_of_the_name_of_the_minerals_management_service_to_the_bureau_of_ocean_energy_management_regulation_and_enforcement.pdf

On October 1, 2011, BOEMRE rules and regulations that now applied to the BOEM were recodified in a new chapter by reorganization of 30 CFR. The establishment of the BOEM and its sibling the BSEE and the recodification of their respective rules and regulations in a revised second chapter and a newly added fifth chapter marked the completion of the reorganization of the former MMS. https://www.govinfo.gov/content/pkg/FR-2011-10-18/pdf/2011-22675.pdf

The BOEM posts an organizational chart on its website. https://www.boem.gov/about-boem/boem-organizational-chart

Statutory and Regulatory Authorities

Statutory material that affects mineral lands and mining is codified in 30 U.S.C. Chapter 26 of that title deals with deep seabed hard mineral resources. https://uscode.house.gov/view.xhtml?path=/prelim@title30/chapter26&edition=prelim

Statutory material that affects public lands is codified in 43 U.S.C. Chapter 36 of that title deals with management of OCS resources. https://uscode.house.

Bureau of Ocean Energy Management

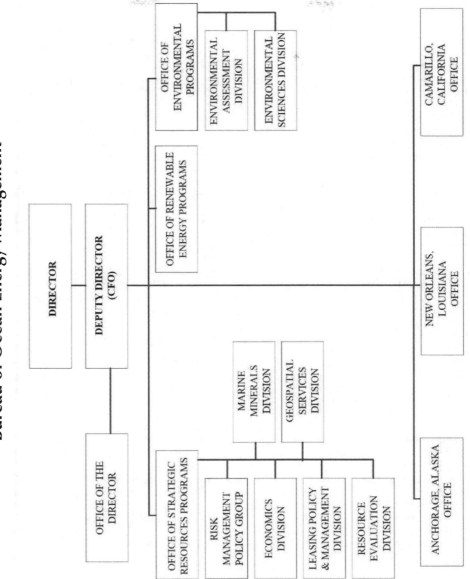

gov/view.xhtml?path=/prelim@title43/
chapter36&edition=prelim

BOEM rules and regulations are codified
in chapter V, parts 500–599, of 30 CFR.
https://www.ecfr.gov/cgi-bin/text-idx?SID=9e
abfe008f51a5c2935452c280fb4160&mc=tr
ue&tpl=/ecfrbrowse/Title30/30chapterV.tpl

Activities

The BOEM manages the exploration
and development of offshore energy and
marine mineral resources on the OCS. The
BOEM supports energy independence,
environmental protection, and economic
development by responsibly managing these
offshore resources in ways that comport with
the best available science.

The OCS is a significant source of oil and
gas for the Nation's energy supply. OCS
production accounts for about 18 percent
of domestic crude oil and 4 percent of
domestic natural gas supply. The BOEM
manages about 2,674 active oil and gas
leases on more than 14.2 million OCS
acres. In fiscal year 2019, offshore Federal
production reached approximately 683
million barrels of oil and 1.03 trillion
cubic feet of gas, almost all of which was
produced in the Gulf of Mexico. https://
www.boem.gov/oil-gas-energy

The BOEM manages offshore development
of renewable energy in Federal waters.
The renewable energy program began in
2009, when the Department of the Interior
announced the final regulations for the
OCS Renewable Energy Program, which the
Energy Policy Act of 2005 had authorized.
The regulations provide a framework for all
of the activities that support the production
and transmission of energy from sources
other than oil and natural gas. The BOEM
anticipates managing the development of
more hydrokinetic and more offshore wind
and solar energy on the OCS. https://www.
boem.gov/renewable-energy

The BOEM's environmental program
covers the three major areas that the
agency regulates on the OCS: oil and gas,
renewable energy, and nonenergy minerals
like sand, gravel, and hard minerals. The
Office of Environmental Programs develops
national policy, provides guidance, and
coordinates with regional activities. The
environmental program's two key functions

are to support science and to conduct
environmental assessments, which include
consultations with stakeholders and other
regulatory agencies to strengthen decision
making. The Chief Environmental Officer
also manages and leads engagement and
consultation at the national and regional
levels with federally recognized Tribes.
https://www.boem.gov/environment

The BOEM partners with communities
through its marine minerals program to
address erosion along the Nation's barrier
islands, coastal beaches, dunes, and
wetlands. Erosion affects defense, energy,
natural resources, public infrastructure, and
tourism. To mitigate the effects of erosion,
the BOEM leases gravel and sand and shell
resources for nourishing beaches, protecting
shorelines, and restoring wetlands. These
resources are extracted from Federal waters
on the OCS with environmental and safety
oversight. The Outer Continental Shelf Lands
Act (PL 83–212) provides the authority
to manage minerals on the OCS and the
requirement to provide environmental
oversight. BOEM is the only Federal agency
with the authority to lease marine minerals
from the OCS. https://www.boem.gov/
marine-minerals

Sources of Information

Archived Records   The "Guide to Federal
Records in the National Archives of the
United States" indicates that MMS records
have been assigned to record group 473.
The MMS is the predecessor agency to the
BOEM. See the above "Establishment and
Organization" section. https://www.archives.
gov/research/guide-fed-records/groups/473.
html

Business Opportunities   Information on
doing business with the BOEM and related
links are available on the "Procurement
Business Opportunities" website. http://
www.boem.gov/Doing-Business-with-BOEM

Calendar   The BOEM maintains an online
events calendar. http://www.boem.gov/
Upcoming-Events

Career Opportunities   The BOEM relies on
professionals with engineering and science
backgrounds for ensuring the safe and
environmentally responsible development
of the Nation's offshore energy and marine

mineral resources. http://www.boem.gov/employment

In 2020, the BOEM ranked 58th among 411 agency subcomponents in the Partnership for Public Service's Best Places To Work Agency Rankings. https://bestplacestowork.org/rankings/detail/IN12

Contact Information Information is available on the "Contact Us" web page. https://www.boem.gov/about-boem/contact-us

Educational Resources BOEM teacher resources are available online. http://www.boem.gov/Environmental-Studies-Program-Teacher-Resources

Factsheets The BOEM posts factsheets on the following topics: about the agency, environment, marine minerals, oil and gas energy, and renewable energy. https://www.boem.gov/newsroom/boem-fact-sheets

Federal Register Significant documents, from 1995 (volume 60) to the present, and recent documents that the BOEM has published in the Federal Register are available online. https://www.federalregister.gov/agencies/ocean-energy-management-bureau

Freedom of Information Act (FOIA) Effective on July 5, 1967, the FOIA gives any person a right to obtain access to Federal agency records; however, nine exemptions and three special law enforcement exclusions shield certain records, or parts of them, from public disclosure. A FOIA request may be made for any agency record. Instructions for submitting a BOEM record request under the FOIA are available online. The BOEM operates a FOIA requester service center. Phone, 703-787-1128. https://www.boem.gov/foia

Frequently Asked Questions (FAQs) The BOEM posts answers to FAQs. https://www.boem.gov/newsroom/frequently-asked-questions

Glossaries The BOEM has posted a glossary of ecological terms. https://www.boem.gov/sites/default/files/boem-newsroom/Technical-Announcements/2016/Chapter-7-Glossary-of-Ecological-Terms.pdf

The BOEM has posted a glossary of terms that are associated with wind energy. https://www.boem.gov/sites/default/files/renewable-energy-program/Studies/FEIS/Section12.0Glossary.pdf

Greenhouse Gas Emissions BOEM OCS Report 2016–065, whose authors are E. Wolvovsky. and W. Anderson, is titled "OCS Oil and Natural Gas: Potential Lifecycle Greenhouse Gas Emissions and Social Cost of Carbon." The report's key findings are the following: Most lifecycle greenhouse gas (GHG) emissions are the result of oil and gas products consumption; the price of oil and gas and production volume have a large effect on the amount of oil and gas lifecycle GHG emissions; the magnitude of emissions and their related social costs are comparable for the 2017–2022 program and the 2017–2022 program's "No Action Alternative"; the production of oil and gas from other global sources can be more carbon-intense relative to oil and gas that are produced on the OCS; absent policy changes or technological advancements, OCS emissions could consume a measurable increment of the remaining worldwide and domestic GHG emissions budget. https://www.boem.gov/sites/default/files/oil-and-gas-energy-program/Leasing/Five-Year-Program/2017-2022/OCS-Report-BOEM-2016-065---OCS-Oil-and-Natural-Gas---Potential-Lifecycle-GHG-Emissions-and-Social-Cost-of-Carbon.pdf

Historic Preservation Archaeologists in Office of Renewable Energy Programs coordinate studies and conduct National Historic Preservation Act reviews to identify and protect archaeological sites and other historic properties. OCS historic properties include aircraft, lighthouses, precontact (European contact with Native Americans) archaeological sites, and shipwrecks. Historic properties onshore come under review when a proposed renewable energy project may affect them. To learn more about investigating the steamship "City of Houston" and German submarine "U–576" and other preservation activities, visit the "Historic Preservation Activities" web page. https://www.boem.gov/Renewable-Energy/Historic-Preservation-Activities

Library The BOEM website has an electronic library. http://www.boem.gov/Library

Marine Minerals Mineral resources from the OCS are used in coastal restoration projects to address erosion. The BOEM has conveyed rights to millions of cubic yards of

OCS sand for coastal restoration projects in multiple States. These projects have restored hundreds of miles of the Nation's coastline, protecting both infrastructure and ecological habitat. The BOEM posts key marine mineral statistics on its website. https://www.boem.gov/marine-minerals/current-statistics/current-marine-minerals-statistics | Email: MarineMinerals@boem.gov

Oil / Gas   The BOEM has posted the 2017–2022 lease sale schedule and 2017–2022 quicklinks on its "Leasing" web page. https://www.boem.gov/oil-gas-energy/leasing/2017-2022-lease-sale-schedule

Posters   Colorful BOEM posters that promote maritime history, ocean science and stewardship, and awareness of marine animals and their habitats are available from the Gulf of Mexico Public Information Office. Phone, 800-200-4853. http://www.boem.gov/BOEM-Posters

Press Releases   The BOEM posts press releases. https://www.boem.gov/newsroom/news-items?news_type=11

Regional Offices   The BOEM operates three regional offices, one for the Alaska Outer Continental Shelf (OCS) region, one for the Pacific OCS region, and one for the Gulf of Mexico and Atlantic OCS regions. Phone, 907-334-5200 (Alaska). Phone, 805-384-6305 (Pacific). Phone, 800-200-4853 (Gulf of Mexico and Atlantic). https://www.boem.gov/regions

Renewable Energy   A list of leases that the BOEM has executed since the inception of its renewable energy program is available online. http://www.boem.gov/Lease-and-Grant-Information

The BOEM collaborates with States on offshore energy development and is in the process of coordinating Federal-State task forces in certain coastal States. A summary of the status of activity in the various States is available online. https://www.boem.gov/Renewable-Energy-Program/State-Activities/Index.aspx

Science / Technology   "Ocean Science" is BOEM's science and technology journal. The agency is a leading contributor to the growing body of scientific knowledge on the Nation's marine and coastal environments. https://www.boem.gov/newsroom/library/ocean-science

Shipwrecks   The BOEM Alaskan shipwreck table is the most comprehensive compilation of Alaskan shipwrecks to date. The table offers a list of wrecks that occurred in Alaskan waters from 1741 to 2011. The "Shipwrecks Off Alaska's Coast" web page also features maritime history, ship, and shipwreck links to external websites. https://www.boem.gov/about-boem/shipwrecks-alaskas-coast

Site Map   The website map helps visitors find specific topics or allows them to browse the site's contents. https://www.boem.gov/sitemap

Social Media   The BOEM maintains a Facebook account. https://www.facebook.com/BureauOfOceanEnergyManagement

The BOEM tweets announcements and other newsworthy items on Twitter. https://twitter.com/BOEM

The BOEM has a YouTube channel. https://www.youtube.com/channel/UCXL807nkJMCuxNj5kF09LLQ/featured

Statistics / Facts   BOEM collects data on its offshore oil and gas energy programs and makes them available in multiple formats. https://www.boem.gov/newsroom/statistics-and-facts

The above Sources of Information were updated 7–2021.

Bureau of Reclamation
Department of the Interior, 1849 C Street NW., Washington, DC 20240
Phone, 202-513-0575. Internet, http://www.usbr.gov

Commissioner *   BRENDA W. BURMAN
https://www.usbr.gov/newsroom/presskit/bios/index.cfm

* The Commissioner reports to the Assistant Secretary of Water and Science.

The above list of key personnel was updated 5–2020.

The Bureau of Reclamation develops, manages, and protects water and related resources in a way that is environmentally and economically responsible and that benefits the American public.

Establishment and Organization
On June 17, 1902, President Theodore Roosevelt, Jr., approved an act to appropriate "the receipts from the sale and disposal of public lands in certain States and Territories to the construction of irrigation works for the reclamation of arid lands." Pursuant to Public Law 161 (32 Stat. 388), which is popularly known as the Reclamation Act or National Irrigation Act of 1902, former Secretary of the Interior Ethan A. Hitchcock established the U.S. Reclamation Service (USRS) in the Geological Survey in July. http://www.loc.gov/law/help/statutes-at-large/57th-congress/session-1/c57s1ch1093.pdf

In 1907, the USRS separated from the Geological Survey and became an independent bureau within the Department of the Interior. Sixteen years later, the independent USRS was renamed the Bureau of Reclamation. https://www.usbr.gov/history/2019%20NEW%20BRIEF%20HISTORY%20V1.pdf

On August 4, 1977, President James E. Carter approved Public Law 95–91, which is also cited as the Department of Energy Organization Act. The law transferred the Bureau's power marketing functions to the Department of Energy (91 STAT. 578) as part of an effort "to secure effective management to assure a coordinated national energy policy" (STAT. 565). https://www.govinfo.gov/content/pkg/STATUTE-91/pdf/STATUTE-91-Pg565.pdf

On November 6, 1979, former Secretary of the Interior Cecil D. Andrus issued Secretarial Order 3042, which changed the Bureau's name to the Water and Power Resources Service (WPRS). On May 18, 1981, former Secretary of the Interior James G. Watt issued Secretarial Order 3064, which renamed the WPRS the Bureau of Reclamation (BR).

The BR posts its organizational chart in Portable Document Format (PDF) for viewing and downloading. https://www.usbr.gov/main/images/br_org_chart.pdf

Statutory and Regulatory Authorities
Codified statutory material dealing the Federal Government's reclamation and irrigation of public lands is found in 43 U.S.C. chapter 12. The Reclamation Act of 1902 is classified generally to this chapter. https://uscode.house.gov/view.xhtml?path=/prelim@title43/chapter12&edition=prelim

Rules and regulations that affect public lands and that are associated with the BR are codified in 43 CFR 400–999 (subtitle B, chapter I). https://www.ecfr.gov/cgi-bin/text-idx?SID=f90eabe3636e1549dfc39643c94595c2&mc=true&tpl=/ecfrbrowse/Title43/43chapterI.tpl

Activities
The BR is the largest wholesaler of water in the United States. It brings water to more than 31 million people and provides 140,000 Western farmers with irrigation water for 10 million acres of farmland. This irrigated farmland produces 60% of the Nation's vegetables and 25% of its fruits and nuts.

The Bureau is also the second largest producer of hydroelectric power in the United States. Its 53 powerplants produce annually more than 40 billion kilowatt hours

Bureau of Reclamation

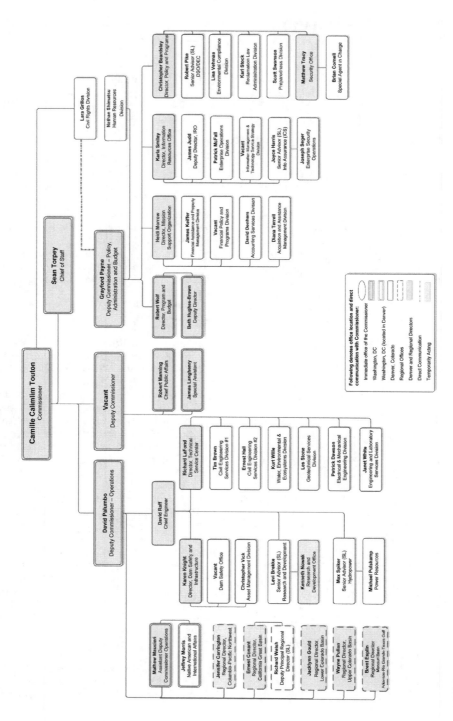

of electricity, earning nearly $1 billion in revenues and generating enough energy for 3.5 million homes. http://www.usbr.gov/main/about/mission.html

The BR's approach to water resource development has evolved over the years: from single-purpose agricultural projects to projects of multipurpose whose scope includes promoting water-based outdoor recreation. Recreation sites that are developed as a result of BR water projects rank among the Nation's most popular places for water-based outdoor recreation. These projects include approximately 6.5 million acres of land and water that are, for the most part, open to the public for recreation. https://www.usbr.gov/recreation

The BR also engages in conservation activities to support native species and their habitats. In partnership with Arizona, California, and Nevada, the BR implemented a program to conserve native species and habitats across the Colorado River Basin. In partnership with the Bonneville Power Administration, Confederated Tribes of the Umatilla Indian Reservation, and U.S. Forest Service, the BR implemented a project to increase mainstem and off-channel habitat in a segment of the Grand Ronde River. The BR also tries to prevent invasive quagga and zebra mussels from spreading. These bivalve mollusks adversely affect the natural ecology, which harms endangered native species. The disruption that they visit upon ecosystems can cause new listings under the Endangered Species Act. Mussel infestations threaten agriculture, navigation locks, and biodiversity that supports the Western outdoor recreation industry. https://www.usbr.gov/conservation/

BR operations and facilities support flood control. Its programs also mitigate the effects of drought through contingency planning, resiliency projects, and emergency response actions. https://www.usbr.gov/drought/

Sources of Information

A–Z Index The BR website has an A–Z index to help visitors navigate its content. https://www.usbr.gov/main/index/

Archived Records The "Guide to Federal Records in the National Archives of the United States" indicates that BR records

have been assigned to record group 115. https://www.archives.gov/research/guide-fed-records/groups/115.html

Art Collection In the late 1960s, the BR launched a program to present its accomplishments through art. The Bureau commissioned 40 of America's most prominent artists to visit BR water resource development sites and record their impressions on canvas. When the project was completed, the artists had created more than 375 pieces of artwork. In the early 1970s, the public had an opportunity to view much of the work in a traveling exhibition that was circulated by the Smithsonian Institution and entitled "The American Artist and Water Reclamation." The BR maintains about 200 pieces of the original artwork. Many of the paintings are on display at the Main Interior Building and some regional offices. https://www.usbr.gov/museumproperty/art/homepage.html

Business Opportunities The BR purchases a wide range of products and services and supports various Federal socioeconomic development programs by assisting businesses. The Bureau also provides financial assistance for programs related to conservation, Endangered Species Act mitigation, rural water, and water management and reclamation and reuse. Phone, 303-445-2431. http://www.usbr.gov/mso/aamd/doing-business.html

Career Opportunities The BR relies on professionals with expertise in administration, engineering and design, environmental protection, research, wildlife management, and other disciplines to carry out its mission. Career-related information is available from the nearest regional office or from the Diversity and Human Resources Office, Denver, CO. Phone, 303-445-2684. https://www.usbr.gov/hr/contact.html

In 2019, the BR ranked 121st among 420 agency subcomponents in the Partnership for Public Service's Best Places To Work Agency Rankings. https://bestplacestowork.org/rankings/detail/IN07

Climate Change Risks The SECURE Water Act (123 STAT. 1329) is part of Public Law 111–11 (123 STAT. 991–1456), whose short title is the Omnibus Public Land Management Act of 2009. Section 9503(c) authorizes the BR to assess climate change risks for water and environmental resources in major river basins that it manages. Section 9503(c) also authorizes the BR to evaluate potential climate change effects on water resource management and development of strategies. Since the law's enactment on March 30, 2009, the BR has prepared two "SECURE Water Act Section 9503(c)—Reclamation Climate Change and Water" reports for the U.S. Congress. https://www.govinfo.gov/content/pkg/STATUTE-123/pdf/STATUTE-123-Pg991.pdf

"SECURE Water Act Section 9503(c)—Reclamation Climate Change and Water 2016" is the second and most recent report that the BR has prepared for Congress. In the report's first chapter, its authors wrote: "[The Act] recognizes that climate change poses a significant challenge to the protection of adequate and safe supplies of water, which are fundamental to the health, economy, security, and ecology of the United States." The next SECURE Water Act report is scheduled for preparation and delivery to the U.S. Congress in 2021. https://www.usbr.gov/climate/secure/docs/2016secure/2016SECUREReport.pdf

Contact Information   Contact information for the Washington, DC, and Denver, CO, based offices and Upper Colorado, Great Plains, Lower Colorado, Mid-Pacific, and Pacific Northwest regional offices is available on the "Addresses and Contacts" web page. http://www.usbr.gov/main/offices.html

Media contact information is posted online. https://www.usbr.gov/newsroom/presskit/mediacontact.html

Contact information for the Acquisition and Assistance Management Division is posted online. https://www.usbr.gov/mso/aamd/org-contact.html

Cooperative Agricultural Weather Network (AgriMet))   In cooperation with local, State, and other Federal sponsors, the BR promotes energy and water conservation through AgriMet, which is a network of more than 90 automated weather stations that collect and telemeter site-specific weather data. The original AgriMet program started in the Pacific Northwest in the 1980s and was expanded into the Great Plains region.

Great Plains Region— https://www.usbr.gov/gp/agrimet/index.html

Pacific Northwest— https://www.usbr.gov/pn/agrimet/

Environmental Resources and Reports   The BR maintains a list of links to online resources that provide environmental information. http://www.usbr.gov/environmental

Factsheet   The BR posts a factsheet on its website. https://www.usbr.gov/main/about/fact.html

Federal Register   Significant documents, from 1995 (volume 60) to the present, and recent documents that the BR has published in the Federal Register are available online. https://www.federalregister.gov/agencies/reclamation-bureau

The BR maintains a "Federal Register Notices and Rulemaking" web page. https://www.usbr.gov/fedreg/index.html

Freedom of Information Act (FOIA)   The FOIA establishes a presumption that records in the possession of Federal agencies are accessible to the public. Before the law was passed in 1966, the individual had to establish a right to examine Government records. Passage of the FOIA shifted the burden of proof from the individual to the Government: A "right to know" doctrine replaced a "need to know" standard. The law established standards for determining records that must be disclosed and records that can be withheld. The law also provided administrative and judicial remedies for information seekers who have been denied access to records. http://www.usbr.gov/foia/contacts.html

The BR maintains an electronic reading room that contains frequently requested records and documents that are currently of special interest. Information seekers should avail themselves of this online resource to determine if the information that they seek is immediately available and readily accessible without the additional step of filing a FOIA request. http://www.usbr.gov/foia/readroom.html

Glossaries   Definitions for terms commonly used by the BR are accessible in its online glossary. http://www.usbr.gov/library/glossary

The BR maintains a separate online glossary of recreation-related terms. http://www.usbr.gov/recreation/glossary.html

Hydrologic and Meteorologic Monitoring (HydroMet)   The BR operates a network of automated Hydromet stations, including their communications and computer systems, throughout the Great Plains and the Pacific Northwest regions. The Hydromet network collects remote environmental and water data and transmits them via radio and satellite. The Hydromet network provides cost-effective, near-real-time water management capability. Streamflow forecasts and current river and resevoir operations conditions are then calculated by combining Hydromet data with other information.

Great Plains Region— https://www.usbr. gov/gp/hydromet

Pacific Northwest— https://www.usbr.gov/pn/hydromet/

Invasive Mussels Two species of dreissenid mussels, namely quagga and zebra, have become established in U.S. freshwater lakes, reservoirs, and rivers. Invasive dreissenid mussels pose significant challenges for all agencies and industries that manage water because they are prolific breeders and settle on or within water facility infrastructure. https://www.usbr.gov/mussels

Library The BR's website has an online search tool that allows visitors to search the electronic library catalog. External patrons may use the library, which is located in Denver, CO, by appointment only, 8:00 a.m.–3:00 p.m. Phone, 303-445-2072. https://www.usbr.gov/library/ | Email: library@usbr.gov

Multimedia Media Links to BR's historic photographs and photograph database are available on the "Reclamation Multimedia" web page. Other links that lead to podcasts on water management and to Really Simple Syndication (RSS) feeds also are available. BR Social Media links include Facebook, Flickr, Instagram, Twitter, and YouTube. https://www.usbr.gov/main/multimedia/index.html#social

News The BR posts news releases and stories, as well as congressional testimony, factsheets, photos, and speeches. http://www.usbr.gov/newsroom/newsrelease

The Sources of Information were updated 2–2020.

Outdoor Recreation / Cultural Activities The BR participates in Recreation.gov. This partnership of twelve Government agencies provides information on all recreation facilities on Federal lands, including those owned and managed by the BR. Online visitors may use the Recreation.gov website to make reservations at facilities requiring them. https://www.recreation.gov/about-us

Publications The BR posts publications on its website. https://www.usbr.gov/library/reclamationpubs.html

Reclamation Manual The BR's website has an online tool that allows users to search for keywords and terms in the "Reclamation Manual." The manual comprises a series of policy and directives and standards, which collectively assign program responsibility and establish and document agencywide methods of doing business. http://www.usbr.gov/recman

Research / Science The Research and Development Office publishes the quarterly magazine "Knowledge Stream," whose content centers on mission-critical news about research and science and on the challenges of managing water and generating power in the American West. https://www.usbr.gov/research/ks.html

Water Conservation The WaterSMART program allows all Department of the Interior bureaus to work with States, tribes, local governments, and nongovernmental organizations to pursue a sustainable water supply for the Nation by establishing a framework that provides Federal leadership and assistance on the efficient use of water, that integrates water and energy policies to support the sustainable use of all natural resources, and that coordinates the water conservation activities of the various departmental offices. https://www.usbr.gov/watersmart

Bureau of Safety and Environmental Enforcement

Department of the Interior, 1849 C Street NW., Washington, DC 20240
Phone, 202-208-3985. Internet, http://www.bsee.gov

Director *	Scott A. Angelle
https://www.bsee.gov/who-we-are/our-organization/ leadership	

* The Director reports to the Assistant Secretary of Land and Minerals Management.

The above list of key personnel was updated 5–2020.

The Bureau of Safety and Environmental Enforcement promotes safety, protects the environment, and conserves resources offshore by overseeing the regulatory process and enforcing Federal rules and regulations.

Establishment and Organization

In April of 2010, the Deepwater Horizon oil rig explosion and resulting oil spill in the Gulf of Mexico exposed inadequacies in the Federal offshore energy regulatory system. In response to the disaster, former Secretary of the Interior Kenneth L. Salazar issued two secretarial orders. On May 19, 2010, he issued Order 3299 "to separate and reassign the responsibilities that had been conducted by the Minerals Management Service [MMS] into new management structures that will improve the management, oversight, and accountability of activities on the Outer Continental Shelf [OCS]." https://www.doi.gov/sites/doi.gov/files/elips/documents/3299a2-establishment_of_the_bureau_of_ocean_energy_management_the_bureau_of_safety_and_environmental_enforcement_and_the_office_of_natural_resources_revenue.pdf

Within the Department of the Interior, Order 3299 initiated the establishment of the new Bureau of Safety and Environmental Enforcement (BSEE), whose director would report to the Assistant Secretary–Land and Minerals Management. The order also initiated the establishment of the new Bureau of Ocean Energy Management (BOEM), whose director also would report to the same Assistant Secretary. A third new agency, the Office of Natural Resources Revenue (ONRR), formerly the MMS's minerals revenue management program, would be established within the Department, and its director would report to the Assistant Secretary–Policy, Management and Budget.

On June 18, 2010, former Secretary Salazar issued Order 3302, which announced that the MMS would be renamed the Bureau of Ocean Energy Management, Regulation and Enforcement (BOEMRE) for the duration of the reorganization period. https://www.federalregister.gov/agencies/safety-and-environmental-enforcement-bureau

On October 1, 2010, the functions of the MMS's minerals revenue management program were transferred to the ONRR. A few days later, the ONRR published a final rule in the Federal Register to move the regulations associated with its royalty and revenue functions from chapter II in 30 CFR to chapter XII in the same title. https://www.govinfo.gov/content/pkg/FR-2010-10-04/pdf/2010-24721.pdf

A year later, in October of 2011, 30 CFR was reorganized. BOEMRE rules and regulations that now applied to the BOEM were recodified in a new fifth chapter; the rules and regulations that now applied to the BSEE were recodified in a revised second chapter. The establishment of the BSEE and its sibling the BOEM and the reorganization of 30 CFR marked the completion of separating and reassigning the responsibilities of the former MMS. https://www.govinfo.gov/content/pkg/FR-2011-10-18/pdf/2011-22675.pdf

The BSEE posts an organizational chart on its website. https://www.bsee.gov/who-we-are/our-organization

Statutory and Regulatory Authorities

Statutory material affecting "Deep Seabed Hard Mineral Resources" is codified in chapter 26, sections 1401–1473, of 30 U.S.C. https://uscode.house.gov/view.xhtml?path=/prelim@title30/chapter26&edition=prelim

BSEE rules and regulations are codified in chapter II, parts 200–299, of 30 CFR. https://www.ecfr.gov/cgi-bin/text-idx?SID=e5dd58 63d76dc4809df5de6afce53bf6&mc=true&t pl=/ecfrbrowse/Title30/30chapterII.tpl

Activities

The BSEE promotes safety, protects the environment, and conserves resources on the Outer Continental Shelf (OCS) through regulatory oversight and enforcement. The Offshore Regulatory Program develops standards and regulations to improve operational safety and to strengthen environmental protection. The Oil Spill Preparedness Division develops standards and guidelines for offshore operators. It also collaborates with sister agencies on spill response technologies and capabilities.

Three regional offices support the Bureau. Their personnel inspect gas and oil drilling rigs and production platforms to ensure compliance with safety requirements. Inspection teams are multiperson, and the expertise of their members spans a range of disciplines. https://www.bsee.gov/what-we-do

Sources of Information

Archived Records The "Guide to Federal Records in the National Archives of the United States" indicates that MMS records have been assigned to record group 473. The MMS is the predecessor agency to the BSEE. See the above "Establishment and Organization" section. https://www.archives.gov/research/guide-fed-records/groups/473.html

Business Opportunities Information on doing business with the BSEE is available online. http://www.bsee.gov/About-BSEE/Doing-Business-with-BSEE/index

Career Opportunities The BSEE relies on professionals with backgrounds in biology, geology, geophysics, engineering, and other fields to carry out its mission. http://www.bsee.gov/careers

In 2019, the BSEE ranked 128th among 420 agency subcomponents in the Partnership for Public Service's Best

Places To Work Agency Rankings. https://bestplacestowork.org/rankings/detail/IN11

Contact Information To contact the BSEE, visit the "Connect With Us" web page, where addresses (email and postal) and phone numbers are available. https://www.bsee.gov/who-we-are/connect

Director's Corner Director Scott A. Angelle posts his thoughts and views on issues facing the BSEE and America's offshore oil and gas industry. "Energy Dominance Requires New Thinking" (SEP 2017) was the first piece that he posted. https://www.bsee.gov/newsroom/directors-corner

Federal Register Significant documents, from 1995 (volume 60) to the present, and recent documents that the BSEE has published in the Federal Register are available online. https://www.federalregister.gov/agencies/safety-and-environmental-enforcement-bureau

Freedom of Information Act (FOIA) The FOIA gives the public the right to request Federal agency records and requires Federal agencies to make certain records available. The BSEE website serves as the portal to the agency's FOIA program. The FOIA is based on the principle of openness in Government: Any person has a right of access to Federal agency records, except to the extent that such records or portions of them are protected from disclosure by exemption or by special law-enforcement record exclusion. https://www.bsee.gov/newsroom/library/foia

The BSEE maintains an electronic FOIA reading room. https://www.bsee.gov/newsroom/library/FOIA-Reading-Rooom

Frequently Asked Questions (FAQs) The BSEE promotes safety, protects the environment, and conserves resources offshore through regulatory oversight and enforcement. To carry out its mission, the BSEE relies on a wide range of world-class professionals. The BSEE posts answers to questions that its experts are asked frequently. https://www.bsee.gov/newsroom/library/frequently-asked-questions | Email: webmaster@bsee.gov

Glossary This glossary contains common oil and gas exploration and leasing terms, many of which are unique to the drilling industry. https://www.bsee.gov/newsroom/library/glossary

News   The BSEE newsroom contains feature stories, media advisories, news briefs, photos and videos, press releases, and posts from the Director. The briefing room contains annual reports, congressional testimony, factsheets, speeches, statements, and technical presentations. https://www.bsee.gov/newsroom

Offshore Statistics   The BSEE posts offshore statistics and facts on its website. https://www.bsee.gov/stats-facts

Reading Room   The Bureau's Deepwater Horizon electronic reading room contains documents that deal with the BP/Deepwater Horizon explosion and ensuing oil spill and that have been cleared for public release. https://www.bsee.gov/newsroom/library/archive/deepwater-horizon-reading-room

The Sources of Information were updated 4–2020.

Regional Offices   Information on the BSEE's three geographic regions—Alaska OCS, Gulf of Mexico OCS, and Pacific OCS—and their respective regional offices is available on the "BSEE Regions" web page. http://www.bsee.gov/About-BSEE/BSEE-Regions/BSEE-Regions

Site Map   The website map helps visitors find specific topics or allows them to browse the site's contents. https://www.bsee.gov/sitemap

Social Media   The BSEE has a Facebook account. https://www.facebook.com/BSEEgov/

The BSEE tweets announcements and other newsworthy items on Twitter. https://twitter.com/BSEEgov

---

National Park Service

Department of the Interior, 1849 C Street NW., Washington, DC 20240
Phone, 202-208-6843. Internet, http://www.nps.gov

Director *   R. David Vela, Acting
https://www.nps.gov/aboutus/director.htm

* The Director reports to the Assistant Secretary of Fish and Wildlife and Parks.

The above list of key personnel was updated 5–2020.

The National Park Service (NPS) was established in the Department of the Interior on August 25, 1916 (16 U.S.C. 1). http://www.nps.gov/aboutus/index.htm

The National Park Service protects the natural and cultural resources and values of the National Park System for the benefit of present and future generations. The National Park System comprises 401 units. These units include national parks, monuments and memorials, battlefield sites and national military parks, scenic parkways, preserves and reserves, trails and riverways, rivers and lakeshores and seashores, recreation areas, and historic sites of American or international importance. The Service also manages a variety of national and international programs to promote natural and cultural resource conservation and to expand the benefits of outdoor recreation.

The NPS develops and implements park management plans and staffs the areas under its administration. Through exhibits, films, publications talks, tours, and other interpretive media, it promotes the natural values of these areas and communicates their historical significance to the public. The NPS operates a range of visitor facilities, including campgrounds, and provides a variety of food, lodging, and transportation services.

The National Park Service also administers the State portion of the Land and Water Conservation Fund, State comprehensive outdoor recreation planning, nationwide outdoor recreation coordination and information, the National Register of Historic Places and the National Trails System, natural area programs, national historic landmarks and historic preservation, technical preservation services, the historic

American engineering record and buildings survey, interagency archeological services, and planning and technical assistance for the national wild and scenic rivers system.

Sources of Information

America the Beautiful Passes A pass may be used at more than 2,000 Federal recreation sites. A pass covers entrance fees at national parks and national wildlife refuges, as well as standard amenity fees and day use fees at national forests and grasslands and at lands managed by the Bureaus of Land Management and Reclamation and the U.S. Army Corps of Engineers. Five types of America the Beautiful passes are available: access, annual, annual fourth grade, senior, and volunteer. https://www.nps.gov/planyourvisit/passes.htm

Business Opportunities Visit the "Doing Business With Us" Web page to find information on commercial tours, contracts and procurement, National Park concessions, and special park uses, including commercial filming. http://www.nps.gov/aboutus/doingbusinesswithus.htm

Career Opportunities To find permanent and seasonal NPS career opportunities online, visit USAJobs, the Federal Government's official source for Federal job listings. https://my.usajobs.gov

Additional information on internships, permanent careers, seasonal opportunities, and volunteering is available on the "Work With Us" Web page. http://www.nps.gov/aboutus/workwithus.htm

Directories An online text box allows Internet visitors to search for NPS employees by last name. https://www.nps.gov/directory

A park directory (SEP 2016) that includes park addresses, codes, phone numbers, and superintendents is available online in Portable Document Format (PDF). https://www.nps.gov/aboutus/upload/NPS-Park-Listing-09-01-16.pdf

Find a Park NPS website visitors may search for a park by name or by State. https://www.nps.gov/findapark/index.htm

Freedom of Information Act (FOIA) Instructions for submitting a FOIA request to obtain NPS records are available online. https://www.nps.gov/aboutus/foia/index.htm

The NPS maintains an electronic FOIA library on its website. https://www.nps.gov/aboutus/foia/foia-reading-room.htm

Frequently Asked Questions (FAQs) The NPS posts answers to FAQs on its website. https://www.nps.gov/aboutus/faqs.htm

Glossaries The NPS's National Center for Preservation Technology and Training maintains an extensive glossary of building stone terms. https://ncptt.nps.gov/buildingstone/glossary

The online series "Defining the Southwest" includes a glossary of terms that are often encountered in discussions of the cultures and environments of the American Southwest. https://www.nps.gov/articles/southwest-glossary.htm

A glossary of geologic terms that the NPS and U.S. Geological Survey western Earth surface processes team compiled is available on the NPS website. http://www.nature.nps.gov/geology/usgsnps/misc/glossaryAtoC.html | Email: parkgeology@den.nps.gov

Grants Information is available online for grants authorized under the Land and Water Conservation Fund. Phone, 202-354-6900. http://www.nps.gov/lwcf/index.htm

Information is also available online for grants authorized under the Historic Preservation Fund. Phone, 202-354-2067. http://www.nps.gov/preservation-grants

News The NPS posts new releases online. https://www.nps.gov/aboutus/news/news-releases.htm

The NPS website has a multimedia section that includes audio, photographs, videos, and webcam. https://www.nps.gov/media/multimedia-search.htm

The NPS tweets announcements and other newsworthy items on Twitter. https://twitter.com/natlparkservice

The NPS maintains a Facebook page. https://www.facebook.com/nationalparkservice

Publications To explain decisions, document information, and disseminate knowledge, the NPS uses a variety of publications, many of which are accessible online. For example, "The National Parks: Index 2012–2016" can be downloaded as a PDF. The "Publications" Web page offers online access to contemporary and historic reports, periodicals, virtual stacks, and public databases. http://www.nps.gov/aboutus/publications.htm

Some publications are available for purchase in hardcopy from the U.S. Government Bookstore. Phone, 202-512-1800. Phone, 866-512-1800.

https://bookstore.gpo.gov/agency/222 | Email: contactcenter@gpo.gov
Regional Offices   Contact information is available online for NPS regional offices and parks and the Washington office. http://www.nps.gov/aboutus/contactinformation.htm
https://www.nps.gov/aboutus/contactus.htm

For further information, contact the Office of Communications, National Park Service, Department of the Interior, 1849 C Street NW., Washington, DC 20240. Phone, 202-208-6843.

Office of Surface Mining Reclamation and Enforcement

Department of the Interior, 1951 Constitution Avenue NW., Washington, DC 20240
Phone, 202-208-2565. TDD, 202-208-2694. Internet, http://www.osmre.gov

Director *	Lanny E. Erdos, Acting
https://www.osmre.gov/about/Director.shtm	

* The Director reports to the Assistant Secretary of Land and Minerals Management.

The above list of key personnel was updated 5–2020.

The Office of Surface Mining Reclamation and Enforcement (OSMRE) was established in the Department of the Interior by the Surface Mining Control and Reclamation Act of 1977 (30 U.S.C. 1211). http://www.osmre.gov/about.shtm

The OSMRE carries out the requirements of the Surface Mining Control and Reclamation Act in cooperation with States and tribes. The Office protects people and the environment from the adverse effects of coal mining. The OSMRE assures that land is restored to beneficial use after mining operations cease, and it mitigates the effects of past operations by reclamation of abandoned coal mines. The Office mainly oversees State mining regulatory and abandoned-mine reclamation programs, assists States in meeting the objectives of surface mining law, and regulates mining and reclamation activities on Federal and Indian lands and in those States opting not to assume primary responsibility for regulating coal mining and reclamation activities within their borders.

The Office establishes national policy for the surface mining control and reclamation program, reviews and approves amendments to previously approved State programs, and reviews and recommends approval of new State program submissions. It also

manages the collection, disbursement, and accounting of abandoned-mine land reclamation fees; administers civil penalties programs; establishes technical standards and regulatory policy for reclamation and enforcement; offers guidance for environmental considerations, research, training, and technology transfers; and monitors and evaluates State and tribal regulatory programs, cooperative agreements, and abandoned-mine land reclamation programs.

Sources of Information

Abandoned Mine Land Inventory System   To provide information for implementing the Surface Mining Control and Reclamation Act of 1977, the OSMRE maintains an inventory of land and water affected by past mining. The inventory contains information on the location, type, and extent of abandoned mine land impacts, as well as information on the reclamation costs. The inventory is based on field surveys by State, tribal, and OSMRE program officials. https://amlis.osmre.gov/About.aspx

Business Opportunities   Information to assist small business operators and owners is available online. For additional information, contact the Acquisition Management

Branch. Phone, 202-208-2902. http://www.osmre.gov/contacts/business.shtm

Career Opportunities   To find employment opportunities at the OSMRE, visit the "Jobs at OSMRE" Web page and click on the USAJobs quick link. http://www.osmre.gov/contacts/jobs.shtm

Freedom of Information Act (FOIA)   A FOIA request for OSMRE records may be submitted via electronic or postal mail or by using the Department of the Interior's electronic request form and selecting "Office of Surface Mining" in the drop-down menu. http://www.osmre.gov/lrg/foia.shtm | Email: foia@osmre.gov

Frequently Asked Questions (FAQs)   The OSMRE posts answers to FAQs online. http://www.osmre.gov/resources/FAQs.shtm

The OSMRE website also has a "How Do I?" section. http://www.osmre.gov/howdoi.shtm

Grants   Information on regulatory program grants and abandoned mine land grants is available on the OSMRE website. http://www.osmre.gov/resources/grants.shtm

Library   The general public may use the OSMRE online library catalog to locate legal and technical information. http://o10007.eos-intl.net/O10007/OPAC/Index.aspx

Mine Maps   The National Mine Map Repository collects and maintains mine map information and images for the entire country. http://mmr.osmre.gov

An index that includes over 180,000 maps of closed and abandoned mines is available online. The index serves as an inventory for determining which maps are available. To obtain actual copies of maps, contact the National Mine Map Repository. Fax, 412-937-2888. http://mmr.osmre.gov/MultiPub.aspx

Most Requested Content   The OSMRE website maintains a collection of links for its most frequently requested web pages. http://www.osmre.gov/resources/mostRequested.shtm

Newsroom   The newsroom features OSMRE stories and news releases. http://www.osmre.gov/resources/newsroom.shtm

The OSMRE tweets announcements and other newsworthy items on Twitter. https://twitter.com/OSMRE

The OSMRE has a Facebook page. https://www.facebook.com/Office.of.Surface.Mining.Reclamation.Enforcement

Regional Offices   Appalachian Region Office http://www.arcc.osmre.gov/contacts.shtm

Mid-Continent Region Office http://www.mcrcc.osmre.gov/contacts.shtm

Western Region Office http://www.wrcc.osmre.gov/contacts.shtm

Resources   The OSMRE website has a section that is dedicated to electronic, informational resources. http://www.osmre.gov/resources.shtm

Site Map   The website map allows visitors to look for specific topics or to browse content that aligns with their interests. http://www.osmre.gov/resources/sitemap.shtm

An A–Z index is also available to help visitors find the information that they seek. http://www.osmre.gov/resources/AtoZ.shtm

Top Priorities   The OSMRE website has a section highlighting the agency's major programs. https://www.osmre.gov/programs.shtm http://www.osmre.gov/contacts.shtm | Email: getinfo@osmre.gov

For further information, contact the Office of Communications, Office of Surface Mining Reclamation and Enforcement, Department of the Interior, 1951 Constitution Avenue NW., Washington, DC 20240. Phone, 202-208-2565. TDD, 202-208-2694.

United States Fish and Wildlife Service

Department of the Interior, 1849 C Street NW., Washington, DC 20240
Phone, 703-358-4545. Internet, http://www.fws.gov

Director *	(vacancy)
Principal Deputy Director	Margaret Everson
https://www.fws.gov/OFFICES/margaret_everson.html	

* The Director reports to the Assistant Secretary of Fish and Wildlife and Parks.

The above list of key personnel was updated 5–2020.

The U.S. Fish and Wildlife Service (USFWS) is the principal Federal agency dedicated to fish and wildlife conservation. The Service's history spans 145 years, dating from the establishment of its predecessor agency, the Bureau of Fisheries, in 1871. First created as an independent agency, the Bureau of Fisheries was later placed in the Department of Commerce. A second predecessor agency, the Bureau of Biological Survey, was established in 1885 in the Department of Agriculture. In 1939, the two Bureaus and their functions were transferred to the Department of the Interior. In 1940, they were consolidated into one agency and redesignated the Fish and Wildlife Service by Reorganization Plan No. 3 (5 U.S.C. app.). http://training.fws.gov/history/USFWS-history.html

The USFWS statement of organization may be found in subchapter A, part 2, of 50 CFR. https://www.ecfr.gov/cgi-bin/text-idx?SID=fd 103790cdbf5f4aa28f53fa458756ca&mc=tru e&node=pt50.1.2&rgn=div5

The USFWS works with others to conserve, protect, and enhance fish, wildlife and plants and their habitats for the continuing benefit of the American people. The Service manages the 150-million-acre National Wildlife Refuge System, which comprises 563 refuges and 38 wetland management districts. It operates 72 national fish hatcheries, a historic national fish hatchery, 65 fishery resource offices, and 81 ecological service field stations. The USFWS enforces Federal wildlife laws, administers the Endangered Species Act, manages migratory bird populations, restores nationally significant fisheries, conserves and restores wildlife habitats, and assists foreign governments with conservation. It also collects excise taxes on fishing and hunting equipment and distributes the revenues to State fish and wildlife agencies.

The Service improves and maintains fish and wildlife resources by proper management of wildlife and habitat. It also helps meet public demand for wildlife dependent recreational activities by maintaining public lands and restoring native fish and wildlife populations.

Wildlife and fishery resource programs support the management of wildlife refuges on public lands. Wildlife-related activities include population control, migration and harvest surveys, and law and gaming enforcement for migratory and nonmigratory birds and mammals. Fishery-related activities include hatchery production monitoring, stocking, and fishery management. Fishery resource programs also provide technical assistance for coastal anadromous, Great Lakes, and other inland fisheries.

The USFWS identifies, protects, and restores endangered fish, wildlife, and plant species. It maintains Federal lists of endangered and threatened wildlife and plants that are published in the Code of Federal Regulations (50 CFR 17.11 et seq.), conducts status surveys, prepares recovery plans, and coordinates national and international wildlife refuge operations.

The Service protects and improves land and water environments to benefit living natural resources and to enhance the quality of human life. It administers grant programs that help imperiled species, assists private landowners restore habitat, asses environmental impact and reviews potential environmental threats, manages Coastal Barrier Resource System mapping, monitors potential wildlife contaminants, and studies fish and wildlife population trends.

Public use and information activities include preparing informational brochures and maintaining public websites; coordinating environmental studies on USFWS lands; operating visitor centers, self-guided nature trails, observation towers, and display ponds; and promoting birdwatching, fishing, hunting, wildlife photography, and other forms of wildlife-dependent outdoor recreation.

The Wildlife and Sport Fish Restoration Program supports the conservation and enhancement of the Nation's fish and wildlife resources. Excise taxes on sporting arms and fishing equipment fund these efforts.

Sources of Information

Archived Records   The "Guide to Federal Records in the National Archives of the United States" indicates that USFWS records have been assigned to record group 022. https://www.archives.gov/research/guide-fed-records/groups/022.html
Blog   "Open Spaces—A Talk on the Wild Side" is the name of the official USFWS blog. https://www.fws.gov/news/blog
Business Opportunities   An online guide explains how to find business opportunities and to compete for them. Information is also available from regional offices and from the Division of Contracting and General Services in Falls Church, VA. Phone, 703-358-2500. http://www.fws.gov/cfm/Small%20Business/BusinessWith.html | Email: small_business_opts@fws.gov
Career Opportunities   Information on careers in conservation is available on the USFWS website. Additional information is available from USFWS regional offices and the Human Capital Office in Falls Church, VA. Phone, 703-358-1743. https://www.fws.gov/humancapital

In 2019, the USFWS ranked 157th among 420 agency subcomponents in the Partnership for Public Service's Best Places To Work Agency Rankings. https://bestplacestowork.org/rankings/detail/IN15
Climate Change   The USFWS website provides a collection of links and informational sources for learning about

climate science and conservation in a changing climate. https://www.fws.gov/home/climatechange/resources.html
Crimes Against Wildlife   To report a violation of wildlife laws or to learn about enforcement of them, visit the "Office of Law Enforcement" website, contact the nearest regional law enforcement office, or call the Office of Law Enforcement in Falls Church, VA. Phone, 703-358-1949. http://www.fws.gov/le | Email: lawenforcement@fws.gov

The USFWS forensic laboratory is unique in its dedication to crimes against wildlife. Forensic experts examine, identify, and compare physical evidence to connect crime scenes, suspects, and victims with it. https://www.fws.gov/lab
Endangered Species   The USFWS website features a search tool for learning about and identifying endangered species. The text boxes can search for an endangered species based on the State, U.S. Territory, or county where it lives, or according to its common or scientific name. https://www.fws.gov/endangered/?ref=topbar

An online subscription form is available to receive breaking news affecting endangered species, endangered species news stories, and the "Endangered Species Bulletin" via email. https://visitor.r20.constantcontact.com/manage/optin?v=001ip3iEJ-xkvrgM_ZzpwhxaKQXTq4Cp14J
Energy Development   The USFWS website has a section that is dedicated to the development of domestic energy sources and its effect on wildlife. https://www.fws.gov/ecological-services/energy-development/energy.html
Federal Register   Significant documents, from 1995 (volume 60) to the present, and recent documents that the USFWS has published in the Federal Register are available online. https://www.federalregister.gov/agencies/fish-and-wildlife-service
Freedom of Information Act (FOIA)   The USFWS makes records available, by law, to the public to the greatest extent possible. The records that are being sought already may be posted online. If the information cannot be found online or if the location of the desired records is uncertain, consider contacting the USFWS FOIA public liaison before submitting a FOIA request. https://www.fws.

gov/irm/bpim/foia.html | Email: fwhq_foia@fws.gov

The USFWS maintains an electronic FOIA library and FOIA reading room on its website. https://www.fws.gov/irm/bpim/foiaread.html

Glossaries   Ecological Services maintains an online glossary of terms found in environmental legislation. https://www.fws.gov/ecological-services/about/glossary.html

The Midwest Region maintains an online glossary of terms associated with endangered species. https://www.fws.gov/midwest/endangered/glossary/index.html

The USFWS website features a short glossary of National Environmental Policy Act (NEPA) terms in Portable Document Format (PDF). https://www.fws.gov/r9esnepa/Intro/Glossary.PDF

National Wildlife Refuges   For information on the National Wildlife Refuge System, including information on specific wildlife refuges and wetland management districts, visit the "National Wildlife Refuge System" website. Phone, 800-344-9453. http://www.fws.gov/refuges/index.html

News Media Inquiries   Journalists, reporters, and other media professionals seeking information or to arrange an interview should contact a regional public affairs officer or the Division of Public Affairs in Falls Church, VA. Phone, 703-358-2220. http://www.fws.gov/external-affairs/contacts.html

Newsroom   The USFWS posts news releases online. https://www.fws.gov/news

Permits   Visit the "Do I Need a Permit" web page to learn the rules for importing, exporting, and reexporting protected species. Information on Convention on International Trade in Endangered Species of Wild Fauna and Flora (CITES) permits and certificates is also available from the Division of Management Authority. Phone, 800-358-2104 or 703-358-2093. http://www.fws.gov/international/permits/do-i-need-a-permit.html | Email: managementauthority@fws.gov

Publications   The USFWS national publications unit is headquartered at the National Conservation Training Center in Shepherdstown, WV. It is the primary distribution center for printed material published by the USFWS. The publications unit handles requests from Federal and State agencies, businesses, educators, and the general public. USFWS publications include booklets, brochures, posters, and reports. Phone, 800-344-9543. http://nctc.fws.gov/resources/knowledge-resources

Some publications may need to be ordered from the U.S. Government Bookstore, which the Government Publishing Office operates. Phone, 866-512-1800 (customer contact center). Phone, 202-512-0132 (store phone). https://bookstore.gpo.gov | Email: ContactCenter@gpo.gov

Regional Offices   USFWS has regional offices that represent each of its geographic regions. Contact information for each of these regional offices is available on the USFWS website. https://www.fws.gov/external-affairs/contacts.html

The Office of Law Enforcement, in addition to its national office in Falls Church, VA, maintains regional offices. Contact information for these offices is available on the USFWS website. https://www.fws.gov/le/regional-law-enforcement-offices.html

A State list of other USFWS offices and their contact information is also available online. https://www.fws.gov/offices

Social Media   The USFWS uses social media to communicate and connect with Internet users worldwide. The agency tweets from its Twitter accounts; maintains an Instagram feed and Pinterest board; posts videos on its YouTube channel and photographs on Flickr; and has Facebook, LinkedIn, and Google+ pages. http://www.fws.gov/home/socialmedia/index.html?ref=topbar

Water Resource Development   The ecological services program includes USFWS participation in projects to develop water resources for meeting the needs of local communities and for conserving fish and wildlife. The USFWS works alongside the U.S. Army Corps of Engineers and the Bureau of Reclamation when participating in these development projects. https://www.fws.gov/ecological-services/energy-development/water.html

The Sources of Information were updated 5–2020.

United States Geological Survey

12201 Sunrise Valley Drive, Reston, VA 20192
Phone, 703-648-4000. Internet, http://www.usgs.gov | Email: ASK@usgs.gov

Director *	JAMES F. REILLY
https://www.usgs.gov/about/key-officials	
Deputy Directors	
Administration and Policy	ROSEANN C. GONZALES-SCHREINER
Operations	CYNTHIA L. LODGE
https://www.usgs.gov/media/images/usgs-organizational-chart	

* The Director reports to the Assistant Secretary of Water and Science.

The above list of key personnel was updated 12–2020.

The United States Geological Survey (USGS) was established by the Organic Act of March 3, 1879 (Ch. 182 / 20 Stat. 394 / 43 U.S.C. 31). Since March 3, 1879, the Survey has provided the United States with science information needed to make important land use and resource management policy decisions. https://www.loc.gov/law/help/statutes-at-large/45th-congress/session-3/c45s3ch182.pdf

The USGS serves as the Earth and natural science research bureau for the Department of the Interior. It is the only integrated natural resources research agency in the Federal Government. USGS research and data support the Department's resource and land management information needs. Other Federal, State, tribal, and local government agencies rely on USGS research and data for their biological, climate, energy, mineral resources, natural hazards, and water information needs. Emergency response organizations, natural resource managers, land use planners, and other customers use USGS research and data to protect lives and property, to address environmental health issues, and to promote the public weal. http://www.usgs.gov/about/about-us/who-we-are

The USGS conducts research, monitoring, and assessments to increase understanding of America's biological, land, and water resources. The Service informs American citizens and members of the global community by producing data, maps, and reports containing analyses and interpretations. These analyses and interpretations cover a range of topics: biological, energy, mineral, and water resources; land surfaces; marine environments; geologic structures; natural hazards; and dynamic processes of the Earth. Citizens, managers, and planners regularly use USGS data, analytical, and interpretive products to respond to and plan for changes in ecosystems and the environment.

The USGS has over 140 years of experience generating science-based data. In more than 400 science centers across the United States, the Service employs approximately 10,000 science and science-support staff, who work on locally, regionally, and nationally scaled studies, on research projects, and at sampling and monitoring sites. https://www.usgs.gov/about/organization

Sources of Information

Archived Records The "Guide to Federal Records in the National Archives of the United States" indicates that USGS records have been assigned to record group 057. https://www.archives.gov/research/guide-fed-records/groups/057.html

Business Opportunities General information on contracting is available from the Office of Acquisition and Grants. Phone, 703-648-7376. https://www.usgs.gov/about/organization/science-support/administration/office-acquisition-and-grants

The "Small Business Program" web page has resources to help small-business owners. https://www.usgs.gov/about/organization/science-support/administration/office-acquisition-and-grants/small-business?qt-

science_support_page_related_con=1#qt-
science_support_page_related_con |
Email: gs_smallbusiness@usgs.gov

Career Opportunities   The USGS relies on
professionals with a range of expertise and
diverse skills to carry out its mission. Many of
these professionals have been educated and
trained in various scientific disciplines: biology,
cartography, chemistry, ecology, geology,
geography, hydrology, and physics. https://
www.usgs.gov/about/organization/science-
support/human-capital/employment-and-
information-center | Email: hcweb@usgs.gov

In 2019, the USGS ranked 168th
among 420 agency subcomponents in
the Partnership for Public Service's Best
Places To Work Agency Rankings. https://
bestplacestowork.org/rankings/detail/IN08

Contact Information   The "Contact USGS"
web page has an electronic message form,
as well as information on social media and
web chat. Phone, 888-275-8747. https://
answers.usgs.gov

Critical Minerals List   On May 18, 2018,
the Department of the Interior's Office of
the Secretary published the notice "Final
List of Critical Minerals 2018" in the Federal
Register (83 FR 23295). The expertise of
USGS staff plays a key role in reducing the
Nation's vulnerability to disruptions in the
supply of these minerals. On its website, the
USGS posted the announcement "Interior
Releases 2018's Final List of 35 Minerals
Deemed Critical to U.S. National Security
and the Economy." Each of the critical
minerals is hyperlinked to a web page with
statistics and other information on that
particular mineral. Although the list is a
final version, it should not be characterized
as a permanent, but as a dynamic, list that
will be updated. https://www.usgs.gov/
news/interior-releases-2018-s-final-list-
35-minerals-deemed-critical-us-national-
security-and

Earthquakes for Kids   Earthquakes for kids
provides online resources to help children
and adults learn about earthquakes and
earthquake science. http://earthquake.usgs.
gov/learn/kids

Federal Register   Documents that the
USGS recently published in the Federal
Register are accessible online. https://www.
federalregister.gov/agencies/geological-
survey

Freedom of Information Act (FOIA)   The
FOIA electronic reading room contains
documents related to the Flow Rate
Technical Group in response to the
Deepwater Horizon oil spill. These
documents have been cleared for public
release, and the USGS expects to publish
additional documents to this collection.
Before submitting a FOIA request for
agency records, an information seeker
should search this reading room and other
Federal Government Deepwater Horizon
electronic reading rooms for documents and
information. https://www.usgs.gov/about/
organization/science-support/foia

Frequently Asked Questions (FAQs)   The
USGS posts answers to FAQs on its website.
https://www.usgs.gov/faq

Glossaries   A landslides glossary is
available on the USGS website. https://www.
usgs.gov/natural-hazards/landslide-hazards/
science/landslides-glossary?qt-science_
center_objects=0#qt-science_center_objects

The earthquake hazards program includes
an online glossary. http://earthquake.usgs.
gov/learn/glossary

The Office of Budget, Planning, and
Integration maintains an online glossary of
common terms and financial terms. https://
www.usgs.gov/about/organization/science-
support/budget/glossary

A glossary of collections management
terms is available online. https://www.usgs.
gov/products/scientific-collections/glossary-
terms

A Landsat glossary and list of acronyms
are available online. https://www.usgs.gov/
core-science-systems/nli/landsat/landsat-
glossary

The USGS published a glossary of
glacier-related terms. https://pubs.usgs.gov/
of/2004/1216/a/a.html

A list of water-related terms and their
definitions are available online. https://www.
usgs.gov/special-topic/water-science-school/
science/dictionary-water-terms?qt-science_
center_objects=0#qt-science_center_objects

History   Mary C. Rabbitt's "The United
States Geological Survey: 1879–1989" is
available in electronic form on the USGS
website. It is a 110-year history of the
relation of geology to the development of
policies for public land, Federal science, and
mapping, and to the development of mineral

resources in the United States. http://pubs.usgs.gov/circ/c1050

Landsat Satellite Missions   In 1966, former Secretary of the Interior Stewart Udall announced the launching of the Earth Resources Observation Satellites (EROS) project. His vision was to observe the Earth for the benefit of all. One of the purposes of the ongoing project is to collect valuable resource data and use them to improve the environmental quality of the biosphere. https://www.usgs.gov/core-science-systems/nli/landsat/landsat-satellite-missions?qt-science_support_page_related_con=0#qt-science_support_page_related_con

Library   Established in 1879, the USGS library is now the largest library for earth sciences in the world. Professional librarians develop and maintain USGS library guides to connect users to relevant resources and research strategies. https://usgs.libguides.com/home | Email: library@usgs.gov

National Map   The National Map website offers Internet users a trove of topographical information. https://www.usgs.gov/core-science-systems/national-geospatial-program/national-map

Natural Hazards   Information on the programs and activities of the natural hazards mission—including information on earthquakes, flooding, landslides, volcanoes, and wildfires—is available online. https://www.usgs.gov/mission-areas/natural-hazards

News   The USGS posts national and State news items. https://www.usgs.gov/news/news-releases

Publications   The USGS publications warehouse provides access to over 130,000 publications written by USGS scientists throughout the agency's history. https://pubs.er.usgs.gov

The Sources of Information were updated 12–2020.

Science Snippets   The USGS posts fun facts and interesting snippets of science. https://www.usgs.gov/news/science-snippets

Site Map   The Website map allows visitors to look for specific topics or to browse content that aligns with their interests. https://www.usgs.gov/sitemap

USGS Store   Educational materials, Federal recreation passes, maps, scientific reports, and more are available from the online USGS Store. https://store.usgs.gov

Social Media   The USGS maintains a presence on social media. https://www.usgs.gov/connect/social-media

Volcanic Activity Alerts   Information on U.S. volcanoes and current activity alerts are available on the "Volcano Hazards" web page. https://www.usgs.gov/volcano

Water Resources   Reliable, impartial, and timely information on the Nation's water resources is available on the "Water Resources" web page. Phone, 888-275-8747. http://www.usgs.gov/water

A nationwide list of all of the USGS water resources mission area science centers and regions and hubs for critical water science that Federal, State, and other partners and stakeholders fund is available online. https://www.usgs.gov/mission-areas/water-resources/about/water-resources-mission-area-science-centers-and-regions

Wetlands and Aquatics Research   The Wetlands and Aquatics Research Center conducts research, develops new approaches and technologies, and disseminates scientific information that is needed for understanding, managing, conserving, and restoring wetlands and other aquatic and coastal ecosystems and their associated plant and animal communities throughout the Nation and the world. https://www.usgs.gov/centers/wetland-and-aquatic-research-center-warc

DEPARTMENT OF THE TREASURY

1500 Pennsylvania Avenue NW., Washington, DC 20220
Phone, 202-622-2000. Internet, http://www.treasury.gov

Secretary of the Treasury	JANET YELLEN
Deputy Secretary of the Treasury	ADEWALE O. ADEYEMO
Chief of Staff	DIDEM NISANCI
https://home.treasury.gov/about/general-information/officials/ janet-yellen	

Under Secretaries

Domestic Finance	(VACANCY)
International Affairs	(VACANCY)
Terrorism and Financial Intelligence	(VACANCY)
https://home.treasury.gov/about/general-information/ organizational-chart	
Treasurer of the United States	JOVITA CARRANZA
https://www.moneyfactory.gov/treasureroftheunitedstates.html	

Assistant Secretaries

Economic Policy	(VACANCY)
Legislative Affairs	BRAD BAILEY, ACTING
Management	(VACANCY)
Public Affairs	CALVIN MITCHELL
Tax Policy	(VACANCY)

Domestic Finance

Financial Institutions Policy	KIPP KRANBUHL, ACTING
Financial Markets	(VACANCY)
Financial Stability	(VACANCY)
Fiscal Service	DAVID A. LEBRYK

International Affairs

International Finance	GEOFFREY OKAMOTO, ACTING
International Markets	(VACANCY)

Terrorism and Financial Intelligence	
Foreign Asset Control	(VACANCY)
Intelligence and Analysis	(VACANCY)
Terrorist Financing and Financial Crimes	(VACANCY)
https://home.treasury.gov/about/general-information/officials	

Chief Officers

Information	(VACANCY)
Risk	KENNETH J. PHELAN
General Counsel	(VACANCY)
https://home.treasury.gov/about/offices	

Inspector General

Deputy	RICHARD K. DELMAR
https://oig.treasury.gov/about	

Department of the Treasury

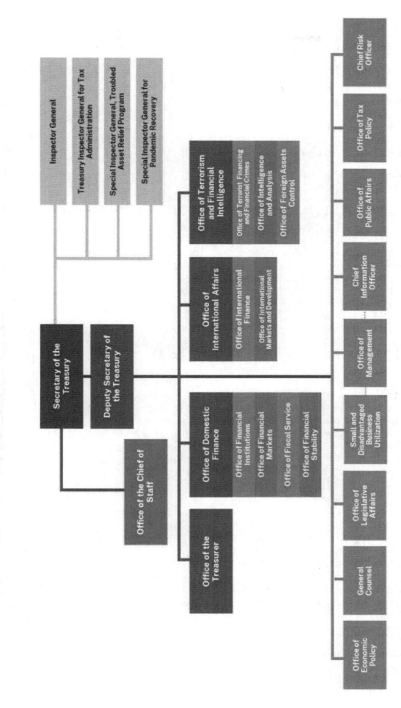

Special Inspectors General
Pandemic Recovery   Brian D. Miller
https://www.sigpr.gov/about-sigpr/meet-special-inspector-general

Troubled Asset Relief Program   Christy G. Romero
https://www.sigtarp.gov/about-us

Treasury Inspector General
Tax Administration   J. Russell George
https://www.treasury.gov/tigta/about_ig.shtml

The above list of key personnel was updated 4–2021.

The Department of the Treasury enforces financial laws, manufactures coins and currency, and recommends economic, fiscal, and tax policies.

Establishment and Organization
On September 2, 1789, a few months after taking his oath of office as the Nation's first President, George Washington signed into law an act establishing a Department of Treasury. Subsequent acts have figured in the development of the Department, delegating new duties to its charge and establishing the numerous bureaus and divisions that constitute today's Department of the Treasury. https://www.loc.gov/law/help/statutes-at-large/1st-congress/session-1/c1s1ch12.pdf

The Department of the Treasury's organizational structure has two major components: departmental offices and operating bureaus. Departmental offices are primarily responsible for the formulation of policy and management of the Department as a whole. Operating bureaus carry out the specific operations that have been assigned to the Department. https://home.treasury.gov/about/general-information/role-of-the-treasury

The Department's organizational chart is posted on the "Organizational Structure" web page. https://home.treasury.gov/about/general-information/organizational-chart

Statutory and Regulatory Authorities
Codified statutory material affecting the Department of the Treasury has been assigned to Chapter 3 of 31 U.S.C. That chapter of Title 31 is divided into two subchapters: "Subchapter I—Organization" runs from section 301 to 315; "Subchapter II—Administrative" runs from section 321 to 333. https://uscode.house.gov/view.

xhtml?path=/prelim@title31/subtitle1/chapter3&edition=prelim

Codified rules and regulations that affect money and finance and that are associated with the Department of the Treasury have been assigned to "Subtitle A—Office of the Secretary of the Treasury" and "Subtitle B—Regulations Relating to Money and Finance" of 31 CFR. https://www.ecfr.gov/cgi-bin/text-idx?SID=f0074465e4c35d4ec9ff9754831610dd&mc=true&tpl=/ecfrbrowse/Title31/31tab_02.tpl

Activities
As a major policy adviser to the President, the Secretary recommends domestic and international financial, economic, and tax policy; formulates broad fiscal policies that have general significance for the economy; and manages the public debt. The Secretary oversees the activities of the Department in carrying out its major law enforcement responsibility; in serving as the financial agent for the U.S. Government; and in manufacturing coins, currency, and other products for customer agencies. The Secretary also acts as the Government's chief financial officer.

Domestic Finance The Office of Domestic Finance maintains confidence in the U.S. Treasury market, manages Federal fiscal operations, and strengthens financial institutions and markets; promotes access to credit; and improves financial access and education in service of America's long-term economic strength and stability. https://home.treasury.gov/about/offices/domestic-finance

Economic Policy   The Office of the Assistant Secretary for Economic Policy helps policymakers determine economic policies. The Office analyzes domestic and international economic issues and developments in the financial markets, assists in forming official economic projections, and works closely with Federal Government agencies to make economic forecasts supporting the yearly budget process. https://home.treasury.gov/policy-issues/economic-policy

Enforcement   The Department's law enforcement activities are carried out by its offices and bureaus, including the Alcohol and Tobacco Tax and Trade Bureau, the Internal Revenue Service, and the Office of Terrorism and Financial Intelligence (TFI). The Office of Foreign Assets Control, which is part of the TFI, plays a key role in controlling the assets of "blocked" countries in the United States and restricting the flow of funds and trade with them.

Alcohol and Tobacco Tax and Trade Bureau https://www.ttb.gov/enforcement

Internal Revenue Service https://www.irs.gov/compliance/criminal-investigation

Office of Terrorism and Financial Intelligence https://home.treasury.gov/about/offices/terrorism-and-financial-intelligence

Financial Institutions   The Office of Financial Institutions coordinates the Department's efforts regarding financial institutions legislation and regulation, legislation affecting Federal agencies that regulate or insure financial institutions, and securities markets legislation and regulation. The Office also coordinates the Department's financial education policy efforts and ensures the resiliency of the financial services sector. https://home.treasury.gov/about/offices/domestic-finance/financial-institutions

Financial Markets   The Office of Financial Markets serves to formulate policy on Federal debt management, State and local finance (including the Federal debt), Federal Government credit policies, and lending and privatization. This Office also oversees the Federal Financing Bank, and the Assistant Secretary serves as the senior member of the Treasury Financing Group and coordinates the President's Working Group on Financial Markets. https://home.treasury.gov/about/offices/domestic-finance/financial-markets

Financial Stability   The Office of Financial Stability within the U.S. Treasury was created by the Emergency Economic Stabilization Act of 2008 (12 U.S.C. 5201 et seq.) to administer the Troubled Asset Relief Program (TARP). The purpose of the TARP was to help restore liquidity and stability to the U.S. financial system following the 2008 financial crisis. The Treasury's authority to make financial commitments under TARP ended on October 3, 2010. The Office continues to wind down the TARP investments in a manner that balances exit speed with maximizing taxpayer returns. It also helps homeowners prevent avoidable foreclosures. https://www.treasury.gov/initiatives/financial-stability/Pages/about-ofs.aspx

Fiscal Affairs   The Office of the Fiscal Assistant Secretary provides policy oversight of the Fiscal Service bureaus and develops policy on payments, collections, debt financing operations, electronic commerce, Governmentwide accounting, Government investment fund management, and other related issues. The Office also performs two critical functions for the Department: It manages the daily cash position of the Government, and it produces the cash and debt forecasts used to determine the size and timing of the Government's financing operations. https://home.treasury.gov/about/offices/domestic-finance/fiscal-service

International Finance   The Office of the Assistant Secretary for International Finance conducts macroeconomic analyses to advise the Under Secretary for International Affairs and other policymakers. The Office also helps them formulate and execute financial and economic policy affecting or involving the International Monetary Fund, the U.S.-China Strategic and Economic Dialogue, the G–20, and other major multilateral and bilateral engagements. https://home.treasury.gov/about/offices/international-affairs

International Markets and Development   The Office of the Assistant Secretary of International Markets and Development manages the work of the Committee on Foreign Investment in the United States and the Treasury's Office of Technical Assistance. The Office also advises the Under Secretary for International Affairs and other policymakers on financial and economic policies relevant to major bilateral and multilateral engagements, and it assists them with these engagements. The Office plays a similar role in the formulation and execution of policies affecting export finance, financial services, trade, and multilateral development, including the World Bank, the regional development banks, and emerging global issues like food security and climate finance.

Committee on Foreign Investment in the United States https://home.treasury.gov/policy-issues/international/the-committee-on-foreign-investment-in-the-united-states-cfius

Office of Technical Assistance https://home.treasury.gov/about/offices/international-affairs/technical-assistance

Tax Policy   The Office of the Assistant Secretary for Tax Policy advises and assists the Secretary and the Deputy Secretary in the formulation and execution of domestic and international tax policies and programs. These functions include analysis of proposed tax legislation and tax programs; projections of economic trends affecting tax bases; studies of effects of alternative tax measures; preparation of official estimates of Government receipts for the President's annual budget messages; legal advice and analysis on domestic and international tax matters; assistance in the development and review of tax legislation and domestic and international tax regulations and rulings; and participation in international tax treaty negotiations and in maintenance of relations with international organizations on tax matters. https://home.treasury.gov/about/offices/tax-policy

Treasurer of the United States   The Office of the Treasurer of the United States was established on September 6, 1777. The Treasurer was originally charged with the receipt and custody of Government funds, but many of these functions have been assumed by different bureaus of the Department. In 1981, the Treasurer was assigned responsibility for oversight of the Bureau of Engraving and Printing and the United States Mint. The Treasurer reports to the Secretary through the Assistant Secretary for Management. https://home.treasury.gov/about/offices/treasurer

Treasury Inspector General for Tax Administration   The Treasury Inspector General for Tax Administration (TIGTA), in accordance with the Internal Revenue Service Restructuring and Reform Act of 1998 (26 U.S.C. 1 note), independently oversees Internal Revenue Service programs and activities. TIGTA monitors the Nation's tax laws to ensure that the Internal Revenue Service (IRS) acts with efficiency, economy, and effectiveness; ensures compliance with applicable laws and regulations; prevents, detects, and deters fraud, waste, and abuse; investigates activities or allegations related to fraud, waste, and abuse by IRS personnel; and protects the IRS against attempts to corrupt or threaten its employees. https://www.treasury.gov/tigta

Sources of Information

Archived Records   The "Guide to Federal Records in the National Archives of the United States" indicates that Department of the Treasury records have been assigned to record group 056. https://www.archives.gov/research/guide-fed-records/groups/056.html?_ga=2.232359263.1725271782.16046 88789-1741997824.1566513831

Assistance for Small Businesses   The paycheck protection program provides small businesses with resources for maintaining payroll, hiring back employees who may have been laid off, and covering overhead that is applicable. https://home.treasury.gov/policy-issues/cares/assistance-for-small-businesses

For information on small and disadvantaged business activities, visit the Office of Small and Disadvantaged Business Utilization's web pages. Phone, 202-622-5666. https://home.treasury.gov/policy-issues/small-business-programs/small-and-disadvantaged-business-utilization-0

Bureaus   The Bureaus carry out specific operations assigned to the Department of the Treasury. Bureau employees constitute 98% of its workforce. The Department's website has a "Bureaus" web page that provides easy access to the websites of each of them. https://home.treasury.gov/about/bureaus

Careers Opportunities   The Department of the Treasury employs over 100,000 professionals nationwide and around the world. https://home.treasury.gov/about/careers-at-treasury

In 2019, the Department of the Treasury ranked number 9 among 17 large Government agencies in the Best Places To Work Agency Rankings. https://bestplacestowork.org/rankings/detail/TR00

Contact Information The "Contact" web page contains information for contacting bureaus, offices, programs, services, and for making inquiries, providing feedback, reporting concerns, and replacing damaged currency. https://home.treasury.gov/utility/contact

Members of the media may contact the Department of the Treasury by phone or email. Phone, 202-622-2960. https://home.treasury.gov/contacts-for-members-of-the-media | Email: press@treasury.gov

Data / Charts A trove of economic information—charts, data, and tables—is available online. https://www.treasury.gov/resource-center/data-chart-center/Pages/index.aspx

Educational Resources The Department of the Treasury's website has learning resources that are suitable for children and parents, for students and teachers, as well as college students and other curious adults. https://home.treasury.gov/services/education

Environment The "Office of Management and Budget Scorecard on Sustainability/Energy" (2016) for the Department of the Treasury is accessible online in Portable Document Format (PDF). https://www.treasury.gov/about/budget-performance/annual-performance-plan/Documents/TREASURY%20Final%20Jan%202016%20OMB%20Scorecard.public%20version.pdf

On October 5, 2009, President Barack Obama signed Executive Order 13514, "Federal Leadership in Environmental, Energy, and Economic Performance," which required scorecards to provide "periodic evaluation of Federal agency performance in implementing" the order and publication of the evaluation results on a public website to support transparency and accountability. https://www.govinfo.gov/content/pkg/FR-2009-10-08/pdf/E9-24518.pdf

Federal Register Significant documents and documents that the Department of the Treasury recently published in the Federal Register are accessible online. https://www.federalregister.gov/agencies/treasury-department

Financing Government The Department of the Treasury's debt management policy prioritizes financing the Government at the lowest cost, over time. To learn more about policymaking for financing the Government, explore the debt management resources that the Department has posted. https://home.treasury.gov/policy-issues/financing-the-government

Forms The "Forms" web page contains links to Government forms that are accessible online. https://home.treasury.gov/services/forms

Freedom of Information Act (FOIA) The FOIA gives a right to request access to records of the U.S. Government's executive branch to any person. The records must be disclosed unless they are shielded from request by one or more of the exempt categories of information found in the statute. https://home.treasury.gov/footer/freedom-of-information-act

The Department of the Treasury maintains an electronic reading room whose holdings are governed by the FOIA. https://home.treasury.gov/footer/freedom-of-information-act/electronic-reading-room

A FOIA request may be submitted electronically. An information seeker who wants to submit his or her request electronically may choose one of two options: using the governmentwide national FOIA portal or submitting a request directly to the appropriate departmental bureau. https://home.treasury.gov/footer/freedom-of-information-act/submit-a-request

Frequently Asked Questions (FAQs) The Department of the Treasury posts answers to FAQs. https://www.treasury.gov/resource-center/faqs/Pages/default.aspx

General Property Auctions Information on upcoming sales of aircraft, vehicles, vessels, and general property is posted online. https://www.treasury.gov/auctions/treasury/gp/

Glossary The Department of the Treasury maintains a list of acronyms and terms that recur on its website. https://www.treasury.gov/initiatives/financial-stability/glossary/pages/default.aspx

History A trove of historical information on the Department of the Treasury and its building is available online. https://home.treasury.gov/about/history

A visual and audio tour of the Treasury Building's points of interest is available online. The points of interest on the map are hyperlinked to brief audio descriptions. https://m.treasury.gov/about/history/m/m.html#map

Nero was purchased in 1793 to serve as "a Dog for the Yard." He—and his successor watchdogs—accompanied the night watchman, whose duties required him to visit all sectors of the Mint premises every hour. To learn more about these early and faithful Treasury employees, see the "Watchdogs of the Treasury" web page. https://www.treasury.gov/about/history/Pages/watchdogs.aspx

Library   The Treasury Library is housed in the Freedman's Bank Building, room 1020. The entrance to the building is located at 720 Madison Place NW., Washington, DC. Members of the public may access the library's holdings by appointment. Visitors must receive clearance from the Secret Service to enter the library. A clearance request must be made at least one business day before a scheduled visit. Consulting with a Treasury librarian in advance of a visit can save time because it helps ensure that relevant materials are readily accessible and available for use. Phone, 202-622-0990. https://home.treasury.gov/services/tours-and-library/library

Press Releases   The Department of the Treasury posts press releases online. https://home.treasury.gov/news/press-releases

Site Map   The website map allows visitors to look for specific topics or to browse content that aligns with their interests. https://www.treasury.gov/Pages/site-map.aspx

Slam the Scam   The Treasury Inspector General for Tax Administration has produced a flyer that explains a scam involving the impersonation of an Internal Revenue Service employee. The flyer is available in English or Spanish. Phone, 800-366-4484. https://www.treasury.gov/tigta/docs/Slam%20the%20Scam%20Flyer.pdf | Email: complaints@tigta.treas.gov

Social Media   The Department of the Treasury maintains a social media presence on Facebook, Flickr, Twitter, and YouTube. https://www.treasury.gov/connect/Pages/default.aspx

Social Security / Medicare   The Secretary of the Treasury chairs the Boards of Trustees of the Social Security and Medicare trust funds. He or she serves with five other trustees: three trustees from the Federal Government and two public trustees whom the President appoints and the

Senate confirms. Each year the trustees provide the U.S. Congress with an accounting of the current and projected financial status of the Social Security and Medicare trust funds. Two reports are issued: One is for Social Security; the other is for Medicare; and both reports are posted on the "Social Security and Medicare Trustee Reports" web page. https://home.treasury.gov/policy-issues/economic-policy/social-security-and-medicare-trustee-reports

Tax Analysis   The staff of the Office of Tax Analysis (OTA) posts original research online in its working papers series. The OTA staff also develops datasets, methods, and models that its uses for policy analysis and estimates. The technical papers series, which is also posted online, presents documentation of these datasets, methods, and models. https://home.treasury.gov/policy-issues/tax-policy/office-of-tax-analysis

Tribal Affairs   The "Tribal Affairs" web page contains links to the "Tribal Consultations" and "Treasury Tribal Advisory Committee" web pages. https://home.treasury.gov/policy-issues/tribal-affairs

Works Progress Administration (WPA) Artwork   A serendipitous consequence of the economic hardship that was caused by the Great Depression, which followed the 1929 stock market collapse, was that Americans started visiting public museums in droves. Having little money for anything other than necessities, they took advantage of free museum admissions, and many were, for the first time, exposed to works of art and responded with appreciation for them. In a cultural moment that the New Deal initiatives of President Franklin D. Roosevelt were shaping, the confluence of a heightened awareness of public art, employment-relief needs of artists, and creation of artwork for new Federal buildings stimulated the establishment of three public arts programs that the Treasury Department administered. https://home.treasury.gov/about/history/collection/paintings/wpa-art-collection

Yield Curves   Information on Treasury Yield Curves for nominal and real coupon issues and its breakeven inflation curve and on the corporate bond yield curve and its relationship to the Pension Protection Act is available on the "Treasury Coupon Issues and Corporate Bond Yield Curves" web page. https://home.treasury.gov/data/treasury-coupon-issues-and-corporate-bond-yield-curves

The above Sources of Information were updated 4–2021.

Alcohol and Tobacco Tax and Trade Bureau

1310 G Street NW., Box 12, Washington, DC 20005
Phone, 202-453-2000. Internet, http://www.ttb.gov

Administrator	MARY G. RYAN
Deputy Administrator	DAVID M. WULF
https://www.ttb.gov/offices/executive-offices	

The above list of key personnel was updated 4–2021.

The Alcohol and Tobacco Tax and Trade Bureau enforces the laws regulating alcohol production, importation, and wholesale businesses; tobacco manufacturing and importing businesses; and alcohol labeling and advertising.

Establishment and Organization

On November 25, 2002, President George W. Bush approved Public Law 107–296, which is also cited as the Homeland Security Act of 2002 (116 Stat. 2135). Title XI—Department of Justice Divisions contains a subtitle (116 Stat. 2274–2280) that transferred the Bureau of Alcohol, Tobacco and Firearms to the Department of Justice, while providing that the tax collection functions were to remain with the Department of the Treasury and be administered by a newly established Tax and Trade Bureau (TTB). https://www.govinfo.gov/content/pkg/STATUTE-116/pdf/STATUTE-116-Pg2135.pdf

The statute became effective 60 days after the President signed it (116 Stat. 2142) thereby establishing the TTB on January 24, 2003. https://www.ttb.gov/about-ttb/history

The TTB posts an organizational chart on its website. https://www.ttb.gov/about-ttb/organizational-chart-for-ttb

Statutory and Regulatory Authorities

Codified material from Public Law 107–296 has been assigned to section 531 of 6 U.S.C. https://uscode.house.gov/view.xhtml?path=/prelim@title6/chapter1/subchapter11&edition=prelim

Codified statutory material affecting taxation of distilled spirits, wines, and beer has been assigned to chapter 51 of 26 U.S.C. https://uscode.house.gov/view.xhtml?path=/prelim@title26/subtitleE/chapter51&edition=prelim

Codified statutory material affecting taxation of tobacco products and cigarette papers and tubes has been assigned to chapter 52 of 26 U.S.C. https://uscode.house.gov/view.xhtml?path=/prelim@title26/subtitleE/chapter52&edition=prelim

Codified rules and regulations that are associated with the Alcohol and Tobacco Tax and Trade Bureau (TTB) have been assigned to chapter 1 of 27 CFR. https://www.ecfr.gov/cgi-bin/text-idx?gp=&SID=f00ed00e5660d6413f0783a84be97e50&mc=true&tpl=/ecfrbrowse/Title27/27chapterI.tpl

Activities

The TTB collects Federal alcohol, tobacco, firearms, and ammunition excise taxes; regulates the production, labeling, and advertising of alcohol beverages; and investigates unfair or unlawful trade in alcohol and tobacco products. The Bureau regulates alcohol and tobacco producers, importers, and wholesalers. Regulation of retailers takes place on State and local levels. https://www.ttb.gov/consumer/about-us-what-we-do

Sources of Information

Archived Records   The "Guide to Federal Records in the National Archives of the United States" indicates that records of the TTB have been assigned to record group 564. The TTB was created when the Bureau of Alcohol, Tobacco and Firearms was split into two new bureaus and its functions were reassigned and distributed between them. The new Bureau of Alcohol, Tobacco, Firearms, and Explosives (ATFE) and its functions became part of the Department of Justice. The new TTB and its function remained within the Department of the Treasury. Record group 564 does not have a description that currently is associated with it. Records of the ATFE have been assigned to record group 436. https://www.archives.gov/research/guide-fed-records/index-numeric/501-to-600.html

Advertising, Labeling, and Formulation   For information on the advertising, labeling, and formulation of alcohol beverages, contact the Advertising, Labeling and Formulation Division. Phone, 202-453-2250 or 866-927-2533. http://www.ttb.gov/advertising/alfd.shtml | Email: alfd@ttb.treas.gov

Business Opportunities   The Bureau procures a variety of commercial goods and services each year, using appropriated and nonappropriated funds. The "Contracting with TTB" web page has more information. https://www.ttb.gov/public-information/contracting

Career Opportunities   The TTB has offices nationwide, including in Puerto Rico. Many TTB employees telework full time. To carry out its mission, the Bureau relies on alcohol and tobacco tax specialists, analysts, attorneys, auditors, chemists, investigators,labeling specialists, writers, and other professionals. https://www.ttb.gov/careers

Among 420 agency subcomponents, the TTB placed 4th in the Partnership for Public Service's 2019 Best Places To Work rankings! https://bestplacestowork.org/rankings/detail/TR40

Consumer Protection   The TTB protects the public by promulgating rules and regulations, collecting information on suspicious activities, and helping to create and enforce laws that promote industry compliance. https://www.ttb.gov/consumer | Email: Market.Compliance@ttb.gov

Contact Information   The "Contact the Alcohol and Tobacco Tax and Trade Bureau" web page contains phone numbers and links to relevant online resources. https://www.ttb.gov/about-ttb/contact-us

Federal Register   Significant documents and documents that the TTB recently published in the Federal Register are accessible online. https://www.federalregister.gov/agencies/alcohol-and-tobacco-tax-and-trade-bureau

Fraud Tipline   To report fraud, diversion, and illegal activity by producers, importers, or wholesalers of alcohol and tobacco, contact the Bureau's tipline. Phone, 855-882-8477. TTD, 202-882-9914. https://www.ttb.gov/contact-id | Email: tips@ttb.gov

Freedom of Information Act (FOIA)   The TTB adheres to the policy and disclosure regulations of the Department of the Treasury for implementing the Freedom of Information Act (FOIA) consistently and uniformly and for providing maximum allowable disclosure of agency records upon request. Requests are processed within the time limits defined by the FOIA. https://www.ttb.gov/foia

The TTB's website has an electronic reading room containing materials that the FOIA requires the Bureau to maintain. Some records are accessible, by appointment, in the public reading room located at 1310 G Street NW., Washington, DC 20005. Phone, 202-882-9904. https://www.ttb.gov/foia/electronic-reading-room

Frequently Asked Questions (FAQs)   The TTB posts answers to FAQs. http://www.ttb.gov/faqs | Email: TTBInternetQuestions@ttb.gov

Glossary   The TTB maintains a glossary on its website. https://www.ttb.gov/glossary/glossary-a

Language Links   Information is available on the TTB website in Chinese, Spanish, and French.

In Chinese https://www.ttb.gov/itd-chinese-index/welcome

En Español https://www.ttb.gov/itd-spanish-index/enespanol

En Français https://www.ttb.gov/itd-french/welome

Name that Grape   Using a grape variety name on an American wine label is optional. Nevertheless, many wineries and bottlers show this information on their labels. The TTB designed its "Grape Variety Designations on American Wine Labels" web page to help explain the rules. https://www.ttb.gov/wine/grape-variety-designations-on-american-wine-labels

The TTB Administrator has approved a list of grape variety names for use as American wine type designations. This list has been assigned to "Subpart J—American Grape Variety Names" of part 4 in 27 CFR. https://www.ecfr.gov/cgi-bin/text-idx?SID=58ae6192e0aa4245e7ebe64227e4d126&mc=true&node=pt27.1.4&rgn=div5#sp27.1.4.j

National Revenue Center The National Revenue Center operates a call center that is open on weekdays, 8 a.m.–11:30 a.m. and 12:30 p.m.–5 p.m., eastern standard time. It can provide information on applications, claims, filing excise tax returns, permits, and other tax collection topics. Phone, 877-882-3277. https://www.ttb.gov/offices/national-revenue-center

News / Events The TTB posts newsletters, press releases, and other newsworthy items on its website. https://www.ttb.gov/press-room/news-and-events

Online Help Center The "Online Help Center" web page has links to information that is relevant for TTB online applications and tools for making certain transactions with TTB easier to complete online. https://www.ttb.gov/about-ttb/online-help-center

Publications The "Publications" web page provides convenient access to TTB publications that are found on various pages of the website. https://www.ttb.gov/publications

Resources for Research The "Research Resources" web page provides convenient access to information on the regulatory process, the laws and regulations that the TTB enforces, and on other subjects. It also has industry statistics and historical information. https://www.ttb.gov/researcher-resources

Startup Tutorial The TTB posted a tutorial on its website to help entrepreneurs get started in the beer, distilled spirits, tobacco, and wind industries. https://www.ttb.gov/industry-startup-tutorial

Statistics / Data The "TTB Statistics and Data" web page provides convenient access to accurate and timely statistics and data. The page has statistics on industry production and operations, TTB tax collections, and processing times for applications, labeling approval, permits, and requests for information. It also has tax rates and analysis tools like conversion charts and the Bureau's formula approval tool. https://www.ttb.gov/statistics

The above Sources of Information were updated 4–2021.

Bureau of Engraving and Printing

Fourteenth and C Streets SW., Washington, DC 20228
Phone, 202-874-4000. Internet, http://www.moneyfactory.com

Director	LEONARD R. OLIJAR
Deputy Director	(VACANCY)
http://www.moneyfactory.com/about/officeofthedirector.html	

The above list of key personnel was updated 04–2021.

The Bureau of Engraving and Printing operates on basic authorities conferred by act of July 11, 1862 (31 U.S.C. 303), and on additional authorities contained in past appropriations made to the Bureau that are still in force. A revolving fund established in 1950, in accordance with Public Law 81–656, finances the Bureau's operations. The Secretary of the Treasury selects the Director who heads the Bureau.

The Bureau designs, prints, and finishes all of the Nation's paper currency and many other security documents, including White House invitations and military identification cards. It also is responsible for advising and assisting Federal agencies in the design and production of other Government documents that, because of their innate value or for other reasons, require security or counterfeit-deterrence characteristics.

The Bureau also operates a second currency manufacturing plant at 9000 Blue Mound Road, Fort Worth, TX. Phone, 817-231-4000. https://www.moneyfactory.gov/about.html

Sources of Information

Archived Records The "Guide to Federal Records in the National Archives of the

United States" indicates that BEP records have been assigned to record group 318. https://www.archives.gov/research/guide-fed-records/groups/318.html?_ga=2.91357530.1147691139.1619118271-898747230.1618953560

Business Opportunities   For information on contracts and small business activities, visit the "Doing Business with the BEP" Web page or contact the Office of Acquisition. Phone, 202-874-2065. http://www.moneyfactory.com/about/dobusinesswithbep.html

Career Opportunities   The BEP relies on acquisition specialists, administrative staff, attorneys, chemists, engineers, police officers, security specialists, and other professionals to carry out its mission. http://www.moneyfactory.com/about/careers.html

Among 420 agency subcomponents, the BEP placed 113th in the Partnership for Public Service's 2019 Best Places To Work rankings. https://bestplacestowork.org/rankings/detail/TRAI

Contact Information   Email and postal addresses and phone numbers for the BEP facilities in Washington, DC, and Fort Worth, TX, are posted on the "Contact Us" web page. http://www.moneyfactory.com/contactus.html

Currency Production   The production of U.S. currency involves highly trained and skilled craftspeople, specialized equipment, and a combination of traditional old world printing techniques merged with sophisticated, cutting edge technology. To learn more about the process, visit the "How Money is Made" Web page. http://www.moneyfactory.com/uscurrency/howmoneyismade.html

Educational Resources   The U.S. currency education program offers free educational and training resources online. https://uscurrency.gov/resource-center

Federal Register   Documents that the BEP recently published in the Federal Register are accessible online. https://www.federalregister.gov/agencies/engraving-and-printing-bureau

Federal Reserve   The BEP provides answers to some common questions about the Federal Reserve. https://www.federalreserve.gov/faqs/about-the-fed.htm

Freedom of Information Act (FOIA)   All Federal agencies, including the BEP, create and receive records when carrying out their missions. The FOIA gives the right to access executive branch agency records to the public. The BEP makes available, upon written request, records or extracts of records in accordance with the FOIA, the Privacy Act, and certain regulations of the Department of the Treasury. The FOIA contains, however, exemptions that shield some records from request and disclosure. Phone, 202-874-2500. Fax, 202-874-2951. http://www.moneyfactory.com/foia.html

The BEP maintains an electronic FOIA library. http://www.moneyfactory.com/bepfoialibrary.html

History   The BEP posted a 11-page booklet in Portable Document Format (PDF) for viewing and downloading. "About BEP" contains a section on the Bureau's history and has images illustrating the activities, history, and products of the Bureau. https://moneyfactory.gov/images/about_bep_S508_web.pdf

The "Image Gallery" web page contains four sections: artwork, engravings, photographs, and products. http://www.moneyfactory.com/resources/imagegallery.html

Lifespan of Paper Money   The estimated lifespans of one, five, ten, twenty, fifty and one hundred dollar notes are posted in an online table. https://www.federalreserve.gov/faqs/how-long-is-the-life-span-of-us-paper-money.htm

Mail Order Sales   Uncut sheets of currency, engraved Presidential portraits, historical engravings of national landmarks, and other souvenirs and mementos are available for purchase by phone and online. Phone, 800-456-3408. https://catalog.usmint.gov

News   The BEP posts press releases online. https://www.moneyfactory.gov/presscenter/pressreleases.html

Serial Numbers   A short explanation of the serial numbers that are printed on notes is available in the "Resources" section. http://www.moneyfactory.com/resources/serialnumbers.html

Tours   BEP public tours have been suspended as a precaution to limit the spread of COVID–19. https://moneyfactory.gov/services/takeatour.html

The above Sources of Information were updated 4–2021.

Bureau of the Fiscal Service

401 Fourteenth Street SW., Washington, DC 20227
Phone, 202-874-6950. Internet, http://www.fiscal.treasury.gov

Commissioner	MATTHEW J. MILLER, ACTING
Deputy Commissioners	
Accounting and Shared Services	DARA SEAMAN, ACTING
Finance and Administration	DARA SEAMAN, ACTING
Financial Services and Operations	JEFFREY J. SCHRAMEK
https://www.fiscal.treasury.gov/about.html	

The above list of key personnel was updated 4–2021.

The Bureau of the Fiscal Service provides central payment services to Federal program agencies, operates the Federal Government's collections and deposit systems, provides Governmentwide accounting and reporting services, manages the collection of delinquent debt owed to the Federal Government, borrows the money needed to operate the Federal Government, accounts for the resulting public debt, and gives reimbursable support to Federal agencies.

Accounting   The Fiscal Service gathers and publishes Governmentwide financial information that is used by the public and private sectors to monitor the Government's financial status and establish fiscal and monetary policies. These publications include the "Daily Treasury Statement," "Monthly Treasury Statement," "Treasury Bulletin," "U.S. Government Annual Report," and "Financial Report of the U.S. Government."

Collections   The Fiscal Service administers the world's largest collection system, processing more than 400 million transactions through the support of six Federal Reserve Banks and a network of over 100 financial institutions. In Fiscal Year 2012, the Fiscal Service collected over $3.16 trillion in Federal revenues from individual and corporate income tax deposits, customs duties, loan repayments, fines, proceeds from leases, as well as from other revenue sources.

The Fiscal Service and Internal Revenue Service manage the Electronic Federal Tax Payment System (EFTPS), which allows individuals and businesses to pay Federal taxes online. The EFTPS website has printable acknowledgment features for documenting transactions, advance payment scheduling, and payment history access.

The Treasury Offset Program is one of the methods used to collect delinquent debt. The Fiscal Service uses the program to withhold Federal payments, such as Federal income tax refunds, Federal salary payments, and Social Security benefits, to recipients with delinquent debts, including past-due child support obligations and State and Federal income tax debt.

Debt Financing   The Bureau auctions and issues Treasury bills, notes, and bonds and manages the sales and redemption of savings bonds. It provides daily and other periodic reports to account for the composition and size of the debt. In addition, the Bureau implements the regulations for the Government securities market. These regulations provide for investor protection while maintaining a fair and liquid market for Government securities.

Do Not Pay   The Do Not Pay Business Center has a two-part vision for programs administered or funded by the Federal Government: to help prevent and stop improper payments from being made and to identify and mitigate fraud, waste, and abuse. The goal of the program is to integrate Do Not Pay into existing business processes by providing agencies with access to current data that are relevant for making an award or payment decision.

Electronic Commerce   Through its electronic money programs, the Fiscal Service offers new payment and collection technologies to help Federal agencies modernize their cash management activities.

Examples include stored-value cards used on military bases, point-of-sale check conversion, and online credit card collection programs.

Payments   Each year, the Fiscal Service disburses more than one billion non-Defense payments to a wide variety of recipients, such as those individuals who receive Social Security, IRS tax refunds, and veterans' benefits. In Fiscal Year 2012, the Fiscal Service issued more than $2.4 trillion in payments, 88 percent of which were issued electronically.

Shared Services   The Administrative Resource Center delivers franchise services on a reimbursable basis to more than 85 Treasury and Federal Government agencies. The Center provides services in six areas: financial management, investment accounting, human resources, information technology, procurement, and travel.

Sources of Information

A–Z Index   The Fiscal Service's website has an alphabetical and comprehensive list of links to the Bureau's major programs and services. https://fiscal.treasury.gov/all-programs-services.html

Career Opportunities   The Fiscal Service relies on accountants, administrators, business and finance experts, information technology specialists, and others to carry out mission. https://www.fiscal.treasury.gov/careers

Among 411 agency subcomponents, the Fiscal Service placed 50th in the Partnership for Public Service's 2020 Best Places To Work rankings. https://bestplacestowork.org/rankings/detail/TRFD

Do Not Pay   The Do Not Pay Business Center supports Federal agencies in their efforts to reduce the number of improper payments. Data, information, and resources are available on its website. https://fiscal.treasury.gov/DNP

Electronic Federal Tax Payment System (EFTPS)   The EFTPS professionals post answers to frequently asked questions (FAQs) online. https://www.eftps.gov/eftps/direct/FAQGeneral.page

Federal Register   Documents that the Fiscal Service recently published in the Federal Register are accessible online. https://www.federalregister.gov/agencies/bureau-of-the-fiscal-service

Freedom of Information Act (FOIA)   The FOIA gives the right to request information from the Federal Government's executive branch agencies to any person. It is sometimes referred to as the law that keeps citizens in the know about their Government. The Fiscal Service posts a lot of information on its website for the public's benefit and convenience. Before submitting a FOIA request in writing, information seekers should search the website for the desired information. It may be accessible immediately and free of charge. https://www.fiscal.treasury.gov/foia.html

The Fiscal Service maintains an electronic reading room to support the FOIA. https://www.fiscal.treasury.gov/foia-readingroom.html

Glossaries   A governmentwide treasury account symbol glossary is available online. https://fiscal.treasury.gov/gtas/glossary.html

The EFTPS website has a glossary of terms and common acronyms. https://www.eftps.gov/eftps/direct/HelpGlossary.page

The Treasury Direct website has a glossary of terms. http://www.treasurydirect.gov/indiv/research/res_glossary/glossary.htm

Government-to-Government Shared Services   The Administrative Resource Center provides Federal agencies with cost-effective, customer-focused, responsive administrative support. https://arc.fiscal.treasury.gov

History   A short history of the Fiscal Service is available at the bottom of the "About Us" webpage. https://www.fiscal.treasury.gov/about.html

The Treasury Direct website uses historical images to tell the story of U.S. Savings Bonds from their introduction in 1935 to the second decade of the 21st century. https://www.treasurydirect.gov/timeline.htm?src=td&med=banner&loc=consumer

News   The Fiscal Service posts news items and press releases online. https://www.fiscal.treasury.gov/fsnews/fs_news.htm

Public Debt Outstanding   The Treasury Direct website has monthly statements of the public debt. For example, on October 31, 2021, the total public debt outstanding was approximately $28,908,765,000,000. https://www.treasurydirect.gov/govt/reports/pd/mspd/mspd.htm

Reports / Publications The monthly "Statement of the Public Debt of the United States" and "Treasury Statement of Receipts and Outlays of the U.S. Government," as well as the annual "Financial Report of the U.S. Government," and other publications are available on the Fiscal Service's website. https://fiscal.treasury.gov/reports-statements
Savings Bonds Savings bonds may be purchased and held in an online account. Current rate information is available online or by calling 800-487-2663. Requests for information on all series of savings bonds, savings notes, and retirement plans

or individual retirement bonds should be addressed to the Bureau of the Fiscal Service, Division of Customer Assistance, PO Box 7012, Parkersburg, WV 26106-7012. Phone, 304-480-7711. https://www.treasurydirect.gov/indiv/products/prod_eebonds_glance.htm
Treasury Securities For information on the purchase of Treasury bills, bonds, and notes, contact the Bureau of the Fiscal Service, Division of Customer Assistance, PO Box 7015, Parkersburg, WV 26106-7015. Phone, 800-722-2678. http://www.treasurydirect.gov/indiv/products/products.htm

The Sources of Information were updated 11–2021.

Internal Revenue Service
1111 Constitution Avenue NW., Washington, DC 20224
Phone, 202-622-5000. Internet, http://www.irs.gov

Commissioner of Internal Revenue	Charles P. Rettig
Chief of Staff	Kevin Q. McIver
https://www.irs.gov/about-irs/todays-irs-organization	
Deputy Commissioners	
Operations Support	Jeffrey Tribiano
Services and Enforcement	Sunita Lough

The above list of key personnel was updated 7–2021.

The Office of the Commissioner of Internal Revenue was established by act of July 1, 1862 (26 U.S.C. 7802). The Internal Revenue Service (IRS) administers and enforces the internal revenue laws and related statutes, except those relating to alcohol, tobacco, firearms, and explosives. It collects the proper amount of tax revenue, at the least cost to the public, by efficiently applying the tax law with integrity and fairness. The IRS aims for the highest possible degree of voluntary compliance in accordance with the tax laws and regulations; advises the public of their rights and responsibilities; determines the extent of compliance and the causes of noncompliance; properly administers and enforces the tax laws; and continually searches for and implements new, more efficient ways of accomplishing its mission. The IRS ensures satisfactory resolution of taxpayer complaints; provides

taxpayer service and education; determines, assesses, and collects internal revenue taxes; determines pension plan qualifications and exempt organization status; and prepares and issues rulings and regulations to supplement the provisions of the Internal Revenue Code.

Most of the collected revenues depend on the individual income tax and the social insurance and retirement taxes. Other major revenue sources are corporate income, excise, estate, and gift taxes. The 16th Amendment of the Constitution, ratified on February 3, 1913, gave Congress the authority to levy taxes on the income of individuals and corporations.

Sources of Information

Business Opportunities Information on and resources for doing business with the IRS are available on its "Procurement" Web page. https://www.irs.gov/about-irs/procurement | Email: AWSSPROCCustomerService@irs.gov

Career Opportunities   To carry out its mission, the IRS relies on accountants, appeals officers, artificial intelligence analysts, attorneys, budget analysts, computer research analysts, contact representatives, data transcribers, engineers, human resources specialists, information technology specialists, internal revenue agents and officers, mathematical statisticians, operations research analysts, policy analysts, program analysts, risk analysts, special agents, tax compliance officers, tax examiners, tax law specialists, and other professionals. https://jobs.irs.gov

In 2020, the IRS ranked 223d among 411 agency subcomponents in the Partnership for Public Service's Best Places To Work Agency Rankings. https://bestplacestowork.org/rankings/detail/?c=TR93

Charities / Nonprofits   Tax information for charities and nonprofit organizations is available online. https://www.irs.gov/charities-and-nonprofits

Contact Information   At the bottom of its "Let Us Help You" web page, the IRS posts phone numbers for those who seek assistance. https://www.irs.gov/help/telephone-assistance

Forms / Publications   Current forms, instructions, and publications may be downloaded from the IRS's website. https://www.irs.gov/forms-instructions

Freedom of Information Act (FOIA)   In 1966, President Lyndon B. Johnson's approval of the FOIA gave the right to access documents or records belonging to the executive branch of the Federal Government to any person. The statute is based on the presumption that the Government and its information belong to the public. The IRS may withhold, however, documents or records shielded from disclosure by one of the statute's nine exemptions, and it must withhold them when disclosure is prohibited by law. https://www.irs.gov/uac/irs-freedom-of-information

The IRS maintains an online library whose contents are arranged by subject category. https://www.irs.gov/privacy-disclosure/foia-library

Frequently Asked Questions (FAQs)   The IRS posts answers to FAQs. https://www.irs.gov/faqs

Identity Theft   The IRS responds to tax-related identity theft with an aggressive strategy of prevention, detection, and victim assistance. The IRS continues to make progress against this crime, and it remains one of the agency's highest priorities. The IRS is committed to helping victims of identity theft resolve their cases as quickly as possible. https://www.irs.gov/identity-theft-central

Language Resources   Assistance in additional languages is available on the "Languages" web page. https://www.irs.gov/help/languages

News   The IRS posts news items online. https://www.irs.gov/newsroom

Reading Rooms   Public reading rooms are located in the national office and in each territory office.

Retirement Plans   The IRS website has resources for and a trove of information on retirement plans. https://www.irs.gov/retirement-plans

Tax Assistance   The IRS provides taxpayers with year-round tax information and assistance, primarily through its website and toll-free telephone system. Answers to many tax-related questions can be found on the IRS's website. The toll-free telephone numbers are listed in local telephone directories and in the annual tax form packages. The telephone system can accommodate the needs of taxpayers who are deaf or hearing-impaired. Taxpayers may also visit IRS offices to find answers to their tax questions. Individual preparation is available for handicapped or other individuals unable to use the group preparation method. Tax assistance in a foreign language is also available at many locations. https://www.irs.gov/help/telephone-assistance

To find the nearest taxpayer assistance center, type a ZIP Code in the text box of the online locator tool. Before going to a taxpayer assistance center for help, call and schedule an appointment. https://apps.irs.gov/app/officeLocator/index.jsp

Taxpayer Advocate Service   Each district has problem resolution personnel to address taxpayer complaints that cannot be resolved

through regular channels. https://www.irs.gov/advocate
Taxpayer Rights The taxpayer bill of rights is available on the IRS's website. https://www.irs.gov/taxpayer-bill-of-rights
Tax Statistics The IRS posts articles, data, and tables that describe and measure elements of the U.S. tax system. https://www.irs.gov/statistics
Tax Tools Tax tools are available for individual taxpayers, businesses, and tax

professionals on the "Tools" web page. https://www.irs.gov/help/tools
Where's My Refund? Once the IRS processes a tax filer's return and approves a refund, he or she can check the refund date online. The IRS usually issues a refund in fewer than 21 days after receiving a tax filer's return. Some returns, however, require additional review and, therefore, additional time to process. https://www.irs.gov/refunds

The above Sources of Information were updated 7–2021.

Office of the Comptroller of the Currency

400 7th Street SW., Washington, DC 20219
Phone, 202-649-6800. Internet, http://www.occ.gov

Comptroller https://www.occ.gov/about/who-we-are/leadership/bio-michael-hsu.html	MICHAEL J. HSU, ACTING
Senior Deputy Comptrollers	GREGORY J. COLEMAN
	GROVETTA N. GARDINEER
	LARRY L. HATTIX
	BENJAMIN W. MCDONOUGH
	SYDNEY MENEFEE
	KATHY K. MURPHY
	BLAKE PAULSON

https://www.occ.gov/about/who-we-are/leadership/index-leadership.html

The above list of key personnel was updated 8–2021.

Establishment and Organization
The Office of the Comptroller of the Currency (OCC) was created on February 25, 1863 (12 Stat. 665), as a bureau of the Department of the Treasury. In 1929, with the issuance of the last national bank notes, the OCC essentially became an organization of national bank examiners with a singular mission: to maintain the safety and soundness of the banks under its supervision. In 2011, when the Office of Thrift Supervision integrated into the OCC, the bureau also assumed responsibility for regulating Federal savings associations, also referred to as Federal thrifts. https://www.loc.gov/collections/united-states-statutes-at-large/about-this-collection/73rd-congress/session-2/c73s2ch668.pdf

The Comptroller of the Currency, whom the President appoints to a 5-year term by the advice of the Senate and with its consent, administers the Federal banking system and serves as the chief officer of the OCC and as a director of the Federal Deposit Insurance Corporation.

The OCC's statement of organization has been codified in the Code of Federal Regulations (CFR) and assigned to part 4 of 12 CFR. https://www.ecfr.gov/cgi-bin/text-idx?SID=7c57a800de8e85e36874c72aa364ac10&mc=true&node=pt12.1.4&rgn=div5

A number of departments and offices that are under the leadership of the Comptroller and senior deputy comptrollers provide the organizational structure for carrying out the OCC's mission. https://occ.gov/about/who-

we-are/organizations/index-organization.
html

Statutory and Regulatory Authorities
Statutory material affecting the
Comptroller of the Currency has been
consolidated and codified in the United
States Code (U.S.C.). This material has
been assigned to the first chapter, sections
1–16, of 12 U.S.C. https://uscode.house.
gov/view.xhtml?path=/prelim@title12/
chapter1&edition=prelim

Rules and regulations that are associated
with the Comptroller of the Currency have
been consolidated and codified in the Code
of Federal Regulations (CFR). These rules and
regulations have been assigned to the first
chapter, parts 1–199, of 12CFR. https://www.
ecfr.gov/cgi-bin/text-idx?SID=9239dee7caf
69de5910e02babdd4547c&mc=true&tpl=/
ecfrbrowse/Title12/12chapterI.tpl

Activities
The OCC regulates national banks and
Federal thrifts by examining them; approving
or denying applications for new charters,
branches, capital, and other changes in
corporate or banking structure; taking
enforcement actions—removing officers and
directors, negotiating agreements to change
practices, and issuing cease and desist orders
and civil monetary penalties—when national
banks and Federal thrifts fail to comply with
laws and regulations or when they engage
in unsound practices; and issuing rules,
regulations, interpretations, and corporate
decisions that govern investments, lending,
and other practices.

The bureau supervises over 1,100
national banks, Federal savings
associations, and Federal branches,
including their trust activities and overseas
operations. A nationwide team of bank
examiners works under the supervision of
four district offices. National banks and
Federal thrifts pay for their examinations, as
well as for the processing of their corporate
applications.

Assessments on national banks and
Federal savings associations cover most OCC
operating expenses. The OCC also benefits
from some investment income, primarily
from U.S. Treasury securities. https://occ.gov/
about/what-we-do/index-what-we-do.html

Sources of Information
Alerts   The OCC posts counterfeiting,
fictitious correspondence, fraudulent
issuances, misrepresentation, and
unauthorized banking activity alerts. https://
occ.gov/news-events/newsroom/index.
html?nr=Alert
Alphabetical Topics List   Online visitors
may browse the contents of the "Topics"
web page by using an alphabetized list or by
subject area. https://occ.gov/topics/topics-
sitemap.html#T|tab-accordion-wrpr2
Annual Reports   The "2020 Annual Report"
is available online in Portable Document
Format (PDF) for downloading. Starting
with the year 2003, earlier annual reports
are available, too. https://www.occ.gov/
publications-and-resources/publications/
annual-report/index-annual-report.html
Answers / Solutions   The
"HelpWithMyBank" website has information
and resources to help customers of national
banks and Federal savings associations
find answers to questions and solutions for
problems. https://www.helpwithmybank.gov/
about/index-about.html
Archived Records   The "Guide to Federal
Records in the National Archives of the
United States" indicates that OCC records
have been assigned to record group
101. https://www.archives.gov/research/
guide-fed-records/groups/101.html?_
ga=2.154427440.926928378.1628716780-
2085205018.1628716780
Bulletins   Starting with the year 1994 and
continuing to the present, OCC bulletins
are accessible online. Rescinded and some
pre-1994 bulletins are also included in the
collection. https://occ.gov/news-events/
newsroom/index.html?nr=Bulletin
Business Opportunities   Procurement
awards typically fall within the following
service categories: computer-related
services; computer facilities management
services; computer systems design services;
data processing, hosting, and related
services; real estate agent and broker
services; insurance agency and brokerage
services; and administrative management
and general management consulting
services. https://occ.gov/about/connect-
with-us/doing-business-with-the-occ/
index-doing-business-with-the-occ.html |

Email: OCCAcquisitionManagement@occ.treas.gov

Career Opportunities The OCC relies on accountants, attorneys, economists, financial analysts, human resources specialists, information technology specialists, project management analysts, and other professionals, particularly bank examiners, to carry out its mission. For more information, contact the Director for Human Resources Operations. Phone, 202-649-6590. Fax, 202-649-5998. https://careers.occ.gov/index.html

National bank examiners work to ensure the safety and soundness of America's national banking system, to provide fair access to financial services and equal treatment, and to establish and maintain a flexible regulatory framework that allows the Nation's banks to be competitive. The OCC generally hires examiners at the entry level through college recruitment. https://www.youtube.com/watch?v=RPrQmIcF0s0

In 2020, the OCC ranked 87th among 411 agency subcomponents in the Partnership for Public Service's Best Places To Work Agency Rankings. https://bestplacestowork.org/rankings/detail/?c=TRAJ

Consumer Protection The OCC posts information and resources on its website to protect consumers. https://occ.gov/topics/consumers-and-communities/consumer-protection/index-consumer-protection.html

Contact Information The "Contact the OCC" web page has informational resources for contacting the agency. https://occ.gov/about/connect-with-us/contact-the-occ/index-contact-the-occ.html

Customer Complaints An online form is available for submitting a complaint against a national bank or Federal savings association. https://appsec.helpwithmybank.gov/olcc_form/intro.aspx

District and Field Offices Contact information for district and field offices is available online. https://occ.gov/about/who-we-are/locations/index-locations.html

Federal Register Significant documents and documents that the OCC recently published in the Federal Register are accessible online. https://www.federalregister.gov/agencies/comptroller-of-the-currency

Freedom of Information Act (FOIA) The FOIA serves as the vehicle for obtaining Federal agency documents and records. The statute does contain, however, nine exemptions and three special law enforcement exclusions that shield some documents and records, or parts of them, from disclosure. https://www.occ.gov/about/connect-with-us/foia/index-foia.html

The electronic reading room contains documents that attract public interest and have been the subject of FOIA requests in the past. https://foia-pal.occ.gov/app/ReadingRoom.aspx

Frequently Asked Questions (FAQs) Answers to FAQs on checking accounts, credit cards, credit reports, mortgages, overdraft fees, and more are posted on the "HelpWithMyBank" website. https://www.helpwithmybank.gov/help-topics/index-help-topics.html

Glossary A dictionary of banking terms and phrases is available on the "HelpWithMyBank" website. https://www.helpwithmybank.gov/dictionary/index-dictionary.html

A list of abbreviations and acronyms is available on the OCC's website in Portable Document Format (PDF). https://www.occ.gov/annual-report/download-the-full-report/abbreviations.pdf

History The OCC's role in the Federal banking system started in a tumultuous year, near the midpoint of the American Civil War. On January 1, 1863, President Abraham Lincoln emancipated over 3 million men, women, and children by signing the Emancipation Proclamation. Fifty-five days later, he added his signature to the National Currency Act, which established the OCC and charged it with responsibility for organizing and administering a system of nationally chartered banks and a uniform national currency. After 1913, its mission increasingly centered on the safety and soundness of national banks. To learn more about the agency's development over the past 155 years, see the "Founding of the OCC and the National Banking System" web page. https://occ.gov/about/who-we-are/history/founding-occ-national-bank-system/index-founding-occ-national-banking-system.html

On March 3, 1865, Congress enacted legislation to establish the Bureau of Refugees, Freedmen and Abandoned Lands, which came to be known as the Freedmen's Bureau. On that same day, it chartered the Freedman's Savings and Trust Company, or Freedman's Savings Bank (FSB), to meet a growing need for financial services among African Americans. To learn more about the intertwining histories of the OCC and FSB, read the online article by former OCC historian Jesse Stiller. https://www.occ.gov/about/what-we-do/history/freedman-savings-bank.html

Minority Outreach   The OCC's External Outreach and Minority Affairs division maintains a "Minority Outreach" web page. https://www.occ.gov/topics/consumers-and-communities/minority-outreach/index-minority-outreach.html

News   The OCC posts news releases on its website. https://occ.gov/news-issuances/news-releases/index.html

Publications   The "Publications" web page allows visitors to browse OCC publications by collection, subject area, or recent dates of publication. https://occ.gov/publications-and-resources/publications/index-publications.html

Public Information on Banks   Federal bank regulators post public information on individual banks. The OCC's website provides convenient access to the websites of these regulators. https://occ.gov/about/contact-us/public-information/public-information.html

The Federal Financial Institutions Examination Council's website has a searchable database for identifying the Federal bank regulatory agency that oversees a particular bank or financial institution. https://www.ffiec.gov/consumercenter/default.aspx

Site Map   The careers section has a site map of its web pages. https://careers.occ.gov/sitemap/sitemap-page.html

The "HelpWithMyBank" website has its own site map. https://www.helpwithmybank.gov/site-map/index-sitemap.html

Social Media   The OCC tweets announcements and other newsworthy items on Twitter. https://twitter.com/usocc

The OCC has a Facebook account. https://www.facebook.com/US-Comptroller-of-the-Currency-213254918823/

The OCC posts videos on its YouTube channel. https://www.youtube.com/user/OCCChannel#p/c/2BAA3C3A20C2630E

Tools   The "Tools" web page brings together in one place all of the tools that are available on the OCC website. https://occ.gov/publications-and-resources/tools/index-tools.html

The above Sources of Information were updated 8–2021.

United States Mint

801 Ninth Street NW., Washington, DC 20220
Phone, 202-354-7200. Internet, http://www.usmint.gov

Director	DAVID J. RYDER
Deputy Director	FRANCIS O'HEARN, ACTING
https://www.usmint.gov/about/directors-office	

The above list of key personnel was updated 8–2021.

The establishment of a mint was authorized by act of April 2, 1792 (1 Stat. 246). The Bureau of the Mint was established by act of February 12, 1873 (17 Stat. 424), and recodified on September 13, 1982 (31 U.S.C. 304, 5131). The name was changed to United States Mint by Secretarial order on January 9, 1984.

The primary mission of the Mint is to produce an adequate volume of circulating coinage for the Nation to conduct its trade and commerce. The Mint also produces and sells numismatic coins, American Eagle gold and silver bullion coins, and national medals. The Fort Knox Bullion Depository is the primary storage facility for the Nation's gold bullion.

The U.S. Mint maintains sales centers at the Philadelphia and Denver Mints and at its headquarters on 9th Street in Washington, DC. Public tours are conducted, with free admission, at the Philadelphia and Denver Mints. https://www.usmint.gov/about_the_mint/index.html

Sources of Information

Archived Records   The "Guide to Federal Records in the National Archives of the United States" indicates that Mint records have been assigned to record group 104. https://www.archives.gov/research/guide-fed-records/groups/104.html

Artists   The artistic infusion program enriches and invigorates coin and medal designs by contracting with a pool of American artists from diverse backgrounds and having a variety of interests. These artists collaborate with the Mint's sculptor-engravers to create and submit new designs for U.S. coins and medals. https://www.usmint.gov/learn/artists

Bullion Dealers   The Mint's website has a locator tool for finding U.S. Mint bullion sellers by city and State or by ZIP Code. http://catalog.usmint.gov/bullion-dealer-locator

Career Opportunities   The Mint offers a wide range of career opportunities. An innovative, progressive bureau in the Department of the Treasury, it operates six facilities nationwide and employees professionals with backgrounds in financial management, information technology, manufacturing, protection, sales and marketing, workforce solutions, and other fields. https://www.usmint.gov/about/careers

Among 411 agency subcomponents, the Mint placed 148th in the Partnership for Public Service's 2020 Best Places To Work rankings. https://bestplacestowork.org/rankings/detail/?c=TRAD

Coin of the Year   The Mint celebrated its 225th anniversary in 2017. To mark the occasion, it created the 2017 American Liberty 225th Anniversary Gold Coin, which features a modern rendition of Lady Liberty. Emblematic figures of liberty have graced American coins since the Mint's founding in 1792. The newest Lady Liberty is a modern rendition of this iconic figure, who embodies equality and freedom, ideals that the Nation's Declaration of Independence enshrined. https://catalog.usmint.gov/american-liberty-225th-anniversary-gold-coin-17XA.html?cgid=null&q=coin%2520of%2520the%2520year&navid=search#q=coin%2520of%2520the%2520year&start=1

Contact Information   The Mint's "Contact Us" web page has phone numbers and postal addresses. It also provides convenient access to an electronic "Contact Us" form that has a comment box. https://catalog.usmint.gov/customer-service/contact-us.html | Email: usmint-support@usmcatalog.com

Customer Service   Mint employees work hard to provide exceptional customer service. To contact the Mint, with questions or concerns about shopping, an order, or another matter, please use the "Live Chat" feature or call customer service. Answers to questions also are provided on the "Frequently Asked Questions" web page. Phone, 800-872-6468. https://catalog.usmint.gov/customerservice | Email: usmint-support@usmcatalog.com

Educational Resources   The Mint's website offers learning resources for children, educators, and parents. https://www.usmint.gov/learn/educators

Facilities   The U.S. Mint operates four mints (CA, CO, NY, PA), one depository (KY), and maintains its headquarters in Washington, DC. https://www.usmint.gov/about/mint-tours-facilities

Federal Register   Documents that the Mint recently published in the Federal Register are accessible online. https://www.federalregister.gov/agencies/united-states-mint

Freedom of Information Act (FOIA)   To any person, the FOIA gives a statutory right for obtaining access to Government information in the records of executive branch agencies. This right to access is limited, however, when the requested information is shielded from disclosure by any of nine exemptions contained within the statute. https://www.usmint.gov/foia

The Mint's electronic reading room contains records that are frequently requested under the FOIA. https://www.usmint.gov/foia/reading-room

Frequently Asked Questions (FAQs)   The Mint posts answers to FAQs on its website. https://catalog.usmint.gov/customer-service/faqs/?_ga=2.162013182.373647902.1628186014-2053548025.1628186014

Glossary   The H.I.P. Pocket Change website features a coin glossary. https://www.usmint.gov/learn/kids/collecting/coin-glossary

History   On April 2, 1792, the U.S. Congress passed the Coinage Act, establishing the first national mint in the United States. Over two centuries later, one of the Federal Government's oldest agencies continues to serve the American public. To learn more about the U.S. Mint, visit its "History" web page. https://www.usmint.gov/learn/history

A timeline of the Mint that stretches from the 18th to 21st century is available online. https://www.usmint.gov/learn/history/timeline-of-the-united-states-mint

How Are Coins Made?   An animated overview of the six-step coin manufacturing process—blanking, annealing, upsetting, striking, inspecting, and counting and bagging—is available on the "Coins" web page.. https://www.usmint.gov/learn/kids/coins

Image Library   High-resolution images of coins and medals are available on the Mint's website. For information on the use of these images, contact the Office of Licensing. Phone, 202-354-7350. Fax, 202-756-6585. https://www.usmint.gov/news/image-library | Email: licensing@usmint.treas.gov

Medals   National medals commemorate significant historical events or sites and honor individuals whose superior deeds and achievements have enriched American history or the world. Some national medals are bronze duplicates of Congressional Gold Medals that Congress authorizes under separate Public Laws, and others are produced under the Secretary of the Treasury's authority to strike them. https://www.usmint.gov/learn/coin-and-medal-programs/medals

The above Sources of Information were updated 8–2021.

News   The Mint posts articles and press releases online. The Mint maintains a public inquiry phone line for its Office of Corporate Communications. Phone, 202-354-7227. https://www.usmint.gov/news | Email: inquiries@usmint.treas.gov

Online Resources   The "Website Resources" web page has a collection of helpful internal and external links. https://www.usmint.gov/policies/website-resources

Production / Sales   The Mint produces circulating coins for commerce, numismatic coins for collectors, and bullion coins for investors. Quantities are measured in terms of production figures when referring to circulating coins, sales figures when referring to numismatic products, and sales and mintage figures when referring to bullion. https://www.usmint.gov/about/production-sales-figures

Reports   Annual and special reports are available online in Portable Document Format (PDF). https://www.usmint.gov/about/reports

Seigniorage   The Mint returned nearly $550 million in seigniorage—the difference between the face value and the manufacturing cost of a circulating coin—to the Department of the Treasury's general fund in 2020. The Mint publishes seigniorage information each year in its annual report. https://www.usmint.gov/wordpress/wp-content/uploads/2021/02/2020-Annual-Report.pdf

Site Map   The website map allows visitors to look for specific topics or to browse content that aligns with their interests. https://www.usmint.gov/about/site-map

Social Media   The Mint maintains a Facebook account. https://www.facebook.com/UnitedStatesMint

The Mint tweets announcements and other newsworthy items on its Twitter account. https://twitter.com/usmint

The Mint posts videos on its YouTube channel. https://www.youtube.com/user/USMINT

EXECUTIVE BRANCH: INDEPENDENT AGENCIES AND GOVERNMENT CORPORATIONS

Administrative Conference of the United States

1120 Twentieth Street NW., Suite 706 South, Washington, DC 20036
Phone, 202-480-2080. Fax, 202-386-7190. Internet, http://www.acus.gov | Email: info@acus.gov

Staff

Chairman https://www.acus.gov/staff	MATTHEW L. WIENER, ACTING
Executive Director Research Director https://www.acus.gov/contacts/matthew-l-wiener	MATTHEW L. WIENER REEVE T. BULL
Chief Financial and Operations Officer https://www.acus.gov/contacts/harry-m-seidman	HARRY M. SEIDMAN
General Counsel https://www.acus.gov/contacts/shawne-mcgibbon	SHAWNE C. MCGIBBON

Council

Chair	MATTHEW L. WIENER, ACTING
Vice Chair	MATTHEW L. WIENER
Government Official	NICHOLAS T. MATICH IV
Private Citizens	RONALD A. CASS JEFFREY M. HARRIS DONALD F. MCGAHN II MICHAEL H. MCGINLEY THEODORE B. OLSON JANE C. SHERBURNE GEOVETTE E. WASHINGTON (VACANCY)

https://www.acus.gov/directory/council

The above list of key personnel was updated 12–2019.

The Administrative Conference of the United States develops recommendations for improving the fairness and effectiveness of procedures by which Federal agencies administer regulatory, benefit, and other Government programs.

ADMINISTRATIVE CONFERENCE OF THE UNITED STATES (ACUS)

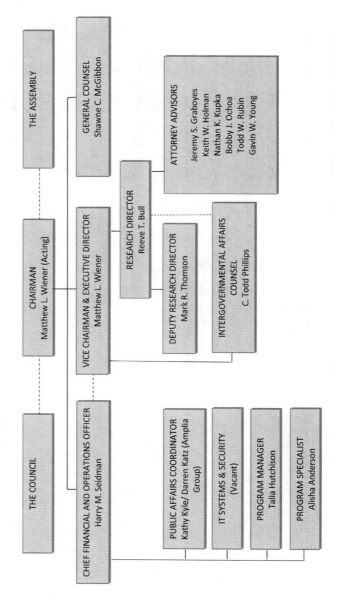

THE ASSEMBLY

THE COUNCIL

CHAIRMAN
Matthew L. Wiener (Acting)

GENERAL COUNSEL
Shawne C. McGibbon

VICE CHAIRMAN & EXECUTIVE DIRECTOR
Matthew L. Wiener

RESEARCH DIRECTOR
Reeve T. Bull

DEPUTY RESEARCH DIRECTOR
Mark R. Thomson

INTERGOVERNMENTAL AFFAIRS COUNSEL
C. Todd Phillips

ATTORNEY ADVISORS
Jeremy S. Graboyes
Keith W. Holman
Nathan K. Kupka
Bobby J. Ochoa
Todd W. Rubin
Gavin W. Young

CHIEF FINANCIAL AND OPERATIONS OFFICER
Harry M. Seidman

PUBLIC AFFAIRS COORDINATOR
Kathy Kyle/ Darren Katz (Amplia Group)

IT SYSTEMS & SECURITY
(Vacant)

PROGRAM MANAGER
Talia Hutchison

PROGRAM SPECIALIST
Alisha Anderson

UPDATED October 2019

Establishment and Organization

The Administrative Conference of the United States (ACUS) was established as a permanent independent agency by the Administrative Conference Act (PL 88–499) enacted in 1964. The Conference is the successor to two temporary Administrative Conferences during the Eisenhower and Kennedy administrations. https://www.govinfo.gov/content/pkg/STATUTE-78/pdf/STATUTE-78-Pg615.pdf

The Conference ceased operations on October 31, 1995, due to termination of funding by Congress. From its beginning in 1968 until its defunding in 1995, the ACUS adopted approximately 200 recommendations, based on research and the deliberations of its members in an open process that encouraged public input. The ACUS published a complete list of these recommendations in the "Federal Register" (60 FR 56312). https://www.govinfo.gov/content/pkg/FR-1995-11-08/pdf/95-27473.pdf#page=1

Congress reauthorized the Conference in 2004 and again in 2008. The 2004 legislation expanded its responsibilities to include specific attention to achieving more effective public participation and efficiency, reducing unnecessary litigation, and improving the use of science in the rulemaking process (5 U.S.C. 591–596). Funding was approved in 2009, and the Conference was officially reestablished in March 2010. https://uscode.house.gov/view.xhtml?path=/prelim@title5/part1/chapter5/subchapter5&edition=prelim

By statute, the Administrative Conference has no fewer than 75 and no more than 101 members, a majority of whom are Government officials. The President appoints the Chairman of the Conference with the advice and consent of the Senate for a 5-year term. The Council, which acts as an executive board, comprises the Chairman and 10 other members whom the President appoints for 3-year terms. Federal officials named to the Council may not constitute more than half of the total Council membership. The Chairman, the only full-time, compensated member of the Conference, appoints members representing the private sector with the approval of the Council for 2-year terms.

The entire membership is divided into committees. Each committee is assigned a broad area of interest such as adjudication, administration and management, judicial review, regulation, or rulemaking. The membership meeting in plenary session constitutes the Assembly of the Conference, which by statute must meet at least once, and customarily meets twice, each year. https://www.acus.gov/history

The agency's organizational chart is available in Portable Document Format (PDF) for viewing and downloading on the "Staff" web page. https://www.acus.gov/sites/default/files/documents/ACUS%20Organization%20Chart_Oct%202019.pdf

The Establishment and Organization paragraphs were updated 12–2019.

Activities

The Chairman develops subjects for inquiry, and the Council approves them. Government and nongovernment experts in administrative procedure often contribute to the development and approval process. The committees conduct thorough reviews of these subjects for inquiry and propose draft recommendations, which are based on supporting reports that expert consultants typically prepare for the ACUS.

Following the proposal process of the committees, the Council considers the supporting reports and the draft recommendations. The Council may then place them on the agenda for an upcoming plenary session of the Assembly. Members of the Assembly debate draft recommendations that the Council has placed on the agenda, and the Assembly's voting members then vote on their final adoption. The general public may attend deliberations of the committees and Assembly.

Recommendations adopted by the Conference may be addressed to administrative agencies, Congress, the President, or the Judicial Conference. Most recommendations call for action on the part of affected agencies or for new legislation. While a substantial number of recommendations have been implemented, implementation activities are continually ongoing.

The Chairman may make independent inquiries into procedural matters, including matters proposed by individuals inside or outside the Government. These inquiries help determine whether the problems should be made the subject of Conference study in the interest of developing fairer or more effective or efficient procedures.

Upon the request of a department or agency head, the Chairman is authorized to advise and assist on matters of administrative procedure. The Conference may collect information and statistics from departments and agencies and publish reports and sourcebooks that it considers useful for evaluating and improving administrative processes. The Conference also serves as a forum for the interchange among departments and agencies of information that may be useful for improving administrative practices and procedures.

The Activities were updated 12–2019.

Sources of Information

Archived Records   The "Guide to Federal Records in the National Archives of the United States" indicates that ACUS records have been assigned to record group 451. The Guide is accessible online, but no description is associated with this record group. https://www.archives.gov/research/guide-fed-records/groups/000.html

Assembly Membership   When the 101 statutory voting members of the ACUS meet in plenary session, they are referred to as the Assembly. The Assembly comprises three types of voting members: Council members, Government members, and public members. Nonvoting members—liaison representatives, special counsels, and senior fellows—may not make motions during plenary sessions and are not reckoned as part of the Assembly. https://www.acus.gov/members

Blog   "Administrative Fix" is the agency's official blog. https://www.acus.gov/administrative-fix-blog

Calendar   A calendar of meetings and events is available online. https://www.acus.gov/meetings-and-events/calendar

Career Opportunities   Current job openings and information on internships and the research fellow program are accessible on the "Opportunities" web page. https://www.acus.gov/opportunities

Committees   The ACUS currently has standing committees on adjudication, administration and management, judicial review, regulation, and rulemaking. https://www.acus.gov/committees

Documents   The ACUS maintains a database of electronic documents that are accessible and searchable. https://www.acus.gov/documents/advanced-search

Freedom of Information Act (FOIA)   The FOIA generally provides that any person has the right to obtain access to Federal agency records, except to the extent that those records are shielded from disclosure by the FOIA or another statute. Formal FOIA requests are unnecessary when seeking information that is publicly available. Before filing a formal FOIA request, an information seeker should search the ACUS website for relevant documents that are already accessible in the public domain and without charge. If the desired document cannot be found on the ACUS website, consider contacting the FOIA liaison. Getting assistance prior to filing a formal request may shorten the response time. Phone, 202-480-2080. https://www.acus.gov/foia

News   The ACUS posts news items on its "Latest News" web page. https://www.acus.gov/newsroom

Press Kit   The ACUS posted a press kit on its website. https://www.acus.gov/press-kit

Publications   Articles, books, papers, reports, and bibliographies are accessible online. https://www.acus.gov/publications

Recommendations   The ACUS maintains an online searchable database of recommendations. The 19 statements that the ACUS has adopted are also included in the database. A statement is adopted when the ACUS seeks to express its views on a matter without making a formal recommendation on the subject. https://www.acus.gov/recommendations

Site Map   The website map allows visitors to look for specific topics or to browse content that aligns with their interests. https://www.acus.gov/sitemap

Social Media   The ACUS maintains a Facebook account. https://www.facebook.com/ACUSgov

The ACUS tweets announcements and other newsworthy items on Twitter. https://twitter.com/ACUSgov

The Sources of Information were updated 12–2019.

Staff Directory   The ACUS maintains a staff directory on its website. https://www.acus.gov/directory/staff

---

Central Intelligence Agency

Washington, DC 20505
Phone, 703-482-0623. Internet, http://www.cia.gov

Director	GINA C. HASPEL
Deputy Director	VAUGHN F. BISHOP
Chief Operating Officer	ANDREW MAKRIDIS
Director of Public Affairs	BRITTANY BRAMELL
General Counsel	COURTNEY SIMMONS ELWOOD
https://www.cia.gov/about-cia/leadership	

Office of Inspector General
Inspector General   (VACANCY)
https://www.cia.gov/offices-of-cia/inspector-general

The above list of key personnel was updated 8–2020.

The Central Intelligence Agency collects, evaluates, and disseminates vital information on economic, military, political, scientific, and other developments abroad to safeguard national security.

Establishment and Organization
On July 26, 1947, President Harry S. Truman approved Public Law 80–253, which is commonly cited as the National Security Act of 1947. The Act established the Central Intelligence Agency (CIA). https://www.loc.gov/law/help/statutes-at-large/80th-congress/session-1/c80s1ch343.pdf

The President appoints the Director by the advice and with the consent of the Senate. The Director serves as the head of the CIA and reports to the Director of National Intelligence (DNI) regarding the activities of the Agency. https://www.cia.gov/about-cia/todays-cia

The National Security Act has been amended since its enactment in 1947 (50 U.S.C. 3001 et seq.). The CIA now functions under the original Act, as amended; Executive Order 12333 of December 4, 1981; the Intelligence Reform and Terrorism Prevention Act of 2004; and other laws, Executive orders, regulations, and directives. https://www.govinfo.gov/content/pkg/

USCODE-2017-title50/pdf/USCODE-2017-title50-chap44.pdf

The CIA's statement of organization is found in 32 CFR 1900. https://www.govinfo.gov/content/pkg/CFR-2018-title32-vol6/pdf/CFR-2018-title32-vol6-subtitleB-chapXIX.pdf

The CIA posts its organizational graphic online in Portable Document Format (PDF). https://www.cia.gov/about-cia/todays-cia/Offices_of_CIA.pdf

Activities
The CIA uses human source collection and other means to gather intelligence; however, it neither carries out internal security functions nor exercises police, subpoena, or other law enforcement powers. The Agency correlates, evaluates, and disseminates national security intelligence. It also directs and coordinates intelligence collecting outside the United States by U.S. intelligence community elements authorized to engage in human source collection. https://www.cia.gov/about-cia

In coordination with other departments, agencies, and authorized elements of the U.S. Government, the CIA ensures that resources are used effectively and that adequate consideration is given to the risks, both to the United States and to those involved in collecting intelligence abroad. The Agency carries out other intelligence-related tasks that are necessary for safeguarding national security, as the President or the DNI may indicate. Under the direction of the DNI and consistent with section 207 of the Foreign Service Act of 1980, the CIA coordinates relationships between elements of the U.S. intelligence community and the security or intelligence services of foreign governments or international organizations in matters of national security and clandestine intelligence. https://www.cia.gov/library/publications/resources/cia-at-a-glance/what-we-do.html

Sources of Information

Agency Offices   The CIA comprises seven components: directorate of analysis, directorate of operations, directorate of science and technology, directorate of support, directorate of digital innovation, mission centers, and offices of the Director. https://www.cia.gov/offices-of-cia

Archived Records   The "Guide to Federal Records in the National Archives of the United States" indicates that CIA records have been assigned to record group 263. https://www.archives.gov/research/guide-fed-records/groups/263.html

Bibliography of Intelligence Literature   The CIA's online bibliography contains works representing a wide spectrum of views on intelligence and the Agency. The readings cover history, opinion, technology, and some of the key figures who are associated with intelligence. https://www.cia.gov/library/intelligence-literature/index.html

Blog   The CIA maintains a blog on its website. https://www.cia.gov/news-information/blog

Career Opportunities   To carry out its mission, the CIA relies on analysts, attorneys, engineers, graphic designers, foreign language instructors, mechanics and truck drivers, physicians and psychiatrists, and other professionals. https://www.cia.gov/careers

Chiefs of State   The CIA updates its online directory of "Chiefs of State and Cabinet Members of Foreign Governments" regularly. https://www.cia.gov/library/publications/resources/world-leaders-1

Contact Information   The CIA posts contact information on its website. https://www.cia.gov/contact-cia

Federal Register   Documents that the CIA has published in the Federal Register are accessible online. https://www.federalregister.gov/agencies/central-intelligence-agency

Foreign Languages   Abridged versions of the CIA's website content is available in several foreign languages. https://www.cia.gov/foreign-languages

Freedom of Information Act (FOIA)   The FOIA gives a right to obtain access to Federal agency records to any person, except to a fugitive from the law. Some records, or portions of them, are, however, shielded from disclosure by one or more of nine statutory exemptions or by specific harm that disclosure may cause. The CIA shields classified national security information, information relating to intelligence sources and methods, and organizational information from release under the FOIA. An information seeker may submit a FOIA request for records by sending it to the FOIA Requester Service Center, Central Intelligence Agency, Washington, DC 20505. A request also may be submitted by facsimile. Fax, 703-613-3007. https://www.cia.gov/library/readingroom/foia-annual-report

The CIA maintains an online FOIA reading room. https://www.cia.gov/library/readingroom

Frequently Asked Questions (FAQs)   The CIA posts answers to FAQs. https://www.cia.gov/about-cia/faqs

History   President Harry S. Truman approved the National Security Act of 1947, creating a permanent central agency for intelligence. His approval was not the beginning of the story: 6 years prior to the formal establishment of the CIA, various renditions of an intelligence agency had occurred. To learn more of the story that underlies today's CIA, visit the "History of the CIA" web page. https://www.cia.gov/about-cia/history-of-the-cia

Maps By country, maps of administration, physiography, and transportation are posted on the CIA website. https://www.cia.gov/library/publications/resources/cia-maps-publications

Museum The CIA Museum's online collection allows visitors to learn more about the Agency through an interactive timeline, historical artifacts, and stories. https://www.cia.gov/about-cia/cia-museum/experience-the-collection

Press Releases / Statements The CIA posts press releases and statements on its website. https://www.cia.gov/news-information/press-releases-statements

Publications The "Publications" web page provides convenient access to resources like "The World Factbook," "Chiefs of State and Cabinet Members of Foreign Governments," and "Maps of the CIA." It also provides easy access to a variety of publications on diverse subjects. https://www.cia.gov/library/publications

Site Map The website map allows visitors to look for specific topics or to browse for content that aligns with their interests. https://www.cia.gov/sitemap.html

Social Media The CIA has a Facebook account. https://www.facebook.com/Central.Intelligence.Agency

The CIA tweets announcements and other newsworthy items on Twitter. https://twitter.com/CIA

The CIA posts videos on its YouTube channel. https://www.youtube.com/user/ciagov

Spy Kids The "Spy Kids" website has materials that are suitable for K–5th grade, 6–12th grade, and parents and teachers. The website's main sections are "Games," "Spy Dogs," and "Stories." A spy dog is a member of the CIA's K9 Corps, whose dogs sniff out explosives and protect CIA officers and buildings from bombs and other explosive threats. https://www.cia.gov/kids-page

World Factbook For 267 world entities, the CIA posts information on their histories, peoples and societies, governments, economies, energy sources, geographies, communications, modes of transportation, militaries, and transnational issues. https://www.cia.gov/library/publications/resources/the-world-factbook

The Sources of Information were updated 8–2020.

Commodity Futures Trading Commission

1155 Twenty-first Street NW, Washington, DC 20581
Phone, 202-418-5000. 202-418-5514 (TTY). Fax, 202-418-5521. Internet, http://www.cftc.gov/index.htm

Commissioners

Chair	Heath P. Tarbert
	Rostin Behnam
	Daniel M. Berkovitz
	Dawn DeBerry Stump
	Brian D. Quintenz

https://www.cftc.gov/About/Commissioners/index.htm

Divisions

Directors	
Clearing and Risk	M. Clark Hutchison III
Enforcement	James M. McDonald
Market Oversight	Amir R. Zaidi
Swap Dealer and Intermediary Oversight	Joshua B. Sterling

https://www.cftc.gov/About/CFTCOrganization/index.htm

Offices

Executive Director	ANTHONY C. THOMPSON
Chief Economist	BRUCE TUCKMAN
Chief Information Officer	JOHN L. ROGERS
General Counsel	DANIEL J. DAVIS
Directors	
External Affairs	MICHAEL C. SHORT
International Affairs	MAURICIO MELARA, ACTING
Legislative and Intergovernmental Affairs	ANN WRIGHT, ACTING
Minority and Women Inclusion	SARAH J. SUMMERVILLE

https://www.cftc.gov/Contact/index.htm

Office of Inspector General

Inspector General	A. ROY LAVIK

https://www.cftc.gov/About/OfficeoftheInspectorGeneral/
index.htm

The above list of key personnel was updated 8–2019.

The Commodity Futures Trading Commission avoids systemic risk; fosters open, transparent, competitive, and financially sound markets; and protects the market users and their funds, consumers, and the public from fraud, manipulation, and abusive practices related to derivatives and other products that are subject to the Commodity Exchange Act.

Establishment and Organizational

On October 23, 1974, President Gerald R. Ford approved Public Law 93–463, which is commonly cited as the Commodity Futures Trading Commission Act of 1974 (7 U.S.C. 2). The Act established the Commodity Futures Trading Commission (CFTC), which became operational in April of 1975. The U.S. Congress renewed the CFTC's authority to regulate futures trading in 1978, 1982, 1986, 1992, 1995, 2000, and 2008. https://www.govinfo.gov/content/pkg/STATUTE-88/pdf/STATUTE-88-Pg1389.pdf

In 2010, Title VII of the Dodd-Frank Wall Street Reform and Consumer Protection Act (Public Law 111–203) gave the CFTC new and expanded responsibilities and authorities for regulating the swaps marketplace. https://www.govinfo.gov/content/pkg/STATUTE-124/pdf/STATUTE-124-Pg1376.pdf

The President appoints the CFTC's five Commissioners by the advice and with the consent of the Senate. The President designates one Commissioner, also by the Senate's advice and with its consent, to serve as the Chair. The Commissioners serve staggered 5-year terms, and no more than three of them may belong to the same political party. https://www.cftc.gov/About/Commissioners/index.htm

The Commission has nine major operating components: the Divisions of Market Oversight, Clearing and Risk, Swap Dealer and Intermediary Oversight, Enforcement, and the Offices of the Executive Director, the General Counsel, the Chief Economist, International Affairs, and Data and Technology. The Office of Inspector General is an independent organizational unit at the CFTC.

The CFTC's statement of organization is found in 17 CFR 140. https://www.ecfr.gov/cgi-bin/retrieveECFR?gp=&SID=ad2cd54a43272e3456dfc1088505c4e4&mc=true&n=pt17.2.140&r=PART&ty=HTML

The CFTC posts it organizational chart online in Portable Document Format (PDF). https://www.cftc.gov/media/2261/cftcorgchart071519/download

Activities

The CFTC regulates trading on the U.S. futures and options markets that offer commodity futures and options contracts, as well as the swaps marketplace in the United States. Oversight of the derivatives marketplace is accomplished through various CFTC activities.

The CFTC oversees derivatives clearing organizations and other market participants in the clearing process, including futures commission merchants, swap dealers, major swap participants, and large traders. The CFTC oversees the registration and compliance of intermediaries and futures industry self-regulatory organizations, including U.S. derivatives exchanges and the National Futures Association. It also oversees trade execution facilities and data repositories, conducts surveillance, reviews new exchange applications, and examines existing exchanges to ensure compliance with applicable core principles. https://www.cftc.gov/About/MissionResponsibilities/index.htm

Exercising the agency's authority, its staff also investigates and prosecutes alleged violations of the Commodity Exchange Act and CFTC regulations. Potential violations include fraud, manipulation, and other abuses concerning commodity derivatives and swaps that threaten market integrity, market participants, and the general public. https://www.cftc.gov/LawRegulation/CommodityExchangeAct/index.htm

Under the Dodd-Frank Wall Street Reform and Consumer Protection Act, the CFTC develops and monitors compliance with regulations addressing registration, business conduct standards, capital adequacy, and margin requirements for swap dealers and major swap participants. https://www.cftc.gov/LawRegulation/DoddFrankAct/index.htm

Sources of Information

Business Opportunities The Commission has recurring requirements for the following goods: furniture, office equipment and supplies, and telecommunications equipment and supplies. It also has recurring requirements for copying and printing services and minor construction. http://www.cftc.gov/About/ProcurementOpportunities/index.htm

Career Opportunities The Commission hires professionals with strong academic records and superior analytical and problem solving skills. http://www.cftc.gov/About/Careers/index.htm

In 2018, the CFTC ranked 23d among 29 small Government agencies in the Partnership for Public Service's Best Places To Work Agency Rankings. https://bestplacestowork.org/rankings/detail/CT00

Climate-Related Market Risk The CFTC has established a subcommittee to prepare a report that identifies and examines climate change-related financial and market risks for the agency's Market Risk Advisory Committee. The climate-related market risk subcommittee will bring experts from academia, industry, and the public sector together to identify and examine the risks that climate change poses to the stability of the U.S. financial system. The subcommittee will propose future actions for policymakers and market participants to consider for mitigating these risks. https://www.cftc.gov/PressRoom/PressReleases/7963-19

Cotton Futures The "Cotton On-Call Report" shows the quantity of bought or sold call cotton on which the price has not been fixed, together with the respective futures on which the purchase or sale is based. Call cotton refers to physical cotton bought or sold, or contracted for purchase or sale at a price to be fixed later based upon a specified delivery month future's price. https://www.cftc.gov/MarketReports/CottonOnCall/index.htm

Disciplinary History Making the CFTC's disciplinary history accessible is part of the agency's ongoing effort to protect market participants and the public from fraud, manipulation, and abusive practices. https://www.cftc.gov/ConsumerProtection/DisciplinaryHistory/index.htm

Forms / Submissions Forms and submissions information for designated contract markets, filing tips and complaints, future commissions merchants, and ownership and control reporting are available online. https://www.cftc.gov/Forms/index.htm

Freedom of Information Act (FOIA) The FOIA gives the right to request access to Federal agency records or information to any person. All agencies of the U.S. Government must disclose records upon receiving a written request for them, except for records that the FOIA's nine exemptions and three exclusions shield from disclosure. This right of access is enforceable in court. http://www.cftc.gov/FOI/index.htm | Email: FOIAsubmissions@cftc.gov

In addition to maintaining a physical, onsite reading room in Washington, DC, the CFTC also has an electronic reading room. Information seekers should see if the records that they seek are immediately available and accessible free of charge in the electronic reading room before submitting a FOIA request. https://www.cftc.gov/FOI/foiareadingrooms.html

Frequently Asked Questions (FAQs)   The "Ask CFTC" web page provides answers to some basic questions regarding the futures markets and how they work, where to go for help, as well as answers to other FAQs. https://www.cftc.gov/ConsumerProtection/EducationCenter/index.htm

Glossary   The online glossary defines specialized words and phrases that are used in the futures industry. Standard reference works do not include some of them. http://www.cftc.gov/ConsumerProtection/EducationCenter/CFTCGlossary/index.htm

History   Futures contracts for agricultural commodities have been traded in the country for more than 150 years. The Federal Government has regulated them since the 1920s. When the CFTC was created in 1974, most futures trading took place in the agricultural sector. Over the years, the futures industry has become increasingly varied and complex. To learn more of the history of the futures trading industry and the Federal Government's role in regulating it, visit the "History of the CFTC" web page. https://www.cftc.gov/About/HistoryoftheCFTC/index.htm

LabCFTC   LabCFTC is the hub for the CFTC's engagement with financial technology innovators. https://www.cftc.gov/LabCFTC/index.htm

Learning Resources   The Office of Consumer Outreach makes information and tools available to help consumers avoid fraud. The "Learning Resources" web page has brochures, reports, videos, and a book to educate consumers on this topic. https://www.cftc.gov/ConsumerProtection/

Resources/index.htm | Email: consumers@cftc.gov

The "Avoid Fraud" web page has additional resources. https://www.cftc.gov/ConsumerProtection/FraudAwarenessPrevention/index.htm

Money Laundering   A general outline of important anti-money laundering topics with links to general information and resources is available on the CFTC website. https://www.cftc.gov/IndustryOversight/AntiMoneyLaundering/index.htm

Press Room   The press room provides convenient access to news, podcasts, press releases, remarks, statements, testimonies, webcasts, and information on public events. http://www.cftc.gov/PressRoom/index.htm

Regional Offices   The Commission maintains regional offices in Chicago, IL, and New York, NY, where many of the Nation's designated contract markets are located. Phone, 312-596-0700 (IL); Phone, 646-746-9700 (NY). A third regional office is located in Kansas City, MO. Phone, 816-960-7700.

Site Map   The Web site map allows visitors to look for specific topics or to browse content that aligns with their interests. http://www.cftc.gov/SiteMap/index.htm

Swaps Report   The "CFTC Swaps Report" is published every Wednesday at 3:30 p.m., unless otherwise noted. https://www.cftc.gov/MarketReports/SwapsReports/index.htm | Email: swapsreport@cftc.gov

Virtual Currencies   One of the most recent marketplace developments driving a lot of interest is the rise in prominence of virtual currencies, specifically bitcoin. The "Bitcoin and Other Virtual Currencies" web page has resources for market participants and customers on virtual currency and on the CFTC's role in overseeing this emerging innovation. https://www.cftc.gov/Bitcoin/index.htm

Whistleblower Program   The Commission gives monetary incentives to whistleblowers who report possible Commodity Exchange Act violations that lead to a successful enforcement action. The Commission also provides antiretaliation protections, confidentiality, and privacy. https://www.whistleblower.gov

The Sources of Information were updated 8–2019.

Consumer Financial Protection Bureau

1700 G Street NW., Washington, DC 20552
Phone, 202-435-7000. Internet, http://www.consumerfinance.gov

Office of the Director

Director	KATHLEEN L. KRANINGER
Deputy Director	BRIAN JOHNSON, ACTING
Chief Communications Officer / Spokesperson	JOHN CZWARTACKI
Chief of Staff	KIRSTEN SUTTON
Principal Policy Director	BRIAN JOHNSON
Associate Director	
Equal Opportunity and Fairness	ALTHEA KIREILIS
ASSISTANT DIRECTORS	
Civil Rights	M. STACEY BACH
Minority and Women Inclusion	(VACANCY)
https://www.consumerfinance.gov/about-us/the-bureau/about-director/	
Administrative Law Judge	CHRISTINE KIRBY
Ombudsman	WENDY KAMENSHINE

Consumer Education and Engagement Division

Policy Associate Director	SHEILA GREENWOOD
Associate Director	GAIL HILLEBRAND
Assistant Directors	
Community Affairs	DANIEL DODD-RAMIREZ
Consumer Engagement	GENE KOO
Consumer Response	CHRISTOPHER JOHNSON
Financial Education	JANNEKE RATCLIFFE
Financial Education—Students and Young Consumers	(VACANCY)
Older Americans	STACY CANAN
Servicemember Affairs	PATRICK CAMPBELL, ACTING
https://www.consumerfinance.gov/about-us/the-bureau/bureau-structure/consumer-education-engagement	

External Affairs Division

Policy Associate Director	ANTHONY WELCHER
Associate Director	ZIXTA MARTINEZ
Assistant Directors	
Advisory Board and Councils	DELICIA HAND
Financial Institutions and Business Liaison	DANIEL SMITH
Intergovernmental Affairs	CHERYL PARKER ROSE
Legislative Affairs	CATHERINE GALICIA
Public Engagement and Community Liaison	KEO CHEA
https://www.consumerfinance.gov/about-us/the-bureau/bureau-structure/external-affairs	

Legal Division

General Counsel	MARY MCLEOD
Principal Deputy General Counsel	RICHARD LEPLEY
Deputy General Counsels	
General Law and Ethics	SONYA WHITE
Law and Policy	STEPHEN VAN METER

Consumer Financial Protection Bureau

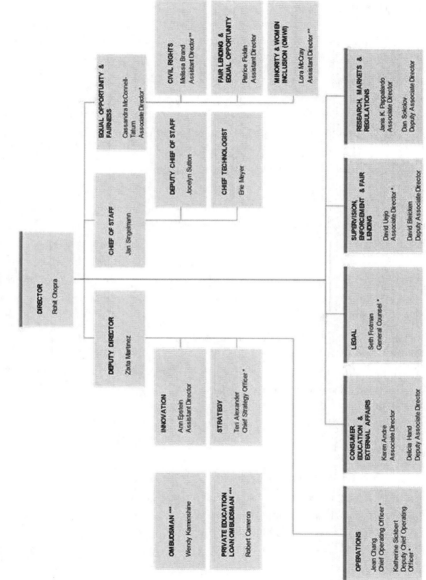

DIRECTOR
Rohit Chopra

CHIEF OF STAFF
Jen Singelmann

DEPUTY DIRECTOR
Zixta Martinez

EQUAL OPPORTUNITY & FAIRNESS
Cassandra McConnell-Tatum
Associate Director*

DEPUTY CHIEF OF STAFF
Jocelyn Sutton

CHIEF TECHNOLOGIST
Erie Meyer

CIVIL RIGHTS
Melissa Brand
Assistant Director***

FAIR LENDING & EQUAL OPPORTUNITY
Patrice Ficklin
Assistant Director

MINORITY & WOMEN INCLUSION (OMWI)
Lora McCray
Assistant Director***

INNOVATION
Ann Epstein
Assistant Director

STRATEGY
Teri Alexander
Chief Strategy Officer*

OMBUDSMAN*
Wendy Kamenshine

PRIVATE EDUCATION LOAN OMBUDSMAN*
Robert Cameron

OPERATIONS
Jean Chang
Chief Operating Officer*
Katherine Sickbert
Deputy Chief Operating Officer*

CONSUMER EDUCATION & EXTERNAL AFFAIRS
Karen Andre
Associate Director
Delicia Hand
Deputy Associate Director

LEGAL
Seth Frotman
General Counsel*

SUPERVISION, ENFORCEMENT & FAIR LENDING
David Uejio
Associate Director*
David Bleicken
Deputy Associate Director

RESEARCH, MARKETS & REGULATIONS
Janis K. Pappalardo
Associate Director
Dan Sokolov
Deputy Associate Director

Litigation and Oversight
https://www.consumerfinance.gov/about-us/the-bureau/
  bureau-structure/legal

JOHN COLEMAN

Operations Division

Chief Operating Officer

KATE FULTON, ACTING

Chief Officers
Administrative Officer
Human Capital
Information
Financial
Procurement
https://www.consumerfinance.gov/about-us/the-bureau/
  bureau-structure/operations

MARTIN MICHALOSKY
JEFFREY SUMBERG
JERRY HORTON
ELIZABETH REILLY
DAVID GRAGAN

Research, Markets, and Regulations Division

Policy Associate Director
Associate Director

THOMAS PAHL
DAVID SILBERMAN

Assistant Directors

Card, Payment and Deposit Markets
Consumer Lending, Reporting and Collection Markets
Mortgage Markets
Small Business Lending Markets
Regulations
Research
https://www.consumerfinance.gov/about-us/the-bureau/
  bureau-structure/research-markets-regulation

WILLIAM WADE-GERY
JOHN MCNAMARA
MARK MCARDLE
GRADY HEDGESPETH
KELLY COCHRAN
RON BORZEKOWSKI

Supervision, Enforcement and Fair Lending Division

Policy Associate Director
Associate Director

ERIC BLANKENSTEIN
CHRISTOPHER D'ANGELO

Assistant Directors
Enforcement
Fair Lending and Equal Opportunity
Supervision Examinations
Supervision Policy

KRISTEN DONOGHUE
PATRICE FICKLIN
PAUL SANFORD
PEGGY TWOHIG

Regional Directors
Midwest region
Northeast region
Southeast region
West region
https://www.consumerfinance.gov/about-us/the-bureau/
  bureau-structure/supervision-enforcement-fair-lending
Office of Inspector General

JOHN SCHROEDER
MITCHELL KENT
JAMES L. CARLEY
EDWIN CHOW

Inspector General
https://oig.federalreserve.gov/the-inspector-general.htm

MARK BIALEK

The above list of key personnel was updated 12–2018.

The Consumer Financial Protection Bureau (CFPB) helps consumer finance markets work by making rules more effective, by consistently and fairly enforcing those rules, and by empowering consumers to take more control over their economic lives.

The Consumer Financial Protection Bureau (CFPB) is an independent Federal agency established by title X of the Dodd-Frank Wall Street Reform and Consumer Protection Act of 2012 (12 U.S.C. 5491). The CFPB is headed by a Director whom the President appoints and the Senate confirms.

Activities

The Bureau regulates the offering and provision of consumer financial products and services under Federal consumer financial laws. It gives consumers the information they need to understand the terms of their agreements with financial companies. It also makes regulations and guidance as clear and streamlined as possible so providers of consumer financial products and services can understand and follow the rules without assistance.

The CFPB's principal activities center on writing rules, supervising companies, and enforcing Federal consumer financial protection laws; restricting unfair, deceptive, or abusive acts or practices; taking consumer complaints; promoting financial education; researching consumer behavior; monitoring financial markets for new risks to consumers; and enforcing laws that prohibit discrimination and other unfair treatment in consumer finance. http://www.consumerfinance.gov/the-bureau

Sources of Information

Blog   The CFPB maintains a blog on its website. https://www.consumerfinance.gov/about-us/blog/?filter_blog_category=At+the+CFPB&filter_range_date_gte=&filter_range_date_lte=

Bureau Structure / Organizational Chart   The "Bureau Structure" web page offers visitors a two-dimensional representation of the CFPB's organizational structure, which also includes the names of officials filling key leadership positions. https://www.consumerfinance.gov/about-us/the-bureau/bureau-structure

Business Opportunities   Information on doing business with the CFPB is available online. http://www.consumerfinance.gov/doing-business-with-us

Career Opportunities   The CFPB posts new job openings online, as well as information on the application process and opportunities for students and recent graduates. http://www.consumerfinance.gov/about-us/careers | Email: jobs@consumerfinance.gov

In 2018, the CFPB ranked 26th among 27 midsize Government agencies in the Partnership for Public Service's Best Places To Work Agency Rankings. https://bestplacestowork.org/rankings/detail/FRFT

Consumer Help   The CFPB forwards financial product or service complaints to the company offering the product or service and then works to get an appropriate response. A form for filing a complaint and a searchable complaint database are accessible online. Assistance by phone is available on weekdays, excluding Federal holidays, 8 a.m.–8 p.m., eastern standard time. Phone, 855-411-2372. TTY/TDD, 855-729-2372. http://www.consumerfinance.gov/complaint

Data   The CFPB publishes research and posts consumer financial marketplace information online. http://www.consumerfinance.gov/data-research

Educational Resources   Resources for educators, librarians, parents, and those who manage someone else's money are available online. http://www.consumerfinance.gov/adult-financial-education

Fraud / Scams   The CFPB's online resources can help consumers prevent, recognize, and report scams and fraud. https://www.consumerfinance.gov/consumer-tools/fraud

Freedom of Information Act (FOIA)   A FOIA request may be submitted by email, fax, or letter. The CFPB recommends using email for making a submission. http://www.consumerfinance.gov/foia-requests/submit-request | Email: CFPB_FOIA@consumerfinance.gov

Frequently Asked Questions (FAQs)   The CFPB website has clear and impartial answers to hundreds of financial questions. The topics covered include auto loans, bank accounts and services, credit cards, credit reports and scores, debt collection, families and money, money transfers, mortgages, payday loans, prepaid cards, and student loans. https://www.consumerfinance.gov/ask-cfpb | Email: info@consumerfinance.gov

Home Mortgage Disclosure Act (HMDA) The CFPB's website features a 3-minute video that explains the purpose of the HMDA. https://www.consumerfinance.gov/data-research/hmda

Invite the CFPB Send an email to invite a CFPB employee to contribute to a publication or participate in a discussion, forum, or other event. Email: invitations2cfpb@consumerfinance.gov

In Your Language In the United States, the most widely spoken foreign languages are Chinese, French, Haitian Créole, Korean, Spanish, Tagalog (Filipino), and Vietnamese. To help those who speak these languages, the CFPB provides information in them for accessing common products and making basic transactions. Assistance by phone is available in more than 180 languages. Phone, 855-411-2372. https://www.consumerfinance.gov/language

Newsroom Blog posts, press releases, and speeches are accessible online. An online subscription form is available to receive press releases via email. http://www.consumerfinance.gov/about-us/newsroom

Open Government The CFPB supports the Open Government initiative by promoting the principles of collaboration, participation, and transparency. http://www.consumerfinance.gov/open-government

Organizational Chart The CFPB is currently revising its organizational chart. https://www.consumerfinance.gov/about-us/the-bureau/bureau-structure/

Plain Writing CFPB editors and writers apply plain language principles in all of their consumer-oriented materials. They want to know if something on the CFPB website or in its printed materials is unclear. http://www.consumerfinance.gov/plain-writing | Email: CFPB_Plain_Writing_Act@consumerfinance.gov

Publications CFPB publications, in English and Spanish, may be ordered in bulk online. http://promotions.usa.gov/cfpbpubs.html

Social Media The CFPB maintains a Facebook account. https://www.facebook.com/CFPB

The CFPB tweets announcements and other newsworthy items on Twitter. https://twitter.com/cfpb

The CFPB posts videos on its YouTube channel. https://www.youtube.com/user/cfpbvideo

Whistleblowers The CFPB wants to know about companies that may be breaking Federal consumer financial laws. A current or former employee of such a company, an industry insider who knows of such a company, or a competitor being unfairly undercut by such a company—people like these should report alleged violations to the CFPB. Phone, 855-695-7974. http://www.consumerfinance.gov/blog/the-cfpb-wants-you-to-blow-the-whistle-on-lawbreakers | Email: whistleblower@cfpb.gov http://www.consumerfinance.gov/contact-us | Email: info@consumerfinance.gov

For further information, contact the Consumer Financial Protection Bureau, 1700 G Street NW., Washington, DC 20552. Phone, 202-435-7000.

Consumer Product Safety Commission

4330 East-West Highway, Bethesda, MD 20814
Phone, 301-504-7923. Internet, http://www.cpsc.gov

Commissioners

Chair
https://www.cpsc.gov/About-CPSC/Chairman/Robert-Adler

ROBERT S. ADLER, ACTING

DANA BAIOCCO
ANN MARIE BUERKLE
PETER A. FELDMAN
ELLIOT F. KAYE

https://www.cpsc.gov/About-CPSC/Commissioners

Independent Offices

Directors	
Communications	JOSEPH MARTYAK
Equal Employment Opportunity and Minority Enterprise	BRITTANY WOOLFOLK
Legislative Affairs	CHRISTOPHER HUDGINS
General Counsel	PATRICIA HANZ
Secretary	ALBERTA MILLS
Offices of the Executive Director	
Executive Director	MARY T. BOYLE
Operations Support	
Deputy Executive Director	MONICA SUMMITT
Assistant Executive Director	
Information and Technology Services	JAMES C. ROLFES
Chief Officers	
Financial	JAY HOFFMAN
Information	JAMES C. ROLFES
Directors	
Facilities Services	MARK OEMLER
Financial Management, Planning, and Evaluation	JAY HOFFMAN
Human Resources Management	DONNA M. SIMPSON
Safety Operations	
Deputy Executive Director	DEWANE RAY
Assistant Executive Directors	
Compliance and Field Operations	ROBERT KAYE
Hazard Identification and Reduction	DUANE BONIFACE
Directors	
International Programs	RICHARD O'BRIEN
Import Surveillance	JAMES JOHOLSKE
Small Business Ombudsman	SHELBY MATHIS
https://www.cpsc.gov/s3fs-public/cpscorgchartMM_081919_0.pdf?o.qldWd.ny4Xw2xhWhRJT7Ju.5KEsS_5	
Inspector General	CHRISTOPHER W. DENTEL
https://www.cpsc.gov/About-CPSC/Inspector-General	

The above list of key personnel was updated 10–2019.

The Consumer Product Safety Commission protects the public by reducing the risk of injury and death from consumer products.

Establishment and Organization

On October 27, 1972, President Richard M. Nixon approved Public Law 92–573, which is commonly cited as the Consumer Product Safety Act (15 U.S.C. 2051 et seq.). The Act established the Consumer Product Safety Commission (CPSC) as an independent regulatory agency. The CPSC became operational on May 14, 1973. https://www.govinfo.gov/content/pkg/STATUTE-86/pdf/STATUTE-86-Pg1207.pdf

Thirty six years later, President George W. Bush approved the reauthorization and modernization of the CPSC by signing the Consumer Product Safety Improvement Act of 2008 (PL 110–314) on August 14. https://www.govinfo.gov/content/pkg/STATUTE-122/pdf/STATUTE-122-Pg3016.pdf

The Commission comprises a maximum of five commissioners. The President appoints each commissioner by the advice and with the consent of the Senate for a term of 7 years. The President also designates one commissioner to serve as Chair. No more than three of the commissioners may be affiliated with the same political party (15 USC 2053). https://uscode.house. gov/view.xhtml?path=/prelim@title15/ chapter47&edition=prelim

The CPSC implements provisions of the Flammable Fabrics Act (15 U.S.C. 1191), Poison Prevention Packaging Act of 1970 (15 U.S.C. 1471), Federal Hazardous Substances Act (15 U.S.C. 1261), Children's Gasoline Burn Prevention Act (15 U.S.C. 2056 note), Virginia Graeme Baker Pool and Spa Safety Act (15 U.S.C. 8001 et seq.), and an act of 2 August 1956 (15 U.S.C. 1211) prohibiting the transportation of refrigerators without door safety devices. https://uscode. house.gov/view.xhtml?path=/prelim@ title15&edition=prelim

The CPSC's organization and functions are found in 16 CFR 1000. https://www.ecfr. gov/cgi-bin/text-idx?gp=&SID=09442eace6 033ddfb202786dac3646bf&mc=true&tpl=/ ecfrbrowse/Title16/16CIIsubchapA.tpl

The agency's organizational chart is available in Portable Document Format (PDF) for viewing and downloading on the "About CPSC" web page. https://www.cpsc. gov/About-CPSC

Activities

To protect the public from risk of injury, the CPSC requires manufacturers to report defects in products presenting substantial hazards; conducts outreach programs for consumers, industry, and local governments; collects information on consumer product-related injuries and maintains the National Injury Information Clearinghouse; conducts research on consumer product hazards; and encourages and assists in the development of voluntary standards affecting the safety of consumer products. When appropriate, the CPSC requires manufacturers to correct hazards associated with specific consumer products already in circulation, establishes mandatory consumer product standards, and bans hazardous products. http://www.

cpsc.gov/en/about-cpsc/national-injury-information-clearinghouse

The Commission also has a special project to reach as many Americans as possible with lifesaving safety information. The Neighborhood Safety Network disseminates safety information to hard-to-reach populations by partnering with other organizations already active within their communities. http://www.cpsc.gov/en/safety-education/neighborhood-safety-network

Sources of Information

All-Terrain Vehicles (ATVs) ATVs are powerful, fast, and potentially dangerous. The CPSC posts ATV safety information online. http://www.cpsc.gov/en/Safety-Education/Safety-Education-Centers/ATV-Safety-Information-Center

Annual Reports The CPSC posts its annual reports online. https://www.cpsc.gov/About-CPSC/Agency-Reports/Annual-Reports

Archived Records The records of the CPSC are referenced in the "Guide to Federal Records in the National Archives of the United States." The Guide is accessible online, and CPSC records have been assigned to Record Group 424. https://www.archives.gov/research/guide-fed-records/groups/424.html

Blog The CPSC maintains a blog on its "OnSafety" website. https://onsafety.cpsc.gov

Career Opportunities To carry out its mission, the CPSC relies on attorneys and paralegal specialists, compliance officers, economists, engineers, IT specialists, product safety investigators, program analysts, statisticians, toxicologists and pharmacologists and chemists, and other skilled professionals. http://www.cpsc.gov/en/About-CPSC/Job

In 2018, the CPSC ranked 14th among 29 small agencies in the Partnership for Public Service's Best Places To Work Agency Rankings. http://bestplacestowork.org/BPTW/rankings/detail/SK00

Contact Information Contact information for specific offices and other public information are available on the CPSC's website. https://www.cpsc.gov/About-CPSC/Contact-Information/Contact-Specific-Offices-and-Public-Information

Data The CPSC makes it data, deliberations, and decisions accessible to consumers, developers, and stakeholders. https://www.cpsc.gov/Data

Fire Safety   Several generations living in a home increases the need for fire safe practices. To learn more, download the multigenerational fire safety toolkit from the "Neighborhood Safety Network Toolkit" web page. https://www.cpsc.gov/safety-education/neighborhood-safety-network/toolkits/fire-safety

Freedom of Information Act (FOIA)   The Electronic Freedom of Information Act Amendments of 1996 require Federal agencies to use electronic information technology to foster access to and availability of FOIA documents. https://www.cpsc.gov/Newsroom/FOIA | Email: cpsc-foia@cpsc.gov

The CPSC informs the public by using various means: local and national media coverage, publication of booklets and product alerts, responses to FOIA requests, and the National Injury Information Clearinghouse. The agency also maintains its public information center, website, and telephone hotline for the same purpose. http://www.cpsc.gov/newsroom/foia/guide-to-public-information

Frequently Asked Questions (FAQs)   The CPSC posts answers to FAQs on its website. https://www.cpsc.gov/About-CPSC/Contact-Information

Hotline   The Commission operates a toll-free consumer product safety hotline in English and Spanish, on weekdays from 8 a.m. to 5:30 p.m. Phone, 800-638-2772. TTY, 301-595-7054.

Injury Statistics   The CPSC posts injury statistics and technical reports by product category and by hazard category on its website. https://www.cpsc.gov/Research--Statistics

Language Assistance   Read Spanish more easily than English? Visit the en Español version of the CPSC website. https://www.cpsc.gov/es/SeguridadConsumidor

Read Vietnamese more easily than English? Visit the Tiếng Việt web pages of the CPSC website. https://www.cpsc.gov/vi-VN/business-and-manufacturing-landing

Newsroom   The online newsroom features CPSC data, Freedom of Information Act documents, press statements, recent news releases, videos, and a public calendar. http://www.cpsc.gov/en/Newsroom

Open Government   The CPSC supports the Open Government initiative by promoting collaboration, participation, and transparency. https://www.cpsc.gov/About-CPSC/Agency-Reports/open | Email: feedback@cpsc.gov

Recalls   Six Federal agencies with different jurisdictions are collaborating to make the American people more aware of defective, hazardous, and unsafe products. http://www.recalls.gov

Safety Publications   Safety guides, safety alerts, and Neighborhood Safety Network posters are available online to download. https://www.cpsc.gov/Safety-Education/Safety-Guides/General-Information/Publications-Listing

Site Map   The website map allows visitors to look for specific topics or to browse content that aligns with their interests. https://www.cpsc.gov/sitemap

Social Media   The CPSC has a Facebook account. https://www.facebook.com/USCPSC

The CPSC tweets announcements and other newsworthy items on Twitter. https://twitter.com/USCPSC

The CPSC posts videos on its YouTube channel. https://www.youtube.com/uscpsc

Swimming Pools / Spas   Pool and spas safety information is available online. http://www.poolsafely.gov

Toolkits   The Neighborhood Safety Network has toolkits for all-terrain vehicle (ATV) safety, carbon monoxide (CO) awareness, child safety, multigenerational fire safety, and older adults, who are the fastest growing segment of the U.S. population. https://www.cpsc.gov/Safety-Education/Neighborhood-Safety-Network/Neighborhood-Safety-Network-Toolkits

The Sources of Information were updated 10–2019.

Corporation for National and Community Service

250 E Street NW., Washington, DC 20525
Phone, 202-606-5000. Internet, http://www.nationalservice.gov

Chair	SHAMINA SINGH
Vice Chair	DEAN A. REUTER
Member	RICHARD CHRISTMAN
Member	ROMONIA S. DIXON
Member	VICTORIA A. HUGHES
Member	ERIC P. LIU
Member	(VACANCY)
Member	(VACANCY)
Member	(VACANCY)
Member	(VACANCY)
Member	(VACANCY)
Member	(VACANCY)
Member	(VACANCY)
Member	(VACANCY)
Member	(VACANCY)
Chief Executive Officer	WENDY SPENCER
Chief Operating Officer / Chief Financial Officer	JEFFREY PAGE
Chief Human Capital Officer	SUSAN BRADBERRY
Chief Information Officer	THOMAS HANLEY
Chief of External Affairs	THEODORE S. MILLER
Chief of Program Operations	KIMBERLY MANSARAY
Chief of Staff	ASIM MISHRA
Chief Risk Officer	LORI GIBLIN
Director, AmeriCorps NCCC	GINA CROSS, ACTING
Director, AmeriCorps State and National	WILLIAM C. BASL
Director, AmeriCorps VISTA	MAX FINBERG
Director, Government Relations	KIMBERLY L. ALLMAN
Director, Office of Field Liaison	MIKEL HERRINGTON
Director, Office of Research and Evaluation	MARY HYDE
Director, Senior Corps	MIKEL HERRINGTON, ACTING
Director, Social Innovation Fund	DAMIAN THORMAN
General Counsel	JEREMY JOSEPH
Inspector General	DEBORAH J. JEFFREY

The Corporation for National and Community Service improves lives, strengthens communities, and fosters civic engagement through service and volunteering.

The Corporation for National and Community Service (CNCS) was established on October 1, 1993, by the National and Community Service Trust Act of 1993 (42 U.S.C. 12651 et seq.). The CNCS is a Federal corporation governed by a bipartisan board of directors whom the President appoints with the advice and consent of the Senate. The Board sets policies and direction for the Corporation and is responsible for all actions taken by the Chief Executive Officer with respect to standards, policies, procedures, programs, and initiatives as necessary to carry out the CNCS's mission.

As the Nation's largest grantmaker for service and volunteering, the CNCS engages millions of Americans in service through its core programs—AmeriCorps, Senior Corps, the Social Innovation Fund, and the Volunteer Generation Fund—and leads President Obama's nationwide service initiative, United We Serve. The CNCS harnesses America's most powerful resource: the energy and talents of its citizens. From grade school through retirement, the CNCS empowers Americans and fosters a lifetime of service to improve lives, strengthen communities, and foster civic engagement. http://www.nationalservice.gov/about

AmeriCorps   AmeriCorps provides opportunities for more than 75,000 Americans each year to serve their communities. AmeriCorps members recruit, train, and supervise community volunteers; tutor and mentor youth; build affordable housing; teach computer skills; clean parks and streams; run afterschool programs; help nonprofit groups become self-sustaining; and assist communities responding to disasters. In exchange for a year of full-time service, AmeriCorps members earn an education award that can be used for college or graduate school tuition or for repaying qualified student loans. Since 1994 nearly 1 million Americans have served in AmeriCorps, which includes AmeriCorps State and National, AmeriCorps NCCC, and AmeriCorps VISTA.

AmeriCorps State and National supports a wide range of local service programs that engage thousands of Americans in community service each year, providing grants to a network of local and national organizations and agencies committed to using national service to address critical community needs in education, public safety, health, and the environment. Each of these organizations and agencies, in turn, uses its AmeriCorps funding to recruit, place, and supervise AmeriCorps members nationwide.

AmeriCorps State and National operates through national and local nonprofit organizations, public agencies, and faith-based and community groups. More than three-quarters of AmeriCorps grant funding goes to Governor-appointed State service commissions, which in turn award grants to nonprofit groups to respond to local needs. AmeriCorps NCCC (National Civilian Community Corps) is a team-based, residential program for men and women from age 18 to 24 that combines the best practices of civilian service, including leadership and team building. AmeriCorps VISTA (Volunteers in Service to America) members serve full-time for 1 year in nonprofit and faith-based organizations and public agencies to fight poverty, improve health services, increase housing opportunities, and bridge the digital divide. http://www.nationalservice.gov/programs/americorps

Senior Corps   Senior Corps taps the skills, talents, and experience of more than 270,000 Americans age 55 and older to meet a wide range of community challenges through three programs: Retired and Senior Volunteers Program (RSVP), Foster Grandparents, and Senior Companions. RSVP volunteers help local police departments conduct safety patrols, participate in environmental projects, provide educational services to children and adults, respond to natural disasters, and recruit other volunteers. Foster Grandparents serve as tutors and mentors to young people with special needs. Senior Companions help homebound seniors and other adults maintain independence in their own homes. Senior Corps volunteers have served 1.5 million Americans, including 560,000 veterans and 300,000 children. http://www.nationalservice.gov/programs/senior-corps

Social Innovation Fund   The Social Innovation Fund is an approach to transforming lives and communities that allows the Federal Government to serve as a catalyst for promoting community solutions with evidence of strong results. A key White House initiative and CNCS program, the Fund identifies solutions that work and makes them work for more people. It combines public and private resources to foster innovative community-based solutions that have produced results in low-income communities in three priority areas: economic opportunity, health, and youth development. http://www.nationalservice.gov/programs/social-innovation-fund | Email: innovation@cns.gov

Other Initiatives   As the Federal agency for service and volunteerism, the CNCS carries out the Call to Service authority in multiple ways. CNCS initiatives include the Martin Luther King, Jr., National Day of Service; September 11th National Day of Service and Remembrance; President's Higher Education Community Service Honor Roll; National Mentoring Month; and United We Serve, a nationwide effort launched with the White House in 2009 to engage Americans in service to meet community needs. As a result of United We Serve, hundreds of thousands of Americans have joined with friends and neighbors to replenish food banks, provide health services, support veterans and military families, restore public lands, and more. The CNCS has also partnered with other agencies and nonprofit organizations on Let's Read! to reduce summer reading loss and Let's Move! to combat childhood obesity. Other initiatives include the Task Force on Expanding National Service, Mayors Day of Recognition, County Day of Recognition, and Joining Forces, an effort led by First Lady Michelle Obama and Dr. Jill Biden to engage Americans in supporting veterans and military families.

Sources of Information

Blog   The National Service blog features posts of interest to students, recent graduates, retirees, senior citizens, veterans, and others. The range of discussion is expansive—conservation, disaster recovery, nonprofit sector career pathways, voluntarism, and more. http://nationalservice.tumblr.com
Data   The CNCS posts datasets and other information online to support the principles of open government. http://www.nationalservice.gov/about/open-government-initiative/transparency/data-sources

Its Open Government Gallery is a demonstration of the CNCS's commitment to collaboration, participation, and transparency. http://www.nationalservice.gov/about/open-government-initiative/open-government-gallery
Employment   Most CNCS career opportunities are volunteer AmeriCorps and Senior Corps positions. The agency hires full-time employees at its Washington, DC, headquarters and at CNCS offices located across the country. http://www.nationalservice.gov/about/careers | Email: jobs@cns.gov https://www.usajobs.gov/JobSearch/Search/GetResults?OrganizationID=KS00
Grants   To find discretionary funding opportunities that Federal agencies have posted, visit the "Funding Opportunities" Web page. http://www.nationalservice.gov/build-your-capacity/grants/funding-opportunities
Newsroom   The newsroom features media advisories, official statements, press releases, and proclamations. http://www.nationalservice.gov/newsroom#menu-newsroom-dropdown-area
Online Courses   Self-paced instructional courses that subject matter experts created on topics aligning with CNCS strategic initiatives are available online. http://www.nationalservice.gov/resources/online-courses
Site Map   The Web site map allows visitors to look for specific topics or to browse content that aligns with their interests. https://www.nationalservice.gov/sitemap http://www.nationalservice.gov/about/contact-us

For further information, contact the Corporation for National and Community Service, 250 E Street NW., Washington, DC 20525. Phone, 202-606-5000.

Defense Nuclear Facilities Safety Board

625 Indiana Avenue NW., Suite 700, Washington, DC 20004
Phone, 202-694-7000. Fax, 202-208-6518. Internet, http://www.dnfsb.gov

Chair	SEAN P. SULLIVAN
Vice Chair	BRUCE HAMILTON
Member	JOYCE L. CONNERY
Member	JESSIE H. ROBERSON

Member	SEAN P. SULLIVAN
General Counsel	JAMES P. BIGGINS
General Manager	GLENN SKLAR
Technical Director	STEVEN STOKES
Deputy General Counsel	(VACANCY)
Deputy General Manager	(VACANCY)
Deputy Technical Director	ADAM POLOSKI

The above list of key personnel was updated 07–2017.

The Defense Nuclear Facilities Safety Board identifies the nature and consequences of public health and safety threats at the Department of Energy's defense nuclear facilities, elevates awareness of and information on such threats to the highest levels of governmental authority, and keeps the public informed.

The Defense Nuclear Facilities Safety Board was established as an independent agency on September 29, 1988, by the Atomic Energy Act of 1954, as amended (42 U.S.C. 2286 et seq.).

The Board comprises five members whom the President appoints with the advice and consent of the Senate. Appointees to the Board must be U.S. citizens and experts in the field of nuclear safety. http://www.dnfsb. gov/about/who-we-are

Activities

The Defense Nuclear Facilities Safety Board reviews and evaluates the content and implementation of standards for the design, construction, operation, and decommissioning of the Department of Energy's defense nuclear facilities; investigates any incident or practice at these facilities that may adversely affect public health and safety; and reviews and monitors their design, construction, and operation. The Board makes recommendations to the Secretary of Energy to ensure adequate protection of public health and safety. When the Board determines that any aspect of operations, practices, or occurrences at these Department of Energy defense nuclear facilities presents an imminent or severe threat to public health and safety, the Board transmits its recommendations directly to the President. http://www.dnfsb.gov/about/ what-we-do

Sources of Information

Employment   Information on career opportunities is available online. http://www. dnfsb.gov/careers/opportunities | Email: jobs@dnfsb.gov http://www.dnfsb.gov/ careers/employee-survey-results

Freedom of Information Act (FOIA)   An information seeker may submit a FOIA request by email, mail, or telephone for records held or believed to be held by the Board. To make a request by mail, write to the Information / FOIA Officer, Defense Nuclear Facilities Safety Board, 625 Indiana Avenue NW., Suite 700, Washington, DC 20004. Phone, 202-694-7000. http://www. dnfsb.gov/foia-reading-room | Email: foia@ dnfsb.gov

Open Government   The Defense Nuclear Facilities Safety Board supports the Open Government initiative to strengthen the principles of collaboration, participation, and transparency. http://www.dnfsb.gov/ open

Safety Management   The Victor Stello, Jr., Award was established by the Board to recognize Department of Energy employees for exemplary leadership in promoting safety management in the Department's defense nuclear complex. http://www.dnfsb.gov/ about/what-we-do/victor-stello-jr-award- safety-leadership

Site Representative Offices   Site representatives produce a weekly report summarizing the pertinent activities and events that occurred during that week at their site. Five Defense Nuclear Facilities locations—Hanford, Los Alamos National Laboratory, Pantex, Savannah River Site, and Y–12 National Security Complex / Oak Ridge National Laboratory—have at least one site representative currently assigned to them. http://www.dnfsb.gov/about/where-we-work/our-site-representative-offices; http://www.dnfsb.gov/website-tools/contact

For further information, contact the Defense Nuclear Facilities Safety Board, 625 Indiana Avenue NW., Suite 700, Washington, DC 20004. Phone, 202-694-7000.

Environmental Protection Agency

1200 Pennsylvania Avenue NW., Washington, DC 20460
Phone, 202-272-0167. Internet, http://www.epa.gov

Office of the Administrator

Administrator	MICHAEL S. REGAN
Deputy Administrator	JANET G. MCCABE
Chief of Staff	DANIEL UTECH
Special Assistant to the Administrator	JOHN LUCEY
https://www.epa.gov/aboutepa/about-office-administrator	
Agency Science Advisor	JENNIFER ORME-ZAVALETA
https://www.epa.gov/aboutepa/about-office-research-and-development-ord	
Chief Financial Officer	DAVID A. BLOOM, ACTING
https://www.epa.gov/aboutepa/about-office-chief-financial-officer-ocfo	
General Counsel	MELISSA HOFFER, ACTING
https://www.epa.gov/aboutepa/about-office-general-counsel-ogc	

Assistant Administrators

Air and Radiation	JOSEPH GOFFMAN, ACTING
Chemical Safety and Pollution Prevention	MICHAL I. FREEDHOFF
Enforcement and Compliance Assurance	LAWRENCE STARFIELD, ACTING
International and Tribal Affairs	MARK KASMAN, ACTING
Land and Emergency Management	BARRY BREEN, ACTING
Mission Support	DONNA J. VIZIAN, ACTING
Research and Development	JENNIFER ORME-ZAVALETA, ACTING
Water	RADHIKA FOX

Regional Administrators

Region 1—Boston (CT, ME, MA, NH, RI, VT, and Tribal Nations)	DEBORAH SZARO, ACTING
Region 2—New York (NJ, NY, and Tribal Nations, as well as Puerto Rico, U.S. Virgin Islands)	WALTER MUGDAN, ACTING
Region 3—Philadelphia (DE, MD, PA, VA, WV, and Tribal Nations, as well as DC)	DIANA ESHER, ACTING

Region 4—Atlanta (AL, FL, GA, KY, MS, NC, SC, TN, and Tribal Nations)	(VACANCY)
Region 5—Chicago (IL, IN, MI, MN, OH, WI, and Tribal Nations)	CHERYL NEWTON, ACTING
Region 6—Dallas (AR, LA, NM, OK, TX, and Tribal Nations)	DAVID W. GRAY, ACTING
Region 7—Kansas City (IA, KS, MO, NE, and Tribal Nations)	EDWARD H. CHU, ACTING
Region 8—Denver (CO, MT, ND, SD, UT, WY, and Tribal Nations)	DEBRA H. THOMAS, ACTING
Region 9—San Francisco (AZ, CA, HI, NV, and Tribal Nations, as well as American Samoa, Federated States of Micronesia, Guam, Marshall Islands, Northern Mariana Islands, Republic of Palau)	DEBORAH JORDAN, ACTING
Region 10—Seattle (AK, ID, OR, WA, and Tribal Nations)	MICHELLE PIRZADEH, ACTING

https://www.epa.gov/aboutepa/epa-organization-chart

Inspector General	SEAN W. O'DONNELL

https://www.epa.gov/office-inspector-general/about-epas-office-inspector-general#IG_bio

The above list of key personnel was updated 7–2021.

The Environmental Protection Agency protects human health and safeguards the environment.

Establishment and Organization

On July 9, 1970, Richard M. Nixon signed Reorganization Plan No. 3 of 1970, which became effective on December 2d of that same year and established the Environmental Protection Agency (EPA) as an independent agency in the executive branch. https://uscode.house.gov/view.xhtml?req=granuleid:USC-prelim-title5a-node84-leaf178&num=0&edition=prelim

President Nixon also sent his "Message to the Congress Transmitting Reorganization Plan 3 of 1970: Environmental Protection Agency" to accompany the plan. The message was published on page 587 of the "Public Papers of the Presidents of the United States" (1970). https://www.govinfo.gov/app/collection/ppp/president-37_Nixon,%20Richard%20M./1970/01%21A%21January%201%20to%20December%2031%2C%201970

The reorganization plan was published in the Federal Register on October 6, 1970 (35 FR 15623–15626). https://www.govinfo.gov/content/pkg/FR-1970-10-06/pdf/FR-1970-10-06.pdf

The Administrator serves as head of the EPA. The President appoints the Administrator by the advice and with the consent of the Senate. The Administrator is responsible to the President for providing overall supervision to the EPA. The Deputy Administrator, whom the President also appoints by the advice and with the consent of the Senate, assists the Administrator and serves as the Acting Administrator in the absence of the Administrator.

The EPA's statement of organization and general information on the agency has been assigned to first part of 40 CFR. https://www.ecfr.gov/cgi-bin/text-idx?SID=0bdc970c644f5ea3d05ff15f7f3c8500&mc=true&node=pt40.1.1&rgn=div5

The EPA website includes an "EPA Organizational Chart" web page. https://www.epa.gov/aboutepa/epa-organization-chart

Regulatory Authorities

Statutory material on "The Public Health and Welfare" has been assigned to 42 U.S.C. For example, that title contains chapters on "National Environmental Policy" (Ch. 55) and "Environmental Quality Improvement" (Ch. 56), as well as a subchapter on the "Safety of Public Water Systems" (Ch. 6A). https://uscode.house.gov/browse/prelim@title42&edition=prelim

Rules and regulations affecting the protection of the environment have been assigned to 40 CFR. https://www.ecfr.gov/cgi-bin/text-idx?SID=73131f98295736a6ba65a9e05ee063f4&mc=true&tpl=/ecfrbrowse/Title40/40tab_02.tpl

Parts 1–49 of 40 CFR contains rules and regulations that are associated with the EPA. https://www.ecfr.gov/cgi-bin/text-idx?SID=73131f98295736a6ba65a9e05ee063f4&mc=true&tpl=/ecfrbrowse/Title40/40cfrv1_02.tpl#0

Activities

The EPA facilitates coordinated and effective governmental action to protect the environment. It also serves as the public's advocate for a livable environment. https://www.epa.gov/aboutepa/our-mission-and-what-we-do

Air / Radiation   The Office of Air and Radiation develops national programs, policies, and regulations to control air pollution and radiation exposure. The Office administers the Clean Air Act, the Atomic Energy Act, the Waste Isolation Pilot Plant Land Withdrawal Act, and other environmental laws. The Office's core concerns include acid rain, climate change, energy efficiency, indoor and outdoor air quality, industrial air pollution, pollution from engines and vehicles, pollution prevention, radiation protection, radon, and stratospheric ozone depletion. https://www.epa.gov/aboutepa/about-office-air-and-radiation-oar

Phone, 202-564-7400.

Chemical Safety / Pollution Prevention   The Office of Chemical Safety and Pollution Prevention protects people and the environment from potential risks that are associated with pesticides and toxic chemicals. The Office administers the Federal Insecticide, Fungicide, and Rodenticide Act; Federal Food, Drug and Cosmetic Act; Toxic Substances Control Act; Pollution Prevention Act; and portions of other statutes. Through innovative partnerships and collaboration, the Office also works to prevent pollution. Stopping pollution before it is created reduces waste, saves energy and natural resources, and keeps homes, schools, and workplaces cleaner and safer. https://www.epa.gov/aboutepa/about-office-chemical-safety-and-pollution-prevention-ocspp

Phone, 202-564-2902.

Enforcement / Compliance Assurance   The Office of Enforcement and Compliance Assurance addresses pollution problems that affects American communities through vigorous civil and criminal enforcement. Its enforcement activities target the most serious water, air and chemical hazards. The Office works with EPA regional offices; it partners with State and Tribal governments; and it cooperates with other Federal agencies to enforce the Nation's environmental laws. These laws include the Clean Air Act; Clean Water Act; Comprehensive Environmental Response, Compensation and Liability Act; Emergency Planning and Community Right-to-Know Act; Federal Insecticide, Fungicide, and Rodenticide Act; Marine Protection, Research and Sanctuaries Act; National Environmental Policy Act; Oil Pollution Act; Resource Conservation and Recovery Act; Safe Drinking Water Act; and Toxic Substances Control Act. With States and Tribal partners, the Office shares a commitment to a clean and healthy environment. By improving transparency, adopting advanced technologies, and increasing community participation, the Office seeks to further empower the public to play a key role in assuring compliance with environmental laws nationwide and to make the playing field more level for entities and organizations that abide by those laws. https://www.epa.gov/aboutepa/about-office-enforcement-and-compliance-assurance-oeca

Phone, 202-564-2440.

International Affairs / Tribal Affairs   The Office of International and Tribal Affairs leads the EPA's international and Tribal engagements. Agencywide and nationwide in scope, the Office's activities cut across EPA programs and regions as it develops and implements policy and programs that protect public health and the environment. Pollution does not respect international borders; therefore, the Office collaborates with other Federal agencies, international organizations, and individual countries to address bilateral, regional, and global environmental challenges and to advance the Nation's foreign policy objectives. The Office honors the government-to-government Federal–Tribal relationship and respects Tribal treaty rights as it guides the agencywide effort to strengthen public health and environmental protection in Indian country. Special efforts are made to enable federally recognized Tribes administer their own environmental programs. https://www.epa.gov/aboutepa/about-office-international-and-tribal-affairs-oita

Phone, 202-564-6400.

Mission Support   The Office of Mission Support leads the core mission support functions of the EPA to improve efficiency, coordination, and customer experience for internal customers, stakeholders, and the general public. https://www.epa.gov/aboutepa/about-office-mission-support

Phone, 202-564-4600.

Research / Development   The Office of Research and Development conducts the research that provides the foundation for EPA decision-making to safeguard human health and ecosystems from environmental pollutants. With input from other EPA offices, external partners, and stakeholders, the Office's six research programs identify the most pressing environmental health research needs. Its "Strategic Research Action Plans," which are updated every few years, outline the current activities of the research programs. The Office also serve as the Agency's national program manager for regional laboratories. https://www.epa.gov/aboutepa/about-office-research-and-development-ord#what

Phone, 202-564-6620.

Waste Programs / Emergency Response   The Office of Land and Emergency Management makes policy, guides, and directs the EPA's emergency response and waste programs. More specifically, the Office develops guidelines for the land disposal of hazardous waste and underground storage tanks; provides technical assistance to all levels of government for establishing safe waste

management practices; supports State and local governments in redeveloping and reusing potentially contaminated sites; responds to abandoned and active hazardous waste sites, as well as to accidental chemical releases; and encourages innovative technologies to address contaminated soil and groundwater. https://www.epa.gov/aboutepa/about-office-land-and-emergency-management

Phone, 202-566-0200.

Water Quality   The Office of Water ensures that drinking water is safe. It also protects human health; supports economic and recreational activities; and provides healthy habitat for fish, plants, and wildlife, by restoring and maintaining oceans, watersheds, and aquatic ecosystems. The Office administers the Clean Water Act; Safe Drinking Water Act; and portions of the Coastal Zone Act Reauthorization Amendments of 1990; Resource Conservation and Recovery Act; Ocean Dumping Ban Act; Marine Protection, Research and Sanctuaries Act; Shore Protection Act; Marine Plastics Pollution Research and Control Act; London Dumping Convention; the International Convention for the Prevention of Pollution from Ships, and several other statutes. The Office works with the 10 EPA regional offices, other Federal agencies, State and local governments, American Indian Tribes, the regulated community, organized professional and interest groups, landowners and managers, and the public-at-large. The Office provides guidance, specifies scientific methods and data collection requirements, performs oversight, and facilitates communication among participants in its work. It also helps States and American Indian Tribes build capacity, and, in some cases, water programs can be delegated to them for implementation. https://www.epa.gov/aboutepa/about-office-water

Phone, 202-564-5700.

Sources of Information

A–Z Index   The EPA website has an alphabetical topic index on its "Web Topics Published" web page. https://www.epa.gov/topics-epa-web

Air Quality Forecasts   The EPA's Office of Air Quality Planning and Standards manages the "AirNow" website, which allows visitors to get air quality data for cities, States, and Zip Codes. https://www.airnow.gov

Archived Records   The "Guide to Federal Records in the National Archives of the United States" indicates that EPA records have been assigned to record group 412. https://www.archives.gov/research/guide-fed-records/groups/412.html

Blogs / Discussion Forums   In addition to its official blog, the EPA has several other blogs. These blogs deal with a range of EPA-related and environmental topics. Two discussion forums center on the topics of data and data sources. https://www.epa.gov/web-policies-and-procedures/list-social-media-platforms-epa-uses#blogs

Business Opportunities   Acquisition management information, the procurement status of projects across the Agency's procurement divisions, and an acquisition forecast database of future EPA procurement opportunities are available on the EPA website. Contact the Office of Acquisition Management for more information. Phone, 202-564-4310. https://www.epa.gov/contracts

Career Opportunities   The EPA relies on professionals from diverse backgrounds and with a wide range of skill sets to carry out its mission. The Agency posts current job openings on its website. For more information, contact the Office of Human Resources. Phone, 202-564-4606. http://www.epa.gov/careers | Email: recruit_inquiries@epa.gov

In 2020, the EPA ranked 20th among 25 midsize Government agencies in the Partnership for Public Service's Best Places To Work Agency Rankings. https://bestplacestowork.org/rankings/detail/?c=EP00

Climate Change Effects   Climate change continues to affect water resources. The "Regional Actions To Address Climate Change Impacts on Water" web page provides links for information on regional actions that are being taken to address this growing problem. https://www.epa.gov/climate-change-water-sector/regional-actions-address-climate-change-impacts-water

Contact Information   Information for accessing libraries; commenting on regulations; connecting on social media; finding mailing addresses; locating an employee, lab, or office; reporting a problem; submitting a Freedom of Information Act request; and subscribing to alerts, blogs, newsletters, and news releases, is available on the "Contact EPA" web page. https://www.epa.gov/home/forms/contact-epa

The EPA maintains a "Mailing Addresses and Phone Numbers" web page. https://www.epa.gov/aboutepa/mailing-addresses-and-phone-numbers

The EPA maintains a "Media Contacts" web page for reporters. https://www.epa.gov/newsroom/media-contacts

Education   Educators and students can access homework resources, lesson plans, and project ideas on the EPA's website. Environmental education incorporates a multidisciplinary approach to learning, builds critical thinking skills, and helps students make informed and responsible decisions that sustain Earth's ecosystems. https://www.epa.gov/students

Energy Efficient Products   The Office of Atmospheric Programs certifies products that help consumers save energy and money through Energy Star. https://www.energystar.gov

Environmental Justice   The website provides access to the EPA's Environmental Justice Screening and Mapping Tool (EJSCREEN) that is based on nationally consistent data and an approach that combines environmental and demographic indicators in maps and reports. The EPA developed its EJSCREEN Tool to help the Agency become a more effective protector of public health and the environment. https://www.epa.gov/ejscreen

Federal Register   Significant documents and documents that the EPA recently published in the Federal Register are accessible online. https://www.federalregister.gov/agencies/environmental-protection-agency

Fire Tools   The EPA's Office of Air Quality Planning and Standards manages the "AirNow" website, which maintains a fire tools web page. https://www.airnow.gov/more-fire-tools

Freedom of Information Act (FOIA)   To any person, the FOIA gives a statutory right for obtaining access to Government information in the records of executive branch agencies. This right to access is limited, however, when the requested information is shielded from disclosure by any of nine exemptions contained within the statute. https://www.epa.gov/foia | Email: hq.foia@epa.gov

The FOIA libraries contain frequently requested information. Before making a FOIA request, search the online FOIA libraries to see if the desired information is immediately available at no cost. https://www.epa.gov/foia/foia-online-libraries

Frequently Asked Questions (FAQs)   Some EPA offices and programs have their own FAQs web pages. The EPA maintains a list of the most often viewed questions, which are drawn from those web pages of FAQs. https://usepa.servicenowservices.com/ecss?id=ecss_kb_home

The EPA maintains a database of FAQs and its answers to them. https://usepa.servicenowservices.com/ecss?id=kb_search&kb_knowledge_base=98a9e8ce1b4858104614ddb6bc4bcb03&spa=1

Glossaries   The "Report on the Environment" glossary defines terms that are used in the report or have particular meaning within the EPA. https://www.epa.gov/report-environment/roe-glossary

An Environmental Justice Screening and Mapping Tool (EJSCREEN) glossary is available on the EPA's website. https://www.epa.gov/ejscreen/glossary-ejscreen-terms

The EPA's Terminology Services maintains a "Terms and Acronyms" web page. A search tool is available on the page. https://sor.epa.gov/sor_internet/registry/termreg/searchandretrieve/termsandacronyms/search.do

The EPA's Terminology Services maintains a "Vocabulary Catalog" web page. A vocabulary search tool is available on the page. https://sor.epa.gov/sor_internet/registry/termreg/searchandretrieve/glossariesandkeywordlists/search.do

Grants   Information to apply for, manage, and understand EPA grants is available online. Contact the Office of Grants and Debarment for more information. Phone, 202-564-5315. https://www.epa.gov/grants

Greenhouse Gas Emissions   The EPA's Office of Atmospheric Programs has released its "DRAFT Inventory of U.S. Greenhouse Gas Emissions and Sinks, 1990–2019" in Portable Document Format (PDF) for viewing and downloading. The final version will be published in April of 2021. https://www.epa.gov/ghgemissions/draft-inventory-us-greenhouse-gas-emissions-and-sinks-1990-2019

Hotlines / Service Lines   Hotline and service line information for specific topics is available on the EPA website. https://www.epa.gov/home/epa-hotlines

Information on region-specific customer service lines is also available. https://www.epa.gov/home/epa-hotlines#RegionSpecificCustomerServiceLines

Laws / Executive Orders   As a regulatory agency, the EPA has received authorization from the U.S. Congress to write regulations that explain environmental laws for proper implementation. A number of Presidential Executive Orders also affect EPA regulatory activities. https://www.epa.gov/laws-regulations/laws-and-executive-orders

Newsroom   The EPA posts news releases online. https://www.epa.gov/newsroom

Non-English Readers   The EPA provides information on its website in Chinese, Korean, Spanish, and Vietnamese. Language tags are visible at the bottom of the EPA's home page. https://www.epa.gov

Open Government   The EPA supports the Open Government initiative by promoting the principles of collaboration, participation, and transparency. https://www.epa.gov/open

Plain Language   The EPA upholds the Plain Writing Act of 2010 by adhering to Federal plain language guidelines. EPA writers and editors want to know if a document or web page contains content that was not written clearly. https://www.epa.gov/home/plain-writing

Protecting Pollinators   The "Protecting Bees and Other Pollinators from Pesticides" web page provides information on helping pollinators stay healthy. In addition to the EPA, advocates, consumers, growers, pesticide manufacturers, and governments have roles to play in protecting pollinators like honeybees and monarch butterflies. https://www.epa.gov/pollinator-protection

Regional Offices   Ten regional offices help develop local programs for pollution abatement. https://www.epa.gov/aboutepa/visiting-regional-office

Regulatory Information EPA regulations address a host of environmental issues that range from acid rain to wetlands ecosystems. The "Regulatory Information By Topic" web page provides convenient access to laws and regulations, to compliance and enforcement information, and to policies and guidance, that are associated with or relevant to the topics listed on it. https://www.epa.gov/regulatory-information-topic

Social Media The EPA has Facebook, Flickr, Instagram, Twitter, and YouTube accounts. Links to these accounts may be found on the "List of Social Media Platforms that EPA Uses" web page. https://www.epa.gov/web-policies-and-procedures/list-social-media-platforms-epa-uses

Staff Directory The EPA maintains an online staff directory. https://cfpub.epa.gov/locator/index.cfm

Superfund Sites The EPA's Superfund program cleans up some of the Nation's most contaminated land and responds to environmental emergencies, oil spills, and natural disasters. The program's website has a search tool for locating Superfund sites. https://www.epa.gov/superfund/search-superfund-sites-where-you-live

Trash-Free Waters Most of the trash that pollutes estuaries, lakes, rivers, and oceans washes into them from land-based sources. Plastic trash, in particular, damages aquatic ecosystems, economic activity, and human health. https://www.epa.gov/trash-free-waters

Website Snapshots Snapshots of the EPA website are available for January 19, 2017, and January 19, 2021. The snapshots capture the content of www.epa.gov at a specific point in time. A new snapshot is made every 4 years, the day before the Presidential Inauguration, and added to the "www.epa.gov Snapshots" web page. https://www.epa.gov/home/wwwepagov-snapshots

The Sources of Information were updated 7–2021.

Equal Employment Opportunity Commission

131 M Street NE., Washington, DC 20507
Phone, 202-663-4900. TTY, 202-663-4444. Internet, http://www.eeoc.gov

The Commission

Chair	JANET L. DHILLON
Vice Chair	KEITH E. SONDERLING
Commissioners	CHARLOTTE A. BURROWS
	ANDREA R. LUCAS
	JOCELYN F. SAMUELS

https://www.eeoc.gov/commission

Executive Officer	BERNADETTE B. WILSON
Chief Officers	
Data	CHRIS HAFFER
Financial	GRACE ZHAO
Human Capital	KEVIN L. RICHARDSON
Information	BRYAN BURNETT
Operating	(VACANCY)
Directors	
Communications and Legislative Affairs	(VACANCY)
Equal Opportunity	STAN PIETRUSIAK, JR.
Federal Operations	CARLTON M. HADDEN
Field Programs	MARTIN S. EBEL
Legal Counsel	ANDREW MAUNZ

EEOC ORGANIZATION

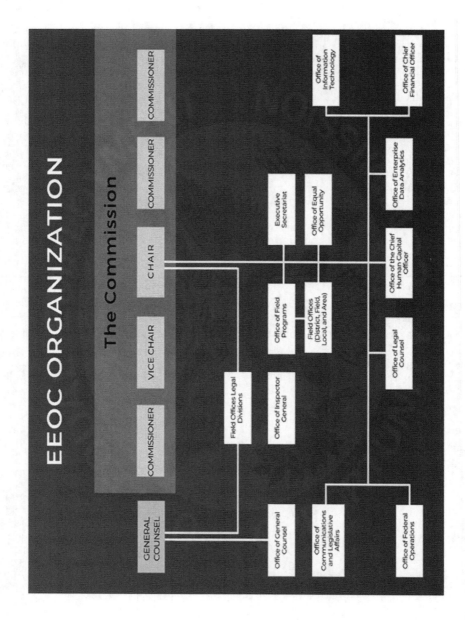

The Commission

COMMISSIONER | VICE CHAIR | CHAIR | COMMISSIONER | COMMISSIONER

GENERAL COUNSEL

Field Offices Legal Divisions
Office of Inspector General

Executive Secretariat
Office of Equal Opportunity

Office of Field Programs
Field Offices (District, Field, Local, and Area)

Office of Information Technology
Office of Chief Financial Officer

Office of Enterprise Data Analytics

Office of the Chief Human Capital Officer

Office of Legal Counsel

Office of General Counsel
Office of Communications and Legislative Affairs
Office of Federal Operations

General Counsel	SHARON F. GUSTAFSON
Inspector General	MILTON A. MAYO, JR.
https://oig.eeoc.gov/about-us	

The above list of key personnel was updated 12–2020.

The Equal Employment Opportunity Commission enforces laws that prohibit employment discrimination based on age, color, disability, gender, genetic information, national origin, race, or religion.

Establishment and Organization

On July 2, 1964, President Lyndon B. Johnson approved Public Law 88–352, which is commonly cited as the Civil Rights Act of 1964" (78 Stat. 241). Title VII of this Act "created a Commission to be known as the Equal Employment Opportunity Commission" (78 Stat. 258). The Equal Employment Opportunity Commission (EEOC), in accordance with the effective date of Title VII, became operational on July 2, 1965 (78 Stat. 266). https://www.govinfo.gov/content/pkg/STATUTE-78/pdf/STATUTE-78-Pg241.pdf

The EEOC is a bipartisan commission comprising five members, whom the President appoints, by the advice and with the consent of the Senate, to staggered 5-year terms. The President also designates one member to serve as Chair of the Commission and another member to service as its Vice Chair (78 Stat. 258).

Public Law 92–261, which is also cited as the Equal Employment Opportunity Act of 1972, provides for the appointment of "a General Counsel of the Commission." The President appoints this General Counsel, by the advice and with the consent of the Senate, to support the Commission and provide direction, coordination, and supervision of the agency's litigation program. The General Counsel serves for a term of 4 years (86 Stat. 110). https://www.govinfo.gov/content/pkg/STATUTE-86/pdf/STATUTE-86-Pg103.pdf

The EEOC included an organizational chart in its "Fiscal Year 2019 Agency Financial Report" in the section "Management's Discussion and Analysis." https://www.eeoc.gov/fiscal-year-2019-agency-financial-report-us-equal-employment-opportunity-commission#h_190127329797157539226499 7

Statutory and Regulatory Authorities

Codified statutory material on civil rights has been assigned to chapter 21 of 42 U.S.C. The chapter runs from section 1981 through 2000h-6. https://uscode.house.gov/view.xhtml?path=/prelim@title42/chapter21&edition=prelim

"Subchapter VI—Equal Employment Opportunities" runs from section 2000e through 2000e–17. Codified statutory material on the EEOC has been assigned to section 2000e–4 of 42 U.S.C. https://uscode.house.gov/view.xhtml?path=/prelim@title42/chapter21/subchapter6&edition=prelim

Codified regulatory material that is associated with the EEOC has been assigned to chapter xiv of 29 CFR. The chapter on the EEOC runs from part 1600 through 1899. Title 29 contains rules and regulations that address labor-related issues. https://www.ecfr.gov/cgi-bin/text-idx?SID=de3741e211c566331cb331784bb63c67&mc=true&tpl=/ecfrbrowse/Title29/29chapterXIV.tpl

Activities

Laws that the EEOC enforces include the Equal Pay Act of 1963 (PL 88–38 / 29 U.S.C. 206); Title VII of the Civil Rights Act of 1964 (PL 88–352 / 42 U.S.C. 2000e et seq.); the Age Discrimination in Employment Act of 1967 (PL 90–202 / 29 U.S.C. 621 et seq.); sections of the Rehabilitation Act of 1973 (PL 93–112 / 29 U.S.C. 791 et seq.); Title I of the Americans with Disabilities Act of 1990 (PL 101–336 / 42 U.S.C. 12101 et seq.); sections of the Civil Rights Act of 1991 (PL 102–166 / 2 U.S.C. 1219); and Title II of the Genetic

Information Nondiscrimination Act of 2008 (PL 110–233 / 42 U.S.C. 2000ff et seq.).

Complaints Against the Federal Government   The EEOC establishes the procedures for Federal employees and job applicants to file complaints of employment discrimination or retaliation. The agency charged with discrimination is responsible for informal counseling and, if a complaint is filed and accepted, for investigating the claims raised therein. At the conclusion of the investigation, a complainant may request a hearing before an EEOC administrative judge or that the agency issue a final decision on the matter. The agency's final decision or final action after a hearing may be appealed to the Commission. https://www.eeoc.gov/federal-sector/overview-federal-sector-eeo-complaint-process

The Office of Federal Operations provides oversight of and technical assistance for equal employment opportunity complaint adjudication and Governmentwide maintenance of affirmative employment programs. Using the guidance and principles contained in its Equal Employment Opportunity Management Directive 715, the Commission monitors and evaluates Federal agencies' affirmative employment programs under Title VII and section 501 of the Rehabilitation Act and ensures that all Federal employees compete on a playing field that is fair and level. https://www.eeoc.gov/federal-sector/management-directive/section-717-title-vii#

Enforcement   The EEOC carries out its statutory, regulatory, policy, and program enforcement responsibilities through its headquarters-based Office of General Counsel, Office of Field Programs, and 53 field offices. The field offices receive charges of discrimination from the public and use a variety of resolution methods, including voluntary mediation and full-scale investigation and conciliation. The field staff seeks to achieve a wide range of objectives that center on the quality, timeliness, and appropriateness of individual, class, and systemic charges; secures relief for victims of discrimination in accordance with EEOC policies; counsels individuals about their rights under the laws that the EEOC enforces; and conducts outreach and

technical assistance programs. The EEOC's Office of General Counsel litigates in U.S. District Courts and Courts of Appeal. https://www.eeoc.gov/laws-guidance-0

Outreach   The Commission promotes voluntary compliance with equal employment opportunity statutes through a variety of educational and technical assistance activities. Its outreach and education programs provide general information on the EEOC, its mission, rights and responsibilities under the statutes that are enforced by the Commission, and the charge (i.e., complaint) process. EEOC representatives are available, on a limited basis and at no cost, to make presentations and to participate in meetings, conferences, and seminars with employee and employer groups, professional associations, students, nonprofit entities, community organizations, and other members of the general public. https://www.eeoc.gov/outreach-education-technical-assistance

For a fee, the EEOC offers in-depth training that it has tailored for employers. The EEOC Training Institute makes additional training available to private employers, to local and State government personnel, and to employees of the Federal Government. Managers and employees receive training on the laws that the Commission enforces and on ways to prevent and reduce discrimination in the workplace. https://eeotraining.eeoc.gov/profile/web/index.cfm?PKwebID=0x2547b105&varPage=home | Email: eeoc.traininginstitute@eeoc.gov

Publication of Data and Statistics   The Commission publishes data on the employment status of minorities and women by conducting four employment surveys that cover private employers (EEO–1), labor unions (EEO–3), State and local governments (EEO–4), and public elementary and secondary schools (EEO–5). The collected data are shared with certain Federal agencies; prepared in aggregated format for major geographic areas and, where possible, also by industry groups (EEO–1), by major trades (EEO–3), or by government types and functions (EEO–4); and after aggregation, released into the public domain for independent analysis and research. https://www.eeoc.gov/statistics/employment

Sources of Information

Archived Records The "Guide to Federal Records in the National Archives of the United States" indicates that EEOC records have been assigned to record group 403. https://www.archives.gov/research/guide-fed-records/groups/403.html

Business Opportunities The "Doing Business With the EEOC" web page has information for contractors and vendors. https://www.eeoc.gov/doing-business-eeoc

Career Opportunities The Commission hires in various job categories: attorneys, information intake representatives, investigators, mediators, office automation assistants, paralegals, program analysts, and social scientists. EEOC employment opportunities are posted on USAJobs—the Federal Government's official source for job listings and employment opportunity information. For more information, contact the Office of Human Resources. Phone, 202-663-4306. https://www.eeoc.gov/jobs-and-internships-eeoc

EEOC Internships offer high school, college, and graduate and law students the opportunity to gain experience working on projects or cases involving issues of Federal antidiscrimination law. Interns work closely with experienced attorneys and specialists on assignments. Work assignments include legal research and writing, research and analysis of public policy developments, correspondence with Commission stakeholders, and assistance with charge intake and investigations. https://www.eeoc.gov/eeoc-internship-program

In 2019, the EEOC ranked 12th among 25 midsize Government agencies in the Partnership for Public Service's Best Places To Work Agency Rankings. https://bestplacestowork.org/rankings/detail/EE00

Contact Information The "Contact EEOC" web page has email addresses, phone numbers, and links to relevant EEOC resources. https://www.eeoc.gov/contact-eeoc

News producers, reporters, writers for news publication and broadcasts, and other people working on news programs or stories may contact the Office of Communications, using the phone number or email address that is provided here. Phone, 202-663-4191.

TTY, 202-663-4494. https://www.eeoc.gov/newsroom/search | Email: newsroom@eeoc.gov

District Offices The EEOC operates 15 district offices. An office list and jurisdictional map are available online. A search tool allows EEOC website visitors to locate field offices by using Zip Codes. https://www.eeoc.gov/field-office

Federal Register Significant documents and documents that the EEOC recently published in the Federal Register are accessible online. https://www.federalregister.gov/agencies/equal-employment-opportunity-commission

Federal Sector Reports The EEOC posts reports that deal with subjects affecting Federal employees. https://www.eeoc.gov/federal-sector/reports

Freedom of Information Act (FOIA) To any person, the FOIA gives a statutory right for obtaining access to Government information that the records of executive branch agencies contain. When the requested information is shielded from disclosure by one or more of nine exemptions that are contained within the statute, this right to access is limited. The EEOC makes many records publicly available on its main website. Documents are also available in an electronic library collection, as well as in physical libraries that are located at EEOC headquarters and district offices. Before submitting a FOIA request, an information seeker should search one of the aforementioned locations to see if the desired information has been released already in the public domain and is accessible free of charge and without the delay of processing a formal request. https://www.eeoc.gov/foia

The EEOC maintains a collection of documents online in its electronic FOIA library. https://www.eeoc.gov/foia/foia-e-library

Frequently Asked Questions (FAQs) The EEOC posts answers to FAQs. https://eeoc.custhelp.com/app/answers/list

Glossary The EEOC maintains a glossary whose content is relevant to small-business owners and employees. https://www.eeoc.gov/employers/small-business/eeoc-glossary-small-businesses

Open Government The EEOC supports the Open Government initiative by implementing principles of collaboration, participation, and transparency. https://www.eeoc.gov/open-government

Poster   An employer is required to post a notice describing the Federal laws that prohibit job discrimination based on age, color, disability, equal pay, genetic information, national origin, race, religion, or sex. The "Equal Employment Opportunity is THE LAW" poster contains a summary of these laws and explains how an employee or applicant can file a discrimination complaint. The EEOC's poster is available in Arabic, Chinese, English, and Spanish. https://www.eeoc.gov/employers/eeo-law-poster

Press Releases   The EEOC posts press releases. https://www.eeoc.gov/newsroom/search

Publications   The EEOC's most popular publications may be downloaded in Portable Document Format (PDF) for easy reproduction. Publications that are unavailable online may be obtained by phone or fax. Phone, 800-669-3362. TTY, 800-800-3302. Fax, 513-489-8692. https://www.eeoc.gov/eeoc-publications

Reading Room   Contact the EEOC Library, 131 M Street NE., Washington, DC 20507. Phone, 202-663-4630.

Reports / Surveys   The EEOC collects workforce data from employers with more than 100 employees. Employers who meet the reporting thresholds are required to provide the information. The data are used for enforcement, research, and self-assessment by employers. Data remain confidential; however, the public can access them in aggregate form. http://www.eeoc.gov/employers/reporting.cfm

Resources   EEOC material on specific discrimination topics that pertain to small businesses is available on the "EEOC Resources" web page. https://www.eeoc.gov/employers/small-business/eeoc-resources

Small Business Resource Center   The Small Business Resource Center provides answers to common questions regarding responsibilities that Federal employment discrimination laws require business owners to meet. It also has tips for preventing discrimination and dealing with issues when they do arise within a business context. https://www.eeoc.gov/employers/small-business

Social Media   The EEOC has a Facebook page. https://www.facebook.com/USEEOC

The EEOC tweets announcements and other newsworthy items, using Twitter. https://twitter.com/useeoc

The EEOC posts videos on its YouTube channel. https://www.youtube.com/user/TheEEOC

Speakers   An agency representative may be available to present an overview of the laws that the EEOC enforces and EEOC charge (i.e., complaint) processing procedures—including mediation—at a conference or seminar. Contact an outreach program coordinator for more information. Phone, 800-669-4000. https://www.eeoc.gov/no-cost-outreach-programs

Statistics   The EEOC posts data, reports, and statistics online. https://www.eeoc.gov/statistics

The Sources of Information were updated 12–2020.

Export-Import Bank of the United States

811 Vermont Avenue NW., Washington, DC 20571
Phone, 202-565-3946. Fax, 800-565-3946. Internet, http://www.exim.gov

President / Chair	CHARLES J. HALL, ACTING
First Vice President / Vice Chair	SCOTT SCHLOEGEL, ACTING
Director	(VACANCY)
Director	(VACANCY)
Director	(VACANCY)
Chief Financial Officer	DAVID M. SENA
Chief Information Officer	HOWARD SPIRA
Chief Risk Officer / Executive Vice President	JEFF GOETTMAN, ACTING

Chief of Staff / Senior Vice President	JESSE LAW
Deputy Chief of Staff	RYAN CAUDELLE
General Counsel / Senior Vice President	ANGELA MARIANA FREYRE
Senior Vice President and Chief Strategy Officer	ANTHONY SCARAMUCCI
Senior Vice President, Export Finance / Chief Banking Officer	TROY FUHRIMAN
Senior Vice President, Communications	JENNIFER HAZELTON
Senior Vice President, Congressional and Intergovernmental Affairs	KEVIN WARNKE, ACTING
Senior Vice President, Credit and Risk Management	KENNETH M. TINSLEY
Senior Vice President, Policy and Planning	JAMES C. CRUSE
Senior Vice President, Resource Management	MICHAEL CUSHING
Senior Vice President, Small Business	JAMES BURROWS
Deputy Chief Banking Officer	MADOLYN PHILLIPS
Vice President, Asset Management	WALTER F. KEATING
Vice President, Business Credit	PAMELA S. BOWERS
Vice President, Business Processes, Total Enterprise Modernization	MICHELE A. KUESTER
Vice President, Communications	REBECCA ROSE
Vice President, Congressional and Intergovernmental Affairs	KEVIN WARNKE
Vice President, Controller	PATRICIA WOLF
Vice President, Country Risk and Economic Analysis / Chief Economist	WILLIAM A. MARSTELLER
Vice President, Credit Review and Compliance	WALTER HILL, JR.
Vice President, Credit Underwriting	DAVID W. CARTER
Vice President, Customer and Business Solutions	ROCHELE BARHAM
Vice President, Engineering and Environment	JAMES A. MAHONEY, JR.
Vice President, Finance / Treasurer	NATHALIE HERMAN
Vice President, International Relations	ISABEL GALDIZ
Vice President, Operations and Data Quality	NICOLE M.B. VALTOS
Vice President, Policy Analysis	HELENE WALSH
Vice President, Sales and Marketing	SEAN LUKE
Vice President, Structured Finance	HALA EL MOHANDES
Vice President, Transportation	ROBERT F.X. ROY

The Export-Import Bank helps finance the export of U.S. goods and services to international markets.

The Export-Import Bank of the United States (ExIm Bank), established in 1934, operates as an independent agency of the U.S. Government under the authority of the Export-Import Bank Act of 1945, as amended (12 U.S.C. 635 et seq.). Its Board of Directors comprises the President and Chair, the First Vice President and Vice Chair, and three directors—a total of five members. With the advice and consent of the Senate, the President appoints all of them.

The ExIm Bank helps American exporters adjust to government-supported financing competition from other countries. The assistance allows U.S. exports to compete for overseas business on the basis of price, performance, and service, which protects U.S. jobs. The Bank also fills gaps in the availability of commercial financing for creditworthy export transactions by providing a variety of financing mechanisms, including working capital guarantees, export-credit insurance, and financing for the purchase of U.S. goods and services.

The Bank is required to find a reasonable assurance of repayment for each transaction it supports. Its legislation requires it to meet the financing terms of competitor export credit agencies, but not to compete with commercial lenders. Restrictions also apply to the Bank's support for military goods and services and to its operation in some countries.

A self-sustaining agency, EXIM operates at no cost to taxpayers. Since 2009, EXIM has contributed nearly $3.8 billion to American taxpayers. http://www.exim.gov/about

Activities

The ExIm Bank is authorized to have loans, guarantees, and insurance outstanding at any one time in aggregate amount not exceeding $120 billion. A variety of Ex-Im Bank programs offered under broad export financing categories—working capital guarantees, export credit insurance, loan guarantees, and direct loans—support U.S. exporters.

The Bank's regional offices focus on small business outreach and support. Its Small Business Committee makes recommendations on and coordinates and evaluates Bank functions necessary for an effective small-business strategy. http://www.exim.gov/what-we-do#by-name

Sources of Information

Electronic Updates   An online subscription form is available to sign up for email updates from the Ex-Im Bank. https://public.govdelivery.com/accounts/USEXIM/subscriber/new

Employment   To carry out its mission, the Bank relies on professionals with a range of skills and expertise: attorney-advisors, business development and loan specialists, economists, engineers, and resource managers in accounting, finance, human resources, and information technology. http://www.exim.gov/about/careers

Freedom of Information Act (FOIA)   A FOIA request must be made in writing. It may be submitted using the online request form or by email, fax, or postal mail. http://www.exim.gov/about/foia | Email: foia@exim.gov

News   ExIm Bank posts board agendas and meeting minutes, reports, and speeches online. http://www.exim.gov/news

The Chair writes a quarterly newsletter that includes information on the Bank's performance over the previous 3 months. The newsletter also includes analysis of global economic trends, customer stories, practical export tips, upcoming Bank events, and other resources. http://www.exim.gov/learning-resources/newsletters

Office of the Inspector General (OIG)   The OIG investigates complaints of abuse, fraud, and waste. Phone, 888-644-3946. http://www.exim.gov/about/oig/oig-hotline | Email: IGhotline@exim.gov

Open Government   The ExIm Bank is becoming more collaborative, participatory, and transparent by making data available in an open format and by providing a mechanism for the public to submit feedback. http://www.exim.gov/open-government-directive

Project Information and Concerns   The "Environmental and Social Project Information and Concerns" Web page provides an online form for expressing project-specific concerns, requesting project-specific information, or submitting information on a particular project. http://www.exim.gov/policies/ex-im-bank-and-the-environment/environmental-and-social-project-information-and-concerns

Regional Offices   The ExIm Bank operates regional export finance centers and field offices nationwide. A List of these centers, with their contact information, is available online. http://www.exim.gov/contact/regional-export-finance-centers http://www.exim.gov/contact/headquarters

For further information, contact the Business Development Office, Export-Import Bank, 811 Vermont Avenue NW., Washington, DC 20571. Phone, 202-565-3946 or 800-565-3946.

Farm Credit Administration

1501 Farm Credit Drive, McLean, VA 22102-5090
Phone, 703-883-4000. Fax, 703-790-3260. Internet, http://www.fca.gov

Board

Chair	DALLAS P. TONSAGER
Member	JEFFERY S. HALL
Member	(VACANCY)
https://www.fca.gov/about/fca_board.html	

Officials

Chief Executive Officer	DALLAS P. TONSAGER
https://www.fca.gov/about/board/tonsager.html	
Chief Operating Officer	WILLIAM J. HOFFMAN
Designated Agency Ethics Official	PHILIP J. SHEBEST
General Counsel	CHARLES R. RAWLS
Secretary to the Board	DALE L. AULTMAN

Directors

Office of Agency Services	A. JEROME FOWLKES
Office of Congressional and Public Affairs	MICHAEL A. STOKKE
Office of Equal Employment Opportunity and Inclusion	THAIS BURLEW
Office of Examination and Chief Examiner	S. ROBERT COLEMAN
Office of Information Technology	JERALD GOLLEY
Office of Regulatory Policy	GARY K. VAN METER
Office of Secondary Market Oversight	LAURIE A. REA
Office of the Chief Financial Officer	STEPHEN G. SMITH
https://www.fca.gov/about/offices/officials.html	
Inspector General	WENDY R. LAGUARDA
https://www.fca.gov/home/inspector.html	

[For the Farm Credit Administration statement of organization, see the Code of Federal Regulations, Title 12, Parts 600 and 611]

The above list of key personnel was updated 09–2017.

The Farm Credit Administration ensures the safe and sound operation of the banks, associations, affiliated service organizations, and other entities of the Farm Credit System, and protects the interests of the public and those who borrow from Farm Credit institutions or invest in Farm Credit securities.

The Farm Credit Administration (FCA) was established as an independent financial regulatory agency in the executive branch of the Federal Government by Executive Order 6084 on March 27, 1933. The FCA carries out its responsibilities by conducting examinations of the various Farm Credit lending institutions: Agricultural Credit Associations, Farm Credit Banks, Federal Land Credit Associations, and the Agricultural Credit Bank.

The FCA also examines the service organizations owned by the Farm Credit lending institutions, as well as the National Consumer Cooperative Bank. http://www.fca.gov/info/organization.html#service

FCA policymaking is vested in the Farm Credit Administration Board, whose three full-time members the President appoints to 6-year terms with the advice and consent of the Senate. One member of the Board is designated by the President as Chair and serves as the FCA's chief executive officer. The Board approves rules and regulations, provides for the examination and regulation of and reporting by Farm Credit institutions, and establishes the policies under which the Administration operates. Board meetings are regularly held on the second Thursday of the month and are subject to the Government in the Sunshine Act. Public announcements of these meetings are published in the "Federal Register." http://www.fca.gov/about/fca_board.html

Authority for the organization and activities of the Farm Credit System may be found in the Farm Credit Act of 1971, as amended.

The lending institutions of the Farm Credit System were established to provide adequate and dependable credit and closely related services to farmers, ranchers, and producers or harvesters of aquatic products; persons engaged in providing on-the-farm services; rural homeowners; and associations of farmers, ranchers, and producers or harvesters of aquatic products, or federations of such associations that operate on a cooperative basis and are engaged in marketing, processing, supply, or business service functions for the benefit of their members. Initially capitalized by the U.S. Government, the Farm Credit lending institutions are organized as cooperatives—their borrowers completely own them. The loan funds provided to borrowers by these institutions are obtained primarily through the sale of securities to investors in the Nation's capital markets. http://www.fca.gov/rpts/information.html

The Agricultural Credit Act of 1987, as amended (12 U.S.C. 2279aa-1), established the Federal Agricultural Mortgage Corporation, commonly known as Farmer Mac. The Corporation, designated as part of the Farm Credit System, is a federally chartered instrumentality of the United States and promotes the development of a secondary market for agricultural real estate and rural housing loans. Farmer Mac also provides guarantees for the timely payment of principal and interest on securities representing interests in or obligations backed by pools of agricultural real estate loans. The Administration examines and regulates Farmer Mac to ensure the safety and soundness of its operations. http://www.fca.gov/info/farmer_mac.html

The FCA manages regulations under which Farm Credit institutions operate. These regulations implement the Farm Credit Act of 1971, as amended (12 U.S.C. 2001), and have the force and effect of law. Similar to the authorities of other Federal regulators of financial institutions, the Administration's authorities include the power to issue cease-and-desist orders, to levy civil monetary penalties, to remove officers and directors of Farm Credit institutions, and to establish financial and operating reporting requirements. Although it is prohibited from participation in routine management or operations of Farm Credit institutions, the Administration is authorized to become involved in these institutions' management and operations when the Farm Credit Act or its regulations have been violated, when taking an action to correct an unsafe or unsound practice, or when assuming a formal conservatorship over an institution.

The Administration does not operate on funds appropriated by Congress: It derives income from assessments collected from the institutions that it regulates and examines. In addition to its headquarters in McLean, VA, the Administration maintains four field offices located in Bloomington, MN; Greenwood Village, CO; Irving, TX; and Sacramento, CA.

Sources of Information

A–Z Index   The FCA Web site has an A–Z index to help visitors navigate its content. https://www.fca.gov/home/atozindex.html
Business Opportunities   The Office of Agency Services manages the FCA's procurement opportunities. Phone, 703-883-4378. TTY, 703-883-4056. https://www.fca.gov/about/procurement.html
Career Opportunities   To carry out its mission, the FCA relies on attorneys, examiners, information technology specialists, and other professionals. Examiners play a prominent role at the FCA: They plan, organize, and conduct examinations of Farm Credit System institutions. The FCA hires examiners who hold university degrees in a variety of disciplines. The ideal candidate has a background in agriculture, business, finance, or information technology. Adaptability, teamwork, and communication skills are essential. Contact the Office of Agency

Services for more information. Phone, 703-883-4135. TTY, 703-883-4056. https://www.fca.gov/browse/fca_careers.html

In 2016, the FCA ranked 10th among 29 small agencies in the Partnership for Public Service's Best Places To Work Agency Rankings. http://bestplacestowork.org/BPTW/rankings/overall/small

Cooperative Principles Farm Credit System institutions generally adhere to three core cooperative principles: user-ownership, user-control, and user-benefits. These principles support the System's cooperative practices. To learn more about them, visit the "Cooperative Way" Web page. https://www.fca.gov/info/cooperativeway.html

Economics / Policy FCA economists monitor conditions in the U.S. farm, national, and global economies. They write economic and policy reports that provide perspective for FCA examiners, leaders, and policy analysts. The FCA posts these reports on its Web site to make them available to a broader audience. https://www.fca.gov/rpts/economistreports.html

En Español The FCA posts information in Spanish on its Web site. https://www.fca.gov/browse/espanol.html

Financial Indicators The FCA posts data on selected financial performance indicators for Farm Credit System institutions. https://www.fca.gov/rpts/fcsindicators.html

Flood Disaster Protection The FCA posts links to resources that help Farm Credit System lenders understand flood insurance rules. https://www.fca.gov/info/flooddisasterprotection.html

Freedom of Information Act (FOIA) A written submission must clearly indicate that it is a "FOIA Request." The FCA may require payment for searching for, reviewing, and reproducing a document. A submitter must provide a detailed description—date, subject matter, title—of the record sought and indicate the maximum amount he or she is willing to pay in fees. A request may be submitted by email or fax, or by mail and addressed to the Freedom of Information Act Officer, Farm Credit Administration, 1501 Farm Credit Drive, McLean, VA 22102-5090. Phone, 703-883-4020. TTY, 703-883-4056. Fax, 703-790-0052. http://www.fca.gov/home/freedom_info.html | Email: foiaofficer@fca.gov

The FCA maintains a FOIA reading room on its Web site. Before submitting a FOIA request, search the reading room to see which documents are already accessible. https://www.fca.gov/home/FOIA_index.html

Frequently Asked Questions (FAQs) The FCA posts answers to FAQs on its Web site. https://www.fca.gov/about/faqs.html

Glossary The FCA maintains an online glossary. http://www.fca.gov/info/glossary.html

Handbook The FCA Handbook database includes regulations, statutes, and FCA Board policy guidance that are applicable to the FCA, Farm Credit System, and Farm Credit System Insurance Corporation. The handbook is accessible free of charge in two formats: a searchable electronic database and files in Portable Document Format (PDF). https://www.fca.gov/exam/handbook.html

History For centuries, North American farmers have sought reliable sources of credit to acquire land and to develop and expand farms. Their need to access long-term, fixed-rate credit has continued to the present. While 19th-century commercial banks made long-term credit available at reasonable rates to businessmen and industrial capitalists, they provided less of the same service to farmers. Presidents Theodore Roosevelt, William Howard Taft, and Woodrow Wilson saw the problem and sought solutions. To learn what they did to help 20th-century American farmers, visit the "History of FCA" Web page. https://www.fca.gov/about/history/historyFCA_FCS.html

Institution Directory and Map The Farm Credit System institution directory contains information on each institution and its chartered territory. https://www.fca.gov/info/directory.html

Lender Locator The Farm Credit System has 70 lending associations. To find an association, use the online locator tool by entering a street address or ZIP Code. Search results include all branch offices for a particular association. More than one lending association may serve a location. Phone, 703-883-4056. https://apps.fca.gov/Locator | Email: info-line@fca.gov

News / Events The FCA announces events and posts news releases, rulemaking factsheets, speeches and statements, and testimonies online. http://www.fca.gov/news/index.html

Office of Inspector General (OIG)   The OIG conducts audits, evaluations, inspections, and investigations; reviews proposed legislation and regulations; informs the FCA Board and Congress of fraud or other serious problems; recommends policies to promote economy and efficiency and to prevent abuse, fraud, and waste; recommends corrective actions and reports on progress made in implementing them; and refers criminal matters to appropriate agencies for prosecution. Hotline, 800-437-7322 or 703-883-4316. Phone, 703-883-4030. https://www.fca.gov/home/inspector.html

Open Government   The FCA supports the Open Government initiative by promoting collaboration, participation, and transparency. https://www.fca.gov/home/opengovernment.html

Organizational Chart   The FCA posts its organizational chart online. https://www.fca.gov/about/offices/orgchart.html

The FCA's organizational chart is available in Portable Document Format (PDF) for viewing and downloading. https://www.fca.gov/Download/FCAorgchart.pdf

Plain Writing   Feedback on the clarity of documents and other items on the Web site helps improve the guidance that the FCA gives to institutions and the services that it offers to Americans. If a document or Web page is unclear, contact the Office of Congressional and Public Affairs. Phone, 703-883-4056. http://www.fca.gov/home/plainwriting.html

Publications   FCA documents are posted online, including publications about the Farm Credit Administration and information on the Farm Credit System. To find an older document, one that is over 5 years old, search in the archives. More information is available from the Office of Congressional and Public Affairs. Phone, 703-883-4056 (voice and TTY). Fax, 703-790-3260. http://www.fca.gov/rpts/index.html | Email: info-line@fca.gov

Site Map   The Web site map allows visitors to look for specific topics or to browse content that aligns with their interests. https://www.fca.gov/home/sitemap.html http://www.fca.gov/home/contact.html | Email: info-line@fca.gov

For further information, contact the Office of Congressional and Public Affairs, Farm Credit Administration, 1501 Farm Credit Drive, McLean, VA 22102-5090. Phone, 703-883-4056.

Federal Communications Commission

445 Twelfth Street SW., Washington, DC 20554
Phone, 888-225-5322. TTY, 888-835-5322. Internet, http://www.fcc.gov

Commissioners	
Chair	AJIT PAI
	BRENDAN CARR
	MICHAEL O'RIELLY
https://www.fcc.gov/about/leadership	JESSICA ROSENWORCEL
Bureau Chiefs	
Consumer and Governmental Affairs	PATRICK WEBRE
Enforcement	ROSEMARY HAROLD
International	THOMAS SULLIVAN
Media	MICHELLE CAREY
Public Safety and Homeland Security	LISA M. FOWLKES
Wireline Competition	KRIS MONTEITH
Wireless Telecommunications	DONALD STOCKDALE
https://www.fcc.gov/offices-bureaus#block-menu-block-4	

Federal Communications Commission

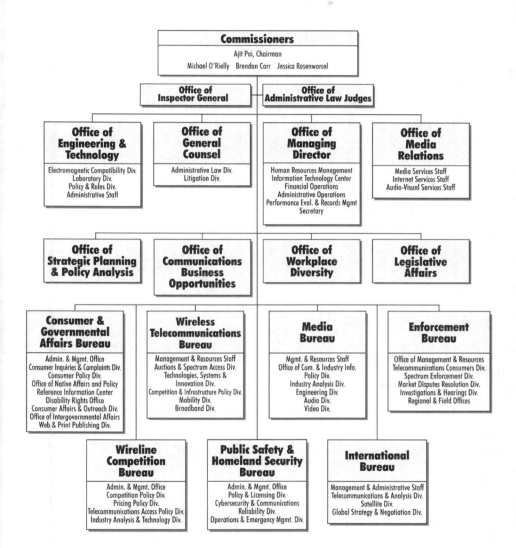

Commissioners
Ajit Pai, Chairman
Michael O'Rielly   Brendan Carr   Jessica Rosenworcel

Office of Inspector General

Office of Administrative Law Judges

Office of Engineering & Technology
Electromagnetic Compatibility Div.
Laboratory Div.
Policy & Rules Div.
Administrative Staff

Office of General Counsel
Administrative Law Div.
Litigation Div.

Office of Managing Director
Human Resources Management
Information Technology Center
Financial Operations
Administrative Operations
Performance Eval. & Records Mgmt
Secretary

Office of Media Relations
Media Services Staff
Internet Services Staff
Audio-Visual Services Staff

Office of Strategic Planning & Policy Analysis

Office of Communications Business Opportunities

Office of Workplace Diversity

Office of Legislative Affairs

Consumer & Governmental Affairs Bureau
Admin. & Mgmt. Office
Consumer Inquiries & Complaints Div.
Consumer Policy Div.
Office of Native Affairs and Policy
Reference Information Center
Disability Rights Office
Consumer Affairs & Outreach Div.
Office of Intergovernmental Affairs
Web & Print Publishing Div.

Wireless Telecommunications Bureau
Management & Resources Staff
Auctions & Spectrum Access Div.
Technologies, Systems &
Innovation Div.
Competition & Infrastructure Policy Div.
Mobility Div.
Broadband Div.

Media Bureau
Mgmt. & Resources Staff
Office of Com. & Industry Info.
Policy Div.
Industry Analysis Div.
Engineering Div.
Audio Div.
Video Div.

Enforcement Bureau
Office of Management & Resources
Telecommunications Consumers Div.
Spectrum Enforcement Div.
Market Disputes Resolution Div.
Investigations & Hearings Div.
Regional & Field Offices

Wireline Competition Bureau
Admin. & Mgmt. Office
Competition Policy Div.
Pricing Policy Div.
Telecommunications Access Policy Div.
Industry Analysis & Technology Div.

Public Safety & Homeland Security Bureau
Admin. & Mgmt. Office
Policy & Licensing Div.
Cybersecurity & Communications
Reliability Div.
Operations & Emergency Mgmt. Div.

International Bureau
Management & Administrative Staff
Telecommunications & Analysis Div.
Satellite Div.
Global Strategy & Negotiation Div.

Office Heads

General Counsel	THOMAS M. JOHNSON, JR.
Managing Director	MARK STEPHENS

Chiefs

Administrative Law Judges	RICHARD L. SIPPEL
Engineering and Technology	JULIUS KNAPP
Strategic Planning and Policy Analysis	WAYNE LEIGHTON

Directors

Communications Business Opportunities	SANFORD S. WILLIAMS
Legislative Affairs	TIMOTHY STRACHAN
Media Relations	BRIAN HART
Workplace Diversity	LARRY HUDSON

https://www.fcc.gov/about-fcc/organizational-charts-fcc

Inspector General	DAVID L. HUNT

https://www.fcc.gov/inspector-general#block-menu-block-4

[For the Federal Communications Commission statement of organization, see the Code of Federal Regulations, Title 47, Part 0]

The above list of key personnel was updated 10–2018.

The Federal Communications Commission regulates interstate and foreign communications by radio, television, wire, satellite, and cable.

The Federal Communications Commission (FCC) was established by the Communications Act of 1934 (47 U.S.C. 151 et seq.) and is charged with regulating interstate and foreign communications by wire and radio in the public interest. The scope of FCC regulation includes radio and television broadcasting; telephone and cable television operation; two-way radio and radio operators; and satellite communication.

The Commission comprises five members whom the President appoints with the advice and consent of the Senate. One of the members is designated by the President as the Chair. https://www.fcc.gov/about/overview

Activities

Consumer and Governmental Affairs Bureau   The Consumer and Governmental Affairs Bureau develops and administers the FCC's consumer and governmental affairs policies and initiatives. The Bureau facilitates public participation in the Commission's decisionmaking process; represents the Commission on consumer and Government committees, working groups, task forces,

and conferences; works with public, Federal, State, local, and tribal agencies to develop and coordinate policies; oversees the Consumer Advisory Committee, the Disability Advisory Committee, and the Intergovernmental Advisory Committee; offers expert advice on applicable disability and accessibility requirements, rules, and regulations, and assists with compliance; resolves informal complaints; and conducts consumer outreach and education programs. https://www.fcc.gov/consumer-governmental-affairs#block-menu-block-4

For further information, contact the Consumer and Governmental Affairs Bureau. Phone, 202-418-1400 or 888-225-5322.

Enforcement Bureau   The Enforcement Bureau serves as the FCC's primary agency for enforcing the Communications Act, other communications statutes, and the FCC's rules. The Bureau investigates and resolves complaints regarding common carriers (wireline, wireless, and international) and noncommon carriers subject to the Commission's jurisdiction under Title II of the Communications Act; radio frequency interference, equipment, and devices; accessibility to communications services and equipment for persons with disabilities; noncompliance with the lighting and marking of radio transmitting towers and pole attachment regulations; and unauthorized construction and operation of communication facilities and false distress signals. https://www.fcc.gov/enforcement#block-menu-block-4

For further information, contact the Enforcement Bureau. Phone, 202-418-7450 or 888-225-5322.

International Bureau The International Bureau serves as the FCC's principal representative at international conferences and in international negotiations. The Bureau promotes procompetitive policies abroad, coordinating the FCC's global spectrum activities and advocating U.S. interests in international communications and competition. It provides advice and technical assistance to U.S. trade officials in the negotiation and implementation of telecommunications trade agreements. It also encourages the international coordination of spectrum allocation and of frequency and orbital assignments to minimize cases of international radio interference involving U.S. licenses. https://www.fcc.gov/international#block-menu-block-4

For further information, contact the International Bureau. Phone, 202-418-0437 or 888-225-5322.

Media Bureau The Media Bureau oversees broadcast radio, television, and cable policy and licensing, as well as post-licensing matters for satellite services. The Bureau also conducts rulemaking proceedings and studies, resolves waiver petitions, and processes applications for authorization, assignment, transfer, and renewal of radio, television, and cable television relay services. https://www.fcc.gov/media#block-menu-block-4

For further information, contact the Media Bureau. Phone, 202-418-7200 or 888-225-5322.

Public Safety and Homeland Security Bureau The Public Safety and Homeland Security Bureau develops, recommends, and administers the FCC's policies on public safety communication. This includes 911 and E911, operability and interoperability of public safety communications,

communications infrastructure protection and disaster response, and network security and reliability. The Bureau also disseminates public safety communication information for emergency communication programs; alerting and warning U.S. citizens; continuity of government operations and operational planning; public safety outreach (e.g., first-responder organizations and hospitals); disaster management coordination and outreach; and studies and reports of public safety, homeland security, and disaster management issues. https://www.fcc.gov/public-safety-and-homeland-security#block-menu-block-4 | Email: pshsbinfo@fcc.gov

For further information, contact the Public Safety and Homeland Security Bureau. Phone, 202-418-1300 or 888-225-5322.

Wireless Telecommunications Bureau The Wireless Telecommunications Bureau administers all domestic commercial and private wireless communication programs and rules. It addresses present and future wireless communication and spectrum needs; promotes access, efficiency, and innovation in the allocation, licensing, and use of electromagnetic spectrum; ensures choice, opportunity, and fairness in the development of wireless communication services and markets; and encourages the development and widespread availability of wireless communication devices, facilities, and services. The Bureau also develops, recommends, administers, and coordinates policy for wireless communication services, including rulemaking, interpretations, and equipment standards; advises the public on FCC rules; serves as the FCC's principal policy and administrative resource for all spectrum auctions; and processes wireless service and facility authorization applications. https://www.fcc.gov/wireless-telecommunications#block-menu-block-4

For further information, contact the Wireless Telecommunications Bureau. Phone, 202-418-0600 or 888-225-5322.

Wireline Competition Bureau The Wireline Competition Bureau advises and makes recommendations to the FCC on policies affecting telephone landlines and fixed broadband. Its programs protect affordable communications access for health care providers, libraries, schools, and lifeline and rural consumers. The Bureau also ensures choice, opportunity, and fairness in the development of wireline communications; assesses the present and future wireline communication needs of the Nation; encourages the development and widespread availability of wireline communication services; and promotes investment in wireline communication infrastructure. https://www.fcc.gov/wireline-competition#block-menu-block-4

For further information, contact the Wireline Competition Bureau. Phone, 202-418-1500 or 888-225-5322.

Sources of Information

Blog The FCC maintains a blog. https://www.fcc.gov/news-events/blog

Business Opportunities The FCC relies on contractors for goods and services to carry out its mission. Many of these procurements are suitable for small businesses, and some offer opportunities for subcontracting. https://www.fcc.gov/about-fcc/contracting | Email: EACHelp@fcc.gov

Career Opportunities The FCC maintains a web-based recruitment system that allows employees and outside job seekers to apply for job opportunities online. https://www.fcc.gov/general/fcc-jobs

In 2017, the FCC ranked 20th among 25 midsize Government agencies in the Partnership for Public Service's Best Places To Work Agency Rankings. http://bestplacestowork.org/BPTW/rankings/detail/FC00

Consumer Assistance For general information on FCC operations, contact the FCC Consumer Center, 445 Twelfth Street SW., Washington, DC 20554. Phone, 888-225-5322. TTY, 888-835-5322. https://www.fcc.gov/consumers

Equal Employment Practices by the Communications Industry For more information, contact the FCC Consumer Center. Phone, 888-225-5322. https://www.fcc.gov/consumers

Ex-Parte Presentations For more information, contact the Commission's Office of General Counsel. Phone, 202-418-1720. https://www.fcc.gov/proceedings-actions/ex-parte

Federal Advisory Committee Management For more information, contact the Office of Managing Director. Phone, 202-418-2178. https://www.fcc.gov/about-fcc/advisory-committees-fcc

Fees Information on the FCC's fee programs is available online or from the Registration System / Fee Filer Help Desk. Phone, 877-480-3201 (option 4). https://www.fcc.gov/licensing-databases/fees | Email: ARINQUIRIES@fcc.gov

Freedom of Information Act For more information, contact the FOIA Requester Service Center. Phone, 202-418-1379. https://www.fcc.gov/general/foia | Email: foia@fcc.gov

Internal Equal Employment Practices For more information, contact the Office of Workplace Diversity. Phone, 202-418-1799. https://www.fcc.gov/workplace-diversity

Internships Information on FCC internships is available online. https://www.fcc.gov/general/internships-available-fcc

Licensing Information on the FCC's licensing systems is available online. http://www.fcc.gov/licensing

News The Office of Media Relations distributes public notices and press releases and makes them available online. https://www.fcc.gov/media-relations

Offices / Bureaus The "Offices and Bureaus" web page includes a brief description of FCC offices and bureaus, as well as links to related webpages with additional information. https://www.fcc.gov/offices-bureaus#block-menu-block-4

Organizational Chart The FCC's organizational chart is available in Portable Document Format (PDF) for viewing and downloading. https://www.fcc.gov/sites/default/files/fccorg-06072018.pdf

The organizational charts of FCC offices and bureaus are available online in Portable Document Format (PDF) for viewing and downloading. https://www.fcc.gov/about-fcc/organizational-charts-fcc

Podcast The official FCC podcast "More Than Seven Dirty Words" features interviews with FCC staff and others in the field of communications. https://www.fcc.gov/news-events/podcast

Public Inspection Records that are deemed nonconfidential by law can be viewed on the FCC's Web site. Each broadcasting station maintains a current copy of its application for license, operational information, and nonconfidential FCC reports for public inspection.
Publications The Consumer and Governmental Affairs Bureau maintains an

online consumer publications library. https://www.fcc.gov/consumers
Social Media To inform and to connect and engage with the general public, the FCC uses social media: Disqus, Facebook, Flickr, GitHub, Instagram, Scribd, Twitter, and YouTube. https://www.fcc.gov/social-media
https://www.fcc.gov/about/contact

For further information, contact the Consumer Center, Federal Communications Commission, 445 Twelfth Street SW., Washington, DC 20554. Phone, 888-225-5322. TTY, 888-835-5322.

Federal Deposit Insurance Corporation

550 Seventeenth Street NW., Washington, DC 20429
Phone, 703-562-2222. Internet, http://www.fdic.gov

Board of Directors

Chair	Martin J. Gruenberg
Vice Chair	Thomas M. Hoenig
Director (Consumer Financial Protection Bureau)	J. Michael Mulvaney, Acting
Director (Office of the Comptroller of the Currency)	Joseph M. Otting
Director	(vacancy)

https://www.fdic.gov/about/learn/board
Headquarters–Washington, DC

Chair	Martin J. Gruenberg
Vice Chair	Thomas M. Hoenig
Chief of Staff	Barbara A. Ryan
Special Advisor for Supervisory Matters	Jason C. Cave
Deputies	
Deputy to the Chair	Kymberly K. Copa
Deputy to the Chair / Chief Financial Officer	Steven O. App
Deputy to the Chair / Chief Operating Officer	Barbara A. Ryan
Deputy to the Vice Chair	Michael Spencer, Acting
Division Heads	
Chief Information Officer / Chief Privacy Officer	Howard Whyte, Acting
Chief Information Security Officer	Noreen Padilla, Acting
Director, Administration	Arleas Upton Kea
Director, Corporate University / Chief Learning Officer	Suzannah L. Susser
Director, Depositor and Consumer Protection	Mark E. Pearce
Director, Finance	Craig R. Jarvill
Director, Information Technology	Russell G. Pittman
Director, Insurance and Research	Diane Ellis
Director, Resolution and Receiverships	Bret D. Edwards
Director, Risk Management Supervision	Doreen R. Eberley
General Counsel	Charles Yi
Office Heads	
Chief Risk Officer	Kenyon Kilber, Acting
Deputy to the Chair for Communications	Barbara Hagenbaugh

Director, Complex Financial Institutions	Ricardo R. Delfin
Director, Legislative Affairs	M. Andy Jiminez
Director, Minority and Women Inclusion	Saul Schwartz, Acting
Ombudsman	M. Anthony Lowe
Inspector General	Jay N. Lerner
https://www.fdicoig.gov	

The above list of key personnel was updated 02–2018.

The Federal Deposit Insurance Corporation preserves and promotes public confidence in U.S. financial institutions by insuring bank and thrift deposits, examining State-chartered banks, and liquidating assets of failed institutions.

The Federal Deposit Insurance Corporation (FDIC) was established under the Banking Act of 1933 after numerous banks failed during the Great Depression. The FDIC began insuring banks on January 1, 1934. The basic insurance coverage per depositor at each insured bank and savings association is $250,000. https://www.fdic.gov/about/history

The FDIC is managed by a five-member Board of Directors, all of whom the President appoints and the Senate confirms. No more than three of the Directors can be affiliated with the same political party.

The FDIC insures approximately 5,850 institutions. It receives no congressional appropriations. FDIC funding comes from insurance premiums on deposits held by insured banks and savings associations and from interest on the investment of those premiums in U.S. Government securities. FDIC has authority to borrow up to $100 billion from the Treasury for insurance purposes. https://www.fdic.gov/about/strategic/strategic/mission.html

Activities

The FDIC insures about $13 trillion of U.S. bank and thrift deposits. As required by law, the fund relies on two sources of income: premiums paid by banks and savings associations, and the interest on the investment of those premiums in U.S. Government securities. An institution's level of capitalization and potential risk to the insurance fund determines its premiums. https://www.fdic.gov/deposit

The FDIC examines about 3,600 State-chartered commercial and savings banks that are not members of the Federal Reserve System, called State nonmember banks. The FDIC also has authority to examine other types of FDIC-insured institutions for deposit insurance purposes. The two types of examinations conducted are for safety and soundness and for compliance with applicable consumer laws such as the Truth in Lending Act, the Home Mortgage Disclosure Act, the Equal Credit Opportunity Act, the Fair Housing Act, and the Community Reinvestment Act. FDIC examiners work onsite at the institution as well analyze bank data offsite. https://www.fdic.gov/regulations

A failed bank or savings association is generally closed by its chartering authority, and the FDIC is named receiver. The FDIC is required to resolve the closure in a manner that is least costly to its Deposit Insurance Fund. Ordinarily, the FDIC attempts to locate a healthy institution to acquire the failed entity. If such an entity cannot be found, the FDIC pays depositors the amount of their insured funds, usually by the next business day following the closure. Depositors with funds that exceed the insurance limit often receive an advance dividend, which is a portion of their uninsured funds that is determined by an estimate of the future proceeds from liquidating the failed institution's remaining assets. Depositors with funds in a failed institution that exceed the insurance limit receive a receivership certificate for those funds and partial payments of their uninsured funds as asset disposition permits.

As part of its insurance, supervisory, and receivership responsibilities, the FDIC approves or disapproves mergers, consolidations, and acquisitions where the resulting bank is an insured State nonmember; approves or disapproves proposals by banks to establish and operate a new branch, close an existing branch, or move its main office from one location to another; and approves or disapproves requests to engage as principal in activities and investments that are not permissible for a national bank. It also issues enforcement actions, including cease-and-desist orders, for specific violations or practices requiring corrective action and reviews changes in ownership or control of a bank.

Sources of Information

Assistance for Bank Customers An electronic form is available for filing a complaint against a particular financial institution. The form also may be used to inquire about FDIC deposit insurance coverage or to ask a question about a particular financial institution. https://www5.fdic.gov/starsmail/index.asp

Bank Failures The FDIC maintains a failed bank list that contains information on how accounts and loans are affected, how vendors can file claims against the receivership, and the acquiring bank—if applicable. The list covers from October 1, 2000, to the present. https://www.fdic.gov/bank/individual/failed/banklist.html

Starting with the year 2001, the FDIC maintains a brief summary of each bank failure. For additional information on recent failures, call the customer service hotline. Phone, 888-206-4662. https://www.fdic.gov/bank/historical/bank

A search tool is available online to help the public find the point of contact information of failed institutions. https://www5.fdic.gov/drrip/cs/index.asp

Detailed information on bank and thrift failures since 1934 is available on the FDIC website. https://www5.fdic.gov/hsob/SelectRpt.asp?EntryTyp=30

Bank Finder The FDIC website has an online tool for locating insured banking institutions. https://research.fdic.gov/bankfind

Call Center The call center is open every day of the week: Monday–Friday, 8 a.m.–8 p.m., eastern standard time; Saturday and Sunday, 9 a.m.–5 p.m., eastern standard time. Phone, 877-275-3342. Phone, 800-925-4618 (hearing impaired).

Career Opportunities FDIC job openings and information on career transition assistance, student employment opportunities, and submitting an application are available online. https://www.fdic.gov/about/jobs

In 2017, the FDIC ranked 3d among 25 midsize Government agencies in the Partnership for Public Service's Best Places To Work Agency Rankings. http://bestplacestowork.org/BPTW/rankings/detail/FD00

Electronic Deposit Insurance Estimator (EDIE) Consumers and bankers can use EDIE to determine, on a per-bank basis, how the insurance rules and limits apply to a depositor's specific group of deposit accounts—what is insured and what portion, if any, exceeds coverage limits. https://www.fdic.gov/edie/index.html

Enlaces en Español Links to information and resources in Spanish are available on the FDIC website. https://www.fdic.gov/quicklinks/spanish.html

Freedom of Information Act (FOIA) The FDIC operates a FOIA service center that is open on weekdays, 8:30 a.m.–5:00 p.m., excluding Federal holidays. Phone, 202-898-7021. https://www.fdic.gov/about/freedom | Email: efoia@fdic.gov

The FDIC's FOIA guide offers a concise explanation of the FOIA and how it can be used to access Government records. It also explains the process for submitting a request to the FDIC. The guide also provides links to helpful reference guides and describes how additional information may be obtained from the FDIC. https://www.fdic.gov/about/freedom/guide.html

The FDIC accepts electronic FOIA requests. https://efoiarequest.fdic.gov/palMain.aspx

History "On March 3 banking operations in the United States ceased . . . the government has been compelled to step in." These words, President Franklin D. Roosevelt spoke to the U.S. Congress in 1933, 6 days after the banks had closed, when the Nation's banking system still lay dormant. The U.S. economy was in the throes of deep and widespread depression. Three months later, in response to the crisis, President Roosevelt approved the Banking Act of 1933, giving birth to the FDIC and Federal depositor protection, which the general public supported. To learn about the antecedents to Federal deposit insurance and the creation of the FDIC and its general history, see "A History of the FDIC 1933–1983." https://www.fdic.gov/bank/analytical/firstfifty

In 2008 and 2009, FDIC agents were active seizing failed banks. To learn about the process of a bank seizure and the efforts made by the FDIC to shield employees and depositors from the ill effects of a failure, watch the CBS 60 Minutes video "Your Bank Has Failed." https://www.fdic.gov/news/letters/60minutes.html

News / Events   The FDIC posts conferences and events, financial institution letters, opinion editorials, press releases, speeches, and testimonies on its website. https://www.fdic.gov/news

The FDIC offers an online subscription service for email alerts. A subscriber may opt to receive various types of alerts: financial institution letters, news releases, statistical publications, and other types. https://service.govdelivery.com/accounts/USFDIC/subscriber/new

The FDIC disseminates information and news using RSS feeds. https://www.fdic.gov/rss.html

The FCC tweets news items and other information on Twitter. https://twitter.com/FDICgov

Office of Inspector General (OIG)   The OIG operates a toll-free, nationwide hotline to provide a way for FDIC employees, its contractors, financial institution staff, and other members of the public to report incidents of abuse, fraud, mismanagement,

and waste within FDIC programs and activities or its contractor operations. A person can file a report anonymously, confidentially, or openly by using the hotline; however, filing a report by email guarantees neither anonymity nor confidentiality. Phone, 800-964-3342. Fax, 703-562-6444. https://www.fdicig.gov | Email: ighotline@fdic.gov

Open Government   The FDIC supports the Open Government initiative by promoting the principles of collaboration, participation, and transparency. https://www.fdic.gov/open | Email: opengov@fdic.gov

Plain Language   The FDIC welcomes comment on it's compliance with the Plain Writing Act of 2010 and suggestions for improving communication between the agency and the public. https://www.fdic.gov/plainlanguage | Email: PlainWriting@fdic.gov

Publications   The FDIC website has an online product catalog and ordering system. https://catalog.fdic.gov

Publications, press releases, congressional testimony, directives to financial institutions, and other documents are available through the Public Information Center. Phone, 877-275-3342 (press 1, then press 5). http://www.fdic.gov/news/publications/PIChardcopies.html | Email: publicinfo@fdic.gov

Site Map   The website map allows visitors to look for specific topics or to browse for content that aligns with their interests. https://www.fdic.gov/sitemap

Social Media   The FDIC has a Facebook account. https://www.facebook.com/FDICgov

The FDIC tweets announcements and other newsworthy items on Twitter. https://twitter.com/FDICgov

The FDIC posts videos on its YouTube channel. https://www.youtube.com/user/FDICchannel https://www.fdic.gov/about/contact/ask | Email: communications@fdic.gov

For further information and media inquiries, contact the Office of Communications, Federal Deposit Insurance Corporation, 550 Seventeenth Street NW., Washington, DC 20429. Phone, 202-898-6993.

Federal Election Commission

999 E Street NW., Washington, DC 20463
Phone, 202-694-1100. Fax, 800-424-9530. Internet, http://www.fec.gov

Chair	STEVEN T. WALTHER
Vice Chair	CAROLINE C. HUNTER
Commissioner	LEE E. GOODMAN
Commissioner	MATTHEW S. PETERSEN
Commissioner	ELLEN L. WEINTRAUB
Commissioner	VACANT
Staff Director	ALEC PALMER
Chief Financial Officer	GILBERT FORD, ACTING
General Counsel	LISA J. STEVENSON, ACTING
Inspector General	VACANT

The Federal Election Commission provides public disclosure of campaign finance activities and ensures compliance with campaign finance laws and regulations.

The Federal Election Commission is an independent agency established by section 309 of the Federal Election Campaign Act of 1971, as amended (52 U.S.C. 30106). It comprises six Commissioners whom the President appoints with the advice and consent of the Senate. The Act also provides for three statutory officers—the staff director, the general counsel, and the inspector general—whom the Commissioners appoint. https://transition.fec.gov/about/offices/offices.shtml

Activities

The Commission administers and enforces the Federal Election Campaign Act of 1971, as amended (52 U.S.C. 30101 et seq.), and the Revenue Act, as amended (26 U.S.C. 1 et seq.). These laws provide for the public funding of Presidential elections, public disclosure of the financial activities of political committees involved in Federal elections, and limitations and prohibitions on contributions and expenditures made to influence Federal elections.

Public Funding of Presidential Elections The Commission oversees the public financing of Presidential elections by certifying Federal payments to primary candidates and general election nominees. It also audits recipients of Federal funds and may require repayment to the U.S. Treasury if a committee has made nonqualified campaign expenditures.

Disclosure The Commission ensures public disclosure of the campaign finance activities reported by political committees supporting Federal candidates. These committees regularly file reports disclosing the sources of campaign money and how that money is spent. The Commission places these reports on the public record within 48 hours after they are received and digitizes the data contained in them. http://www.fec.gov/ans/answers_disclosure.shtml

Sources of Information

Congressional Affairs This Office of Congressional, Legislative, and Intergovernmental Affairs serves as the Commission's primary congressional and executive branch liaison. Phone, 202-694-1006. https://transition.fec.gov/about/offices/cong_affairs/cong_affairs.shtml | Email: congress@fec.gov

Data Data tables summarizing campaign financial activity by filer type, election cycle, and reporting period are available online. http://www.fec.gov/press/campaign_finance_statistics.shtml

Career Opportunities The Commission posts available positions on its Web site. Sign up online to receive email updates regarding employment opportunities. Information is also available from the Office of Human Resources. Phone, 202-694-1080. http://www.fec.gov/pages/jobs/jobs.shtml | Email: fecjobs@fec.gov

Filing Information is available online to help filers comply with the disclosure requirements of the Federal campaign finance law. http://www.fec.gov/info/filing.shtml

Freedom of Information Act (FOIA) FOIA requests may be submitted by email or fax or sent by mail to the Federal Election Commission, Attn: FOIA Requester Service Center, Room 408, 999 E Street NW., Washington, DC 20463. Fax, 202-219-1043. http://www.fec.gov/press/foia.shtml | Email: FOIA@fec.gov

General Inquiries The Information Division informs and assists Federal candidates, political committees, and the public. It answers questions on campaign finance laws, conducts workshops and seminars on these laws, and distributes publications and forms. Phone, 202-694-1100 or 800-424-9530. TDD, 202-219-3336. http://www.fec.gov/pages/contact.shtml | Email: info@fec.gov

Law Library The library contains a collection of basic legal research resources on political campaign financing, corporate and labor political activity, and campaign finance reform. It is open to the public on weekdays, 9 a.m.–5 p.m., except on Federal holidays. Phone, 202-694-1516 or 800-424-9530. http://www.fec.gov/general/library.shtml

Media Inquiries The Press Office answers questions from media sources, issues press releases on Commission actions and statistical data, responds to requests for information, and distributes other materials. Phone, 202-694-1220. http://www.fec.gov/press/index.shtml | Email: press@fec.gov

Public Records The Public Records Branch, located at 999 E Street NW., Washington, DC, provides space for public inspection of campaign finance reports and statements after 1971. It is open to the public on weekdays, 9 a.m.–5 p.m., except on Federal holidays. Phone, 202-694-1120 or 800-424-9530. http://www.fec.gov/pubrec/publicrecordsoffice.shtml | Email: pubrec@fec.gov http://www.fec.gov/pages/contact.shtml

For further information, contact the Information Division, Federal Election Commission, 999 E Street NW., Washington, DC 20463. Phone, 202-694-1100 or 800-424-9530 (option 6).

Federal Housing Finance Agency

400 7th Street SW., Washington, DC 20219
Phone, 202-649-3800. Internet, http://www.fhfa.gov

Director	MELVIN L. WATT
Chief Operating Officer	LAWRENCE STAUFFER, ACTING
Director, Office of Minority and Women Inclusion	SHARRON P. A. LEVINE
Deputy Director, Division of Conservatorship	BOB RYAN, ACTING
Deputy Director, Division of Federal Home Loan Bank Regulation	FRED C. GRAHAM
Deputy Director, Division of Enterprise Regulation	NINA NICHOLS
Deputy Director, Division of Housing Mission and Goals	SANDRA THOMPSON
General Counsel	ALFRED M. POLLARD
Inspector General	LAURA S. WERTHEIMER
Obmbudsman	JANELL BYRD-CHICHESTER, ACTING

The Federal Housing and Finance Agency ensures that the housing Government-Sponsored Enterprises operate safely and soundly and serve as a reliable source of liquidity and funding for housing finance and community investment.

FHFA Organizational Chart

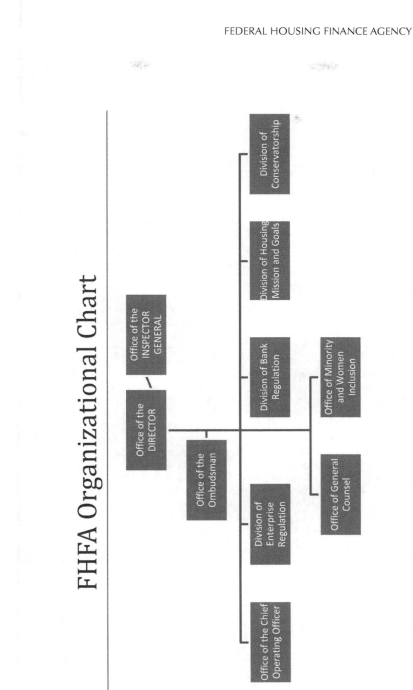

The Federal Housing and Finance Agency (FHFA) was established by the Housing and Economic Recovery Act of 2008 (42 U.S.C. 4501 note) as an independent agency in the executive branch. The merger of the Federal Housing Finance Board and the Office of Federal Housing Enterprise Oversight, combined with the transfer of the Department of Housing and Urban Development's Government-Sponsored Enterprise mission team, formed the FHFA.

The FHFA is managed by a Director whom the President appoints and the Senate confirms. FHFA's Director also serves as the Chairman of the Federal Housing Oversight Board. The Secretary of the Treasury, the Secretary of Housing and Urban Development, and the Chairman of the Securities and Exchange Commission are also members of the Board. http://www.fhfa.gov/AboutUs

Activities

The FHFA provides research and data, supervision, and policies for strengthening and securing the U.S. secondary mortgage markets. It oversees vital components of those markets: the housing Government-Sponsored Enterprises of Fannie Mae, Freddie Mac, and the Federal Home Loan Bank System. Combined, these entities make available more than $5.6 trillion in funding for financial institutions and the U.S. mortgage markets. The FHFA also acts as the conservator of Fannie Mae and Freddie Mac. http://www.fhfa.gov/PolicyProgramsResearch

Sources of Information

Blog   Agency experts share their insights into housing finance issues on the blog "FHFA Insights." https://www.fhfa.gov/Media/Pages/Insights.aspx
Business Opportunities   FHFA contracting operations is responsible for procuring all goods and services, including information technology, that the agency requires. http://www.fhfa.gov/AboutUs/Business
Career Opportunities   The Agency's mission-critical professionals include accountants, attorneys, economists, examiners, financial analysts, and information technology specialists. The

FHFA also relies on budget and procurement and human resource specialists, facilities managers, policy experts, and student interns, to fill important support roles. The Agency advertises opportunities for employment on its "Careers" Web page. Contact the Office of Human Resources Management for additional information. Phone, 202-649-3807. http://www.fhfa.gov/AboutUs/Careers
Dodd–Frank Act Stress Tests   The FHFA requires Fannie Mae and Freddie Mac and Federal Home Loan Banks to conduct stress tests pursuant to the Dodd-Frank Wall Street Reform and Consumer Protection Act of 2010. https://www.fhfa.gov/SupervisionRegulation/DoddFrankActStressTests

The FHFA is categorized as a small agency in the Partnership for Public Service's Best Places To Work in the Federal Government rankings. In 2016, the Agency improved its index score. http://bestplacestowork.org/BPTW/rankings/detail/FY00
Freedom of Information Act (FOIA)   The FOIA established a statutory right of public access to executive branch information in the Federal Government. It gives a right to any person to obtain access to Federal agency records; however, nine exemptions and three special law enforcement exclusions shield certain records from public disclosure. https://www.fhfa.gov/AboutUs/FOIAPrivacy/Pages/FOIA.aspx | Email: foia@fhfa.gov
Frequently Asked Questions (FAQs)   The FHFA posts answers to FAQs on various topics: the Home Affordable Refinance Program (HARP), housing price index (HPI), servicing alignment initiative, as well as on conservatorship, Federal Home Loan Bank membership, principal reduction modification, and private mortgage insurer draft eligibility requirements, https://www.fhfa.gov/Media/Pages/FAQs.aspx
History   On September 6, 2008, the FHFA placed Fannie Mae and Freddie Mac into conservatorship because they could no longer carry out their mission without Government intervention. To learn more about this extraordinary action and this critical moment in the history of the Nation's mortgage market, visit the "History of Fannie Mae and Freddie Mac Conservatorships"

Web page. https://www.fhfa.gov/ Conservatorship/Pages/History-of-Fannie-Mae--Freddie-Conservatorships.aspx

A timeline of significant events in the history of the FHFA is available on its Web site. https://www.fhfa.gov/AboutUs/Timeline

Key Topics These Web pages contain information on the FHFA's work on a range of national issues. They highlight relevant news releases, reports, statements, and web pages on the key topics. https://www.fhfa. gov/KeyTopics

Meet the Experts The "Meet the Experts" page contains brief professional biographies of experienced, well-educated FHFA personnel. https://www.fhfa.gov/ PolicyProgramsResearch/Pages/Meet-the-Experts.aspx

Navigate by Audience The "Government" Web page contains consolidated resources for Federal, State, and local government personnel seeking information related to the Nation's housing finance system. https:// www.fhfa.gov/Government

The "Homeowners and Homebuyers" Web page guides homeowners and buyers to resources and tools: information on avoiding foreclosure, buying a new home, refinancing an existing home, shopping for a mortgage, understanding the housing markets, and more. https://www.fhfa.gov/ Homeownersbuyer

The "Industry" Web page contains consolidated resources for advocacy organizations, investors, mortgage insurers, originators, servicers, small and large companies, trade groups, vendors, and others with an interest in the Nation's housing finance system. https://www.fhfa. gov/Industry

The "Media" Web page gives members of the media and general public access to FHFA expertise on and insight into housing finance. https://www.fhfa.gov/Media | Email: MediaInquiries@fhfa.gov

News The FHFA posts news releases on its Web site. https://www.fhfa. gov/Media/Pages/News-Releases. aspx?k=ContentType%3APublic-Affairs%20 AND%20PublicAffairsCategoryOWSCHCS% 3A%22News%20Release%22%20AND%20 FHFAPublishedDateOWSDATE%3D01%2F0 1%2F2017%2E%2E12%2F31%2F2017

Open Government The FHFA supports the Open Government initiative by promoting the principles of collaboration, participation, and transparency. https://www.fhfa.gov/ AboutUs/Policies/Pages/Open-Government. aspx

Plans / Reports The FHFA posts performance and strategic plans and various types of reports on its Web site. https://www. fhfa.gov/AboutUs/reportsplans

Privacy Act of 1974 Fair information practices govern the collection, maintenance, use, and dissemination of an individual's personally identifiable information that a Federal agency maintains in a system of records—in a group of records that an agency controls and from which its staff may retrieve information by using the individual's name or an assigned identifier. https://www.fhfa.gov/ AboutUs/FOIAPrivacy/Pages/Privacy.aspx | Email: Privacy@fhfa.gov

Site Map The Web site map allows visitors to look for specific topics or to browse content that aligns with their interests. https://www.fhfa.gov/AboutUs/Sitemap

Social Media The FHFA tweets announcements and other newsworthy items on Twitter. https://twitter.com/FHFA

The FHFA posts videos on its YouTube channel. https://www.youtube.com/channel/ UCoKP7Om6nsRkEav9yInFekw

Tools A borrower assistance map, conforming loan limits map, and housing price index (HPI) calculator and motion chart, as well as HPI maps (county, four-quarter appreciation, ZIP5) and summary tables, are available online. https://www. fhfa.gov/DataTools/Tools https://www.fhfa. gov/AboutUs/Contact | Email: fhfainfo@fhfa. gov

For further information, contact the Office of Congressional Affairs and Communications, Federal Housing Finance Agency, 400 7th Street SW., Washington, DC 20219. Phone, 202-649-3802.

Federal Labor Relations Authority

1400 K Street NW., Washington, DC 20005
Phone, 202-218-7770. Internet, http://www.flra.gov

Agency Support	
Chief Executive Officer	ERNEST DUBESTER
Chief Administrative Officer	ERNEST DUBESTER
Directors	
Collaboration and Alternative Dispute Resolution	MICHAEL WOLF
Equal Employment Opportunity	(VACANCY)
Solicitor	NOAH PETERS
Office of Executive Director	
Executive Director	MICHAEL W. JEFFRIES
Directors	
Administrative Services	XAVIER STORR
Budget and Finance	GREGORY MISTER
Human Resources	PAULA CHANDLER
Information Resources Management	DAVID FONTAINE
Legislative Affairs and Program Planning	ALOYSIUS HOGAN
https://www.flra.gov/components-offices/offices/office-executive-director	
Authority Component	
Chair	ERNEST DUBESTER
Members	JAMES T. ABBOTT
	COLLEEN D. KIKO
Case Intake and Publication	(VACANCY)
Chief Administrative Law Judge	DAVID L. WELCH
Solicitor	NOAH PETERS
https://www.flra.gov/about/flra-leadership	
Federal Service Impasses Panel	
Chair	(VACANCY)
Members	(VACANCY)
	(VACANCY)
	(VACANCY)
	(VACANCY)
	(VACANCY)
	(VACANCY)
	(VACANCY)
	(VACANCY)
	(VACANCY)
	(VACANCY)
https://www.flra.gov/components-offices/components/federal-service-impasses-panel-fsip-or-panel	
Foreign Service Impasse Disputes Panel	
Chair	(VACANCY)
Members	RICHARD T. MILLER
	(VACANCY)
	(VACANCY)
	(VACANCY)

https://www.flra.gov/components-offices/components/
   federal-service-impasses-panel-fsip-or-panel/foreign-
   service-impasse

Foreign Service Labor Relations Board

Chair	Ernest DuBester
Members	Dennis K. Hays
	Thomas J. Miller

https://www.flra.gov/components-offices/components/
   authority/foreign-service-labor-relations-board

General Counsel Component

General Counsel	Charlotte A. Dye, Acting

https://www.flra.gov/OGC_bios

Regional Offices

Directors	
Atlanta	Richard Jones
Chicago	Greg A. Weddle, Acting
Denver	Timothy J. Sullivan
San Francisco	John Pannozzo
Washington	Jessica Bartlett

https://www.flra.gov/components-offices/components/office-
   general-counsel-ogc/office-general-counsel-ogc-regional-
   offices

Office of Inspector General

Inspector General	Dana A. Rooney

https://www.flra.gov/components-offices/offices/office-
   inspector-general

The above list of key personnel was updated 7–2021.

The Federal Labor Relations Authority oversees labor-management relations between the Federal Government and its employees.

Establishment and Organization

On May 23, 1978, President James E. Carter transmitted his reorganizational plan that consolidated central policymaking functions in Federal labor-management relations to the Senate and the House of Representatives in the U.S. Congress. Part III of Reorganization Plan No. 2 of 1978 "established, as an independent establishment in the Executive Branch, the Federal Labor Relations Authority [FLRA]." https://www.govinfo.gov/content/pkg/STATUTE-92/pdf/STATUTE-92-Pg3783.pdf

The reorganization plan was printed in the Federal Register on August 15, 1978 (43 FR 36037). https://www.govinfo.gov/content/pkg/FR-1978-08-15/pdf/FR-1978-08-15.pdf

The reorganization became effective January 1, 1979, pursuant to Executive Order 12107 of December 28, 1978 (44 FR 1055). https://www.govinfo.gov/content/pkg/FR-1979-01-03/pdf/FR-1979-01-03.pdf

The FLRA's duties and authority are specified in "Title VII—Federal Service Labor-Management Relations" (92 Stat. 1191) of the Civil Service Reform Act of 1978 (PL 95–454). https://www.govinfo.gov/content/pkg/STATUTE-92/pdf/STATUTE-92-Pg1111.pdf

The FLRA comprises three members whom the President nominates and the Senate confirms to 5-year terms. The Chair of the Authority serves as its Chief Executive and Chief Administrative Officer. The Chair also presides over the Foreign Service Labor Relations Board. The General Counsel investigates alleged unfair labor practices, files and prosecutes unfair labor practice

Federal Labor Relations Authority

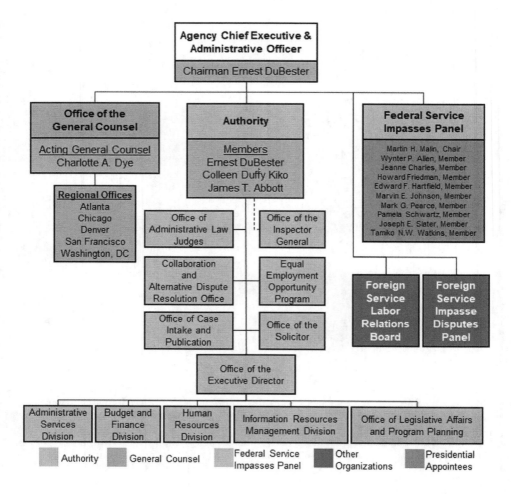

complaints before the Authority, and exercises other powers that the Authority may prescribe. https://www.flra.gov/about/introduction-flra

The FLRA is organized into three statutory components: the Authority, the Office of the General Counsel, and the Federal Service Impasses Panel. Each of the components has its own unique adjudicative or prosecutorial roles. The agency also provides program and staff support to two other organizations: the Foreign Service Impasse Disputes Panel and the Foreign Service Labor Relations Board. https://www.flra.gov/components-offices

The FLRA has a number of offices within its three components. https://www.flra.gov/components-offices/offices

The FLRA posts its organizational chart online. https://www.flra.gov/about/organizational-chart

The FLRA posted a press release describing highlights of its updated organizational chart (June 2020). https://www.flra.gov/system/files/webfm/FLRA%20Agency-wide/Public%20Affairs/Press%20Releases/Press%20Release%20-%20FLRA%20RELEASES%20UPDATED%20ORGANIZATIONAL%20CHART%206-29-2020.pdf

Statutory and Regulatory Authorities
Reorganization Plan No. 2 of 1978 has been codified in the United States Code (U.S.C.) and assigned to the Appendix of 5 U.S.C. https://uscode.house.gov/view.xhtml?req=granuleid:USC-prelim-title5a-node84-leaf186&num=0&edition=prelim

Statutory material that affects the FLRA has been codified and assigned to Chapter 71, sections 7101–7106, of 5 U.S.C. Chapter 71 has the title "Labor-Management Relations" and runs from section 7101 through 7154. https://uscode.house.gov/view.xhtml?path=/prelim@title5/part3/subpartF/chapter71&edition=prelim

Rules and regulations that are associated with the FLRA, General Counsel of the FLRA, and Federal Service Impasse Panel have been codified and assigned to Chapter XIV, parts 2400–2499, of 5 CFR. https://www.ecfr.gov/cgi-bin/text-idx?SID=cd49c395b33e34776afc1b9dce26710e&mc=true&tpl=/ecfrbrowse/Title05/5chapterXIV.tpl

Rules and regulations that are associated with the Foreign Service Labor Relations Board, Federal Labor Relations Authority, General Counsel of the FLRA, and the Foreign Service Impasse Disputes Panel have been codified and assigned to Chapter XIV, parts 1400–1499, of 22 CFR. https://www.ecfr.gov/cgi-bin/text-idx?SID=00ab5d289e663071e5fe1e32170fe541&mc=true&tpl=/ecfrbrowse/Title22/22chapterXIV.tpl

Activities
The Authority adjudicates disputes arising under the Federal Labor-Management Relations Program, deciding cases concerning the negotiability of collective bargaining agreement proposals, appeals concerning unfair labor practices and representation petitions, and exceptions to grievance arbitration awards. It also assists Federal agencies and unions in understanding their rights and responsibilities under the program.

The Federal Service Impasses Panel, an entity within the FLRA, assists in resolving negotiation impasses between agencies and unions. The Panel can either recommend procedures to the parties for the resolution of the impasse or assist the parties in resolving the impasse through whatever methods and procedures it considers appropriate, including fact-finding and mediation-arbitration. If the parties do not arrive at a voluntary settlement after receiving Panel assistance, the Panel may take whatever action is necessary to resolve the impasse, including the imposition of contract terms.

The Foreign Service Labor Relations Board and the Foreign Service Impasse Disputes Panel administer provisions of chapter 2 of the Foreign Service Act of 1980 (22 U.S.C. 3921) concerning labor-management relations. This chapter establishes a statutory labor-management relations program for Foreign Service employees of the U.S. Government. Administrative and staff support is provided by the Federal Labor Relations Authority and the Federal Service Impasses Panel. https://www.flra.gov/about/mission

Sources of Information

Career Opportunities The FLRA posts announcements for job openings on USAJobs. For more information, contact the

Human Resources Division. Phone, 202-218-7979. https://www.usajobs.gov

In 2020, the FLRA ranked 24th among 29 small agencies in the Partnership for Public Service's Best Places To Work Agency Rankings. https://bestplacestowork.org/rankings/detail/?c=AU00

Electronic Filing   To use the FLRA's electronic case filing system, register online and create a user profile. Email addresses are the case filing system's primary means of identifying electronic filers. https://efile.flra.gov/representatives/sign_in

Federal Register   Documents that the FLRA recently published in the Federal Register are accessible online. https://www.federalregister.gov/agencies/federal-labor-relations-authority

Freedom of Information Act (FOIA)   To any person, the FOIA gives a statutory right for obtaining access to Government information in the records of executive branch agencies. This right to access is limited, however, when the requested information is shielded from disclosure by any of nine exemptions that the statute contains. https://www.flra.gov/freedom-information-act-program

The FLRA maintains an electronic FOIA reading room. https://www.flra.gov/elibrary

Media   Members of the media should contact the Counsel for Regulatory and Public Affairs if they have questions or seek information. Phone, 202-218-7776. https://www.flra.gov/about/public-affairs

News   The FLRA posts press releases on its website. The online archives contain press releases from 2009 through 2014. https://www.flra.gov/press_releases

Open Government   The FLRA supports the Federal Government's efforts to increase collaboration, participation, and transparency. https://www.flra.gov/open-government

Plain Language   The FLRA adheres to Federal plain language guidelines. To comply with the Plain Writing Act of 2010, the agency relies on the general public. If a document or web page is difficult to understand, alert the FLRA editorial team to the lack of clarity by sending an email. https://www.flra.gov/plain_language | Email: engagetheFLRA@flra.gov

Regional Offices   Contact information for each of the five Office of the General Counsel Regional Offices is available online. https://www.flra.gov/components-offices/components/office-general-counsel-ogc/office-general-counsel-ogc-regional-offices

The above Sources of Information were updated 7–2021.

Federal Mine Safety and Health Review Commission

1331 Pennsylvania Avenue NW., Suite 520N, Washington, DC 20004-1710
Phone, 202-434-9900. TTY/TDD, 202-434-4000, ext. 293. Internet, http://www.fmshrc.gov |
Email: fmshrc@fmshrc.gov

Commission	
Chair	Marco M. Rajkovich, Jr.
Commissioners	William I. Althen
	Mary Lucille Jordan
	Arthur R. Traynor III
	Michael G. Young
https://www.fmshrc.gov/about/commissioners	
Administration	
Executive Director	Lisa M. Boyd
Chief Administrative Law Judge	(vacancy)
General Counsel	Michael A. McCord
Senior Policy Advisor	Timothy A. Greten

The above list of key personnel was updated 4–2019.

The Federal Mine Safety and Health Review Commission ensures compliance with occupational safety and health standards in the Nation's surface and underground coal, metal, and nonmetal mines.

The Federal Mine Safety and Health Act of 1977 (30 U.S.C. 801 et seq.), as amended, established the Federal Mine Safety and Health Review Commission as an independent and adjudicative agency.

The Commission comprises five members whom the President appoints and the Senate confirms. Each Commissioner serves a 6-year term, and all the terms are staggered. The President appoints one of the Commissioners to serve as the Chair. At the trial level, the FMSHRC's administrative judges decide cases. The Commissioners are responsible for appellate review of a decision made by an administrative law judge.

Activities

FMSHRC provides administrative trial and appellate review of legal disputes arising from enforcement actions taken by the Department of Labor.

The FMSHRC and its administrative law judges decide cases brought before it by the Department of Labor's Mine Safety and Health Administration, mine operators, and miners or their representatives. These cases generally involve review of the Administration's enforcement actions, including citations, mine-closure orders, and proposals for civil penalties issued for violations of the act or the mandatory safety and health standards promulgated by the Secretary of Labor. The FMSHRC also has jurisdiction over discrimination complaints filed by miners or their representatives regarding their safety and health, complaints for compensation filed on behalf of miners idled as a result of mine closure orders issued by the Administration, and disputes involving mine emergency response plans.

Cases brought before the FMSHRC are assigned to a judge in the Office of Administrative Law Judges, and hearings are conducted pursuant to the requirements of the Administrative Procedure Act (5 U.S.C. 554, 556) and the FMSHRC's procedural rules (29 CFR 2700).

A judge's decision becomes a final, nonprecedential order of the FMSHRC 40 days after issuance unless it has directed the case for review in response to a petition or on its own motion. If a review is conducted, a decision of the FMSHRC becomes final 30 days after issuance unless a party adversely affected seeks review in the U.S. Court of Appeals for the District of Columbia Circuit or the circuit within which the mine subject to the litigation is located.

As far as practicable, hearings are held at locations convenient to the affected mines. In addition to its District of Columbia offices, the Office of Administrative Law Judges maintains offices in Colorado and Pennsylvania. https://www.fmshrc.gov/about

Sources of Information

Administrative Law Judges To ask a question regarding a case before an administrative law judge, send an email to the address below or call the Office of the Administrative Law Judges. Phone, 202-434-9950. https://www.fmshrc.gov/about/aljs | Email: docket@fmshrc.gov

Contact Information The "Contact Us" web page has contact information for the Office of the Executive Director and Office of the Administrative Law Judges. The FMSHRC maintains offices in Washington, DC; Denver, CO; and Pittsburgh, PA. Washington—phone, 202-434-9905; fax, 202-434-9906. Denver—phone, 303-844-5267; fax, 303-844-5268. Pittsburgh—phone, 412-920-7240; fax, 412-928-8689. https://www.fmshrc.gov/contact | Email: fmshrc@fmshrc.gov

Decisions Searchable databases of FMSHRC decisions and decisions of administrative law judges are available online. http://www.fmshrc.gov/decisions

The "Cases on Review" web page includes links to cases currently on review before the FMSHRC and to decisions on appeal before the U.S. Courts of Appeals. http://www.fmshrc.gov/content/cases-review

Federal Mine Safety and Health Act   The FMSHRC has prepared a version of the Federal Mine Safety and Health Act of 1977 that reflects changes made to it by the Mine Improvement and New Emergency Response Act of 2006. This unofficial document is available in Portable Document Format (PDF) for viewing and downloading. https://www.fmshrc.gov/content/federal-mine-safety-and-health-act-1977

Filing   Electronic filing may be done through the FMSHRC's electronic case management system (e-CMS). To use the e-CMS, a filer must register at the FMSHRC-eCMS website. The e-CMS support team is available to provide assistance. http://www.fmshrc.gov/guides/instructions-electronic-filing | Email: e-CMS.Support@fmshrc.gov

Freedom of Information Act (FOIA)   The FOIA requires Federal agencies to disclose records after receiving a properly written request. The law does include provisions that shield certain records, or parts of them, from disclosure. The FOIA Service Center assists those seeking information through the FOIA. For more information, write to the Federal Mine Safety and Health Review Commission, FOIA Service Center, 1331 Pennsylvania Avenue NW., Suite 520N, Washington, DC 20004-1710. Phone, 202-434-9935. Fax, 202-434-9944. http://www.fmshrc.gov/foia | Email: foia@fmshrc.gov

Frequently Asked Questions (FAQs)   The FMSHRC posts answers to FAQs. https://www.fmshrc.gov/guides/faq

Guidance   The "Guides" web page includes links to guidance on proceedings, case procedures, reopening a case, electronic filing, and the Freedom of Information Act, https://www.fmshrc.gov/guides

Meetings   The FMSHRC posts audio files of decisional public meetings on its website. https://www.fmshrc.gov/meetings-arguments/meetings

News   The latest FMSHRC news is available online. http://www.fmshrc.gov/about/news

Oral Arguments   The FMSHRC posts audio files of oral arguments on its website. https://www.fmshrc.gov/meetings-arguments/arguments

Organizational Chart   The FMSHRC publishes its organizational chart as part of its "Congressional Budget Justification and Annual Performance Plan." In the budget justification and performance plan for fiscal year 2020 (18 MAR 2019), the chart is on page 5. The key personnel list of commissioners and administrators, which appears at the top of this entry, relies on the organizational chart published in the budget justification and performance plan. https://www.fmshrc.gov/plans/fy2020-justification#

Procedural Rules (29 CFR 2700)   The FMSHRC posts its procedural rules online in Portable Document Format (PDF) for viewing and downloading. https://www.fmshrc.gov/rules/Procedural%20Rules%20Booklet%20Jan%202014.pdf

Reports / Budget Submissions   The "Reports and Budget Submissions" web page includes links to the FMSHRC's current and past strategic plans, sustainability report, reports to Congress, as well as to its budget and annual performance, buy American, and performance accountability reports. http://www.fmshrc.gov/reports-budget-submissions

The Sources of Information were updated 4–2019.

Federal Maritime Commission

800 North Capitol Street NW., Washington, DC 20573
Phone, 202-523-5707. Internet, http://www.fmc.gov

The Commission
Chair

Commissioners

MICHAEL A. KHOURI

REBECCA F. DYE
DANIEL B. MAFFEI
LOUIS E. SOLA
(VACANCY)

https://www.fmc.gov/commissioners

Bureaus and Offices

Managing Director — Karen V. Gregory

Bureau Directors
Certification and Licensing — Sandra L. Kusumoto
Enforcement — Benjamin K. Trogdon
Trade Analysis — Florence A. Carr

Office Director
Consumer Affairs and Dispute Resolution Services — Rebecca A. Fenneman

Chief Administrative Law Judge — Erin M. Wirth
Equal Employment Opportunity Director — Ebony Jarrett
General Counsel — Tyler J. Wood
Secretary — Rachel E. Dickon
https://www.fmc.gov/about-the-fmc/bureaus-offices

Office of Inspector General

Inspector General — Jonathan Hatfield
https://www.fmc.gov/about-the-fmc/bureaus-offices/office-
of-inspector-general | Email: OIG@fmc.gov

The above list of key personnel was updated 6–2019.

The Federal Maritime Commission promotes an efficient, fair, and reliable supply system of international ocean transportation; protects the public from deceptive, unfair, and unlawful practices; and contributes to the integrity and security of the Nation's supply chain and transportation system.

Establishment and Organization

The Federal Maritime Commission (FMC) was established by Reorganization Plan No. 7 of 1961 (46 U.S.C. 301–307), effective August 12, 1961. The FMC is an independent establishment, regulating shipping under the the Shipping Act of 1984, as amended (46 U.S.C. 40101–41309); Section 19 of the Merchant Marine Act, 1920 (46 U.S.C. 42101–42109); the Foreign Shipping Practices Act of 1988 (46 U.S.C. 42301–42307); and Public Law 89–777, approved on November 6, 1966 (46 U.S.C. 44101–44106). https://www.fmc.gov/about-the-fmc/fmc-regulations-statutes

The Commission is composed of five Commissioners, whom the President appoints by the advice and with the consent of the Senate. The President may not appoint more than three Commissioners who are from the same political party. The term of each Commissioner is 5 years. When his or her term ends, the Commissioner may continue to serve until a successor is appointed and qualified, but only for 1 year or less. A vacancy is filled in the same manner as the original appointment, which may be extended to include a second term. An individual appointed to fill a vacancy is appointed for the unexpired term of the person being succeeded. That individual may serve two complete terms in addition to the remainder of the term for which the predecessor of that individual was appointed. https://www.govinfo.gov/content/pkg/USCODE-2017-title46/pdf/USCODE-2017-title46-subtitleI-chap3.pdf

The FMC posts its organizational chart online. https://www.fmc.gov/about-the-fmc/organizational-chart

Activities

Adjudicatory Procedures The FMC conducts formal investigations and hearings on its own motion and adjudicates formal complaints in accordance with the Administrative Procedure Act (5 U.S.C. note prec. 551). https://www.fmc.gov/about-the-fmc/bureaus-offices/administrative-law-judges | Email: judges@fmc.gov

Federal Maritime Commission

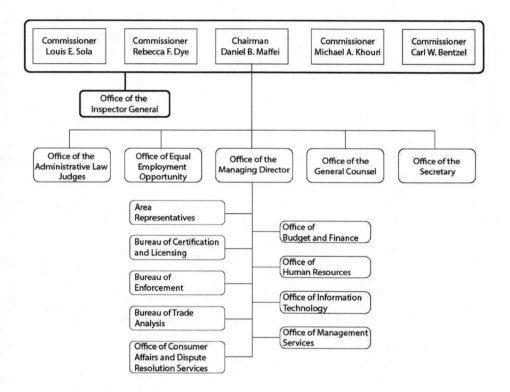

Agreements The FMC reviews agreements by and among ocean common carriers or marine terminal operators or by and among carriers and operators, which are filed under section 5 of the Shipping Act of 1984, for statutory compliance and for their likely effect on competition. It also monitors activities under all effective agreements for compliance with the provisions of law and its rules, orders, and regulations. https://www.fmc.gov/resources-services/vessel-operating-common-carriershttps://www.fmc.gov/resources-services/marine-terminal-operators

Alternative Dispute Resolution The FMC reviews informal complaints and assists parties in resolving disputes. Mediation and other dispute resolution services are available to assist parties in achieving a more acceptable resolution to a dispute at less cost than may be possible in litigation. These services are available before and after the commencement of litigation. The Commission also provides an informal process to adjudicate certain complaints involving less than $50,000 in damages. https://www.fmc.gov/databases-services/alternative-dispute-resolution-services | Email: complaints@fmc.gov

Complaints The FMC reviews alleged or suspected violations of the shipping statutes and rules and regulations of the Commission and may take administrative action to institute formal proceedings, to refer matters to other governmental agencies, or to bring about voluntary agreement between the parties. https://www.fmc.gov/databases-services/consumer-affairs-dispute-resolution-services | Email: complaints@fmc.gov

Economic Analyses The FMC relies on the Office of Economics and Competition Analysis (OECA) for support in antitrust economics and competition policy. OECA staff analyzes and monitors agreements that are filed with the FMC and that are between ocean carriers or marine terminal operators or between carriers and operators. These agreements are monitored for effects that inhibit competition and for compliance with FMC regulations and U.S. shipping laws. https://www.fmc.gov/about-the-fmc/bureaus-offices/bureau-of-trade-analysis | Email: tradeanalysis@fmc.gov

Enforcement The FMC relies on the Bureau of Enforcement (BOE) to serve as its prosecutorial component. Its attorneys participate in formal proceedings as trial counsel and, with the assistance of FMC area representatives, they investigate potential violations of the Shipping Act and FMC regulations. BOE attorneys also negotiate settlements and informal compromises of civil penalties and may participate in factfinding investigations that are initiated under the Shipping Act or the Foreign Shipping Practices Act. https://www.fmc.gov/about-the-fmc/bureaus-offices/bureau-of-enforcement | Email: boe@fmc.gov

International Affairs The FMC conducts investigations of foreign governmental and carrier practices that adversely affect the U.S. shipping trade. In consultation with other executive agencies, the FMC takes action to effect the elimination of discriminatory practices on the part of foreign governments against shipping in the United States foreign trade and to achieve comity between the United States and its trading partners. https://www.fmc.gov/about-the-fmc/bureaus-offices/general-counsel | Email: generalcounsel@fmc.gov

Licenses The FMC issues licenses to those persons and entities in the United States who wish to carry out the business of providing freight forwarding services and non-vessel-operating common carrier services. https://www.fmc.gov/about-the-fmc/bureaus-offices/bureau-of-certification-and-licensing | Email: bcl@fmc.gov

Non-Vessel-Operating Common Carrier Service Arrangements The FMC receives and reviews service arrangements entered into by non-vessel-operating common carriers and their customers. Cargo moving under these service arrangements is exempt from the tariff publication and adherence requirements of the Shipping Act, on the condition that the service arrangements must be filed with the Commission. https://www.fmc.gov/resources-services/ocean-transportation-intermediaries

Passenger Indemnity The FMC administers the passenger indemnity provisions of the act of November 6, 1966, which require shipowners and operators to obtain certificates of financial responsibility to pay judgments for personal injury or death or to refund fares in the event of nonperformance of voyages. https://www.fmc.gov/resources-services/passenger-vessel-operators | Email: pvo@fmc.gov

Rulemaking   The FMC promulgates rules and regulations to interpret, enforce, and ensure compliance with shipping and related statutes by common carriers and other persons subject to the Commission's jurisdiction. https://www.ecfr.gov/cgi-bin/text-idx?SID=77cce38e9b335eb5c0f5f515f1bbe2a2&c=ecfr&tpl=/ecfrbrowse/Title46/46cfrv9_02.tpl

Service Contracts   The FMC receives and reviews filings of confidential service contracts between shippers and ocean common carriers. It also monitors publication of certain essential terms of those service contracts. https://www.fmc.gov/about-the-fmc/bureaus-offices/bureau-of-trade-analysis

Tariffs   The FMC monitors and prescribes requirements to ensure accessibility and accuracy of electronic tariff publications of common carriers engaged in the foreign commerce of the United States. Special permission applications may be submitted for relief from statutory and/or Commission tariff requirements. https://www.fmc.gov/about-the-fmc/bureaus-offices/bureau-of-trade-analysis

Sources of Information

Career Opportunities   To carry out its mission, the FMC relies on attorneys, economists, and other professionals. https://www.fmc.gov/about-the-fmc/employment-opportunities

In 2018, the FMC ranked 9th among 29 small agencies in the Partnership for Public Service's Best Places To Work Agency Rankings. http://bestplacestowork.org/rankings/detail/MC00

Contact Information   Contact and other general information is available on the "Contact Us" web page. https://www.fmc.gov/contact | Email: Inquiries@fmc.gov

Cruise Vacations   The FMC has posted the brochure "Cruise Vacations: Know Before You Go" on its website to help potential passengers select an appropriate cruise

before purchasing their tickets. https://www.fmc.gov/wp-content/uploads/2018/09/PVO2014-508.pdf

General information and additional resources to help cruise passengers are available on the FMC website. https://www.fmc.gov/resources-services/cruise-passenger-assistance

Events   The FMC posts events upcoming events on its website. https://www.fmc.gov/events

Freedom of Information Act (FOIA)   Enacted in 1966, the FOIA took effect on July 4, 1967. The law gives a right to obtain access to Federal agency records to any person, except a fugitive from the law. Some records, or portions of them, are, however, shielded from disclosure by one or more of nine statutory exemptions or by specific harm that disclosure may cause. The FMC makes a lot of information publicly available to reduce the need of filing an official FOIA request. https://www.fmc.gov/about-the-fmc/freedom-of-information-act-requests-reports | Email: FOIA@fmc.gov

The FMC maintains an electronic reading room on its website. https://www2.fmc.gov/readingroom/ProceedingSearch

Greenhouse Gas Reduction / Sustainable Development   The "Federal Maritime Commission 2017 Strategic Sustainability Performance Plan" is available online. Greenhouse gas reduction is part of the plan. https://www.fmc.gov/wp-content/uploads/2018/10/2017SustainabilityPlan.pdf | Email: omd@fmc.gov

"The maritime industry realized years ago that sustainable development is necessary to the survival of people and businesses—whether it is related to maritime transportation, port development, or infrastructure. Any discussion in the industry now necessarily involves mention of sustainability principles. We know that a cleaner environment means economic growth, job creation, and reduced costs with greater efficiency." (excerpted from Chair Mario Cordero's statement on Earth Day 2016) https://www.fmc.gov/chairmans-statement-on-earth-day

History   In 1961, the White House and Congress made a decision that affected international liner shipping companies and the U.S. merchant marine. To learn more about that decision and the establishment of two new maritime agencies by President John F. Kennedy's Executive order, visit the "History" page on the FMC website. https://www.fmc.gov/about-the-fmc/our-history

The FMC maintains an online archive of maritime decisions that are associated with the Department of Commerce, Federal Maritime Board, U.S. Maritime Commission, U.S. Shipping Board, and itself. The archive's content begins with the year 1919. https://www.fmc.gov/fmc-reports

Library The FMC's law and reference library contains books, directories, encyclopedias, journals, magazines, microforms, reports, and videos. It has specialized material that covers the various segments of the international shipping industry and historical and contemporary regulatory materials that cover all phases of shipping in the U.S. foreign trades. It also has material on economics, engineering, political science, and a collection of legal publications. The library's holdings comprise approximately 8,700 volumes and numerous microfiches, CD–ROMs, and online services. Members of the public may visit the library and use the collection; however, all materials must be used in the library during its hours of operation. Materials are released only through an interlibrary loan request. A librarian is available from 8 a.m. to 4:30 p.m., eastern standard time, Monday–Friday. The library is closed on weekends and Federal Holidays. Phone, 202-523-5762. https://www.fmc.gov/about-the-fmc/bureaus-offices/law-reference-library | Email: LibraryInquiries@fmc.gov

All effective vessel-operating common carrier (VOCC) and marine terminal operator (MTO) agreements on file with the FMC are accessible in its electronic agreement library.

The Sources of Information were updated 6–2019.

https://www2.fmc.gov/FMC.Agreements. Web/Public

Moving Overseas The FMC posts tips for protecting property when shipping goods internationally by sea. https://www.fmc.gov/resources-services/protect-your-international-move

Before shipping a car overseas, become familiar with the laws and regulations of the United States and the destination country regarding which vehicles may be imported and the fees that must be paid. https://fmc2.fmc.gov/resources-services/shipping-your-vehicle-overseas

News The "FMC Newsroom" posts recent headlines. https://www.fmc.gov/news-events

Notices of Agreements Recent notices of agreements filed are posted on the "Federal Register" website. https://fmc2.fmc.gov/about-the-fmc/weekly-agreement-notices

Open Government The FMC supports the Open Government initiative by promoting collaboration, participation, and transparency. https://www.fmc.gov/open-government

Resources / Services The FMC has gathered its resources and services in one place, on a single web page, for its stakeholders. In the "Audiences" section, resources and services are grouped by audience: public, attorneys and litigants, ocean transportation intermediaries (OTIs), passenger vessel operators (PVOs), vessel-operating common carriers (VOCCs), and marine terminal operators (MTOs). https://www.fmc.gov/resources-services

Social Media The FMC tweets announcements and other newsworthy items on Twitter. https://twitter.com/FMC_gov

The FMC posts videos on its YouTube channel. https://www.youtube.com/channel/UCwKTAIGGHIA0xcN3bDt_Uqg

Federal Mediation and Conciliation Service

250 E Street SW., Washington, DC 20427
Phone, 202-606-8100. Internet, http://www.fmcs.gov

Office of the Director

Director	(vacancy)
Deputy Director	Richard R. Giacolone
Assistant Director	Gary Hattal
Attorney-Advisor	Dawn Starr
Equal Employment Opportunity Director	Denise McKenney
Senior Advisor	David Thaler
https://www.fmcs.gov/aboutus/agency-departments/office-of-the-director	
Deputy Directors	
Field Operations	D. Scott Blake
National Representative	Scot Beckenbaugh
Chief Operating Officer	Gregory Goldstein

The above list of key personnel was updated 8–2019. https://www.fmcs.gov/aboutus/agency-departments

The Federal Mediation and Conciliation Service helps labor and management resolve disputes in industries affecting commerce, offers training in cooperative processes to promote workplace stability and economic growth, and provides alternative dispute resolution services, training, negotiated rulemaking, and public policy facilitation to government entities.

Establishment and Organization

On June 23, 1947, the "Labor Management Relations Act, 1947," became Public Law 80–101 after the Congress enacted it over a veto by President Harry S. Truman. This Act is also referred to as the Taft-Hartley Act because Senator Robert A. Taft and Representative Fred A. Hartley, Jr., sponsored the bill. The Act amended the National Labor Relations Act of 1935, commonly known as the Wagner Act, and established the The Federal Mediation and Conciliation Service (FMCS) as an independent agency of the U. S. Government to prevent or minimize the effects of labor-management disputes on the free flow of commerce. https://catalog.archives.gov/id/299855

The FMCS "may proffer its services in any labor dispute in any industry affecting commerce, either upon its own motion or upon the request of one or more of the parties to the dispute, whenever in its judgment such dispute threatens to cause a substantial interruption of commerce" (29

U.S.C. 173). Subsequent emendations to the original Labor Management Relations Act have expanded the scope of the agency's dispute resolution services. https://www.govinfo.gov/content/pkg/USCODE-2017-title29/pdf/USCODE-2017-title29-chap7-subchapIII-sec173.pdf

The President appoints the Director by the advice and with consent of the Senate. The Director is prohibited from engaging in any other business, employment, or vocation (29 U.S.C. 172). https://www.govinfo.gov/content/pkg/USCODE-2017-title29/pdf/USCODE-2017-title29-chap7-subchapIII-sec172.pdf

The FMCS is headquartered in Washington, DC, and it has 10 regional offices and more than 60 field and local offices. It provides mediation and conflict resolution services to industry, government agencies, and communities. https://www.fmcs.gov/aboutus

The agency's organizational chart (AUG 2019) is available in Portable Document Format (PDF) for viewing and downloading.

Federal Mediation and Conciliation Service

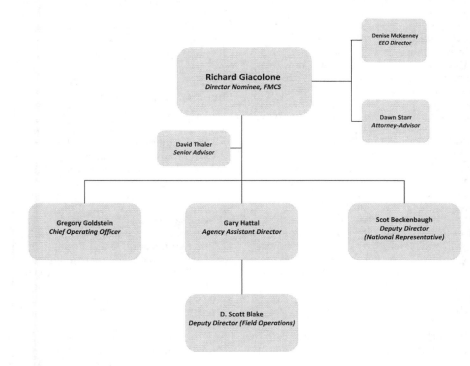

https://www.fmcs.gov/wp-content/
uploads/2019/08/FMCS-Org-Structure-
August-2019.pdf

Activities

The FMCS reduces disruptions to interstate
commerce and improves government
efficiency by providing skilled mediators
to resolve workplace disputes and conflicts
arising under the statutory jurisdiction of
government entities. FMCS mediators do
not enforce laws: They rely on innovative
mediation, communication, and relationship
building techniques to help disputants
achieve consensus.

The FMCS offers its labor mediation and
training services in a variety of industries
and sectors of the economy, including the
private sector (except airlines and railroads),
the Federal sector, and the public sector (in
States without labor mediation agencies).
The Labor-Management Cooperation
Act of 1978 recognized the economic
benefits of a more proactive approach
to workplace stability. The FMCS awards
grants to encourage the establishment of
local, regional, and industrywide labor
management committees to improve
labor management relationships,
organizational effectiveness, and economic
development. The FMCS also promotes
workplace innovation, productivity, and
competitiveness through collaboration,
good labor-management relationships, and
problem solving between companies and
their workers.

The Administrative Dispute Resolution
and Negotiated Rulemaking Acts of 1996
recognized the broader value of FMCS
conflict resolution services for government
efficiency. The agency was designated as a
key resource to help government entities
resolve individual employment disputes,
design conflict management systems,
achieve stakeholder consensus on new
regulations, and conduct more effective
multi-stakeholder public policy dialogues.
https://www.fmcs.gov/services

Mediation / Training   FMCS mediators
help parties resolve workplace disputes
and establish sound, stable, and enduring
labor-management relations. In addition to
mediating collective bargaining disputes,

mediators facilitate better day-to-day
workplace relations through a variety of
joint training programs. FMCS mediators
also assist other government entities with
resolving disputes arising under their
jurisdictions. https://www.fmcs.gov/services/
resolving-labor-management-disputes

Arbitration   Voluntary arbitration and
factfinding are widely used in labor-
management relations. Upon request, the
FMCS can provide panels of arbitrators
who are experienced in labor relations
issues. Requests can be tailored, in terms
of expertise, fees, geography, and other
considerations, to accommodate a variety
of requirements. https://www.fmcs.gov/
services/arbitration

Sources of Information

Calendar   A day-by-day listing of important
FMCS events is available on online. https://
www.fmcs.gov/resources/calendar

Career Opportunities   Stationed in offices
nationwide, FMCS mediators are full-time
excepted service employees of the Federal
Government. They perform duties in five
major areas: advocacy, education, and
outreach; alternative dispute resolution
services to government entities; collective
bargaining mediation; grievance mediation;
and relationship development training.
The ideal applicant seeking to become an
FMCS mediator has full-time experience
in the collective bargaining process. U.S.
citizenship is required. https://www.fmcs.
gov/careers

In 2018, the FMCS ranked 1st among
29 small agencies in the Partnership for
Public Service's Best Places To Work Agency
Rankings! http://bestplacestowork.org/
rankings/detail/FM00

Conflict Management   The FMCS Institute
for Conflict Management offers practical
and experience-based conflict resolution
training for individuals and groups. Course
descriptions and enrollment information
are available online. https://www.fmcs.gov/
services/education-and-outreach/fmcs-institute

Contact   To ask a question or leave a
comment, use the electronic "Feedback
Form." https://www.fmcs.gov/feedback

Documents / Data   Budgets and
performance information, regulations

and policies, speeches and presentations, publications (some in Spanish), and reports are available online. Collective bargaining notice data and work stoppage data are also posted online. https://www.fmcs.gov/resources/documents-and-data

Electronic Updates   The FMCS uses email updates to disseminate information on its dispute resolution services and to announce training opportunities. A sign-up form is available online. https://public.govdelivery.com/accounts/USFMCS/subscriber/new

Find a Mediator   An online search tool is available to find a mediator by city, State, or Zip Code, as well as by name, email, or phone number. https://www.fmcs.gov/aboutus/locations/find-a-mediator

Forms / Applications   Forms and applications needed to obtain FMCS services and funding—arbitration, Freedom of Information Act (FOIA) requests, labor-management cooperation grants, and notice of bargaining (F–7)—are available online. https://www.fmcs.gov/resources/forms-applications

Freedom of Information Act (FOIA)   The FOIA requires Federal agencies to disclose records after receiving a proper written request for them. Certain records, however, are shielded from disclosure by provisions contained within the statute. The FMCS has an online FOIA requester center. The specific procedures for requesting its records, FOIA-related contact information, and a link to records that are already accessible online may be found on the "FOIA Requestor Center" web page. https://www.fmcs.gov/foia | Email: foia@fmcs.gov

Subsequent amendments to the FOIA of 1966 require publicly accessible, electronic reading rooms that contain FOIA response documents and other information that is routinely available to the public. Before submitting a FOIA request, see if the FMCS already has placed the desired information in its electronic reading room. https://www.fmcs.gov/resources/documents-and-data

The Sources of Information were updated 8–2019.

Frequently Asked Questions (FAQs)   The FMCS posts answers to FAQs on its website. https://www.fmcs.gov/resources/faqs

History   A timeline of events in modern American labor relations is available online. The timeline starts with the first Government-mediated settlement in 1838, continues through the creation of the FMCS in 1947 and the West Coast port mediation of 2002, to end currently with President Donald J. Trump's appointment of Richard Giacolone to serve as the agency's acting Director. https://www.fmcs.gov/aboutus/our-history

News   The FMCS maintains an online news archive. https://www.fmcs.gov/news

Regional Offices   Headquartered in Washington, DC, the FMCS delivers services nationwide through its 10 regional and numerous field offices. Contact information for the FMCS national office and its regional and field offices is available online. https://www.fmcs.gov/aboutus/locations/regional-offices

Shared Neutrals   Shared Neutrals, also known as Sharing Neutrals, is an interagency mediation program in the National Capital Region, including the Washington, DC, area and Baltimore. The Shared Neutrals program assists participating Federal agencies through a pool of trained, collateral-duty Federal employees who provide mediation services to an agency, other than their own, in exchange for like services to the program from the recipient agency. https://www.fmcs.gov/sharedneutrals

Site Map   The site map allows visitors to look for specific topics or to browse content that aligns with their interests. https://www.fmcs.gov/site-map

Social Media   The FMCS has a Facebook account https://www.facebook.com/fmcs.usa

The FMCS tweets announcements and other newsworthy items on Twitter. https://twitter.com/FMCS_USA

The FMCS posts videos on its YouTube channel. https://www.youtube.com/user/FMCSInfo

Federal Reserve System

Twentieth Street and Constitution Avenue NW., Washington, DC 20551
Phone, 202-452-3000. Internet, http://www.federalreserve.gov

Board of Governors of the Federal Reserve System

Chair	JEROME H. POWELL
Vice Chair	RICHARD H. CLARIDA
Vice Chair for Supervision	RANDAL K. QUARLES
Governors	
	MICHELLE W. BOWMAN
	LAEL BRAINARD
	CHRISTOPHER J. WALLER
	(VACANCY)
Assistant to the Board and Director	MICHELLE A. SMITH

https://www.federalreserve.gov/aboutthefed/bios/board/default.htm

Federal Reserve Bank Presidents

New York	JOHN C. WILLIAMS
Atlanta	RAPHAEL W. BOSTIC
Boston	ERIC S. ROSENGREN
Chicago	CHARLES L. EVANS
Cleveland	LORETTA J. MESTER
Dallas	ROBERT S. KAPLAN
Kansas City	ESTHER L. GEORGE
Minneapolis	NEEL T. KASHKARI
Philadelphia	PATRICK T. HARKER
Richmond	THOMAS I. BARKIN
San Francisco	MARY C. DALY
St. Louis	JAMES B. BULLARD

https://www.federalreserve.gov/aboutthefed/federal-reserve-system-new-york.htm

Official Staff

Chief Operating Officer	PATRICK J. MCCLANAHAN
General Counsel	MARK E. VAN DER WEIDE
Secretary	ANN E. MISBACK
Directors of Divisions	
Consumer and Community Affairs	ERIC S. BELSKY
Financial Management	RICARDO A. AGUILERA
Financial Stability	ANDREAS W. LEHNERT
Information Technology	SHARON L. MOWRY
International Finance	BETH ANNE WILSON
Management	WINONA VARNON
Monetary Affairs	TREVOR A. REEVE
Research and Statistics	STACEY M. TEVLIN
Reserve Bank Operations and Payment Systems	MATTHEW J. EICHNER
Supervision and Regulation	MICHAEL S. GIBSON

https://www.federalreserve.gov/aboutthefed/officialstaff.htm

Inspector General	MARK BIALEK

https://oig.federalreserve.gov/the-inspector-general.htm

The above list of key personnel was updated 4–2021.

The Federal Reserve System keeps the Nation's monetary and financial system flexible, safe, and stable.

Establishment and Organization

On December 23, 1913, President Woodrow Wilson approved Public Law 63–43, whose short title is the "Federal Reserve Act." The Act provided "for the establishment of Federal reserve banks, to furnish an elastic currency, to afford means of rediscounting commercial paper, to establish a more effective supervision of banking in the United States." Pursuant to the Act, the Secretary of Agriculture, Secretary of the Treasury, and Comptroller of the Currency, constituting The Reserve Bank Organization Committee, designated "not less than eight nor more than twelve cities to be known as Federal reserve cities" and divided "the continental United States, excluding Alaska, into districts, each district to contain only one of such Federal reserve cities" (38 Stat. 251). http://www.loc.gov/law/help/statutes-at-large/63rd-congress/session-2/c63s2ch6.pdf

On August 23, 1935, President Franklin D. Roosevelt approved Public Law 74–305, which is also cited as the Banking Act of 1935. The new law provided "for the sound, effective, and uninterrupted operation of the banking system" (49 Stat. 684), amending parts of the Federal Reserve Act. One of the amendments to the earlier Act renamed the Federal Reserve Board: It now became "known as the 'Board of Governors of the Federal Reserve System.'" The Federal Reserve Board's "governor" and "vice governor" also became "known as the 'chairman' and the 'vice chairman,' respectively, of the Board of Governors of the Federal Reserve System" (49 Stat. 704). http://www.loc.gov/law/help/statutes-at-large/74th-congress/session-1/c74s1ch614.pdf

An organizational chart is accessible in Portable Document Format (PDF) on the "Structure of the Federal Reserve System" web page under "Board Responsibilities." https://www.federalreserve.gov/aboutthefed/structure-federal-reserve-board.htm

Statutory and Regulatory Authorities

Statutory material on the subject of banks and banking is codified in 12 U.S.C. The third chapter, sections 221–522, of title 12 is dedicated to the Federal Reserve System. https://uscode.house.gov/view.xhtml?path=/prelim@title12/chapter3&edition=prelim

Rules and regulations whose subject matter is banks or banking are codified in 12 CFR. https://www.ecfr.gov/cgi-bin/text-idx?SID=267f2409cd6deeef4d6a0875bc7f21bb&mc=true&tpl=/ecfrbrowse/Title12/12tab_02.tpl

Subchapter A, parts 200–269b, of 12 CFR is dedicated to codified subject matter associated with the Board of Governors of the Federal Reserve System. https://www.ecfr.gov/cgi-bin/text-idx?SID=f90a95ecd3b26b1b4cf2f8d82c26abaa&mc=true&tpl=/ecfrbrowse/Title12/12chapterII.tpl

Subchapter B, parts 270–281, of 12 CFR is dedicated to codified subject matter associated with the Federal Open Market Committee. https://www.ecfr.gov/cgi-bin/text-idx?SID=4c219c3266afff42e7efd18cf82f1135&mc=true&tpl=/ecfrbrowse/Title12/12CIIsubchapB.tpl

Structure

The FRS comprises the Board of Governors; the 12 Federal reserve banks and their branches and other facilities; the Federal Open Market Committee; the Federal Advisory Council; the Consumer Advisory Council; the Thrift Institutions Advisory Council; and the Nation's financial institutions, including commercial banks, savings and loan associations, mutual savings banks, and credit unions. https://www.federalreserve.gov/aboutthefed/structure-federal-reserve-system.htm

Board of Governors The Board comprises seven members whom the President appoints by the advice and with the consent of the Senate. The President also designates a chair and two vice chairs by the advice and with the consent of the Senate. The Chair of the Board is a member of the National Advisory Council on International Monetary and Financial Policies, which is chaired by the Secretary of the Department of the Treasury. The Board determines general monetary, credit, and operating policies for the FRS as a whole and formulates the rules and regulations for carrying out the purposes of the Federal Reserve Act. The Board's principal duties consist of monitoring credit conditions; supervising the Federal reserve banks, member banks, and bank holding companies; and regulating the implementation of some consumer credit protection laws.

Within statutory limitations, the Board has the power to fix the requirements for reserves that depository institutions maintain on transaction accounts or nonpersonal time deposits (an interest-bearing bank deposit account that has a date of maturity, such as a certificate of deposit). The Board reviews and determines the discount rate charged by the Federal reserve banks. For the purpose of preventing excessive credit use for the purchase or carrying of securities, the Board regulates the amount of credit that may be initially extended and subsequently maintained on securities (with certain exceptions). http://www.federalreserve.gov/aboutthefed/bios/board/boardmembership.htm

Federal Open Market Committee (FOMC)   The Committee comprises the Board of Governors and five of the presidents of the Federal reserve banks. The Chair of the Board of Governors is traditionally the Chair of the FOMC. The president of the Federal Reserve Bank of New York serves as a permanent member. Four of the other 11 reserve bank presidents rotate annually as voting members of the FOMC.

The Federal reserve banks carry out open market operations in accordance with regulations that the FOMC adopts and pursuant to specific policy directives that it issues. Purchases and sales of securities in the open market are undertaken to supply bank reserves for supporting the credit and money needed for long-term economic growth, for offsetting cyclical economic swings, and for accommodating seasonal business and consumer demand for money and credit. These operations are carried out principally in U.S. Government obligations, but they also include purchases and sales of Federal agency obligations. The Federal Reserve Bank of New York executes transactions for the FRS open market account.

Under the FOMC's direction, the Federal Reserve Bank of New York also undertakes transactions in foreign currencies for the FRS open market account. These operations are meant to safeguard the value of the dollar in international exchange markets and facilitate growth in international liquidity in accordance with the needs of an expanding world economy. https://www.federalreserve.gov/aboutthefed/structure-federal-open-market-committee.htm

Federal Reserve Banks   The 12 reserve banks and their branches function as the operating arms of the FRS. Each reserve bank operates within its own geographic area, or district, of the United States and gathers data and other information on the businesses and the needs of local communities in that district. The FOMC and Board of Governors then factor that information into monetary policy and other decisions. https://www.federalreserve.gov/aboutthefed/structure-federal-reserve-banks.htm

Activities

By influencing the lending and investing of depository institutions and the cost and availability of money and credit, the FRS promotes use of human and capital resources, growth of productivity, relatively stable prices, and equilibrium in the Nation's international balance of payments. The agency's supervisory and regulatory banking functions help maintain a commercial banking system that responds to the Nation's financial needs and objectives. https://www.federalreserve.gov/aboutthefed/pf.htm

Conducting Monetary Policy   The FRS seeks price stability, moderate long-term interest rates, and maximum employment. Under normal economic conditions, the FOMC sets monetary policy by selecting an interest rate. To a bank, that interest rate is the cost of holding reserves. (Reserves are funds held by depository institutions as cash in their vaults or as deposits with their regional Federal reserve bank.) In recent years, the FRS has set a target, or target range, for the Federal funds rate, which is the interest rate that commercial banks charge each other for borrowing reserves for short periods. The open market desk at the Federal Reserve Bank of New York then conducts open market operations—buying or selling U.S. Treasury securities—to change the amount of reserves in the banking system to adjust the Federal funds rate. Since the Federal funds rate is the price of borrowing reserves, open market operations bring the actual Federal funds rate in line with the FOMC's target. The strategy to vary the quantity or the price of reserves in the banking system defines FRS monetary policy. https://www.federalreserve.gov/monetarypolicy.htm

Financial Supervision and Regulation   Supervision refers to the oversight and enforcement of regulations to ensure safe and sound banking behavior. The FRS's supervisory and regulatory actions help to build confidence in the banking system. Protecting the integrity of the Nation's financial institutions, fostering stability in financial markets, ensuring compliance with applicable laws and regulations, and encouraging banking institutions to meet responsibly the financial needs of their communities, promote financial stability. The FRS supervises and regulates State member banks (State chartered banks that have chosen to become members of the FRS) and bank and financial holding companies (companies that own banks). The agency also supervises overseas and international operations of regulated financial institutions. Foreign banks with U.S. branches, agencies, and nonbank operations are also subject to supervision. The FRS's banking supervision and regulation units work with other regulators and authorities to ensure that regulations are uniformly applied and consistently enforced throughout the banking system. https://www.federalreserve.gov/supervisionreg.htm

Payment Services   The FRS provides payment services, including processing checks and electronic payments, to commercial banks and other depository institutions. The FRS operates a nationwide check clearing system. Traditionally, depository institutions sent the actual paper checks that they had received to reserve banks, which processed and routed them to the originating depository institution for collection. These institutions used their Federal reserve accounts to settle the transactions. Since enactment of the Check Clearing for the 21st Century Act, which is also cited as the Check 21 Act, institutions have been using electronic check clearing options. The Check 21 Act enabled reserve banks to employ electronic image-based solutions for the exchange of check data between depository institutions. Ongoing industry advances continue to improve the process of check clearing and to renew the FRS's role in that process. https://www.govinfo.gov/content/pkg/STATUTE-117/pdf/STATUTE-117-Pg1177.pdf

The FRS provides two types of electronic payment services: fund transfers (Fedwire) and the Automated Clearinghouse (ACH). Fedwire processes payments of all sizes up to a maximum of just less than $10 billion. ACH is used mostly for recurring payments, such as business payrolls, consumer insurance payments, and the U.S. Government's military and civilian payrolls and Social Security benefits. https://www.federalreserve.gov/paymentsystems.htm

Protecting and Educating Consumers   The FRS has consumer protection responsibilities. The agency writes consumer protection regulations for the financial industry and enforces consumer protection and civil rights laws and regulations at the banks that it supervises. Community affairs offices across the FRS promote community development and fair and impartial access to credit. In each district of the FRS, economic education offices increase the public's understanding of the role that the FRS plays in the economy.

Services for the Department of the Treasury   As banker and fiscal agent for the Department of the Treasury, the FRS provides services for the Government, primarily through depository institutions. Federal reserve banks provide the Treasury with a checking account. When the Government makes a payment by check or electronically, that payment is usually cashed by or deposited in a commercial bank or similar institution. The FRS processes the payment and deducts the amount from the Treasury's account. Although the Treasury usually keeps the money received from tax payments on deposit at commercial banks, it transfers funds to a Federal reserve bank as needed to make payments. The Federal Government has reduced costs and improved service to the public by using the FRS's electronic payments network. Most regular Federal Government payments, such as Social Security benefits and the Government payroll, are direct deposits made through the FRS's automated clearinghouse service.

Acting as the U.S. fiscal agent, reserve banks sell, transfer, and redeem Government securities; make interest payments on these securities; and assist the Treasury and other Federal Government agencies with their securities in other ways. These actions are done electronically through a system called "Treasury Direct." The Treasury and Federal agencies reimburse the reserve banks for expenses associated with these fiscal agency functions.

Most currency enters circulation and exits circulation through the Federal reserve banks. As the public demands currency from the banking system, depository institutions draw down their accounts at the reserve banks in exchange for additional currency. When currency from the public flows back into depository institutions, those institutions deposit the surplus in their reserve banks. The Department of the Treasury designs and produces U.S. paper money and coin. As the Treasury produces currency, reserve banks put the new money into circulation to meet public needs. The FRS also destroys money that is no longer fit for circulation. By crediting the Government's account, reserve banks "buy" new paper money and coin from the Treasury to replace the notes that they destroy and coin that they return to the U.S. Mint.

Sources of Information

A–Z Index   An alphabetical subject index helps visitors navigate the website's content. https://www.federalreserve.gov/azindex.htm

Archived Records   The "Guide to Federal Records in the National Archives of the United States" indicates that FRS records have been assigned to record group 082. https://www.archives.gov/research/guide-fed-records/groups/082.html

Beige Book   The "Summary of Commentary on Current Economic Conditions by Federal Reserve District" is published eight times per year. Each Federal reserve bank gathers anecdotal information on current economic conditions in its district through reports from bank and branch directors and interviews with key business contacts, economists, market experts, and other sources. The "Summary" or "Beige Book" summarizes this information by district and sector. The Federal Reserve Bank of Minneapolis maintains an online "Beige Book" archives whose content goes back to 1970. https://www.minneapolisfed.org/region-and-community/regional-economic-indicators/beige-book-archive

Business Opportunities   The FRS generally relies on competitive bidding procedures for purchasing supplies and acquiring services. The process involves issuing a solicitation. Companies respond by submitting bids. The agency awards contracts after evaluating the bidders' prices, and in some cases, their technical abilities. http://www.federalreserve.gov/aboutthefed/procurement/about.htm

Calendar   An electronic calendar of FRS events, past and future, is available online. https://www.federalreserve.gov/newsevents/calendar.htm

Career Opportunities   The FRS relies on attorneys, economists, financial analysts, research assistants, information technology experts, and other skilled professionals to carry out its mission. https://www.federalreserve.gov/careers.htm

Consumer Help   The FRS can help a consumer who is having a problem with a bank or other financial institution. Phone, 888-851-1920. TTY, 877-766-8533. Fax, 877-888-2520. https://www.federalreserveconsumerhelp.gov/

Contact Information   To speak with an FRS operator, call 202-452-3000. TDD, 202-263-4869. https://www.federalreserve.gov/aboutthefed/contact-us-topics.htm

Coronavirus Disease 2019 (COVID–19)   The FRS has published a "Coronavirus Disease 2019 (COVID–19)" web page where it posts informational resources and its most recent actions to mitigate the economic effects of the pandemic. https://www.federalreserve.gov/covid-19.htm

Currency Academy   The U.S. Currency Education Program website runs the online Currency Academy, where learning about U.S. currency, or money, is fun. https://

www.uscurrency.gov/educational-materials/
classrooms/currency-academy

Federal Register   Significant documents and documents that the FRS recently published in the Federal Register are accessible online. https://www.federalregister.gov/agencies/federal-reserve-system

Fine Arts   Like all Federal agencies, the Board of Governors may receive gifts of artwork and funds to purchase art. In 1975, former Chairman Arthur F. Burns established the agency's fine arts program. He was responding to President Richard Nixon's urgent desire to continue the development of "the growing partnership between Government and the arts." Chairman Burns created the program to collect and care for artwork and to organize exhibitions in the historic Marriner S. Eccles building. The collection holds more than 1,000 works of art that private individuals have donated. To view a gallery of the Board's permanent collection, visit the "Fine Arts Program" page. https://www.federalreserve.gov/aboutthefed/aroundtheboard/fine-arts.htm

Freedom of Information Act (FOIA)   A request for information may be submitted online with an electronic request form; made in writing and mailed to the Information Disclosure Section, Board of Governors of the Federal Reserve System, 20th and Constitution Avenue NW., Washington, DC 20551; or sent by facsimile to the Information Disclosure Section. Fax, 202-872-7565. https://www.federalreserve.gov/foia/request.htm

The FRS has a FOIA service center to help information seekers learn about the status of a FOIA request or get answers to questions regarding the freedom of information process. The center is open from 9:00 a.m. to 5:00 p.m., Monday–Friday. Phone, 202-452-3684. https://www.federalreserve.gov/foia/servicecenter.htm

The FRS maintains electronic FIOA reading rooms. Before submitting a FOIA request, a requester should browse or search the content of the online reading rooms to ensure that the desired information is not already accessible immediately and free of charge. https://www.federalreserve.gov/foia/readingrooms.htm

Frequently Asked Questions (FAQs)   The FRS posts answers to FAQs on its website. https://www.federalreserve.gov/faqs.htm

Glossary   The Federal Reserve Bank of Richmond included a short glossary in its 16th edition (2012) of "The Federal Reserve Today." The glossary starts on page 35. https://www.richmondfed.org/-/media/richmondfedorg/education/for_teachers/resources/federal_reserve_today/frtoday.pdf#page=40

History   "Hello! This is Liberty speaking—billions of dollars are needed and needed NOW." That message came from Lady Liberty, according to a World War I era depiction of her. To learn more about the role that the FRS played in financing U.S. participation in World War I, visit the "Federal Reserve History" website. https://www.federalreservehistory.org/essays/liberty_bonds

In 1957, shortly after the U.S. Congress had enacted a law making "In God We Trust" the official national motto, the first dollar bills bearing the same four words entered circulation. To learn more about the history of American currency, visit the U.S. Currency Education Program's history section. https://www.uscurrency.gov/history

Interest Rates   As part of the "Fed Listens" series, the Federal Reserve Bank of Chicago hosted a conference (June 2019) on monetary policy strategy, tools, and communication practices. Chair of the Board of Governors Jerome H. Powell gave the opening remarks and spoke about the effective lower bound of interest rates and monetary policy tools. https://www.chicagofed.org/conference-sessions/opening-remarks-1

Monetary Policy   The Federal Reserve Board prepares a semiannual report that discusses monetary policy management, economic developments, and future prospects. It submits this report, which is called the "Monetary Policy Report," to the Senate Committee on Banking, Housing, and Urban Affairs and to the House Committee on Financial Services. https://www.federalreserve.gov/monetarypolicy/mpr_default.htm

As part of the "Fed Listens" series, Governor Lael Brainard participated in a community listening session at the Federal Reserve Bank of Richmond (May 2019). Her short presentation was titled "How Does Monetary Policy Affect Your Community?" https://www.federalreserve.gov/newsevents/speech/brainard20190508a.htm

Money-Financed Fiscal Programs   William B. English, Christopher J. Erceg, and David Lopez-Salido published the staff working paper "Money-Financed Fiscal Programs: A Cautionary Tale" in the Finance and Economics Discussion Series (2017–060) to stimulate discussion and critical comment. In the paper's abstract they wrote: "A number of prominent economists and policymakers have argued that money-financed fiscal programs (helicopter drops) could be efficacious in boosting output and inflation in economies facing persistent economic weakness, very low inflation, and significant fiscal strains. . . . While we do find that money-financed fiscal programs, if communicated successfully and seen as credible by the public, could provide significant stimulus, we underscore the risks that would be associated with such a program." https://www.federalreserve.gov/econres/feds/files/2017060pap.pdf

News / Events   The FRS posts press releases, speeches, and testimonies online. https://www.federalreserve.gov/newsevents.htm

Open Government   The FRS supports the Open Government initiative by promoting collaboration, participation, and transparency. https://www.federalreserve.gov/open/open.htm

Photo Gallery   The FRS posts photographs on its website. High resolution images are available on its Flickr photostream. https://www.federalreserve.gov/photogallery.htm

Publications   The FRS posts its publications online. The agency's most requested publications are its annual report, "Monetary Policy Report," supervision manuals, and "The Federal Reserve System Purposes and Functions." http://www.federalreserve.gov/publications/default.htm

Quantitative Easing   Michael T. Kiley's working paper "Quantitative Easing and the 'New Normal' in Monetary Policy" is meant to stimulate discussion and critical comment on the economic effects of applying this monetary policy tool. https://www.federalreserve.gov/econres/feds/files/2018004pap.pdf

Recent Postings   The most recent postings of the FRS are available on a single web page. https://www.federalreserve.gov/recentpostings.htm

Site Map   The website map allows visitors to look for specific topics or to browse for content that aligns with their interests. https://www.federalreserve.gov/sitemap.htm

Social Media   The FRS maintains a presence on Facebook, Flickr, LinkedIn, Twitter, and YouTube. https://www.federalreserve.gov/aboutthefed/contact-us-topics.htm

What Is The Fed?   The Federal Reserve, which is often referred to as "the Fed," serves as the central bank of the United States. The U.S. Congress created the Fed in 1913 to promote a safer and sounder monetary and financial system for the Nation. To learn more about the Fed, watch the 3-minute video. https://www.youtube.com/watch?v=wLyh5fSTLLw

The Sources of Information were updated 4–2021.

Federal Retirement Thrift Investment Board

77 K Street NE., Washington, DC 20002
Phone, 202-942-1600. Fax, 202-942-1676. Internet, http://www.frtib.gov

Board Members

Chair

David A. Jones, Acting
Dana K. Bilyeu
William S. Jasien
Ronald D. McCray
(Vacancy)

https://www.frtib.gov/BoardMembers/index.html

Management

Executive Director

RAVINDRA DEO

Chief Officers
Financial
Investment
Operating
Risk
Technology

SUSAN C. CROWDER
SEAN MCCAFFREY
SUZANNE TOSINI
(VACANCY)
VIJAY DESAI

Directors
Communications and Education
Enterprise Planning
External Affairs
Participant Services
Resource Management

JAMES COURTNEY
RENÉE C. WILDER GUERIN
KIMBERLY A. WEAVER
TEE RAMOS
GISILE GOETHE

General Counsel

DHARMESH VASHEE, ACTING

https://www.frtib.gov/MeetingMinutes/index.html

The above list of key personnel was updated 5–2021.

The Federal Retirement Thrift Investment Board administers the Thrift Savings Plan in the interest of its participants and beneficiaries.

Establishment and Organization

On June 6, 1986, Ronald W. Reagan approved Public Law 99–335, which is also cited as the Federal Employees' Retirement System Act of 1986. The Act established the Federal Retirement Thrift Investment Board (FRTIB) as an independent agency in the executive branch of the Government (100 Stat. 514). https://www.govinfo.gov/content/pkg/STATUTE-100/pdf/STATUTE-100-Pg514.pdf

The Board includes three members whom the President appoints, and one of them, the President designates to serve as its Chair. The President also appoints two additional members: one is appointed after considering "the recommendation made by the Speaker of the House of Representatives" in consultation with the minority leader of that Chamber; the other is appointed after considering "the recommendation made by the majority leader of the Senate" in consultation with the the minority leader of that Chamber (100 Stat. 578). Board members serve on a part-time basis.

The Act vests responsibility for the agency in six named fiduciaries: the Executive Director and the five Board members. "By action agreed to by a majority of the members," the Board appoints the Executive

Director, who is required to have "substantial experience, training, and expertise in the management of financial investments and pension benefit plans." The Director oversees the agency and invests and manages "the Thrift Savings Fund in accordance with the investment policies and other policies established by the Board" (100 Stat. 580).

The FRTIB does not post an organizational chart on its website.

Statutory and Regulatory Authorities

Statutory material that is associated with the Federal Employees' Retirement System is codified and has been assigned to Chapter 84 (sections 8401–8480) of 5 U.S.C. https://uscode.house.gov/view.xhtml?path=/prelim@title5/part3/subpartG/chapter84&edition=prelim

Statutory material affecting "Government Organization and Employees" is codified and has been assigned to 5 U.S.C. The heading "Participation in the Thrift Savings Plan" describes section 8351. https://uscode.house.gov/view.xhtml?req=granuleid:USC-prelim-title5-section8351&num=0&edition=prelim

Rules and regulations that govern the FRTIB are codified and have been assigned to

Chapter VI (parts 1600–1699) of 5 CFR. https://www.ecfr.gov/cgi-bin/text-idx?SID=381bec672672e2c9d813a8633bd18d00&mc=true&tpl=/ecfrbrowse/Title05/5cfrv3_02.tpl#1600

Activities

The TSP is a tax-deferred, defined contribution plan that constitutes one of the three components of the Federal Employees' Retirement System (FERS). Employees participating in the FERS accumulate savings through the TSP and combine those savings with retirement income from the two other components: Social Security benefits and the FERS Annuity. Employees participating in the Civil Service Retirement System (CSRS) and members of the uniformed services also may take advantage of the TSP to supplement their annuities. https://www.youtube.com/watch?v=XnlQZa7g_d4

The FRTIB operates the TSP and manages the investments of the Thrift Savings Fund for the benefit of participants and their beneficiaries. These operational and management responsibilities include maintaining an account for each TSP participant, making loans, purchasing annuity contracts, and providing for the payment of benefits. https://www.tsp.gov

Sources of Information

Annuities The TSP posts a periodically updated factsheet that explains life annuities. The "Annuities" factsheet (MAR 2020) is posted in Portable Document Format (PDF) for viewing and downloading. https://www.tsp.gov/publications/tspfs24.pdf

Archived Records The "Guide to Federal Records in the National Archives of the United States" indicates that FRTIB records have been assigned to record group 474. Record group 474 does not have a description that is associated with it. It was created in anticipation of the transfer of archival records; however, no transfer had been made before the "Guide to Federal Records in the National Archives of the United States" was updated. https://www.archives.gov/research/guide-fed-records/index-numeric/401-to-500.html

Business Opportunities The FRTIB purchases products and services through contracts and agreements with private-sector entities and other Federal agencies. Due to its unique status—a self-funded Federal agency with independent budgetary authority that receives no annual appropriations from the U.S. Congress—the FRTIB is not strictly bound by the Federal Acquisition Regulation. While subject to many of the same procurement laws as other Government agencies, the FRTIB also works under the mandate of the Federal Employees' Retirement System Act. FRTIB fiduciaries are required by that law to manage Thrift Savings Fund assets in the sole interest of the TSF participants and beneficiaries, expending funds to provide benefits to participants and beneficiaries and defraying reasonable expenses of administering the TSP. https://www.frtib.gov/Procurement/DoingBusiness.html

Calculators / Estimators The TSP website's "Calculators" web page provides convenient access to a collection of calculating and estimating tools. https://www.tsp.gov/calculators

Career Opportunities To carry out its mission, the FRTIB relies on financial experts, tax attorneys, and other professionals who possess diverse skills and expertise. https://www.frtib.gov/Careers/index.html

In 2019, the FRTIB ranked 19th among 28 small agencies in the Partnership for Public Service's Best Places To Work Agency Rankings. http://bestplacestowork.org/rankings/detail/RF00

Contact Information Information for contacting the FRTIB and the TSP is available on the FRTIB website. https://www.frtib.gov/contacts.html

TSP contact information also is available from the "We're Here To Help" web page on the TSP website. https://www.tsp.gov/contact

Federal Register Significant documents and documents that the FRTIB recently published in the Federal Register are accessible online. https://www.federalregister.gov/agencies/federal-retirement-thrift-investment-board

Freedom of Information Act (FOIA) The FOIA gives a right to access Federal Government records to any person. The FOIA is designed to make Government actions and operations more transparent. It applies to existing records and does not require an agency to create new records for compliance. The FOIA also does not require an agency to collect information that it does not have or to do research or analyze data to fulfill a request. Certain records, or parts of them, may be exempt from disclosure by the Act if one of nine exemptions shields their content. In some cases, the FRTIB provides copies of all of the records that a requester seeks. In other cases, part or all of the information falls under an exemption and is withheld, as the law permits. Before making a FOIA request, browse the holdings of the electronic reading room to see what records already are available and consult the FRTIB's "Freedom of Information Act Guide," which is accessible online in Portable Document Format (PDF). https://www.frtib. gov/ReadingRoom/FOIA/e-read_guide.pdf | Email: foiarequest@tsp.gov

Frequently Asked Questions (FAQs) TSP staff posts answers to questions that are asked frequently. https://www.tsp.gov/ frequently-asked-questions

Funds TSP participants may opt to invest their retirement dollars in one or more of five individual funds: the Common Stock Index Investment Fund (C), Fixed Income Index Investment Fund (F), Government Securities Investment Fund (G), International Stock Index Investment Fund (I), and Small Cap Stock Index Investment Fund (S). https:// www.tsp.gov/funds-individual

Each of the TSP's 10 lifecycle (L) funds is a diversified blend of the 5 individual core funds (C, F, G, I, and S). https://www.tsp.gov/ funds-lifecycle

Glossary The January 2021 edition of the "Summary of the Thrift Savings Plan" has a glossary of terms that starts on page 23. The summary is posted in Portable Document Format (PDF) for viewing and downloading. https://www.tsp.gov/publications/tspbk08. pdf

The Sources of Information were updated 5–2021.

History of Share Prices The TSP website's "Share Price History" web page allows visitors to retrieve share prices for all of the individual and lifecycle funds from a specified range of dates. https://www.tsp. gov/fund-performance/share-price-history

Meeting Minutes Starting with the year 2007 and continuing to the present, minutes of the meetings of FRTIB members are available online. https://www.frtib.gov/ MeetingMinutes/index.html

News / Resources To keep abreast of TSP announcements, news, and popular resources, visit the "News and Resources" web page. https://www.tsp.gov/whatsnew/ index.html

Rates of Return Annual and monthly rates of return for each of the individual and life cycle funds are available on the TSP website's "Rates of Return" web page. https://www.tsp.gov/fund-performance

Reading Room Benchmark evaluation and investment option review reports, employee and participant surveys, financial statements, FOIA reports, frequently requested records, press releases, regulations, reports to the U.S. Congress, strategic plans, and other documents are available online in the FRTIB's reading room. https://www.frtib.gov/ ReadingRoom/index.html

Social Media The TSP has a Facebook account. https://www.facebook.com/tsp4gov

The TSP tweets announcements and other newsworthy items on Twitter. https://twitter. com/tsp4gov

The TSP posts videos on its YouTube channel. https://www.youtube.com/user/ tsp4gov

TSP Basics The "TSP Basics" web page highlights the following topics: fitting the TSP into a comprehensive plan for retirement, moving money into the TSP, administrative and investment expenses, and designating beneficiaries. https://www.tsp.gov/tsp-basics

Federal Trade Commission

600 Pennsylvania Avenue NW., Washington, DC 20580
Phone, 202-326-2222. Internet, http://www.ftc.gov

Commission

Chair	LINA KHAN
Commissioners	ROHIT CHOPRA
	NOAH J. PHILLIPS
	REBECCA K. SLAUGHTER
	CHRISTINE S. WILSON
Chief of Staff	JENNIFER HOWARD
Chief Technologist	ERIE MEYER

https://www.ftc.gov/about-ftc/commissioners

Bureaus

Competition	HOLLY VEDOVA, ACTING
Consumer Protection	SAMUEL LEVINE, ACTING
Economics	MARTA WOSIŃSKA

Offices

Executive Director	DAVID B. ROBBINS

Directors
Equal Employment Opportunity and Workplace Inclusion	NAMON C. FRIENDS, ACTING
Congressional Relations	JEANNE BUMPUS
International Affairs	RANDOLPH W. TRITELL
Public Affairs	LINDSAY KRYZAK
Policy Planning	SARAH MACKEY, ACTING

Chiefs
Administrative Law Judge	D. MICHAEL CHAPPELL
Legal Officer	REILLY DOLAN, ACTING
Privacy Officer	JOHN KREBS
General Counsel	REILLY DOLAN, ACTING
Secretary of the Commission	APRIL TABOR

https://www.ftc.gov/about-ftc/bureaus-offices

Office of Inspector General	
	ANDREW KATSAROS

https://www.ftc.gov/about-ftc/office-inspector-general

The above list of key personnel was updated 7–2021.

The Federal Trade Commission protects America's consumers and enforces laws prohibiting anticompetitive, deceptive, or unfair business practices.

Establishment and Organization

The Federal Trade Commission (FTC) was established in 1914 by the Federal Trade Commission Act (15 U.S.C. 41-58). The Commission comprises five members whom the President appoints with the advice and consent of the Senate for 7-year terms. No more than three of the Commissioners may be members of the same political party. The President designates one of them as Chair of the Commission to oversee its administrative management.

The FTC's statement of organization has been codified in the Code of Federal Regulations (CFR) and assigned to Part 0 of 16 CFR. https://www.ecfr.gov/cgi-bin/text-idx

FEDERAL TRADE COMMISSION

Organization Chart

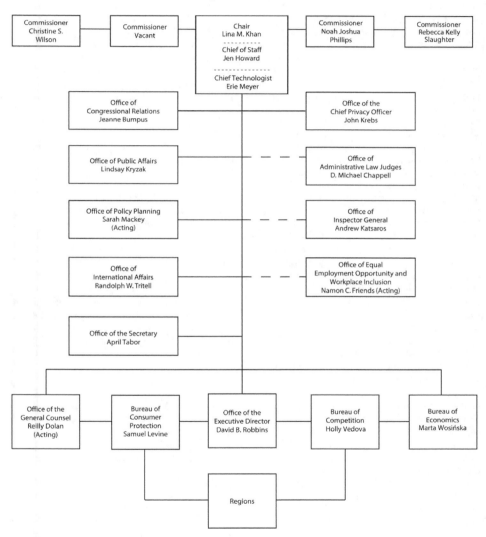

?SID=1eef003b863924b104aa3a379a1a8b5
c&mc=true&node=pt16.1.0&rgn=div5

The FTC posts its organizational chart
(JUN 2021) in Portable Document Format
for viewing and downloading. https://www.
ftc.gov/system/files/attachments/about-ftc/
ftc_org_chart_0.pdf

Activities

The FTC protects consumers and promotes
competition in broad sectors of the economy.
It safeguards and strengthens free and
open markets and helps consumers make
informed choices. The FTC carries out its
mission by using a variety of tools: consumer
and business education, law enforcement,
research, rulemaking, and studies of
marketplace trends and legal developments.
The FTC envisions a vigorously competitive
U.S. economy offering accessible and
accurate information to consumers, an
economy yielding high-quality products at
competitive prices and fostering efficiency,
innovation, and consumer choice. https://
www.ftc.gov/about-ftc

Competition The FTC prevents
anticompetitive mergers and works to keep
the marketplace free from anticompetitive
business practices. To promote competition,
the FTC engages in six law enforcement-
related activities: premerger notification,
merger and joint venture enforcement,
merger and joint venture compliance,
nonmerger enforcement, nonmerger
compliance, and antitrust policy. Policy
initiatives, research, and business guidance
and education also play a role in promoting
competition. https://www.ftc.gov/about-ftc/
bureaus-offices/bureau-competition

Consumer Protection The FTC brings a
variety of consumer protection cases and
works with State attorneys general and
other State and local consumer protection
officials. To protect consumers, it relies on
five law enforcement functions: privacy
and identity protection, financial practices,
marketing practices, advertising practices,
and enforcement. Policy initiatives, research,
and business and consumer education also
enhance protection. https://www.ftc.gov/about-
ftc/bureaus-offices/bureau-consumer-protection

Enforcement The FTC's law enforcement
activities foster voluntary compliance with the
law, but also include formal administrative or
Federal court litigation leading to mandatory
orders against offenders.

The FTC can issue an administrative
complaint or authorize the filing of a Federal
district court complaint charging a person,
partnership, or corporation with violating
one or more of the statutes that the FTC
enforces. If the charges are not contested,
settled by consent of the parties, or found
to be true after an administrative hearing
or a Federal court trial, an administrative
law judge or Federal court judge will
issue an order requiring discontinuance
of the unlawful practices. The FTC also
may request that a U.S. district court issue
preliminary relief to halt allegedly unfair
or deceptive practices, to prevent an
anticompetitive merger or unfair methods
of competition from taking place, or to
prevent violations of any statute that the FTC
enforces, pending the full adjudication of the
matter. In Federal court, the FTC may obtain
other relief, including monetary redress.
An order issued after an administrative or
Federal court proceeding that requires the
respondent to cease and desist or take other
corrective action may be appealed. https://
www.ftc.gov/enforcement

International Affairs With other nations
and international organizations, the FTC
promotes sound competition and consumer
protection policies and provides technical
assistance to nurture competition and enable
consumer protection agencies to perform
their missions. https://www.ftc.gov/policy/
international

Sources of Information

Antitrust Violations To report an
antitrust violation, contact the Bureau
of Competition's Office of Policy and
Coordination. Phone, 202-326-3300.
https://www.ftc.gov/faq/competition/report-
antitrust-violation | Email: antitrust@ftc.gov

Business Opportunities For information
on contracts and procurement, contact
the Assistant Chief Financial Officer for
Acquisitions. Phone, 202-326-2339. Fax,
202-326-3529. https://www.ftc.gov/about-
ftc/bureaus-offices/office-executive-director/
financial-management-office/acquisitions

Career Opportunities To carry out its
mission, the FTC relies on attorneys,

investigators, and specialists in financial management, information technology, public affairs, public policy, and in other fields. The agency posts current job vacancies on its Web site. Information on benefits, diversity, working at the FTC, and the application process is also accessible online. For additional information, contact the Human Capital Management Office. Phone, 202-326-2021. TTY, 202-326-3422. https://www.ftc.gov/about-ftc/careers-ftc

The Partnership for Public Service categorizes the FTC as a midsize agency. In the Partnership's 2020 Best Places To Work in the Federal Government rankings, the FTC placed second in its 25-agency category https://bestplacestowork.org/rankings/detail/?c=FT00

Consumer Complaints The FTC relies on complaints from consumers to detect patterns of abuse and fraud. A complaint may be filed in English or Spanish and online or by phone. The FTC enters complaints into Consumer Sentinel, a secure online database that civil and criminal law enforcement agencies in the U.S. and abroad can access. Phone, 877-382-4357. https://www.ftccomplaintassistant.gov

Contact Information Addresses (electronic and postal), links, and phone numbers are available on the "Contact the Federal Trade Commission" web page. https://www.ftc.gov/contact

Credit Reports The Fair Credit Reporting Act requires each of the nationwide credit reporting companies to provide a free credit report, upon request, once every 12 months. https://www.consumer.ftc.gov/articles/0155-free-credit-reports

Do Not Call Registry Register a home or mobile phone for free on the National Do Not Call Registry to eliminate most telemarketing calls. https://www.donotcall.gov

Federal Register Significant documents and documents that the FTC recently published in the Federal Register are accessible online. https://www.federalregister.gov/agencies/federal-trade-commission

The above Sources of Information were updated 7–2021.

Freedom of Information Act (FOIA) Enacted in 1966, the FOIA generally provides that any Individual has the right to make a request for Federal agency records or information; all Federal Government agencies are required to disclose records upon receiving a written request for them; nine exemptions, in addition to limits to FOIA, shield certain records from disclosure. The Federal FOIA does not provide access to records that State or local government agencies hold, or that private businesses or individuals hold. https://www.ftc.gov/about-ftc/foia

History American Presidents are a part of the FTC's history. To learn which President helped pave the way toward the Commission's creation, whose signature approved the Federal Trade Commission Act, which President literally helped with the building, and which 21st-century President paid a visit to the FTC, see the "Our History" Web page. https://www.ftc.gov/about-ftc/our-history

Identity Theft Use IdentiftyTheft.gov to report identity theft and formulate a personal recovery plan. https://www.identitytheft.gov

Open Government The FTC supports the Open Government initiative by promoting the principles of collaboration, participation, and transparency. https://www.ftc.gov/site-information/open-government

Regional Offices A map of the seven FTC regions—East Central, Midwest, Northeast, Northwest, Southeast, Southwest, and Western—and contact information for the regional offices representing them are available online. https://www.ftc.gov/about-ftc/bureaus-offices/regional-offices

Scam Alerts Stay abreast of new scams with the latest information and practical tips. An online subscription form is available to receive scam alerts by email. https://www.consumer.ftc.gov/scam-alerts

Workshops Information on conferences and workshops is available online. https://www.ftc.gov/news-events

General Services Administration

1800 F Street NW., Washington, DC 20405
Internet, http://www.gsa.gov

Administrator	ROBIN CARNAHAN
Deputy Administrator	KATY KALE
Chief of Staff	BRETT PRATHER
https://www.gsa.gov/about-us/organization/office-of-the-administrator/administrator-bio	

National Services

Commissioners	
Federal Acquisition	SONNY HASHMI
Public Buildings	NINA M. ALBERT

Regional Services

Region 1–New England	GLENN C. ROTONDO, ACTING
Region 2–Northeast and Caribbean	MICHAEL GELBER, ACTING
Region 3–Mid-Atlantic	JOANNA ROSATO, ACTING
Region 4–Southeast Sunbelt	KEVIN KERNS, ACTING
Region 5–Great Lakes	JOHN COOKE, ACTING
Region 6–Heartland	MARY A. RUWWE, ACTING
Region 7–Greater Southwest	GIANCARLO BRIZZI, ACTING
Region 8–Rocky Mountain	PENNY GROUT, ACTING
Region 9–Pacific Rim	DANIEL R. BROWN, ACTING
Region 10–Northwest / Arctic	CHAUN BENJAMIN, ACTING
Region 11–National Capital	DARREN BLUE, ACTING
https://www.gsa.gov/about-us/gsa-regions	

Staff Offices

Associate Administrators	
Civil Rights	ALUANDA DRAIN, ACTING
Congressional and Intergovernmental Affairs	GIANELLE RIVERA
Government-wide Policy	KRYSTAL BRUMFIELD
Mission Assurance	ROBERT J. CARTER
Small and Disadvantaged Business Utilization	EXODIE C. ROE III
Strategic Communication	TERESSA WYKPISZ-LEE
Chief Officers	
Administrative Services	ROBERT STAFFORD
Customer	ED WALTERS
Financial	GERARD BADORREK
Human Capital	TRACI DIMARTINI
Information	DAVID A. SHIVE
General Counsel	NITIN SHAH
https://www.gsa.gov/about-us/organization/gsa-leadership-directory	

Independent Offices

Civilian Board of Contract Appeals	
Chair	ERICA S. BEARDSLEY
https://www.gsa.gov/about-us/organization/leadership-directory/chair-civilian-board-of-contract-appeals	
Inspector General	CAROL F. OCHOA
https://www.gsaig.gov/content/meet-ig	

The above list of key personnel was updated 7–2021.

The General Services Administration delivers value and savings in real estate, acquisition, technology, and other mission-support services across Government.

Establishment and Organization

The General Services Administration (GSA) streamlined the Federal Government's administrative work. Its creation involved consolidating the Federal Works Agency, the National Archives Establishment, and the Public Buildings Administration; the Bureau of Federal Supply and the Office of Contract Settlement; and the War Assets Administration into a single Federal agency that would administer supplies and provide workplaces for Federal employees. https://www.gsa.gov/about-us/background-and-history

On June 30, 1949, President Harry S. Truman approved Public Law 81–152, which also is cited as the Federal Property and Administrative Services Act of 1949. Section 101 of Title I of that statute deals with the organization of the General Services Administration (GSA). To head the new agency, the statute provides for the office of an Administrator of General Services, whom the President appoints by the advice and with the consent of the Senate (63 Stat. 379). https://www.loc.gov/law/help/statutes-at-large/81st-congress/session-1/c81s1ch288.pdf

Pursuant to Public Law 81–109, which is also cited as the Reorganization Act of 1949, President Truman transmitted Reorganization Plan No. 18 of 1950 to the U.S. Congress on March 13 of that same year. The plan transferred functions of building and space management to the Administrator of General Services. https://uscode.house.gov/view.xhtml?req=granuleid:USC-prelim-title5a-node84-leaf122&num=0&edition=prelim

The Reorganization Act of 1949 also required that each ensuing plan of reorganization be published in the Federal Register (63 Stat. 206). On May 25, 1950, Reorganization Plan No. 18 was one of 16 reorganization plans published in the daily issue (15 FR 3177). https://www.govinfo.gov/content/pkg/FR-1950-05-25/pdf/FR-1950-05-25.pdf

The GSA posts its organizational chart online. https://www.gsa.gov/about-us/gsa-organization

Statutory and Regulatory Authorities

Subtitle I of 40 U.S.C. is dedicated to statutory material affecting Federal property and administrative services. Chapter 3, which comprises sections 301–323, is dedicated to the organization of the GSA. https://uscode.house.gov/view.xhtml?path=/prelim@title40/subtitle1&edition=prelim

Part 105–53 of 41 CFR is dedicated to the GSA's statement of organization and functions. https://www.ecfr.gov/cgi-bin/text-idx?SID=43d7a5329a09931825fc019b64f070b8&mc=true&node=pt41.3.105_653&rgn=div5

Activities

The GSA started out, disposing of war surplus goods, managing and storing Government records, handling emergency preparedness, and stockpiling strategic supplies for wartime. It also regulated the sale of various office supplies to Federal agencies and managed a few unexpected operations (e.g., abacá plantations abroad). Today, the GSA provides the spaces, technical innovations, and goods and services that are essential for operating the Federal Government. It provides workplaces by constructing, managing, and preserving Government buildings and by leasing and managing commercial real estate. Its acquisition solutions offer private sector professional services, equipment, supplies, telecommunications, and information technology to Government organizations and the U.S. military. GSA leadership in technology helps agencies buy, build, and use technology in ways that support their missions and better serve the public. The GSA also implements Governmentwide policies to promote best practices of management and efficiency in operations. **Governmentwide Policymaking** The Office of Government-wide Policy (OGP) uses policies, data, and strategy to achieve efficiency and effective management across the Federal Government for key administrative areas: acquisition, fleet

GSA Organization

General Services Administration

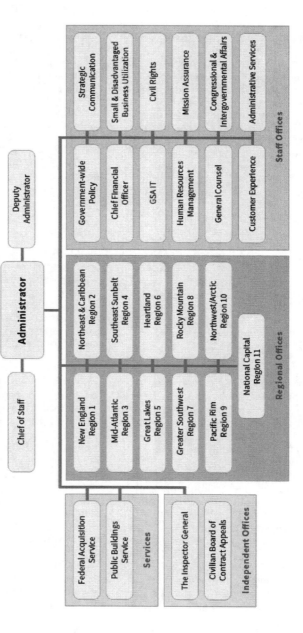

management travel and transportation, information technology modernization, and real estate management. The OGP influences agency behavior in these areas through the development of Governmentwide policy, performance standards, data analysis and benchmarking, and reporting of Governmentwide data. https://www.gsa.gov/about-us/organization/office-of-governmentwide-policy-overview

Product Acquisition / Service Management   The Federal Acquisition Service (FAS) offers more than 28 million different products and services to Federal agencies and delivers annually over $60 billion in information technology products, services, and solutions; telecommunication services; assisted acquisition services; travel and transportation management solutions; motor vehicle and fleet services; and charge card services. The FAS manages over 219,000 vehicles, more than 3.5 million charge cards, and provides personal property disposal services that facilitate the reuse of $1 billion in excess and surplus personal property every year. The FAS leverages the buying power of the Federal Government to negotiate prices on products and services that agencies require for daily operations. By arranging a network of service providers for information technology and total solutions for law enforcement, including security and facility management systems, the FAS meets the operating and mission requirements of an array of Federal agencies and State, Tribal, and local governments. Leveraging its technology transformation services and information technology portfolios, the FAS is developing and deploying Centers of Excellence to improve the public's experience with Government by obtaining and sharing technology applications, platforms, and processes that make Federal services more accessible, efficient, and effective. https://www.gsa.gov/about-us/organization/federal-acquisition-service

Workspace Acquisition / Property Management   The Public Buildings Service (PBS) provides quality facility and workspace solutions to more than 50 Federal agencies, disposes of excess or unneeded Federal properties, and promotes the adoption of innovative workplace solutions and technologies. It acquires space on behalf of the Federal Government through new construction and leasing and acts as a caretaker for Federal properties across the country. As the largest public real estate organization in the United States, the PBS owns or leases more than 8,800 assets and maintains an inventory of nearly 370 million square feet of rentable workspace. This inventory includes more than 413 buildings that are on the National Register of Historic Places. The PBS works with its Federal customers to reduce, overall, the need for workspace and the costs that are associated with acquiring and managing it. https://www.gsa.gov/about-us/organization/public-buildings-service

Sources of Information

A–Z Index   An alphabetized list of frequently visited web pages on the GSA website is available online. https://www.gsa.gov/website-information/az-index

Annual Reports   To enable a more informed assessment of performance, the GSA posts its annual financial report and performance report on the "Annual Reports" web page. https://www.gsa.gov/reference/reports/budget-performance/annual-reports

Archived Records   The "Guide to Federal Records in the National Archives of the United States" indicates that GSA records have been assigned to record group 269. https://www.archives.gov/research/guide-fed-records/groups/269.html

Auctions   The GSA Auctions website is a final part of the agency's transition to becoming an entirely electronic asset management system. The site allows the general public to bid electronically on a wide selection of Federal assets. The auctions are web-enabled: All registered participants may bid on items within specified timeframes. Federal personal property assets, such as airplanes, furniture, heavy machinery, office equipment, scientific equipment, vehicles, vessels, and other items, which may be located anywhere nationwide, can be purchased by online bidders whose physical location is restricted only by Internet access. https://gsaauctions.gov | Email: gsaauctionshelp@gsa.gov

Blogs   The "GSABlog" is available on the agency's main website. Ten other blogs that are associated with the GSA also are accessible on the "GSABlog" web page. These blogs include the 18F Blog, Citizenscience.gov Blog, Code.gov Blog, Data.gov Blog, DigitalGov Blog, FedRAMP Blog, IT Accessibility Blog, and USA.gov Blog, as well as the blogs "Around the Corner" and "Great Government Through Technology." https://www.gsa.gov/blog

Business Opportunities   The GSA serves as the Federal Government's procurement arm. It offers facilities, products, and services that Federal agencies use to benefit the public. The GSA also gives businesses the opportunity to sell billions of dollars worth of products and services to Federal agencies. https://www.gsa.gov/buying-selling/getting-started-with-gsa-purchasing-programs

The Office of Small Business Utilization web pages has information on opportunities, resources, and training for owners of small businesses. Phone, 855-672-8472. https://www.gsa.gov/small-business

Career Opportunities   The GSA relies on professionals with diverse academic backgrounds, life experiences, and skills to carry out its mission. It encourages Federal and private sector employees, Peace Corps volunteers and staff, persons with disabilities, recent retirees, students and recent graduates, veterans, and others to apply for job openings. For more information, contact the national recruitment center. Phone, 816-823-2006. https://www.gsa.gov/about-us/careers | Email: NRC@gsa.gov

In 2019, the GSA ranked 7th among 25 midsize Government agencies in the Partnership for Public Service's Best Places To Work Agency Rankings. https://bestplacestowork.org/rankings/detail/GS00

Consumer Rights   The "Consumer Action Handbook" is a free resource guide that provides general information on shopping for goods and services, information for filing a complaint about a purchase, and tips on consumer rights. Its contents also include a sample complaint letter and a consumer assistance directory that contains contact information for Government agencies and national corporations. The handbook is available in English and Spanish. A digital version in Portable Document Format (PDF) may be downloaded from the USA.gov website. A hardcopy may be ordered online; over the phone, weekdays, 8 a.m.–8 p.m., excluding Federal holidays; or by writing to USAGov–Handbook, Pueblo, CO 81009. Phone, 844-872-4681. https://www.usa.gov/handbook

Contact GSA   The "Contact Us" web page has live chat, an electronic form for submitting questions, a phone number, and a link that leads to an electronic agencywide staff directory. https://www.gsa.gov/about-us/contact-us | Email: press@gsa.gov

Federal Register   Significant documents and documents that the GSA recently published in the Federal Register are accessible online. https://www.federalregister.gov/agencies/general-services-administration

Federal Relay (FedRelay)   FedRelay provides telecommunications services to Federal agencies and tribal governments for conducting official business with people who struggle with deafness, hearing impairments, or speech disabilities. The general public also may use FedRelay for conducting business with Federal agencies. Phone, 855-482-4348. https://www.gsa.gov/technology/technology-purchasing-programs/telecommunications-and-network-services/federal-relay-fedrelay | Email: ITCSC@gsa.gov

Forms   An electronic forms library is available on the GSA website. The library has an easily accessible collection of the forms that are most frequently downloaded. https://www.gsa.gov/reference/forms | Email: forms@gsa.gov

Freedom of Information Act (FOIA)   To any person, the FOIA gives a statutory right for obtaining access to Government information in the records of executive branch agencies. This right to access is limited, however, when the requested information is shielded from disclosure by any of nine exemptions contained within the statute. The GSA participates in FOIAonline, which enables users to submit a FOIA request to all participating agencies, track the status of a request, search for requests submitted by others, access previously released records, and generate agency-specific FOIA processing reports. https://foiaonline.gov/foiaonline/action/public/home#participatingAgencies | Email: gsa.foia@gsa.gov

Governmentwide Initiatives The GSA is involved with dozen of initiatives whose scope is governmentwide. https://www.gsa.gov/governmentwide-initiatives

Help Government Find Answers The GSA maintains the Challenge.gov website, which is the official hub for prize competitions and challenges across the Federal Government. It is a web platform that assists Federal agencies with inviting the public to submit ideas and solutions for solving specific problems. https://www.challenge.gov

Historic Preservation The GSA posts historic preservation resources and tools on its website. https://www.gsa.gov/real-estate/historic-preservation/historic-preservation-policy-tools/preservation-tools-resources

History The GSA has posted a brief history that describes its establishment, original mission, accomplishments through the decades, and changes that it has undergone. https://www.gsa.gov/about-us/background-history/a-brief-history-of-gsa

"GSA70—Supporting Modernization, Innovation, and Efficiency" is a video timeline that celebrates the agency's 70th anniversary and highlights 7 decades of achievements, which include renovating the Presidential residence, starting a Governmentwide motor pool, creating a Federal telecommunications system, introducing the first Government charge card, opening childcare centers in Federal buildings, creating the Government's first official web portal (FirstGov.gov), moving email to a cloud-based system, and more. https://www.youtube.com/watch?v=czy4eQ5iGhU

Inspector General The Office of Inspector General operates a fraud hotline for reporting abuse, fraud, and waste in GSA programs or mismanagement or violations of law, regulations, and rules by GSA employees or contractors. Phone, 202-501-1780 or 800-424-5210. https://www.gsaig.gov/hotline | Email: fraudnet@gsa.gov

Newsroom The GSA posts congressional testimonies, news releases, and photo galleries on its website. https://www.gsa.gov/about-us/newsroom | Email: press@gsa.gov

Open Government The GSA supports the Open Government initiative by promoting the principles of collaboration, participation, and transparency. https://www.gsa.gov/governmentwide-initiatives/gsas-open-government-initiatives | Email: Open.Government@gsa.gov

Payroll Calendars The payroll services branch of the Office of the Chief Financial Officer posts payroll calendars in Portable Document Format (PDF) on the GSA website for viewing and downloading. Phone, 844-303-6515. https://www.gsa.gov/buying-selling/purchasing-programs/shared-services/payroll-shared-services/payroll-calendars

Per Diem Rates The GSA sets the per diem rates for Federal travel within the continental United States. Per diem is the allowance for incidental expenses, lodging, and meals. The GSA website features a search tool for finding current rates in the continental United States by State or ZIP Code or by clicking on a map. https://www.gsa.gov/travel/plan-book/per-diem-rates | Email: travelpolicy@gsa.gov

Plain Language The "Plain Writing Act of 2010" was passed by Congress and approved by the President to improve the effectiveness of Federal agencies and increase their accountability to the public "by promoting clear Government communication that the public can understand and use." The GSA is committed to writing agency documents and its website content in plain language. https://www.gsa.gov/governmentwide-initiatives/plain-language

Presidential Transition Directory The 2020 directory connects the people who are helping plan and design the next Federal Government with information and resources that are relevant to their efforts. https://www.gsa.gov/governmentwide-initiatives/presidential-transition-directory

Properties The GSA owns and leases over 376.9 million square feet of space in 9,600 buildings in more than 2,200 communities nationwide. In addition to office buildings, GSA properties include courthouses, data processing centers, laboratories, land ports of entry, and post offices. https://www.gsa.gov/real-estate/gsa-properties

Real Property Disposal The Office of Real Property Utilization and Disposal is a governmentwide realty services provider. It provides information on the handling of excess real property and on properties that are being offered for sale. https://disposal.gsa.gov

Regional Offices   The GSA operates 11 regional offices. https://www.gsa.gov/about-us/gsa-regions

Site Map   The website map allows visitors to look for specific topics or to browse content that aligns with their interests. http://www.gsa.gov/portal/site/map

Social Media   In addition to a main Facebook page, the GSA has other pages that are associated with its component organizations and programs and its activities and services. The "Social Media at GSA" web page allows visitors to see GSA's entire Facebook presence on social media. https://www.gsa.gov/about-us/newsroom/social-media-at-gsa#Facebook | Email: socialmedia@gsa.gov

The GSA tweets announcements and other newsworthy items on its Twitter accounts. In addition to a main Twitter feed, the GSA has other feeds that are associated with its component organizations and programs and its activities and services. The "Social Media at GSA" web page allows visitors to see GSA's entire Twitter presence on social media. https://www.gsa.gov/about-us/newsroom/social-media-at-gsa#Twitter

The Sources of Information were updated 7–2020.

The GSA posts videos on its YouTube channel. https://www.youtube.com/usgsa

Staff Directory   The GSA maintains an electronic staff directory on its website. After August 1, 2020, the staff directory will be accessible only as a Comma-Separated Values (CSV) file, which allows users to view, search, and download the directory's content. https://www.gsa.gov/staff-directory

Sustainable Facilities (SF) Tool   The SFTool supports the efforts of designers, facility managers, purchasing agents, tenants, and others to make buildings healthier and more efficient and to become more environmentally-responsible in their purchasing. https://sftool.gov | Email: sustainability@gsa.gov

Upcoming Events and Training   The GSA posts upcoming events and training on its "GSA Events" web page. https://www.gsa.gov/about-us/events-and-training/gsa-events

USA.gov   USA.gov is a governmentwide guide to information and services. https://www.usa.gov

Inter-American Foundation

1331 Pennsylvania Avenue, NW., Suite 1200 North, Washington, DC 20004
Phone, 202-360-4530. Internet, http://www.iaf.gov

Chair	EDUARDO ARRIOLA
Vice Chair	JUAN CARLOS ITURREGUI
Secretary	JACK C. VAUGHN, JR.
Director	J. KELLY RYAN
Director	LUIS A. VIADA
Director	ROGER W. WALLACE
Director	(VACANCY)
Director	(VACANCY)
Director	(VACANCY)
President / Chief Executive Officer	PALOMA ADAMS-ALLEN
Chief Operating Officer	LESLEY DUNCAN
General Counsel	PAUL ZIMMERMAN

MANAGING DIRECTORS

Grant-Making and Portfolio Management	Marcy Kelley
Networks and Strategic Initiatives	Stephen Cox
Office of External and Government Affairs	(vacancy)

The above list of key personnel was updated 09–2017.

The Inter-American Foundation supports social and economic development in Latin America and the Caribbean.

The Inter-American Foundation (IAF) was created in 1969 (22 U.S.C. 290f) as an experimental U.S. foreign assistance program. The Foundation is governed by a nine-person Board of Directors whom the President appoints with the advice and consent of the Senate. Six members are drawn from the private sector and three from the Federal Government. The Board of Directors appoints the president of the Foundation. http://www.iaf.gov/about-the-iaf/at-a-glance-3798

In Latin America and the Caribbean, the IAF promotes equitable, participatory, and sustainable self-help development by awarding grants and giving other technical assistance directly to local organizations throughout the region. It also partners with the public and private sectors to build support and to mobilize local, national, and international resources for grassroots development. http://www.iaf.gov/about-the-iaf/more-about-the-iaf

Sources of Information

Blog The IAF blogs in four languages: English, Kreyol, Portuguese, and Spanish. http://www.iaf.gov/resources/blog

Career Opportunities The IAF posts employment opportunities online. http://www.iaf.gov/about-the-iaf/iaf-jobs/vacancies

The IAF posts information on student internships on its Web site. http://www.iaf.gov/about-the-iaf/iaf-jobs/internships

Corporate Partners Contact the Office of External and Government Affairs for information on participating in the program for corporate partners. Phone, 202-688-3051. http://www.iaf.gov/partners/corporate | Email: partnerships@iaf.gov

Country Portfolios A list of the countries where the IAF currently works is available on its Web site. Country pages include descriptions of active IAF grants. http://www.iaf.gov/our-work/where-we-work/country-portfolios

Freedom of Information Act (FOIA) The IAF generally discloses documents or records upon receiving a properly submitted request in writing. Records, or parts of them, that one or more of the nine FOIA exemptions shield will not be released. http://www.iaf.gov/about-the-iaf/legal-notices-and-reports/freedom-of-information-act-foia | Email: foia@iaf.gov

The IAF maintains an electronic FOIA reading room. http://www.iaf.gov/about-the-iaf/legal-notices-and-reports/freedom-of-information-act-foia/foia-e-reading-room

Frequently Asked Questions (FAQs) The IAF posts answers to FAQs online. http://www.iaf.gov/about-the-iaf/faq

Grants The IAF funds the self-help efforts of grassroots groups in Latin America and the Caribbean. It welcomes proposals for its grant program. http://www.iaf.gov/apply-for-grants/call-for-proposals

Multilingual Resources Español http://spanish.iaf.gov/home-spanish
Kreyol http://kreyol.iaf.gov/home-kreyol
Português http://portugues.iaf.gov/home-portuguese

News The IAF posts news items on its Web site. http://www.iaf.gov/resources/news

The IAF posts newsletters on its Web site. http://www.iaf.gov/resources/newsletters

Open Government The IAF's Open Government Web page has shortcuts to items of interest to the public. http://www.iaf.gov/about-the-iaf/legal-notices-and-reports/open-government-initiative | Email: inquiries@iaf.gov

Organizational Chart The IAF includes a small organizational chart on its "Our People" Web page. http://www.iaf.gov/about-the-iaf/our-people

Project Achievements The "From the Field" Web page presents highlights and milestones of

projects that the IAF has supported. http://www.iaf.gov/our-work/results/stories-from-the-field
Publications   The IAF produces print and digital publications in English, Spanish, and Portuguese. http://www.iaf.gov/resources/publications
Site Map   The Web site map allows visitors to look for specific topics or to browse content that aligns with their interests. http://www.iaf.gov/about-the-iaf/new-advanced-components/site-map

Social Media   The IAF has a Facebook account. https://www.facebook.com/iafgrassroots

The IAF tweets announcements and other newsworthy items on Twitter. https://twitter.com/IAFgrassroots

The IAF uploads videos to Vimeo. https://vimeo.com/user15989133/videos http://www.iaf.gov/about-the-iaf/contact-us | Email: inquiries@iaf.gov

For further information, contact the Office of the President, Inter-American Foundation, 1331 Pennsylvania Avenue, NW., Suite 1200 North, Washington, DC 20004. Phone, 202-360-4530.

Merit Systems Protection Board

1615 M Street NW., Fifth Floor, Washington, DC 20419
Phone, 202-653-7200 or 800-209-8960. Fax, 202-653-7130. Internet, http://www.mspb.gov

Chair	MARK ROBBINS, ACTING
Vice Chair	MARK ROBBINS
Member	(VACANCY)
Director, Office of Equal Employment Opportunity	JERRY BEAT
Executive Director	JAMES M. EISENMANN
Clerk of the Board	JENNIFER EVERLING, ACTING
Director, Financial and Administrative Management	KEVIN NASH
Director, Information Resources Management	WILLIAM D. SPENCER, ACTING
Director, Office of Appeals Counsel	SUSAN M. SWAFFORD
Director, Office of Policy and Evaluation	JAMES M. READ
Director, Office of Regional Operations	DEBORAH MIRON
General Counsel	BRYAN G. POLISUK
Legislative Counsel	ROSALYN L. COATES

[For the Merit Systems Protection Board statement of organization, see the Code of Federal Regulations, Title 5, Part 1200]

The Merit Systems Protection Board protects the integrity of the Federal personnel merit systems and the rights of Federal employees.

The Merit Systems Protection Board (MSPB) is a successor agency to the United States Civil Service Commission, established by act of January 16, 1883 (22 Stat. 403). Reorganization Plan No. 2 of 1978 (5 U.S.C. app.) redesignated part of the Commission as the Merit Systems Protection Board. The Board comprises three members whom the President appoints with the advice and consent of the Senate.

Activities

The Board has responsibility for hearing and adjudicating appeals by Federal employees of adverse personnel actions, such as removals, suspensions, and demotions. It also resolves cases involving reemployment rights, denial of periodic step increases in pay, actions against administrative law judges, and charges of prohibited personnel practices, including charges in connection with whistleblowing.

The Board has the authority to enforce its decisions and to order corrective and disciplinary actions. An employee or applicant for employment involved in an appealable action that also involves an allegation of discrimination may ask the Equal Employment Opportunity Commission to review a Board decision. Final decisions and

MERIT SYSTEMS PROTECTION BOARD

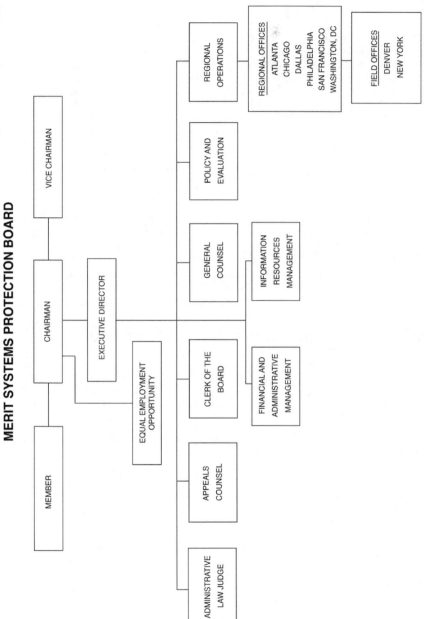

orders of the Board can be appealed to the U.S. Court of Appeals for the Federal Circuit.

The Board reviews regulations issued by the Office of Personnel Management and has the authority to require agencies to cease compliance with any regulation that could constitute a prohibited personnel practice. It also conducts special studies of the civil service and other executive branch merit systems and reports to the President and the Congress on whether the Federal workforce is being adequately protected against political abuses and prohibited personnel practices. http://www.mspb.gov/About/about.htm

Sources of Information

Electronic Filing   An appeal may be filed online using the e-Appeal process. https://e-appeal.mspb.gov
Career Opportunities   The MSPB posts current job openings on USAJobs. http://www.mspb.gov/contact/jobs.htm

Freedom of Information Act (FOIA)   The MSPB participates in FOIAonline, which allows an information seeker to submit FOIA requests to participating agencies, track the status of requests, search for requests that others have submitted, access previously released records, and generate agency-specific FOIA processing reports. http://www.mspb.gov/foia/request.htm https://foiaonline.regulations.gov/foia/action/public/home
Interviews   The MSPB posts external links to MSPB-related interviews on its Web site. http://www.mspb.gov/radio.htm http://www.mspb.gov/video.htm
Public Affairs   The MSPB posts "Federal Register" notices, press releases, reports, and the results of its annual Federal Employee Viewpoint Survey online. http://www.mspb.gov/publicaffairs/publicaffairs.htm http://www.mspb.gov/contact/contact.htm | Email: mspb@mspb.gov

For further information, contact the Merit Systems Protection Board, 1615 M Street NW., Washington, DC 20419. Phone, 202-653-7200 or 800-209-8960. TDD, 800-877-8339. Fax, 202-653-7130.

National Aeronautics and Space Administration

300 E Street SW., Washington, DC 20546
Phone, 202-358-0000. Internet, http://www.nasa.gov

Office of the Administrator
Administrator   C. William Nelson
Deputy Administrator   Pamela A. Melroy

Associate Administrators   Robert D. Cabana
Strategic Engagement and Assessment   Thomas E. Cremins

Chief of Staff   Susan P. Quinn
Deputy Associate Administrator   Melanie W. Saunders
https://www.nasa.gov/nasa-leadership

Administrator Staff Offices

Associate Administrators
Communications   Marc Etkind
Diversity and Equal Opportunity   Stephen T. Shih
International and Interagency Relations   Karen Feldstein
Legislative and Intergovernmental Affairs   Alicia Brown
Small Business Programs   Glenn A. Delgado
STEM Engagement   Michael A. Kincaid

Chiefs
Financial Officer   Margaret V. Schaus
Information Officer   Jeffrey M. Seaton

General Counsel	SUMARA M. THOMPSON-KING
https://www.nasa.gov/about/org_index.html	

Administrator Staff Offices

Senior Climate Advisor	GAVIN A. SCHMIDT

Chiefs
Engineer	RALPH R. ROE
Health and Medical Officer	JAMES D. POLK
Safety and Mission Assurance Officer	W. RUSS DELOACH
Scientist	JAMES L. GREEN
Technologist	DOUGLAS A. TERRIER
https://www.nasa.gov/press-release/nasa-announces-new-role-of-senior-climate-advisor	

Mission Directorates

Associate Administrators
Aeronautics Research	ROBERT PEARCE
Human Exploration and Operations	KATHRYN LUEDERS
Science	THOMAS ZURBUCHEN
Space Technology	JAMES L. REUTER

Mission Support Directorate

Associate Administrator	ROBERT GIBBS

Assistant Administrators
Human Capital Management	JANE DATTA
Procurement	KARLA SMITH JACKSON
Protective Services	JOSEPH S. MAHALEY
Strategic Infrastructure	BURTON R. SUMMERFIELD, ACTING

Executive Directors
NASA Shared Services Center	ANITA F. HARRELL
https://www.nasa.gov/msd/msd-leadership	

Centers and Facilities

Directors
Ames Research Center	EUGENE L. TU
Armstrong Flight Center	DAVID D. MCBRIDE
Glenn Research Center	MARLA PÉREZ-DAVIS
Goddard Space Flight Center	DENNIS ANDRUCYK
Jet Propulsion Laboratory	MICHAEL M. WATKINS
Johnson Space Center	VANESSA WYCHE, ACTING
Kennedy Space Center	JANET PETRO, ACTING
Langley Research Center	CLAYTON TURNER
Marshall Space Flight Center	JOAN A. SINGER, ACTING
Stennis Space Center	RICHARD J. GILBRECH

NASA Management Office	MARCUS A. WATKINS
https://www.nasa.gov/about/sites/index.html	

Inspector General	PAUL K. MARTIN
https://oig.nasa.gov/orgCharts/inspector_general.html	

The above list of key personnel was updated 6–2021.

National Aeronautics and Space Administration

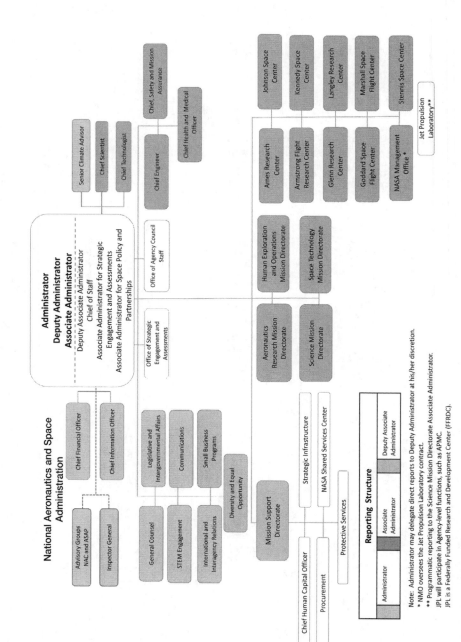

Note: Administrator may delegate direct reports to Deputy Administrator at his/her discretion.

* NMO oversees the Jet Propulsion Laboratory contract.

** Programmatic reporting to the Science Mission Directorate Associate Administrator.

JPL will participate in Agency-level functions, such as APMC.

JPL is a Federally Funded Research and Development Center (FFRDC).

The National Aeronautics and Space Administration advances aeronautic research, explores space, and makes scientific discoveries for the benefit of humankind.

Establishment and Organization

On July 29, 1958, President Dwight D. Eisenhower approved Public Law 85–568, which also is cited as the National Aeronautics and Space Act of 1958, "to provide for research into problems of flight within and outside the earth's atmosphere." In the Act's declaration of policy and purpose, the U.S. Congress declared "that it is the policy of the United States that activities in space should be devoted to peaceful purposes for the benefit of all mankind" (72 Stat. 426). https://www.govinfo.gov/content/pkg/STATUTE-72/pdf/STATUTE-72-Pg426-2.pdf

By approving this Act of Congress, President Eisenhower "established the National Aeronautics and Space Administration" (72 Stat. 429). The newly created executive branch agency has become widely known by its acronym NASA.

The National Advisory Committee for Aeronautics (NACA) was NASA's predecessor organization. The Committee was established on March 3, 1915, as a part of Public Law 63–271, which made appropriations for the naval service and established the Advisory Committee for Aeronautics (38 Stat. 930). After serving four decades as the Nation's premier aeronautical research institution, the NACA was dissolved in 1958, and its laboratories became the nucleus of NASA. https://www.loc.gov/law/help/statutes-at-large/63rd-congress/session-3/c63s3ch83.pdf

NASA's statement of organization and general information on the agency have been codified and assigned to Part 1201 of 14 CFR. The Administration is headed by a civilian Administrator whom the President appoints by the advice and with the consent of the Senate. The Administrator, whom the President supervises and directs, is responsible for exercising all NASA powers and discharging all of its duties. https://www.ecfr.gov/cgi-bin/text-idx?SID=e7061af8ea4349271e3601ceda1fbcdd&mc=true&node=pt14.5.1201&rgn=div5

NASA posts its organizational chart (FEB 2021) in Portable Document Format for viewing and downloading. https://www.nasa.gov/sites/default/files/atoms/files/nasa_organizational_chart_feb_2021.pdf

Statutory and Regulatory Authorities

Statutory material on national and commercial space programs has been codified and assigned to 51 U.S.C. Statutory material on the coordination of aeronautical and space activities has been assigned to Subchapter II of Chapter 201. Subchapter II includes sections 20111–20117. https://uscode.house.gov/view.xhtml?path=/prelim@title51/subtitle2/chapter201/subchapter2&edition=prelim

Rules and regulations concerning aeronautics and space have been assigned to 14 CFR. Chapter V of Title 14 contains codified rules and regulations that are associated with NASA. https://www.ecfr.gov/cgi-bin/text-idx?gp=&SID=e7061af8ea4349271e3601ceda1fbcdd&mc=true&tpl=/ecfrbrowse/Title14/14chapterV.tpl

Activities

Earth and Space Exploration The Science Mission Directorate explores Earth and space to advance Earth science, heliophysics, planetary science, and astrophysics. Using in situ and space-based observations, the Directorate seeks a better understanding of the Sun and its influence on the solar system, climate change, the solar system's origin and evolution, whether life is limited to Earth, and the universe beyond. https://science.nasa.gov/about-us

For further information, call 202-358-3889.

Increasing Efficiency and Safety / Reducing Environmental Harm The Aeronautics Research Mission Directorate conducts research, ground tests, and flight demonstrations to develop technologies and tools that reduce the adverse effects of aviation on the environment, increase efficiency while maintaining safety in skies that are becoming more crowded, and prepare the way for the emergence of new aircraft shapes and propulsion. The Directorate's four research programs partner with industry, other government agencies, and universities to develop technologies, converge breakthroughs from other fields, and ensure that the next generation workforce has the vision and skills for maintaining U.S. leadership in aviation. https://www.nasa.gov/aeroresearch/about-armd

For further information, call 202-358-2047.

Institutional Support for Mission Objectives   The Mission Support Directorate provides overall leadership, stewardship, advocacy, integration, and optimization of Agency institutional activities. These activities include management of human capital and strategic infrastructure, procurement, protective services, headquarters operations, shared services, partnerships, external audits, and management of Agency directives. To enable successful operations, the Directorate focuses on three major goals: to provide stewardship of major institutional operations; to integrate resources, infrastructure, and processes and to advocate for institutional capabilities and needs; and to optimize mission support services through strategic analysis and business services assessments to achieve greater operational efficiency. https://www.nasa.gov/msd/aboutus

For further information, call 202-358-2789.

Space Technology for Missions   The Space Technology Mission Directorate develops crosscutting and pioneering technologies and capabilities that the agency needs to carry out current and future missions. Through transparent, collaborative partnerships, the Directorate rapidly develops and demonstrates high-payoff technologies. It uses a merit-based competition model with a portfolio approach, spanning a range of discipline areas and technology readiness levels. https://www.nasa.gov/directorates/spacetech/about_us/index.html

For further information, call 202-358-0454.

Supporting Human Exploration   The Human Exploration and Operations Mission

Directorate oversees NASA space systems development and operations that support human exploration in and beyond low-Earth orbit. It also oversees low-level requirements development, policy, and programmatic oversight. The International Space Station represents the agency's exploration activities in low-Earth orbit. Beyond low-Earth orbit, exploration activities include the management of exploration systems development, human space flight capabilities, advanced exploration systems, and space life sciences research and applications. The Directorate also provides agency leadership and management of NASA space operations related to launch services and space communications and navigation in support of both human and robotic exploration programs. https://www.nasa.gov/directorates/heo/index.html

For further information, call 202-358-1562.

Nasa Centers

Ames Research Center   Located in California's Silicon Valley, the Center enables exploration through selected developments, innovative technologies, and interdisciplinary scientific discovery. It provides leadership in astrobiology; small satellites; technologies for CEV, CLV, and HLV; the search for habitable planets; supercomputing; intelligent-adaptive systems; advanced thermal protection; and airborne astronomy. The Center also develops tools for a safer, more efficient national airspace, and it cultivates partnerships that benefit NASA's mission. https://www.nasa.gov/ames

Armstrong Flight Research Center   Located at Edwards Air Force Base, CA, the Center carries out flight research and technology integration, validates space exploration concepts, conducts airborne remote sensing and science missions, enables airborne astrophysics observation missions to study the universe, and supports International Space Station operations. It also supports activities of the Agency's four Mission Directorates. https://www.nasa.gov/centers/armstrong/home/index.html

Glenn Research Center   Located on two campuses—at Lewis Field, next to Cleveland

Hopkins International Airport, and at Neil A. Armstrong Test Facility (formerly the Plum Brook Station) in Sandusky, OH—the Center is associated with cutting edge technologies that will enable human exploration to Mars, the design of environmentally friendlier commercial hybrid electric aircraft, and the development of more advanced high-temperature materials. Its 3,200 scientists, engineers, and other specialized employees work in partnership with U.S. companies, universities, and other Government institutions to produce and improve new technologies that are useful on and above and beyond Earth. The Center's specialized staff focuses on air-breathing and in-space propulsion, power and energy storage, aerospace communications, extreme environment materials, biomedical technologies, and high-value space experiments in the physical sciences. https://www.nasa.gov/centers/glenn/home/index.html

Goddard Space Flight Center   Located in Greenbelt, MD, the Center expands humankind's knowledge of Earth and its environment, the solar system, and the universe by observing them from space. It also conducts scientific investigations, develops and operates space systems, and advances essential technologies. https://www.nasa.gov/goddard

Johnson Space Center   Located in Houston, TX, the Center specializes in human space flight. It hosts and staffs program and project offices; selects and trains astronauts; manages and conducts projects that build, test, and integrate human-rated systems for transportation, habitation, and working in space; and plans and operates human space flight missions. This work requires a comprehensive understanding of space and planetary environments, as well as research into the effects of those environments on human physiology. It also requires development of technology to sustain and preserve life; maintenance of a supply chain to design, manufacture, and test flight products; selection, training, and provision of medical care to those who fly space missions; and ongoing administrative mission support services. The Center is currently hosting the International Space Station Program, the Multi-Purpose

Crew Vehicle Program, and the Human Research Program. It plays a lead role in developing, operating, and integrating human exploration missions that include commercial, academic, international, and U.S. Government partners. https://www.nasa.gov/centers/johnson/home/index.html

Kennedy Space Center   Located on Florida's east coast, the Center is responsible for space launch operations and spaceport and range technologies. Home to the launch services program, it manages the processing and launching of astronaut crews and associated payloads. Its management activities include the International Space Station segments, research experiments and supplies, and NASA's scientific and research spacecraft. These scientific and research spacecraft range from robotic landers to Earth observation satellites and space-based telescopes on a variety of launch vehicles.

Innovative technology experts at the Center support NASA's current programs and future exploration missions by developing new products and processes that benefit the Agency and consumers. The Center remains a leader in cutting-edge research and development in the areas of physics, chemistry, technology, prototype designing, engineering, environmental conservation, and renewable energy. https://www.nasa.gov/centers/kennedy/home/index.html

Langley Research Center   Located in Hampton, VA, and established in 1917 as an aeronautics lab, the Center is renowned for its scientific and technological expertise in aerospace research, atmospheric science, systems analysis and integration, and planetary entry, descent and landing. Its researchers and engineers conduct research in structures and materials, applied sciences, space technology development, and aerosciences across the hyper, super, and subsonic flight regimes. Langley researchers and engineers have developed and validated technologies to improve the effectiveness, safety, environmental compatibility, and efficiency of the Nation's air transportation system. The Center supports space exploration and operations, and it plays a major role in expanding science-based knowledge of Earth and its environment. By determining appropriate preventative and corrective action for problems, trends, and issues across agency programs and projects, its engineering and safety personnel at the NASA Engineering Safety Center have improved mission safety and execution. https://www.nasa.gov/langley

Marshall Space Flight Center   Located in Huntsville, AL, the Center oversees complex engineering, technology development, and scientific research for making human space exploration a reality. The Center is building the space launch system and developing advanced technologies that are necessary for the human journey to Mars. It also manages a number of programs and projects: the International Space Station's environmental control and life support system, its payload operations, and numerous other facilities and experiments; the Chandra X-ray Observatory; the Discovery and New Frontiers programs; space technology demonstration missions; and the Michoud Assembly Facility, where space vehicles are manufactured and assembled. https://www.nasa.gov/centers/marshall/home/index.html

Stennis Space Center   Located near Bay St. Louis, MS, the Center serves as the agency's rocket propulsion testing ground. It provides test services not only for America's space program, but also for the Department of Defense and private sector. Its unique rocket propulsion test capabilities will be used for testing the engines and stages of NASA's space launch system rocket. The Advanced Technology and Technology Transfer Branch develops and licenses state-of-the-art components, processes, sensors, and software. https://www.nasa.gov/centers/stennis/home/index.html

Jet Propulsion Laboratory   The Laboratory is a Federally Funded Research and Development Center (FFRDC) managed under contract by the California Institute of Technology (Caltech) in Pasadena, CA. This FFRDC is a unique nongovernment entity sponsored and funded by the Agency to meet specific long-term technical needs that cannot be met by other organizations within the Agency. As part of this special relationship, the Laboratory must operate in the public interest with objectivity and independence, avoid organizational conflicts of interest, and fully disclose its affairs to NASA. The Laboratory develops and maintains technical and managerial competencies to perform the following missions in support of the Agency's strategic goals: to explore the solar system to understand its formation and evolution; to establish a continuous and permanent robotic presence on Mars to discover its history and habitability; to make critical measurements and models to understand the global and regional integrated Earth system; to conduct observations to search for neighboring solar systems and Earth-like planets and help understand formation, evolution, and composition of the Universe; to conduct communications and navigation for deep space missions; to provide support, particularly in robotic infrastructures and precursors, that enables human exploration of the Moon, Mars, and beyond; and, under Caltech's initiative, to collaborate with other Federal and State government agencies and commercial endeavors in areas synergistic with the Laboratory's work performed for NASA. https://www.nasa.gov/centers/jpl/home/index.html

Sources of Information

A–Z Index   NASA maintains an online index of all topics to help visitors browse or search for specific information. https://www.nasa.gov/topics

Albedo   A completely iced over Earth would have an albedo of about 0.84, which means that its surface would reflect 84 percent of the sun's light. A completely forested over Earth, on the other hand, would have an albedo of about 0.14, which means that Earth's surface would absorb 86 percent of the sun's light. Changes that affect airborne pollution, cloudiness, ice cover, or land cover (e.g., forest to farmland) also affect the global albedo. Using satellite measurements that have been collected since the late 1970s, scientists estimate that Earth's average albedo is about about 0.30, which means that its surface reflects about 30 percent of the sun's light. https://earthobservatory.nasa.gov/images/84499/measuring-earths-albedo

Archived Records   The "Guide to Federal Records in the National Archives of the United States" indicates that NASA records have been assigned to record group 255. https://www.archives.gov/research/guide-fed-records/groups/255.html

Business Opportunities   Information on business opportunities is available on NASA's Office of Procurement website. https://www.nasa.gov/office/procurement

NASA offers contracting and subcontracting opportunities to small businesses. Contact the Office of Small Business Programs. Phone, 202-358-2088. https://www.osbp.nasa.gov | Email: smallbusiness@nasa.gov

Career Opportunities   In addition to astronauts, the agency relies on accountants, engineers, human resources specialists, IT specialists, scientists, technicians, writers, and other skilled professionals, to carry out its mission. To learn more about employment opportunities and programs, visit the "Careers at NASA" web page. https://www.nasa.gov/careers

In 2020, NASA ranked the highest among 17 large Government agencies in the Best Places To Work Agency Rankings! https://bestplacestowork.org/rankings/detail/?c=NN00

Contact Infomation   NASA Communications Office personnel work hard, answering questions and responding to requests in a timely manner. Before relying on the "Contact Page" or directing an email to the public inquiries inbox, search NASA's website to see if the desired information is already accessible. NASA also has communication tools that make it easy to keep abreast of the agency's announcements and exciting achievements. https://www.nasa.gov/about/contact/index.html | Email: public-inquiries@hq.nasa.gov

The "Media Contacts and Information" web page was designed with journalists and reporters in mind. https://www.nasa.gov/news/media/info/index.html

Earth Images   The "Earth Observatory" website contains various collections of images of Earth. https://earthobservatory.nasa.gov/images

Federal Register   Significant documents and documents that NASA recently published in the Federal Register are accessible online. https://www.federalregister.gov/agencies/national-aeronautics-and-space-administration

Freedom of Information Act (FOIA)   Any person has a court-enforceable right to request and obtain access to Federal agency records. That right has restrictions and does not extend to records, or portions of them, that are shielded from public disclosure by one of nine statutory exemptions or by one of three special law enforcement record exclusions. The FOIA established a statutory right that affects the process for accessing executive branch information in the Federal Government. https://www.nasa.gov/FOIA/index.html | Email: foia@hq.nasa.gov

NASA maintains a hyperlinked list of FOIA websites for each of its centers. https://www.nasa.gov/FOIA/NASA-Centers.html

NASA maintains a hyperlinked list of its centers' electronic libraries. https://www.nasa.gov/content/nasa-e-libraries

Glossary   NASA;s Earth Observatory maintains an online glossary. https://earthobservatory.nasa.gov/glossary/all

The Science Mission Directorate website has a glossary. https://science.nasa.gov/glossary

Greenland's Melting Glaciers   NASA's Oceans Melting Greenland (OMG) mission investigates the role that warm ocean water plays in accelerating the melting of Greenland's glaciers. The OMG mission gathers data on water temperatures and Greenland's glaciers to improve the science on the melting ice and the global sea level rise that it is causing. https://omg.jpl.nasa.gov/portal

NASA has posted a short animated video on YouTube that shows how a glacier melts. https://www.youtube.com/watch?v=0QVVzFPChAU

History   Students of aeronautical and space history can find a treasure trove of resources on the the "NASA History" web page, which includes links to audio and written sources and image and video collections. https://www.nasa.gov/topics/history/index.html | Email: hq-histinfo@nasa.gov

The History Program Office maintains its own topical index. https://history.nasa.gov/tindex.html

Library   The NASA Headquarters Library welcomes visitors. Located in the East Lobby of NASA Headquarters in Washington, DC, the library is open Monday–Friday, 8 a.m.–4:30 p.m. It is closed on Federal holidays. Phone, 202-358-0168. https://www.nasa.gov/centers/hq/library | Email: library@hq.nasa.gov

Maps NASA's Earth Observatory maintains a collection of maps on its "Global Gaps" web page. https://earthobservatory.nasa.gov/global-maps

Missions A hyperlinked list of NASA missions is maintained on the "NASA Missions A–Z" web page. https://www.nasa.gov/missions

The "Mission Key" assigns a color code to NASA's science missions and groups them in the following categories: universe, solar system, Sun, and Earth. https://science.nasa.gov/missions-page

NASA posts science mission posters for downloading. Posters are grouped in the following four categories: astrophysics, solar system, Sun, and Earth. https://science.nasa.gov/toolkits/nasa-science-mission-posters

Open Government NASA supports the Open Government initiative by promoting collaboration, participation, and transparency. https://www.nasa.gov/open

Picture of the Day Discover something new about the universe each day by visiting NASA's "Astronomy Picture of the Day" web page. A professional astronomer provides a brief explanation for each daily image or photograph. A picture of the day archives is also accessible from the same page. https://apod.nasa.gov/apod/astropix.html

Plain Writing The Plain Writing Act of 2010 requires Federal agencies to communicate clearly. NASA editors and writers aim to use plain language in any document that is necessary for obtaining agency benefits or services, that provides information on agency benefits or services, or that explains how to comply with a requirement that the agency administers or enforces. https://www.nasa.gov/open/plainlanguage.html

Publications The "NASA Headquarters Library" website includes a "Find Publications" web page. The web page contains a section for bibliographies, one for books, one for databases, and another for journals. https://www.nasa.gov/centers/hq/library/find

The NASA scientific and technical information program makes conference papers and research reports accessible online. https://sti.nasa.gov | Email: nasa-dl-sti-id@mail.nasa.gov

The scientific and technical information program website has a site map to make browsing its contents easier. https://sti.nasa.gov/site-map/#.YInEW2dKiUk

Social Media NASA maintains a presence on popular social media websites. The "Social Media at NASA" page provides easy access to the agency's social media accounts. https://www.nasa.gov/socialmedia

Space Technology Explore space technology by visiting the "Technology Overview" web page. https://www.nasa.gov/topics/technology/overview/index.html

Students / Teachers A feast of educational resources for educators and learners is available on the "NASA STEM Engagement" web page. https://www.nasa.gov/stem

Sun / Earth NASA has web pages whose content is dedicated to educating people about our star, the Sun. https://www.nasa.gov/sun

Learn more about our home from a planetary perspective by visiting the "Explore Earth" web page. https://www.nasa.gov/topics/earth/index.html

Sustainability NASA is making its workplaces nationwide more sustainable. Its facilities cover 47 million square feet and include 5,000 buildings. While working to fulfill its mission of exploration and revealing the unknown, NASA is reducing its demand on Earth and lessening its consumption of her finite resources. https://www.nasa.gov/feature/goddard/2021/on-a-changing-planet-nasa-goes-green

The above Sources of Information were updated 6–2021.

National Archives and Records Administration

700 Pennsylvania Avenue NW., Washington, DC, 20408-0001
Phone, 866-272-6272. Internet, http://www.archives.gov

Archivist of the United States https://www.archives.gov/about/archivist/archivist-biography- ferriero.html	DAVID S. FERRIERO
Deputy Archivist of the United States	DEBRA STEIDEL WALL
Chief Innovation Officer	PAMELA S. WRIGHT
Chief of Staff	MARIA CAROSA STANWICH
Directors	
Congressional Affairs	JOHN O. HAMILTON
Equal Employment Opportunity Program	ERICA PEARSON
Executive Director, National Historical Publications and Records Commission	CHRISTOPHER R. ECK
General Counsel	GARY M. STERN
Chief Operating Officer	WILLIAM J. BOSANKO
Director	
Office of the Federal Register	OLIVER A. POTTS
Executives	
Agency Services	JAY A. TRAINER
Legislative Archives, Presidential Libraries, and Museum Services	SUSAN K. DONIUS
Research Services	ANN A. CUMMINGS
Chief of Management and Administration	MICAH M. CHEATHAM
Chief Officers	
Acquisition	LA VERNE FIELDS
Financial	COLLEEN V. MURPHY
Human Capital	VALORIE FINDLATER
Information	SWARNALI HALDAR
Executive for Business Support Services https://www.archives.gov/about/organization/senior-staff	MARK A. SMITH, ACTING
Inspector General https://www.archives.gov/oig/about	BRETT M. BAKER

The above list of key personnel was updated 7–2021.

The National Archives and Records Administration safeguards and preserves the records of the U.S. Government and provides public access to them, ensuring that the American people can discover, learn from, and use their documentary heritage to support democracy.

Establishment and Organization

The National Archives and Records Administration (NARA) is the successor agency to the National Archives Establishment (NAE). The National Archives was officially established in 1934, during a time of expanding Federal reforms, regulations, and work projects. The National Archives also recognizes April 1, 1985, as its "other birthday." On that day, NARA became an independent Federal agency. https://prologue.blogs.archives.gov/2015/04/01/happy-other-birthday-national-archives

On June 19, 1934, President Franklin D. Roosevelt approved Public Law 73–432 "to establish a National Archives of the United

States Government." The statute "created the Office of Archivist of the United States," empowered the President to appoint the Archivist by the advice and with the consent of the Senate, and empowered the Archivist to appoint "all persons to be employed in the National Archives Establishment" (48 Stat. 1122). https://www.loc.gov/law/help/statutes-at-large/73rd-congress/session-2/c73s2ch668.pdf

On June 30, 1949, President Harry S. Truman approved Public Law 81–152, which also is cited as the Federal Property and Administrative Services Act of 1949. Section 104 of Title I of that statute deals with records management. The statute transferred "the National Archives Establishment and its functions, records, property, personnel, obligations, and commitments" to the newly created General Services Administration. It also empowered the Administrator of the new agency to appoint the Archivist of the United States (63 Stat. 381). The new arrangement transformed the NAE into the National Archives and Records Service. More than three decades passed before the National Archives reemerged as an independent agency within the Federal Government's executive branch. https://www.loc.gov/law/help/statutes-at-large/81st-congress/session-1/c81s1ch288.pdf

On October 19, 1984, President Ronald W. Reagan approved Public Law 98–497 "to establish the National Archives and Records Administration" as "an independent establishment in the executive branch of the Government" (98 Stat. 2280). President Reagan issued a statement on signing the Senate bill into law. The new statute's provisions became effective on April 1, 1985, a day that is like a second birthday for the agency (98 Stat. 2295). https://www.govinfo.gov/content/pkg/STATUTE-98/pdf/STATUTE-98-Pg2280.pdf

On June 25, 1985, NARA published a notice in the Federal Register (50 FR 26278). It promulgated the agency's statement of organization. Functions that had been assigned to the General Services Administration were being performed now by NARA. https://www.govinfo.gov/content/pkg/FR-1985-06-25/pdf/FR-1985-06-25.pdf

NARA posts an organizational chart on its "NARA Organization" web page. https://www.archives.gov/about/organization

Statutory and Regulatory Authorities

Chapter 21 of 44 U.S.C., which includes sections 2101–2120, contains codified statutory material affecting NARA. https://uscode.house.gov/view.xhtml?path=/prelim@title44/chapter21&edition=prelim

Chapter XII of 36 CFR is dedicated to codified regulatory material associated with NARA. The chapter comprises parts 1200–1299. https://www.ecfr.gov/cgi-bin/text-idx?SID=284fe0a169d8d22863ef40cfec0c2dcc&mc=true&tpl=/ecfrbrowse/Title36/36chapterXII.tpl

Activities
Classified and Controlled Information Management   The Information Security Oversight Office (ISOO) oversees programs for classified national security information and controlled unclassified information in both Government and industry and reports on their status annually to the President. It receives policy and program guidance from the National Security Council and operates under the authority of Executive Orders 12829, 13549, 13587, 13526, and 13556. As a NARA component, ISOO's goals are fourfold: holding classification activities to the minimum necessary standard for protecting national security; promoting consistency and transparency in how controlled unclassified information is handled; efficiently and cost-effectively safeguarding classified national security information; and encouraging declassification of and public access to information as soon as security considerations permit. https://www.archives.gov/isoo/about

In 2010, ISOO was named the Executive agent for administering Executive Order 13556, "Controlled Unclassified Information." The order establishes consistent information sharing and protection practices by replacing the ad hoc, agency-specific policies and procedures with an Executive branchwide program to manage unclassified information that requires safeguarding or dissemination controls pursuant to and consistent with applicable law, regulations, and Governmentwide policies. https://www.govinfo.gov/content/pkg/DCPD-201000942/

pdf/DCPD-201000942.pdfhttp://www.
archives.gov/isoo | Email: isoo@nara.gov

For further information, contact the Information Security Oversight Office. Phone, 202-357-5250.

Declassification of Records   The National Declassification Center (NDC) was established by Executive Order 13526 and began operations in January of 2010. The Center is responsible for the timely and appropriate processing of referrals between agencies for accessioned Federal records and transferred Presidential records; general interagency declassification activities necessary to fulfill the requirements of sections 3.3 and 3.4 of the Order; the exchange among agencies of detailed declassification guidance to support equity recognition; the development of effective, transparent, and standard declassification work processes, training, and quality assurance measures; the development of solutions to declassification challenges posed by electronic records, special media, and emerging technologies; and the linkage and effective utilization of existing agency databases and the use of new technologies to support declassification activities under the purview of the Center. http://www.archives.gov/declassification | Email: ndc@nara.gov

For further information, contact the National Declassification Center. Phone, 301-837-0405.

Federal Records Storage and Retrieval   NARA's Federal Records Centers Program (FRCP) stores and services active and inactive records for Federal agencies. A national network of 18 facilities, the FRCP system currently stores more than 30 million cubic feet of records. Since 1999, the FRCP system has operated as a reimbursable program that provides the Federal community with services on a fee-for-service basis. These services include storage of textual and special media records; management of classified and nonclassified records; retrieval of records needed by customers to conduct daily business or fulfill statutory requirements; expedited responses to congressional inquiries, litigation, and urgent business needs; disposition services, including the disposal of temporary records that have reached the end of their required retention period and the transfer of permanent records to the legal custody of the National Archives; and a variety of special projects based on customer needs. https://www.archives.gov/frc

The National Personnel Records Center (NPRC) in St. Louis, MO, is the largest facility in the FRCP system. This facility stores and services the civilian personnel, medical, and pay records of former U.S. Civil Service employees and the personnel, medical, and related records of discharged military personnel. The NPRC maintains research rooms where Federal employees and the general public can review official military and civilian personnel folders and other related records. It also supports Federal agencies by providing them with technical advice on and services relating to records disposition, filing and classification schemes, document conversion, and protection of civilian and military records. https://www.archives.gov/st-louis Email: frc@nara.gov

For further information, contact the Federal Records Centers. Phone 314-801-9300.

Federal Register Publications and Services   The Federal Register system is an official legal information service of the U.S. Government. The Federal Register system operates under the general authority of the Administrative Committee of the Federal Register (ACFR), as well as under statutory and regulatory authority that is specific to the Office of the Federal Register (OFR). The OFR is a component of NARA, which is obliged by statute to partner with the Government Publishing Office (GPO) to provide Federal Register publications and services to the public. The OFR's mission centers on informing citizens of their rights and obligations, documenting the actions of Federal agencies, and providing a public forum for participation in the democratic process. https://www.archives.gov/federal-register/about

The OFR makes the official text of several document types publicly accessible: administrative regulations and notices, Presidential documents, and Federal laws. In partnership with the GPO, its editors prepare and publish the "Code of Federal Regulations," "Compilation of Presidential Documents," "Federal Register," "Public

Papers of the Presidents," and "United States Statutes at Large," as well as additional publications.

The OFR coordinates the functions of the Electoral College on behalf of the American people, the Archivist of the United States, the Congress, and the States. It also administers the constitutional amendment process. https://www.archives.gov/federal-register | Email: fedreg.info@nara.gov

For further information, contact Information Services and Technology, Office of the Federal Register. Phone, 202-741-6000. TTY, 202-741-6086. Fax, 202-741-6012.

Freedom of Information Act (FOIA) Compliance   Established under the OPEN Government Act of 2007 (5 U.S.C. 101), the Office of Government Information Services (OGIS) works with agencies across the Executive branch to improve the Government's ability to respond to FOIA requests. OGIS serves as liaison between individuals making FOIA requests and administrative agencies, providing mediation services to resolve disputes as an alternative to litigation. It reviews policies and procedures of administrative agencies under FOIA. OGIS also reviews agency compliance with FOIA and recommends policy changes to the President and Congress. https://www.archives.gov/ogis | Email: ogis@nara.gov

For further information, contact the Office of Government Information Services. Phone, 202-741-5770.

Grant Making   The National Historical Publications and Records Commission (NHPRC) is NARA's grant-making affiliate. NHPRC supports the preservation and promotes the use of America's documentary heritage that is essential for understanding American culture, democracy, and history. NHPRC grants help State and local archives, universities, historical societies, and other nonprofit organizations preserve and manage electronic records, improve training and techniques, strengthen archival programs, preserve and process records collections, and provide access to them through the publication of finding aids and documentary editions of the papers of the Founding Era and other themes and historical figures in American history.

NHPRC works in partnership with a national network of State historical records advisory boards. It also provides Federal leadership in public policy affecting the preservation of and access to America's documentary heritage. http://www.archives.gov/nhprc | Email: nhprc@archives.gov

For further information, contact the National Historical Publications and Records Commission. Phone, 202-357-5010.

Innovation   The Office of Innovation finds innovative ways to serve its customers and to increase access to and delivery of records through all forms of media. Its mission includes demonstrating leadership in the archival and information access field. The Office coordinates NARA's efforts for Open Government and the National Digital Strategy. It comprises several divisions: digitization; digital engagement, including Internet, social media, and NARA's online catalog; business architecture, standards, and authorities; and the Innovation Hub. http://www.archives.gov/innovation-hub

National Archives Trust Funding   The National Archives Trust Fund Board receives funds from the sale of historic document reproductions and publications based on historic records, as well as from gifts and bequests. The Board invests these funds and uses income to support archival functions such as the preparation of publications that make historic records information more widely available. Members of the Board are the Archivist of the United States, the Secretary of the Treasury, and the Chair of the National Endowment for the Humanities. https://www.archives.gov/files/publications/general-info-leaflets/29-trust-fund.pdf

For further information, contact the Secretary, National Archives Trust Fund Board. Phone, 301-837-3165.

Presidential Records Act Compliance   NARA operates the Libraries of Presidents Herbert Hoover through George W. Bush. While such records were once considered personal papers, all Presidential records created on or after January 20, 1981, are declared by law to be owned and controlled by the United States and are required to be transferred to NARA at the end of an administration, pursuant to the Presidential Records Act of

1978 (44 U.S.C. 2201 et seq.). The Office of Presidential Libraries within the National Archives oversees the archival, museum, and education programs of the 14 Presidential Libraries, including the fully digital Barack Obama Presidential Library. https://www.obamalibrary.gov/about-us

Through the Presidential Libraries, which are located at sites selected by the Presidents and built with private funds, NARA preserves and makes available the records, personal papers, and artifacts of a President's administration. Each Library operates a research room and offers reference services for Presidential papers and other historical materials. The Libraries display artifacts and other holdings in museum exhibits illustrating the life and times of a President. The Presidential Libraries also promote citizen engagement by providing programs for students of all ages. http://www.archives.gov/presidential-libraries

For further information, contact the Office of Presidential Libraries. Phone, 301-837-3250. Fax, 301-837-3199.

Providing Access to Archival
Records   NARA maintains the U.S. Government's most historically valuable records, ranging from the Revolutionary War era to the recent past; arranges and preserves records and prepares finding aids to facilitate their use; makes records publicly accessible online and in its research rooms; answers requests for information contained in its holdings; and provides, for a fee, copies of records. NARA holdings include the records of the U.S. House of Representatives and Senate, which are preserved and administered by the Center for Legislative Archives. Many important records are available in microfilm and accessible online. Archival records are maintained in NARA facilities in the Washington, DC, area. Records of exceptional local or regional interest are maintained in NARA archives located in other parts of the country. There are also nine NARA-affiliated archives facilities that hold NARA-owned records and make them available to the public. https://www.archives.gov/research

Research Services provides world-class services to customers seeking access to NARA's accessioned Federal records.

Records are available for research purposes in reading rooms at the National Archives Building (Archives I) in Washington, DC; the National Archives (Archives II) in College Park, MD; and various regional facilities throughout the Nation. https://www.archives.gov/locations#research-facilities

Records Management   To ensure proper documentation of the organization, policies, and activities of the Government, NARA develops standards and guidelines for nationwide management and disposition of recorded information. It appraises Federal records and approves disposition schedules. NARA also inspects agency records and management practices, develops records management training programs, provides guidance and assistance on records management, and stores inactive records.

The Office of the Chief Records Officer assists Government agencies with their records management programs and the lifecycle management of Federal records. The Office formulates recommendations for Governmentwide policies, procedures, regulations, and guidance on the creation, management, and disposition of records in various media. It conducts inspections, evaluations, and surveys of records and records management programs in agencies; reports its findings; and recommends improvements or necessary corrective actions. The Office also provides records management services, including appraisal and scheduling, technical assistance, training, consultation, and analysis regarding policy matters, as well as identifying permanent records eligible for transfer to the National Archives. https://www.archives.gov/records-mgmt | Email: rm.communications@nara.gov

Sources of Information

A–Z Index   NARA's website has an alphabetical subject index to help visitors navigate its content. https://www.archives.gov/global-pages/subject-index.html
Amending the Constitution   NARA's website describes the roles played by the Archivist of the United States and the Office of the Federal Register in the ratification process of a constitutional amendment. https://www.archives.gov/federal-register/constitution

Archived Records   The "Guide to Federal Records in the National Archives of the United States" indicates that NARA records have been assigned to record group 064. https://www.archives.gov/research/guide-fed-records/groups/064.html

Blogs   NARA maintains multiple blogs. https://www.archives.gov/social-media/blogs

Business Opportunities   Resources for doing business with NARA, as well as an inventory of service contracts awarded by the agency, are available online. http://www.archives.gov/contracts

Calendar   NARA maintains a calendar of public events on its website. A recorded announcement of events in Washington, DC, and College Park, MD, also is available. Phone, 202-357-5000. TDD, 301-837-0482. http://www.archives.gov/calendar

Career Opportunities   NARA has a nationwide network of facilities. The agency relies on professionals with administrative, archival, editorial, technical, and other skills to carry out its mission. For more information, visit the "Careers at NARA" web page or contact the Office of Human Capital in St. Louis, MO. Phone, 800-827-0885. https://www.archives.gov/careers

In 2020, NARA ranked 17th among 25 midsize Government agencies in the Partnership for Public Service's Best Places To Work Agency Rankings. https://bestplacestowork.org/rankings/detail/?c=NQ00

Catalog   The National Archives catalog is accessible online. https://catalog.archives.gov

Charters of Freedom   The Declaration of Independence, Constitution, and Bill of Rights have secured the rights of Americans for over two centuries. High resolution images of these three documents, transcriptions of their texts, and articles written on them are available online. https://www.archives.gov/founding-docs

Climate Change   As part of NARA's policy statement for its "Climate Action Plan—September 2021," Archivist of the United States David S. Ferriero wrote that NARA is "committed to integrating climate information that reflects an understanding of global climate change (based on best available science) into its mission and programs via employee training and management functions." https://www.archives.gov/files/about/plans-reports/sustainability/climate-action-plan.pdf

Congressional Affairs   The Congressional Affairs Office maintains liaison with congressional staffs and responds to their inquiries. Phone, 202-357-5100. Fax, 202-357-5959. https://www.archives.gov/congress | Email: congress.affairs@nara.gov

Congressional Records   The Center for Legislative Archives houses the official records of the U.S. Congress from 1789 to the present. These records are in the permanent legal custody of the Senate and House of Representatives, and their rules govern them. The Center responds to congressional committee requests for records to support congressional business needs. It is a full-service archive that assists the Senate and House archivists with managing records, that processes congressional and legislative branch records and provides public access to them, and that creates exhibits, public programs, and educational materials and workshops on the history of the Congress and representative government. Phone, 202-357-5350. Fax, 202-357-5911. http://www.archives.gov/legislative | Email: legislative.archives@nara.gov

Contact Information   Send postal correspondence to the National Archives and Records Administration, 8601 Adelphi Road, College Park, MD 20740-6001. Phone, 866-272-6272. https://www.archives.gov/contact | Email: inquire@nara.gov

Democracy Starts Here   The National Archives contains over 9 billion records—some frivolous, some funny, but others serious, even repellent. More than a national scrapbook, this repository of records gives Americans the opportunity to gain unfiltered, unmediated glimpses of their shared national history, to consider their Government's achievements and shortcomings, to reflect on the praiseworthy and shameful, and to engage in the civic responsibilities of renewing their Nation and fortifying and expanding its democratic institutions. In an 11-minute video, Discovery Channel captures this fundamental concept that sustains NARA's mission. https://www.youtube.com/watch?v=7n3ZZ-UpiR4

The National Historical Publications and Records Commission (NHPRC)

awards grants for projects that publish the American story. The Commission also funds projects that preserve and make accessible the records of all types that are housed in historical repositories across the Nation. The American story is more diverse and unexpected than the Nation's Founding Fathers and 45 Presidents. It includes abolitionists, civil rights leaders, progressives, radicals, and reformers like Chief of the Cherokee Nation John Ross, Presidential candidate Eugene V. Debs of the Socialist Party of America, escaped slave and orator Frederick Douglass, freedom of speech champion and anarchist Emma Goldman, labor organizer Mary Harris "Mother" Jones, Vice President Henry A. Wallace, and Baptist minister Martin Luther King, Jr., whose collections and papers the NHPRC has made more accessible. https://www.archives.gov/publications/prologue/2004/fall/nhprc-sidebar.html

Electoral College The "U.S. Electoral College" web page offers a trove of information on the Electoral College, as well as external resources for learning about elections and voting in the United States. Phone, 202-741-6030. https://www.archives.gov/electoral-college | Email: electoral.college@nara.gov

Exhibits The National Archives in Washington, DC, and the Presidential Libraries and several regional facilities regularly host onsite exhibits. NARA also has national traveling exhibits that bring documents and records of the National Archives to communities nationwide. NARA's website features dozens of online exhibits on a range of topics: gifts that Presidents received, Government drawings, New Deal-era Federal art projects, work and the workplace in the 19th and 20th centuries, the influenza epidemic of 1918, and more. https://www.archives.gov/exhibits | Email: National_Archives_Exhibits_Staff@nara.gov

Federal Register Significant documents and documents that NARA recently published in the Federal Register are accessible online. https://www.federalregister.gov/agencies/national-archives-and-records-administration

Forms Some of the most commonly used forms for obtaining National Archives historical records—Eastern Cherokee applications, Federal census records, Federal land entry files, military pension / bounty land warrant applications, passenger arrival records, post-World War I military records, and pre-World War I military service records—are available online. https://www.archives.gov/forms

Founders Online The National Historical Publications and Records Commission and The University of Virginia Press have collaborated to create the "Founders Online" website, which gives the public free electronic access to the historical documents of the Founders of the United States. The site contains over 176,000 searchable and fully annotated documents from the Founding Fathers Papers projects. These documents include the correspondence and other writings of Benjamin Franklin, Alexander Hamilton, President John Adams and his family, and Presidents George Washington, Thomas Jefferson, and James Madison. https://founders.archives.gov/ | Email: foundersonline@nara.gov

Freedom of Information Act (FOIA) To any person, the FOIA gives a statutory right for obtaining access to Government information in the records of executive branch agencies. This right to access is limited, however, when the requested information is shielded from disclosure by any of nine exemptions contained within the statute. https://www.archives.gov/foia

Frequently Asked Questions (FAQs) NARA posts answers to FAQs on its website. https://www.archives.gov/faqs

History In the early 1930s, the Nation had a records management problem: Federal records were being housed in abandoned buildings, attics, and basements, where security and storage conditions were inadequate. In 1934, the U.S. Congress acted. To learn what it did to solve the problem, visit the "National Archives History" web page. https://www.archives.gov/about/history | Email: archives.historian@nara.gov

History Hub This crowdsourcing platform is a place for asking questions, finding people of particular experiences and interests, sharing information, and working together. The hub allows citizen archivists, American history enthusiasts, and experts from NARA and other organizations to pool their knowledge in support of historical research. https://historyhub.history.gov/docs/DOC-1012 | Email: historyhub@nara.gov

Know Your Records   To assist genealogical and historical researchers with using Federal Government records held at the National Archives, NARA hosts Know Your Records events. Phone, 202-357-5260. http://www.archives.gov/calendar/know-your-records/index.html | Email: kyr@nara.gov

Museum Shops   The National Archives Store sells merchandise highlighting the holdings of the National Archives. Document facsimiles, publications, and souvenirs and gifts are available for sale at each Presidential Library and at the National Archives in Washington, DC. Phone, 202-357-5271. https://www.nationalarchivesstore.org/

News   NARA posts press releases on its website. https://www.archives.gov/press

Open Government   NARA supports the Open Government initiative by promoting the principles of collaboration, participation, and transparency. https://www.archives.gov/open

Páginas en Español   The NARA website features a collection of pages whose content is in Spanish. https://www.archives.gov/espanol

Plain Language   NARA supports the Plain Writing Act of 2010 by "promoting clear Government communication that the public can understand and use." If a document or web page contains content that is unclear, please contact NARA via email and suggest a way to enhance clarity. https://www.archives.gov/open/plain-writing | Email: plainwriting@nara.gov

Publications   The "Publications" web page contains a hyperlinked list of NARA's most requested publications: "Code of Federal Regulations," "Federal Register," "Guide to Federal Records in the National Archives of the United States," "Military Service Records at the National Archives," "Prologue" magazine, and eBooks and more. https://www.archives.gov/publications

The Office of Records Services in Washington, DC, and the Office of Regional Records Services produce most of the publications on the "Publications" web page; however, other NARA offices also publish materials and a few of them do so

extensively. These other offices include the Information Security Oversight Office, Office of the Federal Register, Office of Presidential Libraries, and public affairs staff. https://www.archives.gov/publications/organization.html

NARA units enter into cooperative arrangements with other organizations to produce and sell publications. To become acquainted with these partnership publications, visit the "NARA Publications" web page. https://www.archives.gov/publications/partnerships.html

"Presidential Perspectives from the National Archives" highlights modern American Presidents and the National Archives Presidential Libraries System. https://www.archives.gov/publications/presidential-materials.html

Some print versions of NARA publications are no longer in stock. To inquire about a publication, contact the National Archives Foundation. Phone, 202-357-5271. https://www.archivesfoundation.org/contact-us

Recorded Utterances of Presidents   The Franklin D. Roosevelt Presidential Library and Museum maintains a collection of digitized recordings of the former President's speeches and recordings from 1920 to 1945. Each audio file may be streamed or downloaded directly from the "Utterances" web page. The collection contains the State of the Union address that the President delivered before the U.S. Congress on January 6, 1941. In the speech, he famously enumerated the four freedoms—of speech and expression, to worship God, from want, and from fear (32:45)—and defined freedom generally as "the supremacy of human rights everywhere" (36:17). http://www.fdrlibrary.marist.edu/archives/collections/utterancesfdr.html

The Dwight D. Eisenhower Presidential Library, Museum, and Boyhood Home maintains an audio collection (1943–1961) of the 34th President's speeches that reflect his accomplishments and values. His "Chance for Peace" speech, which is also known as the "Cross of Iron" speech, was given a few weeks after the death of Russian Premier Joseph Stalin on April 16, 1953. In that speech, he said: "Every gun that is made, every warship launched, every rocket fired, signifies, in the final sense, a theft from those who hunger and are not fed, those who are cold and are not clothed" (11:15). The collection also contains his "Farewell Address to the American People," which he addressed to the Nation on January 17, 1961. In that oft quoted address, he spoke of the implications of a growing arms industry and defense establishment. https://www. eisenhowerlibrary.gov/eisenhowers/speeches

Records Management   Records management brochures and pamphlets, posters, and publications are available online. https://www.archives.gov/publications/records-mgmt.html

The national records management training program provides records management instruction to Federal employees and contractors. http://www.archives.gov/records-mgmt/training/index.html | Email: NARA.RecordsMgtTraining@nara.gov

Researcher Newsletter   "Researcher News" covers relevant and the most up-to-date information for conducting research at the National Archives. The newsletter is available online in Portable Document Format (PDF) and also disseminated via email subscription. http://www.archives.gov/research/newsletter | Email: kyr@nara.gov

Resources for Educators   NARA's website has a trove of information and resources to assist teachers. https://www.archives.gov/education

DocsTeach is an online tool that helps educators use National Archives documents for teaching their students. https://www.docsteach.org | Email: docsteach@nara.gov

Resources for Genealogists   NARA's website has a trove of information and resources to assist genealogy researchers. https://www.archives.gov/research/genealogy

Service Records   The "Veterans' Service Records" web page explains how to request service records online, to conduct research using military records, to replace lost medal and awards, and to browse World War II photographs. https://www.archives.gov/veterans

Social Media   NARA has pages on Facebook. https://www.archives.gov/social-media/facebook

NARA and its component organizations tweet announcements and other newsworthy items, using their Twitter accounts. https://www.archives.gov/social-media/twitter

Organizations within NARA post videos on YouTube channels. https://www.archives.gov/social-media/youtube

Today's Document   Each day a different American historical document is featured on NARA's website. https://www.archives.gov/historical-docs/todays-doc

Visitors' Information   The "Visit Us" web page has a nationwide list of NARA facilities—Federal records centers, Presidential Libraries, and research facilities. The list includes directions to, hours for, and details on each facility. https://www.archives.gov/locations

The Sources of Information were updated 6–2021.

National Capital Planning Commission

401 Ninth Street NW., Suite 500, Washington, DC 20004
Phone, 202-482-7200. Internet, http://www.ncpc.gov

Chair	L. Preston Bryant, Jr.
Member	Arrington Dixon
Member	Thomas Gallas
Member	Geoffery Griffis
Member	Elizabeth White
Administrator of General Services (ex officio)	Emily W. Murphy
Chair, Council of the District of Columbia (ex officio)	Philip Mendelson
Chair, House Committee on Oversight and Government Reform (ex officio)	Trey Gowdy
Chair, Senate Committee on Homeland Security and Governmental Affairs (ex officio)	Ron Johnson

NATIONAL CAPITAL PLANNING COMMISSION

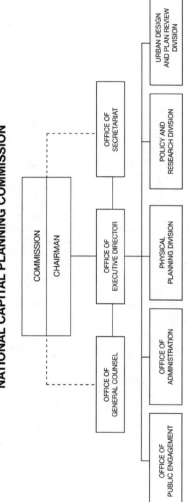

COMMISSION

CHAIRMAN

OFFICE OF GENERAL COUNSEL

OFFICE OF EXECUTIVE DIRECTOR

OFFICE OF SECRETARIAT

OFFICE OF PUBLIC ENGAGEMENT

OFFICE OF ADMINISTRATION

PHYSICAL PLANNING DIVISION

POLICY AND RESEARCH DIVISION

URBAN DESIGN AND PLAN REVIEW DIVISION

Mayor of the District of Columbia (ex officio)	MURIEL BOWSER
Secretary of Defense (ex officio)	JIM MATTIS
Secretary of the Interior (ex officio)	RYAN ZINKE STAFF
EXECUTIVE DIRECTOR	MARCEL C. ACOSTA
Chief Operating Officer	BARRY S. SOCKS
Director, Office of Public Engagement / Secretary to the Commission	JULIA A. KOSTER
Director, Physical Planning	ELIZABETH MILLER
Director, Policy and Research	MICHAEL A. SHERMAN
Director, Urban Design and Plan Review	DIANE SULLIVAN
Director, Office of Administration	DEBRA. DICKSON
General Counsel	ANNE R. SCHUYLER

[For the National Capital Planning Commission statement of organization, see the Code of Federal Regulations, Title 1, Part 456.2]

The National Capital Planning Commission conducts planning and development activities for Federal lands and facilities in the National Capital Region—the District of Columbia, the City of Alexandria, and all land areas within the boundaries of Montgomery, Prince George's, Fairfax, Loudoun, Prince William, and Arlington Counties.

The National Capital Planning Commission was established as a park planning agency by act of June 6, 1924, as amended (40 U.S.C. 8701 et seq.). Two years later, its role was expanded to include comprehensive planning. In 1952, the National Capital Planning Act designated the Commission as the central planning agency for the Federal and District of Columbia governments. https://www.ncpc.gov/ncpc/Main(T2)/About_Us(tr2)/About_Us(tr3)/History.html

In 1973, the National Capital Planning Act was amended by the District of Columbia Home Rule Act, which made the mayor of the District of Columbia the chief planner for the District and gave the Commission specific authority for reviewing certain District decisions. The Commission continues to serve, however, as the central planning agency for the Federal Government in the National Capital Region.

The Commission comprises five appointed and seven ex officio members. Three citizen members, including the Chair, are appointed by the President. The mayor of the District of Columbia appoints the other two members. The Presidential appointees include one resident from Maryland, one resident from Virginia, and one from anywhere else in the United States. The two mayoral appointees must be District of Columbia residents. https://www.ncpc.gov/ncpc/Main(T2)/About_Us(tr2)/AboutUs.html

Sources of Information

Business Opportunities   The Commission posts contracting opportunities on its Web site. http://www.ncpc.gov/ncpc/Main(T2)/About_Us(tr2)/About_Us(tr3)/Opportunities.html

Career Opportunities   The Commission posts employment opportunities on its Web site. http://www.ncpc.gov/ncpc/Main(T2)/About_Us(tr2)/About_Us(tr3)/Opportunities.html

Events   The Commission posts upcoming events that are open to the public online. https://www.ncpc.gov/ncpc/Main(T2)/PublicParticipation(Tr2)/Public%20Participation(Tr3)/UpcomingEvents.html

Freedom of Information Act (FOIA)   FOIA requests should be addressed to the Chief FOIA Officer, National Capital Planning Commission, 401 9th Street NW., Suite 500, Washington, DC 20004. Requests also may be submitted by fax or email. Fax, 202-482-7272 https://www.ncpc.gov/open/home.html

Internships   The Commission offers internships for students at accredited colleges and universities. Students with various educational backgrounds—architecture, communications, community planning, computer aided design, geography and geographic information systems, historic preservation, landscape architecture, law, urban design—are encouraged to apply. http://www.ncpc.gov/ncpc/Main(T2)/About_Us(tr2)/About_Us(tr3)/Opportunities.html

Memorial Map   The Commission, in conjunction with the National Park Service, offers Internet users an interactive map of commemorative works in the Nation's capital. https://www.ncpc.gov/memorials

Newsletters   Monthly newsletters are available online. https://www.ncpc.gov/ncpc/Main(T2)/Publications(Tr2)/Publications(Tr3)/CompleteCatalogue.html?ccpage=1

An archive of quarterly newsletters running from 1998 to 2009 is available online. https://www.ncpc.gov/ncpc/Main(T2)/Publications(Tr2)/Publications(Tr3)/CompleteCatalogue.html?ccpage=3

News   The Commission posts recent news releases on its Web site. Starting with the year 2001, an online archive contains releases from previous years. https://www.ncpc.gov/ncpc/Main(T2)/Media(Tr2)/Media(Tr3)/NewsReleaseArchive.html

Open Government   The Commission supports the Open Government initiative by promoting the principles of collaboration, participation, and transparency. https://www.ncpc.gov/open/home.html

Plain Language   The Commission's writers and editors are committed to using plain language in new communications and revising confusing or unclear language in existing material. If a sentence or paragraph's clarity needs improvement, send them a note using the online form. https://www.ncpc.gov/open/home.html

Publications   Recently released and frequently requested publications are accessible online. https://www.ncpc.gov/ncpc/Main(T2)/Publications(Tr2)/Publications.html

Reports   Starting with the year 2004, the Commission's annual reports are accessible online. https://www.ncpc.gov/ncpc/Main(T2)/Publications(Tr2)/Publications(Tr3)/CompleteCatalogue.html?ccpage=4

Site Map   Web site visitors may use the site map to look for specific topics or to browse for content that aligns with their interests. https://www.ncpc.gov/ncpc/Main(T2)/siteMap.html https://www.ncpc.gov/ncpc/Main(T2)/About_Us(tr2)/About_Us(tr3)/Contactus.html | Email: info@ncpc.gov

For further information, contact the National Capital Planning Commission, 401 Ninth Street NW., Suite 500, Washington, DC 20004. Phone, 202-482-7200. Fax, 202-482-7272.

National Credit Union Administration

1775 Duke Street, Alexandria, VA 22314
Phone, 703-518-6300. Internet, http://www.ncua.gov

Board of Directors

Chair	J. Mark McWatters
Member	Richard T. Metsger
Member	(vacancy)

Headquarters–Washington, DC

Chair	J. Mark McWatters
Member of the Board	Richard T. Metsger
Chief of Staff	Sarah D. Vega
Office Heads	
Chief Economist	Ralph Monaco
Chief Financial Officer	Rendell L. Jones
Chief Information Officer	Edward Dorris

Director, Consumer Protection	GAIL LASTER
Director, Continuity and Security Management	JOY MILLER
Director, Examination and Insurance	LARRY FAZIO
Director, Human Resources	CHERYL EYRE
Director, Minority and Women Inclusion	MONICA DAVY
Director, National Examinations and Supervision	SCOTT HUNT
Director, Public and Congressional Affairs	ALFRED V. GARESCHÉ, ACTING
Director, Small Credit Union Initiatives	MARTHA NINICHUK
Executive Director	MARK A. TREICHEL
General Counsel	MICHAEL MCKENNA
Inspector General	JAMES W. HAGEN

https://www.ncua.gov/about/leadership/Pages/default.aspx

[For the National Credit Union Administration statement of organization, see the Code of Federal Regulations, Title 12, Part 720]

The above list of key personnel was updated 09–2017.

The National Credit Union Administration provides a trustworthy credit union system that builds confidence in the Nation's system of cooperative credit.

The National Credit Union Administration (NCUA) was established by act of March 10, 1970 (12 U.S.C. 1752), and reorganized by act of November 10, 1978 (12 U.S.C. 226), as an independent agency in the executive branch of the Federal Government. It regulates and insures all Federal credit unions and insures State-chartered credit unions that apply and qualify for share insurance.

The Administration's Board comprises three members whom the President appoints and the Senate must confirm. Members serve staggered terms of 6 years, and no more than two of them can belong to the same political party. https://www.ncua.gov/about/leadership/Pages/default.aspx

Activities

Chartering The NCUA grants Federal credit union charters to groups sharing a common bond of occupation or association or to groups within a well-defined neighborhood, community, or rural district. Before granting a Federal charter, the NCUA conducts a preliminary investigation to determine if certain standards are met. https://www.ncua.gov/services/Pages/field-of-membership-chartering.aspx

Examinations The NCUA regularly examines Federal credit unions to assess their solvency, to ensure their compliance with laws and regulations, and to assist credit union management and improve operations.

For further information, contact the Director, Office of Examination and Insurance. Phone, 703-518-6360.

Share Insurance The act of October 19, 1970 (12 U.S.C. 1781 et seq.), provides for a program of share insurance, in which participation is mandatory for Federal credit unions. In some States, State-chartered credit unions must participate in the share insurance program. In other States, State-chartered credit unions may opt to participate in the insurance program. The National Credit Union Share Insurance Fund requires each participating credit union to place and maintain a 1-percent deposit of its insured savings with the Fund. Credit union members' accounts are insured up to $250,000. http://www.mycreditunion.gov/protect/Pages/SI.aspx

Supervision Supervisory activities are carried out through regular examiner contacts and by periodic policy and regulatory releases from the Administration. The NCUA also identifies emerging problems and monitors operations between examinations.

NCUA central offices include examination and supervision programs. Five regional offices manage the oversight of credit unions. http://www.ncua.gov/about/pages/Contact.aspx

Sources of Information

A–Z Index   The NCUA Web site has an A–Z index to help visitors navigate its content. https://www.ncua.gov/Pages/SiteIndex.aspx

Business Opportunities   The NCUA selects vendors who offer the best value to help the agency meet its mission. The Division of Procurement and Facilities Management is responsible for procuring goods and services. Phone, 703-518-6410. Fax, 703-518-6662. https://www.ncua.gov/About/Pages/business-opportunities.aspx | Email: ocfoprocurement@ncua.gov

Career Opportunities   Career information is available from the Office of Human Resources. Phone, 703-518-6510. Fax, 703-518-6539. http://www.ncua.gov/about/Leadership/Pages/page_hr.aspx | Email: ohrmail@ncua.gov

The NCUA relies heavily on credit union examiners to carry out its mission. Watch the video "A Day in the Life of a Credit Union Examiner" to learn about the training required and the role a fully trained examiner plays in safeguarding the stability of the Nation's credit union system. https://www.youtube.com/watch?v=iP-dgprNGnw&feature=youtu.be

The NCUA ranks among the top midsize Government agencies in the Best Places To Work Agency Rankings. http://bestplacestowork.org/BPTW/rankings/overall/mid

Closed Credit Unions   The Asset Management and Assistance Center conducts credit union liquidations and performs asset management and recovery. It also participates in the operational phases of a failed credit union's conservatorship and assists with record reconstruction. The Center posts up-to-date information on closed, conserved, liquidated, and merged credit unions on the NCUA Web site. https://www.ncua.gov/services/Pages/closed-credit-unions.aspx | Email: amacmail@ncua.gov

Consumer Assistance   For answers to questions on credit union insurance and other consumer matters or to submit a complaint, contact the NCUA Consumer Assistance Center on weekdays, 8 a.m.–5 p.m., eastern standard time. After regular business hours, callers may leave a recorded message. Phone, 800-755-1030. http://www. mycreditunion.gov/consumer-assistance-center/Pages/default.aspx

Español   Read Spanish better than English? Visit the Spanish version of the NCUA Web site. https://espanol.ncua.gov/newsroom/Pages/newsroom.aspx

Federally Insured Credit Unions   A directory of federally insured credit unions that includes addresses, asset levels, and membership numbers is available online and for review at central and regional offices. Copies of the directory are available for a nominal fee: Write NCUA, Publications, 1775 Duke Street, Alexandria, VA 22314-3428. Phone, 703-518-6340. http://www.ncua.gov/Legal/GuidesEtc/Pages/CUDirectory.aspx

Financial Literacy   The NCUA offers financial literacy and educational resources to help consumers increase their savings and achieve their financial goals. https://www.ncua.gov/consumers/Pages/financial-literacy-resources.aspx

Fraud Hotline   The NCUA operates a hotline for reporting illegal or suspicious activity associated with credit union employees, members, or officials in federally insured credit unions. Phone, 800-827-9650 or 703-518-6550 (Washington, DC, area). https://www.ncua.gov/services/Pages/fraud-hotline.aspx

Freedom of Information Act (FOIA)   The act allows any person to obtain records of a Federal agency. A record may be withheld only if it carries an exemption under the FOIA. The NCUA operates a FOIA requester service center to answer questions related to the FOIA process, to provide information on the status of a request, and to answer questions about documents that a requester has received from the NCUA. Phone, 703-518-6540. Fax, 703-518-6569. https://www.ncua.gov/services/Pages/freedom-of-information-act.aspx | Email: FOIA@ncua.gov

Games / Activities   Games for testing and activities for exercising financial knowledge are available on the Web site MyCreditUnion.gov. https://www.mycreditunion.gov/tools-resources/Pages/Games-and-Activities.aspx

Glossaries   The NCUA maintains a glossary of the common terms associated with the corporate system resolution costs. https://

www.ncua.gov/regulation-supervision/Pages/corporate-system-resolution/glossary.aspx

The Web site MyCreditUnion.gov has a glossary of common terms associated with the share insurance coverage. http://www.mycreditunion.gov/estimator/Pages/glossary_calculator.aspx

History Court reporter Alphonse Desjardins knew loan sharks were charging outrageous rates of interest in Quebec. He did not like their predatory lending and responded by organizing La Caisse Populaire de Levis, the first credit union in North America, to provide affordable credit to working class families. Nearly a decade later, on April 6, 1909, with the assistance of Desjardins, the St. Mary's Cooperative Credit Association, the first credit union in the United States, opened its doors in Manchester, New Hampshire. Yet the moniker "Father of U.S. Credit Unions" would be earned by another. To learn who this person was and what he did for credit unions, visit the NCUA "History" Web page. https://www.ncua.gov/About/Pages/history.aspx

Learning NCUA webinars and Learning Management Service provide free educational materials. Webinars help credit union professionals stay current on important topics affecting the credit union community. Generally 90 minutes in length, live webinars are scheduled throughout the year. Archived webinars may be viewed on demand approximately three weeks after the live event. The Learning Management Service educates people on building community partnerships, credit union operations, how credit unions are governed, how the credit union system works, and products and services. Phone, 703-518-6610. https://www.ncua.gov/services/Pages/small-credit-union-initiatives/learning.aspx | Email: OSCUImail@ncua.gov

Locate a Credit Union The NCUA Web site features a credit union locator tool, which complements the research a credit union tool. The locator provides a graphical map of credit unions based on an address search. The locator also allows the user to view a credit union's contact information, the services that it offers, and directions to it. http://mapping.ncua.gov

Newsroom The NCUA posts annual reports, events, press releases, speeches, testimonies, and its newsletter "The NCUA Report." https://www.ncua.gov/newsroom/Pages/newsroom.aspx

Open Government NCUA supports the Open Government initiative by promoting the principles of collaboration, participation, and transparency. The NCUA regards openness, in terms of budget, policy, and operations, as essential to fulfilling its statutory mission and maintaining public trust. https://www.ncua.gov/about/Pages/open-government.aspx

Organizational Chart The NCUA posts a Joint Photographic Group (JPG) file of its organizational chart online for viewing and downloading. https://www.ncua.gov/Style%20Library/MainTheme/images/offices/org-chart-download.jpg

Plain Language The Plain Writing Act of 2010 promotes clear Government communication "to improve the effectiveness and accountability of Federal agencies to the public." Members of the public are welcome to comment on the NCUA's compliance with the act and to make suggestions for improving communication. Contact the NCUA via email if content in documents or on web pages is difficult to understand. https://www.ncua.gov/About/Pages/open-government/plain-writing.aspx | Email: PlainWriting@ncua.gov

Proposed Regulations The NCUA encourages the public to submit a comment on its proposed rules. Fax, 703-518-6319. https://www.ncua.gov/regulation-supervision/Pages/rules/proposed.aspx | Email: regcomments@ncua.gov

Publications To order publications, contact the Office of the Chief Financial Officer. Payment by check, credit card, or money order is acceptable and prepayment is required. Phone, 703-518-6340. https://www.ncua.gov/services/Pages/order-publications.aspx

Manuals and guides are available online to facilitate compliance with NCUA rules and regulations and with those from other agencies. The manuals and guides are not definitive and should be used in conjunction with other supervisory guidance and information provided by the NCUA and other Federal financial services regulators. https://www.ncua.gov/regulation-supervision/Pages/manuals-guides.aspx

Research a Credit Union The NCUA Web site features a credit union research tool, which complements the credit union locator. The research tool is text-based, and it can find a credit union and its profile by using a variety of search parameters. http://mapping. ncua.gov/ResearchCreditUnion.aspx

RSS Feeds / Email Subscriptions RSS services provide updates on NCUA Board actions, regulatory alerts, and supervisory guidance. Credit unions, members of the media, and general stakeholders can opt to receive notifications on Board actions, events, and general agency news. https:// www.ncua.gov/Pages/rss.aspx

NCUA Express gives email users another option for receiving electronic NCUA communications. Within hours of a letter, press release, regulatory alert, or other communication being published, a message describing it and a link for downloading it are sent to a subscriber's inbox. https://www. ncua.gov/Pages/ncuaexpress.aspx

Share Insurance Estimator The Web site MyCreditUnion.gov features a share insurance estimator to help consumers, credit unions, and their members know how NCUA share insurance rules apply to member share accounts—what is insured and what portion, if any, exceeds coverage limits. http://www.mycreditunion. gov/estimator/Pages/default.aspx | Email: DCAMail@ncua.gov

Site Map The Web site map allows visitors to look for specific topics or to browse for content that aligns with their interests. https://www.ncua.gov/Pages/ SiteMap.aspx

Social Media The NCUA has a Facebook account. https://www.facebook.com/ NCUAgov

The NCUA tweets announcements and other newsworthy items on Twitter. https:// twitter.com/TheNCUA

The NCUA posts educational videos, quarterly economic updates, and speeches on its YouTube channel. https://www. youtube.com/user/NCUAchannel

Starting a Federal Credit Union Groups interested in forming a Federal credit union may obtain free information from the appropriate regional office. Information is also available on the "How to Start a Credit Union" Web page. https://www.ncua. gov/services/Pages/field-of-membership-chartering/start-a-credit-union.aspx | Email: NewFCU@ncua.gov https://www. ncua.gov/About/Pages/contact.aspx

For further information, contact the Office of Public and Congressional Affairs, National Credit Union Administration, 1775 Duke Street, Alexandria, VA 22314-3428. Phone, 703-518-6330.

NATIONAL FOUNDATION ON THE ARTS AND THE HUMANITIES

National Endowment for the Arts

400 7th Street SW., Washington, DC 20506
Phone, 202-682-5400. TDD, 202-682-5496. Internet, http://www.arts.gov

Chair	R. JANE CHU
Senior Deputy Chairman	MARY ANNE CARTER
Chief Information Officer	VACANT
Chief of Staff	MIKE GRIFFIN
Deputy Chairman, Management and Budget	VACANT
Director, Accessibility	BETH BIENVENU
Director, Administrative Services	KATHY DAUM
Director, Artist Communities and Presenting and Multidisciplinary Works / International Activities Coordinator	MICHAEL ORLOVE
Director, Arts Education	AYANNA N. HUDSON

Director, Budget	JOHN SOTELO
Director, Civil Rights and Equal Employment Opportunity	MIKE GRIFFIN
Director, Dance	JENNIFER KARELIUSSON, ACTING
Director, Design Programs / Visual Arts Division Team Leader	VACANT
Director, Finance	HEIDI REN
Director, Folk and Traditional Arts	CLIFFORD MURPHY
Director, Grants and Contracts	NICKI JACOBS
Director, Guidelines and Panel Operations	JILLIAN L. MILLER
Director, Human Resources	CRAIG M. MCCORD, SR.
Director, Literature	AMY STOLLS
Director, Local Arts Agencies and Challenge America	VACANT
Director, Media Arts	JAX DELUCA
Director, Museums, Visual Arts, and Indemnity	WENDY CLARK
Director, Music and Opera	ANN MEIER BAKER
Director, Public Affairs	JESSAMYN SARMIENTO
Director, Research and Analysis	SUNIL IYENGAR
Director, State and Regional Partnerships	LAURA SCANLAN
Director, Theater and Musical Theater	GREG REINER
Federal Partnerships Coordinator	TONY TIGHE
General Counsel	INDIA PINKNEY
Inspector General	RONALD STITH

The National Endowment for the Arts supports artistic excellence and promotes creativity and innovation to benefit individuals and communities.

Through its grants and programs, the Arts Endowment brings art to all 50 States and six U.S. jurisdictions, including rural areas, inner cities, and military bases. The Arts Endowment awards competitive matching grants to nonprofit organizations, to units of State or local government, and to federally recognized tribal communities or tribes for projects, programs, or activities in the fields of artist communities, arts education, dance, design, folk and traditional arts, literature, local arts agencies, media arts, museums, music, musical theater, opera, presenting, theater, and visual arts. It also awards competitive, nonmatching individual fellowships in literature and honorary fellowships in jazz, folk and traditional arts, and opera. Forty percent of the Arts Endowment's grant funds go to the 56 State and jurisdictional arts agencies and their regional arts organizations in support of arts projects in thousands of communities nationwide.

Sources of Information

Employment Job announcements are posted online. https://www.arts.gov/about/employment-opportunities-nea
Grants Application forms and guidelines and listings of grants recently made to individuals and organizations are accessible online. http://www.arts.gov/grants
Podcasts Podcasts feature actors, authors, composers, musicians, playwrights, poets, and other artists and professionals who support and strengthen the arts. https://www.arts.gov/podcasts
Publications Publications, including annual reports and "NEA Arts" magazine, are available online. http://arts.gov/publications https://www.arts.gov/about/annual-reports https://www.arts.gov/NEARTS https://www.arts.gov/staff

For further information, contact the Public Affairs Office, National Endowment for the Arts, 400 7th Street SW., Washington, DC 20506-0001. Phone, 202-682-5400. TDD, 202-682-5496.

National Endowment for The Humanities

400 7th Street SW., Washington, DC 20506
Phone, 202-606-8400. Fax, 800-634-1121. Internet, http://www.neh.gov | Email: info@neh.gov

Chair	PEGGY PLYMPTON, ACTING
Deputy Chair	VACANT
Assistant Chair, Partnership and Strategic Initiatives	VACANT
Assistant Chair, Planning and Operations	JEFFREY THOMAS
Assistant Chair, Programs	ADAM WOLFSON
Chief Information Officer	BRETT BOBLEY
Chief of Staff	VACANT
General Counsel	MICHAEL MCDONALD
Inspector General	LAURA M.H. DAVIS

The National Endowment for the Humanities supports research, education, preservation, and public programs in the humanities.

According to the agency's authorizing legislation, the term "humanities" includes, but is not limited to, the study of the following: language, both modern and classical; linguistics; literature; history; jurisprudence; philosophy; archeology; comparative religion; ethics; the history, criticism, and theory of the arts; and those aspects of the social sciences that employ historical or philosophical approaches.

To increase understanding and appreciation of the humanities, the Endowment makes grants to individuals, as well as to groups and institutions: colleges, libraries, museums, nonprofit private groups, public television stations and agencies, schools, and universities. http://www.neh.gov/about

Challenge Grants   The Office of Challenge Grants offers matching funds to help nonprofit institutions develop new sources of long-term support for educational, scholarly, preservation, and public programs in the humanities. http://www.neh.gov/divisions/challenge/about

For further information, call 202-606-8309.

Digital Humanities   The Office of Digital Humanities supports projects that use digital technology or study how it affects education, preservation, public programming, and research in the humanities. http://www.neh.gov/divisions/odh/about | Email: odh@neh.gov

For further information, call 202-606-8401.

Education Programs   The Division of Education Programs strengthens sustained, thoughtful study of the humanities at all educational levels. It makes grants to educational institutions and gives fellowships to teachers and scholars. http://www.neh.gov/divisions/education/about

For further information, call 202-606-8500.

Federal/State Partnership   Humanities committees in each of the 50 States, the District of Columbia, Puerto Rico, the Virgin and Northern Mariana Islands, Guam, and American Samoa receive grants from the Endowment. These committees then make grants to humanities programs at the local level. http://www.neh.gov/divisions/fedstate/about

For further information, call 202-606-8254.

Preservation and Access   The Division of Preservation and Access supports creating, preserving, and increasing the availability of resources that are important for research, education, and public programming in the humanities. http://www.neh.gov/divisions/preservation/about

For further information, call 202-606-8570.

Public Programs   The Division of Public Programs supports institutions and organizations that develop and present humanities programming for general

NATIONAL ENDOWMENT FOR THE HUMANITIES

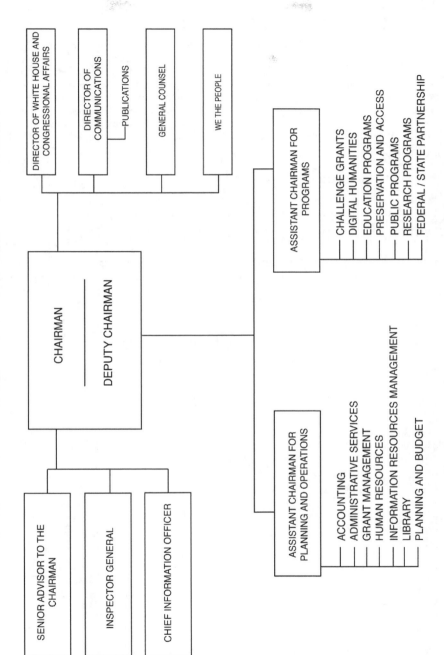

audiences. Its activities center on the Endowment's mandate "to increase public understanding of the humanities." http://www.neh.gov/divisions/public/about

For further information, call 202-606-8268.

Research Programs   The Division of Research Programs promotes original research in the humanities. It provides grants for significant research projects. http://www.neh.gov/divisions/research/about

For further information, call 202-606-8389.

Sources of Information

Employment   The National Endowment for the Humanities posts job opportunities on USAJobs, the Federal Government's official source for Federal job listings and employment opportunity information. https://www.usajobs.gov

Grants   Information on managing a grant, the application review process, and other topics is available on the "NEH Grants" Web page. http://www.neh.gov/grants

Publications   The Endowment's in-house, quarterly magazine "HUMANITIES" is available by subscription from the U.S. Government Publishing Office, P.O. Box 979050, St. Louis, MO 63197–9000. Phone, 202-512-1800. http://www.neh.gov/humanities/staff | Email: publications@neh.gov http://www.neh.gov/about/contact | Email: info@neh.gov

For further information, contact the Office of Communications, National Endowment for the Humanities, 400 7th Street SW., Washington, DC 20506. Phone, 202-606-8400 or 800-634-1121. TDD, 202-606-8282 or 866-372-2930.

The Institute of Museum and Library Services did not meet the publication deadline for submitting updated information of its activities, functions, and sources of information as required by the automatic disclosure provisions of the Freedom of Information Act (5 U.S.C. 552(a)(1)(A)).

Institute of Museum and Library Services

955 L'Enfant Plaza North SW., Suite 4000, Washington, DC 20024-2135
Phone, 202-653-4657. Internet, http://www.imls.gov | Email: imlsinfo@imls.gov

Director	CROSBY KEMPER
Deputy Directors	
Library Services	CYNDEE LANDRUM
Museum Services	PAULA GANGOPADHYAY
https://www.imls.gov/about-us/leadership-staff/crosby-kemper	
Associate Deputy Director for Library Services	ANTHONY SMITH
Chief Administrator for Museum Services	CHRISTOPHER J. REICH
Chief Officers	
Financial	CHRIS CATIGNANI
Information	SCOTT CAREY
Operating	CHRIS CATIGNANI, ACTING
Communications Manager	ELIZABETH HOLTAN
Director of Grants Policy and Management	CONNIE COX BODNER
General Counsel	NANCY E. WEISS
Senior Evaluation Officer for Digital and Information Strategy	MATTHEW BIRNBAUM
https://imls.gov/contact/staff-directory	

The above list of key personnel was updated 10–2020.

The Institute of Museum and Library Services helps libraries and museums enhance cultural and civic engagement, embrace innovation, and further lifelong learning.

The Institute of Museum and Library Services (IMLS) was established within the National Foundation on the Arts and the Humanities by the Museum and Library Services Act of September 30, 1996 (110 Stat. 3009), which amended the Museum Services Act (20 U.S.C. 961 et seq.). The Institute combines the administration of Federal museum programs, which the Institute of Museum Services formerly managed, and Federal library programs, which the Department of Education formerly managed. The Institute's Director, whom the President appoints with the advice and consent of the Senate, is authorized to make grants to museums and libraries. The Director receives policy advice on museum and library programs from the National Museum and Library Services Board. Its 20 voting members are appointed by the President; its three nonvoting members include the Director, Deputy Director for Museum Services, and Deputy Director for Library Services.

The IMLS is the primary source of Federal support for the Nation's 35,000 museums and 123,000 libraries. Its grant making, policy development, and research help museums and libraries offer services that make people and their communities prosper. The IMLS awards grants to art, children's, general, history, natural history, science, and technology museums, as well as to aquariums, arboretums, botanical gardens, nature centers, planetariums, zoos, and historic houses. It also awards grants to academic, public, research, school, and special libraries. IMLS grants improve electronic sharing of information and expand public access to information and services. https://www.imls.gov/about-us

African American History and Culture Museum Grants   The IMLS awards these grants at two funding levels to improve care of collections, develop professional management, and provide internship and fellowship opportunities. https://www.imls. gov/grants/available/museum-grants-african-american-history-and-culture

Laura Bush 21st Century Librarian Program   This program supports recruitment and education of library students, continuing education for those already working in the profession, and new programs and curricula. https://www.imls.gov/grants/available/laura-bush-21st-century-librarian-program

Museum Assessment Program   The IMLS supports the cost of this program through a cooperative agreement with the American Alliance of Museums. The program helps museums strengthen operations, plan for the future, and meet national standards through self-study and a site visit from a peer reviewer. https://www.imls.gov/grants/available/museum-assessment-program-map

Museums for America   The IMLS awards grants at two funding levels to help museums expand their role as lifelong learning resources, increase the vital contributions they make to livable communities, and become better stewards of the Nation's collections. https://www.imls.gov/grants/available/museums-america

National Arts and Humanities Youth Program Awards   This is a project of the President's Committee on the Arts and the Humanities in partnership with the IMLS and the National Endowments for the Arts and for the Humanities. These awards acknowledge museums and libraries for their afterschool and out-of-school arts and humanities programs for young Americans. https://www.imls.gov/grants/available/national-arts-and-humanities-youth-program-awards

National Leadership Grants for Libraries   These grants help library and archive professionals address the challenges and needs of their fields. Projects supported by these grants stimulate research, develop new tools, and produce innovative alliances, models, practices, and services that broadly affect the library and archival fields. https://www.imls.gov/grants/available/national-leadership-grants-libraries

National Leadership Grants for Museums   These grants help museum professionals address the challenges and needs of their field. Projects supported by these grants promote innovation and collaboration and typically produce results that broadly affect the museum field. https://www.imls.gov/grants/available/national-leadership-grants-museums

National Medal for Museum and Library Service   This award acknowledges institutions for providing exceptional and meaningful public service in their communities. https://www.imls.gov/grants/available/national-medal-museum-and-library-service

Native American and Native Hawaiian Museum Services Program These grants to federally recognized tribes and organizations that represent and serve Native Hawaiians help sustain indigenous culture, heritage, and knowledge through improved museum services. https://www.imls.gov/grants/available/native-americannative-hawaiian-museum-services-program

Native American Library Services: Basic Grants and the Education/Assessment Option These noncompetitive grants to federally recognized tribes help them purchase library materials, acquire computers and provide Internet connectivity, and fund salaries. The Education/Assessment option is supplemental to the basic grants and also noncompetitive. It funds library staff participation in continuing education courses, training workshops, and conferences. It also allows libraries to hire a consultant for an onsite professional assessment. https://www.imls.gov/grants/available/native-american-library-services-basic-grants

Native American Library Services: Enhancement Grants These grants to federally recognized tribes expand services for access to information, learning, and partnerships. https://www.imls.gov/grants/available/native-american-library-services-enhancement-grants

Native Hawaiian Library Services This program supports grants that implement new library services or enhance existing ones. https://www.imls.gov/grants/available/native-hawaiian-library-services

Sparks! Ignition Grants for Libraries These grants promote exploration and expansion of the frontiers of archival and library practices and services. https://www.imls.gov/grants/available/sparks-ignition-grants-libraries

Sparks! Ignition Grants for Museums These grants promote exploration and expansion of the frontiers of museum practices and services. https://www.imls.gov/grants/available/sparks-ignition-grants-museums

State Program Grants The Grants to States program is the largest Federal source of funding to support library services in the United States. The IMLS uses a population-based formula to distribute annual grants among the State Library Administrative Agencies—official agencies charged by law with the extension and development of library services. Each year, thousands of Grants to States projects promote the priorities and assist the purposes of the Library Services and Technology Act. https://www.imls.gov/grants/grants-states

Sources of Information

Employment The IMLS offers a unique opportunity to work with the Nation's libraries and museums at the national level and in coordination with State and local organizations. The IMLS posts employment and internship opportunities on its Web site. https://www.imls.gov/about-us/jobs-imls/employment-opportunities https://www.imls.gov/about-us/jobs-imls/internship-opportunities

Freedom of Information Act (FOIA) An online guide answers frequently asked FOIA-related questions. https://www.imls.gov/about-us/agency-reports/freedom-information-act-foia

Grants Search tools are available online to search for available grants and awarded grants. https://www.imls.gov/grants/apply-grant/available-grants https://www.imls.gov/grants/awarded-grants

News The IMLS posts news releases and project profiles online, as well as its "UpNext" blog and "Primary Source" monthly newsletter. https://www.imls.gov/news-events

Open Government The IMLS supports the Governmentwide initiative to promote openness in the work of Federal agencies. It posts datasets on Data.gov and maintains a data catalog that makes IMLS data accessible to developers, researchers, and to the general public. https://www.imls.gov/about-us/open-government

Publications Publications are accessible in Portable Document Format (PDF) on the "Publications List" Web page. https://www.imls.gov/publications

Videos A collection of IMLS videos is available online. https://www.imls.gov/publications/imls-videos http://www.imls.gov | Email: imlsinfo@imls.gov

For further information, contact the Office of Communications and Government Affairs, Institute of Museum and Library Services, 955 L'Enfant Plaza North SW., Suite 4000, Washington, DC 20024. Phone, 202-653-4757.

National Labor Relations Board

1015 Half Street SE., Washington, DC 20570
Phone, 202-273-1000. TDD, 202-273-4300. Internet, http://www.nlrb.gov

Board	
Chair	PHILIP A. MISCIMARRA
Member	MARVIN E. KAPLAN
Member	LAUREN MCFERRAN
Member	MARK G. PEARCE
Member	(VACANCY)
https://www.nlrb.gov/who-we-are/board	
General Counsel	RICHARD F. GRIFFIN, JR.
https://www.nlrb.gov/who-we-are/general-counsel/richard-f-griffin-jr	
Deputy General Counsel	JENNIFER ABRUZZO
Associate General Counsel, Division of Advice	JAYME SOPHIR
Associate General Counsel, Division of Enforcement Litigation	JOHN H. FERGUSON
Associate General Counsel, Division of Legal Counsel	BARBARA O'NEILL
Associate General Counsel, Division of Operations-Management	ANNE G. PURCELL
Chief Financial Officer	MEHUL PAREKH
Chief Information Officer	PREM ABURVASAMY
Chief Judge, Division of Judges	ROBERT A. GIANNASI
Director, Division of Administration	LASHARN HAMILTON
Director, Office of Congressional and Public Affairs	CARMEN SPELL
Director, Office of Equal Employment Opportunity	BRENDA V. HARRIS
Director, Office of Representation Appeals	(VACANCY)
Executive Secretary	GARY W. SHINNERS
Solicitor	(VACANCY)
Inspector General	DAVID P. BERRY
https://www.nlrb.gov/who-we-are/inspector-general	

The National Labor Relations Board remedies unfair labor practices and safeguards employees' rights to organize and to determine whether to have unions as their bargaining representative.

Establishment and Organization

The National Labor Relations Board (NLRB) is an independent agency created by Congress to administer the National Labor Relations Act of 1935 (Wagner Act; 29 U.S.C. 167). The Board is authorized to designate appropriate units for collective bargaining and to conduct secret ballot elections to determine whether employees desire representation by a labor organization. https://www.nlrb.gov/who-we-are/our-history

The NLRB's statement of organization was published on June 14, 1979, in the Federal Register (44 FR 34215). https://www.govinfo.gov/content/pkg/FR-1979-06-14/pdf/FR-1979-06-14.pdf

The NLRB posts its organization chart online. https://www.nlrb.gov/about-nlrb/who-we-are/organization-chart

Statutory and Regulatory Authorities

Statutory material that affects the NLRB has been codified in the United States Code (U.S.C.) and assigned to the subchapter on national labor relations in Chapter 7 of 29 U.S.C. Chapter 7 has the title "Labor-Management Relations" and runs from section 141 to section 197. The subchapter on national labor relations runs from section

151 to section 169. https://uscode.house.gov/view.xhtml?path=/prelim@title29/chapter7/subchapter2&edition=prelim

Rules and regulations that are associated with the NLRB have been codified and assigned to Chapter I, parts 100–199, of 29 CFR. https://www.ecfr.gov/cgi-bin/text-idx?SID=8a8e5d024cddda6d70fbfd8264ee49c0&mc=true&tpl=/ecfrbrowse/Title29/29chapterI.tpl

Activities

In addition to preventing and remedying unfair labor practices, the NLRB conducts secret ballot elections among employees in appropriate collective-bargaining units to determine whether or not they desire to be represented by a labor organization in bargaining with employers over wages, hours, and working conditions. It also conducts secret ballot elections among employees who have been covered by a union-security agreement to determine whether or not they wish to revoke their union's authority to make such agreements. In jurisdictional disputes between two or more unions, the Board determines which competing group of workers is entitled to perform the work involved.

The regional directors and their staffs process representation, unfair labor practice, and jurisdictional dispute cases. They issue complaints in unfair labor practice cases, seek settlement of unfair labor practice charges, obtain compliance with Board orders and court judgments, and petition district courts for injunctions to prevent or remedy unfair labor practices. The regional directors conduct hearings in representation cases, hold elections pursuant to the agreement of the parties or the decisionmaking authority delegated to them by the Board or pursuant to Board directions, and issue certifications of representatives when unions win or certify the results when they lose employee elections. The regional directors process petitions for bargaining unit clarification, for amendment of certification, and for rescission of a labor organization's authority to make a union-shop agreement. They also conduct national emergency employee referendums.

Administrative law judges conduct hearings in unfair labor practice cases, make findings of fact and conclusions of law, and recommend remedies for violations found. Their decisions can be appealed to the Board for a final agency determination. The Board's decisions are subject to review in the U.S. courts of appeals. https://www.nlrb.gov/what-we-do

Sources of Information

Archived Records   The "Guide to Federal Records in the National Archives of the United States" indicates that NLRB records have been assigned to record group 025. https://www.archives.gov/research/guide-fed-records/groups/025.html

Business Opportunities   Businessmen and women who seek to sell products and services to the NLRB can find information on procurement procedures and policies that are generally applicable to NLRB purchasing practices. The NLRB has posted an electronic document that describes the types of items purchased, who procures them, and where they are purchased. The document also includes information that is relevant for small, disadvantaged, service-disabled veteran-owned businesses, and women-owned businesses. https://www.nlrb.gov/about-nlrb/who-we-are/acquisitions

Career Opportunities   The NLRB appoints administrative law judges from a register that the Office of Personnel Management established. The NLRB hires attorneys for all its offices, field examiners for its field offices, and administrative personnel for its Washington and field offices. https://www.nlrb.gov/about-nlrb/who-we-are/careers

In 2020, the NLRB ranked 24th among 25 midsize Government agencies in the Partnership for Public Service's Best Places To Work Agency Rankings. https://bestplacestowork.org/rankings/detail/?c=NL00

Cases / Decisions / Digests   The "Cases and Decisions" web page offers convenient access to cases, decisions, and digests of cases. The NLRB is also developing a list of special cases for organizations that are of interest to the public. Organizations will be added or removed as circumstances warrant. At the moment, the list starts with Bridgewater Associates and ends with Yale University. http://www.nlrb.gov/cases-decisions

The weekly summary of decisions is a digest of decisions that the NLRB issues each week. The summary includes short descriptions of the issues and facts of the cases and links to the decisions. It also has a list of case names and links to decisions by NLRB Administrative Law Judges and to decisions by appellate courts that involve NLRB cases. https://www.nlrb.gov/cases-decisions/decisions/weekly-summaries-decisions

Contact Information   The "Contact Us" web page includes links to the NLRB's headquarters, judges division, and regional office directories and to FOIA, Inspector General, and media sections for inquiries. https://www.nlrb.gov/contact-us | Email: publicinfo@nlrb.gov

Electronic Filing   Parties or other persons may use the e-filing program to file selected documents in unfair labor practice and representation cases with the NLRB's Office of Executive Secretary, the Division of Judges, the General Counsel's Office of Appeals, and regional, subregional, and resident offices. https://apps.nlrb.gov/MyAccount/#/FileCaseDocument/TermsConditions?type=pdfForm%2F

Employees' Rights   The "What's the Law?" web page provides information on rights during union organizing; the right to form a union and the right to refrain; strikes, pickets, and protests; concerted activity; social media; enforcing employees' rights; hiring halls and union dues; and the right to fair representation. https://www.nlrb.gov/about-nlrb/rights-we-protect/whats-law

Español   A Spanish version of the NLRB website is available for Spanish speakers. https://www.nlrb.gov/es

Factsheets   Factsheets on significant cases, on issues pending before the NLRB, and on initiatives undertaken by the General Counsel are posted online. https://www.nlrb.gov/news-publications/publications/fact-sheets

Federal Register   Significant documents and documents that the NLRB recently published in the Federal Register are accessible online. https://www.federalregister.gov/agencies/national-labor-relations-board

Freedom of Information Act (FOIA)   To any person, the FOIA gives a statutory right for obtaining access to Government information in the records of executive branch agencies. This right to access is limited, however, when the requested information is shielded from disclosure by any of nine exemptions contained within the statute. https://www.nlrb.gov/guidance/freedom-of-information-act-foia

The NLRB posts materials that are frequently requested or are of general interest to the public. The FOIA requires agencies to be proactive and make available to the public nonexempt information from certain record categories. These categories include final agency opinions and orders that have been rendered in the adjudication of cases; specific policy statements that are not published in the Federal Register; administrative staff manuals and instructions to staff that affect a member of the public; and frequently requested records or records that are likely to become the subject of subsequent requests. Before submitting a FOIA request, an information seeker should visit the NLRB's FOIA electronic library to ensure that the desired information is not already accessible online and free of charge. https://www.nlrb.gov/guidance/freedom-of-information-act-foia/foia-e-library

Frequently Asked Questions (FAQs)   The NLRB posts answers to FAQs on its website. https://www.nlrb.gov/who-we-are/careers/job-descriptions-and-listings/student-positions-law-non-legal

History   In a time of economic hardship and widespread labor unrest, President Franklin D. Roosevelt created the National Labor Board (NLB). With limited power, the NLB managed to settle over 1,000 strikes and avert nearly 500 additional ones by the time that its authority expired in June of 1934. These events are the background from which the NLRB emerged as part of a new national labor policy trend that began with Senator Robert F. Wagner's National Labor Relations Act of 1935. To learn more about this important chapter of U.S. labor history, visit the NLRB's "Our History" web page. https://www.nlrb.gov/about-nlrb/who-we-are/our-history

News   The NLRB posts announcements and news on its website. https://www.nlrb.gov/news-publications/news

Open Government   The NLRB supports the Open Government initiative by incorporating the principles of collaboration, participation, and transparency in its plans for agency information and systems. https://www.nlrb.gov/open

Publications   NLRB publications are available online. https://www.nlrb.gov/news-publications/publications

Recent Charges / Petitions Filings   The NLRB maintains a database of recent charges and petition filings on its website. https://www.nlrb.gov/reports/graphs-data/recent-filings

Regional Offices   Contact information for NLRB regional, subregional, and resident offices is available on the "Regional Offices" Web pages. https://www.nlrb.gov/about-nlrb/who-we-are/regional-offices

Request a Speaker   A centralized speakers' bureau schedules requests for NLRB representatives to give presentations on agency activities and programs. https://www.nlrb.gov/guidance/fillable-forms/request-speaker

The above Sources of Information were updated 7–2021.

Right To Strike   Sections 7, 8, and 13 of the National Labor Relations Act (NLRA) address issues that protect and limit employees' right to strike. "Employees shall have the right . . . to engage in other concerted activities for the purpose of collective bargaining or other mutual aid or protection"—strikes are included among "concerted activities" that the NLRA protects for employees. More statutory information is available on the "The Right To Strike" web page. https://www.nlrb.gov/strikes

Site Map   Online visitors may use the site map to look for specific topics on the NLRB website or to browse for content that aligns with their interests. https://www.nlrb.gov/sitemap

Social Media   The NLRB has a Facebook page. https://www.facebook.com/NLRBpage/

The NLRB tweets announcements and other newsworthy items on Twitter. https://twitter.com/nlrb

National Mediation Board

1301 K Street NW., Suite 250 East, Washington, DC 20005
Phone, 202-692-5000. Internet, http://www.nmb.gov

Board Members	
Chair	Linda A. Puchala
Member	Harry R. Hoglander
Executive Directors	
Chief of Staff	Daniel Rainey
General Counsel, Office of Legal Affairs	Mary L. Johnson
Assistant Chief of Staff, Administration	Samantha T. Jones
Director, Arbitration Services	Roland Watkins
Deputy Chief of Staff, Mediation	Michael Kelliher

The National Mediation Board facilitates labor-management relations within the railroad and airline industries.

The National Mediation Board (NMB) is an independent agency established by the 1934 amendments to the Railway Labor Act of 1926 (45 U.S.C. 151-158, 160-162, 1181-1188). The Board comprises three members whom the President appoints and the Senate confirms. The Board designates a Chair on a yearly basis.

NMB dispute-resolution processes are designed to resolve disputes over the negotiation of new or revised collective bargaining agreements and the interpretation or application of existing agreements. The Board also effectuates employee rights of self-organization where a representation dispute exists. http://www.nmb.gov/about-nmb/nmb-overview

Activities

Mediation and Alternative Dispute Resolution
Following receipt of an application for mediation, the NMB assigns a mediator to assist the parties in reaching an agreement. The NMB is obligated to use its best efforts to bring about a peaceful resolution to the dispute. If such efforts do not settle the dispute, the NMB advises the parties and offers interest arbitration as an alternative approach to resolve the remaining issues. If either party rejects this offer, the NMB releases the parties from formal mediation. This release triggers a 30-day cooling off period. During this period, the NMB continues to work with the parties to achieve a consensual resolution. If, however, an agreement is not reached by the end of the 30-day period, the parties are free to exercise lawful self-help, such as carrier-imposed working conditions or a strike by the union or organization.

In addition to traditional mediation services, the NMB also provides voluntary Alternative Dispute Resolution (ADR) services. ADR services include facilitation, training, grievance mediation, and an online dispute resolution component, which applies technology to the dispute resolution process. The purpose of the ADR program is to assist the parties in learning and applying more effective, less confrontational methods for resolving their disputes and to help them resolve more of them without outside intervention. http://www.nmb.gov/services/mediation

Presidential Emergency Board
If the NMB determines that a dispute threatens to deprive substantially any section of the country of essential transportation service, it notifies the President. The President, at his discretion, may establish a Presidential Emergency Board (PEB) to investigate and report back within 30 days. After the PEB has been created and for 30 days after it has made its report to the President, neither party to the dispute may exercise self-help.

There are also special emergency procedures for unresolved disputes affecting publicly funded and operated commuter railroads and their employees. If the mediation procedures are exhausted, the parties to the dispute or the Governor of any State where the railroad operates may request that the President establish a PEB. The President is required to establish such a board if requested. If no settlement is reached within 60 days following the creation of the PEB, the NMB is required to conduct a public hearing on the dispute. If there is no settlement within 120 days after the creation of the PEB, either party or the Governor of any affected state may request a second, final-offer PEB. No self-help is permitted pending the exhaustion of these emergency procedures. http://www.nmb.gov/services/pebmenu

Representation
When a labor organization or individual files an application with the NMB to represent employees, the Agency assigns an investigator to conduct a representation investigation. Should the applicant meet the requirements, the NMB continues the investigation, usually with a secret telephone or Internet election. The NMB is responsible for ensuring that the requirements for a fair election process have been maintained. If the employees vote to be represented, the NMB issues a certification that commences the carrier's statutory duty to bargain with the certified representative. http://www.nmb.gov/services/representation

Arbitration
The NMB provides both grievance arbitration and interest arbitration. Grievance arbitration is a process for resolving disputes regarding the interpretation or application of an existing collective bargaining agreement. Grievances must be handled through grievance arbitration if not otherwise resolved, and they cannot be used by the parties to trigger self-help actions. The NMB has significant administrative responsibilities for grievance arbitration in the railroad industry, which includes those before the National Railroad Adjustment Board (NRAB), as well as the two types of arbitration panels established by the labor-management parties at each railroad: public law boards (PLBs) and special boards of adjustment (SBAs). Grievance arbitration in the airline industry is accomplished at the various system boards of adjustment created jointly by labor and management at the parties' expense.

The NMB furnishes panels of prospective arbitrators for the parties' selection in both the airline and railroad industries. The NMB also pays the salary and travel expenses of the arbitrators for railroad arbitration proceedings. Grievance arbitration decisions are final and binding with very limited grounds for judicial review.

Interest arbitration is a process to establish the terms of a new or modified collective bargaining agreement through arbitration rather than through negotiations. Unlike grievance arbitration, its use is not statutorily required. The NMB offers the parties the opportunity to use binding interest arbitration when the agency has determined that further mediation efforts will not be successful. In addition, the parties may directly agree to resolve their collective bargaining dispute or portions of their dispute through interest arbitration. The NMB generally provides the parties with panels of potential arbitrators from which they choose an individual to resolve their dispute. In some instances, however, the parties agree to allow the NMB to appoint an arbitrator directly. Interest arbitration decisions are final and binding with very narrow grounds for judicial appeal. http:// www.nmb.gov/services/arbitration

Sources of Information

Employment   Job openings are posted online. http://www.nmb.gov/about-nmb/jobs
Knowledge Store   The Knowledge Store contains over 100,000 documents— including arbitration awards, representation decisions, annual reports, PEB reports, industry contracts, and union constitutions and bylaws—in an easily searchable format. http://knowledgestore.nmb.gov/ks/build.html
Open Government   The NMB supports the Open Government initiative, which requires Federal executive departments and agencies to implement principles of collaboration, participation, and transparency. http://www. nmb.gov/resources/open
Publications   The annual reports of the National Mediation Board are available on its "NMB Documents On-Line" Web page and in the Knowledge Store. http://www. nmb.gov/resources/docs
Virtual Reading Room   Copies of collective bargaining agreements between labor and management of various rail and air carriers and NMB Determinations dating from October 1, 1998, and some even earlier, are available in the Knowledge Store. http:// knowledgestore.nmb.gov/ks/build.html
http://www.nmb.gov/press-and-contacts/key-contacts

For further information, contact the Public Information Officer, National Mediation Board, Suite 250 East, 1301 K Street NW., Washington, DC 20005-7011. Phone, 202-692-5050.

National Railroad Passenger Corporation (AMTRAK)

1 Massachusetts Avenue NW., Washington, DC 20001
Phone, 202-906-3000. Internet, http://www.amtrak.com

Board of Directors

Chair
Vice Chair

Member
Member
Member
Member
Member
Member

Amtrak President / Amtrak Co-Chief Executive Officer (ex officio)
Secretary of Transportation (ex officio)

https://www.amtrak.com/servlet/ContentServer?c=Page&p
   agename=am%2FLayout&cid=1241245669142

Executive Committee

President / Co-Chief Executive Officer
Co-Chief Executive Officer

Executive Vice Presidents
Administration
Chief Financial Officer
Chief Legal Officer / Corporate Secretary / General
   Counsel
Chief Operations Officer
Marketing and Business Development
Planning, Technology, and Public Affairs
https://www.amtrak.com/servlet/ContentServer?c=Page&p
   agename=am%2FLayout&cid=1241245669145

Inspector General
http://www.amtrakoig.gov

[For the National Railroad Passenger Corporation statement of organization, see the Code of Federal Regulations, Title 49, Part 700]

The above list of key personnel was updated 09–2017.

The National Railroad Passenger Corporation provides intercity rail passenger service in the United States.

The National Railroad Passenger Corporation (Amtrak) was created by the Rail Passenger Service Act of 1970, as amended (49 U.S.C. 241), and was incorporated under the laws of the District of Columbia. By developing, operating, and improving U.S. intercity rail passenger service, Amtrak provides a balanced nationwide transportation system.

Amtrak operates approximately 300 trains per day, serving over 500 stations in 46 States, over a system of 22,000 route miles. Of this route system, Amtrak owns about 530 route miles in the Northeast and several other small track segments elsewhere in the country.

Amtrak owns or leases its stations and owns its repair and maintenance facilities. The Corporation employs a total workforce of approximately 20,000 and provides all reservation, station, and onboard service staffs, as well as train and engine operating crews. Outside the Northeast Corridor, Amtrak has contracts with privately and publicly owned railroads to operate on their track. These railroads are responsible for the condition of the roadbed and for coordinating the flow of traffic.

In fiscal year 2016, Amtrak transported over 31 million people, 85,000 passengers traveling per day. On behalf of 21 agencies in 18 States, Amtrak is a contract operator for corridor services on 29 routes. It also runs commuter trains under contract with several commuter agencies.

Although Amtrak's basic route system was originally designated by the Secretary of Transportation in 1971, modifications have been made to the Amtrak system and to individual routes that have resulted in more efficient and cost-effective operations. Increased capital funding in recent years has allowed Amtrak to reduce its debt load and make progress in bringing its network to a state of good repair. https://www.amtrak.com/about-amtrak

Sources of Information

Business Opportunities Amtrak provides an online procurement portal to foster business partnerships. https://procurement.amtrak.com
Career Opportunities Amtrak employs more than 20,000 professionals in a variety of career fields. https://jobs.amtrak.com

**Freedom of Information Act
(FOIA)** Amtrak maintains an online FOIA library. Phone, 202-906-3741. https://www.amtrak.com/servlet/ContentServer?c=Page&pagename=am%2FLayout&cid=1241267362261
Great American Stations The Great American Stations Project educates communities on the benefits of redeveloping train stations, offers tools to community leaders for preserving their stations, and provides the appropriate Amtrak resources. http://www.greatamericanstations.com
History For a fast way to learn how the U.S. Congress and its passage of key legislation have affected Amtrak, how Amtrak's environmental efforts have evolved, and when Amtrak added service to a local or regional community, visit Amtrak's "Historic Timeline" web page. https://history.amtrak.com/amtraks-history/historic-timeline
Kids Depot "The Kids Depot" website features a learning zone, park, playground, station, treehouse, workshop, and movies! https://www.amtrak.com/media/KidsDepot/KidsDepot.html

Oversight Amtrak's Office of the Inspector General posts reports and data on Oversight.gov, a text-searchable repository of reports that Federal Inspectors General publish. The Council of the Inspectors General on Integrity and Efficiency operates and maintains the website to increase public access to independent and authoritative information on the Federal Government. https://oversight.gov
Social Media Amtrak has a Facebook account. http://www.facebook.com/Amtrak
  Amtrak posts photos on its Instagram web page. http://www.instagram.com/amtrak
  Amtrak tweets announcements and other newsworthy items on Twitter. http://twitter.com/Amtrak
Store Official Amtrak merchandise—adult apparel, calendars, headwear, posters, and toys—may be purchased online. http://store.amtrak.com
Train Tracker A train may be tracked online by using the train name, train number, or train station. https://www.amtrak.com/trainlocationmap http://www.amtrak.com

For further information, contact the Government Affairs Department, Amtrak, 1 Massachusetts Avenue NW., Washington, DC 20001. Phone, 202-906-3918.

National Science Foundation

4201 Wilson Boulevard, Arlington, VA 22230
Phone, 703-292-5111. TDD, 800-281-8749. Internet, http://www.nsf.gov | Email: info@nsf.gov

National Science Board
https://www.nsf.gov/nsb/members/index.jsp

Ex officio member
Terms Expiring in 2020

Chair
Terms Expiring in 2022

FRANCE A. CÓRDOVA

JOHN L. ANDERSON
ROGER N. BEACHY
VICKI L. CHANDLER
ROBERT M. GROVES
JAMES S. JACKSON
SETHURAMAN PANCHANATHAN
GEORGE P. PETERSON
DIANE L. SOUVAINE

ARTHUR BIENENSTOCK
W. KENT FUCHS
W. CARL LINEBERGER
VICTOR R. MCCRARY
EMILIO F. MORAN

Vice Chair

ELLEN OCHOA
JULIA M. PHILLIPS
ANNEILA I. SARGENT

Terms Expiring in 2024

MAUREEN L. CONDIC
SURESH V. GARIMELLA
STEVEN LEATH
DANIEL A. REED
GERALDINE L. RICHMOND
S. ALAN STERN
STEPHEN H. WILLARD
MARIA T. ZUBER

https://www.nsf.gov/nsb/members/terms.jsp

Executive Officer to the National Science Board

JOHN J. VEYSEY II

Inspector General
https://www.nsf.gov/staff/staff_bio.jsp?lan=alerner

ALLISON C. LERNER

National Science Foundation
https://www.nsf.gov/staff/execlist.jsp

Office of the Director (OD)

Director
Deputy Director

FRANCE A. CÓRDOVA
(VACANCY)

Chief Officers
Information
Operating

DOROTHY ARONSON
F. FLEMING CRIM

Office Heads
Diversity and Inclusion
General Counsel
Integrative Activities
International Science and Engineering
Legislative and Public Affairs
https://www.nsf.gov/od
OAD Directorates *

RHONDA J. DAVIS
LAWRENCE RUDOLPH
SUZANNE IACONO
REBECCA S. KEISER
AMANDA H. GREENWELL

Assistant Directors
Biological Sciences
Computer and Information Science and Engineering
Education and Human Resources
Engineering
Geosciences
Mathematical and Physical Sciences
Social, Behavioral, and Economic Sciences
https://www.nsf.gov/staff/orglist.jsp
OAD Offices *

JOANNE S. TORNOW
ERWIN GIANCHANDANI
KAREN A. MARRONGELLE
DAWN TILBURY
WILLIAM E. EASTERLING
ANNE KINNEY
ARTHUR W. LUPIA

Chief Officers
Financial
Human Capital

TERESA GRANCORVITZ
WONZIE L. GARDNER

Office Heads
Budget, Finance, and Award Management
Information and Resource Management

TERESA GRANCORVITZ
WONZIE L. GARDNER

* OAD is an abbreviation for Office of Assistant Director.

National Science Foundation

The above list of key personnel was updated 11–2019.

The National Science Foundation supports research and education to advance science and engineering.

Establishment and Organization

On May 10, 1950, President Harry S. Truman approved "an act to promote the progress of science; to advance the national health, prosperity, and welfare; to secure the national defense; and for other purposes." This statute, which is commonly cited as the National Science Foundation Act of 1950 (Public Law 81–507), established the National Science Foundation (NSF) as an independent and executive branch agency. The NSF consists of a National Science Board (NSB) and a Director. http://www.loc.gov/law/help/statutes-at-large/81st-congress/session-2/c81s2ch171.pdf

Descriptions of the NSF's establishment, composition, functions, purpose, research facilities, and other statutory information are codified in chapter 16, sections 1861–1887, of 42 U.S.C. https://uscode.house.gov/view.xhtml?path=/prelim@title42/chapter16&edition=prelim

The NSB establishes the policies of the NSF. The President appoints each of the 24 members of the Board to a term of 6 years. Appointees have earned distinguished reputations of service in the fields of agriculture, education, engineering, research management, public affairs, and the basic, medical, or social sciences. They also have an outlook that broadly represents that of national science and engineering leadership. The membership is divided into three groups of eight members; the terms of each group are staggered and expire every 2 years. Any member, other than the Director, who has served on the Board for 12 consecutive years is ineligible for reappointment during the 2-year period following the 12th year. The Board elects its Chair and vice chair every 2 years. The election takes place in an even-numbered year at the annual meeting (42 U.S.C. 1863). https://uscode.house.gov/view.xhtml?req=granuleid:USC-prelim-title42-section1863&num=0&edition=prelim

The President, by the advice and with the consent of the Senate, appoints the Director for a term of 6 years. Before making his or her selection, the President must give the Board an opportunity to recommend candidates for consideration (42 U.S.C. 1864). As an ex officio member of the Board, the NSF Director is coordinate with the other Board members, except with respect to compensation and tenure. The Director is a voting member of the Board and is eligible to serve as its Chair or vice chair if elected (42 U.S.C. 1863). https://uscode.house.gov/view.xhtml?req=granuleid:USC-prelim-title42-section1864&num=0&edition=prelim

The NSF publishes its statements of organization in the "Federal Register" as notices:

58 FR 7587–7595 (8 FEB 1993) https://www.govinfo.gov/content/pkg/FR-1993-02-08/pdf/FR-1993-02-08.pdf#page=121

58 FR 30819 (27 MAY 1993) https://www.govinfo.gov/content/pkg/FR-1993-05-27/pdf/FR-1993-05-27.pdf#page=135

59 FR 22690 (2 MAY 1994) https://www.govinfo.gov/content/pkg/FR-1994-05-02/pdf/FR-1994-05-02.pdf#page=210

60 FR 52431 (6 OCT 1995) https://www.govinfo.gov/content/pkg/FR-1995-10-06/pdf/95-24895.pdf#page=1

The agency's organizational chart is available in Portable Document Format (PDF) for viewing and downloading on the "NSF Organization List" web page. https://www.nsf.gov/staff/organizational_chart.pdf

Activities

The NSF initiates and supports fundamental, long-term, merit-selected research in the scientific and engineering disciplines through grants, contracts, and other agreements that are awarded to universities, colleges, academic consortia, and nonprofit and small business institutions. Most of this research attempts to answer scientific and engineering questions of fundamental life processes, natural laws and phenomena, fundamental processes that influence the human environment, and the forces that affect people as members of society, as well as the behavior of society as a whole. https://www.nsf.gov/about

The NSF encourages cooperative efforts involving universities, industries, and government. It also promotes research and development for better products and services that improve the quality of life and stimulate economic growth. https://www.nsf.gov/about/what.jsp

The NSF cultivates talent by supporting undergraduate and graduate students and postdoctoral researchers. It administers special programs to identify and encourage participation of underrepresented groups in science and technology and to strengthen research capability at small institutions and businesses and at colleges and universities. https://www.nsf.gov/od/broadeningparticipation/bp.jsp

It supports major national and international science and engineering activities, including the U.S. Antarctic program, ocean drilling program, and global geoscience studies. Cooperative scientific and engineering research activities support exchange programs for American and foreign scientists and engineers, execution of jointly designed research projects, participation in international science and engineering organizational activities, and travel to international conferences. https://www.nsf.gov/dir/index.jsp?org=OISE

Contracts and cooperative agreements with national centers allow qualified scientists and engineers access to large facilities. The NSF supports national centers that are associated with astronomy and atmospheric sciences, biological and engineering research, science and technology, supercomputers, and long-term ecological research sites.

The agency's science and engineering education activities include grants for research and development of instructional materials for students and teachers and the application of advanced technologies to education. Grants also are available for teacher preparation and enhancement and informal science education activities. Funding is provided for college science instrumentation, course and curriculum improvement, faculty and student activities, and minority resource centers. The NSF also supports studies of the status of math, science, and engineering education. https://www.nsf.gov/funding/aboutfunding.jsp

The Vannevar Bush Award is given annually to an outstanding contributor to the welfare of the Nation and mankind through public service in science and technology. The Alan T. Waterman Award is given annually to a promising young scientist or engineer to support research and study. The NSF also presents its Public Service Award to one individual and to one company, corporation, or organization for increasing public understanding of science or engineering through public service in areas other than research. The NSF administratively supports the President's Committee on the National Medal of Science. https://www.nsf.gov/awards/presidential.jsp

Sources of Information

A–Z Index An A–Z index to find funding opportunities by title is available on the NSF website. https://www.nsf.gov/funding/azindex.jsp

Archived Records NSF records are referenced in the "Guide to Federal Records in the National Archives of the United States." The Guide is accessible online, and NSF records have been assigned to Record Group 307. https://www.archives.gov/research/guide-fed-records/groups/307.html

At a Glance The "At a Glance" web page provides a convenient overview of NSF activities, partners, and personnel. https://www.nsf.gov/about/glance.jsp

Awards The NSF funds science and engineering research and education through contracts, cooperative agreements, and grants. The Foundation provides approximately 20 percent of the Federal support that academic institutions receive for basic research. http://www.nsf.gov/awards/about.jsp

The abstract, institutions, names, programs, title, and other information associated with an award may be found using one search box on the NSF website. https://www.nsf.gov/awardsearch

Board and Committee Meetings Webcasts of NSB open sessions and committee meetings that are held in Arlington, VA, remain available for at least 1 year after the event. Transcripts of closed sessions of the NSB, its committees, and other subentities are available upon request by email. http://www.nsf.gov/nsb/meetings | Email: nationalsciencebrd@nsf.gov

Business Opportunities The NSF publicizes contracting and subcontracting opportunities in the "Commerce Business Daily" and other appropriate publications. Organizations seeking contract work should contact either the Division of Acquisition and Cooperative Support or the Division of Administrative Services, National Science Foundation, Arlington, VA 22230.

Division of Acquisition and Cooperative Support. Phone, 703-292-8240. http://www.nsf.gov/bfa/dcca/index.jsp

Division of Administrative Services. Phone, 703-292-8190. http://www.nsf.gov/oirm/das

Career Opportunities To carry out its mission, the NSF relies on educators, engineers, mathematicians, program directors, and statisticians, as well as on professionals with administrative, business, and management backgrounds. The NSF also offers career opportunities—internship and recent graduates programs and the Presidential Management Fellows program—for students and recent graduates. http://www.nsf.gov/careers

In 2018, the NSF ranked 8th among 27 midsize Government agencies in the Best Places To Work Agency Rankings. https://bestplacestowork.org/rankings/detail/NF00

Climate Change NSF Public Affairs publishes current research news on the effects of climate change on diverse ecosystems like coral reefs, grasslands, and the Southern Ocean of the Antarctic.

—on coral reefs https://www.nsf.gov/discoveries/disc_summ.jsp?cntn_id=299144

—on grasslands https://www.nsf.gov/discoveries/disc_summ.jsp?cntn_id=299102

—on the Southern Ocean https://www.nsf.gov/discoveries/disc_summ.jsp?cntn_id=297719

Contact The "Contact NSF" web page has email addresses and phone numbers. https://www.nsf.gov/help/contact.jsp | Email: info@nsf.gov

The NSF has a separate web page for media inquiries. Phone, 703-292-7090. https://www.nsf.gov/news/newsroom.jsp | Email: media@nsf.gov

Fellowships Consult the online "Guide to Programs / Browse Funding Opportunities" and appropriate announcements and brochures for postdoctoral fellowship opportunities that may be available through some NSF divisions. Beginning graduate and minority graduate students wanting to apply for fellowships should contact the Directorate for Education and Human Resources. Phone, 703-292-8600. http://www.nsf.gov/funding/browse_all_funding.jsp

Freedom of Information Act (FOIA) A request for agency records should be submitted in accordance with the NSF's FOIA regulation (45 CFR 612). A request should be clearly labeled as "FOIA REQUEST" and be addressed to the FOIA Officer, Office of General Counsel, National Science Foundation, Room 1265, Arlington, VA 22230. Phone, 703-292-8060. Fax, 703-292-9242. http://www.nsf.gov/policies/foia.jsp | Email: foia@nsf.gov

Grants The "Grants.gov Application Guide" helps applicants prepare NSF applications and submit them using Grant.gov. The current guide is available in Portable Document Format (PDF) for viewing and downloading. https://www.nsf.gov/publications/pub_summ.jsp?ods_key=grantsgovguide

Mobile Software Applications (Apps) The NSF Science Zone app and Science360 Radio app are accessible through the NSF website. https://www.nsf.gov/news/special_reports/apps/index.jsp

Multimedia Gallery The NSF maintains an online multimedia gallery. https://www.nsf.gov/news/mmg

News Search A visitor to the NSF website may search an assortment of news types by keyword or title. https://www.nsf.gov/news/search.jsp

Office of Inspector General (OIG) NSF employees, grantees, principal investigators, and others working on NSF programs, grants, or contracts are well-positioned to detect problems. Providing information about allegations or suspicions of abuse, fraud, mismanagement, research misconduct, unnecessary Government expenditures, and waste helps the OIG improve management and reduce fraud. https://www.nsf.gov/oig/report-fraud | Email: oig@nsf.gov

Open Government   To increase collaboration, public participation, and transparency, the NSF maintains an Open Government web page and welcomes ideas and suggestions from the public. https://www.nsf.gov/open

Proposal Status   The proposal status service of Research.gov makes a single online site available for principal investigators and sponsored projects office staff to check current status information for proposals that have been submitted to the NSF via Grants.gov or FastLane. https://www.research.gov/research-portal/appmanager/base/desktop?_nfpb=true&_pageLabel=research_node_display&_nodePath=/researchGov/Service/Desktop/grantsapplicationstatus.html

Publications   The NSF maintains an online document system to support the electronic dissemination of its documents. The online library contains thousands of documents that may be downloaded free of charge. Some NSF publications are available only in print, and others (e.g., the "Grant Proposal Guide" and "Award and Administration Guide") may be inconvenient to download. To obtain these publications in hardcopy, contact the NSF Publications Clearinghouse in Arlington, VA. Phone, 703-292-7827. http://www.nsf.gov/publications | Email: pubinfo@nsf.gov

Search or browse the online document library. http://www.nsf.gov/publications/ods

Reading Room   NSF policy documents and staff instructions, as well as current indexes, are available to the public for inspection and copying. To gain access to the collection, a visitor must schedule an appointment in advance with the library, which is open on weekdays, excluding Federal holidays, 8:00 a.m.–4 p.m. The reading room is located in the National Science Foundation Library, Room 225, Arlington, VA 22230. Phone, 703-292-7830. Email: library@nsf.gov

Small Business Support   The Office of Small Business Research and Development informs small businesses with science and technology research capabilities about NSF support that could benefit them. The Office of Small and Disadvantaged Business Utilization oversees agency compliance with the provisions of the Small Business Act and the Small Business Investment Act of 1958, as amended. Phone, 703-292-8050.

The Small Business Innovation Research and Technology Transfer program helps startups and small businesses carry out scientific research and development. http://www.nsf.gov/eng/iip/sbir/home.jsp

Social Media   The NSF uses social media sites and tools to disseminate news about research funds, funding opportunities, job openings, and more. Follow the NSF on Facebook, Instagram, LinkedIn, OpenNSF, Pinterest, Twitter, Wordpress, and YouTube. https://www.nsf.gov/social

Staff Directory   The "Staff Directory" web page has a search box that visitors can use to locate NSF employees in an electronic database. A visitor also can browse staff by NSF organization. https://www.nsf.gov/staff

The Sources of Information were updated 11–2019.

National Transportation Safety Board

490 L'Enfant Plaza SW., Washington, DC 20594
Phone, 202-314-6000. Internet, http://www.ntsb.gov

Board Members

Chair	Robert L. Sumwalt III
Vice Chair	Bruce Landsberg
	Thomas B. Chapman
	Michael E. Graham
	Jennifer L. Homendy

https://www.ntsb.gov/about/board/Pages/default.aspx

Office Heads Reporting to the Board

Chief Financial Officer	EDWARD BENTHALL
Directors	
Office of Equal Employment Opportunity, Diversity, and Inclusion	FARA D. GUEST
Office of Safety Recommendations and Communications	DOLLINE HATCHETT
General Counsel	KATHLEEN SILBAUGH
Managing Director	SHARON BRYSON
Office Heads Reporting to the Managing Director	
Chiefs	
Administrative Law Judge	ALFONSO J. MONTAÑO
Information Officer	MICHAEL ANTHONY
Directors	
Office of Administration	SUSAN KANTROWITZ
Office of Aviation Safety	DANA SCHULZE
Office of Highway Safety	ROBERT J. MOLLOY
Office of Marine Safety	MORGAN TURRELL
Office of Railroad, Pipeline, and Hazardous Materials Investigations	ROBERT J. HALL
Office of Research and Engineering	JAMES RITTER

https://www.ntsb.gov/about/organization/Pages/default.aspx

The above list of key personnel was updated 6–2021.

The National Transportation Safety Board investigates accidents, conducts studies, and makes recommendations on safety to Government agencies, the transportation industry, and others.

Establishment and Organization

The National Transportation Safety Board (NTSB) was established in 1967. On April 1, 1975, the Independent Safety Board Act of 1974 (49 U.S.C. 1111) reestablished the NTSB as an independent agency outside the Department of Transportation. https://www.govinfo.gov/content/pkg/STATUTE-88/pdf/STATUTE-88-Pg2156.pdf

The NTSB consists of five members whom the President appoints for 5-year terms with the advice and by the consent of the Senate. The President designates two of these members as Chair and Vice Chair of the Board for 2-year terms. The President designates the Chair also with the advice and by the consent of the Senate. https://www.ntsb.gov/about/organization/Pages/default.aspx

The NTSB's statement of organization has been assigned to part 800 of 49 CFR. https://www.ecfr.gov/cgi-bin/text-idx?SID=276925d 8bae986aa729b404e5fe1ac4b&mc=true&node=pt49.7.800&rgn=div5

The NTSB posts its organizational chart (NOV 2020) in Portable Document Format (PDF) for viewing and downloading. https://www.ntsb.gov/about/organization/Documents/NTSB-org-chart.pdf

Statutory and Regulatory Authorities

Statutory material affecting the NTSB has been codified and assigned to sections 1111–1155 of 49 U.S.C. Chapter 11 of Title 49 is dedicated to the "National Transportation Safety Board." https://uscode.house.gov/view.xhtml?path=/prelim@title49/subtitle2/chapter11&edition=prelim

Rules and regulations that are associated with the NTSB have been codified and assigned to Chapter VIII of Subtitle B in 49 CFR. https://www.ecfr.gov/cgi-bin/text-idx?SID=0f3dbab2ad23e6338a8ed9

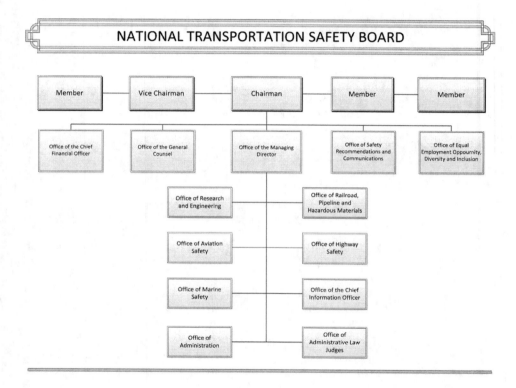

6af83a7895&mc=true&tpl=/ecfrbrowse/
Title49/49chapterVIII.tpl

Activities

Accident Investigation   The NTSB
investigates, determines probable cause,
makes safety recommendations, and
reports the facts and circumstances of the
following types of accidents: U.S. civil
aviation and certain public-use aircraft
accidents; railroad accidents involving a
fatality, substantial property damage, or a
passenger train; pipeline accidents involving
a fatality, substantial property damage,
or significant harm to the environment;
highway accidents (including railroad
grade-crossing accidents) that the NTSB
selects in cooperation with the States; major
marine casualties and accidents involving a
public vessel and a nonpublic vessel; certain
accidents involving hazardous materials;
and other transportation accidents that are
catastrophic, caused by recurring problems,
or otherwise should be investigated in the
judgment of the Board. https://www.ntsb.
gov/investigations/process/Pages/default.aspx

**Certificate, Civil Penalty, and License
Appeal**   On appeal, the NTSB reviews
the suspension, amendment, modification,
revocation, or denial of certain certificates,
licenses, and assessments of civil penalties
issued by the Secretary of Transportation.
The NTSB also reviews, on appeal from
the orders of any administrative law judge,
decisions of the Commandant of the Coast
Guard that revoke, suspend, or deny certain
licenses, certificates, documents, and
registers. http://www.ntsb.gov/legal/alj/Pages/
default.aspx

Disaster Assistance   The NTSB coordinates
the resources of the Federal Government
and other organizations to support the
efforts of local and State governments and
transportation carriers to meet the needs of
disaster victims and their families. It assists
in making Federal resources available to
local authorities and to air, rail, and other
transportation carriers. https://www.ntsb.gov/
tda/Pages/default.aspx

Safety Problem Identification   The NTSB
makes recommendations on matters
of transportation safety. It reduces the
severity and number of transportation

accidents by conducting safety studies
and special investigations; assessing
accident investigation techniques and
publishing recommended procedures;
establishing regulatory requirements
for reporting accidents; evaluating the
transportation safety consciousness and
efficacy of other Government agencies in
accident prevention; evaluating safeguards
and procedures for the transportation of
hazardous materials and the performance
of other Government agencies charged with
ensuring the safe transportation of such
materials; and reporting annually to the
Congress on its activities. http://www.ntsb.
gov/safety/Pages/default.aspx

Sources of Information

Advocacy Priorities   The "Most Wanted
List" raises awareness of what may be done
to reduce the number of transportation
accidents and the loss of life caused by
them. https://www.ntsb.gov/safety/mwl/
Pages/default.aspx

Archived Records   The "Guide to Federal
Records in the National Archives of the
United States" indicates that NTSB records
have been assigned to record group 400.
The guide does not contain, however, a
description that is currently associated with
this record group. https://www.archives.
gov/research/guide-fed-records/index-
numeric/301-to-400.html

The Department of Transportation (DOT)
administered the NTSB until the U.S.
Congress designated it as an independent
agency by passing the Independent Safety
Board Act of 1974 on January 3, 1975.
General records of the DOT have been
assigned to record group 398. https://www.
archives.gov/research/guide-fed-records/
groups/398.html

Business Opportunities   Contractors must
be registered with the Federal Contractor
Registry to do business with the NTSB.
https://www.ntsb.gov/about/organization/
Pages/acquisitions.aspx

Career Opportunities   Information on
career paths at the NTSB is available on
its website. For more information, contact
the Human Resources Division, National
Transportation Safety Board, Washington,
DC 20594. Phone, 202-314-6230. http://

www.ntsb.gov/about/employment/Pages/
Careers.aspx

In 2019, the NTSB ranked 8th among 28 small Government agencies in the Partnership for Public Service's Best Places To Work Agency Rankings. https://bestplacestowork.org/rankings/detail/TB00

Contact Information   The "Contact the National Transportation Safety Board" web page contains general contact information and regional contact information for aviation safety offices. https://www.ntsb.gov/about/Pages/OfficeLocation.aspx

The "Media Resources" web page contains contact information and resources for members of the media. https://www.ntsb.gov/news/Pages/media_resources.aspx

Federal Register   Documents that the NTSB recently published in the Federal Register are accessible online. https://www.federalregister.gov/agencies/national-transportation-safety-board

Freedom of Information Act (FOIA)   To any person, the FOIA gives a statutory right for obtaining access to Government information that the records of executive branch agencies contain. This right to access is limited, however, when the desired information is shielded from disclosure by any of nine exemptions contained within the statute or three special law enforcement record exclusions. https://www.ntsb.gov/about/foia/Pages/default.aspx

History   On December 17, 1903, the Wright "Flyer" became the first powered, heavier-than-air, piloted machine to achieve flight that was controlled and sustained. Twenty-three years later, the U.S. Congress charged the Department of Commerce with investigating the causes of aircraft accidents. Today, NTSB investigators are on call around-the-clock, every day of the year, to investigate significant aviation and surface transportation accidents wherever they may occur. To learn more of the NTSB's story, visit the "History of the National Transportation Safety Board" web page. https://www.ntsb.gov/about/history/Pages/default.aspx

Investigations   The NTSB maintains a database of major aviation, highway, marine, pipeline, and railroad investigations, both ongoing and completed, on its website. https://www.ntsb.gov/investigations/Pages/All-Investigations.aspx

Open Government   The NTSB supports the Open Government initiative by promoting the principles of collaboration, participation, and transparency. https://www.ntsb.gov/about/employment/Pages/open.aspx

Publications   Publications are free of charge for the following categories of subscribers: Federal, State, or local transportation agencies; international transportation organizations or foreign governments; educational institutions or public libraries; nonprofit public safety organizations; and the news media. To receive copies of NTSB publications, persons in these categories should contact the Records Management Division, National Transportation Safety Board, Washington, DC 20594. Phone, 202-314-6551. All other persons may download NTSB publications from the agency's website, or purchase NTSB publications from the National Technical Information Service, 5285 Port Royal Road, Springfield, VA 22161. To place an order, call the subscription unit at 703-487-4630 or the sales desk at 703-487-4768. More information is available on the NTSB website. http://www.ntsb.gov/publications/Pages/default.aspx

Reading Room   The NTSB's public reference room is available for record inspection and photocopying. It is located on the 6th floor at the Board's Washington, DC, headquarters and is open on weekdays from 8:45 a.m. to 4:45 p.m. Requests for access to public records should be made in person at the guard desk. Phone, 202-314-6551 or 800-877-6799.

Site Map   The website map allows visitors to look for specific topics or to browse content that aligns with their interests. https://www.ntsb.gov/Pages/sitemap.aspx

Social Media   The NTSB has a Facebook account. https://www.facebook.com/NTSBgov

The NTSB tweets announcements and other newsworthy items on Twitter. https://twitter.com/ntsb

The NTSB posts videos on its YouTube channel. https://www.youtube.com/user/NTSBgov

Training Center   NTSB investigators and others from the transportation community improve their practice of accident investigation techniques at the training center. Its curriculum promotes independent, objective, and technically advanced accident investigations to raise levels of safety in all modes of transportation. Forums and symposia are open to the public; however, certain courses are limited to those who may be involved in an NTSB accident investigation or who

are members of the emergency response community. Governmental and public organizations may reserve the training and conference center for events. Phone, 571-223-3900. https://www.ntsb.gov/Training_Center/Pages/TrainingCenter.aspx | Email: TCReservations@ntsb.gov

The Sources of Information were updated 6–2021.

Nuclear Regulatory Commission

Washington, DC 20555
Phone, 301-415-7000. Internet, http://www.nrc.gov | Email: opa.resource@nrc.gov

Chair	KRISTINE L. SVINICKI
Commissioner	JEFFREY M. BARAN
Commissioner	STEPHEN G. BURNS
Commissioner	(VACANCY)
Commissioner	(VACANCY)
Chief Administrative Judge, Atomic Safety and Licensing Board Panel	E. ROY HAWKENS
Chief Financial Officer	MAUREEN E. WYLIE
Chief Information Officer	DAVID NELSON
Deputy Executive Director for Materials, Waste, Research, State, Tribal and Compliance Programs	FREDRICK BROWN
Deputy Executive Director for Reactor and Preparedness Programs	MICHAEL R. JOHNSON
Director, Office of Commission Appellate Adjudication	BROOKE POOLE CLARK
Director, Office of Congressional Affairs	EUGENE DACUS
Director, Office of International Programs	NADER L. MAMISH
Director, Office of Public Affairs	DAVID A. CASTELVETER
Executive Director, Advisory Committee on Reactor Safeguards	ANDREA VEIL
Executive Director for Operations	VICTOR M. MCCREE
General Counsel	MARGRET M. DOANE
Inspector General	HUBERT T. BELL, JR.
Secretary of the Commission	ANNETTE L. VIETTI-COOK

[For the Nuclear Regulatory Commission statement of organization, see the Code of Federal Regulations, Title 10, Part I]

The above list of key personnel was updated 06–2017.

The Nuclear Regulatory Commission licenses and regulates civilian use of nuclear energy to protect public health and safety and the environment.

The Nuclear Regulatory Commission (NRC) was established as an independent regulatory agency under the provisions of the Energy Reorganization Act of 1974 (42 U.S.C. 5801 et seq.) and Executive Order 11834 of January 15, 1975. All licensing and related regulatory functions formerly

assigned to the Atomic Energy Commission were transferred to the Nuclear Regulatory Commission. http://www.nrc.gov/about-nrc/governing-laws.html

Five Commissioners whom the President appoints and Senate confirms for 5-year terms govern the NRC. The President appoints one of them to be the Commission's Chair and official spokesperson.

The NRC's major program components are the Office of Nuclear Reactor Regulation, the Office of New Reactors, the Office of Nuclear Material Safety and Safeguards, the Office of Federal and State Materials and Environmental Management Programs, and the Office of Nuclear Regulatory Research. Headquartered in Rockville, Maryland, the NRC has four regional offices.

The Commission ensures that nuclear materials and facilities for civilian use are managed in a manner consistent with public health and safety, environmental quality, national security, and antitrust laws. The NRC centers most of its efforts on regulating the use of nuclear energy to generate electric power. http://www.nrc.gov/about-nrc/organization.html

Activities

The NRC is primarily responsible for the following functions: licensing the construction, operation, and closure of nuclear reactors and other nuclear facilities, such as nuclear fuel cycle facilities, low-level radioactive waste disposal sites under NRC jurisdiction, the geologic repository for high-level radioactive waste, and nonpower test and research reactors; licensing the possession, use, processing, handling, and export of nuclear material; licensing the operators of nuclear power and nonpower test and research reactors; inspecting licensed facilities and activities; conducting the U.S. Government research program on light-water reactor safety; developing and implementing rules and regulations that govern licensed nuclear activities; investigating nuclear incidents and allegations concerning any matter regulated by the Commission; maintaining the NRC Incident Response Program; collecting, analyzing, and disseminating information on the operational safety of commercial nuclear power reactors and certain nonreactor activities; developing working relationships with the States regarding reactor operations and the regulation of nuclear material; and assuring that adequate regulatory programs are maintained by States exercising regulatory control over certain nuclear

materials located within their borders. http://www.nrc.gov/about-nrc/regulatory.html

Sources of Information

Active Regulatory Guides   Regulatory guides provide guidance to licensees and applicants for implementing parts of the Commission's regulations, techniques used by NRC staff to evaluate problems or postulated accidents, and data needed by NRC staff to review applications for permits or licenses. Regulatory guides are issued in 10 broad divisions: antitrust and financial review, environmental and siting, fuels and materials facilities, materials and plant protection, occupational health, power reactors, products, research and test reactors, transportation, and general. Active regulatory guides may be downloaded from the NRC's online library. http://www.nrc.gov/reading-rm/doc-collections/reg-guides
Business Opportunities   The NRC awards contracts to commercial firms, nonprofit organizations, and universities. The agency buys products and services, including technical assistance and research in nuclear fields, information technology, facility management, and administrative support. http://www.nrc.gov/about-nrc/contracting.html
Draft Regulatory Guides   The NRC issues regulatory guides in draft form to solicit public comment and participation in developing regulatory positions. Draft regulatory guides have not received complete staff review, and, therefore, they do not represent official NRC staff positions. The public may comment on draft guides and other documents issued in draft form online. NRC staff considers all comments received during the public comment period. Draft regulatory guides may be downloaded from the NRC's online library. http://www.nrc.gov/public-involve/doc-comment.html http://www.nrc.gov/reading-rm.html
Employment   To carry out its mission, the NRC relies heavily on engineers, scientists, and security professionals. http://www.nrc.gov/about-nrc/employment/opportunities.html http://bestplacestowork.org/BPTW/rankings/overall/mid
Freedom of Information Act (FOIA)   To request copies of records, use the online

"FOIA Request Submittal Form" or contact the FOIA / Privacy Act Officer, Mail Stop T–5 F09, Nuclear Regulatory Commission, Washington, DC 20555-0001. Phone, 301-415-7169. Fax, 301-415-5130. http://www.nrc.gov/reading-rm/foia/foia-submittal-form.html

Glossary The NRC maintains an online glossary. http://www.nrc.gov/reading-rm/basic-ref/glossary.html

Microfiche Collections Selected regional libraries of the U.S. Government Publishing Office Federal Depository Library Program maintain permanent microfiche collections of Nuclear Regulatory Commission documents released between January 1981 and October 1999. Contact the Public Document Room for more information. Phone, 301-415-4737 or 800-397-4209. Fax, 301-415-3548. http://www.nrc.gov/reading-rm/pdr.html | Email: pdr.resource@nrc.gov

Publications The NRC publishes information on licensing and regulation of civilian nuclear facilities and materials, as well as annual and periodic reports. Publications and many documents are accessible on the NRC Web site. The U.S. Government Publishing Office (GPO) and the National Technical Information Service (NTIS) sell single copies of and subscriptions to NRC publications. Contact the GPO bookstore (phone, 202-512-0132) or the NTIS (phone, 888-584-8332 or 703-605-6050) for more information. http://www.nrc.gov/reading-rm.html http://www.gpo.gov/about/bookstore.htm | Email: mainbks@gpo.gov http://www.ntis.gov | Email: customerservice@ntis.gov

Public Documents The Public Document Room—located on the first floor at One White Flint North, 11555 Rockville Pike, Rockville, MD—is open on weekdays, 8 a.m.–4 p.m., except on Federal holidays. The NRC maintains a large collection of documents on licensing proceedings and other significant actions. Documents issued prior to October 1999 are available in paper or microfiche. After October 1999, documents are available online from the NRC's full-text document management system. Most public documents may be reproduced on CD–ROM, microfiche, or paper for a nominal fee. Phone, 301-415-4737 or 800-397-4209. Fax, 301-415-3548. http://www.nrc.gov/reading-rm/pdr.html | Email: pdr.resource@nrc.gov http://www.nrc.gov/reading-rm/adams.html http://www.nrc.gov/about-nrc/contactus.html | Email: opa.resource@nrc.gov

For further information, contact the Office of Public Affairs, Nuclear Regulatory Commission, Washington, DC 20555-0001. Phone, 301-415-8200.

Occupational Safety and Health Review Commission

1120 Twentieth Street NW., Washington, DC 20036-3457
Phone, 202-606-5100. Fax, 202-418-3017. Internet, http://www.oshrc.gov

Commissioners

Chair	CYNTHIA L. ATTWOOD
	AMANDA W. LAIHOW
	(VACANCY)

https://www.oshrc.gov/about/current-commissioners

Administrative Staff

Executive Director	DEBRA A. HALL
Chief Administrative Law Judge	COVETTE ROONEY
Executive Secretary	JOHN X. CERVENY
General Counsel	NADINE N. MANCINI

The above list of key personnel was updated 5–2021.

The Occupational Safety and Health Review Commission ensures the timely and fair resolution of cases involving the alleged exposure of American workers to unsafe or unhealthy working conditions.

The Occupational Safety and Health Review Commission is an independent, quasi-judicial agency established by the Occupational Safety and Health Act of 1970 (29 U.S.C. 651–678).

The Commission rules on cases when disagreements arise over the results of safety and health inspections performed by the Department of Labor's Occupational Safety and Health Administration (OSHA). Employers have the right to dispute alleged job safety or health violations that OSHA inspectors find, the penalties that OSHA proposes, and the time given to correct a hazardous situation.

The Commission posts it organizational chart online in Portable Document Format (PDF) for viewing and downloading. https://www.oshrc.gov/assets/1/6/Org_Chart_May_12,__2021.pdf

The Occupational Safety and Health Act covers virtually every employer in the country. Its purpose is to reduce employment-related injuries, illnesses, and deaths of working men and women in the United States. It requires employers to provide a work environment free from recognized hazards that cause or are likely to cause death or serious physical harm to their employees. It also requires employers to comply with occupational safety and health standards promulgated under the act. http://www.oshrc.gov/about/how-oshrc.html

Activities

The Commission adjudicates enforcement actions initiated under the act when they are contested by employers, employees, or representatives of employees. A case arises when a citation, issued to an employer as the result of an OSHA inspection, is contested within 15 working days of receipt of the report.

There are two levels of adjudication within the Commission. All cases are first assigned to an administrative law judge. A hearing is generally held in the community or as close as possible to where the alleged violation occurred. After the hearing, the judge issues

a decision based on findings of fact and conclusions of law.

A substantial number of these decisions become final orders of the Commission. Commission members, however, will issue the final order if a party petitions the Commission members for review of the judge's decision and the petition is granted.

After a final order is issued, any party to the case may seek a review of the decision in the U.S. courts of appeals.

The Commission's principal office is in Washington, DC. Administrative law judges are also located in the Atlanta and Denver regional offices.

Sources of Information

Career Opportunities   Vacancy announcements are posted online. http://www.oshrc.gov/job_opportunities/job_opport.html

Decisions   The "Decisions" page contains two online search tools, one for the final decisions of administrative law judges and the other for the final decisions of the Commission. The administrative law judge decisions start with the year 1993, and the Commission decisions start with the year 1972. Decisions are available in the form of Hypertext Markup Language (HTML) and Portable Document Format (PDF) files. http://www.oshrc.gov/decisions/index.html

Freedom of Information Act (FOIA)   The FOIA requires Federal agencies to disclose records after receiving a proper written request for them. Certain records, however, are shielded from disclosure by provisions contained within the statute. The Commission's online FOIA information includes the specific procedures for requesting its records, FOIA-related contact information, and links to records that are already accessible online. The Commission operates a FOIA requester service center that can provide information on the status of a submitted request. Phone, 202-606-5724. Fax, 202-606-5417. http://www.oshrc.gov/foia/index.html

Frequently Asked Questions (FAQs)   The Commission posts answers to FAQs on its

Web site. http://www.oshrc.gov/FAQ/index.html

News   The Commission posts press releases on its Web site. http://www.oshrc.gov/press/press.html

Open Government   The Commission supports the Open Government initiative by promoting the principles of collaboration, participation, and transparency. http://www.oshrc.gov/open.html | Email: opengov@oshrc.gov

Plain Language   The Plain Writing Act of 2010 requires all Federal agencies to write in a way that produces "clear Government communication that the public can understand and use." The Commission solicits public assistance in support of plain language: If a document or Web page is unclear, contact the Commission by email and point out the lack of clarity. The Commission seeks to ensure that any document that is necessary for obtaining services, that provides information on services, or that explains how to comply with a requirement that the Commission administers or enforces is plainly written. http://www.oshrc.gov/open/plain_writing.html | Email: plain@oshrc.gov

Publicaciónes en Español   Publications in Spanish are available online. Phone, 202-606-5400. http://www.oshrc.gov/publications/publications_spanish.html

Publications   The Commission's publications are accessible online. Copies of them and decisions are also available from the Office of the Executive Secretary. Phone, 202-606-5400. Fax, 202-606-5050. http://www.oshrc.gov/publications/index.html

Related Sites   The Commission posts helpful and informative links to State Internet and other research sites. The Commission is not affiliated with the organizations whose links are on its "Related Web Sites" page. http://www.oshrc.gov/relatedsites/relatedsites.html http://www.oshrc.gov/about/phone-numbers.html

For further information, contact the Office of the Executive Director, Occupational Safety and Health Review Commission, 1120 Twentieth Street NW., Washington, DC 20036-3457. Phone, 202-606-5100. Fax, 202-418-3017.

Office of Government Ethics

1201 New York Avenue NW., Suite 500, Washington, DC 20005-3917
Phone, 202-482-9300. (TTY) 800-877-8339. Fax, 202-482-9237. Internet, http://www.oge.gov

Director	EMORY A. ROUNDS III
Chief of Staff / Program Counsel	SHELLEY K. FINLAYSON
Deputy Director, Compliance	DALE A. CHRISTOPHER
General Counsel	DAVID J. APOL

[For the Office of Government Ethics statement of organization, see the Code of Federal Regulations, Title 5, Part 2600]

The above list of key personnel was updated 10–2020. https://www.oge.gov/web/oge.nsf/about_leadership

The Office of Government Ethics leads and oversees the executive branch program for preventing and resolving conflicts of interest.

The Office of Government Ethics (OGE) is an executive branch agency established under the Ethics in Government Act of 1978, as amended (5 U.S.C. app. 401).

With the advice and consent of the Senate, the President appoints the Director for a 5-year term. https://www.oge.gov/web/oge.nsf/Organization

Activities

The OGE provides overall leadership and oversight of the executive branch ethics program, which prevents and resolves conflicts of interest. To carry out its leadership and oversight responsibilities, the Office promulgates and maintains enforceable standards of ethical conduct for approximately 2.7 million employees in over 130 executive branch agencies and the White House; oversees a financial disclosure system that reaches approximately 26,000 public and 380,000 confidential financial disclosure report filers; ensures that executive branch agency ethics programs are in compliance with applicable ethics laws and regulations; provides education and training to the more than 4,500 ethics officials throughout the executive branch; conducts outreach to the general public, the private sector, and civil society; and provides technical assistance to State, local, and foreign governments and international organizations. https://www.oge.gov/web/oge.nsf/Mission+and+Responsibilities

Sources of Information

Advisories   The OGE posts written guidance to executive branch ethics officials and employees online. https://www.oge.gov/web/oge.nsf/All%20Advisories

Education   Educational resources for ethics officials—including Institute for Ethics in Government training videos—are available online. https://www.oge.gov/web/oge.nsf/Education%20Resources%20for%20Ethics%20Officials

Career Opportunities   The OGE posts vacancy announcements on USAJobs. The Compliance Division seeks agency ethics officials to participate in rotational details for increasing financial disclosure review proficiency. A detail assignment typically lasts 4–8 weeks, and arrangements can be made to accommodate commitment and schedule. https://www.oge.gov/web/oge.nsf/Careers

Conflict of Interest   The OGE Web site provides links to opinions and other guidance that interpret the conflict of interest laws. https://www.oge.gov/web/OGE.nsf/Legal%20Interpretation

Dates / Deadlines   The schedule of ethics dates helps executive branch agency ethics officials identify key dates and meet important deadlines throughout the calendar year. https://www.oge.gov/web/oge.nsf/Dates%20and%20Deadlines

Executive Orders   A list of Executive orders that significantly affected or continue to affect the executive branch ethics program is available on the OGE's Web site. https://www.oge.gov/web/OGE.nsf/Executive%20Orders

Financial Disclosure   Appointee, nominee, Presidential, and Vice Presidential public financial disclosure reports and ethics agreements are available online. https://www.oge.gov/web/oge.nsf/Presidential%20Appointee%20&%20Nominee%20Records

Resources for public financial disclosure are available on the OGE Web site. https://www.oge.gov/web/OGE.nsf/Public%20Financial%20Disclosure/F8C35F18BF846D1C85257E96006B95B1?opendocument

Forms   All forms created by the OGE and instructions for downloading them are available online. https://www.oge.gov/web/oge.nsf/OGE+Forms

Freedom of Information Act (FOIA)   Information on how to submit a FOIA request is available online. https://www.oge.gov/Web/OGE.nsf/Freedom+of+Information+Act+(FOIA)

An electronic reading room contains documents that the OGE has released after multiple FOIA requests or disclosed proactively. Before making a FOIA request, search the electronic reading room for relevant records that already may be accessible. https://www.oge.gov/web/OGE.nsf/Freedom%20of%20Information%20Act%20(FOIA)/B9B880B7B93AF8EF85257EF5006DAAB6?opendocument

Frequently Asked Questions (FAQs)   The OGE answers media FAQs on its Web site. https://www.oge.gov/web/oge.nsf/Media%20Resources/C82EAE759C7C631885257EBC0043366C?opendocument

International Support   The OGE conducts international work under the auspices of the Department of State. In addition to descriptions of its bilateral and multilateral activities and onsite briefings, the "International Activities" Web pages contain documents that international visitors most often request, international conference papers and speeches, documents prepared for anticorruption meetings, links to other information on the fight against public corruption, and a selection of documents translated into Arabic, Chinese, French, Portuguese, Russian, and Spanish. https://www.oge.gov/web/oge.nsf/International+Activities

Legislative Affairs   The OGE posts budget submissions, correspondence with Congress, information on legislation affecting the executive branch ethics program, and other legislative materials on its Web site. https://www.oge.gov/web/oge.nsf/Legislative%20Affairs%20&%20Budget

Media   The OGE posts documents and information that members of the media request often. A media liaison is available to provide additional assistance. https://www.oge.gov/web/oge.nsf/Media%20Resources | Email: ContactOGE@oge.gov

Open Government   The OGE supports the Open Government initiative by promoting the principles of collaboration, participation, and transparency. https://www.oge.gov/web/oge.nsf/OPEN+GOVERNMENT

Organizational Chart   An organizational chart is available on the "Contact Us" Web page. https://www.oge.gov/Web/OGE.nsf/Resources/Contact+Us

RSS Feeds   The dates and deadlines RSS feed streams the dates of events like training and deadlines that are relevant to the management of agency ethics programs. The latest advisories RSS feed streams new education, legal, and program management advisories. https://www.oge.gov/web/oge.nsf/Resources/RSS%20Feeds

Site Map   A site index presents document categories based on their appearance in the Web site's drop-down menus. https://www.oge.gov/web/oge.nsf/Information/Site+Index?opendocument

Social Media   The OGE tweets announcements and other newsworthy items on Twitter. https://twitter.com/OfficeGovEthics

The Institute for Ethics in Government posts videos on the OGE's YouTube channel. https://www.youtube.com/user/OGEInstitute https://www.oge.gov/web/oge.nsf/Organization/Contact%20Us? | Email: contactoge@oge.gov

For further information, contact the Office of Government Ethics, Suite 500, 1201 New York Avenue NW., Washington, DC 20005-3917. Phone, 202-482-9300. TTY, 800-877-8339. Fax, 202-482-9237.

Office of Personnel Management

1900 E Street NW., Washington, DC 20415-0001
Phone, 202-606-1800. TTY, 202-606-2532. Internet, http://www.opm.gov

Executive Offices

Director	KIRAN AHUJA
Deputy Director	(VACANCY)
Chief of Staff	ANNE HARKAVY
Chief Officers	
Management	DENNIS COLEMAN
Privacy	KELLIE COSGROVE RILEY
Directors	
Communications	CAROLINE CICCONE
Congressional, Legislative and Intergovernmental Affairs	ALETHEA PREDEOUX
Executive Secretariat / Resource Management	JOHN PETTIT, ACTING
Human Capital Data Management and Modernization	DAVID PADRINO
Chief Human Capital Officers Council	
Executive Director	MARGOT CONRAD
General Counsel	LYNN D. EISENBERG

https://www.opm.gov/about-us/our-people-organization/organizational-contacts/office-of-the-director

Program Offices

Associate Directors	
Employee Services	ROBERT SHRIVER

Human Resources Solutions	PETER BONNER
Merit System Accountability and Compliance	MARK W. LAMBERT
Retirement Services	NICHOLAS ASHENDEN
Directors	
Healthcare and Insurance	LAURIE BODENHEIMER
Suitability Executive Agent Programs	LISA M. LOSS
Mission Support Services	
Chief Officers	
Financial	MARGARET PEARSON, ACTING
Human Capital	TYSHAWN THOMAS
Information	GUY CAVALLO
Directors	
Equal Employment Opportunity	LASHONN M. WOODLAND
Facilities, Security and Emergency Management	REID HILLIARD
Human Resources	TYSHAWN THOMAS
Small and Disadvantaged Business Utilization	DESMOND BROWN
Senior Procurement Executive	TODD ANTHONY

https://www.opm.gov/about-us/our-people-organization/
organizational-contacts

Office of the Inspector General

Inspector General	NORBERT E. VINT, ACTING

https://www.opm.gov/about-us/our-people-organization/
organizational-contacts/office-of-inspector-general

Federal Prevailing Rate Advisory Committee

Chair	(VACANCY)

https://www.opm.gov/about-us/our-people-organization/
organizational-contacts/federal-prevailing-rate-advisory-
committee

The above list of key personnel was updated 8–2021.

The Office of Personnel Management administers a merit system to ensure compliance with personnel laws and regulations and assists agencies with recruiting, examining, and promoting on the basis of skills and knowledge irrespective of race, religion, sex, political influence, or other factors not based on merit.

Establishment and Organization

The Office of Personnel Management (OPM) was created as an independent establishment by Reorganization Plan No. 2 of 1978, pursuant to Executive Order 12107, which President James E. Carter signed on December 28, 1978. The Executive order designated January 1, 1979, as the effective date for the establishment of the OPM. The plan and the order transferred many of the U.S. Civil Service Commission's former functions to the OPM.

Reorganization Plan No. 2 of 1978 (92 Stat. 3783) https://www.govinfo.gov/content/pkg/STATUTE-92/pdf/STATUTE-92-Pg3783.pdf

Executive Order 12107 (44 FR 1055–1064) https://www.govinfo.gov/content/pkg/FR-1979-01-03/pdf/FR-1979-01-03.pdf

The OPM published its statement of organization as a notice in the Federal Register on January 5, 1979 (44 FR 1501–1502). https://www.govinfo.gov/content/pkg/FR-1979-01-05/pdf/FR-1979-01-05.pdf

The OPM included an organizational chart on page 12 of its "Annual Performance Report—Fiscal Year 2020," which was published in January of 2021. https://www.opm.gov/about-us/budget-performance/

performance/2020-annual-performance-report.pdf

Statutory and Regulatory Authorities

Reorganization Plan No. 2 of 1978 has been codified and assigned to the appendix of 5 U.S.C. https://uscode.house.gov/view.xhtml?req=granuleid:USC-prelim-title5a-node84-leaf186&num=0&edition=prelim

Statutory material affecting the OPM has been codified and assigned to Chapter 11 (sections 1101–1105) of 5 U.S.C. Title 5 is dedicated to the topic of "Government Organization and Employees," and Chapter 11 of that title deals with the "Office of Personnel Management." https://uscode.house.gov/view.xhtml?path=/prelim@title5/part2/chapter11&edition=prelim

Rules and regulations that are associated with the OPM have been codified and assigned to Chapter I (parts 1–1199) of 5 CFR. Title 5 is dedicated to rules and regulations affecting "Administrative Personnel." https://www.ecfr.gov/cgi-bin/text-idx?SID=c4cab023af8b5d797b0dd7bfa99c9969&mc=true&tpl=/ecfrbrowse/Title05/5chapterI.tpl

Activities

Employee Benefits OPM manages numerous activities that directly affect the well-being of the Federal employee and indirectly enhance employee effectiveness. These include health benefits, life insurance, and retirement benefits. https://www.opm.gov/healthcare-insurance

Examining / Staffing The OPM provides departments and agencies with technical assistance and guidance in examining competitive positions in the Federal civil service for General Schedule grades 1 through 15 and Federal Wage system positions. In addition, OPM is responsible for the following duties: providing testing and examination services, at the request of an agency, on a reimbursable basis; establishing basic qualification standards for all occupations; certifying agency delegated examining units to conduct examining; providing employment information for competitive service positions; and providing policy direction and guidance on promotions, reassignments, appointments in the excepted and competitive services, reinstatements, temporary and term employment, veterans preference, workforce planning and reshaping, organizational design, career transition, and other staffing provisions. https://www.opm.gov/services-for-agencies/recruiting-staffing-solutions/

Executive Resources OPM leads in the selection, management, and development of Federal executives. OPM provides policy guidance, consulting services, and technical support on Senior Executive Service (SES) recruitment, selection, succession planning, mobility performance, awards, and removals. It reviews agency nominations for SES career appointments and administers the Qualifications Review Boards that certify candidates' executive qualifications. It manages SES, senior-level, and scientific and professional space allocations to agencies, administers the Presidential Rank Awards program, and conducts orientation sessions for newly appointed executives. In addition, OPM manages three interagency residential development and training centers for executives and managers. https://www.opm.gov/policy-data-oversight/senior-executive-service

Investigations The Office of the Inspector General conducts comprehensive and independent audits, investigations, and evaluations relating to OPM programs and operations. It is responsible for administrative actions against health care providers who commit sanctionable offenses with respect to the Federal Employees' Health Benefits Program or other Federal programs. https://www.opm.gov/our-inspector-general/

For further information, contact the Office of the Inspector General. Phone, 202-606-1200.

Oversight OPM assesses human capital management Governmentwide and within agencies to gather information for policy development and program refinement, ensure compliance with law and regulation, and enhance agency capability for human resources management accountability. Agency accountability systems help ensure that human capital decisions are consistent with merit principles and that human capital strategies are aligned with mission accomplishment. OPM also works with agencies to find better and more strategic ways to manage Federal human capital. https://www.opm.gov/policy-data-oversight/oversight-activities

Personnel Systems   OPM provides leadership and guidance to agencies on systems to support the manager's personnel management responsibilities. These include the following: white- and blue-collar pay systems, including SES and special occupational pay systems; geographical adjustments and locality payments; special rates to address recruitment and retention problems; allowances and differentials, including recruitment and relocation bonuses, retention allowances, and hazardous duty/environmental pay; and premium pay; annual and sick leave, court leave, military leave, leave transfer and leave bank programs, family and medical leave, excused absence, holidays, and scheduling of work, including flexible and compressed work schedules; performance management, covering appraisal systems, performance pay and awards, and incentive awards for suggestions, inventions, and special acts; classification policy and standards for agencies to determine the series and grades for Federal jobs; labor-management relations, including collective bargaining, negotiability, unfair labor practices, labor-management cooperation, and consulting with unions on Governmentwide issues; systems and techniques for resolving disputes with employees; quality of work-life initiatives, such as employee health and fitness, work and family, AIDS in the workplace, and employee assistance programs; human resources development, including leadership and administration of the Human Resources Development Council and the Government Performance and Results Act interest group; the Training and Management Assistance program, to help agencies develop training and human resources management solutions, including workforce planning and succession management strategies, e-learning applications, traditional classroom training materials, compensation and performance management systems, and other customized products; information systems to support and improve Federal personnel management

decisionmaking; and Governmentwide instructions for personnel processing and recordkeeping and for release of personnel data under the Freedom of Information Act and the Privacy Act.

OPM also provides administrative support to special advisory bodies, including the Federal Prevailing Rate Advisory Committee, the Federal Salary Council, and the Presidential Advisory Committee on Expanding Training Opportunities.

Workforce Diversity   OPM provides leadership, direction, and policy for Governmentwide affirmative recruiting programs for women, minorities, individuals with disabilities, and veterans. It also provides leadership, guidance, and technical assistance to promote merit and equality in systemic workforce recruitment, employment, training, and retention. In addition, OPM gathers, analyzes, and maintains statistical data on the diversity of the Federal workforce and prepares evaluation reports for Congress and others on individual agency and Governmentwide progress toward full workforce representation for all Americans in the Federal sector. https://www.opm.gov/policy-data-oversight/diversity-and-inclusion/

Other Programs

OPM coordinates the temporary assignment of employees between Federal agencies and State, local, and Indian tribal governments, institutions of higher education, and other eligible nonprofit organizations for up to 2 years, for work of mutual benefit to the participating organizations. It administers the Presidential Management Intern Program, which provides 2-year, excepted appointments with Federal agencies to recipients of graduate degrees in appropriate disciplines. In addition, the Office of Personnel Management administers the Federal Merit System Standards, which apply to certain grant-aided State and local programs.

Federal Executive Boards   Federal Executive Boards (FEBs) were established by Presidential memorandum on November 10, 1961, to improve internal Federal management practices and to provide a central focus for Federal participation in civic affairs in major metropolitan centers of Federal activity. They carry out their functions under OPM supervision and control.

FEBs serve as a means for disseminating information within the Federal Government and for promoting discussion of Federal policies and activities of importance to all Federal executives in the field. Each Board is composed of heads of Federal field offices in the metropolitan area. A chairman is elected annually from among the membership to provide overall leadership to the Board's operations. Committees and task forces carry out interagency projects consistent with the Board's mission.

Located in places where Federal activity is concentrated, FEBS can be found in 28 metropolitan areas. Federal executive associations or councils, which are locally organized, can be found in approximately 65 other metropolitan areas. They perform functions similar to the FEBs, but on a lesser scale of organization and activity. https://www.feb.gov/board-locations

For further information, contact the Director for Federal Executive Board Operations. Phone, 202-606-1000.

Sources of Information

A–Z Index   The OPM's website has an alphabetical subject index to help visitors navigate its content. https://www.opm.gov/a-z-index/

Archived Records   The "Guide to Federal Records in the National Archives of the United States" indicates that OPM records have been assigned to record group 478. https://www.archives.gov/research/guide-fed-records/groups/478.html

The "Guide to Federal Records in the National Archives of the United States" indicates that U.S. Civil Service Commission records have been assigned to record group 146. https://www.archives.gov/research/guide-fed-records/groups/146.html

Blog   The OPM has a blog on its website. https://www.opm.gov/blogs/Director/

Business Opportunities   The "Doing Business with OPM" web pages provide information on finding contracting opportunities, registering to do business with the OPM, and connecting with the OPM's

small business program. https://www.opm.gov/about-us/doing-business-with-opm

Staff contact information is available online. https://www.opm.gov/about-us/doing-business-with-opm/contact-us/

Career Opportunities   To help fulfill its mission, the OPM relies on a professional workforce with energy, expertise, personality, and skill. https://www.opm.gov/about-us/careers-at-opm/

In 2020, the OPM ranked 15th among 25 midsize Government agencies in the Partnership for Public Service's Best Places To Work Agency Rankings. https://bestplacestowork.org/rankings/detail/?c=OM00

Contact Information   General contact information is available online. Contact information for specific OPM organizations also is posted. https://www.opm.gov/about-us/contact-us

Coronavirus Disease 2019 (COVID–19)   The OPM works closely with other Federal agencies to keep information current and make it available to Federal agencies and their employees. To learn more, visit the "Coronavirus Disease 2019 (COVID–19)" web page. https://www.opm.gov/policy-data-oversight/covid-19

Federal Holidays   Federal law (5 U.S.C. 6103) establishes the public holidays for Federal employees. Most Federal employees work on weekdays. For these employees, when a holiday falls on a nonworkday—Saturday or Sunday—the Federal holiday usually is observed on Friday or Monday. https://www.opm.gov/policy-data-oversight/snow-dismissal-procedures/federal-holidays/#url=Overview

Federal Register   Significant documents and documents that the OPM recently published in the Federal Register are accessible online. https://www.federalregister.gov/agencies/personnel-management-office

Forms   The "Forms" web page serves as the single source of information for forms belonging to and used by the OPM. Links are also available to browse forms used by other Federal agencies. https://www.opm.gov/forms | Email: formsmanager@opm.gov

Freedom of Information Act (FOIA)   To any person, the FOIA gives a statutory right for obtaining access to Government information in the records of executive branch agencies.

This right to access is limited, however, when the requested information is shielded from disclosure by any of nine exemptions contained within the statute. A FOIA request must be made in writing and clearly labeled "Freedom of Information Act Request." Instructions for making a request are available online. https://www.opm.gov/information-management/freedom-of-information-act

The electronic reading room contains documents that the FOIA identifies for inclusion. This electronic collection also contains records that FOIA users have requested multiple times. https://www.opm.gov/information-management/freedom-of-information-act#url=Electronic-Reading-Room

Frequently Asked Questions (FAQs)   The OPM posts answers to FAQs on its website. https://www.opm.gov/FAQs

Glossaries   A glossary is available on the "Healthcare—Reference Materials" web page. https://www.opm.gov/healthcare-insurance/healthcare/reference-materials/reference/glossary/

A glossary is available on the "Benefits Officers Center—Reference Materials" web page. https://www.opm.gov/retirement-services/benefits-officers-center/reference-materials/#url=Glossary

An insurance glossary of terms that are used on the "Federal Benefits Programs" website is available online. If a term is absent from the glossary, please email a request for its inclusion. https://www.opm.gov/healthcare-insurance/insurance-glossary | Email: fehb@opm.gov

History   On October 27, 1992, the agency's Washington headquarters was dedicated to a former Civil Service Commissioner, who later became the 26th President of the United States. To find out more about this dedicated civil servant, visit the "Theodore Roosevelt" web page. https://www.opm.gov/about-us/our-mission-role-history/theodore-roosevelt/

Insurance   Information on the Federal health benefits open season; flexible spending accounts; and dental and vision, health, life, and long-term care insurance programs, is available online. https://www.opm.gov/healthcare-insurance

Integrity / Efficinecy   The OPM's Office of the Inspector General posts reports and data on Oversight.gov, a text-searchable repository of reports that Federal Inspectors General publish. The Council of the Inspectors General on Integrity and Efficiency operates and maintains the website to increase public access to independent and authoritative information on the Federal Government. https://www.oversight.gov/about

News   The OPM posts news items on its website. https://www.opm.gov/news/latest-news/

Open Government   The OPM supports the Open Government initiative by promoting the principles of collaboration, participation, and transparency. The agency is committed to increasing accountability, effectiveness, efficiency, and innovation; building trust with American citizens; empowering the public; fostering a culture in which everyone's contribution is valued; making better decisions; and tracking how agency money is used. https://www.opm.gov/about-us/open-government

Operating Status   The "Current Status" web page provides the operating status of Federal offices nationwide. https://www.opm.gov/policy-data-oversight/snow-dismissal-procedures/current-status

The OPM sponsors the Operating Status listserv. Subscribers receive an email when the operating status of the Federal Government within the Capital Region changes. https://apps.opm.gov/listserv_apps/list-sub.cfm?targetlist=operatingstatus

Publications   An electronic database allows users to search for operating manuals, periodicals, and other OPM publications. For more information on Federal personnel management publications, contact OPM Publications Management. Phone, 202-606-1822. http://www.opm.gov/news/reports-publications/publications-database

Retirement Information Center   The Retirement Information Center provides information on retirement benefits for current, new, and prospective Federal employees, as well as for Federal retirees, their survivors, and benefits officers. The information includes recent changes, events, and other issues affecting Federal retirement benefits. https://www.opm.gov/Blogs/Retire/

Civil Service Retirement System (CSRS) information on retirement eligibility is

posted online. https://www.opm.gov/
retirement-services/csrs-information/
eligibility
   Federal Employees Retirement System
(FERS) information on retirement eligibility
is posted online. https://www.opm.gov/
retirement-services/fers-information/
eligibility
Salaries / Wages   General schedule locality
pay tables are posted online. https://www.

opm.gov/policy-data-oversight/pay-leave/
salaries-wages/2018/general-schedule/
Social Media   The OPM maintains pages
on Facebook, tweets on Twitter, and posts
videos on its YouTube channel. https://www.
opm.gov/news/social-media-presence
Telework   The OPM maintains the Federal
Government's official telework program
website. https://www.telework.gov/about/ |
Email: teleworkpolicy@opm.gov

The above Sources of Information were updated 8–2021.

Office of the Director of National Intelligence

Washington, DC 20511
Phone, 703-733-8600. Internet, http://www.dni.gov

Director	JOHN L. RATCLIFFE
Principal Deputy Director	(VACANCY)
Principal Executive	NEIL WILEY
Chief Operating Officer	(VACANCY)

https://www.dni.gov/index.php/who-we-are/leadership

Agency Oversight

Chief of Civil Liberties, Privacy, and Transparency	BENJAMIN T. HUEBNER
Chief of Equal Employment Opportunity and Diversity	RITA SAMPSON
General Counsel	BRADLEY BROOKER, ACTING

https://www.odni.gov/index.php/who-we-are/organizations

Directorates:

Enterprise Capacity

Deputy Director of National Intelligence	KEVIN MEINERS

Assistant Directors of National Intelligence / Chief Officers

Finance	JAMES D. TREADWELL
Human Capital	SHERRY VAN SLOUN
Information	JOHN B. SHERMAN

https://www.dni.gov/index.php/who-we-are/organizations/
   enterprise-capacity/enterprise-capacity-who-we-are

Mission Integration

Deputy Director of National Intelligence	BETH SANNER

https://www.dni.gov/index.php/who-we-are/organizations/
   mission-integration/mission-integration-who-we-are

National Security Partnerships

Deputy Director of National Intelligence	LT. GEN. KAREN H. GIBSON

https://www.odni.gov/index.php/who-we-are/organizations/
   national-security-partnerships/national-security-partnerships-
   who-we-are

Strategy and Engagement

Deputy Director of National Intelligence	CORIN R. STONE

Assistant Directors

Legislative Affairs	RYAN CRUMPLER

Office of the Director of National Intelligence

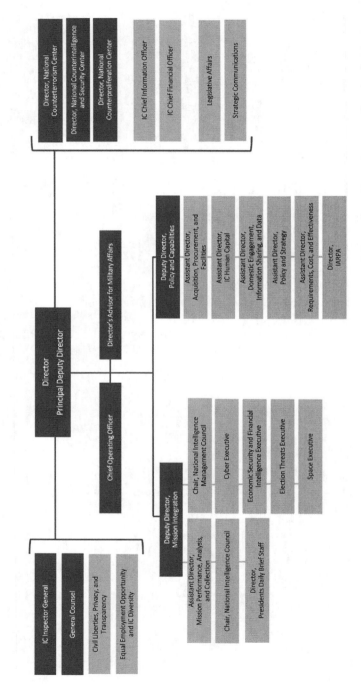

Policy and Strategy	JAMES A. SMITH
Strategic Communications	AMANDA SCHOCH
Transformation and Innovation	PAMELA DUKE

Director of Intelligence Advanced Research Projects Activity   CATHERINE MARSH
https://www.dni.gov/index.php/who-we-are/organizations/
   strategy-engagement/strategy-engagement-who-we-are

Centers:

Cyber Threat Intelligence Integration

Director   ERIN JOE
https://www.dni.gov/index.php/ctiic-who-we-are/leadership
National Counterproliferation

Director   ALAN S. MACDOUGALL
https://www.dni.gov/index.php/ncpc-who-we-are/director-ncpc
National Counterintelligence and Security

Director   WILLIAM R. EVANINA
https://www.dni.gov/index.php/ncsc-who-we-are/ncsc-leadership
National Counterterrorism

Director   LORA SHIAO, ACTING
https://www.dni.gov/index.php/nctc-who-we-are/director-nctc

Intelligence Community Oversight

Inspector General   THOMAS A. MONHEIM, ACTING
https://www.dni.gov/index.php/who-we-are/organizations/icig/
   icig-about-us/icig-leadership/icig-ig-bio | Email: ICIGHotline@
   dni.gov

The above list of key personnel was updated 7–2020.

The Office of the Director of National Intelligence oversees and coordinates the foreign and domestic activities of the Intelligence Community across the Federal Government.

Establishment and Organization

On December 17, 2004, President George W. Bush approved Public Law 108–458, which is also cited as the Intelligence Reform and Terrorism Prevention Act of 2004. This Act established the Office of the Director of National Intelligence (ODNI), which opened on April 22, 2005. https://www.govinfo.gov/content/pkg/STATUTE-118/pdf/STATUTE-118-Pg3638.pdf

The President appoints the Director of National Intelligence by the advice and with the consent of the Senate. The Director is required to "have extensive national security expertise" and "shall not be located within the Executive Office of the President." The President exercises authority, control, and direction over the Director, who serves as head of the Intelligence Community and who acts as the principal adviser to the President, to the National Security Council, and to the Homeland Security Council for intelligence matters involving national security (118 Stat. 3644).

While serving as the Director of National Intelligence, the head of the Intelligence Community may not serve concurrently as "the Director of the Central Intelligence Agency or as the head of any other element of the Intelligence Community" (118 Stat. 3644).

The Law Revision Counsel editorially reclassified section 102 of the National Security Act of 1947. The reclassified statutory material remains part of 50 U.S.C., but has been moved from chapter 15 to chapter 44, Subchapter I—Coordination for National Security (sections 3021–3058). https://uscode.house.gov/view.

xhtml?path=/prelim@title50/chapter44/
subchapter1&edition=prelim

National Defense rules and regulations
that have been published in the Federal
Register are codified in 32 CFR. Chapter
XVII, parts 1700–1799, contain codified
material dealing with the ODNI. https://
www.ecfr.gov/cgi-bin/text-idx?SID=1122b31
df7e7a61c659b0cb96027c179&mc=true&t
pl=/ecfrbrowse/Title32/32chapterXVII.tpl

The ODNI posts an organizational chart
in Portable Document Format (PDF) on its
"Organization" web page. https://www.dni.
gov/files/ODNI/documents/ODNI_Org_
Chart.pdf

Activities

The ODNI provides executive branch
agency and department heads, the Chairman
of the Joint Chiefs of Staff and senior military
commanders, and the U.S. Congress and
President with timely and objective national
intelligence. The agency also establishes
goals and priorities for collection, analysis,
production, and dissemination of national
intelligence; ensures the availability of and
access to intelligence information within
the Intelligence Community; develops
the annual budget for the National
Intelligence Program; oversees coordination
of relationships with the intelligence or
security services of foreign governments and
international organizations; ensures that
accurate analysis of intelligence information
is derived from all sources that are relevant
for supporting national security needs;
develops personnel policies and programs
to increase the capacity for joint operations
and to facilitate staffing of community
management functions; and jointly
oversees, with the Secretary of Defense,
the development and implementation of
an acquisition program management plan.
https://www.dni.gov/index.php/who-we-are/
mission-vision

Sources of Information

Archived Records The "Guide to Federal
Records in the National Archives of the
United States" indicates that ODNI records
have been assigned to record group 576.
ODNI records belong to the "Homeland

Security" cluster. https://www.archives.
gov/research/guide-fed-records/index-
numeric/501-to-600.html
**Biological and Chemical Warfare
/ Nuclear Weapons** The National
Counterproliferation Center has web
pages that introduce readers to the current
challenges of containing the spread of
equipment, information, material, and
technologies that are used for producing
weapons of mass destruction and their
delivery systems. https://www.dni.gov/index.
php/ncpc-features
Career Opportunities The ODNI hires
acquisitions and financial managers,
engineers, foreign language experts,
scientists, security experts, software and
hardware developers, technology specialists,
and other career professionals. https://www.
dni.gov/index.php/careers

In 2019, the Intelligence Community
ranked third among 17 large agencies in
the Partnership for Public Service's Best
Places To Work Agency Rankings. https://
bestplacestowork.org/rankings/detail/IC00
Climate Change "Global Trends:
Paradox of Progress," which the National
Intelligence Council published in January
of 2017, addressed climate change as
part of the report's global trends and key
implications: "A range of global hazards
pose imminent and longer-term threats that
will require collective action to address—
even as cooperation becomes harder. More
extreme weather, water and soil stress,
and food insecurity will disrupt societies.
Sea-level rise, ocean acidification, glacial
melt, and pollution will change living
patterns. Tensions over climate change
will grow. Increased travel and poor health
infrastructure will make infectious diseases
harder to manage." https://www.dni.gov/
files/images/globalTrends/documents/GT-
Main-Report.pdf

"Global Trends 2030: Alternative Worlds,"
which the National Intelligence Council
published in December of 2012, addressed
climate change as part of its "megatrend"
discussion on food, water, and energy:
"Demand for food, water, and energy will
grow . . . owing to an increase in the global
population and the consumption patterns of
an expanding middle class. Climate change
will worsen the outlook for the availability

of these critical resources. . . . the severity of existing weather patterns will intensify, with wet areas getting wetter and dry and arid areas becoming more so. Much of the decline in precipitation will occur in the Middle East and northern Africa as well as western Central Asia, southern Europe, southern Africa, and the US Southwest." https://www.dni.gov/files/documents/ GlobalTrends_2030.pdf

Contact Information   The "Connect with ODNI" web page has a phone number and mailing address for contacting the agency. https://www.odni.gov/index.php/contact-the-odni

Economic Espionage   The National Counterintelligence and Security Center's "Economic Espionage" web page introduces visitors to the efforts of foreign intelligence services, criminals, and private sector spies to compromise American industrial and private sector intellectual property, technology, and trade secrets. Their efforts, which are increasingly carried out within the cyber environment, undermine the Nation's security and long-term prosperity. https:// www.odni.gov/index.php/ncsc-what-we-do/ncsc-threat-assessments-mission/ncsc-economic-espionage

Election Security   The ODNI partners with Federal departments and agencies, State and local governments, election officials, and others to protect U.S. elections and to maintain public transparency about its efforts. Related content and links are accessible on the "Election Security" web page. https://www.odni.gov/index.php/who-we-are/organizations/mission-integration/es/election-security-who-we-are

Factsheets   The ODNI has posted a factsheet (FEB 2017) online. https://www. dni.gov/files/documents/FACTSHEET_ODNI_ History_and_Background_2_24-17.pdf

The National Counterterrorism Center posted a factsheet on its "NCTC At a Glance" web page. https://www.dni.gov/ index.php/nctc-features/1542-nctc-at-a-glance

The Cyber Threat Intelligence Integration Center posted "quick facts" about its activities on the "CTIIC Quick Facts" web page. https://www.dni.gov/index.php/ctiic-features/1722-ctiic-quick-facts

Federal Register   Significant documents and documents that the ODNI recently published in the Federal Register are accessible online. https://www.federalregister.gov/agencies/ national-intelligence-office-of-the-national-director

Freedom of Information Act (FOIA)   Enacted in 1966, the FOIA took effect on July 4, 1967. The Act gives a right for accessing Federal agency records to any person, except a fugitive from the law. Some records, or portions of them, are, however, shielded from disclosure by one or more of nine statutory exemptions or by specific harm that disclosure could cause. The Electronic Freedom of Information Act Amendments of 1996 require Federal agencies to use electronic information technology to expand access to and availability of FOIA documents. https://www. dni.gov/index.php/foia

History   A Director of National Intelligence for coordinating the overall intelligence effort is an idea that predates the establishment of the ODNI by five decades. The attacks of September 11, 2001, against the World Trade Center and the subsequent report by the National Commission on Terrorist Attacks Upon the United States (better known as the 9/11 Commission) increased the momentum for major intelligence reform. To learn more of the story, visit the "History" web page. https://www.odni.gov/index.php/who-we-are/history

Kids   The "Information for Kids" web page has a collection of links that lead to portals on other Intelligence Community websites: Central Intelligence Agency, Departments of Energy and State, Department of the Treasury, Federal Bureau of Investigation, National Reconnaissance Office, and National Security Agency. https://www.odni. gov/index.php/for-kids

Newsroom   The ODNI posts congressional testimonies, news articles, press releases, recent news, reports and publications, and speeches and interviews online. https:// www.dni.gov/index.php/newsroom

Organization   The "Organization" web page has links for the ODNI's four directorates, four mission centers, four oversight offices, and its organizational chart. https://www.odni.gov/index.php/who-we-are/organizations

Private Sector Engagement The ODNI promotes collaboration with the private sector to advance national security interests, while protecting the freedoms, civil liberties, and privacy rights that the U.S. Constitution guarantees. https://www.dni.gov/index.php/who-we-are/organizations/national-security-partnerships/ps-engagement | Email: DNI-NSP-PrivateSector-Info@dni.gov

Reports / Publications Reports and other ODNI publications are available online.

The Sources of Information were updated 3–2020.

https://www.dni.gov/index.php/newsroom/reports-publications

National Intelligence Council publications are available online. https://www.dni.gov/index.php/who-we-are/organizations/mission-integration/nic/nic-related-menus/nic-related-content/nic-publications

Social Media The "Connect with ODNI" web page has links to the ODNI's social media pages on Facebook, Twitter, Tumblr, and YouTube. https://www.odni.gov/index.php/contact-the-odni

---

Overseas Private Investment Corporation

1100 New York Avenue NW., Washington, DC 20527
Phone, 202-336-8400. Fax, 202-336-7949. Internet, http://www.opic.gov

President / Chief Executive Officer	DEV J. JAGADESAN, ACTING
Executive Vice President	(VACANCY)
Chief Information Officer	ROBERT DELUCA
Chief of Staff	CAMERON ALFORD, ACTING
Director, Office of Accountability	WILLIAM KENNEDY
Vice President, Department of Legal Affairs / General Counsel	CINDY SHEPARD, ACTING
Vice President, Department of Management and Administration	MICHELE PEREZ
Vice President, Financial and Portfolio Management	MILDRED CALLEAR
Vice President, Human Resources	MICHELE PEREZ, ACTING
Vice President, Investment Funds	LYNN NGUYEN, ACTING
Vice President, Office of External Affairs	EDWARD BURRIER
Vice President, Office of Investment Policy	MERRYL BURPOE, ACTING
Vice President, Small and Medium Enterprise Finance	JAMES C. POLAN
Vice President, Structured Finance and Insurance	TRACEY WEBB

[For the Overseas Private Investment Corporation statement of organization, see the Code of Federal Regulations, Title 22, Chapter VII]

The above list of key personnel was updated 07–2017.

The Overseas Private Investment Corporation promotes economic growth and job opportunities both at home and abroad by encouraging U.S. private investment in developing countries and emerging markets.

The Overseas Private Investment Corporation (OPIC) was established in 1971 as an independent agency by the Foreign Affairs Reform and Restructuring Act (112 Stat. 2681-790). The Corporation helps U.S. businesses invest overseas, fosters economic development in new and emerging markets, complements the private sector in managing risks associated with foreign direct investment, and supports U.S. foreign policy. It charges market-based fees for its products and operates on a self-sustaining basis at no net cost to American taxpayers. https://www.opic.gov/who-we-are/overview

Activities

The agency serves as the U.S. Government's development finance institution. It mobilizes private capital to help solve critical development challenges. This mobilization of capital advances U.S. foreign policy and national security objectives. Working with the U.S. private sector, the agency helps U.S. businesses gain footholds in emerging markets thereby catalyzing revenues, jobs, and growth opportunities both at home and abroad. Consistent with its mission, the Corporation provides financing guarantees, insures against political risk, and supports private equity investment funds to stimulate investment. https://www.opic.gov/what-we-offer/overview

OPIC projects adhere to high environmental and social standards and uphold human rights. By its adherence to high standards, the agency tries to raise the industry and regional standards of the countries where it operates. OPIC services are available for new and expanding business enterprises in more than 160 countries. https://www.opic.gov/opic-action/overview

Sources of Information

Eligibility   To determine whether a business owner or company is eligible for OPIC insurance or finance products, visit the online applicant screener. Some eligibility requirements are the same across all OPIC products; however, some vary by product. https://www.opic.gov/doing-business-us/applicant-screener

Employment   Most OPIC career opportunities fall within the following professional categories: attorney-advisors, business development specialists, economists, finance specialists, and managers. New hires must be U.S. citizens. https://www.opic.gov/who-we-are/careers

In 2015 and 2016, the OPIC was ranked number two among small Government agencies in the Best Places To Work Agency Rankings. http://bestplacestowork.org/BPTW/rankings/overall/small

Media   Annual reports, newsletters, and public notices, as well as the OPIC blog and media library are available online. https://www.opic.gov/media-events/media-library

Workshops   Participants learn how American small businesses use OPIC finance and insurance products to gain access to emerging markets overseas, as well as how they can take advantage of OPIC products to expand their businesses abroad and support growth at home. https://www.opic.gov/outreach-events/upcoming-workshops https://www.opic.gov/doing-business-us/contact-us | Email: info@opic.gov

For further information, contact the Overseas Private Investment Corporation, 1100 New York Avenue NW., Washington, DC 20527. Phone, 202-336-8400. Fax, 202-336-7949.

Peace Corps

1111 Twentieth Street NW., Washington, DC 20526
Phone, 855-855-1961; 202-692-2000. Fax, 202-692-2231. Internet, http://www.peacecorps.gov

Director	Josephine K. Olsen
Deputy Director	(vacancy)
Chief of Staff	Michelle K. Brooks
https://files.peacecorps.gov/documents/jody-olsen-bio.pdf	
Chief Officers	
Financial	Richard Swarttz
Information	Scott Knell
Director	
Civil Rights and Diversity	John W. Burden
Victim Advocacy	Da Shawna Townsend

General Counsel	ROBERT SHANKS
White House Liaison	MATTHEW MCKINNEY
Associate Directors	
Global Operations	PATRICK YOUNG
Health Services	KAREN BECKER
Safety and Security	SHAWN BARDWELL
Volunteer Recruitment and Selection	DAVID WALKER
Directors	
Global Health and HIV	MARIE MCLEOD
Overseas Programming and Training Support	STEPHANIE RUST
Peace Corps Response	KWEKU BOAFO
Strategic Information, Research, and Planning	JEFFREY KWIECINSKI, ACTING
Regional Directors	
Africa	JOHNATHAN MILLER
Europe, Mediterranean and Asia	JEANNETTE WINDON
Inter-America and the Pacific	GREGORY HUGER
Associate Directors	
External Affairs	RACHEL KAHLER
Management	JEFFREY HARRINGTON
Chief Compliance Officer	ANNE HUGHES
Directors	
Communications	MATTHEW SHEEHEY
Congressional Relations	NANCY HERBOLSHEIMER
Grants and Gifts Management	KAREN ROBERTS
Strategic Partnerships and Intergovernmental Affairs	SHANNON KENDRICK
Third Goal and Returned Volunteer Services	KEITH HONDA
Executive Secretary	SYLVIE MORTIMER, ACTING
https://www.peacecorps.gov/about/leadership	
Inspector General	KATHY A. BULLER
https://www.peacecorps.gov/about/inspector-general	

The above list of key personnel was updated 8–2019.

The Peace Corps gives the peoples of host countries increased access to volunteers who are qualified, skilled, and trained, and it strengthens mutual understanding between Americans and the peoples of the countries served.

Establishment and Organization

President John F. Kennedy approved the Peace Corps Act on September 22, 1961. This Public Law became effective on that same day. Its declaration of purpose states: "It is the policy of the United States and the purpose of this Act to promote world peace and friendship through a Peace Corps, which shall make available to interested countries and areas men and women of the United States qualified for service abroad and willing to serve, under conditions of hardship if necessary, to help the peoples of such countries and areas in meeting their needs for trained manpower, and to help promote a better understanding of the American people on the part of the peoples served and a better understanding of other peoples on the part of the American people." https://www.govinfo.gov/content/pkg/STATUTE-75/pdf/STATUTE-75-Pg612.pdf

The Peace Corps Act has been amended since its enactment (22 U.S.C. 2501). Title VI of the International Security and Development Cooperation Act of 1981 (22

U.S.C. 2501–1) made the Peace Corps an independent agency. https://www.govinfo. gov/content/pkg/USCODE-2017-title22/pdf/ USCODE-2017-title22-chap34.pdf

The President appoints the Director and Deputy Director of the agency by the advice and with the consent of the Senate.

Activities

The Peace Corps consists of a Washington, DC, headquarters, six regional offices, and overseas operations in 62 countries, relying on more than 7,350 volunteers and trainees.

To fulfill the Peace Corps mandate, men and women are trained for a 9- to 14-week period in the appropriate local language, the technical skills necessary for their particular jobs, and the cross-cultural skills needed to adjust to a society with traditions and attitudes different from their own. Volunteers serve for a period of 2 years, living among the people with whom they work. Volunteers are expected to become a part of the community through their service.

Thousands of volunteers serve worldwide and work in six program areas: agriculture, business development, education, environment, health and HIV/AIDS, and youth development. Community-level projects are designed to match the skills of volunteers with the resources of host-country agencies and other international assistance organizations to solve specific development problems, often in conjunction with private volunteer organizations.

In the United States, the Peace Corps is working to promote an understanding of people in other countries. Through its World Wise Schools program, volunteers partner with elementary and junior high school students in the United States to encourage an exchange of letters, pictures, music, and artifacts. Participating students increase their knowledge of geography, languages, and different cultures, while gaining an appreciation for voluntarism.

The Peace Corps offers other domestic programs that rely on former volunteers. Working together with universities, local public school systems, and private businesses and foundations, these former volunteers help solve some of our Nation's most pressing domestic problems. http:// www.peacecorps.gov/about

Sources of Information

Age Limit The Peace Corps does not have an upper age limit, and spouses and partners can serve together. To learn more, visit the "Volunteering at 50–Plus" web page. https:// www.peacecorps.gov/volunteer/is-peace- corps-right-for-me/50plus
Becoming a Volunteer The volunteer program has an online application portal. http://www.peacecorps.gov/apply
Career Opportunities Peace Corps vacancy announcements are posted online. Additional information is available from the Office of Human Resource Management. Phone, 202-692-1200. http://www. peacecorps.gov/about/jobs

The Peace Corps consistently ranks high among midsize agencies in the Partnership for Public Service's Best Places To Work Agency Rankings. In 2018, it ranked 6th among 27 midsize agencies. http:// bestplacestowork.org/rankings/detail/PU00
Climate Change / Sustainability The 2016 Strategic Sustainability Performance Plan identifies greenhouse gas reduction as one of its principal goals and includes an appendix on climate change resilience. https:// files.peacecorps.gov/documents/open- government/2016_Strategic_Sustainability_ Performance_Plan.pdf
Contact Information The "Contact Us" web page has key phone numbers and email addresses for contacting the Peace Corps. https://www.peacecorps.gov/contact/#email_ form | Email: dcinfo@peacecorps.gov
Countries Peace Corps volunteers serve in more than 60 countries. https://www. peacecorps.gov/countries
Donate The "Donate" web page lists and describes projects that donors can support. https://www.peacecorps.gov/donate
Educator Resources The Paul D. Coverdell World Wise Schools program provides online educational resources based on the Peace Corps experience. https://www. peacecorps.gov/educators/resources/?search_ text=climate&list=educators-resources
Events The "Events" web page has a search tool for locating a nearby event by ZIP Code. https://www.peacecorps.gov/events
Facts Curious to know how many Americans have been in the Peace Corps? On which continent most volunteers serve?

To learn the answers to these questions and others, visit the "Fast Facts" web page. https://www.peacecorps.gov/news/fast-facts

Freedom of Information Act (FOIA)   The FOIA (5 USC 552) gives the public right to request records from a Federal agency. An agency must disclose the requested record as long as one of the law's nine exemptions does not shield the information from public disclosure. https://www.govinfo.gov/content/pkg/USCODE-2017-title5/pdf/USCODE-2017-title5-partI-chap5-subchapII.pdf

The Peace Corps posts certain types of records that it creates on its website. A formal FOIA request is not necessary to access them. The Peace Corps also maintains a FOIA requester service center that can provide information on the status of a person's FOIA request. https://www.peacecorps.gov/about/open-government/foia

Frequently Asked Questions (FAQs)   The Peace Corps posts answers to FAQs on its website. https://www.peacecorps.gov/faqs/all

Global Initiatives   These programs promote AIDS relief, work to eliminate malaria, help local people assure their own food security, economically empower women, and support development projects in local communities. https://www.peacecorps.gov/about/global-initiatives

History   At 2 a.m., before a crowd of 10,000 students, then Senator and Presidential candidate John F. Kennedy launched a new experiment in public service from the steps of the Michigan Union at the University of Michigan in Ann Arbor. To learn more about what happened early that morning of October 14, 1960, visit "The Founding Moment" web page. https://www.peacecorps.gov/about/history/founding-moment

News   The Office of Press Relations posts news—agency statements, media advisories, and press releases—on the Peace Corps website. https://www.peacecorps.gov/news | Email: pressoffice@peacecorps.gov

Open Government   The Peace Corps supports the Open Government initiative by promoting the principles of collaboration, participation, and transparency. https://www.peacecorps.gov/about/open-government

Oversight   The Office of the Inspector General from the Peace Corps posts reports and data on Oversight.gov, a text-searchable repository of reports that Federal Inspectors General publish. The Council of the Inspectors General on Integrity and Efficiency operates and maintains the website to increase public access to independent and authoritative information on the Federal Government. https://oversight.gov/reports

Recruitment Offices   Contact information for Peace Corps recruitment offices is available online. http://www.peacecorps.gov/recruiters/offices

Social Media   The Peace Corps tweets announcements and other newsworthy items on Twitter. https://twitter.com/peacecorps

The Peace Corps has a Facebook account. https://www.facebook.com/peacecorps

The Peace Corps posts videos on its YouTube channel. https://www.youtube.com/peacecorps

Stories   Peace Corps volunteers have stories to tell. Read and listen to them on the Peace Corps' website. https://www.peacecorps.gov/stories

The Sources of Information were updated 8–2019.

Pension Benefit Guaranty Corporation

1200 K Street NW., Washington, DC 20005
Phone, 202-326-4000. Fax, 800-400-7242. Internet, http://www.pbgc.gov

Board of Directors
CHAIR (Secretary of Labor)
Member (Secretary of the Treasury)
Member (Secretary of Commerce)

ALEXANDER ACOSTA
STEVEN MNUCHIN
WILBER ROSS OFFICIALS

Director
Chief, Benefits Administration

THOMAS REEDER
DAVID FOLEY

Chief Counsel	ISRAEL GOLDOWITZ
Chief Financial Officer	PATRICIA KELLY
Chief Information Officer	ROBERT SCHERER
Chief Investment Officer	JOHN GREENBERG
Chief Management Officer	ALICE MARONI
Chief, Negotiations and Restructuring	KAREN MORRIS
Chief of Staff	ANN ORR
Chief Policy Officer	(VACANCY)
Deputy Chief, Benefits Administration	(VACANCY)
Deputy Chief, Negotiations and Restructuring	(VACANCY)
Deputy Chief Policy Officer	MICHAEL RAE
Deputy General Counsel	PHILIP HERTZ
Director, Department of Budget	EDGAR BENNETT
Director, Department of Communications Outreach and Legislative Affairs	MARTHA THREATT, ACTING
Director, Department of Corporate Controls and Reviews	MARTIN BOEHM
Director, Department of Corporate Finance and Restructuring	ADI BERGER, ACTING
Director, Department of Financial Operations	THEODORE WINTER
Director, Department of Human Resources	ARRIE ETHERIDGE
Director, Department of Information Technology and Business Modernization	VIDHYA SHYAMSUNDER
Director, Department of Information Technology Infrastructure Operations	JOSHUA KOSSOY
Director, Department of Policy Research and Analysis	CHRISTOPHER BONE
Director, Department of Procurement	STEVE BLOCK
Director, Department of Quality Management	DIANE BRAUNSTEIN
Director, Department of Workplace Solutions	ALISA COTTONE
General Counsel	JUDITH STARR
Inspector General	ROBERT A. WESTBROOKS

The Pension Benefit Guaranty Corporation protects the retirement incomes of American workers in private-sector defined benefit pension plans.

The Pension Benefit Guaranty Corporation (PBGC) is a self-financing, wholly owned Government corporation subject to the Government Corporation Control Act (31 U.S.C. 9101-9109). The Corporation, established by title IV of the Employee Retirement Income Security Act of 1974 (29 U.S.C. 1301-1461), operates in accordance with policies established by its Board of Directors.

The Board comprises the Secretaries of Labor, Commerce, and the Treasury. The Secretary of Labor serves as Chair of the Board. A seven-member advisory committee, comprising two labor, two employer, and three general public representatives whom the President appoints, advises the PBGC on investment issues. The President also appoints the PBGC's Director, whom the

Senate then confirms. http://www.pbgc.gov/about/who-we-are.html

Activities

Coverage The Corporation insures most private sector defined-benefit pension plans that provide a pension benefit based on factors such as age, years of service, and salary.

It administers two insurance programs, separately covering single-employer and multiemployer plans. More than 40 million workers and retirees participate in nearly 24,000 covered plans.

Single-Employer Insurance Under the single-employer program, the Corporation guarantees payment of basic pension benefits if an insured plan terminates without sufficient assets to pay those

PENSION BENEFIT GUARANTY CORPORATION

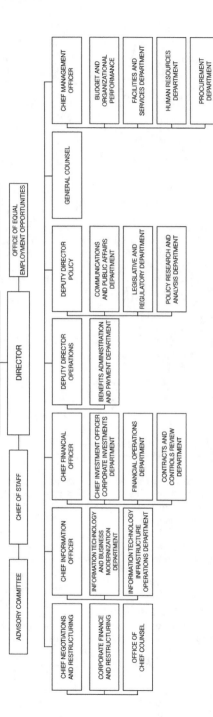

benefits. The law limits, however, the total monthly benefit that the PBGC may guarantee for one individual to $5,011.36 per month for a 65-year-old individual in a pension plan that terminates in 2015. The law also sets other restrictions on PBGC's guarantee, including limits on the insured amount of recent benefit increases. In certain cases, the Corporation may pay some benefits above the guaranteed amount depending on the funding level of the plan and amounts recovered from employers.

A plan sponsor may terminate a single-employer plan in a standard termination if the plan has sufficient assets to purchase private annuities to cover all benefit liabilities. If a plan does not have sufficient assets, the sponsor may seek to transfer the pension liabilities to the PBGC by demonstrating that it meets the legal criteria for a distress termination. In either termination, the plan administrator must inform participants in writing at least 60 days prior to the date the administrator proposes to terminate the plan. Only a plan that has sufficient assets to pay all benefit liabilities may terminate in a standard termination. The Corporation also may institute termination of underfunded plans in certain specified circumstances. http://www.pbgc.gov/wr/benefits/guaranteed-benefits.html

Multiemployer Insurance   Under title IV, as revised in 1980 by the Multiemployer Pension Plan Amendments Act (29 U.S.C. 1001 note), which changed the insurable event from plan termination to plan insolvency, the Corporation provides financial assistance to multiemployer plans that are unable to pay nonforfeitable benefits. The plans are obligated to repay such assistance. The act also made employers withdrawing from a plan liable to the plan for a portion of its unfunded vested benefits. http://www.pbgc.gov/prac/multiemployer.html

Premium Collections   All defined-benefit pension plans insured by the PBGC are required to pay premiums to the Corporation according to rates set by Congress. The per-participant flat-rate premium for plans starting in 2015 is $57.00 for single-employer plans and $26.00 for multiemployer plans. Underfunded single-employer plans must also pay an additional

premium equal to $24 per $1,000 of unfunded vested benefits. A termination premium of $1,250 per participant per year applies to certain distress and involuntary plan terminations, payable for 3 years after the termination. http://www.pbgc.gov/prac/prem/premium-rates.html

Sources of Information

Blog   The PBGC Web site features the "Retirement Matters" blog. http://www.pbgc.gov/about/who-we-are/retirement-matters
Business Opportunities   The PBGC tries to give a fair share of its procurement awards and subcontracting opportunities to small businesses. The PBGC regularly procures accounting, actuarial, auditing, benefits administration, legal, and information technology services.

The agency utilizes various types of contract vehicles that are outlined in the "Federal Acquisition Regulation". These types of contract vehicles include agreements, commercial contracts, major contracts, orders against other Government contracts, and purchase orders. http://www.pbgc.gov/about/procurement.html
Career Opportunities   The PBGC relies on accountants, actuaries, administrative personnel, analysts, attorneys, auditors, employee benefits law specialists, information technology experts, public affairs specialists, and other professionals to carry out its mission. http://www.pbgc.gov/about/jobs.html
Fraud Alerts   The PBGC, with support from its Office of the Inspector General, posts fraud alerts to spread awareness of scams. http://www.pbgc.gov/wr/other/pg/fraud-alerts.html
Freedom of Information Act (FOIA)   The PBGC participates in FOIAonline, which allows information seekers to submit electronic FOIA requests, to track the status of requests, to search for requests submitted by others, to access released records, and to generate agency-specific processing reports. https://foiaonline.regulations.gov/foia/action/public/home

FOIA requests must be in writing and may be submitted also by email, fax, or by regular mail to the Disclosure Officer, Pension Benefit Guaranty Corporation, 1200

K Street NW., Suite 11101, Washington, DC 20005. Fax, 202-326-4042. http://www.pbgc.gov/about/pg/footer/foia.html | Email: disclosure@pbgc.gov
Glossary   The PBGC maintains a glossary of terms with simplified definitions. Some terms and their definitions are PBGC-specific in usage. http://www.pbgc.gov/about/pg/header/glossary.html
Insured Pension Plans   A list of pension plans that recently paid premiums to the PBGC is available online. http://www.pbgc.gov/wr/find-an-insured-pension-plan/pbgc-protects-pensions.html
Open Government   The PBGC posts datasets that are useful for increasing agency accountability, public knowledge of the agency and its operations, and economic opportunity. http://www.pbgc.gov/open/index.html | Email: opengov@pbgc.gov

Plain Language   PBGC writers and editors are committed to using plain language in new communications and revising confusing or unclear language in existing material. Send them a note via email if a sentence or paragraph's clarity could be improved. http://www.pbgc.gov/about/pbgc-in-plain-english.html | Email: webmaster@pbgc.gov
Press Room   The PBGC posts press releases on its Web site. http://www.pbgc.gov/news/press.html
An online subscription form is available to sign up for the latest news, delivered via email, from the PBGC. http://www.pbgc.gov/about/stay-informed.html
Site Map   PBGC Web site visitors may use the site map to look for specific topics or to browse for content that aligns with their interests. http://www.pbgc.gov/pbgc-sitemap.html http://www.pbgc.gov/about/pg/contact/contact.html

For further information, contact the Pension Benefit Guaranty Corporation, 1200 K Street NW., Washington, DC 20005-4026. Phone, 202-326-4000 or 800-400-7242 .

Postal Regulatory Commission

901 New York Avenue NW., Suite 200, Washington, DC 20268-0001
Phone, 202-789-6800. Fax, 202-789-6861. Internet, http://www.prc.gov

Chair	Robert G. Taub
Vice Chair	Mark Acton
Commissioner	Nanci E. Langley
Commissioner	Tony Hammond
Commissioner	(vacancy)
Director, Office of Accountability and Compliance	Margaret Cigno
Director, Office of Public Affairs and Government Relations	Ann Fisher
Director, Office of Secretary and Administration	Stacy L. Ruble
General Counsel	David A. Trissell
Inspector General	John F. Callender

[For the Postal Regulatory Commission statement of organization, see the Code of Federal Regulations, Title 39, Part 3002]

The above list of key personnel was updated 06–2017.

The Postal Regulatory Commission develops and implements a modern system of postal rate regulation.

The Postal Regulatory Commission is the successor agency to the Postal Rate Commission, which was created by the Postal Reorganization Act, as amended (39 U.S.C. 101 et seq.). The Commission was established as an independent agency in the executive branch of Government by the Postal Accountability and Enhancement

Act (39 U.S.C. 501). It comprises five Commissioners, appointed by the President with the advice and consent of the Senate, one of whom is designated as Chair.

The Commission promulgates rules and regulations, establishes procedures, and takes other actions necessary to carry out its obligations. It considers complaints received from interested persons relating to United States Postal Service rates, regulations, and services. The Commission also has certain reporting obligations, including a report on universal postal service and the postal monopoly. http://www.prc.gov/about

Sources of Information

Case Information Active cases and daily listings are accessible online. A docket search tool is also available. http://www.prc.gov/dockets/active http://www.prc.gov/dockets/daily http://www.prc.gov/dockets/search | Email: prc-dockets@prc.gov
Employment The Commission relies on the professional services of accountants, attorneys, economists, industrial engineers, marketing specialists, statisticians, and administrative and clerical personnel to fulfill its mission. http://www.prc.gov/employment-opportunities
Freedom of Information Act (FOIA) A FOIA request form is available online. http://www.prc.gov/foia/onlinerequest
Newsroom The Commission posts congressional submissions, papers, press releases, speeches, and upcoming events online. http://www.prc.gov/press-releases
Reading Room Facilities for inspection and copying of records, viewing automated daily lists of docketed materials, and accessing the Commission's Web site are located at 901 New York Avenue NW., Suite 200, Washington, DC. The room is open on weekdays, excluding legal holidays, 8 a.m.–4:30 p.m.
Practice / Procedure Practice and procedure rules governing the conduct of proceedings before the Commission may be found in parts 3001, 3010, 3015, 3020, 3025, 3030, 3031, 3050, and 3060 of title 39 of the "Code of Federal Regulations." http://www.ecfr.gov/cgi-bin/text-idx?SID=a34266c229a4a7b3c470845f8da08605&node=39:1.0.2.15.2&rgn=div5 http://www.prc.gov/offices/osa

For further information, contact the Secretary, Postal Regulatory Commission, 901 New York Avenue NW., Suite 200, Washington, DC 20268-0001. Phone, 202-789-6840.

Railroad Retirement Board

844 North Rush Street, Chicago, IL 60611-1275
Phone, 312-751-4777. Fax, 312-751-7154. Internet, http://www.rrb.gov | Email: opa@rrb.gov

Board

Chairman	ERHARD R. CHORLÉ
Members	
Labor	JOHN BRAGG
Management	THOMAS R. JAYNE
https://www.rrb.gov/OurAgency/TheBoard	
Bureaus	
Actuary	
Chief	KEITH T. SARTAIN
https://www.rrb.gov/OurAgency/BureauofActuary	
Field Service	
Director	(VACANCY)
https://www.rrb.gov/OurAgency/BureauofFieldService/Director	

Fiscal Operations

Chief   SHAWNA R. WEEKLEY

Divisions
Accounting and Budget   JOHN WALTER
Audit Affairs and Compliance   TIMOTHY HOGUEISSON
Treasury, Debt Recovery and Financial Systems   (VACANCY)
https://rrb.gov/OurAgency/bfo_org
Information Services

Chief   TERRYNE F. MURPHY

Divisions
Enterprise Applications   FRANCESCO RESTIVO
Information Technology Strategy and Technology Management ROBERT LABERRY
Infrastructure Services   (VACANCY)
Policy and Compliance   TIMOTHY GRANT
https://rrb.gov/OurAgency/BureauofInformationServices

Offices

Administration

Director   DANIEL J. FADDEN *

Components
Acquisition Management   PAUL T. AHERN
Human Resources   NANCY L. BITZER
Public Affairs   MICHAEL P. FREEMAN
Real Property Management   SCOTT L. RUSH
* also serves as the Senior Executive Officer
https://rrb.gov/OurAgency/OfficeofAdministration

Equal Opportunity

Director   PAMELA M. TATE
https://rrb.gov/OurAgency/OfficeofEqualOpportunity

General Counsel

                                                               ANA M. KOCUR

Components
Hearings and Appeals   SPIRIDOULA MAVROTHALASITIS
Law   ANA M. KOCUR
Legislative Affairs   BEVERLY BRITTON-FRASER

Secretary to the Board   STEPHANIE HILLYARD
https://www.rrb.gov/OurAgency/OfficeofGeneralCounsel
Programs

Director   (VACANCY)

Components
Disability Benefits   SHERITA P. BOOTS
Policy and Systems   KIMBERLY PRICE
Program Evaluation and Management Services   JANET M. HALLMAN
Retirement–Survivor Benefits   VALERIE ALLEN
Unemployment and Programs Support   MICHEAL T. PAWLAK
https://rrb.gov/OurAgency/OfficeofPrograms

Inspector General

                                                               MARTIN J. DICKMAN

https://www.rrb.gov/OurAgency/InspectorGeneral/OIG

Railroad Retirement Board

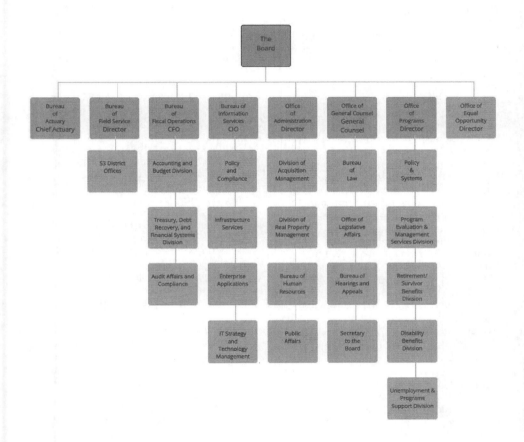

The above list of key personnel was updated 5–2021.

The Railroad Retirement Board administers comprehensive retirement-survivor and unemployment-sickness benefit programs for the Nation's railroad workers and their families.

Establishment and Organization

On June 27, 1934, President Franklin D. Roosevelt approved Public Law 73–485, which is commonly cited as the Railroad Retirement Act, "to provide a retirement system for railroad employees" (48 Stat. 1283). https://www.loc.gov/law/help/statutes-at-large/73rd-congress/session-2/c73s2ch868.pdf

President Roosevelt's approval "established as an independent agency in the executive branch of the Government a Railroad Retirement Board, to be composed of three members appointed by the President, by and with the advice and consent of the Senate" (48 Stat. 1287). One member of the Board, representatives of the railroad employees recommend for appointment; another member, representatives of the carriers (i.e., railroad employers) recommend for appointment. The Chair of the Board, neither representatives of the employees nor representatives of the carriers recommend. The Chair is a public member of the Board and cannot have a pecuniary or other interest in any employee organization or carrier.

The RRB's statement of organization has been assigned to part 200 in 20 CFR. https://www.ecfr.gov/cgi-bin/text-idx?SID=3afc816f2022258c6f160753cdceb5a7&mc=true&node=pt20.1.200&rgn=div5

The RRB posts an "Organization Chart" on its website. https://www.rrb.gov/OurAgency/OrganizationChart

Statutory and Regulatory Authorities

The RRB derives statutory authority from the Railroad Unemployment Insurance Act of 1938 (PL 75–772) and administers its provisions. https://www.loc.gov/law/help/statutes-at-large/75th-congress/session-3/c75s3ch680.pdf

The RRB also derives statutory authority from the Railroad Retirement Act of 1974 (PL 93–445) and administers its provisions. https://www.govinfo.gov/content/pkg/STATUTE-88/pdf/STATUTE-88-Pg1305.pdf

The RRB participates in the administration of the Social Security Act and the Health Insurance for the Aged Act. Certain provisions of these two Acts affect railroad retirement beneficiaries.

Statutory material that emanates from the Railroad Retirement Acts of 1934, 935, 1937, and 1974, has been codified and assigned to Chapter 9 of 45 U.S.C. Title 45 is dedicated to the subject of "Railroads." https://uscode.house.gov/view.xhtml?path=/prelim@title45/chapter9&edition=prelim

Statutory material that deals with railroad unemployment insurance is codified and and has been assigned to Chapter 11 of 45 U.S.C. https://uscode.house.gov/view.xhtml?path=/prelim@title45/chapter11&edition=prelim

Rules and regulations that are associated with the RRB are codified and have been assigned to Chapter II of 20 CFR. Chapter II includes parts 200–399. https://www.ecfr.gov/cgi-bin/text-idx?SID=b110236db6c2db55807fc3d0edf12814&mc=true&tpl=/ecfrbrowse/Title20/20chapterII.tpl

Activities

The RRB's activities center on administering comprehensive retirement-survivor and unemployment-sickness benefit programs for the Nation's railroad workers and their families in accordance with the provisions of railroad retirement and railroad unemployment insurance laws. The RRB also administers certain benefit payments and Medicare coverage that the Social Security Act provides.

RRB field offices manage a placement service for unemployed railroad personnel. https://www.rrb.gov/OurAgency/AgencyOverview

Sources Of Information

Archived Records   The "Guide to Federal Records in the National Archives of the United States" indicates that RRB records have been assigned to record group 184.

https://www.archives.gov/research/guide-fed-records/groups/184.html

Automatic Increases The RRB posts automatic increases—cost of living adjustments and wage indexed amounts—that are associated with Medicare, the Railroad Retirement Act, and the Railroad Unemployment Insurance Act on its website. https://www.rrb.gov/FinancialReporting/FinancialActuarialStatistical/EarningLimits/COLAs#medicare

Benefits The "Benefits" web page has sections on benefits that are associated with disability, Medicare, retirement, sickness, survivorship, and unemployment. The "Benefits" page also has secure service options for conducting personal business with the RRB online and information on Federal income taxes that are withheld form railroad retirement benefit payments. https://www.rrb.gov/Benefits

Some information on benefits is available in Spanish. https://www.rrb.gov/Benefits/Espanol

Career Opportunities Contact the RRB's Bureau of Human Resources. Phone, 312-751-4580. Email: recruit@rrb.gov

In 2019, the RRB ranked 18th among 28 small agencies in the Partnership for Public Service's Best Places To Work Agency Rankings. https://bestplacestowork.org/rankings/detail/RR00

The RRB maintains a job vacancy list of openings that hiring railroad employers report. The list includes job postings that are not expected to be filled locally. https://www.rrb.gov/Resources/Jobs

Contact Information The "Contact Us" web page has an email directory and phone numbers. https://www.rrb.gov/ContactUs

The RRB's Director of Public Affairs coordinates responses to inquiries from members of the media. https://www.rrb.gov/NewsRoom/MediaContact | Email: opa@rrb.gov

Data The RRB posts datasets on the website Data.gov. https://catalog.data.gov/organization/rrb-gov

External Links An extensive collection of links to Government, railroad industry, railroad union, and other websites is available on the RRB website. https://www.rrb.gov/ExternalLinks

Federal Register Significant documents and documents that the RRB recently published in the Federal Register are accessible online. https://www.federalregister.gov/agencies/railroad-retirement-board

Field Offices Field offices are located throughout the country. Staff members answer questions about Medicare and Social Security benefits for railroad workers and their families, retirement benefits, sickness and unemployment benefits, survivor benefits, and tax withholding and statements. A Zip Code locator is available online for finding the nearest field office. https://www.rrb.gov/Field-Office-Locator

Freedom of Information Act (FOIA) The FOIA requires the RRB to disclose records to which a person has requested access in writing. Note, however, that certain exemptions and exclusions that the statute contains shield certain records, or parts of them, from disclosure. The FOIA applies to Federal agencies and does not create a right of access to records that are held by the U.S. Congress, the courts, or by State or local government agencies. https://www.rrb.gov/FOIA

Before submitting a formal FOIA request in writing, browse the electronic FOIA reading room or search specific documents that are part of its collection to confirm that the desired information is not immediately and freely available. https://www.rrb.gov/Resources/FOIA%20Reading%20Room | Email: LAW@rrb.gov

Glossary A glossary of RRB terms is available online. https://www.rrb.gov/Resources/GlossaryofRailroadRetirementTerms

Hotline The illegal receiving of RRB benefits or suspected misconduct affecting or involving the RRB, its programs, or its employees, should be reported to the Office of Inspector General. https://www.rrb.gov/OurAgency/InspectorGeneral/Hotline | Email: hotline@oig.rrb.gov

News The RRB posts news items on its website. https://www.rrb.gov/NewsRoom/NewsReleases

Open Government The USAGM supports the Open Government initiative by promoting collaboration, participation, and transparency. https://www.rrb.gov/OpenGov

Publications   The "Publications" web page provides convenient access to the employer exchange newsletter, program and circular letters, and additional published information. https://www.rrb.gov/Employers/Publications

Resources   RRB online resources include information on appeals, equal opportunity and civil rights, legal opinions and Board decisions, rules and regulations, and paying debts electronically. The "Resources" web page also provides convenient access to a glossary, reading room, retirement handbook, video library, and opportunities for railroad employment. https://www.rrb.gov/Resources

Site Map   The website map allows visitors to look for specific topics or to browse content that aligns with their interests. https://www.rrb.gov/sitemap

The above Sources of Information were updated 5–2021.

Securities and Exchange Commission

100 F Street NE., Washington, DC 20549
Phone, 202-551-7500. Internet, http://www.sec.gov

Chair	W. Jay Clayton
Commissioner	Michael S. Piwowar
Commissioner	Kara M. Stein
Commissioner	(vacancy)
Commissioner	(vacancy)
Division Heads	
Codirector, Enforcement	Stephanie Avakian
Codirector, Enforcement	Steven Peikin
Director, Corporation Finance	William Hinman
Director, Economic and Risk Analysis / Chief Economist	Jeffrey Harris
Director, Investment Management	Dalia Blass
Director, Trading and Markets	Heather Siedel, Acting
Office Heads	
Associate Executive Director, Human Resources	Lacey Dingman
Chief Accountant	Wesley Bricker
Chief Administrative Law Judge	Brenda P. Murray
Chief Financial Officer	Caryn Kauffman, Acting
Chief FOIA Officer	Barry D. Walters
Chief Operating Officer	Kenneth Johnson, Acting
Chief Technology Officer	Pamela Dyson
Director, Acquisitions	Vance Cathell
Director, Compliance Inspections and Examinations	Peter Driscoll, Acting
Director, Credit Ratings	Thomas Butler
Director, Equal Employment Opportunity	Peter Henry, Acting
Director, International Affairs	Paul Leder
Director, Investor Education and Advocacy	Lori J. Schock
Director, Legislative and Intergovernmental Affairs	Keith Cassidy
Director, Minority and Women Inclusion	Pamela Gibbs
Director, Municipal Securities	Jessica Kane
Director, Public Affairs	John Nester
Director, Strategic Initiatives	Mark Ambrose
Director, Support Operations	Barry D. Walters
Ethics Counsel	Shira P. Minton
General Counsel	Robert Stebbins

Securities and Exchange Commission

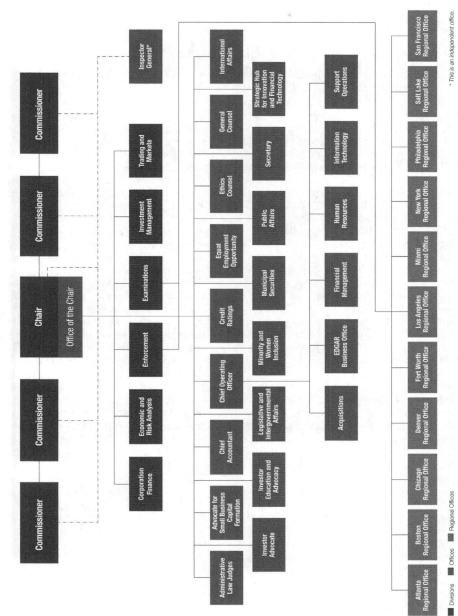

* This is an independent office.

Inspector General   CARL W. HOECKER
Investor Advocate   RICK A. FLEMING
Secretary   BRENT J. FIELDS

[For the Securities and Exchange Commission statement of organization, see the Code of Federal Regulations, Title 17, Part 200]

The above list of key personnel was updated 09–2017.

The Securities and Exchange Commission protects investors, facilitates capital formation, and maintains efficient, fair, and orderly markets.

The Securities and Exchange Commission (SEC) was created under authority of the Securities Exchange Act of 1934 (15 U.S.C. 78a-78jj) and was organized on July 2, 1934. The Commission serves as adviser to United States district courts in reorganization proceedings for debtor corporations in which a substantial public interest is involved. The Commission also has certain responsibilities under section 15 of the Bretton Woods Agreements Act of 1945 (22 U.S.C. 286k-1) and section 851(e) of the Internal Revenue Code of 1954 (26 U.S.C. 851(e)). https://www.sec.gov/about/laws.shtml

The Commission is vested with quasi-judicial functions. Persons aggrieved by its decisions in the exercise of those functions have a right of review by the United States courts of appeals. https://www.sec.gov/about/whatwedo.shtml

Activities

Full and Fair Disclosure   The Securities Act of 1933 (15 U.S.C. 77a) requires issuers of securities and their controlling persons making public offerings of securities in interstate commerce or via mail to file registration statements containing financial and other pertinent data about the issuer and the securities being offered with the SEC. There are limited exemptions, such as government securities, nonpublic offerings, and intrastate offerings, as well as certain offerings not exceeding $1.5 million. The effectiveness of a registration statement may be refused or suspended after a public hearing if the statement contains material misstatements or omissions, thus barring sale of the securities until it is appropriately amended.

Regulation of Investment Advisers   Persons who, for compensation, engage in the business of advising others with respect to securities must register with the Commission. The Commission is authorized to define what practices are considered fraudulent or deceptive and to prescribe means to prevent those practices.

Regulation of Mutual Funds and Other Investment Companies   The Commission registers investment companies and regulates their activities to protect investors. The regulation covers sales load, management contracts, composition of boards of directors, and capital structure. The Commission must also determine the fairness of various transactions of investment companies before they actually occur.

The Commission may institute court action to enjoin the consummation of mergers and other plans of reorganization of investment companies if such plans are unfair to securities holders. It may impose sanctions by administrative proceedings against investment company management for violations of the act and other Federal securities laws. It also may file court actions to enjoin acts and practices of management officials involving breaches of fiduciary duty and personal misconduct and to disqualify such officials from office.

Regulation of Securities Markets   The Securities Exchange Act of 1934 assigns to the Commission broad regulatory responsibilities over the securities markets, the self-regulatory organizations within the securities industry, and persons conducting a business in securities. Persons who execute transactions in securities generally are required to register with the Commission as broker-dealers. Securities exchanges and certain clearing agencies are required to register with the Commission, and associations of brokers or dealers are permitted to register with the Commission.

The act also provides for the establishment of the Municipal Securities Rulemaking Board to formulate rules for the municipal securities industry.

The Commission oversees the self-regulatory activities of the national securities exchanges and associations, registered clearing agencies, and the Municipal Securities Rulemaking Board. In addition, the Commission regulates industry professionals, such as securities brokers and dealers, certain municipal securities professionals, Government securities brokers and dealers, and transfer agents.

Rehabilitation of Failing Corporations In cases of corporate reorganization proceedings administered in Federal courts, the Commission may participate as a statutory party. The principal functions of the Commission are to protect the interests of public investors involved in such cases through efforts to ensure their adequate representation and to participate in legal and policy issues that are of concern to public investors generally.

Representation of Debt Securities Holders The Commission safeguards the interests of purchasers of publicly offered debt securities issued pursuant to trust indentures.

Enforcement Activities The Commission's enforcement activities are designed to secure compliance with the Federal securities laws administered by the Commission and the rules and regulations adopted thereunder. These activities include measures to do the following: compel compliance with the disclosure requirements of the registration and other provisions of the relevant acts; prevent fraud and deception in the purchase and sale of securities; obtain court orders enjoining acts and practices that operate as a fraud upon investors or otherwise violate the laws; suspend or revoke the registrations of brokers, dealers, investment companies, and investment advisers who willfully engage in such acts and practices; suspend or bar from association persons associated with brokers, dealers, investment companies, and investment advisers who have violated any provision of the Federal securities laws; and prosecute persons who have engaged in fraudulent activities or other willful violations of those laws.

In addition, attorneys, accountants, and other professionals who violate the securities laws face possible loss of their privilege to practice before the Commission.

To this end, private investigations are conducted into complaints or other indications of securities violations. Established evidence of law violations is used in appropriate administrative proceedings to revoke registration or in actions instituted in Federal courts to restrain or enjoin such activities. Where the evidence tends to establish criminal fraud or other willful violation of the securities laws, the facts are referred to the Attorney General for criminal prosecution of the offenders. The Commission may assist in such prosecutions. https://www.sec.gov/litigation.shtml

Sources of Information

Business Opportunities The Office of Acquisitions' web page features links to help those who seek business opportunities with the SEC. Phone, 202-551-7300. https://www.sec.gov/oacq

Career Opportunities The SEC relies on accountants, attorneys, economists, examiners, industry specialists, information technology specialists, and other professionals to carry out its mission. Applicants must apply for a specific vacancy and complete a process of competitive selection. This process does not apply, however, to attorney vacancies. The Commission runs a college and law school recruitment program that relies on campus visits and student interviews. http://www.sec.gov/careers

For more information, contact the Office of Human Resources. Phone, 202-551-7500. Fax, 202-777-1028. https://www.sec.gov/ohr

Electronic Data Gathering, Analysis, and Retrieval (EDGAR) The EDGAR database provides free public access to corporate information such as prospectuses, registration statements, and quarterly and annual reports. https://www.sec.gov/edgar.shtml

Events A schedule of upcoming SEC meetings, public appearances by SEC officials, and public hearings is available online. http://www.sec.gov/about/upcoming-events.htm

Fast Answers   The SEC maintains a list of the terms for which SEC website visitors search most frequently. https://www.sec.gov/fast-answers

Freedom of Information Act (FOIA)   The Office of Freedom of Information Act Services makes SEC records available to the public to the greatest extent possible under the FOIA. The Office receives nearly 17,000 requests per year for Commission documents and records. For more information, contact the FOIA public service center. Phone, 202-551-7900. Fax, 202-772-9337. https://www.sec.gov/page/foia

Many records—no-action and interpretive letters, public comments on proposed rules, registration statements and reports filed by regulated companies and individuals, SEC decisions and releases, and staff manuals—can be read and printed for free by using the SEC online search feature. An electronic request form is available for obtaining nonpublic records: consumer complaints, records compiled in investigations, and staff comment letters. The SEC will release nonpublic records, except when they are protected by a FOIA exemption. The electronic request form may be used also for obtaining older records that the SEC has not posted on its website—records usually dated before 1996. https://tts.sec.gov/cgi-bin/request_public_docs

Glossary   The Office of Investor Education and Advocacy maintains an online glossary. https://investor.gov/glossary

Investment Adviser Public Disclosure   The SEC provides an online tool to search for an investment adviser firm and to view the registration or reporting form (Form ADV) that the adviser filed. The tool also allows an investor to search for an individual investment adviser representative and to view his or her professional background and conduct. http://www.adviserinfo.sec.gov/IAPD/default.aspx#

Investor Education   The Office of Investor Education and Advocacy offers services to and provides tools for investors. The Office cannot tell an investor how or where to invest money, but it can help him or her invest knowledgeably and avoid fraud. Phone, 800-732-0330. Fax, 202-772-9295. https://www.investor.gov | Email: help@sec.gov

The Office of Investor Education and Advocacy tweets on Twitter. https://twitter.com/SEC_Investor_Ed

The SEC maintains a list of external educational websites. https://www.sec.gov/investor/links.shtml

The SEC maintains a list of investor calculators and tools that are available on external websites. https://www.sec.gov/investor/tools.shtml

Links   The SEC web page "Other Links" contains links to other websites—government and nongovernment—that may be of interest to Internet visitors. https://www.sec.gov/links

Newsroom   The SEC posts press releases, public statements, speeches, testimonies, and webcasts on its website. A subscription form is available online to receive news alerts via email. https://www.sec.gov/news | Email: news@sec.gov

Open Government   The SEC supports the Open Government initiative by promoting the principles of collaboration, participation, and transparency. https://www.sec.gov/open | Email: opengov@sec.gov

Organizational Chart   The SEC's organizational chart is available in Portable Document Format (PDF) for viewing and downloading. https://www.sec.gov/images/secorg.pdf

A text version of the SEC's organizational chart also is available. https://www.sec.gov/about/orgtext.htm

Plain Language   Like other Federal agencies, the SEC must compose documents in plain writing. According to the Plain Writing Act of 2010, writing should be "clear, concise, well-organized" and follow "other best practices appropriate to the subject or field or audience." SEC writers and editors want to know if agency documents and web pages are difficult to understand. Contact them by email to leave a comment or make a suggestion. https://www.sec.gov/plainwriting.shtml | Email: PlainWriting@sec.gov

Publications   SEC publications are available in Chinese, English, and Spanish in Portable Document Format (PDF). https://www.investor.gov/publications-research-studies/publications

Regional Offices   Regional offices can provide investors with information and assist them with complaints. Contact information for the SEC's 11 regional offices is available online. https://www.sec.gov/page/sec-regional-offices

RSS Feeds RSS feeds are an online resource for keeping abreast of the most recent materials posted to the SEC website. https://www.sec.gov/about/secrss.shtml

Site Map The website map allows visitors to look for specific topics or to browse content that aligns with their interests. https://www.sec.gov/sitemap.shtml

Small Business Activities Information for small businesses—information on legal obligations when they sell securities and on financial and other reporting obligations when their securities are traded publicly—is available online. Contact the Office of Small Business Policy for more information. Phone, 202-551-3460. http://www.sec.gov/info/smallbus.shtml

Social Media The SEC maintains a presence on Flickr, LinkedIn, Pinterest, Twitter, and YouTube. https://www.sec.gov/opa/social_media.html

Tips / Complaints Members of the public can inform the SEC of possible violations of U.S. securities laws by completing the online questionnaire. https://www.sec.gov/complaint.shtml

Votes The final votes of SEC Commissioners on decisions, orders, rules and similar actions are posted online. https://www.sec.gov/about/commission-votes.shtml
https://www.sec.gov/contact.shtml

For further information, contact the Office of Public Affairs, Securities and Exchange Commission, 100 F Street NE., Washington, DC 20549. Phone, 202-551-4120. Fax, 202-777-1026.

Selective Service System

National Headquarters, Arlington, VA 22209-2425
Phone, 703-605-4100. Internet, http://www.sss.gov

National Headquarters—Arlington, VA

Director	DONALD M. BENTON
Deputy Director	JOHN P. PRIGMORE
Chief Officers	
Financial	RODERICK R. HUBBARD
Information Security	ANTHONY CLARK
Chief of Staff	WADI A. YAKHOUR
General Counsel	RUDY G. SANCHEZ, JR.
https://www.sss.gov/About/Directors-Biography	
Associate Directors	
Information Technology	ANTHONY CLARK
Operations	CRAIG T. BROWN
Public and Intergovernmental Affairs	MATTHEW H. TITTMANN
Support Services	RODERICK R. HUBBARD
Data Management Center—Palatine, IL	
Manager	NICOLE F. HARRIS
Regional Headquarters	
Directors	
Region I—North Chicago, IL	THOMAS J. KENNEY
Region II—Marietta, GA	CARLOS M. PEREZ
Region III—Denver, CO	JOHN J. WILBER
https://www.sss.gov/About	

The above list of key personnel was updated 7–2019.

The Selective Service System supplies the Armed Forces with manpower in an emergency and operates an Alternative Service Program for men classified as conscientious objectors.

Establishment and Organization

On June 24, President Harry Truman approved the Selective Service Act of 1948, which established the Selective Service System. https://www.loc.gov/rr/frd/Military_Law/Morgan-Papers/Vol-I_PL-759.pdf

The SSS is an independent agency within the executive branch. The President appoints the Director, who is directly responsible to the President. The agency is not part of the Department of Defense. The agency's statement of organization is found in the Code of Federal Regulations (32 CFR 1605). https://www.govinfo.gov/content/pkg/CFR-2018-title32-vol6/pdf/CFR-2018-title32-vol6-part1605.pdf

By the enactment of a later amendment, the original Act became known as the Military Selective Service Act (50 U.S.C. 3801 et seq.). It requires the registration of male U.S. citizens and other male persons who are in the United States. The Act exempts members of the active Armed Forces and nonimmigrant aliens. https://www.sss.gov/About/Agency-Mission/Military-Selective-Service-Act

From 1948 until 1973, men were drafted to fill Armed Forces vacancies that could not be filled through voluntary means. When the authority of induction expired in 1973, the SSS continued and maintained readiness to support the all-volunteer force in case an emergency should require Congress to authorize a resumption of inductions. Registration was suspended early in 1975, and the SSS assumed a standby posture. Beginning in late 1979, efforts were made to upgrade the System's capability for rapid mobilization in an emergency. In the summer of 1980, the registration requirement was reinstated. https://www.sss.gov/About/History-And-Records/Background-Of-Selective-Service

Proclamation 4771 of July 20, 1980 (45 FR 45247), requires, unless exempted by the Military Selective Service Act, male citizens and other males residing in the country born on or after January 1, 1960, and who have attained age 18, but have not attained age 26, to register. A young man may register at a post office within the United States and at a U.S. Embassy or consulate outside the United States. Today, registering online at the SSS's website is also possible. https://www.govinfo.gov/content/pkg/FR-1980-07-03/pdf/FR-1980-07-03.pdf#page=1

Activities

The Selective Service System (SSS) is a proven way to expand the U.S. Armed Forces in a national emergency. The SSS operates at low cost; it ensures that a future draft will be fair and equitable; and it can respond to the Nation's needs for manpower in a timely manner. Registration is the only mission component that is publicly visible during peacetime; however, readiness to respond is crucial. It fosters timeliness, fairness, and the equity that is expected of the agency if it is directed to reestablish conscription.

The Military Selective Service Act imposes liability for training and service in the Armed Forces upon registrants who are ages 18–26, except those who are exempt or deferred. Persons who have been deferred remain liable for training and service until age 35. Aliens are not liable for training and service until they have remained in the United States for more than 1 year. Conscientious objectors who are opposed to all service in the Armed Forces are required to perform civilian work in lieu of induction into the Armed Forces. https://www.sss.gov/About

Readiness   The SSS maintains readiness to manage a conscription program for the U.S. Armed Forces if authorized by Congress and directed by the President. The agency must be ready to execute a national draft lottery, to issue induction orders to those registrants who are selected through the lottery, and to arrange transportation to relocate them to a military entrance processing station for testing and evaluation before induction into military service. The agency also must maintain the ability to operate an alternative service program for the men who request and are granted conscientious objector status.

Three regional headquarters keep the agency connected with its hundreds of part-time employees and thousands of volunteers throughout the country and U.S. Territories. The regional headquarters maintain the SSS's readiness at the grassroots level. They manage the activities of the agency's 56 State directors; conduct training for them, regional field offices, and civilian board members; and ensure that the local and district appeals boards have sufficient numbers of people serving on them. They also directly support the agency's goal of increasing registration compliance through local registration awareness programs.

The board member program relies on uncompensated civilian volunteers who serve as local, district, and national appeals board members. The SSS trains board members to prepare them for adjudicating claims filed by registrants seeking postponements, exemptions, and deferments in accordance with the Military Selective Service Act, the Code of Federal Regulations, and other policies and procedures. Readiness training, operational planning, and policies for the agency are continually updated to reflect changes that may be occurring in real-time.

Registration Registration is a critical component of readiness. The agency is responsible for providing trained and untrained manpower to the Department of Defense in the event of a national emergency. If conscription becomes necessary, the maximum number of eligible men must be registered to assure the public of a fair and equitable lottery and induction process. By registering, male citizens comply with Federal law and remain eligible for student financial aid, job training, and Government employment opportunities. Immigrant men protect their eligibility for U.S. citizenship by being registered.

Data Management Center employees process registrations and operate the agency's database system. If directed by Congress and the President, the SSS's registration database would be used to facilitate the induction of men into the U.S. Armed Forces. The agency's database is constantly maintained to ensure accuracy, accessibility, and network security.

Sources of Information

Alternative Service The "Alternative Service Program" brochure is available online. https://www.sss.gov/Portals/0/PDFs/ASP%20Brochure%20-%20Web.pdf

Annual Reports The SSS posts it annual reports to the U.S. Congress online. https://www.sss.gov/Reports/Annual-Report-to-Congress

Career Opportunities The Selective Service System offers competitive wages, the Thrift Savings Plan with matching funds, health care benefits, paid vacation time, and work-life benefit options that include telework, as well as alternate and flexible work schedules for most positions. https://www.sss.gov/Careers

In 2018, the SSS ranked 26th among 29 small agencies in the Partnership for Public Service's Best Places To Work Agency Rankings. http://bestplacestowork.org/rankings/detail/SS00

Contact Information The SSS posts helpful email addresses and phone numbers for contacting the agency. https://www.sss.gov/About/ContactInformation | Email: information@sss.gov

Facts / Figures Quick facts and figures are available online. https://www.sss.gov/About/Quick-Facts-and-Figures

Forms Frequently requested forms are available online. https://www.sss.gov/Forms

Freedom of Information Act (FOIA) Enacted in 1966, the FOIA took effect on July 4, 1967. The law gives a right to obtain access to Federal agency records to any person, except a fugitive from the law. Some records, or portions of them, are, however, shielded from disclosure by one or more of nine statutory exemptions or by specific harm that disclosure may cause. https://www.sss.gov/Reports/FOIA

The electronic reading room contains documents that the SSS has posted proactively. Before making a FOIA request, search the electronic reading room for relevant records that may be accessible without a formal FOIA request. https://www.sss.gov/Reports/FOIA/FOIA-Electronic-Reading-Room

Frequently Asked Questions (FAQs) The SSS posts answers to FAQs. https://www.sss.gov/QA

Newsletter   The SSS posts its quarterly newsletter "The Register" online. https://www.sss.gov/Public-Affairs/The-Register-Newsletter

Noncitizens / Dual Nationals   U.S. noncitizens and dual nationals are required by law to register with the SSS. More information is available on the "Non-Citizens and Dual Nationals" web page. https://www.sss.gov/About/History-And-Records/Non-Citizens-and-Dual-Nationals

Performance / Accountability   The agency's performance and accountability reports are available online. https://www.sss.gov/Reports/Financial-Reports/Performance-Accountability-Report

Plain Language   The Selective Service System adheres to Federal plain language guidelines. If a document or web page contains poorly written prose or is difficult to understand, contact the agency by email. https://www.sss.gov/Reports-and-Notices/Plain-Language | Email: Information@sss.gov

Registration   Men, age 18–25, with a valid social security number, may register online using an electronic form. A fillable registration form that can be returned by mail is also available for immigrant males (documented or undocumented), for men who cannot use the online registration form because of a faulty social security number, and for men without a social security number. https://www.sss.gov/Home/Registration

Registration resources that have been adapted for various audiences and made suitable for blogs, websites, and electronic and print newsletters, are available on the agency's website. https://www.sss.gov/Resources/Resources

Return to the Draft   Learn how the SSS would conduct a return to the draft. https://www.sss.gov/About/Events-after-Draft

Social Media   The SSS has a Facebook account. https://www.facebook.com/SSSregistration?ref=ts&fref=ts

The SSS tweets announcements and other newsworthy items on Twitter. https://twitter.com/SSS_gov

The SSS posts videos on its YouTube channel. https://www.youtube.com/user/SelectiveServ?feature=watch

Women   Women are not required to register with the SSS. To learn the reasons for their exemption, visit the "Women and the Draft" web page. https://www.sss.gov/Registration/Women-And-Draft

The Sources of Information were updated 7–2019.

Small Business Administration

409 Third Street SW., Washington, DC 20416
Phone, 202-205-6600. Fax, 202-205-7064. Internet, http://www.sba.gov

SBA Headquarters

Administrator	Christopher M. Pilkerton, Acting
Deputy Administrator	(vacancy)
Chief Counsel	Major Clark, Acting
Senior Advisor	Patricia Gibson
https://www.sba.gov/person/chris-pilkerton	
Associate Administrators	
Capital Access	William Manger
Communications and Public Liaison	Jimmy F. Billimoria
Congressional and Legislative Affairs	Michael Hershey
Disaster Assistance	James Rivera
Entrepreneurial Development	Allen Gutierrez
Field Operations	Michael Vallante, Acting
Government Contracting and Business Development	Robb Wong
International Trade	David M. Glaccum
Investment and Innovation	Joseph Shepard

Small Business Development Centers   GEORGE KOKLANARIS
Veterans Business Development   LARRY STUBBLEFIELD

Assistant Administrator
Hearings and Appeals   DELORICE PRICE FORD

Chief Officers
Financial   DORRICE ROTH
Information   MARIA A. ROAT
Operating   (VACANCY)

General Counsel   CHRISTOPHER M. PILKERTON
National Ombudsman   STEFANIE WEHAGEN
https://www.sba.gov/about-sba/organization/sba-leadership

Regional Administrators

Regions
I   WENDELL G. DAVIS
II   STEVE BULGER
III   MICHELLE CHRISTIAN
IV   ASHLEY DANIEL BELL
V   ROBERT SCOTT
VI   JUSTIN CROSSIE
VII   THOMAS SALISBURY
VIII   DANIEL NORDBERG
IX   MICHAEL VALLANTE
X   JEREMY FIELD
https://www.sba.gov/local-assistance/find/?type=SBA%20
    Regional%20Office&pageNumber=1

Office of Inspector General
Inspector General   H. MIKE WARE
https://www.sba.gov/content/hannibal-mike-ware

The above list of key personnel was updated 6–2019.

The Small Business Administration aids, assists, and counsels entrepreneurs and protects their business interests; preserves free and competitive enterprise; and maintains and strengthens the overall economy.

Establishment and Organization

On July 30, 1953, President Dwight D. Eisenhower approved Public Law 83–163, which is also cited as the "Small Business Act of 1953." This Act created the Small Business Administration (SBA), whose present existence and authority are derived from the Small Business Act (15 U.S.C. 631 et seq.) and the Small Business Investment Act of 1958 (15 U.S.C. 661). https://www.govinfo.gov/content/pkg/STATUTE-67/pdf/STATUTE-67-Pg230.pdf

For the SBA statement of organization, see the Code of Federal Regulations, Title 13, Part 101. https://www.ecfr.gov/cgi-bin/text-idx?SID=d38ae405ec8120025c2a65388e249f57&mc=true&node=pt13.1.101&rgn=div5

The SBA included an organizational chart in its "Agency Financial Report—Fiscal Year 2018" on page 12. https://www.sba.gov/sites/default/files/2018-11/SBA%20FY%202018%20AFR.pdf

Activities

Advocacy   The Office of Advocacy (OA) promotes the views and elevates the concerns of small business before Congress, White House officials, representatives of Federal agencies, Federal court judges, and policymakers on the State level. Within the Federal government, the OA speaks independently on behalf of small business and is the source of small business statistics. The OA also has watchdog responsibilities, ensuring that small business receives the support and consideration that the "Regulatory Flexibility Act of 1980" (Public Law 96–354), as amended, provides. https://advocacy.sba.gov | Email: advocacy@sba.gov

For further information, contact the Office of Advocacy. Phone, 202-205-6533.

Bonding for Contractors   The Surety Bond Guarantee program helps small and emerging contractors obtain the bonding necessary for bidding on and receiving non-Federal contracts up to $6.5 million and Federal contracts up to $10 million. The SBA guarantees bonds that participating surety companies issue and reimburses between 70–90 percent of losses and expenses incurred should a business default on the contract. Construction, service, and supply contractors are eligible for the program if they meet certain standards. https://www.sba.gov/funding-programs/surety-bonds

For further information, contact the Office of Surety Guarantees. Phone, 202-205-6540.

Business Development   The Office of Business Development (OBD) oversees the 8(a) Business Development program. The Office assists with contracts and loans, counsels, expands access to capital and credit, gives technical guidance, and offers training workshops. Eligible 8(a) program participants may receive Federal surplus property on a priority basis. One of the OBD's principal development tools is the Mentor-Protégé program, which allows participants to benefit from business development assistance provided by successful companies. https://www.sba.gov/offices/headquarters/obd/resources

For further information, contact the Office of Business Development. Phone, 202-205-5852.

Capital Access   The Office of the Associate Administrator for Capital Access increases the availability of capital through banks and other lending partners. It oversees SBA programs that help small businesses gain access to capital. These programs include the 7(a) general business guarantee, 504 Certified Development Company, SBA surety bond guarantee, and microlending. https://www.sba.gov/offices/headquarters/oca

For further information, contact the Office of Capital Access. Phone, 202-205-6657.

Disaster Assistance   The SBA serves as the Federal disaster bank for nonfarm, private sector losses. It lends money to disaster survivors for repairing or replacing their most damaged property. The agency makes direct loans with subsidized interest rates to individuals, homeowners, businesses of all sizes, and nonprofit organizations. https://www.sba.gov/content/disaster-assistance | Email: disastercustomerservice@sba.gov

For further information, contact the Office of Disaster Assistance. Phone, 202-205-6734.

Field Operations   The Office of Field Operations is responsible for the provision of SBA services and availability of its products: It serves as the critical link between SBA policymakers and businessmen and women who operate small businesses. The Office provides policy guidance and oversight to regional administrators and district directors for achieving agency goals and objectives and for solving problems in specific operational areas. It plays a liaison role and expedites issues for the regional and district offices when dealing with the central office, coordinating the presentation of views from the field. It also establishes and monitors district performance goals and organizes reviews of the field offices. https://www.sba.gov/about-sba/sba-locations

For further information, contact the Office of Field Operations. Phone, 202-205-6808.

Financial Assistance   The SBA does not lend money directly to owners of small businesses, but it supports lenders in their efforts to make loans to them. The SBA sets guidelines for loans made by lending partners, community development organizations, and micro-lending institutions. The SBA reduces the risk of lending and makes it easier for lenders to access capital, which allows owners and operators of small business to receive loans more easily. The SBA gives its guarantee to lending institutions and certified development companies that make loans to small businesses. Small businesses use the borrowed money for working capital and financing the acquisition of land and buildings, for constructing new and improving existing facilities, and for purchasing equipment and machinery. https://www.sba.gov/funding-programs/loans

For further information, contact the nearest Small Business Administration district office.

Government Contracting   Through various programs and services, the SBA assists small businesses—including HUBZone certified firms and disadvantaged, women-owned, and service-disabled veteran-owned small businesses—with receiving Government procurement. The contracting liaison helps small-scale entrepreneurs secure an equitable share of the natural resources that the Federal Government sells. The Administration also works with the Office of Management and Budget and other Federal agencies to establish policy and regulations affecting small business access to Government contracts. https://www.sba.gov/category/navigation-structure/contracting

For further information, contact the nearest Office of Government Contracting. Phone, 202-205-6460.

Historically Underutilized Business Zone Development   The Historically Underutilized Business Zone (HUBZone) program was part of the Small Business Reauthorization Act of 1997. The program fosters economic development and employment in HUBZones, which include Indian reservations, through the establishment of preferences. The program provides greater access to Federal contracting opportunities for qualified businesses. The SBA regulates and implements the program, determining which businesses are eligible to receive contracts, maintaining a list of qualified businesses that Federal agencies may use for locating vendors, adjudicating protests of eligibility, and reporting to the Congress on the program's effect on employment and investment. https://www.sba.gov/content/understanding-hubzone-program | Email: HUBZone@sba.gov

For further information, contact the HUBZone Help Desk. Phone, 202-205-8885.

International Trade   The Office of International Trade (OIT) makes American small businesses more competitive worldwide by developing international trade opportunities for them. It collaborates with other Federal agencies and with public and private sector groups to promote the exports of small businesses and to help entrepreneurs who seek export opportunities. Through 21 U.S. Export Assistance Centers, SBA district offices, and service-provider partners, the OIT coordinates and directs the Administration's export initiatives. https://www.sba.gov/offices/headquarters/oit

For further information, contact the Office of International Trade. Phone, 202-205-6720.

Local Assistance   The SBA supports business centers for women (WBCs), business outreach centers for veterans (VBOCs), small-business development centers (SBDCs), and the Service Corps of Retired Executives (SCORE). These programs and others help the SBA further its reach beyond the regional, to the local level. https://www.sba.gov/local-assistance

For further information, contact the Small Business Administration. Phone, 202-205-6600.

Native American Affairs   The Office of Native American Affairs assists and encourages the creation, development, and expansion of small businesses that Native Americans own. It develops and implements initiatives designed to address specific business challenges encountered by Native American entrepreneurs. https://www.sba.gov/offices/headquarters/naa

For further information, contact the Office of Native American Affairs. Phone, 202-205-7364.

Regulatory Fairness   Congress established the National Ombudsman and 10 Regulatory Fairness (RegFair) Boards in 1996 as part of the Small Business Regulatory Enforcement Fairness Act. The National Ombudsman assists owners of small businesses when they experience excessive or unfair Federal regulatory enforcement action. The National Ombudsman receives comments from small businesses and acts as a liaison between them and Federal agencies. These comments are forwarded to the appropriate Federal agencies for review and consideration of the fairness of the enforcement actions. The National Ombudsman sends a copy of an agency's response to the business owner. In some cases, fines are reduced or eliminated and decisions changed in favor of the owner.

Each of the RegFair Boards comprises five volunteer members who are owners, operators, or officers of small enterprises. The SBA Administrator appoints board members for 3-year terms. Each RegFair Board meets at least annually with the Ombudsman, reports to the Ombudsman on substantiated instances of excessive or unfair enforcement, and comments on the annual report to Congress prior to its publication. https://www.sba.gov/ombudsman | Email: ombudsman@sba.gov

For further information, contact the Office of the National Ombudsman. Phone, 888-734-3247.

Research Investment / Technology Transfer   The Office of Investment and Innovation manages the Small Business Investment Research (SBIR) and Small Business Technology Transfer (STTR) programs. Together, they provide billions of dollars each year for small enterprises to participate in federally funded research and development and to cooperate with Government agencies and research institutions and universities. The SBIR and STTR programs stimulate the creation of intellectual property with potential for commercialization and with applications in a broad range of sectors in the Nation's economy. https://www.sba.gov/offices/headquarters/ooi/about-us

For further information, contact the Office of Investment and Innovation. Phone, 202-205-6510.

Small Business Development   The Office of Small Business Development Centers funds, oversees, and supports the nationwide Small Business Development Center (SBDC) network. The SBDC program provides one-stop management assistance to current and prospective owners of small businesses in central and easily accessible branch locations. The program relies on the cooperation of the private sector, the educational community, and Federal, State, and local governments.

The SBDC program delivers up-to-date counseling, technical help, and training in all aspects of managing a small business. Its services include assistance with feasibility studies and with engineering, financial,

marketing, organization, production, and technical challenges. SBDC activities include international trade assistance, procurement assistance, rural development, venture capital information, and technical assistance. https://www.sba.gov/offices/headquarters/osbdc

For further information, contact the Office of Small Business Development Centers. Phone, 202-205-6766.

Venture Capital   The Small Business Investment Company (SBIC) program was created in 1958 to connect venture capital with the needs of startups and expanding small businesses. SBICs are privately owned and managed venture capital funds, which the SBA licenses and regulates. They use their own capital, combined with SBA guaranteed funds, to make equity and debt investments in qualifying small businesses. Fund managers may invest up to 75 percent of total capital in small businesses that have no more than 49 percent of their employees oversees, a tangible net worth of between $6 and $19.5 million, and an aftertax income averaged over the previous 2 years of between $2 and $6.5 million. At least 25 percent of the fund's total capital must be invested in smaller U.S. enterprises that have no more than 49 percent of their employees oversees, a tangible net worth of less than $6 million, and an aftertax income averaged over the previous 2 years of less than $2 million. https://www.sba.gov/partners/sbics/apply-be-sbic#section-header-6 | Email: askSBIC@sba.gov

For further information, contact the Investment Division. Phone, 202-205-6510.

Veterans Business Development   The Office of Veterans Business Development (OVBD) formulates, executes, and advances policies and programs that provide assistance to small businesses that veterans own and control. Exclusively promoting veteran entrepreneurship, the OVBD helps veterans, service-disabled veterans, reservists, active-duty servicemembers, transitioning servicemembers, and their dependents or survivors, to avail themselves of all SBA programs and their benefits. The OVBD is involved in each SBA program, ensuring that veterans receive special consideration in each program's operation. The Veterans Business

Outreach Program is an OVBD initiative that oversees Veterans Business Outreach Centers nationwide. https://www.sba.gov/content/veteran-service-disabled-veteran-owned

For further information, contact the Office of Veterans Business Development. Phone, 202-205-6773.

Women's Business Empowerment The Office of Women's Business Ownership (OWBO) enables and empowers female entrepreneurs through advocacy, education, outreach, and support. OWBO programs provide business training and counseling, access to credit and capital, and marketing opportunities, including Federal contracts. The Women's Business Center (WBC) program offers SBA services in almost every State. A WBC tailors its services according to the needs of its individual community. Each WBC provides training in finance, management, marketing, and the Internet, as well as offering access to all financial and procurement assistance programs of the SBA. https://www.sba.gov/offices/headquarters/wbo | Email: owbo@sba.gov

For further information, contact the Women's Business Ownership representative in your SBA district office. Phone, 202-205-6673.

Sources of Information

Blog The SBA blog offers information, news, and perspectives that deal with doing business on a small scale. https://www.sba.gov/blogs

Business Opportunities Information on selling to the Government and qualifying for Government contracts is available online. The SBA also provides online resources for small businesses and posts information on Government contracting programs on its Web site. https://www.sba.gov/contracting

Career Opportunities To carry out its mission, the SBA relies on professionals who are culturally astute, have strong communication and presentation skills, can write effectively, and posses technological proficiency. https://www.sba.gov/about-sba/sba-team/jobs-sba

In 2018, the SBA ranked 20th among 27 midsize agencies in the Partnership for Public Service's Best Places To Work Agency Rankings. http://bestplacestowork.org/BPTW/rankings/detail/SB00

Climate / Sustainability The SBA's Strategic Sustainability Performance Plan (effective, 30 June 2017) presents a blueprint and a framework for the agency to carry out its mission in a way that helps the biosphere and demonstrates a commitment to the creation of a clean energy economy The plan addresses reducing greenhouse gases, pollution, waste, and water use. It also discusses strategies, targets, and metrics for climate change adaptation and resilience planning. https://www.sba.gov/document/support--strategic-sustainability-performance-plan

Contact Information Email addresses and phone numbers are available on the "Contact the SBA" web page (and on the "SBA Locations" web page). https://www.sba.gov/about-sba/organization/contact-sba?interiorpage2015

The SBA public affairs team responds to questions from the media and general public, arranges interviews with appropriate program staff, and provides referrals and other information. To find an SBA local or regional spokesperson, visit the "Regional and Local Media" web page. https://www.sba.gov/about-sba/sba-newsroom/regional-local-media

The Press Office team's contact information is available on the "Press Office Contacts" web page. That team includes staff from the Office of Communications and Public Liaison, Office of Advocacy, Office of Inspector General, and the Freedom of Information Act Office. https://www.sba.gov/about-sba/sba-newsroom/press-office-contacts

Events The "Find Events" page lists upcoming SBA events nationwide. https://www.sba.gov/events/find/?dateRange=all&distance=200&pageNumber=1

Glossary The SBA maintains an online glossary. https://www.sba.gov/offices/headquarters/obd/resources/13240

Freedom of Information Act (FOIA) Enacted in 1966, the FOIA took effect on July 4, 1967. The statute makes all existing Federal Government records available to the public; however, a record may be shielded from disclosure by one or more of nine exemptions or by specific harm that its disclosure may cause. Any person, except a fugitive from the law, has a right to request access to Federal agency records. https://www.sba.gov/about-sba/sba-performance/open-government/foia | Email: FOIA@sba.gov

Introduction to the SBA   A short video explaining the SBA's principal services is available online. https://www.sba.gov/videos/introduction-sba?interiorpage2015

Learning Center   The SBA offers online courses to help entrepreneurs start and run businesses. https://www.sba.gov/learning-center

Locations   The "SBA Locations" page helps visitors find contact and other information for disaster offices, district offices, headquarters offices, regional offices, and loan and guaranty centers. https://www.sba.gov/about-sba/sba-locations

Newsroom   The SBA newsroom features congressional testimonies, disaster press releases, media advisories and other press releases, speeches, and weekly lending reports. https://www.sba.gov/about-sba/sba-newsroom

Open Data   The SBA makes data resources and application programming interfaces (APIs) available to the public. The "Open Data Sources" web page lists all the SBA datasets that the general public can access. https://www.sba.gov/about-sba/sba-performance/open-government/digital-sba/open-data/open-data-sources

Open Government   The SBA supports the Open Government initiative by promoting the principles of collaboration, participation, and transparency. https://www.sba.gov/about-sba/sba-performance/open-government

Plain Language   SBA writers and editors are committed to communicating in plain language. If a document or web pages lacks clarity or is difficult to understand, contact the SBA by email. https://www.sba.gov/about-sba/sba-performance/open-government/other-plans-reports/plain-language-page | Email: plain.language@sba.gov

Resource Guide   The Winter 2019 edition of the "Small Business Resource Guide" is available online in Portable Document Format (PDF). https://www.sba.gov/about-sba/what-we-do/resource-guides

Site Map   The Web site map allows visitors to look for specific topics or to browse content that aligns with their interests. https://www.sba.gov/sitemap

Social Media   The SBA maintains social media accounts on Facebook, Instagram, LinkedIn, Twitter, and YouTube. https://www.sba.gov/about-sba/open-government/about-sbagov-website/social-media

Videos   The SBA has a collection of online videos. The collection includes a 2-minute video series and other videos that are grouped by topic: financing, Government contracting, managing a business, marketing, and starting a business. https://www.sba.gov/videos

The Sources of Information were updated 6–2019.

Social Security Administration

6401 Security Boulevard, Baltimore, MD 21235
Phone, 410-965-1234 / 800-772-1213. 800-325-0778 (TTY). Internet, http://www.socialsecurity.gov

Commissioner	Nancy A. Berryhill, Acting
Deputy Commissioner	(vacancy)
Chief of Staff	Beatrice M. Disman, Acting
Counselor to the Commissioner	(vacancy)
Director, Equal Employment Opportunity	Claudia J. Postell, Acting
Executive Secretary	Darlynda K. Bogle
https://www.ssa.gov/org/coss.htm	
Offices	
Chief Actuary	Stephen C. Goss
General Counsel	Asheesh Agarwal

Deputy Commissioners	
Analytics, Review, and Oversight	Patricia A. Jonas
Budget, Finance, Quality, and Management	Michelle A. King
Communications	James C. Borland, Acting
Hearings Operations	Theresa L. Gruber
Human Resources	Marianna LaCanfora
Legislation and Congressional Affairs	Royce B. Min, Acting
Operations	Mary L. Horne, Acting
Retirement and Disability Policy	Mark J. Warshawsky
Systems / Chief Information Officer	Rajive K. Mathur
https://www.ssa.gov/org/ssachart_access.pdf	
Inspector General	Gale S. Stone, Acting
http://oig.ssa.gov	

[For the Social Security Administration statement of organization, see the Code of Federal Regulations, Title 20, Part 422]

The above list of key personnel was updated 02–2018.

The Social Security Administration manages the retirement, survivors, and disability insurance programs that are known as Social Security; it administers the Supplemental Security Income program for the aged, blind, and disabled; and it assigns Social Security numbers to U.S. citizens and maintains earnings records based on those numbers.

The Social Security Administration (SSA) was established by Reorganization Plan No. 2 of 1946 (5 U.S.C. app.), effective July 16, 1946. It became an independent agency in the executive branch by the Social Security Independence and Program Improvements Act of 1994 (42 U.S.C. 901), effective March 31, 1995. https://www.ssa.gov/history

The SSA is headed by a Commissioner whom the President appoints with the advice and consent of the Senate.

The Deputy Commissioner assists in administering the programs necessary to accomplish the Administration's mission. The Deputy Commissioner performs duties that the Commissioner, Chief Financial Officer, Chief Information Officer, General Counsel, Chief Actuary, and Inspector General assign or delegate to him or her. https://www.ssa.gov/OP_Home/ssact/title07/0702.htm

The Administration's operations are decentralized to provide local services. Each of the 10 SSA regions has a network of field offices and call centers. These offices and centers provide liaison between the SSA and public. The Administration operates 10 regional offices, approximately 1,230 field offices, 33 teleservice centers, 15 Social Security card centers, 6 processing centers, and 2 additional processing centers in its central office. https://www.ssa.gov/org/index.htm

Activities

Black Lung By agreement with the Department of Labor, the SSA assists in the administration of the black lung benefits provisions of the Federal Coal Mine Health and Safety Act of 1969, as amended (30 U.S.C. 901). https://www.ssa.gov/OP_Home/rulings/di/09/SSR73-24-di-09.html

Hearings and Appeals The SSA administers a nationwide hearings and appeals program that offers a way for those who are dissatisfied with determinations affecting their rights to and amounts of benefits or their participation in programs to seek remedy through the Social Security Act. The act allows for administrative appeals of these determinations in accordance with the requirements of the Administrative Procedure and Social Security Acts. The SSA operates approximately 166 hearing offices, including 2 satellite offices; 5 national hearing centers; and 4 national case assistance centers within in its 10 administrative regions. http://www.ssa.gov/appeals/about_odar.html

Social Security Administration

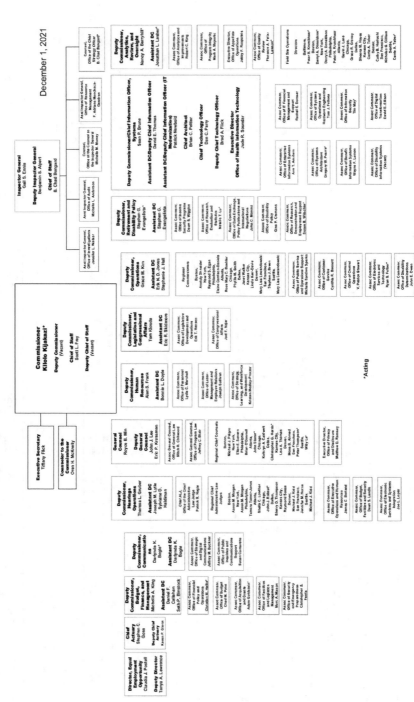

December 1, 2021

*Acting

Medicare While the administration of Medicare is the responsibility of the Centers for Medicare and Medicaid Services, the SSA provides Medicare assistance to the public through SSA field offices and call centers. It adjudicates requests for hearings and appeals of Medicare claims. http://www.ssa.gov/medicare

Old-Age, Survivors, and Disability Insurance The SSA administers social insurance programs that provide monthly benefits to retired and disabled workers, to their spouses and children, and to survivors of insured workers. Financing is under a system of contributory social insurance, whereby employees, employers, and the self-employed pay contributions that are pooled in special trust funds. When earnings stop or decrease because the worker retires, dies, or becomes disabled, monthly cash benefits are paid to supplement the family's reduced income. https://faq.ssa.gov/ics/support/splash.asp

Supplemental Security Income The SSA administers this needs-based program for the aged, blind, and disabled. A basic Federal monthly payment is financed by general revenue, rather than from a special trust fund. Some States, choosing to provide payments to supplement the benefits, have agreements with the Administration under which it administers the supplemental payments for those States. http://www.ssa.gov/disabilityssi/ssi.html

Sources of Information

Business Opportunities The Office of Acquisition and Grants serves as the SSA's principal procurement office. http://www.ssa.gov/oag

Career Opportunities The SSA offers opportunities for various career paths: acquisitions, contracts, and grants; administrative support; facilities and physical security; finance and accounting; human resources; information technology; law enforcement; legal; and public contact. http://www.ssa.gov/careers

In 2017, the SSA ranked 12th among 18 large agencies in the Partnership for Public Service's Best Places To Work Agency Rankings. http://bestplacestowork.org/BPTW/rankings/detail/SZ00

Fraud Hotline The Office of the Inspector General (OIG) operates a toll-free hotline, 10 a.m.–4 p.m., eastern standard time, for reporting allegations of abuse, fraud, and waste affecting SSA programs and operations. Phone, 800-269-0271. TTY, 866-501-2101. Fax, 410-597-0118. https://oig.ssa.gov/report-fraud-waste-or-abuse

An online form also is available to file a report. https://www.ssa.gov/fraudreport/oig/public_fraud_reporting/form.htm

Freedom of Information Act (FOIA) An online guide discusses important FOIA-related topics: how to request information and records, information that the SSA cannot disclose, and the fees associated with making a request. https://www.ssa.gov/foia

Frequently Asked Questions (FAQs) The SSA posts answers to FAQs and offers information on popular help-topics. https://faq.ssa.gov/ics/support/default.asp?deptID=34019&_referrer=https://www.ssa.gov/ask

Glossary A glossary of Social Security terms is available online. https://www.ssa.gov/agency/glossary

History In 1795, the unflagging colonial and revolutionary pamphleteer Thomas Paine wrote about Americans entering adulthood and their welfare in retirement. To the new Republic, he issued a challenge: Establish a public system of economic security that would give a one-time stipend to each citizen upon attaining age 21, as well as annual benefits starting at age 50. To learn more about this patriot's bold proposal, see the "Historical Background and Development of Social Security" web page. https://www.ssa.gov/history/briefhistory3.html

Multilanguage Gateway The SSA tries to eliminate or reduce, as much as possible, barriers of language that impede the delivery of its services. Social Security information is available on the SSA website in the following languages: American Sign Language, Arabic, Armenian, Chinese, Farsi, French, Greek, Haitian Creole, Hmong, Italian, Korean, Polish, Portuguese, Russian, Somali, Spanish, Tagalog, and Vietnamese. The SSA provides free interpreter services for conducting Social Security-related business. https://www.ssa.gov/multilanguage

News   The SSA posts press releases online. https://www.ssa.gov/news/press/releases
   An online newsletter also is available. https://www.ssa.gov/news/newsletter

Online Services   The SSA offers a growing number of services electronically through its website. https://www.ssa.gov/onlineservices

Open Government   The SSA supports the Open Government initiative to create a more open and transparent Government by promoting the principles of collaboration, participation, and transparency. https://www.ssa.gov/open | Email: open.government@ssa.gov

Organizational Chart   The SSA's organizational chart is available in Portable Document Format (PDF) for viewing and downloading. https://www.ssa.gov/org/ssachart.pdf

Plain Language   The Plain Writing Act of 2010 requires Federal agencies to communicate in a manner that the public can understand and use. SSA writers and editors welcome suggestions for improving agency forms, notices, pamphlets, or pages from its website. https://www.ssa.gov/agency/plain-language | Email: PlainWriting@ssa.gov

Publications   Many SSA publications in English, Spanish, and other languages are accessible online. http://www.socialsecurity.gov/pubs

Site Map   The website map allows visitors to look for specific topics or to browse content that aligns with their interests. https://www.ssa.gov/sitemap.htm

Speakers   Under certain circumstances, the SSA can provide a speaker free of charge, generally available during business hours, to explain benefits, programs, and services. An online form is available to initiate a request. http://www.ssa.gov/agency/ask-for-a-speaker.html https://www.ssa.gov/agency/contact | Email: OPI.Policy.Coordination@ssa.gov

For further information, contact the Office of Public Inquiries, Social Security Administration, 6401 Security Boulevard, 1106 West High Rise Building, Baltimore, MD 21235. Phone, 410-965-0709. Fax, 410-965-0695.

Surface Transportation Board

395 E Street SW., Washington, DC 20423
Phone, 202-245-0245. Internet, http://www.stb.gov/stb/index.html

Board

Chair	Martin J. Oberman
Vice Chair	Robert E. Primus
Members	Ann D. Begeman
	Patrick J. Fuchs
	Michelle A. Schultz

https://www.stb.gov/about-stb/board-members

Office Directors

Economics	William J. Brennan
Environmental Analysis	Danielle Gosselin, Acting
Management	Rachel D. Campbell
Proceedings	Scott Zimmerman, Acting
Public Assistance, Governmental Affairs, and Compliance	Michael Higgins, Acting
	Jannie Sheng, Acting
Chief Economist	William J. Brennan
Equal Employment Opportunity	Camella Woodham
General Counsel	Craig Keats

https://www.stb.gov/about-stb/offices

The above list of key personnel was updated 11–2021.

The Surface Transportation Board adjudicates and resolves railroad rate and service disputes and reviews proposals for railroad mergers.

The Surface Transportation Board (STB) is the successor agency to the Interstate Commerce Commission (ICC), which was created in 1887. The ICC Termination Act of 1995 established the STB as an independent adjudicatory body within the Department of Transportation. It remained administratively aligned with the Department for nearly two decades. On December 18, 2015, the Surface Transportation Board Reauthorization Act of 2015 established the STB as a wholly independent Federal agency (49 USC 1301 et seq.). https://www.stb.gov/about-stb

The STB comprises five members, whom the President appoints and the Senate confirms for 5-year terms. The President also designates one of the members to serve as the Board's chair. https://www.stb.gov/about-stb/board-members

The STB posts its organizational chart at the bottom of the "Offices" web page. https://www.stb.gov/about-stb/offices

Activities

The STB adjudicates disputes and regulates interstate surface transportation through various laws governing the different modes of surface transportation. Its general responsibilities include the oversight of firms engaged in interstate and foreign commercial transportation—to the extent that it takes place within the United States, or between or among points in the contiguous United States and points in Alaska, Hawaii, or U.S. Territories or possessions. The STB's jurisdiction generally extends over railroad rate and service issues, rail restructuring transactions, including mergers and line abandonments, construction, and sales, and labor matters related thereto; some moving van, trucking, and noncontiguous ocean shipping company rate matters; some intercity passenger bus company financial, operational, and structural matters; and pipeline matters that the Federal Energy Regulatory Commission does not regulate.

The STB promotes substantive and procedural regulatory reform, provides a forum for the resolution of disputes, and facilitates appropriate market-based business transactions. Through rulemakings and case disposition, it develops improved and efficient ways of analyzing problems, reducing costs associated with regulatory oversight, and encouraging private sector negotiations and resolutions.

Sources of Information

Administrative Issuances The STB posts administrative issuances that may apply to or affect the public. https://www.stb.gov/about-stb/administrative-issuances

Agricultural Contracts Rail carriers must file a summary of each contract entered into for the transportation of agricultural products. Beginning with the first quarter of 2008, filed contract summaries are available on the STB's website in Portable Document Format (PDF) and grouped by railroad. https://www.stb.gov/reports-data/agricultural-contract-summaries | Email: rcpa@stb.gov

Archived Records The "Guide to Federal Records in the National Archives of the United States" indicates that Interstate Commerce Commission (ICC) records have been assigned to record group 134. The ICC's successor agency is the STB. https://www.archives.gov/research/guide-fed-records/groups/134.html

Career Opportunities The STB maintains an employment web page. https://www.stb.gov/about-stb/jobs

In 2020, the STB ranked 13th among 29 small Government agencies in the Partnership for Public Service's Best Places To Work Agency Rankings. https://bestplacestowork.org/rankings/detail/?c=TX00

Contact Information The STB's address is 395 E Street SW., Washington, DC 20423. Phone, 202-245-0245. TTY, 800-877-8339. Email: rcpa@stb.gov

Environmental Comments Correspondence and documents that the Office of Environmental Analysis has issued and comments that are part of environmental reviews are accessible online. https://www.

stb.gov/proceedings-actions/environmental-comments

Federal Register   Significant documents and documents that the STB recently published in the Federal Register are accessible online. https://www.federalregister.gov/agencies/surface-transportation-board

Freedom of Information Act (FOIA)   The FOIA provides that a person may request access to Federal agency records or information. The STB must disclose records that any person properly requests in writing. Pursuant, however, to one or more of nine exemptions and three exclusions that the Act contains, a Federal agency may withhold certain records or parts of them. The FOIA applies only to Federal agencies and does not create a right of access to records held by the U.S. Congress, the courts, State or local government agencies, and private entities. https://www.stb.gov/foia | Email: foia.privacy@stb.gov

Glossary   The STB website has a glossary of terms associated with environmental issues. https://www.stb.gov/resources/environmental/environmental-glossary

Historic Preservation   The National Environmental Policy and National Historic Preservation Acts and other Federal environmental laws require the STB to consider the impact of its licensing decisions on historic properties. The Office of Environmental Analysis develops guidance that clarifies the STB's historic preservation review requirements and posts it on the STB's website. https://www.stb.gov/resources/environmental/historic-preservation-overview

Maps   The "Railroad Map Depot" web page has links to railroad maps. The railroad map information is based on publicly available maps and data that government agencies, railroads, and other stakeholders produce.

The Sources of Information were updated 11–2021.

https://www.stb.gov/resources/railroad-map-depot

Moving Companies   A moving company is responsible if it loses or damages a customer's household possessions during the move. The customer may file a claim with the mover to request financial compensation for the loss or damage. If the moving company denies the claim—in whole or in part—the customer may need to file a lawsuit or pursue arbitration to obtain compensation. In this type of situation, the customer may need to hire an attorney. https://www.stb.gov/resources/need-assistance/hhg-moving/hhg-lost-or-damaged-items

News   The STB posts press releases online. https://www.stb.gov/news-communications/latest-news

Open Government   The STB supports the three principles of Open Government: collaboration, participation, and transparency. https://www.stb.gov/about-stb/open-government

Performance / Accountability   Starting with the year 2016, the STB posts these annual reports on its "Strategic Plan and Performance & Accountability Reports" web page. https://www.stb.gov/about-stb/agency-materials/strategic-plan-and-pars

Rail Customer and Public Assistance   The Rail Customer and Public Assistance Program handles questions on rates and other charges, railroad-car supply and service issues, claims for damage, interchange issues, employee complaints, and community concerns. https://www.stb.gov/resources/need-assistance/rcpa

Reports / Data   Information on the economic data, service data, and other materials that the STB collects or prepares is posted online. https://www.stb.gov/reports-data

Tennessee Valley Authority

400 West Summit Hill Drive, Knoxville, TN 37902
Phone, 865-632-2101. Internet, http://www.tva.com

Board of Directors

Chair	(VACANCY)
Directors	KENNETH E. ALLEN
	A.D. FRAZIER, JR.
	WILLIAM B. KILBRIDE
	JOHN L. RYDER
	JEFFREY W. SMITH
	(VACANCY)
	(VACANCY)
	(VACANCY)

https://www.tva.com/About-TVA/Our-Leadership/Board-of-
   Directors

Executive Leadership

President / Chief Executive Officer	JEFFREY J. LYASH
Senior Vice President	SUSAN E. COLLINS
Executive Vice Presidents	JEANNETTE M. MILLS
	SHERRY A. QUIRK
	JOHN M. THOMAS III

Chief Officers

External Relations	JEANNETTE M. MILLS
Financial	JOHN M. THOMAS III
Human Resources	SUSAN E. COLLINS
Nuclear	TIMOTHY RAUSCH
Operating	MICHAEL D. SKAGGS
General Counsel	SHERRY A. QUIRK

https://www.tva.com/About-TVA/Our-Leadership/Executives

Inspector General	RICHARD W. MOORE

http://oig.tva.gov/igmoore.html

The above list of key personnel was updated 8–2020.

The Tennessee Valley Authority conducts a unified program of resource development to advance economic growth in the Tennessee Valley region.

Establishment and Members of the Board

The Tennessee Valley Authority Act of 1933 created the Tennessee Valley Authority (TVA). This act of May 18, 1933 (16 U.S.C. 831-831dd), established the TVA as a wholly owned Government corporation. https://www.tva.com/file_source/TVA/Site%20Content/About%20TVA/TVA_Act.pdf

All functions of this public corporation are vested in its nine-member Board of Directors, whose members the President appoints by the advice and with the consent of the Senate. At least seven of the nine members must be legal residents of the TVA's service area. The Board designates one of its members to serve as the Chair. https://www.tva.com/About-TVA/Our-History

Activities

TVA activities range from economic development and environmental stewardship to electric power production and transmission; to flood control, navigation, and recreation improvement; and to water supply and water quality management.

The TVA's electric power program is financially self-supporting and operates as part of an independent system with the Authority's system of dams on the Tennessee River and its larger tributaries. These dams provide flood regulation on the Tennessee River and contribute to regulation of the lower Ohio and Mississippi Rivers. The system maintains a continuous 9-foot-draft navigation channel for the length of the 650-mile Tennessee River main stream, from Paducah, KY, to Knoxville, TN. The dams harness the power of the rivers to produce electricity. They also provide other benefits, notably outdoor recreation and water supply.

The Authority operates the river management system and provides assistance to State and local governments in reducing local flood problems. It also works with other agencies to encourage full and effective use of the navigable waterway by industry and commerce.

The TVA is the wholesale power supplier for 154 local municipal and cooperative electric systems serving customers in parts of 7 States. It supplies power to 60 industries and Federal installations whose power requirements are large or unusual. Power to meet these demands is supplied from dams, coal-fired powerplants, nuclear powerplants, natural gas combined-cycle powerplants, combustion turbine and diesel installations, solar energy sites, wind turbines, a methane gas facility, and a pumped-storage hydroelectric plant; U.S. Corps of Engineers dams in the Cumberland Valley; and Brookfield Renewable Energy Partners dams, whose operations are coordinated with the TVA's system.

Economic development is at the heart of the TVA's mission of making the Tennessee Valley a better place to live. A healthy economy means quality jobs, more investment in the region, sustainable growth, and opportunities for residents in the southeastern region to build more prosperous lives. TVA economic development takes a regional approach to economic growth by partnering with power distributors and both public and private organizations to attract new investments and quality jobs, supporting retention and growth of existing businesses and industries, preparing communities for leadership and economic growth, and providing financial and technical services. https://www.tva.com/About-TVA

Sources of Information

Archived Records   The "Guide to Federal Records in the National Archives of the United States" indicates that TVA records have been assigned to record group 142. https://www.archives.gov/research/guide-fed-records/groups/142.html

Birdwatching   With birds living in and migrating through the area year-round, TVA lands offer plenty of opportunities for birdwatchers. https://www.tva.com/environment/recreation/birdwatching | Email: plic@tva.gov

Business Opportunities   The TVA partners with power distributors, suppliers, and other individuals and organizations. It seeks business relationships with firms offering reliable products and services at competitive prices. The TVA encourages businessmen and women of diverse backgrounds—minorities, service-disabled-veterans, veterans, as well as small business owners and entrepreneurs in historically underutilized business zones—to learn about available opportunities. For more information, contact Supply Chain, BR 4A–C, 1101 Market Street, Chattanooga, TN 37402. Phone , 423-751-7903. https://www.tva.com/Information/Doing-Business-with-TVA

Career Opportunities   The TVA is a service-oriented agency whose mission covers 86,000 square miles and depends on professionals with expertise in diverse fields. Some of those fields include archaeology, aviation, economics, engineering, environmental law, hydrology, law enforcement, library science, marketing, program management, water quality, and zoology. https://www.tva.com/Careers | Email: careers@tva.gov

In 2019, the Office of Inspector General ranked first among 420 agency subcomponents in the Partnership for Public Service's Best Places To Work Agency Rankings! http://bestplacestowork.org/BPTW/rankings/detail/TV01

Climate Change The "TVA Climate Change Adaptation and Resiliency Plan—2020 Update" is available in Portable Document Format (PDF) for viewing and downloading. https://tva-azr-eastus-cdn-ep-tvawcm-prd.azureedge.net/cdn-tvawcma/docs/default-source/about-tva/guidelines-reports/climate-change-adaptation-plan.pdf?sfvrsn=ea883571_2

Contact Information The TVA benefits from engaged citizens. It encourages comments, feedback, and input. Contact TVA Communications, 400 W. Summit Hill Drive, Knoxville, TN 37902-1499. Phone, 865-632-2101. https://www.tva.gov/About-TVA/Contact-Us | Email: tvainfo@tva.gov

Economic Development TVA Economic Development serves the seven States of the TVA service area—AL, GA, KY, MS, NC, TN, and VA. Through partnerships with other economic development organizations, the TVA fosters capital investment and job growth in its service area. Information is available online, or contact TVA Economic Development, 26 Century Boulevard, Suite 100, Nashville, TN 37214. Phone, 615-232-6051. https://www.tva.com/Economic-Development

Environmental Reviews The TVA conducts environmental reviews to consider the effects of its proposed projects on the human and natural environment before making final decisions. The TVA's environmental projects are open for public review. https://www.tva.com/Environment/Environmental-Stewardship/Environmental-Reviews

Federal Register Documents that the TVA has published in the Federal Register are accessible online. https://www.federalregister.gov/agencies/tennessee-valley-authority

Fishing Tips The TVA helps ambitious fishermen and women meet their numbers. The "Where the Sport Fish Are" page lists the largest populations of Tennessee Valley sport fish and the reservoirs that they inhabit. https://www.tva.com/Environment/Recreation/Where-the-Sport-Fish-Are | Email: plic@tva.gov

Anglers developed the "Angler's Aquatic Plant ID" as a guide for anglers. The online guide contains seasonal tips for fishing near aquatic plants, starting with American Lotus and ending with Southern Naiad. https://www.tva.com/Environment/Environmental-Stewardship/Anglers-Aquatic-Plant-ID

Freedom of Information Act (FOIA) Like all Federal agencies, the TVA is required to disclose records that any person requests in writing. The statute contains, however, nine exemptions and three exclusions that may shield some records or parts of them from disclosure. The TVA operates a FOIA requester service center. Phone, 865-632-6945. https://www.tva.com/Information/Freedom-of-Information | Email: foia@tva.gov

Green Power The Green Power Providers program offers Tennessee Valley homeowners and businessmen and women an opportunity to help the TVA generate clean, renewable energy. Participants in the program agree to install a small-scale renewable energy system on their property, and the TVA pays them for every kilowatt hour generated by that system. https://www.tva.com/Energy/Valley-Renewable-Energy/Green-Power-Providers

Historic Photographs From the earliest days of the TVA, photographers captured images of the agency's work and the cultural changes that followed. The TVA collection contains over 20,000 black-and-white negatives and over 5,000 original file prints. Its images span half a century, from 1933 to 1983. https://www.tva.com/about-tva/our-history

Lake Levels Current information on ecological health ratings, fish population surveys, planned generation releases at the dams, recreation facilities, reservoir operations, today's levels, and predicted elevations for each TVA reservoir is available online. https://www.tva.com/Environment/Lake-Levels

Library Services Visitors may use the TVA Research Library by appointment. Contact the TVA Research Library, 400 W. Summit Hill Drive, Knoxville, TN 37902-1499. Phone, 865-632-3464. https://tva.com/Our-TVA-Story/Nancy-Proctor | Email: corplibknox@tva.gov

Native American Tribes   Native Americans have a cultural and historical interest in the Tennessee Valley. The TVA consults with 21 federally recognized Tribes when it undertakes projects that could affect their cultural sites. https://www.tva.com/environment/environmental-stewardship/land-management/cultural-resource-management/tribal-relations

Newsroom   The TVA posts news stories and press releases online. https://www.tva.com/Newsroom

Oversight   The Office of the Inspector General from the TVA posts reports and data on Oversight.gov, a text-searchable repository of reports that Federal Inspectors General publish. The Council of the Inspectors General on Integrity and Efficiency operates and maintains the website to increase public access to independent and authoritative information on the Federal Government. https://oversight.gov

Public Relations   The TVA Public Relations team is available to help representatives of the media. https://www.tva.com/newsroom/public-relations

The Sources of Information were updated 8–2020.

Site Map   The website map allows visitors to look for specific topics or to browse content that aligns with their interests. https://www.tva.com/Index

Social Media   The TVA has a Facebook account. https://www.facebook.com/TVA

The TVA posts photos and short videos on Instagram. https://www.instagram.com/TVA/

The TVA publishes business-oriented information on LinkedIn. https://www.linkedin.com/company/tva

The TVA tweets announcements and other newsworthy items on Twitter. https://twitter.com/tvanews

The TVA posts videos on its YouTube channel. https://www.youtube.com/user/TVANewsVideo

TVA Kids   The TVA maintains the website tvakids.com, which is a colorful online resource for students and teachers. The site covers topics like green power, making electricity, and saving energy. It also has a section of "Cool Stuff" that includes games, videos, and warnings about energy vampires. https://www.tvakids.com

Trade and Development Agency

1000 Wilson Boulevard, Suite 1600, Arlington, VA 22209-3901
Phone, 703-875-4357. Fax, 703-875-4009. Internet, http://www.ustda.gov

Director	Enoh T. Ebong, Acting
Deputy Director	Enoh T. Ebong
Administrative Officer	Carolyn Hum
Chief of Staff	Vacant
Chief, Office of Acquisition Management	Garth Hibbert
Director, Congressional Affairs and Public Relations	Thomas R. Hardy
Director, Finance	Kathleen Neumann
General Counsel	Kendra Link, Acting
Chief Information Officer	Benjamin Bergersen
Special Advisor to the Director	Clark Jennings

Regional Directors

East Asia	Carl B. Kress
Latin America and Caribbean	Nathan Younge
Middle East, North Africa, Europe and Eurasia	Carl B. Kress
South and Southeast Asia	Henry D. Steingass
Sub-Saharan Africa	Lida Fitts
Director, Global Programs	Andrea Lupo
Director, Office of Program Monitoring and Evaluation	Diana Harbison

Trade and Development Agency

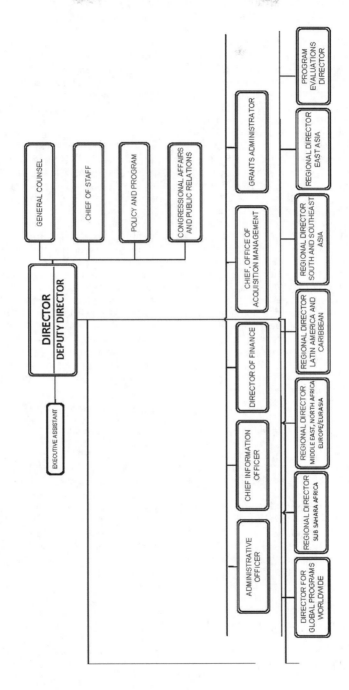

The Trade and Development Agency advances economic development and U.S. commercial interest in developing and middle-income countries.

The Trade and Development Program was established on July 1, 1980, as a component organization of the International Development Cooperation Agency. Section 2204 of the Omnibus Trade and Competitiveness Act of 1988 (22 U.S.C. 2421) made it a separate component agency. The organization was renamed the Trade and Development Agency (USTDA) and made an independent agency within the executive branch of the Federal Government on October 28, 1992, by the Jobs Through Exports Act of 1992 (22 U.S.C. 2421).

The USTDA is a foreign assistance agency that delivers its program commitments through overseas grants and contracts with U.S. firms. The Agency helps companies create U.S. jobs through the export of U.S. goods and services for priority development projects in emerging economies. The Agency links U.S. businesses to export opportunities by funding project planning activities, pilot projects, and reverse trade missions while creating sustainable infrastructure and economic growth in partner countries.

The USTDA provides grant funding to overseas project sponsors for the planning of projects that support the development of modern infrastructure and an open trading system. The hallmark of USTDA development assistance is building partnerships between U.S. companies and overseas project sponsors. These partnerships facilitate the application of proven private sector solutions to developmental challenges.

The Agency works with other U.S. Government agencies to bring their particular expertise and resources to a development objective. These agencies include the Departments of Commerce, Energy, State, Transportation, and the Treasury; Office of the U.S. Trade Representative; Export-Import Bank of the United States; and Overseas Private Investment Corporation. https://www.ustda. gov/about/mission

Activities The USTDA funds various forms of technical assistance, training, early investment analysis, reverse trade missions, and business workshops that support the development of a modern infrastructure and a fair and open trading environment. The Agency works closely with foreign project sponsors and makes its funds available to them for contracting with U.S. businesses. This arrangement gives American firms market entry, exposure, and access to information. It helps them establish positions in markets that are otherwise difficult to penetrate. The USTDA is involved in many sectors, including energy, transportation, and information and communications technologies.

USTDA-funded studies evaluate the technical, economic, and financial aspects of a development project. They provide the host nation with information on the availability of U.S. goods and services. Financial institutions also use these studies for assessing the creditworthiness of an undertaking. Grants are based on an official request for assistance: Either the sponsoring government or a private sector organization in a developing or middle-income nation can make the request. https://www.ustda. gov/program

Sources of Information

Business Opportunities Overseas project sponsors can select U.S. firms to carry out USTDA-funded work through a competitive proposal process that relies on the Federal Business Opportunities Web site (FedBizOpps.gov) or through "sole-source" grants, which allow an overseas project sponsor to identify a U.S. firm as a partner or preferred supplier. More information is available on the "Project Proposals" Web page. https://www.ustda.gov/program/ project-proposals

Employment Job openings and information on internships are posted online. https:// www.ustda.gov/about/career-opportunities https://www.ustda.gov/about/career-opportunities/internships

Freedom of Information Act (FOIA) A FOIA request must be submitted in writing by email, fax, or mail, and clearly identified as a "FOIA REQUEST." Staff is available to answer questions and help formulate a request over the phone; however, the USTDA does not accept phone requests. Mail a request to the FOIA Requester Service Center, U.S. Trade and Development Agency, 1000 Wilson Boulevard, Suite 1600, Arlington, VA 22209-3901. Phone, 703-875-4357. Fax, 703-875-4009. https://www. ustda.gov/about/resources/foia | Email: foia@ ustda.gov

Library The USTDA maintains a collection of reports on infrastructure development projects from emerging economies worldwide. Contact the library by email to obtain a report: Most reports can be sent electronically. These reports are accessible also online. Phone, 703-875-4357. https:// www.ustda.gov/ustda-library | Email: library@ustda.gov

Newsletter To provide timely information on Agency supported activities, the USTDA distributes an electronic newsletter containing business opportunities, events, and updates. A subscription form is available online. https://www.ustda.gov/connect/subscribe-ustda-news-and-alerts

Regional Programs The USTDA is organized into five international regions. Information on each region is available on the Agency's Web site. Questions should be addressed to the appropriate regional director or country manager. Phone, 703-875-4357. http://www.ustda.gov/program/regions/index.asp; https://www.ustda.gov/about/contact | Email: info@ustda.gov

For further information, contact the U.S. Trade and Development Agency, 1000 Wilson Boulevard, Suite 1600, Arlington, VA 22209-3901. Phone, 703-875-4357. Fax, 703-875-4009.

United States African Development Foundation

330 Independence Avenue SW., Washington, DC 20237
Phone, 202-203-4545. Internet, http://www.usagm.gov

Board of Directors

Chair	John W. Leslie, Jr.
Vice Chair	John O. Agwunobi
Members	Ward Brehm
	Morgan M. Davis
	Iqbal Paroo
	(vacancy)
	(vacancy)

http://www.usadf.gov/board-of-directors

Staff

President / Chief Executive Officer	Travis Adkins
Chief of Staff / Director of External Affairs	Brandi James

Chief Officers

Program	Elisabeth Feleke
Strategy	Kwasi Donkor
General Counsel	Mateo Dunne
Managing Director of Finance and Administration	Mathieu Zahui

https://www.usadf.gov/leaderships

The above list of key personnel was updated 02–2022.

The United States African Development Foundation provides seed capital and technical assistance to support African-led development that grows community enterprises.

Establishment and Organization

On December 16, 1980, President James E. Carter approved Public Law 96–533, which contains the "African Development Foundation Act" (94 Stat. 3151). The Act established the United States African Development Foundation (USADF) as a Government corporation with its principal office in the United States and with branch offices, as necessity requires for carrying out its functions, in Africa (94 Stat. 3152, 3153). https://www.govinfo.gov/content/pkg/STATUTE-94/pdf/STATUTE-94-Pg3131.pdf

"To enable the people of African countries to develop their potential, fulfill their aspirations, and enjoy better, more productive lives," the Act described the purposes of the USADF as fourfold: strengthening friendly bonds between Africans and Americans, supporting local self-help activities that enlarge community development opportunities, promoting effective and expansive African participation in their development process, and promoting development institutions that are indigenous to particular African countries and responsive to the requirements of those countries' poor people (94 Stat. 3152).

The management responsibilities of the USADF are vested in seven members who constitute its Board of Directors. The President appoints each of the members by the advice and with the consent of the Senate. The President designates one board member to serve as its Chairperson and another one of the seven to serve as its Vice Chairperson. The President makes his or her appointment based on the appointee's "understanding of and sensitivity to community level development processes." Five of the board members are "appointed from private life"; the two other members are "appointed from among officers and employees of agencies of the United States concerned with African affairs." A member is appointed for a term of 6 years (94 Stat. 3154). https://www.govinfo.gov/content/pkg/STATUTE-94/pdf/STATUTE-94-Pg3131.pdf

The USADF's statement of organization has been assigned to part 1501 of 22 CFR. https://www.ecfr.gov/cgi-bin/text-idx?SID=b295cbf93a8249fce4299d34cd24d414&mc=true&node=pt22.2.1501&rgn=div5

Statutory and Regulatory Authorities

Codified statutory material affecting the USADF has been assigned to the seventh chapter of 22 U.S.C. See "Subchapter XXIII—United States African Development Foundation." https://uscode.house.gov/view.xhtml?path=/prelim@title22/chapter7/subchapter23&edition=prelim

Codified rules and regulations associated with the USADF have been assigned to the 15th chapter of 22 CFR. See "Chapter XV—African Development Foundation" (parts 1500–1599). https://www.ecfr.gov/cgi-bin/text-idx?SID=db2ff5965204ffe475554b1b1daa53a6&mc=true&tpl=/ecfrbrowse/Title22/22chapterXV.tpl

Activities

The USADF invests in African grassroots organizations, entrepreneurs, and small and medium-sized enterprises. The agency's investments promote local economic development by creating jobs, raising incomes, and increasing revenues. These investments also help to empower marginalized populations and underserved communities to leave behind economic insecurity and to reach for stability and prosperity. https://www.usadf.gov/mission

Sources of Information

Agriculture / Food Security Agriculture and food security constitute one of the USADF's key programmatic areas for its transformative programs. https://www.usadf.gov/sectors/2

Archived Records The records of the "African Development Foundation" are referenced in the "Guide to Federal Records in the National Archives of the United States." The guide is accessible online, and USADF records have been assigned to Record Group 487. This record group currently does not have a description because no transfer of archival records had been made before the time of the guide's last update. https://www.archives.gov/research/guide-fed-records/index-numeric/401-to-500.html?_ga=2.185314729.1809565798.1643669212-1043139313.1643669212

Career Opportunities The USADF posts career opportunities on its website. https://www.usadf.gov/career-opportunities

Contact Information The "Contact Us" web page has an electronic form for sending a message. Postal correspondence may be sent to the USADF, 1400 I Street NW., Washington, DC 20005. Phone, 202-233-8800. https://www.usadf.gov/contact-us | Email: info@usadf.gov

Country Portfolios The Foundation has 21 country programs and special initiatives that have extended its reach to a total of 40 African countries. https://www.usadf.gov/countries

Development Model The USADF uses a community-led development approach and a pan-African network of local implementing partners to support African-designed and African-delivered solutions. https://www.usadf.gov/development-model

Entrepreneurship / Job Creation Employment through job training and placement and entrepreneurship grants for women and youth constitute one of the USADF's key programmatic areas for its transformative programs. https://www.usadf.gov/sectors/4

Events The USADF posts information on its events. http://www.usadf.gov/events

Federal Register Recent documents that the USADF published in the Federal Register are accessible online. https://www.federalregister.gov/agencies/african-development-foundation

Freedom of Information Act (FOIA) Information on USADF FOIA policies can be obtained from the agency by using the "Contact Us" web page or by sending an email. https://www.usadf.gov/contact-us | Email: info@usadf.gov

Annual and quarterly FOIA reports are posted on the "Legal Notices and Reports" web page. https://www.usadf.gov/oversight

Frequently Asked Questions (FAQs) The USADF posts answers to FAQs on its website. http://www.usadf.gov/faq

Grants Information on grants is available online. An applicant may download an application in English or French. Once completed, the application may be submitted by email or postal mail. http://www.usadf.gov/apply

History The "Celebrating 40 Years" web page has an annotated timeline that highlights the notable achievements of the past 40 years. https://www.usadf.gov/celebrating-40-years

In the News For news items, see the "USADF in the News" web page. https://www.usadf.gov/usadf-in-the-news

Open Government The USADF supports the Open Government initiative by promoting collaboration, participation, and transparency. https://www.usadf.gov/oversight

Partners The USADF partners with African governments, corporations, foundations, and nongovernmental organizations, as well as with other agencies of the U.S. Government and their initiatives. https://www.usadf.gov/partnerships

Renewable Energy / Energy Access Off the Grid Off-grid renewable energy access is one of the USADF's key programmatic areas for its transformative programs. https://www.usadf.gov/sectors/3

Reports The USADF posted its "Impact Report 2015–2019." The report describes USADF's work and the effects of that work. https://www.usadf.gov/reports

Resources The USADF posts its congressional budget justifications and operating plans. The "Resources" web page also has bar and pie graphs: annual revenues, annual expenditures, and a 5-year revenue source profile. https://www.usadf.gov/resources

Social Media The USADF has a Facebook account. https://www.facebook.com/USADF

The Foundation tweets announcements and other newsworthy items on Twitter. https://twitter.com/USADF

The USADF posts videos on its YouTube channel. https://www.youtube.com/channel/UCvhwYYAN6WGK4rImiWAfEAA

Videos The USADF maintains a large collection of videos on its website. The topics of those videos range from onion farming to transforming the lives of former child soldiers. https://www.usadf.gov/videos

The Sources of Information were updated 02–2022.

United States Agency for Global Media

330 Independence Avenue SW., Washington, DC 20237
Phone, 202-203-4545. Internet, http://www.usagm.gov

Office of the Chief Executive Officer	
Chief Executive Officer	Kelu Chao, Acting
Deputy Director	Brian Conniff
Deputy Director for Operations	Matthew Walsh
Executive Director	H. Oanh Tran
Heads of Offices	
Chief Officers	
Financial	Grant K. Turner
Information	James Reeves
Risk	Nnake Nweke
Strategy	Shawn Powers
Directors	
Congressional Affairs	(vacancy)
Management Services	(vacancy)
Public Affairs	(vacancy)
Technology, Services, and Innovation	P. Terry Balazs
General Counsel	David Kligerman
https://www.usagm.gov/who-we-are/management-team	

Federal Networks

Directors	
Office of Cuba Broadcasting	Sylvia Rosabal
Voice of America	Yolanda Lopez, Acting
Grantee Networks	
Presidents	
Middle East Broadcasting Networks	Kelley Sullivan, Acting
Radio Free Asia	Bay Fang
Radio Free Europe / Radio Liberty	Jamie M. Fly
https://www.usagm.gov/networks	
Open Technology Fund	
President	Laura Cunningham
https://www.opentech.fund/about/people/laura-cunningham	
Office of Inspector General	
Inspector General for the U.S. Department of State	Diana Shaw, Acting
https://www.stateoig.gov/about/IG	

The above list of key personnel was updated 4–2021.

The U.S. Agency for Global Media informs, engages, and connects people around the world in support of freedom and democracy.

Establishment and Organization

On April 30, 1994, President William J. Clinton approved Public Law 103–236, which includes the United States International Broadcasting Act of 1994. The Act "established within the United States Information Agency a Broadcasting Board of Governors." The first Broadcasting Board of Governors (BBG) was sworn in on August

11, 1995. https://www.govinfo.gov/content/pkg/STATUTE-108/pdf/STATUTE-108-Pg382.pdf

Four years later, on October 21, 1998, President Clinton approved Public Law 105–277, which includes the Foreign Affairs Reform and Restructuring Act of 1998 (112 Stat. 2681–761). On October 1, 1999, the BBG became an independent and autonomous entity as a result of the legislation. https://www.govinfo.gov/content/pkg/STATUTE-112/pdf/STATUTE-112-Pg2681.pdf

On December 23, 2016, President Barack H. Obama approved Public Law 114–328, which also is cited as the National Defense Authorization Act for Fiscal Year 2017. Title XII, which is dedicated to matters relating to foreign nations, contains a section that modifies the United States International Broadcasting Act of 1994. The modifications included terminating the position of the Director of the International Broadcasting Bureau and transferring the responsibilities, offices, authorities, and immunities of that position to the Chief Executive Officer of the Broadcasting Board of Governors (130 Stat. 2549). Another modification authorized the agency to rename itself after giving notification to the U.S. Congress of the intended change (130 Stat. 2551). https://www.govinfo.gov/content/pkg/PLAW-114publ328/pdf/PLAW-114publ328.pdf

On August 22, 2018, as part of a modernization effort, the agency changed its name from the BBG to the United States Agency for Global Media (USAGM). The USAGM continued to use the name BBG when referring to its nine-member board until its dissolution in 2020. https://www.usagm.gov/who-we-are/history

The USAGM posts an organizational chart on its website. https://www.usagm.gov/who-we-are/organizational-chart

Statutory and Regulatory Authorities

"Chapter 71—United States International Broadcasting" is assigned to 22 U.S.C. The chapter comprises sections 6201–6216 and contains codified statutory material affecting Radio Free Afghanistan, Radio Free Asia, Radio Free Europe, Radio Free Liberty, and the Chief Executive Officer of the Broadcasting Board of Governors. https://uscode.house.gov/view.xhtml?path=/prelim@title22/chapter71&edition=prelim

"Chapter V—Broadcasting Board of Governors" is assigned to 22 CFR. The chapter comprises parts 500–599 and contains codified regulatory material associated with the agency. https://www.ecfr.gov/cgi-bin/text-idx?SID=44d20bb4bea6e9db09b28364c465d15c&mc=true&tpl=/ecfrbrowse/Title22/22chapterV.tpl

Activities

USAGM broadcast services adhere to the broadcasting standards and principles of the United States International Broadcasting Act of 1994 (108 Stat. 433). https://www.govinfo.gov/content/pkg/STATUTE-108/pdf/STATUTE-108-Pg382.pdf

The statute's principles and standards support reliable, accurate, and comprehensive news; balanced and comprehensive presentations of U.S. thought, institutions, and policies, as well as discussions on those policies; information on developments throughout the world; and a variety of opinions from nations around the world. https://www.usagm.gov/who-we-are

Middle East Broadcasting Networks The Middle East Broadcasting Networks, Inc. (MBN) is a nonprofit news organization that operates Alhurra and Alhurra-Iraq Television, Radio Sawa, and MBN Digital under a grant from the USAGM. Alhurra Television, Radio Sawa, and MBN Digital offer an open line of communication between the people of the Middle East and the United States. These networks deliver accurate information on the United States, its policies, and its people, from a range of perspectives and with an exchange of ideas on relevant issues. They reach an audience of nearly 25 million Arabic-speakers in 22 countries across the Middle East and North Africa. https://www.usagm.gov/networks/mbn

Alhurra TV http://www.alhurra.com

Radio Sawa https://www.radiosawa.com

Office of Cuba Broadcasting The Office of Cuba Broadcasting operates the Martís from its headquarters in Miami, FL. The Martís are a multimedia hub of news, information, and analysis that provides the people of Cuba with interactive programs each day of the week. To broadcast their message, the Martís rely on a combination of high- and low-tech approaches: DVDs, emails, flash drives, Internet, satellite television, shortwave and AM radio, and SMS text. Combined with martinoticias.com, they constitute a unique service that brings accurate information to the Cuban people. https://www.usagm.gov/networks/ocb

Martinoticias http://www.martinoticias.com

Radio Free Asia Radio Free Asia (RFA) is a private nonprofit news organization that operates under a grant from the USAGM. Broadcasting daily in nine languages to Asian audiences whose governments restrict media, RFA delivers award-winning, reliable news and information. It also allows a range of voices and opinions from within Asia to be heard as a demonstration of freedom of expression over the airwaves, on television, and online. Through shortwave, medium wave, satellite and transmission television, social media, and the Internet, RFA broadcasts in Cantonese, Khmer, Korean, Lao, Mandarin, Myanmar, Uyghur, Vietnamese, and in three Tibetan dialects. Headquartered in Washington, DC, it has eight overseas bureaus and a network of correspondents around the world. https://www.usagm.gov/networks/rfa

Radio Free Asia—English https://www.rfa.org/english

Radio Free Europe / Radio Liberty Radio Free Europe/Radio Liberty (RFE/RL) is a private nonprofit multimedia broadcasting corporation whose funding comes from a USAGM grant. It reaches nearly 34 million people in 23 countries—including Afghanistan, Iran, Pakistan, Russia, and Ukraine—in 26 languages. Its journalists provide what many people cannot get locally: uncensored news, responsible discussion, and open debate. RFE/RL uses digital technologies—the Internet, SMS text messaging, online video, satellite radio, and popular social media networks—and conventional broadcast radio to reach people in some of the most closed societies on Earth. With nearly 70 years of surrogate broadcasting experience, it continues to bring diverse, immediate, and interactive content to audiences. https://www.usagm.gov/networks/rferl

Radio Free Europe / Radio Liberty—English https://www.rferl.org

Voice of America The Voice of America (VOA) is a multimedia international broadcasting service funded by the U.S. Government through the USAGM. It began broadcasting in 1942 and now reaches more than 275 million people worldwide. The VOA provides accurate, comprehensive, and trustworthy news and information, as well as informed discussion on the United States and the world. It engages audiences in regions deemed critical to the United States through whatever medium—radio, television, Internet, or digital media—the people of those regions prefer. It broadcasts approximately 1,800 hours of news, information, educational, and cultural programming every week to a global audience. Programs are produced in 46 languages. https://www.usagm.gov/networks/voa

Voice of America—English https://www.voanews.com

Sources of Information

Archived Records The "Guide to Federal Records in the National Archives of the United States" indicates that BBG records have been assigned to record group 517. The BBG is the predecessor agency to the USAGM. See the above "Establishment and Organization" section. Record group 517 does not have a description currently associated with it. https://www.archives.gov/research/guide-fed-records/index-numeric/501-to-600.html

At a Glance The "Who We Are" web page features a 60-second video that captures the essence of USAGM core activities: informing people, engaging them in support of democracy, and connecting with them on a global scale. https://www.usagm.gov/who-we-are

Awards The USAGM has won awards for its productions in a variety of categories: documentary, education, investigative journalism, promotional programming, special reporting, video, and more. https://www.usagm.gov/awards

Business Opportunities Information on contract opportunities and instructions on how to do business with the USAGM are available online. https://www.usagm. gov/who-we-are/partnerwithus/contract-opportunities

Career Opportunities   The USAGM work environment is diverse, multicultural, and professional. In addition to American citizens, the agency also hires non-U.S. citizens for positions that require foreign language skills. Internships are available in the fields of engineering, public affairs, public diplomacy, and research. https:// www.usagm.gov/work-with-us

The USAGM provides training opportunities for reporters and students of media on five continents. https://www. usagm.gov/our-work/media-development

In 2019, the USAGM ranked 23d among 25 midsize agencies in the Partnership for Public Service's Best Places To Work Agency Rankings. https://bestplacestowork.org/rankings/detail/IB00

Climate Change   The USAGM is committed to developing a better understanding of the effects of climate change and to addressing climate change adaptation. https://www. usagm.gov/our-work/strategy-and-results/strategic-priorities/research-reports/strategic-sustainability-performance-plan

The USAGM has provided media training aimed at equipping journalists in the Latin America and the Caribbean region with skills and practices needed to report accurately and effectively on changes in the climate. https://www.usagm.gov/2016/09/29/covering-climate-change

Federal Register   Documents that the USAGM recently published in the Federal Register are accessible online. https://www. federalregister.gov/agencies/united-states-agency-for-global-media

Documents that the BBG published in the Federal Register are accessible online. https://www.federalregister.gov/agencies/broadcasting-board-of-governors

Freedom of Information Act (FOIA)   The FOIA provides a statutory basis for public access to official agency information previously restricted from public view. Through the FOIA, Congress affirmed that citizens have the right to know what their Government does. Under the act, official information is available to "any person" without regard to need for or interest in the material. The USAGM and its FOIA staff are committed to ensuring the fullest possible disclosure that is consistent with the letter and spirit of the law. https://www.usagm.gov/foia | Email: foia@usagm.gov

The FOIA requires agencies to disclose, proactively and electronically, certain categories of records to the public. Records that the USAGM has previously released to the public under the FOIA and that are the subject of subsequent requests or likely to be the subject of subsequent requests are proactively disclosed in the USAGM's electronic reading room for public access. Records that the USAGM determines are of sufficient public interest to warrant automatic disclosure are also proactively disclosed in the electronic reading room. https://www.usagm.gov/foia/electronic-reading-room

History   "The news may be good for us. The news may be bad. But we shall tell you the truth." These words, American journalist and writer William Harlan Hale spoke during the Voice of America's first radio show. For 75 years, U.S. international media have been broadcasting to audiences abroad. Visit the "History" web page to learn more about a story that continues to be heard around the world today. https://www.usagm.gov/who-we-are/history

Learn English   The Voice of America's website features resources for learning American English. https://learningenglish. voanews.com

Legislation / Congressional Committees   The USAGM receives its mandate to supervise all broadcasting activities and to provide strategic management for the agency from various public laws. The U.S. Congress oversees the USAGM, which is an independent executive branch agency, by monitoring, reviewing, and supervising its activities, programs, and policy implementation. https://www.usagm. gov/who-we-are/oversight

Networks   The USAGM's website provides convenient access to the home pages of all of its networks. https://www.usagm.gov/networks

News   USAGM-related news and information are available online. https:// www.usagm.gov/news-and-information

The latest press releases from the USAGM and its networks are available online. https://

www.usagm.gov/news-and-information/press-releases

Open Government   The USAGM supports the Open Government initiative by promoting collaboration, participation, and transparency. https://www.usagm.gov/our-work/strategy-and-results/strategic-priorities/research-reports/open-government | Email: opengov@bbg.gov

Pronunciation Guide   The VOA "Pro • nounce" website is a pronunciation guide with an audio feature. The guide helps people from around the globe pronounce challenging words that have been or are currently trending in media sources. https://pronounce.voanews.com

Services and Technology To Evade Censorship   The Open Technology Fund advances global Internet freedom by supporting research and development and the implementation and sustainability of technologies that facilitate the free flow of information, increase digital security, and enable freedom of expression online. https://www.opentech.fund/about

Site Map   The website map allows visitors to look for specific topics or to browse content that aligns with their interests. https://www.usagm.gov/sitemap

Social Media   The USAGM has a Facebook account. https://www.facebook.com/USAGMgov

The USAGM tweets announcements and other newsworthy items on Twitter. https://twitter.com/USAGMgov

The USAGM posts videos on its YouTube channel. https://www.youtube.com/channel/UCvYge67D7cpRJ6aYn2E9pPw

Students and Youth Worldwide   Voice of America's "Student Union" section offers students and youth international news that relates to them. https://www.voanews.com/student-union

The above Sources of Information were updated 4–2021.

United States Agency for International Development

1300 Pennsylvania Avenue NW., Washington, DC 20523
Phone, 202-712-0000. Internet, http://www.usaid.gov

Administrator	SAMANTHA POWER
Deputy Administrator	(VACANCY)
Chief of Staff	GIDEON MALTZ
Counselor	T. CHRISTOPHER MILLIGAN
Chiefs	
Financial Officer	REGINALD W. MITCHELL
Information Officer	JAY MAHANAND
Directors	
Acquisition and Assistance	MARK A. WALTHER
Executive Secretary	JEREMY BERNTON
General Counsel	MARGARET L. TAYLOR
https://www.usaid.gov/who-we-are/organization/leadership-listing	

Central Bureaus

Assistant Administrators	
Foreign Assistance	(VACANCY)
Legislative and Public Affairs	(VACANCY)
Management	COLLEEN R. ALLEN, ACTING
Assistant to the Administrator	
Policy, Planning and Learning	MICHELE SUMILAS
Functional Bureaus	

Assistant Administrator
Development, Democracy, and Innovation   KARL FICKENSCHER, ACTING
Global Health   KERRY PELZMAN, ACTING

Assistant to the Administrator
Conflict Prevention and Stabilization   ROBERT JENKINS, ACTING
Humanitarian Assistance   SARAH CHARLES
Resilience and Food Security   JIM BARNHART
Geographic Bureaus

Assistant Administrators
Africa   PETER MALNAK, ACTING
Asia   KAREN L. FREEMAN, ACTING
Europe and Eurasia   MARGOT ELLIS, ACTING
Latin America and the Caribbean   PETER NATIELLO, ACTING
Middle East   ANDREW PLITT, ACTING
https://www.usaid.gov/who-we-are/organization/bureaus

Independent Offices
Directors
Budget and Resource Management   TRICIA SCHMITT
Civil Rights and Diversity   ISMAEL MARTINEZ, ACTING
Security   JOHN VOORHEES
Small and Disadvantaged Business Utilization   JOHN M. WATSON, ACTING

Chief Officer
Human Capital   ROBERT LEAVITT
https://www.usaid.gov/who-we-are/organization/independent-
    offices

Office of Inspector General
Inspector General   THOMAS J. ULLOM, ACTING
https://oig.usaid.gov/leadership

The above list of key personnel was updated 6–2021.

The United States Agency for International Development seeks to eradicate extreme global poverty and enables resilient and democratic societies to realize their potential.

Establishment and Organization
The United States Agency for International Development (USAID) is an independent Federal agency established by 22 U.S.C. 6563. https://uscode.house.gov/view.xhtml?path=/prelim@title22/chapter74/subchapter4&edition=prelim

Its principal statutory authority is the Foreign Assistance Act of 1961, as amended (22 U.S.C. 2151 et seq.). https://uscode.house.gov/view.xhtml?path=/prelim@title22/chapter32&edition=prelim

Its statement of organization was published as a notice in the Federal Register on August 26, 1987, (52 FR 32174). https://www.govinfo.gov/content/pkg/FR-1987-08-26/pdf/FR-1987-08-26.pdf

USAID serves as the focal point within the Government for economic matters affecting U.S. relations with developing countries. It administers international economic and humanitarian assistance programs. The Administrator is under the direct authority and foreign policy guidance of the Secretary of State. https://www.usaid.gov/who-we-are/mission-vision-values

The Agency posts its organizational chart online. The chart includes independent offices and central, functional, and geographic bureaus. https://www.usaid.gov/who-we-are/organization

Activities

The Agency works in over 100 countries to promote broadly shared economic prosperity, strengthen democracy and good governance, protect human rights, improve global health, advance food security and agriculture, increase environmental sustainability, further education, help societies prevent and recover from conflicts, and provide humanitarian assistance in the wake of natural and manmade disasters. https://www.usaid.gov/what-we-do

Democracy   The Agency promotes the transition to and consolidation of democratic regimes throughout the world. Programs focus on such problems as human rights abuses; misperceptions of democracy and free-market capitalism; lack of experience with democratic institutions; the absence or weakness of intermediary organizations; nonexistent, ineffectual, or undemocratic political parties; disenfranchisement of women, indigenous peoples, and minorities; failure to implement national charter documents; powerless or poorly defined democratic institutions; tainted elections; and inability to resolve conflicts peacefully. https://www.usaid.gov/democracy

Economic Growth   The Agency promotes broad-based economic growth by addressing factors that enhance the capacity for growth and by working to remove obstacles that obstruct individual opportunity. Programs concentrate on strengthening market economies, expanding economic opportunities for the disadvantaged in developing countries, and building human skills and capacities to facilitate broad participation. https://www.usaid.gov/economic-growth-and-trade

Environment   Environmental programs support two strategic goals: 1) reducing long-term threats to the biosphere, particularly loss of biodiversity and change in climate; 2) promoting sustainable economic growth locally, nationally, and regionally by addressing shortsighted economic, environmental, and developmental practices. Globally, USAID programs focus on reducing sources of greenhouse gas emissions and enhancing greenhouse gas sinks and on promoting innovative approaches to the conservation and sustainable use of Earth's biological diversity.

The approach adopted to address national environmental problems differs from county to country, depending on its environmental priorities. Strategies may include improving agricultural, industrial, and natural resource management practices; strengthening public policies and institutions; being in dialogue with governments and international agencies; and environmental research and education. https://www.usaid.gov/what-we-do/environment-and-global-climate-change

Global Health and Population   The Agency improves access and quality of services for maternal and child health, nutrition, voluntary family planning, and reproductive health. It prevents and treats HIV/AIDS, malaria, and tuberculosis. It assists countries in the design and implementation of state-of-the-art public health approaches to end preventable child-maternal deaths and achieve an AIDS-free generation. The Agency takes advantage of economies of scale in procurement, technical services, and commodities. To promote sustainability, the Agency helps expand health systems and the health workforce by adopting and scaling-up proven health interventions across programs and countries. It also contributes to a cooperative global effort to stabilize world population growth and support women's reproductive rights. The types of population and health programs supported vary with the particular needs of individual countries and the kinds of approaches that local communities initiate and support. https://www.usaid.gov/global-health

Humanitarian Assistance / Post-Crisis Transitions   The Agency gives humanitarian assistance to save lives, reduce suffering, help victims return to self-sufficiency, and reinforce democracy. Programs focus on disaster prevention, preparedness, and mitigation; timely delivery of disaster relief and short-term rehabilitation supplies and services; preservation of basic institutions of civil governance during a disaster crisis; support for democratic institutions during periods of national transition; and building and reinforcement of local capacity to anticipate disasters and better cope with their aftermath. http://www.usaid.gov/what-we-do/working-crises-and-conflict

Overseas Organizations   USAID country organizations are located in countries where a bilateral program is being implemented. The in-country organizations are subject to the direction and guidance of the chief U.S. diplomatic representative in the country, usually the Ambassador. The organizations report to the appropriate assistant administrators according to geographic bureaus: Africa, Asia and the Near East, Europe and Eurasia, and Latin America and the Caribbean.

Overseas program activities that involve more than one country are administered by regional offices. These offices may also have country organizational responsibilities for assigned countries. Generally, the offices are headed by a regional development officer.

Coordination and representative offices for development assistance provide liaison with various international organizations and represent U.S. interests in development assistance matters. These offices may be only partially staffed by USAID personnel and may be headed by employees of other U.S. Government agencies. http://www.usaid.gov/where-we-work

Sources of Information

Archived Records The "Guide to Federal Records in the National Archives of the United States" indicates that USAID records have been assigned to record group 286. https://www.archives.gov/research/guide-fed-records/groups/286.html

Blog "Impact" is the name of the official USAID blog. https://blog.usaid.gov/

Bureaus Geographic bureaus are responsible for the overall activities in countries; functional bureaus conduct Agency programs that are worldwide in nature or that cross geographic boundaries. https://www.usaid.gov/who-we-are/organization/bureaus

Business Opportunities Through worldwide partnerships, USAID seeks to find innovative and cost-effective ways of addressing global challenges. The Agency partners with educational institutions, faith-based and community organizations, non-governmental organizations, and individuals and organizations in the private sector. https://www.usaid.gov/work-usaid/how-to-work-with-usaid

Career Opportunities USAID employs professionals with a variety of managerial, operational, and technical skills to achieve its international development goals. Its workforce includes direct-hire and contract employees based in the United States and at field missions worldwide. http://www.usaid.gov/careers

The Partnership for Public Service ranked USAID 14th among 25 midsize agencies in its Best Places To Work in the Federal Government 2019 rankings. https://bestplacestowork.org/rankings/detail/AM00

Climate Change Deforestation and reliance on fossil fuels accelerate climate disruption. As the climate changes, it undermines the efforts of poor communities to be self-supporting. USAID shares data, knowledge, and tools with developing countries to help people predict, prepare for, and adapt to more frequent and more destructive weather-related events. The Agency also helps countries grow in sustainable ways by promoting clean and reliable energy and healthy landscapes. Watch the 3-minute video to learn more about USAID global climate action. https://www.usaid.gov/climate/usaid-global-climate-action

Contact Information The "Contact Us" web page has an electronic form for submitting comments and questions, phone numbers, and links to relevant USAID web pages. https://www.usaid.gov/contact-us | Email: open@usaid.gov

Federal Register Significant documents and documents that USAID recently published in the Federal Register are accessible online. https://www.federalregister.gov/agencies/agency-for-international-development

Foreign Aid Explorer The Foreign Aid Explorer website offers a multidimensional picture of U.S. foreign assistance to help users find and retrieve the data that they seek. Interactive maps and graphics displaying the historical details of U.S. foreign assistance allow users to explore foreign aid data across countries, sectors, and over time. Advanced users can quickly download data by using data query tools or by selecting a prepared file. https://foreignassistance.gov/consolidation

Forms An electronic forms page features a selection of up-to-date USAID forms that are arranged according to form number. https://www.usaid.gov/forms

Freedom of Information Act (FOIA)   FOIA requests must be submitted in writing: email, fax, mail, or via the Public Access Link web portal. The Agency does not accept verbal FOIA requests. USAID Government information specialists are available to answer questions. Phone, 202-712-0960. Fax, 202-216-3070. https://www.usaid.gov/foia-requests | Email: foia@usaid.gov

USAID adds records that information seekers request repeatedly to its electronic FOIA library. If the desired record or document is not part of the FOIA library, consider submitting a written FOIA request to obtain the desired information. Please search the electronic reading room before submitting an official request for information. https://foiarequest.usaid.gov/app/ReadingRoom.aspx

History   President John F. Kennedy approved the Foreign Assistance Act of 1961 and created USAID by Executive order. Two years later, in a commencement address, he proclaimed: "Our problems are man-made; therefore, they can be solved by man. For in the final analysis, our most basic common link is that we all inhabit this small planet; we all breathe the same air; we all cherish our children's futures—and we are all mortal." President Kennedy's actions and words helped characterize the years of his administration and the one that followed, years that became known as the "decade of development." To learn more about the role that USAID played in expanding international development assistance opportunities, visit the "USAID History" web page. https://www.usaid.gov/who-we-are/usaid-history

Mission Directory   The online mission directory allows users to filter their searches by region: Afghanistan and Pakistan, Africa, Asia, Europe and Eurasia, Latin America and the Caribbean, and the Middle East. https://www.usaid.gov/mission-directory

The Sources of Information were updated 6–2021.

News   USAID posts news and information: congressional testimonies, events, factsheets, photographs and videos, podcasts, press releases, speeches, and success stories, as well as its "Frontlines" magazine, "Impact" newsletter, and "Impact" blog. https://www.usaid.gov/news-info

Offices   USAID has several independent offices that carry out discrete functions. https://www.usaid.gov/who-we-are/organization/independent-offices

Open Government   USAID supports the Open Government initiative by posting data, records, and reports online. https://www.usaid.gov/open

Plain Language   USAID adheres to the principles of transparency and openness that the Plain Writing Act of 2010 promotes. Plain writing plays a key role in achieving Open Government initiative goals and in improving collaboration, public participation, and transparency. https://www.usaid.gov/plain-writing

SERVIR Global   A joint initiative of USAID and the National Aeronautics and Space Administration, SERVIR partners with leading regional organizations worldwide to help developing countries use information from Earth observing satellites and geospatial technologies for managing climate risks and land use. SERVIR products, services, and tools empower decisionmakers to act locally on agriculture, ecosystems, land use, natural disasters, water, and other climate-sensitive issues. https://servirglobal.net/

Social Media   USAID maintains a YouTube channel and has a presence on Facebook, Twitter, and other social media. https://www.usaid.gov/stayconnected

Water / Sanitation   Nearly 2.1 billion people cannot access safe drinking water in their homes, and about 4.4 billion people live exposed to sewage, trash, or both. Inadequate water and sanitation and poor hygiene combine to spread disease and elevate death rates worldwide. https://www.usaid.gov/what-we-do/water-and-sanitation

United States Commission on Civil Rights

1331 Pennsylvania Avenue NW., Suite 1150, Washington, DC 20425
Phone, 202-376-8128. Fax 800-977-8339 (FedRelay). Internet, http://www.usccr.gov

Chair	CATHERINE E. LHAMON
Vice Chair	PATRICIA TIMMONS-GOODSON
Commissioner	DEBO P. ADEGBILE
Commissioner	GAIL HERIOT
Commissioner	PETER N. KIRSANOW
Commissioner	DAVID KLADNEY
Commissioner	KAREN K. NARASAKI
Commissioner	MICHAEL YAKI
Staff Director	MAURO A. MORALES

[For the Commission on Civil Rights statement of organization, see the Code of Federal Regulations, Title 45, Part 701]

The Commission on Civil Rights informs the development of national civil rights policy and enhances enforcement of Federal civil rights laws.

The Commission on Civil Rights was first created by the Civil Rights Act of 1957, as amended, and reestablished by the United States Commission on Civil Rights Act of 1994, as amended (42 U.S.C. 1975). http://www.usccr.gov/about/index.php

Activities

The Commission conducts hearings on important civil rights issues, including issuing subpoenas for the production of documents and the attendance of witnesses; publishes studies and reports on a wide range of civil rights issues to inform and advise policymakers; holds public briefings, issues press releases, makes information publicly available online, and provides a complaint referral service to promote greater public awareness of civil rights issues, protections, and enforcement; and sustains advisory committee involvement in the national program planning to strengthen factfinding. http://www.usccr.gov/about/powers.php

Regional Programs The Commission maintains 51 State Advisory Committees (SACs), one for each State and the District of Columbia. Each SAC is composed of citizen volunteers who are familiar with local and State civil rights issues. SAC members assist the Commission with factfinding, investigating, and disseminating information. The Commission ensures that advisory committees are diverse and represent a variety of backgrounds, skills, experiences, and perspectives. This diversity promotes debate and broadens exploration of the issues. All appointments are made in a nondiscriminatory manner. http://www.usccr.gov/about/sac.php

Sources of Information

Complaints The complaint referral service helps place individuals in contact with the appropriate office for obtaining information on the complaint process. Phone, 202-376-8513 or 800-552-6843. http://www.usccr.gov/filing/complaint.php | Email: referrals@usccr.gov

Employment Career opportunities— vacancy announcements and available internships—are posted online. Contact the Human Resources Division for more information. Phone, 202-376-8364. http://www.usccr.gov/about/careers.php | Email: careers@usccr.gov

Freedom of Information Act (FOIA) Information on how to file a FOIA request is available online. A request may be sent by email or fax, or by mail to the FOIA Officer, U.S. Commission on Civil Rights, 1331 Pennsylvania Avenue NW., Suite 1150,

Washington, DC 20425. Phone, 202-376-8351. Fax, 202-376-1163. http://www.usccr.gov/foia/index.php | Email: foia@usccr.gov

Library   The Robert S. Rankin Memorial Library welcomes visitors. It is open on weekdays, 10 a.m.–4 p.m. (except on Federal holidays). For more information, contact the Robert S. Rankin Memorial Library, 1331 Pennsylvania Avenue NW., Washington, DC 20425. Phone, 202-376-8110. Fax, 202-376-7597. http://www.usccr.gov/about/library.php | Email: publications@usccr.gov

Publications   For a complete list of Commission publications, consult the online catalog. It includes briefings; clearinghouse publications; hearings, consultations, and conferences; periodicals; publications in Spanish; staff reports; State advisory committee reports; and statutory and interim reports. To order a publication, contact the U.S. Commission on Civil Rights, 1331 Pennsylvania Avenue, NW., Suite 1150, Washington, DC 20425. Phone: 202-376-8128. http://www.usccr.gov/pubs/index.php | Email: publications@usccr.gov

Regional Offices   A list of the six regional offices—including addresses, telephone numbers, and areas served—is available online. http://www.usccr.gov/contact/regional.php http://www.usccr.gov/contact/index.php

For further information, contact the Office of the Staff Director, U.S. Commission on Civil Rights, 1331 Pennsylvania Avenue NW., Suite 1150, Washington, DC 20425. Phone, 202-376-7700. Phone, 800-977-8339 (FedRelay).

United States International Trade Commission

500 E Street SW., Washington, DC 20436
Phone, 202-205-2000. Internet, http://www.usitc.gov

Commissioners	
Chair	David S. Johanson
Vice Chair	(Vacancy)
	Meredith M. Broadbent
	Jason E. Kearns
	Rhonda K. Schmidtlein
	Irving A. Williamson
https://www.usitc.gov/press_room/bios.htm	
Chief Administrative Law Judge	Charles E. Bullock
Chief Information Officer	Keith B. Vaughn
General Counsel	Dominic L. Bianchi
Administrative Services Offices	
Chief Administrative Officer	Stephen McLaughlin
Directors	
Human Resources	Eric Mozie
Security and Support Services	Robert N. Riess
Secretary to the Commission	Lisa R. Barton
Financial Offices	
Chief Financial Officer	John M. Ascienzo
Directors	
Budget	Chris Swetz
Finance	Derek Henderson
Procurement	Debra Bridge
Independent Offices	
Directors	
Equal Employment Opportunity	Altivia R. Jackson

External Relations	Jennifer Andberg
Operating Offices	
Director of Operations	Catherine B. DeFilippo
Chief Data Officer	Jeremy Wise

Directors
Analysis and Research Services	Jeremy Wise
Economics	William M. Powers
Industries	Jonathan R. Coleman
Investigations	Nannette M. Christ
Tariff Affairs and Trade Agreements	James R. Holbein
Unfair Import Investigations	Margaret D. Macdonald

Office of Inspector General
Inspector General	Philip M. Heneghan
https://www.usitc.gov/oig.htm	

The above list of key personnel was updated 7–2019.

The United States International Trade Commission provides the President, the U.S. Trade Representative, and the Congress with independent analysis of and information on tariffs, international trade, and the Nation's competitiveness; makes determinations in proceedings involving imports that may harm a domestic industry or violate U.S. intellectual property rights; and maintains the Harmonized Tariff Schedule of the United States.

Establishment and Organization

The United States International Trade Commission (USITC) is an independent agency created by the Revenue Act (39 Stat. 795) and originally named the United States Tariff Commission. The name was changed to the United States International Trade Commission by section 171 of the Trade Act of 1974 (19 U.S.C. 2231). https://www.govinfo.gov/content/pkg/USCODE-2017-title19/pdf/USCODE-2017-title19-chap12.pdf

With the advice and consent of the Senate, the President appoints six commissioners for 9-year terms, unless the appointment is made to fill an unexpired term. The Chair and Vice Chair are designated by the President for 2-year terms, and succeeding Chairs may not be of the same political party. The Chair generally is responsible for the administration of the Commission. Not more than three Commissioners may be members of the same political party (19 U.S.C. 1330). https://www.govinfo.gov/content/pkg/USCODE-2017-title19/pdf/USCODE-2017-title19-chap4-subtitleII.pdf

The USITC posts its organizational chart (2017) online. https://www.usitc.gov/documents/usitc_org_2017_revised.pdf

Activities

The USITC engages in various activities pursuant to the previously mentioned statutes. Under the Tariff Act of 1930, it has broad powers of investigation to scrutinize the following competitive factors: U.S. customs laws and those of foreign countries; the proportional relationship between the volume of imported articles and domestic production and domestic consumption; the conditions, causes, and effects of foreign industries competing with U.S. industries; and any other factor affecting competition between imported articles and U.S. articles. Upon request, the USITC is required to convey its available information to the President, the House Committee on Ways and Means, and the Senate Committee on Finance. The President, the Congress, or the two committees mentioned can direct the USITC to undertake investigations and studies. To carry out its research and conduct its specialized studies, the USITC maintains expertise in all matters relating to the commercial and international trade policies of the United States. https://www.usitc.gov/press_room/about_usitc.htm

Foreign Subsidization / Selling at Less Than Fair Value   The USITC conducts preliminary-phase investigations to determine whether imports of foreign merchandise that are alleged to be subsidized or sold at less than fair value injure or threaten to injure an industry in the United States. If its determination is affirmative and the Secretary of Commerce concludes that unfair practices are occurring or suspects that they may be occurring, then the USITC conducts final-phase investigations to determine the injury or threat of injury to an industry. https://www.usitc.gov/press_room/usad.htm

Under the Uruguay Round Agreements Act, the USITC also conducts sunset reviews. In these reviews, the it evaluates whether material injury to a U.S. industry would continue or recur if the antidumping duty or countervailing duty order under review were revoked. Injury reviews must be conducted on all antidumping duty and countervailing duty orders every 5 years for as long as the orders remain in effect. https://www.usitc.gov/press_room/us_sunset.htm

Generalized System of Preferences   With respect to articles that may be considered for preferential removal of the duty on imports from designated developing countries, the USITC advises the President of the economic consequences that removal may have on the domestic industry and on consumers. https://www.usitc.gov/glossary/term/generalized-system-preferences-gsp

Harmonized Tariff Schedule   The U.S. Congress enacted the "Harmonized Tariff Schedule of the United States" (HTS). The HTS became effective on January 1, 1989, replacing the Nation's former tariff schedules. The USITC publishes the HTS, which contains the U.S. tariff schedules and related matters. The agency also considers questions affecting the arrangement of tariff schedules and the classification of articles. https://www.usitc.gov/tariff_affairs/about_hts.htm

Import Relief for Domestic Industries   The USITC conducts global safeguard investigations upon petition, on behalf of an industry, a firm, a group of workers, or other entity representative of an industry, to determine whether an article is being imported in increased quantities that injure, or threaten to injure, the domestic industry producing a similar article or an article that competes with the imported one. If its determination is affirmative, the USITC recommends to the President action that would address the threat and be most effective in facilitating positive adjustment by the industry to import competition. The President determines if import relief is an appropriate response. The USITC also reports on developments within an industry that has been granted import relief. It advises the President of the probable economic effect of reducing or eliminating the tariff increase that was previously granted. The President may continue, modify, or terminate the import relief. https://www.usitc.gov/press_room/us_safeguard.htm

Imports From NAFTA Countries   Pursuant to section 302 of the NAFTA Implementation Act, the USITC conducts bilateral safeguard investigations. https://www.govinfo.gov/content/pkg/BILLS-103hr3450enr/pdf/BILLS-103hr3450enr.pdf

These investigations seek to determine whether, as a result of the reduction or elimination of a duty that the North American Free Trade Agreement (NAFTA) facilitates, a Canadian or Mexican export to the United States in increased quantities and under certain conditions may damage, or threaten to damage, a U.S. industry that produces a similar article competing with the Canadian or Mexican export. If the USITC makes an affirmative determination, it advises the President on the relief needed to prevent or to remedy serious harm. USITC investigations of this kind resemble procedurally investigations that are conducted under the global safeguard-action provisions of the Trade Act of 1974. https://www.usitc.gov/press_room/us_safeguard.htm

Interference With Agricultural Programs   The USITC conducts investigations, at the direction of the President, to determine whether products are being imported into the United States under conditions and in quantities that render, or tend to render, ineffective or that materially interfere with a Department of Agriculture program. The USITC communicates its findings to the President and makes recommendations. The President then may impose a fee or quota on the imports in question; however, no fee or quota may be imposed on any article that a member of the World Trade Organization produces. https://www.usitc.gov/press_room/statutory_resp.htm

Market Disruption From Communist Countries The USITC conducts investigations to determine whether increased imports of an article produced in a Communist country are causing market disruption in the United States. If the USITC'S determination is in the affirmative, the President may take the same action as in the case of serious injury to an industry, except that the action would apply only to imports of the article from the Communist country. Commission investigations conducted under this provision are similar procedurally to those conducted under the global safeguard action provisions. https://www.usitc.gov/press_room/statutory_resp.htm

Trade Negotiations When duties and other trade barriers are being considered for modification as part of a proposed trade agreement with a foreign county, the USITC advises the President of the potential economic consequences on U.S. industries and on consumers. https://www.usitc.gov/press_room/statutory_resp.htm

Unfair Import Trade Practices The USITC applies U.S. statutory and common law of unfair competition to the importation of products into the United States and their sale. If it determines that there is a violation of law, it will direct that the articles involved be excluded from entry into the United States, or it may issue cease-and-desist orders directing the person engaged in such violation to stop. https://www.usitc.gov/intellectual_property/about_section_337.htm

Uniform Statistical Data The USITC cooperates with the Secretary of the Treasury and the Secretary of Commerce to establish an enumeration of articles imported into and exported from the United States for statistical purposes. It also seeks to establish comparability of these statistics with statistical programs for domestic production. https://www.usitc.gov/press_room/statutory_resp.htm

Sources of Information

Business Opportunities Most USITC contract opportunities are reserved for small businesses. They are typically for experienced contractors in the areas of administrative services, facilities management, information technology, and management consulting. The Office of Procurement oversees all procurements. Phone, 202-205-2252. https://usitc.gov/procurement/doing_business_with_usitc.htm

Career Opportunities The USITC relies on accountants, analysts and specialists, attorneys, economists, and other professionals to carry out its mission. For more information, contact the Director, Office of Human Resources. Phone, 202-205-2651. https://www.usitc.gov/employment/positions.htm | Email: hr@usitc.gov

The USITC ranked 2d among 29 small agencies in the Partnership for Public Service's 2018 Best Places To Work Agency Rankings. http://bestplacestowork.org/rankings/detail/TC00

Contact Information The USITC website has an electronic form for submitting a comment or question. https://www.usitc.gov/contact_us.htm

External Links The "Related External Links" web page has a collection of external links to make locating additional information more convenient. https://www.usitc.gov/related_sites.htm

Freedom of Information Act (FOIA) Enacted in 1966, the FOIA took effect on July 4, 1967. The statute makes all existing Federal Government records available to the public; however, a record may be shielded from disclosure by one or more of nine exemptions or by specific harm that its disclosure may cause. Any person, except a fugitive from the law, has a right to request access to Federal agency records. The FOIA strengthens democratic governance by giving access to Government records to anyone who submits a proper FOIA request. https://www.usitc.gov/secretary/foia/index.htm

The USITC posts answers to frequently asked FOIA-related questions. https://www.usitc.gov/secretary/foia/foia_faq.htm

Glossary The USITC maintains an online glossary. https://usitc.gov/glossary.htm

The "USITC Acronyms" web page enables the nonspecialist to navigate in an acronym-rich environment. https://www.usitc.gov/acronyms.htm

Harmonized Tariff Schedule   The "Harmonized Tariff Schedule of the United States," which includes general notes and rules of interpretation, is available online in Portable Document Format (PDF). The HTS is used to classify imported merchandise for rate of duty and statistical purposes. https://hts.usitc.gov/current

History   The USITC has developed a timeline of U.S. tariffs and trade and posted it online. https://www.usitc.gov/flash/dynamic_timeline.htm

The USITC celebrated its 100th birthday in September of 2016. To mark that milestone, it published a 453-page history of the agency called "A Centennial History of the United States International Trade Commission" (2017). The entire history is available online in Portable Document Format (PDF). https://www.usitc.gov/documents/final_centennial_history_508_compliant_v2.pdf

How To Find It   Try the "How Do I Find" web page, which has a collection of links to help online visitors use the USITC website. https://www.usitc.gov/press_room/how_to_find.htm

Investigations   A list of active antidumping and countervailing duty investigations is available online. https://www.usitc.gov/trade_remedy/731_ad_701_cvd/investigations.htm

337Info is an information retrieval system containing data on USITC Section 337 investigations. https://pubapps2.usitc.gov/337 external | Email: 337InfoHelp@usitc.gov

The Electronic Document Information System (EDIS) contains all documents that have been filed in relation to USITC investigations. EDIS provides the capabilities to file documents for an investigation and to search for documents that have been submitted to the USITC. https://edis.usitc.gov | Email: EDIS3Help@usitc.gov

Low-Carbon Energy / Sustainable Products   European Union climate regulations, which treat wood pellets as a low-carbon energy source, play a principal role in supporting the wood pellet industry's growth. To learn more, see Robert Ireland's 2018 executive briefing, in which he expresses his views on international trade in this energy source. https://www.usitc.gov/publications/332/executive_briefings/wood_pellets_ebot_final.pdf

In their 2018 working paper "Exporting Ecolabels: Is Demand for Certified Sustainable Products Affecting International Trade?" coauthors Renee Berry and Marin Weaver explore the influence of sustainability certifications on trade patterns in food and agricultural products. USITC working papers express the views of their authors and may not represent the views of the U.S. International Trade Commission or its individual Commissioners. https://www.usitc.gov/publications/332/working_papers/exporting_ecolabels_final_with_cover_mjs_071718.pdf

News   The USITC posts news releases on its website. https://www.usitc.gov/press_room/news_release/news_release_index.htm

Open Data   The USITC helps increase the Federal Government's efficiency and transparency by making its operational information more accessible and useful. https://www.usitc.gov/data/index.htm

Reading Rooms   Reading rooms are open to the public in the Office of the Secretary and the USITC Main Library. The USITC Law Library is publicly accessible by prior arrangement. Call 202-205-3287 to schedule a visit.

Popular Topics   The "Popular Topics" web page has links to frequently visited USITC pages. Popular topics include calendar events, commissioner biographies, "Federal Register" notices, hearing protocols, jobs, and news releases. https://usitc.gov/popular_topics.htm

Publications   The Commission publishes results of investigations on various commodities and subjects. Other publications include an annual report to the Congress on the operation of the trade agreements program and an annual review of Commission activities. Specific information on these publications may be obtained from the Office of the Secretary. https://usitc.gov/research_and_analysis/commission_publications.htm

Site Map   The USITC site map allows visitors to look for specific topics or to browse content that aligns with their interests. https://www.usitc.gov/sitemap

Trade Seminars   The research division of the Office of Economics posts the International Trade Seminar Series on the USITC website. https://www.usitc.gov/research_and_analysis/seminars_economics.htm

The Sources of Information were updated 7–2019.

United States Office of Special Counsel

1730 M Street NW., Suite 218, Washington, DC 20036-4505
Phone, 202-804-7000, 800-872-9855, 202-653-5151. Internet, http://www.osc.gov

Leadership Tables
Special Counsel — HENRY J. KERNER
Principal Deputy Special Counsel — ELLEN C. EPSTEIN

Deputy Special Counsels
Legal Affairs — PATRICK HARTOBEY
Public Policy — TRAVIS MILLSAPS

General Counsel — SUSAN K. ULLMAN
https://osc.gov/Pages/Leadership.aspx

Administrative Services Division
Chief Operating Officer — BRUCE GIPE

Chief Officers
Administrative Services — DERRICK MCDUFFIE
Data — SMITA PATEL
Financial — KARL P. KAMMANN
Human Capital — KATHY MCDUFFIE
Information — SMITA PATEL

Clerk — MAHALA DAR

General Law Division

Associate Special Counsel — ANNE WAGNER

Unit Chiefs
Alternative Dispute Resolution — JANE JULIANO
Complaints Examining — BARBARA J. WHEELER
Disclosure — CATHERINE A. MCMULLEN
Diversity, Outreach, and Training — SHIRINE MOAZED

Investigation and Prosecution Division—Field
Associate Special Counsel — BRUCE D. FONG

Field Office Chiefs
Dallas — ANNE GULLICK
Detroit — CHRISTOPHER T. TALL
San Francisco Bay Area — JOSEPH SIEGELMAN

Investigation and Prosecution Division—Headquarters
Associate Special Counsel — LOUIS LOPEZ

Division Chiefs — KIMBERLEY BAXTER
EMILEE COLLIER
DARSHAN SHETH
RACHEL VENIER

Unit Chiefs
Hatch Act — ANA GALINDO-MARRONE
Retaliation and Disclosure — ELIZABETH MCMURRAY
Uniformed Services Employment and Reemployment Rights Act — PATRICK H. BOULAY

The above list of key personnel was updated 11–2019.

The United States Office of Special Counsel investigates allegations of certain activities prohibited by civil service laws, rules, or regulations and litigates before the Merit Systems Protection Board.

Establishment and Organization

The U.S. Office of Special Counsel (OSC) was established on January 1, 1979, by Reorganization Plan No. 2 of 1978 (5 U.S.C. app.). https://uscode.house. gov/view.xhtml?req=granuleid:USC-prelim-title5a-node84-leaf186&num=0&edition=prelim

Public Law 95–454, which is also cited as the Civil Service Reform Act of 1978, was approved on October 13, 1978, and became effective on January 11, 1979. This statute enlarged the agency's functions and powers (92 Stat. 1112). https://www.govinfo.gov/content/pkg/STATUTE-92/pdf/STATUTE-92-Pg1111.pdf

Pursuant to provisions of Public Law 101–12, which is also cited as the Whistleblower Protection Act of 1989, the OSC functions as an independent investigative and prosecutorial executive branch agency that litigates before the Merit Systems Protection Board (103 Stat. 16). https://www.govinfo.gov/content/pkg/STATUTE-103/pdf/STATUTE-103-Pg16.pdf

Statutory material associated with the OSC is codified in sections 1211—1219 of 5 U.S. C. https://uscode.house.gov/view.xhtml?path=/prelim@title5/part2/chapter12/subchapter2&edition=prelim

Additional statutory material that affects the OSC and that derives from the Civil Service Reform Act of 1978 is codified in section 1101, note, of 5 U.S.C. https://uscode.house.gov/view.xhtml?path=/prelim@title5/part2/chapter11&edition=prelim

The OSC included an organizational chart in its "Performance and Accountability Report for Fiscal Year 2018" on page 107. https://osc.gov/Documents/Resources/Statutory%20Reports%20and%20Notices/Performance%20and%20Accountability%20Reports%20(PAR)/Performance%20Reports/FY%202018%20Performance%20and%20Accountability%20Report.pdf

Activities

The OSC safeguards the merit system in Federal employment by protecting employees and applicants from prohibited personnel practices, especially from reprisal for whistleblowing. The Office operates a secure channel for Federal whistleblower disclosures of gross waste of funds or mismanagement, substantial and specific danger to public health and safety, and violations of laws, regulations, or rules. The OSC also issues advice on the Hatch Act and enforces its restrictions on political activity by Government employees. It protects the civilian employment and reemployment rights of military servicemembers under the Uniformed Services Employment and Reemployment Act. The OSC enhances Government accountability and performance by the realization of a diverse, inclusive Federal workplace where employees embrace excellence in service, uphold merit system principles, are encouraged to disclose wrongdoing, and are protected against reprisals and other unlawful employment practices. https://osc.gov/Services

Sources of Information

Archived Records   The "Guide to Federal Records in the National Archives of the United States" indicates that OSC records have been assigned to record group 481. The Guide is accessible online, but no description is associated with this record group. https://www.archives.gov/research/guide-fed-records/groups/000.html

Business Opportunities   The OSC relies on the Department of Interior for performing assisted procurements. The OSC posts contract opportunities online by using Government acquisition vehicles like GSA Ebuy. It posts open market opportunities on the Federal Business Opportunities Web site. https://osc.gov/Careers

Career Opportunities The agency employs approximately 110 employees who work in Washington, DC, or in the Dallas, Detroit, and Oakland field offices. To carry out its mission, the OSC relies heavily on attorneys, investigators, and personnel management specialists.

The OSC seeks law students year-round for internships in Dallas, TX; Detroit, MI; Oakland, CA; and Washington, DC. https://osc.gov/Careers

In 2018, the OSC ranked 14th among 29 small agencies in the Partnership for Public Service's Best Places To Work Agency Rankings. http://bestplacestowork.org/BPTW/rankings/detail/FW00

Contact Information The "Contact OSC" web page has postal and email addresses and phone numbers. https://osc.gov/Pages/contact.aspx | Email: info@osc.gov

Electronic Filing The E–Filing System makes filing a complaint with the OSC easier and faster. https://osc.gov/pages/file-complaint.aspx

En Español The OSC posts information in Spanish on its "Para Información En Español" web page. https://osc.gov/Espanol

Freedom of Information Act (FOIA) FOIA requests must be submitted in writing by email, fax, or U.S. postal mail or other delivery service. The OSC provides a Public Access Link portal that allows information seekers to submit a request online and to receive confirmation of and updates on a pending request. https://osc.gov/Pages/FOIA-Resources.aspx

Frequently Asked Questions (FAQs) The OSC posts answers to FAQs on its website. https://osc.gov/FAQ

The Sources of Information were updated 11–2019.

Hatch Act Advisory Opinions Advice that the OSC has given to individuals on the Hatch Act is publicly accessible online. https://osc.gov/Services/Pages/HatchAct-AdvisoryOpinion.aspx

News The OSC posts press releases online. https://osc.gov/PressReleases

Open Government The OSC supports the Open Government initiative by promoting the principles of collaboration, participation, and transparency. https://osc.gov/OpenGov

Prohibited Personnel Practices The OSC provides information on personnel practices that are prohibited within the Federal workplace. https://osc.gov/Services/Pages/PPP.aspx

Reports The OSC posts reports on its website. https://osc.gov/Reports

Site Map The website map allows visitors to look for specific topics or to browse content that aligns with their interests. https://osc.gov/Pages/SiteMap.aspx

Social Media The OSC tweets announcements and other newsworthy items on Twitter. https://twitter.com/US_OSC

Speakers To request a speaker, contact the OSC by phone or fax. Phone, 202-804-7000. Fax, 202-254-3711.

Whistleblower Files The OSC posts documents from closed investigations on its website. These documents are based on whistleblower disclosures. https://osc.gov/PublicFiles

2302(c) Program Certification The White House has required all Federal agencies to certify that they are educating their employees about the rights of whistleblowers. Phone, 703-466-0259. https://osc.gov/Services/Pages/Outreach-2302Cert.aspx | Email: 2302c@osc.gov

---

United States Postal Service

475 L'Enfant Plaza SW., Washington, DC 20260
Phone, 202-268-2000. Internet, http://www.usps.gov

Board of Governors

Chair	Robert M. Duncan
Vice Chair	(vacancy)
Governor	John M. Barger
Governor	Ronald A. Bloom

Governor	Roman Martinez IV
Governor	Donald L. Moak
Governor	William D. Zollars
Governor	(vacancy)
Governor	(vacancy)
Postmaster General / Chief Executive Officer	Louis DeJoy
Deputy Postmaster General / Chief Government Relations Officer	(vacancy)
Secretary	Michael J. Elston

http://about.usps.com/who-we-are/leadership/board-governors.htm

Officers

Postmaster General / Chief Executive Officer	Louis DeJoy
Deputy Postmaster General	(vacancy)
Executive Vice Presidents	Scott Bombaugh, Acting
	Joseph Corbett
	Isaac Cronkhite
	Thomas J. Marshall
	Pritha Mehra, Acting
	Steve Monteith, Acting
	Kristin Seaver
	Jacqueline Krage Strako
	David E. Williams
Chief Postal Inspector	Gary Barksdale
General Counsel	Thomas J. Marshall
Vice President	
Corporate Communications	Jeffery A. Adams

http://about.usps.com/who-we-are/leadership/pmg-exec-comm.htm#p=1

Commerce and Business Solutions

Chief Commerce and Business Solutions Officer	Jacqueline Krage Strako
Vice Presidents	
Facilities	Thomas Samra
Business Development	(vacancy)
Business Solutions	(vacancy)
Transportation Strategy	Kelly Abney, Acting
Customer Affairs and Marketing	
Chief Customer and Marketing Officer	Steve Monteith, Acting
Vice Presidents	
Customer Experience	Kelly M. Sigmon
Marketing	(vacancy)
Product Innovation	Gary Reblin
Sales	Timothy R. Costello, Acting
Financial Affairs	
Chief Financial Officer	Joseph Corbett
Senior Vice President	
Finance and Strategy	Luke Grossman

Vice Presidents
Controller   Cara Greene
Pricing and Costing   Sharon Owens
Supply Management   Mark Guilfoil
Government Relations

Chief Government Relations Officer   (vacancy)

Judicial Officer   Alan R. Caramella, Acting
https://about.usps.com/who/judicial
Human Resources

Chief Human Resources Officer   Isaac Cronkhite

Labor Relations   Douglas Tulino
Employee Resource Management   Simon Storey
Information

Chief Information Officer   Pritha Mehra, Acting

Vice Presidents
Mail Entry and Payment Technology   Randy Workman, Acting
Information Security   Gregory S. Crabb
Information Technology   Marc McCrery, Acting

Chief Information Security Officer   Gregory S. Crabb
Logistics and Processing Operations

Chief Logistics and Processing Operations Officer   David E. Williams

Vice Presidents
Logistics   Robert Cintron
Processing and Maintenance Operations   Mike Barber

Vice Presidents—Regional Operations
Eastern   Dane Coleman
Western   Larry Muñoz
Retail and Delivery

Chief Retail and Delivery Officer   Kristin Seaver

Vice Presidents
Delivery Operations   Joshua D. Colin
Retail and Post Office Operations   Angela Curtis

Vice Presidents—Area Operations
Atlantic   Salvatore Vacca
Central   Krista Finazzo, Acting
Southern   Shaun E. Mossman
Western Pacific   Gregory Graves
Technology

Chief Technology Officer   Scott Bombaugh, Acting

Vice Presidents
Engineering Systems   Linda M. Malone, Acting
Enterprise Analytics   Jeffrey C. Johnson
http://about.usps.com/who-we-are/leadership/officers.htm

Inspector General   Tammy L. Whitcomb
https://www.uspsoig.gov/about-us/tammy-whitcomb

The above list of key personnel was updated 9–2020.

The United States Postal Service binds the Nation together through the people's personal, educational, literary, and business correspondence by providing prompt, reliable, and efficient services to patrons in all areas and by rendering postal services to all communities.

Establishment and Organization

Three weeks after the battles of Lexington and Concord, the Second Continental Congress met in Philadelphia and planned for the defense of the colonies against Great Britain. The conveyance of letters and intelligence was essential for winning the war for independence. A committee, which Benjamin Franklin chaired, was named to consider the creation of a postal system. The committee reported back to the Continental Congress in July of 1775. The Continental Congress agreed to the committee's recommendations, quickly created the position of Postmaster General, and named the committee's chair to fill the new position. Under Franklin and his immediate successors, the postal system mainly carried communications between Congress and the Continental Army. To ensure reliable service, postmasters and post riders were exempt from military duties. Franklin served as Postmaster General until November of 1776. He held the office when the Declaration of Independence created the United States in July of that year, which means that Franklin had the distinction of serving as the first Postmaster General of the United States. America's present Postal Service descends from the system Franklin placed in operation. https://about.usps.com/publications/pub100.pdf

The Articles of Confederation were ratified in 1781. Article IX addressed the establishment and regulation of "post offices from one State to another, throughout all the United States" and the exaction of "postage on the papers passing" from State to State, throughout the United States, "as may be requisite to defray the expenses of the said office." https://www.ourdocuments.gov/doc.php?flash=false&doc=3&page=transcript

The Constitution of the United States gives the U.S. Congress the power "to establish Post Offices and post Roads" (ART. I, Sec. 8). https://www.ourdocuments.gov/doc.php?flash=false&doc=9&page=transcript

On September 22, 1789, President George Washington approved an "Act for the temporary establishment of the Post-Office" (1 Stat. 70). This temporary piece of legislation provided that "the regulations of the post-office shall be the same as they last were under the resolutions and ordinances of the late Congress." It also provided for the appointment of a Postmaster General, who would "be subject to the direction of the President . . . in performing the duties of his office, and in forming contracts for the transportation of the mail." The Act remained in force "until the end of the next session of Congress," and its provisions were continued by subsequent acts. https://www.loc.gov/law/help/statutes-at-large/1st-congress/session-1/c1s1ch16.pdf

On June 8, 1872, President Ulysses S. Grant approved an "Act to revise, consolidate, and amend the Statutes relating to the Post-office Department" (17 Stat. 283). Even before the passage of this law, the Post Office, or General Post Office, as it sometimes was called, had acquired the additional epithet of Post-office Department, which inaccurately implied its prior establishment as an executive branch department. This law "established, at the seat of government of the United States of America, a department to be known as the Post-office Department." The Post Office was now officially named the Post-office Department, and it had acquired departmental status within the executive branch of Government. https://www.loc.gov/law/help/statutes-at-large/42nd-congress/session-2/c42s2ch335.pdf

Pursuant to the provisions of the Reorganization Act of 1949 (PL 81–109), President Harry S. Truman prepared Reorganization Plan No. 3 of 1949 and transmitted it to the Senate and the House of Representatives on June 20, 1949. The provisions of the Reorganization Act of 1949 became effective on August 20, 1949. https://uscode.house.gov/view.

xhtml?req=granuleid:USC-prelim-title5a-node84-leaf99&num=0&edition=prelim

On August 23, 1949, the National Archives published President Truman's reorganization plan in the Federal Register (14 FR 5225). The plan "established an Advisory Board for the Post Office Department." In addition to the Chair and Vice Chair, the Board comprised seven other members who were representative of the public. It also provided that these seven members "shall be appointed by the President by and with the advice and consent of the Senate"; that this same process shall be applied to the appointment of the Deputy Postmaster General; and that the Post Office Department's Postmaster General and Deputy Postmaster General shall serve as the Board's Chair and Vice Chair. https://www.govinfo.gov/content/pkg/FR-1949-08-23/pdf/FR-1949-08-23.pdf

On August 12, 1970, President Richard M. Nixon approved Public Law 91–375, which is commonly cited as the Postal Reorganization Act. Senators and Representatives passed this piece of legislation "to improve and modernize the postal service" and "to reorganize the Post Office Department." Regarding postal policy, the Act stated: "The United States Postal Service shall be operated as a basic and fundamental service provided to the people by the Government of the United States, authorized by the Constitution, created by Act of Congress, and supported by the people . . . . shall have as its basic function the obligation to provide postal services to bind the Nation together through the personal, educational, literary, and business correspondence of the people . . . . shall provide prompt, reliable, and efficient services to patrons in all areas and shall render postal services to all communities. The costs of establishing and maintaining the Postal Service shall not be apportioned to impair the overall value of such service to the people" (84 Stat. 719). The present United States Postal Service (USPS) commenced operations on July 1, 1971. https://www.govinfo.gov/content/pkg/STATUTE-84/pdf/STATUTE-84-Pg719.pdf

The most comprehensive postal legislation since the Nation's founding, the Postal Reorganization Act transformed the Post Office Department into the USPS, an independent establishment of the executive branch of the Federal Government. The Act did not change, however, the mission of the Postal Service, as stated in section 101 of 39 U.S.C. The new USPS began operations on July 1, 1971, the same day that the President's Cabinet no longer included the Postmaster General among its membership. The Act affected postal rates and mail classifications, terms and conditions of employment, labor and management relations, laws that govern mail transportation, and compensation and benefits for USPS officers and employees.

Regarding labor and management relations, the Postal Reorganization Act authorized collective bargaining on wages and working conditions under laws that apply to private industry and provided for binding arbitration if an impasse persists 180 days after the start of bargaining. The strike ban, which is applicable to all Federal employees, remained in effect. The Act authorized the National Labor Relations Board to determine proper bargaining units, supervise representative elections, and enforce the unfair labor practices provisions. It also protected the rights of all employees to form, join, or assist a labor organization or to refrain from such activity. Today, the USPS is the only Federal agency whose employment policies are governed by a process of collective bargaining that the National Labor Relations Act prescribes. https://about.usps.com/publications/pub100.pdf

On December 20, 2006, President George W. Bush signed Public Law 109–435, which is cited usually as the Postal Accountability and Enhancement Act (120 Stat. 3198). https://www.govinfo.gov/content/pkg/STATUTE-120/pdf/STATUTE-120-Pg3198.pdf

This piece of legislation made more than 150 changes to Federal law, affecting the Postal Service. https://about.usps.com/transforming-business/postal-act-2006.htm

Changes included the categorization of postal products, the replacement of the Postal Rate Commission by the Postal Regulatory Commission, transferring the obligation to pay military pension costs, and the establishment of the Postal Service Retiree Health Benefits Fund, into which the Postal Service was required to prepay benefits for 10 years into the future. https://about.usps.com/publications/pub100.pdf

Spanning two full centuries and parts of two others, congressional action and Presidential approval have shaped the general organization of the Postal Service into what it is today. The Board of Governors directs the exercise of USPS powers, reviews its practices and policies, and directs and controls USPS expenditures. The Board comprises 11 members, 9 of whom the President appoints by the advice and with the consent of the Senate. Not more than five governors may belong to the same political party. The governors are chosen to represent the public interest, and they may not be representatives of specific interests that use the Postal Service. The Postmaster General and Deputy Postmaster General are also voting members of the Board. https://www.ecfr.gov/cgi-bin/text-idx?SID=ac56841027cf753f6ab20c24468d6fa3&mc=true&node=pt39.1.221#se39.1.221_12

The chief executive officer of the Postal Service is the Postmaster General, who is responsible responsible for the overall operation of the Postal Service. The Board of Governors appoints the Postmaster General. The Postmaster General and the governors appoint the Deputy Postmaster General. https://www.ecfr.gov/cgi-bin/text-idx?SID=ac56841027cf753f6ab20c24468d6fa3&mc=true&node=pt39.1.221&rgn=div5#se39.1.221_14

The USPS posts its organizational chart in Portable Document Format (PDF) for viewing and downloading. https://about.usps.com/who/leadership/hq-org.pdf

The USPS statement of organization has been assigned to part 221 in 39 CFR. https://www.ecfr.gov/cgi-bin/text-idx?SID=ac56841027cf753f6ab20c24468d6fa3&mc=true&node=pt39.1.221&rgn=div5

Statutory and Regulatory Authorities

Statutory material affecting the Postal Service has been codified and assigned to 39 U.S.C. The title comprises four parts: General, Personnel, Modernization and Fiscal Administration, Mail Matter, and Transportation of Mail. https://uscode.house.gov/view.xhtml?path=/prelim@title39&edition=prelim

Regulatory material that is associated with the USPS is codified and assigned to 39 CFR. The title comprises parts 1–3099. https://www.ecfr.gov/cgi-bin/text-idx?SID=ac56841027cf753f6ab20c24468d6fa3&mc=true&tpl=/ecfrbrowse/Title39/39tab_02.tpl

Activities

The USPS provides business, Government, mailing, shipping, and sustainability services, as well as law enforcement. As a Federal agency, the USPS has been a sustainability leader through policies and programs like its renewable energy and recycling initiatives. https://about.usps.com/what/welcome.htm

The USPS is the only delivery service that reaches every mailbox—including APO, FPO, DPO, and post office box addresses—nationwide. This comprehensive reach allows the USPS to support Government activities through its services like the distribution of tax forms and the delivery of ballots overseas. https://about.usps.com/what/government-services

USPS programs support communities through disseminating information, educating, and participating in worthwhile causes. Examples of these types of programs include National Dog Bite Awareness Week, the Stamp Out Hunger National Food Drive, and a partnership with the National Center for Missing and Exploited Children. https://about.usps.com/what/corporate-social-responsibility/activities

The U.S. Postal Inspection Service has jurisdiction in criminal matters affecting the integrity and security of the mail. Postal inspectors protect all postal employees and enforce Federal statutes involving mail fraud, mail bombs, child pornography, illegal drugs, mail theft, and other postal crimes. https://www.uspis.gov

To expand and improve its services, the USPS engages in customer cooperation activities, including the development of programs for both the general public and major customers. To provide services that are responsive to public needs, the Postal Service operates its own planning, research, engineering, real estate, and procurement programs, and it maintains close ties with international postal organizations.

Sources of Information

Annual Food Drive   On the second Saturday of May, in more than 10,000 cities and towns nationwide, letter carriers collect food that postal customers donate, as part of the National Association of Letter Carriers' (NALC) one-day Stamp Out Hunger National Food Drive, which is the largest in the Nation. Led by letter carriers who are represented by the NALC (AFL–CIO), with help from rural letter carriers, other postal employees, and volunteers, the drive has delivered more than one billion pounds of food over the past 25 years. Carriers collect nonperishable food donations in post offices and at mailboxes and deliver them to local community food banks, pantries, and shelters. Nearly 1,500 NALC branches in all 50 States, the District of Columbia, Puerto Rico, Guam, and the Virgin Islands participate. https://about.usps.com/what/corporate-social-responsibility/activities/nalc-food-drive.htm

Annual Reports / Strategic Plans   Documents that are required by law and regularly published by the Office of Strategic Planning are available in Portable Document Format (PDF) for viewing online and downloading. https://about.usps.com/strategic-planning/future-postal-service/publications.htm

Archived Records   The "Guide to Federal Records in the National Archives of the United States" indicates that USPS records have been assigned to record group 488. The guide is accessible online, but it does not contain a description that is associated with record group 488. https://www.archives.gov/research/guide-fed-records/index-numeric/401-to-500.html

Blog   "Postal Posts" is the USPS's official blog. https://uspsblog.com

Business Customers   The Business Customer Gateway website supports USPS online services for mailers, shippers, and business. https://gateway.usps.com/eAdmin/view/signin

Business Opportunities   Suppliers can learn about doing business with the Postal Service online. Information on rights and permissions (the use of trademarked material) and licensing products is also available online. http://about.usps.com/doing-business/welcome.htm

Career Opportunities   Information on careers—including information for veterans and reservists, for students and recent graduates—is available on the USPS website or at the nearest post office. https://about.usps.com/careers

In 2019, the Office of Inspector General ranked 57th among 420 agency subcomponents in the Partnership for Public Service's Best Places To Work Agency Rankings. https://bestplacestowork.org/rankings/detail/PS01

Change of Address   A family member, individual, or business owner may change his or her address online, using the "Official USPS Change-of-Address" web page. https://moversguide.usps.com/mgo/disclaimer?referral=MG14

Contact Information   The USPS posts contact information online. It also operates a customer care center. Phone, 800-275-8777. https://www.usps.com/help/contact-us.htm

USPS media relations specialists can answer questions that journalists and reporters may have. https://about.usps.com/newsroom/national-releases/welcome.htm#national-media-contacts

Election Mail   Americans rely on the USPS to fulfill its role in the electoral process. The Postal Service provides an effective, efficient, and secure way for citizens to participate in democracy when policymakers decide to use mail as part of elections. https://about.usps.com/what/government-services/election-mail

The USPS Office of Inspector General website has a section that is devoted to "Election and Political Mail." https://www.uspsoig.gov/election-and-political-mail

Federal Register   Significant documents and documents that the USPS recently published in the Federal Register are accessible online. https://www.federalregister.gov/agencies/postal-service

Forms / Publications   The "Resources" web page provides convenient access to USPS forms and publications, including the "Postal Bulletin," which was started in 1880. http://about.usps.com/periodicals-publications/welcome.htm

Freedom of Information Act (FOIA)   The FOIA is a Federal law that provides the public a right of access to Government documents and records, the premise being that the public has a right to know what the Federal Government is doing. The FOIA applies to executive branch agencies, which includes the USPS. Any person may request a copy of USPS records. The USPS must provide copies of such records, unless a FOIA exemption exists that shields the information from disclosure. https://about. usps.com/who/legal/foia

The Postal Service maintains an electronic FOIA library. Frequently requested records— previously released records that have been or are likely to become the subject of repeated requests—are part of the FOIA library. Before submitting a formal FOIA request, check the online library to see if the desired information is already accessible without charge and without delay. https:// about.usps.com/who-we-are/foia/readroom/ welcome.htm

History   Benjamin Franklin and the Postal Service, what was the nature of their association? It was closer than many Americans may know. To learn more about the role Franklin played in the early years of the Postal Service, see the 149-page and poignantly illustrated publication "The United States Postal Service: An American History." The publication is available in Portable Document Format (PDF) for viewing online and downloading. https:// about.usps.com/publications/pub100.pdf | Email: phistory@usps.gov

The National Postal Museum houses one of the largest and most significant philatelic and postal history collections in the world and one of the most comprehensive library resources on philately and postal history. The museum's exhibition galleries present America's postal history from Colonial times to the present. Its collections contain prestigious international and U.S. postal issues and specialized collections, archival postal documents, and three-dimensional objects. https://postalmuseum.si.edu

Mail Hold   Before submitting a "USPS Hold Mail" request, the requester must create a USPS account. Once an account is created, an account holder may print shipping labels, purchase stamps, print custom forms online, and manage a post office box. https://reg. usps.com/login?app=HOLDMAIL&app URL=https%3A%2F%2Fholdmail.usps. com%2Fholdmail%2F

News   The USPS posts national news items on its "Newsroom" web page. https://about. usps.com/newsroom

Passports   Thousands of post offices accept passport applications on behalf of the Department of State. These post offices offer the products and services needed to acquire a first-time passport or renewal. At some locations, a passport photograph can be taken for an additional fee. https://www. usps.com/international/passports.htm

Philatelic Sales   For information on available stamps, philatelic items, and collectibles, visit the "Stamps" web page. https://store.usps.com/store/results/stamps/_/ N-9y93lv#content

Photo Galleries   Photo galleries are found in the "Our History" section of the USPS website. The galleries are six in number: airmail, buildings, equipment, people, railroads, and vehicles. Students of history can find some arresting images in the galleries. https://about.usps.com/who-we-are/postal-history/pho-gallery.htm

Postal Certainty   The 30-second video highlights the long-standing culture of service associated with USPS mail carriers. https://www.youtube.com/watch?v=uuNLLZcSTKE

Postal Explorer   The Postal Explorer website is a virtual library of postal information and tools for USPS customers, business mailers, and employees. It brings a wealth of postal requirements for mailing and shipping together, in one place, in an easy-to-use format. https://pe.usps.com

Postal Facts   The history of the USPS reaches back to the founding of the Nation. The "Postal Facts" web page has information on postal operations and revenue, as well as other information of a more trivial character. https://facts.usps.com

Postal Money Orders   Using a money order for sending money by mail is a safe alternative to cash and personal checks. A USPS money orders is affordable, widely accepted, and never expires. The money order receipt helps with tracking the payment and shows proof of value in case the money order is damaged or stolen or goes missing. https://www.usps.com/international/money-transfers.htm

Postmaster and Post Officer Finder   Most postmasters who were appointed after 1986

and some postmasters who were appointed before that year, going back to the 18th century, are included in the database. Currently, complete information on more than 15,000 post offices is available, and the number increases weekly. https://about.usps.com/who-we-are/postmasterfinder/welcome.htm

Public Opinion On page 10 of its "FY2019 Annual Report to Congress," the USPS reported: "Public interest and opinion of our organization remain strong. In a poll released in September 2019, the Pew Research Center found that 90 percent of Americans held a favorable opinion of the Postal Service, a higher rating than any other Federal Government agency. Additionally, an April 2019 Gallup Poll found that three in four Americans (74 percent) rated the job performance of the organization as 'excellent' or 'good,' placing [it] as the highest rated Governmental agency. The Postal Service has achieved this top ranking every year Gallup has measured it (2014, 2017, and 2019)." https://about.usps.com/what/financials/annual-reports/fy2019.pdf

Reading Areas Reading areas are maintained in the library at USPS Headquarters on the 11th Floor. The library's holdings include historic, legal, regulatory, and other documents. Visitors must schedule an appointment before accessing the library. Phone, 202-268-2906.

Semipostal Stamps Semipostal stamps are postage stamps with a postage value equal to the First-Class Mail single-piece, 1-ounce, stamp rate, plus an amount to fund a designated cause. Revenue from sales of semipostal stamps, less the postage paid and the costs incurred by the Postal Service, is distributed to designated agencies for support of the particular cause. https://about.usps.com/what/corporate-social-responsibility/activities/semipostals.htm

Site Indices and Maps The USPS site index allows visitors to look for specific topics or to browse for content that aligns with their interests. https://www.usps.com/globals/site-index.htm

The PostalPro site index allows visitors to look for specific topics or to browse for content that aligns with their interests. https://postalpro.usps.com/site-index

The U.S. Postal Inspection Service site map allows visitors to look for specific topics or to browse for content that aligns with their interests. https://www.uspis.gov/sitemap

The Smithsonian's National Postal Museum site map allows visitors to look for specific topics or to browse for content that aligns with their interests. https://postalmuseum.si.edu/site-map

Social Media The USPS has a Facebook account. https://www.facebook.com/USPS

The Postal Service tweets announcements and other newsworthy items on Twitter. https://twitter.com/usps

The Postal Service posts videos on its YouTube channel. https://www.youtube.com/user/uspstv/custom

Stamp Collecting Stamps are miniature gateways to the world. Collectors learn about art, biography, culture, geography, and history as they pursue their interests and build their collections. Stamp collecting has very few rules, and expensive equipment is not required to participate. https://postalmuseum.si.edu/introduction-to-stamp-collecting

Sustainability The USPS is committed to environmental stewardship and leading by example to ensure that we leave behind a healthy biosphere and habitable planet for future generations. https://facts.usps.com/sustainability

The USPS 40-page "Annual Sustainability Report—2020" is available in Portable Document Format (PDF) for viewing online and downloading. https://about.usps.com/what/corporate-social-responsibility/sustainability

Zip Codes Looking for a Zip Code? Visit the "Look Up a Zip Code" web page. https://tools.usps.com/go/ZipLookupAction!input.action

The Sources of Information were updated 9–2020.

QUASI-OFFICIAL AGENCIES

Legal Services Corporation

3333 K Street NW., Washington, DC 20007
Phone, 202-295-1500. Fax, 202-337-6797. Internet, http://www.lsc.gov

Board of Directors

Chair	JOHN G. LEVI
Vice-Chair	FR. PIUS PIETRZYK, O.P.
	ROBERT J. GREY, JR.
	MATTHEW KEENAN
	ABIGAIL LAWLIS KUZMA
	VICTOR B. MADDOX
	JOHN G. MALCOLM
	LAURIE MIKVA
	FRANK X. NEUNER, JR.
	JULIE A. REISKIN
	GLORIA VALENCIA-WEBER

https://www.lsc.gov/about-lsc/board-members

Leadership

President	RONALD S. FLAGG
Chief of Staff	REBECCA FERTIG COHEN

Vice Presidents

Government Relations and Public Affairs	CAROL A. BERGMAN
Grants Management	LYNN A. JENNINGS
Legal Affairs	WILLIAM A. GUNN
Corporate Secretary	REBECCA FERTIG COHEN
General Counsel	WILLIAM A. GUNN
Treasurer	DEBORAH MOORE

Chief Officers

Data	(VACANCY)
Financial	DEBORAH MOORE
Information	JADA BREEGLE

Office Directors

Compliance and Enforcement	LORA RATH
Data Governance and Analysis	(VACANCY)
Human Resources	TRACI HIGGINS
Institutional Advancement	NADIA ELGUINDY
Program Performance	JOYCE MCGEE

https://www.lsc.gov/about-lsc/lsc-leadership

Inspector General	JEFFREY E. SCHANZ

https://www.oig.lsc.gov/about-oig/meet-the-ig

The above list of key personnel was updated 6–2021.

The Legal Services Corporation promotes equal access to justice and provides civil legal assistance to low-income persons.

Establishment and Organization

On July 25, 1974, President Richard M. Nixon approved Public Law 93–355 "to amend the Economic Opportunity Act of 1964 to provide for the transfer of the legal services program from the Office of Economic Opportunity to a Legal Services Corporation." The Legal Services Corporation Act of 1974, as amended (42 U.S.C. 2996 et seq.), established a private, nonprofit corporation to promote equal access to justice under the law for all Americans. https://www.govinfo.gov/content/pkg/STATUTE-88/pdf/STATUTE-88-Pg378.pdf

The President appoints, by the advice and with the consent of the Senate, the 11 members who constitute the Board of Directors, which heads the LSC. By law, it is bipartisan and no more than six members may be of the same political party. A member is appointed to a term of 3 years. A majority of the Board members must be members of the bar of the highest court of any State. The Board meets four or more times per year. https://www.govinfo.gov/content/pkg/USCODE-2017-title42/pdf/USCODE-2017-title42-chap34.pdf

An organizational chart is available on the "LSC Leadership" web page. https://www.lsc.gov/about-lsc/lsc-leadership

Activities

Congressional appropriations fund the LSC to provide legal services through grants to independent, local legal services provider programs. These programs are selected through a system of competition. In 2017, the LSC funded 133 programs. Together, they serve every county and congressional district in the Nation, as well as the U.S. Territories. Some of these programs address the particular needs of Native Americans and migrant farmworkers. http://www.lsc.gov/what-legal-aid/how-we-work

The legal services delivery system is based on several principles: local priorities, national accountability, competition for grants, and a strong public-private partnership. Local programs are governed by their own boards of directors, which set priorities and determine the types of cases that will be handled subject to restrictions set by Congress. A majority of each local board is appointed by local bar associations, and one-third of each local board is composed of client representatives appointed by client groups. Each board hires its own executive director. Programs may supplement their LSC grants with additional funds from State and local governments and other sources. They further leverage Federal funds by involving private attorneys in the delivery of legal services for the poor, mostly through volunteer pro bono work.

LSC-funded programs neither handle criminal cases nor accept fee-generating cases that private attorneys are willing to accept on a contingency basis. In addition, in 1996, a series of new limitations were placed upon activities in which LSC-funded programs may engage on behalf of their clients, even with non-LSC funds. All programs must comply with laws enacted by Congress and the implementing regulations promulgated by the LSC. http://www.lsc.gov/about-lsc/what-we-do

Sources of Information

Blog   The LSC maintains a blog. http://www.lsc.gov/media-center/blog

Board Meetings   Board meeting documents and information are available online. http://www.lsc.gov/about-lsc/board/board-meetings

Business Opportunities   The LSC regularly seeks the assistance of vendors to purchase products and contractors to carry out special projects. The LSC is eligible for General Services Administration schedule pricing and posts requests for proposals on eBuy and FedBizOpps.gov. http://www.lsc.gov/about-lsc/doing-business-lsc-rfps

Career Opportunities   The LSC is an organization of socially aware professionals who serve the unrepresented and promote equal justice. Information on career opportunities and working at the LSC is available online. http://www.lsc.gov/about-lsc/careers

Civil Legal Outcomes The LSC developed its civil legal outcomes toolkit to help legal aid programs with defining, collecting, and reporting on metrics that describe their effectiveness. The toolkit includes detailed instructions, electronic learning modules, examples, and additional resources for implementing an outcomes management system. https://www.lsc.gov/grants-grantee-resources/civil-legal-outcomes

Client Success Stories An interactive map allows website visitors to browse client success stories by State. http://www.lsc.gov/what-legal-aid/client-success-stories

Contact Us To make a media inquiry, submit a Freedom of Information Act request, ask a grant submission question, or need to contact the LSC for another reason, use the electronic form on the "Contact Us" web page. https://www.lsc.gov/about-lsc/contact-us

Data The LSC seeks to increase the accessibility of data that can help grantees, the media, and the public better understand the nature of civil legal needs and the services that are available for addressing the legal needs of individuals and families. https://www.lsc.gov/what-legal-aid/data

Donations Tax-deductible donations to the LSC support the use of technology innovations in legal services, provide law fellows for civil legal aid programs in need, raise public awareness of the legal aid system crisis, and support research into the effectiveness and need of civil legal aid. http://www.lsc.gov/support-lsc/donate-now

Events A list of upcoming events is available online. http://www.lsc.gov/meetings-and-events/calendar

Facts What percentage of the population is eligible for LSC-funded assistance? What is the average annual salary of LSC grantee staff attorneys? To learn the answers to these questions and others, visit the "Quick Facts" web page. http://www.lsc.gov/quick-facts

Federal Register Documents that the Legal Services Corporation recently published in the Federal Register are accessible online. https://www.federalregister.gov/agencies/legal-services-corporation

Find Legal Aid An online search tool is available to find the nearest LSC-funded

legal aid organization by address, city, or ZIP Code. http://www.lsc.gov/what-legal-aid/find-legal-aid

Freedom of Information Act (FOIA) The FOIA grants any person the right to request access to Federal agency records or information. U.S. Government agencies are required to disclose records after they receive a written request for them; however, the statute shields certain records from disclosure. The LSC complies with the FOIA and releases records to information seekers, as long as the desired records are not shielded. A FOIA request must be made in writing and may be submitted by electronic submission form, email, fax, or postal service. The request should be clearly marked: "Freedom of Information Act Request." Fax, 202-337-6519. http://www.lsc.gov/about-lsc/foia | Email: FOIA@lsc.gov

The LSC maintains a FOIA reading room online. Before submitting a FOIA request, information seekers should search the reading room for records that are immediately accessible. http://www.lsc.gov/about-lsc/foia/foia-electronic-public-reading-room

Grant Programs Descriptions of the LSC's seven grant programs—basic field, disaster relief emergency, technology initiative, and veterans appeals pro bono grants; leadership development and loan repayment assistance programs; and pro bono innovation fund—are available online. http://www.lsc.gov/grants-grantee-resources/our-grant-programs

Justice Gap The justice gap represents the difference between the level of civil legal assistance that is available and the level that is necessary to meet the legal needs of low-income individuals and families. To learn more about the justice gap, visit the "The Unmet Need for Legal Aid" web page. http://www.lsc.gov/what-legal-aid/unmet-need-legal-aid

Maps The LSC posts maps that provide a visual representation of nationwide statistics on poverty, disaster risks, flood zones, social vulnerability, and on other topics. https://www.lsc.gov/what-legal-aid/maps

News The LSC posts press releases on its website. http://www.lsc.gov/media-center/press-releases

Oversight The Office of the Inspector General from the LSC posts reports and data on Oversight.gov, a text-searchable repository of reports that Federal Inspectors General publish. The Council of the Inspectors General on Integrity and Efficiency operates and maintains the website to increase public access to independent and authoritative information on the Federal Government. https://oversight.gov

Publications   Annual reports, budget requests, factbooks, and reports are accessible online. http://www.lsc.gov/media-center/publications

Public Commentary   The LSC seeks public comments on a variety of proposals affecting grants and operations. https://www.lsc.gov/about-lsc/matters-comment

The Sources of Information were updated 6–2021.

Sharing Best Practices   The "Model Practices and Innovations" web page has a collection of resources: ideas, innovations, projects, and best practices. The legal aid community has contributed these resources as examples, models, or guidance in the quest to provide the highest quality and most effective legal services to low-income communities. https://www.lsc.gov/grants-grantee-resources/model-practices-innovations

Social Media   The LSC has a Facebook account. https://www.facebook.com/LegalServicesCorporation

The LSC tweets announcements and other newsworthy items on Twitter. https://twitter.com/lsctweets

Smithsonian Institution

1000 Jefferson Drive SW., Washington, DC 20560
Phone, 202-633-1000. Internet, http://www.si.edu

Board of Regents

Citizen Regents

Chair	David M. Rubenstein
Vice Chair	Steve M. Case
	Barbara M. Barrett
	John Fahey
	Roger W. Ferguson
	Michael Govan
	Risa J. Lavizzo-Mourey
	Michael M. Lynton
	John W. McCarter, Jr.

Congressional Regents

Representatives	Thomas J. Cole
	Samuel Johnson
	Doris Matsui
Senators	John Boozman
	Patrick J. Leahy
	David Perdue

Ex Officio Regents

Chief Justice of the United States	John G. Roberts, Jr.
Vice President of the United States	Michael R. Pence
Chief of Staff to the Regents	Porter Wilkinson

https://www.si.edu/regents/members

Senior Executives

Secretary https://www.si.edu/about/secretary-david-skorton	DAVID J. SKORTON
Chief Financial Officer	ALBERT G. HORVATH
Provost	JOHN H. DAVIS, ACTING
Assistant Secretary, Advancement	ZULLY DORR, ACTING
Assistant Secretary, Communications and External Affairs	CAROLYN MARTIN, ACTING
Assistant Secretary, Education and Access	PATTY BARTLETT, ACTING
Director, Equal Employment and Minority Affairs	ERA L. MARSHALL
General Counsel	JUDITH E. LEONARD

Administration / Program Directors

Under Secretary for Finance and Administration	ALBERT G. HORVATH
Chief Information Officer	DERON BURBA
Chief Investment Officer	AMY CHEN
Director, Contracting and Personal Property Management	THOMAS DEMPSEY
Director, Finance and Accounting	JEAN GARVIN
Director, Human Resources	WALTRUNETTE GARDNER, ACTING
Director, Planning, Management and Budget	DAVID VOYLES
Director, Policy and Analysis	H. WHITNEY WATRISS, ACTING
Director, Smithsonian Exhibits	SUSAN ADES
Director, Smithsonian Facilities	NANCY BECHTOL
Director, Sponsored Projects	TRACEY FRASER
President, Smithsonian Enterprises	CHRIS LIEDEL

Museums / Research Centers

Under Secretary for Museums and Research	JOHN H. DAVIS, ACTING

Directors

Anacostia Community Museum	LORI D. YARRISH, ACTING
Archives of American Art	KATE HAW
Center for Astrophysics	CHARLES R. ALCOCK
Center for Folklife and Cultural Heritage	MICHAEL A. MASON
Cooper Hewitt, Smithsonian Design Museum	CAROLINE BAUMANN
Freer Gallery of Art and Arthur M. Sackler Gallery	JULIAN RABY
Hirshhorn Museum and Sculpture Garden	MELISSA CHIU
National Air and Space Museum	JOHN R. DAILEY
National Museum of African American History and Culture	LONNIE G. BUNCH III
National Museum of African Art	CHRISTINE KREAMER, ACTING
National Museum of American History	JOHN GRAY
National Museum of Natural History	KIRK JOHNSON
National Museum of the American Indian	KEVIN GOVER
National Portrait Gallery	KIM SAJET
National Postal Museum	ELLIOT GRUBER
National Zoological Park	DENNIS KELLY
Smithsonian American Art Museum and Renwick Gallery	STEPHANIE STEBICH
Smithsonian Asian Pacific American Center	LISA SASAKI
Smithsonian Environmental Research Center	ANSON H. HINES
Smithsonian Institution Archives	ANNE VAN CAMP
Smithsonian Institution Traveling Exhibition Service	MYRIAM SPRINGUEL
Smithsonian Latino Center	EDUARDO DÍAZ
Smithsonian Libraries	NANCY E. GWINN
Smithsonian Marine Station	VALERIE J. PAUL

Smithsonian Museum Conservation Institute	ROBERT J. KOESTLER
Smithsonian Tropical Research Institute	MATTHEW LARSEN
https://www.si.edu/about/people	
Inspector General	CATHY L. HELM
https://www.si.edu/oig	

The above list of key personnel was updated 09–2017.

The Smithsonian Institution increases the fund of human knowledge and diffuses that knowledge among people.

The Smithsonian Institution was created by an act of Congress on August 10, 1846 (20 U.S.C. 41 et seq.), to carry out the terms of the will of British scientist James Smithson (1765–1829), who in 1826 had bequeathed his entire estate to the United States "to found at Washington, under the name of the Smithsonian Institution, an establishment for the increase and diffusion of knowledge among men." On July 1, 1836, Congress accepted the legacy and pledged the faith of the United States to the charitable trust. http://www.loc.gov/law/help/statutes-at-large/29th-congress/session-1/c29s1ch178.pdf

In September 1838, Smithson's legacy, which amounted to more than 100,000 gold sovereigns, was delivered to the mint at Philadelphia. Congress vested responsibility for administering the trust in the Secretary of the Smithsonian and the Smithsonian Board of Regents, composed of the Chief Justice, the Vice President, three Members of the Senate, three Members of the House of Representatives, and nine citizen members appointed by joint resolution of Congress. To carry out Smithson's mandate, the Institution executes the following functions: conducts scientific and scholarly research; publishes the results of studies, explorations, and investigations; preserves for study and reference more than 137 million artifacts, works of art, and scientific specimens; organizes exhibits representative of the arts, the sciences, American history, and world culture; shares Smithsonian resources and collections with communities throughout the Nation; and engages in educational programming and national and international cooperative research.

The Smithsonian Institution is an independent trust instrumentality of the United States that comprises the world's largest museum and research complex. It includes 19 museums and galleries, the National Zoo, and nine research facilities in several States and the Republic of Panama. The Institution is dedicated to public education, national service, and scholarship in the arts, sciences, history, and culture. Smithsonian activities are supported by its trust endowments and revenues; gifts, grants, and contracts; and funds appropriated to it by Congress. Admission to the museums in Washington, DC, is free. http://www.si.edu/About/History

Activities

Anacostia Community Museum   The Museum, located in the historic Fort Stanton neighborhood of Southeast Washington, serves as a national resource for exhibitions, historical documentation, and interpretive and educational programs relating to the impact of history and contemporary social issues on urban communities. http://anacostia.si.edu | Email: ACMinfo@si.edu

For further information, contact the Anacostia Community Museum, 1901 Fort Place SE., Washington, DC 20020. Phone, 202-633-4820.

Archives of American Art   The Archives contains the Nation's largest collection of documentary materials reflecting the history of visual arts in the United States. On the subject of art in America, it is the largest archives in the world, holding more than 16 million documents. The Archives gathers, preserves, and microfilms the papers of artists, craftsmen, collectors, dealers, critics, and art societies. These papers include manuscripts, letters, diaries, notebooks, sketchbooks, business records, clippings, exhibition catalogs, transcripts of tape-recorded interviews, and photographs of artists and their work. http://www.aaa.si.edu

For further information, contact the Archives of American Art, Suite 2200, 750 Ninth Street NW., Washington, DC 20001. Phone, 202-633-7940.

Arthur M. Sackler Gallery This Asian art museum opened in 1987 on the National Mall. Changing exhibitions drawn from major collections in the United States and abroad, as well as from the permanent holdings of the Sackler Gallery, are displayed in the distinctive below-ground museum. The Gallery's growing permanent collection is founded on a group of art objects from China, South and Southeast Asia, and the ancient Near East that were given to the Smithsonian by Arthur M. Sackler (1913–1987). The Museum's current collection features Persian manuscripts; Japanese paintings; ceramics, prints, and textiles; sculptures from India; and paintings and metalware from China, Korea, Japan, and Southeast Asia. The Sackler Gallery is connected by an underground exhibition space to the neighboring Freer Gallery. http://www.asia.si.edu | Email: publicaffairsAsia@si.edu

For further information, contact the Arthur M. Sackler Gallery, 1050 Independence Avenue SW., Washington, DC 20560. Phone, 202-633-4880.

Center for Astrophysics The Smithsonian Astrophysical Observatory and the Harvard College Observatory have coordinated research activities under a single director in a cooperative venture, Harvard-Smithsonian Center for Astrophysics. The Center's research activities are organized in the following areas of study: atomic and molecular physics, radio and geoastronomy, high-energy astrophysics, optical and infrared astronomy, planetary sciences, solar and stellar physics, and theoretical astrophysics. Research results are published in the Center Preprint Series and other technical and nontechnical bulletins and distributed to scientific and educational institutions around the world. http://www.cfa.harvard.edu/sao

For more information, contact the Smithsonian Astrophysical Observatory, 60 Garden Street, Cambridge, MA 02138. Phone, 617-495-7463.

Center for Folklife and Cultural Heritage The Center is responsible for research, documentation, and presentation of grassroots cultural traditions. It maintains a documentary collection and produces Smithsonian Folkways Recordings, educational materials, documentary films, publications, and traveling exhibits, as well as the annual Smithsonian Folklife Festival on the National Mall. Recent Folklife festivals have featured a range of American music styles, a number of State tributes, and performers from around the world. Admission to the festival is free. The 2-week program includes Fourth of July activities on the National Mall. http://www.folklife.si.edu

For further information, contact the Center for Folklife and Cultural Heritage, Capital Gallery, Suite 2001, 600 Maryland Avenue SW., Washington, DC 20024. Phone, 202-633-1000.

Cooper Hewitt, Smithsonian Design Museum The Museum is the only museum in the country devoted exclusively to historical and contemporary design. Collections include objects in such areas as applied arts and industrial design, drawings and prints, glass, metalwork, wallcoverings, and textiles. Changing exhibits and public programs seek to educate by exploring the role of design in daily life. http://cooperhewitt.org

For further information, contact the Cooper Hewitt, Smithsonian Design Museum, 2 East Ninety-First Street, New York, NY 10128. Phone, 212-849-8400.

Freer Gallery of Art The building, the original collection, and an endowment were the gift of Charles Lang Freer (1854–1919). The Gallery houses one of the world's most renowned collections of Asian art, an important group of ancient Egyptian glass, early Christian manuscripts, and works by 19th- and early 20th-century American artists. The objects in the Asian collection represent the arts of East Asia, the Near East, and South and Southeast Asia, including paintings, manuscripts, scrolls, screens, ceramics, metalwork, glass, jade, lacquer, and sculpture. Members of the staff conduct research on objects in the collection and publish results in scholarly journals and books for general and scholarly audiences. http://www.asia.si.edu | Email: publicaffairsAsia@si.edu

For further information, contact the Freer Gallery of Art, Jefferson Drive at Twelfth Street SW., Washington, DC 20560. Phone, 202-633-4880.

Hirshhorn Museum and Sculpture Garden

From cubism to minimalism, the Museum houses major collections of modern and contemporary art. The nucleus of the collection is the gift and bequest of Joseph H. Hirshhorn (1899–1981). Supplementing the permanent collection are loan exhibitions. The Museum houses a collection research facility, a specialized art library, and a photographic archive, available for consultation by prior appointment. The outdoor sculpture garden is located nearby on the National Mall. There is an active program of public service and education, including docent tours, lectures on contemporary art and artists, and films of historic and artistic interest. http://www.hirshhorn.si.edu | Email: hmsginquiries@si.edu

For further information, contact the Hirshhorn Museum and Sculpture Garden, Seventh Street and Independence Avenue SW., Washington, DC 20560. Phone, 202-633-4674.

Museum Conservation Institute

The Institute researches preservation, conservation, and technical study and analysis of collection materials. Its researchers investigate the chemical and physical processes that are involved in the care of art, artifacts, and specimens and attempt to formulate conditions and procedures for storage, exhibit, and stabilization that optimize the preservation of these objects. In interdisciplinary collaborations with archeologists, anthropologists, and art historians, natural and physical scientists study and analyze objects from the collections and related materials to expand knowledge and understanding of their historical and scientific context. http://www.si.edu/mci

For further information, contact the Museum Conservation Institute, Museum Support Center, Suitland, MD 20746. Phone, 301-238-1240.

National Air and Space Museum

Created to memorialize the development and achievements of aviation and spaceflight, the Museum collects, displays, and preserves aeronautical and space flight artifacts of historical significance, as well as documentary and artistic materials related to air and space. Among its artifacts are full-size planes, models, and instruments. Highlights of the collection include the Wright brothers' "Flyer," Charles Lindbergh's "Spirit of St. Louis," a Moon rock, and Apollo spacecraft. The exhibitions and study collections record the human leap into the air, the sky, and space beyond. They offer a concentrated presentation of flight craft of all types, spaceflight vehicles, and propulsion systems. The Museum's IMAX Theater and domed Einstein Planetarium are popular attractions. The Museum's Steven F. Udvar-Hazy Center, at Washington Dulles International Airport, features artifacts that include a space shuttle and the "Enola Gay" World War II bomber. http://airandspace.si.edu | Email: NASMVisitorServices@si.edu

For further information, contact the National Air and Space Museum, Sixth Street and Independence Avenue SW., Washington, DC 20560. Phone, 202-633-2214.

National Museum of African American History and Culture

Established in 2003, the Museum is the first national museum that documents exclusively African American art, culture, history, and life. http://www.nmaahc.si.edu | Email: NMAAHCinfo@si.edu

For further information, contact the National Museum of African American History and Culture, Capital Gallery, Suite 7001, 600 Maryland Avenue SW., Washington, DC 20024. Phone, 202-633-1000.

National Museum of African Art

This is the only art museum in the United States that portrays exclusively Africa's creative, visual traditions. Its research components, collection, exhibitions, and public programs make the Museum a primary source for the examination and discovery of African arts and culture. The collection includes works in wood, metal, fired clay, ivory, and fiber. The Eliot Elisofon Photographic Archives includes slides, photos, and film segments on Africa. There is also a specialized library. http://africa.si.edu

For further information, contact the National Museum of African Art, 950 Independence Avenue SW., Washington, DC 20560. Phone, 202-633-4600.

National Museum of American History

In pursuit of its fundamental mission to inspire a broader understanding of the

United States and its people, the Museum provides learning opportunities, stimulates the imagination of visitors, and presents challenging ideas about the Nation's past. The Museum's exhibits provide a unique view of the American experience. Emphasis is placed upon innovative individuals representing a wide range of cultures, who have shaped our heritage, and upon science and the remaking of our world through technology. Exhibits draw upon strong collections in the sciences and engineering, agriculture, manufacturing, transportation, political memorabilia, costumes, musical instruments, coins, Armed Forces history, photography, computers, ceramics, and glass. Classic cars, icons of the American Presidency, First Ladies' gowns, the Star-Spangled Banner flag, Whitney's cotton gin, Morse's telegraph, the John Bull locomotive, Dorothy's ruby slippers from "The Wizard of Oz," and other American icons are highlights of the collection. http://www. americanhistory.si.edu | Email: info@si.edu

For further information, contact the National Museum of American History, Fourteenth Street and Constitution Avenue NW., Washington, DC 20560. Phone, 202-633-1000.

National Museum of Natural

History Dedicated to understanding the natural world and the place of humans in it, the Museum's permanent exhibitions focus on human cultures, Earth sciences, biology, and anthropology, with the most popular displays featuring gem stones such as the Hope Diamond, dinosaurs, insects, marine ecosystems, birds, and mammals. In 2010, the Museum celebrated its 100th anniversary with the opening of a new permanent exhibition, the David H. Koch Hall of Human Origins. An IMAX theater offers large-format films. The Museum's encyclopedic collections comprise more than 126 million specimens, making the Museum one of the world's foremost facilities for natural history research. The Museum's seven departments are anthropology, botany, entomology, invertebrate zoology, mineral sciences, paleobiology, and vertebrate zoology. Doctorate-level staff researchers ensure the continued growth and value of the collection by conducting studies in the field

and laboratory. http://www.mnh.si.edu | Email: naturalexperience@si.edu

For further information, contact the National Museum of Natural History, Tenth Street and Constitution Avenue NW., Washington, DC 20560. Phone, 202-633-1000.

National Museum of the American

Indian The Museum was established in 1989, and the building on the National Mall opened September 2004. Much of the collection of the Museum is comprised of the collection of the former Heye Foundation in New York City. It is an institution of living cultures dedicated to the collection, preservation, study, and exhibition of the life, languages, literature, history, and arts of the Native peoples of the Americas. Highlights include Northwest Coast carvings; dance masks; pottery and weaving from the Southwest; painted hides and garments from the North American Plains; goldwork of the Aztecs, Incas, and Maya; and Amazonian featherwork. The National Museum of the American Indian also operates the George Gustav Heye Center at the Alexander Hamilton U.S. Custom House in New York City. http://americanindian.si.edu | Email: NMAI-info@si.edu

For further information, contact the National Museum of the American Indian, Fourth Street and Independence Avenue SW., Washington, DC 20560. Phone, 202-633-1000.

National Portrait Gallery The Gallery was established in 1962 for the exhibition and study of portraiture depicting men and women who have made significant contributions to the history, development, and culture of the United States. The Gallery contains more than 19,000 works, including photographs and glass negatives. The first floor of the Gallery is devoted to changing exhibitions from the Gallery's collection of paintings, sculpture, prints, photographs, and drawings as well as to special portrait collections. Featured on the second floor are the permanent collection of portraits of eminent Americans and the Hall of Presidents, including the famous Gilbert Stuart portrait-from-life of George Washington. The two-story American Victorian Renaissance Great Hall on the third floor of the Gallery houses an exhibit of 20th-century Americans and is used for special events and public programs. The Gallery shares a large library with the Smithsonian American Art Museum and the Archives of American Art. The education department offers public programs; outreach programs for adult groups; and walk-in and group tours. http://www.npg.si.edu | Email: npgnews@si.edu

For further information, contact the National Portrait Gallery, Eighth and F Streets NW., Washington, DC 20001. Phone, 202-633-8300.

National Postal Museum   The Museum houses the Nation's postal history and philatelic collection, the largest of its kind in the world, with more than 13 million objects. The Museum is devoted to the history of America's mail service, and major galleries include exhibits on mail service in colonial times and during the Civil War, the Pony Express, modern mail service, automation, mail transportation, and the art of letters, as well as displays of the Museum's priceless stamp collection. Highlights include three mail planes, a replica of a railway mail car, displays of historic letters, handcrafted mail boxes, and rare U.S. and foreign-issue stamps and covers. http://postalmuseum.si.edu

For further information, contact the National Postal Museum, 2 Massachusetts Avenue NE., Washington, DC 20001. Phone, 202-633-1000.

National Zoological Park   The National Zoo is an international leader in wildlife conservation, education, and research. Home to more than 2,000 animals, the Zoo encompasses 163 acres along Rock Creek Park in Northwest Washington. Exhibits include the David M. Rubenstein Family Giant Panda Habitat, where the giant pandas Mei Xiang and Tian Tian reside with their cub Bao Bao. Built to mimic the animals' natural habitat in China, it is part of the Zoo's Asia Trail, which also takes visitors through the habitats of red pandas, Asian small-clawed otters, fishing cats, sloth bears, and clouded leopards. Other highlights include the Elephant Trails, home to the Asian elephant Kandula, who was born at the Zoo in 2001; Amazonia, a 15,000-square-foot rain forest habitat; the Reptile Discovery Center, featuring African pancake tortoises and the world's largest

lizards, Komodo dragons; and the Great Ape House, home to gorillas, orangutans, and other primates. http://nationalzoo.si.edu

For further information, contact the National Zoo, 3001 Connecticut Avenue NW., Washington, DC 20008. Phone, 202- 633-4888.

Renwick Gallery   The Gallery, a branch of the Smithsonian American Art Museum, is dedicated to exhibiting crafts of all periods and to collecting 20th-century American crafts. It offers changing exhibitions of American crafts and decorative arts, both historical and contemporary, and a rotating selection from its permanent collection. The Gallery's grand salon is elegantly furnished in the Victorian style of the 1860s and 1870s. http://www.americanart.si.edu/renwick | Email: AmericanArtRenwick@si.edu

For further information, contact the Renwick Gallery, Seventeenth Street and Pennsylvania Avenue NW., Washington, DC 20006. Phone, 202-633-7970.

Smithsonian American Art Museum   The Museum's art collection spans centuries of American painting, sculpture, folk art, photography, and graphic art. A major center for research in American art, the Museum has contributed to such resources as the Inventory of American Paintings Executed Before 1914, the Smithsonian Art Index, and the Inventory of American Sculpture. The library, shared with the National Portrait Gallery, contains volumes on art, history, and biography, with special emphasis on the United States. The Donald W. Reynolds Center for American Art and Portraiture is home to the Smithsonian American Art Museum, the National Portrait Gallery, and the Archives of American Art. Hundreds of images from the collection and extensive information on its collections, publications, and activities are available on the Museum's Web site. http://www.americanart.si.edu | Email: AmericanArtInfo@si.edu

For further information, contact the Smithsonian American Art Museum, Eighth and F Streets NW., Washington, DC 20006. Phone, 202-633-7970.

Smithsonian Asian Pacific American Center   The Center seeks to enrich the appreciation of America's Asian Pacific heritage and empower Asian Pacific American communities in their sense of inclusion within the national culture. http://smithsonianapa.org | Email: apac@si.edu

For further information, contact the Asian Pacific American Center's administrative office, Capital Gallery, Suite 7065, MRC 516, P.O. Box 37012, Washington, DC 20013-7012. Phone, 202-633-2691.

Smithsonian Environmental Research Center (SERC) The Center is the leading national research center for understanding environmental issues in the coastal zone. SERC is dedicated to increasing knowledge of the biological and physical processes that sustain life on Earth. The Center, located near the Chesapeake Bay, trains future generations of scientists to address ecological questions of the Nation and the globe. http://www.serc.si.edu

For further information, contact the Smithsonian Environmental Research Center, 647 Contees Wharf Road, Edgewater, MD 21037. Phone, 443-482-2200.

Smithsonian Institution Archives The Smithsonian Institution Archives acquires, preserves, and makes available for research the official records of the Smithsonian Institution and the papers of individuals and organizations associated with the Institution or with its work. These holdings document the growth of the Smithsonian and the development of American science, history, and art. http://siarchives.si.edu

For further information, contact the Smithsonian Institution Archives, Capital Gallery, Suite 3000, 600 Maryland Avenue SW., Washington, DC 20024. Phone, 202-633-5870.

Smithsonian Institution Traveling Exhibition Service (SITES) Since 1952, SITES has been committed to making Smithsonian exhibitions available to millions of people who cannot view them firsthand at the Smithsonian museums. Exhibitions on art, history, and science travel to more than 250 locations each year. http://www.sites.si.edu

For further information, contact the Smithsonian Institution Traveling Exhibition Service, Suite 7103, 470 L'Enfant Plaza SW., Washington, DC 20024. Phone, 202-633-3120.

Smithsonian Latino Center The Center promotes Latino presence within the Smithsonian Institution. It is not represented in one physical location; rather, it works collaboratively with the Institution's museums and research centers to ensure that the

contributions of the Latino community in the arts, history, national culture, and scientific achievement are celebrated, explored, presented, and preserved. The Center supports collections and archives, exhibitions, public and educational programs, research, and Web-based content and virtual platforms. It also manages leadership and professional development programs for emerging scholars, museum professionals, and Latino youth. http://latino.si.edu/Home

For further information, contact the Smithsonian Latino Center at Capital Gallery, 600 Maryland Avenue SW., MRC 512, Washington, DC 20013-7012. Phone, 202-633-1240.

Smithsonian Libraries The Smithsonian Institution Libraries include more than 1 million volumes (among them, 40,000 rare books) with strengths in natural history, art, science, humanities, and museology. Many volumes are available through interlibrary loan. http://library.si.edu

For further information, contact the Smithsonian Institution Libraries, Tenth Street and Constitution Avenue NW., Washington, DC 20560. Phone, 202-633-2240.

Smithsonian Marine Station at Fort Pierce The research institute features a state-of-the-art laboratory where Station scientists catalog species and study marine plants and animals. Among the most important projects being pursued at the site is the search for possible causes of fishkills, including Pfiesteria and other organisms. http://www.sms.si.edu

For further information, contact the Smithsonian Marine Station–Fort Pierce, 701 Seaway Drive, Fort Pierce, FL 34949. Phone, 772-462-6220.

Smithsonian Tropical Research Institute (STRI) The Institute is a research organization for advanced studies of tropical ecosystems. Headquartered in the Republic of Panama, STRI maintains extensive facilities in the Western Hemisphere tropics. It is the base of a corps of tropical researchers who study the evolution, behavior, ecology, and history of tropical species of systems ranging from coral reefs to rain forests. http://www.stri.org

For further information, contact the Smithsonian Tropical Research Institute, 1100 Jefferson Drive SW., Suite 3123, Washington, DC 20560. Phone, 202-633-4700. Phone, 011-507-212-8000 (Panama).

Sources of Information

Business Opportunities   Information on procurement of supplies, property management and utilization services for Smithsonian Institution organizations, and construction contracts may be obtained from the Director, Office of Contracting, Smithsonian Institution, 2011 Crystal Drive, Suite 350, Arlington, VA 22202. Phone, 202-633-7290. http://www.si.edu/se/seproductsubmissions.aspx

Career Opportunities   Employment information is available from the Office of Human Resources, Smithsonian Institution, Capital Gallery, Suite 5060, 600 Maryland Avenue SW., Washington, DC 20560. Phone, 202-633-6370. http://www.sihr.si.edu

In 2016, the Smithsonian Institution ranked 7th among 27 midsize Government agencies in the Best Places To Work Agency Rankings. http://bestplacestowork.org/BPTW/rankings/detail/SM00

Education / Research   Write to the Directors of the following offices at the Smithsonian Institution, Washington, DC 20560: Office of Fellowships and Internships, Smithsonian Center for Folklife and Cultural Heritage, Smithsonian Science Education Center, and Smithsonian Center for Learning and Digital Access. http://www.smithsonianofi.com http://www.folklife.si.edu https://ssec.si.edu http://smithsonianeducation.org

Frequently Asked Questions (FAQs)   The Smithsonian Institution posts answers to FAQs on its website. https://www.si.edu/faqs

Media Affairs   Members of the press may contact the Smithsonian Office of Public Affairs, 1000 Jefferson Drive SW., Washington, DC 20560. Phone, 202-633-2400. http://newsdesk.si.edu/contacts

Memberships   For information on the Friends of the Smithsonian, write to PO Box 37012, MRC 712 Washington, DC 20013-7012. Phone, 202-633-6300. http://smithsonianmembership.com | Email: membership@si.edu

For information on the Resident Associate Program, write to Smithsonian Associates, PO Box 23293, Washington, DC 20026-3293. Phone, 202-633-3030. http://residentassociates.org

For information on the Smithsonian National Associate Program, call 800-766-2149. http://www.si.edu/Membership

For information on the National Air and Space Society, call 202-633-2603. http://www.nasm.si.edu/getinvolved/membership | Email: MembershipNASM@si.edu

For information on the Friends of the National Zoo, call 202-633-3038. http://nationalzoo.si.edu/Audiences/Members

For information on National Museum of the American Indian membership, call 800-242-6624. http://americanindian.si.edu | Email: NMAImember@si.edu

Organizational Chart   The Smithsonian Institution's organizational chart is accessible online in Portable Document Format (PDF) for viewing and downloading. https://www.si.edu/Content/Pdf/About/Smithsonian-organizational-chart.pdf

Photographs   Photographs and slides from the Smithsonian photographic archives are available to researchers, publishers, Government agencies, and the general public. A searchable database of images is available online. Purchase or use of images may require permission from the Smithsonian curatorial unit that holds copyright. For assistance, contact Smithsonian Photographic Services. Phone, 202-633-1933. http://www.si.edu/Collections | Email: photos@si.edu

Publications   The Smithsonian Institution's annual reports, starting with the year 2004, are available online as Portable Document Format (PDF) files. For information on acquiring hardcopies of reports, call 202-633-1000. http://www.si.edu/About/Annual-Report | Email: info@si.edu

Smithsonian Books, in collaboration with the Smithsonian Institution, publishes narrative nonfiction books on culture, history, science and technology, and the arts, as well as signature illustrated books based on Smithsonian museums and their collections. Random House Publisher Services distribute these titles. http://www.smithsonianbooks.com

Smithsonian Institution Scholarly Press, in conjunction with Rowman and Littlefield Publishing Group, Inc., publishes the research and other scholarly contributions of Smithsonian authors. http://www.scholarlypress.si.edu

Subscribe to the "Smithsonian Magazine" online. Phone, 800-766-2149. http://www. smithsonianmag.com | Email: smithsonian@customersvc.com

Subscribe to "Air and Space Magazine" online. Phone, 800-513-3081. http://www.airspacemag.com/?no-ist | Email: airandspace@customersvc.com

Social Media   The Smithsonian Institution has a Facebook account. https://www.facebook.com/Smithsonian

The Smithsonian Institution tweets announcements and other newsworthy items on Twitter. https://twitter.com/smithsonian

The Smithsonian Institution posts videos on its YouTube channel. https://www.youtube.com/user/SmithsonianVideos

Tours   For information on museum and gallery tours, contact the Smithsonian Information Center, 1000 Jefferson Drive SW., Washington, DC 20560. Phone, 202-633-1000. School groups are welcome. The benefits of various memberships and their levels include special guided tours. http://www.si.edu/Visit/GroupTours

Visitor Information   The Smithsonian Information Center, located in the original Smithsonian building, commonly known as The Castle, provides general orientation through films, computer interactive programs, and visitor information specialists to help members and the public learn about the national collections, museum events, exhibitions, and special programs. Write to the Smithsonian Information Center, 1000 Jefferson Drive SW., Washington, DC 20560. Phone, 202-633-1000. http://www.si.edu/Visit/Hours

An accessibility map of Smithsonian museums on and near the National Mall is available online. https://www.si.edu/content/ovs/accessmapsindd.pdf

Volunteer Opportunities   The Smithsonian Institution welcomes volunteers and offers a variety of service opportunities. For information, write to the Office of Visitor Services, 1000 Jefferson Drive SW., Washington, DC 20560. Phone, 202-633-1000. http://www.si.edu/Volunteer http://www.nga.gov/content/ngaweb/contact-us/department-list

For further information, contact the Smithsonian Information Center, 1000 Jefferson Drive SW., Washington, DC 20560. Phone, 202-633-1000. TDD, 202-357-1729.

John F. Kennedy Center for the Performing Arts

John F. Kennedy Center for the Performing Arts, Washington, DC 20566
Phone, 202-467-4600. Internet, http://www.kennedy-center.org

Chair	DAVID M. RUBENSTEIN
President	DEBORAH F. RUTTER
http://www.kennedy-center.org/pages/about/ourpeople	
National Symphony Orchestra	
Music Director	GIANANDREA NOSEDA
http://www.kennedy-center.org/artist/A58901	
The Suzanne Farrell Ballet	
Artistic Director	SUZANNE FARRELL
http://www.kennedy-center.org/sfb/biography	
Washington National Opera	
Artistic Director	FRANCESCA ZAMBELLO
http://www.kennedy-center.org/wno/MTO/ArtDir	

The above list of key personnel was updated 09–2017.

The Kennedy Center is the only official memorial to President John F. Kennedy in Washington, DC. The Center presents a year-round program of dance, drama, music, and opera from the United States and abroad.

Sources of Information

Business Opportunities   Opportunities are posted on the Federal Business Opportunities Web site. For more information, contact The John F. Kennedy Center for the Performing Arts, Washington, DC 20566. https://www.fbo.gov

Career Opportunities   Job descriptions of open positions are available online. http://www.kennedy-center.org/jobs

The John F. Kennedy Center for the Performing Arts offers internships for undergraduate and graduate students and for recent college graduates. http://education.kennedy-center.org/education/internships/overview.html

In partnership with American University, the Center offers a merit-based, 9-month fellowship in art management. http://education.kennedy-center.org/education/internships/fellowships.html

Education / Research   For information on education programs, contact The John F. Kennedy Center for the Performing Arts, Washington, DC 20566. Phone, 202-416-8000. http://www.kennedy-center.org/education

Free Performances   Free performances are given every day at 6 p.m. on the Millennium Stage in the Grand Foyer. https://www.kennedy-center.org/video/upcoming

History   In January of 1964, not long after the death of President John F. Kennedy, Congress designated the National Cultural Center as a "living memorial" to the slain President and authorized 23 million dollars to help build what is known today as the John F. Kennedy Center for the Performing Arts. Before the end of that year, enough artwork, building materials, and additional funds had been donated to start construction. With a gold-plated spade that had been used to break ground at both the Lincoln and Jefferson Memorials, President Lyndon B. Johnson symbolically removed the first soil from the new site. The Center opened to the public in 1971, more than a decade after President Dwight D. Eisenhower and legislators, from both parties, had taken initial steps toward realizing this vision. To learn more about the people who imagined a cultural center

for the Nation, those who supported its realization, and the emergence of the John F. Kennedy Center for the Performing Arts as an iconic institution of the arts, visit the "History" Web page. http://www.kennedy-center.org/pages/about/history

Live Streaming   The Center live streams artists while they perform. http://www.kennedy-center.org/video/live

Memberships   For information on national and local activities, including the bimonthly "Kennedy Center News" for members, visit an information desk inside The John F. Kennedy Center for the Performing Arts. Or, contact Member Services, The John F. Kennedy Center for the Performing Arts, Washington, DC 20566. Phone, 202-416-8310. http://www.kennedy-center.org/membership | Email: membership@kennedy-center.org

Social Media   John F. Kennedy Center for the Performing Arts has a Facebook account. https://www.facebook.com/KennedyCenter

The Center tweets announcements and other newsworthy items on Twitter. https://twitter.com/KenCen

The Center posts videos on its YouTube channel. https://www.youtube.com/user/TheKennedyCenter

Special Functions   For information on using the facilities for special functions, contact the Office of Special Events, The John F. Kennedy Center for the Performing Arts, Washington, DC 20566. Phone, 202-416-8000. https://www.kennedy-center.org/rental

Theater Operations   For information on using the theaters, contact the booking manager at The John F. Kennedy Center for the Performing Arts, Washington, DC 20566. Phone, 202-416-8032. http://www.kennedy-center.org/pages/theaterrental

Tickets   Tickets for admission to performances may be purchased at the box office, by mail, by phone using instant-charge, or online. Phone, 202-467-4600. TTY, 202-416-8524. https://www.kennedy-center.org/tickets

The Center posts answers to frequently asked ticket-related questions. http://www.kennedy-center.org/contact/topic/1

Tours   The Friends of the Kennedy Center volunteers provide visitor services. Tours are available free of charge on weekdays, 10 a.m.–5 p.m., and on weekends, 10 a.m.–1

p.m. https://www.kennedy-center.org/pages/visitor/tours

Videos The Center regularly posts short videos of artists performing. Its Web site has an expanding collection of over 2,000 selections. http://www.kennedy-center.org/Video/recentVideos

Volunteer Opportunities For information on volunteer opportunities, contact Friends of the Kennedy Center, 2700 F Street NW, Washington, DC 20566. Phone, 202-416-8000. http://www.kennedy-center.org/support/volunteers http://www.kennedy-center.org/contact

For further information, contact The John F. Kennedy Center for the Performing Arts. Phone, 202-467-4600.

National Gallery of Art

4th and Constitution Avenue NW., Washington, DC 20565
Phone, 202-737-4215. Internet, http://www.nga.gov

Executive Officers

Director	KAYWIN FELDMAN
Secretary / General Counsel	NANCY R. BREUER

https://www.nga.gov/about/directors-welcome.html

General Trustees

President	MITCHELL P. RALES
Chair	SHARON P. ROCKEFELLER

https://www.nga.gov/about/leadership.html

The above list of key personnel was updated 10–2020.

Activities

The National Gallery of Art administers a world-class collection of painting, sculpture, and the graphic arts. The West Building includes European (13th–early 20th century) and American (18th–early 20th century) works. An extensive survey of Italian painting and sculpture, including the only painting by Leonardo da Vinci in the Americas, is on display in the Gallery. Rich in Dutch masters and French impressionists, the collection offers superb surveys of American, British, Flemish, Spanish, and 15th- and 16th-century German art, as well as Renaissance medals and bronzes, Chinese porcelains, and about 117,000 works of graphic art from the 12th century to the present day. The East Building collections and Sculpture Garden contain important works by major 20th-century artists. The Gallery relies on public and private resources. Federal appropriations support its operations and maintenance. Private donations and funds allow it to acquire artwork, as well as to offer a variety of special programs. For example, a fellowship program promotes graduate and postgraduate research, an extension service provides free education resources to millions of people each year, and other programs educate schoolchildren and the public.

Sources of Information

Business Opportunities For more information, contact the National Gallery of Art, Office of Procurement and Contracts, 2000B South Club Drive, Landover, MD 20785. Phone, 202-842-6745. Fax, 202-312-2792. https://www.fbo.gov/index?s=main&mode=list&tab=list

Calendar The full calendar of events is available online. To subscribe to the quarterly brochure of seasonal exhibition and programming highlights, visit the Gallery's Web site or call 202-842-6662. http://www.nga.gov/content/ngaweb/calendar.html | Email: calendar@nga.gov

Career Opportunities The National Gallery of Art relies on approximately 1,000 employees to carry out its mission.

Some positions require a background in art history or design; however, other positions—like salesperson, security guard, and visitor services aide—support the museum's daily operations and are less specialized. The National Gallery of Art also employs accountants, administrators, facilities managers, fundraisers, information systems specialists, librarians, and other professionals with technical expertise. Phone, 202-842-6282. http://www.nga.gov/content/ngaweb/opportunities/employment-opportunities.html | Email: staffing@nga.gov

The National Gallery of Art offers internships and opportunities for fellows. Conservation and curatorial fellowships are available, as well as Center for Advanced Study in the Visual Arts (CASVA) fellowships. http://www.nga.gov/content/ngaweb/opportunities/interns-and-fellows.html

The National Gallery of Art offers a range of volunteer opportunities. Volunteers serve as docents, manage the information desks at the entrances to the East and West Buildings, work in the library, and help in the horticulture division. Local high school students can participate in the teen volunteer program. http://www.nga.gov/content/ngaweb/opportunities/volunteer-opportunities.html

Center for Advanced Study in the Visual Arts (CASVA)   The CASVA is a research institute that supports study of the production, use, and cultural meaning of architecture, art, artifacts, film, photography, and urbanism. It offers fellowships, organizes scholarly meetings, produces publications, and supports research. These activities are privately funded through endowments and grants to the National Gallery of Art. Phone, 202-842-6480. http://www.nga.gov/content/ngaweb/research/casva.html | Email: casva@nga.gov

Concerts   Concerts by accomplished musicians are open to the public without charge. Seating starts 30 minutes before the performance on a first-come, first-seated basis. Phone, 202-842-6941. http://www.nga.gov/content/ngaweb/calendar/concerts.html

Educational Resources   The Gallery's free loan program allows community groups, educational institutions, individuals, and nonprofit television stations nationwide to borrow teaching packets and DVDs. Dozens of lessons and activities are also accessible on the Gallery's Web site. For more information, including the free catalog of education resources, contact the Department of Education Resources, National Gallery of Art, 2000B South Club Drive, Landover, MD 20785. Phone, 202-842-6273. http://www.nga.gov/content/ngaweb/education/learningresources.html | Email: edresources@nga.gov

Family Programs   The Gallery offers free family programs—children's films, music performances, storytelling, and workshops—that are suitable for children ages 4 and up. Phone, 202-789-3030. http://www.nga.gov/content/ngaweb/education/families.html | Email: family@nga.gov

Films   An ongoing program of classic cinema, documentary, avant-garde, and area premieres takes place each weekend. Seating is on a first-come, first-seated basis, and admission is free. Doors open approximately 30 minutes before each show. Visiting filmmakers and scholars discuss films with the audiences following some screenings. Phone, 202-842-6799. http://www.nga.gov/content/ngaweb/calendar/film-programs.html | Email: film-department@nga.gov

Frequently Asked Questions (FAQs)   The National Gallery of Art posts answers to FAQs on its Web site. http://www.nga.gov/content/ngaweb/contact-us.html

Ice-Skating Rink   Each winter, the National Gallery of Art opens its ice rink in the Sculpture Garden. The seasonal skating schedule is posted online in November. http://www.nga.gov/content/ngaweb/visit/ice-rink.html

Image Collections   The Department of Image Collections serves as the National Gallery of Art's research center for images of Western art and architecture. The collections now contain over 14 million digital images, microforms, negatives, photographs, and slides, making this resource one of the largest of its kind. Gallery staff, Center for Advanced Study in the Visual Arts (CASVA) members, visiting scholars, and serious adult researchers regularly use the collections. The library is accessible by appointment every Monday, noon–4:30 p.m., and Tuesday–Friday, 10 a.m.–4:30 p.m., except on Federal holidays. Phone, 202-842-6026. http://www.nga.gov/content/ngaweb/research/library/imagecollections.html

Lectures   Lecture events are open to the public, and admission is free. Seating is available on a first-come, first-seated basis. http://www.nga.gov/content/ngaweb/calendar/lectures.html

Library   The National Gallery of Art Library maintains a collection of more than 400,000 books and periodicals on the history, theory, and criticism of art and architecture. The collection's holdings emphasize Western art from the Middle Ages to the present and American art from the colonial era to the present. The library is accessible by appointment every Monday, noon–4:30 p.m., and Tuesday–Friday, 10 a.m.–4:30 p.m., except on Federal holidays. Phone, 202-842-6511. http://www.nga.gov/content/ngaweb/research/library/About.html

Memberships   The Gallery offers three membership levels of annual giving: The Circle, The Tower Project, and The Exhibition Circle. Circle members contribute to conservation programs, special exhibitions, and research. Tower Project members promote contemporary artists by supporting modern and contemporary exhibitions in the Tower Gallery of the East Building. Exhibition Circle members provide funding for exhibitions. For more information on membership levels and their benefits, contact The Circle, National Gallery of Art, 2000B South Club Drive, Landover, MD 20785. Phone, 202-842-6450. Fax, 202 789-4577. http://www.nga.gov/content/ngaweb/support/membership.html | Email: circle@nga.gov

News   The National Gallery of Art posts recent news releases on its Web site. http://www.nga.gov/content/ngaweb/press.html | Email: pressinfo@nga.gov

An online subscription form is available to sign up for announcements, newsletters, notifications, and updates on acquisitions and exhibitions; activities, projects, and programs; and other topics. http://subscribe.nga.gov/subscription_form_ngart.cfm

NGAkids   NGAkids offers interactive activities and adventures with artwork from the Gallery's collection and an animated tale set in the Gallery's Sculpture Garden. http://www.nga.gov/content/ngaweb/education/kids.html

Photographs   Photographs that are not on display may be viewed by appointment. Phone, 202-842-6144. **Email: photographs@nga.gov**

Publications   The Gallery Shops sell publications on the Gallery's collections and quality reproductions of artwork. Purchases may be made online or by calling 800-697-9350. https://shop.nga.gov

Public Wi-Fi   Wireless internet service is available throughout the Gallery to visitors who are 18 years old and older or at least 13 years old with permission from a parent or guardian. The network name is "NGA_Public_WiFi," and a password is not needed. A user must, however, supply his or her own Internet device and agree to the "Terms and Conditions of Use." http://www.nga.gov/content/ngaweb/visit/public-wifi.html

Tours   The education division offers daily guided talks and tours in the galleries. Phone, 202-842-6247. http://www.nga.gov/content/ngaweb/visit/tours-and-guides.html

Visitor Services   The Visitor Services Office assists those with special needs, responds to written and telephone requests, and helps visitors plan their stay in the Washington, DC, area. For more information, contact the National Gallery of Art, Office of Visitor Services, 2000B South Club Drive, Landover, MD 20785. Phone, 202-842-6691. http://www.nga.gov/content/ngaweb/visit.html

Works on Paper   Works of art on paper that are not on display may be viewed by appointment. Phone, 202-842-6380 (European works). Phone, 202-842-6605 (American works). http://www.nga.gov/content/ngaweb/research/make-an-appointment.html | Email: printstudyrooms@nga.gov http://www.nga.gov/content/ngaweb/contact-us.html

For further information, contact the National Gallery of Art. Phone, 202-737-4215.

Woodrow Wilson International Center for Scholars

Scholar Administration Office, Woodrow Wilson Center, One Woodrow Wilson Plaza, 1300 Pennsylvania Avenue NW., Washington, DC 20004-3027
Phone, 202-691-4000. Fax, 202-691-4001. Internet, http://www.wilsoncenter.org

Director / President / Chief Executive Officer https://www.wilsoncenter.org/person/jane-harman	JANE L. HARMAN
Board of Trustees Chair https://www.wilsoncenter.org/leadership	WILLIAM E. HASLAM

The above list of key personnel was updated 10–2020.

Activities

Created by an Act of Congress in 1968, the Woodrow Wilson International Center for Scholars is a national, living memorial honoring the legacy of President Woodrow Wilson. The Wilson Center, headquartered in Washington, DC, and supported by both public and private funds, provides a strictly nonpartisan space for scholars and policymakers to interact. By conducting relevant, timely research and promoting dialogue from diverse perspectives, the Center works to address critical current and emerging challenges confronting the United States and the world. https://www.wilsoncenter.org/about-the-wilson-center

Sources of Information

Career Opportunities   Career opportunities at the Center are posted online. For more information, contact the Office of Human Resources, One Woodrow Wilson Plaza, 1300 Pennsylvania Avenue NW., 3d Floor, Washington, DC 20004-3027. http://www.wilsoncenter.org/opportunities/Job | Email: jobs@wilsoncenter.org
Contact Information   In addition to a "Get In Touch" electronic form, the "Contact Us" web page contains the general phone number and email address for and the hours of operation of and directions to the Woodrow Wilson International Center for Scholars. https://www.wilsoncenter.org/contact-us | Email: wwics@wilsoncenter.org
Donations   An online form is available for making tax-deductible contributions to support dialogue and scholarship in public policy. Gifts may be directed to a specific program by using the "Designation" drop-down menu. "Unrestricted" gifts allow the Center to build its overall capacity and meet areas of greatest need. Phone, 202-691-4171. https://engage.wilsoncenter.org/onlineactions/KxzFKoOYTk2W8uYVKK5HKg2 | Email: development@wilsoncenter.org
Experts   The Center convenes scholars to create a dialogue of ideas that the U.S. Congress, the President's administration, and the international policy community may adopt for implementation. https://www.wilsoncenter.org/experts
Fellowships   The Center offers residential fellowships that allow academics, public officials, journalists, business professionals, and others to pursue their research and writing at the Center while interacting with policymakers in Washington. The Center also invites public policy scholars and senior scholars from a variety of disciplines to conduct research for varying lengths of time in residence. Phone, 202-691-4000. http://www.wilsoncenter.org/fellowships-grants
Internships   The Center has a year-round need for interns to assist the program and projects staff and to act as research assistants for scholars and fellows. Phone, 202-691-4053. http://www.wilsoncenter.org/opportunities/Internship
Media Affairs   Members of the press may contact the Center at 202-691-4217. http://www.wilsoncenter.org/media-access-to-the-wilson-center
Multimedia   Wide ranging in scope, "Wilson Center On Demand" serves

as a hub for insightful analysis of and commentary on ideas and issues. https://www.wilsoncenter.org/wilson-center-demand

President Woodrow Wilson To learn about President Wilson's life and which of the Center's scholars are researching and writing about him, visit the "About Woodrow Wilson" web page. The page also contains a bibliography, a list of other institutions that are dedicated to the former President, and some of his quotations. https://www.wilsoncenter.org/about-woodrow-wilson

Press Statements The Center posts press statements. https://www.wilsoncenter.org/press-statements

Publications The Center publishes policy briefs and research reports, as well as books written by staff and visiting scholars and fellows, through the Wilson Center Press. Phone, 202-691-4000. http://www.wilsoncenter.org/publications

Every 3 months, "The Wilson Quarterly" magazine releases a cluster of content

exploring a single topic from diverse perspectives. This free, online magazine examines culture, current events, ideas, and the people affected by them. http://wilsonquarterly.com/quarterly | Email: wq@wilsoncenter.org

Social Media The Center maintains an account on Facebook. https://www.facebook.com/woodrowwilsoncenter

The Center posts openings for jobs and internships on its LinkedIn page. https://www.linkedin.com/company/woodrow-wilson-international-center-for-scholars

The Center tweets announcements, news, and other noteworthy items on Twitter. https://twitter.com/thewilsoncenter

The Center posts videos on its YouTube channel. https://www.youtube.com/user/woodrowwilsoncenter

Visitor Services Events, unless otherwise noted, are free and open to the public. Photo identification is required for entry. A listing of events at the Center is available online. http://www.wilsoncenter.org/events

The Sources of Information were updated 10–2020.

State Justice Institute

11951 Freedom Drive, Suite 1020, Reston, VA 20190
Phone, 571-313-8843. Internet, http://www.sji.gov | Email: contact@sji.gov

Board of Directors

Judges
Treasurer

Chair
Secretary

Public Sector Members

State Court Administrator
Vice Chair
http://www.sji.gov/about-sji/board-of-directors

Executive Director
http://www.sji.gov/about-sji/executivedirector

DAVID V. BREWER
JONATHAN LIPPMAN
WILFREDO MARTINEZ
JOHN D. MINTON, JR.
GAYLE A. NACHTIGAL
CHASE T. ROGERS

ISABEL FRAMER
MARSHA J. RABITEAU
HERNÁN D. VERA
(VACANCY)

DANIEL J. BECKER

JONATHAN D. MATTIELLO

The above list of key personnel was updated 10–2019.

The State Justice Institute supports the Nation's judicial system and the public that it serves.

Establishment and Organization

On November 8, 1984, President Ronald W. Reagan approved Public Law 98–620. Title II of that statute, which is commonly cited as the State Justice Institute Act of 1984, established the State Justice Institute as a private nonprofit corporation whose purpose is "to further the development and adoption of improved judicial administration in State courts in the United States" (98 Stat. 3336). http://www.sji.gov/wp/wp-content/uploads/SJI_Authorization.pdf

Statutory descriptions of the SJI's duties, Board of Directors, officers and employees, grants and contracts, activities, administrative provisions, Presidential coordination, records and reports, and audits, are codified in chapter 113, sections 10701–10713, of 42 U.S.C. https://uscode.house.gov/view.xhtml?path=/prelim@title42/chapter113&edition=prelim

A Board of Directors that comprises 11 members—six judges, a State court administrator, and four members from the public sector— supervises the SJI. The President appoints the members, by the advice and with the consent of the Senate, to 3-year terms. A member cannot be reappointed to more than two consecutive terms immediately following his or her initial term. The Chair of the Board is selected from among the members, by the members. No more than two of the public sector members can affiliate with the same political party. https://uscode.house.gov/view.xhtml?req=granuleid:USC-prelim-title42-section10703&num=0&edition=prelim

The SJI does not post an organizational chart on its website.

Activities

The SJI develops solutions to common issues faced by State courts; provides practical products to judges and court staff; ensures that effective approaches in one State are quickly and economically shared with other courts nationwide; and supports national, regional, and instate educational programs to accelerate the transfer of solutions. To accomplish these broad objectives, the SJI is authorized to provide funds through grants, cooperative agreements, and contracts to the State courts and to organizations that support them. http://www.sji.gov/about-sji

Sources of Information

Archived Records   "Records of the State Justice Institute, 1990 - 2013" have been accessioned by the National Archives and Records Administration. The collection identifier is SJI. https://catalog.archives.gov/id/7459146

Budget Request   The SJI posted its "Fiscal Year 2019 Budget Request" to Congress in Portable Document Format (PDF) on its website. http://www.sji.gov/wp/wp-content/uploads/FY-2019-SJI-Budget-Request.pdf

Forms   Documents to view and print are posted online in Portable Document Format (PDF). These documents include a number of forms: assurances, consultant rate, disclosure of lobbying activities, grant application, project budget, reimbursement request, and State approval certificate. http://www.sji.gov/forms

Grants   Information on various award and grant types—curriculum adaptation and training grants, the education support program, project grants, and technical assistance grants—is available online. http://www.sji.gov/grants

History   In 2014, the SJI published its 30th Anniversary Report, which offers a retrospective overview of achievements over the past three decades. http://www.sji.gov/wp/wp-content/uploads/SJI-30th-Anniversary-Report.pdf

Investment   The SJI has posted its priority investment areas for fiscal year 2020. http://www.sji.gov/priority-investment-areas

News   The SJI posts news items on its website. http://www.sji.gov/news

Newsletter   Readers may subscribe to the monthly "SJI Newsletter" online. http://www.sji.gov/newsletter-archives

Social Media   The SJI has a Facebook account. https://www.facebook.com/SJI.gov

The SJI tweets announcements and other newsworthy items on Twitter. https://twitter.com/statejustice

The Sources of Information were updated 10–2019.

United States Holocaust Memorial Museum

100 Raoul Wallenberg Place, SW., Washington, DC 20024-2126
Phone, 202-488-0400. TTY, 202-488-0406. Internet, http://www.ushmm.org

U.S. Holocaust Memorial Council
Arizona

ANDREW M. COHN
SUSAN G. LEVINE

California

LAURENCE M. BAER
SUSAN E. LOWENBERG
DEBORAH A. OPPENHEIMER
ERIC P. ORTNER
ELLIOT J. SCHRAGE
CLEMANTINE WAMARIYA
JEREMY M. WEINSTEIN
DANIEL G. WEISS

District of Columbia
Vice Chair

ALLAN M. HOLT

JOSHUA B. BOLTEN
NORMAN L. EISEN
RAFFI FREEDMAN-GURSPAN
DAVID M. MARCHICK
BENJAMIN J. RHODES

Florida

WALTER R. ALLEN, JR.
JEFFREY P. FEINGOLD
MURRAY J. LAULICHT
ANDREW J. WEINSTEIN

Illinois

JORDAN T. GOODMAN
SAMUEL N. GORDON
PRISCILLA LEVINE KERSTEN
TAMAR NEWBERGER
MICHAEL P. POLSKY
RICHARD S. PRICE
MAUREEN SCHULMAN

Indiana

LEE A. FEINSTEIN
CINDY SIMON SKJODT

Maryland

EDWARD P. LAZARUS
BRADLEY D. WINE

New Jersey

ETHEL C. BROOKS
BETTY PANTIRER SCHWARTZ

New York

Chair

HOWARD M. LORBER
TOM A. BERNSTEIN
MICHAEL S. BOSWORTH
JONATHAN W. BURKAN
SARA DAREHSHORI
HELENE FELDMAN
DAVID M. FLAUM
MICHAEL H. POSNER
DANIEL J. ROSEN
MENACHEM Z. ROSENSAFT
HOWARD D. UNGER

Other States

Massachusetts	JONATHAN S. LAVINE
Missouri	SAM M. DEVINKI
New Hampshire	DANIEL BENJAMIN
Ohio	RONALD RATNER
Texas	FRED S. ZEIDMAN
Virginia	MELISSA ROGERS
Washington	ERIC A. LEVINE
West Virginia	IRVIN N. SHAPELL

England

STUART A. LEVEY

https://www.ushmm.org/information/about-the-museum/
council

Congressional Members

Florida	REP. THEODORE E. DEUTCH
Georgia	REP. JOHN R. LEWIS
Illinois	REP. BRADLEY S. SCHNEIDER
New York	REP. LEE M. ZELDIN
Tennessee	REP. DAVID F. KUSTOFF
Florida	SEN. MARCO A. RUBIO
Maryland	SEN. BENJAMIN L. CARDIN
South Carolina	TIMOTHY E. SCOTT
Vermont	SEN. BERNARD SANDERS

Ex Officio Members—Nonvoting

Executive Branch Departments

Education	PHILIP H. ROSENFELT
Interior	(VACANCY)
State	THOMAS K. YAZDGERDI

General Counsel to the Council — GERARD LEVAL

Council Staff

Museum Director — SARA J. BLOOMFIELD

Internal Auditor — MEL SCHWARTZ
https://www.ushmm.org/information/about-the-museum/
executive-biographies/bloomfield

Museum Administration

Museum Director	SARA J. BLOOMFIELD
Deputy Museum Director	SARAH OGILVIE

General Counsel	RONALD F. CUFFE
Senior Advisors	
Marketing	MICHELLE STEIN
Strategy	CAMERON HUDSON
Chief Officers	
Development	JORDAN TANNENBAUM
Financial Officer	POLLY POVEJSIL HEATH
Information	JOSEPH KRAUS
Museum Operations	TANELL COLEMAN
Program Officer	SARAH OGILVIE
Directors	
Constituency Engagement	DIANE SALTZMAN
International Affairs	PAUL SHAPIRO
Levine Institute for Holocaust Education	YARIV LAPID
Mandel Center for Advanced Holocaust Studies	WENDY LOWER, ACTING
National Institute for Holocaust Documentation	MICHAEL GRUNBERGER
Planning	DARA GOLDBERG
Simon-Skjodt Center for the Prevention of Genocide	JILL SAVITT, ACTING

The above list of key personnel was updated 7–2019.

The United States Holocaust Memorial Museum promotes documentation, study, and interpretation of the Holocaust and maintains a permanent living memorial to its victims.

Establishment and Organization

On October 7, 1980, President James E. Carter approved Public Law 96–388, which established the U.S. Holocaust Memorial Council. This Act made the Council responsible for planning, constructing, and overseeing "the operation of, a permanent living memorial museum to the victims of the holocaust." It established the United States Holocaust Memorial Museum (USHMM) (36 U.S.C. 1401-1408). https:// www.govinfo.gov/content/pkg/STATUTE-94/ pdf/STATUTE-94-Pg1547.pdf

The United States Holocaust Memorial Council, which serves as a board of trustees, governs the USHMM. The Council's 55 members are appointed by the President to staggered 5-year terms. Additionally, five members are appointed from each Chamber of the Congress. There are also three nonvoting ex-officio members from the Departments of Education, State, and the Interior.

On October 12, 2000, President William J. Clinton approved Public Law 106–292 "to authorize appropriations" for the USHMM and "for other purposes." The Act gave the

Museum permanent authorization as an independent establishment (36 U.S.C. 2301 et seq.). https://www.govinfo.gov/content/ pkg/STATUTE-114/pdf/STATUTE-114-Pg1030.pdf

The USHMM operates as a public-private partnership. Its activities and programs are supported by planned giving, endowments, and revenues; gifts, grants, and contracts; and Federal funding. https://www.ushmm. org/information/about-the-museum

The Museum's organizational chart is available in its "Performance and Accountability Report—FY 2018" on page 35. https://www.ushmm.org/m/ pdfs/20181116-ushmm-par-fy18.pdf

Activities

Advanced Holocaust Studies   The Jack, Joseph and Morton Mandel Center for Advanced Holocaust Studies works with the United States Holocaust Memorial Council's Academic Committee to support research projects and publications on the Holocaust, provide access to Holocaust-related archival materials for study and new research, sponsor fellowship opportunities for pre- and postdoctoral researchers, and offer seminars, summer research workshops, conferences, lectures, and symposia. https://www.ushmm.org/research/about-the-mandel-center

For further information, contact the Jack, Joseph, and Morton Mandel Center for Advanced Holocaust Studies. Phone, 202-488-0400. TTY, 202-488-0406.

Holocaust Education   The William Levine Family National Institute for Holocaust Education promotes a variety of resources and programs to help educators, professionals, and students increase their knowledge of Holocaust history and understand its relevance today. Educational outreach programs provide teachers with classroom strategies and resources for teaching students about the Holocaust. http://www.ushmm.org/educators/teaching-about-the-holocaust

For further information, contact the National Institute for Holocaust Education.

Prevention of Genocide   The Simon-Skjodt Center for the Prevention of Genocide raises awareness of genocide, influences policymaking on genocide prevention, and stimulates worldwide action to prevent genocide and related mass atrocities. It seeks to make genocide prevention a national and international priority by increasing public awareness and mobilizing worldwide support to avert these crimes against humanity. http://www.ushmm.org/confront-genocide/about | Email: genocideprevention@ushmm.org

For further information, contact the Simon-Skjodt Center for the Prevention of Genocide. Phone, 202-488-0400. TTY, 202-488-0406.

Programs

Civic and Defense Initiatives   This program explores the ways in which the military can work to prevent genocide today. http://www.ushmm.org/professionals-and-student-leaders/military-professionals

Ethics, Religion, and the Holocaust   These programs focus on the response of churches to the Holocaust and the ways in which religious institutions, leaders, and theologians have addressed this history and its legacy. https://www.ushmm.org/research/about-the-mandel-center/initiatives/ethics-religion-holocaust

For further information, contact the Programs on Ethics, Religion, and the Holocaust.

Law Enforcement and Society: Lessons of the Holocaust   This program examines the role that law enforcement professionals played in the Holocaust. It also challenges them to reflect on their professional and personal responsibilities in a democracy today. http://www.ushmm.org/professionals-and-student-leaders/law-enforcement

For further information, contact the Lessons of the Holocaust Program.

Law, Justice, and the Holocaust   This program examines the decisions German jurists made and the pressures they faced under the Nazi regime. This is a one-day program for judges, prosecutors, and court administrators. http://www.ushmm.org/professionals-and-student-leaders/judiciary

For further information, contact the Law, Justice, and the Holocaust Program.

Youth and Community Initiatives   This program introduces students to Holocaust history and helps them develop leadership skills for confronting hatred and promoting human dignity. http://www.ushmm.org/professionals-and-student-leaders/student-leaders

For further information, contact the Student Leaders Program.

Sources of Information

Café   The Museum Café is open daily, 8:30 a.m.–4:30 p.m., except on Yom Kippur and Christmas Day. Visitors may not bring food into it or the Museum. The café serves breakfast, salads, sandwiches, and soups, including vegetarian and kosher options. Kosher food is prepared and sealed offsite under rabbinical supervision. https://www.ushmm.org/information/visit-the-museum/museum-cafe

Calendar of Events   For information on upcoming events, see the Museum's online calendar. http://www.ushmm.org/online/calendar

Career Opportunities   The museum employs people with diverse professional experience: collections, education, exhibits, fundraising, marketing, programming, and other areas. A list of current job openings is available on the "Careers" web page. https://www.ushmm.org/information/career-volunteer-opportunities/careers

Paid and unpaid internship opportunities are available. https://www.ushmm.org/information/career-volunteer-opportunities/internships

Collections / Exhibitions The Museum's holdings include art, books, pamphlets, advertisements, maps, film and video historical footage, audio and video oral testimonies, music and sound recordings, furnishings, architectural fragments, models, machinery, tools, microfilm and microfiche of government documents and other official records, personal effects, personal papers, photographs, photo albums, and textiles. The self-guided permanent exhibition spans three floors and presents a narrative history of the Holocaust with historical artifacts, photographs, and film footage. Special exhibitions include Remember the Children: Daniel's Story (for children 8 and up) and Some Were Neighbors: Collaboration and Complicity in the Holocaust. The Museum's traveling exhibitions have gone to numerous cities, States, and countries. These exhibitions extend the history of the Holocaust beyond the Museum's walls. More information on the Museum's collections and exhibitions is available on its website. http://www.ushmm.org/information/exhibitions

Contact Information The "Press Room" web page has phone numbers and email addresses for contacting the Museum's communications staff. https://www.ushmm.org/information/press

Encyclopedia An encyclopedia of the Holocaust is available on the Museum's website. https://www.ushmm.org/learn/holocaust-encyclopedia

Frequently Asked Questions (FAQs) The Museum posts answers to FAQs on its website. https://www.ushmm.org/research/ask-a-research-question/frequently-asked-questions

Multilingual Resources At the top of the Museum's home page is a "Language" drop-down menu that allows non-English readers to access resources in a number of languages: Arabic, Bahasa, Chinese, French, Greek, Hungarian, Italian, Japanese, Korean, Portuguese, Russian, Spanish, and Turkish. https://www.ushmm.org

News The Museum posts press releases on its website. https://www.ushmm.org/information/press/press-releases

To receive electronic Museum news, invitations to special programs and exhibitions, and updates on genocide prevention and other initiatives, subscribe using the online form. https://engage.ushmm.org/subscribe.html

Plan a Visit The Museum is open every day, except on Yom Kippur and Christmas. Admission is free; however, timed passes are required to enter the permanent exhibition from March through August. No passes are required for other Museum exhibitions. The "Plan Your Visit" web pages contain a trove of useful information on accessibility, admission and tickets, group reservations, hours, location, transportation, and more. https://www.ushmm.org/information/visit-the-museum/plan-your-visit

Reports Strategic plans and annual, budget, and FAIR Act reports are available on the "Reports" web page. https://www.ushmm.org/copyright-and-legal-information/annual-reports

Starting with the year 2004, performance and accountability reports are available online. https://www.ushmm.org/copyright-and-legal-information/performance-and-accountability

Social Media The Museum relies on social media to share information on its programs and resources; to memorialize the victims of Nazism; to launch discussion on the Holocaust and its relevance today; and to raise awareness that antisemitism, genocide, and hatred are persistent threats and that everybody has a role in combating them. https://www.ushmm.org/information/connect-with-the-museum#guidelines

Support the Mission Annual membership gifts help the Museum confront antisemitism and answer Holocaust denial, expand educational outreach, and preserve historical artifacts. https://www.ushmm.org/support

The Museum uses its resources to confront hatred and genocide, to educate students and provide classroom resources for teachers, and to rescue Holocaust evidence and make additional historic documents available in digital format. An online contribution, one-time or monthly, supports these activities immediately and directly. https://engage.ushmm.org/support.html

The Sources of Information were updated 7–2019.

Volunteer Opportunities   The Museum welcomes volunteers and offers a variety of service opportunities. http://www.ushmm.org/information/career-volunteer-opportunities/volunteering

---

United States Institute of Peace

2301 Constitution Avenue NW., Washington, DC 20037
Phone, 202-457-1700. Fax, 202-429-6063. Internet, http://www.usip.org

Board of Directors
Appointees from Outside Federal Service

Chair	GEORGE E. MOOSE
Vice Chair	JUDY ANSLEY
Members	ERIC S. EDELMAN
	JOSEPH ELDRIDGE
	STEPHEN J. HADLEY
	KERRY KENNEDY
	IKRAM U. KHAN
	STEPHEN D. KRASNER
	JOHN A. LANCASTER
	JEREMY A. RABKIN
	J. ROBINSON WEST
	NANCY ZIRKIN

Ex–Officio Members

Department of State	SECRETARY ANTONY J. BLINKEN
Department of Defense	UNDER SECRETARY FOR POLICY COLIN H. KAHL
National Defense University	PRESIDENT AND LT. GEN. MICHAEL T. PLEHN, USAF
U.S. Institute of Peace (nonvoting)	PRESIDENT LISE GRANDE

https://www.usip.org/about/leadership/board-directors

Senior Staff

President	LISE GRANDE

Chief Officers

Administrative	KATHLEEN T. ROSS
Executive	LISE GRANDE
Financial	JOSEPH LATAILLE

Director of Overseas Safety and Security	PAUL HUGHES
Special Advisor	PAUL HUGHES

Vice Presidents

Africa Center	JOSEPH SANY
Applied Conflict Transformation	DAVID W. YANG
Asia Programs	ANDREW WILDER
Finance	JOSEPH LATAILLE
Middle East and North Africa Center	MICHAEL YAFFE
Policy, Learning and Strategy	JOSEPH HEWITT

Strategic Stability and Security
https://www.usip.org/about/senior-staff

WILLIAM B. TAYLOR

The above list of key personnel was updated 1–2022.

The United States Institute of Peace prevents, mitigates, and resolves violent conflicts around the world.

Establishment and Organization
On October 19, 1984, President Ronald W. Reagan approved Public Law 98–525, which also is cited as the "Department of Defense Authorization Act, 1985" (98 Stat. 2492). One hundred and sixty-nine pages in length, this new law authorized appropriations for the Department of Defense and the Department of Energy, as well as having other purposes, which included the establishment of "the United States Institute of Peace" (98 Stat. 2651). https://www. govinfo.gov/content/pkg/STATUTE-98/pdf/STATUTE-98-Pg2492.pdf

On the same day that President Reagan approved the Department of Defense Authorization Act, 1985, he released a signing statement. In that statement, he noted the establishment of the United States Institute of Peace (USIP) within the context of affirming the "President's constitutional power to remove [members of the Board of Directors]." https://www.reaganlibrary.gov/archives/speech/statement-signing-department-defense-authorization-act-1985

The Department of Defense Authorization Act, 1985, contains within it Title XVII, which also is cited as the "United States Institute of Peace Act" (98 Stat. 2649–2660). The Act established the USIP as an independent nonprofit corporation for developing, applying, and fostering cost-effective strategies and tools to prevent, mitigate, and resolve violent international conflicts, particularly those that threaten or harm America's strategic and security interests. https://www.usip.org/about-us/history/usip-act

Title 22 of the United States Code (U.S.C.) contains codified statutory material on the topics of foreign relations and intercourse. Chapter 56 (sections 4601–4611) of 22 U.S.C. is dedicated to codified material that affects the United States Institute of Peace. https://uscode.house.gov/view.xhtml?path=/prelim@title22/chapter56&edition=prelim

By the advice and with the consent of the Senate, the President appoints the Institute's bipartisan Board of Directors. It comprises 12 members from outside Federal service; plus four ex officio members from inside Federal service: one from the State Department, one from the Department of Defense, one from the National Defense University, and the USIP President, who serves on the Board as a nonvoting member. The Board governs the Institute and appoints its President. No more than eight voting members may be from the same political party. http://www.usip.org/aboutus/board.html

Activities
The USIP supports U.S. national security and foreign affairs through conflict management and peacebuilding operations, training in conflict management and peacebuilding tradecraft and best practices, and conflict research and analysis. The USIP operates on the ground in conflict zones. It facilitates dialogue among parties in conflict, builds conflict management skills and capacity, identifies and disseminates best practices in conflict management, promotes the rule of law, reforms and strengthens education systems, strengthens civil society, and educates the public through media and other outreach activities. https://www.usip.org/regions-countries

The USIP works in partnership with the State and Defense Departments, the U.S. Agency for International Development, nongovernmental organizations, higher and secondary educational institutions, foreign governments, and international organizations, to promote collaborative problem-solving through conflict management operations, training and analysis, facilitated dialogue, Track 1.5

diplomacy, and special events. The Institute conducts practitioner training in conflict management, including mediation and negotiating skills for government and military personnel, civil society leaders, and staff of nongovernmental and international organizations. The USIP extends its reach through grants, fellowships, and scholarships, to nonprofit organizations in the United States and overseas. http://www. usip.org/issue-areas

Sources of Information

Archived Records   The "Guide to Federal Records in the National Archives of the United States" indicates that USIP records have been assigned to record group 573. The guide does not contain, however, a description that is associated with USIP records. https://www.archives.gov/research/guide-fed-records/index-numeric/501-to-600.html

Blog   The USIP's official blog is called "The Olive Branch." https://www.usip.org/blog

Career Opportunities   The USIP relies on knowledgeable, talented professionals to carry out its mission. A recent graduate typically starts as a program assistant. The ideal candidate is a high academic achiever; has a background in international relations or a related field; and possesses administrative, computer, research, and writing skills. Regional specialization and language skills may be required for some positions. https://www.usip.org/about/careers-usip

Climate Change   The USIP posted a short piece on the outcomes of the 26th Conference of Parties of the U.N. Framework Convention on Climate Change, which took place in Glasgow, in 2021. A senior USIP advisor on the environment and conflict provided the following analysis and commentary: "Glasgow yielded a sobering, honest recognition of the injustices of climate change . . . . The impacts of climate change are agonizingly unfair, with richer countries responsible for the historic build-up of greenhouse gases that cause climate change in the atmosphere, while climate change harms most those who can protect themselves least, including the poorest communities in the world's fragile states. In addition, our responses to climate change can exacerbate inequities within and between countries. The agreement reached at Glasgow takes a big step in recognizing the world's need to address these injustices. It elevates the global focus on seeking climate equity, and in particular intergenerational equity." https://www.usip.org/publications/2021/11/glasgows-summit-will-spur-change-climate-and-conflicts

Contact Information   The "Contact Us" web page has an electronic message box that allows visitors to send a comment or suggestion or to ask a question. Replies from the USIP are sent via email. The USIP postal address and phone number are also located at the bottom of the "Contac Us" page. https://www.usip.org/contact

Education / Training   The USIP runs an academy for peacebuilders seeking to learn more about transforming violent conflict in their communities to peaceful coexistence. It also has nationwide programs that teach students and teachers about American approaches to peacebuilding. https://www.usip.org/education-training

Electoral Violence   The USIP seeks to prevent election violence. Worldwide, 20 percent of elections become marred by violence. No continent is immune from and no level of development can prevent efforts to intimidate voters, to shut down polling stations, or to use police force excessively. To counter these threats to democracy, the USIP promotes civic education, election observation, police training, and preventative diplomacy. https://www.usip.org/issue-areas/electoral-violence

Events   The USIP maintains an events web page. https://www.usip.org/events

Experts   Working with governments and civil society groups worldwide, USIP experts conduct research and provide analysis, resources, and training for partners in conflict zones and in Washington, DC. They specialize in violent conflicts around the world and in issues such as advancing rule of law, countering violent extremism, electoral violence, governance, peace processes, and the roles of religion and technology in promoting peace or supporting conflict. https://www.usip.org/experts

Federal Register Documents that the USIP recently published in the Federal Register are accessible online. https://www.federalregister.gov/agencies/united-states-institute-of-peace

Grants / Fellowships Information on USIP grants and fellowship programs is available online. https://www.usip.org/grants-fellowships

History In the 1960s and 1970s, veterans of the Second World War were assuming important roles in the U.S. Congress. Several of them were men of peace with a vision. To learn who they were and what they did to promote their vision, visit "The Origins of USIP" web page. https://www.usip.org/about/origins-usip

Issue Areas The "Issues Areas" web page allows visitors to explore USIP analysis, programs and publications within a topical framework. https://www.usip.org/issue-areas

News The USIP posts news items on its "Press" web page. https://www.usip.org/press

Newsletter / Bulletin The USIP publishes a weekly newsletter (i.e., "The Weekly Bulletin") and a monthly bulletin (i.e., "Public Education News"). https://www.usip.org/connect

Podcast Network "USIP Events" presents same-day audio of USIP events that feature global leaders, policymakers, and practitioners, as they offer peaceful solutions for mitigating conflict in dangerous zones around the world. Additional audio productions include "Culturally Attuned" (podcast), "On Peace" (weekly discussions), and "The Peace Frequency" (in-depth interviews). https://www.usip.org/podcasts

Publications USIP articles, publications, and tools are accessible online. https://www.usip.org/publications

Regions The USIP is active in 52 countries and has staff in 18 of them. https://www.usip.org/regions-countries

Social Media The USIP has a Facebook account. https://www.facebook.com/usinstituteofpeace

The USIP tweets announcements and other newsworthy items on Twitter. https://twitter.com/USIP

The USIP posts video on its YouTube channel. https://www.youtube.com/user/usinstituteofpeace

Speakers Bureau The Speakers Bureau connects national networks and local organizations in the United States with leading USIP experts for virtual and in-person speaking events on themes that are relevant to the Institute's mission. https://www.usip.org/connect/usip-public-outreach

Strategic Plan The 2020–2022 USIP Strategic Plan has been posted online for viewing and downloading. https://www.usip.org/sites/default/files/USIP-Strategic-Plan-2020-2022.pdf

The Sources of Information were updated 1–2022.

INTERNATIONAL ORGANIZATIONS

African Development Bank

Avenue Jean-Paul II, 01 BP 1387, Abidjan 01, Côte d'Ivoire
Phone, +225 20 26 10 20. Internet, http://www.afdb.org | Email: afdb@afdb.org

President	AKINWUMI A. ADESINA
https://www.afdb.org/en/about-us/organisational-structure/the-president	

The above list of key personnel was updated 10–2020.

The African Development Bank reduces poverty in Arica, improves living conditions for Africans, and mobilizes resources for economic and social development throughout the continent.

Establishment and Organization

The African Development Bank (AFDB) was founded following an agreement that the member states signed on August 14, 1963, in Khartoum, Sudan. The agreement became effective on September 10, 1964. By charter amendment, the AFDB expanded its membership to include nonregional countries in 1982. The admission of nonregional member countries more than doubled AFDB capital resources. https://www.afdb.org/en/about-corporate-information-history/afdb-group-first-50-years

The African Development Bank (AFDB) group is a regional multilateral development finance institution. It was established to help the institution's regional member countries, all of which are African countries, develop economically and to promote their social progress. With its headquarters officially in Abidjan, Côte d'Ivoire, the AFDB is the premier development finance institution on the continent of Africa. https://www.afdb.org/en/about/mission-strategy

The AFDB comprises three entities: a development bank, a development fund, and a trust fund. AFDB membership totals 81 countries: 54 regional (African) and 27 nonregional countries. The United Arab Emirates is a contributor to the African Development Fund (ADF), but is not a nonregional member country. https://www.afdb.org/en/about-us/corporate-information/members

AFDB has posted 11 organograms (i.e., organizational charts) in Portable Document Format (PDF) for viewing and downloading. https://www.afdb.org/en/about-us/organisational-structure

Activities

The AFDB's mandate centers on the economic development and social progress of its regional members. Development banks promote the investment of public and private capital in projects and programs that are likely to contribute to the economic development of their stakeholders. Development banks finance projects that are run either by the government or the private sector. The AFDB is one of the world's five major multilateral development banks that provides assistance to its regional member countries to help them achieve

their development goals. https://www.afdb.
org/en/about/corporate-information/african-
development-bank-afdb

The ADF complements AFDB operations
by providing concessional financing
for high-priority development projects.
Contributing countries provide the ADF
with resources to improve economic and
social conditions in beneficiary countries.
These beneficiaries include countries that
are increasing in economic capacity and
en route to becoming the new emerging
markets or that are regarded as fragile states
and require special assistance for basics
levels of service delivery. https://www.afdb.
org/en/about-us/corporate-information/
african-development-fund-adf

The Nigeria Trust Fund (NTF) is a self-
sustaining and revolving fund. It assists
the development efforts of the AFDB's
low-income regional member countries
whose economic and social conditions and
prospects require concessional financing.
https://www.afdb.org/en/about-us/corporate-
information/nigeria-trust-fund-ntf

Sources of Information

Business Opportunities   The General
Services and Procurement Department
administrates the AFDB's internal
procurement. https://www.afdb.org/en/
about-us/corporate-procurement
Career Opportunities   Grade and salary
data and information on current job
vacancies are available online. http://www.
afdb.org/en/about-us/careers
Climate Change   The AFDB promotes
building greater capacity for African
countries to address climate change
risks. The AFDB finances investments
that are "climate-proof," meaning that
these investments are designed, installed,
implemented, and managed to reduce to
a minimal level global warming's adverse
effects, while maintaining the most cost-
effective ratio as possible. https://www.afdb.
org/en/topics-and-sectors/sectors/climate-
change
Contact Information   The AFDB maintains
some operations in Abidjan, Côte d'Ivoire,
and some functions in Tunis, Tunisia.
Addresses and phone numbers are available

on the AFDB group's website, on the
"Contact Us" page. https://www.afdb.org/en/
about/contact-us
Documents   The AFDB posts documents
on its website. https://www.afdb.org/en/all-
documents
Evolution of an African Institution   In the
1960s, a group of African leaders designed
a new institution to be 100 percent African.
These leaders were expressing a strong and
spreading desire for Africans to be in charge
of their own destiny. To learn more about the
institution that they eventually established
and its growth over time, visit the "Bank
Group's Evolution" web page. https://www.
afdb.org/en/about-corporate-information-
history/bank-groups-evolution
Financial Crisis   The AFDB has knowledge
products on the youth unemployment crisis
in Africa and on systemic banking crises in
low income countries. https://www.afdb.org/
en/topics-and-sectors/topics/financial-crisis
Français   The AFDB website offers
information and resources for visitors who
read French. https://www.afdb.org/fr
Frequently Asked Questions (FAQs)   The
AFDB posts answers to FAQs on its website.
http://www.afdb.org/en/about-us/frequently-
asked-questions
Glossary   The AFDB website features a
glossary of acronyms. http://www.afdb.org/
en/glossary
History   A short history of the AFDB is
available online. https://www.afdb.org/en/
about-us/corporate-information/history
News / Events   The AFDB website
features events, interviews, loan and grant
announcements, multimedia, news, press
releases, project stories, and speeches. http://
www.afdb.org/en/news-and-events
Site Map   The website map allows visitors
to look for specific topics or to browse
content that aligns with their interests. http://
www.afdb.org/en/sitemap
Social Media   The AFDB has a Facebook
account. https://www.facebook.com/
AfDBGroup/?ref=ts

The AFDB tweets announcements and
newsworthy items in English and French on
Twitter. https://twitter.com/AfDB_Group

The AFDB posts videos on its YouTube
channel. https://www.youtube.com/user/
afdbcomu

Statistics Defining achievable goals and setting realistic targets, as well as evaluating the effects of projects, depend heavily on reliable data. The AFDB promotes improvement in the quality and quantity of statistical data on all aspects of development. https://www.afdb.org/en/knowledge/statistics

The Sources of Information were updated 10–2020.

Web TV The AFDB's Web TV features programs in English and French. https://www.afdb.org/en/news-events/afdb-tv
Where the AFDB Works The AFDB's website features a list of African countries where the Bank is active. http://www.afdb.org/en/countries

Asian Development Bank

Headquarters: 6 ADB Avenue, Mandaluyong City, 1550 Metro Manila, Philippines
Phone, +632 632-4444. Fax, +632 636-2444. Internet, http://www.adb.org | Email: information@adb.org

ADB North American Representative Office: 900 17th Street NW., Suite 900, Washington DC 20006
Phone, 202-728-1500. Fax, 202 728 1505

President   TAKEHIKO NAKAO
https://www.adb.org/about/management/takehiko-nakao

The above list of key personnel was updated 09–2017.

The Asian Development Bank stimulates sustainable economic development and social progress in member countries to mitigate poverty and its effects.

The Asian Development Bank (ADB) commenced operations on December 19, 1966. It comprises 67 members: 48 regional and 19 nonregional countries.

The ADB works to eradicate poverty in Asia and the Pacific. As a multilateral development finance institution, it provides grants, loans, and technical assistance. The Bank serves its member countries, which are also its shareholders. Through equity investments and loans, the ADB also provides direct assistance to private enterprises of developing member countries.

To maximize the effects of its assistance on development, the ADB facilitates policy dialogues, offers advisory services, and mobilizes financial resources through cofinancing operations involving official, commercial, and export sources of credit. ABD operations promote three complementary agendas: environmentally sustainable growth, inclusive economic growth, and regional integration. The Bank's core areas of development activity are education, environment, finance, infrastructure, and regional cooperation and integration. http://www.adb.org/print/node/179940

Sources of Information

Business Opportunities ADB projects rely on the goods and services of consultants, contractors, manufacturers, and suppliers. http://www.adb.org/site/business-opportunities/main
Career Opportunities The "Careers" Web page features access to the ABD career and employment system, information on its young professional program and internships, descriptions of current job vacancies, and a summary of what the ADB looks for in a potential employee. http://www.adb.org/site/careers/main
Chinese The ADB website offers information and resources for visitors who read Chinese. https://www.adb.org/zh
Climate Change Production and use of energy from nonrenewable sources and the unsustainable development and consumption of other natural resources destabilize the climate and undermine long-term prosperity in Asia and the Pacific. Devastating storms, droughts, floods, and rising sea levels disproportionately affect poor communities. While climatologists

forecast that extreme climate events will become more frequent and intense, the ADB continues its support of sustainable growth in the region through financing and innovative technologies. https://www.adb.org/themes/climate-change-disaster-risk-management/main

History   Conceived in the early 1960s as a financial institution that would be Asian in character and foster economic growth and cooperation in one of the poorest regions in the world, the ADB opened in the Philippine capital of Manila in 1966. To learn about the Bank's initial achievements and those of more recent decades, visit the "ADB History" web page. https://www.adb.org/about/history

Members   The ADB posts a list of its regional and nonregional members and descriptions of them on its website. https://www.adb.org/about/members

Organizational Chart   The ADB's organizational chart is available in Portable Document Format (PDF) for viewing and downloading. https://www.adb.org/sites/default/files/page/203876/adb-org-chart-20170720.pdf

Publications   The ADB website offers information on books, brochures and flyers, conference proceedings, guides, papers and briefs, policies and plans, reports, and statutory reports and official records. http://www.adb.org/publications

Social Media   The ADB has a Facebook account. https://www.facebook.com/AsianDevBank

The ADB tweets announcements and other newsworthy items on Twitter. https://twitter.com/ADB_HQ

The ADB posts videos on its YouTube channel. https://www.youtube.com/user/AsianDevelopmentBank

Statistical Database System   The ADB maintains a central statistical database to store macroeconomic and social data of its developing member countries. https://sdbs.adb.org/sdbs | Email: sdbs@adb.org

---

European Bank for Reconstruction and Development

One Exchange Square, London EC2A 2JN, United Kingdom
Phone, +44 20 7338 6000. Internet, http://www.ebrd.com

President	SIR SUMA CHAKRABARTI
http://www.ebrd.com/who-we-are/ebrd-president-sir-suma-chakrabarti.html	

The above list of key personnel was updated 09–2017.

The European Bank for Reconstruction and Development develops open and sustainable market economies in democratic countries.

The European Bank for Reconstruction and Development (EBRD) is a multilateral development bank that supports projects in over 30 countries, from central Europe to central Asia and to the southern and eastern Mediterranean. Investing primarily in private sector clients whose needs cannot be met fully by commercial credit and equity markets, the EBRD promotes entrepreneurship and fosters transition toward open and sustainable market economies.

The London-based EBRD has a political mandate: It assists countries that are committed to and apply the principles of multiparty democracy and pluralism. The Bank also conducts its affairs with a commitment to environmental protection and sustainable energy development. In addition to benefiting the countries that receive its investments, the Bank also serves its shareholders' interests: 66 countries from five continents, the European Union, and the

European Investment Bank. http://www.ebrd.com/who-we-are/history-of-the-ebrd.html

Sources of Information

Business Opportunities   Information on opportunities for consultants, contractors, and suppliers is available on the EBRD website. http://www.ebrd.com/work-with-us/procurement.html
Career Opportunities   Information on job locations and types, benefits and rewards, and internships is available on the EBRD website. http://www.ebrd.com/careers-at-the-ebrd.html
Contact Information   Department and country contacts are listed on the "EBRD Contacts" Web page. http://www.ebrd.com/contacts.html
Economic Data   Economic teams publish macroeconomic and structural data series, and they survey data affecting the Bank's countries of operation. http://www.ebrd.com/what-we-do/economic-research-and-data/data.html
Environmental and Social Sustainability   EBRD financing supports sustainable development projects that are designed and operated in compliance with good international practices. To help clients meet sustainability goals, the EBRD posts downloads and resources on its website. http://www.ebrd.com/key-sustainability-downloads.html
Green Economy Transition (GET)   By 2020, the GET approach seeks to increase the volume of green financing to 40 per cent of EBRD annual business investment. Safeguarding the environment and strengthening ecosystems help market economies function better and, therefore, are central to the transition process that the EBRD has promoted since its inception. http://www.ebrd.com/what-we-do/get.html

History   In October of 1989, a month before German citizens dismantled parts of the Berlin Wall, President François Mitterrand of France proposed the establishment of a European bank to meet the challenges of emergent economic and political realities. In less than 2 years, the EBRD opened for business with its headquarters in London. To learn more about the role played by the EBRD in the transition from the end of the Cold War to a new European era, visit the "History of the EBRD" web page. http://www.ebrd.com/who-we-are/history-of-the-ebrd.html
Organizational Chart   The EBRD's organizational chart is available on the "Structure and Management" web page in Portable Document Format (PDF) for viewing and downloading. http://www.ebrd.com/who-we-are/our-structure.html
Products / Services   Information on the EBRD's advisory services, policy reform dialogue services, and financial products is available online. http://www.ebrd.com/what-we-do/products-and-services.html
Reports   The EBRD posts annual, donor, financial, sustainability, and transition reports on its website. http://www.ebrd.com/news/publications.html
Sectors / Topics   The EBRD website features a section that brings together the topics that most concern the Bank and the sectors in which it is most active. http://www.ebrd.com/what-we-do/sectors-and-topics.html
Social Media   The EBRD tweets announcements and other newsworthy items on Twitter. https://twitter.com/ebrd

The EBRD maintains a Facebook account. https://www.facebook.com/ebrdhq
Where EBRD Works   The EBRD website features the list of countries where the Bank is active. http://www.ebrd.com/where-we-are.html

---

Inter-American Defense Board

2600 Sixteenth Street NW., Washington, DC 20441
Phone, 202-939-6041. Fax, 202-319-2791. Internet, http://iadb.jid.org | Email: protocol@jid.org

Chair	VICE ADM. GONZALO NICOLÁS RÍOS POLASTRI

The Inter-American Defense Board is the oldest permanently constituted, international military organization in the world. It was founded by Resolution XXXIX of the Meeting of Foreign Ministers at Rio de Janeiro in January 1942. The Board is governed according to Statutes that the General Assembly of the Organization of American States approved in March 2006. Senior armed forces officers from the member nations staff the various agencies of the Board. Its three major components are the Council of Delegates, the Secretariat, and the Inter-American Defense College. http://iadb.jid.org/quienes-somos/resena-historica-de-la-sede-de-la-jid

The Board studies and recommends to member governments measures it deems necessary for the safety and security of the hemisphere. It also acts as a technical military adviser for the Organization of American States and is involved in projects such as disaster preparedness and humanitarian demining programs in Central and South America.

Established in 1962, the Inter-American Defense College is located on Fort Lesley J. McNair, whose buildings and furnishings the United States Government donated. The United States hosts the College, which prepares senior military officers and civilian functionaries for positions in their respective governments. The College offers an 11-month, professionally-oriented, and fully accredited Masters of Science degree. Multidisciplinary in content, the curriculum centers on the Western Hemisphere's most pressing defense and security issues. http://www.colegio-id.org/index.php

Sources of Information

Documents   Documents are posted online to increase the transparency of Inter-American Defense Board activities. http://iadb.jid.org/documents-and-publications

Events   Symposia and seminars are posted on the Board's Web site. A calendar of meetings also is available on the Web site's home page. https://sites.google.com/a/jid.org/iadb/eventos/simposios-y-seminarios

News   News items are available on the home page of the Board's Web site. http://iadb.jid.org

Regional Organizations   Links to regional organizations are accessible on the "Strategic Links" Web page. http://iadb.jid.org/strategic-links http://iadb.jid.org/quienes-somos/contactos | Email: jid@jid.org

For further information, contact the Inter-American Defense Board, 2600 Sixteenth Street NW., Washington, DC 20441. Phone, 202-939-6041. Fax, 202-319-2791.

Inter-American Development Bank

Headquarters: 1300 New York Avenue NW., Washington, DC 20577
Phone, 202-623-1000. Fax, 202-623-3096. Internet, http://www.iadb.org

President   LUIS A. MORENO
http://www.iadb.org/en/about-us/office-of-the-president,19639.html

---

The above list of key personnel was updated 09–2017.

The Inter-American Development Bank (IDB) was established in 1959 to help accelerate economic and social development in Latin America and the Caribbean.

The Bank has 48 member countries, 26 of which are borrowing members in Latin America and the Caribbean. http://www.iadb.org/en/about-us/about-the-inter-american-development-bank,5995.html

Sources of Information

Business Opportunities   IDB projects in Latin America and the Caribbean create contract opportunities for businesses and consultants. http://www.iadb.org/en/projects/project-procurement,8148.html

Career Opportunities   The IDB relies on professionals with expertise in economics, education, energy, environmental sustainability, financial markets, institutional capacity, investment funds, rural development and disaster risk, science and technology, social protection and health, transport, water and sanitation, and other fields to carry out its mission. http://www.iadb.org/en/careers/careers-at-the-idb,1165.html

Data The IDB posts datasets on its Web site. https://data.iadb.org

Glossary The IDB maintains a glossary on its Web site. http://www.iadb.org/en/projects/glossary,18952.html

Key Facts To learn at glance who leads the IDB, how many people it employs, how many countries are members, who are its clients, and recent annual levels of its approved lending, visit the "Key Facts" section. http://www.iadb.org/en/about-us/key-facts,18246.html

Learning Resources Online courses are accessible on the IDB Web site. http://www.iadb.org/en/courses/home,20468.html

Looking for Something? Try finding it by using the "What Are You Looking For" Web page. http://www.iadb.org/en/projects/what-are-you-looking-for,18944.html?

Publications A variety of publications—annual reports, books, catalogs and brochures, databases and datasets, discussion and working papers, journals, magazines, monographs, newsletters—is available online. https://publications.iadb.org/facet-view?field=type_view

Social Media The IDB tweets announcements and other newsworthy items on Twitter. https://twitter.com/the_IDB

The IDB has a Facebook account. https://www.facebook.com/IADB.org

---

Inter-American Investment Corporation

Headquarters: 1350 New York Avenue NW., Washington, DC 20577
Phone, 202-623-3901. Internet, http://www.iic.org/en

Chair, Board of Executive Directors	LUIS A. MORENO
Chief Executive Officer	JAMES P. SCRIVEN

http://www.iic.org/en/who-we-are/structure-and-management#.WYiXZOauhs0

The above list of key personnel was updated 09–2017.

The Inter-American Development Bank promotes development in Latin America and the Caribbean through the private sector.

The Inter-American Investment Corporation (IIC), an affiliate of the Inter-American Development Bank based in Washington, DC, was established in 1985 to promote the economic development of its Latin American and Caribbean members by financing small- and medium-size private enterprises. The IIC provides project financing in the form of direct loans and equity investments, lines of credit to local financial intermediaries, and investments in local and regional investment funds. http://www.iic.org/en/who-we-are/about-us#.WGLh5H0rLIU

The IIC has 45 member countries, of which 28 are in the Western Hemisphere, including Canada and the United States, and

17 are outside the region. http://www.iic.org/en/what-we-offer#.VumT0H0rLIU

Sources of Information

Career Opportunities The ICC relies on talent and experience to carry out its mission. It recruits, hires, and maintains a staff of diverse, motivated, and qualified professionals with expertise, leadership potential, and strong interpersonal and teamwork skills. Current job opportunities are posted online. http://www.iic.org/en/about-us/careers

History A three-part history, from 1985 to 1999, from 2000 to 2012, and from 2013

to the present, is available on the IIC's Web site. http://www.iic.org/en/who-we-are/our-history-timeline#.WD9-D30rLIV

Key Initiatives   The IIC's Web site features a section on its most important initiatives. http://www.iic.org/en/initiatives

Library   The IIC's Web site features a photo library. http://www.iic.org/en/media/photo-library#.WD94730rLIU

Member Countries   The IIC Web site features two lists of member countries: regional members and other members. An interactive map complements the two lists. http://www.iic.org/en/countries

News   The IIC posts news items on its Web site.

Projects   IIC projects may be searched by country or year. http://www.iic.org/en/projects

Publications   Brochures, factsheets, and reports—some in English and Spanish, some also in French and Portuguese—are available online. http://www.iic.org/en/media/publications#.VumPI30rLIU

Transaction Cycle   A description of the five stages of a successful IIC transaction—business origination, eligibility review, due diligence and approval, closing and disbursement, and supervision and evaluation—is available online. http://www.iic.org/en/what-we-offer/transaction-cycle#.WD9_p30rLIU

Social Media   The IIC tweets announcements and other newsworthy items in Spanish on Twitter. https://twitter.com/GrupoBID_CII

The IIC has a Facebook account. https://www.facebook.com/CIIGrupoBID

International Monetary Fund

700 Nineteenth Street NW., Washington, DC 20431
Phone, 202-623-7000. Fax, 202-623-4661. Internet, http://www.imf.org

Managing Director / Chair of the Executive Board https://www.imf.org/en/About/senior-officials/Bios/kristalina-georgieva	KRISTALINA GEORGIEVA
First Deputy Managing Director https://www.imf.org/en/About/senior-officials/Bios/geoffrey-w-s-okamoto	GEOFFREY W.S. OKAMOTO
Chief Administrative Officer	(VACANCY)
Deputy Managing Directors	
	MITSUHIRO FURUSAWA
	ANTOINETTE M. SAYEH
	TAO ZHANG
https://www.imf.org/en/About/senior-officials	

The above list of key personnel was updated 10–2020.

The International Monetary Fund fosters global monetary cooperation, secures financial stability, facilitates international trade, promotes employment and sustainable economic growth, and reduces poverty worldwide.

Establishment and Organization
The Final Act of the United Nations Monetary and Financial Conference, signed at Bretton Woods, NH, on July 22, 1944, set forth the original Articles of Agreement of the International Monetary Fund (IMF). The Agreement became effective on December

27, 1945, when the President, authorized by the Bretton Woods Agreements Act (22 U.S.C. 286), accepted membership for the United States in the IMF. The inaugural meeting of the Board of Governors was held in March 1946, and the first meeting of the Executive Directors was held May 6,

1946. https://www.govinfo.gov/content/pkg/USCODE-2017-title22/html/USCODE-2017-title22-chap7-subchapXV-sec286.htm

On May 31, 1968, the Board of Governors approved an amendment to the Articles of Agreement for the establishment of a facility based on Special Drawing Rights (SDR) and for modification of certain rules and practices. The amendment became effective on July 28, 1969, and the Special Drawing Account opened on August 6, 1969. The Special Drawing Rights Act (22 U.S.C. 286 et seq.) authorized the United States to accept the amendment and participate in the Special Drawing Account. https://www.imf.org/en/About/Factsheets/Sheets/2016/08/01/14/51/Special-Drawing-Right-SDR

On April 30, 1976, the Board of Governors approved a second amendment to the Articles of Agreement, which became effective on April 1, 1978. This amendment gave members the right to adopt exchange arrangements of their choice while placing certain obligations on them regarding their exchange rate policies, which the IMF was to monitor closely. The official price of gold was abolished, and the Special Drawing Account was promoted as the principal reserve asset of the international monetary system. The Bretton Woods Agreements Act Amendments (22 U.S.C. 286e-5) authorized the United States to accept this amendment. https://www.govinfo.gov/content/pkg/USCODE-2017-title22/pdf/USCODE-2017-title22-chap7-subchapXV-sec286e-5.pdf

On June 28, 1990, the Board of Governors approved a third amendment to the Articles of Agreement, which became effective on November 11, 1992. Under this amendment, a member's voting rights and certain related rights may be suspended by a 70-percent majority of the executive board if the member country has been declared ineligible to use the Fund's general resources and persists in its failure to fulfill any of its obligations under the Articles.

The IMF posts its organizational chart online. https://www.imf.org/external/np/obp/orgcht.htm

Activities

The IMF has 189 member countries. It promotes international monetary cooperation through a permanent forum for consultation and collaboration on international monetary problems; facilitates the expansion and balanced growth of international trade; promotes exchange rate stability; assists in the establishment of an open multilateral system of payments for current transactions among members; and gives confidence to members by making IMF resources temporarily available to them under adequate safeguards.

The IMF helps member countries correct imbalances in their international balances of payments. It periodically examines the economic developments and policies of its members, offers policy advice, and at a member's request and upon executive board approval, provides financial assistance through a variety of financial facilities designed to address specific problems. These financing mechanisms provide access to the Fund's general resources and offer short-term assistance during crises of market confidence, compensatory financing to countries suffering declines in export earnings, emergency assistance for countries recovering from natural disasters or armed conflict, and low-interest rate resources to support structural adjustment and promote growth in the poorest countries. The IMF also provides technical assistance and training to member countries. https://www.imf.org/en/About

Sources of Information

A–Z Index The IMF's website has an alphabetical index to help visitors search for specific topics or browse content that aligns with their interests. https://www.imf.org/external/siteindex.htm

Archives A catalog of the IMF's archives is available online. https://archivescatalog.imf.org/search/simple

At a Glance Fast facts and an overview of the IMF's founding and mission, governance and organization, and core activities are available on "The IMF at a Glance" web page. https://www.imf.org/en/About/Factsheets/IMF-at-a-Glance

Blog The IMF's blog offers insightful and analytical posts on economics and finance. https://blogs.imf.org

Bretton Woods Moment   In her video speech of October 15, 2020, Managing Director Kristalina Georgieva spoke of the necessity to seize "this new Bretton Woods moment" (approximately 4:20 into the video). The length of the entire speech is a little over 12 minutes. https://www.imf.org/en/News/Articles/2020/10/15/sp101520-a-new-bretton-woods-moment

Career Opportunities   In addition to economists and research assistants, the IMF relies on professionals with skills and expertise in a range of other fields: communications, facilities management, finance and accounting, human resources, information technology, language services, law, library science and archives, office assistance, procurement, security, and transportation and hospitality. Information on careers, current job vacancies, and recruitment programs is available online. http://www.imf.org/external/np/adm/rec/recruit.htm

Climate Change   The IMF counts "Climate Change" as one of its six key issues. https://www.imf.org/external/np/fad/environ/index.htm

Commodity Prices   The "IMF Primary Commodity Prices" web page offers easy access to data on primary commodity prices, the interactive commodity data portal, and the commodity terms of trade database. https://www.imf.org/en/Research/commodity-prices

Contact Information   Contact information for general, media, and other types of inquiries is available online. https://www.imf.org/external/np/exr/contacts/contacts.aspx | Email: publicaffairs@imf.org

Country Information   The IMF is an organization comprising 189 countries that, together, work to promote monetary cooperation, financial stability, international trade, employment and sustainable economic growth, and to reduce poverty. An alphabetical index of the participating countries and information on those countries are available on the IMF's website. https://www.imf.org/en/Countries

Data   The IMF publishes data on IMF lending, exchange rates, and other economic and financial indicators. https://www.imf.org/en/Data

Gender   The IMF counts the division along gender lines in labor markets worldwide as one of its six key issues. https://www.imf.org/external/themes/gender/

Glossary   The IMF maintains an online glossary of financial terms and acronyms. http://www.imf.org/external/np/exr/glossary/index.asp

History   James M. Boughton's "Silent Revolution: The International Monetary Fund 1979–1989" is accessible online. https://www.imf.org/external/pubs/ft/history/2001/index.htm

A chronological history of the IMF is available online. https://www.imf.org/external/np/exr/chron/chron.asp

Language Resources   The IMF provides information on its website in Arabic, Chinese, French, Japanese, Russian, and Spanish. Language tags are visible at the top and bottom of the IMF's home page. https://www.imf.org

Negative Interest Rate Policy   IMF Working Papers describe research in progress and are published to elicit comments and encourage debate. The views expressed in working papers belong to the authors and do not necessarily represent the views of the IMF, its executive board, or IMF management. In their recent working paper "Enabling Deep Negative Rates to Fight Recessions: A Guide" (April 2019), Ruchir Agarwal and Miles S. Kimball wrote that "the option to enable deep negative rates will be critical for central banks to maintain effectiveness of monetary policy in the future and will help mitigate the hardships associated with prolonged recessions" (page 84). https://www.imf.org/en/Publications/WP/Issues/2019/04/29/Enabling-Deep-Negative-Rates-A-Guide-46598

News   The IMF posts podcasts, newsworthy items about various countries, and the latest news on its website. https://www.imf.org/en/news

The "What's New Archive" allows easy access to recently posted items of interest. https://www.imf.org/external/what/whatsnewenglish/what.aspx

Publications   The IMF's "Finance and Development" magazine and "Fiscal Monitor" biannual report are available online in Portable Document Format (PDF). Its "New and Noteworthy" newsletter and other publications are also accessible online. https://www.imf.org/en/publications

Site Map   The IMF site map allows visitors to look for specific topics or to browse for content that aligns with their interests. https://www.imf.org/external/sitemap.htm

Social Media   The "IMF Social Hub" allows easy access to the IMF's Facebook page, Instagram photos and videos, LinkedIn account, Tweets and replies, and YouTube channel. https://www.imf.org/external/social.htm

Special Drawing Rights (SDRs)   A 5-minute video explaining the SDR, the international reserve asset that the IMF created to supplement the official reserves of its member countries, is available online. https://www.imf.org/external/mmedia/view.aspx?vid=5027851809001

U.S. Economy   On June 24, 2019, the IMF published its "United States: 2019 Article IV Consultation." The staff report for the consultation noted that the U.S. economy is undergoing the longest expansion in recorded history, unemployment is low, real wages are rising, and inflationary pressures remain subdued. It also notes that "the benefits from this decade-long expansion have not been shared as widely as they could. . . . Average life expectancy is falling, income and wealth polarization have increased, poverty has fallen but remains higher than in other advanced economies, social mobility has steadily eroded, and education and health outcomes are discouraging." https://www.imf.org/en/Publications/CR/Issues/2019/06/24/United-States-2019-Article-IV-Consultation-Press-Release-Staff-Report-and-Statement-by-the-47019

Videos   The IMF posts videos in Arabic, Chinese, English, French, Russian, and Spanish on its website. http://www.imf.org/external/mmedia/index.aspx

The Sources of Information were updated 10–2020.

International Organization for Migration

Headquarters: 17 Route des Morillons, C.P. 17, CH–1211 Geneva 19, Switzerland. Mailing address, P.O. Box 71, CH–1211, Geneva 19, Switzerland
Phone, 011-41-22-717-9111. Internet, http://www.iom.int | Email: hq@iom.int

Washington Office: Suite 700, 1752 N Street NW., Washington, DC 20036
Phone, 202-862-1826. Email: IOMWashington@iom.int

New York Office: 122 E. 42d Street, 48th Floor, New York, NY 10168
Phone, 212-681-7000. Email: newyork@iom.int

Director General	William Lacy Swing
Deputy Director General	Laura Thompson
Chief of Mission–Washington, DC	Luca Dall'Oglio
Director, IOM Office to the United Nations	Ashraf El Nour

The above list of key personnel was updated 09–2017.

The International Organization for Migration addresses the underlying issues of migration, answers the operational challenges of migration management, promotes economic and social development through migration, champions the dignity and well-being of migrants, and challenges the xenophobic narrative directed at them.

Established in 1951, the International Organization for Migration (IOM) is the leading intergovernmental organization in the field of migration. With 166 member states, an additional 8 states holding observer status, and offices in over 100 countries, the IOM promotes humane and orderly migration for the benefit of all. It does so by providing services and advice to migrants and governments, while working in close cooperation with governmental, intergovernmental, and nongovernmental

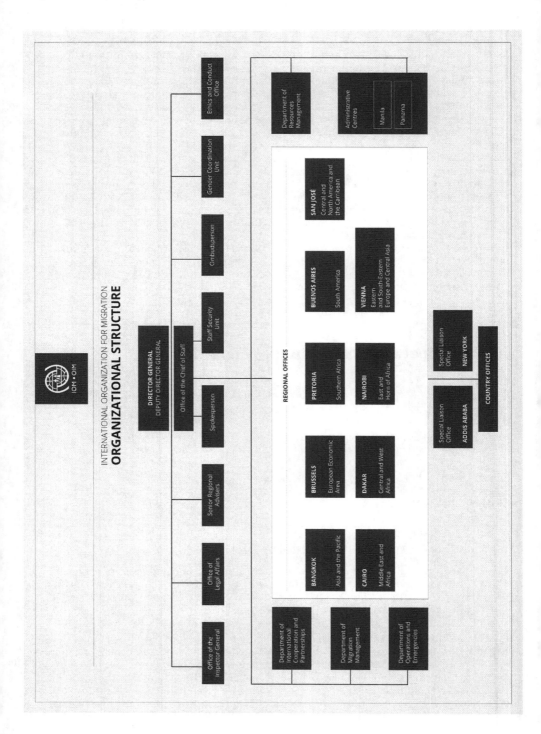

INTERNATIONAL ORGANIZATION FOR MIGRATION
ORGANIZATIONAL STRUCTURE

partners. The IOM has observer status to the United Nations.

The Organization works with its partners in the following areas: meeting the operational challenges of migration management, increasing understanding of migration issues, encouraging social and economic development through migration, and upholding the human dignity and well-being of migrants.

The Organization has been at the forefront of emergency response to ensure assistance and protection to stranded migrants and displaced persons. It has a lead role under the UN Cluster Approach in camp coordination and management in natural disasters and is a key partner in emergency shelter, logistics, health, protection, and early recovery.

IOM expertise and services support the following activities: secure, reliable, and cost-effective assistance for migrating persons; humane and orderly management of migration and the effective respect for migrants' human rights; technical cooperation and operational assistance for building national capacities and facilitating cooperation on issues relevant to migration; helping states to integrate migrants into their new environment and to engage diasporas as development partners; advising states in the development and delivery of programs and technical expertise to combat migrant smuggling and human trafficking; working with national health systems to reduce mortality, morbidity, and disabilities and to enhance access to rights-based health and well-being services throughout the migration cycle; and partnering with states to address labor migration. http://www.iom.int/about-iom

Sources of Information

Blog The IOM maintains a blog on its Web site. http://weblog.iom.int
Business Opportunities Information on procurement opportunities is available online. https://www.iom.int/procurement-opportunities
Career Opportunities Current job vacancies in various countries are posted online. https://recruit.iom.int/

sap/bc/webdynpro/sap/hrrcf_a_unreg_job_search?sap-client=100&sap-language=EN&sap-wd-configid=ZHRRCF_A_UNREG_JOB_SEARCH#
Countries IOM maintains more than 480 country offices and sub-offices worldwide. http://www.iom.int/countries
Español / Français Spanish and French versions of the Web site can be accessed by using language links at the top of the home page. http://www.iom.int
Glossary A list of key migration terms that is based on the IOM's "Glossary on Migration" is available online. http://www.iom.int/key-migration-terms
History Originally known as the Provisional Intergovernmental Committee for the Movement of Migrants from Europe, the IOM got its start amidst the chaos and displacement caused by WWII. Today, the IOM is the leading international agency working to advance the understanding of migration issues, encourage social and economic development through migration, and uphold the human dignity and well-being of migrants. To learn more of the IOM story, which began in 1951, visit the "IOM History" page. http://www.iom.int/iom-history
Organizational Chart The IOM's organizational chart is available in Portable Document Format (PDF) for viewing and downloading. http://www.iom.int/sites/default/files/Organigram.pdf
Press Room The IOM posts featured stories, news, radio and television interviews, and more on its Web site. http://www.iom.int/press-room
Publications Visit the online bookstore to see IOM publications in English, French, and Spanish. http://publications.iom.int
Regional Geographic Coverage A map of IOM regional geographic coverage is available online. http://www.iom.int/sites/default/files/about-iom/IOM_Regional_Geographical_Coverage.jpg

A list of IOM regional geographic coverage also is available online. http://www.iom.int/sites/default/files/about-iom/Coverage-of-ROs-Feb2016.pdf
Regional Offices Regional office staff reviews and endorses projects and provides technical support to Country Offices.

Descriptions of and contact information for the IOM's nine regional offices are available online. http://www.iom.int/regional-offices

Social Media   The IOM has a Facebook account. https://www.facebook.com/IOM

The IOM tweets announcements and other newsworthy items on Twitter. https://twitter.com/UNmigration

The IOM posts videos on its YouTube channel. https://www.youtube.com/user/IOMMigration

United Nations   Information on the IOM's Office to the United Nations is available online. http://unofficeny.iom.int | Email: unofficeny@iom.int http://www.iom.int/contact-us | Email: hq@iom.int

For further information, contact the International Organization for Migration–Headquarters, P.O. Box 71, CH–1211, Geneva 19, Switzerland.

Organization of American States

Seventeenth Street and Constitution Avenue NW., Washington, DC 20006
Phone, 202-370-5000. Fax, 202-458-3967. Internet, http://www.oas.org/en

Secretary General http://www.oas.org/en/about/secretary_general.asp	LUIS ALMAGRO LEMES
Assistant Secretary General http://www.oas.org/en/about/assistant_secretary_general.asp	NESTOR MENDEZ

The above list of key personnel was updated 9–2018.

The Organization of American States seeks an order of peace and justice among its member states, promotes their solidarity and strengthens their collaboration, and defends their sovereignty, territorial integrity, and independence.

The Organization of American States (OAS) brings together the countries of the Western Hemisphere to strengthen cooperation and advance common interests. At the core of the OAS mission is a commitment to democracy. Building on this foundation, OAS works to promote good governance, strengthen human rights, foster peace and security, expand trade, and address the complex problems caused by poverty, drugs, and corruption. Through decisions made by its political bodies and programs carried out by its General Secretariat, OAS promotes greater inter-American cooperation and understanding.

OAS member states have intensified their cooperation since the end of the cold war, taking on new and important challenges. In 1994, the region's 34 democratically elected presidents and prime ministers met in Miami for the First Summit of the Americas, where they established broad political, economic, and social development goals. They have continued to meet periodically since then

to examine common interests and priorities. Through the ongoing Summits of the Americas process, the region's leaders have entrusted the OAS with a growing number of responsibilities to help advance the countries' shared vision.

With four official languages—English, Spanish, Portuguese, and French—the OAS reflects the rich diversity of peoples and cultures across the Americas. The OAS has 35 member states: the independent nations of North, Central, and South America, and of the Caribbean. Since 1962, Cuba has been barred from participation by resolution of the Eighth Meeting of Consultation of Ministers of Foreign Affairs. Countries from all around the world are permanent observers, closely following the issues that are critical to the Americas and often providing key financial support for OAS programs.

Member states set major policies and goals through the General Assembly, which gathers the hemisphere's foreign ministers once a year in regular session.

Organization of American States

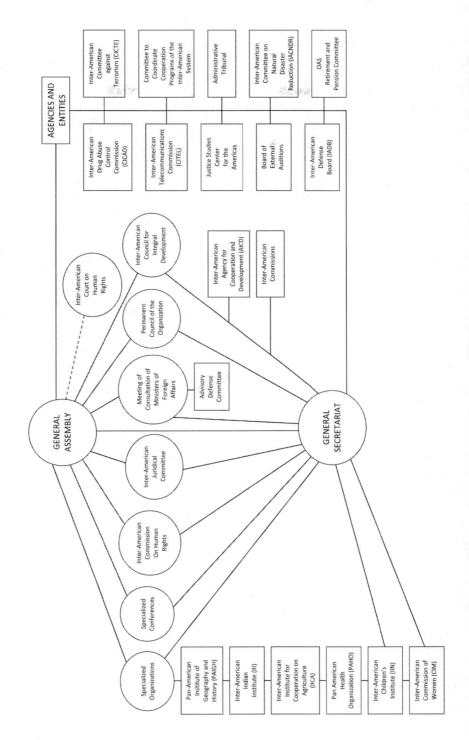

The Permanent Council, made up of ambassadors appointed by member states, meets regularly at OAS headquarters in Washington, DC, to guide ongoing policies and actions. The chairmanship of the Permanent Council rotates every 3 months, in alphabetical order of countries. Each member state has an equal voice, and most decisions are made through consensus.

Also under the OAS umbrella are several specialized agencies that have considerable autonomy: the Pan American Health Organization in Washington, DC; the Inter-American Children's Institute in Montevideo, Uruguay; the Inter-American Institute for Cooperation on Agriculture in San Jose, Costa Rica; and the Pan American Institute of Geography and History and the Inter-American Indian Institute, both in Mexico City.

In 1948, at the Ninth International Conference of American States, 21 nations of the hemisphere signed the OAS Charter: Argentina, Bolivia, Brazil, Chile, Colombia, Costa Rica, Cuba (barred from participation), Dominican Republic, Ecuador, El Salvador, Guatemala, Haiti, Honduras, Mexico, Nicaragua, Panama, Paraguay, Peru, United States of America, Uruguay, and Venezuela.

Subsequently, 14 other countries joined the OAS by signing and ratifying the Charter. They were Barbados, Trinidad and Tobago, Jamaica, Grenada, Suriname, Dominica, Saint Lucia, Antigua and Barbuda, Saint Vincent and the Grenadines, the Bahamas, Saint Kitts and Nevis, Canada, Belize, and Guyana. This brings the number of member states to 35. http://www.oas.org/en/about/who_we_are.asp

Sources of Information

A–Z Index   The "Topics" web page presents a collection of popular topics in alphabetical order. http://www.oas.org/en/topics/default.asp

Career Opportunities   Information on employment, consultancies, and internships is available online. http://www.oas.org/dhrs/dhr/employment_opportunities.asp

Conferences   A calendar of conferences is available online. http://www.apps.oas.org/oasmeetings/default.aspx?Lang=EN

Documents   The most important OAS documents, including its founding Charter and the Inter-American Democratic Charter, are available on its website. Along with these essential documents, links to other key reference material—such as annual reports of the Secretary General, OAS resolutions, agreements, and treaties—are also available. http://www.oas.org/en/information_center/default.asp

History   A short history of the OAS is available. http://www.oas.org/en/about/our_history.asp

Language Assistance   The OAS maintains English and Spanish versions of its website. Some web pages are also available in French and Portuguese. Language tags appear above the search box in the top right corner of most of the site's pages. http://www.oas.org/en

Media Center   Newsletters, press releases, and speeches by OAS leaders are posted in the media center. http://www.oas.org/en/media_center/press_releases.asp

Members States   Information on the 35 independent states of the Americas—all of which have ratified the OAS Charter and are member states—is available on the OAS website. http://www.oas.org/en/member_states/default.asp

Organizational Chart   The OAS posts its organizational chart in Portable Document Format (PDF) online. http://www.oas.org/legal/english/organigramaOEAeng.pdf

Organizational List   The "Organizational List" web page brings informational resources on the OAS's component parts together in one place. http://www.oas.org/en/about/organizational_list.asp

Permanent Representatives   A list of permanent representatives to the OAS is available on its website. http://www.oas.org/en/about/authorities.asp

Publications   OAS publications in English and Spanish are available online. http://www.oas.org/en/information_center/publications.asp

Scholarships   Information on OAS scholarships is available online. http://www.oas.org/en/scholarships

Social Media   The OAS tweets announcements, news, and other noteworthy items on Twitter. https://twitter.com/oas_official

The OAS has a Facebook account. https://www.facebook.com/OASofficial

The OAS posts video news on its Vimeo channel. https://vimeo.com/channels/oasvideonews

Staff Directory   The OAS maintains an online staff directory. To see the complete directory, leave all fields blank and click on the search button. http://www.oas.org/teldir http://www.oas.org/en/contactus.asp

For further information, contact the Organization of American States, Seventeenth Street and Constitution Avenue NW., Washington, DC 20006. Phone, 202-370-5000. Fax, 202-458-3967.

United Nations

United Nations, New York, NY 10017
Phone, 212-963-1234. Internet, http://www.un.org

United Nations Office at Geneva: Palais des Nations, 1211 Geneva 10, Switzerland

United Nations Office at Vienna: Vienna International Centre, P.O. Box 500, A–1400, Vienna, Austria

Washington, DC: United Nations Information Centre, Suite 500, 1775 K Street NW., Washington, DC 20006
Phone, 202-331-8670. Fax, 202-331-9191. Internet, http://www.unicwash.org | Email: unicdc@unic.org

Secretary–General https://www.un.org/sg/en/content/sg/biography	António Guterres
Deputy Secretary-General https://www.un.org/sg/en/dsg/index.shtml	Amina J. Mohammed
Director-General, United Nations Office at Geneva Director-General, United Nations Office at Vienna Director-General, United Nations Office at Nairobi https://www.un.org/sg/en/content/senior-management-group	Tatiana Valovaya Ghada Fathi Waly Zainab Hawa Bangura
Officer in Charge, Washington DC Information Centre http://www.unicwash.org/staff	Stefania Piffanelli

The above list of key personnel was updated 12–2021.

The United Nations supports tolerance and peaceful coexistence among the nations; seeks to maintain peace and security among them; opposes the use of armed force, except in the common interest; and promotes the economic and social advancement of all peoples.

Establishment and Organization

The United Nations is an international organization that was set up in accordance with the Charter drafted by governments represented at the Conference on International Organization meeting at San Francisco. The Charter was signed on June 26, 1945, and came into force on October 24, 1945, when the required number of ratifications and accessions had been made by the signatories. Amendments increasing membership of the Security Council and the Economic and Social Council came into effect on August 31, 1965.

The United Nations now consists of 193 member states, of which 51 are founding members.

A chart of the United Nations System's principal organs is available in Portable Document Format (PDF) for downloading and online viewing. https://www.un.org/en/pdfs/18-00159e_un_system_chart_17x11_4c_en_web.pdf

The purposes of the United Nations set out in the Charter are to maintain international peace and security; to develop friendly relations among nations; to achieve international cooperation in solving international problems of an economic, social, cultural, or humanitarian character and in promoting respect for human rights; and to be a center for harmonizing the actions of nations in the attainment of these

common ends. https://www.un.org/en/
sections/about-un/overview/index.html

Principal Organs

The principal organs of the United Nations
are the Economic and Social Council,
General Assembly, International Court of
Justice, Secretariat, Security Council, and
Trusteeship Council.

Economic and Social Council   This organ
is responsible, under the authority of the
General Assembly, for the economic and
social programs of the United Nations.
Its functions include making or initiating
studies, reports, and recommendations on
international economic, social, cultural,
educational, health, and related matters;
promoting respect for and observance of
human rights and fundamental freedoms for
all; calling international conferences and
preparing draft conventions for submission
to the General Assembly on matters within
its competence; negotiating agreements
with the specialized agencies and
defining their relationship with the United
Nations; coordinating the activities of the
specialized agencies; and consulting with
nongovernmental organizations concerned
with matters within its competence. The
Council consists of 54 members of the
United Nations elected by the General
Assembly for 3-year terms; 18 are elected
each year.

The Council usually holds two regular
sessions a year. It has also held a number of
special sessions. https://www.un.org/ecosoc/en

General Assembly   All states that are
members of the United Nations are members
of the General Assembly. Its functions are
to consider and discuss any matter within
the scope of the Charter of the United
Nations and to make recommendations to
the members of the United Nations and
other organs. It approves the budget of the
organization, the expenses of which are
borne by the members as apportioned by the
General Assembly.

The General Assembly may call the
attention of the Security Council to situations
likely to endanger international peace and
security, may initiate studies, and may
receive and consider reports from other
organs of the United Nations. Under the
"Uniting for Peace" resolution adopted by

the General Assembly in November 1950,
if the Security Council fails to act on an
apparent threat to or breach of the peace
or act of aggression because of lack of
unanimity of its five permanent members,
the Assembly itself may take up the matter
within 24 hours—in emergency special
session—and recommend collective
measures, including, in case of a breach of
the peace or act of aggression, use of armed
force when necessary to maintain or restore
international peace and security.

The General Assembly normally meets
in regular annual session from September
through December. It also has met in special
sessions and emergency special sessions.
http://www.un.org/en/ga

International Court of Justice   The
International Court of Justice is the principal
judicial organ of the United Nations. It has
its seat at The Hague, the Netherlands. All
members of the United Nations are ipso facto
parties to the Statute of the Court. Nonmembers
of the United Nations may become parties
to the Statute of the Court on conditions
prescribed by the General Assembly on the
recommendation of the Security Council.

The jurisdiction of the Court comprises
all cases that the parties refer to it and all
matters specially provided for in the Charter
of the United Nations or in treaties and
conventions in force.

The Court consists of 15 judges known as
members of the Court. They are elected for
9-year terms by the General Assembly and
the Security Council, voting independently,
and may be reelected. http://www.icj-cij.org/
homepage/index.php?lang=en

Secretariat   The Secretariat consists of a
Secretary-General and "such staff as the
Organization may require." The Secretary-
General, who is appointed by the General
Assembly on the recommendation of the
Security Council, is the chief administrative
officer of the United Nations. He acts in
that capacity for the General Assembly, the
Security Council, the Economic and Social
Council, and the Trusteeship Council. Under
the Charter, the Secretary-General "may
bring to the attention of the Security Council
any matter that in his opinion may threaten
the maintenance of international peace and
security." http://www.un.org/en/sections/
about-un/secretariat/index.html

Security Council   The Security Council consists of 15 members, of which 5—the People's Republic of China, France, Russia, the United Kingdom, and the United States of America—are permanent members. The 10 nonpermanent members are elected for 2-year terms by the General Assembly. The primary responsibility of the Security Council is to act on behalf of the members of the United Nations in maintenance of international peace and security. Measures that may be employed by the Security Council are outlined in the Charter.

The Security Council, together with the General Assembly, also elects the judges of the International Court of Justice and makes a recommendation to the General Assembly on the appointment of the Secretary-General of the organization.

The Security Council first met in London on January 17, 1946, and is so organized as to be able to function continuously. http://www.un.org/en/sc

Trusteeship Council   The Trusteeship Council was initially established to consist of any member states that administered trust territories, permanent members of the Security Council that did not administer trust territories, and enough other nonadministering countries elected by the General Assembly for 3-year terms to ensure that membership would be equally divided between administering and nonadministering members. Under authority of the General Assembly, the Council considered reports from members administering trust territories, examined petitions from trust territory inhabitants, and provided for periodic inspection visits to trust territories.

With the independence of Palau, the last remaining United Nations trust territory, the Trusteeship Council formally suspended operations after nearly half a century. The Council will henceforth meet only on an extraordinary basis, as the need may arise. http://www.un.org/en/decolonization/trusteeship.shtml

Sources of Information

A–Z Index   An alphabetical index is available on the United Nations' website to help visitors search for specific topics or browse content that aligns with their interests. https://www.un.org/en/site-index

Career Opportunities   United Nations staff members coordinate relief in humanitarian crises, disarm child soldiers, monitor elections, provide administrative and logistical support for carrying out complex mandates, and carry out a host of other functions around the world. https://careers.un.org/lbw/Home.aspx

Children in Detention   Many children are held in inhuman conditions and in adult facilities—in violation of their human rights—where they are at high risk of violence, rape, and sexual assault, including acts of torture and cruel, inhuman, or degrading treatment or punishment. The Office of the High Commissioner for Human Rights recently released the "Global Study on Children Deprived of Liberty" (OCT 2019). https://www.ohchr.org/EN/HRBodies/CRC/StudyChildrenDeprivedLiberty/Pages/Index.aspx

Climate Change   The Intergovernmental Panel on Climate Change (IPCC) has published "Climate Change 2021: The Physical Science Basis," which is the contribution of Working Group I to the sixth assessment report. Working Group I members have compiled the most up-to-date physical assessment of the climate system and climate change. They brought together the latest advances in climate science and combined multiple lines of evidence from paleoclimate, observations, process understanding, and global and regional climate simulations. In the summary for policymakers, the report states: "Observed increases in well-mixed greenhouse gas concentrations since around 1750 are unequivocally caused by human activities. . . . concentrations have continued to increase in the atmosphere, reaching annual averages of 410 ppm for carbon dioxide, 1866 ppb for methane, and 332 ppb for nitrous oxide in 2019." https://www.ipcc.ch/report/sixth-assessment-report-working-group-i

In southern Madagascar, an ongoing drought that started in 2019 has eliminated nearly all sources of food. The drought has brought severe hunger, and climate change is causing the drought. The World Food Programme of the United Nations has sounded the alarm to raise awareness and stimulate action to provide relief from the catastrophe. https://www.wfp.org/stories/dont-look-other-way-madagascar-grip-drought-and-famine

On December 13, 2021, Secretary-General António Guterres released a statement on the conclusion of the United Nations Climate Change Conference COP26. He wrote: "Our fragile planet is hanging by a thread. We are still knocking on the door of climate catastrophe. It is time to go into emergency mode." https://www.un.org/sg/en/node/260645

On December 2, 2020, Secretary-General António Guterres gave an address at Columbia University in New York City on "The State of the Planet." As part of the address, the Secretary-General warned: "Human activities are at the root of our descent towards chaos." https://www.un.org/sg/en/content/sg/speeches/2020-12-02/address-columbia-university-the-state-of-the-planet

Coronavirus Disease 2019 (COVID–19)   The United Nations maintains "COVID–19 Response" web pages where it posts informational resources and its most recent updates on the pandemic. https://www.un.org/en/coronavirus

The Department of Global Communications has posted the photo essay "We're All in This Together" as part of the United Nations' "COVID–19 Response" section on its website. https://www.un.org/en/coronavirus/covid-19-photo-essay-we%E2%80%99re-all-together

Documents   Launched in 1993 and updated in 2016, the Official Document System (ODS) is an online database of United Nations documents that has full-text, born-digital documents published from 1993 onward. The ODS also includes scanned documents that were published between 1946 and 1993. Documents are available in the official languages of the United Nations. Some documents are also available in German. https://documents.un.org/prod/ods.nsf/home.xsp

Empowering the Next Generation   In the face of crises whose effects are global in scale and scope, the Department of Economic and Social Affairs identifies an important source of hope: the next generation because it is different. https://www.un.org/development/desa/dspd/2019/02/the-generation-that-can-change-the-world-if-we-let-them

Essential UN Information   "The Essential UN" web page brings together in one place the most important information on United Nations activities, funding, priorities, and programs. https://www.un.org/en/essential-un

Food Loss and Waste   The Food and Agriculture Organization maintains the "Food Loss and Waste Database," which is the largest online collection of data on food loss, food waste, and the causes that are reported for the loss and waste. The data and information come from openly accessible reports and studies that measure food loss and waste across food products, stages of the value chain, and geographical areas. The database may be used by anyone who seeks information on food loss and waste and who has Internet access. http://www.fao.org/platform-food-loss-waste/flw-data/en

Frequently Asked Questions (FAQs)   Dag Hammarskjöld Library staff members post answers to FAQs. https://ask.un.org

Global Issues   The "Global Issues" web page offers convenient access to a trove of information on aging, atomic energy, children, climate change, decolonization, democracy, food, population, refugees, water, women, and more. https://www.un.org/en/global-issues

History   More than 75 years after its creation, the United Nations continues to support international peace and security efforts, give humanitarian assistance to those in need, protect human rights, and uphold international law. "The History of the United Nations" web page tells the story of those efforts. https://www.un.org/en/about-us/history-of-the-un

Human Rights   The Universal Declaration of Human Rights and a short history of this document are posted on the United Nation's website. https://www.un.org/en/about-us/universal-declaration-of-human-rights

International Maritime Organization (IMO)   The IMO is a specialized United Nations agency whose responsibilities include shipping safety and security and preventing ships from polluting the atmosphere and marine environment. The work of the IMO supports the United Nations' Sustainable Development Goals. The "Affiliated Bodies and Programmes" web page has a collection of links that provide convenient access to the websites of IMO affiliates and IMO programs. http://www. imo.org/en/About/Pages/Affiliated-Bodies-and-Programmes.aspx

Library   The Dag Hammarskjöld Library is accessible online. https://www.un.org/library

Mine Awareness   The United Nations Mine Action Service observes International Mine Awareness Day each year on April 4th. To hear the United Nation's global advocate's 2019 message, watch the 3-minute video. https://www.youtube.com/watch?v=LcWiyvxpkwE

News   The News Centre provides breaking news coverage of developments around the United Nations system, offering quick access to news-related products and resources. https://news.un.org/en

Non-English Readers   The United Nations provides versions of its website in Arabic, Chinese, French, Russian, and Spanish. Language options are available on the site's welcome page. http://www.un.org

Official Languages   The United Nations has designated six languages as official languages: Arabic, Chinese, English, French, Russian, and Spanish. The work of the United Nations includes communicating issues of global importance clearly and concisely. Accuracy in interpretation and translation makes the difference between communication that is clear and concise and communication that distorts and rambles. https://www.un.org/en/our-work/official-languages

Plastic Pollution   The Food and Agriculture Organization of the United Nations released its "Assessment of Agricultural Plastics and Their Sustainability—A Call For Action" (2021). In the assessment's foreword, the organization's Deputy Director Maria Helena Semedo wrote: "Soils are one of the main receptors of agricultural plastics and are known to contain larger quantities of microplastics than oceans. . . . This report serves as a loud call to coordinated and decisive action to facilitate good management practices and curb the disastrous use of plastics across the agricultural sectors." https://www.fao.org/publications/card/en/c/CB7856EN

Publications   Books, reports, and data are available from the online bookshop. https://shop.un.org

Social Media   Official United Nations social media include Facebook, Flickr, Tumblr, Twitter, YouTube, and other accounts. https://www.un.org/en/get-involved/social-media

Sustainable Development   The United Nations promotes 17 sustainable development goals to end poverty, to ensure prosperity for all people, and to protect Earth's biosphere, as part of a development agenda. https://sdgs.un.org/goals

System Organizations Directory   The Charter of the United Nations established the organizations that constitute the United Nations system. The directory presents these organizations in categories with links to their web pages. https://unsceb.org/structure

Web TV / Video   The United Nation's Web TV Channel is accessible around the clock. Its programming includes selected live broadcasts of United Nations meetings and events and prerecorded video features and documentaries on various global issues. https://media.un.org/en/webtv

The Sources of Information were updated 12–2021.

World Bank Group

Headquarters: 1818 H Street NW., Washington, DC 20433
Phone, 202-473-1000. Fax, 202-477-6391. Internet, http://www.worldbank.org

President   DAVID R. MALPASS
http://www.worldbank.org/en/about/leadership/managers

The above personnel table was updated 7–2021.

The World Bank Group promotes shared global prosperity and seeks to end extreme poverty.

The World Bank Group (WBG) comprises five institutions: the International Bank for Reconstruction and Development (IBRD), the International Development Association (IDA), the International Finance Corporation (IFC), the Multilateral Investment Guarantee Agency (MIGA), and the International Centre for the Settlement of Investment Disputes (ICSID). These WBG institutions work together to help developing countries find answers to tough global and local development challenges that range from climate change adaptation to food security, to fighting corruption and more. http://www.worldbank.org/en/about/what-we-do

The IBRD and the IDA serve as the WBG's primary economic and social development institutions. Together, these two development banks constitute the World Bank. Donor countries and countries with borrowing rights, a total of 189 countries, support and benefit from the World Bank. The activities of the IFC, MIGA, and ICSID complement those of the IBRD and IDA. http://www.worldbank.org/en/about/leadership

Sources of Information

A–Z Topics   An alphabetical list of topics helps visitors learn about the WBG's many and diverse activities. http://www.worldbank.org/en/topic

Access to Information   In 2010, the World Bank adopted its landmark disclosure policy: The World Bank Policy on Access to Information. It also has undertaken numerous initiatives to inform and educate the public. These open access initiatives include Open Data, Open Finances, and Open Knowledge Repository. http://www.worldbank.org/en/access-to-information

Blog   The World Bank posts items by featured bloggers on its website. http://blogs.worldbank.org

Career Opportunities   The WBG typically hires people with strong academic backgrounds, a broad understanding of development issues, and international work experience. In more than 170 countries, it employees professionals who specialize in economics, education, engineering, finance, public health, and many other fields. About 40 percent of World Bank staff members work in more than 110 developing countries. http://www.worldbank.org/en/about/careers

Climate Investment Funds   Since the inception of this climate finance mechanism, donor countries have contributed over 8 billion dollars in support of scaling up mitigation and adaptation action in developing and middle-income countries. The World Bank holds these public resources in trust and disburses them as grants, concessional loans, and risk mitigation instruments to recipient countries through multilateral development banks. https://www.climateinvestmentfunds.org/

Climate Migration   The World Bank report "Groundswell: Preparing for Internal Climate Migration" (2018) found that by midcentury the adverse effects of climate change in three densely populated regions of the world could force more than 140 million people to relocate within their respective countries. Concerted action, including global reductions in greenhouse gas emissions and development planning, could reduce internal migration by as much as 80 percent. http://www.worldbank.org/en/news/feature/2018/03/19/meet-the-human-faces-of-climate-migration

Contact Information   General information for contacting the World Bank is available on its website. http://www.worldbank.org/en/about/contacts

Countries / Regions   The "Where We Work" web page allows visitors to browse WGB locations by region or country group. http://www.worldbank.org/en/country

Data   The World Bank's website allows free and open access to global development data. http://data.worldbank.org

The microdata library facilitates access to data collected through sample surveys of households, business establishments, and other facilities. These sets of microdata may also be derived from agricultural, housing, or population censuses or through an administrative data collection processes. The Library also contains supporting documentation from censuses and surveys that the World Bank and other international organizations, statistical agencies, and other agencies in low and middle-income countries conducted or supported. http://microdata.worldbank.org/index.php/home

World Bank Group

Organizational Chart
Effective January 1, 2022

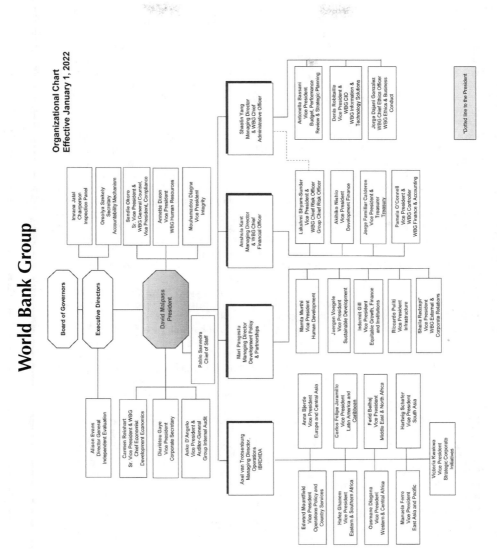

Board of Governors

Executive Directors

David Malpass
President

Imrana Jalal
Chairperson
Inspection Panel

Orsolya Szekely
Secretary
Accountability Mechanism

Sandie Okoro
Sr. Vice President &
WBG General Counsel,
Vice President, Compliance

Annette Dixon
Vice President
WBG Human Resources

Mouhamadou Diagne
Vice President
Integrity

Shaolin Yang
Managing Director
& WBG Chief
Administrative Officer

Antonella Bassani
Vice President
Budget, Performance
Review & Strategic Planning

Denis Robitaille
Vice President &
WBG CIO
WBG Information &
Technology Solutions

Jorge Dajani Gonzalez
WBG Chief Ethics Officer
WBG Ethics & Business
Conduct

*Dotted line to the President

Alison Evans
Director General
Independent Evaluation

Carmen Reinhart
Sr. Vice President & WBG
Chief Economist
Development Economics

Diariétou Gaye
Vice President
Corporate Secretary

Anke D'Angelo
Vice President &
Auditor-General
Group Internal Audit

Pablo Saavedra
Chief of Staff

Mari Pangestu
Managing Director
Development Policy
& Partnerships

Mamta Murthi
Vice President
Human Development

Juergen Voegele
Vice President
Sustainable Development

Indermit Gill
Vice President
Equitable Growth, Finance
and Institutions

Riccardo Puliti
Vice President
Infrastructure

Sheila Redzepi*
Vice President
WBG External &
Corporate Relations

Anshula Kant
Managing Director
& WBG Chief
Financial Officer

Lakshmi Shyam-Sunder
Vice President &
WBG Chief Risk Officer
Group Chief Risk Officer

Akihiko Nishio
Vice President
Development Finance

Jorge Familiar Calderon
Vice President &
Treasurer
Treasury

Pamela O'Connell
Vice President &
WBG Controller
WBG Finance & Accounting

Axel van Trotsenburg
Managing Director
Operations
IBRD/IDA

Edward Mountfield
Vice President
Operations Policy and
Country Services

Hafez Ghanem
Vice President
Eastern & Southern Africa

Ousmane Diagana
Vice President
Western & Central Africa

Manuela Ferro
Vice President
East Asia and Pacific

Victoria Kwakwa
Vice President
Strategic Corporate
Initiatives

Anna Bjerde
Vice President
Europe and Central Asia

Carlos Felipe Jaramillo
Vice President
Latin America and
Caribbean

Ferid Belhaj
Vice President
Middle East & North Africa

Hartwig Schafer
Vice President
South Asia

History   Founded in 1944, and not long thereafter referred to as the World Bank, the International Bank for Reconstruction and Development (IBRD) expanded to become a group of five development institutions. In the aftermath of World War II, IBRD loans helped countries overcome the devastation and rebuild. Over time, the Bank's focus shifted from reconstruction to development, particularly to development of infrastructure: dams, electrical grids, irrigation systems, and roads. To learn more about the inception and growth of the World Bank, visit the "History" web page. http://www.worldbank.org/en/about/history

The "World Bank Group Archives" website supports the institutional memory of the World Bank Group and provides access to records of the International Bank for Reconstruction and Development and the International Development Association. The website also features online historical resources and information products: exhibits on the Archives' collection and World Bank history, General International Standard Archival Description (ISAD(G)) finding aids, and transcripts of oral history interviews. http://www.worldbank.org/en/about/archives

Indicators   The WBG's Global Indicators Group produces indicators and datasets. http://www.doingbusiness.org/about-us/global-indicators

Libraries   The WBG and International Monetary Fund libraries collaborate to provide information services and make available resources to World Bank Group and International Monetary Fund staff. These libraries provide limited services to external researchers and visitors. http://jolis.worldbankimflib.org/external.htm

News   The World Bank posts press releases and other newsworthy items on its website. http://www.worldbank.org/en/news

Open Learning Campus   The Open Learning Campus offers educational opportunities that allow diverse audiences to learn at their own pace. It helps prepare people seeking to address the tough development challenges of the 21st century. https://olc.worldbank.org

Organizational Chart   The World Bank posts its organizational chart in Portable Document Format (PDF) for viewing and downloading. http://pubdocs.worldbank.org/en/404071412346998230/wbg-org-chart.pdf

Partnerships   The World Bank participates in global partnerships. Visit the "Partners" web page to learn about some of them. http://www.worldbank.org/en/about/partners

Podcasts   The World Bank's "All Multimedia" web page allows visitors to access a trove of podcasts on diverse topics: climate change, energy development, food, indigenous communities, immigration and forced displacement, pollution, sanitation, sustainability, tourism and more. http://www.worldbank.org/en/news/multimedia?multimedia_class_exact=Audio&qterm=&lang_exact=English

Poverty and Equity   The "Poverty and Equity Data Portal" web page allows visitors to access the World Bank Group's most recent data on inequality, poverty, and shared prosperity. http://povertydata.worldbank.org/poverty/home/

Projects   The "Projects and Operations" web page allows visitors to browse or search for projects by country or area, sector, or theme. http://projects.worldbank.org

Publications / Research   The "Open Knowledge Repository" allows users to browse and search for thousands of publications. http://www.worldbank.org/en/publication/reference

Social Media   The World Bank tweets announcements and other newsworthy items on Twitter. https://twitter.com/worldbank

The World Bank has a Facebook account. https://www.facebook.com/worldbank

The World Bank posts videos on its YouTube channel. https://www.youtube.com/WorldBank

Speaker's Bureau   The Speaker's Bureau serves as the official liaison between the World Bank Group and its visitors, who include business leaders, governmental representatives, students and teachers, youth organizations, and other professionals. http://www.worldbank.org/en/about/speakers-bureau | Email: speakersbureau@worldbank.org

International Bank for Reconstruction and Development

The International Bank for Reconstruction and Development (IBRD) officially came into existence in 1944. It promotes economic, social, and environmental progress in developing nations by reducing poverty.

The Bank lends funds at market-determined interest rates, provides advice, and serves as a catalyst to stimulate outside investments. Its resources come primarily from funds raised in the world capital markets, its retained earnings, and repayments on its loans. http://www.worldbank.org/en/about/what-we-do/brief/ibrd

Sources of Information

Activities and Achievements   The IBRD helps countries craft policies and shape investments, manage crises and prevent them, and create markets and access additional resources. To learn about the results of these IBRD activities, visit the "Results" web page. http://www.worldbank.org/en/who-we-are/news/campaigns/2018/ibrd-results-page

Countries   The Governments of the 189 member countries own the IBRD. http://www.worldbank.org/en/about/leadership/members

Organizational Chart   The IBRD and International Development Association are represented on the World Bank's organizational chart, which is available in Portable Document Format (PDF) for viewing and downloading. http://pubdocs.worldbank.org/en/404071412346998230/wbg-org-chart.pdf

---

International Centre for Settlement of Investment Disputes

Headquarters: 1818 H Street NW., MSN J2-200, Washington, DC 20433
Phone, 202-458-1534. Fax, 202-522-2615. Internet, http://icsid.worldbank.org/en |
Email: ICSIDsecretariat@worldbank.org

President	David R. Malpass
Secretary-General	Megan Kinnear
https://icsid.worldbank.org/about/secretariat/staff	

The above personnel table was updated 7–2021.

The International Centre for Settlement of Investment Disputes (ICSID) is an autonomous international institution and a World Bank Group affiliate that provides an independent forum for conciliation and arbitration of international investment disputes. By providing an impartial system for dispute settlement, it facilitates foreign investment. The Convention on the Settlement of Investment Disputes Between States and Nationals of Other States established the ICSID, setting forth its mandate, organization, and core functions. The executive directors of the International Bank for Reconstruction and Development formulated this multilateral treaty, which entered into force in 1966, to further the World Bank's goal of promoting international investment.

The ICSID has a composite structure comprising an administrative council and secretariat. Each member state holds one seat on the Administrative Council, whose mandate is to address organizational matters related to ICSID's institutional framework. The Secretariat consists of about 70 professionals who administer arbitration and conciliation cases and support other ICSID activities. https://icsid.worldbank.org/en/Pages/about/default.aspx

Sources of Information

Archives   The ICSID archives contain annual reports, events, featured videos, model clauses, and news and announcements. https://icsid.worldbank.org/en/Pages/resources/Archives.aspx

Contact Information   General information for contacting ICSID is available online. https://icsid.worldbank.org/en/Pages/about/Contact-us.aspx

Convention   The ICSID Convention is available in 20 languages; however, its official version is available in 3 languages: English, French, and Spanish. https://icsid.worldbank.org/en/Pages/resources/ICSID-Convention-in-other-Languages.aspx

Member States   A database of ICSID member states is available online. https://icsid.worldbank.org/en/Pages/about/Database-of-Member-States.aspx

Publications   The ICSID publishes specialized texts on international investment law and investment dispute resolution procedures. https://icsid.worldbank.org/en/Pages/resources/ICSID-Publications.aspx

Related Websites   A list of links to public and commercial websites that may be useful for research in the field of international investment law and practice is available on the ICSID website. https://icsid.worldbank.org/en/Pages/resources/Other-Related-Websites.aspx

Resources Overview   The ICSID Secretariat promotes greater awareness of the ICSID dispute settlement process and the development of international law on foreign investment by posting information resources on its website. https://icsid.worldbank.org/en/Pages/Resources/default.aspx

Social Media   The ICSID tweets announcements and other newsworthy items on Twitter. https://twitter.com/icsid

Structure   This separation of functions within the ICSID enhances impartiality and independence in the resolution of disputes. https://icsid.worldbank.org/en/Pages/about/Structure.aspx

---

International Development Association

Established in 1960, the International Development Association (IDA) reduces poverty by providing loans, or "credits," and grants for programs that boost economic growth, improve living conditions, and reduce inequalities. The IDA complements the International Bank for Reconstruction and Development (IBRD), which is the original lending arm of the World Bank. The IDA and IBRD share the same staff and headquarters and evaluate projects using the same standards.

The IDA lends money on concessional terms, which means that IDA loans, or credits, have a zero or very low interest charge and repayments extend from 25 to 38 years. The IDA also provides grants to countries at risk of debt distress. In addition to loans and grants, the IDA provides significant levels of debt relief. http://ida.worldbank.org/about/who-we-are

Sources of Information

Articles of Agreement   The IDA's Articles of Agreement became effective in 1960. They are available online in Portable Document Format. http://ida.worldbank.org/sites/default/files/IDA-articles-of-agreement.pdf

Climate   Climate change threatens poorer people globally, with the potential to force more than 100 million people back into poverty by 2030. The IDA is making plans to help manage this threat of enormous scope and scale. http://ida.worldbank.org/theme/climate

Countries   Seventy-five countries are eligible to receive IDA resources. http://ida.worldbank.org/about/borrowing-countries

A list of the approximately 50 contributor countries is available on the IDA's website. http://ida.worldbank.org/about/contributor-countries

Crisis Financing   The IDA has a history of involvement in various aspects of crisis response, including providing financial support. http://ida.worldbank.org/financing/crisis-financing

History   Australia, Canada, China, Germany, India, Italy, Malaysia, Norway, Pakistan, Sudan, Sweden, Thailand, United Kingdom, United States, and Vietnam launched the IDA on September 24, 1960, with an initial funding of 912.7 million dollars. http://ida.worldbank.org/about/history

News / Publications   The IDA posts press releases and other newsworthy items online. http://ida.worldbank.org/news

Organizational Chart   The IDA and International Bank for Reconstruction and Development are included on the World Bank's organizational chart, which is available in Portable Document Format (PDF) for viewing and downloading. http://pubdocs.worldbank.org/en/404071412346998230/wbg-org-chart.pdf

Resources / Policy   Every 3 years, donors meet to replenish IDA resources and review its policy framework. The replenishment process typically consists of four formal meetings over the course of 1 year. Four IDA18 replenishment meetings were held in 2016. http://ida.worldbank.org/financing/replenishments/ida18-overview

Results   The IDA's website features an overview of the results of the IDA's efforts in the world's poorest countries by country, theme, and topic. http://ida.worldbank.org/results

Social Media   The IDA has a Facebook account. https://www.facebook.com/IDA.WBG/?ref=nf

The IDA posts videos on its YouTube channel. https://www.youtube.com/playlist?list=PL6A79B12D02618711&feature=plcp

---

International Finance Corporation

Headquarters: 2121 Pennsylvania Avenue NW., Washington, DC 20433
Phone, 202-473-7711. Fax, 202-974-4384. Internet, http://www.ifc.org

President	DAVID R. MALPASS
Managing Director	MAKHTAR DIOP
https://www.ifc.org/wps/wcm/connect/CORP_EXT_Content/IFC_External_Corporate_Site/About+IFC_New/Leadership/	

The above personnel table was updated 7–2021.

The International Finance Corporation (IFC), a World Bank Group institution, was established in 1956 to promote productive private enterprise in developing member countries.

The Corporation pursues its objective principally through direct debt and equity investments in projects that establish new businesses or expand, modify, or diversify existing businesses. It also encourages cofinancing by other investors and lenders.

Additionally, to developing member countries, the IFC provides advisory services and technical assistance in capital market development, corporate restructuring, foreign investment, and privatization. https://www.ifc.org/wps/wcm/connect/corp_ext_content/ifc_external_corporate_site/about+ifc_new

Sources of Information

Articles of Agreement   The official version of the IFC Articles of Agreement is the English version that each member country signs. Translations of the official version are available in Arabic, Chinese, French, Japanese, Portuguese, Russian, and Spanish. https://www.ifc.org/wps/wcm/connect/CORP_EXT_Content/IFC_External_Corporate_Site/About+IFC_New/IFC+Governance/Articles/

Bonds   In 2013, the IFC helped transform the green bond market by issuing a 1 billion dollar global benchmark green bond. The IFC is currently investing in the Green Cornerstone Bond Fund, which buys green bonds issued by banks in Africa, Asia, Central Asia, Eastern Europe, Latin America, and the Middle East. The Green Cornerstone Bond Fund is a partnership involving the IFC and the European asset manager Amundi. http://www.worldbank.org/en/results/2017/12/01/green-bonds

Career Opportunities   The IFC posts career opportunities. http://www.ifc.org/wps/wcm/connect/Careers_Ext_Content/IFC_External_Corporate_Site/IFC+Careers

Climate   The IFC is increasing its climate-related investments to address climate change—a fundamental threat to development, with the potential to impact millions, threatening agricultural livelihoods, increasing the incidence of natural disasters and affecting water, energy, and food supplies. http://www.ifc.org/wps/wcm/connect/Topics_Ext_Content/IFC_External_Corporate_Site/Climate+Business

Contact Information   General information is available on the IFC's website. http://www.ifc.org/wps/wcm/connect/corp_ext_content/ifc_external_corporate_site/about+ifc_new/contacts

Countries   The IFC operates in more than 100 countries. http://www.ifc.org/wps/wcm/connect/corp_ext_content/ifc_external_corporate_site/about+ifc_new/Where+We+Work

Expertise   The IFC's areas of expertise include agribusiness and forestry; financial institutions; funds; health and education; infrastructure; manufacturing; oil, gas, and mining; public-private partnerships; telecoms, media, and technology; and tourism, retail, and property. https://www.ifc.org/wps/wcm/connect/CORP_EXT_Content/IFC_External_Corporate_Site/solutions/expertise

Frequently Asked Questions (FAQs)   The IFC posts answers to FAQs online. https://www.ifc.org/wps/wcm/connect/corp_ext_content/ifc_external_corporate_site/about+ifc_new/faqs

Funding   The IFC raises funds for lending activities by issuing debt obligations in international capital markets. IFC borrowings are diversified by country, currency, source, and maturity to enhance flexibility and cost effectiveness. https://www.ifc.org/wps/wcm/connect/CORP_EXT_Content/IFC_External_Corporate_Site/About+IFC_New/IFC+Governance/Funding/

History   Opened in 1956 with $100 million in capital, the IFC has been creating jobs and raising living standards for six decades. https://www.ifc.org/wps/wcm/connect/CORP_EXT_Content/IFC_External_Corporate_Site/About+IFC_New/IFC+History/

Media   The "Communications Contacts" page contains communications and public affairs contact information, as well as contact information associated with IFC accountability and the various spheres of IFC expertise and regional activity. https://www.ifc.org/wps/wcm/connect/NEWS_EXT_CONTENT/IFC_External_Corporate_Site/News+and+Events/Media+Contacts/

Organizational Chart   The IFC posts its organizational chart in Portable Document Format (PDF) for viewing and downloading. https://www.ifc.org/wps/wcm/connect/7973ac004a4483708622bf10cc70d6a1/IFC+organization+chart.pdf?MOD=AJPERES

Press Releases   The IFC posts press releases in Arabic, Bahasa Indonesia, Chinese, English, French, German, Japanese, Montenegrin, Portuguese, Russian, Spanish, Tajik, Turkish, and Ukranian. https://ifcextapps.ifc.org/ifcext/pressroom/ifcpressroom.nsf/MorePressReleases/?OpenView&Start=1&Count=25

Publications   A search tool allows visitors to search IFC publications by language, region, and topic. The advanced option allows users to refine their search by IFC department, industry, and publication type. https://www.ifc.org/wps/wcm/connect/publications_ext_content/ifc_external_publication_site/publications

Social Media   The IFC has a Facebook account. https://www.facebook.com/IFCwbg

The IFC tweets announcements and other newsworthy items on Twitter. https://twitter.com/IFC_org

The IFC posts videos on its YouTube channel. https://www.youtube.com/user/IFCvideocasts

Stories   The IFC posts stories highlighting the achievements of its clients who affect people's lives in a favorable and notable way. https://www.ifc.org/wps/wcm/connect/NEWS_EXT_CONTENT/IFC_External_Corporate_Site/News+and+Events/News/Impact-Stories

Sustainability   The IFC partners with industry and other stakeholders to find ways that open opportunities for economically, socially, and environmentally sustainable private investment. https://www.ifc.org/wps/wcm/connect/Topics_Ext_Content/IFC_External_Corporate_Site/Sustainability-At-IFC

Multilateral Investment Guarantee Agency

Headquarters: 1818 H Street NW., Washington, DC 20433
Phone, 202-458-2538. Fax, 202-522-0316. Internet, http://www.miga.org

President   DAVID R. MALPASS
Executive Vice President   HIROSHI MATANO
https://www.miga.org/about/management

The above personnel table was updated 7–2021.

The Multilateral Investment Guarantee
Agency (MIGA), a World Bank Group
institution, was formally constituted in 1988.

Working with public and private insurers,
MIGA promotes foreign direct investment in
developing countries to support economic
growth, reduce poverty, and improve the
quality of people's lives. Due to its status
as a World Bank Group institution, MIGA's
guarantees protect investments against
noncommercial risks and help investors gain
access to funding sources with improved
financial terms and conditions. https://www.
miga.org/who-we-are

Sources of Information

Access to Information   MIGA's policy on
accessing information defines its obligations
to disclose information on itself and its
activities. https://www.miga.org/projects/
access-to-information/
Career Opportunities   The MIGA advertises
available positions on the World Bank's job
vacancies page. https://www.miga.org/who-
we-are/careers
Contact Information   General information
is available on the MIGA's website. https://
www.miga.org/contact
Convention   The "Convention Establishing
the Multilateral Investment Guarantee
Agency" went into effect on April 12, 1988.
The Council of Governors amended it in
2010. The Convention is available online in
Portable Document Format (PDF). https://
www.miga.org/who-we-are/miga-
convention
Frequently Asked Questions (FAQs)   The
MIGA posts answers to FAQs on its
website. https://www.miga.org/who-we-are/
frequently-asked-questions

History   A timeline and short history of the
MIGA are available on its website. https://
www.miga.org/who-we-are/history
Member Countries   The names of the 181
member countries—156 developing, 25
industrialized—are available on the MIGA's
website. https://www.miga.org/who-we-are/
member-countries
News   The MIGA posts press releases on its
website. https://www.miga.org/news/press-
releases
Organizational Chart   The MIGA
posts its organizational chart in Portable
Document Format (PDF) for viewing and
downloading. http://pubdocs.worldbank.org/
en/268791412196376513/miga.pdf
Projects   The MIGA provides investment
insurance, or guarantees, for projects in a
variety of sectors, covering all regions of the
world. https://www.miga.org/projects
Reports   The MIGA posts its annual
reports online. https://www.miga.org/Pages/
Resources/Reports/AnnualReports.aspx
Small Investment   The small investment
program facilitates investment in small and
medium-size enterprises that are active in
the agribusiness, finance, manufacturing,
and services sectors. This MIGA program
has a streamlined approval process, which
allows investors to acquire MIGA coverage
quickly.. https://www.miga.org/investment-
guarantees/small-investment-program/

The application for the small investment
program is available online. https://www.
miga.org/Documents/SIP_Application.
pdf#search=SIP%20Application
Social Media   The MIGA tweets
announcements and other newsworthy items
on Twitter. https://twitter.com/miga

The MIGA posts videos on its YouTube
channel. https://www.youtube.com/
migaworldbank

Multilateral Investment Guarantee Agency

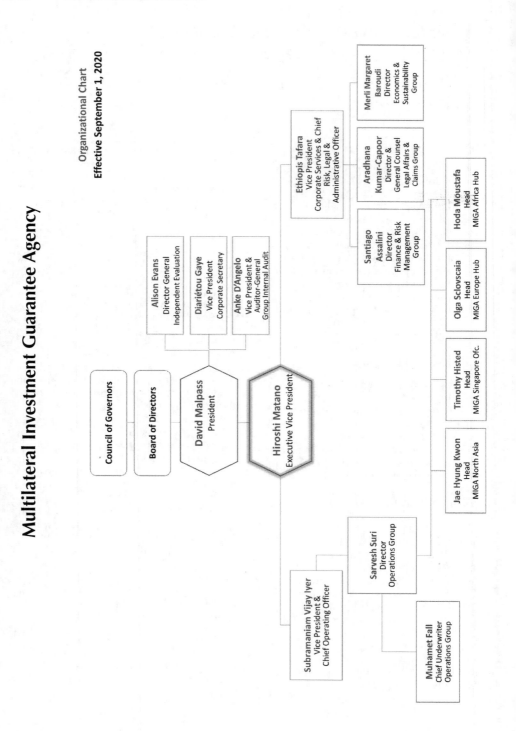

Organizational Chart
Effective September 1, 2020